The United States Government Manual 2019

Bernan Press

Lanham • Boulder • New York • London

Published by Bernan Press
An imprint of The Rowman & Littlefield Publishing Group, Inc.
4501 Forbes Boulevard, Suite 200, Lanham, Maryland 20706
www.rowman.com
800-462-6420

6 Tinworth Street, London, SE11 5AL, United Kingdom

ISBN: 978-1-64143-465-2

♾™ The paper used in this publication meets the minimum requirements of American National Standard for Information Sciences—Permanence of Paper for Printed Library Materials, ANSI/NISO Z39.48-1992.

Preface

As the official handbook of the Federal Government, *The United States Government Manual* provides comprehensive information on the agencies of the legislative, judicial, and executive branches. The *Manual* also includes information on quasiofficial agencies; international organizations in which the United States participates; and boards, commissions, and committees.

A typical agency description includes a list of principal officials, a summary statement of the agency's purpose and role in the Federal Government, a brief history of the agency, including its legislative or executive authority, a description of its programs and activities, and a "Sources of Information" section. This last section provides information on consumer activities, contracts and grants, employment, publications, and many other areas of public interest.

Contents

DECLARATION OF INDEPENDENCE 1

CONSTITUTION OF THE UNITED STATES 5

CHART: The Government of the United States 21

LEGISLATIVE BRANCH
Congress.. 25
    The Senate.. 27
    The House of Representatives.. 34
Architect of the Capitol.. 49
Congressional Budget Office 52
Government Accountability Office 56
Government Publishing Office 59
Library of Congress.. 64
    Congressional Research Service 69
United States Botanic Garden... 69

JUDICIAL BRANCH
The Supreme Court of the United States... 75
Lower Courts 78
    United States Courts of Appeals... 78
    United States Court of Appeals for the Federal Circuit.. 79
    United States District Courts.. 79
    Territorial Courts.. 80
    United States Court of International Trade.. 80
    Judicial Panel on Multidistrict Litigation... 81
Special Courts 81
    United States Court of Appeals for the Armed Forces 81
    United States Court of Appeals for Veterans Claims 82
    United States Court of Federal Claims.. 82
    United States Tax Court 83
Administrative Office of the United States Courts.. 84
Federal Judicial Center... 86
United States Sentencing Commission 89

EXECUTIVE BRANCH
The President... 95
The Vice President 95
The Executive Office of the President... 96
    White House Office 96
    Office of the Vice President 97

Council of Economic Advisers 97
Council on Environmental Quality 98
National Security Council 99
Office of Administration 100
Office of Management and Budget 101
Office of National Drug Control Policy 104
Office of Policy Development 105
    Domestic Policy Council 105
    National Economic Council 105
Office of Science and Technology Policy 105
Office of the United States Trade Representative 107

EXECUTIVE BRANCH: DEPARTMENTS

Department of Agriculture 113
Department of Commerce 135
    Bureau of Industry and Security 137
    Economic Development Administration 139
    Economics and Statistics Administration 140
    International Trade Administration 141
    Minority Business Development Agency 143
    National Oceanic and Atmospheric Administration 143
    National Telecommunications and Information Administration 147
    National Institute of Standards and Technology 148
    National Technical Information Service 149
    United States Patent and Trademark Office 150
Department of Defense 152
Department of the Air Force 159
Department of the Army 167
Department of the Navy 176
    United States Marine Corps 183
    United States Naval Academy 185
Defense Agencies 185
    Defense Advanced Research Projects Agency 185
    Defense Commissary Agency 186
    Defense Contract Audit Agency 186
    Defense Contract Management Agency 187
    Defense Finance and Accounting Service 187
    Defense Information Systems Agency 188
    Defense Intelligence Agency 188
    Defense Legal Services Agency 189
    Defense Logistics Agency 189
    Defense Security Cooperation Agency 190
    Defense Security Service 190
    Defense Threat Reduction Agency 191
    Missile Defense Agency 191
    National Geospatial-Intelligence Agency 192
    National Security Agency / Central Security Service 192
    Pentagon Force Protection Agency 193
    Joint Service Schools 193
        Defense Acquisition University 193
        National Intelligence University 194
        National Defense University 194
        Uniformed Services University of the Health Sciences 196

Department of Education......197
   Federally Aided Corporations 202
      American Printing House for the Blind......202
      Gallaudet University 202
      Howard University......203
      National Technical Institute for the Deaf / Rochester Institute of Technology......204
Department of Energy......205
   Federal Energy Regulatory Commission......213
Department of Health And Human Services 215
   Administration for Children and Families......219
   Administration for Community Living......220
   Agency for Healthcare Research and Quality 220
   Agency for Toxic Substances and Disease Registry......221
   Centers for Disease Control and Prevention......222
   Centers for Medicare and Medicaid Services......224
   Food and Drug Administration......225
   Health Resources and Services Administration 225
   Indian Health Service......226
   National Institutes of Health......227
   Substance Abuse and Mental Health Services Administration 232
Department of Homeland Security 234
Department of Housing And Urban Development......242
Department of Justice 248
   Bureaus......258
      Bureau of Alcohol, Tobacco, Firearms and Explosives......258
      Bureau of Prisons 259
      Drug Enforcement Administration 260
      Federal Bureau of Investigation 261
      International Criminal Police Organization (INTERPOL)–Washington 262
      Office of Justice Programs 262
      United States Marshals Service......263
   Offices / Boards......264
      Executive Office for Immigration Review......264
      Foreign Claims Settlement Commission of the United States......265
      Office of Community Oriented Policing Services......266
      Office on Violence Against Women......266
      United States Parole Commission 267
Department of Labor 268
   Bureau of International Labor Affairs 275
   Bureau of Labor Statistics 276
   Employee Benefits Security Administration 277
   Employment and Training Administration 278
   Mine Safety and Health Administration 280
   Occupational Safety and Health Administration 281
   Veterans' Employment and Training Service......282
   Wage and Hour Division......284
   Women's Bureau 285
Department of State......286
Department of Transportation 300
   Federal Aviation Administration......304
   Federal Highway Administration......307
   Federal Motor Carrier Safety Administration 310
   Federal Railroad Administration......312
   Federal Transit Administration......314

Maritime Administration 318
National Highway Traffic Safety Administration 319
Pipeline and Hazardous Materials Safety Administration 322
Saint Lawrence Seaway Development Corporation 324
Department of Veterans Affairs 326
Department of the Interior 333
Bureau of Indian Affairs 337
Bureau of Indian Education 341
Bureau of Land Management 342
Bureau of Ocean Energy Management 344
Bureau of Reclamation 346
Bureau of Safety and Environmental Enforcement 347
National Park Service 348
Office of Surface Mining Reclamation and Enforcement 350
United States Fish and Wildlife Service 352
United States Geological Survey 355
Department of the Treasury 357
Alcohol and Tobacco Tax and Trade Bureau 362
Bureau of Engraving and Printing 363
Bureau of the Fiscal Service 365
Internal Revenue Service 367
Office of the Comptroller of the Currency 369
United States Mint 372

EXECUTIVE BRANCH: INDEPENDENT AGENCIES AND GOVERNMENT CORPORATIONS

Administrative Conference of the United States 375
Central Intelligence Agency 379
Commodity Futures Trading Commission 381
Consumer Financial Protection Bureau 384
Consumer Product Safety Commission 388
Corporation for National and Community Service 391
Defense Nuclear Facilities Safety Board 394
Environmental Protection Agency 396
Equal Employment Opportunity Commission 400
Export-Import Bank of the United States 404
Farm Credit Administration 406
Federal Communications Commission 409
Federal Deposit Insurance Corporation 414
Federal Election Commission 418
Federal Housing Finance Agency 419
Federal Labor Relations Authority 423
Federal Mine Safety and Health Review Commission 425
Federal Maritime Commission 427
Federal Mediation and Conciliation Service 431
Federal Reserve System 435
Federal Retirement Thrift Investment Board 441
Federal Trade Commission 443
General Services Administration 446
Inter-American Foundation 453
Merit Systems Protection Board 455
National Aeronautics and Space Administration 457
National Archives and Records Administration 463

National Capital Planning Commission 471
National Credit Union Administration 474
National Foundation on the Arts and the Humanities.. 478
 National Endowment for the Arts.. 478
 National Endowment for the Humanities... 479
 Institute of Museum and Library Services... 481
National Labor Relations Board.. 484
National Mediation Board 486
National Railroad Passenger Corporation (AMTRAK) 488
National Science Foundation... 490
National Transportation Safety Board.. 496
Nuclear Regulatory Commission 500
Occupational Safety and Health Review Commission 503
Office of Government Ethics... 504
Office of Personnel Management... 506
Office of the Director of National Intelligence 512
Overseas Private Investment Corporation.. 514
Peace Corps... 515
Pension Benefit Guaranty Corporation.. 518
Postal Regulatory Commission.. 522
Railroad Retirement Board.. 523
Securities and Exchange Commission 525
Selective Service System.. 529
Small Business Administration 533
Social Security Administration 539
Surface Transportation Board 542
Tennessee Valley Authority 545
Trade and Development Agency 548
United States Agency for Global Media 551
United States African Development Foundation.. 555
United States Agency for International Development... 556
United States Commission on Civil Rights 561
United States International Trade Commission 562
United States Office of Special Counsel... 567
United States Postal Service... 570

QUASI-OFFICIAL AGENCIES

Legal Services Corporation 575
Smithsonian Institution 578
 John F. Kennedy Center for the Performing Arts... 587
 National Gallery of Art 589
 Woodrow Wilson International Center for Scholars 591
State Justice Institute 593
United States Holocaust Memorial Museum... 594
United States Institute of Peace... 600

INTERNATIONAL ORGANIZATIONS

African Development Bank... 603
Asian Development Bank 604
European Bank for Reconstruction and Development.. 605
Inter-American Defense Board.. 607
Inter-American Development Bank... 607
Inter-American Investment Corporation 608

International Monetary Fund 609
International Organization for Migration 612
Organization of American States 615
United Nations 617
World Bank Group 621
    International Bank for Reconstruction and Development 624
    International Centre for Settlement of Investment Disputes 624
    International Development Association 625
    International Finance Corporation 626
    Multilateral Investment Guarantee Agency 628

Declaration of Independence

Action of Second Continental Congress, July 4, 1776

IN CONGRESS, JULY 4, 1776.

THE UNANIMOUS DECLARATION of the thirteen united STATES OF AMERICA,

WHEN in the Course of human events, it becomes necessary for one people to dissolve the political bands which have connected them with another, and to assume among the powers of the earth, the separate and equal station to which the Laws of Nature and of Nature's God entitle them, a decent respect to the opinions of mankind requires that they should declare the causes which impel them to the separation.

We hold these truths to be self-evident, that all men are created equal, that they are endowed by their Creator with certain unalienable Rights, that among these are Life, Liberty and the pursuit of Happiness.—That to secure these rights, Governments are instituted among Men, deriving their just powers from the consent of the governed,—That whenever any Form of Government becomes destructive of these ends, it is the Right of the People to alter or to abolish it, and to institute new Government, laying its foundation on such principles and organizing its powers in such form, as to them shall seem most likely to effect their Safety and Happiness. Prudence, indeed, will dictate that Governments long established should not be changed for light and transient causes; and accordingly all experience hath shewn, that mankind are more disposed to suffer, while evils are sufferable, than to right themselves by abolishing the forms to which they are accustomed. But when a long train of abuses and usurpations, pursuing invariably the same Object evinces a design to reduce them under absolute Despotism, it is their right, it is their duty, to throw off such Government, and to provide new Guards for their future security.—Such has been the patient sufferance of these Colonies; and such is now the necessity which constrains them to alter their former Systems of Government. The history of the present King of Great Britain is a history of repeated injuries and usurpations, all having in direct object the establishment of an absolute Tyranny over these States. To prove this, let Facts be submitted to a candid world.

He has refused his Assent to Laws, the most wholesome and necessary for the public good.

He has forbidden his Governors to pass Laws of immediate and pressing importance, unless suspended in their operation till his Assent should be obtained; and when so suspended, he has utterly neglected to attend to them.

He has refused to pass other Laws for the accommodation of large districts of people, unless those people would relinquish the right of Representation in the Legislature, a right inestimable to them and formidable to tyrants only.

He has called together legislative bodies at places unusual, uncomfortable, and distant from the depository of their public Records, for the sole purpose of fatiguing them into compliance with his measures.

He has dissolved Representative Houses repeatedly, for opposing with manly firmness his invasions on the rights of the people.

1

He has refused for a long time, after such dissolutions, to cause others to be elected; whereby the Legislative powers, incapable of Annihilation, have returned to the People at large for their exercise; the State remaining in the mean time exposed to all the dangers of invasion from without, and convulsions within.

He has endeavoured to prevent the population of these States; for that purpose obstructing the Laws for Naturalization of Foreigners; refusing to pass others to encourage their migrations hither, and raising the conditions of new Appropriations of Lands.

He has obstructed the Administration of Justice, by refusing his Assent to Laws for establishing Judiciary powers.

He has made Judges dependent on his Will alone, for the tenure of their offices, and the amount and payment of their salaries.

He has erected a multitude of New Offices, and sent hither swarms of Officers to harrass our people, and eat out their substance.

He has kept among us, in times of peace, Standing Armies without the Consent of our legislatures.

He has affected to render the Military independent of and superior to the Civil power.

He has combined with others to subject us to a jurisdiction foreign to our constitution, and unacknowledged by our laws; giving his Assent to their Acts of pretended Legislation:

For Quartering large bodies of armed troops among us:

For protecting them, by a mock Trial, from punishment for any Murders which they should commit on the Inhabitants of these States:

For cutting off our Trade with all parts of the world:

For imposing Taxes on us without our Consent:

For depriving us in many cases, of the benefits of Trial by Jury:

For transporting us beyond Seas to be tried for pretended offences

For abolishing the free System of English Laws in a neighbouring Province, establishing therein an Arbitrary government, and enlarging its Boundaries so as to render it at once an example and fit instrument for introducing the same absolute rule into these Colonies:

For taking away our Charters, abolishing our most valuable Laws, and altering fundamentally the Forms of our Governments:

For suspending our own Legislatures, and declaring themselves invested with power to legislate for us in all cases whatsoever.

He has abdicated Government here, by declaring us out of his Protection and waging War against us.

He has plundered our seas, ravaged our Coasts, burnt our towns, and destroyed the lives of our people.

He is at this time transporting large Armies of foreign Mercenaries to compleat the works of death, desolation and tyranny, already begun with circumstances of Cruelty & perfidy scarcely paralleled in the most barbarous ages, and totally unworthy the Head of a civilized nation.

He has constrained our fellow Citizens taken Captive on the high Seas to bear Arms against their Country, to become the executioners of their friends and Brethren, or to fall themselves by their Hands.

He has excited domestic insurrections amongst us, and has endeavoured to bring on the inhabitants of our frontiers, the merciless Indian Savages, whose known rule of warfare, is an undistinguished destruction of all ages, sexes and conditions.

In every stage of these Oppressions We have Petitioned for Redress in the most humble terms: Our repeated Petitions have been answered only by repeated injury. A Prince whose character is thus marked by every act which may define a Tyrant, is unfit to be the ruler of a free people.

Nor have We been wanting in attentions to our Brittish brethren. We have warned them from time to time of attempts by their legislature to extend an unwarrantable jurisdiction over us. We have reminded them of the circumstances of our emigration and settlement here. We have appealed to their native justice and magnanimity, and we have conjured them by the ties of our common kindred to disavow these usurpations, which, would inevitably interrupt our connections and correspondence. They too have been deaf to the voice of justice and of consanguinity. We must, therefore, acquiesce in the necessity, which denounces our Separation, and hold them, as we hold the rest of mankind, Enemies in War, in Peace Friends.

WE, THEREFORE, THE REPRESENTATIVES OF THE UNITED STATES OF AMERICA, in General Congress, Assembled, appealing to the Supreme Judge of the world for the rectitude of our intentions, do, in the Name, and by Authority of the good People of these Colonies, solemnly publish and declare, That these United Colonies are, and of Right ought to be FREE AND INDEPENDENT STATES; that they are Absolved from all Allegiance to the British Crown, and that all political connection between them and the State of Great Britain, is and ought to be totally dissolved; and that as Free and Independent States, they have full Power to levy War, conclude Peace, contract Alliances, establish Commerce, and to do all other Acts and Things which Independent States may of right do. And for the support of this Declaration, with a firm reliance on the protection of divine Providence, we mutually pledge to each other our Lives, our Fortunes and our sacred Honor.

The 56 signatures on the Declaration appear in the positions indicated:

Column 1

Georgia:
Button Gwinnett
Lyman Hall
George Walton

Column 2

North Carolina:
William Hooper
Joseph Hewes
John Penn
South Carolina:
Edward Rutledge
Thomas Heyward, Jr.
Thomas Lynch, Jr.
Arthur Middleton

Column 3

Massachusetts:
John Hancock
Maryland:
Samuel Chase
William Paca
Thomas Stone
Charles Carroll of
Carrollton
Virginia:
George Wythe
Richard Henry Lee
Thomas Jefferson
Benjamin Harrison
Thomas Nelson, Jr.
Francis Lightfoot Lee
Carter Braxton

Column 4

Pennsylvania:
Robert Morris
Benjamin Rush
Benjamin Franklin
John Morton
George Clymer
James Smith
George Taylor
James Wilson
George Ross
Delaware:
Caesar Rodney
George Read
Thomas McKean

Column 5

New York:
William Floyd
Philip Livingston
Francis Lewis
Lewis Morris
New Jersey:
Richard Stockton
John Witherspoon
Francis Hopkinson
John Hart
Abraham Clark

Column 6

New Hampshire:
Josiah Bartlett
William Whipple
Massachusetts:
Samuel Adams
John Adams
Robert Treat Paine
Elbridge Gerry
Rhode Island:
Stephen Hopkins
William Ellery
Connecticut:
Roger Sherman
Samuel Huntington
William Williams
Oliver Wolcott
New Hampshire:
Matthew Thornton

For more information on the Declaration of Independence and the Charters of Freedom, see http://archives.gov/exhibits/charters/declaration.html

Constitution of the United States

Note: The following text is a transcription of the Constitution in its original form. Items that are hyperlinked/underlined have since been amended or superseded.

Preamble

WE THE PEOPLE of the United States, in order to form a more perfect union, establish justice, insure domestic tranquility, provide for the common defense, promote the general welfare, and secure the blessings of liberty to ourselves and our posterity, do ordain and establish this Constitution for the United States of America.

Article I

Section 1. All legislative powers herein granted shall be vested in a Congress of the United States, which shall consist of a Senate and House of Representatives.

Section 2. The House of Representatives shall be composed of members chosen every second year by the people of the several states, and the electors in each state shall have the qualifications requisite for electors of the most numerous branch of the state legislature.

No person shall be a Representative who shall not have attained to the age of twenty five years, and been seven years a citizen of the United States, and who shall not, when elected, be an inhabitant of that state in which he shall be chosen.

Representatives and direct taxes shall be apportioned among the several states which may be included within this union, according to their respective numbers, which shall be determined by adding to the whole number of free persons, including those bound to service for a term of years, and excluding Indians not taxed, three fifths of all other Persons. The actual Enumeration shall be made within three years after the first meeting of the Congress of the United States, and within every subsequent term of ten years, in such manner as they shall by law direct. The number of Representatives shall not exceed one for every thirty thousand, but each state shall have at least one Representative; and until such enumeration shall be made, the state of New Hampshire shall be entitled to chuse three, Massachusetts eight, Rhode Island and Providence Plantations one, Connecticut five, New York six, New Jersey four, Pennsylvania eight, Delaware one, Maryland six, Virginia ten, North Carolina five, South Carolina five, and Georgia three.

When vacancies happen in the Representation from any state, the executive authority thereof shall issue writs of election to fill such vacancies.

The House of Representatives shall choose their speaker and other officers; and shall have the sole power of impeachment.

Section 3. The Senate of the United States shall be composed of two Senators from each state, chosen by the legislature thereof, for six years; and each Senator shall have one vote.

Immediately after they shall be assembled in consequence of the first election, they shall be divided as equally as may be into three classes. The seats of the Senators of the first class shall be vacated at the expiration of the second year, of the second class at the expiration of the fourth year, and the third class at the expiration of the sixth year, so that one third may be chosen every second year; and if vacancies happen by resignation, or otherwise, during the recess of the legislature of any state, the executive thereof may make temporary appointments until the next meeting of the legislature, which shall then fill such vacancies.

No person shall be a Senator who shall not have attained to the age of thirty years, and been nine years a citizen of the United States and who shall not, when elected, be an inhabitant of that state for which he shall be chosen.

The Vice President of the United States shall be President of the Senate, but shall have no vote, unless they be equally divided.

The Senate shall choose their other officers, and also a President pro tempore, in the absence of the Vice President, or when he shall exercise the office of President of the United States.

The Senate shall have the sole power to try all impeachments. When sitting for that purpose, they shall be on oath or affirmation. When the President of the United States is tried, the Chief Justice shall preside: And no person shall be convicted without the concurrence of two thirds of the members present.

Judgment in cases of impeachment shall not extend further than to removal from office, and disqualification to hold and enjoy any office of honor, trust or profit under the United States: but the party convicted shall nevertheless be liable and subject to indictment, trial, judgment and punishment, according to law.

Section 4. The times, places and manner of holding elections for Senators and Representatives, shall be prescribed in each state by the legislature thereof; but the Congress may at any time by law make or alter such regulations, except as to the places of choosing Senators.

The Congress shall assemble at least once in every year, and such meeting shall be on the first Monday in December, unless they shall by law appoint a different day.

Section 5. Each House shall be the judge of the elections, returns and qualifications of its own members, and a majority of each shall constitute a quorum to do business; but a smaller number may adjourn from day to day, and may be authorized to compel the attendance of absent members, in such manner, and under such penalties as each House may provide.

Each House may determine the rules of its proceedings, punish its members for disorderly behavior, and, with the concurrence of two thirds, expel a member.

Each House shall keep a journal of its proceedings, and from time to time publish the same, excepting such parts as may in their judgment require secrecy; and the yeas and nays of the members of either House on any question shall, at the desire of one fifth of those present, be entered on the journal.

Neither House, during the session of Congress, shall, without the consent of the other, adjourn for more than three days, nor to any other place than that in which the two Houses shall be sitting.

Section 6. The Senators and Representatives shall receive a compensation for their services, to be ascertained by law, and paid out of the treasury of the United States. They shall in all cases, except treason, felony and breach of the peace, be privileged from arrest during their attendance at the session of their respective Houses, and in going to and returning from the same; and for any speech or debate in either House, they shall not be questioned in any other place.

No Senator or Representative shall, during the time for which he was elected, be appointed to any civil office under the authority of the United States, which shall have been created, or the emoluments whereof shall have been increased during such time: and no person holding any office under the United States, shall be a member of either House during his continuance in office.

Section 7. All bills for raising revenue shall originate in the House of Representatives; but the Senate may propose or concur with amendments as on other Bills.

Every bill which shall have passed the House of Representatives and the Senate, shall, before it become a law, be presented to the President of the United States; if he approve he shall sign it, but if not he shall return it, with his objections to that House in which it shall have originated, who shall enter the objections at large on their journal, and proceed to reconsider it. If after such reconsideration two thirds of that House shall agree to pass the bill, it shall be sent, together with the objections, to the other House, by which it shall likewise be reconsidered, and if approved by two thirds of that House, it shall become a law. But in all such cases the votes of both Houses shall be determined by yeas and nays, and the names of the persons voting for and against the bill shall be entered on the journal of each House respectively. If any bill shall not be returned by the President within ten days (Sundays excepted) after it shall have been presented to him, the same shall be a law, in like manner as if he had signed it, unless the Congress by their adjournment prevent its return, in which case it shall not be a law.

Every order, resolution, or vote to which the concurrence of the Senate and House of Representatives may be necessary (except on a question of adjournment) shall be presented to the President of the United States; and before the same shall take effect, shall be approved by him, or being disapproved by him, shall be repassed by two thirds of the Senate and House of Representatives, according to the rules and limitations prescribed in the case of a bill.

Section 8. The Congress shall have power to lay and collect taxes, duties, imposts and excises, to pay the debts and provide for the common defense and general welfare of the United States; but all duties, imposts and excises shall be uniform throughout the United States;

To borrow money on the credit of the United States;

To regulate commerce with foreign nations, and among the several states, and with the Indian tribes;

To establish a uniform rule of naturalization, and uniform laws on the subject of bankruptcies throughout the United States;

To coin money, regulate the value thereof, and of foreign coin, and fix the standard of weights and measures;

To provide for the punishment of counterfeiting the securities and current coin of the United States;

To establish post offices and post roads;

To promote the progress of science and useful arts, by securing for limited times to authors and inventors the exclusive right to their respective writings and discoveries;

To constitute tribunals inferior to the Supreme Court;

To define and punish piracies and felonies committed on the high seas, and offenses against the law of nations;

To declare war, grant letters of marque and reprisal, and make rules concerning captures on land and water;

To raise and support armies, but no appropriation of money to that use shall be for a longer term than two years;

To provide and maintain a navy;

To make rules for the government and regulation of the land and naval forces;

To provide for calling forth the militia to execute the laws of the union, suppress insurrections and repel invasions;

To provide for organizing, arming, and disciplining, the militia, and for governing such part of them as may be employed in the service of the United States, reserving to the states respectively, the appointment of the officers, and the authority of training the militia according to the discipline prescribed by Congress;

To exercise exclusive legislation in all cases whatsoever, over such District (not exceeding ten miles square) as may, by cession of particular states, and the acceptance of Congress, become the seat of the government of the United States, and to exercise like authority over all places purchased by the consent of the legislature of the state in which the same shall be, for the erection of forts, magazines, arsenals, dockyards, and other needful buildings;—And

To make all laws which shall be necessary and proper for carrying into execution the foregoing powers, and all other powers vested by this Constitution in the government of the United States, or in any department or officer thereof.

Section 9. The migration or importation of such persons as any of the states now existing shall think proper to admit, shall not be prohibited by the Congress prior to the year one thousand eight hundred and eight, but a tax or duty may be imposed on such importation, not exceeding ten dollars for each person.

The privilege of the writ of habeas corpus shall not be suspended, unless when in cases of rebellion or invasion the public safety may require it.

No bill of attainder or ex post facto Law shall be passed.

No capitation, or other direct, tax shall be laid, unless in proportion to the census or enumeration herein before directed to be taken.

No tax or duty shall be laid on articles exported from any state.

No preference shall be given by any regulation of commerce or revenue to the ports of one state over those of another: nor shall vessels bound to, or from, one state, be obliged to enter, clear or pay duties in another.

No money shall be drawn from the treasury, but in consequence of appropriations made by law; and a regular statement and account of receipts and expenditures of all public money shall be published from time to time.

No title of nobility shall be granted by the United States: and no person holding any office of profit or trust under them, shall, without the consent of the Congress, accept of any present, emolument, office, or title, of any kind whatever, from any king, prince, or foreign state.

Section 10. No state shall enter into any treaty, alliance, or confederation; grant letters of marque and reprisal; coin money; emit bills of credit; make anything but gold and silver coin a tender in payment of debts; pass any bill of attainder, ex post facto law, or law impairing the obligation of contracts, or grant any title of nobility.

No state shall, without the consent of the Congress, lay any imposts or duties on imports or exports, except what may be absolutely necessary for executing it's inspection laws: and the net produce of all duties and imposts, laid by any state on imports or exports, shall be for the use of the treasury of the United States; and all such laws shall be subject to the revision and control of the Congress.

No state shall, without the consent of Congress, lay any duty of tonnage, keep troops, or ships of war in time of peace, enter into any agreement or compact with another state, or with a foreign power, or engage in war, unless actually invaded, or in such imminent danger as will not admit of delay.

Article II

Section 1. The executive power shall be vested in a President of the United States of America. He shall hold his office during the term of four years, and, together with the Vice President, chosen for the same term, be elected, as follows:

Each state shall appoint, in such manner as the Legislature thereof may direct, a number of electors, equal to the whole number of Senators and Representatives to which the State may be entitled in the Congress: but no Senator or Representative, or person holding an office of trust or profit under the United States, shall be appointed an elector.

The electors shall meet in their respective states, and vote by ballot for two persons, of whom one at least shall not be an inhabitant of the same state with themselves. And they shall make a list of all the persons voted for, and of the number of votes for each; which list they shall sign and certify, and transmit sealed to the seat of the government of the United States, directed to the President of the Senate. The President of the Senate shall, in the presence of the Senate and House of Representatives, open all the certificates, and the votes shall then be counted. The person having the greatest number of votes shall be the President, if such number be a majority of the whole number of electors appointed; and if there be more than one who have such majority, and have an equal number of votes, then the House of Representatives shall immediately choose by ballot one of them for President; and if no person have a majority, then from the five highest on the list the said House shall in like manner choose the President. But in choosing the President, the votes shall be taken by States, the representation from each state having one vote; A quorum for this purpose shall consist of a member or members from two thirds of the states, and a majority of all the states shall be necessary to a choice. In every case, after the choice of the President, the person having the greatest number of votes of the electors shall be the Vice President. But if there should remain two or more who have equal votes, the Senate shall choose from them by ballot the Vice President.

The Congress may determine the time of choosing the electors, and the day on which they shall give their votes; which day shall be the same throughout the United States.

No person except a natural born citizen, or a citizen of the United States, at the time of the adoption of this Constitution, shall be eligible to the office of President; neither shall any person be eligible to that office who shall not have attained to the age of thirty five years, and been fourteen Years a resident within the United States.

In case of the removal of the President from office, or of his death, resignation, or inability to discharge the powers and duties of the said office, the same shall devolve on the Vice President, and the Congress may by law provide for the case of removal, death, resignation or inability, both of the President and Vice President, declaring what officer shall then act as President, and such officer shall act accordingly, until the disability be removed, or a President shall be elected.

The President shall, at stated times, receive for his services, a compensation, which shall neither be increased nor diminished during the period for which he shall have been elected, and he shall not receive within that period any other emolument from the United States, or any of them.

Before he enter on the execution of his office, he shall take the following oath or affirmation:—"I do solemnly swear (or affirm) that I will faithfully execute the office of President of the United States, and will to the best of my ability, preserve, protect and defend the Constitution of the United States."

Section 2. The President shall be commander in chief of the Army and Navy of the United States, and of the militia of the several states, when called into the actual service of the United States; he may require the opinion, in writing, of the principal officer in each of the executive departments, upon any subject relating to the duties of their respective offices, and he shall have power to grant reprieves and pardons for offenses against the United States, except in cases of impeachment.

He shall have power, by and with the advice and consent of the Senate, to make treaties, provided two thirds of the Senators present concur; and he shall nominate, and by and with the advice and consent of the Senate, shall appoint ambassadors, other public ministers and consuls, judges of the Supreme Court, and all other officers of the United States, whose appointments are not herein otherwise provided for, and which shall be established by law: but the Congress may by law vest the appointment of such inferior officers, as they think proper, in the President alone, in the courts of law, or in the heads of departments.

The President shall have power to fill up all vacancies that may happen during the recess of the Senate, by granting commissions which shall expire at the end of their next session.

Section 3. He shall from time to time give to the Congress information of the state of the union, and recommend to their consideration such measures as he shall judge necessary and expedient; he may, on extraordinary occasions, convene both Houses, or either of them, and in case of disagreement between them, with respect to the time of adjournment, he may adjourn them to such time as he shall think proper; he shall receive ambassadors and other public ministers; he shall take care that the laws be faithfully executed, and shall commission all the officers of the United States.

Section 4. The President, Vice President and all civil officers of the United States, shall be removed from office on impeachment for, and conviction of, treason, bribery, or other high crimes and misdemeanors.

Article III

Section 1. The judicial power of the United States, shall be vested in one Supreme Court, and in such inferior courts as the Congress may from time to time ordain and establish. The judges, both of the supreme and inferior courts, shall hold their offices during good behaviour, and shall, at stated times, receive for their services, a compensation, which shall not be diminished during their continuance in office.

Section 2. The judicial power shall extend to all cases, in law and equity, arising under this Constitution, the laws of the United States, and treaties made, or which shall be made, under their authority;—to all cases affecting ambassadors, other public ministers and consuls;—to all cases of admiralty and maritime jurisdiction;—to controversies to which the United States shall be a party;—to controversies between two or more states;—between a state and citizens of another state;—between citizens of different states;—between citizens of the same state claiming lands under grants of different states, and between a state, or the citizens thereof, and foreign states, citizens or subjects.

In all cases affecting ambassadors, other public ministers and consuls, and those in which a state shall be party, the Supreme Court shall have original jurisdiction. In all the other cases before mentioned, the Supreme Court shall have appellate jurisdiction, both as to law and fact, with such exceptions, and under such regulations as the Congress shall make.

The trial of all crimes, except in cases of impeachment, shall be by jury; and such trial shall be held in the state where the said crimes shall have been committed; but when not committed within any state, the trial shall be at such place or places as the Congress may by law have directed.

Section 3. Treason against the United States, shall consist only in levying war against them, or in adhering to their enemies, giving them aid and comfort. No person shall be convicted of treason unless on the testimony of two witnesses to the same overt act, or on confession in open court.

The Congress shall have power to declare the punishment of treason, but no attainder of treason shall work corruption of blood, or forfeiture except during the life of the person attainted.

Article IV

Section 1. Full faith and credit shall be given in each state to the public acts, records, and judicial proceedings of every other state. And the Congress may by general laws prescribe the manner in which such acts, records, and proceedings shall be proved, and the effect thereof.

Section 2. The citizens of each state shall be entitled to all privileges and immunities of citizens in the several states.

A person charged in any state with treason, felony, or other crime, who shall flee from justice, and be found in another state, shall on demand of the executive authority of the state from which he fled, be delivered up, to be removed to the state having jurisdiction of the crime.

No person held to service or labor in one state, under the laws thereof, escaping into another, shall, in consequence of any law or regulation therein, be discharged from such service or labor, but shall be delivered up on claim of the party to whom such service or labor may be due.

Section 3. New states may be admitted by the Congress into this union; but no new states shall be formed or erected within the jurisdiction of any other state; nor any state be formed by the junction of two or more states, or parts of states, without the consent of the legislatures of the states concerned as well as of the Congress.

The Congress shall have power to dispose of and make all needful rules and regulations respecting the territory or other property belonging to the United States; and nothing in this Constitution shall be so construed as to prejudice any claims of the United States, or of any particular state.

Section 4. The United States shall guarantee to every state in this union a republican form of government, and shall protect each of them against invasion; and on application of the legislature, or of the executive (when the legislature cannot be convened) against domestic violence.

Article V

The Congress, whenever two thirds of both houses shall deem it necessary, shall propose amendments to this Constitution, or, on the application of the legislatures of two thirds of the several states, shall call a convention for proposing amendments, which, in either case, shall be valid to all intents and purposes, as part of this Constitution, when ratified by the legislatures of three fourths of the several states, or by conventions in three fourths thereof, as the one or the other mode of ratification may be proposed by the Congress; provided that no amendment which may be made prior to the year one thousand eight hundred and eight shall in any manner affect the first and fourth clauses in the ninth section of the first article; and that no state, without its consent, shall be deprived of its equal suffrage in the Senate.

Article VI

All debts contracted and engagements entered into, before the adoption of this Constitution, shall be as valid against the United States under this Constitution, as under the Confederation.

This Constitution, and the laws of the United States which shall be made in pursuance thereof; and all treaties made, or which shall be made, under the authority of the United States, shall be the supreme law of the land; and the judges in every state shall be bound thereby, anything in the Constitution or laws of any State to the contrary notwithstanding.

The Senators and Representatives before mentioned, and the members of the several state legislatures, and all executive and judicial officers, both of the United States and of the several states, shall be bound by oath or affirmation, to support this Constitution; but no religious test shall ever be required as a qualification to any office or public trust under the United States.

Article VII

The ratification of the conventions of nine states, shall be sufficient for the establishment of this Constitution between the states so ratifying the same.

Signers

Done in convention by the unanimous consent of the states present the seventeenth day of September in the year of our Lord one thousand seven hundred and eighty seven and of the independence of the United States of America the twelfth. *In witness whereof We have hereunto subscribed our Names,*

G. Washington—Presidt.
and deputy from Virginia

New Hampshire	John Langdon
	Nicholas Gilman
Massachusetts	Nathaniel Gorham
	Rufus King
Connecticut	Wm: Saml. Johnson
	Roger Sherman
New York	Alexander Hamilton
New Jersey	Wil: Livingston
	David Brearly
	Wm. Paterson
	Jona: Dayton
Pennsylvania	B. Franklin
	Thomas Mifflin
	Robt. Morris
	Geo. Clymer
	Thos. FitzSimons
	Jared Ingersoll
	James Wilson
	Gouv Morris
Delaware	Geo: Read
	Gunning Bedford jun
	John Dickinson
	Richard Bassett
	Jaco: Broom
Maryland	James McHenry
	Dan of St Thos. Jenifer
	Danl Carroll
Virginia	John Blair—
	James Madison Jr.

North Carolina	Wm. Blount
	Richd. Dobbs Spaight
	Hu Williamson
South Carolina	J. Rutledge
	Charles Cotesworth Pinckney
	Charles Pinckney
	Pierce Butler
Georgia	William Few
	Abr Baldwin

Amendments

Note: The first ten Amendments were ratified December 15, 1791, and form what is known as the Bill of Rights.

Amendment 1

Congress shall make no law respecting an establishment of religion, or prohibiting the free exercise thereof; or abridging the freedom of speech, or of the press; or the right of the people peaceably to assemble, and to petition the government for a redress of grievances.

Amendment 2

A well regulated militia, being necessary to the security of a free state, the right of the people to keep and bear arms, shall not be infringed.

Amendment 3

No soldier shall, in time of peace be quartered in any house, without the consent of the owner, nor in time of war, but in a manner to be prescribed by law.

Amendment 4

The right of the people to be secure in their persons, houses, papers, and effects, against unreasonable searches and seizures, shall not be violated, and no warrants shall issue, but upon probable cause, supported by oath or affirmation, and particularly describing the place to be searched, and the persons or things to be seized.

Amendment 5

No person shall be held to answer for a capital, or otherwise infamous crime, unless on a presentment or indictment of a grand jury, except in cases arising in the land or naval forces, or in the militia, when in actual service in time of war or public danger; nor shall any person be subject for the same offense to be twice put in jeopardy of life or limb; nor shall be compelled in any criminal case to be a witness against himself, nor be deprived of life, liberty, or property, without due process of law; nor shall private property be taken for public use, without just compensation.

Amendment 6

In all criminal prosecutions, the accused shall enjoy the right to a speedy and public trial, by an impartial jury of the state and district wherein the crime shall have been committed, which district shall have been previously ascertained by law, and to be informed of the nature and cause of the accusation; to be confronted with the witnesses against him; to have compulsory process for obtaining witnesses in his favor, and to have the assistance of counsel for his defense.

Amendment 7

In suits at common law, where the value in controversy shall exceed twenty dollars, the right of trial by jury shall be preserved, and no fact tried by a jury, shall be otherwise reexamined in any court of the United States, than according to the rules of the common law.

Amendment 8

Excessive bail shall not be required, nor excessive fines imposed, nor cruel and unusual punishments inflicted.

Amendment 9

The enumeration in the Constitution, of certain rights, shall not be construed to deny or disparage others retained by the people.

Amendment 10

The powers not delegated to the United States by the Constitution, nor prohibited by it to the states, are reserved to the states respectively, or to the people.

Amendment 11

(Ratified February 7, 1795)

The judicial power of the United States shall not be construed to extend to any suit in law or equity, commenced or prosecuted against one of the United States by citizens of another state, or by citizens or subjects of any foreign state.

Amendment 12

(Ratified July 27, 1804)

The electors shall meet in their respective states and vote by ballot for President and Vice-President, one of whom, at least, shall not be an inhabitant of the same state with themselves; they shall name in their ballots the person voted for as President, and in distinct ballots the person voted for as Vice-President, and they shall make distinct lists of all persons voted for as President, and of all persons voted for as Vice-President, and of the number of votes for each, which lists they shall sign and certify, and transmit sealed to the seat of the government of the United States, directed to the President of the Senate;—The President of the Senate shall, in the presence of the Senate and House of Representatives, open all the certificates and the votes shall then be counted;—the person having the greatest number of votes for President, shall be the President, if such number be a majority of the whole number of electors appointed; and if no person have such majority, then from the persons having the highest numbers not exceeding three on the list of those voted for as President, the House of Representatives shall choose immediately, by ballot, the President. But in choosing the President, the votes shall be taken by states, the representation from each state having one vote; a quorum for this purpose shall consist of a member or members from two-thirds of the states, and a majority of all the states shall be necessary to a choice. And if the House of Representatives shall not choose a President whenever the right of choice shall devolve upon them, before the fourth day of March next following, then the Vice-President shall act as President, as in the case of the death or other constitutional disability of the President. The person having the greatest number of votes as Vice-President, shall be the Vice-President, if such number be a majority of the whole number of electors appointed, and if no person have a majority, then from the two highest numbers on the list, the Senate shall choose the Vice-President; a quorum for the purpose shall consist of two-thirds of the whole number of Senators, and a majority of the whole number shall be necessary to a choice. But no person constitutionally ineligible to the office of President shall be eligible to that of Vice-President of the United States.

Amendment 13

(Ratified December 6, 1865)

Section 1. Neither slavery nor involuntary servitude, except as a punishment for crime whereof the party shall have been duly convicted, shall exist within the United States, or any place subject to their jurisdiction.

Section 2. Congress shall have power to enforce this article by appropriate legislation.

Amendment 14

(Ratified July 9, 1868)

Section 1. All persons born or naturalized in the United States, and subject to the jurisdiction thereof, are citizens of the United States and of the state wherein they reside. No state shall make or enforce any law which shall abridge the privileges or immunities of citizens of the United States; nor shall any state deprive any person of life, liberty, or property, without due process of law; nor deny to any person within its jurisdiction the equal protection of the laws.

Section 2. Representatives shall be apportioned among the several states according to their respective numbers, counting the whole number of persons in each state, excluding Indians not taxed. But when the right to vote at any election for the choice of electors for President and Vice President of the United States, Representatives in Congress, the executive and judicial officers of a state, or the members of the legislature thereof, is denied to any of the male inhabitants of such state, being twenty-one years of age, and citizens of the United States, or in any way abridged, except for participation in rebellion, or other crime, the basis of representation therein shall be reduced in the proportion which the number of such male citizens shall bear to the whole number of male citizens twenty-one years of age in such state.

Section 3. No person shall be a Senator or Representative in Congress, or elector of President and Vice President, or hold any office, civil or military, under the United States, or under any state, who, having previously taken an oath, as a member of Congress, or as an officer of the United States, or as a member of any state legislature, or as an executive or judicial officer of any state, to support the Constitution of the United States, shall have engaged in insurrection or rebellion against the same, or given aid or comfort to the enemies thereof. But Congress may by a vote of two-thirds of each House, remove such disability.

Section 4. The validity of the public debt of the United States, authorized by law, including debts incurred for payment of pensions and bounties for services in suppressing insurrection or rebellion, shall not be questioned. But neither the United States nor any state shall assume or pay any debt or obligation incurred in aid of insurrection or rebellion against the United States, or any claim for the loss or emancipation of any slave; but all such debts, obligations and claims shall be held illegal and void.

Section 5. The Congress shall have power to enforce, by appropriate legislation, the provisions of this article.

Amendment 15

(Ratified February 3, 1870)

Section 1. The right of citizens of the United States to vote shall not be denied or abridged by the United States or by any state on account of race, color, or previous condition of servitude.

Section 2. The Congress shall have power to enforce this article by appropriate legislation.

Amendment 16

(Ratified February 3, 1913)

The Congress shall have power to lay and collect taxes on incomes, from whatever source derived, without apportionment among the several states, and without regard to any census or enumeration.

Amendment 17

(Ratified April 8, 1913)

The Senate of the United States shall be composed of two Senators from each state, elected by the people thereof, for six years; and each Senator shall have one vote. The electors in each state shall have the qualifications requisite for electors of the most numerous branch of the state legislatures.

When vacancies happen in the representation of any state in the Senate, the executive authority of such state shall issue writs of election to fill such vacancies: Provided, that the legislature of any state may empower the executive thereof to make temporary appointments until the people fill the vacancies by election as the legislature may direct.

This amendment shall not be so construed as to affect the election or term of any Senator chosen before it becomes valid as part of the Constitution.

Amendment 18

(Ratified January 16, 1919. Repealed December 5, 1933 by Amendment 21)

Section 1. After one year from the ratification of this article the manufacture, sale, or transportation of intoxicating liquors within, the importation thereof into, or the exportation thereof from the United States and all territory subject to the jurisdiction thereof for beverage purposes is hereby prohibited.

Section 2. The Congress and the several states shall have concurrent power to enforce this article by appropriate legislation.

Section 3. This article shall be inoperative unless it shall have been ratified as an amendment to the Constitution by the legislatures of the several states, as provided in the Constitution, within seven years from the date of the submission hereof to the states by the Congress.

Amendment 19

(Ratified August 18, 1920)

The right of citizens of the United States to vote shall not be denied or abridged by the United States or by any state on account of sex.

Congress shall have power to enforce this article by appropriate legislation.

Amendment 20

(Ratified January 23, 1933)

Section 1. The terms of the President and Vice President shall end at noon on the 20th day of January, and the terms of Senators and Representatives at noon on the 3d day of January, of the years in which such terms would have ended if this article had not been ratified; and the terms of their successors shall then begin.

Section 2. The Congress shall assemble at least once in every year, and such meeting shall begin at noon on the 3d day of January, unless they shall by law appoint a different day.

Section 3. If, at the time fixed for the beginning of the term of the President, the President elect shall have died, the Vice President elect shall become President. If a President shall not have been chosen before the time fixed for the beginning of his term, or if the President elect shall have failed to qualify, then the Vice President elect shall act as President until a President shall have qualified; and the Congress may by law provide for the case wherein neither a President elect nor a Vice President elect shall have qualified, declaring who shall then act as President, or the manner in which one who is to act shall be selected, and such person shall act accordingly until a President or Vice President shall have qualified.

Section 4. The Congress may by law provide for the case of the death of any of the persons from whom the House of Representatives may choose a President whenever the right of choice shall have devolved upon them, and for the case of the death of any of the persons from whom the Senate may choose a Vice President whenever the right of choice shall have devolved upon them.

Section 5. Sections 1 and 2 shall take effect on the 15th day of October following the ratification of this article.

Section 6. This article shall be inoperative unless it shall have been ratified as an amendment to the Constitution by the legislatures of three-fourths of the several states within seven years from the date of its submission.

Amendment 21

(Ratified December 5, 1933)

Section 1. The eighteenth article of amendment to the Constitution of the United States is hereby repealed.

Section 2. The transportation or importation into any state, territory, or possession of the United States for delivery or use therein of intoxicating liquors, in violation of the laws thereof, is hereby prohibited.

Section 3. This article shall be inoperative unless it shall have been ratified as an amendment to the Constitution by conventions in the several states, as provided in the Constitution, within seven years from the date of the submission hereof to the states by the Congress.

Amendment 22

(Ratified February 27, 1951)

Section 1. No person shall be elected to the office of the President more than twice, and no person who has held the office of President, or acted as President, for more than two years of a term to which some other person was elected President shall be elected to the office of the President more than once. But this article shall not apply to any person holding the office of President when this article was proposed by the Congress, and shall not prevent any person who may be holding the office of President, or acting as President, during the term within which this article becomes operative from holding the office of President or acting as President during the remainder of such term.

Section 2. This article shall be inoperative unless it shall have been ratified as an amendment to the Constitution by the legislatures of three-fourths of the several states within seven years from the date of its submission to the states by the Congress.

Amendment 23

(Ratified March 29, 1961)

Section 1. The District constituting the seat of government of the United States shall appoint in such manner as the Congress may direct:
   A number of electors of President and Vice President equal to the whole number of Senators and Representatives in Congress to which the District would be entitled if it were a state, but in no event more than the least populous state; they shall be in addition to those

appointed by the states, but they shall be considered, for the purposes of the election of President and Vice President, to be electors appointed by a state; and they shall meet in the District and perform such duties as provided by the twelfth article of amendment.

Section 2. The Congress shall have power to enforce this article by appropriate legislation.

Amendment 24

(Ratified January 23, 1964)

Section 1. The right of citizens of the United States to vote in any primary or other election for President or Vice President, for electors for President or Vice President, or for Senator or Representative in Congress, shall not be denied or abridged by the United States or any state by reason of failure to pay any poll tax or other tax.

Section 2. The Congress shall have power to enforce this article by appropriate legislation.

Amendment 25

(Ratified February 10, 1967)

Section 1. In case of the removal of the President from office or of his death or resignation, the Vice President shall become President.

Section 2. Whenever there is a vacancy in the office of the Vice President, the President shall nominate a Vice President who shall take office upon confirmation by a majority vote of both Houses of Congress.

Section 3. Whenever the President transmits to the President pro tempore of the Senate and the Speaker of the House of Representatives his written declaration that he is unable to discharge the powers and duties of his office, and until he transmits to them a written declaration to the contrary, such powers and duties shall be discharged by the Vice President as Acting President.

Section 4. Whenever the Vice President and a majority of either the principal officers of the executive departments or of such other body as Congress may by law provide, transmit to the President pro tempore of the Senate and the Speaker of the House of Representatives their written declaration that the President is unable to discharge the powers and duties of his office, the Vice President shall immediately assume the powers and duties of the office as Acting President.

Thereafter, when the President transmits to the President pro tempore of the Senate and the Speaker of the House of Representatives his written declaration that no inability exists, he shall resume the powers and duties of his office unless the Vice President and a majority of either the principal officers of the executive department or of such other body as Congress may by law provide, transmit within four days to the President pro tempore of the Senate and the Speaker of the House of Representatives their written declaration that the President is unable to discharge the powers and duties of his office. Thereupon Congress shall decide the issue, assembling within forty-eight hours for that purpose if not in session. If the Congress, within twenty-one days after receipt of the latter written declaration, or, if Congress is not in session, within twenty-one days after Congress is required to assemble, determines by two-thirds vote of both Houses that the President is unable to discharge the powers and duties of his office, the Vice President shall continue to discharge the same as Acting President; otherwise, the President shall resume the powers and duties of his office.

Amendment 26

(Ratified July 1, 1971)

Section 1. The right of citizens of the United States, who are 18 years of age or older, to vote, shall not be denied or abridged by the United States or any state on account of age.

Section 2. The Congress shall have the power to enforce this article by appropriate legislation.

Amendment 27

(Ratified May 7, 1992)

No law, varying the compensation for the services of the Senators and Representatives, shall take effect, until an election of Representatives shall have intervened.

For more information on the Constitution and the Charters of Freedom, see http://archives.gov/exhibits/charters/constitution.html

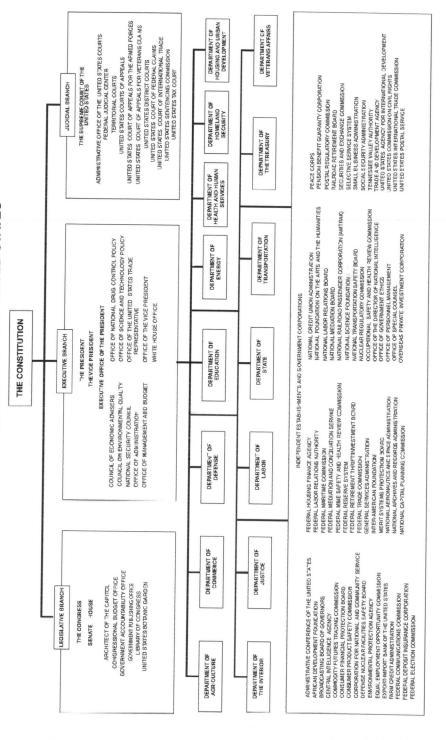

THE GOVERNMENT OF THE UNITED STATES

Legislative Branch

LEGISLATIVE BRANCH

CONGRESS
http://www.congress.gov

The Congress of the United States was created by Article I, section 1, of the Constitution, adopted by the Constitutional Convention on September 17, 1787, providing that "All legislative Powers herein granted shall be vested in a Congress of the United States, which shall consist of a Senate and House of Representatives."

The first Congress under the Constitution met on March 4, 1789, in the Federal Hall in New York City. The membership then consisted of 20 Senators and 59 Representatives.*

Congressional Record Proceedings of Congress are published in the Congressional Record, which is issued each day when Congress is in session. Publication of the Record began March 4, 1873. It was the first record of debate officially reported, printed, and published directly by the Federal Government. The Daily Digest of the Congressional Record, printed in the back of each issue of the Record, summarizes the proceedings of that day in each House and each of their committees and subcommittees, respectively. The Digest also presents the legislative program for each day and, at the end of the week, gives the program for the following week. Its publication was begun March 17, 1947.

Sessions Section 4 of Article I of the Constitution makes it mandatory that "The Congress shall assemble at least once in every Year. . . ." Under this provision, also, the date for convening Congress was designated originally as the first Monday in December, "unless they shall by Law appoint a different Day." Eighteen acts were passed, up to 1820, providing for the meeting of Congress on other days of the year. From 1820 to 1934, however, Congress met regularly on the first Monday in December. In 1934 the 20th amendment changed the convening of Congress to January 3, unless Congress "shall by law appoint a different day." In addition, the President, according to Article II, section 3, of the Constitution "may, on extraordinary Occasions, convene both Houses, or either of them, and in Case of Disagreement between them, with Respect to the Time of Adjournment, he may adjourn them to such Time as he shall think proper. . . ."

Powers of Congress Article I, section 8, of the Constitution defines the powers of Congress. Included are the powers to assess and collect taxes—called the chief power; to regulate commerce, both interstate and foreign; to coin money; to establish post offices and post roads; to establish courts inferior to the Supreme Court; to declare war; and to raise and maintain an army and navy. Congress is further empowered "To provide for calling forth the Militia to execute the Laws of the Union, suppress Insurrections and repel Invasions;" and "To make all Laws which shall be necessary and proper for carrying into Execution the foregoing Powers, and all other Powers vested by this Constitution in the Government of the United States, or in any Department or Officer thereof."

---

*New York ratified the Constitution on July 26, 1788, but did not elect its Senators until July 15 and 16, 1789. North Carolina did not ratify the Constitution until November 21, 1789; Rhode Island ratified it on May 29, 1790.

Amendments to the Constitution Another power vested in the Congress is the right to propose amendments to the Constitution, whenever two-thirds of both Houses shall deem it necessary. Should two-thirds of the State legislatures demand changes in the Constitution, it is the duty of Congress to call a constitutional convention. Proposed amendments shall be valid as part of the Constitution when ratified by the legislatures or by conventions of three-fourths of the States, as one or the other mode of ratification may be proposed by Congress.

Prohibitions Upon Congress Section 9 of Article I of the Constitution also imposes prohibitions upon Congress. "The Privilege of the Writ of Habeas Corpus shall not be suspended, unless when in Cases of Rebellion or Invasion the public Safety may require it." A bill of attainder or an ex post facto law cannot be passed. No export duty can be imposed. Ports of one State cannot be given preference over those of another State. "No money shall be drawn from the Treasury, but in Consequence of Appropriations made by Law. . . ." No title of nobility may be granted.

Rights of Members According to section 6 of Article I, Members of Congress are granted certain privileges. In no case, except in treason, felony, and breach of the peace, can Members be arrested while attending sessions of Congress "and in going to and returning from the same. . . ." Furthermore, the Members cannot be questioned in any other place for remarks made in Congress. Each House may expel a Member of its body by a two-thirds vote.

Enactment of Laws In order to become law, all bills and joint resolutions, except those proposing a constitutional amendment, must pass both the House of Representatives and the Senate and either be signed by the President or be passed over the President's veto by a two-thirds vote of both Houses of Congress. Section 7 of Article I states: "If any Bill shall not be returned by the President within ten Days (Sundays excepted) after it shall have been presented to him, the Same shall be a Law, in like Manner as if he had signed it, unless the Congress by their Adjournment prevent its Return, in which Case it shall not be a Law." When a bill or joint resolution is introduced in the House, the usual procedure for its enactment into law is as follows: assignment to House committee having jurisdiction; if favorably considered, it is reported to the House either in its original form or with recommended amendments; if the bill or resolution is passed by the House, it is messaged to the Senate and referred to the committee having jurisdiction; in the Senate committee the bill, if favorably considered, may be reported in the form as received from the House, or with recommended amendments; the approved bill or resolution is reported to the Senate, and if passed by that body, is returned to the House; if one body does not accept the amendments to a bill by the other body, a conference committee comprised of Members of both bodies is usually appointed to effect a compromise; when the bill or joint resolution is finally approved by both Houses, it is signed by the Speaker (or Speaker pro tempore) and the Vice President (or President pro tempore or acting President pro tempore) and is presented to the President; and once the President's signature is affixed, the measure becomes a law. If the President vetoes the bill, it cannot become a law unless it is re-passed by a two-thirds vote of both Houses.

The Senate

The Capitol, Washington, DC 20510
Phone, 202-224-3121. Internet, http://www.senate.gov

Constitutionally Mandated Officers
President of the Senate / Vice President of the United States MICHAEL R. PENCE
President pro tempore CHARLES E. GRASSLEY

Political Party Leaders
Majority Leader A. MITCHELL MCCONNELL
Minority Leader CHARLES E. SCHUMER

Officers / Officials
Chaplain BARRY C. BLACK
Parliamentarian ELIZABETH C. MACDONOUGH
Secretary for the Majority LAURA C. DOVE
Secretary for the Minority GARY B. MYRICK
Secretary of the Senate JULIE E. ADAMS
Sergeant at Arms MICHAEL C. STENGER
http://www.senate.gov/senators/leadership.htm

The above list of key personnel was updated 5–2019.

Overview The Senate comprises 100 Members, 2 from each State. Senators are elected to serve for a term of 6 years. There are three classes of Senators, and a new class is elected every 2 years. Senators were originally chosen by the State legislatures. The 17th amendment, which became part of the Constitution in 1913, made their election a function of the people.

A Senator must be a resident of the State that he or she represents. A Senator also must be at least 30 years of age and have been a U.S. citizen for at least 9 years.

Officers The Vice President of the United States is the Presiding Officer of the Senate. In the Vice President's absence, the duties are taken over by a President pro tempore, elected by that body, or someone designated by the President pro tempore.

The positions of Senate Majority and Minority Leader have been in existence only since the early years of the 20th century. Leaders are elected at the beginning of each new Congress by a majority vote of the Senators in their political party. In cooperation with their party organizations, Leaders are responsible for the design and achievement of a legislative program. This involves managing the flow of legislation, expediting noncontroversial measures, and keeping Members informed regarding proposed action on pending business. Each Leader serves as an ex officio member of his party's policymaking and organizational

bodies and is aided by an assistant floor leader (whip) and a party secretary.

The Secretary of the Senate, elected by vote of the Senate, performs the duties of the Presiding Officer of the Senate in the absence of the Vice President and pending the election of a President pro tempore. The Secretary is the custodian of the seal of the Senate, draws requisitions on the Secretary of the Treasury for moneys appropriated for the compensation of Senators, officers, and employees, and for the contingent expenses of the Senate, and is empowered to administer oaths to any officer of the Senate and to any witness produced before it. The Secretary's executive duties include certification of extracts from the Journal of the Senate; the attestation of bills and joint, concurrent, and Senate resolutions; in impeachment trials, issuance, under the authority of the Presiding Officer, of all orders, mandates, writs, and precepts authorized by the Senate; and certification to the President of the United States of the advice and consent of the Senate to ratification of treaties and the names of persons confirmed or rejected upon the nomination of the President.

The Sergeant at Arms, elected by vote of the Senate, serves as the executive, chief law enforcement, and protocol officer and is the principal administrative manager for most support services in the Senate. As executive officer, the Sergeant at Arms has custody of the Senate gavel; enforces Senate rules and

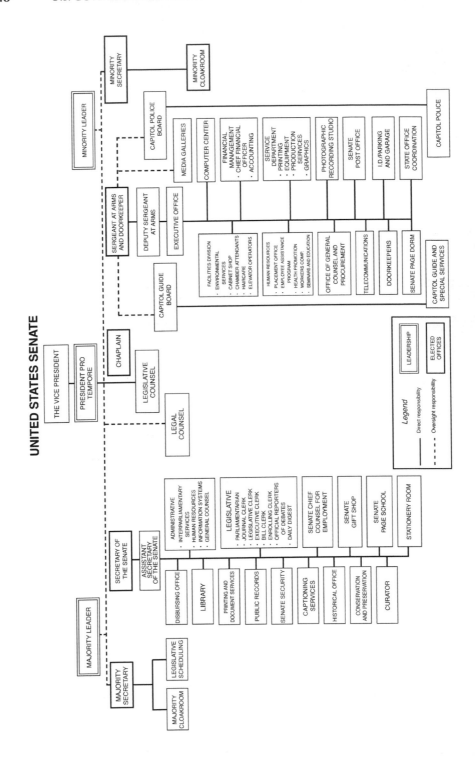

UNITED STATES SENATE

regulations as they pertain to the Senate Chamber, the Senate wing of the Capitol, and the Senate office buildings; and subject to the Presiding Officer, maintains order on the Senate floor, Chamber, and galleries. As chief law enforcement officer of the Senate, the Sergeant at Arms is authorized to maintain security in the Capitol and all Senate buildings, as well as to protect Senators; to arrest and detain any person violating Senate rules; and to locate absentee Senators for a quorum. The Sergeant at Arms serves as a member of the Capitol Police Board and as its chairman each odd year. As protocol officer, the Sergeant at Arms escorts the President and other heads of state or official guests of the Senate who are attending official functions in the Capitol; makes arrangements for funerals of Senators who die in office; and assists in planning the inauguration of the President and organizing the swearing-in and orientation programs for newly elected Senators.

Committees   The work of preparing and considering legislation is done largely by committees of both Houses of Congress. There are 16 standing committees in the Senate. The standing committees of the Senate are shown in the list below. In addition, there are two select committees in each House and various congressional commissions and joint committees composed of Members of both Houses. Each House may also appoint special investigating committees. The membership of the standing committees of each House is chosen by a vote of the entire body; members of other committees are appointed under the provisions of the measure establishing them.

Each bill and resolution is usually referred to the appropriate committee, which may report a bill out in its original form, favorably or unfavorably, recommend amendments, report original measures, or allow the proposed legislation to die in committee without action. http://www.senate.gov/general/common/generic/about_committees.htm

Standing Committees of the Senate

Committee	Chair	Website
Agriculture, Nutrition, and Forestry	C. Patrick Roberts	http://www.agriculture.senate.gov
Appropriations	Richard C. Shelby	http://www.appropriations.senate.gov
Armed Services	James M. Inhofe	http://www.armed-services.senate.gov
Banking, Housing, and Urban Affairs	Michael D. Crapo	http://www.banking.senate.gov
Budget	Michael B. Enzi	http://www.budget.senate.gov
Commerce, Science, and Transportation	Roger F. Wicker	http://www.commerce.senate.gov
Energy and Natural Resources	Lisa A. Murkowski	https://www.energy.senate.gov
Environment and Public Works	John A. Barrasso	https://www.epw.senate.gov
Finance	Charles E. Grassley	https://www.finance.senate.gov
Foreign Relations	James E. Risch	http://www.foreign.senate.gov
Health, Education, Labor, and Pensions	A. Lamar Alexander, Jr.	http://www.help.senate.gov
Homeland Security and Governmental Affairs	Ronald H. Johnson	https://www.hsgac.senate.gov
Indian Affairs	John H. Hoeven III	https://www.indian.senate.gov
Judiciary	Lindsey O. Graham	https://www.judiciary.senate.gov
Rules and Administration	Roy D. Blunt	http://www.rules.senate.gov/public
Small Business and Entrepreneurship	Marco A. Rubio	http://www.sbc.senate.gov
Veterans' Affairs	John H. Isakson	https://www.veterans.senate.gov

The above list of committee chairs was updated 5–2019. https://www.senate.gov/committees/committees_home.htm

Special Powers   Under the Constitution, the Senate is granted certain powers not accorded to the House of Representatives. The Senate approves or disapproves certain Presidential appointments by majority vote, and treaties must be concurred in by a two-thirds vote.

List of U.S. Senators

State	Expiration of Term—Party Affiliation	Contact Information
Alabama		
Richard C. Shelby	2023—Republican	http://www.shelby.senate.gov
G. Douglas Jones	2021—Democrat	https://www.jones.senate.gov
Alaska		
Lisa A. Murkowski	2023—Republican	https://www.murkowski.senate.gov
Daniel S. Sullivan	2021—Republican	http://www.sullivan.senate.gov
Arizona		
Martha E. McSally	2023—Republican	https://www.mcsally.senate.gov
Kyrsten Sinema	2025—Democrat	https://www.sinema.senate.gov
Arkansas		
John N. Boozman	2023—Republican	https://www.boozman.senate.gov
Thomas B. Cotton	2021—Republican	https://www.cotton.senate.gov
California		
Dianne Feinstein	2025—Democrat	http://www.feinstein.senate.gov
Kamala D. Harris	2023—Democrat	https://www.harris.senate.gov
Colorado		
Michael F. Bennet	2023—Democrat	https://www.bennet.senate.gov
Cory S. Gardner	2021—Republican	https://www.gardner.senate.gov
Connecticut		
Richard L. Blumenthal	2023—Democrat	https://www.blumenthal.senate.gov
Christopher S. Murphy	2025—Democrat	https://www.murphy.senate.gov
Delaware		
Thomas R. Carper	2025—Democrat	https://www.carper.senate.gov
Christopher A. Coons	2021—Democrat	https://www.coons.senate.gov
Florida		
Richard L. Scott	2025—Republican	https://www.rickscott.senate.gov
Marco A. Rubio	2023—Republican	http://www.rubio.senate.gov
Georgia		
John H. Isakson	2023—Republican	https://www.isakson.senate.gov
David A. Perdue, Jr.	2021—Republican	http://www.perdue.senate.gov
Hawaii		
Mazie K. Hirono	2025—Democrat	https://www.hirono.senate.gov
Brian E. Schatz	2023—Democrat	http://www.schatz.senate.gov
Idaho		
Michael D. Crapo	2023—Republican	http://www.crapo.senate.gov
James E. Risch	2021—Republican	http://www.risch.senate.gov
Illinois		
L. Tammy Duckworth	2023—Democrat	https://www.duckworth.senate.gov
Richard J. Durbin	2021—Democrat	http://www.durbin.senate.gov
Indiana		
Michael K. Braun	2025—Republican	https://www.braun.senate.gov
Todd C. Young	2023—Republican	https://www.young.senate.gov
Iowa		
Joni K. Ernst	2021—Republican	http://www.ernst.senate.gov
Charles E. Grassley	2023—Republican	http://www.grassley.senate.gov

List of U.S. Senators (*Continued*)

State	Expiration of Term—Party Affiliation	Contact Information
Kansas		
Gerald W. Moran	2023—Republican	http://www.moran.senate.gov
C. Patrick Roberts	2021—Republican	http://www.roberts.senate.gov
Kentucky		
A. Mitchell McConnell	2021—Republican	http://www.mcconnell.senate.gov
Randal H. Paul	2023—Republican	https://www.paul.senate.gov
Louisiana		
William M. Cassidy	2021—Republican	http://www.cassidy.senate.gov
John N. Kennedy	2023—Republican	https://www.kennedy.senate.gov
Maine		
Susan M. Collins	2021—Republican	https://www.collins.senate.gov
Angus S. King, Jr.	2025—Independent	http://www.king.senate.gov
Maryland		
Benjamin L. Cardin	2025—Democrat	https://www.cardin.senate.gov
Christopher Van Hollen, Jr.	2023—Democrat	https://www.vanhollen.senate.gov
Massachusetts		
Edward J. Markey	2021—Democrat	http://www.markey.senate.gov
Elizabeth A. Warren	2025—Democrat	https://www.warren.senate.gov
Michigan		
Gary C. Peters	2021—Democrat	https://www.peters.senate.gov
Deborah A. Stabenow	2025—Democrat	http://www.stabenow.senate.gov
Minnesota		
Tina F. Smith	2021—Democrat	https://www.smith.senate.gov
Amy J. Klobuchar	2025—Democrat	https://www.klobuchar.senate.gov
Mississippi		
Cindy Hyde-Smith	2021—Republican	https://www.hydesmith.senate.gov
Roger F. Wicker	2025—Republican	https://www.wicker.senate.gov
Missouri		
Roy D. Blunt	2023—Republican	http://www.blunt.senate.gov
Joshua D. Hawley	2025—Republican	https://www.hawley.senate.gov/
Montana		
Steven D. Daines	2021—Republican	https://www.daines.senate.gov
R. Jon Tester	2025—Democrat	http://www.tester.senate.gov
Nebraska		
Debra S. Fischer	2025—Republican	http://www.fischer.senate.gov
Benjamin E. Sasse	2021—Republican	http://www.sasse.senate.gov
Nevada		
Catherine Cortez Masto	2023—Democrat	https://www.cortezmasto.senate.gov
Jacklyn S. Rosen	2025—Democrat	http://www.rosen.senate.gov
New Hampshire		
Margaret Wood Hassan	2023—Democrat	https://www.hassan.senate.gov
C. Jeanne Shaheen	2021—Democrat	https://www.shaheen.senate.gov
New Jersey		
Cory A. Booker	2021—Democrat	http://www.booker.senate.gov
Robert Menendez	2025—Democrat	https://www.menendez.senate.gov

List of U.S. Senators *(Continued)*

State	Expiration Of Term—Party Affiliation	Contact Information
New Mexico		
Martin T. Heinrich	2025—Democrat	http://www.heinrich.senate.gov
Thomas S. Udall	2021—Democrat	http://www.tomudall.senate.gov
New York		
Kirsten E. Gillibrand	2025—Democrat	https://www.gillibrand.senate.gov
Charles E. Schumer	2023—Democrat	https://www.schumer.senate.gov
North Carolina		
Richard M. Burr	2023—Republican	http://www.burr.senate.gov
Thomas R. Tillis	2021—Republican	https://www.tillis.senate.gov
North Dakota		
Kevin Cramer	2025—Republican	http://www.cramer.senate.gov
John H. Hoeven III	2023—Republican	https://www.hoeven.senate.gov
Ohio		
Sherrod C. Brown	2025—Democrat	https://www.brown.senate.gov
Robert J. Portman	2023—Republican	http://www.portman.senate.gov
Oklahoma		
James M. Inhofe	2021—Republican	http://www.inhofe.senate.gov
James Lankford	2023—Republican	https://www.lankford.senate.gov
Oregon		
Jeffrey A. Merkley	2021—Democrat	https://www.merkley.senate.gov
Ronald L. Wyden	2023—Democrat	https://www.wyden.senate.gov
Pennsylvania		
Robert P. Casey, Jr.	2025—Democrat	https://www.casey.senate.gov
Patrick J. Toomey	2023—Republican	http://www.toomey.senate.gov
Rhode Island		
John F. Reed	2021—Democrat	https://www.reed.senate.gov
Sheldon Whitehouse	2025—Democrat	https://www.whitehouse.senate.gov
South Carolina		
Lindsey O. Graham	2021—Republican	https://www.lgraham.senate.gov
Timothy E. Scott	2023—Republican	https://www.scott.senate.gov
South Dakota		
M. Michael Rounds	2021—Republican	https://www.rounds.senate.gov
John R. Thune	2023—Republican	https://www.thune.senate.gov
Tennessee		
A. Lamar Alexander, Jr.	2021—Republican	https://www.alexander.senate.gov
Marsha W. Blackburn	2025—Republican	https://www.blackburn.senate.gov
Texas		
John Cornyn III	2021—Republican	https://www.cornyn.senate.gov
R. Edward Cruz	2025—Republican	https://www.cruz.senate.gov
Utah		
W. Milton Romney	2025—Republican	http://www.romney.senate.gov
Michael S. Lee	2023—Republican	https://www.lee.senate.gov
Vermont		
Patrick J. Leahy	2023—Democrat	https://www.leahy.senate.gov
Bernard Sanders	2025—Independent	https://www.sanders.senate.gov

List of U.S. Senators (Continued)

State	Expiration Of Term—Party Affiliation	Contact Information
Virginia		
Timothy M. Kaine	2025—Democrat	http://www.kaine.senate.gov
Mark R. Warner	2021—Democrat	http://www.warner.senate.gov
Washington		
Maria Cantwell	2025—Democrat	https://www.cantwell.senate.gov
Patricia L. Murray	2023—Democrat	http://www.murray.senate.gov
West Virginia		
Shelley Moore Capito	2021—Republican	https://www.capito.senate.gov
Joseph A. Manchin III	2025—Democrat	http://www.manchin.senate.gov
Wisconsin		
Tammy S. Baldwin	2025—Democrat	https://www.baldwin.senate.gov
Ronald H. Johnson	2023—Republican	https://www.ronjohnson.senate.gov
Wyoming		
John A. Barrasso III	2025—Republican	https://www.barrasso.senate.gov
Michael B. Enzi	2021—Republican	http://www.enzi.senate.gov

The Above List of 100 Senators was Updated 5–2019. Republicans are 53; Democrats are 45; Independents are 2; and there are no vacancies. Information on Senate.gov may be more accurate and current. https://www.senate.gov/general/contact_information/senators_cfm.cfm?OrderBy=state&Sort=ASC

Sources of Information

Art   The Senate's collections of ephemera, decorative art, graphic art, paintings, and sculpture can be viewed online. https://www.senate.gov/art/art_hist_home.htm | Email: curator@sec.senate.gov

Biographical Directory   The online "Biographical Directory of the United States Congress, 1774–Present," allows visitors to search for Members of Congress—past and present—by first or last name, political affiliation, position, State, or year or Congress. http://bioguide.congress.gov/biosearch/biosearch.asp

Books by Senators   A bibliography of books that Senators who are currently serving in the U.S. Congress have written is available online. https://www.senate.gov/senators/BooksWrittenbySittingSenators.htm

Campaign Finance   The Federal Election Commission maintains a campaign finance database that contains information on candidates, including senatorial candidates, who file reports with the Commission. Users of the online "Candidate and Committee Viewer" can sort data and download them. The data presentations consist of biennial summaries, report summaries, and report images and downloads. http://www.fec.gov/finance/disclosure/candcmte_info.shtml?tabIndex=1

Campaign Websites   The Library of Congress maintains a database of "Archived Web Sites" that includes thousands of official campaign websites. Former senatorial candidates' websites are part of this collection. https://www.loc.gov/websites

Career Opportunities   Information on fellowships, internships, and job openings is available online. http://www.senate.gov/visiting/employment.htm

Children's Books   Links to educational resources are available on the Senate's website. https://www.senate.gov/reference/bibliography/kids/kids.shtml

Committees   Information on Senate committees is available online. http://www.senate.gov/committees/committees_home.htm

Congressional Record   Starting with the year 1995, the official record of the proceedings and debates of the U.S. Congress is available on Congress.gov. https://www.congress.gov/congressional-record

Starting with the year 1994, the official record of the proceedings and debates of the U.S. Congress is available on the Government Publishing Office's govinfo website. https://www.govinfo.gov/app/collection/crec

Contact Information   The address for sending postal correspondence to a Senator or Senate committee is available online. Secretary of the Senate: Phone, 202-224-2115. U.S. Capitol switchboard: Phone, 202-224-3121. https://www.senate.gov/general/contacting.htm

Phone numbers, postal addresses, and online forms are available for contacting a Senator. http://www.senate.gov/senators/contact

An online list of States also provides web forms for contacting a Senator via email. http://www.senate.gov/senators/states.htm

Glossary   A Senate glossary is available online. http://www.senate.gov/reference/glossary.htm

History   The Senate Historical Office has told the history of the Senate, from the First Federal Congress of 1789 through the early 21st century; explained its traditions; described the individuals who served in its Chamber, and examined the major issues that confronted these national leaders. http://www.senate.gov/pagelayout/history/a_three_section_with_teasers/Explore_Senate_History.htm | Email: historian@sec.senate.gov

How To . . .   Many congressional and other Government documents are available online. The Senate's website has resources that explain how to find materials related to the Senate and the general legislative process. https://www.senate.gov/reference/howto.htm

Legislation / Records   Research guides and resources are available online. http://www.senate.gov/legislative/legislative_home.htm

Member Profiles   The "Members of the U.S. Congress" database contains profiles for Senators who have held office since 1973 or were still serving in the 93d Congress. Users of the database can filter profiles by chamber, Congress, political affiliation, and State or U.S. Territory. A Member profile includes the following: dates of service, State represented, party affiliation, and a picture when available, as well as a link to the Member's entry in the "Biographical Directory of the United States Congress, 1774–Present" and a link to remarks made in the "Congressional Record." A profile also includes the list of legislation that the Member sponsored and cosponsored. https://www.congress.gov/members

Membership / Party Divisions   The Office of the Clerk's "Congressional Profile" Web page keeps a tally of the number of Democrats, Independents, Republicans, and vacant seats in both the Senate and the House of Representatives. http://clerk.house.gov/member_info/cong.aspx

Publications   The "Congressional Directory," the "Senate Manual," and telephone directory for the U.S. Senate are available from the Government Publishing Office's bookstore. Phone, 202-512-0132. https://bookstore.gpo.gov/ | Email: mainbks@gpo.gov

Statistics / Lists   Statistics on and lists regarding a variety of topics—including cloture, nominations, roll call votes, Senate history, senators, and much more—are available online. https://www.senate.gov/reference/stats_and_lists.htm

Websites   More information on legislation and the U.S. Senate is available on Congress.gov. https://www.congress.gov

More information also is available on the Government Publishing Office's govinfo website. https://www.govinfo.gov

The Senate's Sources of Information were updated 5–2019.

The House of Representatives

The Capitol, Washington, DC 20515
Phone, 202-225-3121. Internet, http://www.house.gov

Constitutionally Mandated Officer	
Speaker of the House	NANCY P. PELOSI
Political Party Leaders	
Majority Leader	STENY H. HOYER
Minority Leader	KEVIN O. MCCARTHY
https://www.house.gov/leadership	
Officers / Officials	
Chaplain	PATRICK J. CONROY
Chief Administrative Officer	PHILIP G. KIKO

Clerk	Cheryl L. Johnson
Parliamentarian	Thomas J. Wickham, Jr.
Sergeant at Arms	Paul D. Irving
https://www.house.gov/the-house-explained/officers-and-organizations	

The above list of key personnel was updated 5–2019.

Overview   The House of Representatives comprises 435 Representatives. The number representing each State is determined by population, but every State is entitled to at least one Representative. Members are elected by the people for 2-year terms, all terms running for the same period. Representatives must be residents of the State from which they are chosen. In addition, a Representative must be at least 25 years of age and must have been a citizen for at least 7 years.

A Resident Commissioner from Puerto Rico (elected for a 4-year term) and Delegates from American Samoa, the District of Columbia, Guam, the Northern Mariana Islands, and the Virgin Islands complete the composition of the Congress of the United States. Delegates are elected for a term of 2 years. The Resident Commissioner and Delegates may take part in the floor discussions, but have no vote in the full House. They do, however, vote in the committees to which they are assigned.

Officers   The Presiding Officer of the House of Representatives, the Speaker, is elected by the House. The Speaker may designate any Member of the House to act in the Speaker's absence.

The House leadership is structured essentially the same as the Senate, with the Members in the political parties responsible for the election of their respective leader and whips.

The elected officers of the House of Representatives include the Clerk, the Sergeant at Arms, the Chief Administrative Officer, and the Chaplain.

The Clerk is custodian of the seal of the House and administers the primary legislative activities of the House. These duties include accepting the credentials of the Members-elect and calling the Members to order at the commencement of the first session of each Congress; keeping the Journal; taking all votes and certifying the passage of bills; and processing all legislation. Through various departments, the Clerk is also responsible for floor and committee reporting services; legislative information and reference services;

the administration of House reports pursuant to House rules and certain legislation including the Ethics in Government Act and the Lobbying Disclosure Act of 1995; and the distribution of House documents. The Clerk is also charged with supervision of the offices vacated by Members due to death, resignation, or expulsion.

The Sergeant at Arms maintains the order of the House under the direction of the Speaker and is the keeper of the Mace. As a member of the U.S. Capitol Police Board, the Sergeant at Arms is the chief law enforcement officer for the House and serves as Board Chairman each even year. The ceremonial and protocol duties parallel those of the Senate Sergeant at Arms and include arranging the inauguration of the President of the United States, Joint Sessions of Congress, visits to the House of heads of state, and funerals of Members of Congress. The Sergeant at Arms enforces the rules relating to the privileges of the Hall of the House, including admission to the galleries, oversees garage and parking security of the House, and distributes all House staff identification cards.

Committees   The work of preparing and considering legislation is done largely by committees of both Houses of Congress. There are 19 standing committees in the House of Representatives. The standing committees of the House of Representatives are shown in the list below. In addition, there are two select committees in the House and various congressional commissions and joint committees composed of Members of both Houses. Each House may also appoint special investigating committees. The membership of the standing committees of each House is chosen by a vote of the entire body; members of other committees are appointed under the provisions of the measure establishing them.

Each bill and resolution is usually referred to the appropriate committee, which may report a bill out in its original form, favorably or unfavorably, recommend amendments, report original measures, or allow the proposed legislation to die in committee without action.

Standing Committees of The House Of Representatives

Committee	Chair	Website
Agriculture	Collin C. Peterson	http://agriculture.house.gov
Appropriations	Nita M. Lowey	http://appropriations.house.gov
Armed Services	D. Adam Smith	https://armedservices.house.gov
Budget	John A. Yarmuth	http://budget.house.gov
Education and Labor	Robert C. Scott	https://edlabor.house.gov
Energy and Commerce	Frank J. Pallone, Jr.	https://energycommerce.house.gov
Ethics	Theodore E. Deutch	http://ethics.house.gov
Financial Services	Maxine M. Waters	http://financialservices.house.gov
Foreign Affairs	Eliot L. Engel	https://foreignaffairs.house.gov
Homeland Security	Bennie G. Thompson	https://homeland.house.gov
House Administration	Zoe Lofgren	https://cha.house.gov
Judiciary	Jerrold L. Nadler	https://judiciary.house.gov
Natural Resources	Raúl M. Grijalva	http://naturalresources.house.gov
Oversight and Reform	Elijah E. Cummings	https://oversight.house.gov
Rules	James P. McGovern	https://rules.house.gov
Science, Space, and Technology	Eddie Bernice Johnson	https://science.house.gov
Small Business	Nydia M. Velázquez	http://smallbusiness.house.gov
Transportation and Infrastructure	Peter A. DeFazio	http://transportation.house.gov
Veterans' Affairs	Mark A. Takano	https://veterans.house.gov
Ways and Means	Richard E. Neal	https://waysandmeans.house.gov

The above list of committee chairs was updated 5–2019. | https://www.house.gov/committees

Special Powers   The House of Representatives is granted the power of originating all bills for the raising of revenue. Both Houses of Congress act in impeachment proceedings, which, according to the Constitution, may be instituted against the President, Vice President, and all civil officers of the United States. The House of Representatives has the sole power of impeachment, and the Senate has the sole power to try impeachments.

List of U.S. Representatives

State / District	District—Party Affiliation	Contact Information
Alabama		
Bradley R. Byrne	01—Republican	https://byrne.house.gov
Martha D. Roby	02—Republican	http://roby.house.gov
Michael D. Rogers	03—Republican	https://mikerogers.house.gov
Robert B. Aderholt	04—Republican	https://aderholt.house.gov
Morris J. Brooks, Jr.	05—Republican	https://brooks.house.gov
Gary J. Palmer	06—Republican	https://palmer.house.gov
Terrycina A. Sewell	07—Democrat	https://sewell.house.gov
Alaska		
Donald E. Young	At Large—Republican	http://donyoung.house.gov
American Samoa		
Amata Coleman Radewagen	Delegate—Republican	https://radewagen.house.gov
Arizona		
Thomas C. O'Halleran	01—Democrat	https://ohalleran.house.gov
Ann L. Kirkpatrick	02—Democrat	https://kirkpatrick.house.gov
Raúl M. Grijalva	03—Democrat	https://grijalva.house.gov
Paul A. Gosar	04—Republican	http://gosar.house.gov
Andrew S. Biggs	05—Republican	https://biggs.house.gov

List of U.S. Representatives (*Continued*)

State / District	District—Party Affiliation	Contact Information
David Schweikert	06—Republican	https://schweikert.house.gov
Ruben M. Gallego	07—Democrat	https://rubengallego.house.gov
Debra Kay Lesko	08—Republican	https://lesko.house.gov
Gregory J. Stanton	09—Democrat	https://stanton.house.gov
Arkansas		
Eric A. Crawford	01—Republican	https://crawford.house.gov
J. French Hill	02—Republican	https://hill.house.gov
Stephen A. Womack	03—Republican	https://womack.house.gov
Bruce E. Westerman	04—Republican	https://westerman.house.gov
California		
Douglas L. LaMalfa	01—Republican	http://lamalfa.house.gov
Jared W. Huffman	02—Democrat	https://huffman.house.gov
John R. Garamendi	03—Democrat	https://garamendi.house.gov
Thomas M. McClintock	04—Republican	https://mcclintock.house.gov
Michael C. Thompson	05—Democrat	https://mikethompson.house.gov
Doris O. Matsui	06—Democrat	https://matsui.house.gov
Amerish B. Bera	07—Democrat	https://bera.house.gov
Paul J. Cook	08—Republican	https://cook.house.gov
Gerald M. McNerney	09—Democrat	https://mcnerney.house.gov
Joshua K. Harder	10—Democrat	https://harder.house.gov
Mark J. DeSaulnier	11—Democrat	https://desaulnier.house.gov
Nancy P. Pelosi	12—Democrat	https://pelosi.house.gov
Barbara J. Lee	13—Democrat	https://lee.house.gov
K. Jacqueline Speier	14—Democrat	https://speier.house.gov
Eric M. Swalwell	15—Democrat	https://swalwell.house.gov
James M. Costa	16—Democrat	https://costa.house.gov
Ro Khanna	17—Democrat	https://khanna.house.gov
Anna G. Eshoo	18—Democrat	https://eshoo.house.gov
Zoe Lofgren	19—Democrat	https://lofgren.house.gov
James V. Panetta	20—Democrat	https://panetta.house.gov
Terrance J. Cox	21—Democrat	https://cox.house.gov
Devin G. Nunes	22—Republican	https://nunes.house.gov
Kevin O. McCarthy	23—Republican	https://kevinmccarthy.house.gov
Salud O. Carbajal	24—Democrat	https://carbajal.house.gov
Katherine L. Hill	25—Democrat	https://katiehill.house.gov
Julia A. Brownley	26—Democrat	https://juliabrownley.house.gov
Judy M. Chu	27—Democrat	https://chu.house.gov
Adam B. Schiff	28—Democrat	https://schiff.house.gov
Antonio Cárdenas	29—Democrat	https://cardenas.house.gov
Bradley J. Sherman	30—Democrat	https://sherman.house.gov
Peter R. Aguilar	31—Democrat	https://aguilar.house.gov
Grace F. Napolitano	32—Democrat	https://napolitano.house.gov
Ted W. Lieu	33—Democrat	https://lieu.house.gov
Jimmy Gomez	34—Democrat	https://gomez.house.gov
Norma J. Torres	35—Democrat	https://torres.house.gov
Raul Ruiz	36—Democrat	https://ruiz.house.gov
Karen R. Bass	37—Democrat	https://bass.house.gov
Linda T. Sánchez	38—Democrat	https://lindasanchez.house.gov
Gilbert R. Cisneros, Jr.	39—Democrat	https://cisneros.house.gov
Lucille Roybal-Allard	40—Democrat	https://roybal-allard.house.gov
Mark A. Takano	41—Democrat	https://takano.house.gov

List of U.S. Representatives (Continued)

State / District	District—Party Affiliation	Contact Information
Kenneth S. Calvert	42—Republican	http://calvert.house.gov
Maxine M. Waters	43—Democrat	https://waters.house.gov
Nanette Diaz Barragán	44—Democrat	https://barragan.house.gov
Katherine M. Porter	45—Democrat	https://porter.house.gov
J. Luis Correa	46—Democrat	https://correa.house.gov
Alan S. Lowenthal	47—Democrat	http://lowenthal.house.gov
Harley E. Rouda, Jr.	48—Democrat	https://rouda.house.gov
Michael T. Levin	49—Democrat	https://mikelevin.house.gov
Duncan D. Hunter	50—Republican	https://hunter.house.gov
Juan C. Vargas	51—Democrat	http://vargas.house.gov
Scott H. Peters	52—Democrat	http://scottpeters.house.gov
Susan A. Davis	53—Democrat	https://susandavis.house.gov
Colorado		
Diana L. DeGette	01—Democrat	http://degette.house.gov
Joseph D. Neguse	02—Democrat	https://neguse.house.gov
Scott R. Tipton	03—Republican	http://tipton.house.gov
Kenneth R. Buck	04—Republican	https://buck.house.gov
Douglas L. Lamborn	05—Republican	http://lamborn.house.gov
Jason A. Crow	06—Democrat	https://crow.house.gov
Edwin G. Perlmutter	07—Democrat	https://perlmutter.house.gov
Connecticut		
John B. Larson	01—Democrat	https://larson.house.gov
Joseph D. Courtney	02—Democrat	https://courtney.house.gov
Rosa L. DeLauro	03—Democrat	https://delauro.house.gov
James A. Himes	04—Democrat	https://himes.house.gov
Jahana F. Hayes	05—Democrat	https://hayes.house.gov
Delaware		
Lisa Blunt Rochester	At Large—Democrat	https://bluntrochester.house.gov
District of Columbia		
Eleanor Holmes Norton	Delegate—Democrat	https://norton.house.gov
Florida		
Matthew L. Gaetz II	01—Republican	https://gaetz.house.gov
Neal P. Dunn	02—Republican	https://dunn.house.gov
Theodore S. Yoho	03—Republican	http://yoho.house.gov
John H. Rutherford	04—Republican	https://rutherford.house.gov
Alfred J. Lawson, Jr.	05—Democrat	https://lawson.house.gov
Michael G. Waltz	06—Republican	https://waltz.house.gov
Stephanie N. Murphy	07—Democrat	https://stephaniemurphy.house.gov
William J. Posey	08—Republican	http://posey.house.gov
Darren M. Soto	09—Democrat	https://soto.house.gov
Valdez Butler Demings	10—Democrat	https://demings.house.gov
Daniel A. Webster	11—Republican	http://webster.house.gov
Gus M. Bilirakis	12—Republican	https://bilirakis.house.gov
Charlie J. Crist, Jr.	13—Democrat	https://crist.house.gov
Katherine A. Castor	14—Democrat	http://castor.house.gov
V. Ross Spano	15—Republican	https://spano.house.gov
Vernon G. Buchanan	16—Republican	https://buchanan.house.gov
W. Gregory Steube	17—Republican	https://steube.house.gov
Brian J. Mast	18—Republican	https://mast.house.gov
L. Francis Rooney III	19—Republican	https://francisrooney.house.gov

List of U.S. Representatives (*Continued*)

State / District	District—Party Affiliation	Contact Information
Alcee L. Hastings	20—Democrat	http://alceehastings.house.gov
Lois J. Frankel	21—Democrat	http://frankel.house.gov
Theodore E. Deutch	22—Democrat	http://teddeutch.house.gov
Deborah Wasserman Schultz	23—Democrat	https://wassermanschultz.house.gov
Frederica S. Wilson	24—Democrat	https://wilson.house.gov
Mario R. Díaz-Balart	25—Republican	http://mariodiazbalart.house.gov
Debbie J. Mucarsel-Powell	26—Democrat	https://mucarsel-powell.house.gov
Donna E. Shalala	27—Democrat	https://shalala.house.gov
Georgia		
Earl L. Carter	01—Republican	http://buddycarter.house.gov
Sanford D. Bishop, Jr.	02—Democrat	http://bishop.house.gov
A. Drew Ferguson IV	03—Republican	https://ferguson.house.gov
Henry C. Johnson, Jr.	04—Democrat	https://hankjohnson.house.gov
John R. Lewis	05—Democrat	https://johnlewis.house.gov
Lucia K. McBath	06—Democrat	https://mcbath.house.gov
W. Robert Woodall	07—Republican	https://woodall.house.gov
J. Austin Scott	08—Republican	https://austinscott.house.gov
Douglas A. Collins	09—Republican	https://dougcollins.house.gov
Jody B. Hice	10—Republican	https://hice.house.gov
Barry D. Loudermilk	11—Republican	http://loudermilk.house.gov
Richard W. Allen	12—Republican	http://allen.house.gov
David A. Scott	13—Democrat	http://davidscott.house.gov
J. Thomas Graves, Jr.	14—Republican	http://tomgraves.house.gov
Guam		
Michael F.Q. San Nicolas	Delegate—Democrat	https://sannicolas.house.gov
Hawaii		
Edward E. Case	01—Democrat	https://case.house.gov
Tulsi Gabbard	02—Democrat	https://gabbard.house.gov
Idaho		
Russell M. Fulcher	01—Republican	https://fulcher.house.gov
Michael K. Simpson	02—Republican	http://simpson.house.gov
Illinois		
Bobby L. Rush	01—Democrat	http://rush.house.gov
Robin L. Kelly	02—Democrat	https://robinkelly.house.gov
Daniel W. Lipinski	03—Democrat	https://lipinski.house.gov
Jesús G. García	04—Democrat	https://chuygarcia.house.gov
Michael B. Quigley	05—Democrat	https://quigley.house.gov
Sean T. Casten	06—Democrat	https://casten.house.gov
Danny K. Davis	07—Democrat	https://davis.house.gov
S. Raja Krishnamoorthi	08—Democrat	https://krishnamoorthi.house.gov
Janice D. Schakowsky	09—Democrat	https://schakowsky.house.gov
Bradley S. Schneider	10—Democrat	https://schneider.house.gov
William G. Foster	11—Democrat	http://foster.house.gov
Michael J. Bost	12—Republican	https://bost.house.gov
Rodney L. Davis	13—Republican	http://rodneydavis.house.gov
Lauren Underwood	14—Democrat	https://underwood.house.gov
John M. Shimkus	15—Republican	https://shimkus.house.gov
Adam D. Kinzinger	16—Republican	http://kinzinger.house.gov

List of U.S. Representatives (*Continued*)

State / District	District—Party Affiliation	Contact Information
Cheryl C. Bustos	17—Democrat	https://bustos.house.gov
Darin M. LaHood	18—Republican	https://lahood.house.gov
Indiana		
Peter J. Visclosky	01—Democrat	https://visclosky.house.gov
Jacqueline S. Walorski	02—Republican	http://walorski.house.gov
James E. Banks	03—Republican	https://banks.house.gov
James R. Baird	04—Republican	https://baird.house.gov
Susan W. Brooks	05—Republican	http://susanwbrooks.house.gov
Gregory J. Pence	06—Republican	https://pence.house.gov
André D. Carson	07—Democrat	http://carson.house.gov
Larry D. Bucshon	08—Republican	https://bucshon.house.gov
Joseph A. Hollingsworth III	09—Republican	https://hollingsworth.house.gov
Iowa		
Abby L. Finkenauer	01—Democrat	https://finkenauer.house.gov
David W. Loebsack	02—Democrat	http://loebsack.house.gov
Cynthia L. Axne	03—Democrat	https://axne.house.gov
Steven A. King	04—Republican	https://steveking.house.gov
Kansas		
Roger W. Marshall	01—Republican	https://marshall.house.gov
Stephen D. Watkins	02—Republican	https://watkins.house.gov
Sharice L. Davids	03—Democrat	https://davids.house.gov
Ronald G. Estes	04—Republican	https://estes.house.gov
Kentucky		
James R. Comer	01—Republican	https://comer.house.gov
S. Brett Guthrie	02—Republican	https://guthrie.house.gov
John A. Yarmuth	03—Democrat	https://yarmuth.house.gov
Thomas H. Massie	04—Republican	https://massie.house.gov
Harold D. Rogers	05—Republican	https://halrogers.house.gov
Garland H. Barr IV	06—Republican	https://barr.house.gov
Louisiana		
Stephen J. Scalise	01—Republican	http://scalise.house.gov
Cedric L. Richmond	02—Democrat	https://richmond.house.gov
G. Clay Higgins	03—Republican	https://clayhiggins.house.gov
J. Michael Johnson	04—Republican	https://mikejohnson.house.gov
Ralph L. Abraham	05—Republican	https://abraham.house.gov
Garret N. Graves	06—Republican	https://garretgraves.house.gov
Maine		
Chellie M. Pingree	01—Democrat	https://pingree.house.gov
Jared F. Golden	02—Democrat	https://golden.house.gov
Maryland		
Andrew P. Harris	01—Republican	http://harris.house.gov
C.A. Dutch Ruppersberger	02—Democrat	http://ruppersberger.house.gov
John P. Sarbanes	03—Democrat	https://sarbanes.house.gov
Anthony G. Brown	04—Democrat	https://anthonybrown.house.gov
Steny H. Hoyer	05—Democrat	https://hoyer.house.gov
David J. Trone	06—Democrat	https://trone.house.gov
Elijah E. Cummings	07—Democrat	https://cummings.house.gov
Jamin B. Raskin	08—Democrat	https://raskin.house.gov

List of U.S. Representatives (*Continued*)

State / District	District—Party Affiliation	Contact Information
Massachusetts		
Richard E. Neal	01—Democrat	https://neal.house.gov
James P. McGovern	02—Democrat	http://mcgovern.house.gov
Lori L. Trahan	03—Democrat	https://trahan.house.gov
Joseph P. Kennedy III	04—Democrat	https://kennedy.house.gov
Katherine M. Clark	05—Democrat	https://katherineclark.house.gov
Seth W. Moulton	06—Democrat	http://moulton.house.gov
Ayanna S. Pressley	07—Democrat	https://pressley.house.gov
Stephen F. Lynch	08—Democrat	http://lynch.house.gov
William R. Keating	09—Democrat	https://keating.house.gov
Michigan		
John W. Bergman	01—Republican	https://bergman.house.gov
William P. Huizenga	02—Republican	http://huizenga.house.gov
Justin A. Amash	03—Republican	http://amash.house.gov
John R. Moolenaar	04—Republican	https://moolenaar.house.gov
Daniel T. Kildee	05—Democrat	http://dankildee.house.gov
Frederick S. Upton	06—Republican	http://upton.house.gov
Timothy L. Walberg	07—Republican	http://walberg.house.gov
Elissa B. Slotkin	08—Democrat	https://slotkin.house.gov
Sander M. Levin	09—Democrat	http://levin.house.gov
Paul Mitchell III	10—Republican	https://mitchell.house.gov
Haley M. Stevens	11—Democrat	https://stevens.house.gov
Deborah A. Dingell	12—Democrat	https://debbiedingell.house.gov
Rashida H. Tlaib	13—Democrat	https://tlaib.house.gov
Brenda L. Lawrence	14—Democrat	https://lawrence.house.gov
Minnesota		
James L. Hagedorn	01—Republican	https://hagedorn.house.gov
Angela D. Craig	02—Democrat	https://craig.house.gov
Dean B. Phillips	03—Democrat	https://phillips.house.gov
Betty L. McCollum	04—Democrat	http://mccollum.house.gov
Ilhan A. Omar	05—Democrat	https://omar.house.gov
Thomas E. Emmer, Jr.	06—Republican	https://emmer.house.gov
Collin C. Peterson	07—Democrat	http://collinpeterson.house.gov
Peter A. Stauber	08—Republican	https://stauber.house.gov
Mississippi		
J. Trent Kelly	01—Republican	https://trentkelly.house.gov
Bennie G. Thompson	02—Democrat	https://benniethompson.house.gov
Michael P. Guest	03—Republican	https://guest.house.gov
Steven M. Palazzo	04—Republican	http://palazzo.house.gov
Missouri		
W. Lacy Clay, Jr.	01—Democrat	https://lacyclay.house.gov
Ann L. Wagner	02—Republican	http://wagner.house.gov
W. Blaine Luetkemeyer	03—Republican	http://luetkemeyer.house.gov
Vicky J. Hartzler	04—Republican	https://hartzler.house.gov
Emanuel Cleaver II	05—Democrat	http://cleaver.house.gov
Samuel B. Graves, Jr.	06—Republican	https://graves.house.gov
William H. Long	07—Republican	https://long.house.gov
Jason T. Smith	08—Republican	https://jasonsmith.house.gov
Montana		
Gregory R. Gianforte	At Large—Republican	https://gianforte.house.gov

List of U.S. Representatives (*Continued*)

State / District	District—Party Affiliation	Contact Information
Nebraska		
Jeffrey L. Fortenberry	01—Republican	https://fortenberry.house.gov
Donald J. Bacon	02—Republican	https://bacon.house.gov
Adrian M. Smith	03—Republican	http://adriansmith.house.gov
Nevada		
A. Costandina Titus	01—Democrat	https://titus.house.gov
Mark E. Amodei	02—Republican	https://amodei.house.gov
Suzanne K. Lee	03—Democrat	https://susielee.house.gov
Steven A. Horsford	04—Democrat	https://horsford.house.gov
New Hampshire		
Christopher C. Pappas	01—Democrat	https://pappas.house.gov
Ann McLane Kuster	02—Democrat	http://kuster.house.gov
New Jersey		
Donald W. Norcross	01—Democrat	https://norcross.house.gov
Jefferson H. Van Drew	02—Democrat	https://vandrew.house.gov
Andrew Kim	03—Democrat	https://kim.house.gov
Christopher H. Smith	04—Republican	http://chrissmith.house.gov
Joshua S. Gottheimer	05—Democrat	https://gottheimer.house.gov
Frank J. Pallone, Jr.	06—Democrat	https://pallone.house.gov
Tomasz P. Malinowski	07—Democrat	https://malinowski.house.gov
Albio B. Sires	08—Democrat	https://sires.house.gov
William J. Pascrell, Jr.	09—Democrat	http://pascrell.house.gov
Donald M. Payne, Jr.	10—Democrat	http://payne.house.gov
R. Michelle Sherrill	11—Democrat	https://sherrill.house.gov
Bonnie Watson Coleman	12—Democrat	https://watsoncoleman.house.gov
New Mexico		
Debra A. Haaland	01—Democrat	https://haaland.house.gov
Xochitl Torres Small	02—Democrat	https://torressmall.house.gov/
Ben R. Luján	03—Democrat	https://lujan.house.gov
New York		
Lee M. Zeldin	01—Republican	https://zeldin.house.gov
Peter T. King	02—Republican	http://peteking.house.gov
Thomas R. Suozzi	03—Democrat	https://suozzi.house.gov
Kathleen M. Rice	04—Democrat	http://kathleenrice.house.gov
Gregory W. Meeks	05—Democrat	http://meeks.house.gov
Grace Meng	06—Democrat	http://meng.house.gov
Nydia M. Velázquez	07—Democrat	https://velazquez.house.gov
Hakeem S. Jeffries	08—Democrat	http://jeffries.house.gov
Yvette D. Clarke	09—Democrat	https://clarke.house.gov
Jerrold L. Nadler	10—Democrat	http://nadler.house.gov
Max N. Rose	11—Democrat	https://maxrose.house.gov
Carolyn B. Maloney	12—Democrat	http://maloney.house.gov
Adriano D. Espaillat	13—Democrat	https://espaillat.house.gov
Alexandria Ocasio-Cortez	14—Democrat	https://ocasio-cortez.house.gov
José E. Serrano	15—Democrat	https://serrano.house.gov
Eliot L. Engel	16—Democrat	https://engel.house.gov
Nita M. Lowey	17—Democrat	https://lowey.house.gov
Sean P. Maloney	18—Democrat	http://seanmaloney.house.gov
Antonio Delgado	19—Democrat	https://delgado.house.gov
Paul D. Tonko	20—Democrat	https://tonko.house.gov

List of U.S. Representatives (*Continued*)

State / District	District—Party Affiliation	Contact Information
Elise M. Stefanik	21—Republican	https://stefanik.house.gov
Anthony Brindisi	22—Democrat	https://brindisi.house.gov
Thomas W. Reed II	23—Republican	https://reed.house.gov
John M. Katko	24—Republican	https://katko.house.gov
Joseph D. Morelle	25—Democrat	https://morelle.house.gov
Brian M. Higgins	26—Democrat	http://higgins.house.gov
Christopher C. Collins	27—Republican	https://chriscollins.house.gov
North Carolina		
George K. Butterfield	01—Democrat	http://butterfield.house.gov
George F.B. Holding	02—Republican	http://holding.house.gov
(vacancy)	03—	http://
David E. Price	04—Democrat	https://price.house.gov
Virginia A. Foxx	05—Republican	http://foxx.house.gov
B. Mark Walker	06—Republican	https://walker.house.gov
David C. Rouzer	07—Republican	https://rouzer.house.gov
Richard L. Hudson, Jr.	08—Republican	https://hudson.house.gov
(vacancy)	09—	https://
Patrick T. McHenry	10—Republican	http://mchenry.house.gov
Mark R. Meadows	11—Republican	https://meadows.house.gov
Alma S. Adams	12—Democrat	http://adams.house.gov
Theodore P. Budd	13—Republican	https://budd.house.gov
North Dakota		
Kelly Armstrong	At Large—Republican	https://armstrong.house.gov
Northern Mariana Islands		
Gregorio K.C. Sablan	Delegate—Democrat	http://sablan.house.gov
Ohio		
Steven J. Chabot	01—Republican	http://chabot.house.gov
Brad R. Wenstrup	02—Republican	http://wenstrup.house.gov
Joyce B. Beatty	03—Democrat	http://beatty.house.gov
James D. Jordan	04—Republican	http://jordan.house.gov
Robert E. Latta	05—Republican	http://latta.house.gov
William L. Johnson	06—Republican	http://billjohnson.house.gov
Robert B. Gibbs	07—Republican	https://gibbs.house.gov
Warren E. Davidson	08—Republican	https://davidson.house.gov
Marcia C. Kaptur	09—Democrat	https://kaptur.house.gov
Michael R. Turner	10—Republican	https://turner.house.gov
Marcia L. Fudge	11—Democrat	https://fudge.house.gov
W. Troy Balderson	12—Republican	https://balderson.house.gov
Timothy J. Ryan	13—Democrat	http://timryan.house.gov
David P. Joyce	14—Republican	https://joyce.house.gov
Steven E. Stivers	15—Republican	http://stivers.house.gov
Anthony Gonzalez	16—Republican	https://anthonygonzalez.house.gov
Oklahoma		
Kevin R. Hern	01—Republican	https://hern.house.gov
Markwayne Mullin	02—Republican	http://mullin.house.gov
Frank D. Lucas	03—Republican	http://lucas.house.gov
Thomas J. Cole	04—Republican	https://cole.house.gov
Kendra S. Horn	05—Democrat	https://horn.house.gov
Oregon		
Suzanne M. Bonamici	01—Democrat	http://bonamici.house.gov

List of U.S. Representatives *(Continued)*

State / District	District—Party Affiliation	Contact Information
Gregory P. Walden	02—Republican	https://walden.house.gov
Earl Blumenauer	03—Democrat	https://blumenauer.house.gov
Peter A. DeFazio	04—Democrat	http://defazio.house.gov
W. Kurt Schrader	05—Democrat	http://schrader.house.gov
Pennsylvania		
Brian K. Fitzpatrick	01—Republican	https://fitzpatrick.house.gov
Brendan F. Boyle	02—Democrat	https://boyle.house.gov
Dwight E. Evans	03—Democrat	https://evans.house.gov
Madeleine C. Dean	04—Democrat	https://dean.house.gov
Mary Gay Scanlon	05—Democrat	https://scanlon.house.gov
Christina J. Houlahan	06—Democrat	https://houlahan.house.gov
Susan E. Wild	07—Democrat	https://wild.house.gov
Matthew A. Cartwright	08—Democrat	https://cartwright.house.gov
Daniel P. Meuser	09—Republican	https://meuser.house.gov
Scott G. Perry	10—Republican	https://perry.house.gov
Lloyd K. Smucker	11—Republican	https://smucker.house.gov
(vacancy)	12—	https://
John P. Joyce	13—Republican	https://johnjoyce.house.gov
Guy L. Reschenthaler	14—Republican	https://reschenthaler.house.gov
Glenn W. Thompson	15—Republican	https://thompson.house.gov
George J. Kelly, Jr.	16—Republican	https://kelly.house.gov
Conor J. Lamb	17—Democrat	https://lamb.house.gov
Michael F. Doyle	18—Democrat	https://doyle.house.gov
Puerto Rico		
Jenniffer A. González-Colón	Resident Commissioner— Republican	https://gonzalez-colon.house.gov
Rhode Island		
David N. Cicilline	01—Democrat	http://cicilline.house.gov
James R. Langevin	02—Democrat	http://langevin.house.gov
South Carolina		
Joseph K. Cunningham	01—Democrat	https://cunningham.house.gov
Addison G. Wilson	02—Republican	http://joewilson.house.gov
Jeffrey D. Duncan	03—Republican	http://jeffduncan.house.gov
William R. Timmons	04—Republican	https://timmons.house.gov
Ralph W. Norman, Jr.	05—Republican	https://norman.house.gov
James E. Clyburn	06—Democrat	http://clyburn.house.gov
H. Thompson Rice, Jr.	07—Republican	http://rice.house.gov
South Dakota		
Dustin M. Johnson	At Large—Republican	https://dustyjohnson.house.gov
Tennessee		
D. Phillip Roe	01—Republican	http://roe.house.gov
Timothy F. Burchett	02—Republican	https://burchett.house.gov
Charles J. Fleischmann	03—Republican	http://fleischmann.house.gov
Scott E. DesJarlais	04—Republican	https://desjarlais.house.gov
James H.S. Cooper	05—Democrat	http://cooper.house.gov
John W. Rose	06—Republican	https://johnrose.house.gov
Mark E. Green	07—Republican	https://markgreen.house.gov
David F. Kustoff	08—Republican	https://kustoff.house.gov
Stephen I. Cohen	09—Democrat	https://cohen.house.gov

List of U.S. Representatives (*Continued*)

State / District	District—Party Affiliation	Contact Information
Texas		
Louis B. Gohmert, Jr.	01—Republican	https://gohmert.house.gov
Daniel R. Crenshaw	02—Republican	https://crenshaw.house.gov
N. Vancampen Taylor	03—Republican	https://vantaylor.house.gov
John L. Ratcliffe	04—Republican	https://ratcliffe.house.gov
Lance Gooden	05—Republican	https://gooden.house.gov
Ronald J. Wright	06—Republican	https://wright.house.gov
Elizabeth P. Fletcher	07—Democrat	https://fletcher.house.gov
Kevin P. Brady	08—Republican	http://kevinbrady.house.gov
Alexander N. Green	09—Democrat	http://algreen.house.gov
Michael T. McCaul	10—Republican	http://mccaul.house.gov
K. Michael Conaway	11—Republican	http://conaway.house.gov
Kay M. Granger	12—Republican	http://kaygranger.house.gov
W. McClellan Thornberry	13—Republican	http://thornberry.house.gov
Randy K. Weber, Sr.	14—Republican	http://weber.house.gov
Vicente Gonzalez	15—Democrat	https://gonzalez.house.gov
Veronica Escobar	16—Democrat	https://escobar.house.gov
William H. Flores	17—Republican	http://flores.house.gov
Sheila Jackson Lee	18—Democrat	http://jacksonlee.house.gov
Jodey Cook Arrington	19—Republican	https://arrington.house.gov
Joaquin Castro	20—Democrat	https://castro.house.gov
Charles E. Roy	21—Republican	https://roy.house.gov
Peter G. Olson	22—Republican	https://olson.house.gov
William B. Hurd	23—Republican	https://hurd.house.gov
Kenny E. Marchant	24—Republican	https://marchant.house.gov
J. Roger Williams	25—Republican	http://williams.house.gov
Michael C. Burgess	26—Republican	http://burgess.house.gov
Michael J. Cloud	27—Republican	https://cloud.house.gov
Enrique R. Cuellar	28—Democrat	http://cuellar.house.gov
Sylvia R. Garcia	29—Democrat	https://sylviagarcia.house.gov
Eddie Bernice Johnson	30—Democrat	http://ebjohnson.house.gov
John R. Carter	31—Republican	https://carter.house.gov
Colin Z. Allred	32—Democrat	https://allred.house.gov
Marc A. Veasey	33—Democrat	http://veasey.house.gov
Filemón B. Vela, Jr.	34—Democrat	https://vela.house.gov
Lloyd A. Doggett II	35—Democrat	https://doggett.house.gov
Brian Babin	36—Republican	http://babin.house.gov
Utah		
Robert W. Bishop	01—Republican	http://robbishop.house.gov
Christopher D. Stewart	02—Republican	http://stewart.house.gov
John R. Curtis	03—Republican	https://curtis.house.gov
Benjamin M. McAdams	04—Democrat	https://mcadams.house.gov
Vermont		
Peter F. Welch	At Large—Democrat	https://welch.house.gov
Virgin Islands		
Stacey E. Plaskett	Delegate—Democrat	https://plaskett.house.gov
Virginia		
Robert J. Wittman	01—Republican	http://wittman.house.gov
Elaine G. Luria	02—Democrat	https://luria.house.gov
Robert C. Scott	03—Democrat	http://bobbyscott.house.gov

List of U.S. Representatives (Continued)

State / District	District—Party Affiliation	Contact Information
A. Donald McEachin	04—Democrat	https://mceachin.house.gov
Denver L. Riggleman III	05—Republican	https://riggleman.house.gov
Benjamin L. Cline	06—Republican	https://cline.house.gov
Abigail D. Spanberger	07—Democrat	https://spanberger.house.gov
Donald S. Beyer, Jr.	08—Democrat	http://beyer.house.gov
H. Morgan Griffith	09—Republican	http://morgangriffith.house.gov
Jennifer L. Wexton	10—Democrat	https://wexton.house.gov
Gerald E. Connolly	11—Democrat	https://connolly.house.gov
Washington		
Suzan K. DelBene	01—Democrat	https://delbene.house.gov
Richard R. Larsen	02—Democrat	http://larsen.house.gov
Jaime L. Herrera Beutler	03—Republican	http://herrerabeutler.house.gov
Daniel M. Newhouse	04—Republican	https://newhouse.house.gov
Cathy A. McMorris Rodgers	05—Republican	http://mcmorris.house.gov
Derek C. Kilmer	06—Democrat	https://kilmer.house.gov
Pramila Jayapal	07—Democrat	https://jayapal.house.gov
Kimberly M. Schrier	08—Democrat	https://schrier.house.gov
D. Adam Smith	09—Democrat	https://adamsmith.house.gov
Dennis L. Heck	10—Democrat	http://dennyheck.house.gov
West Virginia		
David B. McKinley	01—Republican	https://mckinley.house.gov
Alexander X. Mooney	02—Republican	https://mooney.house.gov
Carol D. Miller	03—Republican	https://miller.house.gov
Wisconsin		
Bryan G. Steil	01—Republican	https://steil.house.gov
Mark Pocan	02—Democrat	http://pocan.house.gov
Ronald J. Kind	03—Democrat	https://kind.house.gov
Gwendolynne S. Moore	04—Democrat	https://gwenmoore.house.gov
F. James Sensenbrenner, Jr.	05—Republican	http://sensenbrenner.house.gov
Glenn S. Grothman	06—Republican	http://grothman.house.gov
Sean P. Duffy	07—Republican	https://duffy.house.gov
Michael J. Gallagher	08—Republican	https://gallagher.house.gov
Wyoming		
Elizabeth L. Cheney	At Large—Republican	https://cheney.house.gov

The Above List of 435 Representatives Was Updated 5–2019. The Resident Commissioner and Delegates are not counted as Members. Democrats are 235; Republicans are 197; and there are 3 vacancies. Information on House.gov may be more accurate and current. | https://www.house.gov/representatives

Information on the Office of the Clerk's website may be more accurate and current. | https://clerkpreview.house.gov/Members#MemberProfiles

Sources of Information

A–Z Index of Resources   An alphabetical index of help pages, lists, popular saved searches, research guides, and more is available on the Congress.gov website. https://www.congress.gov/resources/display/content/Resources+A+to+Z

Art Competition   Each spring, the Congressional Institute sponsors a nationwide high school visual art competition to recognize and encourage artistic talent. Students submit their entries to their Representative's office, and panels of district artists select the winning artwork, which is displayed at the U.S. Capitol for 1 year. http://www.house.gov/content/educate/art_competition

Campaign Finance   The Federal Election Commission maintains a campaign finance database that contains information on candidates, including congressional candidates, who file reports with the Commission. Users of the online "Candidate and Committee Viewer" can sort data and download them. The data presentations consist of biennial summaries, report summaries, and report images and downloads. http://www.fec.gov/finance/disclosure/candcmte_info.shtml?tabIndex=1

Campaign Websites   The Library of Congress maintains a database of "Archived Web Sites" that includes thousands of official campaign websites. Former congressional candidates' websites are part of this collection. https://www.loc.gov/websites

Career Opportunities   The House Vacancy Announcement and Placement Service assists House Members, committees, and leadership by posting job vacancies and maintaining a resume bank. The Service provides confidential referral of resumes when House offices request them. Information on submitting a resume is available online. http://www.house.gov/content/jobs/members_and_committees.php

To apply for positions with House organizations, read the individual vacancy announcements and follow the instructions. http://www.house.gov/content/jobs/vacancies.php

Committees   Information on House committees is available on House.gov. http://www.house.gov/committees

Additional information is available on the Office of the Clerk's website. http://clerk.house.gov/committee_info/index.aspx

Congressional Record   Starting with the year 1995, the official record of the proceedings and debates of the U.S. Congress is available on Congress.gov. https://www.congress.gov/congressional-record

Starting with the year 1994, the official record of the proceedings and debates of the U.S. Congress is available on the Government Publishing Office's govinfo website. https://www.govinfo.gov/app/collection/crec

Contact the Clerk   Additional information on the House of Representatives is available from the Clerk, U.S. Capitol, Room H-154, Washington, DC 20515-6601. Phone, 202-225-7000. https://clerkpreview.house.gov/About#OverviewContact | Email: info.clerkweb@mail.house.gov

Directories   The website House.gov has a directory that contains the committee assignment, congressional district, name, phone number, political affiliation, and room number of each Member of the U.S. House of Representatives, as well as the Uniform Resources Locator (URL) that leads to his or her website. http://www.house.gov/representatives

The online "Biographical Directory of the United States Congress, 1774–Present," allows visitors to search for Members of Congress—past and present—by first or last name, political affiliation, position, State, or year or Congress. http://bioguide.congress.gov/biosearch/biosearch.asp

Present and former Members of Congress have control numbers associated with their records in the "Biographical Directory of the United States Congress." Member IDs or "BioGuide IDs" serve as metadata within Congress.gov and legislative documents that the Government Publishing Office publishes. https://www.congress.gov/help/field-values/member-bioguide-ids

Find a Representative   A Zip code-based search tool is available on House.gov for locating a representative. http://www.house.gov/representatives/find

Frequently Asked Questions (FAQs)   The Office of the Clerk has posted answers to general legislative questions and to more specific questions related to members and committees. https://clerkpreview.house.gov/Help#MemberFAQs

Glossary   The Office of the Clerk's website has a short glossary for children. https://kids-clerk.house.gov/high-school/glossary.html

House.gov has a glossary of terms for readers of congressional records. http://history.house.gov/Records-and-Research/FAQs/Congressional-Glossary/

House.gov features a glossary of records management terms. http://history.house.gov/Records-and-Research/FAQs/Records-Glossary/

The "Statement of Disbursements" is a quarterly public report of all receipts and expenditures for U.S. House of Representatives committees, leadership, Members, and officers and offices. To help the general public read this report, House.gov maintains an online glossary. https://www.house.gov/the-house-explained/open-government/statement-of-disbursements/glossary-of-terms

History   The House of Representative's "History, Art and Archives" website features resources and a trove of information, including online collections, exhibitions, publications, and records. http://history.house.gov

Learning About the House   The Office of the Clerk's website features educational and entertaining information on the legislative branch of the Government for students of all ages. Its "Kids in the House" site explains the role of the House of Representatives, describes the legislative process, and covers House history. https://kids-clerk.house.gov

Adults seeking to learn about commissions, committees, House history, House leadership, Representatives, rules, or a Representative's schedule may benefit from "The House Explained" section on House.gov. http://www.house.gov/content/learn

Member Profiles   The "Members of the U.S. Congress" database contains profiles for Representatives who have held office since 1973 or were still serving in the 93d Congress. Users of the database can filter profiles by chamber, Congress, political affiliation, and State or U.S. Territory. A Member profile includes the following: dates of service, district number and State, party affiliation, and a picture when available, as well as a link to the Member's entry in the "Biographical Directory of the United States Congress, 1774–Present" and a link to remarks made in the "Congressional Record." A profile also includes the list of legislation that the Member sponsored and cosponsored. https://www.congress.gov/members

The Office of the Clerk's website also maintains a database of Member profiles. https://clerkpreview.house.gov/Members#MemberProfiles

Membership / Party Divisions   The Office of the Clerk's "Congressional Profile" page keeps a tally of the number of Democrats, Independents, Republicans, and vacant seats in both the House of Representatives and the Senate. http://clerk.house.gov/member_info/cong.aspx

Most-Viewed Bills   The top ten most-viewed bills list is compiled each Monday and posted on the Congress.gov website. https://www.congress.gov/resources/display/content/Most-Viewed+Bills

Oath of Office   The constitutional oath of office requires each Member of Congress to swear or affirm that he or she will support and defend the U.S. Constitution against foreign and domestic enemies; bear faith and allegiance to the Constitution; take this obligation freely, with neither mental reservation nor purpose of evasion; and discharge the duties of the office well and faithfully. https://clerkpreview.house.gov/Members#MemberOaths

Publications   The Congressional Directory, Rules and Manual of the House of Representatives, and telephone directory for the House of Representatives are available from the Government Publishing Office's bookstore. Phone, 202-512-0132. https://bookstore.gpo.gov | Email: mainbks@gpo.gov

Schedule   The House's schedule and related resources are available in the "Legislative Activity" section on House.gov. http://www.house.gov/legislative

Site Map   House.gov features a site map that allows visitors to look for a specific topic or to browse content that aligns with their interests. http://www.house.gov/content/site_tools/sitemap.php

Websites   More information on legislation and the U.S. House of Representatives is available on Congress.gov. https://www.congress.gov

More information also is available on House.gov. http://www.house.gov

More information also is available on the Government Publishing Office's govinfo website. https://www.govinfo.gov

The Sources of Information for the House of Representatives were updated 5–2019.

Architect of the Capitol

U.S. Capitol Building, Washington, DC 20515
Phone, 202-228-1793. Internet, http://www.aoc.gov

Architect of the Capitol	THOMAS J. CARROLL III, ACTING
Deputy Architect of the Capitol	(VACANCY)
Directors	
Communications and Congressional Relations	ERIN COURTNEY, ACTING
Safety, Fire and Environmental Programs	PATRICIA WILLIAMS
General Counsel	JASON BALTIMORE

https://www.aoc.gov/organization/acting-architect

Jurisdictions Reporting to the Architect

Chief Executive Officer for Visitor Services	
U.S. Capitol Visitor Center	BETH PLEMMONS

https://www.aoc.gov/jurisdiction/capitol-visitor-center

Executive Director	
U.S. Botanic Garden	SAHARAH MOON CHAPOTIN

https://www.aoc.gov/jurisdiction/botanic-garden

Operations

Chief Operating Officer	(VACANCY)
Chief Officers	
Administrative	WILLIAM R. O'DONNELL
Financial	JONATHAN KRAFT, ACTING
Director	
Planning and Project Management	PETER W. MUELLER

Jurisdictions Reporting to the Chief Operating Officer

Directors	
Capitol Grounds and Arboretum	JAMES KAUFMANN
Capitol Police Buildings, Grounds and Security	VAL HASBERRY, ACTING
Capitol Power Plant	CHRISTOPHER POTTER
Facility Manager	
Supreme Court Building and Grounds	JOSEPH A. CAMPBELL
Superintendents	
Capitol Building	MARK REED
House Office Buildings	MICHELLE KAYON, ACTING
Library Buildings and Grounds	ANTONIO M. EDMONDS
Senate Office Buildings	LAWRENCE BARR, ACTING

https://www.aoc.gov/organizational-directory

Office of Inspector General

Inspector General	CHRISTOPHER P. FAILLA

https://www.aoc.gov/oig/inspector-general

The above list of key personnel was updated 10–2019.

The Architect of the Capitol maintains the U.S. Capitol and the buildings and grounds of the Capitol campus.

Establishment and Organization

The origins of the office of the Architect of the Capitol (AOC) may be traced to the act of July 16, 1790, that established "the temporary and permanent seat of the Government of the United States" (1 Stat. 130). https://www.loc.gov/law/help/statutes-at-large/1st-congress/session-2/c1s2ch28.pdf

The title Architect of the Capitol is the official title of both the agency and the person who heads it. The act of August 15, 1876, that made "appropriations for the legislative, executive, and judicial expenses of the Government . . . and for other purposes" established permanent authority for the care and maintenance of the U.S. Capitol (19 Stat. 147). https://www.loc.gov/law/help/statutes-at-large/44th-congress/session-1/c44s1ch287.pdf

Prior to 1989, the President selected the Architect for an unlimited term and without any formal action by Congress. An act of November 21, 1989, that made "appropriations for the Legislative Branch . . . and for other purposes" changed the procedure. This statute, which is also cited as the "Legislative Branch Appropriations Act, 1990," stipulates that the President appoints the Architect of the Capitol for a term of 10 years, by the advice and with the consent of the Senate, from a list of at least three candidates whom a congressional commission recommends (103 Stat. 1068). Upon confirmation by the Senate, the Architect becomes an official of the legislative branch as an officer of Congress. The Architect is eligible for reappointment at the end of his or her 10-year term. While overseeing the agency, the Architect also serves as the Acting Director of the U.S. Botanic Garden. https://www.govinfo.gov/content/pkg/STATUTE-103/pdf/STATUTE-103-Pg1041.pdf

The Congressional Research Service prepared the report "Architect of the Capitol: Appointment, Duties, and Current Issues," which includes a section on the statutory evolution of the Architect's office. Mildred Amer, a specialist on the Congress, of the Government and Finance Division, prepared the report in October of 2008. https://www.everycrsreport.com/reports/RL32820.html

An organizational directory is available online. https://www.aoc.gov/organizational-directory

Activities

The Architect of the Capitol serves the Congress and Supreme Court in its capacity as the builder and steward of the landmark buildings and grounds of Capitol Hill. AOC employees preserve and maintain the art, historic buildings, monuments, and gardens on the Capitol campus. Comprising more than 2,000 employees and providing around-the-clock service, the AOC team creates a safe environment and inspiring experiences for those who visit or work on Capitol Hill.

The agency oversees the operations and care of more than 17.4 million square feet of facilities, 580 acres of grounds, and thousands of works of art. The Capitol campus accommodates 30,000 daily occupants and hosts more than 3 million visitors annually. https://www.aoc.gov/defining-aoc

Sources of Information

Architecture   A trove of information on columns, materials, styles, and more is available on the AOC website. https://www.aoc.gov/architecture

Art   The AOC website includes pages on AOC art stories, artists, art by State, decorative arts, paintings and murals, and sculptures, as well as on African Americans, Native Americans, and women in art. https://www.aoc.gov/art

Blog   AOC experts write on the architecture, art, and work on the Capitol Hill. http://www.aoc.gov/blog

Business Opportunities   Information for contractors and small businesses—delivery instructions, procedures, procurement opportunities, and programs—is accessible online. https://www.aoc.gov/procurement

Career Opportunities   The AOC relies heavily on architects, carpenters, electricians, engineers, gardeners, masons, mechanics, painters and plasterers, plumbers, and sheet metal workers to maintain the U.S. Capitol and the buildings and grounds of the surrounding campus. https://www.aoc.gov/careers

In 2018, the AOC ranked 9th among 27 midsize Government agencies in the Best Places To Work Agency Rankings. http://bestplacestowork.org/BPTW/rankings/detail/AC00

Events The AOC website contains pages of events associated with the U.S. Capitol and Botanic Garden. Events include Christmas tree displays, concerts, lying in state, Presidential Inaugurations, and State of the Union addresses. https://www.aoc.gov/capitol-campus-events

Facts Capitol Hill facts are posted on the AOC website. https://www.aoc.gov/facts/capitol-hill

Gallery A multimedia gallery is available online. https://www.aoc.gov/multimedia-gallery

Grounds Frederick L. Olmsted planned the late 19th-century expansion and landscaping of the Capitol Grounds. Olmsted, who also designed Central Park in New York City, was regarded as the most talented American landscape architect of his day. The "About the Grounds" web page features an informative 4-minute video on his plan for the U.S. Capitol. https://www.aoc.gov/capitol-grounds/about-grounds

History President George Washington appointed commissioners to provide buildings and accommodations for Congress. The commissioners hired the French artist and engineer Major Pierre Charles L'Enfant, a Revolutionary War veteran, to lay out the new city. They also staged a competition for the design of the Capitol. Dr. William Thornton's entry won the competition. To learn more about the first "architect of the capitol" and the Architects that followed, visit the AOC's history web pages. https://www.aoc.gov/about-aoc/history-architect

Map A map of Capitol Hill is available online. https://www.aoc.gov/us-capitol-map

News The AOC posts news and notices on its website. https://www.aoc.gov/news

Oversight The Office of the Inspector General from the AOC posts reports and data on Oversight.gov, a text-searchable repository of reports that Federal Inspectors General publish. The Council of the Inspectors General on Integrity and Efficiency operates and maintains the website to increase public access to independent and authoritative information on the Federal Government. https://oversight.gov

Planning a Visit Information on accessibility services, activities, tours, visiting hours, and where to shop and eat is available online. http://www.aoc.gov/plan-your-visit

Projects The AOC never lacks things to preserve or restore. Visit the "Projects" web page to learn about ongoing work. https://www.aoc.gov/projects

Publications The AOC publishes a variety of publications that are accessible online. https://www.aoc.gov/publications

Site Map The website map allows visitors to look for specific topics or to browse content that aligns with their interests. https://www.aoc.gov/sitemap

Social Media The AOC has a Facebook account. https://www.facebook.com/ArchitectoftheCapitol

The AOC tweets announcements and other newsworthy items on Twitter. https://twitter.com/uscapitol

The AOC posts videos on its YouTube channel. https://www.youtube.com/user/AOCgov

Trees Approximately 890 trees surround the Capitol Building on Capitol Square, and more than 4,300 trees grow throughout the 274-acre Capitol Grounds. A tree map is available on the "Trees on Capitol Grounds" web page. https://www.aoc.gov/trees

The Sources of Information were updated 10–2019.

Congressional Budget Office

Second and D Streets SW., Washington, DC 20515
Phone, 202-226-2600. Internet, http://www.cbo.gov

Office of the Director

Director	PHILLIP L. SWAGEL
Deputy Director	MARK P. HADLEY
General Counsel	(VACANCY)
Senior Advisor	ROBERT A. SUNSHINE
Associate Directors	
Communications	DEBORAH KILROE
Economic Analysis	WENDY EDELBERG
	JEFFREY KLING
Legislative Affairs	LEIGH ANGRES

Other Divisions

Assistant Directors	
Budget Analysis	THERESA A. GULLO
Financial Analysis	SEBASTIEN GAY
Health, Retirement, and Long-Term Analysis	DAVID WEAVER
Macroeconomic Analysis	JEFFREY F. WERLING
Assistant Director, Microeconomic Studies	JOSEPH KILE
National Security	DAVID E. MOSHER
Tax Analysis	JOHN MCCLELLAND
Chief Administrative Officer	
Management, Business, and Information Services	JOSEPH E. EVANS, JR.
https://www.cbo.gov/about/organization-and-staffing	

The above list of key personnel was updated 7–2019.

The Congressional Budget Office independently analyzes budgetary and economic issues to support the congressional budget process.

The Congressional Budget Office (CBO) was established by the Congressional Budget Act of 1974 (2 U.S.C. 601), which also created a procedure by which the Congress considers and acts on the annual Federal budget. This process enables the Congress to have an overview of the Federal budget and to make overall decisions on spending and taxation levels and on the deficit or surplus these levels generate. https://www.cbo.gov/about/founding

Activities

The CBO assists the congressional budget committees with drafting and enforcing the annual budget resolution, which serves as a blueprint for total levels of Government spending and revenues in a fiscal year. Once completed, the budget resolution guides the action of other congressional committees in drafting subsequent spending and revenue legislation within their jurisdiction.

To support this process, the CBO makes budgetary and economic projections, analyzes the proposals set forth in the President's budget request, and details alternative spending and revenue options for lawmakers to consider. The CBO also provides cost estimates of bills approved by congressional committees and tracks the progress of spending and revenue legislation in a scorekeeping system. CBO cost estimates and scorekeeping help the budget committees determine whether the budgetary effects of individual proposals are

Organization Chart   **July 2019**

consistent with the most recent spending and revenue targets.

Upon congressional request, the CBO also produces reports analyzing specific policy and program issues that are significant for the budget. In keeping with the Office's nonpartisan role, its analyses do not include policy recommendations, and they routinely disclose their underlying assumptions and methods. This open and nonpartisan stance has been instrumental in preserving the credibility of the Office's analyses. https://www.cbo.gov/about/products/RecurringReports

Analysis of the President's Budget   The CBO estimates the budgetary impact of the proposals in the President's budget using its own economic forecast and assumptions. The CBO's independent reestimate allows Congress to compare the administration's spending and revenue proposals with the CBO's baseline projections and other proposals using a consistent set of economic and technical assumptions. https://www.cbo.gov/about/products#2

Baseline Budget Projections and Economic Forecasts   Each year, the CBO issues reports on the budget and economic outlook that cover the 10-year period used in the congressional budget process. Those reports present and explain the CBO's baseline budget projections and economic forecast, which are generally based on current law regarding Federal spending and revenues. The reports also describe the differences between the current projections and previous ones, compare the CBO's economic forecast with those of other forecasters, and show the budgetary impact of some alternative policy assumptions. https://www.cbo.gov/about/products#1

Budgetary and Economic Policy Issues   The CBO also analyzes specific program and policy issues that affect the Federal budget and the economy. Generally, requests for these analyses come from the chair or ranking minority member of a committee or subcommittee or from the leadership of either party in the House or Senate. https://www.cbo.gov/topics/reports-policy-options

Cost Estimates for Bills   The CBO provides cost estimates of every bill to show how it would affect spending or revenues over the next 5 or 10 years, depending on the type of spending involved. The CBO also provides informal estimates at the committee level and other stages in the legislative process. https://www.cbo.gov/publication/54437

Federal Mandates   As required by the Unfunded Mandates Reform Act of 1995, the CBO analyzes the costs that proposed legislation would impose on State, local, and tribal governments and on the private sector. The CBO produces mandate statements with its cost estimates for each committee-approved bill. https://www.cbo.gov/about/products#7

Scorekeeping   The CBO provides the budget and appropriations committees with frequent tabulations of congressional action affecting spending and revenues. Those scorekeeping reports provide information on whether legislative actions are consistent with the spending and revenue levels set by the budget resolution. https://www.cbo.gov/about/products#9

Sources of Information

Blog   The CBO maintains an active blog. https://www.cbo.gov/blog

Business Opportunities   The CBO posts answers to questions that vendors frequently ask. https://www.cbo.gov/about/business-opportunities | Email: procurementservices@cbo.gov

Career Opportunities   CBO employees and interns analyze public policies and their budgetary and economic effects, work with policy analysis experts, support the Congress, and provide nonpartisan and objective analysis. To carry out these activities, the agency relies on professionals with superior academic backgrounds and experience in defense, environmental and resource, financial, health, and labor economics; industrial organization; macroeconomics; public finance; and public-policy analysis. https://www.cbo.gov/about/careers | Email: careers@cbo.gov

According to the Partnership for Public Service, the CBO is an outstanding place to work in the Federal Government. Among 29 small agencies, it placed 3d in the 2018 Best Places To Work rankings. http://bestplacestowork.org/rankings/detail/CB00

Climate   In "Expected Costs of Damage From Hurricane Winds and Storm-Related Flooding" (April 2019), the CBO reports:

"Without limits on emissions, the rise in sea levels is predicted to accelerate in the second half of this century . . . . Those increases, along with other changes caused by warming (such as increases in droughts and the spread of certain invasive species), will adversely affect economic output in the future and have other negative effects that are not captured by change in GDP (such as decreases in biodiversity)." https://www.cbo.gov/topics/climate-and-environment/climate-change

Contact Information   The nature of the inquiry determines the best way to contact the agency. The "Contact Information" page has specific contact information for Members of Congress and congressional staff, members of the public, representatives of the media, job candidates, vendors and contractors, and for those wanting to leave a comment about the CBO website. https://www.cbo.gov/about/contact

Cost Estimates   The Congress relies on CBO cost estimates for implementing budget enforcement rules and procedures. https://www.cbo.gov/cost-estimates

Defense Budget   The CBO analyzes the possible consequences of planned reductions in funding for the military's force structure and acquisitions. It also studies the budgetary implications of Department of Defense plans, including military personnel, weapon systems, and operations plans. https://www.cbo.gov/topics/defense-and-national-security/defense-budget

Frequently Asked Questions (FAQs)   The CBO posts answers to the most common questions that people ask. https://www.cbo.gov/faqs

Glossary   The glossary is available online in Portable Document Format (PDF). It defines terms that are commonly used in CBO reports. Many of the entries conform to those published in "A Glossary of Terms Used in the Federal Budget Process" (Government Accountability Office, 2005). https://www.cbo.gov/publication/42904

History   The CBO was birthed in the crucible of conflict: President Richard M. Nixon had threatened to withhold congressional appropriations for programs whose activities diverged from his policies. Members of Congress responded by enacting the Congressional Budget and Impoundment Control Act of 1974. This law reasserted Congress's constitutional control over the budget and created new legislative institutions for implementing the new budget process. One of these institutions was a new legislative-branch agency. To learn more, visit the CBO "History" web page. https://www.cbo.gov/about/history

Information Products   CBO informational, nonpartisan products include baseline projections for selected programs, budget and economic data, and major recurring reports. https://www.cbo.gov/about/products

Interactive Tools / Workbooks   The "Interactives" web page allows visitors to simulate a variety of budget-relevant scenarios and explore their potential costs. For example, the "Force Structure Tool" determines the costs and capabilities of customized plans for the Armed Forces. https://www.cbo.gov/interactives

Nuclear Forces Costs   The CBO projects the 10-year costs of nuclear forces every 2 years. The report of January 2019 contains projections for the period from 2019 to 2028. https://www.cbo.gov/publication/54914

Organizational Chart   The CBO posts its organizational chart in Portable Document Format (PDF) for viewing and downloading. https://www.cbo.gov/system/files/2019-07/CBO-Organization-Chart-2019-07.pdf

Press Center   The most recent CBO news is available online. Each Thursday, the agency posts a list of key publications that are likely to be released during the coming week or soon thereafter. https://www.cbo.gov/about/press-center

Social Media   The CBO has a SlideShare account. https://www.slideshare.net/cbo

The CBO tweets announcements and other newsworthy items on Twitter. https://twitter.com/uscbo

The CBO posts videos on its YouTube channel. https://www.youtube.com/uscbo

Ten Things To Know   The CBO has posted the 10 most important things that it wants people to know about the agency. https://www.cbo.gov/about/10-things-to-know

Topics   The Topics web page allows visitors to browse subjects ranging from agriculture to veterans' issues. https://www.cbo.gov/topics

Transparency   By prioritizing its commitment to transparency, the CBO seeks to promote better understanding of its work, to help people gauge the potential change

in estimates when policies or circumstances differ, and to enhance the credibility of its analyses and processes. https://www.cbo.gov/about/transparency
Visiting Scholars The CBO welcomes applications from analysts and scholars

The Sources of Information were updated 7–2019.

in all fields; however, it has a special interest in collaborating with experts in macroeconomics and financial, health, and public economics. https://www.cbo.gov/about/careers/visitingscholars | Email: careers@cbo.gov

Government Accountability Office

441 G Street NW., Washington, DC 20548
Phone, 202-512-3000. Internet, http://www.gao.gov

Comptroller General of the United States	GENE L. DODARO
Staff Offices—Managing Directors	
Congressional Relations	ORICE WILLIAMS BROWN
Opportunity and Inclusiveness	EDDA EMMANUELLI-PEREZ
Public Affairs	CHARLES YOUNG
Strategic Planning and External Liaison	JAMES-CHRISTIAN BLOCKWOOD
http://www.gao.gov/cghome/gdbiog.html	
Chief Operating Officer	KATHERINE A. SIGGERUD
Chief Quality Officer	TIMOTHY P. BOWLING
Managing Director of the Continuous Process Improvement Office	PATRICIA MCCLURE
Mission Teams—Managing Directors	
Applied Research and Methods	NANCY KINGSBURY
Contracting and National Security Acquisitions	MICHELE MACKIN
Defense Capabilities and Management	CATHLEEN A. BERRICK
Education, Workforce, and Income Security	BARBARA D. BOVBJERG
Financial Management and Assurance	J. LAWRENCE MALENICH
Financial Markets and Community Investment	LAWRANCE EVANS, JR.
Forensic Audits and Investigative Service	JOHANA R. AYERS
Health Care	A. NICOLE CLOWERS
Homeland Security and Justice	CHARLES M. JOHNSON, JR.
Information Technology and Cybersecurity	VALERIE MELVIN
International Affairs and Trade	THOMAS MELITO
Natural Resources and Environment	MARK E. GAFFIGAN
Physical Infrastructure	DANIEL BERTONI
Strategic Issues	J. CHRISTOPHER MIHM
Chief Administrative Officer / Chief Financial Officer	KARL J. MASCHINO
Deputy Chief Administrative Officer	PAUL R. JOHNSON
General Counsel	THOMAS H. ARMSTRONG
Deputy General Counsel / Ethics Counselor	(VACANCY)
Inspector General	ADAM TRZECIAK
http://www.gao.gov/about/workforce/igbio.html	
https://www.gao.gov/about/careers/our-teams/	

The key personnel table was updated 2–2019.

The Government Accountability Office helps the Congress fulfill its constitutional responsibilities and heightens the Federal Government's accountability and performance.

The Government Accountability Office (GAO) is an independent, nonpartisan agency that works for the Congress. The agency is known as the "congressional watchdog" because it investigates how the Federal Government spends taxpayer dollars. The Budget and Accounting Act of 1921 (31 U.S.C. 702) established the General Accounting Office. Eighty three years later, it was renamed the Government Accountability Office pursuant to the GAO Capital Reform Act of 2004 (31 U.S.C. 702 note).

Activities

The GAO gathers information that the Congress uses to determine how effective executive branch agencies are at carrying out their missions. Its efforts routinely center on answering basic questions: Are Government programs meeting their objectives? Are they providing services of value to the public? Ultimately, the GAO ensures that the Government is accountable to the American people.

To help Senators and Representatives make informed policy decisions, the GAO provides them with accurate, balanced, and timely information. The Office supports congressional oversight by evaluating Government policies and programs; auditing agency operations to ensure effective, efficient, and appropriate spending of Federal funds; investigating allegations of illegal and improper activities; and issuing legal decisions and opinions.

With virtually the entire Federal Government subject to its review, the GAO issues a steady stream of products, including hundreds of reports and testimonies by GAO officials each year. Its reports, which are often called "blue books," meet short-term, immediate needs for information on a wide range of Government operations. These reports help Members of Congress better understand emerging, long-term issues whose effects are far-reaching. The GAO saves billions of American tax dollars by supporting improvements in Government operations and thoughtfulness in legislative actions. http://www.gao.gov/about

Sources of Information

At a Glance   The "GAO at a Glance" web page offers a profile of the agency, including information on the scope and nature of its activities. http://www.gao.gov/about/gglance.html

Bid Protests   Bidders or other interested parties may protest Federal Government procurement contracts. The GAO provides an inexpensive and expeditious forum for the resolution of these protests. Two search tools are available on the "Bid Protests" web page. One allows users to search and access all published bid protest decisions; the other allows users to search the bid protest docket to find status information on cases filed within the past 12 months. http://www.gao.gov/legal/bid-protests/search | Email: ProtestFinder@gao.gov

Blog   The GAO's website features "WatchBlog: Following the Federal Dollar." To receive electronic notifications of new posts, sign up by entering an email address in the appropriate text box on the "WatchBlog" web page. https://blog.gao.gov

Career Opportunities   The GAO relies on attorneys, communications analysts, criminal investigators, economists, financial auditors, information technology analysts, and other professionals to carry out its mission. http://www.gao.gov/careers/index.html

The GAO offers an intern program for students. Appointments for intern positions are 10–16 weeks in length and normally held during summer months. A student must be enrolled on at least a half-time basis, as determined by his or her college or university. A GAO student intern receives an appointment on a nonpermanent basis; however, after completing 400 hours of service and meeting degree requirements, he or she may be eligible for a permanent position. Internships are open to undergraduate and graduate students. http://www.gao.gov/careers/student.html

According to the Partnership for Public Service, the GAO is an outstanding place to work in the Federal Government. Among 27 midsize agencies, it placed fourth in the 2018 Best Places To Work rankings. http://bestplacestowork.org/BPTW/rankings/detail/GA00

Find an Expert   The "Find an Expert" web page is useful for identifying a subject matter expert as a potential speaker for an organizational event. The list of experts includes names, as well as areas of expertise, email addresses, and telephone numbers. https://www.gao.gov/about/contact-us/find-an-expert

FraudNet   FraudNet helps people report suspicion of abuse, fraud, waste, or mismanagement of Federal funds to the appropriate authorities. It refers allegations to Federal, State, and local law enforcement, and to Offices of Inspector General, when appropriate; it supports congressional investigation and audit requests; it provides audit and investigative leads to GAO staff; and it offers support to government at all levels for establishing and operating hotlines. Phone, 800-424-5454. Fax, 202-512-3086. http://www.gao.gov/fraudnet | Email: fraudnet@gao.gov

Freedom of Information Act (FOIA)   The GAO is not subject to the FOIA; however, it discloses information in accordance with the spirit of the Act, while remaining true to its duties and functions as an agency whose primary responsibility is to the Congress. Fax, 202-512-5806. http://www.gao.gov/about/freedom_of_information_act | Email: RecordsRequest@gao.gov

Frequently Asked Questions (FAQs)   The GAO posts answers to general questions about its legal decisions. http://www.gao.gov/legal/more/about

Good Governance   The Center for Audit Excellence promotes good governance and builds the capacity of domestic and international accountability organizations. It provides high-quality training, technical assistance, and related products and services. http://www.gao.gov/resources/centerforauditexcellence/overview

History   After the signing of the armistice agreement of November 11, 1918, the hostilities of the First World War ended. Although the United States had entered the war late as a combatant, it transported millions of troops and their equipment to the Western Front to support the Allies. Wartime spending inflated the national debt, and Congress needed reliable information and enhanced expenditure control. In 1921, to improve managing the Nation's affairs, Congress passed the Budget and Accounting Act. To learn more about this piece of legislation and the role that a new agency was playing in Federal financial management, visit "The History of GAO"

web pages. http://www.gao.gov/about/history

Key Issues   The "Key Issues" web pages allow visitors to explore the GAO's work on a range of national issues by agency or topic. The agency's most relevant reports are highlighted on these web pages. http://www.gao.gov/key_issues/overview#t=0

Organizational Chart   The GAO's organizational chart is available on its website. http://www.gao.gov/about/workforce/orgchart.html

Podcast Gallery   Recorded, hosted, and produced by GAO staff, the "Watchdog Report" features interviews with agency officials on significant issues and new reports. http://www.gao.gov/multimedia/podcast

Press Releases   The GAO posts press releases online. https://www.gao.gov/about/press-center/press-releases/

Publications   Most GAO products and publications are available online, free of charge. Charges for printed copies cover the printing, shipping, and handling costs. Phone, 202-512-6000 or 866-801-7077. TDD, 202-512-2537. http://www.gao.gov/ordering.htm

The GAO's website allows visitors to browse reports and testimonies by date and topic and by agency alphabetically or hierarchically. http://www.gao.gov/browse/date/week

The "Principles of Federal Appropriations Law," also known as the "Red Book," is a multivolume treatise on Federal fiscal law. It provides text discussions with references to specific legal authorities to illustrate legal principles, their applications, and exceptions. These references include GAO decisions and judicial decisions, opinions, statutory provisions, and other relevant sources. http://www.gao.gov/legal/red-book/overview

Recommendations Database   The recommendations database contains report recommendations that still need to be addressed. GAO's recommendations help congressional and agency leaders prepare for appropriations and oversight activities, as well as improve Government operations. Recommendations remain open until designated as "closed-implemented" or "closed-not implemented." The general public may browse or search open recommendations online. http://www.gao.gov/recommendations

Reports / Testimonies The GAO posts an alphabetical listing of significant reports and testimonies each month. https://www.gao.gov/reports-testimonies/month-in-review/top-ten/

Resources The GAO website features resources that auditors and others promoting accountability may find useful. http://www.gao.gov/resources/auditors/overview

The GAO website features resources that Members of Congress and and their staff may find useful. http://www.gao.gov/resources/congress/overview

The GAO website features resources that Federal agency managers may find useful. http://www.gao.gov/resources/federal_managers/overview

The GAO website features resources that journalists may find useful. http://www.gao.gov/resources/journalists/overview

The GAO website features resources—search tips for locating GAO products on its website, information on using the data and images contained in them, suggestions for additional informational sources—that researchers may find useful. http://www.gao.gov/resources/researchers/overview

Site Map The website map allows visitors to look for specific topics or to browse content that aligns with their interests. http://www.gao.gov/sitemap.html

Social Media The GAO uses social media tools—Facebook, Flickr, LinkedIn, Twitter, YouTube—to make its work more accessible to both Congress and the general public. https://www.gao.gov/about/contact-us/stay-connected/

Telephone Directory The "Organizational Telephone Directory" (January 2019), a resource that the agency updates often, contains GAO personnel contact information. It is available online in Portable Document Format (PDF). http://www.gao.gov/about.gao/phonebook/orgphonebook.pdf

Updates A subscription form is available on the GAO's website to sign up for email updates on the latest reports. Daily or monthly electronic updates are options, too, as well as notifications about correspondence, reports, and testimony that fall within a specific topic area. http://www.gao.gov/subscribe/index.php

Video Gallery The GAO website features a video collection that is diverse and extensive, educational and informative. http://www.gao.gov/multimedia/video/#video_id=679942

Widgets Snippets of HTML code for embedding small news widgets that refresh automatically are available on the GAO website. Pasting the code into the desired location on a website makes the most recent reports and testimonies and legal decisions from GAO locally accessible. http://www.gao.gov/widgets_reports_and_legal.html; http://www.gao.gov/about/contact.html | Email: contact@gao.gov

For further information, contact the Office of Public Affairs, Government Accountability Office, 441 G Street NW., Washington, DC 20548. Phone, 202-512-4800.

Government Publishing Office

732 North Capitol Street NW., Washington, DC 20401
Phone, 202-512-1800. Internet, http://www.gpo.gov

Director	(VACANCY)
Deputy Director	JOHN W. CRAWFORD, ACTING
Equal Employment Opportunity Managing Director	MARK A. PARAS

https://www.gpo.gov/who-we-are/our-agency/leadership

Administration

Chief Administrative Officer	LYLE L. GREEN, ACTING
Administrative Services Manager	OKSANA POZDA
Chief Officers	
Acquisition	LORNA E. BAPTISTE-JONES
Human Capital	DAN M. MIELKE
Information	WESAM MUSA

Finance

Chief Financial Officer   William L. Boesch, Jr.

Legal

General Counsel   Kerry L. Miller, Acting

Associate General Counsel—Labor Relations   Melissa Hatfield

Operations

Deputy Director   John W. Crawford, Acting

Managing Directors
Official Journals of Government   Lyle L. Green
Plant Operations   John W. Crawford
Security and Intelligent Documents   Stephen G. LeBlanc
Customer Services   Sandra K. MacAfee

Public Access

Superintendent of Documents   Laurie Hall
Library Services and Content Management Managing   Laurie Hall
   Director
Publications and Information Sales Director   Lisa Williams

Security Services

Chief Security Officer   LaMont R. Vernon

Strategy

Chief of Staff   Richard G. Davis, Acting

Chief Officers
Technology   Richard G. Davis
Public Relations   Gary Somerset

Specialists
Congressional Relations   James McCarthy
Employee Communications   Gary Somerset

Inspector General   Michael P. Leary
https://www.gpo.gov/who-we-are/our-agency/inspector-
   general/overview-and-hotline

The above list of key personnel was updated 10–2019.

The Government Publishing Office produces, procures, and disseminates printed and electronic publications of the Congress, executive departments, and Federal agencies and establishments

Establishment and Organization

On June 23, 1860, the U.S. Congress passed Joint Resolution 25 in "Relation to the Public Printing" (12 Stat. 117). It empowered the Superintendent of Public Printing to execute the printing and binding that the Senate and House of Representatives, the executive and judicial departments, and the Court of Claims authorized. It also directed the Superintendent "to contract for the erection or purchase of the necessary buildings, machinery, and materials for that purpose." The Government Printing Office opened for business on March 4, 1861, the same day that President Abraham Lincoln was sworn into office and a few weeks after the first salvos of the American Civil War, when Confederate guns bombarded Fort Sumter in Charleston Harbor. https://www.loc.gov/law/help/statutes-at-large/36th-congress/c36.pdf

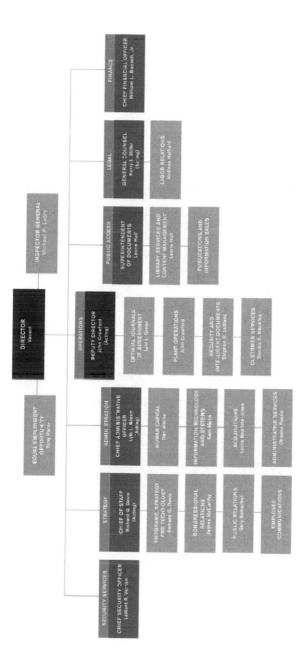

U.S. GOVERNMENT PUBLISHING OFFICE | KEEPING AMERICA INFORMED | OFFICIAL   DIGITAL | SECURE

732 North Capitol Street, NW, Washington, DC 20401 | **www.gpo.gov** | www.fdsys.gov

July 2019

On December 17, 2014, President Barack Obama approved Public Law 113–235, which is commonly cited as the "Consolidated and Further Continuing Appropriations Act, 2015." Section 1301 of that law (128 Stat. 2537) redesignated the Government Printing Office as the Government Publishing Office (GPO). Congress changed the name to reflect the prominent role that the GPO plays in providing access to Government information in digital formats. https://www.congress. gov/113/plaws/publ235/PLAW-113publ235. pdf

The agency's duties are defined in title 44 of the U.S. Code. https://uscode. house.gov/view.xhtml?path=/prelim@ title44&edition=prelim

By the advice and with the consent of the Senate, the President nominates and appoints "a suitable person" as the Director "to take charge of and manage" the agency (44 USC 301). https://uscode. house.gov/view.xhtml?path=/prelim@title44/ chapter3&edition=prelim

The agency's organizational chart is available in Portable Document Format (PDF) for viewing and downloading on the "Leadership" web page. https://www.gpo. gov/docs/default-source/leadership-pdf-file/ gpo_organizationchart_7-18-19

Activities

Headquartered in Washington, DC, with a total employment of approximately 1,700, the Office is responsible for the production and distribution of information products and services for the three branches of the Federal Government. It is the Federal Government's primary centralized resource for producing, procuring, cataloging, indexing, authenticating, disseminating, and preserving the official information products of the U.S. Government in digital and tangible forms.

While many of the informational products, such as the "Congressional Record" and "Federal Register," are produced at the main GPO plant, most of the Government's printing is done in partnership with America's printing industry. The Office procures 75 percent of all printing orders through private sector vendors across the country, competitively buying products and services from thousands of businesses in all 50 States. The contracts cover the entire spectrum of printing and publishing services and are suitable for companies of all sizes.

The agency disseminates Federal information products through a sales program, a nationwide distribution network of Federal depository libraries, the Federal Digital System (FDsys), and the free U.S. Government information service known as govinfo, which is replacing FDsys. The public can already access hundreds of thousands of Federal Government document titles by visiting the govinfo website. https:// www.gpo.gov/who-we-are/our-agency/ mission-vision-and-goals

Sources of Information

Annual Reports / Budget Submissions   An annual report archives and budget submission archives are available on the "Congressional Relations" web page. https:// www.gpo.gov/who-we-are/our-agency/ congressional-relations

Archived Records   The records of the GPO are referenced in the "Guide to Federal Records in the National Archives of the United States." The Guide is accessible online, and GPO records have been assigned to Record Group 149. https://www. archives.gov/research/guide-fed-records/ groups/149.html

Ben's Guide   An educational website for children and young adults, Ben's Guide has learning adventures for the apprentice level (ages 4–8), journeyperson level (ages 9–13), and master level (ages 14 and older). https:// bensguide.gpo.gov

Blog   "Government Book Talk" offers reviews of new and popular publications, talking about forthcoming and out-of-print books. The blog spotlights the variety of Government publications that are available and the scope of their influence. https:// govbooktalk.gpo.gov

Bookstore   Printed copies of many documents, ranging from Supreme Court opinions to reports from the Bureau of Labor Statistics, may be purchased. To order in person, visit the GPO Main Bookstore at 710 North Capitol Street NW., Washington, DC (corner of North Capitol Street NW. and G Street), 8 a.m.–4 p.m. To order online, use the link below. To order by phone or inquire about an order, call 866-512-1800 or 202-512-1800 (Washington, DC–metropolitan area), 8 a.m.–5:30 p.m., eastern standard time. All orders require prepayment by an American Express, Discover/NOVUS, MasterCard, or VISA credit card; check or money order; or Superintendent of Documents (SOD) deposit account, which customers who purchase Government products on a recurring basis can open with the GPO. Fax, 202-512-2104. https://bookstore.gpo.gov | Email: contactcenter@gpo.gov

Business Opportunities   GPO procurement services teams post open term contract and one-time bid solicitations online. https://www.gpo.gov/how-to-work-with-us/vendors/contract-opportunities

Small purchase solicitations are posted on the "Quick Quote" website. https://contractorconnection.gpo.gov/OpenJobs.aspx

Career Opportunities   The GPO provides other Government agencies with services for the printing, publishing, distribution, and storage of digital content. To deliver these services successfully, it relies on creative, energetic, and talented professionals representing diverse trades and administrative fields. https://www.gpo.gov/who-we-are/careers/how-to-apply

Catalog of U.S. Government Publications (CGP)   The CGP is a searchable Federal publications catalog that contains descriptive information on recent and historical publications, as well as links to some complete documents. Users may search the catalog by agency, keywords, subject, and title. https://catalog.gpo.gov/F?RN=785806650

Congressional Relations   The Office of Congressional Relations responds to congressional inquiries and requests. Phone, 202-512-1991. Fax, 202-512-1293. https://www.gpo.gov/who-we-are/our-agency/congressional-relations

Contact Information   To ask a question or report a technical issue, visit the "Contact Us" page. https://www.gpo.gov/contact.htm | Email: ContactCenter@gpo.gov

Federal Depository Libraries   The Federal depository library directory is available online. https://catalog.gpo.gov/fdlpdir/FDLPdir.jsp

Federal Lawmaking   An outline of the Federal lawmaking process—starting with the introduction of a bill by a Member of the Congress, continuing through its passage by both Chambers, and culminating in the President's approval—is available online in Portable Document Format (PDF). https://www.gpo.gov/docs/default-source/media-kit-files/how-a-bill-becomes-a-Law.pdf

Govinfo   Free public access to the full text of official publications from the three branches of the Federal Government is available at govinfo. The website also serves as a standards-compliant preservation repository, offers advanced search engine capabilities, and functions as a content management system to control digital content throughout its lifecycle. https://www.govinfo.gov

History   The GPO opened for business several weeks before Confederate artillery opened fire on a Federal fort in Charleston Harbor. Within 18 months of the first salvo, the GPO had readied one of the most significant documents in American history for President Abraham Lincoln's signature. To learn more about the 1862 war order that acted as a precursor to the Emancipation Proclamation of 1863, watch the video "Lincoln and His Printers: GPO in the Civil War." https://www.gpo.gov/who-we-are/our-agency/history

A GPO timeline and short history of making electronic Government information accessible to the public is available online. https://www.govinfo.gov/about/history

Media Kit   The GPO media kit contains links to access resources and to download information that may be useful for reporters and Federal agency customers. It also has a list of links providing easy access to the agency's social media sites. For additional information, contact the Public Relations team. Phone, 202-512-1957. https://www.gpo.gov/who-we-are/news-media/media-kit

News / Press Releases   The GPO posts the latest news and maintains a news archive, from 1997 to the present, on its website. Phone, 202-512-1957. Fax, 202-512-1998. https://www.gpo.gov/who-we-are/news-media/news-and-press-releases

Offices / Distribution Centers   Contact information for nationwide offices and the Laurel, MD, and Pueblo, CO, distribution centers is available on the GPO website.

https://www.gpo.gov/who-we-are/our-agency/office-locations

Oversight   The Office of the Inspector General from the GPO posts reports and data on Oversight.gov, a text-searchable repository of reports that Federal Inspectors General publish. The Council of the Inspectors General on Integrity and Efficiency operates and maintains the website to increase public access to independent and authoritative information on the Federal Government. https://oversight.gov

The Sources of Information were updated 10–2019.

Social Media   The GPO maintains a presence on six social media sites: Facebook, Twitter, YouTube, LinkedIn, Instagram, and Pinterest. Links to these sites are listed together in one location on the "Media Kit" web page. https://www.gpo.gov/who-we-are/news-media/media-kit

Style Manual   An official guide to the form and style of Federal Government publishing is available online. https://www.govinfo.gov/content/pkg/GPO-STYLEMANUAL-2016/pdf/GPO-STYLEMANUAL-2016.pdf

Library of Congress
101 Independence Avenue SE., Washington, DC 20540
Phone, 202-707-5000. Internet, http://www.loc.gov

Librarian of Congress	CARLA D. HAYDEN
Deputy Librarian for Institutional Advancement	ROBERT R. NEWLEN
Chief of Staff	ELIZABETH C. MORRISON
Chief Operating Officer	EDWARD R. JABLONSKI
General Counsel	ELIZABETH PUGH
Inspector General	KURT W. HYDE
Chief Communications Officer	ROSWELL M. ENCINA
Director of Human Resources Services	RACHEL BOUMAN
Director of Congressional Research Service	MARY B. MAZANEC
Associate Librarian for Library Services	J. MARK SWEENEY
Director of National International Outreach	JANE MCAULIFFE
Law Librarian of Congress	JANE F. SÁNCHEZ
Acting Register of Copyrights	KARYN A. TEMPLE CLAGGETT

Library of Congress Trust Fund Board

Chair (Librarian of Congress)	CARLA D. HAYDEN
(Fiscal Assistant Secretary of the Treasury)	DAVID A. LEBRYK
(Chair, Joint Committee on the Library)	GREGG HARPER
(Vice Chair, Joint Committee on the Library)	RICHARD SHELBY
Member	KATHLEEN L. CASEY
Member	J. RICHARD FREDERICKS
Member	THOMAS GIRARDI
Member	CHRISTOPHER G. LONG
Member	SHEILA MARCELO
Member	GEORGE MARCUS
Member	JOHN MILLER
Member	(VACANCY)
Member	(VACANCY)
Member	(VACANCY)

The Library of Congress is the national library of the United States, offering diverse materials for research, including the world's most extensive collections in areas such as American history, music, and law.

The Library of Congress was established by Act of April 24, 1800 (2 Stat. 56), appropriating $5,000 "for the purchase of such books as may be necessary for the use of Congress . . . ." The Library's scope of responsibility has been widened by subsequent legislation (2 U.S.C. 131-168d). The Librarian, appointed by the President with the advice and consent of the Senate, directs the Library.

The Library's first responsibility is service to Congress. Its Congressional Research Service provides Congress with legislative research and analysis that is authoritative, confidential, objective, and timely during all stages of the legislative process. The Library's Congress.gov Web site serves as a source of legislative information for both Congress and the general public. https://www.congress.gov

As the Library has developed, its range of service has expanded to include the entire governmental establishment and the public at large. The Library serves as a national library for the United States, and its online presence makes it a global resource. https://www.loc.gov/about

Activities

Collections The Library's extensive collections are universal in scope. They include books, serials, and pamphlets on every subject and in more than 470 languages, and research materials in many formats, including maps, photographs, manuscripts, motion pictures, and sound recordings. Among them are the most comprehensive collections of books outside Asia and the former Soviet Union; the largest collection of published aeronautical literature; and the most extensive collection of books in the Western Hemisphere.

The manuscript collections relate to various aspects of American history and civilization and include the personal papers of most of the Presidents from George Washington to Calvin Coolidge. The music collections contain volumes and pieces—manuscript and published—from classic works to the newest popular compositions. Other materials available for research include maps and views; photographic records; recordings, prints, drawings, and posters; government documents, newspapers, and periodicals; and motion pictures, microforms, audio and video tapes, and digital and online materials. https://www.loc.gov/discover

Reference Resources Admission to the various research facilities of the Library is free. The Library's reading rooms are open to persons age 16 and older. Readers must register by presenting valid photo identification with a current address. For some collections, there are additional requirements. While priority is given to inquiries about special materials or to unique resources, the Library provides helpful responses to all inquirers. Online reference service is also available through the "Ask a Librarian" Web page. http://www.loc.gov/rr

Copyrights With the enactment of the second general revision of the U.S. copyright law by Act of July 8, 1870 (16 Stat. 212–217), all activities relating to copyright, including deposit and registration, were centralized in the Library of Congress. The Copyright Act of 1976 (90 Stat. 2541) brought all forms of copyrightable authorship, both published and unpublished, under a single statutory system which gives authors protection upon creation of their works. Exclusive rights granted to authors under the statute include the right to reproduce and prepare derivative works, distribute copies or phonorecords, perform and display the work publicly, and in the case of sound recordings, to perform the work publicly by means of a digital audio transmission. Works eligible for copyright include literary works (books and periodicals), musical works, dramatic works, pantomimes and choreographic works, pictorial, graphic, and sculptural works, motion pictures, sound recordings, vessel hull designs, mask works, and architectural works.

The Copyright Office serves as a National registry for creative works, registering more than 500,000 claims annually. It is also a major source of acquisitions for the Library's collections. Most paper information is also accessible on its Web site. http://www.copyright.gov

Extension of Service The Library offers duplication services; the sale of sound recordings, cataloging data and tools; the exchange of duplicates with other institutions; development of classification schemes; preparation of bibliographic lists for Government and research; maintenance and publication of cooperative publications; and publication of catalogs, bibliographic guides, and lists, and texts of original manuscripts and rare books. It has items for circulation in traveling exhibitions; books in Braille, as well as "talking books on the Internet, and books on tape. The Library distributes electronic materials and provides research and analytical services for a fee. The Library also manages the following programs: centralized and cooperative cataloging; cataloging-in-publication for unpublished books; interlibrary loan system; and the U.S. International Standard Serial Number (ISSN) Center.

Furthermore, the Library provides for the following: the preparation of bibliographical lists responsive to the needs of Government and research; the maintenance and the publication of cooperative publications; the publication of catalogs, bibliographical guides, and lists, and of texts of original manuscripts and rare books in the Library of Congress; the circulation in traveling exhibitions of items from the Library's collections; the provision of books in Braille, electronic access to Braille books on the Internet, "talking books," and books on tape for the blind and the physically handicapped through more than 100 cooperating libraries throughout the Nation; the distribution of its electronic materials via the Internet; and the provision of research and analytical services on a fee-for-service basis to agencies in the executive and judicial branches. https://www.loc.gov/services

American Folklife Center   The American Folklife Center was established in the Library of Congress by Act of January 2, 1976 (20 U.S.C. 2102 et seq.). It supports, preserves, and presents American folklife by receiving and maintaining folklife collections, scholarly research, field projects, performances, exhibitions, festivals, workshops, publications, and audiovisual presentations. The Center administers the Veterans History Project, which records and preserves the first-person accounts of war veterans. It collaborates with the Smithsonian Institution's National Museum of African American History and Culture to maintain the Civil Rights History Project and

its resulting collection of interviews with leaders and participants in the Civil Rights movement. The Center also maintains and administers the American Folklife Center Archive, which is an extensive multi-format collection of ethnographic materials from this country and around the world, and serves as the national repository for folk-related field recordings, manuscripts, and other unpublished materials. The Archive also contains the collections of StoryCorps, a program to record and collect oral histories from people from all walks of life.

The Center's reading room contains over 4,000 books and periodicals; a sizable collection of magazines, newsletters, unpublished theses, and dissertations; field notes; and many textual and some musical transcriptions and recordings. Information on the Center's blog, social media, publications, and collections is available online. https://www.loc.gov/folklife

For further information, call 202-707-5510.

Center for the Book   The Center was established in the Library of Congress by an Act of October 13, 1977 (2 U.S.C. 171 et seq.), to stimulate public interest in books, reading, and libraries, and to encourage the study of books and print culture. The Center promotes and explores the vital role of books, reading, and libraries, nationally and internationally. As a partnership between the Government and the private sector, the Center for the Book depends on tax-deductible contributions from individuals and corporations to support its programs.

The Center's activities are directed toward the general public and scholars. The overall program includes reading promotion projects with television and radio networks, symposia, lectures, exhibitions, special events, and publications. More than 80 national education and civic organizations participate in the Center's annual reading promotion campaign.

The Center provides leadership for 52 affiliated State—including the District of Columbia and the Virgin Islands—centers for the book and nonprofit reading-promotion partners. It oversees the Library's read.gov Web site, administers the Library's Young Readers Center and its Poetry and Literature Center, and plays a key role in the Library's annual National

Book Festival. The Center also administers the position of Poet Laureate Consultant in Poetry, as well as, in collaboration with the Children's Book Council, the position of the National Ambassador for Young People's Literature. http://www.read.gov/cfb | Email: cfbook@loc.gov

For further information, contact the Center for the Book. Phone, 202-707-5221. Fax, 202-707-0269.

National Film Preservation Board The National Film Preservation Board, established by the National Film Preservation Act of 1988 (102 Stat. 1785) and reauthorized by the National Film Preservation Act of 2005 (2 U.S.C. 179l note), serves as a public advisory group to the Librarian of Congress. The Board works to ensure the survival, conservation, and increased public availability of America's film heritage, including advising the Librarian on the annual selection of films to the National Film Registry and counseling the Librarian on development and implementation of the national film preservation plan. https://www.loc.gov/programs/national-film-preservation-board/about-this-program

For further information, call 202-707-5912.

National Sound Recording Preservation Board The National Recording Preservation Board, established by the National Recording Preservation Act of 2000 (2 U.S.C. 1701 note) reviews nominated sound recordings for inclusion in the National Recording Registry and advises the Librarian on the inclusion of such recordings in the Registry to preserve sound recordings that are culturally, historically, or aesthetically significant. The Board comprises three major components: a National Recording Preservation Advisory Board, which brings together experts in the field; a National Recording Registry; and a fundraising foundation, all of which are conducted under the auspices of the Library of Congress. The Board implements a national plan for the long-term preservation and accessibility of the Nation's audio heritage. The national recording preservation program sets standards for future private and public preservation efforts in conjunction with the Library's National Audio-Visual Conservation Center in Culpeper, VA. https://www.loc.gov/programs/national-recording-preservation-board/about-this-program

For further information, call 202-707-5856.

Preservation The Library provides technical information related to the preservation of library and archival material. The Library's Preservation Directorate includes three preservation science laboratories, a Center for the Library's Analytical Science Samples, and a Collections Recovery Room. Information on publications and various preservation and conservation topics is available online. http://www.loc.gov/rr/askalib/ask-preserv.html

For further information, call 202-707-1840.

Sources of Information

Books for the Blind and Physically Handicapped Braille and talking books and magazines, including music materials, are distributed through more than 100 regional and subregional libraries to residents of the United States and its territories who are blind or have a physical disability. Eligible Americans living abroad are also able to participate. Users may also register for the Braille and Audio Reading Download (BARD) online service, enabling them to use the BARD mobile app to read on smart devices. Information is available from the National Library Service for the Blind and Physically Handicapped, Library of Congress, 1291 Taylor Street NW., Washington, DC 20542-4960. Phone, 202-707-5100 or 1-888-NLS-READ (1-888-657-7323). http://www.loc.gov/ThatAllMayRead | Email: nls@loc.gov

Business Opportunities To learn about business opportunities, visit the "Doing Business With the Library" Web page. http://www.loc.gov/about/doing-business-with-the-library

Cataloging Distribution Services Cataloging and bibliographic information in the form of microfiche catalogs, book catalogs, magnetic tapes, CD-ROM cataloging tools, bibliographies, and other technical publications is distributed to libraries and other institutions. Information about ordering materials is available from the Cataloging Distribution Service, Library of Congress,

Washington, DC 20541-4910. Phone, 202-707-6100. TDD, 202-707-0012. Fax, 202-707-1334. Email, cdsinfo@mail.loc. gov. Card numbers for new publications and Electronic Preassigned Control Numbers for publishers are available from the Cataloging in Publication Division, Library of Congress, Washington, DC 20541-4910. Phone, 202-707-6345.

Copyright Services   Information about the copyright law (title 17 of the U.S. Code), the method of securing copyright, and copyright registration procedures may be obtained by writing to the Copyright Office, Library of Congress, 101 Independence Avenue SE., Washington, DC 20559-6000. Phone, 202-707-3000. Registration application forms may be ordered by calling the forms hotline at 202-707-9100. Copyright records may be researched and reported by the Copyright Office for a fee; for an estimate, call 202-707-6850. Members of the public may use the copyright card catalog in the Copyright Office without charge. The database of Copyright Office records cataloged from January 1, 1978, to the present is available online at http://cocatalog.loc.gov/. The Copyright Information Office is located in Room LM-401, James Madison Memorial Building, 101 Independence Avenue SE., Washington, DC 20559-6000. It is open to the public Monday through Friday, 8:30 a.m. to 5 p.m., except for Federal holidays. http://www.loc.gov/copyright

Employment   The Library offers many opportunities for those seeking employment, fellowships or internships, or volunteer positions. Job vacancy announcements and application information are posted online and also available from the Employment Office, Room LM-107, 101 Independence Avenue SE., Washington, DC 20540. Phone, 202-707-4315. http://www.loc.gov/hr/employment

Duplication Services   Copies of manuscripts, prints, photographs, maps, and book material not subject to copyright and other restrictions are available for a fee. Order forms for photo reproduction and price schedules are available from Duplication Services, Library of Congress, 101 Independence Avenue SE., Washington, DC 20540-4570. Phone, 202-707-5640. http://www.loc.gov/duplicationservices

Exhibitions   Throughout the year, the Library offers free exhibitions featuring items from its collections. Library exhibitions may be viewed Monday through Saturday, 8:30 a.m. to 4:30 p.m., in the Thomas Jefferson Building. For more information, call 202-707-4604. To view current and past exhibitions online, use the link below. http://www.loc.gov/exhibits

Federal Agency Research Services   Federal agencies can procure research and analytical products on foreign and domestic topics using the collections of the Library of Congress through the Federal Research Division. Science, technology, humanities, and social science research are conducted by staff specialists exclusively on behalf of Federal agencies on a fee-for-service basis. Research requests should be directed to the Federal Research Division, Marketing Office, Library of Congress, Washington, DC 20540-4840. Phone, 202-707-9133. Fax, 202-707-3920. https://www.loc.gov/rr/frd

Publications   Library of Congress publications are available online. The Library of Congress Magazine (LCM) is published 6 times a year and may be viewed online at http://www.loc.gov/lcm/. The calendar of public events is also available online at www.loc.gov/loc/events and is available by mail to persons within 100 miles of Washington, DC. To be added to the calendar mailing list, send a request to Office Systems Services, Mail and Distribution Management Section, Library of Congress, 101 Independence Avenue SE., Washington, DC 20540-9441 or send an email to pao@loc.gov. http://www.loc.gov/visit/shopping

Reference and Bibliographic Services   Guidance is offered to readers in identifying and using the material in the Library's collections, and reference service is provided to those with inquiries who have exhausted local, State, and regional resources. Persons requiring services that cannot be performed by the Library staff can be supplied with names of private researchers who work on a fee-for-service basis. Requests for information should be directed to the Reference Referral Service, Library of Congress, 101 Independence Avenue SE., Washington, DC 20540-4720. Phone, 202-707-5522. Fax, 202-707-1389. Questions may also be submitted online at the "Ask a Librarian" Web site. http://www.loc.gov/rr/askalib

Research and Reference Services in Science and Technology Requests for reference services should be directed to the Science, Technology, and Business Division, Library of Congress, Science Reference Section, 101 Independence Avenue SE., Washington, DC 20540-4750. Phone, 202-707-5639. http://www.loc.gov/rr/scitech

Tours Guided tours of the Library are available on weekdays, 10:30 a.m.–3:30 p.m., and on Saturdays at 10:30 and 11:30 a.m. and at 1:30 and 2:30 p.m. For more information on scheduling a tour for a group of 10 or more, contact the Visitor Services Office. Phone, 202-707-0919. https://www.loc.gov/visit/tours; http://www.loc.gov | Email: pao@loc.gov

For further information, contact the Public Affairs Office, Library of Congress, 101 Independence Avenue SE., Washington, DC 20540-8610. Phone, 202-707-2905. Fax, 202-707-2905. Fax, 202-707-9199.

Congressional Research Service

101 Independence Avenue SE., Washington, DC 20540
Phone, 202-707-5000

Director, Congressional Research Service — Mary B. Mazanec

The Congressional Research Service (CRS) provides comprehensive research and analysis on all legislative and oversight issues of interest to Congress. The CRS assists Congress by responding to specific questions and by preparing reports on legislative topics in anticipation of questions and emerging issues. The CRS works with Members, committees, and congressional staff to identify and clarify policy problems and assess the implications of proposed policy alternatives. CRS experts play a role in every stage of the legislative process. http://www.loc.gov/crsinfo/about

Sources of Information

Employment Current vacancies and entry-level opportunities are posted online, as well as information on internship programs. http://www.loc.gov/crsinfo/opportunities; http://www.loc.gov/crsinfo/contact

For further information, call 202-707-5700.

United States Botanic Garden

Office of Executive Director, 245 First Street SW., Washington, DC 20024
Phone, 202-226-8333. Internet, http://www.usbg.gov | Email: usbg@aoc.gov
Conservatory, 100 Maryland Avenue SW., Washington, DC 20001
Production Facility, 4700 Shepherd Parkway SW., Washington, DC 20032
Phone, 202-226-4780

Acting Director

(VACANCY)
https://www.aoc.gov/organization/acting-architect

Executive Director

Saharah Moon Chapotin
https://www.usbg.gov/staff/saharah-moon-chapotin-phd

The above list of key personnel was updated 10–2019.

The United States Botanic Garden demonstrates the essential contribution that plants make aesthetically, culturally, ecologically, economically, and therapeutically, to the well-being of humankind, and it supports partnerships, nationally and internationally, by fostering exchanges of information and ideas.

Establishment and Organization   The U.S. Botanic Garden (USBG) has a long root that runs deep in the soil of the Nation's history. On October 21, 1796, while addressing some gentlemen in a letter from Mount Vernon, President George Washington conceived that "a Botanical Garden would be a good appendage to the Institution of a University" in the "Federal City." Twenty-four years later, that conception blossomed, when President James Madison helped establish a botanic garden in the U.S. Capital under the auspices of the Columbian Institute, a society dedicated to promoting the arts and sciences. This early botanic collection served as the core of what would grow to become the Nation's future botanic garden. https://founders.archives.gov/?q=%20 Author%3A%22Washington%2C%20 George%22&s=1211311113&r=2118

The U.S. Congress also supported establishing a national botanic garden. By an act of August 26, 1842, it made provision for the safekeeping and arrangement of dried and living specimens that Lieutenant Charles Wilkes's expedition had collected while exploring the Pacific Rim. Congress enacted that the enlarged collection should be placed under the stewardship of its Joint Committee on the Library and that it should be kept in the upper room of the Patent Office (5 Stat. 534). http://www.loc.gov/ law/help/statutes-at-large/27th-congress/ session-2/c27s2ch205.pdf

When the old Patent Office was expanded in 1849, a new location for the plants and greenhouse had to be found. Congress again intervened and, by an act of May 15, 1850, funded the construction of a new greenhouse and the collection's removal and relocation to a "suitable site on the public grounds" of the Capitol. The Joint Committee on the Library, with supervision

from the Commissioner of Public Buildings, managed the project (9 Stat. 427). A new national botanic garden opened on the National Mall, at the west end of the Capitol Grounds, later that year. http://www.loc. gov/law/help/statutes-at-large/31st-congress/ session-1/c31s1ch10.pdf

By 1856—the collection had been named officially the United States Botanic Garden, Congress was providing an annual appropriation for its upkeep, and the Joint Committee on the Library had assumed responsibility for both its direction and maintenance. To satisfy the McMillan Commission's plan for a large, open mall, the USBG relocated one block south, to its present site, in 1933. The Joint Committee on the Library maintains oversight of the USBG through the Architect of the Capitol, who holds the title of Acting Director. https:// www.usbg.gov/brief-history-us-botanic-garden

Activities
The USBG highlights botanical diversity worldwide and informs people about plants' aesthetic, cultural, ecological, economic, and therapeutic significance. The agency promotes appreciation of plants and stimulates interest in botany through artistic plant displays, education programs, exhibits, and curation of a large plant collection. It supports conservation by serving as a repository for endangered plant species. It also encourages the exchange of ideas and disseminates mission-relevant information to national and international visitors and policymakers. https://www.usbg.gov/about-us

Three USBG sites are open year-round to the public: the Conservatory, the National Garden, and Bartholdi Park. The production facility is periodically open for public programs and tours. https://www.usbg.gov/ hours-and-location-0

Sources of Information

America's Agricultural Experience Based on a meeting that the U.S. Botanic Garden helped to organize of the Nation's leading agricultural and botanical educators, "Agriculture and the Future of Food: The Role of Botanic Gardens" presents a series of educational narratives that promote the reconnection of people and plants through the American agricultural experience. The document is available online in Portable Document Format (PDF). https://www.usbg.gov/sites/default/files/attachments/agriculture_and_the_future_of_food_-_the_role_of_botanic_gardens.pdf

Calendar of Events The USBG offers children and family programs, lectures, special tours, and workshops, as well as free theater, concerts, cooking demonstrations, and more. An events calendar is posted on the "Programs and Events" page, and a Portable Document Format (PDF) version is available for downloading. https://www.usbg.gov/programs-and-events

Carbon Footprint A small step can lead to a big change. A carbon, or ecological, footprint helps demonstrate the effect that lifestyle has on Earth systems. Most people can reduce their carbon footprint (i.e., the amount of emitted greenhouse gases that lifestyle governs) by shifting to sustainable practices and products. The USBG posted a list of suggestions for developing a more sustainable lifestyle, a lifestyle that leaves behind a smaller carbon footprint. The list includes suggestions for bottled water, coffee grounds, driving less, eating locally, junk mail, planting trees, plastic bags, and washing clothes. https://www.usbg.gov/know-your-impact

Career Opportunities Information on career and volunteer opportunities is available online. https://www.usbg.gov/opportunities-us-botanic-garden

Contact Information The USBG welcomes feedback: comments, concerns, and questions. Got a growing plant question? Select the "Plant Hotline" option in the "Inquiry Type" field of the electronic comment form. https://www.usbg.gov/contact-us-botanic-garden

Exhibits The USBG creates exhibits that not only delight and educate visitors, but that inspire them to become more active and better stewards of the plants supporting life on Earth. It posts Information on current and upcoming exhibits online. https://www.usbg.gov/exhibits

Factsheets Gardening factsheets are available online. https://www.usbg.gov/gardening-fact-sheets-0

Kids The USBG is a child-friendly living plant museum. https://www.usbg.gov/kids-are-welcome-us-botanic-garden

Land Development and Management An interdisciplinary partnership led by the USBG, American Society of Landscape Architects, and the Lady Bird Johnson Wildflower Center, the Sustainable Sites Initiative™ improves land development and management practices with a voluntary rating system for sustainable land design, construction, and maintenance practices. Architects, designers, developers, engineers, landscape architects, policymakers, and others use SITES to align land development and management with sustainable design. SITES supports the creation of ecologically resilient communities, and it benefits property owners, local and regional communities and their economies, as well as the environment. Certification covers development projects on land where buildings are absent or present. http://www.sustainablesites.org

Landscaping A collaboration between the USBG and the Lady Bird Johnson Wildflower Center, Landscape For Life™ promotes an approach to landscaping that respects nature. Irrespective of location—downtown, suburbia, or the farm—every landscape or garden can protect and even restore the environment, without sacrificing visual appeal. The Landscape for Life website contains a trove of information—getting started, materials, human health, plants, soil, and water—for transforming an environmentally ambivalent landscape into a healthy, sustainable one. http://landscapeforlife.org

Living Collections Database An online tool is available to search the USBG's living collections database. https://www.usbg.gov/search-collection

Native Plant Recommendations The USBG posts lists of selected plants to grow in the garden. The lists are available in Portable

Document Format (PDF) for downloading. https://www.usbg.gov/national-garden-native-plant-recommendations

Plant Hotline   Questions about a garden plant? Call the Plant Hotline. Phone, 202-226-4785.

Pollinators   Learn about the role birds and bees, as well as other creatures like bats, beetles, butterflies, flies, moths, and even wasps, play in the life cycle of plants. https://www.usbg.gov/pollinator-information

Production Facility   The production facility opens periodically for public programs and tours. An annual open house allows visitors to meet the gardeners, ask questions, and explore the facility. https://www.usbg.gov/us-botanic-garden-production-facility

Rare and Endangered Plants   USBG experts bank seeds of rare plants, introduce rare plants to the horticultural trade, maintain live specimens, and study wild plants at risk of endangerment or extinction. The website maintains a gallery of plants whose threat levels are vulnerable, threatened, and endangered. https://www.usbg.gov/gardens/rare-and-endangered-plants-gallery

Site Map   The website map allows visitors to look for specific topics or to browse content that aligns with their interests. https://www.usbg.gov/sitemap

Social Media   The USBG has a Facebook account. https://www.facebook.com/usbotanicgarden

Staff Directory   Approximately 65 employees work at the USBG in four divisions: Administration, Horticulture, Operations, and Public Programs. https://www.usbg.gov/staff-directory

Visitor Guide   More than a million visitors come to see the USBG each year. A visitor guide is available in Arabic, Chinese, English, French, German, Italian, Japanese, Korean, Russian, and Spanish. https://www.usbg.gov/visit

The Sources of Information were updated 10–2019.

Judicial Branch

JUDICIAL BRANCH

The Supreme Court of the United States

United States Supreme Court Building, One First Street NE., Washington, DC 20543
Phone, 202-479-3000. Internet, http://www.supremecourt.gov

Members

Chief Justice of the United States	JOHN G. ROBERTS, JR.
Associate Justice	CLARENCE THOMAS
Associate Justice	RUTH BADER GINSBURG
Associate Justice	STEPHEN G. BREYER
Associate Justice	SAMUEL A. ALITO, JR.
Associate Justice	SONIA SOTOMAYOR
Associate Justice	ELENA KAGAN
Associate Justice	NEIL M. GORSUCH
Associate Justice	BRETT M. KAVANAUGH

https://www.supremecourt.gov/about/biographies.aspx

Officers

Counselor to the Chief Justice	JEFFREY P. MINEAR
Clerk	SCOTT S. HARRIS
Court Counsel	ETHAN V. TORREY
Curator	CATHERINE E. FITTS
Director of Information Technology	ROBERT J. HAWKINS
Librarian	LINDA S. MASLOW
Marshal	PAMELA TALKIN
Public Information Officer	KATHLEEN L. ARBERG
Reporter of Decisions	CHRISTINE L. FALLON

The above list of key personnel was updated 10–2018.

Article III, section 1, of the Constitution of the United States provides that "[t]he judicial Power of the United States, shall be vested in one supreme Court, and in such Inferior Courts as the Congress may from time to time ordain and establish."

The Supreme Court of the United States was created in accordance with this provision and by authority of the Judiciary Act of September 24, 1789 (1 Stat. 73). It was organized on February 2, 1790. Article III, section 2, of the Constitution defines the jurisdiction of the Supreme Court.

The Supreme Court comprises the Chief Justice of the United States and such number of Associate Justices as may be fixed by Congress, which is currently fixed at eight (28 U.S.C. 1). The President nominates the Justices with the advice and consent of the Senate. Article III, section 1, of the Constitution further provides that "[t]he Judges, both of the supreme and inferior Courts, shall hold their Offices during good Behaviour, and shall, at stated Times, receive for their Services, a

Compensation, which shall not be diminished during their Continuance in Office."

In the performance of its functions, the Court is assisted by nine court officers: the Clerk, the Counselor to the Chief Justice, the Court Counsel, the Curator, the Director of Information Technology, the Librarian, the Marshal, the Public Information Officer, and the Reporter of Decisions. https://www.supremecourt.gov/about/about.aspx

Appellate Jurisdiction   Various statutes, derived from the authority that the Constitution has given to Congress, confer appellate jurisdiction upon the Supreme Court. The basic statute effective at this time in conferring and controlling jurisdiction of the Supreme Court may be found in 28 U.S.C. 1251, 1253, 1254, 1257-1259, and various special statutes. Congress has no authority to change the original jurisdiction of this Court.

Court Term   The term of the Court begins on the first Monday in October and lasts until the first Monday in October of the next year. Over the course of a term, approximately 10,000 petitions are filed for cases to be briefed before the Court. Moreover, each year, about 1,200 applications that can be acted upon by a single Justice while serving in the capacity of a Circuit Justice are filed. http://www.supremecourt.gov/about/procedures.aspx

Rulemaking   From time to time, Congress has conferred upon the Supreme Court power to prescribe rules of procedure to be followed by the lower courts of the United States.

Sources of Information

Art Collections   The Supreme Court has been acquiring artwork since the 1830s. Today, it continues to add to its three collections of decorative art, fine art, and graphic art. These collections include antique furniture, busts, engravings, historic furnishings, lithographs, miniatures, photographs, and portraits. https://www.supremecourt.gov/about/historicCollections.aspx

Audio Recordings of Oral Arguments   Recordings of oral arguments become publicly accessible at the end of each argument week. A listener has the option to download the audio files or to hear the arguments on the Supreme Court's website. Recordings are listed by case name, docket number, and the date of oral argument. https://www.supremecourt.gov/oral_arguments/argument_audio/2018

Calendars / Lists   Supreme Court calendars and argument calendars, as well as day call and hearing lists, are posted in Portable Document Format (PDF) for viewing and downloading. https://www.supremecourt.gov/oral_arguments/calendarsandlists.aspx

Career Opportunities   The Supreme Court posts vacancy announcements online. It also has programs for docents, fellows, and interns. https://www.supremecourt.gov/jobs/jobs.aspx

Chief and Associate Justices   A Chief Justices list and Associate Justices list are available on the "Justices 1789 to Present" web page. The lists include all of the Justices who have served on the Supreme Court. https://www.supremecourt.gov/about/members_text.aspx

A timeline of Chief and Associate Justices is also available. https://www.supremecourt.gov/about/members.aspx

Constitutional Interpretation   See the cornerstone address of Chief Justice Charles E. Hughes: "The Republic Endures and This Is the Symbol of Its Faith." https://www.supremecourt.gov/about/constitutional.aspx

Docket Search   The online docket database contains information on the status of cases filed since the beginning of the 2001 Term. https://www.supremecourt.gov/docket/docket.aspx

The engrossed dockets from 1791 to 1995 have been scanned by the National Archives from its microfilm collection and are available in its catalog. https://catalog.archives.gov/id/1524561

Exhibitions   The Office of the Curator creates exhibitions to highlight the work and history of the Nation's highest court, the lives of individual Justices, and the architecture of the Supreme Court building. Exhibitions are self-guided and located on the ground floor of the building. http://www.supremecourt.gov/visiting/exhibition.aspx

Frequently Asked Questions (FAQs)   The Supreme Court posts answers to FAQs online. https://www.supremecourt.gov/about/faq.aspx

The Public Information Office has answered questions that reporters often ask in its "Reporter's Guide to Applications Pending Before The Supreme Court of the United States." https://www.supremecourt.gov/publicinfo/reportersguide.pdf | Email: pio@supremecourt.gov

Gift Shop   The Supreme Court Historical Society Gift Shop is accessible online and located on the ground floor of the Supreme Court building. Merchandise ranges from books, folders, statues, and woven throws to jewelry, learning games, scarves, ties, and writing instruments. The shop is open Monday–Friday, from 9 a.m. to 4:25 p.m., excluding Federal Holidays. Phone, 888-539-4438. http://supremecourtgifts.org/ | Email: giftshop@supremecourthistory.org

History   The Supreme Court Historical Society, a private nonprofit organization, collects and preserves the history of the Supreme Court. Incorporated in the District of Columbia in 1974, its founder Chief Justice Warren E. Burger served as the first honorary chairman. The Society is headquartered in the Opperman House in Washington, DC, where it maintains The Goldman Library. The books housed therein comprise one of the finest collections of Court histories, Justices' writings, and judicial biographies. The library also has materials relating to U.S. attorneys general, solicitors, and Presidents. http://supremecourthistory.org/index.html

Indigent Petitioners   The "Guide for Filing In Forma Pauperis Cases" assists litigants who may lack the financial resources to pay the filing fee or to submit booklet-format documents under Court Rule 33.1. https://www.supremecourt.gov/guideforIFPcases2017.pdf

Links   The Supreme Court's website has links to other Internet sources of information on the Federal Government, the Judiciary, and the Supreme Court. https://www.supremecourt.gov/links/links.aspx

Minutes of the Court   The "Journal of the Supreme Court" contains the official minutes. It reflects the disposition of each case, identifies the court whose judgment is under review, lists the cases argued that day and the attorneys who presented oral argument, contains miscellaneous announcements by the Chief Justice from the bench, and names the attorneys who have been admitted to the bar of the Supreme Court. https://www.supremecourt.gov/orders/journal.aspx

Press Releases   Press releases are posted online. https://www.supremecourt.gov/publicinfo/press/pressreleases.aspx

Search Tips   Use the search tips to refine a search and find more specific results on the Supreme Court's website. https://www.supremecourt.gov/search_help.aspx

Site Map   The site map allows visitors to look for specific information or to browse content that aligns with their interests. https://www.supremecourt.gov/sitemap.aspx

Slip Opinions   Slip opinions are posted within minutes after the Justices issue their opinions. They remain posted until the opinions for the entire term are published in the bound volumes of the "United States Reports." A slip opinion comprises the majority or principal opinion, concurring or dissenting opinions, and a prefatory syllabus summarizing the decision. https://www.supremecourt.gov/opinions/slipopinion/18

Speeches   Speeches of current and former Supreme Court Justices are available online. https://www.supremecourt.gov/publicinfo/speeches/speeches.aspx

Visiting the Court   The Supreme Court building is open to the public Monday–Friday, from 9:00 a.m. to 4:30 p.m, excluding Federal holidays. http://www.supremecourt.gov/visiting/visiting.aspx

Maps and brochures are available online. The visitors' guide and map are available in translation: Chinese, French, German, Japanese, Russian, and Spanish. https://www.supremecourt.gov/visiting/mapsandbrochures.aspx; http://www.supremecourt.gov/contact/contactus.aspx | Email: pio@supremecourt.gov

For further information concerning the Supreme Court, contact the Public Information Office, United States Supreme Court Building, One First Street NE., Washington, DC 20543. Phone, 202-479-3211.

Lower Courts

Article III of the Constitution declares, in section 1, that the judicial power of the United States shall be invested in one Supreme Court and in "such inferior Courts as the Congress may from time to time ordain and establish." The Supreme Court has held that these constitutional courts ". . . share in the exercise of the judicial power defined in that section, can be invested with no other jurisdiction, and have judges who hold office during good behavior, with no power in Congress to provide otherwise."

United States Courts of Appeals

The courts of appeals are intermediate appellate courts created by act of March 3, 1891 (28 U.S.C. ch. 3), to relieve the Supreme Court of considering all appeals in cases originally decided by the Federal trial courts. They are empowered to review all final decisions and certain interlocutory decisions (18 U.S.C. 3731; 28 U.S.C. 1291, 1292) of district courts. They also are empowered to review and enforce orders of many Federal administrative bodies. The decisions of the courts of appeals are final except as they are subject to review on writ of certiorari by the Supreme Court.

The United States is divided geographically into 12 judicial circuits, including the District of Columbia. Each circuit has a court of appeals (28 U.S.C. 41, 1294). Each of the 50 States is assigned to one of the circuits. The territories and the Commonwealth of Puerto Rico are assigned variously to the first, third, and ninth circuits. There is also a Court of Appeals for the Federal Circuit, which has nationwide jurisdiction defined by subject matter. At present each court of appeals has from 6 to 28 permanent circuit judgeships (179 in all), depending upon the amount of judicial work in the circuit. Circuit judges hold their offices during good behavior as provided by Article III, section 1, of the Constitution. The judge senior in commission who is under 70 years of age (65 at inception of term), has been in office at least 1 year, and has not previously been chief judge, serves as the chief judge of the circuit for a 7-year term. One of the Justices of the Supreme Court is assigned as circuit justice for each of the 13 judicial circuits. Each court of appeals normally hears cases in panels consisting of three judges but may sit en banc with all judges present.

The judges of each circuit (except the Federal Circuit) by vote determine the size of the judicial council for the circuit, which consists of the chief judge and an equal number of circuit and district judges. The council considers the state of Federal judicial business in the circuit and may "make all necessary and appropriate orders for [its] effective and expeditious administration . . ." (28 U.S.C. 332).

The chief judge of each circuit may summon periodically a judicial conference of all judges of the circuit, including members of the bar, to discuss the business of the Federal courts of the circuit (28 U.S.C. 333). The chief judge of each circuit and a district judge elected from each of the 12 geographical circuits, together with the chief judge of the Court of International Trade, serve as members of the Judicial Conference of the United States, over which the Chief Justice of the United States presides. This is the governing body for the administration of the Federal judicial system as a whole (28 U.S.C. 331).

To obtain a complete list of judges, court officials, and official stations of the United States Courts of Appeals for the Federal Circuit, as well as information on opinions and cases before the court, consult the Judicial Circuit Web sites listed below.

List of Judicial Circuit Web Sites—United States Courts of Appeals

Circuit	URL
District of Columbia Circuit	http://www.cadc.uscourts.gov
First Circuit	http://www.ca1.uscourts.gov
Second Circuit	http://www.ca2.uscourts.gov
Third Circuit	http://www.ca3.uscourts.gov
Fourth Circuit	http://www.ca4.uscourts.gov
Fifth Circuit	http://www.ca5.uscourts.gov
Sixth Circuit	http://www.ca6.uscourts.gov
Seventh Circuit	http://www.ca7.uscourts.gov
Eighth Circuit	http://www.ca8.uscourts.gov
Ninth Circuit	http://www.ca9.uscourts.gov
Tenth Circuit	http://www.ca10.uscourts.gov
Eleventh Circuit	http://www.ca11.uscourts.gov

United States Court of Appeals for the Federal Circuit

This court was established under Article III of the Constitution pursuant to the Federal Courts Improvement Act of 1982 (28 U.S.C. 41, 44, 48), as successor to the former United States Court of Customs and Patent Appeals and the United States Court of Claims. The jurisdiction of the court is nationwide (as provided by 28 U.S.C. 1295) and includes appeals from the district courts in patent cases; appeals from the district courts in contract, and certain other civil actions in which the United States is a defendant; and appeals from final decisions of the U.S. Court of International Trade, the U.S. Court of Federal Claims, and the U.S. Court of Appeals for Veterans Claims. The jurisdiction of the court also includes the review of administrative rulings by the Patent and Trademark Office, U.S. International Trade Commission, Secretary of Commerce, agency boards of contract appeals, and the Merit Systems Protection Board, as well as rulemaking of the Department of Veterans Affairs; review of decisions of the U.S. Senate Committee on Ethics concerning discrimination claims of Senate employees; and review of a final order of an entity to be designated by the President concerning discrimination claims of Presidential appointees.

The court consists of 12 circuit judges. It sits in panels of three or more on each case and may also hear or rehear a case en banc. The court sits principally in Washington, DC, and may hold court wherever any court of appeals sits (28 U.S.C. 48). http://www.cafc.uscourts.gov

United States District Courts

The Nation's district courts are the trial courts of general Federal jurisdiction. These courts resolve disputes by determining the facts and applying legal principles to decide which party is right. Each State has at least one district court, and large States have as many as four. There are 89 district courts in the 50 States, plus one in the District of Columbia and another in the Commonwealth of Puerto Rico. Three other U.S. Territories also have courts that hear Federal cases: Guam and the Northern Mariana and Virgin Islands.

At present, each district court has from 2 to 28 Federal district judgeships, depending upon the amount of judicial work within its territory. Only one judge is usually required to hear and decide a case in a district court, but in some limited cases it is required that three judges be called together to comprise the court (28 U.S.C. 2284). The judge senior in commission who is under 70 years of age (65 at inception of term), has been in office for at least 1 year, and has not previously been chief judge, serves as chief judge for a 7-year term. There are 645 permanent district judgeships in the 50 States and 15 in the District of Columbia. There are seven district judgeships in Puerto Rico. District judges hold their offices during good behavior as provided by Article III, section 1, of the Constitution. However, Congress may temporary

judgeships for a court with the provision that when a future vacancy occurs in that district, such vacancy shall not be filled. Each district court has one or more United States magistrate judges and bankruptcy judges, a clerk, a United States attorney, a United States marshal, probation officers, court reporters, and their staffs. The jurisdiction of the district courts is set forth in title 28, chapter 85, of the United States Code and at 18 U.S.C. 3231.

Cases from the district courts are reviewable on appeal by the applicable court of appeals. http://www.uscourts.gov/about-federal-courts/court-role-and-structure

Territorial Courts

Pursuant to its authority to govern the Territories (Art. IV, sec. 3, clause 2, of the Constitution), Congress has established district courts in the territories of Guam and the Virgin Islands. The District Court of the Canal Zone was abolished on April 1, 1982, pursuant to the Panama Canal Act of 1979 (22 U.S.C. 3601 note). Congress has also established a district court in the Northern Mariana Islands, which is administered by the United States under a trusteeship agreement with the United Nations. These Territorial courts have jurisdiction not only over the subjects described in the

judicial article of the Constitution, but also over many local matters that, within the States, are decided in State courts. The District Court of Puerto Rico, by contrast, is established under Article III, is classified like other "district courts," and is called a "court of the United States" (28 U.S.C. 451). There is one judge each in Guam and the Northern Mariana Islands, and two in the Virgin Islands. The judges in these courts are appointed for terms of 10 years. http://www.uscourts.gov/about-federal-courts/court-role-and-structure

For further information concerning the lower courts, contact the Administrative Office of the United States Courts, Thurgood Marshall Federal Judiciary Building, One Columbus Circle NE., Washington, DC 20544. Phone, 202-502-2600.

United States Court of International Trade

This court was originally established as the Board of United States General Appraisers by act of June 10, 1890, which conferred upon it jurisdiction theretofore held by the district and circuit courts in actions arising under the tariff acts (19 U.S.C. ch. 4). The act of May 28, 1926 (19 U.S.C. 405a), created the United States Customs Court to supersede the Board; by acts of August 7, 1939, and June 25, 1948 (28 U.S.C. 1582, 1583), the court was integrated into the United States court structure, organization, and procedure. The act of July 14, 1956 (28 U.S.C. 251), established the court as a court of record

of the United States under Article III of the Constitution. The Customs Court Act of 1980 (28 U.S.C. 251) constituted the court as the United States Court of International Trade.

The Court of International Trade has jurisdiction over any civil action against the United States arising from Federal laws governing import transactions. This includes classification and valuation cases, as well as authority to review certain agency determinations under the Trade Agreements Act of 1979 (19 U.S.C. 2501) involving antidumping and countervailing duty matters. In addition, it has exclusive jurisdiction of civil actions to review determinations as to the eligibility of workers, firms, and communities for adjustment assistance under the Trade Act of 1974 (19 U.S.C. 2101). Civil actions commenced by the United States to recover customs duties, to recover on a customs bond, or for certain civil penalties alleging fraud or negligence are also within the exclusive jurisdiction of the court.

The court is composed of a chief judge and eight judges, not more than five of whom may belong to any one political party. Any of its judges may be temporarily designated and assigned by the Chief Justice of the United States to sit as a court of appeals or district court judge in any circuit or district. The court has a clerk and deputy clerks, a librarian, court reporters, and other supporting personnel. Cases before the court may be tried before a jury. Under the Federal Courts Improvement Act of 1982 (28 U.S.C. 1295), appeals are taken to the U.S. Court of Appeals for the Federal Circuit, and ultimately review may be sought in appropriate cases in the Supreme Court of the United States.

The principal offices are located in New York, NY, but the court is empowered to hear and determine cases arising at any port or place within the jurisdiction of the United States. http://www.cit.uscourts.gov

For further information, contact the Clerk, United States Court of International Trade, One Federal Plaza, New York, NY 10278-0001. Phone, 212-264-2814.

Judicial Panel on Multidistrict Litigation

The Panel, created by act of April 29, 1968 (28 U.S.C. 1407), and consisting of seven Federal judges designated by the Chief Justice from the courts of appeals and district courts, is authorized to temporarily transfer to a single district, for coordinated or consolidated pretrial proceedings, civil actions pending in different districts that involve one or more common questions of fact. http://www.jpml.uscourts.gov

For further information, contact the Clerk, Judicial Panel on Multidistrict Litigation, Room G–255, Thurgood Marshall Federal Judiciary Building, One Columbus Circle NE., Washington, DC 20002-8041. Phone, 202-502-2800.

SPECIAL COURTS
United States Court of Appeals for the Armed Forces

450 E Street NW., Washington, DC 20442-0001
Phone, 202-761-1448. Fax, 202-761-4672. Internet, http://www.armfor.uscourts.gov

This court was established under Article I of the Constitution of the United States pursuant to act of May 5, 1950, as amended (10 U.S.C. 867). Subject only to certiorari review by the Supreme Court of the United States in a limited number of cases, the court serves as the final appellate tribunal to review court-martial convictions of all the Armed Forces. It is exclusively an appellate criminal court, consisting of five civilian judges who are appointed for 15-year terms by the President with the advice and consent of the Senate.

The court is called upon to exercise jurisdiction to review the record in all cases extending to death; certified to the court by a Judge Advocate General of one of the Armed Forces; or petitioned by accused who have received a sentence of confinement for 1 year or more and/or a punitive discharge.

The court also exercises authority under the All Writs Act (28 U.S.C. 1651(a)).

In addition, the judges of the court are required by law to work jointly with the senior uniformed lawyer from each of the Armed Forces and two members of the public appointed by the Secretary of Defense to make an annual comprehensive survey, to report annually to the Congress on the operation and progress of the military justice system under the Uniform Code of Military Justice, and to recommend improvements wherever necessary.

Sources of Information

Career Opportunities   Job openings and available clerkships are posted online.

http://www.armfor.uscourts.gov/newcaaf/ employment.htm; http://www.armfor. uscourts.gov/newcaaf/contact.htm

For further information, contact the Clerk, United States Court of Appeals for the Armed Forces, 450 E Street NW., Washington, DC 20442-0001. Phone, 202-761-1448. Fax, 202-761-4672.

United States Court of Appeals for Veterans Claims

Suite 900, 625 Indiana Avenue NW., Washington, DC 20004-2950
Phone, 202-501-5970. Fax, 202-501-5848. Internet, http://www.uscourts.cavc.gov

The United States Court of Appeals for Veterans Claims, a court of record under Article I of the Constitution, was established on November 18, 1988 (38 U.S.C. 7251) and given exclusive jurisdiction to review decisions of the Board of Veterans' Appeals. Appeals concern veteran disability benefits, dependent educational assistance, survivor benefits, and pension benefits claims. In addition to its review authority, the Court has contempt authority, as well as the authority to compel action by the Secretary of Veterans Affairs, the authority to grant a petition for extraordinary relief under the All Writs Act (28 U.S.C. 1651), and the authority to make attorney fee determinations under the Equal Access to Justice Act (28 U.S.C. 2412). Decisions of the Court of Appeals for Veterans Claims are subject to review by the United States Court of Appeals for the Federal Circuit on questions of law and on writ of certiorari by the United States Supreme Court.

The Court consists of nine judges whom the President appoints with the advice and consent of the Senate for 15-year terms. One of the judges serves as chief judge.

The Chief Judge generally conducts a judicial conference every 2 years. The primary purpose of the conference, which involves the active participation of members of the legal community, attorneys, and practitioners admitted to practice before the Court, is to consider the business of the Court and to recommend means of improving the administration of justice within the Court's jurisdiction.

The Court is located in Washington, DC, but it is a court of national jurisdiction and may sit at any location within the United States.

Opinions issued by the Court, case information, and a current list of judges and officials of the United States Court of Appeals for Veterans Claims are available online.

Sources of Information

Employment   Job opportunities are posted online. http://www.uscourts.cavc.gov/ employment.php; http://www.uscourts.cavc. gov/contact.php

For further information, contact the Clerk, United States Court of Appeals for Veterans Claims, Suite 900, 625 Indiana Avenue NW., Washington, DC 20004-2950. Phone, 202-501-5970. Fax, 202-501-5848

United States Court of Federal Claims

717 Madison Place NW., Washington, DC 20439
Phone, 202-357-6400. Internet, http://www.uscfc.uscourts.gov

The United States Court of Federal Claims has jurisdiction over claims seeking money judgments against the United States. A claim must be founded upon the Constitution, an act of Congress, an Executive order, a contract with the United States, or Federal regulations. Judges are appointed by the President for 15-year terms, subject to Senate confirmation. Appeals are to the U.S. Court of Appeals for the Federal Circuit.

Sources of Information

Career Opportunities   Information on job opportunities and internships is available online. http://www.uscfc.uscourts.gov/job-opportunitiesemployment; http://www.uscfc.uscourts.gov/court-directory

For further information, contact the Clerk's Office, United States Court of Federal Claims, 717 Madison Place NW., Washington, DC 20439. Phone, 202-357-6400.

United States Tax Court

400 Second Street NW., Washington, DC 20217-0002
Phone, 202-521-0700. Internet, http://www.ustaxcourt.gov

The United States Tax Court is a court of record under Article I of the Constitution of the United States (26 U.S.C. 7441). The court was created as the United States Board of Tax Appeals by the Revenue Act of 1924 (43 Stat. 336). The name was changed to the Tax Court of the United States by the Revenue Act of 1942 (56 Stat. 957). The Tax Reform Act of 1969 (83 Stat. 730) established the court under Article I and then changed its name to the United States Tax Court.

The court comprises 19 judges who are appointed by the President to 15-year terms and subject to Senate confirmation. The court also has varying numbers of both senior judges (who may be recalled by the chief judge to perform further judicial duties) and special trial judges (who are appointed by the chief judge and may hear and decide a variety of cases). The court's jurisdiction is set forth in various sections of title 26 of the U.S. Code.

The offices of the court and its judges are in Washington, DC. However, the court has national jurisdiction and schedules trial sessions in more than 70 cities in the United States. Each trial session is conducted by one judge, senior judge, or special trial judge. Court proceedings are open to the public and are conducted in accordance with the court's rules of practice and procedure and the rules of evidence applicable in trials without a jury in the U.S. District Court for the District of Columbia. A fee of $60 is charged for the filing of a petition. Practice before the court is limited to practitioners admitted under the court's rules of practice and procedure.

Decisions entered by the court, other than decisions in small tax cases, may be appealed to the regional courts of appeals and, thereafter, upon the granting of a writ of certiorari, to the Supreme Court of the United States. At the option of petitioners, simplified procedures may be used in small tax cases. Small tax cases are final and not subject to review by any court. http://www.ustaxcourt.gov/about.htm

Sources of Information

Career Opportunities   Vacancy announcements and information on the court's law clerk program are available online. http://www.ustaxcourt.gov/employment.htm
Forms   Applications, certificates, notices, and other forms can be completed online and then printed. http://www.ustaxcourt.gov/forms.htm
Taxpayer Information   An online guide provides information—not legal advice—that may be helpful for those representing themselves before the Tax Court. It answers frequent questions that taxpayers ask and explains the process of filing a petition to begin a Tax Court case and things that occur before, during, and after trial. It also features a glossary. http://www.ustaxcourt.gov/taxpayer_info_intro.htm | Email: info@ustaxcourt.gov; http://www.ustaxcourt.gov/phone.htm

For further information, contact the Office of the Clerk of the Court, United States Tax Court, 400 Second Street NW., Washington, DC 20217-0002. Phone, 202-521-0700.

Administrative Office of the United States Courts

One Columbus Circle NE., Washington, DC 20544
Phone, 202-502-2600. Internet, http://www.uscourts.gov

Director	JAMES C. DUFF
Deputy Director	LEE ANN BENNETT
Associate Directors	
Departments	
Administrative Services	JAMES R. BAUGHER
Program Services	MARY LOUISE MITTERHOFF
Technology Services	JOSEPH R. PETERS, JR.
Officers	
Judicial Conference Secretariat	KATHERINE H. SIMON
Legislative Affairs	DAVID T. BEST
Public Affairs	DAVID A. SELLERS
General Counsel	SHERYL L. WALTER

https://www.uscourts.gov/statistics-reports/
profile-administrative-office-us-courts-annual-
report-2017

The above list of key personnel was updated 2–2019.

The Administrative Office of the United States Courts supports and serves the nonjudicial, administrative business of the United States Courts.

The Administrative Office of the United States Courts was created by act of August 7, 1939 (28 U.S.C. 601). It was established on November 6, 1939. The Chief Justice of the United States, after consultation with the Judicial Conference, appoints the Director and Deputy Director of the Administrative Office.
Administering the Courts   The Director is the administrative officer of the courts of the United States—except of the Supreme Court. Under the guidance of the Judicial Conference of the United States, the Director supervises all administrative matters relating to the offices of clerks and other clerical and administrative personnel of the courts; examines the state of the dockets of the courts, secures information as to the courts' need of assistance, and prepares statistical data and reports each quarter and transmits them to the chief judges of the circuits; submits an activities report of the Administrative Office and the courts' state of business to the annual meeting of the Judicial Conference of the United States; fixes the compensation of court employees whose compensation is not otherwise fixed by law; regulates and pays annuities to widows and surviving dependent children of judges; disburses moneys appropriated for the maintenance and operation of the courts; examines accounts of court officers; regulates travel of judicial personnel; provides accommodations and supplies for the courts and their clerical and administrative personnel; establishes and maintains programs for the certification and utilization of court interpreters and the provision of special interpretation services in the courts; and performs such other duties as may be assigned by the Supreme Court or the Judicial Conference of the United States.

The Director also prepares and submits the budget of the courts, which the Office of Management and Budget transmits to Congress without change. http://www.uscourts.gov/about-federal-courts/judicial-administration
Probation Officers   The Administrative Office exercises general supervision of the accounts and practices of the Federal probation offices, which are subject to primary control by the respective district courts that they serve. The Administrative Office publishes, in cooperation with the

Department of Justice's Bureau of Prisons, the "Federal Probation Journal." This online, quarterly publication presents current thought, research, and practice in corrections, community supervision, and criminal justice.

In accordance with the Pretrial Services Act of 1982 (18 U.S.C. 3152), the Director establishes pretrial services in the district courts. The offices of these district courts report information on pretrial release of persons charged with Federal offenses and supervise such persons who are released to their custody. http://www.uscourts.gov/services-forms/probation-and-pretrial-services

Bankruptcy   According to the Bankruptcy Amendments and Federal Judgeship Act of 1984 (28 U.S.C. 151), the bankruptcy judges for each judicial district constitute a unit of the district court known as the bankruptcy court. The courts of appeals appoint bankruptcy judges in such numbers as authorized by Congress. These judges serve for a term of 14 years as judicial officers of the district courts.

This act placed jurisdiction in the district courts over all cases under title 11, United States Code, and all proceedings arising in or related to cases under that title (28 U.S.C. 1334). The district court may refer such cases and proceedings to its bankruptcy judges (as authorized by 28 U.S.C. 157).

The Director of the Administrative Office recommends to the Judicial Conference the duty stations of bankruptcy judges and the places they hold court, surveys the need for additional bankruptcy judgeships to be recommended to Congress, and determines the staff needs of bankruptcy judges and the clerks of the bankruptcy courts. http://www.uscourts.gov/services-forms/bankruptcy

Federal Magistrate Judges   The Director of the Administrative Office exercises general supervision over administrative matters in offices of U.S. magistrate judges, compiles and evaluates statistical data relating to such offices, and submits reports thereon to the Judicial Conference. The Director reports annually to Congress on the business that has come before U.S. magistrate judges and also prepares legal and administrative manuals for the magistrate judges. In compliance with the act, the Administrative Office conducts surveys of the conditions in the judicial districts to make recommendations as to the number, location, and salaries of magistrate judges.

The Judicial Conference then determines their number, location, and salaries, subject to the availability of appropriated funds.

Federal Defenders   The Criminal Justice Act (18 U.S.C. 3006A) establishes the procedure for the appointment of private panel attorneys in Federal criminal cases for individuals who are unable to afford adequate representation, under plans adopted by each district court. The act also permits the establishment of Federal public defender or Federal community defender organizations by the district courts in districts where at least 200 persons annually require the appointment of counsel. Two adjacent districts may be combined to reach this total.

Each defender organization submits to the Director of the Administrative Office an annual report of its activities along with a proposed budget or, in the case of community defender organizations, a proposed grant for the coming year. The Director is responsible for the submission of the proposed budgets and grants to the Judicial Conference for approval. The Director also makes payments to the defender organizations out of appropriations in accordance with the approved budgets and grants, as well as compensating private counsel appointed to defend criminal cases in the United States courts. http://www.uscourts.gov/services-forms/defender-services

Sources of Information

Budget, Accounting, and Procurement   Phone, 202-502-2000. http://www.uscourts.gov/services-forms/business-opportunities

Court Services   Phone, 202-502-1500.

Defender Services   Phone, 202-502 3030. http://www.uscourts.gov/services-forms/defender-services

Educational Resources   Learning resources for students are available online. http://www.uscourts.gov/about-federal-courts/educational-resources

Electronic Filing   Attorneys and others may submit files online using the Federal courts' Case Management and Electronic Case Files system. http://www.uscourts.gov/courtrecords/electronic-filing-cmecf

Frequently Asked Questions (FAQs)   Answers to FAQs on the Federal

Judiciary are available online. http://www.
uscourts.gov/frequently-asked-questions-faqs
General Counsel   Phone, 202-502-1100.
Glossary   A glossary of legal terms is available
online. http://www.uscourts.gov/glossary
Human Resources   Phone, 202-502-3100.
**Judicial Conference Executive
Secretariat**   Phone, 202-502-2400. http://
www.uscourts.gov/about-federal-courts/
governance-judicial-conference/about-
judicial-conference
Judicial Services   Phone, 202-502-1800.
Judiciary Reporting and Analysis   Phone,
202-502-1440.
Legislative Affairs   Phone, 202-502-1700.

Probation and Pretrial Services   Phone, 202-
502-1600. http://www.uscourts.gov/services-
forms/probation-and-pretrial-services
Public Affairs   Phone, 202-502-2600.
Publications   The Federal judiciary and
Administrative Office produce publications
for the Congress, the public, and others to
educate and inform about the work of the
courts. http://www.uscourts.gov/statistics-
reports/publications
Statistical Data   Statistical data on the
business of the Federal Judiciary are
available online. http://www.uscourts.gov/
statistics-reports/caseload-statistics-data-
tables; https://www.uscourts.gov/contact-us

For further information, contact the Administrative Office of the United States Courts, Thurgood Marshall Federal
Judiciary Building, One Columbus Circle NE., Washington, DC 20544. Phone, 202-502-2600.

Federal Judicial Center

Thurgood Marshall Federal Judiciary Building, One Columbus Circle NE., Washington, DC 20002-8003
Phone, 202-502-4000. Internet, http://www.fjc.gov

Director	JOHN S. COOKE
Deputy Director	CLARA J. ALTMAN

Division Directors

Education	DANA K. CHIPMAN
Research	JAMES B. EAGLIN

Office Directors

Administration	NANCY PAYNE
Federal Judicial History	(VACANCY)
International Judicial Relations	MIRA GUR-ARIE
Information Technology	ESTHER DEVRIES
https://www.fjc.gov/about/senior-staff	

Board of the Federal Judicial Center

Chief Justice of The United States *	JOHN G. ROBERTS, JR.
Bankruptcy Judge	BARBARA J. HOUSER
Circuit Judges	DUANE BENTON
	DAVID S. TATEL
District Judges	CURTIS L. COLLIER
	KIMBERLY J. MUELLER
	GEORGE Z. SINGAL
Magistrate Judge	TIMOTHY A. BAKER
Director of the Administrative Office of the U.S. Courts **	JAMES C. DUFF

*The Chief Justice chairs the Board of the Federal Judicial Center. ** The Director of the Administrative Office is an ex
officio member of the Board. https://www.fjc.gov/about/board-members

The above list of key personnel was updated 10–2019.

*The Federal Judicial Center is the judicial branch's agency for policy research and continuing
education.*

Establishment and Organization

On December 20, 1967, President Lyndon B. Johnson approved Public Law 90–219, "an act to provide for the establishment of a Federal Judicial Center [FJC], and for other purposes." The FJC was established "to further the development and adoption of improved judicial administration in the courts of the United States" (81 Stat. 664). https://www.govinfo.gov/content/pkg/STATUTE-81/pdf/STATUTE-81-Pg664.pdf

The FJC's statutory duties are described in chapter 42, sections 620–629, of 28 U.S.C. https://uscode.house.gov/browse/prelim@title28/part3/chapter42&edition=prelim

The Board of the FJC determines the agency's basic policies and activities. The Board comprises the Chief Justice of the United States, who permanently chairs of the Board by statute; two circuit judges of the U.S. courts of appeals; three judges of the U.S. district courts; one bankruptcy judge; and one magistrate judge. The Judicial Conference of the United States elects these eight members of the Board for 4-year terms. The ninth member is the Director of the Administrative Office of the United States Courts, who serves on Board in a permanent capacity. An elected member may serve only for one four-year term on the Board. https://www.fjc.gov/about/statute

The FJC does not post an organizational chart on its website.

Activities

The organization of the FJC reflects its primary statutory mandates. The Education Division plans education and produces training—including curriculum packages for in-district training, in-person programs, publications, video programs, and web-based programs and resources—for judges and court staff. The Research Division examines and evaluates current and alternative Federal court practices and policies. Its research assists Judicial Conference committees in developing policy recommendations. The research also supports the FJC's educational programs. The Federal Judicial History Office helps courts and other parties study and preserve Federal judicial history. The International Judicial Relations Office provides information to judicial and legal officials from foreign countries and informs Federal judicial personnel of developments In international law and other court systems that may affect their work. Two units of the Director's Office—the Editorial and Information Services Office and the Information Technology Office—provide editorial and design assistance, organization and dissemination of FJC resources, and technology. https://www.fjc.gov/about

Sources of Information

Annual Reports   Annual Reports, from 1969 to the present, are available to download as Portable Document Format (PDF) files. https://www.fjc.gov/content/annual-reports

Archived Judicial Records   The FJC record group does not currently have a description associated with it in the "Guide to Federal Records in the National Archives of the United States." The Guide is accessible online, and FJC records have been assigned to Record Group 516. https://www.archives.gov/research/guide-fed-records/groups/000.html

The National Archives does maintain a "Judicial Records" web page that contains information and resources for identifying and locating Federal court documents within its holdings. These documents comprise records of hearings and trials of Federal jurisdiction. https://www.archives.gov/research/court-records/archives.html

Biographical Directory of Judges   The directory includes the biographies of judges appointed by the President to serve during good behavior since 1789 on the U.S. district courts, U.S. courts of appeals, Supreme Court of the United States, and U.S. Court of International Trade, as well as the former U.S. circuit courts, Court of Claims, U.S. Customs Court, and U.S. Court of Customs and Patent Appeals. Also included are judges who received presidential recess appointments to the above named courts but were not confirmed by the Senate to serve during good behavior. https://www.fjc.gov/history/judges

Career Opportunities   The FJC posts job openings online. Contact the Human Resources Office for more information. Phone, 202-502-4165. https://www.fjc.gov/about/job-vacancies | Email: personnel@fjc.gov

Contact Information   The "Contact Us" page has fax and phone numbers for FJC offices and divisions. https://www.fjc.gov/about/contact-us

Educational Materials   Materials that the FJC produces as part of its educational programs for judges and court employees are accessible online. https://www.fjc.gov/education

Environmental Law   The FJC published "International Environmental Law: A Guide for Judges" (2015) that Roger R. Martella, Jr., and James W. Coleman wrote. The guide introduces judges to some of the major areas of international environmental law and examines how the law might arise in Federal litigation involving climate change, hazardous chemicals and materials, protected species, water pollution, air pollution, environmental disaster response, and transborder enforcement of environmental regulations. It also discusses the sources of international environmental laws, such as bilateral investment treaties, international standards and standard-setting organizations, and multilateral trade agreements. The FJC regards the content of the guide as responsible and valuable, but it does not reflect the policy or recommendations of the FJC Board. https://www.fjc.gov/content/309707/international-environmental-law-guide-judges

History   Questions about the history of the Federal judiciary? Submit them to the experts at the Federal Judicial History Office. Phone, 202-502-4180. Fax, 202-502-4077. https://www.fjc.gov/history | Email: history@fjc.gov

Nearly 600 images of historic Federal courthouses and other buildings that have served as the meeting places of Federal courts are available online. https://www.fjc.gov/history/courthouses

Timelines of the structure of the Federal courts, jurisdiction of the Federal courts, administration of the Federal courts, and cases that shaped the them are posted online. https://www.fjc.gov/history/timeline

Integrated Database   Under a working arrangement with the Administrative Office of the U.S. Courts, The FJC provides public access to its Integrated Data Base, which contains data on civil case and criminal defendant filings and terminations in the district courts, as well as bankruptcy court and appellate court case information. https://www.fjc.gov/research/idb

Publications   The online catalog contains records of FJC publications: manuals, monographs, reference guides, and research reports. A bibliographic record, which includes abstract or description, author and title, and additional information, is available for each item. Phone, 202-502-4153. Fax, 202-502-4077. https://www.fjc.gov/publications | Email: publications@fjc.gov

Reports / Studies   The FJC posts studies that were published in the past on its website in Portable Document Format (PDF) for downloading. Its Research Division conducted them. Some Center reports are not published or made publicly available due to restrictions in place from the source of the research request. https://www.fjc.gov/research/reports-and-studies

Resources on Law and Practice   The "Special Topics" web page provides online access to curated collections of FJC resources on discrete areas of law and judicial practice. https://www.fjc.gov/research/special-topics

Site Map   The website map allows visitors to look for specific topics or to browse content that aligns with their interests. https://www.fjc.gov/sitemap

Teaching Resources   Teaching and civic outreach resources are available online. https://www.fjc.gov/education/civic-education-about-courts

Visiting Foreign Judicial Fellows   Foreign judges, court officials, and scholars may apply for the opportunity to conduct research at the FJC on topics concerning the administration of justice in the United States. https://www.fjc.gov/content/visiting-foreign-judicial-fellows-program

The Sources of Information were updated 10–2019.

United States Sentencing Commission

Suite 2-500, One Columbus Circle NE., Washington, DC 20002-8002
Phone, 202-502-4500. Internet, http://www.ussc.gov

Chair	William H. Pryor, Jr., Acting
Vice Chair	(vacancy)
Vice Chair	(vacancy)
Vice Chair	(vacancy)
Commissioner	Charles R. Breyer
Commissioner	Rachel E. Barkow
Commissioner	Danny C. Reeves
Commissioner	William H. Pryor, Jr.
Commissioner (ex officio)	Jonathan Wroblewski
Commissioner (ex officio)	J. Patricia Wilson Smoot
Staff Director	Kenneth P. Cohen
Director, Office of Administration and Planning	Susan M. Brazel
Director, Office of Education and Sentencing Practice	Raquel Wilson
Director, Office of Legislative and Public Affairs	Christine M. Leonard
Director, Office of Research and Data	Glenn R. Schmitt
General Counsel	Kathleen C. Grilli

The United States Sentencing Commission develops sentencing guidelines and policies for the Federal court system.

The United States Sentencing Commission was established as an independent agency in the judicial branch of the Federal Government by the Sentencing Reform Act of 1984 (28 U.S.C. 991 et seq. and 18 U.S.C. 3551 et seq.). The Commission establishes sentencing guidelines and policies for the Federal courts, advising them of the appropriate form and severity of punishment for offenders convicted of Federal crimes.

The Commission comprises seven voting members and two nonvoting members. The President appoints the voting members with the advice and consent of the Senate for 6-year terms. The President also appoints one of the voting members as the Chair and designates three others as Vice Chairs.

The Commission evaluates the effects of the sentencing guidelines on the criminal justice system, advises Congress on the modification or enactment of statutes pertaining to criminal law and sentencing matters, establishes a research and development program on sentencing issues, and performs other related duties.

In executing its duties, the Commission promulgates and distributes to Federal courts and to the U.S. probation system guidelines for determining sentences to be imposed in criminal cases, general policy statements regarding the application of guidelines, and policy statements on the appropriate use of probation and supervised release revocation provisions. These sentencing guidelines and policy statements are intended to support the principles of just punishment, deterrence, incapacitation, and rehabilitation; provide fairness in meeting the purposes of sentencing; avoid unwarranted disparity; and reflect advancement in the knowledge of human behavior as it relates to the criminal justice process.

The Commission also provides training, conducts research on sentencing-related issues, and serves as an information resource for Congress, criminal justice practitioners, and the public. http://www.ussc.gov/about

Sources of Information

Education The Commission offers courses that fulfill continuing legal education requirements in several jurisdictions. http://www.ussc.gov/education/training-resources/continuing-legal-education

UNITED STATES SENTENCING COMMISSION

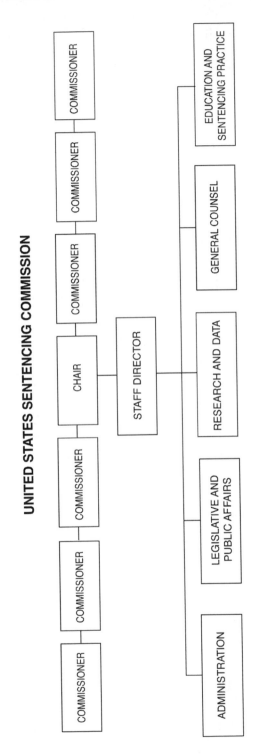

Career Opportunities   The Commission posts job announcements on its Web site. http://www.ussc.gov/employment

Guidelines Manual   The current "USSC Guidelines Manual" is available in Portable Document Format on the Commission's Web site. An electronic archive of the yearly manual starts with the year 1987. http://www.ussc.gov/guidelines/2015-guidelines-manual/archive

Helpline   Attorneys, judges, and probation officers who have questions may call the Commission's helpline for assistance. The helpline also handles data requests. Its hours of operations are 8:30 a.m.–5 p.m., eastern standard time, Monday–Friday, excluding Federal holidays. Phone, 202-502-4545.

News   Press releases are available on the Commission's Web site. http://www.ussc.gov/about/news/press-releases

The Commission also posts amicus curiae briefs, reports, speeches, statements, and testimonies online. http://www.ussc.gov/about/news/testimony-speeches/speeches-and-submissions

Publications   A topical index of publications is available online. http://www.ussc.gov/research/topical-index-publications

Reports   The Commission posts reports to the Congress on its Web site. http://www.ussc.gov/research/reports-congress

Annual overviews of Federal criminal cases are available online. http://www.ussc.gov/topic/year-review

The Office of Research and Data publishes periodic reports on Federal sentencing practices. The reports include information on the types of crimes committed, offenders who commit those crimes, the punishments imposed, and the manner in which the sentencing guidelines were applied. http://www.ussc.gov/topic/data-reports

Site Map   The Web site map allows visitors to look for specific topics or to browse content that aligns with their interests. http://www.ussc.gov/sitemap

Updates   An online subscription form is available to sign up for regular email updates from the USSC. http://www.ussc.gov/sign-regular-updates; http://www.ussc.gov | Email: pubaffairs@ussc.gov

For further information, contact the Office of Legislative and Public Affairs, U.S. Sentencing Commission, Suite 2–500, One Columbus Circle NE., Washington, DC 20002-8002. Phone, 202-502-4500.

Executive Branch

EXECUTIVE BRANCH: THE PRESIDENT

THE PRESIDENT

The President of the United States   DONALD J. TRUMP

Article II, section 1, of the Constitution provides that "[t]he executive Power shall be vested in a President of the United States of America. He shall hold his Office during the Term of four Years, . . . together with the Vice President, chosen for the same Term . . . ." In addition to the powers set forth in the Constitution, the statutes have conferred upon the President specific authority and responsibility covering a wide range of matters (United States Code Index).

The President is the administrative head of the executive branch of the Government, which includes numerous agencies, both temporary and permanent, as well as the 15 executive departments.

The Cabinet The Cabinet, a creation of custom and tradition dating back to George Washington's administration, functions at the pleasure of the President. Its purpose is to advise the President upon any subject, relating to the duties of the respective offices, on which he requests information (pursuant to Article II, section 2, of the Constitution).

The Cabinet is composed of the Vice President and the heads of the 15 executive departments--the Secretaries of Agriculture, Commerce, Defense, Education, Energy, Health and Human Services, Homeland Security, Housing and Urban Development, Interior, Labor, State, Transportation, Treasury, and Veterans Affairs, and the Attorney General. Additionally, in the Obama administration, Cabinet-level rank has been accorded to the Chief of Staff to the President; the Administrator, Environmental Protection Agency; the Chair, Council of Economic Advisers; the Director, Office of Management and Budget; the U.S. Permanent Representative to the United Nations; and the U.S. Trade Representative.

THE VICE PRESIDENT

The Vice President   MICHAEL R. PENCE

Article II, section 1, of the Constitution provides that the President "shall hold his Office during the Term of four Years, . . . together with the Vice President . . . ." In addition to his role as President of the Senate, the Vice President is empowered to succeed to the Presidency, pursuant to Article II and the 20th and 25th amendments to the Constitution.

The executive functions of the Vice President include participation in Cabinet meetings and, by statute, membership on the National Security Council and the Board of Regents of the Smithsonian Institution.

THE EXECUTIVE OFFICE OF THE PRESIDENT

Under authority of the Reorganization Act of 1939 (5 U.S.C. 133-133r, 133t note), various agencies were transferred to the Executive Office of the President by the President's Reorganization Plans I and II of 1939 (5 U.S.C. app.), effective July 1, 1939. Executive Order 8248 of September 8, 1939, established the divisions of the Executive Office and defined their functions. Subsequently, Presidents have used Executive orders, reorganization plans, and legislative initiatives to reorganize the Executive Office to make its composition compatible with the goals of their administrations.

White House Office

1600 Pennsylvania Avenue NW., Washington, DC 20500
Phone, 202-456-1414. Internet, http://www.whitehouse.gov

Assistants to the President

Chief of Staff	GEN. JOHN F. KELLY, USMC (RETIRED)
Chief of Staff to the First Lady	LINDSAY REYNOLDS
Counsel to the President	DONALD F. McGAHN II
Deputy Chief of Staff for Implementation	RICK DEARBORN
Deputy Chief of Staff for Operations	JOE HAGIN
Deputy National Security Adviser	MAJ. GEN. RICKY WADDELL, USA (RETIRED)
Director of the White House Military Office	(VACANCY)
Director of Communications	HOPE C. HICKS
Director of Presidential Personnel	JOHN DeSTEFANO
Director of Scheduling and Advance	(VACANCY)
National Security Adviser	LT. GENERAL H.R. McMASTERS, USA
Press Secretary	SARAH H. SANDERS
Assistant to the President for Homeland Security and Counterterrorism	THOMAS BOSSERT
Counselor to the President	KELLYANNE CONWAY

Senior Advisors

Assistant to the President for Climate, Conservation and Energy Policy	BRIAN C. DEESE
Assistant to the President for Intergovernmental Affairs and Public Engagement	VALERIE B. JARRETT
Assistant to the President for Strategy and Communications	SHAILAGH MURRAY

The above list of key personnel was updated 10–2017.

The White House Office serves the President in the performance of the many detailed activities incident to his immediate office.

The President's staff facilitates and maintains communication with the Congress, the heads of executive agencies, the press and other information media, and the general public. The various Assistants to the President aid the President in such matters as he may direct.

Office of the Vice President

Eisenhower Executive Office Building, Washington, DC 20501
Phone, 202-456-7549. Internet, https://https://www.whitehouse.gov/administration/vice-president-biden

Chief of Staff to the Vice President	NICK AYERS
Chief of Staff to Karen Pence	KRISTAN KING NEVINS
Special Assistant to the Vice President	ZACH BAUER
Counsel / Assistant to the Vice President	MARK PAOLETTA
Deputy Chief of Staff to Karen Pence / Special Assistant to the President	ANTHONY BERNAL
Directors	
Administration / Deputy Assistant to the Vice President	MIKE BOISVENUE
Advance / Deputy Assistant to the Vice President	ROBERT PEEDE
Communications	JARED AGEN
Public Engagement and Intergovernmental Affairs / Special Assistant to the President	ANDELIZ CASTILLO
Legislative Affairs / Assistant to the Vice President	JONATHAN HILAR
Scheduling / Deputy Assistant to the Vice President	MEGAN PATENAUDE
Speechwriting / Special Assistant to the President	STEPHEN FORD
National Security Advisor	ANDREA THOMPSON

The Office of the Vice President serves the Vice President in the performance of the many activities incident to his immediate office.

Council of Economic Advisers

Seventeenth and Pennsylvania Avenue NW., Washington, DC 20502
Phone, 202-456-4779. Internet, http://www.whitehouse.gov/cea

Chairman	KEVIN A. HASSETT
Member	TOMAS J. PHILIPSON
Member	RICHARD V. BURKHAUSER

The Council of Economic Advisers analyzes and appraises the national economy to make policy recommendations to the President.

The Council of Economic Advisers (CEA) was established in the Executive Office of the President by the Employment Act of 1946 (15 U.S.C. 1023). It now functions under that statute and Reorganization Plan No. 9 of 1953 (5 U.S.C. app.), effective August 1, 1953.

The Chair and the two members govern the Council. The President appoints the Chair, whom the Senate must confirm, and the two members.

The Council analyzes the national economy and its various segments; advises the President on economic developments; appraises the economic programs and policies of the Federal Government; recommends policies for economic growth and stability to the President; assists in the preparation of the President's economic reports to the Congress; and prepares the Annual Report of the Council of Economic Advisers.

Sources of Information

Career Opportunities To learn about career opportunities, visit the "Jobs and Internships" Web page. https://www.whitehouse.gov/administration/eop/cea/jobs

History Photographs and brief professional bios of former Council Chairs, beginning with Edwin G. Nourse, who served as the Chair from 1946 to 1949, are available online. https://www.whitehouse.gov/administration/eop/cea/about/former-chairs

Brief professional bios of former Council members, beginning with John D. Clark, who served as a member from 1946 to 1950 and then as the Vice Chair, are available online. https://www.whitehouse.gov/administration/eop/cea/about/Former-Members

Publications   Reports and briefs are available in Portable Document Format (PDF) on the Council's Web site. https://www.whitehouse.gov/administration/eop/cea/factsheets-reports

A monthly publication prepared by the Council for the Joint Economic Committee, "Economic Indicators" provides Congress and the public with information on business activity; credit, money, and prices; Federal finance; gross domestic product; employment, income, and production; international statistics; and security markets.

https://www.whitehouse.gov/administration/eop/cea/economic-indicators

A yearly report written by the Council's Chair, the "Economic Report of the President" presents the administration's domestic and international economic policies. The report surveys the Nation's economic progress with text and data appendices. The full report and individual chapters are accessible in Portable Document Format (PDF) for download on the Council's Web site. Statistical tables are also available for download in Portable Document and Excel formats. https://www.whitehouse.gov/administration/eop/cea/economic-report-of-the-President

Speeches / Testimony   The Council posts Op-Ed pieces, prepared testimonies for congressional hearings, and speeches on its Web site. https://www.whitehouse.gov/administration/eop/cea/speeches-testimony; http://www.whitehouse.gov/cea

For further information, contact the Council of Economic Advisers, Seventeenth and Pennsylvania Avenue NW., Washington, DC 20502. Phone, 202-456-4779.

Council on Environmental Quality

722 Jackson Place NW., Washington, DC 20503
Phone, 202-395-5750 or 202-456-6224. Fax, 202-456-2710. Internet, http://www.whitehouse.gov/administration/eop/ceq

CHAIR	(VACANCY)
Chief of Staff	CHRISTOPHER ADAMO
Associate Directors	
Climate Preparedness	JAINEY BAVISHI
Communications	NOREEN NIELSON
Conservation and Wildlife	TIMOTHY MALE
Energy and Climate Change	RICHARD DUKE
Lands and Water Ecosystems	MICHAEL DEGNAN
Legislative Affairs	STEPHENNE HARDING
NEPA Oversight	EDWARD BOLING
Ocean and Coastal Policy	WHITLEY SAUMWEBER
Deputy Associate Director, Public Engagement and Communications	MARK ANTONIEWICZ
General Counsel	BRENDA MALLORY
Managing Director	CHRISTINA GOLDFUSS

The Council on Environmental Quality formulates and recommends national policies and initiatives for improving the environment.

The Council on Environmental Quality (CEQ) was established within the Executive Office of the President by the National Environmental Policy Act of 1969 (NEPA) (42 U.S.C. 4321 et seq.). The Environmental Quality Improvement Act of 1970 (42 U.S.C. 4371 et seq.) established the Office of Environmental Quality (OEQ) to provide professional and administrative support for the Council. The CEQ and OEQ are referred to, collectively, as the Council on Environmental Quality. The CEQ Chair, whom the President appoints and the Senate confirms, serves as Director of the OEQ.

The Council develops policies that bring together the Nation's economic, social, and environmental priorities to improve Federal decisionmaking. As required by NEPA, the CEQ also evaluates, coordinates, and mediates Federal activities. It advises and assists the President on both national and international environmental policy matters. It oversees Federal agency and departmental implementation of NEPA. https://www. whitehouse.gov/administration/eop/ceq/ initiatives

Sources of Information

Blog The CEQ Web site features a blog. https://www.whitehouse.gov/administration/ eop/ceq/blog

Freedom of Information Act (FOIA) Requests may be submitted by email (without an attachment) or fax or sent by postal mail to the Freedom of Information Officer, Council on Environmental Quality, 722 Jackson Place NW., Washington, DC 20503. Fax, 202-456-0753. https://www. whitehouse.gov/administration/eop/ceq/ foia | Email: efoia@ceq.eop.gov

Internships Most interns work a semester-based schedule (May–August, September–December, or January–April). A position may be customized, however, to accommodate applicant availability and project needs. Application deadlines are February 1 for the summer, June 13 for the fall, and October 1 for the spring. https://www.whitehouse. gov/administration/eop/ceq/internships | Email: internships@ceq.eop.gov

Open Government The CEQ supports the Open Government initiative by promoting the principles of collaboration, participation, and transparency. https://www.whitehouse. gov/administration/eop/ceq/open

Participation The CEQ maintains a social media presence on Twitter and Facebook. An online subscription form is available to sign up for email updates from the CEQ and opportunities to get involved. https://www. whitehouse.gov/administration/eop/ceq/stay-connected

Press Releases The CEQ posts announcements, factsheets, memoranda, statements, and other newsworthy items on its Web site. https://www.whitehouse.gov/ administration/eop/ceq/press_releases; http:// www.whitehouse.gov/administration/eop/ ceq

For further information, contact the Information Office, Council on Environmental Quality, 722 Jackson Place NW., Washington, DC 20503. Phone, 202-395-5750. Fax, 202-456-2710.

National Security Council

Eisenhower Executive Office Building, Washington, DC 20504
Phone, 202-456-1414. Internet, http://www.whitehouse.gov/nsc

Members

The President	DONALD J. TRUMP
The Vice President	MICHAEL R. PENCE
Secretary of State	REX TILLERSON
Secretary of Defense	GEN. JAMES MATTIS, USMC (RETIRED)

Statutory Advisers

Director of National Intelligence	DAN COATS
Chairman, Joint Chiefs of Staff	GEN. JOSEPH F. DUNFORD, JR., USMC

Standing Participants

Secretary of the Treasury	STEVEN MNUCHIN
Chief of Staff to the President	GEN. JOHN KELLY, USMC (RETIRED)
Counsel to the President	DONALD F. MCGAHN, II
National Security Adviser	LT. GEN. H.R. MCMASTERS, USA (RETIRED)
Director of the National Economic Council	GARY D. COHN

Officials

National Security Adviser	LT. GEN. H.R. MCMASTERS, USA (RETIRED)
Deputy National Security Adviser	MAJ. GEN. RICKY WADDELL, USA (RETIRED)

The National Security Council was established by the National Security Act of 1947, as amended (50 U.S.C. 402). The Council was placed in the Executive Office of the President by Reorganization Plan No. 4 of 1949 (5 U.S.C. app.).

The President chairs the National Security Council. Its statutory members, in addition to the President, are the Vice President and the Secretaries of State and Defense. The Chairman of the Joint Chiefs of Staff is the statutory military adviser to the Council, and the Director of National Intelligence serves as its intelligence adviser. The Secretary of the Treasury, the U.S. Representative to the United Nations, the Assistant to the President for National Security Affairs, the Assistant to the President for Economic Policy, and the Chief of Staff to the President are invited to all meetings of the Council. The Attorney General and the Director of National Drug Control Policy are invited to attend meetings pertaining to their jurisdictions, and other officials are invited, as appropriate.

The Council advises and assists the President in integrating all aspects of national security policy as it affects the United States—domestic, foreign, military, intelligence, and economic—in conjunction with the National Economic Council. http://www.whitehouse.gov/nsc

For further information, contact the National Security Council, Eisenhower Executive Office Building, Washington, DC 20504. Phone, 202-456-1414.

Office of Administration

Eisenhower Executive Office Building, 1650 Pennsylvania Avenue, NW., Washington, DC 20503
Phone, 202-456-2861. Internet, http://www.whitehouse.gov/oa

Director / Deputy Assistant to the President	(VACANCY)
Chief Administrative Officer	(VACANCY)
Chief Financial Officer	FAISAL AMIN
Chief Logistics Officer	STEPHEN E. PEARSON, ACTING
General Counsel	HUGH L. BRADY

The Office of Administration was formally established within the Executive Office of the President by Executive Order 12028 of December 12, 1977. https://www.whitehouse.gov/administration/eop/oa/history

The Office is exclusively dedicated to assisting the President in providing uniform administrative support services to all units within the Executive Office of the President. The services provided include facilities, information, personnel, technology, and financial management; digital solutions, library, and research services; security; legislative liaisons; and general office operations such as mail, messenger, printing, procurement, and supply services. https://www.whitehouse.gov/administration/eop/oa

Sources of Information

Career Opportunities The Office of Administration relies on professionals who come from diverse backgrounds and posses a rare blend of education, experience, and skill. The Office announces job vacancies on USAJobs.gov. https://www.whitehouse.gov/administration/eop/oa/jobs

Photo Gallery The Office of Administration contributes to the architectural and historic preservation of the properties associated with the Executive Office of the President. Images of current and past preservation projects are available online. https://www.whitehouse.gov/administration/eop/oa/preservation/projects; http://www.whitehouse.gov/oa

For further information, contact the Office of the Director, Office of Administration, Washington, DC 20503. Phone, 202-456-2861.

Office of Management and Budget

New Executive Office Building, Washington, DC 20503
Phone, 202-395-3080. Internet, http://www.whitehouse.gov/omb

Director	Mick Mulvaney
Deputy Director	Thomas M. Reilly, Acting
Controller, Office of Federal Financial Management	(vacancy)
Deputy Director, Management	Dustin S. Brown, Acting
Executive Associate Director	(vacancy)
General Counsel	(vacancy)
Intellectual Property Enforcement Coordinator	(vacancy)

Administrators

Office of Federal Procurement Policy	(vacancy)
Office of Information and Regulatory Affairs	Dominic J. Mancini, Acting

DIRECTORS
Assistant Directors

Budget	Kelly A. Kinneen, Acting
Legislative Reference	Matthew J. Vaeth
Management and Operations	Sarah W. Spooner

Associate Directors

Communications	John S. Czwartacki
Economic Policy	(vacancy)
Education, Income Maintenance and Labor	John W. Gray
General Government Programs	Kathleen L. Kraninger
Health	Joseph L. Grogan
Information Technology and E–Government	(vacancy)
Legislative Affairs	Jonathan A. Slemrod
National Security Programs	Robert B. Blair
Natural Resource Programs	James P. Herz
Performance Management	(vacancy)

The Office of Management and Budget evaluates, formulates, and coordinates management procedures and program objectives within and among Federal departments and agencies. It also controls the administration of the Federal budget, while routinely providing the President with recommendations regarding budget proposals and relevant legislative enactments.

The Office of Management and Budget (OMB), formerly the Bureau of the Budget, was established in the Executive Office of the President pursuant to Reorganization Plan No. 1 of 1939 (5 U.S.C. app.).

The Office's primary functions are diverse and many: to assist the President in developing and maintaining effective government by reviewing the organizational structure and management procedures of the executive branch to ensure that the intended results are achieved; to assist in developing efficient coordinating mechanisms to implement Government activities and to expand interagency cooperation; to assist the President in preparing the budget and in formulating the Government's fiscal program; to supervise and control the administration of the budget; to assist the President by clearing and coordinating departmental advice on proposed legislation and by making recommendations effecting Presidential action on legislative enactments, in accordance with past practice; to assist in developing regulatory reform proposals and programs for paperwork reduction, especially reporting burdens of the public; to assist in considering, clearing, and, where necessary, preparing proposed Executive orders and proclamations; to plan and develop information systems that provide the President with program performance data; to plan, conduct, and promote evaluation efforts that assist the President in assessing program objectives, performance, and efficiency; to keep the President informed of the progress of activities by Government agencies with respect to work proposed, initiated, and completed, together with the relative timing of work between the several agencies of the Government, all to the end that the work programs of the several agencies of the executive branch of the Government may be coordinated and that the moneys appropriated by the Congress may be expended in the most economical manner, barring overlapping and duplication of effort; and to improve the efficiency and effectiveness of the procurement processes by providing overall direction of procurement policies, regulations, procedures, and forms. https://www. whitehouse.gov/omb/organization_mission

Sources of Information

Career Opportunities The "Join OMB" Web page has links to learn more about career and detail opportunities, student internships, and applying for OMB positions. Questions may be addressed to the Human Resources Division, Office of Administration, Washington, DC 20500. Phone, 202-395-1088. https://www.whitehouse.gov/omb/recruitment_default

Freedom of Information Act (FOIA) Information on how to submit a FOIA request is available online. The OMB's FOIA Request Service Center also provides assistance. Phone, 202-395-3642. https://www.whitehouse.gov/omb/foia_default#reading | Email: OMBFOIA@omb.eop.gov

Publications A copy of the "Budget of the United States Government" may be downloaded from the OMB Web site or purchased from the Government Publishing Office bookstore. Phone, 202-512-0132. https://www.whitehouse.gov/omb/budget/Overview; https://bookstore.gpo.gov/catalog/budget-economy | Email: mainbks@gpo.gov; https://www.whitehouse.gov/omb/contact

For further information, contact the Office of Management and Budget, New Executive Office Building, Washington, DC 20503. Phone, 202-395-3080.

Office of Management and Budget

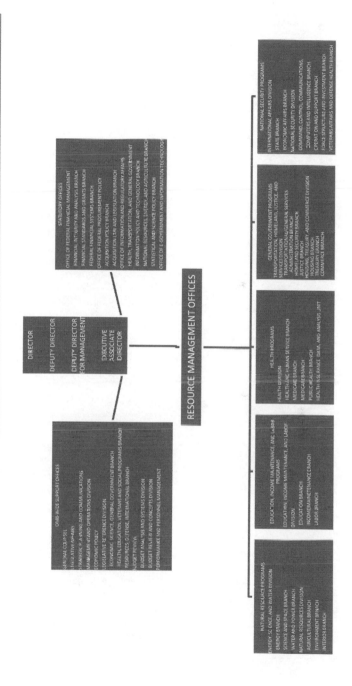

DIRECTOR

DEPUTY DIRECTOR

DEPUTY DIRECTOR FOR MANAGEMENT

EXECUTIVE ASSOCIATE DIRECTOR

RESOURCE MANAGEMENT OFFICES

STATUTORY OFFICES
OFFICE OF FEDERAL FINANCIAL MANAGEMENT
FINANCIAL INTEGRITY AND ANALYSIS BRANCH
FINANCIAL STANDARDS AND GRANTS BRANCH
FEDERAL FINANCIAL SYSTEMS BRANCH
OFFICE OF FEDERAL PROCUREMENT POLICY
ACQUISITION POLICY BRANCH
ACQUISITION LAW AND LEGISLATION BRANCH
OFFICE OF INFORMATION AND REGULATORY AFFAIRS
HEALTH, TRANSPORTATION, AND GENERAL GOVERNMENT
INFORMATION POLICY AND TECHNOLOGY BRANCH
NATURAL RESOURCES, ENERGY, AND AGRICULTURE BRANCH
STATISTICAL AND SCIENCE POLICY BRANCH
OFFICE OF E-GOVERNMENT AND INFORMATION TECHNOLOGY

OMB-WIDE SUPPORT OFFICES
GENERAL COUNSEL
LEGISLATIVE AFFAIRS
STRATEGIC PLANNING AND COMMUNICATIONS
MANAGEMENT AND OPERATIONS DIVISION
ECONOMIC POLICY
LEGISLATIVE REFERENCE DIVISION
ECONOMIC SCIENCE, GENERAL GOVERNMENT BRANCH
HEALTH, EDUCATION, VETERANS AND SOCIAL PROGRAMS BRANCH
RESOURCES, DEFENSE, INTERNATIONAL BRANCH
BUDGET REVIEW
BUDGET ANALYSIS AND SYSTEMS DIVISION
BUDGET REVIEW AND CONCEPTS DIVISION
PERFORMANCE AND PERSONNEL MANAGEMENT

NATURAL RESOURCE PROGRAMS
ENERGY SCIENCE AND WATER DIVISION
ENERGY BRANCH
SCIENCE AND SPACE BRANCH
WATER AND POWER BRANCH
NATURAL RESOURCES DIVISION
AGRICULTURAL BRANCH
ENVIRONMENT BRANCH
INTERIOR BRANCH

EDUCATION, INCOME MAINTENANCE, AND LABOR PROGRAMS
EDUCATION, INCOME MAINTENANCE, AND LABOR DIVISION
EDUCATION BRANCH
INCOME MAINTENANCE BRANCH
LABOR BRANCH

HEALTH PROGRAMS
HEALTH DIVISION
HEALTH CARE HUMAN SERVICE BRANCH
MEDICARE BRANCH
MEDICAID BRANCH
PUBLIC HEALTH BRANCH
HEALTH INSURANCE DATA, AND ANALYSIS UNIT

GENERAL GOVERNMENT PROGRAMS
TRANSPORTATION, HOMELAND, JUSTICE, AND SERVICES DIVISION
TRANSPORTATION/GENERAL SERVICES ADMINISTRATION BRANCH
HOMELAND SECURITY BRANCH
JUSTICE BRANCH
HOUSING, TREASURY, AND COMMERCE DIVISION
HOUSING BRANCH
TREASURY BRANCH
COMMERCE BRANCH

NATIONAL SECURITY PROGRAMS
INTERNATIONAL AFFAIRS DIVISION
STATE BRANCH
ECONOMIC AFFAIRS BRANCH
NATIONAL SECURITY DIVISION
COMMAND, CONTROL, COMMUNICATIONS, COMPUTERS AND INTELLIGENCE BRANCH
CREDIT ON AND SUPPORT BRANCH
FORCE STRUCTURE AND INVESTMENT BRANCH
VETERANS AFFAIRS AND DEFENSE HEALTH BRANCH

Office of National Drug Control Policy

Executive Office of the President, Washington, DC 20503
Phone, 202-395-6700. Fax, 202-395-6708. Internet, http://www.ondcp.gov

Director	RICHARD J. BAUM, ACTING
Chief of Staff	LAWRENCE L. MUIR, ACTING
Deputy Director, Office of Policy, Research and Budget	(VACANCY)
General Counsel	LAWRENCE L. MUIR
Associate Directors	
Office of Intelligence	GERARD K. BURNS
Office of Intergovernmental Public Liaison	(VACANCY)
Office of Legislative Affairs	(VACANCY)
Office of Management and Administration	MICHELE C. MARX
Office of Public Affairs	(VACANCY)
Office of Research / Data Analysis	(VACANCY)

The Office of National Drug Control Policy helps the President establish his National Drug Control Strategy objectives, priorities, and policies and makes budget, program, and policy recommendations affecting National Drug Control Program agencies.

The Office of National Drug Control Policy (ONDCP) was established by the National Narcotics Leadership Act of 1988 (21 U.S.C. 1501 et seq.), effective January 29, 1989, reauthorized through the Office of National Drug Control Policy Reauthorization Act of 1988 (21 U.S.C. 1701 et seq.), and again reauthorized through the Office of National Drug Control Policy Reauthorization Act of 2006 (21 U.S.C. 1701 et seq.).

The President appoints the Director of National Drug Control Policy with the advice and consent of the Senate.

The Director establishes policies, objectives, priorities, and performance measurements for the National Drug Control Program. Each year, the Director promulgates the President's National Drug Control Strategy, other related drug control strategies, supporting reports, and a program budget that the President submits to Congress. The Director advises the President on necessary changes in the organization, management, budgeting, and personnel allocation of Federal agencies that monitor drug activities. The Director also notifies Federal agencies if their policies do not comply with their responsibilities under the National Drug Control Strategy. The ONDCP also has direct programmatic responsibility for the Drug-Free Communities Support and the High Intensity Drug Trafficking Areas programs. https://www.whitehouse.gov/ondcp/office-descriptions

Sources of Information

Career Opportunities   Contact the Personnel Section, Office of National Drug Control Policy. Phone, 202-395-6695. Information on student opportunities is available on the "Working at ONDCP" Web page. https://www.whitehouse.gov/ondcp/working-at-ondcp
Publications   To receive publications on drugs and crime control policies, to access specific drug-related data, to access customized bibliographic searches, and to learn more about data availability and other resources, visit the ONDCP Web site. https://www.whitehouse.gov/ondcp/news-releases; http://www.whitehouse.gov/ondcp

For further information, contact the Office of National Drug Control Policy, Executive Office of the President, Washington, DC 20503. Phone, 202-395-6700. Fax, 202-395-6708.

Office of Policy Development

The Office of Policy Development comprises the Domestic Policy and the National Economic Councils, which advise and assist the President in the formulation, coordination, and implementation of domestic and economic policy. The Office of Policy Development also supports other policy development and implementation activities as directed by the President.

Domestic Policy Council

Room 469, Eisenhower Executive Office Building, Washington, DC 20502
Phone, 202-456-5594. Internet, https://https://www.whitehouse.gov/administration/eop/dpc

Domestic Policy Council
Director / Domestic Policy Advisor to the President   ANDREW P. BREMBERG

The above list of key personnel was updated 10–2018.

The Domestic Policy Council was established August 16, 1993, by Executive Order 12859. The Council oversees development and implementation of the President's domestic policy agenda and ensures coordination and communication among the heads of relevant Federal offices and agencies.

National Economic Council

Room 235, Eisenhower Executive Office Building, Washington, DC 20502
Phone, 202-456-2800. Internet, https://https://www.whitehouse.gov/administration/eop/nec

National Economic Council
Director / Assistant to the President for Economic Policy   LAWRENCE A. KUDLOW

The above list of key personnel was updated 10–2018.

The National Economic Council was created January 25, 1993, by Executive Order 12835, to coordinate the economic policymaking process and advise the President on economic policy. The Council also ensures that economic policy decisions and programs remain consistent with the President's stated goals and monitors the implementation of the President's economic goals.

Office of Science and Technology Policy

Eisenhower Executive Office Building, 1650 Pennsylvania Avenue NW., Washington, DC 20502
Phone, 202-456-4444. Fax, 202-456-6021. Internet, http://www.ostp.gov

Director   JOHN P. HOLDREN
Chief of Staff   CRISTIN DORGELO
Assistant Director, Federal Research and Development   KEI KOIZUMI
Assistant Director, Legislative Affairs   DONNA PIGNATELLI
Communications Director / Senior Policy Analyst   KRISTIN LEE

Deputy Chief of Staff / Assistant Director	TED M. WACKLER
General Counsel	RACHAEL LEONARD

Office of The Chief Technology Officer

Chief Technology Officer	MEGAN SMITH
Deputy Chief Technology Officer	ALEXANDER MACGILLIVRAY
Deputy Chief Technology Officer	CORINNA ZAREK
Deputy Chief Technology Officer	EDWARD W. FELTEN
Deputy Chief Technology Officer, Data Policy / Chief Data Scientist	DHANURAY PATIL

Environment and Energy Division

Associate Director	(VACANCY)
Assistant Director, Clean Energy and Transportation	AUSTIN BROWN
Assistant Director, Climate Adaptation and Ecosystems	LAURA PETES
Assistant Director, Climate Resilience and Information	AMY LUERS
Assistant Director, Climate Resilience and Land Use	RICH POUYAT
Assistant Director, Climate Science	DONALD WUEBBLES
Assistant Director, Earth Observations	DAVID HERMRECK
Assistant Director, Environmental Health	BRUCE RODAN
Assistant Director, Natural Disaster Resilience	JACQUELINE MESZAROS
Assistant Director, Polar Sciences	MARTIN JEFFRIES
Assistant Director, Space Weather	WILLIAM MURTAGH
Principal Assistant Director, Environment and Energy	TAMARA DICKINSON

National Security and International Affairs Division

Associate Director	(VACANCY)
Assistant Director, Biosecurity and Emerging Technologies	GERALD EPSTEIN
Assistant Director, Cybersecurity	TIMOTHY POLK
Assistant Director, Cybersecurity Strategy	GREGORY SHANNON
Assistant Director, Defense Programs	CHRIS FALL
Assistant Director, Global Security	MATTHEW J. HEAVNER
Assistant Director, Special Programs	MARK LEBLANC
Principal Assistant Director, National Security and International Affairs	STEVE FETTER

Science Division

Associate Director	JO EMILY HANDELSMAN
Assistant Director, Bioethics and Privacy	MELISSA GOLDSTEIN
Assistant Director, Broadening Participation	WANDA WARD
Assistant Director, Education and Learning Science	DANIELLE CARNIVAL
Assistant Director, Education and Physical Sciences	MEREDITH DROSBACK
Assistant Director, Research Infrastructure	ALTAF CARIM
Assistant Director, Scientific Data and Information	JERRY SHEEHAN

Technology and Innovation Division

Associate Director	(VACANCY)
Assistant Director, Behavioral Science	MAYA SHANKAR
Assistant Director, Biological Innovation	ROBBIE BARBERO
Assistant Director, Civil and Commercial Space	BENJAMIN ROBERTS
Assistant Director, Education and Telecommunications Innovation	AADIL GINWALA
Assistant Director, Entrepreneurship	DOUGLAS RAND
Assistant Director, Innovation for Growth	JENNIFER ERICKSON
Assistant Director, Learning and Innovation	KUMAR GARG
Assistant Director, Nanotechnology and Advanced Materials	LLOYD WHITMAN
Assistant Director, Open Innovation	CHRISTOFER NELSON
Deputy Director for Technology and Innovation	THOMAS KALIL

Budget and Administration

Operations Manager and Security Officer	STACY MURPHY

Councils
President's Council of Advisors on Science and Technology
Executive Director   ASHLEY PREDITH

National Science and Technology Council
Executive Director   AFUA BRUCE
Director, National Nanotechnology Coordination Office   MICHAEL MEADOR
Director, Networking and Information Technology Research and
    Development National Coordination Office   BRYAN BIEGEL
Director, U.S. Global Change Research Program National
    Coordination Office   MICHAEL KUPERBERG
Director, U.S. Group on Earth Observation Program   TIMOTHY STRYKER

The Office of Science and Technology Policy (OSTP) was established within the Executive Office of the President by the National Science and Technology Policy, Organization, and Priorities Act of 1976 (42 U.S.C. 6611).

The Office supports the President by serving as a source of engineering, scientific, and technological analysis and judgment on plans, policies, and programs of the Federal Government. OSTP experts advise the President on scientific and technological matters that affect areas of national concern like the economy, environment, foreign relations, health, and national security; evaluate the effectiveness, quality, and scale of the Federal effort in science and technology; advise and assist the President, the Office of Management and Budget, and Federal agencies throughout the Federal budget development process; and help the President with leading and coordinating the Federal Government's research and development programs. https://www.whitehouse.gov/administration/eop/ostp/about

Sources of Information

Blog   The OSTP's Web site features a blog. https://www.whitehouse.gov/administration/eop/ostp/blog

Freedom of Information Act (FOIA)   Instructions for submitting a FOIA request are available online. https://www.whitehouse.gov/administration/eop/ostp/library/foia

Internships   Internships offer a unique opportunity to work with senior White House officials and science and technology policy analysts in the OSTP's topic-based divisions or on the OSTP legal team. Applicants may apply for one of three terms: Fall, Spring, or Summer. Each term lasts no more than 90 days; interns receive no remuneration; and students may be eligible to receive academic credit. https://www.whitehouse.gov/administration/eop/ostp/about/student

Library   The OSTP's resource library is an expanding collection of agency materials that includes compliance guidelines, documents, presentations, reports, speeches, and testimonies. An archival section contains materials from past administrations. https://www.whitehouse.gov/administration/eop/ostp/library

Press Room   White House factsheets and science and technology-related remarks, statements, weekly addresses, and other Presidential items are available on the OSTP's Web site. https://www.whitehouse.gov/administration/eop/ostp/pressroom; https://www.whitehouse.gov/administration/eop/ostp/contactus

For further information, contact the Office of Science and Technology Policy, Eisenhower Executive Office Building, 1650 Pennsylvania Avenue NW., Washington, DC 20502. Phone, 202-456-4444. Fax, 202-456-6021.

Office of the United States Trade Representative

600 Seventeenth Street NW., Washington, DC 20508
Phone, 202-395-3230. Internet, http://www.ustr.gov

Office of the U.S. Trade Representative

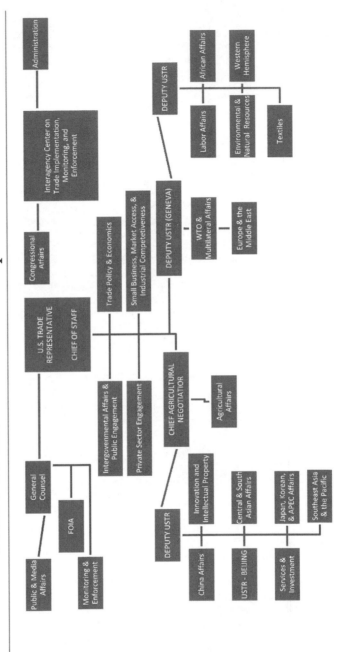

United States Trade Representative	ROBERT E. LIGHTHIZER
Deputy U.S. Trade Representative–Geneva	(VACANCY)
Deputy U.S. Trade Representative–Washington	(VACANCY)
Deputy U.S. Trade Representative–Washington	(VACANCY)
Chief Agricultural Negotiator	(VACANCY)
Chief of Staff	JAMIESON L. GREER
Director, Interagency Center on Trade Implementation, Monitoring and Enforcement	(VACANCY)
General Counsel	STEPHEN VAUGHN

Assistant U.S. Trade Representatives

Administration	FED AMES
African Affairs	(VACANCY)
Agricultural Affairs	SHARON BOMER LAURITSEN
South and Central Asian Affairs	MARK LINSCOTT
China Affairs	TERRENCE J. McCARTIN, ACTING
Congressional Affairs	CHRISTOPHER JACKSON
Environment and Natural Resources	JENNIFER PRESCOTT
Europe and Middle East Affairs	L. DANIEL MULLANEY
Innovation and Intellectual Property	(VACANCY)
Intergovernmental Affairs and Public Engagement	(VACANCY)
Japan, Korea, and Asia Pacific Economic Cooperation (APEC) Affairs	MICHAEL BEEMAN
Labor	LEWIS KARESH
Monitoring and Enforcement	JUAN MILLAN
Private Sector Engagement	(VACANCY)
Public and Media Affairs	(VACANCY)
Services and Investment	DANIEL BAHAR
Small Business, Market Access and Industrial Competitiveness	JAMES SANFORD
Southeast Asia and Pacific Affairs	BARBARA WEISEL
Textiles	WILLIAM JACKSON
Trade Policy and Economic Affairs	EDWARD GRESSER
Western Hemisphere	JOHN MELLE
World Trade Organization (WTO) and Multilateral Affairs	DAWN SHACKLEFORD

The United States Trade Representative formulates trade policy for and directs all trade negotiations of the United States.

The Office of the U.S. Trade Representative was created as the Office of the Special Representative for Trade Negotiations by Executive Order 11075 of January 15, 1963. The Trade Act of 1974 (19 U.S.C. 2171) established the Office as an agency of the Executive Office of the President charged with administering the trade agreements program. https://ustr.gov/about-us/history

The Office sets and administers overall trade policy. The U.S. Trade Representative heads the Office and serves as the President's principal adviser, negotiator, and spokesperson on international trade and investment issues. The Representative acts as the chief representative of the United States in all General Agreement on Tariffs and Trade activities; in Organization for Economic Cooperation and Development discussions, meetings, and negotiations that deal primarily with commodity issues and trade; in U.N. Conference on Trade and Development negotiations and other multilateral institution negotiations that deal primarily with commodity issues and trade; in other bilateral and multilateral negotiations that deal primarily with commodities or trade, including East-West trade; in negotiations under sections 704 and 734 of the Tariff Act of 1930 (19 U.S.C. 1671c and 1673c); and in negotiations on direct investment incentives and disincentives and on bilateral investment issues concerning barriers to investment.

The Omnibus Trade and Competitiveness Act of 1988 codified these authorities and added additional authority, including the implementation of section 301 actions that enforce U.S. rights under international trade agreements.

The U.S. Trade Representative serves as a Cabinet-level official with the rank of Ambassador and reports directly to the President. The Chief Agricultural Negotiator and three Deputy U.S. Trade Representatives also hold the rank of Ambassador—two of the deputies are located in Washington, DC, and the other serves in Geneva, Switzerland.

The U.S. Trade Representative is also an ex officio member on the boards of directors of the Export-Import Bank and the Overseas Private Investment Corporation. The Representative also serves on the National Advisory Council on International Monetary and Financial Policy. https://ustr.gov/about-us

Sources of Information

Blog   "Tradewinds" is the official blog of the U.S. Trade Representative. https://ustr.gov/tradewinds

Factsheets   The U.S. Trade Representative releases factsheets on trade issues. https://ustr.gov/about-us/policy-offices/press-office/fact-sheets

Freedom of Information Act (FOIA)   Requests must be made in writing: Freedom of Information Officer, Office of the U.S. Trade Representative, 1724 F Street NW., Washington, DC 20508. Security procedures can slow down mail receipt and processing. Sending a request by email or fax avoids security-related delays. To facilitate finding the desired information, a record description must contain key details—author, date, recipient, subject matter, title or name. The Office of the U.S. Trade Representative operates a FOIA requestor service center. Phone, 202-395-3419. Fax, 202-395-9458.

https://ustr.gov/about-us/reading-room/freedom-information-act-foia | Email: FOIA@ustr.eop.gov

The electronic reading room contains information that is made available on a routine basis to the public. It also features documents that are frequently requested under the FOIA. This collection of online documents continues to grow as records in which the public expresses an interest are added. https://ustr.gov/about-us/reading-room/freedom-information-act-foia/electronic-reading-room

History   In 1963, President John F. Kennedy created a new Office of the Special Trade Representative in the Executive Office of the President and designated two new Deputies, one in the Nation's capital and the other in Geneva, Switzerland. The rest of the story is available on the Web site of the Office of the U.S. Trade Representative. https://ustr.gov/about-us/history

The Office of the U.S. Trade Representative posted "Facts About Trade" to commemorate its 50th anniversary. https://ustr.gov/50/facts

Key Issues   The Office of the U.S. Trade Representative focuses it's trade policy on 14 issue areas: agriculture, economy and trade, enforcement, environment, government procurement, industry and manufacturing, intellectual property, labor, preference programs, services and investment, small business, textiles and apparel, trade and development, and trade organizations. https://ustr.gov/issue-areas

Map   The United States has trade relations with more than 75 countries worldwide. https://ustr.gov/countries-regions

North American Free Trade Agreement (NAFTA)   The Web site of the Office of the U.S. Trade Representative features facts on the NAFTA. https://ustr.gov/trade-agreements/free-trade-agreements/north-american-free-trade-agreement-nafta

Open Government   The Office of the U.S. Trade Representative supports the Open Government initiative by promoting the principles of collaboration, participation, and transparency. https://www.whitehouse.gov/open/around/eop/ustr

Press Releases   The Office of the U.S. Trade Representative posts press releases on its Web site. https://ustr.gov/about-us/policy-offices/press-office/press-releases

Reports / Publications   The Office of the U.S. Trade Representative posts reports and publications on its Web site. https://ustr.gov/about-us/policy-offices/press-office/reports-and-publications

Social Media   The U.S. Trade Representative tweets announcements and other newsworthy items on Twitter. https://twitter.com/USTradeRep

The Office of the U.S. Trade Representative has a Facebook account. https://www.facebook.com/USTradeRep

Speeches / Transcripts   The Office of the U.S. Trade Representative posts transcriptions of public remarks made by its senior staff. https://ustr.gov/about-us/policy-offices/press-office/speeches

Transatlantic Trade and Investment Partnership (T–TIP)   The Web site of the Office of the U.S. Trade Representative features a T–TIP issue-by-issue information center. https://ustr.gov/trade-agreements/free-trade-agreements/transatlantic-trade-and-investment-partnership-t-tip/t-tip

Trans-Pacific Partnership (TPP)   The Office of the U.S Trade Representative has answered frequently asked questions regarding the TPP on its Web site. https://ustr.gov/tpp/#facts; https://ustr.gov/about-us/policy-offices/press-office

For further information, contact the Office of Public and Media Affairs, Office of the U.S. Trade Representative, 600 Seventeenth Street NW., Washington, DC 20508. Phone, 202-395-3230.

EXECUTIVE BRANCH: DEPARTMENTS

DEPARTMENT OF AGRICULTURE
1400 Independence Avenue SW., Washington, DC 20250
Phone, 202-720-2791. Internet, http://www.usda.gov

Secretary of Agriculture
George E. Perdue III
Deputy Secretary
Michael L. Young, Acting
https://www.usda.gov/our-agency/about-usda/our-secretary

MISSION AREAS
https://www.usda.gov/our-agency/about-usda/mission-areas

Farm Production and Conservation
Under Secretary
(VACANCY)
Deputy Under Secretary
Robert Johansson, Acting
Administrator, Farm Service Agency
Steven J. Peterson, Acting
Chief, Natural Resources Conservation Service
Leonard Jordan
Administrator, Risk Management Agency
Heather Manzano, Acting
https://www.usda.gov/media/press-releases/2017/06/16/perdue-names-leadership-acting-
   roles-usda-reorganization-takes

Food, Nutrition and Consumer Services
Under Secretary
(VACANCY)
Deputy Under Secretary
Brandon Lipps, Acting
Administrator, Food and Nutrition Service
Brandon Lipps
Director, Center for Nutrition Policy and Promotion
Jackie Haven, Acting
https://www.usda.gov/media/press-releases/2017/07/19/secretary-perdue-announces-new-
   leadership-food-nutrition-and

Food Safety
Under Secretary
(VACANCY)
Deputy Under Secretary
Carmen Rottenberg, Acting
Administrator, Food Safety and Inspection Service
Paul Kiecker, Acting
https://www.fsis.usda.gov/wps/portal/informational/aboutfsis/agency-leadership

Marketing and Regulatory Programs
Under Secretary
Gregory Ibach
Administrator, Agricultural Marketing Service
Bruce Summers, Acting
Administrator, Animal and Plant Health Inspection Service
Kevin Shea
Administrator, Grain Inspection, Packers and Stockyards
Randall D. Jones, Acting
   Administration
https://www.ams.usda.gov/about-ams/our-leadership/under-secretary-greg-ibach

Natural Resources and Environment
Under Secretary
(VACANCY)

Deputy Under Secretary	DAN JIRON, ACTING
Chief, Forest Service	TONY TOOKE

https://www.fs.fed.us/about-agency/newsroom/leadership-biographies

Research, Education and Economics

Under Secretary	(VACANCY)
Deputy Under Secretary	CHAVONDA JACOBS-YOUNG, ACTING
Administrator, Agricultural Research Service	CHAVONDA JACOBS-YOUNG
Administrator, Economic Research Service	MARY BOHMAN
Administrator, National Agricultural Statistics Service	HUBERT HAMER, JR.
Director, National Agricultural Library	PAUL WESTER
Director, National Institute of Food and Agriculture	SONNY RAMASWAMY

https://www.ree.usda.gov/about-ree/biographies

Rural Development

Assistant to the Secretary	ANNE HAZLETT
Adminstrator, Rural Business-Cooperative Service	MARK BRODZISKI, ACTING
Administrator, Rural Housing Service	CURTIS ANDERSON, ACTING
Administrator, Rural Utilities Service	CHRIS MCLEAN, ACTING

https://www.rd.usda.gov/about-rd/leadership

Trade and Foreign Agricultural Affairs

Under Secretary	(VACANCY)
Deputy Under Secretary	JASON HAFEMEISTER, ACTING
Administrator, Farm Agricultural Service	HOLLY HIGGINS, ACTING

https://www.fas.usda.gov/about-fas/leadership

Office Heads

Assistant Secretary for Administration	MALCOM SHORTER, ACTING
Assistant Secretary for Civil Rights	(VACANCY)
Chief Economist	ROBERT JOHANSSON
Chief Financial Officer	LYNN M. MOANEY, ACTING
Chief Information Officer	GARY WASHINGTON, ACTING
Chief Scientist	CHAVONDA JACOBS-YOUNG, ACTING
Deputy Assistant Secretary for Congressional Relations	ABBEY FRETZ, ACTING
Deputy Assistant Secretary for External and Intergovernmental Affairs	DOUG CRANDALL, ACTING
Director, Advocacy and Outreach	CAROLYN PARKER
Director, Budget and Program Analysis	DIEM-LINH JONES, ACTING
Director, Communications	TIMOTHY M. MURTAUGH
Director, National Appeals Division	STEVEN C. SILVERMAN
Director, Tribal Relations	BEN KEEL
General Counsel	STEPHEN A. VADEN, ACTING

https://www.usda.gov/our-agency/staff-offices

Inspector General	PHYLLIS K. FONG

https://www.usda.gov/oig

[For the Department of Agriculture statement of organization, see the Code of Federal Regulations, Title 7, Part 2]

The above list of key personnel was updated 06–2017.

The Department of Agriculture develops agricultural markets, fights hunger and malnutrition, conserves natural resources, and ensures food quality standards.

USDA Organization Chart

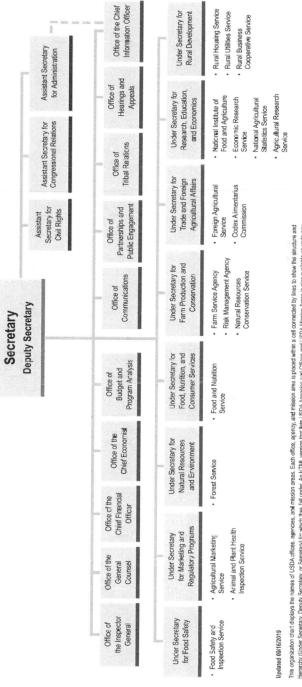

Secretary
Deputy Secretary

Assistant Secretary for Civil Rights

Assistant Secretary for Congressional Relations

Assistant Secretary for Administration

Office of the Inspector General

Office of the General Counsel

Office of the Chief Financial Officer

Office of the Chief Economist

Office of Budget and Program Analysis

Office of Communications

Office of Partnerships and Public Engagement

Office of Tribal Relations

Office of Hearings and Appeals

Office of the Chief Information Officer

Under Secretary for Food Safety
- Food Safety and Inspection Service

Under Secretary for Marketing and Regulatory Programs
- Agricultural Marketing Service
- Animal and Plant Health Inspection Service

Under Secretary for Natural Resources and Environment
- Forest Service

Under Secretary for Food, Nutrition, and Consumer Services
- Food and Nutrition Service

Under Secretary for Farm Production and Conservation
- Farm Service Agency
- Risk Management Agency
- Natural Resources Conservation Service

Under Secretary for Trade and Foreign Agricultural Affairs
- Foreign Agricultural Service
- Codex Alimentarius Commission

Under Secretary for Research, Education, and Economics
- National Institute of Food and Agriculture
- Economic Research Service
- National Agricultural Statistics Service
- Agricultural Research Service

Under Secretary for Rural Development
- Rural Housing Service
- Rural Utilities Service
- Rural Business Cooperative Service

Updated 09/16/2019

This organization chart displays the names of USDA offices, agencies, and mission areas. Each office, agency, and mission area is placed within a cell connected by lines to show the structure and hierarchy (Under Secretary, Deputy Secretary, or Secretary) for which they fall under. An HTML version that lists USDA Agencies and Offices and USDA Mission Areas is also available on usda.gov

The Secretary's Memorandum 1076-031 was signed August 15, 2019 effectuating a change to Rural Development.

The Department of Agriculture (USDA) was created by an act of Congress on May 15, 1862 (7 U.S.C. 2201). In carrying out its work in the program mission areas, the USDA relies on the support of departmental administration staff, as well as on the Offices of Communications, Congressional Relations, the Chief Economist, the Chief Financial Officer, the Chief Information Officer, the General Counsel, and the Inspector General. http://www.usda.gov/wps/portal/usda/usdahome?navid=USDA150

Farm and Foreign Agricultural Services

This mission area centers on helping America's farmers and ranchers deal with the unpredictable nature of weather and markets. These services deliver commodity, conservation, credit, disaster, and emergency assistance programs to strengthen and stabilize the agricultural economy. http://www.usda.gov/wps/portal/usda/usdahome?navid=USDA_MISSION_AREAS

Farm Service Agency (FSA)   The Farm Service Agency administers farm commodity, disaster, and conservation programs for farmers and ranchers. It also makes and guarantees farm emergency, ownership, and operating loans through a network of State and county offices. http://www.fsa.usda.gov/index

Commodity Credit Corporation   The Commodity Credit Corporation, an agency and instrumentality of the United States within the USDA, is under the supervision of the Secretary of Agriculture. The Corporation does not have any employees, but relies on various Federal agencies, principally those in the USDA, to conduct its operations. It carries out a wide array of functions as authorized by the Commodity Credit Corporation Charter Act and as specifically authorized by the Congress in numerous statutes. Corporation funds are used to offer marketing assistance loans to producers of certain commodities, fund conservation programs to protect or enhance natural resources, support the export of agricultural commodities, provide humanitarian assistance abroad, and further economic progress in developing countries. http://www.fsa.usda.gov/about-fsa/structure-and-organization/commodity-credit-corporation/index

Commodity Operations   FSA facilitates the purchase, storage, transportation, and disposition of U.S.-origin commodities acquired as a result of commodity loan forfeiture or through procurement for humanitarian food aid programs. FSA administers the United States Warehouse Act, which authorizes the Secretary of Agriculture to license warehouse operators who store agricultural products. The FSA also enters into agreements with warehouse operators to store commodities owned by the Commodity Credit Corporation or pledged by farmers as security for Commodity Credit Corporation marketing assistance loans. http://www.fsa.usda.gov/about-fsa/structure-and-organization/commodity-operations/index

Conservation Programs   FSA's conservation programs include the Conservation Reserve Program, which is the Federal Government's largest environmental improvement program on private lands. It safeguards millions of acres of topsoil from erosion, improves air quality, increases wildlife habitat, and reduces water runoff and sedimentation. In return for planting a protective cover of grass or trees on environmentally sensitive land, participants receive an annual rental payment. Cost-share payments are available to help establish conservation practices such as the planting of native grass, trees, windbreaks, or plants that improve water quality and give shelter and food to wildlife. http://www.fsa.usda.gov/FSA/webapp?area=home&subject=copr&topic=landing

Farm Commodity Programs

FSA manages farm safety net programs for America's farmers and ranchers. Its Commodity Credit Corporation stabilizes, supports, and protects farm income and prices; helps maintain balanced and adequate supplies of agricultural commodities; and aids in their orderly distribution. http://www.fsa.usda.gov/about-fsa/structure-and-organization/commodity-credit-corporation/index

Farm Loan Programs

FSA makes and guarantees loans to family farmers and ranchers to purchase farmland and finance agricultural production. These programs offer credit on reasonable rates and terms to farmers—those who have suffered financial setbacks from natural disasters, those with limited resources for establishing and maintaining profitable farming operations, and beginners. http://www.fsa.usda.gov/programs-and-services/farm-loan-programs/index

Noninsured Crop Disaster Assistance Program The Noninsured Crop Disaster Assistance Program gives financial assistance to producers of noninsurable crops when yields are low, inventory is lost, or natural disasters prevent planting. http://www.fsa.usda.gov/programs-and-services/disaster-assistance-program/noninsured-crop-disaster-assistance/index

Other Emergency Assistance In counties that are declared disaster areas, low-interest loans for eligible farmers help cover physical and production losses. Eligible producers can be compensated for crop losses, livestock feed losses, tree damage, and for the cost of rehabilitating certain farmlands damaged by natural disaster. http://www.fsa.usda.gov/programs-and-services/disaster-assistance-program/index

For further information, contact the Office of External Affairs, Farm Service Agency, Department of Agriculture, Stop 0506, 1400 Independence Avenue SW., Washington, DC 20250. Phone, 202-720-7807. Or, contact the Information Division, Foreign Agricultural Service, Department of Agriculture, Stop 1004, 1400 Independence Avenue SW., Washington, DC 20250. Phone, 202-720-7115. Fax, 202-720-1727.

Foreign Agricultural Service (FAS) The Foreign Agricultural Service improves foreign market access for U.S. products, builds new markets, improves the competitive position of U.S. agriculture in the global marketplace, and provides food aid and technical assistance to foreign countries.

FAS has the primary responsibility for USDA's activities in the areas of international marketing, trade agreements and negotiations, and the collection and analysis of international statistics and market information. It also administers the USDA's export credit guarantee and food aid programs. FAS helps increase income and food availability in developing nations by mobilizing expertise for agriculturally led economic growth.

FAS also enhances U.S. agricultural competitiveness through a global network of agricultural economists, marketing experts, negotiators, and other specialists. FAS agricultural counselors, attaches, trade officers, and locally employed staff are stationed in over 93 countries to support U.S. agricultural interests and cover 171 countries.

In addition to agricultural affairs offices in U.S. embassies, trade offices operate in a number of key foreign markets. They function as service centers for U.S. exporters and foreign buyers seeking market information.

Reports prepared by FAS overseas offices cover changes in policies and other developments that could affect U.S. agricultural exports. FAS staff in U.S. embassies worldwide assess U.S. export marketing opportunities and respond to the daily informational needs of those who develop, initiate, monitor, and evaluate U.S. food and agricultural policies and programs.

The Service also maintains a worldwide agricultural reporting system based on information from U.S. agricultural traders, remote sensing systems, and other sources. Analysts in Washington, DC, prepare production forecasts, assess export marketing opportunities, and track changes in policies affecting U.S. agricultural exports and imports.

FAS programs help U.S. exporters develop and maintain markets for hundreds of food and agricultural products, from bulk commodities to brand-name items. Formal market promotion activities are carried out chiefly in cooperation with agricultural trade associations, State-regional trade groups, small businesses, and cooperatives that plan, manage, and contribute human and financial resources to these efforts. The Service also advises exporters on locating buyers and provides assistance through a variety of other methods, including supporting U.S. participation in trade shows and single-industry exhibitions each year.http://www.fas.usda.gov

For further information, contact the Public Affairs Division, Foreign Agricultural Service, Stop 1004, 1400 Independence Avenue SW., Department of Agriculture, Washington, DC 20250-1004. Phone, 202-720-7115. Fax, 202-720-1727.

Risk Management Agency (RMA) The Risk Management Agency, on behalf of the Federal Crop Insurance Corporation (FCIC), oversees and administers the Federal crop insurance program under the Federal Crop Insurance Act.

Federal crop insurance is offered to qualifying producers through 16 private sector crop insurance companies. Under the Standard Reinsurance Agreement (SRA), RMA provides reinsurance, pays premium subsidies, reimburses insurers for administrative and operating expenses, and oversees the financial integrity and operational performance of the delivery system. RMA bears much of the noncommercial insurance risk under the SRA, allowing insurers to retain commercial insurance risks or reinsure those risks in the private market.

In 2016, the Federal crop insurance program provided producers with more than $100 billion in protection. Twenty-five insurance plans are available, covering over 550 varieties of crops, 37 reinsured privately developed products, and 18 RMA-developed pilot programs in various stages of operation.

RMA also works closely with the private sector to find innovative ways to expand coverage. The expansion affects risk protection for specialty crops, livestock and forage, and rangeland and pasture. Thus, RMA is able to reduce the need for ad hoc disaster assistance, while providing coverage for production declines that result from adverse weather in many areas.

Additional information is available on the RMA Web site, which features agency news, State profiles, publications, and announcements on current issues. It also has summaries of insurance sales, pilot programs, downloadable crop policies, and agency-sponsored events. Online tools, calculators, and applications are also part of the Web site. http://www.rma.usda.gov

For further information, contact the Office of the Administrator, Risk Management Agency, Department of Agriculture, Stop 0801, 1400 Independence Avenue SW., Washington, DC 20250. Phone, 202-690-2803.

Food, Nutrition and Consumer Services

The mission area of the food, nutrition, and consumer services centers on harnessing the Nation's agricultural abundance to reduce hunger and improve health in the United States. Its agencies administer Federal domestic nutrition assistance programs and the Center for Nutrition Policy and Promotion, which links scientific research to the nutrition needs of consumers through science-based dietary guidance, nutrition policy coordination, and nutrition education. http://www.usda.gov/wps/portal/usda/usdahome?navid=USDA_MISSION_AREAS

Center for Nutrition Policy and Promotion (CNPP)   The Center for Nutrition Policy and Promotion improves the health and well-being

of Americans by developing and promoting dietary guidance that links the latest evidence-based scientific research to consumers' nutrition needs. Initiatives range from setting Federal dietary guidance to consumer-based nutrition education (MyPlate), to cutting-edge personalized electronic tools (SuperTracker), to "report cards" on the status of the American diet. https://www.choosemyplate.gov; https://www.supertracker.usda.gov; http://www.cnpp.usda.gov

For further information, contact the Office of Public Information, Center for Nutrition Policy and Promotion, Suite 200, 1120 20th Street NW., Washington, DC 20036-3406. Phone, 202-418-2312.

Food and Nutrition Service (FNS)   The Food and Nutrition Service administers the USDA domestic nutrition assistance programs, serving one in four Americans in the course of a year. The FNS works in partnership with States and local agencies to increase food security and reduce hunger by providing children and low-income people with access to food, a healthy diet, and nutrition education. http://www.fns.usda.gov

FNS administers the following nutrition assistance programs:

The Supplemental Nutrition Assistance Program (SNAP) gives nutrition assistance to millions of eligible low-income individuals and families, and it provides economic benefits to communities. SNAP is the largest program in the domestic hunger safety net. FNS also works with State partners and the retail community to improve program administration and ensure program integrity. http://www.fns.usda.gov/snap/supplemental-nutrition-assistance-program-snap

The Special Supplemental Nutrition Program for Women, Infants, and Children (WIC) provides Federal grants to States for supplemental foods, health care referrals, and nutrition education for low-income pregnant, breastfeeding, and nonbreastfeeding postpartum women, and to infants and children up to age 5 who are found to be at nutritional risk. WIC and the Seniors' Farmers' Market Nutrition Programs provide WIC participants and senior citizens with increased access to fresh produce through coupons to purchase fresh fruits and vegetables from authorized farmers. http://www.fns.usda.gov/wic/women-infants-and-children-wic

The Farmers' Market Nutrition Program is linked to WIC, which provides supplemental foods, health care referrals, and nutrition education at no cost to low-income pregnant, breastfeeding, and nonbreastfeeding post partum women, and to infants and children who are up to 5 years of age and found to be at nutritional risk. http://www.fns.usda.gov/fmnp/wic-farmers-market-nutrition-program-fmnp

The Senior Farmers' Market Nutrition Program awards grants to States, U.S. Territories, and federally recognized Indian tribal governments for coupons that low-income seniors can use to purchase eligible foods at farmers' markets, roadside stands, and community-supported agriculture programs. http://www.fns.usda.gov/sfmnp/senior-farmers-market-nutrition-program-sfmnp

The Commodity Supplemental Food Program improves the health of low-income pregnant and breastfeeding women, nonbreastfeeding mothers up to 1 year postpartum, infants, and children up to age 6. The program supplements their diets with nutritious USDA commodity foods. It also provides food and administrative funds to States to supplement the diets of these groups. http://www.fns.usda.gov/csfp/commodity-supplemental-food-program-csfp

School districts and independent schools that choose to take part in the National School Lunch Program receive cash subsidies and donated commodities from the USDA. In return, they must serve lunches that meet Federal requirements and must offer free or reduced-price lunches to eligible children. School food authorities can also be reimbursed for snacks served to children through age 18 in afterschool educational or enrichment programs. http://www.fns.usda.gov/nslp/national-school-lunch-program-nslp

The School Breakfast Program operates like the National School Lunch Program. School districts and independent schools that choose to take part in the breakfast program receive cash subsidies from the USDA for each meal they serve. In return, they must serve breakfasts that meet Federal requirements and must offer free or reduced-price breakfasts to eligible children. http://www.fns.usda.gov/sbp/school-breakfast-program-sbp

The Special Milk Program provides milk to schoolchildren and children in childcare institutions who do not participate in other Federal meal service programs. The program reimburses schools for the milk that they serve. Schools in the National School Lunch or School Breakfast Programs may participate so that milk is available to prekindergarten and kindergarten children who may not have access to school meal programs. http://www.fns.usda.gov/smp/special-milk-program

The Child and Adult Care Food Program helps child and adult care institutions and family or group day care homes provide nutritious foods to promote the health and wellness of young children, older adults, and chronically impaired disabled persons. http://www.fns.usda.gov/cacfp/child-and-adult-care-food-program

The Summer Food Service Program ensures that low-income children receive nutritious meals when they are not attending school. http://www.fns.usda.gov/sfsp/summer-food-service-program-sfsp

The Emergency Food Assistance Program helps low-income and elderly Americans access free emergency food and nutrition assistance. The program provides food and administrative funds to States to supplement the diets of these groups. http://www.fns.usda.gov/tefap/emergency-food-assistance-program-tefap

The Food Distribution Program on Indian Reservations helps low-income households—including the elderly living on Indian reservations—and Native American families residing in designated areas in Oklahoma and near reservations elsewhere to access USDA foods. http://www.fns.usda.gov/fdpir/food-distribution-program-indian-reservations-fdpir

The Fresh Fruit and Vegetable Program helps make fruits and vegetables available to students free of charge, during the schoolday, in participating elementary schools. The program is a tool for reducing childhood obesity: It exposes schoolchildren to fresh produce that they otherwise might not have the opportunity to sample. http://www.fns.usda.gov/ffvp/fresh-fruit-and-vegetable-program

For further information, contact the Public Information Officer, Food and Nutrition Service, Department of Agriculture, 3101 Park Center Drive, Alexandria, VA 22302. Phone, 703-305-2286.

Food Safety

This mission area centers on the labeling and packaging, safety, and wholesomeness of the Nation's commercial supply of egg, poultry, and meat. It also contributes significantly to the President's Council on Food Safety and has helped coordinate a nationwide food safety strategic plan. http://www.usda.gov/wps/portal/usda/usdahome?navid=USDA_MISSION_AREAS

Food Safety and Inspection Service

(FSIS)   The Food Safety and Inspection Service was established by the Secretary of Agriculture on June 17, 1981, pursuant to authority contained in 5 U.S.C. 301 and Reorganization Plan No. 2 of 1953 (5 U.S.C. app.). FSIS monitors the Nation's commercial supply of meat, poultry, and processed egg products. http://www.fsis.usda.gov/wps/portal/fsis/home

Meat, Poultry, and Processed Egg Products Inspection   FSIS is the public health regulatory agency in the U.S. Department of Agriculture that ensures commercial meat, poultry, and processed egg products are safe, wholesome, accurately labeled, and properly packaged. FSIS enforces the Federal Meat Inspection Act (FMIA), the Poultry Products Inspection Act (PPIA), and the Egg Products Inspection Act (EPIA), which require Federal inspection and regulation of meat, poultry, and processed egg products prepared for distribution in commerce for use as human food. FSIS is also responsible for administering the Humane Methods of Slaughter Act, which requires that livestock are handled and slaughtered humanely at the FSIS-inspected establishment.

FSIS administers FMIA, PPIA, and EPIA by developing and implementing data-driven regulations, including inspection, testing, and enforcement activities for the products under FSIS's jurisdiction. In addition to mandatory inspection of meat, poultry, and processed egg products, FSIS tests samples of these products for microbial and chemical residues to monitor trends for enforcement purposes and to understand, predict, and prevent contamination. FSIS also ensures that only meat, poultry, and processed egg products that meet U.S. requirements are imported into the United States, and it certifies meat, poultry, and processed egg products for export.

FSIS also monitors meat, poultry, and processed egg products throughout storage, distribution, and retail channels, and it ensures regulatory compliance to protect the public, including detention of products, voluntary product recalls, court-ordered seizures of products, administrative suspension and withdrawal of inspection, and referral of violations for criminal and civil prosecution. To protect against intentional contamination, the Agency conducts food defense activities, as well.

FSIS maintains a toll-free Meat and Poultry Hotline (phone, 888-674-6854; TTY, 800-256-7072) and chat feature to answer questions in English and Spanish about the safe handling of meat, poultry, and egg products. The Hotline's hours are weekdays, from 10 a.m. to 4 p.m., EST, year round. An extensive selection of food safety messages in English and Spanish is available at the same number at all hours of the day. Questions can also be submitted anytime to MPHotline.fsis@usda.gov.

"Ask Karen," an online virtual representative, provides answers to consumer questions on preventing foodborne illness, safe food handling and storage, and safe preparation of meat, poultry, and egg products (http://www.fsis.usda.gov/wps/portal/informational/askkaren). http://www.fsis.usda.gov

For further information, contact the Assistant Administrator, Office of Public Affairs and Consumer Education, Department of Agriculture, 1400 Independence Avenue SW., Washington, DC 20250. Phone, 202-720-3884.

Marketing And Regulatory Programs

The scope of the marketing and regulatory mission area includes marketing and regulatory programs other than those concerned with food safety. http://www.usda.gov/wps/portal/usda/usdahome?navid=USDA_MISSION_AREAS

Agricultural Marketing Service (AMS)   The Agricultural Marketing Service was established by the Secretary of Agriculture on April 2, 1972, under the authority of Reorganization Plan No. 2 of 1953 (5 U.S.C. app.) and other authorities. The Service facilitates the fair and efficient marketing of U.S. agricultural products. It supports agriculture through a variety of programs: cotton and tobacco; dairy; fruit and vegetable; livestock, poultry, and seed; organic products; transportation and marketing, and science and technology. The Service's activities support American agriculture in the global marketplace and help ensure the availability of wholesome food. http://www.ams.usda.gov

Audit and Accreditation Services AMS audit and accreditation programs give producers and suppliers of agricultural products the opportunity to assure customers of their ability to provide consistent quality products and services. The AMS verifies their documented programs through independent, third-party audits. AMS audit and accreditation programs are voluntary and paid through hourly user-fees. http://www.ams.usda.gov/services/auditing

Commodity Purchasing The AMS purchases a variety of domestically produced and processed commodity food products through a competitive process involving approved vendors. The purchasing supports American agriculture by providing an outlet for surplus products and encouraging domestic consumption of domestic foods. The wholesome, high quality products, collectively called USDA Foods, are delivered to schools, food banks, and households across the country and constitute a vital component of the Nation's food safety net. http://www.ams.usda.gov/selling-food

Farmers Markets / Direct-to-Consumer Marketing The AMS regularly collects data and analyzes farmers market operations and other direct-to-consumer marketing outlets—Community Supported Agriculture, food hubs, on-farm markets—to help market managers, planners, and researchers better understand the effect of these outlets on food access and local economic development, and to help the public find sources of fresh, local food. http://www.ams.usda.gov/services/local-regional

Grades / Standards USDA grade shields, official seals, and labels are symbols of the quality and integrity of American agricultural products. Large-volume buyers such as grocery stores, military institutions, restaurants, and foreign governments benfit from the quality grades and standards because they serve as as a common "language" that simplifies business transactions. http://www.ams.usda.gov/AMSv1.0/standards

Grant Programs The AMS administers a series of grant programs that make over $100 million available to support a variety of agricultural activities, including the specialty crop industry and local and regional food system expansion. These grant programs improve domestic and international opportunities for growers and producers and help support rural America. http://www.ams.usda.gov/services/grants

Laboratory Testing and Approval Services The AMS oversees the National Science Laboratories (NSL), a fee-for-service lab network. NSL scientists and technicians conduct chemical, microbiological, and biomolecular analyses on food and agricultural commodities. The network provides testing services for AMS commodity programs, other USDA agencies, Federal and State agencies, research institutions, private sector food and agricultural industries, and the U.S. military. The AMS also approves or accredits labs to perform testing services in support of domestic and international trade. At the request of industry, other Federal agencies, or foreign governments, it develops and administers laboratory approval programs to verify that the analysis of food and agricultural products meet country or customer specified requirements. http://www.ams.usda.gov/services/lab-testing

Marketing Agreements and Orders Marketing agreements and orders are initiated by industry to stabilize markets for dairy products, fruits, vegetables, and specialty crops. An agreement is binding only for handlers who sign the agreement. Marketing orders are a binding regulation for the entire industry in the specified geographical area, once the producers and the Secretary of Agriculture have approved it. http://www.ams.usda.gov/rules-regulations/moa

Market News Market News issues thousands of reports each year, providing the agricultural industry with important wholesale, retail, and shipping data. The reports give farmers, producers, and other agricultural businesses the information they need to evaluate market conditions, identify trends, make purchasing decisions, monitor price patterns, evaluate transportation equipment needs, and accurately assess movement. http://www.ams.usda.gov/market-news

National Organic Program   The National Organic Program is a regulatory program housed within the AMS. It develops national standards for organically-produced agricultural products. The "USDA ORGANIC" seal means that a product met consistent and uniform standards. USDA organic regulations do not address food safety or nutrition. Organic production integrates cultural, biological, and mechanical practices to increase cycling of resources, biodiversity, and ecological balance. http://www.ams.usda.gov/about-ams/programs-offices/national-organic-program

Pesticide Data Program   The Pesticide Data Program (PDP) monitors pesticide residue nationwide. It produces the most comprehensive pesticide residue database in the Nation. The PDP administers the sampling, testing, and reporting of pesticide residues on agricultural commodities in the U.S. food supply—with an emphasis on those commodities regularly consumed by infants and children. The AMS implements the program in cooperation with State agriculture departments and other Federal agencies. The Environmental Protection Agency relies on PDP data to assess dietary exposure, and Food and Drug Administration and other government experts use them for making informed decisions. http://www.ams.usda.gov/datasets/pdp

Plant Variety Protection Program   The Plant Variety Protection Office protects the intellectual property of breeders of new seed and tuber varieties. Implementing the Plant Variety Protection Act, the Office examines new applications and grants certificates that protect varieties for 20 or 25 years. Certificate owners have exclusive rights to market and sell their varieties, manage the use of their varieties by other breeders, and benefit from legal protection of their work. http://www.ams.usda.gov/services/plant-variety-protection

Regulatory Programs   The AMS administers several regulatory programs designed to protect producers, handlers, and consumers of agricultural commodities from financial loss or personal injury resulting from careless, deceptive, or fraudulent marketing practices. These regulatory programs encourage fair trading practices in the marketing of fruits and vegetables, and they require accuracy in seed labeling and in advertising. The AMS also enforces the Country of Origin Labeling law, which requires retailers—full-line grocery stores, supermarkets, club warehouse stores—to notify their customers with information regarding the source of certain foods. http://www.ams.usda.gov/rules-regulations

Research and Promotion Programs   The AMS monitors certain industry-sponsored research, promotion, and information programs authorized by Federal laws. These programs give farmers and processors a means to finance and operate various research, promotion, and information activities for agricultural products. http://www.ams.usda.gov/rules-regulations/research-promotion

Quality Grading / Inspections   Nearly 600 grade standards have been established for some 230 agricultural commodities to help buyers and sellers trade on agreed-upon quality levels. Standards are developed with assistance from individuals outside the Department, particularly from those involved with the industries directly affected. The AMS also participates in developing international commodity standards to facilitate trade. Grading and classing services are provided to certify the grade and quality of products. These grading services are provided to buyers and sellers of live cattle, swine, sheep, meat, poultry, eggs, rabbits, fruits, vegetables, tree nuts, peanuts, dairy products, tobacco, and other miscellaneous food products. Classing services are provided to buyers and sellers of cotton and cotton products. These services are mainly voluntary and are provided upon request and for a fee. The AMS is also responsible for testing seed. http://www.ams.usda.gov/services/grading

Transportation Research and Analysis   The Transportation Services Division (TSD) of the AMS serves as the definitive source for economic analysis of agricultural transportation. TSD experts support domestic and international agribusinesses by giving technical assistance and releasing reports and offering analysis. They track developments in truck, rail, barge, and ocean transportation and provide information on and analysis of these modes of moving food from farm to table, from port to market. http://www.ams.usda.gov/services/transportation-analysis

For further information, contact the Public Affairs Staff, Agricultural Marketing Service, Department of Agriculture, Room 3933, South Agriculture Building, Stop 0273, 1400 Independence Ave, SW., Washington, DC 20250. Phone, 202-720-8998.

Animal and Plant Health Inspection Service (APHIS)   [For the Animal and Plant Health Inspection Service statement of organization, see the Code of Federal Regulations, Title 7, Part 371]

The Animal and Plant Health Inspection Service was originally established in 1972 and reestablished by the Secretary of Agriculture on March 14, 1977, pursuant to authority contained in 5 U.S.C. 301 and Reorganization Plan No. 2 of 1953 (5 U.S.C. app.). The APHIS was established to conduct regulatory and control programs to protect and improve animal and plant health for the benefit of agriculture and the environment. In cooperation with State governments, industry stakeholders, and other Federal agencies, the APHIS works to prevent the entry and establishment of foreign animal and plant pests and diseases. It also regulates certain genetically engineered organisms and supports healthy international agricultural trade and exports of U.S. agricultural products. The agency also works to ensure the humane treatment of certain animals and carries out research and operational activities to mitigate damage caused by birds, rodents, and other wildlife. https://www.aphis.usda.gov/wps/portal/aphis/home

Animal Care   Animal Care upholds and enforces the Animal Welfare Act and the Horse Protection Act. The Animal Welfare Act requires that federally established standards of care and treatment be provided for certain warmblooded animals bred for commercial sale, used in research, transported commercially, or publicly exhibited. The Horse Protection Act seeks to end soring by preventing sored horses from participating in auctions, exhibitions, sales, and shows. The Center for Animal Welfare collaborates with other animal welfare entities to help the USDA build partnerships domestically and internationally, improve regulatory practices, and develop outreach, training, and educational resources. Animal Care's emergency response component provides national leadership on the safety and well-being of pets during disasters—supporting animal safety during emergencies is a significant factor in ensuring the well-being of pet owners. https://www.aphis.usda.gov/wps/portal/aphis/ourfocus/animalwelfare

Biotechnology Regulatory Services   To protect plant health, Biotechnology Regulatory Services implements APHIS regulations affecting the importation, movement, and field release of genetically engineered plants and certain other genetically engineered organisms that may pose a risk to plant health. The APHIS coordinates these responsibilities along with the other designated Federal agencies as part of the Federal coordinated framework for the regulation of biotechnology. https://www.aphis.usda.gov/wps/portal/aphis/ourfocus/biotechnology

International Services   APHIS protects the health and value of American agriculture and natural resources. Its International Services supports this mission in an international environment. The Services collaborate with foreign partners to control pests and diseases, facilitate safe agricultural trade, ensure effective and efficient management of internationally-based programs, and invest in international capacity-building with foreign counterparts to build technical and regulatory skills that prevent diseases and pests from spreading. https://www.aphis.usda.gov/wps/portal/aphis/ourfocus/internationalservices

Plant Protection and Quarantine   APHIS oversees Plant Protection and Quarantine. The program protects U.S. agriculture and natural resources against the entry, establishment, and spread of economically and environmentally significant pests. It also facilitates the safe trade of agricultural products. https://www.aphis.usda.gov/wps/portal/aphis/ourfocus/planthealth

Veterinary Services   Veterinary Services supports APHIS' efforts to protect and improve the health, quality, and marketability of the Nation's animals, animal products, and veterinary biologics. The Service is organized strategically into four sections: surveillance, preparedness, and response; national import export services; science, technology, and analysis; and program support services. https://www. aphis.usda.gov/wps/portal/aphis/ourfocus/ animalhealth

Wildlife Services   Wildlife Services provides Federal leadership and expertise for resolving conflicts between wildlife and people to allow coexistence. It conducts program delivery, research, and other activities through regional and State offices, the National Wildlife Research Center and field stations, as well as through national programs. Contact the APHIS customer service call center for more information. Phone, 844-820-2234. https://www. aphis.usda.gov/wps/portal/aphis/ourfocus/ wildlifedamage

For further information, contact Legislative and Public Affairs, Animal and Plant Health Inspection Service, Department of Agriculture, 1400 Independence Avenue SW., Washington, DC 20250. Phone, 202-799-7030.

Grain Inspection, Packers and Stockyards Administration (GIPSA)

The Grain Inspection, Packers and Stockyards Administration was established in 1994 to facilitate the marketing of livestock, poultry, meat, cereals, oilseeds, and related agricultural products, and to promote fair and competitive trading practices for the overall benefit of consumers and American agriculture. The Packers and Stockyards Program protects fair trade practices, financial integrity, and competitive markets for livestock, meat, and poultry. The Federal Grain Inspection Service facilitates the marketing of U.S. grains, oilseeds, and related agricultural products through its grain inspection and weighing system. The Service also maintains the integrity of the grain marketing system by developing unbiased grading standards and methods for assessing grain quality. http://www.gipsa. usda.gov

Inspection   The United States Grain Standards Act requires most U.S. export grain to be inspected. At export port locations, GIPSA or State agencies that have been delegated authority by the Administrator carry out inspections. For domestic grain marketed at inland locations, the Administrator designates private and State agencies to provide official inspection services upon request. Both export and domestic services are provided on a fee-for-service basis. http://www.gipsa.usda.gov/fgis/ inspectionservices.aspx

Methods Development   GIPSA's methods development activities include applied research or tests to produce new or improved techniques for measuring grain quality. Examples include knowledge gained through the study of how to establish real-time grain inspection, develop reference methods in order to maintain consistency and standardization in the grain inspection system, as well as the comparison of different techniques for evaluation of end-use quality in wheat.

Packers and Stockyards Activities   GIPSA prohibits deceptive, discriminatory, and unfair practices by market agencies, dealers, stockyards, packers, swine contractors, and live poultry dealers in the livestock, meat packing, and poultry industries. According to the provisions of the Packers and Stockyards Act, it fosters fair competition and ensures payment protection for growers and farmers through regulatory activities: investigating alleged violations of the act, auditing regulated entities, verifying the accuracy of scales, and monitoring industry trends to protect consumers and members of the livestock, meat, and poultry industries. The Administration also has certain responsibilities derived from the Truth-in-Lending and the Fair Credit Reporting Acts. GIPSA carries out the Secretary's responsibilities under section 1324 of the Food Security Act of 1985 pertaining to State-established central filing systems to prenotify buyers, commission merchants, and selling agents of security interests against farm products. GIPSA administers the section of the act commonly referred to as the "Clear Title" provision and certifies qualifying State systems. http://www.gipsa. usda.gov/psp/psp.aspx

Standardization   Official inspections of grains, oilseeds, and other agricultural and processed commodities are based on established official U.S. standards. The inspections also rely on sound, proven, and standardized procedures, techniques, and equipment. The official standards and accompanying procedures, techniques, and equipment produce consistent test results and services, from elevator to elevator and State to State. http://www.gipsa.usda.gov/ fgis/standardprocedures.aspx

Weighing GIPSA or State agencies that have been delegated authority the Administrator officially weigh U.S. export grain at port locations. For domestic grain marketed at inland locations, GIPSA or designated private or State agencies provide the weighing services. Weighing services are provided on a fee-for-service basis. http://www.gipsa.usda.gov/fgis/weighingservices.aspx

For further information, contact the Grain Inspection, Packers, and Stockyards Administration, Department of Agriculture, 1400 Independence Avenue SW., Washington, DC 20250. Phone, 202-720-0219.

Natural Resources and Environment

This mission area centers on stewardship of 75 percent of the Nation's total land area. The USDA's operating philosophy in this mission area places a premium on collaboration with diverse partners and on the health and sustainability of ecosystems to maximize stewardship of the Nation's natural resources. This approach ensures that the necessary requirements for maintaining healthy and sustainable systems are in balance with people's priorities and the products and services that they desire. http://www.usda.gov/wps/portal/usda/usdahome?navid=USDA_MISSION_AREAS

Forest Service (FS) [For the Forest Service statement of organization, see the Code of Federal Regulations, Title 36, Part 200.1]

In 1876, Congress created the Office of Special Agent in the Department of Agriculture to assess the condition of the forests in the United States. The Forest Service was created decades later by the Transfer Act of February 1, 1905 (16 U.S.C. 472), which transferred the Federal forest reserves and the responsibility for their management to the USDA from the Department of the Interior. The mission of the Forest Service is to achieve quality land management under the sustainable, multiple-use management concept to meet the diverse needs of people. The Service advocates a conservation ethic in promoting the health, productivity, diversity, and beauty of forests and associated lands; listens to people and responds to their diverse needs in making decisions; protects and manages the National Forests and Grasslands to best demonstrate the sustainable, multiple-use

management concept; provides technical and financial assistance to State, tribal, and private forest landowners, encouraging them to become better stewards and quality land managers; helps cities and communities improve their natural environment by planting trees and caring for their forests; provides international technical assistance and scientific exchanges to sustain and enhance global resources and to encourage quality land management; assists States and communities in using the forests wisely to promote rural economic development and a quality rural environment; develops and disseminates scientific and technical knowledge that helps protect, manage, and improve use of forests and rangelands; and offers employment, training, and educational opportunities to the unemployed, underemployed, disadvantaged, elderly, and youth. http://www.fs.fed.us

Forest Research The Service performs basic and applied research to develop the scientific information and technology needed to protect, manage, use, and sustain the natural resources of the Nation's forests and rangelands, including those on private and tribal lands. Its forest research strategy focuses on three major program components: understanding the structure and functions of forest and range ecosystems; understanding how people perceive and value the protection, management, and use of natural resources; and determining which protection, management, and utilization practices are most suitable for sustainable production and use of natural resources worldwide. http://www.fs.fed.us/research/research-topics

National Forest System Using the principles of multiple-use and sustained yield, the Service manages 154 National Forests, 20 National Grasslands, 1 tall grass prairie, and 8 national monuments on approximately 193 million acres of land in 44 States, the U.S. Virgin Islands, and Puerto Rico. The Nation's need for wood and paper products must be balanced against the other vital, renewable resources or benefits that the National Forests and Grasslands provide: recreation and natural beauty, wildlife habitat, livestock forage, and water supplies. As a guiding principle, the Service tries to achieve greatest good for the greatest number in the long run.

These lands are managed to promote resiliency against catastrophic wildfire, epidemics of disease and insect pests, erosion, and other threats. Burned areas receive emergency seeding treatment to prevent massive erosion and stream siltation. Roads and trails are built where needed to give the public access to outdoor recreation areas and provide scenic drives and hikes. Picnic, camping, skiing, water sport and other recreational areas feature facilities for public convenience and enjoyment. Vegetative management methods protect the land and streams, ensure rapid renewal of the forest, provide food and cover for wildlife and fish, and mitigate human impact on scenic and recreation assets. Local communities benefit from activities on National Forest lands. These lands also provide needed oil, gas, and minerals. Millions of livestock and game animals benefit from improved rangelands. The National Forests serve as a refuge for many species of endangered birds, animals, and fish. Some 34.6 million acres are set aside as wilderness and 175,000 acres as primitive areas where timber will not be harvested. http://www.fs.fed.us/managing-land/national-forests-grasslands

State and Private Forestry   The State and Private Forestry organization of the Forest Service reaches across the boundaries of National Forests to States, tribes, communities, and nonindustrial private landowners. The organization is the Federal leader in giving technical and financial assistance to landowners and resource managers to help sustain the Nation's forests and protect communities and the environment from wildland fires. National priorities for State and private forestry promote four core actions: conserving and managing working forest landscapes for multiple values and uses, protecting forests from threats, enhancing public benefits from trees and forests, and increasing organizational effectiveness. The State and Private Forestry organization supports sustainable stewardship of non-Federal forest land nationwide, including 423 million acres of private forest land, 69 million acres of State forest land, 18 million acres of tribal forests, and over 130 million acres of urban and community forests. The organization offers leadership

in wildland fire management, operations, methods development, risk mapping, forest products utilization, and advanced survey and monitoring, as well as geospatial technologies. http://www.fs.fed.us/spf

Natural Resources Conservation Service (NRCS)   [For the Natural Resources Conservation Service statement of organization, see the Code of Federal Regulations, Title 7, Parts 600 and 601]

The Natural Resources Conservation Service, formerly known as the Soil Conservation Service, helps America's farmers, ranchers, and other private landowners develop and implement voluntary efforts to conserve and protect the Nation's natural resources. http://www.nrcs.usda.gov/wps/portal/nrcs/site/national/home

Agricultural Conservation Easement Program   The Agricultural Conservation Easement Program helps conserve agricultural lands and wetlands by offering financial and technical assistance. Under the program's Agricultural Land Easements component, NRCS supports Indian tribes, State and local governments, and nongovernmental organizations in their efforts to protect working agricultural lands and to limit agricultural land use for nonagricultural purposes. Under the program's Wetlands Reserve Easements component, NRCS supports efforts to restore, protect, and enhance enrolled wetlands. http://www.nrcs.usda.gov/wps/portal/nrcs/main/national/programs/easements/acep

Agricultural Management Assistance   Agricultural Management Assistance, by giving financial and technical assistance to agricultural producers, encourages them to incorporate conversation practices into their farming operations to improve water management and quality, to reduce erosion, and to mitigate risk through production diversification. The assistance supports producers' in their efforts to plant trees for windbreaks, construct irrigation structures, use integrated pest management, and transition to organic farming. NRCS administers the program's conservation components, while AMS and RMA handle the others. http://www.nrcs.usda.gov/wps/portal/nrcs/main/national/programs/financial/ama

Conservation Stewardship Program   The Conservation Stewardship Program helps agricultural producers maintain and improve their existing conservation systems and adopt additional conservation practices that address resource concerns of high priority. Participants earn program payments for conservation performance: Payments are directly proportional to performance. The program offers two types of payments through 5-year contracts: annual payments for adopting new conservation practices and maintaining current ones, and supplemental payments for initiating a resource-conserving crop rotation. Producers may be able to renew a contract if they met the obligations of the initial contract and agree to achieve additional conservation goals. http://www.nrcs.usda.gov/wps/portal/nrcs/main/national/programs/financial/csp

Conservation Technical Assistance   Conservation Technical Assistance makes conservation technology and the delivery system needed to achieve the benefits of a healthy and productive landscape available to land users. The program reduces the loss of soil from erosion; offers solutions for agricultural waste management, air quality, soil, and water conservation and quality problems; mitigates potential water, sedimentation, or drought damage; improves fish and wildlife habitat; assists others in facilitating changes in land use for natural resource protection and sustainability; and increases the long term sustainability of all lands—cropland, forestland, grazing lands, coastal lands, and developing or developed lands. Technical Assistance supports clients in their efforts to address concerns and problems and explore opportunities related to the use of natural resources. NRCS staff and the employees of other agencies or entities under the technical supervision of NRCS provide the assistance. http://www.nrcs.usda.gov/wps/portal/nrcs/main/national/programs/technical/cta

Emergency Watershed Protection Program   The Emergency Watershed Protection Program safeguards lives and property in jeopardy due to sudden watershed impairment caused by natural disasters. Emergency assistance includes quickly establishing a protective plant cover on denuded land and stream banks, opening dangerously restricted channels, and repairing diversions and levees. To be eligible for assistance under this program, an emergency area does not need to be declared a national disaster area. NRCS may bear up to 75 percent of the construction cost of emergency measures. The remaining cost must come from local sources. Funding is subject to Congressional approval. http://www.nrcs.usda.gov/wps/portal/nrcs/main/national/programs/landscape/ewpp

Environmental Quality Incentives Program   The Environmental Quality Incentives Program assists agricultural producers by offering contracts up to a maximum term of 10 years in length. These contracts provide financial assistance for planning and implementing conservation practices that address natural resource concerns and for improving air, animal, plant, soil, water, and related resources on agricultural land and nonindustrial private forestland. Sixty percent of the available funds are for conservation activities related to livestock production. The program also helps producers meet Federal, State, tribal and local environmental regulations. http://www.nrcs.usda.gov/wps/portal/nrcs/main/national/programs/financial/eqip

Healthy Forests Reserve Program   The Healthy Forests Reserve Program helps landowners restore, enhance, and protect forestland resources on private lands through easements, 30-year contracts, and 10-year cost-share agreements. The program supports the efforts of landowners to promote the recovery of endangered or threatened species, increase plant and animal biodiversity, and improve carbon sequestration. http://www.nrcs.usda.gov/wps/portal/nrcs/main/national/programs/easements/forests

National Cooperative Soil Survey   The National Cooperative Soil Survey, a nationwide partnership of Federal, State, regional, and local agencies and private entities and institutions, works cooperatively to investigate, inventory, document, classify, interpret, disseminate, and publish soil information. It informs the public about the uses and capabilities of local soils. The published survey for a county or other designated area includes maps and interpretations that are essential for farm planning, other private land use decisions, and governmental policy development and resource planning. http://www.nrcs.usda.gov/wps/portal/nrcs/main/soils/survey/partnership/ncss

Plant Materials Program   The Plant Materials Program selects conservation plants and develops innovative planting technology for addressing natural resource challenges and maintaining healthy and productive farms and ranches. It focuses on using plants as a natural solution for conservation issues and reestablishing ecosystem function; collects, selects, and releases grasses, legumes, wildflowers, trees and shrubs, working with commercial, private, public, and tribal partners and land managers to apply new plant-based conservation methods; provides plant materials and new applied technologies for national initiatives; offers plant solutions to fight invasive species, heal lands damaged by natural disasters, reduce drought effects, promote air and water quality, and produce alternative energy; and assists Native American tribes with producing and protecting culturally significant plants. http://www.nrcs.usda.gov/wps/portal/nrcs/main/plantmaterials/about

Regional Conservation Partnership Program   The Regional Conservation Partnership Program promotes coordination between NRCS and its partners for the delivery of conservation assistance to producers and landowners. NRCS assists producers through partnership agreements and program contracts or easement agreements. The program combines the authorities of four previous programs: the Cooperative Conservation Partnership Initiative, the Agricultural Water Enhancement, the Chesapeake Bay Watershed, and the Great Lakes Basin Programs. http://www.nrcs.usda.gov/wps/portal/nrcs/main/national/programs/farmbill/rcpp

Small Watershed Program   The Small Watershed Program relies on local government sponsors to help participants solve natural resource and related economic problems on a watershed basis. Projects include efforts to protect watersheds, prevent floods, control erosion and sedimentation, improve water supply and quality, enhance fish and wildlife habitat, create and restore wetlands, and support public recreation in watersheds of 250,000 or fewer acres. The program offers both financial and technical assistance. Through the Small Watershed

Program, NRCS maps flood hazard areas, solves local flooding problems, evaluates potential greenbelts along streams, develops guidelines for erosion control and runoff management, helps farmers control erosion in high priority watersheds, and improves the water quality of ground water and water bodies. http://www.nrcs.usda.gov/wps/portal/nrcs/detail/nd/programs/?cid=nrcs141p2_001682

Snow Survey and Water Supply Forecasts   The Snow Survey is conducted by NRCS to make information on future water supplies available to residents of Alaska and Western States. At more than 1,800 mountain sites, NRCS personnel collect and analyze data on snowpack depth and its water equivalent to estimate annual water availability, spring runoff, and summer streamflows. Federal and State agencies, organizations, and individuals rely on these forecasts for agricultural production, fish and wildlife management, municipal and industrial water supply, urban development, flood control, recreation power generation, and water quality management. The National Weather Service includes the forecasts in their river forecasting function. http://www.nrcs.usda.gov/wps/portal/nrcs/main/national/water/snowsurvey

Watershed Surveys and Planning   The Watershed Surveys and Planning program supports Federal, State, and local agencies and tribal governments in their efforts to protect watersheds from damage caused by erosion, floodwater, and sediment and to conserve and develop water and land resources. The program addresses a number of resource concerns: agricultural drought problems, municipal and industrial water needs, rural development, upstream flood damages, water quality and conservation, wetland and water storage capacity, and water needs for fish, wildlife, and forest-based industries. http://www.nrcs.usda.gov/wps/portal/nrcs/main/national/programs/landscape/wsp

Research, Education and Economics

This mission area centers on creating, applying, and transferring knowledge and technology to make available affordable food and fiber, ensure food safety and nutrition, and support rural development and people's natural resource needs. The creation, application, and transfer of this knowledge and technology are achieved by conducting integrated national and international research and by providing information, education, and statistical programs and services. http://www.usda.gov/wps/portal/usda/usdahome?navid=USDA_MISSION_AREAS

Agricultural Research Service (ARS) The Agricultural Research Service conducts research on agricultural problems of high national priority. It provides information access and dissemination to ensure high-quality, safe food and other agricultural products; to assess the nutritional needs of Americans; to sustain a competitive agricultural economy; to enhance the natural resource base and the environment; and to promote economic opportunities for rural citizens, communities, and society as a whole.

Research activities are carried out at 96 domestic locations, including Puerto Rico and the U.S. Virgin Islands, and five overseas locations. ARS conducts much of this research in cooperation with partners in State universities and experiment stations, other Federal agencies, and private organizations. National Programs, headquartered in Beltsville, MD, plans and coordinates the research programs, and five area offices carry out the day-to-day management of the respective programs for specific field locations.

The National Agricultural Library, the primary resource in the United States for information on food, agriculture, and natural resources, serves as an electronic gateway to a widening array of scientific literature, printed text, and agricultural images. The library supports the USDA and a broad customer base of policymakers, agricultural specialists, research scientists, and the general public. It works with other agricultural libraries and institutions to advance open and democratic access specifically to the Nation's agricultural knowledge and to agricultural information in general. http://www.nal.usda.gov

For further information, contact the Agricultural Research Service, Department of Agriculture, 1400

Independence Avenue SW., Washington, DC 20250. Phone, 202-720-3656. Fax, 202-720-5427.

The National Institute of Food and Agriculture (NIFA) The National Institute of Food and Agriculture invests in and advances agricultural education, extension, and research to address societal challenges. The Institute works with academic institutions, land-grant universities, and other science organizations nationwide. With its partners and customers, NIFA promotes a global system of research, extension, and higher education in the food and agricultural sciences and related environmental and human sciences for the good of people, communities, and the Nation.

The Institute collaborates with scientists, policymakers, experts, and educators in organizations worldwide to find innovative solutions to pressing local and global problems. Scientific discovery and application advance the competitiveness of American agriculture, strengthen the U.S. economy, make the Nation's food supply safer, improve the nutrition and well-being of American citizens, sustain natural resources and the environment, and build energy independence. Partnering with other Federal science agencies, NIFA also makes important contributions to science policy decisionmaking. http://nifa.usda.gov

For further information, contact the Communications Staff, The National Institute of Food and Agriculture , Department of Agriculture, 1400 Independence Avenue SW., Washington, DC 20250-2207. Phone, 202-720-4651. Fax, 202-690-0289.

Economic Research Service (ERS) The Service informs and strengthens public and private decisionmaking on economic and policy issues affecting agriculture, food, rural development, and the environment. ERS also serves as a primary source of economic information and research in the USDA.

Using a variety of means, ERS disseminates economic information and research results. It produces agency-published research reports, economic briefs, data products, and market analysis and outlook reports. "Amber Waves," its award-winning online magazine features articles on the economics of food, farming, natural resources, and rural America (www.ers.usda.gov/amber-waves). The ERS Web site allows access to all agency products, and it connects users directly with ERS analysts. The agency delivers oral briefings, written staff analyses, and congressionally mandated studies to executive and legislative branch policymakers and program administrators. Its experts also write articles for professional journals and present papers at academic conferences and meetings. http://www.ers. usda.gov

For further information, contact the Information Services Division, Economic Research Service, Department of Agriculture, 1400 Independence Avenue SW., Washington, DC 20250. Phone, 202-694-5100. Fax, 202-245-4781.

National Agricultural Statistics Service (NASS)
The National Agricultural Statistics Service prepares estimates and reports on production, supply, price, chemical use, and other items necessary for the orderly operation of the U.S. agricultural economy.

NAAS reports include statistics on field crops, fruits and vegetables, dairy, cattle, hogs, sheep, poultry, aquaculture, and related commodities or processed products. Estimates concern farm numbers, farm production expenditures, agricultural chemical use, prices received by farmers for products sold, prices paid for commodities and services, indexes of prices received and paid, parity prices, farm employment, and farm wage rates.

NASS prepares these estimates through a complex system of sample surveys of producers, processors, buyers, and others associated with agriculture. Information is gathered by mail, electronic data reporting, telephone, and personal interviews.

The Service conducts the Census of Agriculture, which is taken every 5 years and provides comprehensive data on the agricultural economy down to the county level. It also conducts follow-on studies on aquaculture, irrigation, horticultural energy, and organic agriculture.

NASS performs reimbursable survey work and statistical consulting services for other Federal and State agencies. It also helps other countries develop agricultural data systems by offering technical assistance. http://www.nass.usda.gov

For further information, contact the Customer Service Center, National Agricultural Statistics Service,

Department of Agriculture, 1400 Independence Avenue SW., Washington, DC 20250-2000. Phone, 202-720-3878.

Rural Development

The rural development mission area centers on increasing the economic opportunities of rural Americans and improving their quality of life. To achieve these goals, the USDA creates and fosters cooperative relationships among Government, industry, and communities. As a capital investment bank, the USDA provides financing for rural housing and community facilities, business and cooperative development, telephone and high-speed Internet access, and electric, water, and sewer infrastructure. Approximately 3,400 employees in 47 State offices and 477 field offices administer rural development loan and grant programs at the local level. http://www.usda.gov/wps/portal/usda/usdahome?navid=USDA_MISSION_AREAS

Advanced Biofuel Repayment Program   The program provides payments to producers to support and expand production of advanced biofuels refined from sources other than corn kernel starch. http://www.rd.usda.gov/programs-services/advanced-biofuel-payment-program

Biorefinery, Renewable Chemical, and Biobased Product Manufacturing Assistance Program   This program assists in the development, construction, and retrofitting of new and emerging technologies for developing advanced biofuels, renewable chemicals, and biobased product manufacturing by giving loan guarantees. http://www.rd.usda.gov/programs-services/biorefinery-renewable-chemical-and-biobased-product-manufacturing-assistance

Business and Industry Guaranteed Loan Program   This program creates jobs and stimulates the rural economy by financially backing rural businesses. It bolsters the existing private credit structure through the guaranteeing of loans for rural businesses, allowing private lenders to increase the credit that they extend. Borrowers use loan proceeds for working capital, machinery and equipment, buildings, real estate, and certain types of debt refinancing. A borrower may be a cooperative organization, corporation, partnership, nonprofit corporation, Native American tribe, federally recognized tribal group, public body, or individual. http://www.rd.usda.gov/programs-services/business-industry-loan-guarantees

Cooperative Programs USDA Cooperative Programs is the Nation's major source for information on cooperatives. Its library of more than 150 co-op publications—many of which are available in hardcopy, as well as online range from co-op primers, such as "Co-ops 101," to reports on technical topics, such as "Tax Law for Cooperatives," to reports focusing on co-op economic theory, such as "The Nature of the Cooperative." These publications may be accessed on the "Publications for Cooperatives" Web page. http://www.rd.usda.gov/programs-services/all-programs/cooperative-programs

Delta Health Care Services Grant Program This program provides financial assistance to meet ongoing health needs in the Delta Region through cooperation among health care professionals, institutions of higher education, research institutions, and others in the Delta Region. http://www.rd.usda.gov/programs-services/delta-health-care-services-grants

Intermediary Relending Program This program provides capital to rural areas through low-interest and direct loans made to nonprofit corporations, public agencies, Native American groups, and certain corporations (intermediaries). These intermediaries establish revolving loan funds so they can relend the money to businesses in economically and socially disadvantaged rural communities. The process creates a source of capital that promotes job growth and economic development. http://www.rd.usda.gov/programs-services/intermediary-relending-program

Repowering Assistance Program This program funds up to 50 percent of the total eligible costs for biorefineries to install renewable biomass systems for heating and power or to produce new energy from renewable biomass. http://www.rd.usda.gov/programs-services/repowering-assistance-program

Rural Business Development Grant Program This program provides grants for rural projects that promote small

and emerging business development, business incubators, employment, and related adult education programs. It also provides grants for sustainable economic development in rural communities with exceptional needs. Recipients use the grants to fund community- and technology-based economic development projects, feasibility studies, leadership and entrepreneur training, rural business incubators, and long-term business strategic planning. Eligible organizations include Native American tribes, nonprofit corporations, and rural public entities. http://www.rd.usda.gov/programs-services/rural-business-development-grants

Rural Business-Cooperative Service To meet business credit needs in underserved rural areas, USDA's Rural Business-Cooperative Service provides loan guarantees, direct loans, and grants to rural businesses, cooperatives, farmers, and ranchers, often in partnership with private sector lenders. The following is a list and description of USDA's Rural Development business and cooperative programs. http://www.rd.usda.gov/about-rd/agencies/rural-business-cooperative-service

Rural Cooperative Development Grant Program This program improves rural economic conditions by assisting individuals and businesses in the startup, expansion or operational improvement of rural cooperatives and other mutually-owned businesses through Cooperative Development Centers. http://www.rd.usda.gov/programs-services/rural-cooperative-development-grant-program

Rural Economic Development (RED) Loan and Grant Program The RED Loan and Grant programs provide funding to rural projects through local utility organizations. Under the loan program, USDA gives zero-interest loans that local utilities pass through to local businesses for projects that create and retain employment in rural areas. Under the grant program, USDA gives grant funds to local utility organizations that use them to establish revolving loan funds. http://www.rd.usda.gov/programs-services/rural-economic-development-loan-grant-program

Rural Energy for America Program Grant recipients assist rural small businesses and agricultural producers by conducting and promoting energy audits and assisting in the development of renewable energy. http://www.rd.usda.gov/programs-services/rural-energy-america-program-energy-audit-renewable-energy-development-assistance

Rural Housing Programs   USDA Rural Development improves the quality of life in rural America. Its Rural Housing Service offers loans, grants, and loan guarantees to support essential services such as housing, economic development, health care, first-responder equipment and personnel, and water, electric and communications infrastructure. It also helps rural residents buy or rent safe and affordable housing, and make home repairs to improve safety and to create healthier living environments. http://www.rd.usda.gov/about-rd/agencies/rural-housing-service

Rural Microentrepreneur Assistance Program   This program makes loans and gives grants to Microenterprise Development Organizations. These organizations then provide microloans for microenterprise startups and growth through a rural microloan revolving fund. They also offer training and technical assistance to microloan borrowers and microentrepreneurs. http://www.rd.usda.gov/programs-services/rural-microentrepreneur-assistance-program

Rural Utilities Programs   USDA Rural Development strengthens rural economies and makes life better for Americans living in rural areas. Its Rural Utilities Service administers programs that provide infrastructure or infrastructure improvements to nonurban communities. These programs include water and waste treatment and electric power and telecommunications services. Utilities programs connect residents to the global community and its economy by increasing access to broadband and 21st-century telecommunications services, funding sustainable renewable energy development and conservation, financing reliable and affordable electric systems, working to integrate electric smart grid technologies, and developing reliable and affordable rural water and wastewater systems. http://www.rd.usda.gov/about-rd/agencies/rural-utilities-service

Socially-Disadvantaged Groups Grant Program   This program gives technical assistance to small socially-disadvantaged agricultural producers in rural areas. http://www.rd.usda.gov/programs-services/socially-disadvantaged-groups-grant

Value-Added Producer Grant Program   This program helps agricultural producers engage in value-added activities related to the processing and marketing of bio-based, value-added products. The program is designed to generate new products, create and expand marketing opportunities, and increase producer income. http://www.rd.usda.gov/programs-services/value-added-producer-grants

For further information, contact the Rural Development Legislative and Public Affairs Staff, Department of Agriculture, Stop 0705, 1400 Independence Avenue SW., Washington, DC 20250-0320. Phone, 202-690-0498.

Sources of Information

Ask the Expert   This tool helps Web site visitors locate the answers to their USDA-related questions. http://www.usda.gov/wps/portal/usda/usdahome?navid=ASK_EXPERT2

A–Z Index   The USDA Web site has a topical index that is arranged in alphabetical order. http://www.usda.gov/wps/portal/usda/usdahome?navid=AZ_INDEX

Blog   The USDA Web site features a blog that includes contributions on conservation, energy, food and nutrition, forestry, knowing your farmer and your food, rural development, and other topics. http://blogs.usda.gov

Business Opportunities   Marketing to the USDA can be a daunting task. To assist businessmen and women who seek to sell their products and services to the agency, the USDA has collected all of the necessary information and packaged it in one place—in the "Doing Business with USDA Kit" (2005 edition). http://www.dm.usda.gov/procurement/business/index.htm

The USDA awards over 50 percent of eligible contracting dollars to small businesses nationwide. Information on contracting or subcontracting opportunities, attending small business outreach events, or how to do business with the USDA is available on the "Office of Small and Disadvantaged Business Utilization" Web site. Phone, 202-720-7117. http://www.dm.usda.gov/smallbus/index.php

Career Opportunities For information on vacant positions within the USDA and opportunities for students, recent graduates, and veterans, visit the "Careers and Jobs" Web page. http://www.usda.gov/wps/portal/usda/usdahome?navid=CAREERS

In 2017, the USDA ranked 7th among 18 large agencies in the Partnership for Public Service's Best Places To Work Agency Rankings. http://bestplacestowork.org/BPTW/rankings/detail/AG00

Freedom of Information Act (FOIA) Departmental Management oversees the USDA's FOIA program. Twenty-one USDA FOIA officers at the mission area and agency levels work to increase Government transparency through proactive disclosures and the use of technology. http://www.dm.usda.gov/foia

Agency reading rooms are updated frequently and contain commonly requested records. Information seekers should visit the relevant reading rooms before submitting a FOIA request. http://www.dm.usda.gov/foia/agencyfoia.htm

The FOIA public access link (PAL) is a web portal that allows information seekers to create and submit a FOIA request and to check its status. Registration, which requires creating a user name and password, is the first step for using PAL. https://efoia-pal.usda.gov/palMain.aspx

Glossary The USDA maintains a glossary of agency acronyms. http://www.usda.gov/wps/portal/usda/usdahome?navid=glossary#top

Newsroom Announcements, factsheets, reports, and statements are accessible online. http://www.usda.gov/wps/portal/usda/usdahome?navid=NEWSROOM

Open Government The USDA supports the Open Government initiative by promoting the principles of collaboration, participation, and transparency. http://www.usda.gov/wps/portal/usda/usdahome?navid=USDA_OPEN

Organic Agriculture The USDA is committed to increasing organic agriculture. It operates many programs that serve the growing organic sector. The USDA Organic Seal, which has been in use nearly 15 years, is a leading global standard. Visit the "Organic Agriculture" Web pages to learn more. http://www.usda.gov/wps/portal/usda/usdahome?navid=organic-agriculture

Instructions for becoming a certified organic operation are available online. https://www.ams.usda.gov/services/organic-certification/faq-becoming-certified

To receive "USDA Organic Insider" updates via email, use the online subscription form. https://visitor.r20.constantcontact.com/manage/optin/ea?v=001tanuLSmJHqsq1D840Z7eyw%3D%3D

Organizational Chart The USDA's organizational chart is available in Portable Document Format (PDF) for viewing and downloading. https://www.usda.gov/sites/default/files/documents/usda-organization-chart.pdf

Plain Language In support of the Plain Writing Act of 2010, USDA editors and writers strive to provide the public with information that is clear, understandable, and useful in forms, instructions, letters, notices, and publications. If a USDA document or content on the Department's Web site is unclear or difficult to understand, contact the USDA via email. http://www.usda.gov/wps/portal/usda/usdahome?navid=PLAIN_WRITING | Email. plainlanguage@osec.usda.gov

Program Discrimination The Office of the Assistant Secretary for Civil Rights investigates and resolves complaints of discrimination in programs operated or assisted by the USDA. Information on what to include in a letter of complaint is available online. For information on the discrimination complaint process, contact the information research service in the Office of the Assistant Secretary. Phone, 202-260-1026 or 866-632-9992. Federal Relay Service, 800-877-8339 (English) or 800-845-6136 (Spanish). https://www.ascr.usda.gov/filing-program-discrimination-complaint-usda-customer | Email: CR-INFO@ascr.usda.gov

Reports Agency reports, data, and forecasts and outlooks are accessible online. http://www.usda.gov/wps/portal/usda/usdahome?navid=AGENCY_REPORTS

Site Map The Web site map allows visitors to look for specific topics or to browse for topics that align with their interests. http://www.usda.gov/wps/portal/usda/usdahome?navtype=FT&navid=SITE_MAP

Snarge   Birds and other animals occasionally collide with airborne aircraft and planes moving on the ground. These collisions are called wildlife strikes, and snarge is the remaining residue after impact. To learn about efforts to reduce wildlife strikes, visit the Animal and Plant Health Inspection Service's (APHIS) wildlife strike Web page. https://www.aphis.usda.gov/aphis/ourfocus/wildlifedamage/programs/SA_Airport/CT_Wildlife_strike

Watch the USDA's video to see how bird parts and snarge are collected, reported, shipped, and identified. https://www.youtube.com/watch?v=_OhJXexmmTg&list=PLF1BE3AC34367E99E

Social Media   The USDA tweets announcements, events, and other newsworthy items on Twitter. https://twitter.com/usda

Speakers   Contact the nearest USDA office or county extension agent. In the District of Columbia, contact the Office of Communications, U.S. Department of Agriculture, 1400 Independence Avenue SW., Washington, DC 20250. Phone, 202-720-4623. http://www.usda.gov/wps/portal/usda/usdahome?navid=OC_MEDIA_COMMS

Whistleblower Hotline   To file a complaint of alleged improprieties—employee misconduct, conflicts of interest, criminal activity, mismanagement or wasteful use of funds, workplace violence—visit the "OIG Hotline" Web page and use the "Submit a Complaint" feature. Or, contact a regional office or the Office of the Inspector General, U.S. Department of Agriculture, P.O. Box 23399, Washington, DC 20026. Phone, 800-424-9121 or 202-690-1622. TDD, 202-690-1202. Fax, 202-690-2474. http://www.usda.gov/oig/hotline.htm

Wood Pellets   European Union (EU) policies requiring renewable energy sources and energy associated with low greenhouse gas emissions are affecting wood products manufacturing and forests in the United States. Wood pellet production is on the rise as export to the EU increases. The primary U.S. exporting region is the South. To learn more about this topic, see the "Effect of Policies on Pellet Production and Forests in the U.S. South," which was published by the Southern Research Station of the U.S. Forest Service in December of 2014. https://www.srs.fs.usda.gov/pubs/gtr/gtr_srs202.pdf; http://www.usda.gov/wps/portal/usda/usdahome?navid=CONTACT_US

For further information concerning the Department of Agriculture, contact the Office of Communications, Department of Agriculture, 1400 Independence Avenue SW., Washington, DC 20250. Phone, 202-720-4623.

DEPARTMENT OF COMMERCE

Fourteenth Street and Constitution Avenue NW., Washington, DC 20230
Phone, 202-482-2000. Internet, http://www.doc.gov

Secretary of Commerce	WILBUR ROSS
Deputy Secretary	BRUCE H. ANDREWS
Assistant Secretary, Administration / Chief Financial Officer	LISA CASIAS
Assistant Secretary, Legislative and Intergovernmental Affairs	MIKE PLATT
Chief Information Officer	STEVE COOPER
Director, Office of Business Liaison	THEODORE JOHNSTON
Director, Office of Policy and Strategic Planning	JOHN RATLIFF
Director, Office of Public Affairs	MARNI GOLDBERG
Director, Office of the Executive Secretariat	JAMES SLATTERY
Director, Office of White House Liaison	LAUREN LEONARD
General Counsel	PETER DAVIDSON
Inspector General	PEGGY GUSTAFSON

The Department of Commerce promotes the Nation's domestic and international trade, economic growth, and technological advancement by fostering free enterprise worldwide, supporting fair trade, compiling social and economic statistics, protecting Earth's physical resources, granting patents and registering trademarks, and assisting small and minority-owned businesses.

The Department of Commerce was designated as such by act of March 4, 1913 (15 U.S.C. 1501). The act reorganized the Department of Commerce and Labor, created by act of February 14, 1903 (15 U.S.C. 1501), by transferring labor activities into a new, separate Department of Labor.

Office of the Secretary

Secretary The Secretary is responsible for the administration of all functions and authorities assigned to the Department of Commerce and for advising the President on Federal policy and programs affecting the industrial and commercial segments of the national economy. The Secretary is served by the offices of Deputy Secretary, Inspector General, General Counsel, and the Assistant Secretaries of Administration, Legislative and Intergovernmental Affairs, and Public Affairs. Other offices whose public purposes are widely administered are detailed below. https://www.commerce.gov/office-secretary

Business Liaison The Office of Business Liaison directs the business community to the offices and policy experts who can best respond to their needs by promoting proactive, responsive, and effective outreach programs and relationships with the business community. It also informs the Secretary and Department officials of the critical issues facing the business community, informs the business community of Department and administration initiatives and priorities, as well as information regarding Department resources, policies, and programs, and provides general assistance to the business community. https://www.commerce.gov/os/office-business-liaison

For further information, call 202-482-1360.

Sources of Information

Business Opportunities Contact the Office of Small and Disadvantaged Business Utilization. Phone, 202-482-1472. http://www.osec.doc.gov/osdbu

DEPARTMENT OF COMMERCE

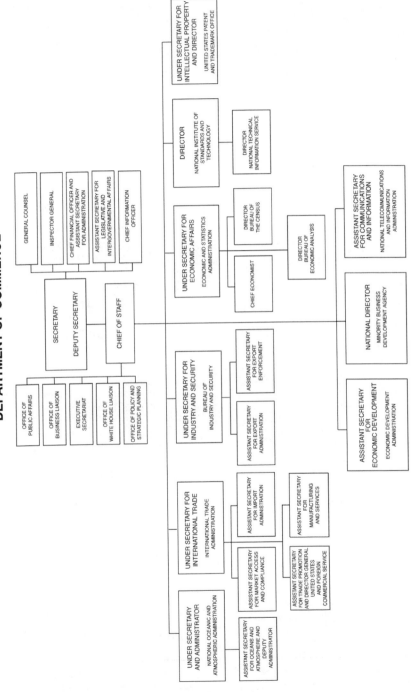

Data Age and sex and citizenship data are available online and from the Personal Census Search Unit, Bureau of the Census, National Processing Center, P.O. Box 1545, Jeffersonville, IN 47131. Phone, 812-218-3046. https://www.census.gov/population/age; https://www.census.gov/programs-surveys/acs/library/keywords/citizenship.html?cssp=SERP

Economic Development Information The Economic Development Administration maintains a clearinghouse for economic development information on its Web site. http://www.eda.gov

Career Opportunities For information on internships and career opportunities throughout the Department, visit the "Career Opportunities and Internships" Web page. https://www.commerce.gov/page/career-opportunities-and-internships

Environment The National Oceanic and Atmospheric Administration conducts research and gathers data on the atmosphere, oceans, space, and Sun, and it applies this knowledge to science and public service: warning of dangerous weather, charting seas and skies, guiding the use and protection of ocean and coastal resources, and improving stewardship of the environment. For more information, contact the Office of Communications, National Oceanic and Atmospheric Administration, Room 6013, Fourteenth Street and Constitution Avenue NW., Washington, DC 20230. Phone, 202-482-6090. Fax, 202-482-3154. http://www.noaa.gov

Inspector General Hotline The Office of Inspector General promotes economy, efficiency, and effectiveness and prevents and detects fraud, waste, abuse, and mismanagement in departmental programs and operations. To file a complaint, contact the Hotline, Inspector General, Complaint Intake Unit, Mail Stop 7886, 1401 Constitution Avenue, NW., Washington, DC 20230. Phone, 202-482-2495 or 800-424-5197. TTD, 202-482-5923 or 856-860-6950. Fax, 855-569-9235. http://www.oig.doc.gov | Email: hotline@oig.doc.gov

Publications The Department's "Find Data" Web page features recent releases of key economic indicators and the "Commerce Data Hub," which allows the general public to access an abundance of data. The titles of selected publications are noted in the appropriate sections below dealing with the operating units responsible for their issuance. These publications and others are announced in the weekly "Business Service Checklist": Contact the Government Publishing Office's Superintendent of Documents. Phone, 202-512-1800. https://www.commerce.gov/economicindicators; https://www.commerce.gov/os/office-public-affairs | Email: publicaffairs@doc.gov

For further Information concerning the Department of Commerce, contact the Office of Public Affairs, Department of Commerce, Fourteenth Street and Constitution Avenue NW., Room 5040, Washington, DC 20230. Phone, 202-482-3263.

Bureau of Industry and Security

Department of Commerce, Washington, DC 20230
Phone, 202-482-2721. Internet, http://www.bis.doc.gov

Under Secretary, Industry and Security	Eric L. Hirschhorn
Deputy Under Secretary, Industry and Security	Daniel O. Hill
Assistant Secretary, Export Administration	Kevin J. Wolf
Assistant Secretary, Export Enforcement	David W. Mills

[For the Bureau of Industry and Security statement of organization, see the Federal Registers of June 7, 1988, 53 FR 20881, and April 26, 2002, 67 FR 20630]

The Bureau of Industry and Security (BIS) advances U.S. national security, foreign policy, and economic objectives by ensuring an effective export control and treaty compliance system and promoting continued U.S. strategic technology leadership. BIS activities include regulating the export of sensitive goods and technologies in an effective and efficient manner; enforcing export control, antiboycott, and public safety laws; cooperating with and assisting other countries on export control and strategic trade issues; assisting U.S. industry to comply with international arms control agreements; monitoring the viability of the U.S. defense industrial base; evaluating the effects on national security of foreign investments in U.S. companies; and supporting continued U.S. technology leadership in industries that are essential to national security. http://www.bis.doc.gov/index.php/about-bis

Export Administration   The Office of the Assistant Secretary for Export Administration is responsible for export licenses, treaty compliance, treaty obligations relating to weapons of mass destruction, and the defense industrial and technology base. The Office regulates the export of dual-use items requiring licenses for national security, nonproliferation, foreign policy, and short supply; ensures that approval or denial of license applications is consistent with economic and security concerns; promotes an understanding of export control regulations within the business community; represents the Department in interagency and international forums relating to export controls, particularly in multilateral regimes; monitors the availability of industrial resources of national defense; analyzes the impact of export controls on strategic industries; and assesses the security consequences of certain foreign investments. http://www.bis.doc.gov/index.php/regulations/export-administration-regulations-ear

Export Enforcement   The Office of the Assistant Secretary for Export Enforcement enforces dual-use export controls. This enables exporters to take advantage of legal export opportunities while ensuring that illegal exports will be detected and either prevented or investigated and sanctioned. The Office also ensures prompt, aggressive action against restrictive trade practices; and conducts cooperative enforcement activities on an international basis. Export Enforcement also enforces U.S. antiboycott laws and regulations by advising U.S. exporters on potential prohibited requests contained in foreign contracts; investigating violations such as the furnishing of boycott-related information, refusing to deal with blacklisted businesses; and pursuing criminal and administrative sanctions for violations.

Contact information for the nine export enforcement field offices is available on the "Investigations" Web page. http://www.bis.doc.gov/index.php/enforcement/oee/investigations

Management and Policy Coordination   The Management and Policy Coordination (MPC) unit establishes and evaluates the Bureau's overall policy agenda, priorities, goals, unit objectives, and key metrics. MPC performs oversight of program operations and expenditures; executes or supervises the President's Management Agenda; and adjudicates appeals of licensing and enforcement decisions as part of an extended legal process involving administrative law judges and the Office of General Counsel. MPC provides guidance and coordination for the Bureau's participation in the Export Control and Related Border Security Assistance Program, which provides technical assistance to strengthen the export and transit control systems of nations that are identified as potential locations for the exporting of weapons of mass destruction, missile delivery systems, or the commodities, technologies, and equipment that can be used to design and build them.

Sources of Information

Business Information   U.S. business information—export news, updates to Export Administration Regulations, export license and enforcement information, compliance and training information, Bureau program information, e-FOIA information, export seminar event schedules, and Denied Persons List information—is available on the Bureau's Web site. http://www.bis.doc.gov/index.php/about-bis/newsroom

Employment   BIS career opportunities are posted on USAJobs, a free web-based job board that serves as the Federal Government's official source of Federal job listings and employment opportunity information. https://my.usajobs.gov

Enforcement For enforcement-related questions, contact the partnership-in-security hotline. Phone, 800-424-2980. http://www.bis.doc.gov/index.php/component/rsform/form/14-reporting-violations-form?task=forms.edit

Outreach / Education The Outreach and Educational Services Division has offices in Washington, DC (phone, 202-482-4811); Irvine, CA (phone, 949-660-0144); and San Jose, CA (phone, 408-998-8806). http://www.bis.doc.gov/index.php/program-offices

Publications Publications available on the Bureau's Web site include the BIS's Annual Report to Congress, the guidance on the Commerce Department's Reexport Controls, and the Exporter User Manual and Licensing FAQ. http://www.bis.doc.gov/index.php/about-bis/newsroom/publications; http://www.bis.doc.gov/index.php/about-bis/newsroom

Rules Subscribers to the Export Administration Regulations can stay informed of the latest rules. Subscriptions typically cost $199 per year. Phone, 301-208-0700 (ext. 112). http://www.bis.doc.gov/index.php/regulations/order-a-hard-copy-of-the-ear | Email: pubs@ocr-inc.com; http://www.bis.doc.gov/index.php/about-bis/contact-bis

For further information, contact the Bureau of Industry and Security, Office of Public Affairs, Room 3895, Fourteenth Street and Constitution Avenue NW., Washington, DC 20230. Phone, 202-482-2721.

Economic Development Administration

Department of Commerce, Washington, DC 20230
Phone, 202-482-5081. Internet, http://www.eda.gov

Assistant Secretary, Economic Development	JAY WILLIAMS
Deputy Assistant Secretary, Economic Development	MATTHEW ERSKINE

The Economic Development Administration (EDA) was created in 1965 under the Public Works and Economic Development Act (42 U.S.C. 3121) as part of an effort to target Federal resources to economically distressed areas and to help develop local economies in the United States. It was mandated to assist rural and urban communities that were outside the mainstream economy and that lagged in economic development, industrial growth, and personal income.

EDA provides grants to States, regions, and communities nationwide to generate wealth and minimize poverty by promoting an attractive business environment for private capital investment and higher skill, higher wage jobs through capacity building, planning, infrastructure, research grants, and strategic initiatives. Through its grant program, EDA uses public sector resources to cultivate an environment where the private sector risks capital and job opportunities are created. https://www.eda.gov/about

Sources of Information

Employment For information on career opportunities, visit the "EDA Job Opportunities" Web page. http://www.eda.gov/careers

Newsroom The online newsroom features blog posts, press releases, an archive of newsletters, and the latest media. https://www.eda.gov/news

Regional Offices Contact information for the Administration's six regional offices—Atlanta, Austin, Chicago, Denver, Philadelphia, Seattle—is available on the "Contact" Web page. http://www.eda.gov/contact; https://www.eda.gov

For further information, contact the Economic Development Administration, Department of Commerce, Washington, DC 20230. Phone, 202-482-5081. Fax, 202-273-4781.

Economics and Statistics Administration

Department of Commerce, Washington, DC 20230
Phone, 202-482-3727. Internet, http://www.esa.doc.gov

Under Secretary, Economic Affairs	JUSTIN ANTONIPILLAI
Deputy Under Secretary, Economic Affairs	KENNETH A. ARNOLD
Chief Economist	ELLEN HUGHES-CROMWICK
Director, Bureau of Economic Analysis	BRIAN C. MOYER
Director, Bureau of the Census	JOHN H. THOMPSON

The Economics and Statistics Administration (ESA), headed by the Under Secretary for Economic Affairs, has three principal components: the Office of the Chief Economist, the Bureau of the Census, and the Bureau of Economic Analysis. ESA develops policy options, analyzes economic developments, manages economic data systems, and produces a major share of U.S. economic and demographic statistics, including the national economic indicators. The Under Secretary is the chief economic adviser to the Secretary and provides leadership and executive management for the Office of the Chief Economist and the Bureaus of Economic Analysis and of the Census. http://www.esa.gov/content/about-economics-statistics-administration

Bureau of Economic Analysis

[For the Bureau of Economic Analysis statement of organization, see the Federal Register of Dec. 29, 1980, 45 FR 85496]

The Bureau of Economic Analysis (BEA) provides the most accurate, relevant, and timely economic accounts data in an objective and cost-effective manner. BEA's economic statistics offer a comprehensive picture of the U.S. economy. BEA prepares national, regional, industry, and international accounts that present essential information on such issues in the world economy.

BEA's national economic statistics provide a comprehensive look at U.S. production, consumption, investment, exports and imports, and income and saving. The international transactions accounts provide information on trade in goods and services (including the balance of payments and trade), investment income, and government and private finances. In addition, the accounts measure the value of U.S.

international assets and liabilities and direct investment by multinational companies.

The regional accounts provide data on total and per capita personal income by region, State, metropolitan area, and county, and on gross State product. The industry economic account provides a detailed view of the interrelationships between U.S. producers and users and the contribution to production across industries. http://www.bea.gov | Email: customerservice@bea.gov

For further information, contact the Public Information Office, Bureau of Economic Analysis, Department of Commerce, Washington, DC 20230. Phone, 202-606-9900. Fax, 202-606-5310.

Bureau of the Census

[For the Bureau of the Census statement of organization, see the Federal Register of Sept. 16, 1975, 40 FR 42765]

The Bureau of the Census was established as a permanent office by act of March 6, 1902 (32 Stat. 51). The major functions of the Census Bureau are authorized by the Constitution, which provides that a census of population shall be taken every 10 years, and by laws codified as title 13 of the United States Code. The law also provides that the information collected by the Census Bureau from individual persons, households, or establishments be kept strictly confidential and be used only for statistical purposes.

The Census Bureau is responsible for the decennial censuses of population and housing; the quinquennial censuses of State and local governments, manufacturers, mineral industries, distributive trades, construction industries, and transportation; current surveys that provide information on many of the subjects covered in the censuses at monthly, quarterly, annual, or other intervals; compilation of current statistics on U.S. foreign trade, including data on imports, exports, and shipping; special censuses at the request and expense of State and local government units; publication of estimates and projections of the population; publication of current data on population and housing characteristics; and current reports on manufacturing, retail and wholesale trade, services, construction, imports and exports, State and local government finances and employment, and other subjects.

The Census Bureau makes available statistical results of its censuses, surveys, and other programs to the public through the Internet, mobile applications, and other media. The Bureau also prepares special tabulations sponsored and paid for by data users. It also produces statistical compendia, catalogs, guides, and directories that are useful in locating information on specific subjects. Upon request, the Bureau makes searches of decennial census records and furnishes certificates to individuals for use as evidence of age, relationship, or place of birth. A fee is charged for searches. http://www.census.gov | Email: PIO@census.gov

For further information, contact the Public Information Office, Bureau of the Census, Department of Commerce, Washington, DC 20233. Phone, 301-763-3030. Fax, 301-763-3762.

Office of the Chief Economist

The economists and analysts of the Office of the Chief Economist analyze domestic and international economic developments and produce in-depth reports, factsheets, briefings, and social media postings.

These tools cover policy issues and current economic events, as well as economic and demographic trends. Department of Commerce and White House policymakers, American businessmen, State and local governments, and news organizations worldwide rely on these tools. http://www.esa.gov/content/chief-economist

Sources of Information

Data   Monthly and quarterly economic indicators are posted online. To receive the most current economic indicators by email, subscribe using the online form. http://www.esa.gov/content/indicators; https://service.govdelivery.com/accounts/USESAEI/subscriber/new

Employment   For information on employment opportunities at the Bureaus of Economic Analysis or the Census, visit the "Working at BEA" or "Census Careers" Web page. http://www.bea.gov/jobs/index.htm; http://www.census.gov/about/census-careers.html

Publications   The BEA posts research papers, its customer guide, and the monthly journal "Survey of Current Business" under the "Publications" section on its Web site. The Census Bureau's most recently released publications are part of its online library. http://www.bea.gov/scb/index.htm; https://www.census.gov/library/publications.html

Regional Offices   Contact information for the Census Bureau's six regional offices—Atlanta, Chicago, Denver, Los Angeles, New York, Philadelphia—is available on its "Regional Offices" Web page. http://www.census.gov/regions; http://www.esa.gov | Email: ESAwebmaster@doc.gov

For further information, contact the Economics and Statistics Administration, Department of Commerce, Washington, DC 20230. Phone, 202-482-6607.

International Trade Administration

Department of Commerce, Washington, DC 20230
Phone, 202-482-3917. Internet, http://www.trade.gov

Under Secretary, International Trade	KENNETH E. HYATT, ACTING
Deputy Under Secretary, International Trade	THOMAS MCGINTY, ACTING
Assistant Secretary, Enforcement and Compliance	PAUL PIQUADO

Assistant Secretary, Global Markets / Director General   ARUN M. KUMAR
  of the U.S. and Foreign Commercial Service
Assistant Secretary, Industry and Analysis   MARCUS D. JADOTTE

[For the International Trade Administration statement of organization, see the Federal Register of Jan. 25, 1980, 45 FR 6148]

The International Trade Administration (ITA) was established on January 2, 1980, by the Secretary of Commerce to promote world trade and to strengthen the international trade and investment position of the United States.

The International Trade Administration (ITA) was established on January 2, 1980, by the Secretary of Commerce to promote world trade and to strengthen the international trade and investment position of the United States. The Under Secretary for International Trade heads the ITA, coordinating all issues concerning trade promotion, international commercial policy, market access, and trade law enforcement. The Administration is responsible for U.S. Government nonagricultural trade operations, and it supports the U.S. Trade Representative's efforts to negotiate trade policy. http://www.trade.gov/about.asp

Enforcement / Compliance   The Office of Enforcement and Compliance defends American industry against injurious and unfair trade practices by administering U.S. antidumping and countervailing duty trade laws. The Office also ensures the proper administration of foreign trade zones and advises the Secretary on establishment of new ones; oversees the administration of the Department's textiles program; and administers programs governing watch assemblies and other statutory import programs. http://www.trade.gov/enforcement

Global Markets   The Global Markets unit assists and advocates for U.S. businesses in international markets. Relying on a network of trade promotion and policy professionals located in over 70 countries and 100 U.S. locations, the unit promotes U.S. exports, especially those of small and medium-sized enterprises; advances and protects U.S. commercial interests overseas; and attracts investment from abroad into the United States. http://www.trade.gov/markets

Industry / Analysis   The Manufacturing and Services unit advises on domestic and international trade and investment policies affecting the competitiveness of U.S. industry. It also researches and analyzes manufacturing and services. Based on this analysis and interaction with U.S. industry, the unit Secretary develops strategies, policies, and programs to strengthen U.S. industry competitiveness domestically and globally. The unit manages an integrated program that includes industry and economic analysis, trade policy development and multilateral, regional, and bilateral trade agreements for manufactured goods and services; administers trade arrangements with foreign governments in product and service areas; and develops and provides business information and assistance to the United States on its rights and opportunities under multilateral and other agreements. http://www.trade.gov/industry

Sources of Information

Data   Trade data and export and import statistics are available online. http://www.trade.gov/data.asp

Employment   For information on career opportunities, visit the "Jobs" Web page. http://www.trade.gov/jobs

Publications   The ITA has an online bookstore. http://www.trade.gov/publications; http://www.trade.gov/contact.asp

For further information, contact the International Trade Administration, Department of Commerce, Washington, DC 20230. Phone, 202-482-3917.

Minority Business Development Agency

Department of Commerce, Washington, DC 20230
Phone, 202-482-2332. Internet, http://www.mbda.gov

National Director ALEJANDRA Y. CASTILLO
National Deputy Director ALBERT K. SHEN

[For the Minority Business Development Agency statement of organization, see the Federal Register of Mar. 17, 1972, 37 FR 5650, as amended]

The Minority Business Development Agency was established by Executive order in 1969. The Agency develops and coordinates a national program for minority business enterprise.

The Agency was created to help minority businesses achieve effective and equitable participation in the American free enterprise system and overcome social and economic disadvantages that limited past participation. The Agency provides policies and leadership supporting a partnership of business, industry, and government with the Nation's minority businesses.

Business development services are provided to the minority business community through three vehicles: the minority business opportunity committees, which disseminate information on business opportunities; the minority business development centers, which provide management and technical assistance and other business development services; and electronic commerce, which includes a Web site that shows how to start a business and use the service to find contract opportunities.

The Agency promotes and coordinates the efforts of other Federal agencies in assisting or providing market opportunities for minority business. It coordinates opportunities for minority firms in the private sector. Through such public and private cooperative activities, the Agency promotes the participation of Federal, State, and local governments, and business and industry in directing resources for the development of strong minority businesses. http://www.mbda.gov/main/who-mbda/about-minority-business-development-agency

Sources of Information

Internships Information on student eligibility and how to apply is available online. http://www.mbda.gov/main/intern-program

Library An online research library serves as a repository for factsheets, reports, statistical data, and other publications. http://www.mbda.gov/pressroom/research-library

Newsletter A free, monthly newsletter is accessible online. http://www.mbda.gov/newsletter

Speakers For information on scheduling a speaker for an organized event, visit the "Speaker Request Form" Web page. http://www.mbda.gov/main/mbda-speaker-request-form; http://www.mbda.gov/contact

For further information, contact the Office of the National Director, Minority Business Development Agency, Department of Commerce, Washington, DC 20230. Phone, 202-482-2332.

National Oceanic and Atmospheric Administration

Department of Commerce, Washington, DC 20230
Phone, 202-482-2985. Internet, http://www.noaa.gov

Under Secretary, Oceans and Atmosphere NEIL JACOBS, ACTING
Deputy NOAA Administrator TIMOTHY GALLAUDET
Deputy Under Secretary, Operations BENJAMIN FRIEDMAN
Assistant Secretary, Environmental Observation and Prediction NEIL JACOBS

Assistant Secretary, Oceans and Atmosphere
Chief Scientist
https://www.noaa.gov/about/organization

TIMOTHY GALLAUDET
CRAIG N. MCLEAN, ACTING

[For the National Oceanic and Atmospheric Administration statement of organization, see the Federal Register of Feb. 13, 1978, 43 FR 6128]

The above list of key personnel was updated 6–2019.

Establishment   On October 3, 1970, Reorganization Plan No. 4 of 1970 (5 U.S.C. app.) formed the National Oceanic and Atmospheric Administration (NOAA).

Science, service, and stewardship characterize NOAA's mission. Its researchers, scientists, and technicians study the atmosphere, the ocean, and the ecosystems associated with them; they integrate research and analysis; they observe and monitor; and they use modeling to predict the future state of complex systems. NOAA serves academic institutions, businesses, communities, and ordinary people by communicating and sharing its data, information, knowledge, and research. NOAA also applies its institutional know-how and science assets to the conservation and management of coastal and marine ecosystems and resources. The agency regulates and sustains marine fisheries and ecosystems, protects endangered species, restores habitats and ecosystems, conserves marine sanctuaries, responds to environmental emergencies, and assists with disaster recovery. http://www.noaa.gov/our-mission-and-vision

Marine and Aviation Operations   The Office of Marine and Aviation Operations manages the aviation safety, the small boat, and the NOAA diving programs. It also operates a fleet of specialized ships and aircraft that collect data and carry out research to support NOAA's mission, the Global Earth Observation System, and the Integrated Ocean Observing System—including flying "hurricane hunter" aircraft into the most turbulent storms to collect data critical for research. http://www.omao.noaa.gov/about.html

For further information, contact Office of Marine and Aviation Operations, Suite 500, 8403 Colesville Rd., Silver Spring, MD 20910. Phone, 301-713-7600. Fax, 301-713-1541.

National Coastal Resources   The National Ocean Service helps balance the Nation's use of coastal resources through research, management, and policy. The Service monitors the health of U.S. coasts by examining how human use and natural events affect coastal ecosystems. Coastal communities rely on the Service for information on natural hazards so they can reduce or eliminate destructive effects of coastal hazards. The Service assesses the damage caused by hazardous material spills and tries to restore or replace the affected coastal resources. The Service also protects beaches, water quality, wetlands, and wildlife. It provides a wide range of navigational products and data that help vessels move safely through U.S. waters, and it supplies the basic information for establishing the latitude, longitude, and elevation framework necessary for the Nation's mapping, navigation, positioning, and surveying activities. https://oceanservice.noaa.gov/

For further information, contact the National Ocean Service, Room 13231, SSMC 4, 1305 East-West Highway, Silver Spring, MD 20910. Phone, 301-713-3074. Fax, 301-713-4307.

National Environmental Satellite, Data, and Information   The National Environmental Satellite, Data, and Information Service operates the Nation's civilian geostationary and polar-orbiting environmental satellites. It also manages the largest collection of atmospheric, climatic, geophysical, and oceanographic data in the world. The Service develops and provides, through various media, environmental data for forecasts, national security, and weather warnings to protect life and property. These data are also used for energy distribution, global food supplies development, natural resources management, and rescuing downed pilots and mariners in distress. https://www.nesdis.noaa.gov/

For further information, contact the National Environmental Satellite, Data, and Information Service, 1335 East-West Highway, Silver Spring, MD 20910-3283. Phone, 301-713-3578. Fax, 301-713-1249.

NOAA HEADQUARTERS ORGANIZATION

CORPORATE FUNCTIONS

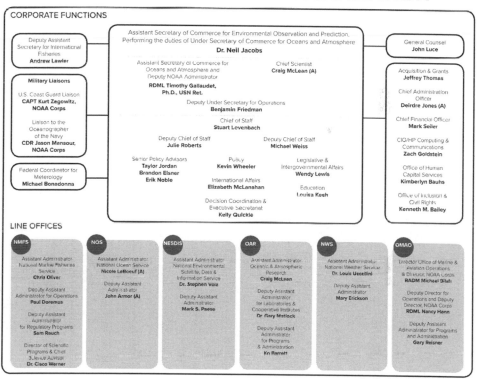

Deputy Assistant Secretary for International Fisheries
Andrew Lawler

Military Liaisons

U.S. Coast Guard Liaison
CAPT Kurt Zegowitz, NOAA Corps

Liaison to the Oceanographer of the Navy
CDR Jason Mansour, NOAA Corps

Federal Coordinator for Meterology
Michael Bonadonna

Assistant Secretary of Commerce for Environmental Observation and Prediction, Performing the duties of Under Secretary of Commerce for Oceans and Atmosphere
Dr. Neil Jacobs

Assistant Secretary of Commerce for Oceans and Atmosphere and Deputy NOAA Administrator
RDML Timothy Gallaudet, Ph.D., USN Ret.

Chief Scientist
Craig McLean (A)

Deputy Under Secretary for Operations
Benjamin Friedman

Chief of Staff
Stuart Levenbach

Deputy Chief of Staff
Julie Roberts

Deputy Chief of Staff
Michael Weiss

Senior Policy Advisors
Taylor Jordan
Brandon Elsner
Erik Noble

Policy
Kevin Wheeler

Legislative & Intergovernmental Affairs
Wendy Lewis

International Affairs
Elizabeth McLanahan

Education
Louisa Koch

Decision Coordination & Executive Secretariat
Kelly Quickie

General Counsel
John Luce

Acquisition & Grants
Jeffrey Thomas

Chief Administration Officer
Deirdre Jones (A)

Chief Financial Officer
Mark Seiler

CIO/HP Computing & Communications
Zach Goldstein

Office of Human Capital Services
Kimberlyn Bauhs

Office of Inclusion & Civil Rights
Kenneth M. Bailey

LINE OFFICES

NMFS
Assistant Administrator National Marine Fisheries Service
Chris Oliver

Deputy Assistant Administrator for Operations
Paul Doremus

Deputy Assistant Administrator for Regulatory Programs
Sam Rauch

Director of Scientific Programs & Chief Science Advisor
Dr. Cisco Werner

NOS
Assistant Administrator National Ocean Service
Nicole LeBoeuf (A)

Deputy Assistant Administrator
John Armor (A)

NESDIS
Assistant Administrator National Environmental Satellite, Data & Information Service
Dr. Stephen Volz

Deputy Assistant Administrator
Mark S. Paese

OAR
Assistant Administrator Oceanic & Atmospheric Research
Craig McLean

Deputy Assistant Administrator for Laboratories & Cooperative Institutes
Dr. Gary Matlock

Deputy Assistant Administrator for Programs & Administration
Ko Barrett

NWS
Assistant Administrator National Weather Service
Dr. Louis Uccellini

Deputy Assistant Administrator
Mary Erickson

OMAO
Director Office of Marine & Aviation Operations & Director, NOAA Corps
RADM Michael Silah

Deputy Director for Operations and Deputy Director, NOAA Corps
RDML Nancy Hann

Deputy Assistant Administrator for Programs and Administration
Gary Reisner

Key. (A) – Acting   Last updated 06/03/19

National Marine Fisheries   The National Marine Fisheries Service supports the management, conservation, and sustainable development of domestic and international living marine resources and the protection and restoration of ecosystems. The Service helps assess the stock of the Nation's multibillion-dollar marine fisheries, protect marine mammals and threatened species, conserve habitats, assist trade and industry, and conduct fishery enforcement activities. http://www.nmfs.noaa.gov

For further information, contact the National Marine Fisheries Service, 1315 East-West Highway, Silver Spring, MD 20910. Phone, 301-713-2239. Fax, 301-713-1940.

National Weather   The National Weather Service (NWS) provides weather, water, and climate warnings and forecasts and data for the United States, its territories, and adjacent waters and ocean areas. Government agencies, the private sector, the general public, and the global community rely on NWS data and products to protect life and property. Working with partners in Government, academic and research institutions, and private industry, the Service responds to the needs of the American public through its products and services. NWS data and information support aviation, maritime activities, and other sectors of the economy, as well as wildfire suppression. The Service also helps national security efforts with long- and short-range forecasts, air quality and cloud dispersion forecasts, and broadcasts of warnings and critical information over the 800-station NOAA Weather Radio network. http://www.weather.gov

For further information, contact the National Weather Service–Executive Affairs, 1325 East-West Highway, Silver Spring, MD 20910-3283. Phone, 301-713-0675. Fax, 301-713-0049.

Oceanic and Atmospheric Research   The Office of Oceanic and Atmospheric Research conducts research on air quality and composition, climate variability and change, weather, and coastal, marine, and Great Lakes ecosystems. The Office uses its own laboratories and offices to run research programs in atmospheric, coastal, marine, and space sciences, as well as relying on networks of university-based programs across the country. http://www.oar.noaa.gov

For further information, contact the Office of Oceanic and Atmospheric Research, Room 11458, 1315 East-West Highway, Silver Spring, MD 20910. Phone, 301-713-2458. Fax, 301-713-0163.

Sources of Information

Arctic Report Cards   Every year, NOAA publishes an Arctic Report Card as part of its efforts to track recent environmental changes relative to historical records. https://arctic.noaa.gov/Report-Card

Atmospheric Carbon Dioxide   Adding to the data record that C. David Keeling of the Scripps Institution of Oceanography started in 1958, NOAA continues to measure atmospheric carbon at the Mauna Loa Observatory in Hawaii. https://www.esrl.noaa.gov/gmd/ccgg/trends/full.html

The Earth System Research Laboratory's Global Monitoring Division has posted a 4-minute video showing 800,000 years of atmospheric carbon dioxide history. https://www.esrl.noaa.gov/gmd/ccgg/trends/history.html

Atmospheric Methane   The Earth System Research Laboratory's Global Monitoring Division has been measuring methane since 1983 at a globally distributed network of air sampling sites. https://esrl.noaa.gov/gmd/ccgg/trends_ch4

A recent NOAA study (APR 2019) concludes that long-term measurements show little evidence for large increases in total U.S. methane emissions over the past decade. https://research.noaa.gov/article/ArtMID/587/ArticleID/2453/US-methane-emissions-flat-since-2006-despite-increased-oil-and-gas-activity-study

Career Opportunities   A career at NOAA is a mission-oriented experience that centers on protecting natural resources, safeguarding the public, and strengthening the economy. https://www.careers.noaa.gov/index.html

Opportunities are available for students, teachers, and volunteers. https://www.noaa.gov/work-with-us

In 2018, NOAA ranked 154th among 415 agency subcomponents in the Partnership for Public Service's Best Places To Work Agency Rankings. https://bestplacestowork.org/rankings/detail/CM54

Climate Change   The National Climate Assessment assesses the science of climate change and variability. It also addresses how a climate in flux is affecting the United States today and how the change will affect the country even more in the future. https://nca2018.globalchange.gov/

Contact Information The "Contact Us" web page has contact information and other frequently requested resources. https://www.noaa.gov/contact-us

Freedom of Information Act (FOIA) Any person has a right to obtain access to Federal agency records; however, some records, or portions of them, may be shielded from disclosure by one of nine FOIA exemptions or by one of three special law enforcement exclusions. https://www.noaa.gov/foia-freedom-of-information-act

Before submitting a FOIA request, an information seeker should search the electronic reading room to determine if the desired information is in the public domain. https://www.noaa.gov/foia-reading-room

Maritime Archaeology Visit the "Maritime Archaeology" web page to learn about discovering shipwrecks and safeguarding them. https://www.noaa.gov/topic-tags/maritime-archaeology

Nautical Charts NOAA has posted the entire suite of U.S. coastal and Great Lakes charts on its "Charting" page for download. https://www.noaa.gov/charting

NOAA's Sources of Information were updated 12–2019.

NOAA Nationwide NOAA facilities—as well as personnel and the activities and programs they manage—are located throughout the Nation in various States and Territories. https://www.legislative.noaa.gov/NIYS/

Organizational Chart NOAA's organizational chart (JUN 2019) is available in Portable Document Format (PDF) for viewing and downloading. https://www.noaa.gov/sites/default/files/atoms/files/NOAA%20-%20Org%20Chart%20-%20June%203%202019.pdf

Podcast The NOAA Ocean podcast explores topics ranging from coastal science to coral reefs with ocean experts. https://oceanservice.noaa.gov/podcast/

Social Media NOAA relies on social media to share information and to promote understanding of its science, service, and stewardship-oriented mission. https://www.noaa.gov/stay-connected

Staff Directory The NOAA staff directory is available online. https://nsd.rdc.noaa.gov/

Weather The NOAA Weather Radio All Hazards network broadcasts continuous weather information nationwide from the nearest National Weather Service office. The network broadcasts official Weather Service forecasts, warnings, watches, and other hazard information around the clock every day. https://www.weather.gov/nwr/

National Telecommunications and Information Administration

Department of Commerce, Washington, DC 20230
Phone, 202-428-1840. Internet, http://www.ntia.doc.gov

Assistant Secretary, Communications and Information / Administrator	LAWRENCE E. STRICKLING
Deputy Assistant Secretary, Communications and Information	ANGELA SIMPSON

[For the National Telecommunications and Information Administration statement of organization, see the Federal Register of June 5, 1978, 43 FR 24348]

The National Telecommunications and Information Administration (NTIA) was established in 1978 by Reorganization Plan No. 1 of 1977 (5 U.S.C. app.) and Executive Order 12046 of March 27, 1978 (3 CFR, 1978 Comp., p. 158), by combining the Office of Telecommunications Policy of the Executive Office of the President and the Office of Telecommunications of the Department of Commerce to form a new agency reporting to the Secretary of Commerce. NTIA operates under the authority of the National Telecommunications and Information Administration Organization Act (47 U.S.C. 901).

NTIA serves as the principal executive branch adviser to the President on telecommunications and information policy; develops and presents U.S. plans and policies at international communications conferences and related meetings; prescribes policies for and manages Federal use of the radio frequency spectrum; serves as the principal Federal telecommunications research and engineering laboratory— NTIA's Institute for Telecommunication Sciences; promotes broadband deployment and adoption through BroadbandUSA (www2.ntia.doc.gov); and assists the First Responder Network Authority (www.firstnet. gov) develop and operate a nationwide broadband network dedicated to public safety. https://www.ntia.doc.gov/about

Sources of Information

Employment To see current NTIA career opportunities on USAJobs, click on the link below, scroll down, and select "NTIA Jobs." https://www.ntia.doc.gov/about

Publications Since 1954, NTIA and its predecessors have published several hundred technical reports and memoranda, special publications, contractor reports, and other information products. For more information, call the Office of Spectrum Management in Washington, DC, at 202-482-1850. Or, contact the publications officer at the Institute for Telecommunication Sciences–Department of Commerce, 325 Broadway, MC ITS.D, Boulder, CO 80305. Phone, 303-497-3572. https://www.ntia.doc. gov/publications

Speakers A speaker request form is available online. https://www.ntia.doc.gov/ webform/speaker-request

Telecommunications Research For information on telecommunications research and engineering services, visit the "Institute for Telecommunication Sciences" Web page. Phone, 303-497-3571. http://www.its. bldrdoc.gov | Email: info@its.bldrdoc.gov; https://www.ntia.doc.gov/contact

For further information, contact the National Telecommunications and Information Administration, Department of Commerce, Washington, DC 20230. Phone, 202-482-1551.

National Institute of Standards and Technology

100 Bureau Drive, Gaithersburg, MD 20899
Phone, 301-975-2000. Internet, http://www.nist.gov

Under Secretary, Standards and Technology / Director	WILLIE E. MAY

The National Institute of Standards and Technology (NIST) operates under the authority of the National Institute of Standards and Technology Act (15 U.S.C. 271), which amends the Organic Act of March 3, 1901 (ch. 872), which created the National Bureau of Standards (NBS) in 1901. In 1988, the Congress renamed NBS as NIST and expanded its activities and responsibilities. http://www.nist.gov/timeline.cfm

NIST is a nonregulatory Federal agency within the Department of Commerce. To carry out its mission, NIST relies on research laboratories, user facilities, innovative manufacturing programs, and its participation in collaborative institutes and centers. NIST research laboratories conduct world-class research to advance the Nation's technological infrastructure and help U.S. companies improve products and services. The Baldrige Performance Excellence Program (www. nist.gov/baldrige) also helps them and other organizations increase operational performance and quality. NIST user facilities include the Center for Nanoscale Science and Technology (www.nist.gov/ cnst) and NIST Center for Neutron Research (www.ncnr.nist.gov). http://www.nist.gov/ programs-projects.cfm

Sources of Information

Employment For information on career opportunities, visit the "Careers at NIST" Web page. http://www.nist.gov/ohrm/careers.cfm

Publications The "Journal of Research of the National Institute of Standards and Technology" and other publications are available online. http://www.nist.gov/nvl/nist_publications.cfm; http://www.nist.gov/public_affairs/contact.cfm | Email: inquiries@nist.gov

For further information, contact the National Institute of Standards and Technology, 100 Bureau Drive, Mail Stop 1070, Gaithersburg, MD 20899-1070. Phone, 301-975-6478. Fax, 301-926-1630.

National Technical Information Service

5301 Shawnee Road, Alexandria, VA 22312
Phone, 703-605-6050. Fax, 888-584-8332. Internet, http://www.ntis.gov

Director	Avi Bender

The National Technical Information Service (NTIS) is the largest central resource for business-related, engineering, Government-funded, scientific, and technical information available. For more than 60 years, the Service has assured businesses, Government, universities, and the public timely access to approximately 3 million publications covering over 350 subject areas. The Service supports the Department of Commerce's mission by providing access to information that stimulates innovation and discovery. The Service receives no appropriations and recovers its costs through fees charged for products and services.

The NTIS promotes economic growth, progress, and science and information. On behalf of the Secretary of Commerce, the Service operates a permanent clearinghouse of scientific and technical information and makes it readily available to industry, business, and the general public—codified as chapter 23 of Title 15 of the United States Code (15 U.S.C. 1151–1157). The Service collects scientific and technical information; catalogs, abstracts, indexes, and permanently archives the information; disseminates information through electronic and other media; and provides information processing services to other Federal agencies.

NTIS also provides information management services to other Federal agencies to help them interact with and better serve the information needs of their own constituents. It develops, plans, evaluates, and implements business strategies for information management and dissemination services and Internet-based service business opportunities for Federal agencies; uses new and existing technologies to ensure optimal access to Government online information services; and manages service projects using in-house capabilities and through joint public-private partnerships. NTIS provides eTraining and Knowledge Management, Web services and cloud computing, distribution and fulfillment, digitization and scanning services for Federal Government agencies. http://www.ntis.gov/about

Sources of Information

Employment Approximately 150 NTIS employees work in Northern Virginia. The Service hires professionals with skills in administration, information technology, and program management. https://www.usajobs.gov

Freedom of Information Act (FOIA) The Office of Director handles Freedom of Information Act (FOIA) requests. The FOIA contact reviews, coordinates, and responds to requests within 20 days under the requirements of the Freedom of Information Act. http://www.ntis.gov/about/FOIA

Products For general information or to place a telephone order, call the Customer Contact Center, 8 a.m.–6 p.m., eastern standard time. Phone, 800-553-6847. TDD, 703-487-4639. Fax, 703-605-6900. http://www.ntis.gov/products | Email: info@ntis.gov

Services   To learn more about NTIS information services for Federal agencies,

call the Office of Federal Services at 703-605-6800. http://www.ntis.gov/services | Email: obdinfo@ntis.gov; http://www.ntis.gov/about/contact

For further information, contact the National Technical Information Service, 5301 Shawnee Road, Alexandria, VA 22312. Phone, 703-605-6000 or 800-553-6847.

United States Patent and Trademark Office

600 Dulany Street, Alexandria, VA 22314
Phone, 571-272-8700. Internet, http://www.uspto.gov

Under Secretary, Intellectual Property / Director	MICHELLE K. LEE
Deputy Under Secretary, Intellectual Property / Deputy Director	RUSSELL D. SLIFER

[For the Patent and Trademark Office statement of organization, see the Federal Register of Apr. 14, 1975, 40 FR 16707]

The United States Patent and Trademark Office (USPTO) was established by the act of July 19, 1952 (35 U.S.C. 1) "to promote the progress of science and useful arts, by securing for limited times to authors and inventors the exclusive right to their respective writings and discoveries" (U.S. Constitution Art. I, sec. 8). The commerce clause provides the constitutional basis for the registration of trademarks.

USPTO examines and issues patents. There are three major patent categories: utility patents, design patents, and plant patents. USPTO also issues statutory invention registrations and processes international patent applications.

Through the registration of trademarks, USPTO assists businessmen and women in protecting their investments, promoting goods and services, and safeguarding consumers against confusion and deception in the marketplace. A trademark includes any distinctive word, name, symbol, device, or any combination thereof adopted and used or intended to be used by a manufacturer or merchant to identify his or her goods or services and distinguish them from those manufactured or sold by others. Trademarks are examined by the Office for compliance with various statutory requirements to prevent unfair competition and consumer deception.

In addition to the examination of patent and trademark applications, issuance of patents, and registration of trademarks, USPTO advises and assists government agencies and officials in matters involving all domestic and global aspects of intellectual property. USPTO also promotes an understanding of intellectual property protection.

USPTO provides public access to patent, trademark, and related scientific and technical information. Patents and trademarks may be reviewed and searched online or at designated Patent and Trademark Depository Libraries. There are 80 Patent and Trademark Depository Libraries located within the United States and Puerto Rico. Additionally, USPTO's Scientific and Technical Information Center in Alexandria, VA, houses over 120,000 volumes of scientific and technical books in various languages; 90,000 bound volumes of periodicals devoted to science and technology; the official journals of 77 foreign patent organizations; and over 40 million foreign patents on paper, microfilm, microfiche, and CD–ROM. http://www.uspto.gov/about-us

Sources of Information

Data   Monthly summaries for patents data and quarterly summaries for trademark data are available online. http://www.uspto.gov/ learning-and-resources/statistics

Employment   Information on employment opportunities is available on the "Careers" Web page. http://careers.uspto.gov

Patents   Information on getting started and applying for and maintaining a patent is available online. http://www.uspto.gov/ patent

Publications   The "Official Gazette" journal, "Inventors Eye" newsletter, and other publications are accessible online. http://www.uspto.gov/learning-and-resources/official-gazette; http://www.uspto. gov/learning-and-resources/newsletter-archives; http://www.uspto.gov/about-us/ news-updates

Speakers   A speaker request form is available online. http://www.uspto.gov/ about-us/organizational-offices/office-chief-communications-officer/speaker-request-form

Trademarks   Information on getting started and applying for and maintaining a trademark is available online. http://www. uspto.gov/trademark; http://www.uspto.gov/ about-us/organizational-offices/office-chief-communications-officer

For further information, contact the Office of the Chief Communications Officer, United States Patent and Trademark Office, 600 Dulany Street, Alexandria, VA 22314. Phone, 571-272-8400.

DEPARTMENT OF DEFENSE

Office of the Secretary, The Pentagon, Washington, DC 20301-1155
Phone, 703-545-6700. Internet, http://www.defense.gov

Secretary of Defense	JAMES M. MATTIS
Deputy Secretary of Defense	PATRICK M. SHANAHAN
Under Secretary of Defense for Acquisition, Technology and Logistics	JAMES MACSTRAVIC, ACTING
Under Secretary of Defense Comptroller / Chief Financial Officer	DAVID L. NORQUIST
Under Secretary of Defense for Intelligence	KARI BINGEN, ACTING
Under Secretary of Defense for Personnel and Readiness	ANTHONY M. KURTA, ACTING
Under Secretary of Defense for Policy	ROBERT KAREM, ACTING
Principal Deputy Under Secretary of Defense Comptroller / DOD Chief Financial Officer	JOHN ZANGARDI, ACTING
Principal Deputy Under Secretary of Defense for Acquisition, Technology and Logistics	(VACANCY)
Principal Under Secretary of Defense for Intelligence	TODD LOWERY, ACTING
Principal Under Secretary of Defense for Personnel and Readiness	(VACANCY)
Principal Under Secretary of Defense for Policy	THERESA WHELAN, ACTING
Assistant Secretary of Defense for Acquisition	DYKE WEATHERINGTON, ACTING
Assistant Secretary of Defense for Asian and Pacific Security Affairs	DAVID HELVY, ACTING
Assistant Secretary of Defense for Health Affairs	DAVID SMITH, ACTING
Assistant Secretary of Defense for Homeland Defense and Global Security	KENNETH RAPUANO
Assistant Secretary of Defense for International Security Affairs	ROBERT KAREM
Assistant Secretary of Defense for Legislative Affairs	PETE GIAMBASTIANI, ACTING
Assistant Secretary of Defense for Logistics and Materiel Readiness	KRISTIN FRENCH, ACTING
Assistant Secretary of Defense for Manpower and Reserve Affairs	STEPHANIE BARNA, ACTING
Assistant Secretary of Defense for Nuclear, Chemical, and Biological Defense Programs	TOM HOPKINS, ACTING
Assistant Secretary of Defense for Operational Energy Plans and Programs	THOMAS E. MOREHOUSE, ACTING
Assistant Secretary of Defense for Personnel and Readiness	ELIZABETH VAN WINKLE, ACTING
Assistant Secretary of Defense for Research and Engineering	MARY MILLER, ACTING
Assistant Secretary of Defense for Special Operations/ Low-Intensity Conflict	CARYN HOLLIS, ACTING
Chief Information Officer	JOHN A. ZANGARDI, ACTING

Chief Operating Officer	STEVEN L. SCHLEIEN
Director, Administration and Management	MICHAEL L. RHODES
Director, Cost Assessment and Program Evaluation	SCOTT COMES, ACTING
Director, Operational Test and Evaluation	DAVID DUMA, ACTING
General Counsel	PAUL S. KOFFSKY, ACTING
Inspector General	GLENN A. FINE, ACTING
Assistant to the Secretary of Defense for Public Affairs	DANA W. WHITE
Deputy Chief Management Officer	DAVID TILLOTSON III, ACTING

Joint Chiefs of Staff

CHAIR	GEN. JOSEPH F. DUNFORD, JR., USMC
Vice Chair	GEN. PAUL J. SELVA, USAF
Senior Enlisted Advisor to the Chair	CSM JOHN W. TROXWELL, USMC
Chief of Naval Operations	ADM. JOHN RICHARDSON, USN
Chief of Staff, Air Force	GEN. DAVID L. GOLDFEIN, USAF
Chief of Staff, Army	GEN. MARK A. MILLEY, USA
Chief of the National Guard Bureau	GEN. JOSEPH L. LENGYEL, USAF
Commandant of the Marine Corps	GEN. ROBERT B. NELLER, USMC

[For the Department of Defense statement of organization, see the Code of Federal Regulations, Title 32, Chapter I, Subchapter R]

The Department of Defense provides the military forces needed to deter war and protect national security. Under the President, the Secretary of Defense directs and exercises authority and control over the separately organized Departments of the Air Force, the Army, and the Navy; over the Joint Chiefs of Staff; over the combatant commands; and over defense agencies and field activities.

The National Security Act Amendments of 1949 redesignated the National Military Establishment as the Department of Defense (DOD) and established it as an executive department (10 U.S.C. 111) headed by the Secretary of Defense.

Structure   The Department of Defense is composed of the Office of the Secretary of Defense; the military departments and the military services within those departments; the Chairman of the Joint Chiefs of Staff and the Joint Staff; the combatant commands; the defense agencies; DOD field activities; and such other offices, agencies, activities, and commands as may be established or designated by law or by the President or the Secretary of Defense.

Each military department is separately organized under its own Secretary and functions under the authority, direction, and control of the Secretary of Defense. The Secretary of each military department is responsible to the Secretary of Defense for the operation and efficiency of his department. Orders to the military departments are issued through the Secretaries of these departments or their designees, by the Secretary of Defense, or under authority specifically delegated in writing by the Secretary of Defense or provided by law.

The commanders of the combatant commands are responsible to the President and the Secretary of Defense for accomplishing the military missions assigned to them and exercising command authority over forces assigned to them. The operational chain of command runs from the President to the Secretary of Defense, to the commanders of the combatant commands. The Chairman of the Joint Chiefs of Staff functions within the chain of command by transmitting the orders of the President or the Secretary of Defense to the commanders of the combatant commands.

Office of the Secretary of Defense

Secretary of Defense   The Secretary of Defense is the principal defense policy adviser to the President and is responsible for the formulation of general defense

DEPARTMENT OF DEFENSE

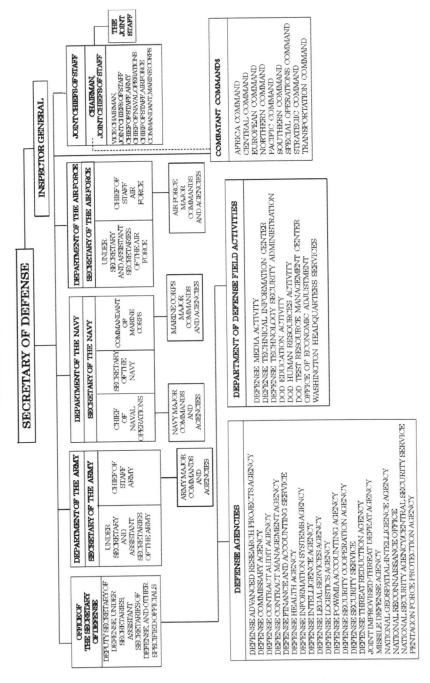

SECRETARY OF DEFENSE

OFFICE OF THE SECRETARY OF DEFENSE
DEPUTY SECRETARY OF DEFENSE UNDER SECRETARIES, ASSISTANT SECRETARIES OF DEFENSE, AND OTHER SPECIFIED OFFICIALS

INSPECTOR GENERAL

JOINT CHIEFS OF STAFF
CHAIRMAN, JOINT CHIEFS OF STAFF

THE JOINT STAFF

VICE CHAIRMAN, JOINT CHIEFS OF STAFF
CHIEF OF STAFF, ARMY
CHIEF OF NAVAL OPERATIONS
CHIEF OF STAFF, AIR FORCE
COMMANDANT, MARINE CORPS

DEPARTMENT OF THE ARMY
SECRETARY OF THE ARMY
UNDER SECRETARY AND ASSISTANT SECRETARIES OF THE ARMY
CHIEF OF STAFF, ARMY
ARMY MAJOR COMMANDS AND AGENCIES

DEPARTMENT OF THE NAVY
SECRETARY OF THE NAVY
CHIEF OF NAVAL OPERATIONS
COMMANDANT OF MARINE CORPS
NAVY MAJOR COMMANDS AND AGENCIES
MARINE CORPS MAJOR COMMANDS AND AGENCIES

DEPARTMENT OF THE AIR FORCE
SECRETARY OF THE AIR FORCE
UNDER SECRETARY AND ASSISTANT SECRETARIES OF THE AIR FORCE
CHIEF OF STAFF, AIR FORCE
AIR FORCE MAJOR COMMANDS AND AGENCIES

COMBATANT COMMANDS
AFRICA COMMAND
CENTRAL COMMAND
EUROPEAN COMMAND
NORTHERN COMMAND
PACIFIC COMMAND
SOUTHERN COMMAND
SPECIAL OPERATIONS COMMAND
STRATEGIC COMMAND
TRANSPORTATION COMMAND

DEPARTMENT OF DEFENSE FIELD ACTIVITIES
DEFENSE MEDIA ACTIVITY
DEFENSE TECHNICAL INFORMATION CENTER
DEFENSE TECHNOLOGY SECURITY ADMINISTRATION
DOD EDUCATION ACTIVITY
DOD HUMAN RESOURCES ACTIVITY
DOD TEST RESOURCE MANAGEMENT CENTER
OFFICE OF ECONOMIC ADJUSTMENT
WASHINGTON HEADQUARTERS SERVICES

DEFENSE AGENCIES
DEFENSE ADVANCED RESEARCH PROJECTS AGENCY
DEFENSE COMMISSARY AGENCY
DEFENSE CONTRACT AUDIT AGENCY
DEFENSE CONTRACT MANAGEMENT AGENCY
DEFENSE FINANCE AND ACCOUNTING SERVICE
DEFENSE HEALTH AGENCY
DEFENSE INFORMATION SYSTEMS AGENCY
DEFENSE INTELLIGENCE AGENCY
DEFENSE LEGAL SERVICES AGENCY
DEFENSE LOGISTICS AGENCY
DEFENSE POW/MIA ACCOUNTING AGENCY
DEFENSE SECURITY COOPERATION AGENCY
DEFENSE SECURITY SERVICE
DEFENSE THREAT REDUCTION AGENCY
JOINT IMPROVISED-THREAT DEFEAT AGENCY
MISSILE DEFENSE AGENCY
NATIONAL GEOSPATIAL-INTELLIGENCE AGENCY
NATIONAL RECONNAISSANCE OFFICE
NATIONAL SECURITY AGENCY/CENTRAL SECURITY SERVICE
PENTAGON FORCE PROTECTION AGENCY

policy and policy related to DOD and for the execution of approved policy. Under the direction of the President, the Secretary exercises authority, direction, and control over the Department of Defense. http://www.defense.gov/osd

Acquisition, Technology and Logistics The Under Secretary of Defense for Acquisition, Technology and Logistics is the principal staff assistant and adviser to the Secretary of Defense for all matters relating to the DOD Acquisition System; research and development; modeling and simulation; systems engineering; advanced technology; developmental test and evaluation; production; systems integration; logistics; installation management; military construction; procurement; environment, safety, and occupational health management; utilities and energy management; business management modernization; document services; and nuclear, chemical, and biological defense programs. http://www.acq.osd.mil

Intelligence The Under Secretary of Defense for Intelligence is the principal staff assistant and adviser to the Secretary and Deputy Secretary of Defense for intelligence, intelligence-related matters, counterintelligence, and security. The Under Secretary of Defense for Intelligence supervises all intelligence and intelligence-related affairs of DOD.

Networks and Information Integration The Assistant Secretary of Defense for Networks and Information Integration is the principal staff assistant and adviser to the Secretary and Deputy Secretary of Defense for achieving and maintaining information superiority in support of DOD missions, while exploiting or denying an adversary's ability to do the same. The Assistant Secretary of Defense for Networks and Information Integration also serves as the Chief Information Officer. http://dodcio.defense.gov

Personnel and Readiness The Under Secretary of Defense for Personnel and Readiness is the principal staff assistant and adviser to the Secretary of Defense for policy matters relating to the structure and readiness of the total force. Functional areas include readiness; civilian and military personnel policies, programs, and systems; civilian and military equal opportunity programs; health policies, programs, and activities; Reserve component programs, policies, and activities; family policy, dependents' education, and personnel support programs; mobilization planning and requirements; language capabilities and programs; and the Federal Voting Assistance Program. The Under Secretary of Defense for Personnel and Readiness also serves as the Chief Human Capital Officer. http://prhome.defense.gov

Policy The Under Secretary of Defense for Policy is the principal staff assistant and adviser to the Secretary of Defense for policy matters relating to overall international security policy and political-military affairs and represents the Department at the National Security Council and other external agencies involved with national security policy. The Under Secretary's areas of activity include homeland defense; NATO affairs; foreign military sales; arms limitation agreements; international trade and technology security; regional security affairs; special operations and low-intensity conflict; stability operations; integration of departmental plans and policies with overall national security objectives; drug control policy, requirements, priorities, systems, resources, and programs; and issuance of policy guidance affecting departmental programs. http://policy.defense.gov

Special Staff A special staff assists the Secretary and Deputy Secretary of Defense. This special staff of assistants includes the Assistant Secretaries of Defense for Legislative Affairs and for Public Affairs; the Under Secretary of Defense (Comptroller), who also functions as the Chief Financial Officer; the General Counsel; the Inspector General; the Assistant to the Secretary of Defense for Intelligence Oversight; the Directors of Administration and Management, of Operational Test and Evaluation, of Business Transformation, of Net Assessment, of Program Analysis and Evaluation; and other officers whom the Secretary of Defense determines are necessary to help carry out his or her duties and responsibilities. http://www.defense.gov/About-DoD/Leaders

Joint Chiefs of Staff

The Joint Chiefs of Staff consist of the Chairman, the Vice Chairman, the Chief of Staff of the Army, the Chief of Naval Operations, the Chief of Staff of the Air Force, and the Commandant of the Marine Corps. The Chairman of the Joint Chiefs of Staff is the principal military adviser to the President, the National Security Council, and the Secretary of Defense. The other members of the Joint Chiefs of Staff are military advisers who may provide additional information upon request from the President, the National Security Council, or the Secretary of Defense. They may also submit their advice when it does not agree with that of the Chairman. Subject to the authority of the President and the Secretary of Defense, the Chairman of the Joint Chiefs of Staff is responsible for assisting the President and the Secretary of Defense in providing strategic direction and planning for the Armed Forces; making recommendations for the assignment of responsibilities within the Armed Forces; comparing the capabilities of American and allied Armed Forces with those of potential adversaries; preparing and reviewing contingency plans that conform to policy guidance; preparing joint logistic and mobility plans; and recommending assignment of logistic and mobility responsibilities.

The Chairman, while so serving, holds the grade of general or admiral and outranks all other officers of the Armed Forces.

The Vice Chairman of the Joint Chiefs performs duties assigned by the Chairman, with the approval of the Secretary of Defense. The Vice Chairman acts as Chairman when there is a vacancy in the office of the Chairman or in the absence or disability of the Chairman. The Vice Chairman, while so serving, holds the grade of general or admiral and outranks all other officers of the Armed Forces except the Chairman of the Joint Chiefs of Staff. http://www.jcs.mil

Joint Staff   The Joint Staff, under the Chairman of the Joint Chiefs of Staff, assists the Chairman and the other members of the Joint Chiefs of Staff in carrying out their responsibilities.

The Joint Staff is headed by a Director who is selected by the Chairman in consultation with the other members of the Joint Chiefs of Staff and with the approval of the Secretary of Defense. Officers assigned to serve on the Joint Staff are selected by the Chairman in approximately equal numbers from the Army, Navy, Marine Corps, and Air Force. http://www.jcs.mil/About.aspx

Combatant Commands

The combatant commands are military commands with broad continuing missions maintaining the security and defense of the United States against attack; supporting and advancing the national policies and interests of the United States and discharging U.S. military responsibilities in their assigned areas; and preparing plans, conducting operations, and coordinating activities of the forces assigned to them in accordance with the directives of higher authority. The operational chain of command runs from the President to the Secretary of Defense, to the commanders of the combatant commands. The Chairman of the Joint Chiefs of Staff serves as the spokesman for the commanders of the combatant commands, especially on the administrative requirements of their commands. http://www.defense.gov/Sites/Unified-Combatant-Commands

Field Activities

Counterintelligence Field Activity   The DOD Counterintelligence Field Activity was established in 2002 to build a Defense counterintelligence (CI) system that is informed by national goals and objectives and supports the protection of DOD personnel and critical assets from foreign intelligence services, foreign terrorists, and other clandestine or covert threats. The desired end is a transformed Defense CI system that integrates and synchronizes the counterintelligence activities of the military departments, defense agencies, Joint Staff, and combatant commands.

Defense Health Agency   The Defense Health Agency (DHA) manages the activities of the Military Health System. It is also the market manager for the National Capital Region enhanced Multi-Service Market, which includes Walter Reed National Military Medical Center and Fort Belvoir Community Hospital. http://www.dha.mil

Defense Media Activity   Defense Media Activity (DMA) gathers Defense news and information from all departmental levels and reports that news and information to DOD audiences worldwide through American Forces Network online, radio, television, and through publications. DMA reports news on individual airmen, marines, sailors, soldiers, and DOD civilian employees to the American public through the Hometown News Service. DMA provides World Wide Web infrastructure and services for DOD organizations. It collects, processes, and stores DOD imagery products created by the Department and makes them available to the American public. It trains the Department's public affairs and visual information military and civilian professionals. DMA also operates Stars and Stripes, a news and information organization, free of Government editorial control and censorship, for military audiences overseas. http://www.dma.mil

Defense Prisoner of War / Missing in Action Accounting Agency The Defense POW / MIA Accounting Agency (DPAA) provides centralized management of prisoner of war and missing personnel affairs within the DOD. DPAA's primary responsibilities include leadership for and policy oversight over all efforts to account for Americans still missing from past conflicts and the recovery of and accounting for those who may become isolated in hostile territory in future conflicts. DPAA also provides administrative and logistical support to the U.S.-Russia Joint Commission on POW / MIAs, conducts research and analysis to help resolve cases of those unaccounted for, examines DOD documents for possible public disclosure, and maintains viable channels of communications on POW / MIA matters between the DOD and Congress, the families of the missing, and the American public. http://www.dpaa.mil

Defense Technical Information Center The Defense Technical Information Center (DTIC) is a field activity in the Office of the Under Secretary of Defense for Acquisition, Technology and Logistics. It operates under the authority, direction, and control of the Director of Defense Research and Engineering. DTIC provides defense scientific and technical information, offers controlled access to defense information, and designs and hosts more than 100 DOD Web sites. DTIC's collections include technical reports, summaries of research in progress, independent research and development material, defense technology transfer agreements, and DOD planning documents. http://www.dtic.mil/dtic/about/about.html

Defense Technology Security Administration The Defense Technology Security Administration (DTSA) is the central DOD point of contact for development and implementation of technology security policies governing defense articles and services and dual-use commodities. DTSA administers the development and implementation of DOD technology security policies on international transfers of defense-related goods, services, and technologies. It does so to ensure that critical U.S. military technological advantages are preserved, transfers that could prove detrimental to U.S. security interests are controlled and limited, weapons of mass destruction and their means of delivery do not proliferate, diversion of defense-related goods to terrorists is prevented, legitimate defense cooperation with foreign friends and allies is supported, and the health of the defense industrial base is assured. http://www.dtsa.mil/SitePages/default.aspx

Education Activity The Department of Defense Education Activity (DODEA) was established in 1992. It consists of two subordinate organizational entities: the Department of Defense Dependents Schools (DODDS) and the Department of Defense Domestic Dependent Elementary and Secondary Schools (DDESS). DODEA formulates, develops, and implements policies, technical guidance, and standards for the effective management of Defense dependents education activities and programs. It also plans, directs, coordinates, and manages the education programs for eligible dependents of U.S. military and civilian personnel stationed overseas and stateside; evaluates the programmatic and operational policies and procedures for DODDS and DDESS; and provides education activity representation at meetings and deliberations of educational panels and advisory groups. http://www.dodea.edu/Americas

Human Resources Field Activity The Department of Defense Human Resources Activity (DODHRA) enhances the operational effectiveness and efficiency of a host of dynamic and diverse programs supporting the Office of the Under Secretary of Defense for Personnel and Readiness. The Field Activity supports policy development, performs cutting-edge research and expert analysis, supports readiness and reengineering efforts, manages the largest automated personnel data repositories in the world, prepares tomorrow's leaders through robust developmental programs, supports recruiting and retaining the best and brightest, and delivers both benefits and critical services to warfighters and their families. http://www.dhra.mil/website/index.shtml

Office of Economic Adjustment   The Office of Economic Adjustment (OEA) assists communities that are adversely affected by base closures, expansions, or realignments and Defense contract or program cancellations. OEA provides technical and financial assistance to those communities and coordinates other Federal agencies' involvement through the Defense Economic Adjustment Program. http://www.oea.gov

Test Resource Management   The Test Resource Management Center (TRMC) is a DOD Field Activity under the authority, direction, and control of the Under Secretary of Defense for Acquisition, Technology and Logistics. The Center develops policy, plans for, and assesses the adequacy of the major range and test facility base to provide adequate testing in support of development, acquisition, fielding, and sustainment of defense systems. TRMC develops and maintains the test and evaluation resources strategic plan, reviews the proposed DOD test and evaluation budgets, and certifies the adequacy of the proposed budgets and whether they provide balanced support of the strategic plan. TRMC manages the Central Test and Evaluation Investment Program, the Test and Evaluation Science and Technology Program, and the Joint Mission Environment Test Capability Program. http://www.acq.osd.mil/dte-trmc

Washington Headquarters Services   Washington Headquarters Services (WHS), established as a DOD Field Activity on October 1, 1977, is under the authority and control of the Deputy Chief Management Officer. WHS provides a range of administrative and operational services to the Office of the Secretary of Defense, specified DOD components, the general public, and for Federal Government activities. WHS services include contracting and procurement; data systems and information technology support; Defense facilities, directives and records, and financial management; enterprise information technology infrastructure, human resource, legal, library, and personnel security services; evaluation and planning functions; Pentagon renovation and construction; and support for advisory boards and commissions. http://www.whs.mil

Sources of Information

Budget Data   The Defense Technical Information Center (DTIC) sponsors a Web site that features congressional budget data pertaining to the DOD. The DTIC posts data from each budget report once it is filed and made available on the Library of Congress' Web site. The data are accessible in Portable Document Format (PDF) and Excel spreadsheet format. http://www.dtic.mil/congressional_budget

Business Opportunities   Information on and resources for acquisition, business, contracting, and subcontracting opportunities are available on the DOD's Web site. http://www.defense.gov/Resources/Contract-Resources

The Office of Small Business Programs supports the participation of small businesses in the acquisition of goods and services for the DOD. http://www.acq.osd.mil/osbp

Career Opportunities   The DOD employs over 718,000 civilian personnel. For additional information on applying for DOD job opportunities, contact Washington Headquarters Services–Human Resources Servicing Team. Phone, 614-692-0252. https://dod.usajobs.gov

Dictionary   The Defense Technical Information Center's Web site features the "DOD Dictionary of Military and Associated Terms," which is commonly called the "DOD Dictionary." The dictionary facilitates communication and mutual understanding within the DOD, with external Federal agencies, and between the United States and its international partners by standardizing military and associated terminology. http://www.dtic.mil/doctrine/dod_dictionary

Freedom of Information Act (FOIA) Approved by President Lyndon B. Johnson in 1966, the statute generally provides that any person has the right to request access to Federal agency information or records. Upon receiving a written request, the Federal agency holding the desired document or record must disclose it. Some records, however, are shielded from disclosure by one of the FOIA's nine exemptions or three exclusions. http://open.defense.gov/Transparency/FOIA.aspx

History A short history of the Pentagon, from construction to completion, is available on the Pentagon Tours Office's Web site. https://pentagontours.osd.mil/Tours/construction.jsp

Joint Chiefs of Staff The Joint Chiefs of Staff maintain a Web site. http://www.jcs.mil

News The DOD posts news releases on its Web site. http://www.defense.gov/News/News-Releases

Plain Language The DOD aims to write documents in readable English by adhering to Federal plain language guidelines. http://www.dtic.mil/whs/directives/plainlanguage.html

Popular Resources A page of popular DOD resources is available on the DOD Web site. http://www.defense.gov/Resources

Social Media The DOD tweets announcements and other newsworthy items on Twitter. https://twitter.com/DeptofDefense

The DOD has a Facebook account. https://www.facebook.com/DeptofDefense

The DOD posts videos on its YouTube channel. https://www.youtube.com/user/DODvClips/featured

Site Index The Web site index allows visitors to look for specific topics or to browse content that aligns with their interests. http://www.defense.gov/Site-Index

Speakers Civilian and military officials from the DOD are available to speak to public and private sector groups interested in defense-related topics, including the global war on terrorism. Requests for speakers should be addressed to the Director for Community Relations and Public Liaison, 1400 Defense Pentagon, Room 2C546, Washington, DC 20310-1400.

Today in the DOD The "Today in the Department of Defense" Web page features contracts, news and casualty releases, photos, press advisories, speeches, and transcripts on a daily basis. http://www.defense.gov/Today-in-DoD

Tours For information on guided tours of the Pentagon, contact the Pentagon Tours Office. Phone, 703-697-1776. http://pentagontours.osd.mil | Email: osd.pentagon.pa.mbx.pentagon-tours-schedule@mail.mil

Web Sites A list of DOD Web site links is available online. http://www.defense.gov/Military-Services/DoD-Websites

An A–Z list of DOD Web site links is available online. http://www.defense.gov/Military-Services/A-Z-List; http://www.defense.gov/Contact

For further information concerning the Department of Defense, contact the Director, Directorate for Public Inquiry and Analysis, Office of the Assistant Secretary of Defense for Public Affairs, 1400 Defense Pentagon, Washington, DC 20301-1400. Phone, 703- 697-9312.

Department of the Air Force

1690 Air Force Pentagon, Washington, DC 20330-1670
Phone, 703-697-6061. Internet, http://www.af.mil

Air Force Secretariat

Secretary of the Air Force	Dr. Heather A. Wilson
Under Secretary of the Air Force	Lisa S. Disbrow
Administrative Assistant	Patricia J. Zarodkifwicz
Auditor General	Daniel F. McMillin
General Counsel	Joseph M. McDade, Jr.

Information Dominance and Chief Information Officer (A6)	LT. GEN. WILLIAM J. BENDER
Inspector General	LT. GEN. ANTHONY J. ROCK
Legislative Liaison	MAJ. GEN. STEVEN L. BASHAM
Assistant Secretary, Acquisition	DARLENE COSTELLO
Assistant Secretary, Financial Management and Comptroller	DOUG BENNETT
Assistant Secretary, Installations, Environment, and Energy	RICHARD K. HARTLEY
Assistant Secretary, Manpower and Reserve Affairs	DANIEL R. SITTERLY
Deputy Under Secretary for Management	MARILYN M. THOMAS
Deputy Under Secretary, International Affairs	HEIDI H. GRANT
Deputy Under Secretary, Space	WINSTON BEAUCHAMP
Director, Air Force Small Business Programs	MARK S. TESKEY
Director, Public Affairs	BRIG. GEN. EDWARD W. THOMAS, JR.

Air Staff

Chief of Staff	GEN. DAVID L. GOLDFEIN
Vice Chief of Staff	GEN. STEPHEN W. WILSON
Chief Master Sergeant of the Air Force	CMSAF KALETH O. WRIGHT
Assistant Vice Chief of Staff	LT. GEN. STAYCE D. HARRIS
Judge Advocate General	LT. GEN. CHRISTOPHER F. BURNE
Surgeon General	LT. GEN. MARK A. EDIGER
Chief of Air Force Reserve	LT. GEN. MARYANNE MILLER
Chief of Chaplains	MAJ. GEN. DONDI CONSTIN
Chief of Safety	MAJ. GEN. ANDREW MUELLER
Chief of Staff, Strategic Deterrence and Nuclear Integration (A10)	LT. GEN. JACK WEINSTEIN
Chief Scientist	GREG L. ZACHARIAS
Deputy Chief of Staff, Intelligence, Surveillance and Reconnaissance (A2)	LT. GEN. VERALINN JAMIESON
Deputy Chief of Staff, Logistics, Engineering and Force Protection (A4)	LT. GEN. JOHN B. COOPER
Deputy Chief of Staff, Manpower, Personnel and Services (A1)	LT. GEN. GINA GROSSO
Deputy Chief of Staff, Operations, Plans and Requirements (A3)	LT. GEN. MARK C. NOWLAND
Deputy Chief of Staff, Strategic Plans and Programs (A5/8)	LT. GEN. JERRY D. HARRIS, JR.
Director, Air Force Sexual Assault Prevention and Response	MAJ. GEN. JAMES C. JOHNSON
Director, Air National Guard	LT. GEN. L. SCOTT RICE
Director, History and Museums Policies and Programs	WALTER A. GRUDZINSKAS
Director, Studies and Analyses, Assessments (A9)	KEVIN E. WILLIAMS
Director, Test and Evaluation	DEVIN CATE

Major Commands

Air Combat Command	GEN. JAMES M. HOLMES
Air Education and Training Command	LT. GEN. DARRYL L. ROBERSON
Air Force Global Strike Command	GEN. ROBIN RAND
Air Force Materiel Command	GEN. ELLEN M. PAWLIKOWSKI
Air Force Reserve Command	LT. GEN. MARYANNE MILLER

Air Force Space Command	GEN. JOHN W. RAYMOND
Air Force Special Operations Command	LT. GEN. MARSHALL B. WEBB
Air Mobility Command	GEN. CARLTON D. EVERHART II
Pacific Air Forces	GEN. TERRENCE J. O'SHAUGHNESSY
U.S. Air Forces in Europe	GEN. TOD D. WOLTERS

The Department of the Air Force defends the United States by providing air, space, and cyberspace capabilities.

The Department of the Air Force (USAF) was established as part of the National Military Establishment by the National Security Act of 1947 (61 Stat. 502) and came into being on September 18, 1947. The National Security Act Amendments of 1949 redesignated the National Military Establishment as the Department of Defense, established it as an executive department, and made the Department of the Air Force a military department within the Department of Defense (63 Stat. 578). The Department of the Air Force is separately organized under the Secretary of the Air Force. It operates under the authority, direction, and control of the Secretary of Defense (10 U.S.C. 8010). The Department comprises the Office of the Secretary of the Air Force, the Air Staff, and field organizations.

Secretary

The Secretary and Secretariat Staff oversee matters of organization, training, logistical support, maintenance, welfare of personnel, administrative, recruiting, research and development, and other activities that the President or Secretary of Defense prescribes. http://www.af.mil/AboutUs/AirForceSeniorLeaders/SECAF.aspx

Air Staff   The Air Staff assists the Secretary, the Under Secretary, the Assistant Secretaries, and the Chief of Staff in carrying out their responsibilities.

Field Organizations   The major commands, field operating agencies, and direct reporting units constitute the field organizations of the Air Force. They are organized primarily on a functional basis in the United States and on a geographic basis overseas. These commands are responsible for accomplishing certain phases of the Air Force's worldwide activities. They also organize, administer, equip, and train subordinate elements to accomplish assigned missions.

Major Commands: Continental U.S. Commands

Air Combat Command   The Air Combat Command operates CONUS-based, combat-coded fighter and attack aircraft. It organizes, trains, equips, and maintains combat-ready forces for rapid deployment and employment while ensuring strategic air defense forces are ready to meet the challenges of peacetime air sovereignty and wartime air defense. http://www.acc.af.mil

Air Education and Training Command   The Air Education and Training Command recruits, assesses, commissions, educates, and trains Air Force enlisted and officer personnel. It provides basic military training, initial and advanced technical training, flying training, and professional military and post-secondary education. The Command also conducts Air Force security assistance, joint, medical service, and readiness training. http://www.aetc.af.mil

Air Force Global Strike Command   The Air Force Global Strike Command is responsible for the Nation's three intercontinental ballistic missile wings; the Air Force's bomber force, including the B–1, B–2, and B–52 wings; the Long Range Strike Bomber program; and operational and maintenance support to organizations within the nuclear enterprise. http://www.afgsc.af.mil

Air Force Materiel Command   The Air Force Materiel Command delivers expeditionary capabilities through research, development, test, evaluation, acquisition, modernization, and sustainment of aerospace weapon systems throughout their life cycles. Those weapon systems include Air Force fighter, bomber, cargo, and attack fleets and armament. They also include net-centric command and control assets; intelligence, surveillance,

Department of the Air Force

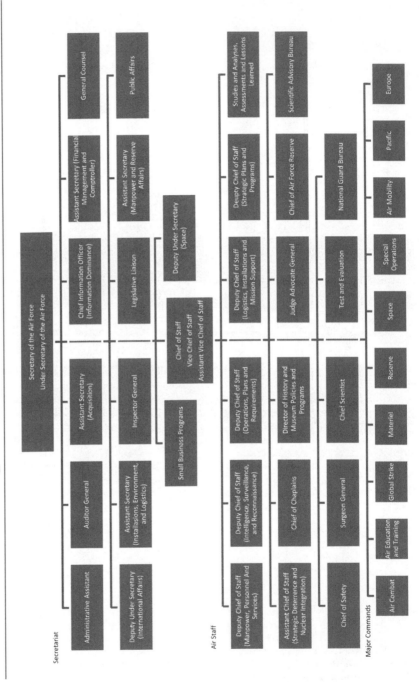

Secretariat

Secretary of the Air Force
Under Secretary of the Air Force

General Counsel

Public Affairs

Assistant Secretary (Financial Management and Comptroller)

Assistant Secretary (Manpower and Reserve Affairs)

Chief Information Officer (Information Dominance)

Legislative Liaison

Deputy Under Secretary (Space)

Assistant Secretary (Acquisition)

Inspector General

Small Business Programs

Auditor General

Assistant Secretary (Installations, Environment, and Logistics)

Administrative Assistant

Deputy Under Secretary (International Affairs)

Air Staff

Chief of Staff
Vice Chief of Staff
Assistant Vice Chief of Staff

Studies and Analyses, Assessments and Lessons Learned

Scientific Advisory Bureau

Deputy Chief of Staff (Strategic Plans and Programs)

Chief of Air Force Reserve

National Guard Bureau

Deputy Chief of Staff (Logistics, Installations and Mission Support)

Judge Advocate General

Test and Evaluation

Deputy Chief of Staff (Operations, Plans and Requirements)

Director of History and Museum Policies and Programs

Chief Scientist

Deputy Chief of Staff (Intelligence, Surveillance, and Reconnaissance)

Chief of Chaplains

Surgeon General

Deputy Chief of Staff (Manpower, Personnel And Services)

Assistant Chief of Staff (Strategic Deterrence and Nuclear Integration)

Chief of Safety

Major Commands

Europe

Pacific

Air Mobility

Special Operations

Space

Reserve

Materiel

Global Strike

Air Education and Training

Air Combat

and reconnaissance assets; and combat support information systems. The command oversees basic research and development that support air, space, and cyberspace capabilities. The command relies on an integrated, efficient life cycle management approach to ensure the best possible support to warfighters. http://www.afmc. af.mil

Air Force Reserve Command The Air Force Reserve Command provides the Air Force with approximately 14 percent of the total force and approximately 4 percent of the manpower budget. Reservists support air, space, and cyberspace superiority; command and control; global integrated intelligence surveillance reconnaissance; global precision attack; nuclear deterrence operations; special operations; rapid global mobility; and personnel recovery. They also perform aircraft flight testing, space operations, as well as communications, civil engineer, military training, mobility support, security forces, services, and transportation missions. http://www.afrc. af.mil

Air Force Space Command The Air Force Space Command provides space and cyberspace capabilities such as missile warning, space control, spacelift, satellite operations, and designated cyberspace activities. http://www.afspc.af.mil

Air Force Special Operations Command The Air Force Special Operations Command provides the air component of U.S. Special Operations Command. The command deploys specialized air power and delivers special operations combat power wherever and whenever needed. It provides agile combat support, combat search and rescue, information warfare, precision aerospace fires, psychological operations, and specialized aerospace mobility and refueling to unified commands. http://www.afsoc. af.mil

Air Mobility Command The Air Mobility Command provides airlift, air refueling, special air missions, and aeromedical evacuation for U.S. forces. It also airlifts forces to theater commands to support wartime tasking. http://www.amc.af.mil

Major Commands: Overseas Commands

Pacific Air Forces The Pacific Air Forces deliver rapid and precise air, space, and cyberspace capabilities to protect the United States, its territories, and its allies and partners; provide integrated air and missile warning and defense; promote interoperability throughout the Pacific area of responsibility; maintain strategic access and freedom of movement across all domains; and posture to respond across the full spectrum of military contingencies to restore regional security. http://www.pacaf. af.mil

U.S. Air Forces in Europe The U.S. Air Forces in Europe (USAFE) execute the Air Force, European Command, and Africa Command missions with forward-based air power and infrastructure to conduct and enable theater and global operations. The USAFE direct air operations in a theater that spans three continents, covers more than 19 million square miles, contains 104 independent states, produces more than a quarter of the world's gross domestic product, and comprises more than a quarter of Earth's population. http://www.usafe.af.mil

Field Operating Agencies

Air Force Agency for Modeling and Simulation The Air Force Agency for Modeling and Simulation provides seamless integration of cross-functional live, virtual, and constructive operational training environments that allow war fighters to maximize performance and optimize decisionmaking. The agency works with combatant commands, major commands, the Air Force Reserve Command, the Air National Guard, the Air Force headquarters, direct reporting units, and field operating agencies to provide the necessary development and implementation standards for common access and interoperability within the live, virtual, and constructive domains for efficient and secure global operations. http://www.afams.af.mil

Air Force Audit Agency The Air Force Audit Agency provides all levels of Air Force management with independent, objective, and quality audit services by reviewing and promoting operational economy, effectiveness, and efficiency; evaluating programs and activities to achieve intended results; and assessing and improving financial reporting. http://www.afaa.af.mil

Air Force Cost Analysis Agency   The Air Force Cost Analysis Agency performs nonadvocate cost analyses for major space, aircraft, and information system programs. The agency supports the departmentwide cost analysis program by developing and maintaining cost-estimating tools, techniques, and infrastructure. It provides guidance, analytical support, quantitative risk analyses, and special studies to improve long-range planning, force structure, analysis of alternatives, and lifecycle cost analyses.

Air Force Flight Standards Agency   The Air Force Flight Standards Agency performs worldwide inspection of airfields, navigation systems, and instrument approaches. It provides flight standards to develop Air Force instrument requirements and certifies procedures and directives for cockpit display and navigation systems. It also provides air traffic control and airlift procedures and evaluates air traffic control systems and airspace management procedures.

Air Force Historical Research Agency   The Air Force Historical Research Agency serves as a repository for Air Force historical records and maintains research facilities for scholars and the general public. http://www.afhra.af.mil/index.asp

Air Force Inspection Agency   The Air Force Inspection Agency provides independent inspection, evaluation, oversight, training and analysis to improve the effectiveness and efficiency of the Air Force. http://www.af.mil/AboutUs/FactSheets/Display/tabid/224/Article/104564/air-force-inspection-agency.aspx

Air Force Legal Operations Agency   The Air Force Legal Operations Agency includes all senior defense, senior trial, appellate defense, and Government counsel in the Air Force, as well as all Air Force civil litigators who defend the Air Force against civil lawsuits that claim damages and seek other remedies in contracts, environmental, labor, and tort litigation.

Air Force Manpower Analysis Agency   The Air Force Manpower Analysis Agency

provides analysis and develops tools for helping Air Force and Department of Defense senior leaders make decisions affecting total force manpower requirements. The agency supports the Under Secretary of the Air Force for Management's efforts to improve processes and carries out departmentwide transformation initiatives. It also oversees human capital planning and training to develop and sustain manpower-specific capabilities at adequate levels. http://www.af.mil/AboutUs/FactSheets/Display/tabid/224/Article/104598/air-force-manpower-agency.aspx

Air Force Medical Operations Agency   The Air Force Medical Operations Agency assists the Air Force Surgeon General in developing plans, programs, and policies for aerospace medicine, bioenvironmental engineering, clinical investigations, family advocacy, health promotion, military public health, quality assurance, radioactive material management, and the medical service. http://www.airforcemedicine.af.mil/afmoa

Air Force Medical Support Agency   The Air Force Medical Support Agency provides consultative support and policy development for the Air Force Surgeon General in medical force management. It also supports ground and air expeditionary medical capabilities used in global, homeland security, and force health protection, as well as all aspects of medical and dental services, aerospace medicine operations, and medical support functions.

Air Force Mortuary Affairs Operations   The Air Force Mortuary Affairs Operations, a field operating agency of the Deputy Chief of Staff for Manpower, Personnel and Services, works to support the entire Department of Defense and other Federal entities ensuring dignity, honor and respect to the fallen, and care, service, and support to their families. http://www.mortuary.af.mil

Air Force Office of Special Investigations   The Air Force Office of Special Investigations identifies, exploits, and neutralizes criminal, terrorist, and intelligence threats to the U.S. Air Force, Department of Defense, and U.S. Government. Its primary responsibilities are criminal investigations and counterintelligence services. It also protects critical technologies and information, detects and mitigates threats, provides global specialized services, conducts major criminal investigations, and offensively engages foreign adversaries and threats. http://www.osi.af.mil

Air Force Operations Group The Air Force Operations Group collects, processes, analyzes, and communicates information, enabling situational awareness of USAF operations worldwide. This awareness facilitates timely, responsive, and effective decisionmaking by senior USAF leaders and combatant commanders.

Air Force Personnel Center The Air Force Personnel Center ensures that commanders around the world have enough skilled Air Force personnel to carry out the mission. The center also runs programs affecting the entire life cycle of military and civilian Air Force personnel from accession through retirement. http://www.af.mil/AboutUs/FactSheets/Display/tabid/224/Article/104554/air-force-personnel-center.aspx

Air Force Program Executive Offices The Air Force Program Executive Offices (PEOs) oversee the execution of a program throughout its entire lifecycle. While the PEOs are not part of USAF headquarters, they report on acquisition and program-specific issues directly to the Air Force Service Acquisition Executive and the Assistant Secretary of the Air Force for Acquisition. Air Force PEOs are currently responsible for diverse programs in a range of areas: aircraft, command and control and combat support systems, Joint Strike Fighter, and weapons. http://ww3.safaq.hq.af.mil/organizations/index.asp

Air Force Public Affairs Agency The Air Force Public Affairs Agency manages the Air Force media center. The center collects, archives, and distributes Air Force imagery; manages licensing and branding of Air Force trademarks; provides policy guidance and oversight for the Air Force's Web site and social media programs; operates the Air Force's official social media program; composes original musical arrangements for Air Force regional bands; and develops training curricula and requirements for the Air Force's nearly 6,000 public affairs practitioners. http://www.publicaffairs.af.mil

Air Force Review Boards Agency The Air Force Review Boards Agency manages various military and civilian appellate processes for the Secretary of the Air Force. http://www.af.mil/AboutUs/FactSheets/Display/tabid/224/Article/104511/air-force-review-boards-agency.aspx

Air Force Safety Center The Air Force Safety Center promotes safety to reduce the number and severity of mishaps. It also supports combat readiness by developing, implementing, executing, and evaluating Air Force aviation, ground, weapons, nuclear surety, space, and system programs. http://www.safety.af.mil

Air National Guard Readiness Center The Air National Guard Readiness Center performs the operational and technical tasks associated with manning, equipping, and training Air National Guard units to meet required readiness levels. http://www.angrc.ang.af.mil

National Air and Space Intelligence Center The National Air and Space Intelligence Center (NASIC) assesses foreign air and space threats. It creates integrated, predictive intelligence in the domains of air, space, and cyberspace to support military operations, force modernization, and policymaking. NASIC analyzes data on foreign aerospace forces and weapons systems to determine performance characteristics, capabilities, vulnerabilities, and intentions. These assessments are used to shape national security and defense policies. NASIC personnel also play a role in weapons treaty negotiations and verification. http://www.nasic.af.mil

Direct Reporting Units

Air Force District of Washington The Air Force District of Washington supports Headquarters Air Force and other Air Force units in the National Capital Region. http://www.afdw.af.mil

Air Force Operational Test and Evaluation Center The Air Force Operational Test and Evaluation Center plans and conducts test and evaluation procedures to determine operational effectiveness and suitability of new or modified USAF systems and their capacity to meet mission needs. http://www.afotec.af.mil

U.S. Air Force Academy   The U.S. Air Force Academy provides academic and military instruction and experience to prepare future USAF career officers. The Academy offers Bachelor of Science degrees in 31 academic majors, and upon completion, graduates receive commissions as second lieutenants. http://www.usafa.af.mil

Sources of Information

Employment   Members of the Air Force civilian service work side by side with active duty airmen. They are a diverse group of professionals: contract specialists, engineers, human resources specialists, intelligence experts, mechanics, scientists, teachers, and more. https://afciviliancareers.com/content/home-air-force-civilian-service

Factsheets   Factsheets contain current information and statistics on Air Force careers, organizations, inventory, and equipment—including aircraft and weapons. http://www.af.mil/AboutUs/FactSheets.aspx | Email: DMAPublicAffairs@mail.mil

Freedom of Information Act (FOIA)   The Freedom of Information and Privacy Act Office manages the policy and procedural guidance for the Freedom of Information Act (FOIA), Privacy Act (PA) and Quality of Information (QIP) programs in accordance with applicable laws. http://www.foia.af.mil/Welcome.aspx

Links to FOIA requester service centers are available online. The service centers are grouped, by base and by command, in two lists. http://www.foia.af.mil/Offices

Frequently Asked Questions (FAQs)   The Air Force provides answers to FAQs on its web-site. http://www.af.mil/Questions.aspx

History   For over a century, the Air Force has relied on the bravery and skill of American airmen to protect the United States in the air, space, and cyberspace. An overview of that history is available online. https://www.airforce.com/mission/history

Inspector General (IG)   The IG receives and investigates complaints of abuse, fraud, and waste involving Air Force personnel or programs. http://www.af.mil/InspectorGeneralComplaints.aspx | Email: usaf.ighotline@mail.mil

Intelligence, Surveillance, and Reconnaissance (ISR)   The Air Force's web-site features a section dedicated to ISR activities and news. http://www.af.mil/ISR.aspx

Joining the Air Force   To learn about its mission, how to join, and about educational, training, and career opportunities that enlistment offers, visit the Air Force's recruitment Web site. https://www.airforce.com/how-to-join

Medal of Honor   Members of the Air Force and its predecessor organizations have earned Medals of Honor. The medal is awarded for conspicuous gallantry and intrepidity at the risk of life above and beyond the call of duty. http://www.af.mil/MedalofHonor.aspx

News   The Air Force posts announcements, art, commentaries, news items, and photos on its Web site. Air Force TV and radio news are also accessible online. http://www.af.mil/News.aspx | Email: DMAPublicAffairs@mail.mil

"Air Force Magazine" is posted online. Beginning in January 2013, full issues are available. Beginning in November 2015, HTML5 versions are available. http://www.airforcemag.com/MagazineArchive/Pages/default.aspx

Reading List   The Air Force Chief of Staff's annual reading list (2016) is available on the Department's Web site. An archives of the reading list, starting with the year 2007, is also available online. http://static.dma.mil/usaf/csafreadinglist/01_books.html

Sexual Assault   The "Sexual Assault Prevention and Response" (SAPR) Web page has information, policies, and reports on sexual assault, as well as links leading to additional resources within the Department of Defense (DOD) community and to external resources. http://www.af.mil/SAPR.aspx

The "SAPR" Web page also provides access to the Safe Helpline—an anonymous, confidential, and free crisis support service for DOD community members who have been affected by sexual assault. Phone, 877-995-5247. https://www.safehelpline.org/about-dod-safe-helpline

Social Media   The Air Force has a blog and maintains a social media presence on Facebook, Flickr, Instagram, Twitter, and YouTube. The Web site provides shortcuts to the different platforms as well as social media resources. http://www.af.mil/AFSites/SocialMediaSites.aspx

Strategic Documents   The site contains various "CSAF Focus Area", and other strategic documents in Portable Document Format (PDF). http://www.af.mil/Airpower4America.aspx

Suicide Prevention   The "Suicide Prevention" Web page promotes resources like the ACE (Ask, Care, and Escort) Card and provides access, by phone or confidential online chat, to the Military Crisis Line. Phone, 800-273-8255. http://www.af.mil/SuicidePrevention.aspx

Web sites   A directory of all registered Air Force Web sites is available online. http://www.af.mil/ContactUs.aspx

For further information concerning the Department of the Air Force, contact the Office of the Director of Public Affairs, Department of the Air Force, 1690 Air Force Pentagon, Washington, DC 20330-1670. Phone, 703-697-6061.

Editorial Note
The Department of the Army did not meet the publication deadline for submitting updated information of its activities, functions, and sources of information as required by the automatic disclosure provisions of the Freedom of Information Act (5 U.S.C. 552(a)(1)(A))

Department of the Army
The Pentagon, Washington, DC 20310
Phone, 703-695-6518. Internet, http://www.army.mil

Executive Office

Secretary of the Army	ROBERT SPEER, ACTING
Under Secretary of the Army	KARL F. SCHNEIDER, ACTING
Administrative Assistant to the Secretary of the Army	GERALD B. O'KEEFF
Auditor General	ANNE L. RICHARDS
Deputy Under Secretary of the Army	THOMAS E. HAWLEY
Director, Small Business Programs	TOMMY L. MARKS
Executive Director, Army National Military Cemeteries	PATRICK K. HALLINAN
General Counsel	(VACANCY)
Inspector General	LT. GEN. DAVID E. QUANTOCK
Assistant Secretary of the Army, Acquisition, Logistics and Technology	STEFFANIE EASTER
Assistant Secretary of the Army, Civil Works	JO-ELLEN DARCY
Assistant Secretary of the Army, Financial Management / Comptroller	ROBERT M. SPEER
Assistant Secretary of the Army, Installations, Energy and Environment	KATHERINE G. HAMMACK
Assistant Secretary of the Army, Manpower and Reserve Affairs	DEBRA S. WADA
Chief Information Officer (G–6)	MAJ. GEN. BRUCE T. CRAWFORD
Chief of Legislative Liaison	MAJ. GEN. LAURA E. RICHARDSON
Chief of Public Affairs	BRIG. GEN. OMAR J. JONES IV

Office of the Chief Of Staff

Chief of Staff of the Army	GEN. MARK A. MILLEY
Vice Chief of Staff of the Army	GEN. DANIEL B. ALLYN
Director of the Army Staff	LT. GEN. GARY H. CHEEK
Vice Director of the Army Staff	STEVEN J. REDMANN

Army Staff

Sergeant Major of the Army	SMA Daniel A. Dailey
Chief of the National Guard Bureau	Gen. Joseph Lengyel
Assistant Chief of Staff, Installation Management	Lt. Gen. Gwen Bingham
Chief of Army Reserve	Lt. Gen. Charles D. Luckey
Chief of Chaplains	Maj. Gen. Paul K. Hurley
Chief of Engineers	Lt. Gen. Todd T. Semonite
Director, Army National Guard	Lt. Gen. Timothy J. Kadavy
Judge Advocate General	Lt. Gen. Flora D. Darpino
Provost Marshal General	Maj. Gen. Mark S. Inch
Surgeon General	Lt. Gen. Nadja Y. West
Deputy Chiefs of Staff	
Financial Management (G–8)	Lt. Gen. John M. Murray
Intelligence (G–2)	Lt. Gen. Robert P. Ashley, Jr.
Logistics (G–4)	Lt. Gen. Gustave F. Perna
Operations (G–3/5/7)	Lt. Gen. Joseph Anderson
Personnel (G–1)	Lt. Gen. James C. McConville

Commands

Commanding Generals	
U.S. Army Forces Command	Gen. Robert B. Abrams
U.S. Army Materiel Command	Gen. Gustave F. Perna
U.S. Army Training and Doctrine Command	Gen. David G. Perkins

Army Service Component Commands

Commanding Generals	
U.S. Army Africa / Southern European Task Force	Maj. Gen. Joseph P. Harrington
U.S. Army Central	Lt. Gen. Michael X. Garrett
U.S. Army Europe	Lt. Gen. Ben Hodges
U.S. Army North	Lt. Gen. Jeffrey S. Buchanan
U.S. Army Pacific	Gen. Robert B. Brown
U.S. Army South	Maj. Gen. Clarence K.K. Chinn
U.S. Army Military Surface Deployment and Distribution Command	Maj. Gen. Susan A. Davidson
U.S. Army Space and Missile Defense Command/Army Strategic Command	Lt. Gen. David L. Mann
U.S. Army Special Operations Command	Lt. Gen. Kenneth E. Tovo

Direct Reporting Units

Commandant, U.S. Army War College	Maj. Gen. William E. Rapp
Commander, Second Army	Lt. Gen. Edward C. Cardon
Commander, U.S. Army Accessions Support Brigade	Col. Janet R. Holliday
Director, U.S. Army Acquisition Support Center	Craig A. Spisak
Executive Director, Arlington National Cemetery	Patrick K. Hallinan
Superintendent, U.S. Military Academy	Lt. Gen. Robert L. Caslen, Jr.
Commanding Generals	
U.S. Army Corps of Engineers	Lt. Gen. Todd T. Semonite
U.S. Army Criminal Investigation Command	Maj. Gen. Mark S. Inch
U.S. Army Installation Management Command	Lt. Gen. Kenneth R. Dahl
U.S. Army Intelligence and Security Command	Maj. Gen. Christopher S. Ballard
U.S. Army Medical Command	Lt. Gen. Nadja Y. West
U.S. Army Military District of Washington	Maj. Gen. Bradley A. Becker
U.S. Army Reserve Command	Lt. Gen. Charles D. Luckey
U.S. Army Test and Evaluation Command	Maj. Gen. Daniel L. Karbler

DEPARTMENT OF THE ARMY

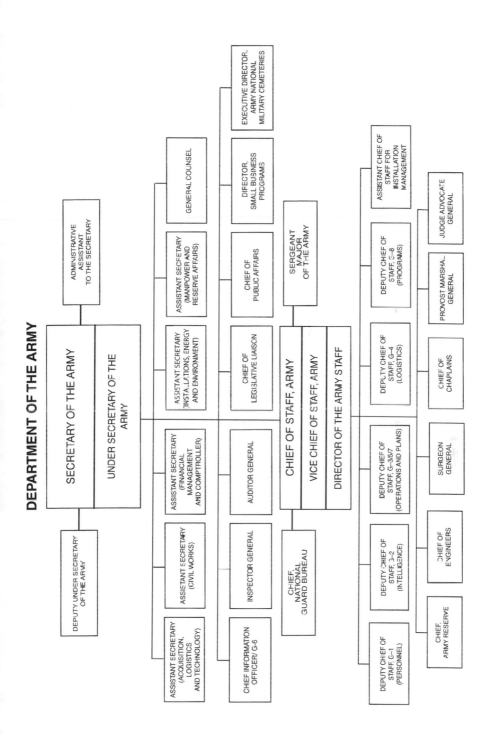

The Department of the Army equips, organizes, and trains active duty and reserve forces to maintain peace and security and to defend the Nation; administers programs to mitigate erosion and flooding, to develop water resources, to improve waterway navigation, and to protect the environment; and provides military and natural disaster relief assistance to Federal, State, and local government agencies.

The Continental Congress established the American Continental Army, now called the United States Army, on June 14, 1775, more than a year before the Declaration of Independence. The Department of War was established as an executive department at the seat of Government by act approved August 7, 1789 (1 Stat. 49). The Secretary of War was established as its head. The National Security Act of 1947 (50 U.S.C. 401) created the National Military Establishment, and the Department of War was designated the Department of the Army. The title of its Secretary became Secretary of the Army (5 U.S.C. 171). The National Security Act Amendments of 1949 (63 Stat. 578) provided that the Department of the Army be a military department within the Department of Defense.

Secretary

The Secretary of the Army is the senior official of the Department of the Army. Subject to the direction, authority, and control of the President as Commander in Chief and of the Secretary of Defense, the Secretary of the Army is responsible for and has the authority to conduct all affairs of the Department of the Army, including its organization, administration, operation, efficiency, and such other activities as may be prescribed by the President or the Secretary of Defense as authorized by law. https://www.army.mil/leaders/sa

For further information, call 703-695-2422.

Army Staff

The Army Staff is the Secretary of the Army's military staff. It makes preparations for deploying the Army, including recruiting, organizing, supplying, equipping, training, mobilizing, and demobilizing it, to support the Secretary or the Chief of Staff in his or her executive capacity; investigates and reports on the efficiency of the Army and its

preparation for military operations; acts as the agent of the Secretary of the Army and the Chief of Staff in coordinating the action of all organizations of the Department of the Army; and performs other nonstatutory duties that the Secretary of the Army may prescribe.

Program Areas

Civil Functions   Civil functions of the Department of the Army include the administration of Arlington and the U.S. Soldiers' and Airmen's Home National Cemeteries and the Civil Works Program—the Nation's principal Federal water resources development activity involving dams, reservoirs, levees, harbors, waterways, locks, and other engineering structures. http://www.army.mil/asacw

History   This area includes advisory and coordination service provided to the Army Secretariat and staff on all historical matters: the formulation and execution of the Army historical program, the maintenance of the organizational history of Army units, the preparation and publication of histories that the Army requires, and historical properties. http://www.history.army.mil | Email: usarmy. mcnair.cmh.mbx.answers@mail.mil

Installations   This area consists of policies, procedures, and resources for the management of installations to ensure the availability of efficient and affordable base services and infrastructure in support of military missions. It includes the identification and validation of resource requirements, the review of facilities requirements and stationing, and program and budget development and justification. Other activities include support for base operations; base realignment and closure; competitive sourcing; energy security and sustainability; environmental programs; housing; military construction; morale, recreation, and welfare; and real property maintenance and repair. https://www.army. mil/info/organization/unitsandcommands/ commandstructure/imcom

Intelligence This area includes management of Army intelligence with responsibility for policy formulation, planning, programming, budgeting, evaluation, and oversight of intelligence activities. The Army Staff is responsible for monitoring relevant foreign intelligence developments and foreign disclosure; imagery, signals, human, open-source, measurement, and signatures intelligence; counterintelligence; threat models and simulations; and security countermeasures. https://www.army.mil/inscom/?from=org

Medical This area includes management of health services for the Army and as directed for other services, agencies, and organizations; health standards for Army personnel; health professional education and training; career management authority over commissioned and warrant officer personnel of the Army Medical Department; medical research, materiel development, testing, and evaluation; policies concerning health aspects of Army environmental programs and prevention of disease; and planning, programming, and budgeting for Armywide health services. https://www.army.mil/armymedicine/?from=org

Military Operations and Plans This includes Army forces strategy formation; mid-range, long-range, and regional strategy application; arms control, negotiation, and disarmament; national security affairs; joint service matters; net assessment; politico-military affairs; force mobilization, demobilization, and planning; programming structuring, development, analysis, requirements, and management; operational readiness; overall roles and missions; collective security; individual and unit training; psychological operations; information operations; unconventional warfare; counterterrorism; operations security; signal security; special plans; equipment development and approval; nuclear and chemical matters; civil affairs; military support of civil defense; civil disturbance; domestic actions; command and control; automation and communications programs and activities; management of the program for law enforcement, correction, and crime prevention for military members of the Army; special operations forces; foreign language and distance learning; and physical security.

Reserve Components This area includes management of individual and unit readiness and mobilization for Reserve Components, which consist of the Army National Guard and U.S. Army Reserve. https://www.army.mil/reserve/?from=org

Religious This area includes departmentwide management of religious and moral leadership and chaplain support activities; religious ministrations, religious education, pastoral care, and counseling for Army military personnel; liaison with ecclesiastical agencies; chapel construction requirements and design approval; and career management of clergymen serving in the Chaplains Corps. http://www.army.mil/chaplaincorps

Army Commands

U.S. Army Forces Command Headquartered at Fort Bragg, NC, U.S. Army Forces Command (FORSCOM) prepares conventional forces to provide a sustained flow of trained and ready land power to combatant commanders in defense of the Nation at home and abroad. https://www.army.mil/info/organization/unitsandcommands/commandstructure/forscom/?from=org

For further information, contact the FORSCOM Public Affairs Office. Phone, 910-570-7200.

U.S. Army Materiel Command U.S. Army Materiel Command (AMC) is the Army's premier provider of materiel readiness—technology, acquisition support, materiel development, logistics power projection, and sustainment—to the total force across the spectrum of joint military operations. Headquartered at Redstone Arsenal, Alabama, AMC's missions include the development of weapon systems, advanced research on future technologies, and maintenance and distribution of spare parts and equipment. AMC works closely with program executive offices, industry, academia, and other Military Services and Government agencies to develop, test, and acquire equipment that soldiers and units need to accomplish their missions. https://www.army.mil/info/organization/unitsandcommands/commandstructure/amc/?from=org

For further information, contact the AMC Public Affairs Office. Phone, 256-450-7978.

U.S. Army Training and Doctrine Command

Headquartered in Fort Eustis, VA, U.S. Army Training and Doctrine Command (TRADOC) develops, educates, and trains soldiers, civilians, and leaders; supports unit training; and designs, builds, and integrates a versatile mix of capabilities, formations, and equipment to strengthen the U.S. Army as a force of decisive action. https://www.army.mil/tradoc/?from=org

For further information, contact the TRADOC Public Affairs Office. Phone, 757-501-5876.

Army Service Component Commands

U.S. Army Africa / Southern European Task Force

U.S. Army Africa (USARAF) / Southern European Task Force (SETAF) is the Army service component command for U.S. Africa Command. It supports U.S. Africa Command operations, employs Army forces as partners, builds sustainable capacity, and supports the joint force to disrupt transnational threats and promote regional security in Africa. http://www.usaraf.army.mil

For further information, contact the USARAF / SETAF Public Affairs Office. Phone, 011-39-0444-71-8341 or 8342.

U.S. Army Central

U.S. Army Central (ARCENT) shapes the U.S. Central Command area of responsibility in 20 countries through forward land power presence and security cooperation engagements that ensure access, build partner capacity, and develop relationships. ARCENT also provides flexible options and strategic depth to the U.S. combatant commander and sets the conditions for improved regional security and stability. http://www.arcent.army.mil | Email: usarmy.shaw.usarcent.mbx.public-affairs@mail.mil

For further information, contact the USARCENT Public Affairs Office. Phone, 803-885-8266.

U.S. Army Europe

U.S. Army Europe (USAREUR) provides the principal land component for U.S. European Command throughout a 51-country area. As the U.S. Army's largest forward-deployed expeditionary force, USAREUR supports NATO and U.S. bilateral, multinational, and unilateral objectives. It supports U.S. Army forces in the European Command area; receives and assists in the reception, staging, and onward movement and integration of U.S. forces; establishes, operates, and expands operational lines of communication; ensures regional security, access, and stability through presence and security cooperation; and supports U.S. combatant commanders and joint and combined commanders. http://www.eur.army.mil

For further information, contact the USAREUR Public Affairs Office. Phone, 011-49-611-143-537-0005 or 0006.

U.S. Army North

U.S. Army North (USARNORTH) supports U.S. Northern Command, the unified command responsible for defending the U.S. homeland and coordinating defense support of civil authorities. USARNORTH helps maintain readiness to support homeland defense, civil support operations, and theater security cooperation activities. http://www.arnorth.army.mil | Email: usarmy.jbsa.arnorth.list.pao-owner@mail.mil

For further information, contact the USARNORTH Public Affairs Office. Phone, 210-221-0015.

U.S. Army South

U.S. Army South (ARSOUTH) is the Army service component command of U.S. Southern Command. ARSOUTH conducts security cooperation and responds to contingencies as part of a whole-of-government approach in conjunction with partner national armies in the U.S. Southern Command area of responsibility, which encompasses 31 countries and 15 areas of special sovereignty in Central and South America and the Caribbean. These activities counter transnational threats and strengthen regional security in defense of the homeland. ARSOUTH maintains a deployable headquarters at Fort Sam Houston, Texas, where it conducts strategic and operational planning. http://www.arsouth.army.mil | Email: usarmy.jbsa.arsouth.mbx.pao@mail.mil

For further information, contact the ARSOUTH Public Affairs Office. Phone, 210-295-6739.

U.S. Army Pacific

U.S. Army Pacific (USARPAC) prepares the force for unified

land operations, responds to threats, sustains and protects the force, and builds military relationships that develop partner defense capacity to contribute to the stability and security of the U.S. Pacific Command area of responsibility. USARPAC commands soldiers in an area spanning from the Northwest Coast and Alaska to the Asia-Pacific region, including Japan. Since September 11, 2001, USARPAC soldiers have played a vital role in homeland defense for Alaska and Hawaii, Guam, and Japan, as well as in supporting operations with our allies elsewhere in the region. https://www.army. mil/info/organization/unitsandcommands/ commandstructure/usarpac/?from=org

For further information, contact USARPAC Public Affairs. Phone, 808-438-9761.

U.S. Army Military Surface Deployment and Distribution Command
U.S. Army Military Surface Deployment and Distribution Command (SDDC) delivers world-class, origin-to-destination distribution. It is the Army service component command of the U.S. Transportation Command and a subordinate command to the Army Materiel Command. This relationship links the Transportation Command's joint deployment and distribution enterprise with the Army Materiel Command's materiel enterprise. The SDDC also partners with the commercial transportation industry as the coordinating link between Department of Defense surface transportation requirements and the capability industry provides. http://www. sddc.army.mil

For further information, contact the SDDC Public Affairs Office. Phone, 618-220-6284.

U.S. Army Space and Missile Defense Command / Army Strategic Command
U.S. Army Space and Missile Defense Command (SMDC / ARSTRAT) conducts space and missile defense operations and provides planning, integration, control, and coordination of Army forces and capabilities in support of U.S. Strategic Command missions. SMDC / ARSTRAT also supports space, high-altitude, and global missile defense modernization efforts; serves as the Army operational integrator for global missile defense; and conducts mission-related research

and development to support the Army's statutory responsibilities. http://www.army. mil/info/organization/unitsandcommands/ commandstructure/smdc

For further information, contact the SMDC Public Affairs Office. Phone, 256-955-3887.

U.S. Army Special Operations Command
U.S. Army Special Operations Command (USASOC) administers, deploys, educates, equips, funds, mans, mobilizes, organizes, sustains, and trains Army special operations forces to carry out missions worldwide, as directed. These special and diverse military operations support regional combatant commanders, American ambassadors, and other agencies. https:// www.army.mil/usasoc/?from=org; http:// www.soc.mil | Email: pao@soc.mil

For further information, contact the USASOC Public Affairs Office. Phone, 910-432-6005.

Sources of Information

Business Opportunities For information on contract procurement policies and procedures, contact the Deputy Assistant Secretary of the Army, Procurement. Phone, 703-695-2488. http://www.micc.army.mil/ contracting-offices.asp

Assistance for small businesses and minority educational institutions to increase participation in the Army contracting program is available through the Office of Small Business Programs. Phone, 703-697-2868. Fax, 703-693-3898. http://www.micc.army.mil/small-business. asp

Cemeteries Arlington National Cemetery is one of the two national military cemeteries that the Army maintains. This cemetery is the final resting place for more than 400,000 active duty servicemembers, veterans, and their families. For more information, visit its Web site or contact the cemetery. Phone, 877-907-8585. http://www. arlingtoncemetery.mil

The U.S. Soldiers' and Airmen's Home National Cemetery is one of the two national military cemeteries that the Army maintains. This cemetery is the final resting place for more than 14,000 veterans, including those that fought in the Civil War.

For more information, visit its Web site or contact the Superintendent. Phone, 877-907-8585. http://www.nps.gov/nr/travel/national_cemeteries/district_of_columbia/us_soldiers_and_airmens_home_national_cemetery.html

Environment   Information is available from the U.S. Army Environmental Command. https://aec.army.mil

Information is also available from the Office of the Deputy Assistant Secretary of the Army for Environment, Safety and Occupational Health. http://www.asaie.army.mil/Public/ESOH

The Army Environmental Policy Institute posts publications on its Web site. "Army Water Security Strategy" (DEC 2011), the results of the first comprehensive study of Army water security management, is available in Portable Document Format (PDF). "Quantifying the Army Supply Chain Water Bootprint" (DEC 2011), an initial step to quantify the amount of water used by suppliers to produce the goods and services that the Army procures through the supply chain, is also available in PDF. http://www.aepi.army.mil

Employment   More than 330,000 Army civilians work in a wide range of diverse professions. These professionals are not active duty military, but serve as an integral part of the Army team to support the defense of the Nation. http://armycivilianservice.com

Films   Address loan requests for Army-produced films to the Visual Information Support Centers of Army installations. Unclassified Army productions are available for sale from the National Audiovisual Center, National Technical Information Service, 5301 Shawnee Road, Alexandria, VA 22312. Phone, 800-553-6847. http://www.ntis.gov/Index.aspx | Email: orders@ntis.gov

Freedom of Information Act (FOIA)   Contact the appropriate information management officer associated with the Army installation or activity managing the desired information. Information is also available on the Records Management and Declassification Agency's Web site. https://www.rmda.army.mil

Frequently Asked Questions (FAQs)   The Army posts answers to FAQs on its Web site. https://www.army.mil/faq

Gold Star Survivors   All Gold Star family members have made a sacrifice to the Nation. The Army recognizes that no one gives more for the Nation than a family member of the fallen. Gold Star Mother's and Family's Day is the last Sunday of September, and Gold Star Spouses Day is April 5. https://www.army.mil/goldstar

History   "Army History" magazine, the professional bulletin of Army history, is available online in Portable Document Format (PDF). http://www.history.army.mil/news/2016/160900a_armyHistoryMag.html

A directory of Army museums is available on the Center of Military History's Web site. http://www.history.army.mil/museums/directory.html

The Office of Historic Properties and Partnerships raises awareness of and explores and tests creative uses for the Army's historic buildings. Its staff also promotes partnerships between the Army and nonprofit organizations, public or private, to preserve, renovate, and restore. http://www.asaie.army.mil/Public/IH/OHP/ohp.htm

Joining the Army   Information on Army life, assignments, benefits, pay, and enlisting or joining in other capacities is available online. Phone, 888-550-2769. http://www.goarmy.com

National Guard   The National Guard responds to domestic emergencies, counterdrug efforts, overseas combat missions, reconstruction missions, and more. The President or a State governor can call on the Guard in a moment's notice. Guard soldiers hold civilian jobs or attend college while maintaining their military training on a part-time basis, and their primary area of operation is their home state. https://www.nationalguard.com

Public Affairs / Community Relations   For official Army and community relations information, contact the Office of the Chief of Public Affairs. Phone, 703-695-0616. Automated assistance is available after normal work hours. Phone, 201-590-6575. http://www.army.mil/info/institution/publicAffairs

Publications   To request a publication, contact either the proponent listed on the title page of the document or the information management officer of the Army activity that publishes the desired publication. If the requester does not know which Army activity published the document, contact the Publishing Division, Army Publishing Directorate. Phone, 703-693-1557. http://www.army.mil/media/publications

Official texts published by Headquarters, Department of the Army, are available from the National Technical Information Service. Phone, 888-584-8332. http://www.ntis.gov

Ranks   Descriptions of officer, warrant officer, and enlisted ranks are available on the Army Web site. https://www.army.mil/symbols/armyranks.html

Reading List   The U.S. Army Chief of Staff's professional reading list comprises three categories—Armies at war: battles and campaigns; the Army profession; and strategy and the strategic environment—and is accessible online. http://www.history.army.mil/html/books/105/105-1-1/index.html

Research   The Research, Development and Engineering Command is the Army's technology leader and largest technology developer. Its Web site features news on and resources related to long-range research and development plans for materiel requirements and objectives. Phone, 443-395-4006 (Public Affairs) or 3922 (Media Relations). http://www.army.mil/info/organization/unitsandcommands/commandstructure/rdecom

Reserve Officers' Training Corps (ROTC)   Available at over 1,100 colleges and universities nationwide, the ROTC offers merit-based scholarships that can cover the full cost of tuition and open educational opportunities. http://www.goarmy.com/rotc.html

Site Index   The Army's Web site features an A–Z index. https://www.army.mil/info/a z

Specialized Careers   Information on how to become an Army chaplain, the chaplain candidate program, and chaplain corps careers and jobs is available online and from the U.S. Army Recruiting Command. Phone, 877-437-6572. http://www.goarmy.com/chaplain

Health care professionals serving as officers in the Army's medical department benefit from a wide range of opportunities and financial incentives. http://www.goarmy.com/amedd.html

Members of the Army Judge Advocate General's corps often represent soldiers during courts-martial; however, they also engage in a wider range of legal activities that include civil litigation, international law, labor law, and tort claims. For more information, contact the Army Judge Advocate Recruiting Office. Phone, 866-276-9524. http://www.goarmy.com/jag

The Army relies on talented musicians to assist with military ceremonies, boost morale, and provide entertainment. http://www.goarmy.com/band.html

Speakers   The Public Affairs Office nearest the event can help provide local Army speakers. The Office of the Chief of Public Affairs can assist with scheduling a general officer to address Army matters at public forums. To request a general officer speaker, writer to the Office of the Chief of Public Affairs, ATTN: Community Relations, Division (Speaker Request), 1500 Army Pentagon, Washington, DC 20310-1500. A lead time of at least 60–90 days is required. Phone, 703-614-1107. http://www.army.mil/comrel/assetrequests

U. S. Military Academy   West Point has been educating, training, and inspiring U.S. Army leaders for more than 200 years. The academy offers a 47-month leader-development program of academic rigor, military discipline, and physical challenges with adherence to a code of honor. http://www.usma.edu | Email. admissions-Info@usma.edu; http://www.army.mil/info/institution/publicAffairs

For further information concerning the Department of the Army, contact U.S. Army Public Affairs, Community Relations Division, Office of the Chief of Public Affairs, 1500 Army Pentagon, Washington, DC 20310-1500.

Department of the Navy

The Pentagon, Washington, DC 20350
Phone, 703-697-7391. Internet, http://www.navy.mil

Secretary of the Navy	SEAN J. STACKLEY, ACTING
Under Secretary of the Navy	THOMAS P. DEE, ACTING
Assistant Secretaries	
Energy, Installations and Environment	STEVEN R. ISELIN, ACTING
Financial Management / Comptroller	JOSEPH B. MARSHALL JR., ACTING
Manpower and Reserve Affairs	ROBERT L. WOODS, ACTING
Research, Development and Acquisition	ALLISON F. STILLER
Auditor General	DONJETTE L. GILMORE, ACTING
Chief Information Officer	ROBERT FOSTER
Chief of Information	REAR ADM. DAWN CUTLER, ACTING
Chief of Legislative Affairs	REAR ADM. CRAIG S. FALLER
Chief of Naval Research	REAR ADM. DAVID J. HAHN
Director, Naval Criminal Investigative Service	ANDREW L. TRAVER
General Counsel	ANNE M. BRENNAN, ACTING
Judge Advocate General	VICE ADM. JAMES W. CRAWFORD III
Naval Inspector General	VICE ADM. HERMAN SHELANSKI
Deputy Under Secretary of the Navy (Management)	SCOTT W. LUTTERLOH
Director, Sexual Assault Prevention and Response Office	JILL VINES LOFTUS
Chief of Naval Operations	ADMIRAL JOHN M. RICHARDSON
Vice Chief of Naval Operations	ADMIRAL BILL MORAN
Master Chief Petty Officer of the Navy	STEVEN S. GIORDANO

Naval Operations

Chief of Naval Operations	ADM. JOHN M. RICHARDSON
Vice Chief of Naval Operations	ADM. WILLIAM F. MORAN
Deputy Chiefs of Naval Operations	
Fleet Readiness and Logistics	VICE ADM. DIXON SMITH
Information Dominance	VICE ADM. JAN TIGHE
Integration of Capabilities and Resources	VICE ADM. WILLIAM LESCHER
Manpower, Personnel, Training Education	VICE ADM. ROBERT P. BURKE
Operations, Plans and Strategy	VICE ADM. JOHN C. AQUILINO
Directors	
Naval Intelligence	VICE ADM. JAN TIGHE
Naval Nuclear Propulsion Program	ADM. JAMES F. CALDWELL
Navy Staff	VICE ADM. JAMES G. FOGGO
Test and Evaluation and Technology Requirements / Chief of Naval Research	REAR ADM. DAVID J. HAHN
Chief of Chaplains of the Navy	REAR ADM. MARGARET G. KIBBEN
Chief of Naval Reserve	VICE ADM. LUKE MCCOLLUM
Master Chief Petty Officer of the Navy	STEVEN GIORDANO
Oceanographer of the Navy / Navigator of the Navy	REAR ADM. TIMOTHY C. GALLAUDET
Surgeon General of the Navy	VICE ADM. C. FORREST FAISON III

Shore Establishment

Chief of Naval Operations	ADM. JOHN M. RICHARDSON
Commanders	
Naval Air Systems Command	VICE ADM. PAUL GROSKLAGS

Naval Education and Training Command	REAR ADM. MICHAEL S. WHITE
Naval Facilities Engineering Command	REAR ADM. KATE L. GREGORY
Naval Legal Service Command	REAR ADM. JOHN G. HANNINK
Naval Meteorology and Oceanography	REAR ADM. TIMOTHY C. GALLUDET
Naval Network Warfare Command	CAPT. JOHN W. CHANDLER
Naval Sea Systems Command	VICE ADM. THOMAS MOORE
Naval Supply Systems Command	REAR ADM. JONATHAN A. YUEN
Naval Warfare Development Command	REAR ADM. BRET C. BATCHELDER
Navy Installations Command	VICE ADM. DIXON SMITH
Space and Naval Warfare Systems Command	REAR ADM. DAVID H. LEWIS
Chief, Bureau of Medicine and Surgery	VICE ADM. C. FORREST FAISON III
Chief, Naval Personnel	VICE ADM. ROBERT P. BURKE
Director, National Maritime Intelligence-Integration Office / Commander, Office of Naval Intelligence	REAR ADM. ELIZABETH L. TRAIN
Director, Strategic Systems Program	REAR ADM. TERRY J. BENEDICT
Superintendent, U.S. Naval Academy	VICE ADM. WALTER E. CARTER, JR.

Operating Forces

Commanders

U.S. Fleet Forces Command	ADM. PHILIP S. DAVIDSON
Pacific Fleet	ADM. SCOTT H. SWIFT
Military Sealift Command	REAR ADM. DEE L. MEWBOURNE
Naval Forces Central Command	VICE ADM. KEVIN M. DONEGAN
Naval Forces Europe	ADM. MICHELLE J. HOWARD
Naval Reserve Forces Command	REAR ADM. THOMAS W. LUSCHER
Naval Special Warfare Command	REAR ADM. TIMOTHY SZYMANSKI
Operational Test and Evaluation Force	REAR ADM. JEFFREY R. PENFIELD

[For the Department of the Navy statement of organization, see the Code of Federal Regulations, Title 32, Part 700]

The Department of the Navy protects the United States and its interests by the prosecution of war at sea, including the seizure or defense of advanced naval bases with the assistance of its Marine Corps component; supports the forces of all military departments of the United States; and safeguards freedom of the seas.

The United States Navy was founded on October 13, 1775, when Congress enacted the first legislation creating the Continental Navy of the American Revolution. The Department of the Navy and the Office of Secretary of the Navy were established by act of April 30, 1798 (10 U.S.C. 5011, 5031). For 9 years prior to that date, by act of August 7, 1789 (1 Stat. 49), the Secretary of War oversaw the conduct of naval affairs.

The National Security Act Amendments of 1949 provided that the Department of the Navy be a military department within the Department of Defense (63 Stat. 578).

The President appoints the Secretary of the Navy as the head of the Department of the Navy. The Secretary is responsible to the Secretary of Defense for the operation and efficiency of the Navy (10 U.S.C. 5031).

The Department of the Navy includes the U.S. Coast Guard when it is operating as a Service in the Navy.

Secretary The Secretary of the Navy is the head of the Department of the Navy, responsible for the policies and control of the Department of the Navy, including its organization, administration, functioning, and efficiency. The members of the Secretary's executive administration assist in the discharge of the responsibilities of the Secretary of the Navy. http://www.navy.mil/secnav

Legal The Office of the Judge Advocate General provides all legal advice and related services throughout the Department of the Navy, except for the advice and services provided by the General Counsel. It also provides legal and policy advice

DEPARTMENT OF THE NAVY

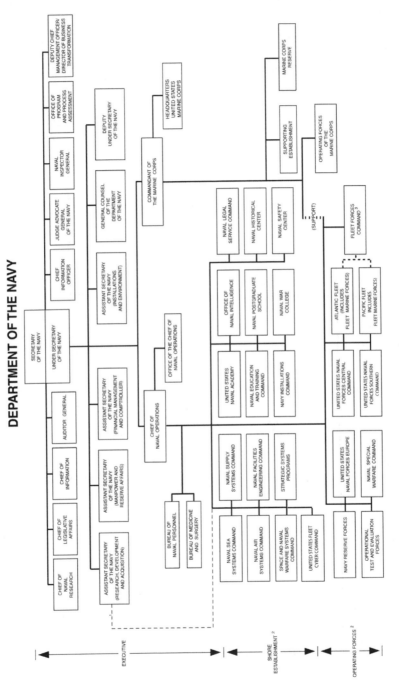

[1] Systems commands and SSP report to ASN (RDA) for acquisition matters only.

[2] Also includes other Echelon 2 commands and subordinate activities under the command or supervision of the designated organizations.

[3] For Interdeployment Training Cycle purposes, Commander, Fleet Forms Command Controls LANFLT and PACFLT assets.

to the Secretary of the Navy on military justice, ethics, administrative law, claims, environmental law, operational and international law and treaty interpretation, and litigation involving these issues. The Judge Advocate General provides technical supervision for the Naval Justice School at Newport, RI. http://www.navy.mil/local/jag/index.asp

For further information, contact the Office of the Judge Advocate General, Department of the Navy, Washington Navy Yard, Suite 3000, 1322 Patterson Avenue SE., Washington Navy Yard, DC 20374-5066. Phone, 202-685-5190.

Criminal Investigations   The Naval Criminal Investigative Service investigates and neutralizes criminal, terrorist, and foreign intelligence threats to the United States Navy and Marine Corps. To carry out its mission, the Service relies on the professionalism and law enforcement expertise of administrative support personnel, forensic specialists, intelligence analysts, investigators, military personnel, security specialists, special agents, and technical investigative specialists. http://www.ncis.navy.mil

For further information, contact the Naval Criminal Investigative Service, 27130 Telegraph Road, Quantico, VA 22134. Phone, 877-579-3648.

Research   The Office of Naval Research initiates, coordinates, plans, and promotes naval research, including the coordination of research and development conducted by other agencies and offices in the Department of the Navy. The Office researches, develops, and delivers decisive naval capabilities by investing in a balanced portfolio of promising scientific research, innovative technology, and talent. It also manages and controls activities within the Department concerning copyrights, inventions, manufacturing technology, patents, royalty payments, small businesses, and trademarks. http://www.onr.navy.mil; | Email: onrpublicaffairs@navy.mil

For further information, contact the Public Affairs Office, Office of Naval Research, One Liberty Center, 875 North Randolph Street, Arlington, VA 22203-1995. Phone, 703-696-5031.

Operating Forces   Operating forces carry out operations that enable the Navy to meet

its responsibility to uphold and advance the national policies and interests of the United States. These forces include the several fleets; seagoing, fleet marine, and other assigned Marine Corps forces; the Military Sealift Command; Naval Reserve forces; and other forces and activities that the President or the Secretary of the Navy may assign. The Chief of Naval Operations administers and commands the operating forces of the Navy.

The Atlantic Fleet is composed of ships, submarines, and aircraft that operate throughout the Atlantic Ocean and Mediterranean Sea.

The Naval Forces Europe includes forces assigned by the Chief of Naval Operations or made available from either the Pacific or Atlantic Fleet to operate in the European theater.

The Pacific Fleet is composed of ships, submarines, and aircraft operating throughout the Pacific and Indian Oceans.

The Military Sealift Command provides ocean transportation for personnel and cargo of all components of the Department of Defense and, as authorized, for other Federal agencies; operates and maintains underway replenishment ships and other vessels providing mobile logistic support to elements of the combatant fleets; and operates ships in support of scientific projects and other programs for Federal agencies.

Other major commands of the operating forces of the Navy are the Naval Forces Central Command, Operational Test and Evaluation Force, Naval Special Warfare Command, and Naval Reserve Force. http://www.navy.mil/navydata/organization/orgoptor.asp

Activities
Air Systems   The Naval Air Systems Command provides full life-cycle support of naval aviation aircraft, weapons, and systems operated by Sailors and Marines. This support includes research, design, development, and systems engineering; acquisition; test and evaluation; training facilities and equipment; repair and modification; and in-service engineering and logistics support. The Command comprises eight "competencies" or communities

of practice: program management, contracts, research and engineering, test and evaluation, logistics and industrial operations, corporate operations, comptroller, and counsel. The Command also supports the affiliated naval aviation program executive officer and the assigned program managers, who are responsible for meeting the cost, schedule, and performance requirements of their assigned programs. It is the principal provider for the Naval Aviation Enterprise, while contributing to every warfare enterprise in the interest of national security. http://www.navair.navy.mil

For further information, contact the Commander, Naval Air Systems Command, 47123 Buse Road, Building 2272, Suite 540, Patuxent River, MD 20670-1547. Phone, 301-757-7825.

Coast Guard   The Commandant of the Coast Guard reports to the Secretary of the Navy and the Chief of Naval Operations when the Coast Guard is operating as a service in the Navy and represents the Coast Guard before the Joint Chiefs of Staff. During such service, Coast Guard operations are integrated and uniform with Department of the Navy operations to the maximum extent possible. The Commandant of the Coast Guard organizes, trains, prepares, and maintains the readiness of the Coast Guard for the performance of national defense missions as directed. The Commandant also maintains a security capability; enforces Federal laws and regulations on and under the high seas and waters subject to the jurisdiction of the United States; and develops, establishes, maintains, and operates aids to maritime navigation, as well as ice-breaking and rescue facilities, with due regard to the requirements of national defense. http://www.uscg.mil

Computers and Telecommunications   Naval Network Warfare Command operates the Navy's networks to achieve effective command and control through optimal alignment, common architecture, mature processes, and functions and standard terminology. The command enhances the Navy's network security posture and improves IT services through standardized enterprise-level management, network information assurance compliance, enterprise management, and root cause

and trend analysis. Naval Network Warfare Command also delivers enhanced space products to operating forces by leveraging Department of Defense, national, commercial, and international space capabilities. The command serves as the Navy's commercial satellite operations manager; it executes tactical-level command and control of Navy networks and leverages Joint Space capabilities for Navy and Joint Operations. http://www.public.navy.mil/fcc-c10f/nnwc/Pages/default.aspx

For further information, contact Public Affairs, Naval Network Warfare Command, 112 Lake View Parkway, Suffolk, VA 23435. Phone, 757-203-0205.

Education and Training   The Naval Education and Training Command provides shore-based education and training for Navy, certain Marine Corps, and other personnel; develops specifically designated education and training afloat programs for the fleet; provides voluntary and dependents education; and participates with research and development activities in the development and implementation of the most effective teaching and training systems and devices for optimal education and training. http://www.navy.mil/local/cnet/ | Email: pnsc.netc.pao@navy.mil

For further information, contact the NETC Office of Public Affairs, 250 Dallas Street, Pensacola, FL 32508-5220. Phone, 850-452-4858.

Facilities   The Naval Facilities Engineering Command provides material and technical support to the Navy and Marine Corps for shore facilities, real property and utilities, fixed ocean systems and structures, transportation and construction equipment, energy, environmental and natural resources management, and support of the naval construction forces. http://www.navy.mil/local/navfachq

For further information, contact the Commander, Naval Facilities Engineering Command and Chief of Civil Engineers, Washington Navy Yard, 1322 Patterson Avenue SE., Suite 1000, Washington, DC 20374-5065. Phone, 202-685-1423.

Intelligence   The Office of Naval Intelligence ensures the fulfillment of the intelligence requirements and responsibilities of the Department of the Navy. http://www.oni.navy.mil | Email: pao@nmic.navy.mil

For further information, contact the Office of Public Affairs, Office of Naval Intelligence, Department of the Navy, 4251 Suitland Road, Washington, DC 20395-5720. Phone, 301-669-5670.

Manpower The Bureau of Naval Personnel directs the procurement, distribution, administration, and career motivation of the military personnel of the regular and reserve components of the U.S. Navy to meet the quantitative and qualitative manpower requirements determined by the Chief of Naval Operations. http://www.navy.mil/cnp/index.asp

For further information, contact the Bureau of Naval Personnel, Department of the Navy, Federal Office Building 2, Washington, DC 20370-5000. Phone, 703-614-2000.

Medicine The Bureau of Medicine and Surgery directs the medical and dental services for Navy and Marine Corps personnel and their dependents; administers the implementation of contingency support plans and programs to effect medical and dental readiness capability; provides medical and dental services to the fleet, fleet marine force, and shore activities of the Navy; and ensures cooperation with civil authorities in matters of public health disasters and other emergencies. http://www.med.navy.mil

For further information, contact the Bureau of Medicine and Surgery, Department of the Navy, 2300 E Street NW., Washington, DC 20373-5300. Phone, 202-762-3211.

Oceanography The Naval Meteorology and Oceanography Command and the Naval Observatory are responsible for the science, technology, and engineering operations that are essential to explore the ocean and the atmosphere and to provide astronomical data and time for naval and related national objectives. To that end, the naval oceanographic program studies astrometry, hydrography, meteorology, oceanography, and precise time. http://www.usno.navy.mil/USNO

For further information, contact the Commander, Naval Meteorology and Oceanography Command, 1100 Balch Boulevard, Stennis Space Center, MS 39529-5005. Phone, 228-688-4384. Internet, http://www.navmetoccom.navy.mil. Or, contact the Oceanographer of the Navy, U.S. Naval Observatory, 3450 Massachusetts Avenue NW., Washington, DC 20392-1800. Phone, 202-762-1026.

Sea Systems The Naval Sea Systems Command provides material support to the Navy and Marine Corps and to the Departments of Defense and Transportation for ships, submarines, and other sea platforms, shipboard combat systems and components, other surface and undersea warfare and weapons systems, and ordnance expendables not specifically assigned to other system commands. http://www.navsea.navy.mil | Email: nssc_public_affairs@navy.mil

For further information, contact the Office of Public Affairs, Naval Sea Systems Command, 1333 Isaac Hull Avenue SE., Washington Navy Yard, DC 20376-1010. Phone, 202-781-4123.

Space and Naval Warfare The Space and Naval Warfare Systems Command develops, delivers, and sustains advanced cyber capabilities for naval warfighters. It helps provide the hardware and software needed to executive Navy missions. With nearly 10,000 active military and civilian professionals worldwide, the Command is at the forefront of research, engineering, and acquisition relevant for keeping U.S. military forces connected around the globe. http://www.spawar.navy.mil

For further information, contact the Commander, Space and Naval Warfare Systems Command, 4301 Pacific Highway, San Diego, CA 92110-3127. Phone, 619-524-3428.

Strategic Systems The Office of Strategic Systems Programs provides development, production, and material support to the Navy for fleet ballistic missile and strategic weapons systems, security, training of personnel, and the installation and direction of necessary supporting facilities. http://www.ssp.navy.mil

For further information, contact the Director, Strategic Systems Programs, Department of the Navy, Nebraska Avenue Complex, 287 Somers Court NW., Suite 10041, Washington, DC 20393-5446. Phone, 202-764-1608.

Supply Systems The Naval Supply Systems Command provides supply management policies and methods and administers related support service systems for the Navy and Marine Corps. http://www.navy.mil/local/navsup | Email: navsuphqQuestions@navy.mil

For further information, contact the Commander, Naval Supply Systems Command, 5450 Carlisle Pike, P.O. Box 2050, Mechanicsburg, PA 17055-0791. Phone, 717-605-3565.

Warfare Development   The Navy Warfare Development Command plans and coordinates experiments employing emerging operational concepts; represents the Department of the Navy in joint and other service laboratories and facilities and tactical development commands; and publishes and disseminates naval doctrine. http://www.navy.mil/local/nwdc

For further information, contact the Commander, Navy Warfare Development Command, 686 Cushing Road, Sims Hall, Newport, RI 02841. Phone, 401-841-2833.

Sources of Information

Business Opportunities   "Open for Business," a short video that gives an overview of the Navy's buying activities and small business programs, is available online. For more information, contact the Office of Small Business Programs. Phone, 202-685-6485. http://www.secnav. navy.mil/smallbusiness/Pages/video-openforbusiness.aspx | Email: osbp.info@navy.mil

Civilian Employment   The possibilities of a civilian career at the Department of the Navy are many and diverse. They include a full range of occupations: from aircraft mechanic to pipefitter, from electrician to engineer, from zoologist to physician, and more. The Navy offers hundreds of different occupations nationwide and around the world. http://www.secnav.navy.mil/donhr/Pages/Default.aspx | Email: donhrfaq@navy.mil

Environment   For information on Navy and Marine Corps environmental protection and natural resources management programs, contact the Deputy Assistant Secretary–Environment, 1000 Navy Pentagon, Room 4A674, Washington, DC 20350-1000. Phone, 703-614-5493. http://www.secnav.navy.mil/eie/Pages/Environment.aspx

The "U.S. Navy Climate Change Roadmap" (April 2010) is available in Portable Document Format (PDF) online. http://www.navy.mil/navydata/documents/CCR.pdf

The Navy has posted its environmental goals and descriptions of its strategies to achieve them. http://greenfleet.dodlive.mil/environment

Glossary   The origins of Navy terminology section explains nautical terminology that has become a part of everyday English. http://www.navy.mil/navydata/traditions/html/navyterm.html

Joining the Navy   Unparalleled opportunities, challenges, and experiences motivate bright and skilled people to join. America's Navy offers careers and jobs that match many backgrounds and interests. Hundreds of distinct roles in dozens of professional fields are part of what the Navy has to offer. http://www.navy.com/joining.html

Naval Oceanography Portal   The U.S. Naval Meteorology and Oceanography Command provides information from the ocean depths to the distant reaches of space to meet the needs of civilian and the military and scientific communities. http://www.usno.navy.mil

The U.S. Naval Observatory offers a wide range of astronomical data and products, and it serves as the official source of time for the Department of Defense and as the official source of a standard of time for the entire United States. http://www.usno.navy.mil/USNO

"The Sky This Week" is a weekly set of pictures and descriptions of the planets, sky, and stars. http://www.usno.navy.mil/USNO/tours-events/sky-this-week/the-sky-this-week

News   The Navy posts recent headline news stories on its Web site. http://www.navy.mil/listStories.asp?x=2

An online subscription form is available to sign up for updates from the Navy news service. https://service.govdelivery.com/accounts/USNAVYDMA/subscriber/new

"All Hands" magazine is an electronic publication for sailors by sailors. It features articles, imagery, information, and videos that are relevant to sailors and their families. http://www.navy.mil/ah_online

Research Programs   Research programs of the Office of Naval Research cover a broad spectrum of scientific fields. The research is primarily for the needs of the Navy and Marine Corps, but some of these programs conduct research that has relevance for the general public. For information on specific research programs, contact the Office of Naval Research–Public Affairs, One Liberty Center 875 N. Randolph Street, Arlington, VA 22203-1995. Phone, 703-696-5031. http://www.onr.navy.mil

Ships The Navy operates and relies on many types of ships to carry out its mission.

Descriptions of these different ships—aircraft carriers, amphibious assault ships, cruisers, destroyers, littoral combat ships, and submarines—are available online. http://www.navy.mil/navydata/our_ships.asp

Site Index An A–Z information index is available on the Navy's Web site. http://www.navy.mil/navydata/infoIndex.asp?id=A; http://www.navy.mil/submit/contacts.asp

For further information concerning the Navy, contact the Office of Information, Department of the Navy, 1200 Navy Pentagon, Washington, DC 20350-1200. For press inquiries, phone 703-697-7391 or 703-697-5342.

United States Marine Corps

Commandant of the Marine Corps, Headquarters, U.S. Marine Corps, 3000 Pentagon, Washington, DC 20380-1775
Phone, 703-614-2500. Internet, http://www.marines.mil

Commandant of the Marine Corps	GEN. ROBERT B. NELLER
Assistant Commandant of the Marine Corps	GEN. GLENN M. WALTERS
Sergeant Major of the Marine Corps	SGT. MAJ. RONALD L. GREEN

The Continental Congress established the United States Marine Corps by resolution on November 10, 1775. Marine Corps composition and functions are detailed in 10 U.S.C. 5063.

The Marine Corps, which is part of the Department of the Navy, is the smallest of the Nation's combat forces. It also is the only service that the Congress has tasked specifically to be able to fight in the air, on land, and at sea. Although Marines fight in each of these dimensions, they are primarily a maritime force linked with the Navy, moving from the sea to fight on land.

The Marine Corps conducts entry-level training for its enlisted marines at two bases: Marine Corps Recruit Depot, Parris Island, SC; and Marine Corps Recruit Depot, San Diego, CA. Officer candidates are evaluated at Officer Candidate School, Marine Corps Combat Development Command, Quantico, VA. Marines train to be first on the scene to respond to attacks on the United States or its interests and to acts of political violence against Americans abroad, to provide disaster relief and humanitarian assistance, and to evacuate Americans from foreign countries.

Sources of Information

DSTRESS Line The DSTRESS Line offers an around-the-clock anonymous phone, live chat, and referral service. The call center is staffed with veteran Marines, Fleet Marine Force Navy Corpsmen who were previously attached to the Marine Corps, Marine spouses and other family members, and licensed behavioral health counselors trained in Marine Corps culture. DSTRESS Line is designed to help callers improve overall fitness and to develop the necessary skills for coping with the challenges of life in the Marine Corps. Phone, 877-476-7734. http://www.usmc-mccs.org/index.cfm/services/support/dstress-line | Email: dstressline@usmc.mil

Electronic Publications Authentic and current digital versions of publications issued by Headquarters Marine Corps staff agencies, major commands, and other Department of Defense and Federal agencies are available online. http://www.marines.mil/News/Publications

Freedom of Information Act (FOIA) Procedures for requesting records that the U.S. Marine Corps controls are available online. Phone, 703-614-4008.

http://www.hqmc.marines.mil/Agencies/
USMC-FOIA | Email: hqmcfoia@usmc.mil

Marine Corps Bands   Marine Corps bands
perform at ceremonies, concerts, festivals,
parades, professional sporting events, and
other public events. Marine Corps bands
perform six types of ensembles: brass/
woodwind quintet, bugler, ceremonial
band, concert band, jazz combo, and jazz/
show band. Phone, 504-697-8184. http://
www.marines.mil/Community-Relations/
Asset-Requests/Band | Email: smb.mfr.pao.
comrel@usmc.mil

News   The Marine Corps posts press
releases on its Web site. http://www.marines.
mil/News/Press-Releases

Marines TV is accessible via the Marine
Corps Web site. http://www.marines.mil/
News/Marines-TV

Reading List   The Commandant's
professional reading list is available
online. http://guides.grc.usmcu.edu/
content.php?pid=408059&sid=3340387 |
Email: Reading@usmc.mil

Sexual Assault   The Marine Corps' Sexual
Assault Prevention and Response program
lowers the incidence of sexual assault
through preventative strategies and provides
care to victims of the crime. http://www.
usmc-mccs.org/index.cfm/services/support/
sexual-assault-prevention

The Safe Helpline provides anonymous
and confidential support for sexual assault
survivors in the military. Phone, 877-995-
5247. https://safehelpline.org

Silent Drill Platoon   The Marine Corps
Silent Drill Platoon is a 24-Marine rifle
platoon that performs a precision drill
exhibition. This disciplined platoon
exemplifies the professionalism associated
with the U.S. Marine Corps. It first performed
in the Sunset Parades of 1948 and received
such a favorable response that it became

a regular part of the parades at Marine
Barracks, Washington, DC. Performance
requests for the Silent Drill Platoon should
be made 30–90 days prior to the event.
Phone, 504-697-8184. http://www.marines.
mil/Community-Relations/Asset-Requests/
Silent-Drill-Platoon | Email: smb.mfr.pao.
comrel@usmc.mil

Site Map   The Web site map allows visitors
to look for specific topics or to browse
content that aligns with their interests. http://
www.marines.mil/Home/SiteMap.aspx

Social Media   The Marine Corps maintains
a social media presence and supports online
communities where people can go to share
and collect information and stories. http://
www.marines.mil/News/Social-Media

Speakers   The Marine Corps supports
speaking engagements for community
events nationwide, ranging from small-
town civic organizations to big-city
national conventions. The Marine Corps
In the Community program helps business
executives, educators, members of civic
organizations, conference organizers, and
others make contact with a Marine Corps
public speaker. Phone, 504-697-8184. http://
www.marines.mil/Community-Relations/
Asset-Requests/Speakers | Email: smb.mfr.
pao.comrel@usmc.mil

Tattoo Regulations   The Marine Corps
tattoo policy seeks to balance personal
taste with the high standards of professional
military appearance and heritage. The
Marine Corps Bulletin 1020 (June 2016)
explains the current tattoo policy, which
replaces previous guidance on the subject.
http://www.marines.mil/Tattoos.aspx

Unit Directory   A complete list of Marine
Corps units with links to their respective
web pages is available online. http://www.
marines.mil/Units.aspx; http://www.marines.
mil/Contact-Us

For further information regarding the Marine Corps, contact the Director of Public Affairs, Headquarters, U.S. Marine
Corps, 2 Navy Annex–Pentagon 5D773, Washington, DC 20380-1775. Phone, 703-614-1492.

United States Naval Academy

Annapolis, MD 21402-5018
Phone, 410-293-1500. Internet, http://www.usna.edu

Superintendent	Vice Adm. Walter E. Carter, Jr., USN
Commandant of Midshipmen	Col. Stephen E. Liszewski, USMC

The U.S. Naval Academy is the undergraduate college of the Naval Service. Through its comprehensive 4-year program, which stresses excellence in academics, physical education, professional training, conduct, and honor, the Academy prepares young men and women morally, mentally, and physically to be professional officers in the Navy and Marine Corps. All graduates receive a Bachelor of Science degree in 1 of 19 majors. https://www.usna.edu/About/index.php

Sources of Information

Armel-Leftwich Visitor Center   From March to December, the visitor center is open daily, 9 a.m.–5 p.m. During January and February, the visitor center is open on weekdays, 9 a.m.–4 p.m. The gift shop, however, is open on the weekends, 9 a.m.–5 p.m. http://www.usnabsd.com/for-visitors | Email: tourinfo@usna.edu

A–Z Index   The Naval Academy's Web site has an alphabetical index to help visitors search for information or browse topics of interest. https://www.usna.edu/TOC/index.php

Career Opportunities   Six sources of employment are associated with the Naval Academy and its supporting organizations. https://www.usna.edu/Employment

Naval Academy Preparatory School   The Naval Academy Preparatory School prepares midshipman candidates for success at the U.S. Naval Academy. The 10-month course of instruction, August–May, centers on preparation in Chemistry, English Composition, Information Technology, Mathematics, and Physics. Phone, 401-841-6966 (administration). Phone, 401-841-2947 (academics). https://www.usna.edu/NAPS

Naval Academy Store   All Profits support the brigade of midshipmen. http://navyonline.com

Nimitz Library   An online tool is available to search the library's collection of articles, books, ebooks, and journals. Phone, 410-293-6945. https://www.usna.edu/Library | Email: askref@usna.edu; https://www.usna.edu/Contact

For further information concerning the U.S. Naval Academy, contact the Superintendent, U.S. Naval Academy, 121 Blake Road, Annapolis, MD 21402-5018.

DEFENSE AGENCIES
The Defense Agencies' personnel tables were updated 09–2017.

Defense Advanced Research Projects Agency

675 North Randolph Street, Arlington, VA 22203-2114
Phone, 703-526-6630. Internet, http://www.darpa.mil

Director	Steven H. Walker, Acting
Deputy Director	Stefanie Tompkins, Acting
https://www.darpa.mil/about-us/people	

The Defense Advanced Research Projects Agency is a separately organized agency within the Department of Defense and is under the authority, direction, and control of the Under Secretary of Defense (Acquisition, Technology and Logistics). The Agency serves as the central research and development organization of the Department of Defense with a primary responsibility to maintain U.S. technological superiority over potential adversaries. It pursues imaginative and innovative research and development projects, and conducts demonstration projects that represent technology appropriate for joint programs, programs in support of deployed forces, or selected programs of the military departments. To this end, the Agency arranges, manages, and directs the performance of work connected with assigned advanced projects by the military departments, other Government agencies, individuals, private business entities, and educational or research institutions, as appropriate. http://www.darpa.mil

For further information, contact the Defense Advanced Research Projects Agency, 675 North Randolph Street, Arlington, VA 22203-2114. Phone, 703-526-6630.

Defense Commissary Agency

1300 E Avenue, Fort Lee, VA 23801-1800
Phone, 804-734-8720. Internet, http://www.commissaries.com

Director / Chief Executive Officer	MICHAEL J. DOWLING, ACTING
Deputy Director / Chief Operating Officer	MICHAEL J. DOWLING
https://www.commissaries.com/our-agency/deca-organization	

The Defense Commissary Agency (DeCA) was established in 1990 and is under the authority, direction, and control of the Under Secretary of Defense for Personnel and Readiness and the operational supervision of the Defense Commissary Agency Board of Directors.

DeCA provides an efficient and effective worldwide system of commissaries that sell quality groceries and household supplies at low prices to members of the Armed Services community. This benefit satisfies customer demand for quality products and delivers exceptional savings while enhancing the military community's quality of life. DeCA works closely with its employees, customers, and civilian business partners to satisfy its customers and to promote the commissary benefit. The benefit fosters recruitment, retention, and readiness of skilled and trained personnel.

Sources of Information

Employment information is available at www.commissaries.com or by calling the following telephone numbers: employment (703-603-1600); small business activities (804-734-8000, extension 4-8015/4-8529); contracting for resale items (804-734-8000, extension 4-8884/4-8885); and contracting for operations support and equipment (804-734-8000, extension 4-8391/4-8830). http://www.commissaries.com

For further information, contact the Defense Commissary Agency, 1300 E Avenue, Fort Lee, VA 23801-1800. Phone, 804-734-8720

Defense Contract Audit Agency

8725 John J. Kingman Road, Suite 2135, Fort Belvoir, VA 22060-6219
Phone, 703-767-3265. Internet, http://www.dcaa.mil | Email: dcaaweb@dcaa.mil

Director	ANITA F. BALES
Deputy Director	KENNETH J. SACCOCCIA

The Defense Contract Audit Agency (DCAA) was established in 1965 and is under the authority, direction, and control of the Under Secretary of Defense (Comptroller)/ Chief Financial Officer. DCAA performs all necessary contract audit functions for

DOD and provides accounting and financial advisory services to all Defense components responsible for procurement and contract administration. These services are provided in connection with the negotiation, administration, and settlement of contracts and subcontracts to ensure taxpayer dollars are spent on fair and reasonable contract prices. They include evaluating the acceptability of costs claimed or proposed by contractors and reviewing the efficiency and economy of contractor operations.

Other Government agencies may request the DCAA's services under appropriate arrangements.

DCAA manages its operations through five regional offices responsible for approximately 104 field audit offices throughout the United States and overseas. Each region is responsible for the contract auditing function in its assigned area. Point of contact information for DCAA regional offices is available at www.dcaa.mil. http://www.dcaa.mil | Email: dcaaweb@dcaa.mil

For further information, contact the Executive Officer, Defense Contract Audit Agency, 8725 John J. Kingman Road, Suite 2135, Fort Belvoir, VA 22060-6219. Phone, 703-767-3265.

Defense Contract Management Agency

3901 A Avenue, Fort Lee, VA 23801
Phone, 804-734-0814. Internet, http://www.dcma.mil

Director	VICE ADM. DAVID H. LEWIS, USN
Deputy Director	(VACANCY)
http://www.dcma.mil/About-Us	

The Defense Contract Management Agency (DCMA) was established by the Deputy Secretary of Defense in 2000 and is under the authority, direction, and control of the Under Secretary of Defense (Acquisition, Technology, and Logistics). DCMA is responsible for DOD contract management in support of the military departments, other DOD components, the National Aeronautics and Space Administration, other designated Federal and State agencies, foreign governments, and international organizations, as appropriate. http://www.dcma.mil

For further information, contact the Office of General Counsel, Defense Contract Management Agency, 3901 A Avenue, Fort Lee, VA 23801. Phone, 804-734-0814.

Defense Finance and Accounting Service

1800 Mark Center Drive, Suite 08J25-01, Alexandria, VA 22350-3000
Phone, 571-372-7883. Internet, http://www.dfas.mil

Director	TERESA A. MCKAY
Principal Deputy Director	AUDREY Y. DAVIS
https://www.dfas.mil/pressroom/dfasleadership.html#	

The Defense Finance and Accounting Service (DFAS) was established in 1991 under the authority, direction, and control of the Under Secretary of Defense (Comptroller)/Chief Financial Officer to strengthen and reduce costs of financial management and operations within DOD.

DFAS is responsible for all payments to servicemembers, employees, vendors, and contractors. It provides business intelligence and finance and accounting information to DOD decisionmakers. DFAS is also responsible for preparing annual financial statements and the consolidation, standardization, and modernization of finance and accounting requirements, functions, processes, operations, and systems for DOD. http://www.dfas.mil

For further information, contact Defense Finance and Accounting Service Corporate Communications, 4800 Mark Center Drive, Suite 08J25-01, Alexandria, VA 22350-3000. Phone, 571-372-7883.

Defense Information Systems Agency

P.O. Box 549, Command Building, Fort Meade, MD 20755
Phone, 301-225-6000. Internet, http://www.disa.mil | Email: dia-pao@dia.mil

Director	Lt. Gen. Alan R. Lynn, USAF
Vice Director	Rear Adm. Nancy A. Norton, USN
http://www.disa.mil/About/Our-Leaders	

The Defense Information Systems Agency (DISA), established originally as the Defense Communications Agency in 1960, is under the authority, direction, and control of the Assistant Secretary of Defense (Networks and Information Integration). DISA is a combat support agency responsible for planning, engineering, acquiring, fielding, operating, and supporting global net-centric solutions to serve the needs of the President, Vice President, Secretary of Defense, and other DOD components. http://www.disa.mil | Email: dia-pao@dia.mil

For further information, contact the Public Affairs Office, Defense Information Systems Agency, P.O. Box 549, Command Building, Fort Meade, MD 20755. Phone, 301-225-6000.

Defense Intelligence Agency

200 MacDill Boulevard, Washington DC 20340-5100
Phone, 202-231-0800. Internet, http://www.dia.mil | Email: dia-pao@dia.mil

Director	Lt. Gen. Vincent R. Stewart, USMC
Deputy Director	Melissa A. Drisko
http://www.dia.mil/About/Leadership	

The Defense Intelligence Agency (DIA) was established in 1961 and is under the authority, direction, and control of the Under Secretary of Defense for Intelligence. DIA provides timely, objective, and cogent military intelligence to warfighters, force planners, as well as defense and national security policymakers. DIA obtains and reports information through its field sites worldwide and the Defense Attache System; provides timely intelligence analysis; directs Defense Human Intelligence programs; operates the Joint Intelligence Task Force for Combating Terrorism and the Joint Military Intelligence College; coordinates and facilitates Measurement and Signature Intelligence activities; manages and plans collections from specialized technical sources; manages secure DOD intelligence networks; and coordinates required intelligence support for the Secretary of Defense, Joint Chiefs of Staff, Combatant Commanders, and Joint Task Forces. http://www.dia.mil | Email: dia-pao@dia.mil

For further information, contact the Public Affairs Office, Defense Intelligence Agency, 200 MacDill Boulevard, Washington DC 20340-5100. Phone, 202-231-0800.

Defense Legal Services Agency

The Pentagon, Washington, DC 20301-1600
Phone, 703-695-3341. Internet, http://www.dod.mil/dodgc

Director / General Counsel of the Department of Defense http://ogc.osd.mil/gc_bio.html	WILLIAM S. CASTLE, ACTING
Principal Deputy General Counsel of the Department of Defense http://ogc.osd.mil/dgc_bio.html	WILLIAM S. CASTLE

The Defense Legal Services Agency (DLSA) was established in 1981 and is under the authority, direction, and control of the General Counsel of the Department of Defense, who also serves as its Director. DLSA provides legal advice and services for specified DOD components and adjudication of personnel security cases for DOD and other assigned Federal agencies and departments. It also provides technical support and assistance for development of the Department's legislative program; coordinates positions on legislation and Presidential Executive orders; provides a centralized legislative and congressional document reference and distribution point for the Department; maintains the Department's historical legislative files; and administers programs governing standards of conduct and alternative dispute resolution. http://www.dod.mil/dodgc

For further information, contact the Administrative Office, Defense Legal Services Agency, Room 3A734, Washington, DC 20301-1600. Phone, 703-697-8343.

Defense Logistics Agency

8725 John J. Kingman Road, Suite 2533, Fort Belvoir, VA 22060-6221
Phone, 703-767-5261. Internet, http://www.dla.mil

Director	LT. GEN. DARRELL K. WILLIAMS, USA
Vice Director http://www.dla.mil/Leaders.aspx	EDWARD J. CASE

The Defense Logistics Agency (DLA) is under the authority, direction, and control of the Under Secretary of Defense for Acquisition, Technology, and Logistics. DLA supports both the logistics requirements of the military services and their acquisition of weapons and other materiel. It provides logistics support and technical services to all branches of the military and to a number of Federal agencies. DLA supply centers consolidate the requirements of the military services and procure the supplies in sufficient quantities to meet their projected needs. DLA manages supplies in eight commodity areas: fuel, food, clothing, construction material, electronic supplies, general supplies, industrial supplies, and medical supplies. Information on DLA's field activities and regional commands is available at www.dla.mil/ataglance.aspx.

Sources of Information

Career Opportunities For the Washington, DC, metropolitan area, all inquiries and applications concerning job recruitment programs should be addressed to Human Resources, Customer Support Office, 3990 East Broad Street, Building 11, Section 3, Columbus, OH, 43213-0919. Phone, 877-352-4762. http://www.dla.mil/Careers.aspx

Environmental Program For information on the environmental program, contact the Staff Director, Environmental and Safety, Defense Logistics Agency, Attn: DSS-E, 8725 John J. Kingman Road, Fort Belvoir, VA 22060-6221. Phone, 703-767-6278.

Procurement / Small Business Activities For information on procurement and small business activities, contact the Director, Small and Disadvantaged

Business Utilization, Defense Logistics Agency, Attn: DB, 8725 John J. Kingman Road, Fort Belvoir, VA 22060-6221. Phone, 703-767-0192. http://www.dla.mil/DoingBusinessWithDLA.aspx
Surplus Sales Program Questions concerning this program should be addressed to DOD Surplus Sales, International Sales Office, 74 Washington Avenue North, Battle Creek, MI 49017-3092. Phone, 877-352-2255. http://dispositionservices.dla.mil/sales/Pages/default.aspx; http://www.dla.mil

For further information, contact the Defense Logistics Agency, 8725 John J. Kingman Road, Fort Belvoir, VA 22060-6221. Phone, 703-767-5264.

Defense Security Cooperation Agency

201 Twelfth Street South, Suite 203, Arlington, VA 22202-5408
Phone, 703-604-6605. Internet, http://www.dsca.mil | Email: info@dsca.mil

Director	Lt. Gen. Charles Hooper, USA
Deputy Director	Gregory M. Kausner
http://www.dsca.mil/about-us/leadership	

The Defense Security Cooperation Agency (DSCA) was established in 1971 and is under the authority, direction, and control of the Under Secretary of Defense (Policy). DSCA provides traditional security assistance functions such as military assistance, international military education and training, and foreign military sales. DSCA also has program management responsibilities for humanitarian assistance, demining, and other DOD programs. http://www.dsca.mil | Email: info@dsca.mil

For further information, contact the Defense Security Cooperation Agency, 201 Twelfth Street South, Suite 203, Arlington, VA 22202-5408. Phone, 703-604-6605.

Defense Security Service

27130 Telegraph Road, Quantico, VA 22134
Phone, 703-617-2352. Internet, http://www.dss.mil

Director	Daniel E. Payne
http://www.dss.mil/about_dss/director.html	
Deputy Director	James J. Kren
http://www.dss.mil/about_dss/Deputy_Director.html	

The Defense Security Service (DSS) is under the authority, direction, and control of the Under Secretary of Defense for Intelligence. DSS ensures the safeguarding of classified information used by contractors on behalf of the DOD and 22 other executive branch agencies under the National Industrial Security Program. It oversees the protection of conventional arms, munitions, and explosives in the custody of DOD contractors; evaluates the protection of selected private sector critical assets and infrastructures (physical and cyber-based systems) and recommends measures needed to maintain operations identified as vital to DOD. DSS makes clearance determinations for industry and provides support services for DOD Central Adjudicative Facilities. It provides security education, training, and proactive awareness programs for military, civilian, and cleared industry to enhance their proficiency and awareness of DOD security policies and procedures. DSS also has a counterintelligence office to integrate counterintelligence principles into security countermeasures missions and to support the national counterintelligence strategy. Information on DSS operating locations and centers is available at www.dss.mil/isp/dss_opor_loc.html. http://www.dss.mil

For further information, contact the Defense Security Service, Office of Public Affairs, 27130 Telegraph Road, Quantico, VA 22134. Phone, 703-617-2352.

Defense Threat Reduction Agency

8725 John J. Kingman Road, MS 6201, Fort Belvoir, VA 22060-6201
Phone, 703-767-7594. Internet, http://www.dtra.mil

Director	VAYL S. OXFORD
Deputy Director	REAR ADM. SCOTT JERABEK, USN
http://www.dtra.mil/About/Our-Leadership	

The Defense Threat Reduction Agency (DTRA) was established in 1998 and is under the authority, direction, and control of the Under Secretary of Defense for Acquisition, Technology, and Logistics. DTRA's mission is to reduce the threat posed by weapons of mass destruction (WMD). DTRA covers the full range of WMD threats (chemical, biological, nuclear, radiological, and high explosive), bridges the gap between the warfighters and the technical community, sustains the nuclear deterrent, and provides both offensive and defensive technology and operational concepts to warfighters. DTRA reduces the threat of WMD by implementing arms control treaties and executing the Cooperative Threat Reduction Program. It uses combat support, technology development, and chemical-biological defense to deter the use and reduce the impact of such weapons. DTRA also prepares for future threats by developing the technology and concepts needed to counter new WMD threats and adversaries. http://www.dtra.mil

For further information, contact the Public Affairs Office, Defense Threat Reduction Agency, 8725 John J. Kingman Road, MS 6201, Fort Belvoir, VA 22060-5916. Phone, 703-767-7594. Email, dtra.publicaffairs@dtra.mil.

Missile Defense Agency

5700 Eighteenth Street, Bldg 245, Fort Belvoir, VA 22060-5573
Phone, 703-695-6420. Email: mda.info@mda.mil

Director	LT. GEN. SAMUEL A. GREAVES, USAF
https://www.mda.mil/about/leadership.html	
Deputy Director	REAR ADM. JON A. HILL , USN
http://www.navy.mil/navydata/bios/navybio.asp?bioID=786	

[For the Missile Defense Agency statement of organization, see the Code of Federal Regulations, Title 32, Part 388]

The Missile Defense Agency's (MDA) mission is to establish and deploy a layered ballistic missile defense system to intercept missiles in all phases of their flight and against all ranges of threats. This capability will provide a defense of the United States, deployed forces, and allies. MDA is under the authority, direction, and control of the Under Secretary of Defense for Acquisition, Technology, and Logistics. MDA manages and directs DOD's ballistic missile defense acquisition programs and enables the Services to field elements of the overall system as soon as practicable. MDA develops and tests technologies and, if necessary, uses prototype and test assets to provide early capability. Additionally, MDA improves the effectiveness of deployed capabilities by implementing new technologies as they become available or when the threat warrants an accelerated capability. https://www.mda.mil | Email: mda.info@mda.mil

For further information, contact the Human Resources Directorate, Missile Defense Agency, 5700 Eighteenth Street, Bldg 245, Fort Belvoir, VA 22060-5573. Phone, 703-695-6420. Email, mda.info@mda.mil.

National Geospatial-Intelligence Agency

7500 Geoint Drive, MS N73-OCCAE, Springfield, Virginia 22150
Phone, 571-557-7300. Internet, http://www.nga.mil

Director	Robert Cardillo
Deputy Director	Justin Poole
https://www.nga.mil/About/Leadership/Pages/	
default.aspx	

The National Geospatial-Intelligence Agency (NGA), formerly the National Imagery and Mapping Agency, was established in 1996 and is under the authority, direction, and control of the Under Secretary of Defense for Intelligence. NGA is a DOD combat support agency and a member of the national intelligence community. NGA's mission is to provide timely, relevant, and accurate geospatial intelligence in support of our national security. Geospatial intelligence means the use and analysis of imagery to describe, assess, and visually depict physical features and geographically referenced activities on the Earth. Headquartered in Bethesda, MD, NGA has major facilities in the Washington, DC, Northern Virginia, and St. Louis, MO, areas with NGA support teams worldwide. http://www.nga.mil | Email: publicaffairs@nga.mil

For further information, contact the Public Affairs Office, National Geospatial-Intelligence Agency,. 7500 Geoint Drive, MS N73-OCCAE, Springfield, Virginia 22150. Phone, 571-557-7300.

National Security Agency / Central Security Service

Fort Meade, MD 20755-6248
Phone, 301-688-6524. Fax, 301-688-6198. Internet, http://www.nsa.gov

Director	Adm. Michael S. Rogers, USN
Deputy Director	George C. Barnes
https://www.nsa.gov/about/leadership	

The National Security Agency (NSA) was established in 1952 and the Central Security Service (CSS) was established in 1972. NSA/CSS is under the authority, direction, and control of the Under Secretary of Defense for Intelligence. As the Nation's cryptologic organization, NSA/CSS employs the Nation's premier codemakers and codebreakers. It ensures an informed, alert, and secure environment for U.S. warfighters and policymakers. The cryptologic resources of NSA/CSS unite to provide U.S. policymakers with intelligence information derived from America's adversaries while protecting U.S. Government signals and information systems from exploitation by those same adversaries. http://www.nsa.gov | Email: nsapao@nsa.gov

For further information, contact the Public Affairs Office, National Security Agency/Central Security Service, Fort Meade, MD 20755-6248. Phone, 301-688-6524. Fax, 301-688-6198.

Pentagon Force Protection Agency

9000 Defense Pentagon, Washington, DC 20301
Phone, 703-697-1001. Internet, http://www.pfpa.mil

Director   JONATHAN H. COFER
http://www.pfpa.mil/director.html

Deputy Director   DANIEL P. WALSH, ACTING
http://www.pfpa.mil/dpy_director.html

The Pentagon Force Protection Agency (PFPA) was established in May 2002 in response to the events of September 11, 2001, and subsequent terrorist threats facing the DOD workforce and facilities in the National Capital Region (NCR). PFPA is under the authority, direction, and control of the Director, Administration and Management, in the Office of the Secretary of Defense. PFPA provides force protection, security, and law enforcement for the people, facilities, infrastructure, and other resources at the Pentagon and for DOD activities and facilities within the NCR that are not under the jurisdiction of a military department. Consistent with the national strategy on combating terrorism, PFPA addresses threats, including chemical, biological, and radiological agents, through a strategy of prevention, preparedness, detection, and response to ensure that the DOD workforce and facilities in the NCR are secure and protected. http://www.pfpa.mil

For further information, contact the Pentagon Force Protection Agency, 9000 Defense Pentagon, Washington, DC 20301. Phone, 703-697-1001.

JOINT SERVICE SCHOOLS
Defense Acquisition University

9820 Belvoir Road, Fort Belvoir, VA 22060-5565
Phone, 703-805-2764. Internet, http://www.dau.mil

President   JAMES P. WOOSLEY
https://www.dau.mil/about

The Defense Acquisition University (DAU), established pursuant to the Defense Acquisition Workforce Improvement Act of 1990 (10 U.S.C. 1701 note), serves as the DOD center for acquisition, technology, and logistics training; performance support; continuous learning; and knowledge sharing. DAU is a unified structure with five regional campuses and the Defense Systems Management College-School of Program Managers, which provides executive and international acquisition training. DAU's mission is to provide the training, career management, and services that enable the acquisition, technology, and logistics community to make smart business decisions and deliver timely and affordable capabilities to warfighters. http://www.dau.mil

For further information, contact the Director, Operations Support Group, Defense Acquisition University, 9820 Belvoir Road, Fort Belvoir, VA 22060-5565. Phone, 800-845-7606.

National Intelligence University

Defense Intelligence Analysis Center, Washington, DC 20340-5100
Phone, 202-231-5466. Internet, http://www.ni-u.edu

President   J. SCOTT CAMERON
http://ni-u.edu/wp/about-niu/leadership-2/office-of-
    the-president

The National Intelligence University, formerly the Joint Military Intelligence College, was established in 1962. The College is a joint service interagency educational institution serving the intelligence community and operates under the authority of the Director, Defense Intelligence Agency. Its mission is to educate military and civilian intelligence professionals, conduct and disseminate relevant intelligence research, and perform academic outreach regarding intelligence matters. The College is authorized by Congress to award the bachelor of science in intelligence, master of science and technology intelligence, and master of science of strategic intelligence. Courses are offered to full-time students in a traditional daytime format and for part-time students in the evening, on Saturday, and in an executive format (one weekend per month and a 2-week intensive summer period). http://www.ni-u.edu

For further information, contact the Admissions Office, National Intelligence University, 200 MacDill Blvd (MCA-2), Washington, DC 20340-5100. Phone, 202-231-5466 or 202-231-3319.

National Defense University

300 Fifth Avenue, Building 62, Fort McNair, DC 20319-5066
Phone, 202-685-2649. Internet, http://www.ndu.edu
College of International Security Affairs: 260 Fifth Avenue, Building 64, Fort McNair, DC 20319-5066
Phone, 202-685-3870. Internet, http://cisa.ndu.edu
Dwight D. Eisenhower School for National Security and Resource Strategy: 408 Fourth Avenue, Building 59, Fort McNair, DC 20319-5062
Phone, 202-685-4333. Internet, http://es.ndu.edu/Home.aspx
Information Resources Management College: 300 Fifth Avenue, Building 62, Fort McNair, DC 20319-5066
Phone, 202-685-6300. Internet, http://icollege.ndu.edu
Joint Forces Staff College: 7800 Hampton Boulevard, Norfolk, VA 23511-1702
Phone, 757-443-6124. Internet, http://jfsc.ndu.edu
National War College: 300 D Street SW., Building 61, Fort McNair, DC 20319-5078
Phone, 202-685-3674. Fax, 202-685-6461. Internet, http://nwc.ndu.edu

PRESIDENT   MAJ. GEN. FREDERICK M. PADILLA, USMC
http://www.ndu.edu/About/Leadership/Article-View/
    Article/572672/major-general-frederick-m-padilla-
    usmc

Senior Vice President   DONALD YAMAMOTO
http://www.ndu.edu/About/Leadership/Article-View/
    Article/572661/ambassador-donald-yamamoto

Commandant, Dwight D. Eisenhower School for   BRIG. GEN. JOHN JANSEN, USMC
    National Security and Resource Strategy
Commandant, Joint Forces Staff College   REAR ADM. JEFFREY RUTH, USN
Commandant, National War College   BRIG. GEN. CHAD T. MANSKE, USAF

| Chancellor, College of International Security Affairs | COL. MICHAEL S. BELL, USA (RETIRED) |
| Chancellor, Information Resources Management College | REAR ADM. JANICE HAMBY, USN (RETIRED) |

http://www.ndu.edu/About/Leadership

National Defense University

The mission of the National Defense University is to prepare military and civilian leaders from the United States and other countries to evaluate national and international security challenges through multidisciplinary educational and research programs, professional exchanges, and outreach.

The National Defense University was established in 1976 and comprises the following colleges and programs: the Dwight D. Eisenhower School for National Security and Resource Strategy, National War College, Joint Forces Staff College, Information Resources Management College, College of International Security Affairs, Institute for National Strategic Studies, Center for the Study of Weapons of Mass Destruction, Center for Technology and National Security Policy, International Student Management Office, Joint Reserve Affairs Center, CAPSTONE, Security of Defense Corporate Fellows Program, NATO Education Center, Institute for National Security Ethics and Leadership, Center for Joint Strategic Logistics Excellence, Center for Applied Strategic Leaders, and Center for Complex Operations. http://www.ndu.edu

For further information, contact the Human Resources Directorate, National Defense University, 300 Fifth Avenue, Building 62, Fort McNair, DC 20319-5066. Phone, 202-685-2169.

College of International Security Affairs

The College of International Security Affairs (CISA) is one of NDU's five colleges. CISA educates students from across the international, interagency, and interservice communities. CISA's primary areas of concentration include counterterrorism, conflict management of stability of operations, homeland security, and defense and international security studies. CISA is also home to NDU's International Counterterrorism Fellowship Program. http://cisa.ndu.edu

For further information, contact the Office of Academic Affairs, College of International Security Affairs, 260 Fifth Avenue, Building 64, Fort McNair, DC 20319-5066. Phone, 202-685-7774.

Dwight D. Eisenhower School for National Security and Resource Strategy

The Dwight D. Eisenhower School for National Security and Resource Strategy provides graduate level education to senior members of the U.S. Armed Forces, Government civilians, foreign nationals, and professionals from the private industrial sector. The School prepares students to contribute to national security strategy and policy, emphasizing the evaluation, marshaling, and managing of national resources. Students who fulfill the degree requirements receive a Master of Science degree in national resource strategy. http://es.ndu.edu/Home.aspx

For further information, contact the Director of Operations, Dwight D. Eisenhower School for National Security and Resource Strategy, 408 Fourth Avenue, Building 59, Fort McNair, DC 20319-5062. Phone, 202-685-4333.

Information Resources Management College

The Information Resources Management College provides graduate-level courses in information resources management. The College prepares leaders to direct the information component of national power by leveraging information and information technology for strategic advantage. The College's primary areas of concentration include policy, strategic planning, leadership/management, process improvement, capital planning and investment, performance- and results-based management, technology assessment, architecture, information assurance and security, acquisition, domestic preparedness, transformation, e-Government, and information operations. http://icollege.ndu.edu

For further information, contact the Office of Student Services, Information Resources Management College, 300 Fifth Avenue, Building 62, Fort McNair, DC 20319-5066. Phone, 202-685-6300.

Joint Forces Staff College   The Joint Forces Staff College (JFSC) is an intermediate- and senior-level joint college in the professional military education system dedicated to the study of the principles, perspectives, and techniques of joint operational-level planning and warfare. The mission of JFSC is to educate national security professionals in the planning and execution of joint, multinational, and interagency operations in order to instill a primary commitment to joint, multinational, and interagency teamwork, attitudes, and perspectives. The College accomplishes this mission through four schools: the Joint Advanced Warfighters School, the Joint and Combined Warfighting School, the Joint Continuing and Distance Education School, and the Joint Command, Control, and Information Operations School. http://jfsc.ndu.edu

For further information, contact the Public Affairs Officer, Joint Forces Staff College, 7800 Hampton Boulevard, Norfolk, VA 23511-1702. Phone, 757-443-6212. Fax, 757-443-6210.

National War College   The National War College provides education in national security policy to selected military officers and career civil service employees of Federal departments and agencies concerned with national security. It is the only senior service college with the primary mission of offering a course of study that emphasizes national security policy formulation and the planning and implementation of national strategy. Its 10-month academic program is an issue-centered study in U.S. national security. The elective program is designed to permit each student to tailor his or her academic experience to meet individual professional development needs. http://nwc.ndu.edu

For further information, contact the Office of Administration, National War College, 300 D Street SW., Building 61, Fort McNair, DC 20319-5078. Phone, 202-685-3674.

Uniformed Services University of the Health Sciences

4301 Jones Bridge Road, Bethesda, MD 20814-4799
Phone, 301-295-3190. Internet, http://www.usuhs.mil

President	Maj. Gen. Richard W. Thomas, USA (retired)
https://www.usuhs.edu/pres/leadership	

Authorized by act of September 21, 1972 (10 U.S.C. 2112), the Uniformed Services University of the Health Sciences was established to educate career-oriented medical officers for the Military Departments and the Public Health Service. The University currently incorporates the F. Edward Hebert School of Medicine (including graduate and continuing education programs) and the Graduate School of Nursing.

Students are selected by procedures recommended by the Board of Regents and prescribed by the Secretary of Defense. The actual selection is carried out by a faculty committee on admissions and is based upon motivation and dedication to a career in the uniformed services and an overall appraisal of the personal and intellectual characteristics of the candidates without regard to sex, race, religion, or national origin. Applicants must be U.S. citizens.

Medical school matriculants will be commissioned officers in one of the uniformed services. They must meet the physical and personal qualifications for such a commission and must give evidence of a strong commitment to serving as a uniformed medical officer. The graduating medical student is required to serve a period of obligation of not less than 7 years, excluding graduate medical education.

Students of the Graduate School of Nursing must be commissioned officers of the Army, Navy, Air Force, or Public Health Service prior to application. Graduate nursing students must serve a commitment determined by their respective service. http://www.usuhs.mil

For further information, contact the President, Uniformed Services University of the Health Sciences, 4301 Jones Bridge Road, Bethesda, MD 20814-4799. Phone, 301-295-3013.

DEPARTMENT OF EDUCATION

400 Maryland Avenue SW., Washington, DC 20202
Phone, 202-401-1000. TTY, 800-437-0833. Internet, http://www.ed.gov

Secretary of Education	BETSY DEVOS
Deputy Secretary	MITCHELL ZAIS
Under Secretary	(VACANCY)

Office of the Secretary

Assistant Deputy Secretary and Director, Office of English Language Acquisition	JOSE VIANA
Assistant Deputy Secretary, Office of Innovation and Improvement	JIM BLEW, ACTING
Assistant Secretary, Office for Civil Rights	KENNETH MARCUS
Assistant Secretary, Office of Communication and Outreach	(VACANCY)
Assistant Secretary, Office of Elementary and Secondary Education	FRANK BROGAN
Assistant Secretary, Office of Legislation and Congressional Affairs	PETER OPPENHEIM
Assistant Secretary, Office of Planning, Evaluation and Policy Development	JIM BLEW
Assistant Secretary, Office of Special Education and Rehabilitative Services	JOHNNY COLLETT
Chief of Staff	JOSHUA VENABLE
Director, International Affairs Office	MAUREEN A. MCLAUGHLIN
Director, Institute of Education Sciences	MARK SCHNEIDER
Inspector General	KATHLEEN S. TIGHE

Office of the Deputy Secretary

Assistant Secretary, Office of Management	DENISE CARTER, ACTING
Chief Financial Officer	DOUGLAS WEBSTER
Chief Information Officer	JASON K. GRAY
Director, Office of Educational Technology	(VACANCY)
General Counsel	CARLOS MUNIZ

Office of the Under Secretary

Assistant Secretary, Office of Career, Technical, and Adult Education	SCOTT STUMP
Assistant Secretary, Office of Postsecondary Education	(VACANCY)
Chief Operating Officer for Federal Student Aid	JAMES MANNING, ACTING
Director, Center for Faith-Based and Neighborhood Partnerships	ANDREA RAMIREZ
Executive Director, White House Initiative on American Indian and Alaska Native Education	(VACANCY)
Executive Director, White House Initiative on Asian Americans and Pacific Islanders	HOLLY HAM
Executive Director, White House Initiative on Educational Excellence for African Americans	(VACANCY)

| Executive Director, White House Initiative on Educational Excellence for Hispanic Americans | AIMEE VIANA |
| Executive Director, White House Initiative on Historically Black Colleges and Universities | JOHNATHAN HOLIFIELD |

The Department of Education ensures equal access to education; promotes educational excellence; and administers, coordinates, and makes policy for most Federal assistance to education with the aim of raising levels of student achievement and readiness for the global future.

The Department of Education was created by the Department of Education Organization Act (20 U.S.C. 3411) and is administered under the supervision and direction of the Secretary of Education. http://www2.ed.gov/about/landing.jhtml?src=ln

Secretary   The Secretary of Education advises the President on education plans, policies, and programs of the Federal Government and serves as the chief executive officer of the Department, supervising all Department activities, providing support to States and localities, and focusing resources to ensure equal access to educational excellence throughout the Nation. http://www2.ed.gov/about/offices/list/os/index.html?src=oc

Activities

Career, Technical, and Adult Education   The Office of Career, Technical, and Adult Education (OCTAE) administers grant, contract, and technical assistance programs for vocational-technical education and for adult education and literacy. It promotes programs that enable adults to acquire the basic literacy skills necessary to function in today's society. The Office also helps students acquire challenging academic and technical skills and prepare for high-skill, high-wage, and high-demand occupations in the 21st-century global economy. OCTAE provides national leadership and works to strengthen the role of community colleges in expanding access to postsecondary education for youth and adults in advancing workforce development. http://www2.ed.gov/about/offices/list/ovae/index.html

Education Sciences   The Institute of Education Sciences was formally established by the Education Sciences Reform Act of 2002 (20 U.S.C. 9501 note). The Institute includes national education centers focused on research, special education, statistics, and evaluation and is the mechanism through which the Department supports the research activities needed to improve education policy and practice. https://ies.ed.gov

Elementary and Secondary Education   The Office of Elementary and Secondary Education directs, coordinates, and formulates policy relating to early childhood, elementary, and secondary education. Included are grants and contracts to State educational agencies and local school districts, postsecondary schools, and nonprofit organizations for disadvantaged, migrant, and Indian children; enhancement of State student achievement assessment systems; improvement of reading instruction; economic impact aid; technology; safe and healthy schools; and after-school learning programs. The Office also focuses on improving K–12 education, providing children with language and cognitive development, early reading, and other readiness skills, and improving the quality of teachers and other instructional staff. http://www2.ed.gov/about/offices/list/oese/index.html

English Language Acquisition   The Office of English Language Acquisition helps children who are limited in their English, including immigrant children and youth, attain English proficiency, develop high levels of academic attainment in English, and meet the same challenging State academic content and student academic achievement standards that all children are expected to meet. http://www2.ed.gov/about/offices/list/oela/index.html

Federal Student Aid   Federal Student Aid partners with postsecondary schools and financial institutions to deliver programs

DEPARTMENT OF EDUCATION

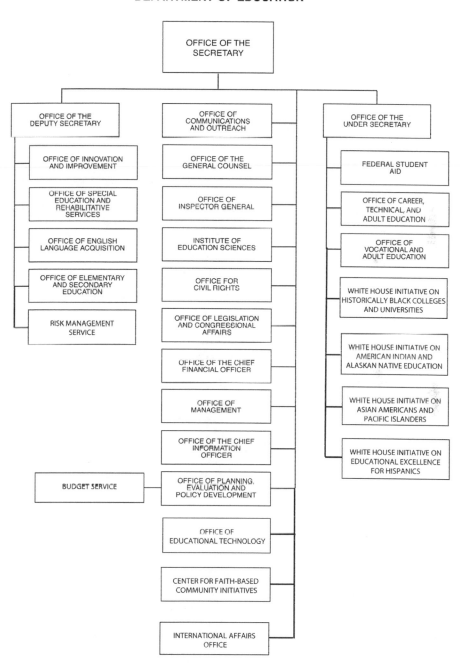

and services that help students finance their education beyond high school. This includes administering postsecondary student financial assistance programs authorized under Title IV of the Higher Education Act of 1965, as amended. https://studentaid.ed.gov

Innovation and Improvement   The Office of Innovation and Improvement (OII) oversees competitive grant programs that support innovations in the educational system and disseminates the lessons learned from these innovative practices. OII administers, coordinates, and recommends programs and policy for improving the quality of activities designed to support and test innovations throughout the K–12 system in areas such as parental choice, teacher quality, use of technology in education, and arts in education. OII encourages the establishment of charter schools through planning, start-up funding, and approaches to credit enhancement for charter school facilities. OII also serves as the Department's liaison and resource to the nonpublic education community. http://innovation.ed.gov

Postsecondary Education   The Office of Postsecondary Education (OPE) formulates Federal postsecondary education policy and administers programs that address critical national needs in support of the mission to increase access to quality postsecondary education. OPE develops policy for Federal student financial programs and support programs that reach out to low-income, first-generation college students and communities. OPE also supports programs that strengthen the capacity of colleges and universities serving a high percentage of disadvantaged students and improve teacher quality. OPE recognizes accrediting agencies that monitor academic quality, promote innovation in higher education, and expand American educational resources for international studies and services. http://www2.ed.gov/about/offices/list/ope/index.html

Special Education and Rehabilitative Services   The Office of Special Education and Rehabilitative Services (OSERS) provides leadership and resources to help ensure that people with disabilities have equal opportunities to learn, work, and live as fully integrated and contributing members of society. OSERS has three components: The Office of Special Education Programs administers the Individuals with Disabilities Education Act legislation, which helps States meet the early intervention and educational needs of infants, toddlers, children, and youth with disabilities. The Rehabilitation Services Administration supports State vocational rehabilitation, independent living, and assistive technology programs that provide people with disabilities the services, technology, and job training and placement assistance they need to gain meaningful employment and lead independent lives. The National Institute on Disability and Rehabilitation Research supports research and development programs that improve the ability of individuals with disabilities to work and live in a barrier-free, inclusive society. OSERS also supports Gallaudet University, the National Technical Institute for the Deaf, the American Printing House for the Blind, and the Helen Keller National Center. http://www2.ed.gov/about/offices/list/osers/index.html

Sources of Information

Blog   "Homeroom" is the official blog of the Department of Education. http://blog.ed.gov

Business Opportunities   Contact the Office of Small and Disadvantaged Business Utilization. Phone, 202-245-6301. http://www.ed.gov/fund/contract-opportunities.html

College Scorecard   The Department of Education's Web site features a tool to help college bound students find colleges and universities based upon their location, size, and the programs and degrees that they offer. https://collegescorecard.ed.gov

Data / Statistics   Information on school accreditation and data on the academic achievement of U.S. students are available on the "Data and Research" Web page. The National Center for Education Statistics collects and analyzes data related to education. Phone, 202-403-5551. http://www2.ed.gov/rschstat/landing.jhtml?src=pn; http://nces.ed.gov

Career Opportunities   For information on employment and the college recruitment program, contact Human Capital and Client Services. Phone, 202-401-0553. http://www.ed.gov/jobs

Freedom of Information Act (FOIA) The FOIA generally provides that any person has the right to request access to Federal agency records or information; all agencies of the Government are required to disclose records upon receiving a written request for them; nine exemptions to the FOIA protect certain records from disclosure; and three special protection provisions or record exclusions authorize Federal law enforcement agencies, under exceptional circumstances, to exclude records from FIOA requirements. The Federal FOIA does not provide access to records held by State or local government agencies, or by private businesses or individuals. http://www2.ed.gov/policy/gen/leg/foia/foiatoc.html?src=ft

Before submitting a request, browse the electronic FOIA Library and search the Department of Education's Web site. The desired records and information may be immediately available online and not require a FOIA request to access them. http://www2.ed.gov/policy/gen/leg/foia/readingroom.html

Frequently Asked Questions (FAQs) The Department of Education provides answers to FAQs on its Web site. https://answers.ed.gov/ics/support/default.asp?deptID=28025&_referrer=http://www.ed.gov/&src=ft

Glossaries The Department of Education's Web site features a glossary of reading terms. https://lincs.ed.gov/research/Glossary.html

The Department of Education's Web site features a glossary of terms related to Federal student aid. https://studentaid.ed.gov/sa/glossary

The Department of Education's Web site features a glossary of terms related to education research. http://www.ics.ed.gov/ncee/wwc/Glossary

The Department of Education's Web site features a glossary of terms related to education statistical standards. http://nces.ed.gov/statprog/2002/glossary.asp

Language Assistance Education resources for Spanish speakers are available on the Department's Web site. http://www2.ed.gov/espanol/bienvenidos/es/index.html?src=ft

Free language assistance services— Chinese, Korean, Spanish, Vietnamese, Tagalog—are available to the public. Phone, 800-872-5327. http://www.ed.gov/notices/english-la | Email: Ed.Language.Assistance@ed.gov

News The Department of Education posts media advisories, press releases, and speeches on its Web site. http://www.ed.gov/news

Press releases in Spanish are also available on the Department's Web site. http://www2.ed.gov/espanol/news/pressreleases/index.html

Open Government The Department of Education supports the Open Government initiative by promoting the principles of collaboration, participation, and transparency. http://www2.ed.gov/about/open.html | Email: opengov@ed.gov

Plain Language Department of Education writers and editors are committed to using Federal plain language guidelines. Publishing clear, useful information on programs and services is a priority and an ongoing effort. To comment on the clarity of a written product or to offer a suggestion for improvement, please communicate via email. http://www.ed.gov/plain-language | Email: plainwriting@ed.gov

Regional Offices Each regional office serves as a center for the dissemination of information and provides technical assistance to State and local educational agencies and other institutions and individuals interested in Federal educational activities. Offices are located in Boston, MA; New York, NY; Philadelphia, PA; Atlanta, GA; Chicago, IL; Cleveland, OH; Dallas, TX; Kansas City, MO; Denver, CO; San Francisco, CA; and Seattle, WA. http://www2.ed.gov/about/contacts/gen/regions.html

Site Map The Web site map allows visitors to look for specific topics or to browse content that aligns with their interests. http://www2.ed.gov/help/site/map/sitemap.jsp

Student Loans Information on student loans is available online. http://www2.ed.gov/fund/grants-college.html?src=pn; http://www2.ed.gov/about/contacts/gen/index.html

For further information, contact the Information Resources Center, Department of Education, Room 5E248 (FB–6), 400 Maryland Avenue SW., Washington, DC 20202. Phone, 800-872-5327.

Federally Aided Corporations

American Printing House for the Blind

P.O. Box 6085, Louisville, KY 40206
Phone, 502-895-2405. Internet, http://www.aph.org

President	CRAIG MEADOR
Chair of the Board	JANE HARDY

Founded in 1858 as a nonprofit organization, the American Printing House for the Blind (APH) received its Federal charter in 1879 when Congress passed the Act to Promote Education of the Blind. This Act designates APH as the official supplier of educational materials adapted for students who are legally blind and who are enrolled in formal educational programs below the college level. Materials produced and distributed by APH include textbooks in Braille and large type, educational tools such as Braille typewriters and computer software and hardware, teaching aides such as tests and performance measures, and other special supplies. The materials are distributed through allotments to the States to programs serving individuals who are blind. http://www.aph.org/about

Sources of Information

Business Opportunities   Requests for proposals are posted online. http://www.aph.org/rfp

Employment   The APH is the world's largest manufacturer of products for people who are blind and visually impaired. It is a drug-free workplace: New hires must pass a drug screening test and background check. http://www.aph.org/careers; http://www.aph.org/contact

For further information, contact the American Printing House for the Blind, P.O. Box 6085, Louisville, KY 40206. Phone, 502-895-2405.

Gallaudet University

800 Florida Avenue NE., Washington, DC 20002
Phone, 202-651-5000. Internet, http://www.gallaudet.edu

President	T. ALAN HURWITZ
Chair, Board of Trustees	HEATHER HARKER

Gallaudet University received its Federal charter in 1864 and is currently authorized by the Education of the Deaf Act of 1986, as amended. Gallaudet is a private, nonprofit educational institution providing elementary, secondary, undergraduate, and continuing education programs for persons who are deaf. The University offers a traditional liberal arts curriculum for students who are deaf and graduate programs in fields related to deafness for students who are deaf and students who are hearing. Gallaudet also conducts a wide variety of basic and applied deafness research and provides public service programs for persons who are deaf and for professionals who work with persons who are deaf.

Gallaudet University is accredited by a number of organizations, among which are the Middle States Association of Colleges and Secondary Schools, the National Council for Accreditation of Teacher Education, and the Conference of Educational Administrators of Schools and Programs for the Deaf. http://www2.gallaudet.edu/attend-gallaudet/about-gallaudet

Laurent Clerc National Deaf Education Center   Gallaudet's Laurent Clerc National Deaf Education Center operates elementary and secondary education programs on the main campus of the University. These programs are authorized by the Education of the Deaf Act of 1986 (20 U.S.C. 4304, as amended) for the primary purpose of developing, evaluating, and disseminating model curricula, instructional strategies, and materials in order to serve individuals who are deaf or hard of hearing. The Education of the Deaf Act requires the programs to include students preparing for postsecondary opportunities other than college and students with a broad spectrum of needs, such as students who are academically challenged, come from non-English-speaking homes, have secondary disabilities, are members of minority groups, or are from rural areas. http://www.gallaudet.edu/clerc-center.html

Model Secondary School for the Deaf The school was established by act of October 15, 1966, which was superseded by the Education of the Deaf Act of 1986. The school provides day and residential facilities for secondary-age students from across the United States from grades 9 to 12, inclusively. http://www.gallaudet.edu/mssd.html

Kendall Demonstration Elementary School The school became the Nation's first demonstration elementary school for the deaf by the act of December 24, 1970 (20 U.S.C. 695), which was also later superseded by the Education of the Deaf Act of 1986. The school is a day program for students from the Washington, DC, metropolitan area from the age of onset of deafness to age 15, inclusively, but not beyond the eighth grade or its equivalent. http://www.gallaudet.edu/kdes.html

Sources of Information

Campus Tour A virtual tour of the University's campus is available online. http://www.gallaudet.edu/visitors-center/virtual-tour.html

Employment Serving deaf and hard of hearing students from many different backgrounds, Gallaudet University seeks to develop a workforce that reflects its diversity. The University is an equal employment opportunity and affirmative action employer, and it encourages members of traditionally underrepresented groups, persons with disabilities, veterans, and women to apply for vacancies. http://www.gallaudet.edu/hrs/employment-opportunities.html; http://www.gallaudet.edu/about-gallaudet/contact-us.html

For further information, contact the Public Relations Office, Gallaudet University, 800 Florida Avenue NE., Washington, DC 20002. Phone, 202-651-5505.

Howard University

2400 Sixth Street NW., Washington, DC 20059
Phone, 202-806-6100. Internet, http://www.howard.edu

President	WAYNE A.I. FREDERICK

Howard University was established by Congress by the act of March 2, 1867 (14 Stat. 438). It offers instruction in 12 schools and colleges, as follows: the colleges of arts and sciences; dentistry; engineering, architecture, and computer sciences; medicine; pharmacy, nursing, and allied health sciences; the graduate school; the schools of business; communications; divinity; education; law; and social work. In addition, Howard University has research institutes, centers, and special programs in the following areas: cancer, child development, computational science and engineering, international affairs, sickle cell disease, and the national human genome project. https://www2.howard.edu/about/howard-glance

Sources of Information

Employment Information is available on the "Career Opportunities" Web page. https://www2.howard.edu/about/careers

Libraries The Howard University Libraries are accessible online. http://library.howard.edu/library; https://www2.howard.edu/contact

For further information, contact the Office of University Communications, Howard University, 2400 Sixth Street NW., Washington, DC 20059. Phone, 202-806-0970.

National Technical Institute for the Deaf / Rochester Institute of Technology

52 Lomb Memorial Drive, Rochester, NY 14623
Phone, 585-475-6317. Internet, http://www.ntid.rit.edu

President, Rochester Institute of Technology	WILLIAM W. DESTLER
President, National Technical Institute for the Deaf / Vice President, Rochester Institute of Technology	GERARD J. BUCKLEY

The National Technical Institute for the Deaf (NTID) was established by act of June 8, 1965 (20 U.S.C. 681) to promote the employment of persons who are deaf by providing technical and professional education. The National Technical Institute for the Deaf Act was superseded by the Education of the Deaf Act of 1986 (20 U.S.C. 4431, as amended). The U.S. Department of Education contracts with the Rochester Institute of Technology (RIT) for the operation of a residential facility for postsecondary technical training and education for individuals who are deaf. The purpose of the special relationship with the host institution is to give NTID's faculty and students access to more facilities, institutional services, and career preparation options than could be provided otherwise by a national technical institute for the deaf operating independently.

NTID offers a variety of technical programs at the certificate, diploma, and associate degree levels. Degree programs include majors in business, engineering, science, and visual communications. In addition, NTID students may participate in approximately 200 educational programs available through RIT.

NTID also conducts applied research in occupational- and employment-related aspects of deafness, communication assessment, demographics of NTID's target population, and learning processes in postsecondary education. In addition, NTID conducts training workshops and seminars related to deafness. These workshops and seminars are offered nationwide to professionals who employ, work with, teach, or serve persons who are deaf. http://www.ntid.rit.edu/about

Sources of Information

Campus Tour A virtual tour of the college's campus is available online. http://www.ntid.rit.edu/virtual-tour; http://www.ntid.rit.edu/contact

For further information, contact the Rochester Institute of Technology, National Technical Institute for the Deaf, Department of Recruitment and Admissions, Lyndon Baines Johnson Building, 52 Lomb Memorial Drive, Rochester, NY 14623-5604. Phone, 716-475-6700.

DEPARTMENT OF ENERGY

1000 Independence Avenue SW., Washington, DC 20585
Phone, 202-586-5000. Internet, http://www.energy.gov

Office of the Secretary

Secretary of Energy	RICHARD PERRY
Deputy Secretary / Chief Operating Officer	VACANT
Associate Deputy Secretary	VACANT
Chief of Staff	BRIAN MCCORMACK
Inspector General	APRIL STEPHENSON, ACTING
Administrator, U.S. Energy Information Administration	HOWARD GRUENSPECHT, ACTING
Assistant Secretary, Congressional and Intergovernmental Affairs	SHARI DAVENPORT, ACTING
Assistant Secretary, International Affairs	ANDREA LOCKWOOD, ACTING
Chief Financial Officer	ALISON DOONE, ACTING
Director, Advanced Research Projects Agency–Energy	ERIC ROHLFING, ACTING
Director, Energy Policy and System Analysis	CAROL BATTERSHELL, ACTING
Director, Enterprise Assessment	GLENN S. PODONSKY
Director, Intelligence and Counterintelligence	STEVEN BLACK
Director, Public Affairs	ROBERT HAUS
Director, Small and Disadvantaged Business Utilization	CHRISTY JACKIEWICZ, ACTING
Executive Director, Loan Programs Office	JOHN SNEED
General Counsel	JOHN LUCAS, DESIGNATED BY POTUS
Ombudsman	RITA FRANKLIN

Office of the Under Secretary for Management and Performance

Assistant Secretary, Environmental Management	SUSAN CANGE, ACTING
Under Secretary	MATTHEW MOURY, ACTING
Deputy Under Secretary	VACANT
Associate Under Secretary, Environment, Health, Safety and Security	ANDREW LAWRENCE, ACTING
Chief Human Capital Officer	TONYA MACKEY, ACTING
Chief Information Officer	STEPHEN EVERETT
Director, Economic Impact and Diversity	ANDRE SAYLES, ACTING
Director, Hearing and Appeals	POLI MARMOLEJOS
Director, Legacy Management	CARMELO MELENDEZ
Director, Management	INGRID KOLB
Director, Project Management Oversight and Assessment	PAUL BOSCO

Office of the Under Secretary for Science and Energy

Under Secretary	PATRICIA A. HOFFMAN, DESIGNATED BY POTUS
Deputy Under Secretary	VACANT
Assistant Secretary, Electricity Delivery and Energy Reliability	PATRICIA A. HOFFMAN, ACTING
Assistant Secretary, Energy Efficiency and Renewable Energy	DANIEL SIMMONS, ACTING
Assistant Secretary, Fossil Energy	DOUGLAS HOLLETT, ACTING
Assistant Secretary, Nuclear Energy	EDWARD MCGINNIS, ACTING
Director, Indian Energy Policy and Programs	WILLIAM BRADFORD

205

Director, Science	STEVE BINKLEY, ACTING
Director, Technology Transitions	ROCHELLE BLAUSTEIN, ACTING

Office of the Under Secretary for Nuclear Security / National Nuclear Security Administration

Under Secretary, Nuclear Security / Administrator, National Nuclear Security Administration	LT. GENERAL FRANK G. KLOTZ, USAF (RETIRED)
Principal Deputy Administrator, National Nuclear Security	WILLIAM WHITE, DESIGNATED BY POTUS
Deputy Under Secretary, Counterterrorism and Counterproliferation	JAY TILDEN
Deputy Administrator, Defense Nuclear Nonproliferation	DAVID HUIZENGA, ACTING
Deputy Administrator, Defense Programs	PHILIP CALBOS, ACTING
Deputy Administrator, Naval Reactors	ADM. JAMES F. CALDWELL, JR., USN
Associate Administrator, Emergency Operations	ERIC SMITH, ACTING
Associate Administrator, Defense Nuclear Security	JEFFREY JOHNSON
Associate Administrator Safety, Infrastructure and Operations	JAMES MCCONNELL
Associate Administrator, Counterterrorism and Counterproliferation	JAY TILDEN

The Department of Energy addresses the Nation's energy, environmental, and nuclear challenges, using transformative science and technology to ensure national security and prosperity.

The Department of Energy (DOE) was established by the Department of Energy Organization Act (42 U.S.C. 7131), effective October 1, 1977, pursuant to Executive Order 12009 of September 13, 1977. The act consolidated the major Federal energy functions into one Cabinet-level department. http://www.energy.gov/management/office-management/operational-management/history/brief-history-department-energy

Secretary The Secretary decides major energy policy and planning issues; acts as the principal spokesperson for the Department; and ensures effective communication and working relationships with the public and with Federal, State, local, and tribal governments. The Secretary also serves as the President's principal adviser on energy policies, plans, and programs. http://www.energy.gov/leadership

Enterprise Assessments The Office of Enterprise Assessments functions as an autonomous organization that assesses nuclear and industrial safety performance, cyber and physical security performance, and other critical functions as directed by the Secretary and his or her leadership team. The Office implements congressionally-mandated enforcement functions, manages the National Training Center, serves as an important check-and-balance that meets the DOE's self-regulating responsibilities. http://www.energy.gov/ea/about-us

For further information, contact the Office of Resources, Communications and Congressional Affairs. Phone, 301-903-3272.

Environment, Health, Safety, and Security The Office of the Associate Under Secretary for Environment, Health, Safety and Security increases the effectiveness and efficiency of DOE primary mission-support organizations and initiates enterprisewide responses to common, widespread challenges. The Office serves as the central organization responsible for health, safety, environment, and security and for coordinating and integrating these vital programs. It develops policy and assists with technical matters, provides safety analysis, and oversees corporate safety and security programs. http://www.energy.gov/ehss/about-us

For further information, contact the Office of Resources Management. Phone, 301-903-5139.

Intelligence and Counterintelligence The Office of Intelligence and Counterintelligence safeguards national security information and technologies that comprise intellectual property of incalculable value. The Office has the ability to leverage the Department's scientific and technological expertise to assist policymakers, as well as national security missions in cyber, energy, and homeland security, and in defense and intelligence. http://www.energy.gov/office-intelligence-and-counterintelligence

For further information, contact the Office of Intelligence and Counterintelligence. Phone, 202-586-2610.

Operations, Field, and Site Offices The Administration of Government-owned, contractor-operated facility contracts is the principal responsibility of the operations, field, and site offices. Contractors who operate Government-owned facilities do most of the DOE's energy and physical research and development, environmental restoration, and waste management.

Department operations offices act as a formal link between Department headquarters and the field laboratories and other operating facilities. They manage programs and projects that the lead headquarters program offices assign. The appropriate assistant secretary, office director, or program officer provides daily, specific program direction for the operations offices. He or she also provides management guidance and coordination for and oversight of them and the field and site offices. http://www.energy.gov/offices

Project Management Oversight and Assessments The Office of Project Management Oversight and Assessments is the Department of Energy's central management organization providing leadership and assistance in developing and implementing departmentwide policies, procedures, programs, and management systems pertaining to project management, and independently monitors, assesses, and reports on project execution performance. http://www.energy.gov/projectmanagement/about_us

Energy Programs

Advanced Research Projects Agency–Energy The Advanced Research Projects Agency–Energy (ARPA–E) advances high-potential, high-impact energy technologies before they attract private-sector investment. ARPA-E awardees pursue new ways of generating, storing, and using energy. The Agency focuses on transformational energy projects that can be advanced with a small investment over a defined period of time. A streamlined awards process allows quick action to stimulate cutting-edge energy research. http://arpa-e.energy.gov/?q=arpa-e-site-page/about

For further information, contact the Office of the Director. Phone, 202-287-1004.

Efficiency and Renewable Energy The Office of Energy Efficiency and Renewable Energy leads the Department's efforts to develop and deliver market-driven solutions for sustainable transportation, renewable electricity generation, and energy-saving homes, buildings, and manufacturing. It supports research and development and technology transfer activities to improve energy efficiency in the transportation, building, industrial, and utility sectors. The Office also administers programs providing financial assistance for State energy planning, weatherizing homes owned by the poor and disadvantaged, implementing State and local energy conservation initiatives, and promoting energy efficient construction and renovation of Federal facilities. http://www.energy.gov/eere/office-energy-efficiency-renewable-energy

For further information, contact the Director of Information and Business Management Systems. Phone, 202-586-7241.

Electricity Delivery and Energy Reliability The Office of Electricity Delivery and Energy Reliability comprises five divisions: Advanced Grid Integration, Energy Infrastructure Modeling and Analysis, Infrastructure Security and Energy Restoration, National Electricity Delivery, and Power Systems Engineering Research and Development. It promotes electric grid modernization and energy infrastructure resiliency and leads the Department's efforts to ensure a resilient, reliable, and flexible electricity system. http://www.energy.gov/oe/about-office-electricity-delivery-and-energy-reliability

For further information, contact the Office of the Director. Phone, 202-586-1411.

Energy Information   The Energy Information Administration collects, processes, and disseminates data on energy consumption, demand, distribution, production, resource reserves, and technology. It also helps government and nongovernment energy users understand trends by offering analyses of the data. http://www.eia.gov/about

For further information, contact the Director, National Energy Information Center. Phone, 202-586-6537.

Fossil Energy   The Office of Fossil Energy is responsible for Federal research, development, and demonstration efforts on advanced carbon capture and storage (CCS) technologies, as well as the development of technological solutions for the prudent and sustainable development of our unconventional oil and gas domestic resources. It also manages the nation's Strategic Petroleum Reserve and Northeast Home Heating Oil Reserve, both key emergency response tools available to the President to protect Americans from energy supply disruptions. http://www.energy.gov/fe/about

For further information, contact the Office of Communications. Phone, 202-586-6803.

Indian Energy Policy and Programs   The Office of Indian Energy Policy and Programs coordinates, directs, fosters, and implements energy planning, education, management, and programs to assist Tribes with energy development, capacity building, energy infrastructure, energy costs, and electrification of Indian lands and homes. The Office works within the Department, across Government agencies, and with tribes and organizations to promote Indian energy policies and initiatives. https://www.energy.gov/indianenergy/about-us-0

For further information, contact the Director. Phone, 202-586-1272.

Loan Programs Office   The Loan Programs Office accelerates the domestic commercial deployment of innovative and advanced clean energy technologies at a scale that contributes significantly to achieving national clean energy objectives: enhanced American global economic competitiveness, job creation, reduced dependency on foreign oil, and an improved environmental legacy. It fulfills this mission by guaranteeing loans to eligible clean energy projects and by providing direct loans to eligible manufacturers of advanced technology vehicles and components. http://www.energy.gov/lpo/about-us-home | Email: lgprogram@hq.doe.gov

For further information, contact Loan Programs Office. Phone, 202-586-8335.

Nuclear Energy   The Office of Nuclear Energy advances nuclear power as a resource capable of meeting the Nation's energy, environmental, and national security needs. It relies on research, development, and demonstration to resolve barriers of cost, proliferation resistance, safety, security, and technology. Four research objectives guide the Office's efforts: developing technologies and other solutions to improve the reliability, maintain the safety, and extend the life of current reactors; making new reactors more affordable so that nuclear energy can play a bigger role in meeting energy security and climate change goals; developing sustainable fuel cycles; and understanding and minimizing the risks of nuclear proliferation and terrorism. http://www.energy.gov/ne/about-us

For further information, contact the Director, Corporate Communications and External Affairs. Phone, 301-903-1636.

Science   The Office of Science delivers scientific discoveries and tools to transform our understanding of nature and to advance national security, including the Nation's economic and energy security. The Office is the lead Federal agency supporting fundamental scientific research for energy and the Nation's largest supporter of basic research in the physical sciences. It supports scientific research and the development, construction, and operation of open-access, state-of-the-art facilities for researchers. For example, it supports research in all 50 States and the District of Columbia—at DOE laboratories and more than 300 universities and institutions of higher learning nationwide. http://science.energy.gov/about

For further information, contact the Director of Human Resources. Phone, 202-586-5430

Technology Transitions   The Office of Technology Transitions oversees and advances the DOE's mission by expanding the commercial impact of its portfolio of research, development, demonstration, and deployment activities in the short, medium, and long term. The Office develops the Department's policy and vision for expanding the commercial results of its research investments, and it streamlines information and access to DOE's national labs and sites to foster partnerships that will move innovations from the labs into the marketplace. http://www.energy.gov/technologytransitions/about-us

Environmental Quality Programs

Environmental Management   The Office of Environmental Management completes the safe cleanup of the environmental legacy after decades of nuclear weapons development and Government-sponsored nuclear energy research. The Office adheres to a mission philosophy based on reducing risk and reducing environmental liability. Current activities include fulfilling commitments to lower risk and complete cleanup across all sites; constructing and operating facilities treating radioactive liquid tank waste in a safe, stable form; securing and storing nuclear material in a safe, stable manner in secure locations; transporting and disposing transuranic and low-level wastes in a safe, cost-effective way; decontaminating and decommissioning facilities without further value; remediating soil and ground water containing radioactive and hazardous contaminants; and planning a facility to manage and store mercury. http://www.energy.gov/em/mission

For further information, contact the Director of Communication/External Affairs. Phone, 202-287-5591.

Legacy Management   The Office of Legacy Management manages DOE post-closure responsibilities and ensures the future protection of human health and the environment. The Office has control and custody for legacy land, structures, and facilities that it maintains at levels consistent with DOE long-term plans. Its activities include protecting human health and the environment through long-term surveillance and maintenance; preserving, protecting, and making accessible legacy records and information; supporting a workforce structured to accomplish DOE missions; implementing departmental policy affecting continuity of worker pension and medical benefits; managing legacy land and assets with an emphasis on safety, reuse, and disposition; mitigating community impacts from the cleanup of legacy waste and changing departmental missions; and coordinating policy issues with appropriate departmental organizations. http://www.energy.gov/lm/mission

For further information, contact the Director of Business Operations. Phone, 202-586-7388.

Nuclear Security Programs

Defense Programs   The Office of Defense Programs ensures that the U.S. nuclear arsenal meets national security requirements and continues to serve as a deterrent. In partnership with the Department of Defense, the Office provides the research, development, secure transportation, and production activities necessary to support the U.S. nuclear weapons stockpile. http://www.nnsa.energy.gov/aboutus/ourprograms/defenseprograms

For further information, contact the Associate Administrator for Management and Budget. Phone, 202-586-5753.

Naval Nuclear Propulsion   The Naval Reactors Office administers the Naval Nuclear Propulsion Program, which provides militarily effective nuclear propulsion plants and maintains their operational safety, reliability, and longevity. This program relies on trained U.S. Navy personnel, fast and stealthy ships, and supply-chain independence to carry out its mission. http://www.nnsa.energy.gov/aboutus/ourprograms/powernavy2

For further information, contact the Deputy Administrator for Naval Reactors. Phone, 202-781-6174.

Nuclear Nonproliferation   The Office of Defense Nuclear Nonproliferation works closely with a range of international partners, U.S. Federal agencies, the U.S. national laboratories, and the private sector.

It secures and safeguards or disposes of dangerous nuclear and radiological material and monitors and controls the proliferation of weapons-of-mass-destruction technology and expertise. http://nnsa.energy.gov/aboutus/ourprograms/nonproliferation-0

For further information, contact the Associate Administrator for Management and Budget. Phone, 202-586-5753.

Nuclear Security Administration The National Nuclear Security Administration (NNSA) was created by Congress through the National Defense Authorization Act for Fiscal Year 2000 (113 Stat. 512) to bring focus to the management of the Nation's defense nuclear security programs. Three existing organizations within the Department of Energy—Defense Programs, Defense Nuclear Nonproliferation, and Naval Reactors—were combined into a new, separately managed agency, headed by an Administrator who reports to the Secretary of Energy. The NNSA seeks to strengthen national security through military application of nuclear energy and by reducing the global threat from terrorism and weapons of mass destruction.

The Administration's service center and eight site offices provide operations oversight and contract administration for NNSA site activities. Federally-run site offices oversee the management and operating contractors for each of NNSA's eight sites. These offices provide the necessary communication between Federal and contractor employees as well as oversight to improve management procedures. http://www.nnsa.energy.gov/ourmission

For further information, contact the Associate Administrator for Management and Budget. Phone, 202-586-5753.

Power Administrations

The Department's four Power Administrations market and transmit electric power produced at Federal hydroelectric projects and reservoirs. The Deputy Secretary provides management oversight of the Power Administrations.

Bonneville Power Administration The Bonneville Power Administration is a nonprofit federal power marketing administration based in the Pacific Northwest. Although BPA is part of the U.S. Department of Energy, it is self-funding and covers its costs by selling its products and services. BPA markets wholesale electrical power from 31 federal hydroelectric projects in the Northwest, one nonfederal nuclear plant and several small nonfederal power plants. BPA promotes energy efficiency, renewable resources and new technologies that improve its ability to deliver on its mission. It also funds regional efforts to protect and rebuild fish and wildlife populations affected by hydropower development in the Columbia River Basin. BPA is committed to public service and makes its decisions with input from all stakeholders. BPA dedicates itself to providing high system reliability, low rates consistent with sound business principles, environmental stewardship, and accountability. http://www.bpa.gov/Pages/home.aspx

For further information, contact the Bonneville Power Administration, 905 Eleventh Avenue NE., Portland, OR 97232-4169. Phone, 503-230-3000 or 800-282-3713.

Southeastern Power Administration This Administration transmits and disposes of surplus electric power and energy generated at reservoir projects in Alabama, Florida, Georgia, Kentucky, Mississippi, North and South Carolina, Tennessee, Virginia, and West Virginia.

It sets the lowest possible rates for consumers consistent with sound business practices and gives preference to public entities. http://www.energy.gov/sepa/about-us

For further information, contact the Southeastern Power Administration, 1166 Athens Tech Road, Elberton, GA 30635-4578. Phone, 706-213-3800.

Southwestern Power Administration This Administration sells and disposes of electric power and energy in Arkansas, Kansas, Louisiana, Missouri, Oklahoma, and Texas.

It transmits and disposes of the electric power and energy generated at Federal reservoir projects, supplemented by power purchased from public and private utilities, in such a manner as to encourage the most widespread and economical use. It sets the lowest possible rates for consumers consistent with sound business practices and gives preference to public entities. It also conducts and participates in the comprehensive planning of water resource development in the Southwest. http://www.swpa.gov/agency.aspx

For further information, contact the Southwestern Power Administration, Suite 1600, Williams Center Tower One, One West Third Street, Tulsa, OK 74103-3532. Phone, 918-595-6600.

Western Area Power Administration   WAPA markets and transmits wholesale electricity from multi-use water projects. Its service area encompasses a 15-state region of the central and western U.S. where more than 17,000 circuit mile transmission system carries electricity from 56 hydropower plants operated by the Bureau of Reclamation, U.S. Army Corps of Engineers and the International Boundary and Water Commission. WAPA also markets power from the Navajo Generating Station coal-fired plant near Page, Ariz. Together, these plants have an installed capacity of 10,504 megawatts. WAPA sells power to preference customers such as Federal and state agencies, cities and towns, rural electric cooperatives, public utility districts, irrigation districts and Native American tribes. In turn, they provide retail electric service to millions of consumers in the West. http://www.wapa.gov/About/Pages/about.aspx

For further information, contact the Western Area Power Administration, 12155 West Alameda Parkway, Lakewood, CO 80228-1213. Phone, 720-962-7000.

Sources of Information

Business Opportunities   To learn about the Office of Small and Disadvantaged Business Utilization and its mission or to find information on the services that it offers and its programs, visit the Office's Web site. Phone, 202-586-7377. http://www.energy.gov/osdbu/office-small-and-disadvantaged-business-utilization | Email: smallbusiness@hq.doe.gov

Useful external links for small businesses are available on the Office of Small and Disadvantaged Business Utilization's Web site. http://www.energy.gov/osdbu/small-business-services/useful-links-small-businesses

Employment   The DOE offers career opportunities that span a broad, diverse range of professions: accounting and contracting, administration, business, communications and information technology, computer science, engineering, mathematics, national security and international affairs, public affairs, science and technology, and more. Most Federal jobs require U.S. citizenship; however, noncitizens may apply for some opportunities at the National Laboratories. http://www.energy.gov/jobs/jobs

Information on opportunities for students and recent graduates, veterans, and those with disabilities is available on the DOE Web site. For more information, contact the Chief Human Capital Officer. Phone, 202-586-1234. http://www.energy.gov/jobs/services/students-recent-graduates

Energy Saver   Energy Saver is the DOE's consumer resource on saving energy and using renewable energy technologies at home. http://www.energy.gov/energysaver/energy-saver

When deciding whether or not to invest in more energy efficiency, consumers can benefit from knowing electricity usages and the associated costs. The online energy use calculator estimates annual energy use and costs associated with operating appliances and home electronics. http://energy.gov/energysaver/estimating-appliance-and-home-electronic-energy-use

Energy Simulation Software   EnergyPlus is cross-platform, free, and open-source software that runs on the Windows, Mac OS X, and Linux operating systems. It is a whole building energy simulation program that architects, engineers, and researchers use to model energy consumption and water use in buildings. The DOE's Building Technologies Office funded the development of EnergyPlus, and the National Renewable Energy Laboratory manages it. http://apps1.eere.energy.gov/buildings/energyplus

Freedom of Information Act (FOIA)   The Office of Information Resources administers policies, procedures, and programs to ensure DOE compliance with the FOIA. The DOE provides resources on its Web site to assist information seekers with finding answers to questions about DOE programs and with locating information that is already publicly available and does not require a

FOIA request to access. Information seekers should use these resources before submitting a FOIA request for DOE records. http://www.energy.gov/management/office-management/operational-management/freedom-information-act

Contact information for FOIA requester service centers and FOIA public liaisons and officers is available online. http://www.energy.gov/management/office-management/operational-management/freedom-information-act/foia-contacts | Email: foia-central@hq.doe.gov

The DOE Web site features an electronic FOIA request form. http://www.energy.gov/doe-headquarters-foia-request-form

Glossaries   The Bioenergy Technologies Office maintains an online biomass glossary. Its short descriptions are intended to help students and researchers understand biomass terminology. http://www.energy.gov/eere/bioenergy/glossary

The waterpower program maintains an online hydropower glossary. It is intended to help readers understand terminology associated with hydroturbine and hydropower plant components. http://www.energy.gov/eere/water/glossary-hydropower-terms

History   The DOE history timeline provides the public with easy access to information on the Department's history and its predecessor agencies. The timeline includes links to press releases, reports, speeches, and other documentation. http://energy.gov/management/office-management/operational-management/history/doe-history-timeline

Maps   The DOE Web site features maps depicting a variety of energy-related topics and trends: alternative fueling stations, carbon capture, climate vulnerabilities, per capita energy expenditure, renewable energy production, solar energy potential, and more. http://www.energy.gov/maps

National Laboratories   For more than 60 years, these Laboratories have been leading institutions for scientific innovation in the United States. To learn more about the Ames Laboratory, Princeton Plasma Physics Laboratory, Thomas Jefferson National Accelerator Facility, and the other 14 National Laboratories, visit the DOE's "About the National Labs" Web page. http://energy.gov/about-national-labs

News   The DOE posts news stories, photos, speeches, and videos on its Web site, which also features a blog. http://www.energy.gov/news-blog

The DOE's online photo galleries are diverse and extensive, as well as captivating for browsers who have an interest in America's energy future. https://www.energy.gov/photos

An online subscription form is available to sign up for DOE advisories and press releases. http://onlinepressroom.net/doe

Office of Inspector General (OIG)   The OIG maintains electronic and telephone hotlines to facilitate the reporting of allegations of abuse, fraud, mismanagement, or waste in DOE programs or operations. Phone, 202-586-4073 or 800-541-1625. http://www.energy.gov/ig/office-inspector-general | Email: ighotline@hq.doe.gov

An online complaint form for reporting allegations is also available on the OIG Web site. http://www.energy.gov/ig/complaint-form

The early alert system is a distribution list used to inform subscribers of significant press releases, publications, and reports the moment that the OIG posts them online. Subscription is free and available to anyone who has an email address and an interest in the OIG's work. http://www.energy.gov/ig/subscription-information | Email: ignewmedia@hq.doe.gov

Open Government   The DOE supports the Open Government initiative to create a more open and transparent Government by promoting the principles of collaboration, participation, and transparency. http://www.energy.gov/open-government | Email: open@hq.doe.gov

Phonebook   A departmentwide phonebook with a text box for entering search requests is available on the DOE Web site. http://www.energy.gov/phonebook

Program and Staff Offices   The "Offices" Web page features links to the program and staff offices' Web sites. It also includes links to the Web sites of the laboratories and technology centers, power marketing administrations, field sites, and Energy Information and National Nuclear Security Administrations. http://www.energy.gov/offices

Renewable Energy The steady expansion of the U.S. renewable energy sector indicates that a clean energy revolution is underway nationwide. The DOE Web site features charts that graphically illustrates trends that will shape America's energy future. http://energy.gov/science-innovation/energy-sources/renewable-energy

Scientific and Technical Information The Office of Scientific and Technical Information (OSTI) advances science and sustains technological creativity by making research and development findings available to and useful for DOE researchers and the public. The OSTI Web site provides access to DOE science resources and to U.S. Federal science (Science.gov) and global science (WorldWideScience.org) information. https://www.osti.gov/home/2014-catalogue-collections

Social Media The DOE tweets announcements and other newsworthy items on Twitter. https://twitter.com/energy

The DOE has a Facebook page. https://www.facebook.com/energygov; http://www.energy.gov/contact-us

For further information, contact the Office of Public Affairs, Department of Energy, 1000 Independence Avenue SW., Washington, DC 20585. Phone, 202-586-4940.

Federal Energy Regulatory Commission

888 First Street NE., Washington, DC 20426
Phone, 202-502-8004. Internet, http://www.ferc.gov

CHAIR	CHERYL A. LEFLEUR, ACTING
Commissioner	(VACANCY)
Commissioner	(VACANCY)
Commissioner	(VACANCY)
Commissioner	(VACANCY)

The Federal Energy Regulatory Commission helps consumers obtain efficient, reliable, and sustainable energy services at fair and reasonable rates through regulatory and market means.

The Federal Energy Regulatory Commission (FERC) is an independent agency within the Department of Energy that regulates the interstate transmission of electricity, natural gas, and oil. The Commission comprises five members whom the President appoints with the advice and consent of the Senate. FERC Commissioners serve 5-year terms and have an equal vote on regulatory matters. The President designates one member to serve as both the Commission's Chair and its administrative head.

Under the authority of the Federal Power, the Natural Gas, and the Interstate Commerce Acts, the FERC regulates the interstate transmission of electricity, natural gas, and oil. That authority also includes review of proposals to build interstate natural gas pipelines, natural gas storage facilities, and liquefied natural gas terminals, and licensing of nonfederal hydropower dams.

The FERC enforces regulatory requirements by imposing civil penalties and other means, monitors and investigates energy markets, and protects the reliability of the high voltage interstate transmission system through mandatory reliability standards. http://www.ferc.gov/about/ferc-does.asp

Sources of Information

Critical Energy Infrastructure Information (CEII) The FERC protects energy facilities by restricting public access to CEII. An electronic CEII request form is available on the Commission's Web site. http://www.ferc.gov/legal/ceii-foia/ceii/eceii.asp

Employment   Information on college recruitment and internship programs, reasons for pursuing career opportunities at the FERC, and a list of job vacancies are available online. http://ferc.gov/careers/careers.asp

In 2016, the FERC was ranked as the #4 best midsize agencies at which to work in the Federal Government, and #1 in Work-Life Balance for three years running. http://bestplacestowork.org/BPTW/rankings/detail/DR00

FERC Online   FERC Online serves as a portal to documents and dockets and provides an easy and efficient way to communicate and do business with the Commission. http://www.ferc.gov/docs-filing/ferconline.asp

Freedom of Information Act (FOIA)   An electronic FOIA request form is available on the Commission's Web site. http://www.ferc.gov/legal/ceii-foia/foia/foia-new-form/FOIARequest.aspx

Frequently Asked Questions (FAQs)   A topical list of FAQs is available on the Commission's Web site. http://www.ferc.gov/resources/faqs.asp

Glossary   The FERC maintains a glossary and list of acronyms on its Web site. http://www.ferc.gov/resources/glossary.asp; http://www.ferc.gov/resources/acronyms.asp

Media   The Commission posts headlines, news releases, photographs, and statements, as well as informational videos and podcasts, congressional testimony, speeches, and interviews. http://www.ferc.gov/media/media.asp

Open Government   The FERC supports the principles of collaboration, participation, and transparency to expand the openness of the Federal Government. https://www.ferc.gov/open.asp

Phone Book   The employee phone directory is available online in Portable Document Form (PDF). http://www.ferc.gov/contact-us/tel-num/phone.pdf

Plain Language   The Commission is committed to the Plain Writing Act of 2010 and adheres to Federal plain language guidelines. Please let FERC editors and writers know if a document or section of the Web site is difficult to understand. https://www.ferc.gov/open/plain-language.asp | Email: customer@ferc.gov

Public Participation   Citizens who may be affected by a proposed natural gas or hydroelectric project that the Commission regulates have certain rights. These rights range from being able to look at project correspondence to becoming an intervener and being able to appeal FERC decisions in Federal court. http://www.ferc.gov/resources/get-involved.asp

Speakers   An online form is available to initiate a request for a FERC representative to serve as a speaker at an organized event. http://ferc.gov/contact-us/speak-req.asp; http://www.ferc.gov/contact-us/tel-num.asp

For further information, contact the Office of External Affairs. Phone, 202-502-8004 or 866-208-3372. Fax, 202-208-2106.

Editorial Note

The Department of Health and Human Services did not meet the publication deadline for submitting updated information of its activities, functions, and sources of information as required by the automatic disclosure provisions of the Freedom of Information Act (5 U.S.C. 552(a)(1)(A)).

DEPARTMENT OF HEALTH AND HUMAN SERVICES

200 Independence Avenue SW., Washington, DC 20201
Phone, 202-690-6343. Internet, http://www.hhs.gov

Secretary of Health and Human Services	THOMAS E. PRICE
Deputy Secretary	MARY K. WAKEFIELD, ACTING
Chief of Staff	ALASTAIR M. FITZPAYNE
Chair, Departmental Appeals Board	CONSTANCE B. TOBIAS
Chief Administrative Law Judge, Office of Medicare Hearings and Appeals	NANCY J. GRISWOLD
Executive Secretary	MADHURA VALVERDE
General Counsel	PEGGY DOTZEL, ACTING
Inspector General	DANIEL R. LEVINSON
National Coordinator for Health Information Technology	KAREN B. DESALVO
Surgeon General	VIVEK H. MURTHY

Assistant Secretaries

Administration	COLLEEN BARROS, ACTING
Financial Resources	ELLEN G. MURRAY
Global Affairs	JIMMY KOLKER
Health	KAREN B. DESALVO, ACTING
Legislation	JIM R. ESQUEA
Planning and Evaluation	KATHRYN MARTIN, ACTING
Preparedness and Response	NICOLE LURIE
Public Affairs	KEVIN GRIFFIS

Directors

Center for Faith-Based and Neighborhood Partnerships	ACACIA BAMBERG SALATTI
Office for Civil Rights	JOCELYN SAMUELS
Office of Health Reform	MEENA SESHAMANI
Office of Intergovernmental and External Affairs	EMILY BARSON

https://www.hhs.gov/about/leadership/index.html

The Department of Health and Human Services strengthens the public health and welfare of the American people by making affordable and quality health care and childcare accessible, ensuring the safety of food products, preparing for public health emergencies, and advancing the diagnosis, treatment, and curing of life-threatening illnesses.

The Department of Health and Human Services (HHS) was created as the Department of Health, Education, and Welfare on April 11, 1953 (5 U.S.C. app.).

Secretary The Secretary of Health and Human Services advises the President on health, welfare, and income security plans, policies, and programs of the Federal Government and directs Department staff in carrying out the programs and activities of the Department and promotes general public understanding of the Department's goals, programs, and objectives. http://www.hhs. gov/about/leadership/index.html#secretary

Office of Intergovernmental and External Affairs The Office of Intergovernmental and External Affairs (IEA) supports the Secretary by serving as the primary liaison between the Department and external stakeholders and governments at the State, local, territorial, and tribal levels. The Office facilitates communication regarding HHS initiatives as they relate to external stakeholders and governments at the State,

DEPARTMENT OF HEALTH AND HUMAN SERVICES

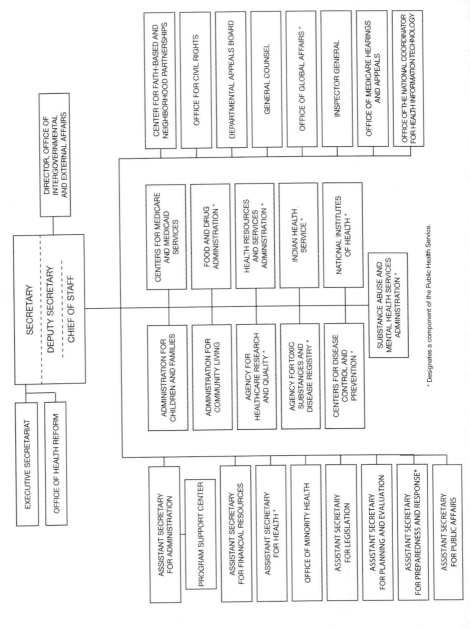

* Designates a component of the Public Health Service.

SECRETARY
DEPUTY SECRETARY
CHIEF OF STAFF

DIRECTOR, OFFICE OF INTERGOVERNMENTAL AND EXTERNAL AFFAIRS

EXECUTIVE SECRETARIAT

OFFICE OF HEALTH REFORM

CENTER FOR FAITH-BASED AND NEIGHBORHOOD PARTNERSHIPS

OFFICE FOR CIVIL RIGHTS

DEPARTMENTAL APPEALS BOARD

GENERAL COUNSEL

OFFICE OF GLOBAL AFFAIRS *

INSPECTOR GENERAL

OFFICE OF MEDICARE HEARINGS AND APPEALS

OFFICE OF THE NATIONAL COORDINATOR FOR HEALTH INFORMATION TECHNOLOGY

CENTERS FOR MEDICARE AND MEDICAID SERVICES

FOOD AND DRUG ADMINISTRATION *

HEALTH RESOURCES AND SERVICES ADMINISTRATION *

INDIAN HEALTH SERVICE *

NATIONAL INSTITUTES OF HEALTH *

SUBSTANCE ABUSE AND MENTAL HEALTH SERVICES ADMINISTRATION *

ADMINISTRATION FOR CHILDREN AND FAMILIES

ADMINISTRATION FOR COMMUNITY LIVING

AGENCY FOR HEALTHCARE RESEARCH AND QUALITY *

AGENCY FOR TOXIC SUBSTANCES AND DISEASE REGISTRY *

CENTERS FOR DISEASE CONTROL AND PREVENTION *

ASSISTANT SECRETARY FOR ADMINISTRATION

PROGRAM SUPPORT CENTER

ASSISTANT SECRETARY FOR FINANCIAL RESOURCES

ASSISTANT SECRETARY FOR HEALTH *

OFFICE OF MINORITY HEALTH

ASSISTANT SECRETARY FOR LEGISLATION

ASSISTANT SECRETARY FOR PLANNING AND EVALUATION

ASSISTANT SECRETARY FOR PREPAREDNESS AND RESPONSE *

ASSISTANT SECRETARY FOR PUBLIC AFFAIRS

local, territorial, and tribal levels. The IEA both represents the State, territorial, and tribal perspective in the process of Federal policymaking and clarifies the Federal perspective to State, territorial and tribal representatives. http://www.hhs.gov/intergovernmental

For further information, contact the Office of Intergovernmental and External Affairs. Phone, 202-690-6060.

Office of the Assistant Secretary for Preparedness and Response

The Office of the Assistant Secretary for Preparedness and Response (ASPR) provides national leadership in the prevention of, preparation for, and response to the adverse health effects of public health emergencies and disasters. It acts as the primary advisor to the HHS Secretary on bioterrorism and other public health emergency matters, strengthens the Nation's health and response systems, and enhances national health security. The ASPR leads a collaborative policy approach to the Department's preparedness, response, and recovery portfolio. It works with partners across Federal, State, local, tribal, and international bodies, in communities, and in the private sector to promote a unified and strategic approach to the challenges of public health and medical preparedness, response, and recovery through programs like the Hospital Preparedness Program. The ASPR coordinates public health and medical support available from across the Federal Government to help prepare communities and to augment local capabilities of overwhelmed communities during and after disasters, which includes providing medical professionals through the ASPR's National Disaster Medical System and the Medical Reserve Corps. The ASPR provides an integrated, systematic approach to the advanced development and acquisition of the necessary vaccines, drugs, therapies, and diagnostic tools for public health medical emergencies. It also coordinates within the Department and among Federal partners on the policy, prioritization, funding, acquisition, and distribution of these medical countermeasures. In addition, offices within the ASPR coordinate within the division, within the Department and with Federal, State, local, territorial, tribal and international bodies on emergency communications, science preparedness, and administrative management to support decisionmakers in emergencies. http://www.phe.gov/preparedness/pages/default.aspx

For further information, contact the Office of the Assistant Secretary for Preparedness and Response. Phone, 202-205-2882.

Office of the Assistant Secretary for Health

The Office of the Assistant Secretary for Health (ASH) comprises 12 offices and 10 Presidential and secretarial advisory committees. The Assistant Secretary for Health heads the Office and serves as the Secretary's senior public health advisor. ASH provides assistance in implementing and coordinating secretarial decisions for the Public Health Service and coordination of population-based health clinical divisions; provides oversight of research conducted or supported by the Department; implements programs that provide population-based public health services; and provides direction and policy oversight, through the Office of the Surgeon General, for the Public Health Service Commissioned Corps. ASH administers a wide array of interdisciplinary programs related to disease prevention, health promotion, the reduction of health disparities, women's health, HIV/AIDS, vaccine programs, physical fitness and sports, bioethics, population affairs, blood supply, research integrity, and human research protections. http://www.hhs.gov/ash

For further information, contact the Office of the Assistant Secretary for Health. Phone, 202-690-7694.

Sources of Information

A–Z Index   The HHS Web site features an alphabetical index to help visitors search for specific topics or browse content that aligns with their interests. http://www.hhs.gov/az/a/index.html

Bullying   The HHS manages StopBullying.gov, a Web site that provides resources for defining, preventing, and responding to bullying, and for identifying who may be at risk. The Web site also features sections for children and teens, educators, parents, and communities. https://www.stopbullying.gov

Information on identifying, preventing, and reporting cyberbullying is also available on the Web site. https://www.stopbullying. gov/cyberbullying/index.html

Business Opportunities   The HHS relies on its contractors and grantees to help protect the health of Americans and provide essential human services. http://www.hhs. gov/grants/index.html#contract

The Office of Small and Disadvantaged Business Utilization helps develop and implement outreach programs to raise awareness of HHS contracting opportunities within the small business community. For information on programs, contact the Office of Small and Disadvantaged Business Utilization. Phone, 202-690-7300. http:// www.hhs.gov/asfr/ogapa/osbdu

Civil Rights   The Office for Civil Rights improves people's health and well-being, ensures equal access to health care and services without discrimination, and protects the privacy and security of people's health information. For information on enforcement of civil rights laws, contact the Director, Office for Civil Rights, 200 Independence Avenue SW.,Room 515–F Washington, DC 20201. Phone, 800-368-1019. TDD, 800-537-7697. http://www.hhs.gov/ocr/civilrights

Departmental Appeals Board   For information, contact the Departmental Appeals Board Immediate Office, MS 6127, Wilbur J. Cohen Building, 330 Independence Avenue SW., Room G–644, Washington, DC 20201. Phone, 202-565-0200. http://www.hhs.gov/dab

Career Opportunities   For information on training opportunities and opportunities for recent graduates and students or to view current job openings, visit the "Why a Career at HHS?" Web page. http://www.hhs. gov/about/careers/index.html

Freedom of Information Act (FOIA)   The FOIA allows individuals to request access to Federal agency records. The statute contains, however, nine exemptions that exempt some records or portions of them from disclosure. The Assistant Secretary for Public Affairs also serves as the Agency Chief FOIA Officer. http://www.hhs.gov/foia | Email: hhs.acfo@hhs.gov

Frequently Asked Questions (FAQs)   The HHS posts answers to FAQs on its Web site. http://www.hhs.gov/answers

Glossary   In the world of organ donation and transplantation, terms are used and topics discussed that many may not recognize. The OrganDonor.gov Web site features a glossary of organ donation terms. http://www.organdonor.gov/about/facts-terms/terms.html

Inspector General   Contact the Office of Inspector General, Wilbur J. Cohen Building, 330 Independence Avenue SW., Washington, DC 20201. http://oig.hhs.gov

To report fraud, waste, or abuse in Department programs, contact the Office of Inspector General, OIG Hotline Operations, P.O. Box 23489, L'Enfant Plaza Station, Washington, DC 20026-3489. TIPS Line, 800-447-8477. OIG Fugitive Line, 888-476-4453. TTY, 800-377-4950. Fax, 800-223-8164. https://forms.oig.hhs.gov/hotlineoperations

Medicare Hearings / Appeals   For information on Medicare hearings before administrative law judges, regarding Medicare coverage and payment determinations that Medicare contractors, Medicare Advantage Organizations, or Part D plan sponsors have made, as well as information on determinations related to Medicare beneficiary eligibility and entitlement, Part B late enrollment penalties, and income-related monthly adjustment amounts that the Social Security Administration has made, contact the Office of Medicare Hearings and Appeals. Phone, 703-235-0635 or 855-556-8475. http://www.hhs.gov/omha | Email: medicare.appeals@hhs.gov

Open Government   The HHS supports the Open Government initiative by promoting the principles of collaboration, participation, and transparency. http://www.hhs.gov/open/index.html

Privacy Rights   For information on the HIPAA privacy, security, and breach notification rules or the Patient Safety Act, contact the Office for Civil Rights. Phone, 800-368-1019. TDD, 800-537-7697. http://www.hhs.gov/ocr/privacy

Public Health Service Commissioned Corps Officer Program   Information on the Commissioned Corps Officer programs is available at the Public Health Service Commissioned Corps Officer Web site. http://www.usphs.gov

Regional Offices   Visit the "Regional Offices" Web page for contact information. http://www.hhs.gov/about/agencies/regional-offices

Support Services (Fee-for-Service Activities)   The Program Support Center provides support services to all components of the Department and Federal agencies worldwide. For information concerning fee-for-service activities in the areas of acquisitions, occupational health,

information technology support and security, human resource systems, financial management, and administrative operations, contact the Program Support Center, 5600 Fishers Lane, Rockville, MD 20857. Phone, 301-443-0034. http://www.psc.gov

Surgeon General   For information on the benefits of active living, healthy eating, mental and emotional well-being, and tobacco-free living, visit the "Surgeon General" Web site. Phone, 240-276-8853. http://www.surgeongeneral.gov; http://www.hhs.gov/contactus.html

For further information, contact the U.S. Department of Health and Human Services, 200 Independence Avenue SW., Washington, DC 20201. Phone, 877-696-6775.

Administration for Children and Families

330 C Street SW., Washington, DC 20201
Phone, 202-401-9200. Internet, http://www.acf.hhs.gov

Assistant Secretary for Children and Families	MARK GREENBERG, ACTING
Chief of Staff	S. JEFFREY HILD

The Administration for Children and Families administers programs and provides advice to the Secretary on issues relevant to children, youth, and families; child support enforcement; community services; developmental disabilities; family assistance; Native American assistance; and refugee resettlement. http://www.acf.hhs.gov/about/what-we-do

Sources of Information

Career Opportunities   The Administration employs professionals with diverse academic and social backgrounds in a broad range of career fields and positions. http://www.acf.hhs.gov/about/jobs-contracts

History   The Administration for Children and Families was created on April 15, 1991. A short history of the Administration is available on its Web site. http://www.acf.hhs.gov

Homelessness   The Administration's Web site features information on its programs and services for the homeless and for those at risk of becoming homeless. http://www.acf.hhs.gov/program-topics/homelessness

Hotlines   The Administration supports nationwide crisis hotlines for child abuse, domestic violence, human trafficking, and runaways. The Health Insurance Marketplace Call Center assists callers with choosing coverage that provides the best protection and benefits for them and family members, as well as for their businesses. http://www.acf.hhs.gov/acf-hotlines

Lesbian, Gay, Bisexual, and Transgender (LGBT) Assistance   The Administration's Web site features information on its programs and services for the LGBT community, especially for LGBT families and youth. http://www.acf.hhs.gov/program-topics/lgbt-0

News   The Administration posts press releases on its Web site. http://www.acf.hhs.gov/media/press

Programs / Services   The Administration's Web site features a page showcasing by topic the programs and services that it provides to support families, children, individuals, and communities. Topics include children and youth, communities, emergency response and recovery, families, financial security, global populations, Hispanic outreach, homelessness, human trafficking, LGBT, Native Americans and tribes, and unaccompanied children. http:// www.acf.hhs.gov/program-topics; http:// www.acf.hhs.gov/media/program-contacts

For further information, contact the Administration for Children and Families, 330 C Street SW., Washington, DC 20201. Phone, 202-401-9200.

Administration for Community Living

330 C Street SW., Washington, DC 20201
Phone, 202-401-4634. TTY, 800-877-8339. Internet, http://www.acl.gov

Administrator	MARY LAZARE, ACTING
Principal Deputy Administrator	MARY LAZARE, ACTING

The Administration for Community Living administers programs and advises the Secretary on issues relevant to people with disabilities, their families and caregivers, and the independence, well-being, and health of older adults. https://acl.gov/About_ACL/Index.aspx

Sources of Information

Blog   The Administration's Blog presents diverse perspectives on trends and issues related to older adults and people with disabilities. https://acl.gov/NewsRoom/blog/Index.aspx

Data / Statistics   Data and statistics on older adults, as well as on persons with intellectual, physical, and developmental disabilities, are available on the Administration's Web site. https://acl.gov/Data_Outcomes/Index.aspx

Elder Care Services   The elder care locator is a public service that provides information on services for older adults and their families. Online chat with an information specialist is also available Monday–Friday, 9 a.m.–8 p.m., eastern time. Phone, 800-677-1116. http://www.eldercare.gov/Eldercare.NET/Public/Index.aspx

Employment   For information on employment opportunities, visit the "Career Opportunities" Web page. http://www.acl.gov/About_ACL/CareerOpportunities/Index.aspx

Help / Resources   The Administration's Web site features resources for connecting caregivers, families, older adults, people with disabilities, and professionals to Federal, national, and local programs and information. https://acl.gov/Get_Help/Index.aspx; http://www.acl.gov

For further information, contact the Administration for Community Living, 330 C Street SW., Washington, DC 20201. Phone, 202-401-4634. TTY, 800-877-8339.

Agency for Healthcare Research and Quality

5600 Fishers Lane, Rockville, MD 20857
Phone, 301-427-1364. Internet, http://www.ahrq.gov

Director	ANDREW BINDMAN
Deputy Director	SHARON B. ARNOLD

The Agency for Healthcare Research and Quality produces evidence to make health care affordable, equitable, more accessible, of a higher quality, and safer. It also works within the Department of Health and Human Services and with other partners to ensure that the evidence is understood and used. http://www.ahrq.gov/cpi/about/profile/index.html

Sources of Information

Data Statistical portraits of health care delivery in the United States are available on the Agency's Web site. http://www.ahrq.gov/research/data/index.html
Career Opportunities For information on employment opportunities, visit the "Job Opportunities" Web page. http://www.ahrq.gov/cpi/about/careers/index.html

Frequently Asked Questions (FAQs) The Agency posts answers to FAQs on is Web site. https://info.ahrq.gov
Site Map The Web site map allows visitors to look for specific topics or to browse content that aligns with their interests. http://www.ahrq.gov/sitemap.html; http://www.ahrq.gov

For further information, contact the Agency for Healthcare Research and Quality, 5600 Fishers Lane, Rockville, MD 20857. Phone, 301-427-1364.

Agency for Toxic Substances and Disease Registry

MS E–61, 4770 Buford Highway NE., Atlanta, GA 30341
Phone, 770-488-0604. Internet, http://www.atsdr.cdc.gov

Administrator	BRENDA FITZGERALD

The Agency for Toxic Substances and Disease Registry (ATSDR), as part of the Public Health Service, tries to prevent exposure to toxic substances—exposure to substances from wastesites, unplanned releases, and other pollution sources present in the environment—which produces adverse health effects and diminishes the quality of life. https://www.atsdr.cdc.gov/about/index.html

Sources of Information

A–Z Index The Agency's Web site features an alphabetical index to help visitors search for specific topics or browse content that aligns with their interests. https://www.atsdr.cdc.gov/az/a.html
ATSDR in 60 Seconds The ATSDR protects people from the health effects of chemical exposures. The Agency's Web site features the 60-second video "Dangerous Discovery" that communicates the importance of its mission. https://www.atsdr.cdc.gov/videos/ATSDR_DangerousDiscovery_h264.mp4
Internships / Training Information on internships and educational and training opportunities is available on the ATSDR

Web site. http://www.atsdr.cdc.gov/environmentaleducation.html
Toxic Frequently Asked Questions (ToxFAQs) ToxFAQs features a series of summaries on hazardous substances that the Agency's Division of Toxicology developed. ATSDR toxicological profiles and public health statements are the sources of information on which the series relies. Each factsheet serves as a guide that is quick to read and easy to understand. ToxFAQs also answers FAQs on exposure to hazardous substances that are encountered near wastesites and their effects on human health. https://www.atsdr.cdc.gov/toxfaqs/index.asp
Toxic Substances Portal The portal offers convenient access to the most relevant information on toxic substances and their effects on human health. The portal's Web pages feature an alphabetical ordering of documents on specific substances, toxicological information by health effect or chemical class, and toxicological information for specific audiences (community members, emergency responders, toxicological and health professionals, and health care providers). https://www.atsdr.cdc.gov/substances/index.asp; http://www.atsdr.cdc.gov

For further information, contact the Agency for Toxic Substances and Disease Registry, 4770 Buford Highway NE., Atlanta, GA 30341. Phone, 770-488-0604.

Centers for Disease Control and Prevention

1600 Clifton Road, Atlanta, GA 30333
Phone, 800-232-4636. Internet, http://www.cdc.gov

Director	BRENDA FITZGERALD
Principal Deputy Director	ANNE SCHUCHAT

The Centers for Disease Control and Prevention (CDC), as part of the Public Health Service, protect the public health of the Nation by providing leadership and direction in the prevention and control of diseases and other preventable conditions and by responding to public health emergencies. Within the CDC, the following seven centers, institutes, and offices lead prevention, diagnosis, and treatment efforts for public health concerns. http://www.cdc.gov/about/default.htm

Center for Global Health   The Center leads the CDC global health strategy, working in partnership with foreign governments and international organizations to help countries worldwide evaluate, manage, and plan global health care programs. The Center works to eradicate chronic diseases and life-threatening injuries, expanding global health care programs to address the leading causes of disability, morbidity, and mortality. http://www.cdc.gov/globalhealth/index.html

National Institute for Occupational Safety and Health   The Institute coordinates, directs, and plans a national program to develop and establish recommended occupational safety and health standards and to conduct research and training, offer technical assistance, and engage in related activities to assure safe and healthy work conditions for every working person. http://www.cdc.gov/NIOSH

Office of Infectious Diseases   The Office facilitates research, programs, and policies to reduce the national and international burden of infectious diseases. The Office includes the following organizational components: the National Center for HIV/AIDS, Viral Hepatitis, STD and TB Prevention; the National Center for Immunization and Respiratory Diseases; and the National Center for Emerging and Zoonotic Infectious Diseases. http://www.cdc.gov/oid

Office of Noncommunicable Diseases, Injury, and Environmental Health   The Office provides strategic direction and leadership for the prevention of noncommunicable diseases, injuries, disabilities, and environmental health hazards. The Office includes the following organizational components: the National Center on Birth Defects and Developmental Disabilities; the National Center for Chronic Disease Prevention and Health Promotion; the National Center for Environmental Health; and the National Center for Injury Prevention and Control. http://www.cdc.gov/maso/pdf/ONDIEHfs.pdf

Office of Public Health Preparedness and Response   The Office helps the Nation prepare for and respond to urgent public health threats by providing strategic direction, coordination, and support for CDC's terrorism preparedness and emergency response activities. http://www.cdc.gov/phpr

Office of Public Health Scientific Services   The Office provides scientific services, knowledge, and resources to promote public health, prepare for potential health threats, and prevent disease, disability, and injury. It includes the following organizational components: the National Center for Health Statistics and the Center for Surveillance, Epidemiology, and Laboratory Services. http://www.cdc.gov/ophss

Office of State, Tribal, Local, and Territorial Support   The Office provides guidance, strategic direction, oversight, and leadership in support of State, local, territorial, and tribal public health agencies, initiatives, and priorities to improve the capacity and performance of a comprehensive public health system. http://www.cdc.gov/stltpublichealth

Sources of Information

Disease of the Week   The "Disease of the Week" Web page features key facts on, prevention tips for, and a quiz to test one's knowledge of common, serious diseases. http://www.cdc.gov/dotw

Career Opportunities   The CDC is the leading national public health protection agency in the United States. It relies on professionals with scientific and nonscientific expertise to protect Earth's human population from the threat of deadly diseases like Ebola, HIV/AIDS, influenza, malaria, and tuberculosis. Most scientific and technical positions at the CDC are filled through the Commissioned Corps of the Public Health Service, a uniformed service of the U.S. Government. http://jobs.cdc.gov

Freedom of Information Act (FOIA)   The CDC posts answers to frequently asked FOIA questions on its Web site. http://www.cdc.gov/od/foia/faqs/index.htm | Email: FOIARequests@cdc.gov

The CDC posts frequently requested agency records in its electronic reading room. http://www.cdc.gov/od/foia/reading/records/index.htm

Influenza (Flu)   The CDC Web site features of trove of influenza information and resources. https://www.cdc.gov/flu/index.htm

Library   The Stephen B. Thacker CDC Library helps the advancement of science and public health and safety through information. It provides a full range of information services and products to support public health research, policy, and action. The Library, which comprises the headquarters library in Atlanta and six branches, serves CDC employees nationwide, as well as employees working in international locations. http://www.cdc.gov/library

Museum   The David J. Sencer CDC Museum features award-winning permanent and changing exhibitions that focus on public health topics, as well as on the history of the CDC. The museum is located in Atlanta, GA, and admission is free. It is open to the public on weekdays, excluding Federal holidays. Phone, 404-639-0830. http://www.cdc.gov/museum/index.htm

Podcasts   CDC podcasts provide reliable health and safety information. https://www2c.cdc.gov/podcasts

Publications   Many publications are accessible on the CDC's Web site. https://www.cdc.gov/publications

Reports   The monthly report "CDC Vital Signs" is released on the first Tuesday of every month. Past editions have addressed topics like colorectal and breast cancer screening, obesity, alcohol and tobacco use, HIV testing, motor vehicle safety, cardiovascular disease, teen pregnancy and infections associated with health care, foodborne disease, and more. The report is also available in Spanish. http://www.cdc.gov/vitalsigns

The CDC prepares the "Morbidity and Mortality Weekly Report," which it uses for scientific publication of accurate, authoritative, objective, reliable, timely, and useful public health information and recommendations. Educators, epidemiologists and other scientists, physicians and nurses, public health practitioners, and researchers and laboratorians regularly read the report. https://www.cdc.gov/mmwr/index.html | Email: mmwrq@cdc.gov

Social Media   CDC uses social media to provide users with access to credible, science-based health information. https://www.cdc.gov/socialmedia/

Stress   The CDC's Web site provides information on managing stress after a traumatic event. https://www.cdc.gov/features/copingwithstress/index.html

Travel Health Notices   The CDC posts travel health notices on its Web site. http://wwwnc.cdc.gov/travel/notices; http://www.cdc.gov

For further information, contact the Centers for Disease Control and Prevention, 1600 Clifton Road, Atlanta, GA 30333. Phone, 800-232-4636. TTY, 888-232-6348.

Centers for Medicare and Medicaid Services

7500 Security Boulevard, Baltimore, MD 21244
Phone, 410-786-3000. Internet, http://www.cms.gov

Administrator	ANDREW SLAVITT, ACTING
Principal Deputy Administrator	PATRICK H. CONWAY, ACTING
Chief Operating Officer / Chief of Staff	MANDY COHEN

The Centers for Medicare and Medicaid Services (CMS) provides health coverage to more than 100 million people through Medicare, Medicaid, the Children's Health Insurance Program, and the Health Insurance Marketplace. The CMS seeks to strengthen and modernize the Nation's health care system, to provide access to high quality care and improved health at lower costs. https://www.cms.gov/About-CMS/About-CMS.html

Sources of Information

Blog   The CMS maintains an official blog on its Web site. https://blog.cms.gov
Career Opportunities   For information on career opportunities, visit the "Careers at CMS" Web page. https://www.cms.gov/About-CMS/Career-Information/CareersatCMS/index.html
Forms   Many CMS forms are accessible on the agency's Web site. https://www.cms.gov/Medicare/CMS-Forms/CMS-Forms/CMS-Forms-List.html
Frequently Asked Questions (FAQs)   The CMS posts answers to FAQs on its Web site. https://questions.cms.gov
Glossary   The CMS maintains a glossary that explains terms found on its Web site. https://www.cms.gov/apps/glossary
History   The CMS Web site features the agency's program history. https://www.cms.

gov/About-CMS/Agency-Information/History/index.html
Medicaid   The CMS manages the Medicaid.gov Web site. https://www.medicaid.gov
Medicare   The CMS manages the Medicare.gov Web site. https://www.medicare.gov
    The Medicare Coverage Database contains all national coverage determinations and local coverage determinations, local articles, and proposed national coverage determination decisions. The database also includes several other types of national coverage policy-related documents, including national coverage analyses, coding analyses for labs, Medicare Evidence Development and Coverage Advisory Committee proceedings, and Medicare coverage guidance documents. https://www.cms.gov/medicare-coverage-database
    The CMS manages the "STOP Medicare Fraud" Web site. To report Medicare fraud, call 800-447-8477. TTY, 800-377-4950. https://www.stopmedicarefraud.gov/index.html
Newsroom   The CMS posts news items on its Web site. https://www.cms.gov/Newsroom/Newsroom-Center.html
Social Media   The CMS tweets announcements and other newsworthy items on Twitter. https://twitter.com/cmsgov
    The CMS posts videos on its YouTube channel. https://www.youtube.com/user/CMSHHSgov; http://www.cms.gov

For further information, contact the Centers for Medicare and Medicaid Services, Department of Health and Human Services, 7500 Security Boulevard, Baltimore, MD 21244. Phone, 410-786-3000.

Food and Drug Administration

10903 New Hampshire Avenue, Silver Spring, MD 20993
Phone, 888-463-6332. Internet, http://www.fda.gov

Commissioner	SCOTT GOTTLIEB
Chief of Staff	LAUREN SILVIS

The Food and Drug Administration (FDA) protects the public health by ensuring the safety, security, and efficacy of human and veterinary drugs, biological products, medical devices, the Nation's food supply, cosmetics, and products that emit radiation. The FDA also advances the public health by accelerating innovations to make medicines more effective and by providing the public with accurate, science-based information on medicines and food to improve health. The agency plays a significant role in the Nation's counterterrorism capability by ensuring the security of the food supply. http://www.fda.gov/AboutFDA/default.htm

Sources of Information

Animal and Veterinary Recalls   The FDA posts animal and veterinary recall information—brand name, date of recall, company name, product description, and the reason or problem—on its Web site. http://www.fda.gov/AnimalVeterinary/SafetyHealth/RecallsWithdrawals/default.htm
A–Z Index   The FDA's Web site features an alphabetical index to help visitors search for specific topics or browse content that aligns with their interests. http://www.fda.gov/SiteIndex/default.htm
Career Opportunities   The FDA relies on attorneys, biologists, chemists, consumer safety officers, engineers, information technology specialists, medical officers, microbiologists, pharmacists, pharmacologists, statisticians, and other professionals to carry out its mission. http://www.fda.gov/AboutFDA/WorkingatFDA/default.htm
Cigarettes   The FDA describes cigarettes with three words: attractive, addictive, and deadly. Cigarettes are designed to be attractive and addictive. The FDA's infographic "How a Cigarette is Engineered" explains the role design plays in attraction and addiction. http://www.fda.gov/TobaccoProducts/NewsEvents/ucm529397.htm
Cosmetics   The FDA posts answers to the questions that consumers frequently ask about cosmetic safety and regulation. http://www.fda.gov/Cosmetics/ResourcesForYou/Consumers/ucm2005206.htm
Foodborne Illnesses   The FDA regulates human and animal food. It posts information on recent foodborne illness outbreaks on its Web site. http://www.fda.gov/Food/RecallsOutbreaksEmergencies/Outbreaks/default.htm
Recalls / Safety Alerts   Information gathered from press releases and other public notices on certain recalls of FDA-regulated products is available online. http://www.fda.gov/Safety/Recalls/default.htm; http://www.fda.gov

For further information contact the Food and Drug Administration, 10903 New Hampshire Avenue, Silver Spring, MD 20993. Phone, 888-463-6332.

Health Resources and Services Administration

5600 Fishers Lane, Rockville, MD 20857
Phone, 301-443-3376. Internet, http://www.hrsa.gov

Administrator	GEORGE SIGOUNAS
Deputy Administrator	DIANA ESPINOSA

The Health Resources and Services Administration (HRSA) improves access to health care by strengthening the health care workforce, building healthy communities, and achieving health equity. HRSA programs make health care accessible to people who are geographically isolated or economically or medically vulnerable. It supports the training of health professionals, the distribution of providers to areas where they are needed most, and improvements in health care delivery. The agency also oversees organ, bone marrow, and cord blood donations; compensates individuals harmed by vaccination; and maintains databases that protect against health care abuse, fraud, malpractice, and waste. https://www.hrsa.gov/about/index.html

Sources of Information

Data   The HRSA maintains an online data warehouse. https://datawarehouse.hrsa.gov
Career Opportunities   The HRSA posts career opportunities on its Web site. https://www.hrsa.gov/hr/

Freedom of Information Act (FOIA)   The FOIA requires the HRSA to disclose documents or records that any person properly requests in writing. Certain documents or records, or parts of them, may be protected, however, from disclosure by one of the nine exemptions contained in the statute. https://www.hrsa.gov/foia/index.html
Organ Donation and Transplantation   The HRSA manages the OrganDonor.gov Web site, which provides the public with U.S. Government information on organ donation and transplantation. http://organdonor.gov/index.html
Social Media   The HRSA tweets announcements and other newsworthy items on Twitter. https://twitter.com/HRSAgov
The HRSA has a Facebook account. https://www.facebook.com/HRSAgov
The HRSA posts videos on its YouTube channel. https://www.youtube.com/user/HRSAtube/videos; http://www.hrsa.gov/about/contact

For further information, contact the Office of Communications, Health Resources and Services Administration, 5600 Fishers Lane, Rockville, MD 20857. Phone, 301-443-3376.

Indian Health Service

5600 Fishers Lane Rockville, MD 20857
Phone, 301-443-3593. Internet, http://www.ihs.gov

Director	(VACANCY)
Principal Deputy Director	MICHAEL WEAHKEE
Deputy Director	CHRISTOPHER BUCHANAN

The Indian Health Service, as part of the Public Health Service, provides a comprehensive health services delivery system for American Indians and Alaska Natives. It helps Native American tribes develop their health programs; facilitates and assists tribes in coordinating health planning and obtaining and utilizing health resources available through Federal, State, and local programs, in operating comprehensive health programs and evaluating them; and provides comprehensive health care services, including hospital and ambulatory medical care, preventive and rehabilitative services,

and development of community sanitation facilities. https://www.ihs.gov/aboutihs

Sources of Information

A–Z Index   The Indian Health Service's Web site features an alphabetical index to help visitors search for specific topics or browse content that aligns with their interests. https://www.ihs.gov/atoz/a/
Career Opportunities   For information on employment, visit the "Career Opportunities" Web page. https://www.ihs.gov/careeropps

Freedom of Information Act (FOIA) The Indian Health Service's Web site features an electronic FOIA requester center. https://www.ihs.gov/FOIA

Newsroom The Newsroom features announcements, congressional testimony, factsheets, press releases, and speeches. https://www.ihs.gov/newsroom | Email: newsroom@ihs.gov

Social Media The Indian Health Service has a Facebook account. https://www.facebook.com/IndianHealthService

The Indian Health Service posts videos on its YouTube channel. https://www.youtube.com/user/IHSgov/feed; http://www.ihs.gov/contact

For further information, contact the Management Policy and Internal Control Staff, Indian Health Service, 5600 Fishers Lane Rockville, MD 20857. Phone, 301-443-3593.

National Institutes of Health

1 Center Drive, Bethesda, MD 20892
Phone, 301-496-4000. Internet, http://www.nih.gov

Director	FRANCIS S. COLLINS
Principal Deputy Director	LAWRENCE A. TABAK

The National Institutes of Health (NIH) support biomedical and behavioral research domestically and abroad, conduct research in NIH laboratories and clinics, train research scientists, and develop and disseminate credible, science-based health information to the public. https://www.nih.gov/about-nih/what-we-do

Aging The National Institute on Aging (NIA) conducts and supports research on the aging process, age-related diseases, and other special problems and needs of older people. It is also the lead NIH Institute for research on age-related cognitive change and Alzheimer's disease. The NIA provides information on aging to the scientific community, health care providers, and the public. http://www.nia.nih.gov

For further information, contact the National Institute on Aging. Phone, 301 496 1752.

Alcohol Abuse and Alcoholism The National Institute on Alcohol Abuse and Alcoholism leads the national effort to reduce alcohol-related problems by conducting and supporting biomedical and behavioral research into the causes, consequences, prevention, and treatment of alcohol-use disorders. http://www.niaaa.nih.gov

For further information, contact the National Institute on Alcohol Abuse and Alcoholism. Phone, 301-443-3885.

Allergy and Infectious Diseases The National Institute of Allergy and Infectious Diseases conducts and supports research to study the causes of infectious diseases and immune-mediated diseases and to develop better means of preventing, diagnosing, and treating these diseases. http://www.niaid.nih.gov

For further information, contact the National Institute of Allergy and Infectious Diseases. Phone, 866-284-4107 or 301-496-5717.

Arthritis and Musculoskeletal and Skin Diseases The National Institute of Arthritis and Musculoskeletal and Skin Diseases supports research on the causes, treatment, and prevention of arthritis and musculoskeletal and skin diseases; the basic and clinical training of scientists to carry out this research; and the dissemination of information on research progress. http://www.niams.nih.gov

For further information, contact the National Institute of Arthritis and Musculoskeletal and Skin Diseases. Phone, 877-226-4267 or 301-496-8190.

Behavioral and Social Sciences Research The Office of Behavioral and Social Sciences Research supports and coordinates health-related behavioral and social sciences research that the NIH conducts or supports, and it integrates these sciences within the larger NIH research enterprise. It also communicates and disseminates research findings to stakeholders within and outside the Federal Government, thereby increasing understanding and improving treatment and prevention of disease. https://obssr.od.nih.gov

For further information, contact the Office of Behavioral and Social Sciences Research. Phone, 301-402-1146.

Biomedical Imaging and Bioengineering   The National Institute of Biomedical Imaging and Bioengineering supports research, training, and the dissemination of research advances for accelerating the development and application of biomedical technologies to improve the detection, treatment, and prevention of disease. It integrates the physical and engineering sciences with the life sciences to advance basic research and medical care. http://www.nibib.nih.gov

For further information, contact the National Institute of Biomedical Imaging and Bioengineering. Phone, 301-496-3500.

Cancer   The National Cancer Institute (NCI) is the Federal Government's principal agency for cancer research and training. It coordinates the National Cancer Program, which conducts and supports research, training, health information dissemination, and other activities associated with diagnosing, preventing, treating, and finding the cause of cancer and with the continuing care of cancer patients and their families. http://www.cancer.gov

For further information, contact the Cancer Information Service. Phone, 800-422-6237.

Center for Information Technology   The Center for Information Technology provides, coordinates, and manages information technology to advance computational science. http://www.cit.nih.gov

For further information, contact the Center for Information Technology. Phone, 301-496-5703.

Child Health and Human Development   The Eunice Kennedy Shriver National Institute of Child Health and Human Development conducts and supports basic, clinical, and epidemiological research on the reproductive, rehabilitative,

neurobiological, developmental, and behavioral processes that determine the health of children, adults, families, and communities. http://www.nichd.nih.gov

For further information, contact the Eunice Kennedy Shriver National Institute of Child Health and Human Development. Phone, 800-370-2943.

Clinical Center   The Clinical Center is the clinical research hospital for the NIH. By doing clinical research, investigators translate laboratory discoveries into better treatments, therapies, and interventions to improve the Nation's health. The Center conducts clinical and laboratory research and trains future clinical investigators. Nearly 500,000 volunteers from across the Nation have participated in clinical research studies since the Center opened in 1953. About 1,500 clinical research studies are currently in progress. http://clinicalcenter.nih.gov

For further information, contact the Clinical Center. Phone, 301-496-4000.

Communications   The Office of Communications and Public Liaison communicates information on consumer health, scientific results, and NIH accomplishments, issues, and research and training programs to the public, media, scientific and medical communities, and other interested groups. http://www.nih.gov/institutes-nih/nih-office-director/office-communications-public-liaison

For further information, contact the Office of Communications and Public Liaison. Phone, 301-496-5787

Complementary and Integrative Health   The National Center for Complementary and Integrative Health defines the utility and safety of complementary and integrative health interventions and their roles in improving health and health care. This science-based information helps the public, health care professionals, and health policymakers make decisions on the use and integration of complementary and integrative health approaches. https://nccih.nih.gov

For further information, contact the National Center for Complementary and Integrative Health. Phone, 888-644-6226.

Deafness and Other Communication Disorders   The National Institute on Deafness and Other Communication Disorders conducts and supports biomedical and behavioral research and training on normal and disordered processes of hearing, balance, taste, smell, voice, speech, and language. The Institute also makes science-based health information publicly available, and it supports efforts to create devices that substitute for lost or impaired sensory and communication function. http://www.nidcd.nih.gov | Email: NIDCDinfo@nidcd.nih.gov

For further information, contact the National Institute on Deafness and Other Communication Disorders. Phone, 800-241-1044. TTY, 800-241-1055.

Dental and Craniofacial Research   The National Institute of Dental and Craniofacial Research funds research on dental, oral, and craniofacial health and disorders. It also conducts research in its own laboratories and clinic, supports research training, and promotes the timely transfer of research-based knowledge and its implications for health to researchers, to health professionals, to patients, and to the general public. http://www.nidcr.nih.gov

For further information, contact the National Institute of Dental and Craniofacial Research. Phone, 301-496-4261.

Diabetes and Digestive and Kidney Diseases   The National Institute of Diabetes and Digestive and Kidney Diseases conducts, supports, and coordinates research and research training. It also offers science-based information on diabetes and other endocrine and metabolic diseases; on digestive diseases, nutritional disorders, weight control, and obesity; and on kidney, urologic and blood diseases. https://www.niddk.nih.gov

For further information, contact the National Institute of Diabetes and Digestive and Kidney Diseases. Phone, 301-496-3583.

Drug Abuse   The National Institute on Drug Abuse supports and conducts basic and clinical research on drug use, its consequences, and the underlying neurobiological, behavioral, and social mechanisms. The Institute also ensures effective translation and dissemination of scientific findings to improve the prevention and treatment of substance-use disorders, and it works at raising the public's awareness that addiction is a type of brain disorder. http://www.drugabuse.gov

For further information, contact the National Institute on Drug Abuse. Phone, 877-643-2644.

Environmental Health Sciences   The National Institute of Environmental Health Sciences supports research that explores how the environment affects people's health. Its research centers on environmental exposures and understanding their effects on human biology and health with an emphasis on disease and disability prevention. The Institute also houses the national toxicology program, a cross-agency organization that coordinates toxicity testing across the Federal Government. http://www.niehs.nih.gov

For further information, contact the National Institute of Environmental Health Sciences. Phone, 919-541-3345.

Eye and Vision Diseases   The National Eye Institute conducts, fosters, and supports research on the causes, natural history, prevention, diagnosis, and treatment of disorders of the eye and visual system. It also directs the National Eye Health Education Program. http://www.nei.nih.gov

For further information, contact the National Eye Institute. Phone, 301-496-5248.

Fogarty International Center   The Fogarty International Center addresses global health challenges through innovative and collaborative research and training programs. It also supports and advances the NIH mission through international partnerships. http://www.fic.nih.gov

For further information, contact the Fogarty International Center. Phone, 301-496-2075.

General Medical Sciences   The National Institute of General Medical Sciences (NIGMS) supports basic research that increases understanding of biological processes and lays the foundation for advances in disease diagnosis, treatment, and prevention. NIGMS-funded scientists investigate how living systems work at a range of levels, from molecules and cells to tissues, to whole organisms and populations. The Institute also supports research in clinical areas, primarily those that affect multiple organ systems. To assure the vitality and productivity of the research enterprise, the NIGMS provides leadership in training the next generation of scientists, in diversifying the scientific workforce, and in developing research capacities throughout the country. http://www.nigms.nih.gov

For further information, contact the National Institute of General Medical Sciences. Phone, 301-496-7301.

Heart, Lung, and Blood Diseases   The National Heart, Lung, and Blood Institute provides leadership for a global program in sleep disorders, blood resources, and diseases of the heart, blood vessels, blood, and lungs. It conducts, fosters, and supports a comprehensive program of basic research, clinical investigations and trials, observational and implementation science studies, as well as demonstration and education projects. http://www.nhlbi.nih.gov

For further information, contact the National Heart, Lung, and Blood Institute. Phone, 301-592-8573.

Human Genome Research   The National Human Genome Research Institute supports research to uncover the role that the genome plays in human health and disease; studies on the ethical, legal, and social implications of genomics research for individuals, families, and communities; and the application of genomics research to medical care. http://www.genome.gov

For further information, contact the National Human Genome Research Institute. Phone, 301-402-0911.

Library of Medicine   The National Library of Medicine, the world's largest biomedical library, serves as the Nation's principal medical information source, providing medical library services and extensive online information resources to scientists, practitioners, and the general public. It conducts, fosters, and supports research and training in biomedical informatics and supports development and dissemination of clinical terminology standards. http://www.nlm.nih.gov

For further information, contact the National Library of Medicine. Phone, 301-496-6308.

Mental Health   The National Institute of Mental Health works to transform the understanding and treatment of mental illnesses. Through basic and clinical research, it advances the prevention, recovery, and cure of mental conditions that disable many Americans. http://www.nimh.nih.gov

For further information, contact the National Institute of Mental Health. Phone, 866-615-6464.

Minority Health and Health Disparities   The National Institute on Minority Health and Health Disparities leads scientific research to improve minority health and eliminate health disparities. The Institute plans, reviews, coordinates, and evaluates all minority health and health disparities research and activities of the NIH; conducts and supports research on minority health and health disparities; promotes and supports the training of a diverse research workforce; translates and disseminates research information; and fosters innovative collaborations and partnerships. http://www.nimhd.nih.gov

For further information, contact the National Institute on Minority Health and Health Disparities. Phone, 301-402-1366.

Neurological Disorders and Stroke   The National Institute of Neurological Disorders and Stroke works to better understand the brain and spinal cord and to use that knowledge to mitigate the effects of neurological disease. It conducts, promotes, coordinates, and guides research and training on the causes, prevention, diagnosis, and treatment of neurological disorders and stroke. It also supports basic, translational, and clinical research in related scientific areas. http://www.ninds.nih.gov

For further information, contact the National Institute of Neurological Disorders and Stroke. Phone, 301-496-5751.

Nursing Research   The National Institute of Nursing Research supports clinical and basic research and research training to build the scientific foundation for clinical practice, to prevent disease and disability, to manage and eliminate symptoms caused by illness, to enhance end-of-life and palliative care, and to train the next generation of nurse scientists. http://www.ninr.nih.gov

For further information, contact the National Institute of Nursing Research. Phone, 301-496-0207.

Program Coordination, Planning, and Strategic Initiatives   The Division of Program Coordination, Planning, and Strategic Initiatives coordinates trans-NIH programs, planning, and strategic scientific initiatives in the Office of the NIH Director. The Division includes major programmatic offices that coordinate and support research and research infrastructure. The Division also serves as a portfolio analysis resource, coordinates evaluation reporting and agency activities under the Government Performance and Results Act, and supports science education partnership awards. http://dpcpsi.nih.gov

For further information, contact the Division of Program Coordination, Planning, and Strategic Initiatives. Phone, 301-402-9852.

Scientific Review   The Center for Scientific Review (CSR) organizes the peer review groups that evaluate the majority of grant applications submitted to the NIH. These groups include experienced and respected researchers from across the country and abroad. Since 1946, CSR has ensured that NIH grant applications receive fair, independent, expert, and timely reviews— free from inappropriate influences—so the NIH can fund the most promising research. CSR also receives all incoming applications and assigns them to the appropriate Centers and Institutes that fund grants. http://public.csr.nih.gov

For further information, contact the Center for Scientific Review. Phone, 301-435-1111.

Translational Sciences   The National Center for Advancing Translational Sciences focuses on what is common across diseases and the translational process. The Center emphasizes innovation and deliverables, relying on data and new technologies to develop, demonstrate, and disseminate advances in translational science that tangibly improve human health. https://ncats.nih.gov

For further information, contact the National Center for Advancing Translational Sciences. Phone, 301-435-0888.

Sources of Information

Employment   For information on employment opportunities, visit the "Jobs at NIH" Web page. http://www.jobs.nih.gov

Events   The NIH posts upcoming events on its Web site. https://www.nih.gov/news-events/events

Freedom of Information Act (FOIA)   The FOIA gives a right to access documents or records in the possession of the Federal Government to any person. The Government may withhold, however, information pursuant to the statute's nine exemptions and three exclusions. For more information, contact the NIH FOIA Office. Phone, 301-496-5633. Fax, 301-402-4541. https://www.nih.gov/institutes-nih/nih-office-director/office-communications-public-liaison/freedom-information-act-office | Email: nihfoia@mail.nih.gov

Frequently Asked Questions (FAQs)   The NIH posts answers to FAQs on its Web site. https://www.nih.gov/about-nih/frequently-asked-questions

History   The story of the agency begins in 1887, and a brief retelling of it is available online. https://www.nih.gov/about-nih/who-we-are/history

The DeWitt Stetten, Jr., Museum of Medical Research, also known as the NIH Stetten Museum, preserves and interprets the material culture of the NIH's scientific work through physical and virtual exhibits. https://history.nih.gov/museum/index.html

News   The NIH posts news releases on its Web site. https://www.nih.gov/news-events/news-releases

The monthly newsletter "NIH News In Health" features practical consumer health news and information that is based on NIH research. https://newsinhealth.nih.gov

Social Media   The NIH tweets announcements and other newsworthy items on Twitter. https://twitter.com/NIH

The NIH has a Facebook account. https://www.facebook.com/nih.gov

The NIH posts videos on its YouTube channel. https://www.youtube.com/user/nihod

Spanish   Important health information is available in Spanish. https://salud.nih.gov

Staff Directory   The NIH enterprise directory allows users to search for staff members by email address, name, or phone number. https://ned.nih.gov/search

Visitor Information   Maps and information on access and security, parking, tours, the campus shuttle, and more are available on the NIH Web site. https://www.nih.gov/about-nih/visitor-information

Weight Management The National Institute of Diabetes and Digestive and Kidney Diseases' Web site has a trove of weight management information and resources. https://www.niddk.nih.gov/health-information/weight-management

The online body weight planner allows users to make personalized calorie and physical activity plans for reaching a target weight within a specific time period—and for maintaining it afterwards. https://www.niddk.nih.gov/health-information/health-topics/weight-control/body-weight-planner/Pages/bwp.aspx; https://www.nih.gov/about-nih/contact-us

For further information, contact the National Institutes of Health, 1 Center Drive, Bethesda, MD 20892. Phone, 301-496-4000.

Substance Abuse and Mental Health Services Administration

5600 Fishers Lane Rockville, MD 20857
Phone, 240-276-2130. Internet, http://www.samhsa.gov

Administrator	Kana Enomoto, Acting
Chief of Staff	Tom Coderre

The Substance Abuse and Mental Health Services Administration mitigates the effects of substance abuse and mental illness on communities nationwide. It provides national leadership, serving as a voice for behavioral health; funds State and local service agencies through grants and formulas; collects data and makes available surveillance reports on the effect of behavioral health on Americans; leads efforts to offer public education on mental illness and substance abuse prevention, treatment, and recovery; regulates and oversees national behavioral health programs; and promotes practice improvement in community-based, primary, and specialty care settings. http://www.samhsa.gov/about-us

Sources of Information

Blog The Administration's Web site features a blog. https://blog.samhsa.gov

Data The Administration maintains five collections of data: Center for Behavioral Health Statistics and Quality reports, client level data, mental health facilities data, population data, and substance abuse facilities data. http://www.samhsa.gov/data

Career Opportunities For information on career opportunities, visit the "Jobs and Internships" Web page. http://www.samhsa.gov/about-us/jobs-internships

Help / Treatment Resources for help and treatment are available on the Administration's Web site. http://www.samhsa.gov/find-help

KSOC–TV KSOC–TV is a web-based technical assistance program featuring behavioral health experts discussing leading issues in children's mental health. http://www.samhsa.gov/children/multimedia

Newsroom Press announcements, quarterly newsletters, and media highlights of initiatives and other activities are available in the newsroom. http://www.samhsa.gov/newsroom

Offices / Centers The agency's offices and centers provide leadership and assistance for quality behavioral health services, as well as support States, territories, tribes, communities, and local organizations through grants and contract awards. Contact information for these offices and centers is available online. http://www.samhsa.gov/about-us/who-we-are/offices-centers

Publications Hundreds of publications are available on the Administration's Web site. http://store.samhsa.gov

Site Map The Web site map allows visitors to look for specific topics or to browse content that aligns with their interests. http://www.samhsa.gov/sitemap

Social Media The Administration uses various forms of social media to connect with the Internet community and engage people. http://www.samhsa.gov/social-media/social-media-accounts

Suicide Prevention The Administration funds the National Suicide Prevention Lifeline. Phone, 800-273-8255. http://suicidepreventionlifeline.org/?WT_ac=AD20110315NSPI #

Treatment Services Locator The behavioral health treatment services locator is a confidential and anonymous source of information for persons seeking treatment facilities in the United States or U.S. Territories for substance abuse, addiction, mental health problems, or a combination of the three. Phone, 800-662-4357. TDD, 800-487-4889. https://findtreatment.samhsa.gov

Underage Drinking Underage drinking accounts for 11 percent of all the alcohol consumed in the United States. Alcohol is the most widely misused substance among America's youth. The Administration disseminates information on the dangers of underage drinking and offers prevention tips. http://www.samhsa.gov/underage-drinking-topic; http://www.samhsa.gov/about-us/contact-us

For further information, contact the Substance Abuse and Mental Health Services Administration, 5600 Fishers Lane Rockville, MD 20857, Rockville, MD 20857. Phone, 240-276-2130.

DEPARTMENT OF HOMELAND SECURITY

Washington, DC 20528
Phone, 202-282-8000. Internet, http://www.dhs.gov

Secretary of Homeland Security	KEVIN K. MCALEENAN, ACTING
Deputy Secretary	(VACANCY)
Chief of Staff	MILES E. TAYLOR
Executive Secretary	CHRISTINA G. BOBB
Military Advisor	REAR ADM. BRENDAN C. MCPHERSON
https://www.dhs.gov/leadership	

Office of the Secretary

Undersecretary	
Strategy, Policy, and Plans	(VACANCY)
Assistant Secretaries	
Legislative Affairs	CHRISTINE CICCONE
Partnership and Engagement	JOHN H. HILL
Public Affairs	ANDREW MEEHAN, ACTING
Chief Privacy Officer	JONATHAN R. CANTOR, ACTING
Citizenship and Immigration Services Ombudsman	JULIE KIRCHNER
Civil Rights and Civil Liberties Officer	CAMERON QUINN
General Counsel	JOHN M. MITNICK
https://www.dhs.gov/office-secretary	

Operational and Support Components

Under Secretaries	
Intelligence and Analysis	DAVID J. GLAWE
Management	CHARLES H. FULGHUM, ACTING
Science and Technology	(VACANCY)
Administrators	
Federal Emergency Management Agency	PETE T. GAYNOR, ACTING
Transportation Security Administration	DAVID P. PEKOSKE
Assistant Secretary	
Countering Weapons of Mass Destruction	JAMES F. MCDONNELL
Chief Officers	
Chief Financial Officer	STACY MARCOTT, ACTING
Chief Information Officer	JOHN A. ZANGARDI
Directors	
Cybersecurity and Infrastructure Security Agency	CHRISTOPHER C. KREBS
Federal Law Enforcement Training Centers	THOMAS J. WALTERS
Operations Coordination	FRANK DIFALCO, ACTING
U.S. Citizenship and Immigration Services	KENNETH T. CUCCINELLI, ACTING
U.S. Immigration and Customs Enforcement	MARK MORGAN, ACTING
U.S. Secret Service	JAMES M. MURRAY
U.S. Coast Guard Commandant	ADM. KARL L. SCHULTZ

U.S. Customs and Border Protection Commissioner   Kevin K. McAleenan
https://www.dhs.gov/operational-and-support-components

Office of Inspector General

Inspector General   Jennifer L. Costello, Acting
https://www.oig.dhs.gov/about/meetActingIG

The above list of key personnel was updated 6–2019.

The Department of Homeland Security prevents terrorism and enhances security, manages the Nation's borders, administers immigration laws, safeguards cyberspace, and ensures resilience in the wake of disaster.

Establishment

On November 25, 2002, President George W. Bush approved the "Homeland Security Act of 2002" (6 U.S.C. 101 note), which established the Department of Homeland Security (DHS). Sixty days after its enactment, on January 24, 2003, the law became effective. By the advice and with the consent of the Senate, the President appoints the Secretary of Homeland Security, who is head of the Department, having direction, authority, and control over it.

The Secretary develops and coordinates a comprehensive strategy to protect the Nation from terrorist attacks. These efforts are undertaken in coordination with Federal, State, local, international, and private sector partners. The Secretary advises the President on border management and protection, cyberspace security, administration and enforcement of immigration laws, intelligence analysis and infrastructure protection, using science and technology for countering weapons of mass destruction, and resilience after a disastrous event. https://www.dhs.gov/sites/default/files/publications/hr_5005_enr.pdf

Administration

Citizenship and Immigration   The Office of the Citizenship and Immigration Services Ombudsman improves the quality of citizenship and immigration services that are delivered to the public by providing individual case assistance. The Offices also makes recommendations for improving the U.S. Citizenship and Immigration Services' administration of immigration benefits. http://www.dhs.gov/topic/cis-ombudsman | Email: cisombudsman@hq.dhs.gov

Civil Rights and Liberties   The Office for Civil Rights and Civil Liberties ensures that while the DHS secures the Nation, it also preserves individual liberty, fairness, and equality under the law. The Office promotes respect for civil rights and civil liberties in policymaking and implementation; advises DHS leadership and personnel, and State and local partners; communicates with communities and individuals whose civil rights and civil liberties may be affected by DHS activities, informing them about policies and avenues of redress and bringing appropriate attention to their experiences and concerns within the Department; investigates civil rights and liberties complaints filed by the public regarding DHS policies or activities, or actions taken by DHS personnel; and leads DHS equal employment opportunity programs and promotes workforce diversity and merit system principles. http://www.dhs.gov/office-civil-rights-and-civil-liberties

Department of Defense Coordination   The Military Advisor counsels and supports the Secretary and Deputy Secretary on matters relating to policy, procedures, preparedness activities, and operations involving the DHS and the Department of Defense. http://www.dhs.gov/about-office-military-advisor

Executive Support   The Office of the Executive Secretary directly supports the Secretary and Deputy Secretary and provides related support to leadership and management agencywide. The Office's activities are diverse, including accurate and timely dissemination of information and written communications to the Secretary and Deputy Secretary from throughout the DHS and its homeland security partners. http://www.dhs.gov/office-executive-secretary

Internal Audits and Investigations   The Office of Inspector General conducts and supervises audits, investigations, and inspections relating to DHS programs and operations. The Office examines, evaluates, and, where necessary, critiques DHS operations and activities. It recommends ways for the agency to carry out its responsibilities in more economical, efficient, and effective ways. The Office also reviews recommendations regarding existing and proposed legislation and regulations affecting DHS programs and operations. https://www.oig.dhs.gov

Legal Compliance   The Office of General Counsel ensures that departmental activities comply with applicable legal requirements. The Office provides legal advice on matters affecting national security, immigration, litigation, international law, maritime safety and security, transportation security, border security law, cybersecurity, fiscal and appropriations law, environmental law, and on matters affecting many more subjects. It also ensures that DHS efforts to secure the Nation are consistent with the civil rights and civil liberties of its citizens and follow the rule of law. The Office also provides legal services in several areas where the law intersects with the achievement of mission goals, such as the coordination of rulemaking activities, managing interdepartmental clearance of proposed legislation, and providing legal training for law enforcement officers. http://www.dhs. gov/office-general-counsel

Legislative Affairs   The Office of Legislative Affairs serves as primary liaison to Members of Congress and their congressional staff. The Office responds to inquiries from Congress; notifies it about DHS initiatives, policies, and programs; and keeps the agency's senior leaders informed about the activities of Congress. The Office also participates in the Senate confirmation process of each DHS nominee whom the President nominates. http://www.dhs.gov/about-office-legislative-affairs

Partnership and Engagement   The Office of Partnership and Engagement includes the following offices and programs: the Office for State and Local Law Enforcement, Private Sector Office, Office of Academic Engagement, Committee Management

Office, Homeland Security Advisory Council, Homeland Security Academic Advisory Council, Blue Campaign, and the "If You See Something, Say Something" public awareness campaign. The Office comprises stakeholder engagement offices that communicate with State, local, tribal, and territorial governments, and with law enforcement, the private sector, academia, and Federal advisory committees. These offices coordinate DHS programs and policies with these same stakeholders. The Office also serves as the liaison between these stakeholders and the Office of the Secretary. It promotes an integrated national approach to homeland security by coordinating and advancing Federal interaction with external stakeholders, and it continues the homeland security dialogue with those partners and with the national associations representing them. http://www. dhs.gov/partnership-engagement

Privacy   The Privacy Office safeguards the collection, disclosure, and use of personally identifiable information and departmental information. It ensures that appropriate access to information is consistent with the core values, mission, and vision of DHS. The Office also implements the agency's policies to defend and protect the individual rights, liberties, and information interests of U.S. citizens. The Office has oversight of privacy and disclosure policy matters, including compliance with the Privacy Act of 1974, the Freedom of Information Act, and the completion of statements addressing the effect of new programs and systems on privacy, as required by the E-Government Act of 2002 and the Homeland Security Act of 2002. http://www.dhs.gov/privacy-office | Email: privacy@dhs.gov

Public Affairs   The Office of Public Affairs coordinates the public affairs activities of DHS components and offices. It also serves as the Federal Government's lead public information office during a national emergency or disaster. The Office is the point of contact for members of the news media, representatives of organizations, and the general public who seek information on DHS policies, procedures, programs, services, and statistics. The Office assists the Secretary with strategic and internal communications and with all matters of public affairs. http://www.dhs.gov/office-public-affairs

Strategy, Policy, and Plans   The Office of Strategy, Policy, and Plans advises the Secretary and Deputy Secretary, develops policy and represents the DHS in interagency fora, coordinates and unifies policy positions, leads and coordinates international engagement and negotiations, operates the REAL ID and Visa Waiver programs, leads the development of operational and resource allocation guidance, develops strategies and operational plans, and collects and maintains and reports immigration data. https://www.dhs.gov/office-policy

Operations and Support

Citizenship and Immigration   The Unites States Citizenship and Immigration Services (USCIS) administers the Nation's legal immigration system. Operating primarily by fee funding, it ensures that information and decisions on citizenship and immigration benefits are provided to applications and petitioners in an accurate, consistent, courteous, professional, and timely manner that is consistent with national security. USCIS also strengthens the integrity of the Nation's legal immigration system by combating the unauthorized practice of immigration law, by helping to combat unauthorized employment in the workplace, and by deterring, detecting, and pursuing immigration-related fraud. http://www.uscis.gov

Customs and Border Protection   The U.S. Customs and Border Protection secures America's borders to protect the public from dangerous people and materials, while enabling legitimate trade and travel to enhance the Nation's global economic competitiveness. http://www.cbp.gov

Cybersecurity and Infrastructure Security   The Cybersecurity and Infrastructure Security Agency (CISA) builds the Nation's capacity to defend against cyber attacks and works with the Federal Government to provide cybersecurity tools, incident response services, and assessment capabilities to safeguard the networks that support the essential operations of partner departments and agencies. The Agency coordinates security and resilience efforts, using trusted partnerships across the private and public sectors, and delivers technical assistance and assessments to Federal stakeholders and to infrastructure owners and operators nationwide. Working with stakeholders nationwide, CISA conducts extensive outreach to support and strengthen the ability of emergency responders and relevant government officials to communicate in the event of a natural disaster, act of terrorism, or other man-made disaster. https://www.dhs.gov/cisa/about-cisa

Emergency Management   Federal Emergency Management Agency (FEMA) administers a nationwide, risk-based, and comprehensive emergency management system of preparedness, protection, response, recovery, and mitigation. The goal is to reduce the loss of life and property and to protect the Nation from all hazards, including natural disasters, acts of terrorism, and other man-made disasters. FEMA coordinates programs to improve the effectiveness of emergency response providers at all levels of the government, initiates proactive mitigation activities, and manages the National Flood Insurance Program and U.S. Fire Administration. It also leads Government continuity planning, guidance, and operations for the Federal executive branch to minimize the disruption of essential operations and to guarantee enduring constitutional governance. http://www.fema.gov

Immigration and Customs Enforcement   U.S. Immigration and Customs Enforcement (ICE) is the principal investigative arm of DHS. It promotes homeland security and public safety through the criminal and civil enforcement of Federal laws governing border control, customs, immigration, and trade. https://www.ice.gov

Intelligence and Analysis   The Office of Intelligence and Analysis, as a member of the U.S. Intelligence Community, is the nexus between the Nation's intelligence apparatus and DHS components and other State, local, and private sector partners. The Office ensures that information is gathered from all relevant DHS field operations and other State, local, and private sector partners and that this information is shared with appropriate stakeholders to produce accurate, timely, and actionable analytical intelligence products and services. https://

www.dhs.gov/office-intelligence-and-analysis

Law Enforcement Training   The Federal Law Enforcement Training Centers (FLETC) is the Nation's largest provider of law enforcement training. It offers career-long training to law enforcement professionals to help them fulfill their responsibilities safely and proficiently. Under a collaborative training model, FLETC's Federal partner organizations provide training unique to their missions, while FLETC provides training in areas common to all law enforcement officers: driving, firearms, investigations, legal training, and tactics.https://www.fletc.gov

Management   The Directorate for Management is responsible for accounting and finance, appropriations, budget, expenditure of funds, and procurement; equipment, facilities, property, and other material resources; human resources, personnel, and their security; identification and tracking of performance measurements relating to the responsibilities of the agency, and information technology and communication systems. The Directorate ensures that DHS employees have well-defined responsibilities and that managers and their employees have effective means of communicating with one another, with other governmental and nongovernmental bodies, and with the public they serve. http://www.dhs.gov/directorate-management

Maritime Safety and Security   The U.S. Coast Guard (USCG) is the principal Federal agency responsible for maritime safety, security, and environmental stewardship in U.S. ports and waterways. The USCG protects and defends more than 100,000 miles of coastline and inland waterways and safeguards an exclusive economic zone that stretches from north of the Arctic Circle to south of the equator, from Puerto Rico to Guam. The USCG is a member of the Intelligence Community and one of the five Armed Services. It is also a first response and humanitarian service provider that aids people in distress or impacted by natural and man-made disasters both at sea and ashore. It is a law enforcement and regulatory agency with broad legal authorities associated with bridge administration, hazardous materials shipping, maritime transportation, oil spill response, pilotage,

and vessel construction and operation. https://www.work.uscg.mil

Nuclear Terrorism   The Domestic Nuclear Detection Office focuses solely on preventing nuclear terrorism, in coordination with domestic and international partners, by improving deterrence, detection, response, and attribution. The Office coordinates development of the global nuclear detection architecture with partners from the private sector and local, State, Federal, and international governments. The Office develops, acquires, and supports the deployment of mechanisms to detect and report attempts to import, possess, store, transport, develop, or use unauthorized nuclear and other radioactive material in the United States. The Office also serves as steward of an enduring national technical nuclear forensics capability and leads efforts to improve national nuclear forensics expertise. Working with the international community, it promotes the development of nuclear detection architectures and nuclear forensics guidance. http://www.dhs.gov/domestic-nuclear-detection-office

Operations Coordination   The Office of Operations Coordination provides decision support and enables the Secretary's execution of responsibilities across the homeland security enterprise by promoting situational awareness and information sharing, integrating and synchronizing strategic operations, and administering the DHS continuity program. At the strategic level, the Office provides a joint operations coordination capability to support DHS operational decision making, departmental leadership, and participation in interagency operations throughout the homeland security enterprise and across all mission areas. http://www.dhs.gov/office-operations-coordination

Presidential Protection / Safeguarding Financial and Payment Systems   The U.S. Secret Service carries out a dual mission of protection and investigation. It protects the President, Vice President, and their families; major Presidential and Vice Presidential candidates; visiting heads of state and government; and National Special Security Events, as well as the White House and other designated buildings within the Washington, DC, area. The Secret Service also safeguards the Nation's financial infrastructure and payment systems to preserve the integrity of the economy. http://www.secretservice.gov

Science and Technology The Science and Technology Directorate is the primary research and development arm of the agency. The Directorate provides Federal, State, and local officials with protective technology and capabilities. Its strategic objectives are developing and deploying systems to prevent, detect, and mitigate the consequences of biological, chemical, explosive, nuclear, and radiological attacks; develop equipment, protocols, and training procedures for response and recovery; enhance the agency's and other Federal, State, local, and tribal government's technical capabilities to fulfill their homeland security-related functions; and develop technical standards and establish certified laboratories to evaluate homeland security and emergency responder technologies for SAFETY Act certification. http://www.dhs.gov/science-and-technology/our-work

Transportation Security The Transportation Security Administration protects the Nation's transportation systems to ensure freedom of movement for people and commerce. https://www.tsa.gov

Sources of Information

A–Z Index The DHS website has an alphabetical index of topics to help visitors navigate its content. https://www.dhs.gov/dhsgov-z-index

Audits, Inspections, and Evaluations The Office of the Inspector General (OIG) posts reports on its website. Starting with the year 2003, the OIG's archives of audits, inspections, and evaluations cover the following areas of oversight: border security, counterterrorism, cybersecurity, disaster recovery, immigration, management, and transportation security. https://www.oig.dhs.gov/reports/audits-inspections-and-evaluations

Blog The DHS maintains a blog on its website. https://www.dhs.gov/news-releases/blog?field_news_type_tid=588

Career Opportunities The DHS is one of the largest agencies in the Federal Government. It offers career opportunities in the areas of immigration and travel security, law enforcement, mission support, and prevention and response. To carry out its mission, the agency relies on attorneys, contract specialists, engineers, intelligence analysts, K–9 officers, pilots, scientists, and many other types of experts and professionals. https://www.dhs.gov/homeland-security-careers

In 2018, the DHS ranked 17th among 17 large Government agencies in the Partnership for Public Service's Best Places To Work Agency Rankings. http://bestplacestowork.org/rankings/detail/HS00

Climate Preparedness and Resilience FEMA's web page on climate change helps visitors learn more about the agency's resources and other Federal Government resources that support climate preparedness and resilience. https://www.fema.gov/climate-change

In "Best Practices & Key Considerations for Enhancing Federal Facility Security and Resilience to Climate-Related Hazards" (2015), the Interagency Security Committee identified threats posed by climate change to the assets, missions, operations, and workforce of the Federal Government. It also provided guidance and security planning considerations for agencies housed in nonmilitary Federal facilities. This document's main purpose is to identify short- and long-term strategies for enhancing physical security and resilience in the face climate-related threats. https://www.dhs.gov/publication/isc-climate-related-hazards-best-practices

Contact Information Contact information for DHS headquarters, DHS components, and specific programs of interest is available on the "Direct Contact Information" web page. https://www.dhs.gov/direct-contact-information

The "Department White Pages" is a listing of key contacts that are organized by component. The listing includes email addresses and phone numbers. https://www.dhs.gov/department-white-pages

Current Issues The "In Focus" web page brings together in one place key current issues that fall within the scope of the Department's mission. https://www.dhs.gov/focus

Data The DHS and its components provide Internet access to statistical reports and datasets: Coast Guard maritime information, Customs and Border Protection intellectual property rights recordations, Federal Emergency Management Agency disaster declarations, immigration data, and more. https://www.dhs.gov/topic/data

Flood Insurance Rate Maps

(FIRMs)   Flooding can occur anywhere in the United States; however, certain areas are prone to serious flooding. To help communities understand their risk, flood maps or FIRMs have been created to show the locations of high-risk, moderate-to-low risk, and undetermined-risk areas. Banks, citizens, insurance agents, and all levels of government rely on FIRMs to determine whether flood insurance is required. https://msc.fema.gov/portal

Freedom of Information Act (FOIA)   To any person, the FOIA gives a statutory right for obtaining access to Government information in the records of executive branch agencies. This right to access is limited, however, when the requested information is shielded from disclosure by any of nine exemptions contained within the statute. Instructions for submitting a FOIA request or filing a Privacy Act request and information on other FOIA-related matters are available on the DHS website. https://www.dhs.gov/how-submit-foia-request

The DHS maintains a FOIA library on its website. Information seekers should avail themselves of this online resource to determine if the desired record is immediately available and readily accessible without the additional effort of filing a FOIA request. https://www.dhs.gov/foia-library

Frequently Requested Pages   Links to the most requested pages on the DHS website are collected in place for convenience. https://www.dhs.gov/frequently-requested-pages

Green Card   A person may obtain authorization to live and work in the United States on a permanent basis in several ways: A family member or employer in the United States may sponsor the Green Card applicant; refugee or asylee status and other humanitarian programs offer additional pathways; and, in some cases, a person may be eligible to file on his or her own initiative for permanent residency. https://www.dhs.gov/how-do-i/get-green-card

How Do I?   The DHS website features a comprehensive section that arranges answers to "how do I" questions according to audience: DHS employees, businessmen and women, travelers, and the general public. Entrepreneurs can learn how to apply for grants, find forms for exporting and importing, and verify employment eligibility; travelers can learn how to check wait times at airports and border crossings; and members of the public can learn how to adopt a child internationally, become a citizen, check the status of an immigration case, prepare for a disaster, and report cyber incidents and suspicious activity. https://www.dhs.gov/how-do-i

Keywords   The DHS website features a long list of keywords that are linked to pages containing information on the DHS, its components, and its mission. https://www.dhs.gov/keywords

Multilingual Resources   The Office of Civil Rights and Civil Liberties identifies documents containing information that is particularly important to diverse communities of limited English proficiency. These documents are often translated into Arabic, Chinese, French, Haitian-Creole, Portuguese, Russian, Somali, Spanish, and Vietnamese. https://www.dhs.gov/dhs-multilingual-resources

Naturalization   Congress has established the requirements that a foreign citizen or national must fulfill to receive U.S. citizenship. The process of being granted citizenship is known as naturalization. The U.S. Citizenship and Immigration Services' website offers resources for those seeking citizenship through naturalization. https://www.uscis.gov/us-citizenship/citizenship-through-naturalization

News   The DHS posts audio items, congressional testimony, factsheets, photos and videos, press releases, and speeches on its website. It also posts news items on national security in Spanish. https://www.dhs.gov/news

Open Government   The DHS supports the Open Government initiative by promoting the principles of collaboration, participation, and transparency.   https://www.dhs.gov/open-government

Operational Components   The DHS comprises 10 operational components: the

U.S. Department of Homeland Security, Cybersecurity and Infrastructure Security Agency (CISA), U.S. Customs and Border Protection (CBP), Federal Emergency Management Agency (FEMA), Federal Law Enforcement Training Center (FLETC), U.S. Immigration and Customs Enforcement (ICE), U.S. Secret Service (USSS), Transportation Security Administration (TSA), U.S. Coast Guard (USCG), and U.S. Citizenship and Immigration Services (USCIS). The DHS website offers easy access to each of their home pages. https://www.dhs.gov/dhs-component-websites

Organizational Chart   The agency's organizational chart is available in Portable Document Format (PDF) for viewing and downloading. https://www.dhs.gov/sites/default/files/publications/18_1204_DHS_Organizational_Chart.pdf

Policy Facts   The information on the regularly updated "Myth vs. Fact" web page responds to misleading characterizations of DHS policies in the public domain. https://www.dhs.gov/myth-vs-fact?utm_source=hp_carousel&utm_medium=web&utm_campaign=dhsgov

Publications   The DHS publications library contains brochures, guidance and policy papers, guidelines, program regulations, reports, strategies, and more. https://www.dhs.gov/publications

Report Cyber Incidents   To protect the Nation's cybersecurity, the DHS has organizations dedicated to collecting information and reporting on cyber incidents, phishing, malware, and other vulnerabilities. https://www.dhs.gov/how-do-i/report-cyber-incidents

Site Links   The "Site Links" web page offers easy access to some of the most helpful resources on the DHS web site. https://www.dhs.gov/site-links

Site Map   The website map allows visitors to look for specific topics or to browse content that aligns with their interests. https://www.dhs.gov/sitemap

Social Media   The DHS maintains accounts on Facebook, Flickr, Instagram, and Twitter. An online subscription form also is available to sign up for email updates. https://www.dhs.gov/social-media-directory

Topics   The "Topics" web page offers convenient access to content that has been arranged topically. https://www.dhs.gov/topics

Transportation Security   The "Transportation Security" web page provides information on transportation and travel: aviation security, cargo screening, domestic travel, electronic passports, visas, and more. https://www.dhs.gov/topic/transportation-security

Travel Alerts   The DHS website offers convenient access to alerts and wait times: airport security checkpoint wait times from the Transportation Security Administration, airport wait times from the U.S. Customs and Border Protection, international travel warnings from the Department of State, and health alerts from the Centers for Disease Control and Prevention. https://www.dhs.gov/travel-alerts

White House Fence   The White House complex fence is in the process of being redesigned. The proposal for the new fence is accessible on the website of the U.S. Secret Service. See the Fine Arts Commission's 35-page presentation (JUN 2016) of the "White House Complex Fence—Phase 1." https://www.secretservice.gov/data/about/faqs/WH-Fence-updated-CFA-061616.pdf

The Sources of Information were updated 6–2019.

DEPARTMENT OF HOUSING AND URBAN DEVELOPMENT

451 Seventh Street SW., Washington, DC 20410
Phone, 202-708-1422. Internet, http://www.hud.gov

Secretary	BENJAMIN S. CARSON, SR.
Chief of Staff	ANDREW HUGHES
General Counsel	J. PAUL COMPTON, JR.
Assistant Secretaries	
Congressional and Intergovernmental Relations	LEONARD WOLFSON
Public Affairs	CAROLINE VANVICK, ACTING
Chief Officers	
Financial	IRVING L. DENNIS
Information	DAVID C. CHOW
Directors	
Faith and Opportunity Initiative	(VACANCY)
Small and Disadvantaged Business Utilization	JEAN LIN PAO
https://www.hud.gov/about/leadership/ben_carson	
Deputy Secretary	(VACANCY)
Assistant Secretaties	
Administration	(VACANCY)
Community Planning and Development	(VACANCY)
Fair Housing and Equal Opportunity	ANNA MARIA FARÍAS
Housing	BRIAN D. MONTGOMERY
Policy Development and Research	SETH APPLETON
Public and Indian Housing	HUNTER KURTZ
Assistant Deputy Secretary	
Field Policy and Management	BENJAMIN E. DEMARZO
Chief Officers	
Administrative	NELSON BREGON
Human Capital	MONICA MATTHEWS
Procurement	RONALD C. FLOM
Commissioner	
Federal Housing	BRIAN D. MONTGOMERY
Directors	
Equal Employment Opportunity	JOHN P. BENISON
Lead Hazard Control and Healthy Homes	MATTHEW E. AMMON
Business Transformation	(VACANCY)
https://www.hud.gov/about/leadership	
Government National Mortgage Association—Ginnie Mae	
President	(VACANCY)
https://www.ginniemae.gov/about_us/who_we_are/pages/ executive_leadership.aspx	
Independent Oversight	

Inspector General
RAE OLIVER DAVIS
https://www.hudoig.gov/about-hud-oig/organization-staff/
    inspector-general-immediate-office/rae-oliver-davis

The above list of key personnel was updated 10–2019.

The Department of Housing and Urban Development oversees housing needs nationwide, ensures fair housing opportunities, and creates strong, sustainable, and inclusive communities.

Establishment and Organization

On September 9, 1965, President Lyndon B. Johnson approved Public Law 89–174, which is also cited as the Department of Housing and Urban Development Act. As part of the statute's declaration of purpose, Congress declared that "the general welfare and security of the Nation and the health and living standards of our people require . . . sound development of the Nation's communities and metropolitan areas in which the vast majority of its people live and work." To support this requirement of sound development, Congress established "an executive department to be known as the Department of Housing and Urban Development [HUD]" (79 Stat. 667). https://www.govinfo.gov/content/pkg/STATUTE-79/pdf/STATUTE-79-Pg667.pdf

HUD's statutory duties are described in chapter 44, sections 3531–3549, of 42 U.S.C. https://www.govinfo.gov/content/pkg/USCODE-2017-title42/pdf/USCODE-2017-title42-chap44.pdf

Regulations relating to the Office of the Secretary and to housing and urban development are found in parts 0–4199 of 24 CFR. https://www.ecfr.gov/cgi-bin/text-idx?tpl=/ecfrbrowse/Title24/24tab_02.tpl

By the advice and with the consent of the Senate, the President appoints the Secretary of HUD. The Secretary supervises and directs the administration of the Department (79 Stat. 667). https://www.hud.gov/about/hud_secretary/powersec

HUD's department structure is presented like an organizational chart in its "Fiscal Year 2020 Annual Performance Plan" and "Fiscal Year 2018 Annual Performance Report" on page 11. The Plan and Report are combined into one document (March 2019). https://www.hud.gov/sites/dfiles/SPM/documents/HUDFY2020APP-FY2018APR-3.22.2019.pdf

Program Areas

HUD administers various programs to facilitate its six core functions: insuring mortgages for single-family and multifamily dwellings and extending loans for home improvement and for the purchasing of mobile homes; channeling funds from investors to the mortgage industry through the Government National Mortgage Association–Ginnie Mae; making direct loans for construction or rehabilitation of housing projects that benefit the elderly and handicapped; providing Federal housing subsidies for low- and moderate-income families; giving community development grants to States and communities; and promoting and enforcing fair housing and equal housing opportunity. https://www.hud.gov/topics

Community Planning and Development The Office of Community and Planning Development administers grant programs to help communities plan and finance growth and development, to increase their governing capacity, and to shelter and provide services for the homeless. The Office is responsible for implementing Community Development Block Grant (CDBG) programs for entitlement communities; the State- and HUD-administered Small Cities Program; community development loan guarantees; special purpose grants for insular areas and historically black colleges and universities; Appalachian Regional Commission grants; the Home Investment in Affordable Housing Program, which provides Federal assistance for housing rehabilitation, tenant-based assistance, first-time homebuyers, and new construction when a jurisdiction is determined to need new rental housing; the Department's programs to address homelessness; the John Heinz Neighborhood Development

Program; community outreach partnerships; the joint community development plan that assists institutions of higher education working in concert with State and local governments to undertake activities under the CDBG program; community adjustment and economic diversification planning grants; empowerment zones and enterprise communities; efforts to improve the environment; and community planning and development efforts of other departments and agencies, public and private organizations, private industry, financial markets, and international organizations. http://portal.hud.gov/hudportal/HUD?src=/program_offices/comm_planning

For further information, contact the Office of Community Planning and Development. Phone, 202-708-2690.

Fair Housing / Equal Opportunity   The Office of Fair Housing and Equal Opportunity administers fair housing laws and regulations prohibiting discrimination in public and private housing; equal opportunity laws and regulations prohibiting discrimination in HUD-assisted housing and community development programs; the fair housing assistance grants program to provide financial and technical assistance to State and local government agencies to implement local fair housing laws and ordinances; and the Community Housing Resources Boards program to provide grants for fair housing activities, including outreach and education, identification of institutional barriers to fair housing, and telephone hotlines for complaints. http://portal.hud.gov/hudportal/HUD?src=/program_offices/fair_housing_equal_opp

For further information, contact the Office of Fair Housing and Equal Opportunity. Phone, 202-708-4252.

Government National Mortgage Association–Ginnie Mae   Ginnie Mae is a Government corporation that makes housing affordable for millions of low- and moderate-income earners by channeling capital into the Nation's housing markets. The Ginnie Mae guaranty allows mortgage lenders to obtain a higher price when selling their mortgage loans in the secondary mortgage market. Lenders can then use the proceeds of these sales to fund new mortgage loans. Without that liquidity, lenders would have to keep all loans in their own portfolios and would not have adequate capital for making new loans. Ginnie Mae guarantees investors the timely payment of principal and interest on mortgage-backed securities that are backed by federally insured or federally guaranteed loans—loans insured by the Federal Housing Administration or guaranteed by the Department of Veterans Affairs. Other guarantors, or issuers, of loans that are eligible as collateral for Ginnie Mae mortgage-backed securities include HUD's Office of Public and Indian Housing and the Department of Agriculture's Rural Development. Ginnie Mae securities are the only mortgage-backed securities to carry the full faith and credit guaranty of the U.S. Government. http://www.ginniemae.gov/pages/default.aspx

For further information, contact the Government National Mortgage Association. Phone, 202-708-0926.

Housing   The Office of Housing oversees aid for construction and financing of new and rehabilitated housing and for preservation of existing housing. The Office underwrites single-family, multifamily, property improvement, and manufactured home loans; administers special purpose programs designed for the elderly, handicapped, and chronically mentally ill; administers housing assistance programs for low-income families having difficulties affording standard housing; administers grants to fund resident ownership of multifamily house properties; and protects consumers against fraudulent land development and promotional practices. http://portal.hud.gov/hudportal/HUD?src=/program_offices/housing

For further information, contact the Office of Housing. Phone, 202-708-3600.

Lead Hazard Control / Healthy Homes   The Office of Lead Hazard Control and Healthy Homes is responsible for lead hazard control policy development, abatement, training, regulations, and research. Activities of the Office include increasing public and building-industry awareness of the dangers of lead-based paint poisoning and the options for detection, risk reduction, and abatement; encouraging the development of safer, more effective, and less costly methods for detection, risk reduction, and abatement; and encouraging State and local governments to develop lead-based paint programs covering contractor certification, hazard reduction, financing, enforcement, and primary prevention, including public education. http://portal.hud.gov/hudportal/HUD?src=/program_offices/healthy_homes

For further information, contact the Office of Lead Hazard Control and Healthy Homes. Phone, 202-755-1785.

Public and Indian Housing

The Office of Public and Indian Housing administers public and Indian housing programs; assists technically and financially with planning, developing, and managing low-income projects; subsidizes the operations of public housing agencies (PHAs) and Indian housing authorities (IHAs) and provides procedures for reviewing the management of public housing agencies; administers the comprehensive improvement assistance and comprehensive grant programs for modernizing low-income housing projects; administers programs for resident participation, resident management, home ownership, economic development and supportive services, and drug-free neighborhood programs; protects low-income tenants from lead-based paint poisoning by requiring PHAs and IHAs to comply with HUD regulations for the testing and removal of lead-based paint; implements and monitors program requirements related to program eligibility and admission of families to public and assisted housing, as well as tenant income and rent requirements for continued occupancy; administers the HOPE VI and vacancy reduction programs; administers voucher and certificate programs and the Moderate Rehabilitation Program; coordinates all departmental housing and community development programs for Indian and Alaskan Natives; and awards grants to PHAs and IHAs for the construction, acquisition, and operation of public and Indian housing projects. http://portal.hud.gov/hudportal/HUD?src=/program_offices/public_indian_housing/ih

For further information, contact the Office of Public and Indian Housing. Phone, 202-708-0950.

Sources of Information

A–Z Index An alphabetical index is available on the HUD website to help visitors search for specific topics or browse content that aligns with their interests. https://portal.hud.gov/hudportal/HUD?src=/siteindex/quicklinks

Archived Records HUD records are referenced in the "Guide to Federal Records in the National Archives of the United States." The Guide is accessible online, and HUD records have been assigned to Record Group 207. https://www.archives.gov/research/guide-fed-records/groups/207.html

Bibliographic Database The HUD USER bibliographic database contains more than 10,000 full-abstract citations to research reports, articles, books, monographs, and data sources in housing policy, building technology, economic development, urban planning, and a host of other relevant fields. https://www.huduser.gov/portal/bibliodb/pdrbibdb.html

Business Opportunities To learn about contracting opportunities, programs, and resources, use the link below. The Office of the Chief Procurement Officer can provide additional information. Phone, 202-708-1290. TDD, 202-708-1455. http://portal.hud.gov/hudportal/HUD?src=/program_offices/cpo

Career Opportunities Information on career opportunities—including opportunities for veterans, students, and people with disabilities—is available online. Information is also available from the Personnel Division at the nearest regional office and from the Office of Human Resources in Washington, DC. Phone, 202-708-0408. http://portal.hud.gov/hudportal/HUD?src=/program_offices/administration/careers

In 2018, HUD ranked 21st among 27 midsize Government agencies in the Partnership for Public Service's Best Places To Work Agency Rankings. https://bestplacestowork.org/rankings/detail/HU00

Contact Information Contact information is available online. https://www.hud.gov/contact

Data / Research The Office of Policy Development and Research posts datasets, publications, research, and information on initiatives on its "HUD User" website. http://www.huduser.org/portal/home.html

Disaster Resilience The Office of Economic Development oversees HUD's preparations to mitigate the effects of climate change on it's mission, operations, and programs. This includes promoting greater capacity in and more utilization of resilient approaches to community development at the local, regional, and State levels. https://www.hud.gov/program_offices/economic_development/resilience/about | Email: EconomicDevelopment@hud.gov

En Español   HUD posts information in Spanish on its website. https://www.hud.gov/espanol

Some contact information is available on the "Información en Español" web page. https://www.hud.gov/directory/800/parainformacion

Field Offices   Visit HUD's online local office directory to find contact information for its field offices. http://portal.hud.gov/hudportal/HUD?src=/program_offices/field_policy_mgt/localoffices

Freedom of Information Act (FOIA)   Many HUD documents are available online. Before submitting a written request, click on the "Frequently Requested Materials" and "E–FOIA Reading Room" links on HUD's FOIA web page to see if the desired information is immediately accessible, free of charge. Phone, 202-708-3054. http://portal.hud.gov/hudportal/HUD?src=/program_offices/administration/foia

Frequently Asked Questions (FAQs)   Answers to FAQs are posted online. https://portal.hud.gov/hudportal/HUD?src=/faqs

Glossary   The Government National Mortgage Association (Ginnie Mae) maintains a glossary on its website. https://www.ginniemae.gov/Pages/Glossary.aspx

History   In the aftermath of assassination that outraged communities of color and sparked protest and violence in American cities, President Lyndon B. Johnson approved Title VIII of the Civil Rights Act of 1968, commonly referred to as the Fair Housing Act. Signing "into law the promises of a century" was his description of that moment. The promises of this legislation included outlawing most housing discrimination and giving enforcement responsibility to HUD. To learn more about HUD's history of overseeing and coordinating Federal housing programs and enforcing fair housing practices, visit the "HUD History" web page. https://portal.hud.gov/hudportal/HUD?src=/about/hud_history

Hotline   The Office of the Inspector General maintains the Hotline to report fraud, mismanagement, and waste. Phone, 202-708-4200 or 800-347-3735. TDD, 202-708-2451. http://www.hudoig.gov/hotline | Email: hotline@hudoig.gov

Human Stories   "The Humans of HUD" web page allows visitors to meet the men and women whom HUD serves. The page contains brief narratives and short videos. https://www.hud.gov/humansofhud

Library   The library is located at HUD headquarters in Washington, DC. Visitors must schedule an appointment to use the library. It is open weekdays, except Federal holidays, from 9:30 a.m. to 5 p.m. Phone, 202-402-2680.

Locate a HUD Employee   To locate a HUD employee or to send a HUD employee an email, visit the "Search for HUD Employees" web page. An automated phone locator service is also available. Phone, 202-708-1112. TDD, 202-708-1455. http://peoplesearch.hud.gov/po/i/netlocator

Organizational Directory   An organization directory of HUD's headquarters is available online. https://www.hud.gov/directory/director

Press Room   HUD posts press releases, remarks, speeches, statements, and testimonies on its website. https://www.hud.gov/press

Program Offices   The "Program Offices" web page provides links for easy access to program information. https://www.hud.gov/program_offices

Property Disposition   For single-family properties, contact the Chief Property Officer at the nearest HUD regional office or the Property Disposition Division. Phone, 202-708-0614. For multifamily properties, contact the Regional Housing Director at the nearest HUD regional office or the Property Disposition Division. Phone, 202-708-0614. http://portal.hud.gov/hudportal/HUD?src=/topics/homes_for_sale

Regional Organization Map   HUD is organized in 10 regions, each of which a regional administrator manages. A field office director manages each field office within a region. Field office directors report to the appropriate regional administrator. https://www.hud.gov/localoffices/regions

Resources The "Resources" web page has a list of helpful links in alphabetical order. https://www.hud.gov/resources

Site Map The website map allows visitors to look for specific topics or to browse content that aligns with their interests. https://portal.hud.gov/hudportal/HUD?src=/siteindex

Social Media HUD's social media directory provides links to all of its official blogs and social media platforms on Facebook, Flickr, Instagram, Twitter, and YouTube. https://portal.hud.gov/hudportal/HUD?src=/program_offices/public_affairs/socialmedia

Veterans HUD's "Veteran Information" page has resources that can help veterans. For example, HUDVet promotes collaboration among Federal agencies and veteran-serving organizations. https://www.hud.gov/program_offices/comm_planning/veteran_information | Email: hudvet@hud.gov

The Sources of Information were updated 10–2019.

Editorial Note

The Department of Justice did not meet the publication deadline for submitting updated information of its activities, functions, and sources of information as required by the automatic disclosure provisions of the Freedom of Information Act (5 U.S.C. 552(a)(1)(A))

DEPARTMENT OF JUSTICE

950 Pennsylvania Avenue NW., Washington, DC 20530
Phone, 202-514-2000. Internet, http://www.justice.gov

Attorney General
Deputy Attorney General

JEFF SESSIONS
ROD J. ROSENSTEIN

Associate Attorney General
Counsel, Office of Professional Responsibility
Inspector General
Pardon Attorney
Solicitor General

RACHEL L. BRAND
ROBIN C. ASHTON
MICHAEL E. HOROWITZ
LAWRENCE KUPERS, ACTING
JEFF WALL, ACTING

Assistant Attorneys General
Criminal Division
Environment and Natural Resources Division
Justice Management Division / Chief Financial Officer
National Security Division
Office of Legislative Affairs
Tax Division

LESLIE RAGON CALDWELL
JOHN C. CRUDEN
LEE J. LOFTHUS
JOHN P. CARLIN
PETER J. KADZIK
CAROLINE D. CIRAOLO, ACTING

Directors
Community Relations Service
Executive Office for Organized Crime and Drug Enforcement Task Force
Executive Office for U.S. Attorneys
Executive Office for U.S. Trustees
Office for Access to Justice
Office of Information Policy
Office of Public Affairs
Office of Tribal Justice and Safety
Professional Responsibility Advisory Office

PAUL MONTEIRO, ACTING
BRUCE G. OHR

MONTY WILKINSON
CLIFFORD J. WHITE III
LISA FOSTER
MELANIE ANN PUSTAY
SARAH ISGUR FLORES
TRACY TOULOU
STACY LUDWIG

Principal Deputy Assistant Attorneys General
Antitrust Division
Civil Division
Civil Rights Division
Office of Legal Counsel
Office of Legal Policy

ANDREW C. FINCH, ACTING
CHAD A. READLER, ACTING
JOHN M. GORE, ACTING
CURTIS E. GANNON, ACTING
RYAN NEWMAN, ACTING

[For the Department of Justice statement of organization, see the Code of Federal Regulations, Title 28, Chapter I, Part 0]

The Department of Justice serves as counsel for U.S citizens and represents them by enforcing the law in the public interest. It deters criminality and subversion, ensures healthy business competition, safeguards consumers, and enforces drug, immigration, and naturalization laws.

The Department of Justice was established by act of June 22, 1870 (28 U.S.C. 501, 503, 509 note), with the Attorney General as its head. The affairs and activities of the Department of Justice are generally directed by the Attorney General.

Attorney General   The Attorney General represents the United States in legal matters

U.S. Department of Justice

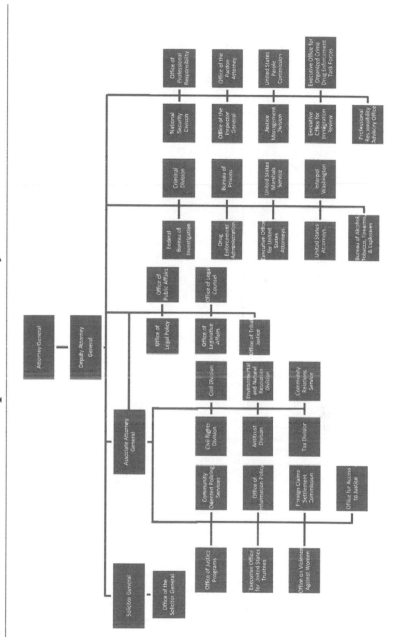

generally and gives advice and opinions to the President and to the heads of the executive departments of the Government when so requested. The Attorney General appears in person to represent the Government before the U.S. Supreme Court in cases of exceptional gravity or importance.

Community Relations Service   The Service offers assistance to communities in resolving disputes relating to race, color, or national origin and facilitates the development of viable agreements as alternatives to coercion, violence, or litigation. It also assists and supports communities in developing local mechanisms as proactive measures to prevent or reduce ethnic and racial tensions.

A list of Community Relations Service regional offices—including contact information—is available online. http://www.justice.gov/crs/about-crs/regional-and-field-offices; http://www.justice.gov/crs/contact-office

For further information, contact any regional office or the Director, Community Relations Service, Department of Justice, Suite 2000, 600 E Street NW., Washington, DC 20530. Phone, 202-305-2935.

Pardon Attorney   The Office of the Pardon Attorney assists the President in the exercise of his pardon power under the Constitution. Generally, all requests for pardon or other forms of executive clemency, including commutation of sentences, are directed to the Pardon Attorney for investigation and review. The Pardon Attorney prepares the Department's recommendation to the President for final disposition of each application. http://www.justice.gov/pardon

For further information, contact the Office of the Pardon Attorney, Department of Justice, Suite 5E–508, 145 N Street NE., Washington, DC 20530. Phone, 202-616-6070.

Solicitor General   The Office of the Solicitor General represents the U.S. Government in cases before the Supreme Court. It decides what cases the Government should ask the Supreme Court to review and what position the Government should take in cases before the Court. It also supervises the preparation of the Government's Supreme Court briefs and other legal documents and the conduct of the oral arguments in the Court. The Solicitor

General also decides whether the United States should appeal in cases that it loses before the lower courts. http://www.justice.gov/osg

For further information, contact the Executive Officer, Office of the Solicitor General, Room 5142, 950 Pennsylvania Avenue NW., RFK Justice Building (Main), Washington, DC 20530-0001.

U.S. Attorneys   The Executive Office for U.S. Attorneys was created on April 6, 1953, to provide liaison between the Department of Justice in Washington, DC, and the U.S. attorneys. It gives general executive assistance to the 94 offices of the U.S. attorneys and coordinates the relationship between the U.S. attorneys and the organization components of the Department of Justice and other Federal agencies. http://www.justice.gov/usao/eousa

For further information, contact the Executive Office for U.S. Attorneys, Department of Justice, Room 2261, 950 Pennsylvania Avenue NW., Washington, DC 20530. Phone, 202-514-1020.

U.S. Trustee Program   The Program was established by the Bankruptcy Reform Act of 1978 (11 U.S.C. 101 et seq.) as a pilot effort in 10 regions comprising 18 Federal judicial districts to promote the efficiency and protect the integrity of the bankruptcy system by identifying and helping to investigate bankruptcy fraud and abuse. It now operates nationwide except in Alabama and North Carolina. The Bankruptcy Abuse Prevention and Consumer Protection Act of 2005 (11 U.S.C. 101 note) significantly expanded the Program's responsibilities and provided additional tools to fight bankruptcy fraud and abuse. The Executive Office for U.S. Trustees provides day-to-day policy and legal direction, coordination, and control. http://www.justice.gov/ust

For further information, contact the Executive Office for U.S. Trustees, Department of Justice, Suite 6150, 441 G Street NW., Washington, DC 20530. Phone, 202-307-1391.

Divisions

Antitrust Division   The Assistant Attorney General in charge of the Antitrust Division is responsible for promoting and maintaining competitive markets by enforcing the Federal antitrust laws. This involves investigating possible antitrust violations, conducting grand jury proceedings, reviewing proposed mergers and acquisitions, preparing and trying antitrust cases, prosecuting appeals, and negotiating and enforcing final judgments. The Division prosecutes serious and willful violations of antitrust laws by filing criminal suits that can lead to large fines and jail sentences. Where criminal prosecution is not appropriate, the Division seeks a court order forbidding future violations of the law and requiring steps by the defendant to remedy the anticompetitive effects of past violations.

The Division also is responsible for acting as an advocate of competition within the Federal Government as well as internationally. This involves formal appearances in Federal administrative agency proceedings, development of legislative initiatives to promote deregulation and eliminate unjustifiable exemptions from the antitrust laws, and participation on executive branch policy task forces and in multilateral international organizations. The Division provides formal advice to other agencies on the competitive implications of proposed transactions requiring Federal approval, such as mergers of financial institutions. http://www.justice.gov/atr

For further information, contact the Office of the Assistant Attorney General, Antitrust Division, Department of Justice, 950 Pennsylvania Avenue NW., Washington, DC 20530. Phone, 202-514-2401.

Civil Division   The Civil Division represents the United States, its departments and agencies, Members of Congress, Cabinet officers, and other Federal employees. Its litigation reflects the diversity of Government activities involving, for example, the defense of challenges to Presidential actions; national security issues; benefit programs; energy policies; commercial issues such as contract disputes, banking, insurance, fraud, and debt collection; all manner of accident and liability claims; and violations of the immigration and consumer protection laws. The Division confronts significant policy issues, which often rise to constitutional dimensions, in defending and enforcing various Federal programs and actions. Each year, Division attorneys handle thousands of cases that collectively involve billions of dollars in claims and recoveries.

The Division litigates cases in the following areas:

Commercial litigation, litigation associated with the Government's diverse financial involvements including all monetary suits involving contracts, express or implied; actions to foreclose on Government mortgages and liens; bankruptcy and insolvency proceedings; suits against guarantors and sureties; actions involving fraud against the Government, including false or fraudulent claims for Federal insurance, loans, subsidies, and other benefits such as Medicare, false or fraudulent claims for payment under Federal contracts, whistleblower suits, and Government corruption; patent, copyright, and trademark cases and suits arising out of construction, procurement, service contracts, and claims associated with contract terminations; claims for just compensation under the Fifth Amendment; claims for salary or retirement by civilian and military personnel; cases assigned by congressional reference or special legislation; and litigation involving interests of the United States in any foreign court, whether civil or criminal in nature.

Consumer litigation, including civil and criminal litigation and related matters arising under various consumer protection and public health statutes.

Federal programs, including constitutional challenges to statutes, suits to overturn Government policies and programs, challenges to the legality of Government decisions, allegations that the President has violated the Constitution or Federal law, suits to enforce regulatory statutes and to remedy or prevent statutory or regulatory violations.

The areas of litigation include:

Suits against the heads of Federal departments and agencies and other Government officials to enjoin official actions, as well as suits for judicial review of administrative decisions, orders, and regulations; suits involving national security, including suits to protect sensitive intelligence sources and materials; suits to prevent interference with Government operations; litigation concerning the constitutionality of Federal laws; and suits raising employment discrimination claims and Government personnel issues.

Immigration litigation, involving civil litigation under the Immigration and Nationality Act and related laws; district court litigation, habeas corpus review and general advice; petitions for removal order review and immigration-related appellate matters; cases pertaining to the issuance of visas and passports; and litigation arising under the legalization and employer sanction provisions of the immigration laws.

Torts, including the broad range of tort litigation arising from the operation of the Federal Government, constitutional tort claims against Federal Government officials throughout the Government, aviation disasters, environmental and occupational disease, and radiation and toxic substance exposure. It defends petitions filed pursuant to the Vaccine Injury Compensation Program and is responsible for administering the Radiation Exposure Compensation Program. It also handles maritime litigation and suits that seek personal monetary judgments against individual officers or employees.

Appellate, having primary responsibility for the litigation of Civil Division cases in the courts of appeal, and on occasion, State appeal courts. The Appellate Staff prepares Government briefs and presents oral arguments for these cases. Additionally, the Appellate Staff works with the Solicitor General's office to prepare documents filed for these cases in the Supreme Court, including briefs on the merits, petitions for certiorari, and jurisdictional statements. The Appellate Staff also works with the Solicitor General's office to obtain authorization for appellate review. http://www.justice.gov/civil

For further information, contact the Office of the Assistant Attorney General, Civil Division, Department of Justice, Tenth Street and Pennsylvania Avenue NW., Washington, DC 20530. Phone, 202-514-3301.

Civil Rights Division   The Civil Rights Division, headed by an Assistant Attorney General, was established in 1957 to secure effective Federal enforcement of civil rights. The Division is the primary institution within the Federal Government responsible for enforcing Federal statutes prohibiting discrimination on the basis of race, sex, disability, religion, citizenship, and national origin. The Division has responsibilities in the following areas:

Coordination and review of various civil rights statutes that prohibit discrimination on the basis of race, color, national origin, sex, and religion in programs and activities that receive Federal financial assistance by Federal agencies.

Criminal cases involving conspiracies to interfere with federally protected rights; deprivation of rights under color of law; the use of force or threat of force to injure or intimidate someone in their enjoyment of specific rights (such as voting, housing, employment, education, public facilities, and accommodations); interference with the free exercise of religious beliefs or damage to religious property; the holding of a worker in a condition of slavery or involuntary servitude; and interference with persons seeking to obtain or provide reproductive services.

Disability rights cases, achieving equal opportunity for people with disabilities in the United States by implementing the Americans with Disabilities Act (ADA). ADA mandates are carried out through enforcement, certification, regulatory, coordination, and technical assistance activities, combined with an innovative mediation program and a technical assistance grant program. The Division also carries out responsibilities under sections 504 and 508 of the Rehabilitation Act, the Help America Vote Act of 2002, the Small Business Regulatory Enforcement Fairness Act, and Executive Order 12250.

Educational opportunities litigation, involving title IV of the Civil Rights Act of 1964, the Equal Educational Opportunities Act of 1974, and title III of the Americans with Disabilities Act. In addition, the Division is responsible for enforcing other statutes such as title VI of the Civil Rights Act of 1964, title IX of the Education Amendments of 1972, section 504 of the Rehabilitation Act of 1973, title II of the Americans with Disabilities Act, and the Individuals with Disabilities Education Act upon referral from other governmental agencies.

Employment litigation enforcing against State and local government employers the provisions of title VII of the Civil Rights Act of 1964, as amended, and other Federal laws prohibiting employment practices that discriminate on grounds of race, sex, religion, and national origin. The Division also enforces against State and local government and private employers the provisions of the Uniformed Services Employment and Reemployment Rights Act of 1994, which prohibits employers from discriminating or retaliating against an employee or applicant for employment because of such person's past, current, or future military obligation.

Housing and Civil Enforcement statutes enforcing the Fair Housing Act, which prohibits discrimination in housing; the Equal Credit Opportunity Act, which prohibits discrimination in credit; title II of the Civil Rights Act of 1964, which prohibits discrimination in certain places of public accommodation, such as hotels, restaurants, nightclubs and theaters; title III of the Civil Rights Act of 1964, which prohibits discrimination in public facilities; and the Religious Land Use and Institutionalized Persons Act, which prohibits local governments from adopting or enforcing land use regulations that discriminate against religious assemblies and institutions or which unjustifiably burden religious exercise.

Immigration-related unfair employment practices enforcing the antidiscrimination provisions of the Immigration and Nationality Act, which protect U.S. citizens and legal immigrants from employment discrimination based upon citizenship or immigration status and national origin, unfair documentary practices relating to the employment eligibility verification process, and retaliation.

Special litigation protecting the constitutional and statutory rights of persons confined in certain institutions owned or operated by State or local governments, including facilities for individuals with mental and developmental disabilities, nursing homes, prisons, jails, and juvenile detention facilities where a pattern or practice of violations exist; civil enforcement of statutes prohibiting a pattern or practice of conduct by law enforcement agencies that violates Federal law; and protection against a threat of force and physical obstruction that injures, intimidates, or interferes with a person seeking to obtain or provide reproductive health services, or to exercise the first amendment right of religious freedom at a place of worship.

Voting cases enforcing the Voting Rights Act, the Help America Vote Act of 2002, the National Voter Registration Act, the Voting Accessibility for the Elderly and Handicapped Act, the Uniformed and Overseas Citizens Absentee Voting Act, and other Federal statutes designed to safeguard citizens' rights to vote. This includes racial and language minorities, illiterate persons, individuals with disabilities, overseas citizens, persons who change their residence shortly before a Presidential election, and persons 18 to 20 years of age. http://www.justice.gov/crt

For further information, contact the Executive Officer, Civil Rights Division, Department of Justice, 950 Pennsylvania Avenue NW., Washington, DC 20035. Phone, 202-514-4224.

Criminal Division   The Criminal Division develops, enforces, and supervises the application of all Federal criminal laws, except those specifically assigned to other divisions. In addition to its direct litigation responsibilities, the Division formulates and implements criminal enforcement policy and provides advice and assistance, including representing the United States before the United States Courts of Appeal. The Division engages in and coordinates a wide range of criminal investigations and prosecutions, such as those targeting individuals and organizations that engage in international and national drug trafficking and money laundering systems or organizations and organized crime groups. The Division also approves or monitors sensitive areas of law enforcement such as participation in the Witness Security Program and the use of electronic surveillance; advises the Attorney General, Congress, the Office of Management and Budget, and the White House on matters of criminal law; provides legal advice, assistance, and training to Federal, State, and local prosecutors and investigative agencies; provides leadership for coordinating international and national law enforcement matters; and provides training and development assistance to foreign criminal justice systems. Areas of responsibility include the following:

Asset forfeiture and money laundering, including the prosecution of complex, sensitive, multidistrict, and international cases; formulating policy and conducting training in the money laundering and forfeiture areas; developing legislation and regulations; ensuring the uniform application of forfeiture and money laundering statutes; participating in bilateral and multilateral initiatives to develop international forfeiture and money laundering policy and promote international cooperation; adjudicating petitions for remission or mitigation of forfeited assets; distributing forfeited funds and properties to appropriate domestic and foreign law enforcement agencies and community groups within the United States; and ensuring that such agencies comply with proper usage of received funds.

Child exploitation and obscenity, including the prosecution of sexual predators, sex trafficking of children, U.S. citizens and resident aliens who travel abroad to sexually abuse foreign children (sex tourism), and the enforcement of sex offender registration laws; providing forensic assistance to Federal prosecutors and law enforcement agents in investigating and prosecuting child exploitation: coordinating nationwide operations targeting child predators; and developing policy and legislative proposals related to these issues.

Computer and intellectual property crimes, including cyberattacks on critical information systems (cyberterrorism); strengthening, domestic and international laws prosecute computer crimes; and directing multidistrict and transnational cyberinvestigations and prosecutions.

Enforcement, including the review of all Federal electronic surveillance requests and requests to apply for court orders permitting the use video surveillance; authorizing or denying the entry of applicants into the Federal Witness Security Program (WSP) and coordinating and administering its program components; reviewing requests for witness immunity ; transfer of prisoners to and from foreign countries to serve the remainder of their prison sentences; attorney and press subpoenas; applications for S-visa status; and disclosure of grand jury information.

Fraud, including the investigation and prosecution of white-collar crimes (corporate, securities, and investment fraud), government program and procurement fraud, and international criminal violations including the bribery of foreign government officials in violation of the Foreign Corrupt Practices Act.

International affairs, including making requests for international extradition and foreign evidence on behalf of Federal, State, and local prosecutors and investigators, fulfilling foreign requests for fugitives and evidence, and negotiating and implementing law enforcement treaties.

Narcotics and dangerous drugs, including domestic and international drug trafficking and narco-terrorism; enforcing laws that criminalize the extraterritorial manufacture or distribution of certain controlled substances; prosecuting drug traffickers who support a person or organization that engages in terrorist activity; and providing targeted intelligence support to the DEA and other law enforcement agencies worldwide.

Organized crime, including combining the resources and expertise of several Federal agencies in cooperation with the Tax Division, U.S. attorneys offices, and State and local law enforcement to identify, disrupt, and dismantle major drug supply and money laundering organizations through coordinated, nationwide investigations targeting the entire infrastructure of these enterprises.

Assistance to foreign law enforcement institutions, including the creation of new and reforming existing police forces in other countries and international peacekeeping operations; enhancing the capabilities of existing police forces in emerging democracies; and assisting nations that are combating terrorism.

Overseas prosecutorial development, assistance, and training for prosecutors and judicial personnel in other countries to develop and sustain democratic criminal justice institutions.

Policy and legislation, developing legislative proposals and reviewing pending legislation affecting the Federal criminal justice system; reviewing and developing proposed changes to the Federal sentencing guidelines and rules; and analyzing crime policy and program issues.

Public integrity efforts to combat corruption of elected and appointed public officials at all levels of government.

Human rights and special prosecutions, investigating and prosecuting human rights violations, international violent crime, immigration violations, and war crimes.

Appellate work, including drafting briefs and certiorari petitions for the Solicitor General for filing in the U.S. Supreme Court; making recommendations to the Solicitor General as to whether further review is warranted on adverse decisions in the district courts and courts of appeals; and preparing briefs and arguing cases in the courts of appeals.

Counterterrorism, including in conjunction with the National Security Division, investigating and prosecuting terrorist financing and material support cases; establishing and maintaining an essential communication network between the Department of Justice and United States Attorneys' Offices for the rapid transmission of information on terrorism threats and investigative activity; providing and serving as trusted liaisons to the intelligence, defense, and immigration communities as well as to foreign government partners on counterterrorism issues and cases. http://www.justice.gov/criminal

For further information, contact the Office of the Assistant Attorney General, Criminal Division, Department of Justice, Tenth Street and Pennsylvania Avenue NW., Washington, DC 20530. Phone, 202-514-2601.

Environment and Natural Resources Division

The Environment and Natural Resources Division is the Nation's environmental lawyer. The Division's responsibilities include enforcing civil and criminal environmental laws that protect America's health and environment. It also defends environmental challenges to Government activities and programs and ensures that environmental laws are implemented in a fair and consistent manner nationwide. It also represents the United States in all matters concerning the protection, use, and development of the Nation's natural resources and public lands, wildlife protection, Indian rights and claims, and the acquisition of Federal property. To carry out this broad mission, the Division litigates in the following areas:

Environmental crimes, prosecuting individuals and corporate entities violating laws designed to protect the environment.

Civil environmental enforcement, on behalf of EPA; claims for damages to natural resources filed on behalf of the Departments of the Interior, Commerce, and Agriculture; claims for contribution against private parties for contamination of public land; and recoupment of money spent to clean up certain oil spills on behalf of the U.S. Coast Guard.

Environmental defense, representing the United States in suits challenging the Government's administration of Federal environmental laws including claims that regulations are too strict or lenient and claims alleging that Federal agencies are not complying with environmental standards.

Wildlife and marine resources protection, including prosecution of smugglers and black-market dealers in protected wildlife.

Use and protection of federally owned public lands and natural resources across a broad spectrum of laws.

Indian resources protection, including establishing water rights, establishing and protecting hunting and fishing rights, collecting damages for trespass on Indian lands, and establishing reservation boundaries and rights to land.

Land acquisition for use by the Federal Government for purposes ranging from establishing public parks to building Federal courthouses. http://justice.gov/enrd

For further information, contact the Office of the Assistant Attorney General, Environment and Natural Resources Division, Department of Justice, Tenth Street and Pennsylvania Avenue NW., Washington, DC 20530. Phone, 202-514-2701.

National Security Division

The National Security Division (NSD) develops, enforces, and supervises the application of all Federal criminal laws related to the national counterterrorism and counterespionage enforcement programs, except those specifically assigned to other divisions. NSD litigates and coordinates a wide range of prosecutions and criminal investigations involving terrorism and violations of the espionage, export control, and foreign agents registration laws. It administers the

Foreign Intelligence Surveillance Act and other legal authorities for national security activities; approves and monitors the use of electronic surveillance; provides legal and policy advice regarding the classification of and access to national security information; performs prepublication review of materials written by present and former DOJ employees; trains the law enforcement and intelligence communities; and advises the Department and legislative and executive branches on all areas of national security law. NSD also serves as the Department's representative on interdepartmental boards, committees, and entities dealing with issues related to national security.

NSD also has some additional counterterrorism, counterespionage, and intelligence oversight responsibilities as follows: to promote and oversee national counterterrorism enforcement programs; develop and implement counterterrorism strategies, legislation, and initiatives; facilitate information sharing between and among the Department and other Federal agencies on terrorism threats; share information with international law enforcement officials to assist with international threat information and litigation initiatives; liaison with the intelligence, defense, and immigration communities and foreign governments on counterterrorism issues and cases; supervise the investigation and prosecution of cases involving national security, foreign relations, the export of military and strategic commodities and technology, espionage, sabotage, neutrality, and atomic energy; coordinate cases involving the application for the Classified Information Procedures Act; enforce the Foreign Agents Registration Act of 1938 and related disclosure laws; supervise the preparation of certifications and applications for orders under the Foreign Intelligence Surveillance Act (FISA); represent the United States before the Foreign Intelligence Surveillance Court; participate in the development, implementation, and review of United States intelligence policies; evaluate existing and proposed national security-related activities to determine their consistency with relevant policies and law; monitor intelligence and counterintelligence activities of other agencies to ensure

conformity with Department objectives; prepare reports evaluating domestic and foreign intelligence and counterintelligence activities; and process requests to use FISA-derived information in criminal, civil, and immigration proceedings and to disseminate that information to foreign governments. http://www.justice.gov/nsd

For further information, contact the Office of the Assistant Attorney General, National Security Division, Department of Justice, Tenth Street and Pennsylvania Avenue NW., Washington, DC 20530. Phone, 202-514-5600.

Tax Division Tax Division ensures the uniform and fair enforcement of Federal tax laws in Federal and State courts. The Division conducts enforcement activities to deter specific taxpayers, as well as the taxpaying public at large, from conduct that deprives the Federal Government of its tax-related revenue. It represents the United States and its officers in all civil and criminal litigation arising under the internal revenue laws, other than proceedings in the U.S. Tax Court. Tax Division attorneys frequently join with assistant U.S. attorneys in prosecuting tax cases. Some criminal tax grand jury investigations and prosecutions are handled solely by Tax Division prosecutors, while others are delegated to assistant U.S. attorneys. Division attorneys evaluate requests by the Internal Revenue Service or U.S. attorneys to initiate grand jury investigations or prosecutions of tax crimes.

The Division handles a wide array of civil tax litigation, including the following: suits to enjoin the promotion of abusive tax shelters and to enjoin activities relating to aiding and abetting the understatement of tax liabilities of others; suits to enforce Internal Revenue Service administrative summonses that seek information essential to determine and collect taxpayers' liabilities, including summonses for records of corporate tax shelters and offshore transactions; suits brought by the United States to set aside fraudulent conveyances and to collect assets held by nominees and egos; tax refund suits challenging the Internal Revenue Service's determination of taxpayers' Federal income, employment, excise, and estate liabilities; bankruptcy litigation raising issues of the validity, dischargeability, and priority of Federal tax claims, and the feasibility of reorganization plans; suits brought by taxpayers challenging determinations made in the collection due process proceedings before the Internal Revenue Service's Office of Appeals; and suits against the United States for damages for the unauthorized disclosure of tax return information or for damages claimed because of alleged injuries caused by Internal Revenue Service employees in the performance of their official duties.

The Division also collects judgments in tax cases. To this end, the Division directs collection efforts and coordinates with, monitors the efforts of, and provides assistance to the various U.S. attorneys' offices in collecting outstanding judgments in tax cases. The Division also works with the Internal Revenue Service, U.S. attorneys, and other Government agencies on policy and legislative proposals to enhance tax administration and handling tax cases assigned to those offices. http://www.justice. gov/tax

For further information, contact the Office of the Assistant Attorney General, Tax Division, Department of Justice, Tenth Street and Pennsylvania Avenue NW., Washington, DC 20530. Phone, 202-514-2901.

Sources of Information

Americans with Disabilities The Civil Rights Division maintains an Americans with disabilities hotline. Phone, 800-514-0301. TDD, 800-514-0383. http://www.usdoj.gov/ crt/ada/adahom1.htm

Business Opportunities / Grants For information on business opportunities, grants, and small and disadvantaged business utilization, visit the "Business and Grants" Web page. http://www.justice.gov/ business

Career Opportunities For general information on career opportunities, visit the "Careers" Web page. http://www.justice.gov/ careers

The "Legal Careers" Web page provides information that is of interest to experienced and entry-level attorneys and law students. http://www.justice.gov/legal-careers

Component Agencies A single Web page contains a convenient collection of links leading to the Web sites of the Department's component agencies. https://www.justice. gov/agencies

Drugs / Crime The Bureau of Justice Statistics' Web page includes criminal justice statistics on drugs and crime. http://www.bjs. gov/index.cfm?ty=tp&tid=35

Forms The Department's Web site features a forms list that can be sorted by form number, form title, or agency. This list does not include Federal Bureau of Prisons forms because they are available on the Bureau's Web site. https://www.justice.gov/forms

Freedom of Information Act (FOIA) The Department manages the Web site FOIA.gov to make information on the FOIA accessible, interactive, and understandable. https:// www.foia.gov/index.html

Instructions for properly submitting a FOIA request to the Department are available online. https://www.justice.gov/oip/make-foia-request-doj

History Historical information on the Attorneys General of the United States, the Department's motto and seal, and the art and architecture of the Robert F. Kennedy Department of Justice Building is available online. https://www.justice.gov/about/history

Housing Discrimination Contact the Civil Rights Division's housing and civil enforcement section. Phone, 800-896-7743. http://www.justice.gov/crt/housing-and-civil-enforcement-section

Immigration-Related Employment Matters The Civil Rights Division maintains a worker hotline. Phone, 800-255-7688. TDD, 800-237-2515. It also offers information for employers. Phone, 800-255-8155. TDD, 800-362-2735. http://www. justice.gov/crt/hotline-technical-assistance-referral-agencies

Open Government The Department supports the Open Government initiative by promoting the principles of collaboration, participation, and transparency. https://www. justice.gov/open

Plain Language The Department supports the Plain Writing Act of 2010. Online visitors who find a document lacking in clarity, should contact the Department via email and include the relevant page title and Uniform Resources Locator (URL). https:// www.justice.gov/open/plain-writing-act | Email: DOJPlainWriting@usdoj.gov

Publications   Department of Justice reports and publications are accessible and arranged alphabetically online. https://www.justice.gov/publications/usdoj-resources-publications-alphabetical-list

Each year, the Department publishes the U.S. Attorney General's annual report and posts it online. http://www.justice.gov/ag/publications.htm

Textbooks on citizenship—teacher manuals and student textbooks at various reading levels—are distributed free to public schools for citizenship applicants. Others may purchase them from the Superintendent of Documents, Government Publishing Office, Washington, DC 20402. Public schools or organizations under the supervision of public schools that are entitled to free textbooks should make their requests to the appropriate Immigration and Naturalization Service regional office.

Reading Rooms   Reading rooms are located in Washington, DC, at the Department of Justice, Tenth Street and Constitution Avenue NW., and at the National Institute of Justice, 633 Indiana Avenue NW., and in Falls Church, VA, at the Board of Immigration Appeals, 5107 Leesburg Pike. Phone, 202-514-3775. http://www.justice.gov/contact-us

For further information, contact the Office of Public Affairs, Department of Justice, Tenth Street and Constitution Avenue NW., Washington, DC 20530. Phone, 202-514-2007. TDD, 202-786-5731.

BUREAUS
Bureau of Alcohol, Tobacco, Firearms and Explosives

99 New York Avenue NE., Washington, DC 20226
Phone, 202-648-8500. Internet, http://www.atf.gov

Director	THOMAS E. BRANDON, ACTING
Associate Deputy Director/Chief Operating Officer	RONALD B. TURK

The Bureau of Alcohol, Tobacco, Firearms and Explosives (ATF) is responsible for enforcing Federal criminal laws and regulating the firearms and explosives industries. ATF, formerly known as the Bureau of Alcohol, Tobacco, and Firearms, was initially established by Department of Treasury Order No. 221, effective July 1, 1972, which transferred the functions, powers, and duties arising under laws relating to alcohol, tobacco, firearms, and explosives from the Internal Revenue Service to ATF. The Homeland Security Act of 2002 (6 U.S.C. 531) transferred certain functions and authorities of ATF to the Department of Justice and established it under its current name. Directly and through partnerships, ATF investigates and deters violent crime involving arson, firearms and explosives, and trafficking of alcohol and tobacco products. The Bureau provides training and support to its Federal, State, local, and international law enforcement partners and works primarily in 25 field divisions across the 50 States, Puerto Rico, the U.S. Virgin Islands, and Guam. It also has foreign offices in Canada, Colombia, France, and Mexico.

Sources of Information

Employment   Information on career opportunities is available online. https://www.atf.gov/careers

Publications   FOIA and regulations libraries and factsheets are accessible online. https://www.atf.gov/resource-center/publications-library https://www.atf.gov/contact

For further information, contact the Office of Public Affairs, Bureau of Alcohol, Tobacco, Firearms and Explosives, Department of Justice, 99 New York Avenue NE., Suite 10W.121, Washington, DC 20530. Phone, 202-648-8500.

Bureau of Prisons

320 First Street NW., Washington, DC 20534
Phone, 202-307-3198. Internet, http://www.bop.gov

Director	THOMAS R. KANE, ACTING
Deputy Director Federal Bureau Of Prisons	JUDI SIMON GARRETT, ACTING

The BOP was established in 1930 to provide more progressive and humane care for Federal inmates, to professionalize the prison service, and to ensure consistent and centralized administration of the 11 Federal prisons in operation at that time. Today, the Bureau comprises more than 100 institutions and 6 regional offices. The Bureau has its headquarters, also known as Central Office, in Washington, DC. The Central Office is divided into 10 divisions, including the National Institute of Corrections.

The Correctional Programs Division (CPD) is responsible for inmate classification and programming, including psychology and religious services, substance abuse treatment, case management, and programs for special needs offenders. CPD provides policy direction and daily operational oversight of institution security, emergency preparedness, intelligence gathering, inmate discipline, inmate sentence computations, receiving and discharge, and inmate transportation, as well as coordinating international treaty transfers and overseeing the special security needs of inmates placed in the Federal Witness Protection Program. CPD administers contracts and intergovernmental agreements for the confinement of offenders in community-based programs, community corrections centers, and other facilities, including privately managed facilities. CPD staff is also involved in the Bureau's privatization efforts.

The Industries, Education, and Vocational Training Division oversees Federal Prison Industries, or UNICOR, which is a wholly owned Government corporation that provides employment and training opportunities for inmates confined in Federal correctional facilities. Additionally, it is responsible for oversight of educational, occupational, and vocational training and leisure-time programs, as well as those related to inmate release preparation.

The National Institute of Corrections (NIC) provides technical assistance, training, and information to State and local corrections agencies throughout the country, as well as the Bureau. It also provides research assistance and documents through the NIC Information Center. https://www.bop.gov/about/agency

Sources of Information

Business Opportunities Information is available on the "Let's Do Business" Web page. http://www.bop.gov/business
Career Opportunities Job openings are posted online. For additional career-related information, contact any regional or field office or the Central Office, 320 First Street NW., Washington, DC 20534. Phone, 202-307-3082. http://www.bop.gov/jobs
Find an Inmate The Department's Web site features a search tool for locating Federal inmates who were incarcerated after 1981. https://www.bop.gov/inmateloc
Locations The "Our Locations" Web page features a list of locations, a search tool that requires the facility's name, and location maps (national, regional, type of facility). https://www.bop.gov/locations
Population Statistics Federal inmate population statistics are online. https://www.bop.gov/about/statistics/population_statistics.jsp
Reading Room The reading room is located at the Bureau of Prisons, 320 First Street NW., Washington, DC 20534. Phone, 202-307-3029.
Resources by Audience Resources to help Bureau of Prisons staff and their families access frequently used services are online. https://www.bop.gov/resources/employee_resources.jsp

Resources to help former inmates make the transition from incarceration to normal life within a community are online. https://www.bop.gov/resources/former_inmate_resources.jsp

The Attorney General and the Secretary of Health and Human Services provide health management guidelines for infectious disease prevention, detection, and treatment of inmates and correctional employees who are exposed to infectious diseases in correctional facilities. https://www.bop.gov/resources/health_care_mngmt.jsp

Resources to help qualified media representatives visit institutions and gather information on programs and activities or conduct interviews are online. https://www.bop.gov/resources/media_resources.jsp

Resources to help victims or witnesses of Federal crimes find information on complaint procedures, notifications, and payments are online. https://www.bop.gov/resources/victim_resources.jsp; http://www.bop.gov/contact

For further information, contact the Public Information Office, Bureau of Prisons, 320 First Street NW., Washington, DC 20534. Phone, 202-514-6551.

Drug Enforcement Administration

8701 Morrissette Drive, Springfield, VA 22152
Phone, 202-307-1000. Internet, http://www.dea.gov/index.shtml

Administrator   CHARLES ROSENBERG, ACTING

The Drug Enforcement Administration (DEA) is the lead Federal agency in enforcing narcotics and controlled substances laws and regulations. The DEA also enforces the Federal money laundering and bulk currency smuggling statutes when the funds involved in the transactions or smuggling are derived from the sale of narcotics. It was created in July 1973 by Reorganization Plan No. 2 of 1973 (5 U.S.C. app.).

The DEA enforces the provisions of the controlled substances and chemical diversion and trafficking laws and regulations of the United States, operating on a worldwide basis. It presents cases to the criminal and civil justice systems of the United States—or any other competent jurisdiction—on those significant organizations and their members involved in cultivation, production, smuggling, distribution, laundering of proceeds, or diversion of controlled substances appearing in or destined for illegal traffic in the United States. The DEA disrupts and dismantles these organizations by arresting their members, confiscating their drugs, and seizing their assets; and it creates, manages, and supports enforcement-related programs—domestically and internationally—to reduce the availability of and demand for illicit controlled substances.

The DEA's responsibilities include: investigation of major narcotic, chemical, drug-money laundering, and bulk currency smuggling violators who operate at interstate and international levels; seizure and forfeiture of assets derived from, traceable to, or intended to be used for illicit drug trafficking; seizure and forfeiture of assets derived from or traceable to drug-money laundering or the smuggling of bulk currency derived from illegal drugs; enforcement of regulations governing the legal manufacture, distribution, and dispensing of controlled substances; management of an intelligence program that supports drug investigations, initiatives, and operations worldwide; coordination with Federal, State, and local law enforcement authorities and cooperation with counterpart agencies abroad; assistance to State and local law enforcement agencies in addressing their most significant drug and drug-related violence problems; leadership and influence over international counterdrug and chemical policy and support for institution building in host nations; training, scientific research, and information exchange in support of drug traffic prevention and control; and education and assistance to the public community on the prevention, treatment, and dangers of drugs.

The DEA maintains liaison with the United Nations, INTERPOL, and other organizations on matters relating to international narcotics control programs. It has 222 offices in 21 divisions throughout the United States and 86 foreign offices located in 67 countries.

Sources of Information

Controlled Substances Act Registration For information on registration under the Controlled Substances Act, contact the Office of Diversion Control, 8701 Morrissette Drive, Springfield, VA 22152. Phone: 800-882-9539. http://www. deadiversion.usdoj.gov/drugreg/index.html | Email: DEA.Registration.Help@usdoj.gov

Employment For career information, contact the nearest DEA field division recruitment office. To learn about searching for job vacancies online and applying, visit the "How To Apply" Web page. http://www. dea.gov/careers/how-to-apply.shtml
Publications A limited selection of pamphlets and brochures is available. The most frequently requested publication is "Drugs of Abuse," an identification manual intended for professional use. Single copies are free. http://www.dea.gov/docs/drugs_of_abuse_2011.pdf; http://www.dea.gov/contact.shtml

For further information, contact the Public Affairs Section, Drug Enforcement Administration, 8701 Morrissette Drive Springfield, VA 22152. Phone, 202-307-7977.

Federal Bureau of Investigation

935 Pennsylvania Avenue NW., Washington, DC 20535
Phone, 202-324-3000. Internet, http://www.fbi.gov

Director	CHRISTOPHER WRAY

The Federal Bureau of Investigation (FBI) is the Department of Justice's principal investigative arm. It is primarily charged with gathering and reporting facts, locating witnesses, and compiling evidence in cases involving Federal jurisdiction. It also provides law enforcement leadership and assistance to State and international law enforcement agencies.

The FBI was established in 1908 by the Attorney General, who directed that Department of Justice investigations be handled by its own staff. The Bureau is charged with investigating all violations of Federal law except those that have been assigned by legislative enactment or otherwise to another Federal agency. Its jurisdiction includes a wide range of responsibilities in the national security, criminal, and civil fields. Priority has been assigned to areas such as counterterrorism, counterintelligence, cybercrimes, internationally and nationally organized crime and drug-related activities, and financial crimes.

The FBI also offers cooperative services to local, State, and international law enforcement agencies. These services include fingerprint identification, laboratory examination, police training, the Law Enforcement Online communication and information service for use by the law enforcement community, the National Crime Information Center, and the National Center for the Analysis of Violent Crime.

Sources of Information

Employment The FBI relies on professionals with diverse expertise and skills to analyze data for the intelligence community, safeguard national security, and support the structure of the Bureau. Information on career opportunities, including student internships, is available online. https://www.fbijobs.gov
Publications The "FBI Law Enforcement Bulletin," reports, and other publications are available online. https://leb.fbi.gov; https://www.fbi.gov/stats-services/publications; https://www.fbi.gov/contact-us

For further information, contact the Office of Public Affairs, Federal Bureau of Investigation, J. Edgar Hoover FBI Building, 935 Pennsylvania Avenue NW., Washington, DC 20535. Phone, 202-317-2727.

International Criminal Police Organization (INTERPOL)–Washington

Department of Justice, Washington, DC 20530
Phone, 202-616-9000. Fax, 202-616-8400. Internet, http://www.justice.gov/interpol-washington

Director	WAYNE SALZGABER, ACTING

INTERPOL–Washington is a separate component under the supervision of the Deputy Attorney G0eneral and comanaged with the Department of Homeland Security. It provides an essential communications link between the U.S. police community and their counterparts in the foreign member countries.

INTERPOL is an association of 190 countries that promotes mutual assistance among law enforcement authorities to prevent and suppress international crime. With no police force of its own, INTERPOL has no powers of arrest or search and seizure and, therefore, relies on the law enforcement authorities of its member countries. Each member country is required to have a national central bureau, such as INTERPOL–Washington, to act as the primary point of contact for police affairs. INTERPOL serves as a channel of communication for its member countries to cooperate in the investigation and prosecution of crime; provides a forum for discussions, working group meetings, and symposia to help police focus on specific areas of criminal activity affecting their countries; and issues information and maintains databases— supplied and used by member countries—on crime, fugitives, humanitarian concerns, missing persons, and stolen passports and vehicles.

INTERPOL–Washington has permanent staff and detailed special agents from numerous Federal law enforcement agencies. It is organized into seven divisions: the Alien and Fugitive, Counterterrorism, Drug, Economic Crimes, Human Trafficking and Child Protection, State and Local Police Liaison, and Violent Crimes Divisions.

Sources of Information

Employment Information on career opportunities is available online. http://www.justice.gov/interpol-washington/employment; http://www.justice.gov/interpol-washington

For further information, contact the INTERPOL–Washington, Department of Justice, Washington, DC 20530. Phone, 202-616-9000.

Office of Justice Programs

810 Seventh Street NW., Washington, DC 20531
Phone, 202-307-0703. Internet, http://www.ojp.gov | Email: askojp@ojp.usdoj.gov

Assistant Attorney General	ANDREW C. FINCH, ACTING

The Office of Justice Programs (OJP) was established by the Justice Assistance Act of 1984 (42 U.S.C. 3711) and reauthorized in 1994 and 2005 to provide Federal leadership, coordination, and assistance needed to make the Nation's justice system more efficient and effective in preventing and controlling crime. OJP is responsible for collecting statistical data and conducting analyses; identifying emerging criminal justice issues; developing and testing promising approaches to address these issues; evaluating program results; and disseminating these findings and other information to State and local governments.

The OJP is comprised of the following bureaus and offices: the Bureau of Justice Assistance provides funding, training, and technical assistance to State and local governments to combat violent and drug-related crime and help improve the criminal justice system; the Bureau of Justice Statistics is responsible for collecting and analyzing data on crime, criminal offenders, crime victims, and the operations of justice systems at all levels of government; the National Institute of Justice sponsors research and development programs, conducts demonstrations of innovative approaches to improve criminal justice, and develops new criminal justice technologies; the Office of Juvenile Justice and Delinquency Prevention provides grants and contracts to States to help them improve their juvenile justice systems and sponsors innovative research, demonstration, evaluation, statistics, replication, technical assistance, and training programs to increase the Nation's understanding of and improve its response to juvenile violence and delinquency; the Office for Victims of Crime administers victim compensation and assistance grant programs and provides funding, training, and technical assistance to victim service organizations, criminal justice agencies, and other professionals to improve the Nation's response to crime victims; and the Office of Sex Offender Sentencing, Monitoring, Apprehending, Registering, and Tracking (SMART) maintains the standards of the Sex Offender Registration and Notification Act as defined by the Adam Walsh Act. The SMART Office also provides technical assistance and supports innovative and best practices in the field of sex offender management.

Sources of Information

Employment For employment information, contact the Human Resources Division, 810 Seventh Street NW., Washington, DC 20531. Phone, 202-307-0730. http://www.ojp.usdoj.gov/about/jobs.htm; http://ojp.gov/home/contactus.htm | Email: askojp@ojp.usdoj.gov

For further information, contact the Department of Justice Response Center. Phone, 800-421-6770.

United States Marshals Service

Department of Justice, Washington, DC 20530
Phone, 703-740-1699. Internet, http://www.usmarshals.gov

Director	DAVID HARLOW, ACTING
Deputy Director	DAVID HARLOW

The United States Marshals Service is the Nation's oldest Federal law enforcement agency, having served as a vital link between the executive and judicial branches of the Government since 1789. The Marshals Service performs tasks that are essential to the operation of virtually every aspect of the Federal justice system.

The Marshals Service has these responsibilities: providing support and protection for the Federal courts, including security for 800 judicial facilities and nearly 2,000 judges and magistrates, as well as countless other trial participants such as jurors and attorneys; apprehending the majority of Federal fugitives; operating the Federal Witness Security Program and ensuring the safety of endangered Government witnesses; maintaining custody of and transporting thousands of Federal prisoners annually; executing court orders and arrest warrants; managing and selling seized property forfeited to the Government by drug traffickers and other criminals and assisting the Justice Department's asset forfeiture program; responding to emergency circumstances, including civil disturbances, terrorist incidents, and other crisis situations through its Special Operations Group; restoring order in riot and mob-violence situations; providing housing, transportation, and medical care of federal detainees; and operating the U.S. Marshals Service Training Academy.

Sources of Information

Business Opportunities   The Marshals Service posts online products and services that it purchases. https://www.usmarshals.gov/business/products.html
Employment   The Marshals Service hires administrative staff, aviation and detention enforcement officers, Deputy U.S. Marshals, and other types of professionals. Information on Deputy U.S. Marshal hiring programs is available online. https://www.usmarshals.gov/careers/index.html; http://www.usmarshals.gov/contacts/index.html

For further information, contact the Office of Public Affairs, U.S. Marshals Service, Department of Justice, Washington, DC 20530. Phone, 703-740-1699.

OFFICES / BOARDS
Executive Office for Immigration Review

Falls Church, VA 22041
Phone, 703-305-0289. Internet, http://www.usdoj.gov/eoir

Director	JAMES MCHENRY, ACTING

The Executive Office for Immigration Review (EOIR), under a delegation of authority from the Attorney General, is charged with adjudicating matters brought under various immigration statutes before its three administrative tribunals: the Office of the Chief Immigration Judge, the Board of Immigration Appeals, and the Office of the Chief Administrative Hearing Officer.

The Office of the Chief Immigration Judge provides overall direction for more than 300 immigration judges located in 58 immigration courts throughout the Nation. Immigration judges are responsible for conducting formal administrative proceedings and act independently in their decision-making capacity. Their decisions are administratively final, unless appealed or certified to the BIA.

In removal proceedings, an immigration judge determines whether an alien should be removed or allowed to remain in the United States. Judges are located throughout the United States, and each judge has jurisdiction to consider various forms of relief available under the law.

The Board of Immigration Appeals (BIA) has nationwide jurisdiction to hear appeals from certain decisions made by immigration judges and by district directors of the Department of Homeland Security (DHS). In addition, the BIA is responsible for hearing appeals involving disciplinary actions against attorneys and representatives before DHS and EOIR.

Decisions of the BIA are binding on all DHS officers and immigration judges unless modified or overruled by the Attorney General or a Federal court. All BIA decisions are subject to judicial review in Federal court. The majority of appeals reaching the BIA involve orders of removal and applications for relief from removal. Other cases before the BIA include petitions to classify the status of alien relatives for the issuance of preference immigrant visas, fines imposed upon carriers for the violation of the immigration laws, and motions for reopening or reconsideration of decisions previously rendered.

The Office of the Chief Administrative Hearing Officer (OCAHO) is headed by a Chief Administrative Hearing Officer (CAHO), who is responsible for the general supervision and management of administrative law judges (ALJs). OCAHO ALJs preside at hearings that are mandated by provisions of immigration law concerning allegations of unlawful employment of aliens, employment eligibility verification violations ("employer sanctions), unfair immigration-related employment practices, and immigration document fraud. ALJ decisions in employer sanctions and document fraud cases may be reviewed by the CAHO and the Attorney General, and all OCAHO cases may be appealed to the appropriate U.S. Circuit Court of Appeals.

Sources of Information

Library A virtual law library that serves as a complement to the Law Library and Immigration Research Center is available online. http://www.justice.gov/eoir/virtual-law-library
Statistics and Publications Agency decisions and plans, instructions and manuals, meeting notes, and reports and

updates are available on the "Statistics and Publications" Web page. http://www.justice.gov/eoir/statistics-and-publications#Top

For further information, contact the Office of Communications and Legislative and Public Affairs, Executive Office for Immigration Review, Department of Justice, 5107 Leesburg Pike, Suite 1902, Falls Church, VA 22041. Phone, 703-305-0289. Fax, 703-605-0365.

For further information, contact the Office of Communications and Legislative Affairs, Executive Office for Immigration Review, Department of Justice, 5107 Leesburg Pike, Suite 1902, Falls Church, VA 22041. Phone, 703-305-0289. Fax, 703-605-0365. http://www.justice.gov/eoir/contact-office

For further information, contact the Office of Legislative and Public Affairs, Executive Office for Immigration Review, Department of Justice, 5107 Leesburg Pike, Suite 1902, Falls Church, VA 22041. Phone, 703-305-0289. Fax, 703-605-0365.

Foreign Claims Settlement Commission of the United States

Suite 6002, 600 E Street NW., Washington, DC 20579
Phone, 202-616-6975. Fax, 202-616-6993. Internet, http://www.justice.gov/fcsc

Commissioner	ANUJ C. DESAI
Commissioner	SYLVIA M. BECKER

The Foreign Claims Settlement Commission of the United States is a quasi-judicial, independent agency within the Department of Justice, which adjudicates claims of U.S. nationals against foreign governments, either under specific jurisdiction conferred by Congress or the Department of State or pursuant to international claims settlement agreements. The decisions of the Commission are final and are not reviewable under any standard by any court or other authority. Funds for payment of the Commission's awards are derived from congressional appropriations, international claims settlements, or the liquidation of foreign assets in the United States by the Departments of Justice and the Treasury.

The Commission also has authority to receive, determine the validity and amount, and provide for the payment of claims by members of the U.S. Armed Services and civilians held as prisoners of war or interned by a hostile force in Southeast Asia during

the Vietnam conflict or by the survivors of such servicemembers and civilians.

The Commission is also responsible for maintaining records and responding to inquiries related to the various claims programs it has conducted against the Governments of Albania, Bulgaria, China, Cuba, Czechoslovakia, Egypt, Ethiopia, the Federal Republic of Germany, the German Democratic Republic, Hungary, Iran, Italy, Panama, Poland, Romania, the Soviet Union, Vietnam, and Yugoslavia, as well as those authorized under the War Claims Act of 1948 and other statutes.

Sources of Information

Employment General information on career opportunities is available on the Department of Justice's "Careers" Web page. For additional information on attorney positions, contact the Office of the Chief Counsel, 600 E Street NW., Suite 6002,

Washington, DC 20579. Phone, 202-616-6975. http://www.justice.gov/careers
Publications   Annual reports, starting with the year 2008, are available on the "Publications" Web page. http://www.justice.gov/fcsc/publications

Reading Room   The reading room is located at 600 E Street NW., Washington, DC 20579. Phone, 202-616-6975. http://www.justice.gov/fcsc/contact-commission

For further information, contact the Office of the Chairman, Foreign Claims Settlement Commission of the United States, Department of Justice, Suite 6002, 600 E Street NW., Washington, DC 20579. Phone, 202-616-6975. Fax, 202-616-6993.

Office of Community Oriented Policing Services

935 N. Street NE., Washington, DC 20530
Phone, 202-514-2058. Internet, http://www.cops.usdoj.gov

Director	Ronald L. Davis

The Office of Community Oriented Policing Services (COPS) was established to assist law enforcement agencies in enhancing public safety through the implementation of community policing strategies. The Office gives assistance by providing training to enhance law enforcement officers' problem-solving and community interaction skills and helping law enforcement and community members develop initiatives to prevent crime; increasing the number of law enforcement officers directly interacting with communities; and supporting the development of new technologies to shift law enforcement's focus to preventing crime and disorder within communities.

Sources of Information

Employment   To sign up to receive email updates on COPS employment opportunities, visit the "Careers" Web page. http://www.cops.usdoj.gov/careers
Grants and Funding   COPS grants and funding opportunities support State, local, and tribal law enforcement efforts to advance community policing. Current applicant and grantee information—announcements, fiscal year grant programs, current funding opportunities, and resources for grantees—is available online. http://www.cops.usdoj.gov/grants; http://www.cops.usdoj.gov/contact

For further information, contact the Office of Community Oriented Policing Services (COPS), Department of Justice, 935 N Street NE., Washington, DC 20530. Phone, 202-514-2058.

Office on Violence Against Women

145 N Street NE., Suite 10W–121, Washington, DC 20530
Phone: 202-307-6026. Internet, http://www.justice.gov/ovw

Director	Nadine M. Neufville, Acting

The Office on Violence Against Women (OVW) was established in 1995 to reduce violence against women through the implementation of the Violence Against Women Act. The Office administers financial and technical assistance to communities that are developing programs, policies, and practices to end domestic and dating violence, sexual assault, and stalking.

Sources of Information

Employment   Information on employment and internship opportunities is available online. http://www.justice.gov/ovw/careers

Publications   Portable Document Format (PDF) files of selected publications are available online. http://www.justice.gov/ ovw/selected-publications; http://www. justice.gov/ovw/contact-office | Email: ovw. info@usdoj.gov

For further information, contact the Office on Violence Against Women, 145 N Street NE., Suite 10W-121, Washington, DC, 20530. Phone, 202-307-6026.

United States Parole Commission

90 K Street NE., Washington, DC 20530
Phone, 202-346-7000. Internet, http://www.usdoj.gov/uspc

Chair   J. PATRICIA WILSON SMOOT

The U.S. Parole Commission (USPC) makes parole release decisions for eligible Federal and District of Columbia prisoners; authorizes methods of release and conditions under which release occurs; prescribes, modifies, and monitors compliance with the terms and conditions governing offenders' behavior while on parole or mandatory or supervised release; issues warrants for violation of supervision; determines probable cause for the revocation process; revokes parole, mandatory, or supervised release; releases from supervision those offenders who are no longer a risk to public safety; and promulgates the rules, regulations, and guidelines for the exercise of USPC's authority and the implementation of a national parole policy.

USPC has sole jurisdiction over the following: Federal offenders who committed offenses before November 1, 1987; DC Code offenders who committed offenses before August 5, 2000; DC Code offenders sentenced to a term of supervised release; Uniform Code of Military Justice offenders who are in Bureau of Prison's custody; transfer treaty cases; and State probationers and parolees in the Federal Witness Protection Program.

Sources of Information

Freedom of Information Act (FOIA)   The Commission maintains an online FOIA library. Information on Freedom of Information Act requests is available online. http://www.justice.gov/uspc/freedom-information-act-foia/foia-library; http://www.justice.gov/uspc/freedom-information-act-foia | Email: USPC.FOIA@usdoj.gov
Reading Room   The reading room is located at 90 K Street NE., Washington, DC 20530. Phone, 202-346-7000. http://www.justice.gov/uspc/contact-commission

For further information, contact the U.S. Parole Commission, Department of Justice, 90 K Street NE., Washington, DC 20530. Phone, 202-346-7000.

DEPARTMENT OF LABOR

200 Constitution Avenue NW., Washington, DC 20210
Phone, 202-693-6000. Internet, http://www.dol.gov

Secretary of Labor	R. Alexander Acosta
Deputy Secretary	Vacant
Chief Economist	Vacant
Chief of Staff	Wayne Palmer
Executive Secretariat Director	Elizabeth Way, Acting

Agencies

Administrator, Wage and Hour Division	Vacant
Chief Administrative Law Judge	Stephen R. Henley
Chief Financial Officer	Geoffrey Kenyon, Acting
Commissioner, Bureau of Labor Statistics	William Wiatrowski, Acting
Deputy Undersecretary, Bureau of International Labor Affairs	Mark Mittelhauser, Acting
Inspector General	Scott S. Dahl
Ombudsman, Energy Employee Occupational Illness Compensation Program	Malcolm Nelson
Solicitor of Labor	Nicholas Geale, Acting

Assistant Secretaries

Employee Benefits Security Administration	Timothy Hauser, Acting
Employment and Training Administration	Byron Zuidema, Acting
Mine Safety and Health Administration	Patricia Silvey, Acting
Occupational Safety and Health Administration	Thomas Galassi, Acting
Office of Congressional and Intergovernmental Affairs	Vacant
Office of Disability Employment Policy	Jennifer Sheehy, Acting
Office of Public Affairs	Vacant
Office of the Assistant Secretary, Administration and Management	Edward C. Hugler, Acting
Office of the Assistant Secretary, Policy	Vacant
Veterans' Employment and Training Services	Sam Shellenberger, Acting

Chief Judges / Chairs

Administrative Review Board	Paul M. Igasaki
Benefits Review Board	Betty Jean Hall
Employees' Compensation Appeals Board	Christopher Godfrey

Directors

Center for Faith-Based and Neighborhood Partnerships	Vacant
Office of Workers' Compensation Programs	Gary Steinberg, Acting
Office of Federal Contract Compliance Programs	Thomas Dowd, Acting
Office of Labor-Management Standards	Andrew Auerbach, Acting
Office of Public Engagement	Vacant
Women's Bureau	Joan Harrigan-Farrelly, Acting

The Department of Labor promotes the welfare of job seekers, wage earners, and retirees by improving working conditions, advancing opportunities for profitable employment, protecting retirement and health care benefits, matching workers to employers, strengthening free collective bargaining, and tracking changes in economic indicators on a national scale.

DEPARTMENT OF LABOR

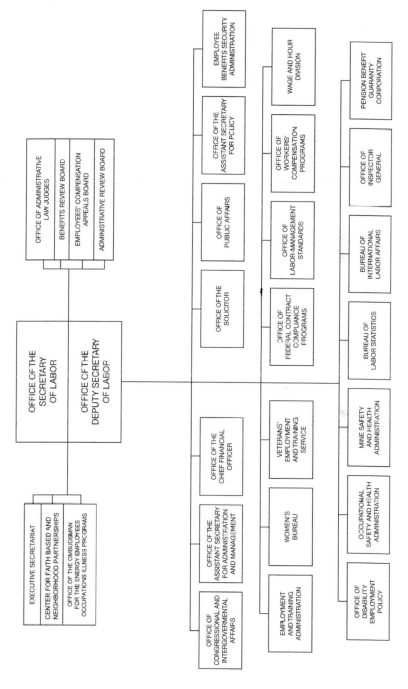

OFFICE OF THE SECRETARY OF LABOR

OFFICE OF THE DEPUTY SECRETARY OF LABOR

OFFICE OF ADMINISTRATIVE LAW JUDGES

BENEFITS REVIEW BOARD

EMPLOYEES' COMPENSATION APPEALS BOARD

ADMINISTRATIVE REVIEW BOARD

EXECUTIVE SECRETARIAT

CENTER FOR FAITH BASED AND NEIGHBORHOOD PARTNERSHIPS

OFFICE OF THE OMBUDSMAN FOR THE ENERGY EMPLOYEES OCCUPATIONS ILLNESS PROGRAMS

OFFICE OF CONGRESSIONAL AND INTERGOVERMENTAL AFFAIRS

OFFICE OF THE ASSISTANT SECRETARY FOR ADMINISTRATION AND MANAGEMENT

OFFICE OF THE CHIEF FINANCIAL OFFICER

OFFICE OF THE SOLICITOR

OFFICE OF PUBLIC AFFAIRS

OFFICE OF THE ASSISTANT SECRETARY FOR POLICY

EMPLOYEE BENEFITS SECURITY ADMINISTRATION

EMPLOYMENT AND TRAINING ADMINISTRATION

WOMEN'S BUREAU

VETERANS' EMPLOYMENT AND TRAINING SERVICE

OFFICE OF FEDERAL CONTRACT COMPLIANCE PROGRAMS

OFFICE OF LABOR-MANAGEMENT STANDARDS

OFFICE OF WORKERS' COMPENSATION PROGRAMS

WAGE AND HOUR DIVISION

OFFICE OF DISABILITY EMPLOYMENT POLICY

OCCUPATIONAL SAFETY AND HEALTH ADMINISTRATION

MINE SAFETY AND HEALTH ADMINISTRATION

BUREAU OF LABOR STATISTICS

BUREAU OF INTERNATIONAL LABOR AFFAIRS

OFFICE OF INSPECTOR GENERAL

PENSION BENEFIT GUARANTY CORPORATION

The Department of Labor (DOL) was created by act of March 4, 1913 (29 U.S.C. 551). Congress first created a Bureau of Labor in the Interior Department by act of June 24, 1884. The Bureau of Labor later became independent as a Department of Labor without executive rank by act of June 13, 1888. It returned to bureau status in the Department of Commerce and Labor, which was created by act of February 14, 1903 (15 U.S.C. 1501; 29 U.S.C. 1 note).

The Department administers a variety of Federal labor laws to guarantee workers' rights to fair, safe, and healthy working conditions, including minimum hourly wage and overtime pay, protection against employment discrimination, and unemployment insurance.

Secretary   The Secretary is the principal adviser to the President on the development and execution of policies and the administration and enforcement of laws relating to wage earners, their working conditions, and their employment opportunities. http://www.dol.gov/_sec

Administrative Law   Administrative law judges from the Office of Administrative Law Judges preside over formal adversarial hearings involving labor-related matters: the Longshore and Harbor Workers' Compensation, the Defense Base, the Black Lung Benefits, the McNamara O'Hara Service Contract, and the Davis Bacon Act; environmental, transportation, and securities whistleblower protection laws; permanent and temporary immigration; child labor law violations; employment discrimination; training; seasonal and migrant workers; and Federal construction and service contracts. The Office is comprised of headquarters in Washington, D.C. and seven district offices. Its judges are nonpolitical appointees: They are appointed under and guaranteed decisional independence by the Administrative Procedure Act. The Administrative Review Board or Benefits Review Board typically reviews appeals of the decisions made by the Office's judges. Depending upon the statute at issue, appeals then go to Federal district or appellate courts and, ultimately, may go to the U.S. Supreme Court. http://www.oalj.dol.gov

For further information, call 202-693-7300.

Administration and Management   The Office of the Assistant Secretary for Administration and Management is responsible for the development and promulgation of policies, standards, procedures, systems, and materials related to the resource and administrative management of the Department and for the execution of such policies and directives at Headquarters and in the field. http://www.dol.gov/oasam

For more information, call 202-693-4040.

Audits / Investigations   The Office of Inspector General (OIG) conducts audits to review the economy, effectiveness, efficiency, and integrity of all DOL programs and operations, including those performed by its contractors and grantees. The Inspector General works to answer the following types of questions: Do Department programs and operations comply with the applicable laws and regulations; are departmental resources being utilized efficiently and economically; and are DOL programs achieving their intended results? The Office also conducts administrative, civil, and criminal investigations relating to violations of Federal laws, regulations, or rules—including violations committed by DOL contractors and grantees—as well as investigations of allegations of misconduct on the part of DOL employees. In addition, the OIG has an "external" program function to conduct criminal investigations to combat the influence of labor racketeering and organized crime in the nation's labor unions. The OIG conducts labor racketeering investigations in three areas: employee benefit plans, labor-management relations, and internal union affairs. The OIG also works with other law enforcement partners on human trafficking matters. http://www. oig.dol.gov

For further information, call 202-693-5100.

Communications / Public Affairs   The Office of Public Affairs (OPA) directs and coordinates all public and employee communications activities. The Assistant Secretary of the Office acts as the chief adviser to the Secretary of Labor and his or her Deputy Secretary and to the agency heads and departmental staff for developing and implementing strategies that engage and connect with the public and educate it about the work and mission of the Department.

The Assistant Secretary also acts as the Secretary's chief adviser on crisis communications. The OPA serves as the first point of contact for news media inquiries, as the clearance and dissemination point for DOL public-facing materials, and it develops and maintains the Department's Web-based, audiovisual, and contact center communications. The OPA also administers "lock ups" when sensitive economic data are released to the press under an embargo. https://www.dol.gov/general/contact/media-contact

For further information, call 202-693-4676.

Disability Employment Policy The Office of Disability Employment Policy (ODEP) is the only non-regulatory federal agency that promotes policies and coordinates with employers and all levels of government to increase workplace success for people with disabilities. ODEP helps employers foster inclusive workplaces where all employees can contribute and succeed, and works to improve government workforce systems so people with disabilities can secure good jobs and excel in the workplace. http://www.dol.gov/odep

For further information, call 202-693-7880. TTY, 202-693-7881.

Energy Employees Occupational Illness Compensation The Office of the Ombudsman for the Energy Employees Occupational Illness Compensation Program was established in 2004 under Part E of the Energy Employees Occupational Illness Compensation Program Act (EEOICPA), as amended (42 U.S.C. 7385s-15). The EEOICPA is a system of Federal payments to compensate certain nuclear workers for occupational illnesses caused by exposure to toxic substances. This small and independent Office is headed by the Ombudsman, whom the Secretary of Labor appoints. It provides information to claimants on the benefits available under Parts B and E of the EEOICPA and issues annual reports to Congress detailing the complaints, grievances, and requests for assistance that the Office receives. http://www.dol.gov/eeombd

For further information, call 202-693-5890.

Federal Contract Compliance The Office of Federal Contract Compliance Programs administers and enforces three equal employment opportunity laws: Executive Order 11246, Section 503 of the Rehabilitation Act of 1973, and the Vietnam Era Veterans' Readjustment Assistance Act of 1974. As amended, these laws prohibit Federal contractors and subcontractors from discriminating based on race, color, religion, sex, sexual orientation, gender identity, national origin, disability, or status as a protected veteran. Executive Order 11246 prohibits Federal contractors and subcontractors, with limited exceptions, from taking adverse employment actions against applicants and employees for asking about, discussing, or sharing information on their pay or the pay of their coworkers. These laws also require Federal contractors and subcontractors to take affirmative action to ensure equal employment opportunity. http://www.dol.gov/ofccp | Email: OFCCP-Public@dol.gov

For further information, call 800-397-6251.

Labor-Management Standards The Office of Labor-Management Standards (OLMS) administers and enforces most provisions of the Labor-Management Reporting and Disclosure Act of 1959 (LMRDA). The LMRDA primarily promotes union democracy and financial integrity in private sector labor unions through standards for union officer elections and union trusteeships and safeguards for union assets. Additionally, the LMRDA promotes labor union and labor-management transparency through reporting and disclosure requirements for labor unions and their officials, employers, labor relations consultants, and surety companies.

OLMS also administers provisions of the Civil Service Reform Act of 1978 and the Foreign Service Act of 1980, which extend comparable protections to Federal labor unions. OLMS does not have jurisdiction over unions representing solely state, county, or municipal employees. In addition, the Division of Statutory Programs (DSP) administers DOL responsibilities under the Federal Transit Act by ensuring that fair and equitable arrangements protecting mass transit employees are in place before the release of Federal transit grant funds. http://www.dol.gov/olms

For further information, call 202-693-0123.

Legal Services   The Office of the Solicitor of Labor (SOL) provides comprehensive legal services to help the Department achieve its mission. More specifically, the Solicitor serves dual roles in the Department. The Solicitor is the Department's chief enforcement officer, pursuing affirmative litigation on behalf of the Secretary before administrative law judges, review boards and commissions, and in the Federal district courts and courts of appeals. The Solicitor is also the Department's general counsel, assisting in the development of regulations, standards, and legislative proposals; providing legal opinions and advice on all of the Department's activities; advising the Solicitor General on Supreme Court litigation; and coordinating with the Department of Justice, as appropriate, to defend the Department in litigation. http://www.dol.gov/sol

For further information, call 202-693-5260.

Policy and Rulemaking   The Office of the Assistant Secretary for Policy advises and assists the Secretary, Deputy Secretary, and Department on policy development, policy evaluation, regulation, and legislation that improve the lives of workers, retirees, and their families. The Office also serves as the DOL's regulatory policy officer and regulatory reform officer to ensure that the Department complies with the regulatory and guidance development requirements of Executive Order 12866, as amended, Executive Order 13777, and any other related Office of Management and Budget circular or bulletin. The Office leads special initiatives and manages department-wide and interdepartmental activities. In its capacity as the DOL's policy innovation arm, it invests in research and analysis of current and emerging labor issues. https://www.dol.gov/asp

For further information, call 202-693-5959.

Workers' Compensation   The Office of Workers' Compensation Programs (OWCP) protects workers who are injured or become ill on the job by making decisions on claims, paying benefits, and helping workers return to their jobs. OWCP administers eight major disability compensation statutes: the Federal Employees' Compensation Act; the Longshore and Harbor Workers' Compensation Act; the Defense Base Act (DBA); the Nonappropriated Fund Instrumentalities Act; the Outer Continental Shelf Lands Act; the War Hazards Compensation Act; the Black Lung Benefits Act; and the Energy Employees Occupational Illness Compensation Act. OWCP serves specific employee groups that are covered under the relevant statutes and regulations by mitigating the financial burden resulting from workplace injury or illness and promoting return to work when appropriate. Dependents or survivors may also be eligible for benefits. http://www.dol.gov/owcp

For further information, call 202-343-5580.

Boards

Administrative Review   The Administrative Review Board (ARB) consists of five members appointed by the Secretary. It issues final agency decisions for appeals cases under a wide range of worker protection laws, including the Service Contract Act (SCA) and the Davis Bacon Act (DBA). The appeals cases primarily address environmental, transportation, and securities whistleblower protection; H-1B immigration provisions; child labor law violations; employment discrimination; job training; seasonal and migrant workers. The Board's cases generally arise upon appeal from decisions of Department of Labor Administrative Law Judges (OALJ) or the Administrator of the Department's Wage and Hour Division (WHD). Depending upon the statute at issue, the parties may appeal the Board's decisions to Federal district or appellate courts and, ultimately, to the U.S. Supreme Court. http://www.dol.gov/arb/welcome.html

For further information, call 202-693-6234.

Benefits Review   The Benefits Review Board (BRB) consists of five members appointed by the Secretary. In 1972, Congress created the Board to review and issue decisions on appeals of workers'

compensation cases arising under the Longshore and Harbor Workers' Compensation Act, and its extensions, and the Black Lung Benefits amendments to the Federal Coal Mine Safety Act of 1969. Board decisions may be appealed to the U.S. Courts of Appeals and to the U.S. Supreme Court. http://www.dol.gov/brb/welcome. html

For further information, call 202-693-6234.

Employees' Compensation Appeals The Employees' Compensation Appeals Board (ECAB) is a five-member quasi-judicial body appointed by the Secretary and delegated exclusive jurisdiction by Congress to hear and make final decisions on appeals filed by Federal workers arising under the Federal Employees' Compensation Act (FECA). The Board was created by Reorganization Plan No. 2 of 1946 (60 Stat. 1095). The Board's decisions are not reviewable and are binding upon the Office of Workers' Compensation Programs (OWCP). http://www.dol.gov/ecab/welcome.html

For further information, call 202-693-6234.

Sources of Information

Agencies / Programs The DOL carries out its mission through a number of offices and agencies, which are organized into major program areas. An Assistant Secretary, Director, or other official oversees each of these offices and agencies. https://www.dol.gov/agencies; https://www.dol.gov/general/dol-agencies

A–Z Index The DOL Web site features an alphabetical index to help visitors search for information or browse topics of interest. https://www.dol.gov/general/siteindex

Business Opportunities The Office of Procurement Services is the primary procurement office for the DOL national office. It carries out most contracting, grants, and related activities. The Office procures a variety of goods and services on a recurring basis: auditors, expert witnesses, moving services, printing and graphics, support services, technical studies, and video productions. It also acts as the central procurement center for the Department's information technology needs. Phone, 202-

693-4570. http://www.dol.gov/oasam/boc/ops/index.htm

The Office of Small and Disadvantaged Business Utilization administers the DOL's small business program in accordance with the Small Business Act. It seeks to ensure a fair share of procurement opportunities for small businesses, as well as for Historically Underutilized Business Zone (HUBZone) certified, service-disabled veteran-owned, small disadvantaged, and woman-owned small businesses. Phone, 202-603-7299. https://www.dol.gov/oasam/boc/osdbu/index.htm

Employment Detailed information on job opportunities with the DOL—including the addresses and telephone numbers of personnel offices in the regions and in Washington, DC—is available online. http://www.dol.gov/dol/jobs.htm

Find It! The "Find It" Web page allows Internet visitors to look for information by audience or by topic. It also contains the following internal links: A–Z index, DOL agencies, DOL forms, DOL services by location, and top 20 requested items. https://www.dol.gov/general/findit

Freedom of Information Act (FOIA) The FOIA provides that anyone can request access to Federal agency records or information. The DOL must disclose records that are properly requested in writing by any person. Pursuant, however, to one or more of nine exemptions and three exclusions contained in the law, a Federal agency may withhold information. The FOIA applies only to Federal agencies and does not create a right of access to records held by Congress, the courts, State or local government agencies, and private entities. https://www.dol.gov/general/foia

Frequently Asked Questions (FAQs) Answers to many FAQs are posted on the DOL's Web site. http://webapps.dol.gov/dolfaq/dolfaq.asp

History A historical timeline is available on the DOL's Web site. https://www.dol.gov/general/aboutdol/history

The history of the DOL in narrative form is available on its Web site. https://www.dol.gov/general/aboutdol/history/webannalspage

Library The Wirtz Labor Library maintains an online card catalog of holdings added to the library after January of 1975. The online catalog also includes collections of historical significance: for example, the Folio and James Taylor Collections. The library is open to the public from 8:15 a.m. to 4:45 p.m. on weekdays, excluding Federal holidays. If the purpose of a visit is to access research material, contact the library in advance: Wirtz Labor Library, 200 Constitution Avenue NW., Frances Perkins Building, Room N–2445, Washington, DC 20210. Phone, 202-693-6600. http://www.dol.gov/oasam/wirtzlaborlibrary | Email: m-Library@dol.gov

Minimum Wage   The DOL Web site features a list of DOL Web pages that deal with the topic of minimum wage. The Wage and Hour Division administers and enforces the federal minimum wage law. https://www.dol.gov/general/topic/wages/minimumwage

Newsroom   The newsroom features the DOL newsletter, news releases, and press resources, including national media contact information. Phone, 202-693-4676. https://www.dol.gov/newsroom

Office of Inspector General (OIG)   To file a complaint of abuse, fraud, or waste, use the online complaint form, call the OIG Hotline, or write to the Office of Inspector General, Department of Labor, 200 Constitution Avenue NW., Room S–5506, Washington, DC 20210. Phone, 202-693-6999 or 800-347-3756. Fax, 202-693-7020. https://www.oig.dol.gov/hotline.htm

The OIG maintains a glossary of terms related to its activities and mission. https://www.oig.dol.gov/hotlineterms.htm

Open Government   The DOL has a comprehensive Open Government plan to support the making of a more accountable, responsive, and transparent Government. https://www.dol.gov/open

Plain Language   The DOL is committed to producing documents whose content complies with Federal plain language guidelines. It trains its employees and has adopted an oversight process to ensure the use of plain language in any document that is necessary for obtaining Federal Government benefits or services or filing taxes, provides information on Federal Government benefits or services, or explains to the public how to comply with a requirement that the Federal Government administers or enforces. https://www.dol.gov/general/plainwriting

Popular Topics   The DOL Web site features a topics page with links for convenient access to popular material. https://www.dol.gov/general/topic

Publications   The Office of Public Affairs distributes factsheets that describe the activities of the major agencies within the Department. See individual agency webpages for more information.

Public Disclosure   The Office of Labor-Management Standards maintains an online disclosure room where online visitors can search for union annual financial reports starting with the year 2000; view and print reports filed by unions, union officers and employees, employers, and labor relations consultants starting with the year 2000; and order copies of reports for the years prior to 2000. Certain collective bargaining agreements are also available. OLMS has public disclosure room: 200 Constitution Avenue NW., Room N–1519, Washington, DC 20210, which offers the same materials. http://www.unionreports.gov | Email: OLMS-Public@dol.gov

Spanish   The DOL supports the Hispanic workforce. An online list highlights some of the Department's Spanish resources. This list is intended for English-speakers who are looking for information in Spanish to share with the Hispanic community.   https://www.dol.gov/general/topic/spanish-speakingtopic; http://www.dol.gov/dol/contact/media-contact-regional.htm

For further information concerning the Department of Labor, contact the Office of Public Affairs, Department of Labor, Room S–1032, 200 Constitution Avenue NW., Washington, DC 20210. Phone, 202-693-4650.

Bureau of International Labor Affairs

200 Constitution Avenue NW., Washington, DC 20210
Phone, 202-693-4770. Internet, http://www.dol.gov/ilab

Deputy Under Secretary	VACANT
Associate Deputy Undersecretary	VACANT
Associate Deputy Undersecretary	MARK MITTELHAUSER

The Bureau of International Labor Affairs (ILAB) promotes a fair global playing field for workers and businesses in the United States by enforcing trade commitments; strengthening labor standards; and combating international child labor, forced labor, and human trafficking. ILAB combines trade and labor monitoring and enforcement, policy engagement, technical assistance, and research to carry out the international responsibilities of the Department. https://www.dol.gov/agencies/ilab/about-us/offices

Sources of Information

Contracts / Grants The Bureau of International Labor Affairs partners with international organizations, non-governmental organizations, universities, research institutions, and others to advance workers' rights and livelihoods through technical assistance projects, research, and project evaluations. These activities are funded through grants, cooperative agreements, and contracts. https://www.dol.gov/agencies/ilab/resources/grants

Laws / Regulations ILAB's work supports the President's and the Secretary of Labor's objectives related to labor and foreign policy and meets all applicable congressional mandates. The Bureau's Web site features a page of laws and regulations that are relevant to its work. https://www.dol.gov/agencies/ilab/about/laws

Newsroom The Bureau posts news releases on its Web site. https://www.dol.gov/agencies/ilab/newsroom

Reports Legislation and delegations from the President mandate that ILAB prepare a number of reports to inform policy deliberations and the public about certain trade and labor issues. ILAB publishes three reports on international child labor and forced labor that serve as valuable resources for research, advocacy, government action and corporate responsibility. These reports are The Department of Labor's Findings on the Worst Forms of Child Labor; the List of Goods Produced by Child Labor or Forced Labor; and the List of Products Produced by Forced or Indentured Child Labor. For each new trade agreement that the President submits to Congress, ILAB prepares reports on the potential employment impacts in the United States and on the labor rights situation in the proposed partner country or countries. https://www.dol.gov/ilab/reports

Research ILAB conducts and funds rigorous research and evaluation projects and uses the results to inform the design and implementation of policy and programs. Our research programs cover the effects of trade on American workers, cross-country comparisons of labor markets, worker livelihoods, and worker rights and related enforcement issues, including with regard to child labor and forced labor around the world. https://www.dol.gov/ilab/research

Web-based Resources The Bureau's Web sites features a toolkit to help responsible entrepreneurs reduce the chance that their products—and the raw materials from which they are made—are harvested, manufactured, or mined by children who should be in school or by workers who are locked in sweatshops or forced to work through threats or false promises. ILAB has also made available to the public a research app, Sweat & Toil: Child Labor, Forced Labor, and Human Trafficking Around the World. This app represents a comprehensive resource, developed by ILAB, documenting child labor and forced labor worldwide, with data and research from ILAB's three flagship reports on child labor and forced labor. https://www.dol.gov/ilab/child-forced-labor/index.htm; http://www.dol.gov/ilab

For further information, contact the Bureau of International Affairs, Department of Labor, Room C–2235, Washington, DC 20201. Phone, 202-693-4770.

Bureau of Labor Statistics

2 Massachusetts Avenue NE., Washington, DC 20212
Phone, 202-691-7800; 800-877-8339 (TDD). Internet, http://www.bls.gov

Commissioner	ERICA L. GROSHEN
Deputy Commissioner	WILLIAM WIATROWSKI

The Bureau of Labor Statistics (BLS) was established, in the Department of the Interior, as the Bureau of Labor by the act of June 27, 1884 (23 Stat. 60). It was renamed the Bureau of Labor Statistics by the act of March 4, 1913 (37 Stat. 737). The BLS measures labor market activity, working conditions, and price changes in the economy. It also collects, analyzes, and disseminates essential economic information to support public and private decisionmaking.

The Bureau strives to have its data satisfy a number of criteria, including: relevance to current social and economic issues, timeliness in reflecting today's rapidly changing economic conditions, accuracy and consistently high statistical quality, and impartiality in both subject matter and presentation.

Basic data are issued in monthly, quarterly, and annual news releases; bulletins, reports, and special publications; and periodicals. Regional offices issue additional reports and releases that often contain content of local or regional relevance. http://www.bls.gov/bls/infohome.htm

Sources of Information

Data Tools Calculators, databases, and tables are available online. http://www.bls.gov/data

Employment Information on career opportunities is available online. http://bls.gov/jobs/home.htm

Frequently Asked Questions (FAQs) The BLS posts answers to FAQs on its Web site. http://www.bls.gov/bls/faqs.htm

Glossary The BLS maintains a glossary on its Web site. http://www.bls.gov/bls/glossary.htm

Green Jobs The BLS received funding to develop and implement the collection of new data on environmentally sustainable jobs. The Quarterly Census of Employment and Wages and Occupational Employment Statistics programs are involved in this effort. Information on the BLS green jobs initiative, the status of survey development, the BLS green jobs definition, as well as a link to career information for selected green jobs, and other information, are available on the "Measuring Green Jobs" Web page. https://www.bls.gov/green/home.htm

The BLS has defined the term "green jobs" for use in data collection and posted its green jobs definition online. https://www.bls.gov/green/home.htm#definition

Publications The BLS publishes bulletins and reports and economic news releases. Its major publications include "Beyond the Numbers," "Career Outlook," "Monthly Labor Review," "Occupational Outlook Handbook," "The Economics Daily", and "Spotlight on Statistics." These publications are available online. For more information, contact the Washington Information Office or one of the Bureau's regional offices. http://www.bls.gov/opub

Regional Information Economic statistics and data according to geographic areas are available on the "Regional Information Offices" Web page. http://www.bls.gov/bls/regnhome.htm

Resources by Audience The BLS Web site contains pages of useful information on the economy for the benefit of specific audiences: business leaders, consumers, developers, economists, investors, job seekers, media, public policymakers, students and teachers, and survey respondents. https://www.bls.gov/audience/home.htm

A–Z Index The BLS Web site features an alphabetical index to help visitors navigate its content. http://www.bls.gov/bls/topicsaz.htm

Unemployment / Employment A local area unemployment statistics map is available on the BLS Web site. http://data.bls.gov/map/MapToolServlet?survey=la

An overview of statistics on unemployment is available on the BLS Web site. http://www.bls.gov/bls/unemployment.htm

An overview of statistics on employment is available on the BLS Web site. http://www.bls.gov/bls/employment.htm

Updates The BLS Web site features an online subscription form to sign up for electronic updates. https://subscriptions.bls.gov/accounts/USDOLBLS/subscriber/new; http://www.bls.gov

For further information, contact the Bureau of Labor Statistics, Department of Labor, Room 4040, 2 Massachusetts Avenue NE., Washington, DC 20212. Phone, 202-691-7800.

Employee Benefits Security Administration

Department of Labor, Washington, DC 20210
Phone, 866-444-3272. Internet, http://www.dol.gov/ebsa

Assistant Secretary	PHYLLIS C. BORZI
Deputy Assistant Secretary for Policy	JUDITH MARES
Deputy Assistant Secretary for Program Operations	TIMOTHY HAUSER

The Employee Benefits Security Administration (EBSA) promotes and protects the retirement, health, and other benefits of the over 141 million participants and beneficiaries in over 5 million private sector employee benefit plans. EBSA develops regulations; assists and educates workers, plan sponsors, fiduciaries, and service providers; and enforces the law. The Employee Retirement Income Security Act is enforced through 13 field offices nationwide and a national office in Washington, DC. https://www.dol.gov/agencies/ebsa/about-ebsa

Sources of Information

Ask EBSA EBSA's workers and families assistance Web page provides accessible information on programs and services, answers to questions, and assistance in cases where a health or retirement benefit has been denied inappropriately. https://www.dol.gov/agencies/ebsa/about-ebsa/ask-a-question/ask-ebsa

Key Topics The EBSA Web site features a page with links to key topics: health and other employee benefits, reporting and filing, and retirement. https://www.dol.gov/agencies/ebsa/key-topics

Offices A list of EBSA regional and district offices is available online. https://www.dol.gov/agencies/ebsa/about-ebsa/about-us/regional-offices#district-offices

Publications The EBSA distributes booklets, factsheets, and pamphlets on employer obligations and employee rights under the Employee Retirement Income Security Act. A list of publications is available online or from the Office of Outreach, Education, and Assistance. Phone, 866-444-3272. http://www.dol.gov/ebsa/publications/main.html

Reading Room The EBSA maintains a disclosure room at Room N–1513, 200 Constitution Avenue NW., Washington, DC 20210. Reports filed under the Employee Retirement Income Security Act may be examined in the public disclosure room and purchased for 15 cents per page. Phone, 202-693-8673. http://www.dol.gov/ebsa/foia/foia.html

Spanish Information is available in Spanish. https://www.dol.gov/es/agencies/ebsa/about-ebsa/our-activities/informacion-en-espanol; http://www.dol.gov/ebsa

For further information, contact the Employee Benefits Security Administration, Department of Labor, Room S-2524, Washington, DC 20210. Phone, 866-444-3272.

Employment and Training Administration

Department of Labor, Washington, DC 20520
Phone, 877-872-5627. Internet, http://www.doleta.gov

Assistant Secretary	PORTIA Y. WU
Deputy Assistant Secretary	GERRI FIALA
Deputy Assistant Secretary	ERIC SELEZNOW
Deputy Assistant Secretary	BYRON ZUIDEMA

The Employment and Training Administration (ETA) provides quality job training, employment, labor market information, and income maintenance services, primarily through State and local workforce development systems. ETA also administers programs to enhance employment opportunities and business prosperity. https://www.doleta.gov/etainfo/mission.cfm

Apprenticeship Programs   The Office of Apprenticeship oversees the National Apprenticeship System, sets standards for apprenticeship, and assists States, industry, and labor in developing apprenticeship programs that meet required standards while promoting equal opportunity and safeguarding the welfare of apprentices. http://www.dol.gov/apprenticeship

For more information, call 202-693-2796.

Contracts Management   The Office of Contracts Management (OCM) provides leadership and direction to ensure acquisition excellence, integrity, accountability, and sound management of procurement resources to support Employment and Training Administration (ETA) and Job Corps goals and guiding principles for the acquisition of goods and services. Job Corps contracts account for 75 percent of the Department's contracting activity. Non-Job Corps contract activity supports ETA grant programs through technical assistance and long-term studies and evaluations. http://www.doleta.gov/contracts

For further information, contact the Office of Contracts Management, Department of Labor, Suite N-4643, Washington, DC 20210. Phone, 202-693-3701.

Financial Administration   The Office of Financial Administration (OFA) is responsible for managing all ETA fiscal resources for programs and activities for which funds are appropriated through its functions of accounting, budget, and financial system oversight. OFA provides critical budgetary, accounting, audit, and internal control management. It coordinates with the Departmental Budget Center and the Office of the Chief Financial Officer to provide financial management supporting the accomplishment of all aspects of ETA's mission. http://www.doleta.gov/budget

For further information, call 202-693-3162.

Foreign Labor Certification   The Office of Foreign Labor Certification (OFLC) carries out the delegated responsibility of the Secretary of Labor under the Immigration and Nationality Act, as amended, concerning the admission of foreign workers into the United States for employment.

In carrying out this responsibility, OFLC administers temporary nonimmigrant and permanent labor certification programs through ETA's National Processing Centers located, respectively, in Chicago and Atlanta.

OFLC also administers nationally the issuance of employer-requested prevailing wage determinations through ETA's National Prevailing Wage and Helpdesk Center located in Washington, DC. Prevailing wage determinations are issued for use in all nonagricultural temporary labor certification programs and the permanent labor certification program. http://www.foreignlaborcert.doleta.gov

For more information, call 202-693-3010.

Job Training   The Office of Job Corps (OJC) teaches young adults relevant skills they need to become employable and independent and helps them secure meaningful jobs or opportunities for further education. OJC has six regional offices responsible for monitoring and oversight of

Job Corps centers, outreach and admissions, and career transition services. http://www.jobcorps.gov/home.aspx

For further information, call 202-693-3000.

Management and Administrative Services

The Office of Management and Administrative Services (OMAS) is responsible for managing administrative and grant management programs for ETA. OMAS provides critical grant-making and human resources management, information technology services, controlled correspondence, emergency preparedness, Freedom of Information Act coordination, facilities management, and facilitates communication and coordination of activities providing strategic advice, counsel, and customer service to ETA's six regions. OMAS provides technological infrastructure and administrative support for critical ETA functions. https://www.doleta.gov/grants

For further information, call 202-693-2800.

Policy Development and Research

The Office of Policy Development and Research (OPDR) supports ETA policies and investments to improve the public workforce system by analyzing, formulating, and recommending legislative changes and options for policy initiatives, including budget justifications. OPDR coordinates ETA's legislative and regulatory activities and their interactions with international organizations and foreign countries. OPDR maintains ETA's portion of the Department's regulatory agenda and disseminates advisories and publications to the public workforce system. OPDR provides ETA with strategic approaches to improve performance and outcomes through research, demonstrations, and evaluation of its major programs. OPDR manages the Workforce Investment Act performance accountability reporting system; oversees the maintenance of wage record exchange systems for State and other grantees; coordinates the development of ETA's Operating Plan; and disseminates workforce program performance results. OPDR also provides policy guidance and technical assistance on the Worker Adjustment and Retraining Notification Act. http://www.doleta.gov/etainfo/opder

For further information, call 202-693-3700.

Trade Adjustment Assistance

The Office of Trade Adjustment Assistance (TAA) is responsible for administering a workers assistance program for those who have lost or may lose their jobs because of foreign trade. The TAA program provides reemployment services and allowances for eligible individuals. http://www.doleta.gov/tradeact

For further information, call 202-693-3560.

Unemployment Compensation

The Office of Unemployment Insurance (OUI) provides national leadership, oversight, policy guidance, and technical assistance to the Federal-State unemployment compensation system. OUI also interprets Federal legislative requirements. http://www.unemploymentinsurance.doleta.gov

For more information, call 202-693-3029.

Workforce Investment

The Office of Workforce Investment (OWI) is responsible for implementing an integrated national workforce investment system that supports economic growth and provides workers with the information, advice, job search assistance, supportive services, and training needed for employment. OWI also helps employers acquire skilled workers. http://www.doleta.gov/etainfo/WrkSys/WIOffice.cfm

For further information, call 202-693-3980.

Sources of Information

Advisories The ETA uses its advisory system to disseminate its interpretations of Federal laws; procedural, administrative, management, and program direction; and other information to the States, direct grant recipients, and other interested parties. https://wdr.doleta.gov/directives

Data Unemployment insurance data are available on the ETA Web site. http://www.ows.doleta.gov/unemploy/DataDashboard.asp

Program data from the Office of Foreign Labor Certification are available on the ETA Web site. https://www.foreignlaborcert.doleta.gov/performancedata.cfm

Statistics, charts, and other information used to analyze the Trade Adjustment Assistance for Workers program are available on the ETA Web site. https://www.doleta. gov/tradeact/StatMap2015.cfm

Job Corps   Answers to frequently asked questions are posted on the Job Corps Web site. http://www.jobcorps.gov/faq.aspx

The six Job Corps regional offices oversee Job Corps centers nationwide. Contact information for these regional offices is available on the Job Corps Web site. http://www.jobcorps.gov/contact.aspx#national

Job Corps trains more than 60,000 students at 125 centers nationwide. Contact information for these training centers is available on the Job Corps Web site. Phone, 800-733-5627. http://www.jobcorps.gov/centers.aspx

Library   A large repository of information is available online at the ETA Library. http://www.doleta.gov/reports

News   The ETA posts news releases on its Web site. https://www.doleta.gov/ETA_News_Releases

Regional Offices   Contact information for the ETA's six regional offices is available on its Web site. https://www.doleta.gov/regions/regoffices/Pages/eta_default.cfm?CFID=847134926&CFTOKEN=31628934

Research   The research publication database provides access to a collection of research and evaluation reports. The ETA commissioned the research and evaluation reports to help guide the workforce investment system in administering effective programs that enhance employment opportunity and business. https://wdr.doleta.gov/research/eta_default.cfm

Youth Services   The Division of Youth Services has a "Resources" Web page. https://www.doleta.gov/Youth_services/resources.cfm; https://www.doleta.gov/etainfo/ETA_Contacts.cfm

For further information, contact the Employment and Training Administration, Department of Labor, Washington, DC 20210. Phone, 877-872-5627.

Mine Safety and Health Administration

201 12th Street South, Suite 400, Arlington, Virginia 22202
Phone, 202-693-9400. Internet, http://www.msha.gov

Assistant Secretary	JOSEPH A. MAIN
Deputy Assistant Secretary for Operations	PATRICIA W. SILVEY
Deputy Assistant Secretary for Policy	LAURA McCLINTOCK

The Mine Safety and Health Administration (MSHA) was created in 1978, when the Federal Mine Safety and Health Act of 1977 transferred the Federal mine safety program from the Department of the Interior to the Department of Labor. https://www.msha.gov/about/history

The MSHA promotes safe and healthful workplaces for the Nation's miners. The MSHA develops and enforces safety and health rules for all U.S. mines. The MSHA also provides technical, educational, and other assistance to mine operators. https://www.msha.gov/about/mission

Sources of Information

Data   Mine safety and health data—information on accidents, air sampling, employment, injuries, illnesses, inspections, production totals, violations, and more—are available on the MSHA Web site. Compliance calculator tools that allow users to find a mine's history of key health and safety violations are also available the Web site. https://www.msha.gov/data-reports/data-sources-calculators

Summaries of MSHA data on annual fatality and injury statistics, most frequently cited standards, number of citations and orders issued, total dollar amount of penalties assessed, and more are available on the MSHA Web site. https://www.msha.gov/data-reports/statistics

Employment   Information on employment opportunities is available online. http://www.msha.gov/about/careers

The MSHA seeks motivated professionals committed to ensuring the health and safety of the Nation's miners. http://arlweb.msha.gov/inspectors/inspectorhiringprogram.asp

Frequently Asked Questions (FAQs) The MSHA posts answers to FAQs on its Web site. https://www.msha.gov/training-education/frequently-asked-questions | Email: mshatraining@dol.gov

News / Media The MSHA posts alerts and hazards, announcements, congressional testimonies, events, news releases, photographs and videos, and speeches on its Web site. https://www.msha.gov/news-media

Offices A complete listing of MSHA district and field offices is available online. http://www.msha.gov/district/disthome.htm

Reports Current and historical preliminary accident reports, fatalgrams, and fatal investigation reports for metal, nonmetal, and coal mines are accessible on the MSHA Web site. Quarterly and annual summaries of mining fatalities along with associated best practices and preventative recommendations are also accessible. https://www.msha.gov/data-reports/fatality-reports

Part 50 of Title 30 of the "Code of Federal Regulation" (30 CFR Part 50) requires mine operators to notify the MSHA of accidents, requires operators to investigate accidents, and restricts disturbance of accident related areas. This part also requires them to file reports with the MSHA pertaining to accidents, occupational injuries, and occupational illnesses, as well as employment and coal production data. These Data are summarized in quarterly and annual reports. https://www.msha.gov/data-reports/reports

Resources / Tools Mine emergency operations information, miners' resources, and technical resources and reports are available on the MSHA Web site. https://www.msha.gov/support-resources/resources-tools

Spanish In the top right corner of the MSHA's home page are an Español option and an Inglés option. Using these options, visitors to the Web site can toggle between content in Spanish or English. https://www.msha.gov; https://www.msha.gov/about/contact-msha | Email: AskMSHA@dol.gov

For further information, contact the Office of Program Education and Outreach Services, Mine Safety and Health Administration, Department of Labor, 201 12th Street South, Suite 400, Arlington, Virginia 22202. Phone, 202-693-9400.

Occupational Safety and Health Administration

Department of Labor, Washington, DC 20210
Phone, 800-321-6742. Internet, http://www.osha.gov

Assistant Secretary — DAVID MICHAELS
Deputy Assistant Secretary — JORDAN BARAB
Deputy Assistant Secretary — DOROTHY DOUGHERTY

The Occupational Safety and Health Administration (OSHA), created pursuant to the Occupational Safety and Health Act of 1970 (29 U.S.C. 651 et seq.), assures safe and healthful working conditions for men and women by promulgating common sense, protective health, and safety standards; enforcing workplace safety and health rules; providing training, outreach, education, and assistance to workers and employers in their efforts to control workplace hazards; prevent work-related injuries, illnesses, and fatalities; and

partnering with States that run their own OSHA-approved programs. https://www.osha.gov/about.html

Sources of Information

Enforcement Cases The OSHA Web site features a nationwide map of enforcement cases with initial penalties above $40,000. https://www.osha.gov/topcases/bystate.html

File a Complaint Information on how to file a safety and health complaint and an electronic complaint form are available on the OSHA Web site. Phone, 800-321-6742. https://www.osha.gov/workers/file_complaint.html

Freedom of Information Act (FOIA)   The OSHA is required to disclose records that are properly requested in writing by any person. An agency may withhold information pursuant to one or more of nine exemptions and three exclusions contained in the FOIA. The act applies only to Federal agencies and does not create a right of access to records held by Congress, the courts, State or local government agencies, and private entities. https://www.osha.gov/as/opa/foia/foia.html

Frequently Asked Questions (FAQs)   The OSHA posts answers to FAQs on its Web site. https://www.osha.gov/OSHA_FAQs.html

Injury and Illness Data   The OSHA Web site features a searchable, establishment-specific database for establishments that provided OSHA with valid data from 1996 through 2011. https://www.osha.gov/pls/odi/establishment_search.html

Workplace injury, illness, and fatality statistics are available on the OSHA Web site. https://www.osha.gov/oshstats/work.html

Make a Report   Employers must notify OSHA when an employee is killed on the job or suffers a work-related amputation, hospitalization, or loss of an eye. A fatality must be reported within 8 hours; an amputation, in-patient hospitalization, or eye loss must be reported within 24 hours. An employer should be prepared to supply the name of the business, the names of employees who were affected, the location and time of the incident, a brief description of the incident, and a contact person and phone number. https://www.osha.gov/report.html

News   The OSHA posts news releases, which can be sorted by subject, date, or region, on its Web site. https://www.osha.gov/newsrelease.html

The "What's New" Web page features news items that are organized chronologically. https://www.osha.gov/whatsnew.html

Offices   A complete listing of OSHA regional and area offices is available online. http://www.osha.gov/html/RAmap.html

Publications   OSHA publications are accessible online. https://www.osha.gov/pls/publications/publication.html

Site Index   An A–Z index is available on the OSHA Web site. https://www.osha.gov/html/a-z-index.html

Spanish   In the top right corner of the OSHA's home page are an Español option and an Inglés option. Using these options, visitors to the Web site can toggle between content in Spanish or English. https://www.osha.gov

Training / Education   Stand-alone, interactive, Web-based training tools—eTools and the eMatrix—are available on the OSHA Web site. These tools are highly illustrated and utilize graphical menus. https://www.osha.gov/dts/osta/oshasoft/index.html

Prevention video training tools (v-tools) on construction hazards are available on the OSHA Web site. These videos show how workers can be injured suddenly or even killed on the job. The videos assist those who are in the construction industry with identifying, reducing, and eliminating hazards. The videos are presented in clear, accessible vocabulary; show common construction worksite activities; and most are 2–4 minutes long. https://www.osha.gov/dts/vtools/construction.html; https://www.osha.gov/html/Feed_Back.html

For further information, contact the Occupational Safety and Health Administration, Department of Labor, Washington, DC 20210. Phone, 202-693-2000 or 800-321-6742.

Veterans' Employment and Training Service

Department of Labor, Washington, DC 20210
Phone, 866-487-2365. Internet, http://www.dol.gov/vets

Assistant Secretary	MIKE MICHAUD
Deputy Assistant Secretary for Policy	TERESA W. GERTON
Deputy Assistant Secretary for Operations and Management	SAM SHELLENBERGER

The Veterans' Employment and Training Service (VETS) is responsible for administering veterans' employment and training programs and compliance activities that help them and servicemembers succeed in their civilian careers. VETS also administers the Jobs for Veterans State Grant program, which provides grants to States to fund personnel dedicated to serving the employment needs of veterans. VETS field staff works closely with and provides technical assistance to State employment workforce agencies to ensure that veterans receive priority of service and gain meaningful employment. VETS has two competitive grants programs: the Homeless Veterans Reintegration Program, and the Incarcerated Veterans Transition Program. VETS also prepares separating servicemembers for the civilian labor market with its Transition Assistance Program Employment Workshop.

VETS has three distinct compliance programs: the Federal Contractor Program, Veterans' Preference in Federal hiring and the Uniformed Services Employment and Reemployment Rights Act of 1994 (USERRA). With respect to Federal contractors, VETS promulgates regulations and maintains oversight of the program by assisting contractors to comply with their affirmative action and reporting obligations. Although the Office of Personnel Management is responsible for administering and interpreting statutes and regulations governing veterans' preference in Federal hiring, VETS investigates allegations that veterans' preference rights have been violated. In addition, VETS preserves servicemembers' employment and reemployment rights through its administration and enforcement of the USERRA statute. VETS conducts thorough investigations of alleged violations and conducts an extensive USERRA outreach program. https://www.dol.gov/vets/aboutvets/aboutvets.htm

Sources of Information

Directories A national office directory is available online. https://www.dol.gov/vets/aboutvets/nationaloffice.htm

A regional and State directory is available online. https://www.dol.gov/vets/aboutvets/regionaloffices/map.htm

Freedom of Information Act (FOIA) Any person has the right to request access to Federal agency records or information. VETS is required to disclose records that are properly requested in writing by any person. An agency may withhold information pursuant to nine exemptions and three exclusions contained in the FOIA. The act applies only to Federal agencies and does not create a right of access to records held by Congress, the courts, or by State or local government agencies. A FOIA request should be submitted to the appropriate national or regional VETS office by email, fax, or mail. The subject line, cover page, or envelope should be clearly labeled "Freedom of Information Act Request." The content of the request should indicate that it is a FOIA request, and it should contain as much information as possible describing the record or records being sought. https://www.dol.gov/vets/foia

Frequently Asked Questions (FAQs) VETS posts answers to FAQs on its Web site. https://www.dol.gov/vets/resources/faqs.htm

Grants Information on grants and other opportunities is available online. http://www.dol.gov/vets/resources/grants.htm

Hire a Veteran Resources to help employers hire veterans are available online. https://www.dol.gov/vets/hire/index.htm

News / Media VETS posts news releases and public service announcements on its Web site. https://www.dol.gov/vets/news.htm

Updates / Reports The VETS Web site features updates and reports, as well as congressional testimonies, factsheets, and infographics. https://www.dol.gov/vets/updates/index.htm; http://www.dol.gov/vets

For further information, contact the Assistant Secretary for Veterans' Employment and Training, Department of Labor, Washington, DC 20210. Phone, 202-693-4700.

Wage and Hour Division

Department of Labor, Washington, DC 20210
Phone, 866-487-9243. Internet, http://www.dol.gov/whd

Administrator	DAVID WEIL
Deputy Administrator	LAURA A. FORTMAN
Deputy Administrator for Program Operations	PATRICIA DAVIDSON

The Wage and Hour Division (WHD) enforces Federal minimum wage, overtime pay, recordkeeping, and child labor law requirements of the Fair Labor Standards Act. WHD also enforces the Migrant and Seasonal Agricultural Worker Protection Act, the Employee Polygraph Protection Act, the Family and Medical Leave Act, wage garnishment provisions of the Consumer Credit Protection Act, and a number of employment standards and worker protections as provided in several immigration-related statutes. Additionally, WHD administers and enforces the prevailing wage requirements of the Davis Bacon Act and the Service Contract Act and other statutes applicable to Federal contracts for construction and for the provision of goods and services. https://www.dol.gov/whd/about/mission/whdmiss.htm

Sources of Information

Evaluations / Studies   The WHD posts evaluations and studies on its Web site in Portable Document Format (PDF). https://www.dol.gov/whd/resources/evaluations.htm
File a Complaint   Instructions for filing a complaint are available online. Phone, 866-487-9243. https://www.dol.gov/wecanhelp/howtofilecomplaint.htm
Freedom of Information Act (FOIA)   The WHD is required to disclose records that are properly requested in writing by any person. The WHD may withhold information pursuant to nine exemptions and three exclusions contained in the FOIA. The WHD does not require a special FOIA request form. A request must reasonably describe the desired record. Providing its name or title is not mandatory, but the more specific the record description, the more likely that WHD staff can locate it. A FOIA request must be made in writing and may be submitted by courier service, email, fax, or postal mail. https://www.dol.gov/whd/foia/index.htm
Frequently Asked Questions (FAQs)   The WHD provides answers to FAQs on its Web site. https://www.dol.gov/wecanhelp/faq.htm
News   The WHD posts national and State news releases on its Web site. https://www.dol.gov/whd/media/press/whdprssToc.asp
Offices   Contact information for WHD area, district, and regional offices is available on the "WHD Local Offices" Web page. https://www.dol.gov/whd/america2.htm
Resources   Resources for workers are available on the WHD Web site. https://www.dol.gov/whd/workers.htm

Resources for employers are available on the WHD Web site. https://www.dol.gov/whd/foremployers.htm

Resources for State and local governments are available on the WHD Web site. https://www.dol.gov/whd/forstatelocalgovernments.htm; https://www.dol.gov/whd/contact_us.htm

For further information, contact the Office of the Administrator, Wage and Hour Division, Department of Labor, Room S-3502, Washington, DC 20210. Phone, 202-693-0051.

Women's Bureau

Department of Labor, Washington, DC 20210
Phone, 202-693-6710. Internet, http://www.dol.gov/wb

Director	LATIFA LYLES
Deputy Director	JOAN HARRIGAN-FARRELLY

The Women's Bureau develops policies and standards and conducts inquiries to safeguard the interests of working women, to advocate for their equality and the economic security of their families, and to promote quality work environments.

The Bureau identifies, researches, and analyzes topics that are relevant for working women; pioneers policies and programs to address those topics; and enhances public education and outreach efforts to raise awareness on key issues and developments affecting women in the workforce. http://www.dol.gov/wb/overview_14.htm

Sources of Information

Blog   The Bureau's Web site features a blog. https://www.dol.gov/wb/media/blog_posts.htm

Data / Statistics   Current and historical statistics on a broad range of topics and subpopulations of women in the labor force are available online. http://www.dol.gov/wb/stats/stats_data.htm

Regional Offices   A complete listing of Women's Bureau regional offices is available online. http://www.dol.gov/wb/info_about_wb/regions/regional_offices.htm

Resources   Resources for women in the labor force produced by or in collaboration with the Bureau are available on its Web site. https://www.dol.gov/wb/resources; https://www.dol.gov/wb/info_about_wb/contact_us.htm

For further information, contact the Women's Bureau, Department of Labor, Room S-3002, NW., Washington, DC 20210. Phone, 202-693-6710.

DEPARTMENT OF STATE

2201 C Street NW., Washington, DC 20520
Phone, 202-647-4000. Internet, http://www.state.gov

Secretary of State	MICHAEL R. POMPEO
Counselor of the Department	T. ULRICH BRECHBUHL
Executive Secretary	LISA D. KENNA
https://www.state.gov/biographies/michael-r-pompeo	
Deputy Secretary of State	JOHN J. SULLIVAN
Director, Office of U.S. Foreign Assistance	JAMES L. RICHARDSON
https://www.state.gov/biographies/john-j-sullivan	
Deputy Secretary of State for Management and Resources	JOHN J. SULLIVAN

Bureaus Reporting to the Secretary
Assistant Secretaries

Intelligence and Research	ELLEN E. MCCARTHY
Legislative Affairs	MARY ELIZABETH TAYLOR

Offices Reporting to the Secretary
Ambassadors-At-Large

Coordinating U.S. Government Activities to Combat HIV/ AIDS	DEBORAH L. BIRX
Global Health Diplomacy	DEBORAH L. BIRX
Global Women's Issues	(VACANCY)

Directors

Civil Rights	GREGORY B. SMITH
Policy Planning	PETER BERKOWITZ
Chief of Protocol	KATHERINE C. HENDERSON
Legal Adviser	MARIK A. STRING, ACTING

Special Envoys and Representatives Reporting to the Secretary
Presidential Envoys

Global Coalition to Defeat ISIS	JAMES F. JEFFREY
Hostage Affairs	HUGH T. DUGAN, ACTING

Representatives

Afghanistan Reconciliation	ZALMAY M. KHALILZAD
Iran	BRIAN H. HOOK
North Korea	STEPHEN E. BIEGUN
Syria Engagement	JAMES F. JEFFREY
Venezuela	ELLIOTT ABRAMS
https://www.state.gov/bureaus-offices/bureaus-and-offices-reporting-directly-to-the-secretary	

Arms Control and International Security

Undersecretary	ANDREA L. THOMPSON

Assistant Secretaries
Arms Control, Verification and Compliance — THOMAS G. DiNANNO
International Security and Nonproliferation — CHRISTOPHER FORD
Political-Military Affairs — R. CLARKE COOPER
https://www.state.gov/bureaus-offices/under-secretary-for-
arms-control-and-international-security-affairs

Civilian Security, Democracy, and Human Rights
Undersecretary — NATHAN A. SALES, ACTING
Ambassadors-At-Large
Counterterrorism and Countering Violent Extremism — NATHAN A. SALES
Global Criminal Justice — (VACANCY)
Monitoring and Combating Trafficking in Persons — JOHN C. RICHMOND

Assistant Secretaries
Conflict and Stabilization Operations — DENISE NATALI
Democracy, Human Rights, and Labor — MICHAEL KOZAK
International Narcotics and Law Enforcement Affairs — KIRSTEN D. MADISON
Population, Refugees, and Migration — CAROL O'CONNELL, ACTING
https://www.state.gov/bureaus-offices/under-secretary-for-
civilian-security-democracy-and-human-rights

Economic Growth, Energy, and the Environment

Undersecretary — KEITH J. KRACH

Assistant Secretaries
Economic and Business Affairs — MANISHA SINGH
Energy Resources — FRANCIS R. FANNON
Oceans and International Environmental and Scientific Affairs (VACANCY)

Chief Economist — SHARON BROWN-HRUSKA
Senior Science and Technology Adviser to the Secretary — MATTHEW CHESSEN
https://www.state.gov/bureaus-offices/under-secretary-for-
economic-growth-energy-and-the-environment

Management

Undersecretary — BRIAN J. BULATAO

Assistant Secretaries
Administration — CARRIE B. CABELKA
Consular Affairs — CARL C. RISCH
Diplomatic Security — MICHAEL T. EVANOFF
Information Resource Management — STUART M. McGUIGAN

Chief Officers
Information — STUART M. McGUIGAN
Medical — MARK J. COHEN

Directors
Budget and Planning — DOUGLAS A. PITKIN
Global Financial Services — JEFFREY C. MOUNTS
Foreign Missions — STEPHEN J. AKARD
Foreign Service Institute — DANIEL B. SMITH
Human Resources — CAROL Z. PEREZ
Management Policy, Rightsizing, and Innovation — JAMES S. SCHWAB
Medical Services — MARK J. COHEN
Overseas Buildings Operations — ADDISON D. DAVIS IV

Comptroller   JEFFREY C. MOUNTS
Director General of the Foreign Service   CAROL Z. PEREZ
https://www.state.gov/bureaus-offices/under-secretary-for-
    management/bureau-of-administration

Political Affairs
Undersecretary   DAVID M. HALE

Assistant Secretaries   TIBOR P. NAGY, JR.
African Affairs   DAVID R. STILWELL
East Asian and Pacific Affairs   PHILIP T. REEKER, ACTING
European and Eurasian Affairs   KEVIN E. MOLEY
International Organization Affairs   DAVID K. SCHENKER
Near Eastern Affairs   ALICE G.WELLS, ACTING
South and Central Asian Affairs   JULIE J. CHUNG, ACTING
Western Hemisphere Affairs
https://www.state.gov/bureaus-offices/under-secretary-for-
    political-affairs

Public Diplomacy and Public Affairs
Undersecretary   (VACANCY)

Assistant Secretaries   MICHELLE S. GIUDA
Global Public Affairs   MARIE T. ROYCE
Educational and Cultural Affairs
https://www.state.gov/bureaus-offices/under-secretary-for-
    public-diplomacy-and-public-affairs

United States Mission to the United Nations
799 United Nations Plaza, New York, NY 10017

AMBASSADORS
Representative of the U.S.A.   KELLY KNIGHT CRAFT
Deputy Representative of the U.S.A.   JONATHAN R. COHEN
United Nations Management and Reform   CHERITH NORMAN CHALET
https://usun.usmission.gov/our-leaders

Inspector General   STEVE A. LINICK
https://oig.state.gov/about/IG

The above list of key personnel was updated 9–2019.

The Department of State advises the President on issues of foreign policy; supports democracy, freedom, and prosperity for all people; and fosters conditions that favor stability and progress worldwide.

Establishment and Organization
The First Congress of the United States held its first session in the City of New York, starting on March 4, 1789, and ending on September 29, 1789. By act of July 27, 1789 (Statute I, Ch. IV), which President George Washington signed, the U.S. Congress enacted the establishment of an executive department "to be denominated the Department of Foreign Affairs." https://www.loc.gov/law/help/statutes-at-large/1st-congress/c1.pdf

During the same session, by act of September 15, 1789 (Statute I, Ch. XIV), which President George Washington also signed, the First Congress renamed the Department of Foreign Affairs as the Department of State, and its principal officer became known as the Secretary of State. https://www.loc.gov/law/help/statutes-at-large/1st-congress/c1.pdf

Subject matter on the establishment and organization of the Department of State is consolidated and codified in Title

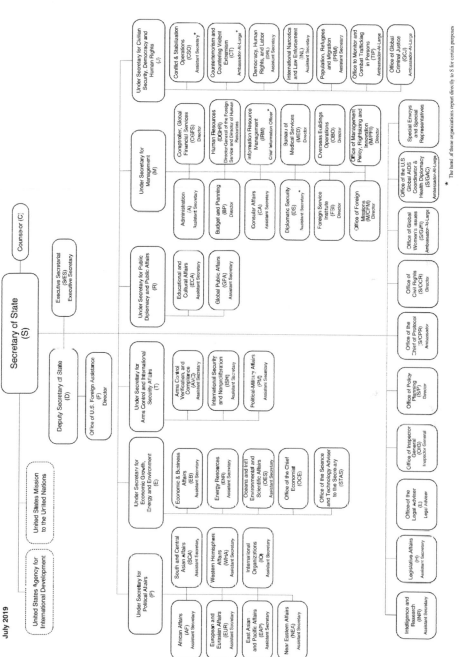

July 2019

Secretary of State (S)

Counselor (C)

Executive Secretariat (SES)
Executive Secretary

United States Agency for International Development

United States Mission to the United Nations

Deputy Secretary of State (D)

Office of U.S. Foreign Assistance (F)
Director

Under Secretary for Political Affairs (P)

African Affairs (AF)
Assistant Secretary

European and Eurasian Affairs (EUR)
Assistant Secretary

East Asian and Pacific Affairs (EAP)
Assistant Secretary

Near Eastern Affairs (NEA)
Assistant Secretary

South and Central Asian Affairs (SCA)
Assistant Secretary

Western Hemisphere Affairs (WHA)
Assistant Secretary

International Organizations (IO)
Assistant Secretary

Under Secretary for Economic Growth, Energy and Environment (E)

Economic & Business Affairs (EB)
Assistant Secretary

Energy Resources (ENR)
Assistant Secretary

Oceans and Int'l Environmental and Scientific Affairs (OES)
Assistant Secretary

Office of the Chief Economist (OCE)

Office of the Science and Technology Adviser to the Secretary (STAS)

Under Secretary for Arms Control and International Security Affairs (T)

Arms Control, Verification, and Compliance (AVC)
Assistant Secretary

International Security and Nonproliferation (ISN)
Assistant Secretary

Political-Military Affairs (PM)
Assistant Secretary

Under Secretary for Public Diplomacy and Public Affairs (R)

Educational and Cultural Affairs (ECA)
Assistant Secretary

Global Public Affairs (GPA)
Assistant Secretary

Under Secretary for Management (M)

Administration (A)
Assistant Secretary

Budget and Planning (BP)
Director

Consular Affairs (CA)
Assistant Secretary

Diplomatic Security (DS)*
Assistant Secretary

Foreign Service Institute (FSI)
Director

Office of Foreign Missions (M/OFM)
Director

Comptroller, Global Financial Services (CGFS)
Director

Human Resources (DGHR)
Director-General of the Foreign Service and Director of Human Resources

Information Resource Management (IRM)*
Chief Information Officer

Bureau of Medical Services (MED)
Director

Overseas Buildings Operations (OBO)
Director

Office of Management Policy, Rightsizing and Innovation (M/PRI)
Director

Under Secretary for Civilian Security, Democracy and Human Rights (J)

Conflict & Stabilization Operations (CSO)*
Assistant Secretary

Counterterrorism and Countering Violent Extremism (CT)*
Ambassador-At-Large

Democracy, Human Rights, and Labor (DRL)
Assistant Secretary

International Narcotics and Law Enforcement (INL)
Assistant Secretary

Population, Refugees and Migration (PRM)
Assistant Secretary

Office to Monitor and Combat Trafficking in Persons (TIP)
Ambassador-At-Large

Office of Global Criminal Justice
Ambassador-At-Large

Intelligence and Research (INR)
Assistant Secretary

Legislative Affairs (H)
Assistant Secretary

Office of the Legal Adviser (L)
Legal Adviser

Office of Inspector General (OIG)
Inspector General

Office of Policy Planning (S/P)
Director

Office of the Chief of Protocol (S/CPR)
Ambassador

Office of Civil Rights (S/OCR)
Director

Office of Global Women's Issues (S/GWI)
Ambassador-At-Large

Office of the U.S. Global AIDS Coordinator & Health Diplomacy (S/GAC)
Ambassador-At-Large

Special Envoys and Special Representatives

* The head of these organizations report directly to S for certain purposes

* The head of these organizations report directly to S for certain purposes

22, Chapter 38, of the U.S. Code (Sec. 2651 and 2651a). https://uscode.house.gov/view.xhtml?path=/prelim@title22/chapter38&edition=prelim

By the advice and with the consent of the Senate, the President appoints the Secretary of State, the Deputy Secretary of State, and the Deputy Secretary of State for Management and Resources. By the Senate's advice and with its consent, the President also appoints, up to a maximum of six, the Department's Undersecretaries (22 USC 2651a). https://uscode.house.gov/view.xhtml?req=granuleid:USC-prelim-title22-section2651a&num=0&edition=prelim

The Department of State's statement of organization is found in 22 CFR 5. https://www.ecfr.gov/cgi-bin/text-idx?SID=9fcaa112da47aad8595acce6fd09ca0e&mc=true&node=pt22.1.5&rgn=div5

The Department's organizational chart is available in Portable Document Format (PDF) for viewing and downloading. https://www.state.gov/department-of-state-organization-chart

Activities

The Secretary of State directs, coordinates, and supervises U.S. foreign relations and the interdepartmental activities of the U.S. Government abroad. The Secretary ranks first in importance among the President's foreign affairs advisers, serves as a Cabinet member and on the National Security Council, and oversees State Department operations, including the Foreign Service. http://www.state.gov/secretary

The future of the United States depends on the relations that its has with other countries. The U.S. Foreign Service is the principal cultivator of those relations. Trained representatives stationed worldwide provide the President and the Secretary of State with many of the building blocks from which foreign policy is constructed. These representatives also offer recommendations to help guide the process of policy building.

Ambassadors are the personal representatives of the President and report to the President through the Secretary of State. Ambassadors have full responsibility for implementation of U.S. foreign policy by U.S. Government personnel within their country of assignment, except those who are under military commands. Responsibilities include negotiating agreements between the United States and the host country, explaining and disseminating official U.S. policy, and maintaining cordial relations with that country's government and people.

Administration   The Bureau of Administration provides support programs and services to Department of State operations worldwide, as well as programs and services to other U.S. Government agencies represented at U.S. Embassies and consulates. These functions include administrative policy; domestic emergency management; management of owned or leased facilities in the United States; procurement, supply, travel, and transportation support; classified pouch, unclassified pouch, and domestic mail distribution; official records, publishing, library, and foreign language interpreting and translating services; and support to the schools abroad that educate dependents of U.S. Government employees assigned to diplomatic and consular missions. Direct services to the public include authenticating documents used abroad for legal and business purposes; responding to requests under the Freedom of Information and Privacy Acts; providing the electronic reading room for public reference to State Department records; and determining use of the diplomatic reception rooms of the Harry S. Truman headquarters building in Washington, DC. https://www.state.gov/about-us-bureau-of-administration

For further information, contact the Bureau of Administration. Phone, 202-485-7000.

Arms Control, Verification, and Compliance   The Bureau of Arms Control, Verification and Compliance is responsible for ensuring and verifying compliance with international arms control, nonproliferation, and disarmament agreements and commitments. The Bureau also leads negotiation and implementation efforts with respect to strategic arms control, most recently the new START Treaty and conventional forces in Europe. The Bureau is the principal policy representative to the intelligence community with regard to verification and compliance matters and uses this role to promote, preserve, and enhance key collection and analytic capabilities and to ensure that intelligence verification, compliance, and implementation requirements are met. The Bureau staffs and manages treaty implementation commissions, creates negotiation and implementation policy for agreements and commitments, and develops policy for future arms control, nonproliferation, and disarmament arrangements. It also provides secure government-to-government communication linkages with foreign treaty partners. The Bureau is also responsible for preparing verifiability assessments on proposals and agreements, and reporting these to Congress as required. The Bureau also prepares the "President's Annual Report to Congress on Adherence to and Compliance With Arms Control, Nonproliferation, and Disarmament Agreements and Commitments," as well as the reports required by the Iran, North Korea, and Syria Nonproliferation Act. http://www.state.gov/t/avc

For further information, contact the Bureau of Arms Control, Verification and Compliance. Phone, 202-647-6830. Fax, 202-647-1321.

Budget and Planning

The Bureau of Budget and Planning manages budgeting and resource management for operation accounts. https://www.state.gov/bureaus-offices/under-secretary-for-management/bureau-of-budget-and-planning

For further information, contact the Bureau of Budget and Planning. Phone, 202-647-8517.

Comptroller and Global Financial Services

The Bureau of the Comptroller and Global Financial Services, led by the Chief Financial Officer, integrates strategic planning, budgeting, and performance to secure departmental resources. The Bureau manages all departmental strategic and performance planning; global financial services, including accounting, disbursing, and payroll; issuance of financial statements and oversight of the Department's management control program; coordination of national security resources and remediation of vulnerabilities within the Department's global critical infrastructure; and management of the International Cooperative Administrative Support Services Program. http://www.state.gov/m/cgfs

For further information, contact the Bureau of the Comptroller and Global Financial Services. Phone, 703-875-4364.

Conflict and Stabilization Operations

The Bureau of Conflict and Stabilization Operations advances U.S. national security by driving integrated, civilian-led efforts to prevent, respond to, and stabilize crises in priority states, setting conditions for long-term peace. The Bureau emphasizes sustainable solutions guided by local dynamics and actors and promotes unity of effort, strategic use of scarce resources, and burden sharing with international partners. http://www.state.gov/j/cso

For further information, contact the Bureau of Conflict Stabilization Operations. Phone, 202-663-0299.

Consular Affairs

The Bureau of Consular Affairs is responsible for the protection and welfare of American citizens and interests abroad; the administration and enforcement of the provisions of the immigration and nationality laws insofar as they concern the Department of State and Foreign Service; the issuance of passports and visas; and related services. Approximately 18 million passports a year are issued by the Bureau's Office of Passport Services at the processing centers in Portsmouth, NH, and Charleston, SC, and the regional agencies in Boston, MA; Chicago, IL; Aurora, CO; Honolulu, HI; Houston, TX; Los Angeles, CA; Miami, Fl ; New Orleans, LA; New York, NY; Philadelphia, PA; San Francisco, CA; Seattle, WA; Norwalk, CT; Detroit, MI; Minneapolis, MN; and Washington, DC. In addition, the Bureau helps secure America's borders against entry by terrorists or narcotraffickers, facilitates international adoptions, and supports parents whose children have been abducted abroad. http://travel.state.gov/content/travel/en.html

More information is available online at the Bureau of Consular Affairs.

Counterterrorism

The Bureau of Counterterrorism leads the Department in the U.S. Government's effort to counter terrorism abroad and secure the United States against foreign terrorist threats. To carry out its mission, the Bureau develops and implements counterterrorism strategies, promotes international cooperation on counterterrorism issues, serves as the Department's key link on counterterrorism to the Department of Homeland Security, focuses efforts to counter violent extremism, and develops international partner counterterrorism capacity. http://www.state.gov/j/ct

For further information, contact CT's Office of Public Affairs. Phone, 202-647-1845.

Democracy, Human Rights, and Labor   The Bureau of Democracy, Human Rights, and Labor (DRL) is responsible for developing and implementing U.S. policy on democracy, human rights, labor, religious freedom, monitoring and combating anti-Semitism, and advocating for inclusion of people with disabilities. DRL practices diplomatic engagement and advocacy to protect human rights and strengthen democratic institutions. Working with governments, civil society, and multilateral organizations to support democratic governance and human rights, the Bureau also participates in multi-stakeholder initiatives to encourage multinational corporations to adhere to human rights standards of conduct, including the elimination of child labor. DRL fulfills the USG reporting responsibilities on human rights and democracy, producing the annual "Country Reports on Human Rights Practices," the annual "International Religious Freedom" report, and the "Advancing Freedom and Democracy" report. Providing targeted program assistance through the Human Rights and Democracy Fund and other funding streams, the Bureau works to protect human rights and strengthen democratic institutions around the world. DRL programs help prosecute war criminals, promote religious freedom, support workers' rights, encourage accountability in governance, as well as facilitate freedom of expression and freedom to access information on the Internet. The Bureau also has a Congressionally mandated responsibility to ensure that foreign military assistance and training is not provided to gross violators of human rights. DRL leads the Secretary of State's Task Force on Global Internet Freedom. http://www.state.gov/j/drl

For further information, contact the Bureau of Democracy, Human Rights, and Labor. Phone, 202-647-2126.

Diplomatic Security   The Bureau of Diplomatic Security provides a secure environment to promote U.S. interests at home and abroad. The Bureau's mission includes protecting the Secretary of State and other senior Government officials, resident and visiting foreign dignitaries, and foreign missions in the United States; conducting criminal, counterintelligence, and personnel security investigations; ensuring the integrity of international travel documents, sensitive information, classified processing equipment, and management information systems; the physical and technical protection of domestic and overseas facilities of the Department of State; providing professional law enforcement and security training to U.S. and foreign personnel; and a comprehensive, multifaceted overseas security program serving the needs of U.S. missions and resident U.S. citizens and business communities. Through the Office of Foreign Missions, the Bureau regulates the domestic activities of the foreign diplomatic community in the areas of taxation, real property acquisitions, motor vehicle operation, domestic travel, and customs processing. http://www.state.gov/m/ds

For further information, contact the Bureau of Diplomatic Security Office of Public Affairs. Phone, 571-345-2502.

Economic and Business Affairs   The Bureau of Economic and Business Affairs (EB) promotes international trade, investment, economic development, and financial stability on behalf of the American people. EB works to build prosperity and economic security at home and abroad by implementing policy related to the promotion of U.S. trade, investment and exports, international development and reconstruction, intellectual property enforcement, terrorism financing and economic sanctions, international communications and information policy, and aviation and maritime affairs. EB formulates and carries out U.S. foreign economic policy and works to sustain a more democratic, secure, and prosperous world. http://www.state.gov/e/eb

For further information, contact the Bureau of Economic and Business Affairs. Phone, 202-647-9204.

Educational and Cultural Affairs   The Bureau of Educational and Cultural Affairs administers the principal provisions of the Mutual Educational and Cultural Exchange Act (the Fulbright-Hays Act), including U.S. international educational and cultural exchange programs. These programs include the prestigious Fulbright Program for students, scholars, and teachers; the International Visitor Leadership Program, which brings leaders and future leaders from other countries to the United States for consultation with their professional colleagues; and professional, youth, sports, and cultural exchanges. Programs are implemented through cooperative relationships with U.S. nongovernmental organizations that support the Bureau's mission. http://exchanges.state.gov

For further information, contact the Bureau of Educational and Cultural Affairs. Phone, 202-632-6445. Fax, 202-632-2701.

Energy Resources   The Bureau of Energy Resources (ENR) leads the State Department in the U.S. Government's promotion of U.S. and international energy policy. ENR works to ensure that international energy markets are secure and predictable in order to mitigate potential disruptions, while also working with international partners to diversify U.S. energy supplies. The Bureau also seeks to encourage the transformation of United States and world production and consumption of energy to confront the limits of a hydrocarbon-based society and rapid increases in energy demand. ENR works to promote good governance, transparency, and reform of energy sectors globally, which will help broaden energy access, further ensure stable energy supplies, and reduce political instability. http://www.state.gov/e/enr

For further information, contact the Bureau of Energy Resources. Phone, 202-647-3423.

Foreign Service Institute   The Foreign Service Institute of the Department of State is the Federal Government's primary foreign affairs-related training institution. In addition to the Department of State, the Institute provides training for more than 47 other Government agencies. The Institute has more than 700 courses, including some 70 foreign language courses, ranging in length from 1 day to 2 years. The courses are designed to promote successful performance in each professional assignment, to ease the adjustment to other countries and cultures, and to enhance the leadership and management capabilities of the foreign affairs community. https://www.state.gov/bureaus-offices/under-secretary-for-management/foreign-service-institute

For further information, contact the Foreign Service Institute. Phone, 703-302-7144. Fax, 703-302-7152.

Information Resource Management   The Bureau of Information Resource Management (IRM) provides the Department with the information technology it needs to carry out U.S. diplomacy in the information age. The IRM Bureau is led by the Department's Chief Information Officer. IRM establishes effective information resource management planning and policies; ensures availability of information technology systems and operations, including information technology contingency planning, to support the Department's diplomatic, consular, and management operations; exercises management responsibility to ensure the Department's information resources meet the business requirements of the Department and provide an effective basis for knowledge sharing and collaboration within the Department and with other foreign affairs agencies and partners; exercises delegated approving authority for the Secretary of State for the development and administration of the Department's computer and information security programs and policies. http://www.state.gov/m/irm

For further information, contact the Bureau of Information Resource Management. Phone, 202-647-2977.

Inspector General   The Office of Inspector General (OIG) conducts independent audits, inspections, and investigations to promote effective management, accountability, and positive change in the Department of State, the Broadcasting Board of Governors (BBG), and the foreign affairs community. OIG provides leadership to promote integrity, efficiency, effectiveness, and economy; prevents and detects waste, fraud, abuse, and mismanagement; identifies vulnerabilities and recommends constructive solutions; offers expert assistance to improve Department and BBG operations; communicates timely, useful information that facilitates decision-making and achieves measurable gains; and keeps the Department, BBG, and Congress informed. https://oig.state.gov

For further information, contact the Office of Inspector General. Phone, 202-663-0340.

Intelligence and Research   The primary mission of the Bureau of Intelligence and Research (INR) is to harness intelligence to serve U.S. diplomacy. Drawing on all-source intelligence, INR provides value-added independent analysis of events to Department policymakers, ensures that intelligence activities support foreign policy and national security purposes, and serves as the focal point in the Department for ensuring policy review of sensitive counterintelligence and law enforcement activities. The Bureau also analyzes geographical and international boundary issues. INR is a member of the U.S. Intelligence Community and serves as the Community's Executive Agent for Analytical Outreach. http://www.state.gov/s/inr

For further information, contact the Bureau of Intelligence and Research. Phone, 202-647-1080.

International Narcotics and Law Enforcement   The Bureau of International Narcotics and Law Enforcement Affairs (INL) is responsible for developing policies and managing programs to combat and counter international narcotics production and trafficking, and for strengthening law enforcement and other rule of law institutional capabilities outside the United States. The Bureau also directs narcotics control coordinators at posts abroad and provides guidance on narcotics control, justice sector reform, and anticrime matters to the chiefs of missions. It supports the development of strong, sustainable criminal justice systems as well as training for police force and judicial officials. INL works closely with a broad range of other U.S. Government agencies. http://www.state.gov/j/inl

For further information, contact the Bureau of International Narcotics and Law Enforcement Affairs. Phone, 202-647-2545. Fax, 202-736-4045.

International Organizations   The Bureau of International Organization Affairs provides guidance and support for U.S. participation in international organizations and conferences and formulates and implements U.S. policy toward international organizations, with particular emphasis on those organizations which make up the United Nations system. It provides direction in the development, coordination, and implementation of U.S. multilateral policy. http://www.state.gov/p/io

For further information, contact the Bureau of International Organization Affairs. Phone, 202-647-9600. Fax, 202-736-4116.

International Security and Nonproliferation   The Bureau of International Security and Nonproliferation (ISN), is responsible for managing a broad range of nonproliferation, counterproliferation, and arms control functions. ISN leads U.S. efforts to prevent the spread of weapons of mass destruction (nuclear, radiological, chemical, and biological weapons) related materials, and their delivery systems. It is responsible for spearheading efforts to promote international consensus on weapons of mass destruction proliferation through bilateral and multilateral diplomacy; addressing weapons of mass destruction proliferation threats posed by nonstate actors and terrorist groups by improving physical security, using interdiction and sanctions, and actively participating in the Proliferation Security Initiative; coordinating the implementation of key international treaties and arrangements, working to make them relevant to today's security challenges; working closely with the U.N., the G–8, NATO, the Organization for the Prohibition of Chemical Weapons, the International Atomic Energy Agency, and other international institutions and organizations to reduce and eliminate the threat posed by weapons of mass destruction; and supporting efforts of foreign partners to prevent, protect against, and respond to the threat or use of weapons of mass destruction by terrorists. http://www.state.gov/t/isn

For further information, contact the Bureau of International Security and Nonproliferation. Phone, 202-647-9868. Fax, 202-736-4863.

Legal Adviser   The Office of the Legal Adviser advises the Secretary of State and other Department officials on all domestic and international legal matters relating to the Department of State, Foreign Service, and diplomatic and consular posts abroad. The Office's lawyers draft, negotiate, and interpret treaties, international agreements, domestic statutes, departmental regulations, Executive orders, and other legal documents; provide guidance on international and domestic law; represent the United States in international organization, negotiation, and treaty commission meetings; work on domestic and foreign litigation affecting the Department's interests; and represent the United States before international tribunals, including the International Court of Justice. http://www.state.gov/s/l

For further information, contact the Office of the Legal Adviser. Phone, 202-647-9598.

Legislative Affairs   The Bureau of Legislative Affairs coordinates legislative activity for the Department of State and advises the Secretary, the Deputy, as well as the Under Secretaries and Assistant Secretaries on legislative strategy. The Bureau facilitates effective communication between State Department officials and the Members of Congress and their staffs. Legislative Affairs works closely with the authorizing, appropriations, and oversight committees of the House and Senate, as well as with individual Members that have an interest in State Department or foreign policy issues. The Bureau also manages Department testimony before House and Senate hearings, organizes Member and staff briefings, facilitates congressional travel to overseas posts for Members and staff throughout the year, reviews proposed legislation, and coordinates Statements of Administration Policy on legislation affecting the conduct of U.S. foreign policy. The Legislative Affairs staff advises individual Bureaus of the Department on legislative and outreach strategies and coordinates those strategies with the Secretary's priorities. https://www.state.gov/bureaus-offices/bureaus-and-offices-reporting-directly-to-the-secretary/bureau-of-legislative-affairs

For further information, contact the Bureau of Legislative Affairs. Phone, 202-647-1714.

Medical Services   The Office of Medical Services (MED) develops, manages, and staffs a worldwide primary health care system for U.S. Government employees and their eligible dependents residing overseas. In support of its overseas operations, MED approves and monitors the medical evacuation of patients, conducts pre-employment and in-service physical clearance examinations, and provides clinical referral and advisory services. MED also provides for emergency medical response in the event of a crisis at an overseas post. https://www.state.gov/bureaus-offices/under-secretary-for-management/bureau-of-medical-services

For further information, contact the Office of Medical Services. Phone, 202-663-1649. Fax, 202-663-1613.

Oceans and International Environmental and Scientific Affairs   The Bureau of Oceans and International Environmental and Scientific Affairs (OES) serves as the foreign policy focal point for International oceans, as well as environmental and scientific efforts. OES projects, protects, and promotes U.S. global interests in these areas by articulating U.S. foreign policy, encouraging international cooperation, and negotiating treaties and other instruments of international law. The Bureau serves as the principal adviser to the Secretary of State on international environment, science, and technology matters and takes the lead in coordinating and brokering diverse interests in the interagency process, where the development of international policies or the negotiation and implementation of relevant international agreements are concerned. The Bureau seeks to promote the peaceful exploitation of outer space, develop and coordinate policy on international health issues, encourage government-to-government scientific cooperation, and prevent the destruction and degradation of the planet's natural resources and the global environment. http://www.state.gov/e/oes

For further information, contact the Bureau of Oceans and International Environmental and Scientific Affairs. Phone, 202-647-3004.

Overseas Buildings Operations   The Bureau of Overseas Buildings Operations (OBO) directs the worldwide overseas buildings program for the Department of State and the U.S. Government community serving abroad under the authority of the chiefs of mission. Along with the input and support of other State Department bureaus, foreign affairs agencies, and Congress, OBO sets worldwide priorities for the design, construction, acquisition, maintenance, use, and sale of real properties and the use of sales proceeds. OBO also serves as the Single Real Property Manager of all overseas facilities under the authority of the chiefs of mission. http://overseasbuildings.state.gov

For further information, contact the Bureau of Overseas Buildings Operations. Phone, 703-875-4131. Fax, 703-875-5043.

Political-Military Affairs   The Bureau of Political-Military Affairs is the principal link between the Departments of State and Defense and is the Department of State's lead on operational military matters. The Bureau provides policy direction in the areas of international security, security assistance, military operations, defense strategy and policy, counterpiracy measures, and defense trade. Its responsibilities include coordinating the U.S. Government's response to piracy in the waters off the Horn of Africa, securing base access to support the deployment of U.S. military forces overseas, negotiating status of forces agreements, coordinating participation in coalition combat and stabilization forces, regulating arms transfers, directing military assistance to U.S. allies, combating illegal trafficking in small arms and light weapons, facilitating the education and training of international peacekeepers and foreign military personnel, managing humanitarian mine action programs, and assisting other countries in reducing the availability of man-portable air defense systems. http://www.state.gov/t/pm

For further information, contact the Bureau of Political-Military Affairs. Phone, 202-647-9022. Fax, 202-736-4413.

Population, Refugees, and Migration   The Bureau of Population, Refugees, and Migration directs the Department's population, refugee, and migration policy development. It administers U.S. contributions to international organizations and nongovernmental organizations for humanitarian assistance- and protection-related programs on behalf of refugees, conflict victims, and internally displaced persons. The Bureau oversees the annual admissions of refugees to the United States for permanent resettlement, working closely with the Department of Homeland Security, the Department of Health and Human Services, and various State and private voluntary agencies. It coordinates U.S. international population policy and promotes its goals through bilateral and multilateral cooperation. It works closely with the U.S. Agency for International Development, which administers U.S. international population programs. The Bureau also coordinates the Department's international migration policy through bilateral and multilateral diplomacy. The Bureau oversees efforts to encourage greater participation in humanitarian assistance and refugee resettlement on the part of foreign governments and uses humanitarian diplomacy to increase access and assistance to those in need in the absence of political solutions. https://www.state.gov/bureaus-offices/under-secretary-for-civilian-security-democracy-and-human-rights/bureau-of-population-refugees-and-migration

For further information, contact the Bureau of Population, Refugees, and Migration. Phone, 202-453-9339. Fax, 202-453-9394.

Protocol   The Chief of Protocol is the principal adviser to the U.S. Government, the President, the Vice President, and the Secretary of State on matters of diplomatic procedure governed by law or international custom and practice. The Office is responsible for arranging visits of foreign chiefs of state, heads of government, and other high officials to the United States; organizing credential presentations of newly arrived Ambassadors, as presented to the President and to the Secretary of State; operating the President's guest house, Blair House; organizing delegations representing the President at official ceremonies abroad; conducting official ceremonial functions and public events; interpreting the official order of precedence; conducting outreach programs of cultural enrichment and substantive briefings of the Diplomatic Corps; accrediting of over 118,000 embassy, consular, international organization, and other foreign government personnel, members of their families, and domestics throughout the United States; determining entitlement to diplomatic or consular immunity; publishing of diplomatic and consular lists; resolving problems arising out of diplomatic or consular immunity, such as legal and police matters; and approving the opening of embassy and consular offices in conjunction with the Office of Foreign Missions. http://www.state.gov/s/cpr

For further information, contact the Office of the Chief of Protocol. Phone, 202-647-1735. Fax, 202-647-1560.

Public Affairs   The Bureau of Public Affairs (PA) supports U.S. foreign policy goals and objectives, advances national interests, and enhances National security by informing and influencing domestic and global public opinion about American interaction with the rest of the world. In addition, PA works to help Americans understand the importance of foreign affairs by conducting press briefings for the domestic and foreign press, pursuing media outreach by other means, arranging townhall meetings and community speakers, and preparing historical studies on U.S. diplomacy and foreign affairs matters. http://www.state.gov/r/pa

For further information, contact the Bureau of Public Affairs. Phone, 202-647-6575.

Sources of Information

Air Quality Worldwide   AirNow–Department of State collects air quality monitoring data globally from U.S. embassies and consulates. https://airnow.gov/index.cfm?action=airnow.global_summary

Archived Records   The records of the Department are referenced in the "Guide to Federal Records in the National Archives of the United States." The Guide is accessible online, and its records belong to Record Group 059. https://www.archives.gov/research/guide-fed-records/groups/059.html

Art in Embassies (AIE)   The Department's AIE program stimulates cross-cultural dialogue and mutual understanding through the visual arts and artist exchanges. The program develops and presents approximately 60 exhibitions per year and has installed over 70 permanent art collections in the Department's diplomatic facilities in over 200 venues in 189 countries. https://art.state.gov

Blog   "DipNote," the Department of State's official blog, offers first-person perspectives from U.S. Government employees who are working to shape and sustain a peaceful, prosperous, just, and democratic world and to foster stability and progress for people of every nation. https://blogs.state.gov

Business Opportunities   Direct Line allows U.S. businessmen and women to hear directly from U.S. Ambassadors and economic and commercial experts at Embassies and consulates in over 190 countries. Direct line can help U.S. businessmen and women identify promising market sectors and U.S. exporters capitalize on new opportunities. https://www.state.gov/direct-line-for-american-business

The Office of Small and Disadvantaged Business Utilization works with industry partners, the acquisition corps, and program offices to increase prime and subcontracting opportunities for U.S. small businesses. Phone, 703-875-6822. http://www.state.gov/s/dmr/sdbu/index.htm

Career Opportunities   To learn about joining the Civil Service, becoming a Foreign Service Specialist, the Consular Fellows Program, and other opportunities, visit the "Job Seekers" web page. Information of interest to students, recent graduates, veterans, and persons with disabilities is also accessible online. State Department personnel are available to answer questions on Federal workdays, 8:30 a.m.–4:30 p.m., eastern standard time. Phone, 202 663-2176. https://www.state.gov/job-seekers

In 2018, the Department of State ranked 14th among 17 large agencies in the Partnership for Public Service's Best Places To Work Agency Rankings. http://bestplacestowork.org/BPTW/rankings/detail/ST00

Climate Change   The Office of Global Change implements and manages U.S. international policy on climate change. It also represents the United States in negotiations under the United Nations Framework Convention on Climate Change and in other international fora that focus on the topic, including the International Civil Aviation Organization and the International Maritime Organization. https://www.state.gov/bureaus-offices/under-secretary-for-economic-growth-energy-and-the-environment/bureau-of-oceans-and-international-environmental-and-scientific-affairs/office-of-global-change

Diplomatic and Official Passports   Those inquiring about these types of passports should contact their respective travel offices. The U.S. Government only issues these types of passports to individuals traveling abroad in connection with official employment. Additional information is available on the Bureau of Consular Affairs website. http://travel.state.gov

DIPLOMATS@work   This experience provides insight into the distinct responsibilities of Foreign Service Officers in each of the five career tracks during a crisis situation in Vendurasaca, a fictitious country designed to represent an overseas location in which a U.S. embassy or consulate is located. https://careers.state.gov/daw/diplomats-at-work

Embassies   Contact information for U.S. Embassies, consulates, and diplomatic missions worldwide is available online. https://www.usembassy.gov

Emergencies Abroad   The Bureau of Consular Affairs posts information for emergency travel-related situations abroad. https://travel.state.gov/content/travel/en/international-travel/emergencies.html

Foreign Affairs Manual (FAM) / Foreign Affairs Handbooks (FAHs)   The (FAM) and (FAHs) are a single, comprehensive, and authoritative source for the Department's organization structures, policies, and procedures that govern the operations of the State Department, the Foreign Service, and, when applicable, other Federal agencies. The FAM, which centers on policy, and the FAHs, which center on procedures, convey codified information to Department staff and contractors, enabling them to carry out their responsibilities in accordance with statutory, executive, and Department mandates. https://fam.state.gov

Freedom of Information Act (FOIA)   To request records, write to the Director, Office of Information Programs and Services, A/GIS/IPS/RL, Department of State, SA–2, Washington, DC 20522-8100. For more information, contact the FOIA Requester Service Center. Phone, 202-261-8484. https://foia.state.gov/Default.aspx

The Department of State maintains an online reading room that contains over 220,000 documents. Before submitting a FOIA request, search the reading room to see if the desired document is accessible immediately and free of charge. https://foia.state.gov/Search/Search.aspx

Frequently Asked Questions (FAQs)   The Department of State posts answers to FAQs. https://careers.state.gov/faqs

The Office of the Historian posts answers to FAQs on its website. https://history.state.gov/about/faq

Geographic Bureaus   The geographic bureaus, which include the Bureaus of African, East Asian and Pacific, European and Eurasian, Near Eastern, South and Central Asian, and Western Hemisphere Affairs handle foreign affairs activities worldwide. https://www.state.gov/bureaus-offices/under-secretary-for-political-affairs

History   The Office of the Historian maintains an online guide to the United States' history of recognition, diplomatic, and consular relations by country. The database begins with the year 1776. https://history.state.gov/countries | Email: history@state.gov

The Office of the Historian also maintains an online index to diplomatic archives worldwide. https://history.state.gov/countries/archives | Email: history@state.gov

International Adoptions   For information on adoption of foreign children by private U.S. citizens, contact the Office of Children's Issues, Bureau of Consular Affairs, Department of State, SA–29, 2201 C Street NW., Washington, DC 20520-4818. Phone, 888-407-4747 or 202-501-4444 (international). http://travel.state.gov/content/adoptionsabroad/en.html

Open Government   The Department of State supports the Open Government initiative by promoting collaboration, participation, and transparency. https://www.state.gov/open-government-initiative

Passports Information on the application process for a new passport and on the renewal process for an expiring passport is available online. Lost or stolen passports may be reported online. Phone, 877-487-2778. TDD/TTY, 888-874-7793. https://travel.state.gov/content/travel/en/passports.html | Email: NPIC@state.gov

Press Releases The Office of the Spokesperson releases factsheets, media notes, notices to the press, and statements on a daily basis. https://www.state.gov/press-releases

Programs by State State Department programs affect American communities. The "Department of State by State" web pages describe some of the effects by offering State-by-State statistics. https://www.state.gov/department-of-state-by-state

Publications The Bureau of Human Resources publishes "State Magazine" monthly, except bimonthly in July and August. The magazine has an informative character and should not be regarded as authority for official action. Views and opinions expressed in "State Magazine" are not necessarily those of the Department of State. https://statemag.state.gov | Email: statemagazine@state.gov

The Sources of Information were updated 9–2019.

Social Media The "Press" web page presents links to the Department's social media accounts under the "Follow Us" section heading. Using the "Press" web page, a visitor can access easily the official blog "Dipnote," Facebook, Flickr, Google+, Instagram, Tumblr, Twitter, YouTube, and a form for subscribing to email updates. https://www.state.gov/press

Telephone Directory The Department's telephone directory can be accessed online. https://www.state.gov/telephone-directory

Tips for U.S. Travelers Information for Americans traveling abroad—including a traveler's checklist and tips on destinations, personal safety, health, and other topics—is available online from the Bureau of Consular Affairs. http://travel.state.gov/content/passports/english/go.html

Travel Advisories and Alerts The Bureau of Consular Affairs website posts travel advisories, alerts, and other information to help Americans travel safely abroad. http://travel.state.gov/content/passports/en/alertswarnings.html

Visas For information on visas for foreigners wishing to enter the United States, visit the Bureau of Consular Affairs online or call 603-334-0700. http://nvc.state.gov

DEPARTMENT OF TRANSPORTATION

1200 New Jersey Avenue SE., Washington, DC 20590
Phone, 202-366-4000. Internet, http://www.dot.gov

Secretary of Transportation	ELAINE L. CHAO
Deputy Secretary	JEFFREY ROSEN
Chief of Staff	GEOFF BURR
Director of Executive Secretariat	RUTH DRINKARD KNOUSE
Director of Operations	J. TODD INMAN
https://www.transportation.gov/key-officials	

Office Heads

Under Secretary	
Policy	DEREK KAN
Assistant Secretaries	
Aviation and International Affairs	(VACANCY)
Transportation Policy	(VACANCY)
https://www.transportation.gov/policy/key-officials	
Assistant Secretaries	
Governmental Affairs	(VACANCY)
Research and Technology	(VACANCY)
Chiefs	
Administrative Law Judge	RONNIE A. YODER
Information Officer	VICTORIA HILDEBRAND
Legal Officer / General Counsel	STEVEN G. BRADBURY
Deputy Assistant Secretaries	
Administration	KEITH WASHINGTON
Budget and Programs	LANA T. HURDLE
Directors	
Departmental Office of Civil Rights	CHARLES E. JAMES, SR.
Drug and Alcohol Policy and Compliance	PATRICE M. KELLY
Intelligence, Security and Emergency Response	MICHAEL W. LOWDER
Public Affairs	MARIANNE MCINERNEY
Small and Disadvantaged Business Utilization	WILLIS A. MORRIS
https://www.transportation.gov/office-of-secretary	
Inspector General	CALVIN L. SCOVEL III
https://www.oig.dot.gov	

[For the Department of Transportation statement of organization, see the Code of Federal Regulations, Title 49, Part 1, Subpart A]

The above list of key personnel was updated 02–2018.

The Department of Transportation establishes national transportation policy for highway planning and construction, motor carrier safety, urban mass transit, railroads, aviation, and the safety of waterways, ports, highways, and pipelines.

300

DEPARTMENT OF TRANSPORTATION

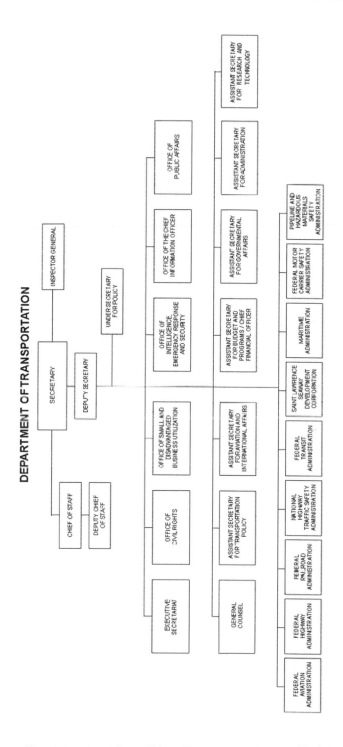

The Department of Transportation (DOT) was established by act of October 15, 1966, as amended (49 U.S.C. 102 and 102 note), "to assure the coordinated, effective administration of the transportation programs of the Federal Government" and to develop "national transportation policies and programs conducive to the provision of fast, safe, efficient, and convenient transportation at the lowest cost consistent therewith." It became operational in April 1967 and comprised elements transferred from eight other major departments and agencies.

Secretary   The Secretary of Transportation, who serves as the principal adviser to the President in all Federal transportation program matters, administers the DOT. https://www.transportation.gov/office-of-secretary

Under Secretary   The Under Secretary for Policy serves as a principal policy adviser to the Secretary and provides leadership in policy development for the DOT. https://www.transportation.gov/policy

Aviation and International Affairs

The Office of the Assistant Secretary for Aviation and International Affairs develops, reviews, and coordinates policy for international transportation and develops, coordinates, and implements policy on economic regulation of the airline industry. The Office licenses U.S. and foreign carriers to serve in international air transportation and conducts carrier fitness determinations for carriers serving the United States. The Office participates in negotiations with foreign governments to develop multilateral and bilateral aviation and maritime policies on international transportation and trade and to coordinate cooperative agreements for the exchange of scientific and technical information. The Office also resolves complaints of unfair competitive practices in domestic and international air transportation, establishes international and intra-Alaska mail rates, determines the disposition of requests for approval and immunization from the antitrust laws of international aviation agreements, and administers the essential air service program. https://www.transportation.gov/policy/assistant-secretary-aviation-international-affairs

For further information, contact the Office of the Assistant Secretary for Aviation and International Affairs. Phone, 202-366-8822.

Drug and Alcohol Policy and Compliance

The Office of Drug and Alcohol Policy and Compliance ensures that the Secretary's national and international drug and alcohol policies and goals are developed and implemented in a consistent, efficient, and effective manner within the transportation industry. Experts from the Office advise, counsel, and give recommendations on drugs and alcohol, as they pertain to the DOT and testing within the industry, to the Secretary. https://www.transportation.gov/odapc

For further information, contact the Office of Drug and Alcohol Policy and Compliance. Phone, 202-366-3784.

Intelligence, Security and Emergency Response

The Office of Intelligence, Security and Emergency Response ensures development, coordination, and execution of plans and procedures for the DOT to balance transportation security requirements with safety, mobility, and the Nation's economic needs. The Office monitors the Nation's transportation network on a continuous basis; advises the Secretary on incidents affecting transportation systems; leads on issues of national preparedness, response, and transportation security; briefs the Secretary on transportation-related intelligence; performs the DOT's National Response Framework Emergency Support Function responsibilities; coordinates departmental participation in emergency preparedness and response exercises under the National Training and Exercise Program; administers the DOT's Continuity of Government and Continuity of Operations programs; and serves as the DOT representative for emergency planning for civil aviation support to NATO and other allies. https://www.transportation.gov/mission/administrations/intelligence-security-emergency-response

For further information, contact the Office of Intelligence, Security and Emergency Response. Phone, 202-366-6525.

Transportation Policy

The Office of the Assistant Secretary for Transportation Policy analyzes, develops, articulates, and reviews policies and plans for all transportation modes. It also develops, coordinates, and evaluates public policy on safety, energy, and environmental initiatives that affect air, surface, marine, and pipeline transportation. It maintains policy and economic oversight of DOT regulatory programs and legislative initiatives. The Office also analyzes the economic and institutional implications of current and emerging transportation policy issues, transportation infrastructure finances, and new transportation technologies. https://www.transportation.gov/policy/assistant-secretary-transportation-policy

For further information, contact the Office of Transportation Policy. Phone, 202-366-8979.

Research and Technology

The Office of the Assistant Secretary for Research and Technology (OST–R) was created by title I, division L, of the Department of Transportation Appropriations Act, 2014 (49 USC 112 note), which transferred the authorities, functions, personnel, and powers and duties of the former Research and Innovative Technology Administration to the OST–R. The Office coordinates, facilitates, and reviews DOT research and development programs and activities; performs transportation statistics research, analysis, and reporting; and promotes innovative technologies for improving transportation systems. The OST–R is composed of the staff from the Bureau of Transportation Statistics, the Volpe National Transportation Systems Center, the Transportation Safety Institute, and the Office of Research, Development, and Technology. http://www.rita.dot.gov/about_rita

Sources of Information

Administrations The "Our Administrations" Web page provides convenient Internet access to the home pages of the DOT's administrations. https://www.transportation.gov/administrations

Aviation Consumer Protection For information on air travelers' rights or for assistance in resolving consumer problems with providers of commercial air transportation services, contact the Consumer Affairs Division. Phone, 202-366-2220. https://www.transportation.gov/airconsumer

The Office of Aviation Enforcement and Proceedings produces the "Air Travel Consumer Report" each month. The report makes information on the quality of airline services accessible to consumers. Issues of the consumer report are posted on the DOT's Web site in Portable Document Format (PDF). Phone, 202-366-2220. TTY, 202-366-0511. https://www.transportation.gov/airconsumer/air-travel-consumer-reports

Blog "Fast Lane" is the DOT's official blog. https://www.transportation.gov/blog/fastlane

Business Opportunities Contact the Office of the Senior Procurement Executive. Phone, 202-366-4263. Information is also available on the "Small Business" Web page. https://www.transportation.gov/osdbu

Career Opportunities The DOT employs administrators and managers, air traffic controllers, aviation safety specialists, clerical staff, electronics maintenance technicians, and engineers—aeronautical, automotive, civil, electrical, highway, and general. For further information, contact the Office of the Secretary–Human Resource Operations, 1200 New Jersey Avenue SE., Room W75–340, Washington, DC 20590. Phone, 202-366-9391 or 800-525-2878. https://www.transportation.gov/careers

In 2017, the DOT ranked 4th among 18 large agencies in the Partnership for Public Service's Best Places To Work Agency Rankings. http://bestplacestowork.org/BPTW/rankings/detail/TD00

In 2017, the Office of the Inspector General ranked 7th among 339 agency subcomponents in the Partnership for Public Service's Best Places To Work Agency Rankings. http://bestplacestowork.org/BPTW/rankings/detail/TD12

Civil Rights For information on equal employment opportunity, nondiscrimination in DOT employment and transportation services, or the Department's disadvantaged business enterprise certification appeals program, contact the Director, Departmental Office of Civil Rights. Phone, 202-366-4648. https://www.civilrights.dot.gov

Freedom of Information Act (FOIA) The FOIA gives information seekers the right to access DOT records, unless the Department determines that releasing the information would harm an interest protected by one or more of the nine FOIA exemptions or that releasing the information would violate the law. After receiving a properly submitted FOIA request, the DOT must provide the requester with copies of the relevant documents and records, or portions of them, that he or she is entitled to access under the law. https://www.transportation.gov/foia

Motor Vehicle Safety   To report vehicle safety problems, get motor vehicle and highway safety information, or request consumer information publications, visit the National Highway Traffic Safety Administration's SafeCar.gov Web site or call its vehicle safety hotline. Phone, 888-327-4236. TTY, 800-424-9153. Complaints also can be filed online. http://www.safercar.gov

News   The DOT posts press releases on its Web site. https://www.transportation.gov/press-releases

Office of Inspector General (OIG)   To report abuse, fraud, or waste, contact the DOT Inspector General, 1200 New Jersey Avenue SE., West Building–7th floor, Washington, DC 20590. Phone, 800-424-9071. https://www.oig.dot.gov/Hotline | Email: hotline@oig.dot.gov

Open Government   The DOT supports the Open Government initiative by promoting the principles of collaboration, participation, and transparency. https://www.transportation.gov/mission/open/open-government

Organizational Chart   The DOT's organizational chart is accessible online. https://www.transportation.gov/sites/dot.gov/files/DOT-Org-Chart-2017_.png

Plain Language   The DOT seeks to comply with the Plain Writing Act of 2010. If a DOT document or Web page is difficult to understand, please contact the Department via email and point out the lack of clarity. https://www.transportation.gov/open/plain-language | Email: PlainLanguage@dot.gov

Policy Initiatives   The DOT posts current policy initiatives on its Web site. https://www.transportation.gov/policy-initiatives

Publications   The DOT and its operating agencies issue publications on a variety of subjects. Some of these publications are available from the issuing administration or from the Government Publishing Office. http://www.gpo.gov/customers/p-i-sales.htm

Other publications are available from the National Technical Information Service, 5285 Port Royal Road, Springfield, VA 22151. https://www.ntis.gov/index.html

Reading Rooms   Contact the Public Docket, Room W12–140, 1200 New Jersey Avenue SE., Washington, DC 20590. Phone, 800-647-5527. DOT administrations and their regional offices maintain reading rooms for public use. Contact the appropriate administration by using the address or phone number indicated in its entry below. Other reading rooms are located at the Technical and Law Libraries: Technical Library, Room 2200, 1200 New Jersey Avenue SE., Washington, DC 20590. Phone, 202-366-0745. Law Library, Room W12–300, 1200 New Jersey Avenue SE., Washington, DC 20590. Phone, 202-366-0746. http://ntl.bts.gov/about_ntl.html | Email: library@dot.gov

Social Media   The DOT has a YouTube channel and maintains Facebook, Flickr, Instagram, LinkedIn, and Twitter accounts. https://www.transportation.gov/social; https://www.transportation.gov/briefingroom/administration-news

For further information, contact the Department of Transportation, Office of Public Affairs, 1200 New Jersey Avenue SE., Washington, DC 20590. Phone, 202-366-5580.

Federal Aviation Administration

800 Independence Avenue SW., Washington, DC 20591
Phone, 202-366-4000. Fax, 866-835-5322. Internet, http://www.faa.gov

Administrator	Daniel K. Elwell, Acting
Deputy Administrator	Carl E. Burleson, Acting
Chief of Staff	Tina Amereihn, Acting
https://www.faa.gov/about/key_officials	

The above list of key personnel was updated 02–2018.

The Federal Aviation Administration (FAA), formerly the Federal Aviation Agency, was established by the Federal Aviation Act of 1958 (72 Stat. 731). The Administration became a component of the Department of Transportation in 1967, pursuant to the Department of Transportation Act (49 U.S.C. 106). The FAA regulates civil aviation and U.S. commercial space transportation, maintains and operates air traffic control and navigation systems for civil and military aircraft, and develops and administers programs involving aviation safety and the National Airspace System.

Activities

Air Navigation Facilities   The FAA locates and positions, constructs or installs, maintains, operates, and assures the quality of Federal air navigation electronic and visual aids. At flight service stations, airport traffic control towers, and air route traffic control centers, the Administration operates and maintains computer systems, radar facilities, and voice-data communications and visual display equipment. http://www.faa.gov/about/safety_efficiency

Airport Programs   The Administration maintains a national plan of airport requirements, administers a grant program for development of public-use airports to assure and improve safety and to meet current and future airport capacity needs, evaluates the environmental effects of airport development, and administers an airport noise compatibility program. It also develops standards for and technical guidance on airport planning, design, operations, and safety and provides grants to assist public agencies in airport system and master planning and airport development and improvement. http://www.faa.gov/airports

Airspace and Air Traffic Management   FAA activities center on the safe and efficient utilization of the navigable airspace. To achieve this goal, the Administration operates a network of airport traffic control towers, air route traffic control centers, and flight service stations. It develops air traffic rules and regulations and allocates airspace use. It also provides air traffic security control that meets national defense requirements. http://www.faa.gov/air_traffic

Civil Aviation Abroad   Under the Federal Aviation Act of 1958 and the International Aviation Facilities Act (49 U.S.C. app. 1151), the FAA promotes aviation safety and supports civil aviation abroad. FAA experts exchange aeronautical information with foreign counterparts; certify foreign airmen, mechanics, and repair shops; provide technical aid and training; negotiate bilateral airworthiness agreements with other countries; and participate in international conferences. http://www.faa.gov/about/safety_efficiency

Commercial Space Transportation   The Administration regulates and supports the U.S. commercial space transportation industry. It licenses commercial space launch facilities and private sector launches of space payloads on expendable vehicles. It also sets insurance requirements for the protection of persons and property and ensures that space transportation activities comply with U.S. domestic and foreign policy. http://www.faa.gov/about/office_org/headquarters_offices/ast/about

Registration   The Aircraft Registry establishes and maintains the record of every U.S. civil aircraft. Buyers seeking information on aircraft they want to acquire, banks that finance aircraft purchases, aviation historians, and law enforcement and security agencies rely on the registry. An aircraft record contains information on the aircraft's registered owner, its airworthiness, and on recorded aircraft security interests. http://www.faa.gov/licenses_certificates/aircraft_certification/aircraft_registry/about_aircraft_records

Research, Engineering, and Development   The research, engineering, and development activities of the FAA provide the systems, procedures, facilities, and devices needed for a safe and efficient air navigation and air traffic control system for civil aviation and air defense. The Administration also performs an aeromedical research function: It applies knowledge gained from its research program and the work of others to improve civil aviation safety and the safety, health, and efficiency of FAA employees. The Administration also supports the development and testing of aircraft and their parts. http://www.faa.gov/data_research/research

Safety Regulation   The FAA issues and enforces regulations and minimum standards affecting the manufacture, operation, and maintenance of aircraft. It also certifies airmen and airports that serve air carriers. http://www.faa.gov/about/safety_efficiency

Test and Evaluation   The FAA tests and evaluates specified items such as aviation systems, subsystems, equipment, devices, materials, concepts, or procedures at any phase in the cycle of their development from conception to acceptance, to implementation. At key decision points, it also carries out assigned independent testing.

Other Programs   The FAA administers the Aviation Insurance Program, which provides insurance products to cover U.S. domestic air transportation industry needs that are not adequately met by the commercial insurance market. The Administration develops specifications for the preparation of aeronautical charts. It also publishes current information on airways and airport service; issues technical publications for the improvement of in-flight safety, airport planning and design, and other aeronautical activities; and serves as the executive administration for the operation and maintenance of the DOT automated payroll and personnel systems. http://www.faa.gov/about/office_org/headquarters_offices/apl/aviation_insurance; http://www.faa.gov/air_traffic/flight_info/aeronav

Sources of Information

A–Z Index   The FAA Web site features an alphabetical index to help visitors browse its content or search for information. https://www.faa.gov/quick_reference

Aircraft Registry   The FAA maintains a registry that allows users to search aircraft registration information online. https://www.faa.gov/licenses_certificates/aircraft_certification/aircraft_registry

Airlines   The Air Traffic Control System Command Center Web site features a list of links for the Web sites of airlines. http://www.fly.faa.gov/FAQ/Airline_Links/airline_links.jsp

Airmen Certification   The FAA posts answers to frequently asked questions dealing with airmen certification on its Web site. https://www.faa.gov/licenses_certificates/airmen_certification/airmen_FAQ

Business Opportunities   Registration with the System for Award Management is required for doing business with the FAA. https://faaco.faa.gov

The FAA's small business development program supports the procurement of goods and services from qualified small businesses. http://www.sbo.faa.gov/Home.cfm

Career Opportunities   The FAA offers civil aviation career opportunities in air traffic control, acquisition, contracts, engineering, information technology, safety and security, and other fields. https://www.faa.gov/jobs/career_fields

In 2016, the FAA ranked 165th among 305 agency subcomponents in the Partnership for Public Service's Best Places To Work Agency Rankings. http://bestplacestowork.org/BPTW/rankings/detail/TD03

Contact the FAA   Information for finding the appropriate point of contact or reporting an issue to the FAA is available online. https://www.faa.gov/contact

Data / Research   The FAA conducts research on commercial and general aviation. It posts information on how the research is carried out, the resulting data and statistics, and grant data and funding information. https://www.faa.gov/data_research

Field and Regional Offices   Contact information for field and regional offices is available on the FAA Web site. https://www.faa.gov/about/office_org

Flight Delays   The FAA's Air Traffic Control System Command Center provides status information, which is not flight specific, for general airport conditions nationwide. http://www.fly.faa.gov/flyfaa/usmap.jsp

Email, personal digital assistants (PDAs), pagers, phones, and wireless devices can be used to monitor the real-time operating status of the Nation's largest airports and receive delay information from the FAA. https://www.fly.faa.gov/ais/jsp/ais.jsp

Freedom of Information Act (FOIA)   The FOIA gives anybody the right to access information from the Federal Government. The law requires agencies to disclose information that is requested, unless that information is protected from public disclosure. https://www.faa.gov/foia

FAA posts a lot of information on its Web site. Before making a formal FOIA request, first look through what is immediately available, particularly through the contents of the FAA's electronic FOIA library. The desired information already may be accessible. https://www.faa.gov/foia/electronic_reading_room

Frequently Asked Questions (FAQs) The FAA posts answers to FAQs on its Web site. https://faa.custhelp.com

Glossary The Air Traffic Control System Command Center maintains a glossary of air traffic control management acronyms and terms. http://www.fly.faa.gov/FAQ/Acronyms/acronyms.jsp

History The FAA's Web site features a timeline of aerospace history that starts on December 17, 1903, with Orville and Wilbur Wright's first self-propelled airplane flight. https://www.faa.gov/about/history/timeline

News The FAA posts factsheets, news items and updates, press releases, speeches, and testimony on its Web site. https://www.faa.gov/news

NextGen NextGen is a comprehensive suite of state-of-the-art technologies and procedures that enable aircraft to move more directly between two distant points. These technologies will help passengers reach their destinations on schedule and mitigate environmental damage by reducing fuel consumption. To learn more about NextGen and the improvements that it will bring to air travel in the United States, visit its Web site. https://www.faa.gov/nextgen

Social Media The FAA has accounts on Facebook, Flickr, Instagram, LinkedIn, and Twitter, as well as a channel on YouTube. https://www.faa.gov/news/stay_connected

Wildlife Strikes Aircraft and wildlife in the United States collide on occasion. Wildlife strikes almost always involve birds; however, the FAA also has received reports of alligator, bat, coyote, deer, skunk, and turtle strikes. The most frequently struck birds are gulls, but ducks and geese cause more damage per strike. The FAA's National Wildlife Strike Database contains the information needed for telling the full story of collisions involving aircraft and animals. http://wildlife.faa.gov

The wildlife strike reporting system helps the FAA collect the information used to build the National Wildlife Strike Database. An online form is available for submitting a strike report. http://wildlife.faa.gov/strikenew.aspx; https://www.faa.gov/about/office_org/headquarters_offices/aoc/contact

For further information, contact the Federal Aviation Administration, Office of Communications, 800 Independence Avenue SW., Washington, DC 20591. Phone, 202-267-3883. Fax, 202-267-5039.

Federal Highway Administration

1200 New Jersey Avenue SE., Washington, DC 20590
Phone, 202-366-0650. Internet, http://www.fhwa.dot.gov

Administrator	BRANDYE L. HENDRICKSON, ACTING
Deputy Administrator	BRANDYE L. HENDRICKSON
Executive Director	WALTER C. WAIDELICH, JR.
https://fhwaapps.fhwa.dot.gov/foisp/hqphone.do	

The above list of key personnel was updated 02–2018.

The Federal Highway Administration (FHWA) was established as an agency of the Department of Transportation by the Department of Transportation Act (49 U.S.C. 104). Title 23 of the United States Code and other supporting legislation authorize the Administration's various activities.

The FHWA improves mobility on our Nation's highways through national leadership, innovation, and program delivery. The Administration works with Federal, State, and local agencies as well as with other stakeholders and partners to maintain and improve the National

Highway System, which includes the Interstate System and other roads of importance for national defense and mobility. The FHWA works to increase the National Highway System's safety and to minimize its traffic congestion. The FHWA ensures that America's roads and highways remain safe, technologically up-to-date, and environmentally friendly.

Through surface transportation programs, innovative and traditional financing mechanisms, and new types of pavement and operational technology, the FHWA helps people and goods move more efficiently throughout the Nation. The Administration also improves the efficiency of highway and road connections to other modes of transportation. The Federal-aid Highway Program's budget is primarily divided between Federal-aid funding and the Federal Lands Highway Program. http://www.fhwa. dot.gov/about

Activities

Federal-aid Highway Program The Federal-Aid Highway Program supports State highway systems, providing financial assistance for the construction, maintenance and operations of the Nation's 3.9 million-mile highway network, which includes the Interstate Highway System, primary highways, and secondary local roads. The FHWA implements the Federal-aid Highway Program in cooperation with State and local governments. http://www.fhwa.dot.gov/federal-aidessentials/federalaid.cfm

Federal Lands Highway Program The Office of Federal Lands Highway promotes effective, efficient, and reliable administration for a coordinated program of Federal public roads and bridges; protects and enhances the Nation's natural resources; and gives transportation access to Native Americans. The Office provides financial resources and engineering assistance for public roads that meet the transportation needs of Federal and Indian lands. These services are provided in all 50 States, Puerto Rico, U.S. Territories, and the District of Columbia through the Office's Headquarters and its eastern, central, and western Federal Lands Highway division offices. http://flh.fhwa.dot.gov/about

Sources of Information

All-American Roads / National Scenic Byways America's Byways—which include the National Scenic Byways and All-American Roads—is an umbrella term referring to the collection of 150 roads that the Secretary of Transportation selects for inclusion based on distinctiveness and diverseness. http://www.fhwa.dot.gov/byways

Business Opportunities FHWA programs generate a large number of contracting and procurement opportunities. http://www.fhwa.dot.gov/about/business.cfm

The Office of Acquisition and Grants Management manages most FHWA contracting opportunities. Phone, 202-366-4232. http://www.fhwa.dot.gov/aaa

Career Opportunities The FHWA operates offices throughout the country and hires professionals with expertise in a variety of fields to carry out its mission. http://www.fhwa.dot.gov/careers

The FHWA consistently ranks high among agency subcomponents in the Partnership for Public Service's Best Places To Work Agency Rankings. http://bestplacestowork.org/BPTW/rankings/detail/TD04

Core Topics The "Core Highway Topics" Web page features a topical, alphabetical list. The topics are categorized according to nine headings: environment, Federal and Indian lands, highway funding, international, research and technologies, road operations and congestion, roads and bridges, road users, and safety. http://www.fhwa.dot.gov/resources/topics

Environment The "Air Quality and Climate Change Highlights" newsletter is available on the FHWA Web site. https://www.fhwa.dot.gov/environment/sustainability/newsletter/index.cfm

Federal-Aid Essentials Federal-aid Essentials offers an online library of informational videos and resources for local public agencies. Each video addresses a single topic and condenses the complex regulations and requirements of the Federal-aid Highway Program into basic concepts and illustrated examples. http://www.fhwa.dot.gov/federal-aidessentials

Field and Division Offices The FHWA comprises a headquarters office in

Washington, DC; a Federal-aid division office in each State, Puerto Rico, and the District of Columbia; four metropolitan offices—Chicago, Los Angeles, New York City, Philadelphia—that serve as extensions of the corresponding Federal-aid division offices; and three Federal Lands Highway division offices. http://www.fhwa.dot.gov/about/field.cfm

Freedom of Information Act (FOIA)   The FOIA establishes a presumption that records in the possession of agencies and departments of the Federal Government's executive branch are available to the public. The statute sets standards for determining when Government records must be made available and which records may be withheld. It also gives information seekers specific legal rights and provides administrative and judicial remedies when access is denied. Most importantly, the FOIA requires that Federal agencies provide, to the fullest extent possible, access to and disclosure of information pertaining to the Government's business. http://www.fhwa.dot.gov/foia

The FHWA maintains an electronic FOIA reading room. It contains records that are often requested under the statute. http://www.fhwa.dot.gov/foia/err.cfm

Glossary   The FHWA Web site features a glossary of transportation planning terms and acronyms. https://www.fhwa.dot.gov/planning/glossary

History   The FHWA Web site features a general highway history. http://www.fhwa.dot.gov/infrastructure/history.cfm

Infrastructure   The FHWA's Web site offers a trove of information on the following infrastructure topics: asset management, bridges and structures, construction, design, Federal-aid Program administration, Federal-aid programs and special funding, geotechnical, hydraulics, pavement, preservation, and transportation performance management. http://www.fhwa.dot.gov/infrastructure

Libraries   The FHWA research library is located in the Turner-Fairbank Highway Research Center in McLean, VA. It is open on weekdays, excluding Federal holidays, 7:30–4 p.m. Phone, 202-493-3172. Fax, 202-493-3495. http://www.fhwa.dot.gov/research/library/ | Email: fhwalibrary@dot.gov

Each FHWA office maintains accessibility information that relates to its own program. The accessibility resource library supports the effort to organize information relating to the Americans with Disabilities Act and other accessibility resources that may affect FHWA projects. http://www.fhwa.dot.gov/accessibility

Newsroom   The FHWA posts press releases, as well as photos and videos, speeches and testimony, on its Web site and YouTube channel. http://www.fhwa.dot.gov/briefingroom

Resource Center / Technical Service Teams   The FHWA's technical service teams are organized into 12 activity areas: air quality, civil rights, construction and program management, environment and realty, finance services, geotechnical, hydraulics, operations, pavement and materials, planning, safety and design, and structures. Contact information for these teams and information on their activities, products, and services are available online in the Resource Center. http://www.fhwa.dot.gov/resourcecenter/index.cfm

Social Media   The FHWA tweets announcements and other newsworthy items on Twitter. https://twitter.com/USDOTFHWA

The FHWA maintains a page on Facebook. https://www.facebook.com/FederalHighwayAdmin

The FHWA posts videos on its YouTube channel. https://www.youtube.com/user/USDOTFHWA

Staff Directories   The headquarters organizational directory, key field personnel directory, and Washington headquarters fax numbers are available on the FHWA's Web site. http://www.fhwa.dot.gov/about/staff.cfm

Sustainability   The FHWA provides technical assistance to local, regional, and State transportation agencies to help them enhance sustainability, improve resilience, and reduce energy use and emissions on the Nation's highway system. https://www.fhwa.dot.gov/environment/sustainability/index.cfm; http://www.fhwa.dot.gov/contact

For further information, contact the Federal Highway Administration, Office of Public Affairs, 1200 New Jersey Avenue, SE., Washington, DC 20590. Phone, 202-366-0660.

Federal Motor Carrier Safety Administration

1200 New Jersey Avenue SE., Washington, DC 20590
Phone, 202-366-2519. Internet, http://www.fmcsa.dot.gov

Administrator	(VACANCY)
Deputy Administrator	CATHY F. GAUTREAUX
https://www.fmcsa.dot.gov/mission/leadership	

The above list of key personnel was updated 02–2018.

The Federal Motor Carrier Safety Administration (FMCSA) was established within the Department of Transportation on January 1, 2000, pursuant to the Motor Carrier Safety Improvement Act of 1999 (49 U.S.C. 113).

Formerly a part of the Federal Highway Administration, the FMCSA reduces commercial motor vehicle-related fatalities and injuries. Administration activities increase the safety of motor carrier operations by enforcing safety regulations—targeting high-risk commercial drivers and carriers; improving safety information systems and commercial motor vehicle technologies; strengthening equipment and operating standards; and increasing safety awareness. When carrying out these activities, the Administration works with representatives of the motor carrier industry, labor safety interest groups, and Federal, State, and local enforcement agencies. https://www.fmcsa.dot.gov/mission/about-us

Activities

Commercial Licensing   The FMCSA develops standards to test and license commercial motor vehicle drivers. https://www.fmcsa.dot.gov/registration/commercial-drivers-license

Data / Analysis   The FMCSA collects and disseminates data on motor carrier safety and directs resources to improve motor carrier safety. https://www.fmcsa.dot.gov/safety/data-and-statistics/motor-carrier-safety-progress-reports

Regulatory Compliance / Enforcement   The FMCSA operates a program to improve safety performance and remove high-risk carriers from the Nation's highways. https://www.fmcsa.dot.gov/regulations

Research / Technology   The FMCSA coordinates research and development to improve the safety of motor carrier operations and commercial motor vehicles and drivers. https://www.fmcsa.dot.gov/safety/research-and-analysis/active-research-projects

Safety Assistance   The FMCSA provides States with financial assistance for roadside inspections and other commercial motor vehicle safety programs. https://www.fmcsa.dot.gov/safety

Other Activities   The FMCSA supports the development of unified motor carrier safety requirements and procedures throughout North America. It participates in international technical organizations and committees to help share best-practices in motor carrier safety worldwide. It enforces regulations ensuring safe highway transportation of hazardous materials and maintains a task force to identify and investigate carriers of household goods that exhibit an unmistakable pattern of consumer abuse.

Sources of Information

Bicyclists / Pedestrians   Bicyclists and pedestrians share roads with large trucks and buses. The FMCSA Web site features resources promoting safety issues affecting riders, walkers, and drivers. https://www.fmcsa.dot.gov/safety/resources-bicyclists-and-pedestrians

Career Opportunities   The FMCSA posts job announcements on the USAJobs Web site. Application tips, information for students and recent graduates, and reasons for pursuing a career at the FMCSA are available on its Web site. Phone, 800-832-5660. https://www.fmcsa.dot.gov/careers

In 2016, the FMCSA ranked 69th among 305 agency subcomponents in the Partnership for Public Service's Best Places To Work Agency Rankings. http://bestplacestowork.org/BPTW/rankings/detail/TD17

Certified Medical Examiners Inclusion in the National Registry of Certified Medical Examiners is limited to medical professionals who complete training and pass an exam on the FMCSA's physical qualification standards. https://nationalregistry.fmcsa.dot.gov/NRPublicUI/home.seam

Commercial Carriers The FMCSA Web site features resources to help carrier companies with registration and safety and regulatory matters. https://www.fmcsa.dot.gov/resources-for-carrier-companies

The FMCSA Web site features resources—regulatory information and safety publications—to help passenger carriers comply with regulations and operate safely. https://www.fmcsa.dot.gov/safety/passenger-safety/safety-information-passenger-carriers

Commercial Drivers The FMCSA Web site features driver resources to promote safety and for registration and licensing. https://www.fmcsa.dot.gov/resources-for-drivers

Company Safety Records The FMCSA maintains Web sites that provide convenient access to safety-related information. To perform a search, a user must know a company's name, USDOT number, or motor carrier number. https://www.fmcsa.dot.gov/safety/company-safety-records

Data / Statistics The annual "Pocket Guide to Large Truck and Bus Statistics" highlights the FMCSA's role in collecting and analyzing data on large trucks and buses. The pocket guide is a compilation of statistics from the overall state of the industry to enforcement activity, details on traffic violations and other incidents, the costs of crashes, and more. https://www.fmcsa.dot.gov/safety/data-and-statistics/commercial-motor-vehicle-facts

The Analysis Division compiles the information used for "Large Truck and Bus Crash Facts," an annual report containing descriptive statistics on fatal, injurious, and property-damage-only crashes involving large trucks and buses. https://www.fmcsa.dot.gov/safety/data-and-statistics/large-truck-and-bus-crash-facts

Freedom of Information Act (FOIA) The FMCSA supports efforts to create a more open and transparent Federal Government, and it conscientiously carries out its FOIA responsibilities. The FMCSA ensures that nonexempt documents or records are accessible to anyone who properly files a FOIA request. Phone, 202-366-2960. Fax, 202-385-2335. https://www.fmcsa.dot.gov/foia | Email: foia@fmcsa.dot.gov

The FMCSA's electronic reading room contains frequently requested records, as well as final opinions and orders, policy statements, and staff manuals. https://www.fmcsa.dot.gov/foia/foia-electronic-reading-room

Frequently Asked Questions (FAQs) The FMCSA provides answers to FAQs on its Web site. https://www.fmcsa.dot.gov/faq

Grants State and local government agencies in the 50 States and the District of Columbia, as well as in American Samoa, Guam, Puerto Rico, and the Northern Mariana and the U.S. Virgin Islands may apply for safety grant funding. https://www.fmcsa.dot.gov/mission/grants

Look Before You Book The FMCSA Web site features resources to assist travel planners or those chartering buses for sport events, field trips, or other group activities. Safety tips and information, software applications (apps) to research bus operators, and information on reporting safety violations are available on the "Look Before You Book" Web pages. https://www.fmcsa.dot.gov/safety/look-you-book/look-you-book

Bus travel safety kits for seniors, students, and those traveling to faith-based events are available on "Look Before You Book." https://www.fmcsa.dot.gov/safety/look-you-book/consumer-safety-resources

Newsroom The FMCSA posts events, news releases, speeches, and testimony on its Web site. https://www.fmcsa.dot.gov/newsroom

Protect Your Move The "Protect Your Move" Web pages feature a trove of information on and resources for planning a move, selecting a mover, and filing a moving fraud complaint. https://www.fmcsa.dot.gov/protect-your-move

Safety Violations Safety, service, or discrimination issues involving a bus or truck or moving company or a cargo tank facility? If so, file a complaint on the National Consumer Complaint Database Web site or by phone on weekdays, 8 a.m.–8 p.m., eastern time. Phone, 888-368-7238. https://nccdb.fmcsa.dot.gov/nccdb/home.aspx

Service Centers / Field Offices   Contact information for service centers and field offices is available on the FMCSA Web site. Phone, 800-832-5660. https://www.fmcsa.dot.gov/mission/field-offices

Social Media   The FMCSA tweets announcements and other newsworthy items on Twitter. https://twitter.com/fmcsa

The FMCSA has a Facebook account. https://www.facebook.com/FMCSA

USDOT Numbers   The FMCSA Web site features an interactive tool that can determine whether or not a commercial vehicle requires a USDOT number. https://www.fmcsa.dot.gov/registration/do-i-need-usdot-number

Veterans   The FMCSA helps veterans find employment in the motor carrier industry. Several provisions in the Fixing America's Surface Transportation (FAST) Act support this effort. https://www.fmcsa.dot.gov/fastact/veteran-drivers; https://www.fmcsa.dot.gov/contact-us

For further information, contact the Federal Motor Carrier Safety Administration, 1200 New Jersey Avenue SE., Washington, DC 20590. Phone, 202-366-2519.

Federal Railroad Administration

1200 New Jersey Avenue, SE., West Building, Washington, DC 20590
Phone, 202-493-6014. Internet, http://www.fra.dot.gov

Administrator	(VACANCY)
Deputy Administrator	JUAN D. REYES III, ACTING
https://www.fra.dot.gov/Page/P1009	

The above list of key personnel was updated 02–2018.

The Federal Railroad Administration (FRA) was created pursuant to section 3(e)(1) of the Department of Transportation Act of 1966 (49 U.S.C. 103). The Administration promulgates and enforces rail safety regulations, administers railroad financial assistance programs, conducts research and development to improve railroad safety and national rail transportation policy, provides for the rehabilitation of Northeast Corridor rail passenger service, and consolidates Government support of rail transportation activities. https://www.fra.dot.gov/Page/P0002

Activities

Passenger and Freight Services   The FRA's passenger rail activities include administering Federal grants and loans to Amtrak, Alaska Railroad, and high-speed rail; supporting the Secretary of Transportation in his or her role as a member of Amtrak's board of directors; providing guidance and analysis of intercity passenger rail services and high-speed rail. Its freight rail activities include supporting current freight rail market share and growth and developing strategies to attract 50 percent of all shipments 500 miles or more to intermodal rail. The Administration's Office of Railroad Policy and Development implements programs that provide financial support, research and development, and analysis and guidance for the freight rail industry and its stakeholders. https://www.fra.dot.gov/Page/P0247; https://www.fra.dot.gov/Page/P0528

Railroad Safety   The Administration administers and enforces the Federal laws and regulations that promote railroad safety, and it exercises jurisdiction over all areas of rail safety under the Rail Safety Act of 1970—track maintenance, inspection standards, equipment standards, operating practices. Railroad and related industry equipment, facilities, and records are inspected and required reports are reviewed. The Administration also educates the public about safety at highway rail grade crossings and the danger of trespassing on rail property. https://www.fra.dot.gov/Page/P0010

Research and Development   The FRA's research and development program relies on basic and applied research and on the development of innovations and solutions to ensure the efficient, reliable, and safe movement of people and goods. Safety is the principal driver of the research and development program. https://www.fra.dot.gov/Page/P0019

Transportation Test Center   The Administration tests and evaluates conventional and advanced railroad systems and components at the Transportation Test Center, Inc. Private sector companies and the Governments of Canada, Japan, and the United States use the facility to study the operation of conventional and advanced systems under controlled conditions. Amtrak tests new high-speed locomotives and trains at the Center, and the Federal Transit Administration uses it for testing urban rapid transit vehicles. https://www.fra.dot.gov/Page/P0153; http://www.ttci.aar.com

Sources of Information

Business Opportunities   The FRA's Web site explains how to become eligible for doing business and how to identify business opportunities with the FRA. The Web site also features a database of small business vendors. https://www.fra.dot.gov/Page/P0009

Career Opportunities   The FRA relies heavily on railroad safety inspectors—hazardous materials, motive power and equipment, operating practices, signals and train control, and track inspectors—to carry out its mission. Safety inspectors inspect for compliance with Federal laws, regulations, rules, and standards; conduct accident investigations and report on their findings; and seek correction of unsafe conditions. They also testify as expert witnesses in civil suits. These jobs require skill in evaluation, factfinding, and report writing; comprehension and application of technical and regulatory standards; an ability to build rapport with individuals and organizations; and knowledge of methods used in installation, operation, and maintenance or manufacturing of railroad equipment and systems. https://www.fra.dot.gov/Page/P0008

In 2016, the FRA ranked 106th among 305 agency subcomponents in the Partnership for Public Service's Best Places To Work Agency Rankings. http://bestplacestowork.org/BPTW/rankings/detail/TD05

Electronic Library (E-library)   An e-library offers convenient access to all the documents that are found on the FRA's public Web site. https://www.fra.dot.gov/eLib/Find

Freedom of Information Act (FOIA)   Any person—U.S. citizens, foreign nationals, as well as those representing organizations, associations, and universities—can file a FOIA request. All FOIA requests must be submitted in writing and are processed in the Office of Chief Counsel at FRA headquarters in Washington, DC. https://www.fra.dot.gov/Page/P0386 | Email: FRAFOIA@dot.gov

To comply with the Electronic Freedom of Information Act (E–FOIA) Amendments of 1996, agencies must make some categories of records available to the public on an ongoing basis. https://www.fra.dot.gov/Page/P0388

Horn Noise   Noise from transportation systems, including rail operations, often produces adverse environmental effects. The FRA posts answers to frequently asked questions on horn noise. https://www.fra.dot.gov/Page/P0599

Maps   The FRA Web site features a Geographic Information System safety map. https://www.fra.dot.gov/Page/P0053

News   The FRA posts news items on its Web site. https://www.fra.dot.gov/Page/P0095

Railroad Crossings / Trespassing   FRA programs have helped to reduce the number of railroad crossing and trespassing fatalities by 60% over the last two decades. The Railroad Crossing Safety and Trespasser Prevention Division seeks to continue this trend. Information on and resources for railroad crossing safety and preventing trespassing along railroad rights-of-way are available online. https://www.fra.dot.gov/Page/P0841

Railroad Safety   The Office of Safety Analysis posts railroad safety information—data related to railroad accidents and incidents, including highway-rail grade crossing accidents, rail equipment accidents, and employee injuries and illnesses—on its Web site. http://safetydata.fra.dot.gov/OfficeofSafety/Default.aspx

The FRA monitors the occurrence of train accidents and incidents and investigates serious events to determine their cause and to assess compliance with safety laws and regulations. Detailed information on these investigations is available on the FRA's Web site. https://www.fra.dot.gov/Page/P0037

Regional Offices   A list of the Federal Railroad Administration's eight regional offices—California, Georgia, Illinois, Massachusetts, Missouri, Pennsylvania, Texas, and the District of Columbia —is available on the "Regional Offices" Web page. https://www.fra.dot.gov/Page/P0244

Research / Development   The Office of Research and Development is organized into four divisions and works in 10 program areas. An online table shows where the four divisions and 10 program areas intersect with the most frequent causes of railroad accidents and incidents. https://www.fra.dot.gov/Page/P0562

Social Media   The FRA posts photographs and tweets announcements and other newsworthy items on Twitter. https://twitter.com/USDOTFRA

The FRA has a Facebook page. https://www.facebook.com/USDOTFRA

The FRA posts videos on its YouTube channel. https://www.youtube.com/user/usdotfra; http://www.fra.dot.gov | Email: FRAPA@dot.gov

For further information, contact the Federal Railroad Administration, Office of Public Affairs, 1200 New Jersey Avenue SE., Washington, DC 20590. Phone, 202-493-6024. Fax, 202-493-6481.

Federal Transit Administration

1200 New Jersey Avenue SE., Washington, DC 20590
Phone, 202-366-4043. Internet, http://www.fta.dot.gov

Administrator	K. Jane Williams, Acting
Deputy Administrator	K. Jane Williams
Executive Director	Matthew J. Welbes
https://www.transit.dot.gov/about/officials/officials	

[For the Federal Transit Administration statement of organization, see the Code of Federal Regulations, Title 49, Part 601]

The above list of key personnel was updated 02–2018.

The Federal Transit Administration (FTA), formerly the Urban Mass Transportation Administration, was established as an operating administration of the U.S. Department of Transportation by section 1 of Reorganization Plan No. 2 of 1968 (5 U.S.C. app. 1), effective July 1, 1968. The FTA helps America's communities by developing improved public transportation and providing financial assistance to State and local governments to finance public transportation systems and carry out national transit goals and policy. https://www.transit.dot.gov/about-fta

Programs

Alternatives Analysis   The Alternatives Analysis program provides grants to help identify public transportation needs and the costs and benefits of various transportation strategies for a defined travel corridor. The results of these studies may be the selection of a locally preferred transportation alternative, which is the first step for developing viable projects for possible future funding under the New Starts and Small Starts program. http://www.fta.dot.gov/grants/13094_7395.html

For further information, call the Office of Program Management. Phone, 202-366-2053.

Capital Investment   The Capital Investment program helps finance the acquisition, construction, reconstruction, and improvement of facilities and equipment for public transportation service in urban areas. The Capital Investment program makes available three types of funds: fixed guideway modernization funds for rolling stock renewal, safety-related improvements, and signal and power modernization; new and small starts funds for construction of new fixed guideway systems or extensions to existing fixed guideway systems or corridor based rapid bus systems; and bus and bus facilities funds for the acquisition of buses and rolling stock, ancillary equipment, and the construction of bus facilities. http://www.fta.dot.gov/12304.html

For further information, call the Office of Program Management. Phone, 202-366-2053.

Clean Fuels Grants   The Clean Fuels Grants program helps nonattainment and maintenance areas achieve or maintain the National Ambient Air Quality Standards for ozone and carbon monoxide, and it supports emerging clean fuel and advanced propulsion technologies for transit buses and markets for those technologies. The program funds purchasing or leasing clean fuel buses, including buses that employ a lightweight composite primary structure and vans for use in revenue service; constructing or leasing clean fuel bus facilities, including electrical recharging facilities and related equipment; and projects involving clean fuel, biodiesel, hybrid electric, or zero emissions technology buses. http://www.fta.dot.gov/cleanfuels

For further information, call the Office of Program Management. Phone, 202-366-2053.

Elderly Persons and Persons With Disabilities   The Transportation for Elderly Persons and Persons With Disabilities program provides financial assistance to private nonprofit agencies for the transportation needs of elderly persons and persons with disabilities in places where public services are unavailable, insufficient, or inappropriate; to public bodies approved by the State to coordinate services for elderly persons or persons with disabilities; and to public bodies that certify to the Governor that no nonprofit corporation or association is readily available in an area to provide the service. Funds are allocated by formula to the States. Local organizations apply for funding through a designated State agency. http://www.fta.dot.gov/grants/13093_3556.html

For further information, call the Office of Program Management. Phone, 202-366-2053.

Job Access and Reverse Commuting   The Job Access and Reverse Commute program addresses the transportation challenges faced by welfare recipients and low-income persons seeking or maintaining employment. The program provides capital and planning and operating expenses for projects that transport low income individuals to and from jobs and employment-related activities and for projects that support reverse commuting. Many new entry level jobs are located in suburban areas: Low-income individuals have difficulty accessing these jobs from their inner city, urban, or rural neighborhoods. Many entry level-jobs also require working late or on weekends when conventional transit services are either reduced or nonexistent. Many employment related-trips also are complex, involving multiple destinations. http://www.fta.dot.gov/grants/13093_3550.html

For further information, call the Office of Program Management. Phone, 202-366-2053.

New Freedom   The New Freedom formula grants program supports new public transportation services that surpass the requirements of the Americans with Disabilities Act (ADA) of 1990. The program makes capital and operating funding available to private nonprofit organizations, State and local governmental authorities, and operators of public transportation services, including private operators of public transportation services. Eligible projects must benefit individuals with disabilities: Projects must assist them with transportation—including transportation to and from jobs and employment services—and remove barriers to transportation. http://www.fta.dot.gov/grants/13093_3549.html

For further information, call the Office of Program Management. Phone, 202-366-2053.

Nonurban Area Assistance   The Other Than Urbanized Areas formula grants program provides funding to States to support public transportation in rural areas—with populations under 50,000. The program enhances people's access in nonurbanized areas to health care, shopping, education, employment, public services, and recreation;

assists in the maintenance, development, improvement, and use of public transportation systems in nonurbanized areas; encourages and facilitates the most efficient use of all transportation funds used to provide passenger transportation in nonurbanized areas through the coordination of programs and services; helps develop and support intercity bus transportation; and promotes the participation of private transportation providers in nonurbanized transportation. http://www.fta.dot.gov/grants/13093_3555.html

For further information, call the Office of Program Management. Phone, 202-366-2053.

Planning   The Office of Planning and Environment supports the development of information that Federal, State, and local officials use to make transportation investment decisions. With FHWA partners, the Office co-administers a national planning program that provides funding, guidance, oversight, and technical support to State and local transportation agencies. The FTA's 10 region offices and FHWA's 52 division offices work to convey the program to State and local governments and other transportation agencies. http://www.fta.dot.gov/about/12347.html

For further information, call the Office of Planning and Environment. Phone, 202-366-4033.

Research and Technology   The FTA conducts research, development, demonstration, deployment, and evaluation projects to improve public transportation services. The FTA administers the Bus Testing, International Public Transportation, National Research and Technology, and Transit Cooperative Research Programs. Through the Transit Investments for Greenhouse Gas and Energy Reduction (TIGGER) program, the Administration works with public transportation agencies to implement new strategies for lowering greenhouse gas emissions and to reduce energy use within transit operations. The FTA has five priority research areas: bicycles and transit, bus rapid transit, environmental sustainability, livable and sustainable communities, and state of good repair. https://www.transit.dot.gov/about/research-innovation

For further information, call the Office of Research, Demonstration and Innovation. Phone, 202-366-4052.

Rural Transit Assistance   The Rural Transit Assistance Program provides a funding source to help design and implement training and technical assistance projects and other support services tailored to meet the needs of transit operators in nonurbanized areas. States, local governments, and providers of rural transit services can receive program funds. States may use the funds to support nonurbanized transit activities in four areas: training, technical assistance, research, and related support services. http://www.fta.dot.gov/grants/13093_3554.html

For further information, call the Office of Program Management. Phone, 202-366-2053.

Safety   The Office of Transit Safety and Oversight administers a national safety program and oversees compliance with it. Based on FTA legislative, policy, and regulatory requirements, the program helps further the nationwide provision of transit service that is equitable, reliable, and safe. http://www.fta.dot.gov/tso.html

For further information, call the Office of Transit Safety and Oversight. Phone, 202-366-1783.

Training and Technical Assistance   The Administration funds the National Transit Institute at Rutgers, The State University of New Jersey. Working with the Institute, the FTA develops and offers training courses on transit operations, planning, workforce performance, and productivity. Institute courses are offered at locations nationwide on a variety of subjects. Current course offerings are posted online. http://www.ntionline.com/courses/list.php

For further information, call the Office of Research, Demonstration and Innovation. Phone, 202-366-4052.

Transit in Parks   The Paul S. Sarbanes Transit in Parks Program provides funding for alternative transportation projects in and around National Parks and other Federal recreation areas. Alternative transportation includes bicycle, ferry, pedestrian trail, shuttle bus, and other forms of public or nonmotorized transportation. These projects reduce congestion, protect sensitive natural and cultural treasures, and enhance visitor experience. Funding is awarded through a competitive process to units of Federal land management agencies and to State, local and tribal government agencies. http://www.fta.dot.gov/transitinparks

For further information, call the Office of Program Management. Phone, 202-366-2053.

Sources of Information

Business Opportunities Procurement-related information and resources are available on the FTA Web site. https://www.transit.dot.gov/funding/procurement/procurement

Career Opportunities FTA fills vacancies in its Washington, DC, headquarters and regional offices. The FTA relies on attorneys, congressional relations specialists, engineers, environmental specialists, planners, program management specialists, research program specialists, and other professionals to carry out its mission. https://www.transit.dot.gov/about/jobs/jobs

In 2016, the FTA ranked 228th among 305 agency subcomponents in the Partnership for Public Service's Best Places To Work Agency Rankings. http://bestplacestowork.org/BPTW/rankings/detail/TD09

Environmental Justice The FTA posts answers to questions related to environmental justice on its Web site. https://www.transit.dot.gov/regulations-and-guidance/environmental-programs/environmental-justice/environmental-justice-faqs

Events The FTA has a calendar of events on its Web site. https://www.transit.dot.gov/about/events

Freedom of Information Act (FOIA) The FOIA grants public access to the content of certain records that are held by the offices, agencies, corporations, administrations, commissions, boards, and services of the Federal Government's executive branch. Some records that contain sensitive commercial, governmental, and personal information are protected from disclosure. https://www.transit.dot.gov/foia/foia-requests | Email: FTA.FOIA@dot.gov

The FTA maintains an electronic reading room. Before submitting a FOIA request, information seekers should search for the desired document or record in the reading room to determine whether it is accessible immediately, without charge. https://www.transit.dot.gov/foia/foia-electronic-reading-room

Glossary The FTA maintains a National Transit Database glossary on its Web site. https://www.transit.dot.gov/ntd/national-transit-database-ntd-glossary

Grants The FTA provides grants to local public transit systems. It invests billions of dollars each year to support and to expand public transit services. It provides annual formula grants to transit agencies nationwide, as well as discretionary funding in competitive processes. https://www.transit.dot.gov/funding/grants/grant-programs

History A brief history of mass transit is available on the FTA Web site. https://www.transit.dot.gov/about/brief-history-mass-transit

National Transit Database U.S. transit ridership has grown by more than 20 percent in the last decade. To keep track of the industry and provide public information and statistics as growth continues, the National Transit Database records the asset, financial, and operating conditions of transit systems. Phone, 888-252-0936. https://www.transit.dot.gov/ntd | Email: NTDhelp@dot.gov

News The FTA posts news releases on its Web site. https://www.transit.dot.gov/about/news

Regional Offices Contact information for the 10 regional offices is available on the FTA's Web site. https://www.transit.dot.gov/about/regional-offices/regional-offices

Research / Innovation Research projects assess new operational processes, expand public-private partnerships, fund demonstration grants for low or no emissions buses, improve traveler experiences, and test systems that monitor safety. Research and innovation reports and publications are available on the FTA Web site. https://www.transit.dot.gov/research-innovation/research-innovation-reports-and-publications

Social Media The FTA maintains a channel on YouTube, as well as accounts on Facebook, LinkedIn, and Twitter. https://www.transit.dot.gov/about/news/social-media

Updates A subscription form is available on the FTA Web site to sign up for email updates. https://public.govdelivery.com/accounts/USDOTFTA/subscriber/new; http://www.fta.dot.gov/newsroom/13006.html

For further information, contact the Federal Transit Administration, Office of Communications and Congressional Affairs, 1200 New Jersey Avenue SE., Washington, DC 20590. Phone, 202-366-4043.

Maritime Administration

1200 New Jersey Avenue SE., Washington, DC 20590
Phone, 202-366-5807. Fax, 800-996-2723. Internet, http://www.marad.dot.gov

Administrator	MARK H. BUZBY
Deputy Administrator	RICHARD BALZANO
https://www.marad.dot.gov/about-us/key-personnel	

The above list of key personnel was updated 2–2018.

The Maritime Administration was established by Reorganization Plan No. 21 of 1950 (5 U.S.C. app.). The Maritime Act of 1981 (46 U.S.C. 1601) transferred the Maritime Administration to the DOT. The Administration manages programs that help develop and promote the U.S. merchant marine and its operations. It also organizes and directs emergency merchant ship operations.

The Administration serves as the DOT's waterborne transportation agency. Its programs promote waterborne transportation use, the seamless integration of waterborne transportation with other parts of the transportation system, and U.S. merchant marine viability. The Administration's activities involve ships and shipping, shipbuilding, port operations, vessel operations, national security, safety, and the environment. It also maintains the health of the merchant marine—commercial mariners, vessels, and intermodal facilities contribute significantly to national security. The Administration, therefore, supports current mariners, helps educate future mariners, and informs Americans about the maritime industry and how it benefits them. Recently, the Administration realigned its functions to be more effective as an industry promoter and to focus more attention on the environment and safety.

The Administration administers the Maritime Security Program, which maintains a core fleet of U.S.-flag, privately-owned ships that operate in international commerce. Under agreement, these ships are available to provide needed capacity, during war and national emergencies, to meet Department of Defense requirements.

It also administers the Ready Reserve Force program to facilitate deployment of U.S. military forces—rapidly and worldwide.

The Force primarily supports transport of Army and Marine Corps unit equipment and combat support equipment. The Force also supports initial resupply during the critical surge period before commercial ships become available. The program provides nearly one-half of the Government-owned surge sealift capability.

For information on the Administration's 10 Gateway Offices, visit the "Gateway Presence" Web page. http://www.marad.dot.gov/about-us/gateway-offices

Sources of Information

Business Opportunities   Links to business services are available on the Administration's Web site. http://www.marad.dot.gov/about-us/links-to-business-services

The Administration uses FedBizOpps.Gov for announcing solicitations and requests for comments. https://www.marad.dot.gov/about-us/office-of-acquisition

Career Opportunities   For information, visit the "Careers" Web page. http://www.marad.dot.gov/about-us/maritime-administration-careers

In 2016, the Maritime Administration ranked 79th among 305 agency subcomponents in the Partnership for Public Service's Best Places To Work Agency Rankings. http://bestplacestowork.org/BPTW/rankings/detail/TD13

Data / Statistics   The Administration's Web site features an open data portal that provides access to maritime data and statistics. https://www.marad.dot.gov/resources/data-statistics

Educational Resources   The Adopt a Ship program allows a class of students to partner with a ship's crew. During the school year, the class and crew correspond and share experiences. The correspondence stimulates interest in English, geography, history, math, science, trade, and transportation. It gives children a unique opportunity for responding to their natural curiosity of the sea and introduces them to the men and women of the American Merchant Marine. https://www.marad.dot.gov/education/adopt-a-ship-program

A video archives is available on the Administration's Web site. https://www.marad.dot.gov/resources/multimedia-gallery

Exhibits / Virtual Tours A shipbuilding exhibit and virtual tours inside cargo and crew spaces and engine rooms are part of the Administration's Web site. https://www.marad.dot.gov/about-us/maritime-administration-history-program/maritime-administrations-artifact-collection/exhibits

Freedom of Information Act (FOIA) Instructions for submitting a FOIA request are available on the Administration's Web site. Fax, 202-366-7485. https://www.marad.dot.gov/about-us/foia | Email: FOIA.Marad@dot.gov

The Administration maintains an electronic reading room. Before submitting a FOIA request, an information seeker should search for the desired document or record in the reading room to determine whether it may be available immediately, without charge. https://www.marad.dot.gov/about-us/foia/electronic-reading-room

Frequently Asked Questions (FAQs) The Administration posts answers to FAQs on its Web site. https://www.marad.dot.gov/about-us/frequently-asked-questions

History Historical documents and resources are available on the Administration's Web site. https://www.marad.dot.gov/about-us/maritime-administration-history-program/historical-documents-and-resources

Newsroom News items and releases, as well as advisories, events, photographs, and speeches, are accessible in the newsroom. https://www.marad.dot.gov/newsroom

Ports Information on the importance of ports to the Nation's economy and the Strong Ports program is available on the Administration's Web site. https://www.marad.dot.gov/ports/strongports | Email: StrongPorts@dot.gov

Publications Factsheets, policy papers, and reports are available on the Administration's Web site. http://www.marad.dot.gov/resources/maritime-publications

Ship Disposal The Administration's Web site provides information on four methods of ship disposal: artificial reefing, domestic recycling, ship donations, and naval sink at sea live-fire training exercises (SINKEX). https://www.marad.dot.gov/ships-and-shipping/ship-disposal; http://www.marad.dot.gov/about-us/contact-us

For further information, contact the Maritime Administration, Office of Congressional and Public Affairs, 1200 New Jersey Avenue SE., Washington, DC 20590. Phone, 202-366-5807.

National Highway Traffic Safety Administration

1200 New Jersey Avenue SE., Washington, DC 20590
Phone, 202-366-9550. Fax, 888-327-4236. Internet, http://www.nhtsa.gov

Administrator	(VACANCY)
Deputy Administrator	HEIDI KING
Executive Director	JACK DANIELSON
https://www.nhtsa.gov/about-nhtsa/nhtsa-leadership	

[For the National Highway Traffic Safety Administration statement of organization, see the Code of Federal Regulations, Title 49, Part 501]

The above list of key personnel was updated 2–2018.

The National Highway Traffic Safety Administration (NHTSA) was established by the Highway Safety Act of 1970 (23 U.S.C. 401 note) to reduce the number of deaths, injuries, and economic losses resulting from motor vehicle crashes on the Nation's highways.

The Administration administers motor vehicle and related equipment safety performance programs; co-administers the State and community highway safety program; regulates the Corporate Average Fuel Economy program; issues Federal Motor Vehicle Safety Standards (FMVSS) that prescribe safety features and levels of safety-related performance for vehicles and vehicular equipment; rates the safety of passenger vehicles in the New Car Assessment Program; monitors and participates in international vehicle safety forums to harmonize the FMVSS where appropriate; investigates and prosecutes odometer fraud; administers the National Driver Register Program; conducts studies and operates programs to reduce economic losses in motor vehicle crashes and repairs; performs studies, conducts demonstration projects, and issues regulations requiring manufacturers to provide motor vehicle consumer information; promotes programs to reduce impaired driving, to reduce risky driver behaviors, and to increase seat belt use; and issues theft prevention standards for passenger motor vehicles.

Activities

Research and Program Development   The Administration helps develop motor vehicle and highway safety program standards. It analyzes data and researches, develops, tests, and evaluates motor vehicles, motor vehicle equipment, and advanced technologies, and it collects and analyzes crash data. NHTSA activities are broad in scope with respect to safety: The Administration encourages industry to adopt advanced motor vehicle safety designs, increases public awareness of safety issues, and provides a base for vehicle safety information. http://www.nhtsa.gov/Research

Regional Operations and Program Delivery   The NHTSA administers State highway safety grant programs that the Safe, Accountable, Flexible, Efficient Transportation Equity Act: A Legacy for Users authorized. The Highway Safety formula grant program provides funds to States, Indian nations, and the territories each year to support safety programs, particularly in the following priority areas: data and traffic records, emergency medical services, impaired driving, motorcycle safety, occupant protection, pedestrian and bicycle safety, police traffic services, roadway safety, and speed control. Incentive grants are also used to encourage States to implement effective data improvement, impaired driving, motorcycle safety, and occupant protection programs. https://www.nhtsa.gov/highway-safety-grants-program

Rulemaking   The Administration issues FMVSS that prescribe safety features and levels of safety-related performance for vehicles and vehicular equipment. The Administration participates in the United Nations World Forum for the Harmonization of Vehicle Regulations (WP.29). It also oversees the New Car Assessment Program and the Government's Five Star Safety Rating Program, which evaluates the safety performance of light trucks, passenger cars, vans, and child seats (https://www.nhtsa.gov/ratings). These evaluations are highly publicized—star ratings must be visible on the price labels of new vehicles. The Administration also educates consumers on topics such as driving while distracted, as well as the proper use of vehicle safety features and child restraint seats. To promote fuel economy, it manages a program establishing and revising fleet average fuel economy standards for passenger car and light truck manufacturers (https://www.nhtsa.gov/laws-regulations/corporate-average-fuel-economy). The Administration also runs an antitheft program. Under this program the NHTSA issues rules requiring that certain passenger motor vehicles meet parts-marking requirements, and it calculates and publishes annual motor vehicle theft rates. https://www.nhtsa.gov/laws-regulations

Enforcement   The Administration's Office of Enforcement assures that all new vehicles sold in the U.S. meet applicable FMVSS. Under its compliance program, the Office conducts random tests and collects consumer complaints to identify and investigate problems with motor vehicles and vehicular equipment. If a vehicle or equipment suffers from a safety-related defect or does not meet all applicable FMVSS, the Office seeks a recall, which requires manufacturers to notify owners and to remedy the defect free of charge. The Office monitors recalls to ensure that owners are notified in a timely manner and that the scope of the recall and the remedy are adequate. The Office also assures that all motor vehicles subject to the Corporate Average Fuel Economy (CAFE) regulations meet their respective targets, and it enforces violations of Federal odometer fraud regulations by criminally prosecuting offenders. https://www.nhtsa.gov/recalls

National Center for Statistics and Analysis   The NHTSA maintains a collection of scientific and technical information on motor vehicle safety. It also operates the National Center for Statistics and Analysis, whose activities include the development and maintenance of national highway-crash data collection systems and related statistical and economic analyses. The public and the private sector and universities and Federal, State, and local agencies rely on these motor vehicle safety information resources for documentation. https://www.nhtsa.gov/research-data/national-center-statistics-and-analysis-ncsa

Communications and Consumer Information   The Office of Communications and Consumer Information develops, directs, and implements communication strategies based on NHTSA policy and programs, including campaigns to support high visibility enforcement efforts. It promotes safety messages for NHTSA vehicle-related issues. The Office also manages NHTSA Web sites and the toll-free Vehicle Safety Hotline. Information received from calls to the hotline forms the basis of investigations, which can lead to recalls if safety-related defects are identified. http://www.trafficsafetymarketing.gov/ciot

Sources of Information

Car Seats   A car seat glossary is available on the Parents Central Web site. http://www.safercar.gov/parents/CarSeats/Car-Seat-Glossary-of-Terms.htm?view=full

The car seat finder is an online tool that uses date of birth, height, and weight to find a car seat type that properly fits a child. http://www.safercar.gov/cpsApp/crs/index.htm

Career Opportunities   Information on job openings is available on the "Jobs at NHTSA" Web page. http://www.nhtsa.gov/Jobs

In 2016, the NHTSA ranked 290th among 305 agency subcomponents in the Partnership for Public Service's Best Places To Work Agency Rankings. http://bestplacestowork.org/BPTW/rankings/detail/TD10

Data   The NHTSA posts factsheets, reports, research notes, statistics, and studies on its Web site. https://www.nhtsa.gov/research-data

Driving Safety   The NHTSA Web site features a trove of safety information and resources. Disabled, older, and teen drivers, as well as motorcyclists and others can find Web pages dedicated to improving their driving habits and addressing their safety needs. http://www.nhtsa.gov/Driving-Safety

Events   The NHTSA hosts meetings and forums to explore new approaches to highway safety. Information and materials from these event are available online. https://www.nhtsa.gov/events

Freedom of Information Act (FOIA)   The NHTSA is required to disclose records that are properly requested in writing by any person. A Government agency may withhold information pursuant to one or more of nine exemptions and three exclusions contained in the FOIA. The act applies only to Federal agencies and does not give a right of access to records held by Congress, the courts, State or local government agencies, and private entities. https://www.nhtsa.gov/about-nhtsa/foia

The NHTSA maintains an electronic reading room. Before submitting a FOIA request, an information seeker should search for the desired document or record in the reading room to determine whether it may be available immediately, without charge. The NHTSA also operates a service center for answering FOIA-related questions. Phone, 202-366-2870. https://www.nhtsa.gov/about-nhtsa/electronic-reading-room

News   The NHTSA posts press releases on its Web site. http://www.nhtsa.gov/About-NHTSA/Press-Releases

The NHTSA posts speeches, press events, and testimonies on its Web site. https://www.nhtsa.gov/speeches-presentations

Publications   The NHTSA disseminates information on traffic safety programs in "Traffic Techs." The publication, starting with the year 1995, is available online. Staring with the years 2005 and 2006, "Traffic Techs" becomes available in Portable Document Format (PDF). http://www.nhtsa.gov/About-NHTSA/Traffic-Techs | Email: TrafficTech@dot.gov

Recalls   The Recalls Spotlight monitors high-profile recalls and provides resources finding and addressing vehicle recalls. http://www.safercar.gov/rs/index.html

The NHTSA's Web site features a search tool that allows the user to enter a vehicle's identification number (VIN) to learn whether it has been repaired as part of a safety recall in the last 15 years. http://www-odi.nhtsa.dot.gov/owners/SearchSafetyIssues

Regional Offices   Contact information for the NHTSA's 10 regional offices is available on the "Regional Offices" Web page. http://www.nhtsa.gov/nhtsa/whatis/regions

Research   The Office of Vehicle Safety Research strategizes, plans, and implements research programs to reduce crashes, fatalities, and injuries. The NHTSA's Web site contains a trove of information related to these programs. http://www.nhtsa.gov/Research

Resources for Parents   The Parents Central Web site features resources to help parents protect their children and educate them on car and road safety and becoming responsible drivers. http://www.safercar.gov/parents/index.htm

Vehicle Safety   The NHTSA Web site features a trove of information on and resources for vehicle safety. Topics include defects and recalls, odometer fraud, theft protection, and tires. http://www.nhtsa.gov/Vehicle-Safety

To report suspected safety defects in vehicles, vehicle equipment, and child restraint seats, call the Vehicle Safety Hotline. English- and Spanish-speaking representatives are available on weekdays, excluding Federal holidays. Phone, 888-327-4236. TTY, 800-424-9153. https://www-odi.nhtsa.dot.gov/VehicleComplaint; https://www.nhtsa.gov/about-nhtsa/contact-us

For further information, contact the National Highway Traffic Safety Administration, Office of Communications and Consumer Information, 1200 New Jersey Avenue SE., Washington, DC 20590. Phone, 202-366-9550.

Pipeline and Hazardous Materials Safety Administration

1200 New Jersey Avenue SE., Washington, DC 20590
Phone, 202-366-4433. Internet, http://www.phmsa.dot.gov

Administrator	HOWARD R. ELLIOTT
Deputy Administrator	DRUE PEARCE
Executive Director	HOWARD W. MCMILLAN
https://www.phmsa.dot.gov/about/key-officials	

The above list of key personnel was updated 02–2018.

The Pipeline and Hazardous Materials Safety Administration (PHMSA) was established on February 20, 2005. It is responsible for hazardous materials transportation and pipeline safety.

Hazardous Materials

The Office of Hazardous Materials Safety develops and issues regulations for the safe and secure transportation of hazardous materials by all modes, except bulk transportation by water. The regulations cover shipper and carrier operations, packaging and container specifications, and hazardous materials definitions. The Office provides training and outreach to help shippers and carriers meet hazardous material regulatory requirements. The Office enforces regulations other than those applicable to a single mode of transportation. It manages a fee-funded grant program to help States plan for hazardous materials emergencies and to assist them and Indian tribes with training for hazardous materials emergencies. The Office also maintains a national safety program to safeguard food and other products from contamination during motor or rail transportation. http://www.phmsa.dot.gov/hazmat/info-center | Email: phmsa.hm-infocenter@dot.gov

For further information, call the Hazardous Materials Information Center. Phone, 800-467-4922.

Pipelines

The Office of Pipeline Safety (OPS) ensures the safety, security, and environmental protection of the Nation's pipeline transportation system. The Office establishes and enforces safety and environmental standards for pipeline transportation of gas and hazardous liquids. The Office analyzes data, educates and trains, promotes damage prevention, and conducts research and development for pipeline safety. Through OPS administered grants, States that voluntarily assume regulatory jurisdiction of pipelines can receive funding for up to 50 percent of the costs for their intrastate pipeline safety programs. OPS engineers inspect most interstate pipelines and other facilities not covered by State programs. In accordance with the Oil Pollution Act of 1990, the Office also approves and tests oil pipeline spill response plans. http://phmsa. dot.gov/pipeline

For further information, call the Pipeline Safety Information Center. Phone, 202-366-4595. Fax, 202-493-2311.

Sources of Information

Business Opportunities Information on the acquisition vehicles that the PHMSA uses to fulfill the requirements for goods and services of its program offices is available online. http://www.phmsa.dot.gov/doing-biz
Career Opportunities The PHMSA relies on accident investigators, accountants, attorneys, auditors, budget analysts, economists, engineers, finance analysts, geographic information systems specialists, grant specialists, human resource specialists, information technology specialists, and other professionals to carry out its mission. http:// www.phmsa.dot.gov/careers
In 2016, the PHMSA ranked 136th among 305 agency subcomponents in the Partnership for Public Service's Best Places To Work Agency Rankings. http:// bestplacestowork.org/BPTW/rankings/detail/ TD16
Data / Statistics The Office of Pipeline Safety makes available data on federally regulated and State regulated natural gas pipelines, hazardous liquid pipelines, and liquefied natural gas plants. The operators of these pipeline facilities report this data

in accordance with PHMSA pipeline safety regulations. The PHMSA provides downloads of the raw data, yearly summaries, multiyear trends of safety performance metrics, and inventories tracking the removal of aging and other higher-risk infrastructure. http://www. phmsa.dot.gov/pipeline/library/data-stats
Environmental Justice The PHMSA Web site provides information for promoting environmental justice and ensuring nondiscrimination in communities. http://phmsa.dot.gov/org/civilrights/ EnvironmentalJustice
Events A calendar of PHMSA events is available online. http://www.phmsa.dot. gov/portal/site/PHMSA/menuitem.c078b89 b7940f5f756f2cee62d9c8789/?vgnextoid= 574ffed8df6ec410VgnVCM100000d2c97 898RCRD&vgnextchannel=574ffed8df6ec 410VgnVCM100000d2c97898RCRD&vgn extfmt=print
Freedom of Information Act (FOIA) The FOIA establishes the public's right to obtain information from Federal Government agencies. Any person may file a FOIA request, including citizens and foreign nationals, as well as associations, organizations, and universities. http://www. phmsa.dot.gov/about/foia
Frequently Asked Questions (FAQs) The PHMSA posts answers to FAQs on its Web site. http://www.phmsa.dot.gov/about/faq
Glossary The PHMSA's Web site features an online glossary. http://www.phmsa.dot. gov/resources/glossary
History Millions of miles of transportation pipelines deliver the energy products that the American public uses to keep homes and businesses running. While rare, pipeline incidents can be fatal and cost millions of dollars in property damage. The Office of Pipeline Safety participated in the investigations of major pipeline incidents in San Bruno, CA; Allentown, PA; and Marshall, MI. In its commitment to safety awareness and outreach, the Office offers a historical look at high-profile pipeline incidents. http://www.phmsa.dot.gov/ pipeline/safety-awareness-and-outreach/ pipeline-incidents
Library The electronic library contains an accessible collection of public documents related to the safe transport of hazardous materials. http://www.phmsa.dot.gov/ hazmat/library

The Pipeline Library is an online resource containing electronic files that stakeholders and pipeline safety industry professionals regularly use. These files include archives, forms, frequently asked questions, glossaries, and Freedom of Information Act information. http://www.phmsa.dot.gov/pipeline/library
Mapping System   The National Pipeline Mapping System public map viewer is a Web-based application designed to assist the general public with displaying and querying data related to gas transmission and hazardous liquid pipelines, liquefied natural gas plants, and breakout tanks under the jurisdiction of the PHMSA. https://www.npms.phmsa.dot.gov/Default.aspx
News   The PHMSA posts announcements, congressional testimony, events, press releases, speeches, videos, and more in its electronic briefing room. http://www.phmsa.dot.gov/media-congress
Site Map   The Web site map allows visitors to look for specific topics or to browse content that aligns with their interests. http://www.phmsa.dot.gov/about/sitemap; http://www.phmsa.dot.gov/about/contact

For further information, contact the Pipeline and Hazardous Materials Safety Administration, Office of Governmental, International and Public Affairs, 1200 New Jersey Avenue SE., East Building—2d Floor, Washington, DC 20590. Phone: 202-366-4831.

Saint Lawrence Seaway Development Corporation

55 M Street SE., Suite 930, Washington, DC 20003.
Phone, 202-366-0091, 202-366-7147. Internet, http://www.seaway.dot.gov

Departmental Postal Address: Saint Lawrence Seaway Development Corporation, 1200 New Jersey Avenue SE., Washington, DC 20590.
Email: slsdc@dot.gov

Postal and Physical Address: Saint Lawrence Seaway Development Corporation–Operations, 180 Andrews Street, Massena, NY 13662
Phone, 315-764-3200, 315-764-3235

Policy Headquarters—Washington, DC

Administrator	(VACANCY)
Deputy Administrator	CRAIG H. MIDDLEBROOK

Operational Headquarters—Massena, NY

Associate Administrator, Seaway Operations	THOMAS A. LAVIGNE
https://www.seaway.dot.gov/about/meet-our-team	

The above list of key personnel was updated 02–2018.

The Saint Lawrence Seaway Development Corporation (SLSDC) was established by the Saint Lawrence Seaway Act of May 13, 1954 (33 U.S.C. 981–990) and became an operating administration of the DOT in 1966.

The SLSDC, working jointly with the Saint Lawrence Seaway Management Corporation (SLSMC) of Canada, operates and maintains a safe, reliable, and efficient deep draft waterway between the Great Lakes and the Atlantic Ocean. It ensures the safe transit of commercial and noncommercial vessels through the two U.S. locks and the navigation channels of the Saint Lawrence Seaway System and engages in economic and trade development activities to stimulate trade and employment in the eight States of the Great Lakes region. The SLSDC and SLSMC work together on all matters related to rules and regulations, overall operations, vessel inspections, traffic control, navigation aids, safety, operating dates, and trade development programs.

The Great Lakes-Saint Lawrence Seaway System extends from the Atlantic Ocean to the Lake Superior ports of Duluth and Superior, a distance of 2,342 miles. The Corporation's main customers are vessel owners and operators, Midwest States and Canadian Provinces, Great Lakes port communities, shippers and receivers of domestic and international cargo, and the maritime and related service industries of the Great Lakes and Saint Lawrence Seaway systems. https://www.seaway.dot.gov/about/what-does-slsdc-do

Sources of Information

Career Opportunities   The SLSDC relies on professionals with expertise in administration, engineering, information technology, management, marine operations, public policy, and other fields. https://www.seaway.dot.gov/about/careers-slsdc

Freedom of Information Act (FOIA)   Any person has the right to a copy of certain records possessed by the Government's executive administrations, agencies, boards, commissions, corporations, offices, and services. Some records, however, are protected from disclosure. https://www.seaway.dot.gov/publications/electronic-reading room

Grants   The SLSDC has an easy-to-use Federal grants toolkit that offers a snapshot of the essential information, resources, and tools needed to identify Federal agencies and processes offering financial assistance to maritime stakeholders seeking to carry out environmental, infrastructural, intermodal, and other development projects. https://www.seaway.dot.gov/publications/slsdc-federal-grants-toolkit

Map   An interactive map of vessels transiting the Great Lakes-St. Lawrence Seaway System is available online. https://www.seaway.dot.gov/explore/interactive-shipping-map-and-shipping-schedule

News   The SLSDC's quarterly newsletter "Seaway Compass" is available online. It features current information and recent news on the Great Lakes-St. Lawrence Seaway System. https://www.seaway.dot.gov/publications/seaway-compass

Publications   The "Great Lakes-St. Lawrence Seaway System Directory" is a comprehensive publication on the ports and shipping-related businesses that are critical throughout the region and beyond.

It features extensive photography and serves as an excellent resource for readers who are interested in the Great Lakes Seaway maritime industry. https://www.seaway.dot.gov/publications/seaway-system-directory

The SLSDC's marketing brochure offers comprehensive information on the waterway and its significance to the Great Lakes region. It is available online in Portable Document Format (PDF). https://www.seaway.dot.gov/publications/slsdc-marketing-brochure

Reports   The SLSDC posts annual reports on its Web site. https://www.seaway.dot.gov/publications/annual-reports

The SLSDC posts Asset Renewal Program reports on its Web site. https://www.seaway.dot.gov/publications/asset-renewal-program-reports

Social Media   The SLSDC maintains a Facebook account. https://www.facebook.com/USDOTSLSDC

Studies   The "Environmental and Social Impacts of Marine Transport in the Great Lakes-St. Lawrence Seaway Region" study provides marine stakeholders, transportation planners, and government policymakers with an assessment of the potential environmental and social consequences that could occur if cargo carried by marine vessels on the Seaway navigation system shifted to rail and road modes of transport. https://www.seaway.dot.gov/publications/social-impact-study

Videos   The SLSDC's Web site features a video gallery. https://www.seaway.dot.gov/explore/video-about-the-seaway

Visitors' Center   The Seaway Visitors' Center at the Eisenhower Lock provides tourists and ship watchers with an observation deck where they can view commercial vessels and cruise ships transiting the lock. Each year, hundreds of ships from all over the globe make thousands of transits through the St. Lawrence Seaway. They carry a wide variety of cargoes: coal, grains, iron ore, steel, steel slabs, stone, and more. https://www.seaway.dot.gov/explore/visitors-center; https://www.seaway.dot.gov/about/contact-us

For further information, contact the Saint Lawrence Seaway Development Corporation, Director of Congressional and Public Relations, 1200 New Jersey Avenue SE., Washington, DC 20590. Phone, 202-366-0091. Fax, 202-366-7147.

DEPARTMENT OF VETERANS AFFAIRS

810 Vermont Avenue NW., Washington, DC 20420
Phone, 202-461-4800. Internet, http://www.va.gov

Office of the Secretary
Secretary of Veterans Affairs — ROBERT WILKIE
Deputy Secretary — JAMES BYRNE, ACTING
Chief of Staff — PAMELA POWERS
https://www.va.gov/opa/bios/secva.asp

Administrations
Executive in Charge
Health — RICHARD A. STONE

Under Secretaries
Benefits — PAUL LAWRENCE
Memorial Affairs — RANDY C. REEVES
https://www.va.gov/opa/bios/index.asp

Staff Offices
Assistant Secretaries
Congressional and Legislative Affairs — BROOKS D. TUCKER
Enterprise Integration — MELISSA S. GLYNN
Human Resources and Administration — JACQUELYN HAYES-BYRD, ACTING
Information and Technology / Chief Information Officer — CAMILO SANDOVAL
Management / Chief Financial Officer — JON J. RYCHALSKI
Public and Intergovernmental Affairs — JOHN ULLYOT

Executive Directors
Accountability and Whistleblower Protection — KIRK M. NICHOLAS
Acquisition, Logistics, and Construction — KAREN L. BRAZELL
Chair, Board of Veterans' Appeals — CHERYL L. MASON
Chief Veterans Experience Officer — LYNDA C. DAVIS
General Counsel — CATHERINE MITRANO, ACTING
https://www.va.gov/landing_organizations.htm

Office of Inspector General
Inspector General — MICHAEL J. MISSAL
https://www.va.gov/oig/about/inspector-general.asp

The above list of key personnel was updated 11–2018.

The Department of Veterans Affairs operates programs benefiting Veterans and members of their families: It offers education opportunities and rehabilitation services and provides compensation payments for disabilities or death related to military service, home loan guaranties, pensions, burials, and health care that includes the services in clinics, medical centers, community living centers (which replace nursing home)s, and home- and community-based settings.

The Department of Veterans Affairs (VA) was established as an executive department by the Department of Veterans Affairs Act (38 U.S.C. 201 note). It is comprised of three organizations that administer Veterans programs: the Veterans Health Administration, the Veterans Benefits Administration, and the National Cemetery Administration. Each organization has field facilities and a central office component. Staff offices support the overall function of the Department and its Administrations. http://www.va.gov/landing2_about.htm

Activities

Acquisition, Logistics, and Construction The Office of Acquisition, Logistics, and Construction (OALC) is a multifunctional organization responsible for directing the acquisition, logistics, construction, and leasing functions within the VA. The Executive Director, OALC, is also the Chief Acquisition Officer for the VA. http://www.va.gov/OALC

Cemeteries The National Cemetery Administration (NCA) is responsible for the management and oversight of 135 national cemeteries in the United States and Puerto Rico, as well as 33 soldiers' lots, Confederate cemeteries, and monument sites. Burial in a national cemetery is available to eligible veterans, certain members of reserve components, and their spouses and dependent children. At no cost to the family, a national cemetery burial includes the gravesite, graveliner, opening and closing of the grave, headstone or marker, and perpetual care as part of a national shrine. If an eligible veteran is buried in an unmarked grave in a private cemetery anywhere in the world, NCA will provide a headstone or marker. A Government-furnished headstone or marker may be provided for eligible Veterans who died on or after Nov. 1, 1990 and whose grave is marked with a privately purchased headstone. A Government-furnished medallion may be provided for eligible Veterans who served on or after Apr. 6, 1917 and whose grave is marked with a privately purchased headstone or marker. NCA's Veterans Cemetery Grants Program provides funds to State and tribal governments to establish, expand, or improve veterans' cemeteries. NCA issues Presidential Memorial Certificates to honor the memory of deceased veterans who are eligible for

burial in a national cemetery. http://www.cem.va.gov

Congressional and Legislative Affairs The mission of the Office of the Assistant Secretary for Congressional and Legislative Affairs (OCLA) is to improve the lives of Veterans and their families by advancing pro-Veteran legislation and maintaining responsive and effective communications with Congress. OCLA coordinates the Department's activities with Congress. It is the Department's focal point for interactions and engagements with Members of Congress, authorization committees, and personal staff. Additionally, the Office is the Department's liaison with the Government Accountability Office (GAO). https://www.va.gov/oca/

Faith-Based and Neighborhood Partnerships The mission of the Center for Faith-Based and Neighborhood Partnerships (CFBNP) is to develop partnerships with, provide relevant information to, and expand participation of faith-based, nonprofit, and community/neighborhood organizations in VA programs in order to better serve the needs of Veterans, their families, survivors, caregivers, and other beneficiaries. https://www.va.gov/cfbnpartnerships/

Field Facilities The Department's operations are handled through the following field facilities: cemeteries, medical centers, outpatient clinics, community living centers, domiciliaries, and regional offices. Cemeteries provide burial services to Veterans, their spouses, and dependent children. Medical centers provide eligible beneficiaries with medical and other health care services equivalent to those provided by private sector institutions, augmented in many instances by services to meet the special requirements of Veterans. Outpatient clinics provide the most common outpatient services, including health and wellness visits, without the hassle of visiting a larger medical center. Community Living Centers (CLC) are skilled nursing facilities, often referred to as nursing homes. Veterans with chronic stable conditions such as dementia, those requiring rehabilitation or those who need comfort and care at the end of life are served within one of our 135 Community Living Centers. Domiciliaries provide a variety of care to Veterans who suffer from a wide range of medical, psychiatric, vocational, educational, or social problems and illnesses in a safe, secure, homelike environment. VHA continues to expand the network of outpatient clinics to include more rural locations, putting access to care closer to home.

Regional offices grant benefits and services provided by law for Veterans, their dependents, and beneficiaries within an assigned territory; furnish information regarding VA benefits and services; adjudicate claims and make awards for disability compensation and pension; conduct outreach and information dissemination; provide support and assistance to various segments of the Veteran population to include former prisoners of war, minorities, the homeless, women, and elderly Veterans; supervise payment of VA benefits to incompetent beneficiaries; provide vocational rehabilitation and employment training; administer educational benefits; guarantee loans for purchase, construction, or alteration of homes; process grants for specially adapted housing; process death claims; and assist Veterans in exercising rights to benefits and services. https://www.va.gov/directory/guide/home. asp

Health Services The Veterans Health Administration (VHA) is the largest integrated health care system in the United States. It provides hospital, long-term services and support in community living centers (which replace nursing homes)- and home- and community- based settings, domiciliary, and outpatient medical and dental care and community care to eligible Veterans of the Armed Forces. In addition to providing health care, VHA performs research, and assists in the education and training of physicians, dentists, and many other health care professionals through its affiliations with educational institutions and organizations. As of March 2017, VHA treated over 8.76 million patients in over 1,700 sites of care. VHA has 1,247 health care facilities, including 170 VA Medical Centers and 1,067 outpatient sites of care of varying complexity (VHA outpatient clinics). In addition, VA purchases medical care when needed from community providers including long-term services and supports

in community nursing homes, State Veterans Homes, and in home and community based settings. In 2016, VA hospitals had about 621,520 inpatient admissions and provided nearly 84 million outpatient visits. In addition to care delivered in the VA system, VA also delivers care to millions of Veterans in the community. The number of women Veterans receiving health care from VA more than tripled between 2000 and 2016, growing from 160,000 in 2000 to 475,000. VA hospitals provide more public data about quality and safety than any health care system in the world and held academic affiliations with more than 1,800 educational institutions. More than 123,552 health care students receive clinical training at a VA facility each year.

Historically, VHA has been at the forefront of medical research. The first electronic health record, cardiac pacemaker, bionic ankle, and successful liver transplant were all developed at VA. VA has also developed new drugs and treatments for acquired immune deficiency syndrome/ human immunodeficiency virus, diabetes, Alzheimer's disease, and osteoporosis. Currently, VHA medical centers provide a wide range of services including traditional services such as primary care, surgery, critical care, mental health, orthopedics, pharmacy, radiology and physical therapy. Additional medical and surgical specialty services, including audiology & speech pathology, dermatology, dental, geriatrics, neurology, palliative medicine, oncology, podiatry, prosthetics, urology, vision care and extended care services; such as facility and community based long-term services and supports and hospice care are available. Some medical centers also offer advanced services such as organ transplants and plastic surgery. VA is also using Telehealth and Telemedicine to improve access to care, especially in remote areas. http://www. va.gov/HEALTH

Management The Advisory Committee Management Office (ACMO) provides administrative and management support to the Department's 29 Federal Advisory Committees (as of July 2017). VA's advisory committees solicit advice and recommendations from outside experts and the public concerning programs for which the Department is responsible for by law. http://www.va.gov/ADVISORY

Minority Veterans   The Center for Minority Veterans (CMV), established by the Veterans' Benefits Improvement Act of 1994, identifies barriers to benefits and health care access, promotes awareness of minority Veteran-related issues, develops strategies for improving minority Veterans' participation in existing VA programs, The CMV focuses on the unique and special needs of African Americans, Hispanics, Asian Americans, Pacific Islanders, and Native Americans, which include American Indians, Native Hawaiians, and Alaska Natives. http://www.va.gov/centerforminorityveterans

Small and Disadvantaged Business Utilization   The Office of Small and Disadvantaged Business Utilization (OSDBU) is the Department's principal liaison to the Small Business Administration (SBA), the Department of Commerce, the General Services Administration (GSA), and the Office of Federal Procurement Policy for matters dealing with small and disadvantaged business activities. OSDBU's mission is to enable Veterans to gain access to economic opportunity by leveraging the federal procurement system and expanding participation of procurement-ready small businesses. http://www.va.gov/osdbu

Survivors Assistance   Office of Survivors Assistance (OSA) provides support to survivors of Veterans by identifying and informing them of the benefits and services offered by VA. https://www.va.gov/survivors/

Veterans' Appeals   The Board of Veterans' Appeals (BVA) renders final decisions on behalf of the Secretary on appeals from decisions of local VA offices. The Board reviews all appeals for entitlement to Veterans' benefits, including claims for service connection, increased disability ratings, total disability ratings, pension, insurance benefits, educational benefits, home loan guaranties, vocational rehabilitation, dependency and indemnity compensation, health care delivery, and fiduciary matters. The Board has jurisdiction over appeals arising from the VA regional offices, VA medical centers, the National Cemetery Administration, and the Office of General Counsel. The Board's mission is to conduct hearings and issue timely,

understandable, and quality decisions for Veterans and other appellants in compliance with the requirements of law. Final BVA decisions are appealable to the U.S. Court of Appeals for Veterans Claims. http://www.bva.va.gov

Veterans Benefits   VBA provides information, advice, and assistance to Veterans, their dependents, beneficiaries, representatives, and others applying for VA benefits. It also cooperates with the Department of Labor and other Federal, State, and local agencies in developing employment opportunities for Veterans and referrals for assistance in resolving socioeconomic, housing, and other related problems.

VBA's Compensation and Pension and Fiduciary Services are responsible for adjudicating claims for disability compensation and pension, specially adapted housing, accrued benefits, adjusted compensation in death cases, reimbursement for headstones or markers, allowances for automobiles and special adaptive equipment, special clothing allowances, emergency officers' retirement pay, Survivors' claims for death compensation, dependency and indemnity compensation, death pension, burial and plot allowances, forfeiture determinations, and a benefits protection program for minors and incompetent adult beneficiaries.

VBA's Education Service administers VA education benefits to Veterans, Servicemembers, National Guard members, Selected Reserve members, and eligible dependents. These benefits provide financial assistance for attending institutions of higher learning, non-college degree programs, on-the-job and apprenticeship training, flight training, distance learning, correspondence training, national testing programs, licensing and certifications, entrepreneurship training, work-study programs, and co-op training. Education Service also performs compliance surveys to ensure that approved programs are compliant with pertinent laws. Additional information is available at www.benefits.va.gov/gibill.

VBA's Insurance Service operates for the benefit of Servicemembers, Veterans, and their beneficiaries. Customers can reach Insurance Service through the

VA Insurance Center (phone, 800-669-8477). The Insurance Center performs a complete range of activities necessary to operate national life insurance programs. Activities include maintenance of individual accounts, underwriting functions, life and death insurance claims awards, and other insurance-related transactions for multiple insurance programs. The Insurance Center administers the Veterans Mortgage Life Insurance Program for those disabled Veterans who receive a VA grant for specially adapted housing, and the Service-Disabled Veterans Insurance program for Veterans who receive a service-connected disability rating. In addition, Insurance Service oversees the Servicemembers' Group Life Insurance (SGLI) and Veterans' Group Life Insurance Programs, as well as the Family Servicemembers' Group Life Insurance and SGLI Traumatic Injury Protection programs.

VBA's Loan Guaranty Service is responsible for administering operations that include establishing the eligibility of Veterans for the program; ensuring VA credit, income, and appraisal requirements are met; managing a panel of appraisers and establishing a property value; approving grants for specially adapted housing; supervising the construction of new residential properties; making direct loans to Native American Veterans to acquire a home on trust land; servicing and liquidating defaulted loans; and disposing of real estate acquired as the consequence of defaulted loans.

VBA's Vocational Rehabilitation and Employment Service (VR&E) program provides assistance to Veterans and Servicemembers with service-connected disabilities and an employment handicap, to prepare for, obtain, and maintain suitable employment. For those persons who are severely disabled and suitable employment is not an option, assistance may be provided to allow each person to live more independently. Through VA's VR&E program, individuals may benefit from individual support, vocational counseling, evaluation of interest, aptitudes and abilities, training, employment assistance, and other rehabilitation services. In some cases, rehabilitation services are available to spouses and children of totally and permanently disabled Veterans as well as Survivors of certain deceased Veterans.

Under 38 U.S.C. Chapter 18, VR&E provides vocational training and rehabilitation services to children with spina bifida having a parent who served in the Republic of Vietnam during the Vietnam era or who served in certain military units in or near the demilitarized zone in Korea between September 1, 1967 and August 31, 1971.

The Appeals Management Office assumes responsibility for and authority over all VBA appeals-related program policy, planning, budgeting, staffing, and other operational control as a separate entity under the VBA Principal Deputy Under Secretary for Benefits (PDUSB). This office works closely with the Board of Veterans Appeals to better service Veterans and their families. http://www.benefits.va.gov/benefits

Women Veterans The Center for Women Veterans (CWV), established by the Veterans' Benefits Improvement Act of 1994, monitors and coordinates VA's health care, benefits, services, and programs for women Veterans. CWV advocates a cultural transformation within VA and the general public to recognize the service and contributions of women Veterans and women in the military, and raises awareness of the responsibility to treat women Veterans with dignity and respect. The CWV Director serves as the primary advisor to the SECVA on all matters related to policy, legislation, programs, issues, and initiatives affecting women Veterans. http://www.va.gov/WOMENVET

Sources of Information

A–Z Index The "Veterans Health A–Z Index" includes frequent inquiries, popular subjects, and topics of critical importance to veterans and their caregivers. https://www.va.gov/health/topics

Blog "VAntage Point" is the VA's official blog. http://www.blogs.va.gov/VAntage | Email: blog.dalcbdt@va.gov

Business Opportunities The VA purchases goods and services on the national, regional, and local level from large and small businesses. Each VA facility has a local acquisition office that handles its procurement process. http://www.va.gov/

oal/business/dbwva.asp | Email: dalcbdt@va.gov

The VA has the authority to award set-aside and sole source contracts to service-disabled veteran-owned small businesses and to veteran-owned small businesses. This procurement authority extends the reach of the agency's mission of caring for the Nation's veterans. Phone, 866-584-2344. https://www.va.gov/osdbu/verification/ | Email: osdbu@va.gov

Career Opportunities The VA employs over 300,000 people in hundreds of professions. To fulfill its mission, the VA relies on claims examiners, dentists, management analysts, nurses, occupational therapists, optometrists, pharmacists, physical therapists, physician assistants, physicians, secretaries, and many additional types of professionals. www.vacareers.gov

In 2017, the VA ranked 17th among 18 large agencies in the Partnership for Public Service's Best Places To Work Agency Rankings. https://bestplacestowork.org/rankings/detail/VA00

Data / Statistics The National Center for Veterans Analysis and Statistics posts reports, statistics, surveys, and other information on its website. https://www.va.gov/vetdata | Email: vancvas@va.gov

Freedom of Information Act (FOIA) The FOIA requires that Federal agencies disclose records that information seekers request; however, some records or parts of them may be shielded from disclosure by one or more of nine statutory exemptions. A FOIA request should be sent by email, fax, or postal mail to the appropriate VA component where the desired document or record is kept. http://www.va.gov/oig/foia

If the information requester does not know which office or component maintains the desired document or record, he or she should contact the Director, FOIA Service, (005R1C), 810 Vermont Avenue NW., Washington, DC 20420. Phone, 877-750-3642. Fax 202-273-0487. https://www.oprm.va.gov/docs/foia/VACO_FOIA_Offices_Contact_List.pdf

Glossaries The VA website has a health benefits glossary. https://www.va.gov/HEALTHBENEFITS/resources/glossary.asp

The VA National Center for Patient Safety has a glossary of patient safety terms on its website. http://www.patientsafety.va.gov/professionals/publications/glossary.asp

Gravesite Locator The "National Cemetery Administration" website has a burial information database that is updated each day. The online locator allows users to search for the burial locations of veterans and their family members in VA National Cemeteries, State veterans cemeteries, and various other military and Department of Interior cemeteries, as well as for the interment sites of veterans who were buried in private cemeteries and whose graves are marked with Government grave markers. http://gravelocator.cem.va.gov/index.html

History The Continental Congress of 1776 encouraged enlistments during the Revolutionary War by providing pensions to disabled soldiers. More than 210 years later, the 40th President of the United States elevated the Veterans Administration to a cabinet-level executive department. The promotion brought with it a new name: the Department of Veterans Affairs. To learn more about the history of the most comprehensive veterans assistance system in world, visit the "VA History" web page. https://www.va.gov/about_va/vahistory.asp?

Homeless Veterans Information and resources to help a homeless veteran find a home are available on the VA website. https://www.va.gov/homeless

Locations This page provides a facility locator that allows users to search for VHA facilities by state or territory, street address, type of facility, and distance. https://www.va.gov/directory/guide/division.asp?dnum=1

Media Room The VA posts news releases online. http://www.va.gov/opa/pressrel

The VA posts speeches online. http://www.va.gov/opa/speeches

My Health The "My HealtheVet" website provides information and tools for veterans to partner with their health care team and improve health care management. The website allows veterans to refill VA prescriptions, track their delivery, and view medication lists; to monitor approaching VA appointments and receive reminders; to communicate online with health care teams; and to access medical records and add information to them. Phone, 877-327-0022. TTY, 800-877-8339. https://www.myhealth.va.gov/mhv-portal-web/home

Office of Inspector General (OIG)   Public documents and information are available on the OIG's website. Complaints may be sent to the VA Inspector General (53E), P.O. Box 50410, Washington, DC 20091-0410. Hotline phone, 800-488-8244. http://www.va.gov/oig/default.asp | Email: page. vaoighotline@va.gov

Organizational Chart   The VA's "2017 Functional Organizational Manual—version 4.0" is available online in Portable Document Format (PDF). The Department's organizational chart may be seen on page 2. https://www.va.gov/landing_organizations.htm

Our Doctors   The "Federation of State Medical Boards" website has an online directory that allows users to search for information about physicians. http://www.docinfo.org/#/search/query

Posttraumatic Stress Disorder (PTSD)   The National Center for PTSD is the world's leading PTSD and traumatic stress research and educational center. The website's home page has a helpful short video titled "What Is PTSD?" to explain the disorder. Information voice mail, 802-296-6300. https://www.ptsd.va.gov/

Public Affairs / News Media   Contact the nearest regional Office of Public Affairs: Atlanta (404-929-5880); Chicago (312-980-4235); Dallas (817-385-3720); Denver (303-914-5855); Los Angeles (310-268-4207); New York (212-807-3429); or Washington, DC (202-530-9360). Representatives of the national media may prefer contacting the Office of Public Affairs in the VA Central Office, 810 Vermont Avenue NW., Washington, DC 20420. Phone, 202-461-7400. http://www.va.gov/opa

Publications   Information on books, factsheets, and other publications is available on the "Office of Public and Intergovernmental Affairs" website. http://www.va.gov/opa/publications

Site Map   The website map allows visitors to look for specific topics or to browse content that aligns with their interests. http://www.va.gov/site_map.htm

Social Media   To see all of the VA's social media accounts, visit the "Social Media Directory" web page. https://www.va.gov/opa/socialmedia.asp

Sports Programs / Special Events   Having fun together by participating in adaptive sports improves health, creates new friends, and elevates the quality of life. Many sports opportunities are available to veterans of all ages and abilities. To get started, visit the "National Veterans Sports Programs and Special Events" website and speak with your VA clinical team about getting involved. https://www.blogs.va.gov/nvspse/ | Email: sports4vets@va.gov

Veterans Service Organizations   The VA maintains an online directory of veterans services organizations in Portable Document Format (PDF). For further information, contact the Office of Public and Intergovernmental Affairs, Department of Veterans Affairs, 810 Vermont Avenue NW., Washington, DC 20420. Phone, 202-273-6000. http://www.va.gov/vso

Women Veterans Call Center   Women veterans, as a demographic, underutilize VA benefits and services. The main reason seems to be a lack of awareness that they are eligible recipients. https://www.womenshealth.va.gov/WOMENSHEALTH/ProgramOverview/wvcc.asp; http://www.va.gov/opa

For further information, contact the Office of Public and Intergovernmental Affairs, Department of Veterans Affairs, 810 Vermont Avenue NW., Washington, DC 20420. Phone, 202-273-6000.

DEPARTMENT OF THE INTERIOR

1849 C Street NW., Washington, DC 20240
Phone, 202-208-3100. Internet, http://www.doi.gov

Secretary of the Interior	DAVID L. BERNHARDT
Deputy Secretary	KATHARINE MACGREGOR, ACTING
https://www.doi.gov/whoweare/secretary-bernhardt	

Assistant Secretaries

Fish and Wildlife and Parks	ROBERT WALLACE
Indian Affairs	TARA KATUK MAC LEAN SWEENEY
Insular and International Affairs	DOUGLAS W. DOMENECH
Land and Mineral Management	(VACANCY)
Policy, Management and Budget	SUSAN COMBS
Water and Science	TIMOTHY R. PETTY

Other Officers

Chief Information Officer	WILLIAM E. VAJDA
Solicitor	(VACANCY)
Special Trustee for American Indians	JEROLD GIDNER, ACTING
https://www.doi.gov/interior-leadership	

Office of the Inspector General

Inspector General	MARK LEE GREENBLATT
https://www.doioig.gov/about-us/inspector general	

The above list of key personnel was updated 12–2019.

The Department of the Interior protects America's heritage and natural resources, honors its cultures and tribal communities, and supplies energy for powering its future.

Establishment and Organization

On March 3, 1849, President James K. Polk approved an act that created the Department of the Interior (DOI) by transferring the Office of Indian Affairs and the General Land, the Patent, and the Pension Offices to a new department. The head of that new department was, and still is, called the Secretary of the Interior. The President appoints the Secretary by the advice of the Senate and with its consent. http://www.loc.gov/law/help/statutes-at-large/30th-congress/session-2/c30s2ch108.pdf

Topics such as the establishment of the DOI and the duties of its Secretary and Deputy Secretary are codified in title 43, chapter 31, of the U.S. Code. https://uscode.house.gov/view.xhtml?path=/prelim@title43/chapter31&edition=prelim

The Secretary of the Interior supervises the public business of the following agencies and subjects: Alaska Railroad, Alaska Road Commission, bounty-lands, Bureau of Land Management, U.S. Bureau of Mines, Bureau of Reclamation, division of Territories and Island Possessions, Fish and Wildlife Service, U.S. Geological Survey, Indians, National Park Service, petroleum conservation, and public lands and the mines that are part of those lands (43 U.S.C. 1457). The Secretary reports directly to the President. https://uscode.house.gov/view.xhtml?req=granuleid:USC-prelim-title43-section1457&num=0&edition=prelim

333

Rules and regulations associated with the Office of the Secretary of the Interior are codified in the Code of Federal Regulations in title 43, parts 1–199. https://www.ecfr.gov/cgi-bin/text-idx?SID=2dff2e4675b2891abcf7c9eb0078703c&mc=true&tpl=/ecfrbrowse/Title43/43cfrv1_02.tpl#0

The DOI was reorganized by Reorganization Plan No. 3 of 1950, as amended (5 U.S.C. app.). https://uscode.house.gov/view.xhtml?req=granuleid:USC-prelim-title5a-node84-leaf107&num=0&edition=prelim

A more recent reorganization has created 12 unified administrative regions to improve coordination among bureaus, effectiveness of relationships with its partners, and customer service. The reorganization delegates authority and accountability closer to field operations and places a greater emphasis on local decision making. https://www.doi.gov/employees/reorg

This reorganization started under the direction of former Secretary Ryan K. Zynke, who led the DOI from March 2, 2017, through January 2, 2019. The reorganization, which became final on August 22, 2018, established unified interior region boundaries that are based on watersheds and generally follow State lines to simplify coordination with external partners. https://www.doi.gov/employees/reorg/unified-regional-boundaries

The "Strategic Plan for Fiscal Years 2018–2022" includes the DOI's organization chart on page 6. https://www.doi.gov/sites/doi.gov/files/uploads/fy2018-2022-strategic-plan.pdf

Mission Areas

A set of six mission areas offers a brief description of DOI activities that are top priorities through the year 2022. They are discussed in detail in the "Strategic Plan for Fiscal Years 2018–2022" on pages 15–47.

Conserving Land and Water The DOI conserves America's lands and waters for the benefit, enjoyment, and use of current and future generations. The DOI's nine technical bureaus rely on the best science that is available, efficient decision-making processes, improved land use planning, modern natural resource management techniques, partnerships, and technology and engineering to balance stewardship with public lands use and the development of natural resources that are part of those lands, including fish species and wildlife. https://www.doi.gov/stewardship

Expanding Outdoor Recreation and Access Every year, more than 330 million people from across the country and around the world visit the national parks. Millions more visit other public lands that the DOI also manages. The DOI works to make outdoor recreation opportunities on public lands more accessible. The DOI's multiple-use policy of land management allows Americans to fish and hunt on public lands, as well as boat, camp, climb, hike, view wildlife, and engage in other outdoor activities. https://www.doi.gov/recreation

Fulfilling Trust and Insular Responsibilities The DOI upholds the U.S. Government's unique trust responsibilities by fostering government-to-government relationships that exist between the Federal Government and federally recognized Tribes. It also upholds those responsibilities by providing services to individual American Indians and Alaskan Natives. https://www.doi.gov/ost/whatwedo/

The U.S. Government also has important relationships with the affiliated insular areas, which include the Territories of American Samoa, Guam, the U.S. Virgin Islands, and the Commonwealth of the Northern Mariana Islands. The DOI administers and oversees Federal assistance to the three Freely Associated States, which comprise the two Republics of Palau and the Marshall Islands and the Federated States of Micronesia. https://edit.doi.gov/oia/what-we-do

Generating Revenue From Utilization of Natural Resources The DOI provides access to and manages energy resources like coal, gas, oil, and woody biomass on public lands, as well as Outer Continental Shelf energy resources like gas and oil. It also provides access to and manages other public land resources like nonenergy minerals, rangelands suitable for grazing, and timber from forests. By responsibly using public lands for extracting resources to achieve multiple use and economic benefits for the Nation, the DOI supports American energy dominance. https://www.doi.gov/sites/doi.gov/files/uploads/fy2019_bib_dh005.pdf

Modernizing Organization and Infrastructure The DOI seeks to ensure more effective operations and service delivery through coordinated organizational alignments in the field, across bureaus, and with other Federal and non-Federal partners, and by putting a larger fraction of DOI employees in the field to serve the public. Expediting environmental analysis and compliance, reducing the cost of space, collocating offices for convenient public service and improved interagency coordination, and common regional boundaries are potential ways to modernize the DOI's infrastructure and improve its effectiveness. https://www.doi.gov/sites/doi.gov/files/site-page/many-bureaus-one-mission.pdf

Protecting People and the Border Inherent in the DOI's management responsibilities of public lands is protecting employees and visitors. Ensuring employee and public safety requires the resources of multiple bureaus and offices covering four disciplines: emergency management, law enforcement, natural hazards science, and wildland fire. Depending on the season, approximately 3,500–4,000 law enforcement officers, rangers, and other employees patrol vast areas of public lands, national parks, wildlife refuges, and Indian communities. They protect people and natural, cultural, and heritage resources from illegal activities.

The U.S. Geological Survey protects lives by monitoring natural hazards like earthquakes, environmental health hazards, landslides, and volcanoes, and by issuing warnings of their potential threat levels. Wildland fires endanger lives and damage property. The Office of Wildland Fire coordinates with the DOI's land management bureaus and the U.S. Forest Service to prevent, respond to, and manage the damage and loss that wildfires cause. The Office of Wildland Fire also shares wildfire management responsibilities with Mexico along the southern border.

The DOI manages land on the Canadian border and the Mexican border, and the Department has a presence in the Pacific, where Americans are exposed to risk from Asia. A considerable amount of DOI land abuts Mexico. Accordingly, DOI law enforcement officers work in partnership with the U.S. Customs and Border Patrol, Immigration and Customs Enforcement, Drug Enforcement Agency, and Tribal, State, and local governments, to address illegal immigration, trafficking in drugs and in guns, and to mitigate these activities' consequences, which adversely affect DOI lands and community partners.

Sources of Information

A–Z Additional Resources The additional resources index contains links to resources that DOI employees may find helpful. https://www.doi.gov/employees/additional-resources

Archived Records The "Guide to Federal Records in the National Archives of the United States" indicates that Office of the Secretary of the Interior records have been assigned to record group 048. https://www.archives.gov/research/guide-fed-records/groups/048.html

Blog "People, Land, and Water" is the DOI's official blog. https://www.doi.gov/blog

Bureaus / Offices The DOI employs resource-management professionals, scientists, and other experts in its nine technical bureaus. https://www.doi.gov/bureaus

In addition to the nine technical bureaus, a number of offices fall under the Offices of the Secretary and Assistant Secretary; Office of Policy, Management, and Budget; Office of the Solicitor; and Office of the Inspector General. https://www.doi.gov/bureaus/offices

Business Opportunities The DOI supports the transition to a clean energy economy and stimulates local economic growth through stewardship. The DOI also procures goods and services from American businesses. The DOI relies on them for bridge, irrigation system, office building, reservoir, road, school, and other types of maintenance. More information is available from the Office of Acquisition and Property Management. Phone, 202-513-7554. https://www.doi.gov/pam

Career Opportunities Information to assist persons with disabilities, students and recent graduates, veterans, and others who are interested in career opportunities is available on the DOI's website. https://www.doi.gov/joinus

In 2019, the DOI ranked 10th among 17 large agencies in the Partnership for Public Service's Best Places To Work Agency Rankings. https://bestplacestowork.org/rankings/detail/IN00

Climate Change Changes in climate are creating new challenges for communities and resource managers nationwide. The U.S. Geological Survey's Climate Adaptation Science Centers help managers of ecosystems, fish, and wildlife better understand the effects of these changes and strategically plan for and adapt to them. https://nccwsc.usgs.gov

Contact Information The DOI has included an electronic feedback form on its "Contact Interior" web page. The DOI also may be contacted by email, phone, or postal correspondence. The contact information is available online. https://www.doi.gov/contact-us

Deepwater Horizon The DOI continues to play a major role in restoration efforts associated with the Deepwater Horizon oil spill that occurred in the Gulf of Mexico in 2010. https://www.doi.gov/deepwaterhorizon

Freedom of Information Act (FOIA) Thirteen bureaus and offices support the DOI's FOIA operations. Its website features a single web page that allows convenient access to those bureaus and offices and to their electronic FOIA libraries. From the same web page, an information seeker may file a request, track the status of a request, learn about the FOIA program's structure, and review FOIA-related guidance and resources. Please note: the Department and its bureaus and offices post a great deal of information online; therefore, an information seeker should visit the appropriate electronic libraries and search for the desired information before submitting a FOIA request. That information already may be accessible, immediately and without charge. https://www.doi.gov/foia

Frequently Asked Questions (FAQs) The DOI has posted answers to FAQs about its reorganization. https://www.doi.gov/employees/reorg/faq

History On March 3, 1849, the last day of the 30th Congress, a bill was passed to create a department to manage the Nation's internal development and the welfare of its people. The responsibilities of the new Department were diverse and came to include the colonization of freed slaves in Haiti, exploration of western wilderness, oversight of the District of Columbia jail, regulation of territorial governments, management of hospitals and universities, and more. To explore the rich history of the "Department of Everything Else"—just about everything else that fell outside the purview of the Departments of Foreign Affairs, War, and the Treasury—visit the "History of the Department of the Interior" web page. https://www.doi.gov/whoweare/history

"There are no words that can tell the hidden spirit of the wilderness that can reveal its mystery, its melancholy and its charm. The Nation behaves well if it treats the natural resources as assets which it must turn over to the next generation increased and not impaired in value. These words belong to President Theodore Roosevelt, a man who loved the outdoors. To learn about the important role this President played in the history of American conservation, visit the "Theodore Roosevelt's Legacy" web page. https://www.doi.gov/blog/theodore-roosevelts-legacy

Library The Interior Library's holdings and its reference and research services support the mission of the Department and its agencies and bureaus. Its holdings cover American history, geology, law, national parks, Native American culture and history, nature, and public lands and wildlife management. The library offers subscription databases and other online data sources that give Interior employees and external researchers nationwide access. A holdings catalog and descriptions of educational programs and training opportunities are available on the library's website. Phone, 202-208-5815. https://www.doi.gov/library | Email: library@ios.doi.gov

Museum The Interior Museum offers exhibits on the history and mission of the Department. Programs highlight bureau management of cultural and natural resources. Museum guides conduct tours of the Interior Building's New Deal era art and architecture. Phone, 202-208-4743. https://www.doi.gov/interiormuseum

News The Department posts press releases online. https://www.doi.gov/pressreleases

The DOI posts news and headlines of the week in video format on the "This Week at

Interior" web page. https://www.doi.gov/video/twai

Open Government The Department of the Interior supports the Open Government initiative by promoting the principles of collaboration, participation, and transparency. Beyond meeting Open Government requirements, the agency intends to create better relationships between citizens and their Government; to become better at understanding citizens' demands for services and more responsive to their needs; to accelerate the rate of innovation by leveraging public knowledge; to increase the Department's ability to carry out its mission more effectively and efficiently by transparently engaging the public in decisionmaking; and to encourage the development of Open Government programs. https://www.doi.gov/open | Email: open@ios.doi.gov

Priorities The "Our Priorities" web page lists the DOI's top 10 priorities. https://www.doi.gov/ourpriorities

Regulatory Reform President Donald J. Trump has placed an emphasis on reforming rules and regulations that negatively affect the U.S. economy while doing little to help the environment. https://www.doi.gov/regulatory-reform

Site Map The website map allows visitors to look for specific topics or to browse content that aligns with their interests. https://www.doi.gov/sitemap

Social Media The DOI maintains a facebook account. https://www.facebook.com/USInterior

The DOI tweets announcements and other newsworthy items on Twitter. https://twitter.com/interior

The DOI posts videos on its YouTube channel. https://www.youtube.com/user/USInterior

Sustainability Programs The Department of the Interior is dedicated to conserving and protecting the Nation's natural and cultural resources now and for future generations. Its employees are passionate about their stewardship responsibility for the resources and properties that they manage for the American People. https://www.doi.gov/stewardship

Water Conservation The WaterSMART program improves water conservation and helps water-resource managers make sound decisions about water use. It identifies strategies to ensure that this and future generations will have sufficient supplies of clean water for drinking, economic activities, ecosystem health, and recreation. The program also identifies adaptive measures to address climate change and its effect on future water demands. https://www.doi.gov/watersmart

The Sources of Information were updated 12–2019.

Bureau of Indian Affairs

Department of the Interior, 1849 C Street NW., Washington, DC 20240
Phone, 202-208-3710. Internet, http://www.bia.gov/bia

Director *   DARRYL LACOUNTE
https://www.bia.gov/as-ia/opa/online-press-
    release/assistant-secretary-sweeney-names-
    darryl-lacounte-director-bureau-of-indian-
    affairs

---

* The Director reports to the Assistant Secretary of Indian Affairs.

The above list of key personnel was updated 12–2019.

The Bureau of Indian Affairs enhances the quality of life, promotes economic opportunity, and protects and improves the trust assets of American Indians, Indian tribes, and Alaska Natives.

Bureau of Indian Affairs

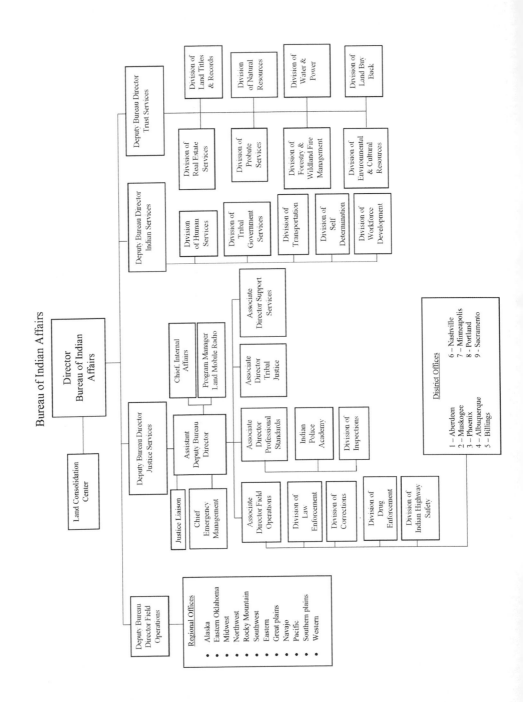

Establishment and Organization

Secretary of War John C. Calhoun established the Bureau of Indian Affairs (BIA) on March 11, 1824, to oversee and carry out the Federal Government's trade and treaty relations with tribes. The BIA remains the oldest Department of the Interior (DOI) agency in continuous existence and one of the oldest in the Federal government. The DOI formally adopted Bureau of Indian Affairs (BIA) as the agency's official name on September 17, 1947. Prior to that time, it was referred to as the Indian office, Indian bureau, Indian department, and Indian service. https://www.doi.gov/blog/193rd-anniversary-bureau-indian-affairs

On March 3, 1849, President James K. Polk approved an act that transferred the "supervisory and appellate powers now exercised by the Secretary of the War Department, in relation to all the acts of the Commissioner of Indian Affairs," to the Secretary of the Interior, who now headed the newly created DOI. http://www.loc.gov/law/help/statutes-at-large/30th-congress/session-2/c30s2ch108.pdf

Codified legislative material on the Bureau of Indian Affairs is found in title 25, chapter 1, sections 1–17, of the U.S. Code. https://uscode.house.gov/view.xhtml?path=/prelim@title25/chapter1&edition=prelim

Rules and regulations that affect Indians are codified in title 25 of the Code of Federal Regulations. Parts 1–299 contain rules and regulations that are associated with the Bureau of Indian Affairs. Parts 900–999 contain rules and regulations that are associated with the Bureau of Indian Affairs and with the Department of Health and Human Service's Indian Health Service. https://www.ecfr.gov/cgi-bin/text idx?SID=2d ff2e4675b2891abcf7c9eb0078703c&mc=tru e&tpl=/ecfrbrowse/Title25/25tab_02.tpl

The Bureau's organizational chart is available in Portable Document Format (PDF) for viewing and downloading. https://www.indianaffairs.gov/sites/bia.gov/files/uploads/bia/bia-org-chart.pdf

Activities

The BIA's mission centers on fulfilling its trust responsibilities and promoting self-determination on behalf of federally recognized tribal governments, American Indians, and Alaska Natives. The BIA provides services to members of 573 federally recognized Indian Tribes in the 48 contiguous United States and Alaska—nearly two million American Indians and Alaska Natives. https://www.bia.gov/bia

The BIA serves the federally recognized Tribes through four Offices:

The Office of Indian Services operates the BIA's general assistance, disaster relief, Indian child welfare, tribal government, Indian self-determination, and reservation roads programs. https://www.bia.gov/bia/ois

The Office of Justice Services directly operates or funds law enforcement, tribal courts, and detention facilities on Federal Indian lands. https://www.bia.gov/bia/ojs

The Office of Trust Services works with tribes and individual American Indians and Alaska Natives in the management of their trust lands, assets, and resources. https://www.bia.gov/bia/ots

Lastly, the Office of Field Operations oversees 12 regional offices and 83 agencies that carry out the mission of the BIA at the tribal level. The regional offices and agencies administer delivery of program services to the federally recognized Tribes, to individual Indians, and to Alaska Natives, either directly or through contracts, grants or compacts. https://www.bia.gov/regional-offices

Sources of Information

Archived Records The "Guide to Federal Records in the National Archives of the United States" indicates that Bureau of Indian Affairs records have been assigned to record group 075. https://www.archives.gov/research/guide-fed-records/groups/075.html
Career Opportunities BIA job opportunities, common job documents, and hiring information for American Indian and Alaska Native veterans are available online. https://www.bia.gov/Jobs/index.htm

In 2019, the BIA ranked 349th among 420 agency subcomponents in the Partnership for Public Service's Best Places To Work Agency Rankings. https://bestplacestowork.org/rankings/detail/IN06
Contact Information The BIA posts its mailing address and fax and phone numbers on the Indian Affairs' website on the

"Contact Us" web page. https://www.bia.
gov/contact-us

Estate Planning   The American Indian
Probate Reform Act of 2004 (AIPRA) made
changes to the way trust or restricted land
and property is inherited. It also made
changes that affected land management and
purchases. The BIA website has information
that explains how AIPRA affects wills and
inheritance. https://www.bia.gov/bia/ots/
dres/estate-planning

Freedom of Information Act (FOIA)   The
FOIA establishes a presumption that the
public may access records in the possession
of Federal agencies. The Act is based on
the principle of openness in government
and generally provides that a person has a
right of access to Federal agency records.
This right of access is restricted, however,
by nine exemptions and three special law
enforcement record exclusions that shield
certain records, or parts of them, from
disclosure. More information on the FOIA
and instructions for submitting a request
to access BIA records are available on the
Indian Affairs website. https://www.bia.gov/
as-ia/foia | Email: foia@bia.gov

Before submitting a FOIA request in
writing with the FOIA officer, the requester
should check that the information being
sought is not already in the public domain.
The DOI maintains FOIA libraries that
include the following record types and
resources: final opinions made in the
adjudication of cases; policy statements and
interpretations that the DOI has adopted,
but not published in the Federal Register;
administrative staff manuals and staff
instructions that affect a member of the
public; records that have been requested
repeatedly by submitters of FOIA requests
or records that the DOI anticipates will be
requested repeatedly in the future; an index
of frequently requested records; and links to
other related sites and reference materials.
https://www.doi.gov/foia/library

Frequently Asked Questions (FAQs)   Indian
Affairs posts answers to FAQs on its website.
https://www.bia.gov/frequently-asked-
questions

Library   Frequently requested documents
and links are accessible on the Indian Affairs
website in the electronic document library.
https://www.bia.gov/bia/document-library

Maps   The Office of Trust Services' Branch
of Geospatial Support (BGS) posts web maps
and static maps, as well as downloadable
data, on the Indian Affairs' website. The BGS
provides geographic information systems
software, training, and system support for
the management of natural resources on
Indian lands. Phone, 877-293-9494. https://
biamaps.doi.gov | Email: geospatial@bia.gov

"Indian Lands of Federally Recognized
Tribes of the United States" is available on
the Office of Trust Services' "Division of
Land Titles and Records" web page. The
Office's web team posted the map file in
Portable Document Format (PDF) for viewing
and downloading. https://www.bia.gov/sites/
bia.gov/files/assets/bia/ots/webteam/pdf/
idc1-028635.pdf

The "National Climate Assessment—
Indigenous People's Resilience Actions"
map, which is posted on the Office of Trust
Services' website, provides an overview of
indigenous people's actions to prepare for
changes in climate by taking steps to increase
resilience. https://biamaps.doi.gov/nca/

Programs / Services   Federally recognized
Tribes look to the BIA for a range of services.
The "Programs and Services" web page,
which is accessible on the Indian Affairs'
website, provides information about them.
https://www.bia.gov/programs-services

Regional Offices   Contact information
for the 12 BIA regional offices is available
online. https://www.bia.gov/regional-offices

Regulations in Development   The
"Regulations and Other Documents in
Development" web page, which is part of
the Indian Affairs' website, allows visitors
to monitor the progress of regulations that
are in development, under review, or in
development and under review. https://www.
bia.gov/as-ia/raca/regulations-and-other-
documents-in-development

Site Map   The site map, which is part of
the Indian Affairs' website, allows visitors to
look for specific topics or to browse content
that aligns with their interests. https://www.
bia.gov/sitemap

Social Media   The BIA posts content on
Facebook. https://www.facebook.com/
USIndianAffairs

The BIA tweets announcements and other
newsworthy items on Twitter. https://twitter.
com/USIndianAffairs

Tribal Leaders Directory The directory, which is part of the Indian Affairs' website, provides contact information for each federally recognized Tribe, as well as for the leadership of the BIA. The electronic and interactive map-based directory contains information on each BIA region and agency that provides services to a specific Tribe. https://www.bia.gov/tribal-leaders-directory

The Sources of Information were updated 12–2019.

Wildland Fire Management Indian Affairs posted a collection of fire prevention and education videos on wildland fire management in Indian country on its website. Note that not all of the videos in the collection were produced by the BIA. https://www.bia.gov/bia/ots/dfwfm/bwfm/Video-Library

---

Bureau of Indian Education

Department of the Interior, 1849 C Street NW., Washington, DC 20240
Phone, 202-208-3710. Internet, http://www.bie.edu

Director   TONY L. DEARMAN
https://www.bie.edu/cs/groups/webteam/
   documents/text/idc2-092903.pdf

---

*The Director reports to the Assistant Secretary of Indian Affairs.
The above list of key personnel was updated 12–2019.

The Bureau of Indian Education provides educational opportunities for eligible American Indian and Alaska Native elementary, secondary, and postsecondary students from federally recognized Tribes

Establishment and Organization

Formerly known as the Office of Indian Education Programs, the Bureau of Indian Education (BIE) was renamed and established on August 29, 2006, to reflect the parallel purpose and organizational structure BIE has in relation to other programs within the Office of the Assistant Secretary–Indian Affairs. https://www.bia.gov/bie

The Director heads the Bureau and is responsible for forming policies and procedures, supervising all program activities, and approving the expenditure of funds that are appropriated for education functions.

The BIE organizational chart is part of the Indian Affairs organizational chart. https://www.indianaffairs.gov/sites/bia.gov/files/OrgChartFY18Greenbook.pdf

Activities

The BIE educates approximately 48,000 American Indian and Alaska Native children at 183 elementary and secondary schools on 64 reservations in 23 States. The Bureau operates 58 of these schools. The other 125 schools are tribally operated under the Indian Self-Determination and Education Assistance Act of 1975 (25 U.S.C. 450 et seq.) or the Tribally Controlled Schools Act of 1988 (25 U.S.C. 2501 et seq.). The BIE oversees two postsecondary schools— Haskell Indian Nations University in Lawrence, KS, and Southwestern Indian Polytechnic Institute in Albuquerque, NM— and it funds the Navajo and United Tribes Technical Colleges. https://www.bia.gov/bie

Sources of Information

Archived Records The "Guide to Federal Records in the National Archives of the United States" indicates that Bureau of Indian Affairs records have been assigned to record group 075. "Records of the Education Division 1874–1972" are part of that record group. https://www.archives.gov/research/guide-fed-records/groups/075.html

Career Opportunities   American Indian children deserve a quality education—and that starts with highly qualified, dedicated staff and educators. The BIE employees nearly 4,500 professionals in careers that offer unique and diverse cultural and lifestyle experiences. Phone, 505-563-5304. https://www.bie.edu/Jobs/index.htm | Email: staffing@bie.edu

Contact Information   The "Contact Us" web page has addresses and phone numbers for contacting the BIE. https://www.bie.edu/ContactUs/index.htm

The BIE "National Staff Directory" (APR 2019) is available in Portable Document Format (PDF) for viewing and downloading. https://www.bie.edu/cs/groups/xbie/documents/text/idc2-093307.pdf

Divisions / Programs   The BIE website features a web page with a list of the agency's divisions and programs and links to their web sites. https://www.bie.edu/Programs/index

Freedom of Information Act (FOIA)   The FOIA establishes a presumption that the public may access records in the possession of Federal agencies. The Act is based on the principle of openness in government and generally provides that a person has a right of access to Federal agency records. This right of access is restricted, however, by nine exemptions and three special law enforcement record exclusions that shield certain records, or parts of them, from disclosure. More information on the FOIA and instructions for submitting a request to access BIE records are available on the Indian Affairs website. https://www.bia.gov/as-ia/foia | Email: foia@bia.gov

Before submitting a FOIA request in writing with the FOIA officer, the requester should check that the information being sought is not already in the public domain. The DOI maintains FOIA libraries that include the following record types and resources: final opinions made in the adjudication of cases; policy statements and interpretations that the DOI has adopted, but not published in the Federal Register; administrative staff manuals and staff instructions that affect a member of the public; records that have been requested repeatedly by submitters of FOIA requests or records that the DOI anticipates will be requested repeatedly in the future; an index of frequently requested records; and links to other related sites and reference materials. https://www.doi.gov/foia/library

News   The BIE posts news items on its website. https://www.bie.edu/NewsEvents/index.htm

Reports   Performance and special education reports and school report cards are accessible online. https://www.bie.edu/HowAreWeDoing/index.htm

Resources   BIE education line officers, school superintendents, principals, teachers, and staff can access program guidance, handbooks, templates, and training provided in various formats—WebEx or PowerPoint—to refresh professional skills. These online documents and presentations are provided to supplement staff training throughout the school year. https://www.bie.edu/Resources/index.htm

Scholarships   The BIE website provides information on scholarship opportunities for American Indian students. https://www.bie.edu/ParentsStudents/Grants/index.htm

Site Map   The website map allows visitors to look for specific topics or to browse content that aligns with their interests. https://www.bie.edu/SiteMap/index.htm

Social Media   The BIE maintains a Facebook account. https://www.facebook.com/Bureauofindianeducation

The BIE tweets announcements and other newsworthy items on Twitter. https://twitter.com/BureauIndianEdu

The Sources of Information were updated 12–2019.

Bureau of Land Management

Department of the Interior, 1849 C Street NW., Washington, DC 20240
Phone, 202-208-3801. Internet, https://https://www.blm.gov

Director   VACANT

The Bureau of Land Management (BLM) was established July 16, 1946, by the consolidation of the General Land Office (created, 1812) and the Grazing Service (formed, 1934). https://www.blm.gov/about

The Bureau sustains the diversity, health, and productivity of America's public lands for the benefit of present and future generations through a mandate of multiple-use and sustained-yield. It manages 1 of every 10 acres of land across the United States, about 245 million acres of land, most of which is located in Alaska and 11 other Western States. The Bureau also manages about 30 percent or 700 million acres of the Nation's subsurface mineral estate. The Bureau oversees conventional and renewable energy development, livestock grazing, recreation, and timber harvesting, and it protects cultural, historical, and natural resources. Many of these resources are found on National Conservation Lands, a subset of BLM lands that are federally designated, that cover 32 million acres, and that include 223 wilderness areas and 25 national monuments. https://www.blm.gov/programs/national-conservation-lands

BLM management responsibilities and activities are broad in scope and diverse. It manages Federal onshore coal, gas, and oil operations—and also vast stretches of public lands that will play a significant role in the Nation's emerging renewable energy portfolio. The BLM is already 75 percent of the way to reaching President Obama's Climate Action Plan goal of approving projects that will generate 20,000 megawatts of renewable energy by 2020. The Bureau also contributes to wildland fire management to protect the public and the Nation's natural resource landscape, recreational areas, and wildlife habitat. https://www.blm.gov/programs/energy-and-minerals

The Bureau manages livestock on 155 million acres of land, administering nearly 18,000 permits and leases held by ranchers who graze mostly cattle and sheep. Under the Wild Free-Roaming Horses and Burros Act of 1971, it also manages herds of wild horses and burros on public rangelands. https://www.blm.gov/programs/natural-resources/rangelands-and-grazing; https://www.blm.gov/programs/wild-horse-and-burro

Recreation is also part of the BLM's portfolio. Birdwatchers, campers, hang gliders, horseback riders, hunters, mountain bikers, photographers, whitewater rafters, and visitors to cultural and natural heritage sites recreate on hundreds of millions of acres of public lands. The Bureau estimates that it receives approximately 62 million recreational visits per year. https://www.blm.gov/programs/recreation

The Bureau's broad management responsibilities require balancing public land uses and protection of public land resources. Working with State and local and tribal governments, stakeholder groups, and the public, the BLM creates land use plans, referred to as Resource Management Plans, to guide decisions for approved uses of and actions affecting public lands. https://www.blm.gov/programs/planning-and-nepa

Sources of Information

Adoption Schedule   The BLM offers wild horses and burros for adoption or purchase at events nationwide throughout the year. The most current adoption event schedule is accessible online. https://www.blm.gov/programs/wild-horse-and-burro/adopton-and-sales/adoption-events

Business Opportunities   The National Operations Center in Denver, Colorado, and the Oregon/Washington State Office handle most procurements over $150,000 and also award and administer all Indefinite Delivery / Indefinite Quantity (IDIQ) contracts that are national in scope.

Government contracting and financial assistance information and resources for small businesses are available online. https://www.blm.gov/services/acquisition/contractingl

Career Opportunities   The BLM relies on people with diverse skills and professional backgrounds—administration and management, biological sciences, business services, cadastral survey and geological sciences, fire and aviation, law and realty, petroleum engineering, and more—to carry out its mission. https://www.blm./careersl

Information on BLM Pathways programs for students and recent graduates is available online. https://www.blm.gov/careers/students-and-grads/pathways-program-coordinators

Freedom of Information Act (FOIA)   Instructions to submit a FOIA request for agency records are available on the BLM Web site. https://www.blabout/foia

General Land Office Records   The General Land Office Records Automation Web site provides access to Federal land conveyance records for the Public Land States, including image access to more than five million Federal land title records issued between 1820 and the present. The Web site also has survey plat- and field note-related images that date back to 1810. Please note: The Web site does not currently contain every Federal title record issued for the Public Land States. https://www.glorecords.blm.gov/default.aspx

Reading Rooms   State offices provide facilities where visitors may examine status records, tract books, and other records of public lands and their resources.

Recreation   The National Conservation Lands program offers online recreational guides for a convenient connection to public lands. https://www.blm.gov/visit

The BLM Web site provides resources for mountain bikers. These resources include the BLM Top 20 Mountain Biking Opportunities list and interactive mountain biking maps for trails on BLM lands. https://www.blm.gov/mountainbike/

Renewable Energy   The BLM Web site features a table that contains the locations and other details of the renewable energy projects approved since 2009 on public lands.

Site Maps   An index of BLM site maps is available online. A site map allows Internet visitors to look for specific topics or to browse content that aligns with their interests.

Speakers   Upon request from organizations within their areas of jurisdiction, local offices will arrange for speakers to explain BLM programs.

Statistics   Public Land Statistics documents according to year and starting with 1996 are accessible online. http://www.blm.gov/public_land_statistics/index.htm

Tables and spreadsheets with data that include the numbers of BLM-administered oil and gas leases, of applications for permit to drill, and of oil and gas wells are accessible on the BLM Web site. Most of the statistics presented cover Fiscal Years 1988–2015. https://www.blm.gov/about/data/public-land-statistics; https://www.blm.gov

For further information, contact the Office of Public Affairs, Bureau of Land Management, Department of the Interior, 1849 C Street NW., Washington, DC 20240. Phone, 202-208-3801.

Bureau of Ocean Energy Management

Department of the Interior, 1849 C Street NW., Washington, DC 20240-0001
Phone, 202-208-6474. Internet, http://www.boem.gov

Director	ABIGAIL ROSS HOPPER

The Bureau of Ocean Energy Management (BOEM) was created on October 1, 2011, as directed by Secretarial Order No. 3299, as amended.

The Bureau assesses marine-related activities on the Outer Continental Shelf (OCS) and the nature, extent, recoverability, and value of energy resources and minerals located there. It promotes responsible marine-related activities, including exploring, inventorying, and developing energy and mineral resources; analyzes the potential environmental effects of proposed resource management operations; conducts and oversees environmental studies to inform policy decisions on OCS energy and marine mineral resources management; develops and implements leasing and resource evaluation and management regulations; and oversees the financial accountability of lessees, operators, and operating-rights holders to ensure that they meet financial and contractual commitments.

The Bureau promotes cooperation among the Federal Government, State and tribal governments, and native communities on national, regional, and local issues relevant to the scope of its responsibilities. BOEM activities also support national policy priorities: energy security, environmental protection, and social and economic development. http://www.boem.gov/About-BOEM

Sources of Information

Business Opportunities   Information on doing business with the Bureau is available online. http://www.boem.gov/Doing-Business-with-BOEM

Calendar   The BOEM Web site features a calendar of upcoming events. http://www.boem.gov/Upcoming-Events

Career Opportunities   The BOEM relies on professionals with engineering and science backgrounds for ensuring the safe and environmentally responsible development of the Nation's offshore energy and marine mineral resources. http://www.boem.gov/employment

The BOEM posts vacancy announcements on its Web site. http://www.boem.gov/vacancies

Educational Resources   BOEM teacher resources are available online. http://www.boem.gov/Environmental-Studies-Program-Teacher-Resources

Freedom of Information Act (FOIA)   Instructions for submitting a request for BOEM records under the FOIA are available online. The BOEM operates a FOIA requester service center. Phone, 703-787-1818. http://www.boem.gov/Requesting-Access-to-BOEM-Records

Glossary   The BOEM maintains an online resource evaluation glossary. http://www.boem.gov/Resource-Evaluation-Glossary

Historic Preservation   Archaeologists in Office of Renewable Energy Programs coordinate studies and conduct National Historic Preservation Act reviews to identify and protect archaeological sites and other historic properties. OCS historic properties include aircraft, lighthouses, precontact (European contact with Native Americans) archaeological sites, and shipwrecks. Historic properties onshore come under

review when a proposed renewable energy project may affect them. To learn more about investigating the steamship "City of Houston" and German submarine "U–576" and other preservation activities, visit the "Historic Preservation Activities" Web page. https://www.boem.gov/Renewable-Energy/Historic-Preservation-Activities

Library   The BOEM Web site has an electronic library. http://www.boem.gov/Library

Marine Minerals   Mineral resources from the OCS are used in coastal restoration projects to address erosion. The BOEM has conveyed rights to millions of cubic yards of OCS sand for coastal restoration projects in multiple States. These projects have restored hundreds of miles of the Nation's coastline, protecting both infrastructure and ecological habitat. The BOEM posts key marine mineral statistics on its Web site. http://www.boem.gov/MMP-Current-Statistics | Email: MarineMinerals@boem.gov

Newsroom   The BOEM newsroom features congressional testimony, factsheets, Frequently Asked Questions (FAQs), leadership presentations, media advisories, notes to stakeholders, science notes, statistics and facts, technical announcements, and videos. http://www.boem.gov/BOEM-Newsroom

Oil and Gas Energy   The BOEM has posted the 2012–2017 lease sale schedule and information on specific lease sales on its Web site. http://www.boem.gov/Oil-and-Gas-Energy-Program/Leasing/Five-Year-Program/Lease-Sale-Schedule/2012---2017-Lease-Sale-Schedule.aspx

Posters   Colorful BOEM posters that promote maritime history, ocean science and stewardship, and awareness of marine animals and their habitats are available from the Gulf of Mexico Public Information Office. Phone, 800-200-4853. http://www.boem.gov/BOEM-Posters

Renewable Energy   The offshore renewable energy guide provides background information on ocean renewable energy resources, the Outer Continental Shelf, and alternate uses for oil and gas platforms. http://www.boem.gov/Offshore-Renewable-Energy-Guide

A list of leases that the BOEM has executed since the inception of its renewable energy program is available online. http://www.boem.gov/Lease-and-Grant-Information

The BOEM collaborates with States on offshore energy development and is in the process of coordinating Federal-State task forces in certain coastal States. A summary of the status of activity in the various States is available online. https://www.boem.gov/Renewable-Energy-Program/State-Activities/Index.aspx

Regional Offices   The BOEM operates three regional offices, one for the Alaska Outer Continental Shelf (OCS) region, one for the Pacific OCS region, and one for the Gulf of Mexico and Atlantic OCS regions. Phone, 907-334-5200 (Alaska). Phone, 805-384-

6305 (Pacific). Phone, 800-200-4853 (Gulf of Mexico and Atlantic).

Shipwrecks   The BOEM Alaskan shipwreck table is the most comprehensive compilation of Alaskan shipwrecks to date. The table offers a list of wrecks that occurred in Alaskan waters from 1741 to 2011. The "Shipwrecks Off Alaska's Coast" Web page also features maritime history, ship, and shipwreck links to external Web sites. http://www.boem.gov/Alaska-Coast-Shipwrecks

Site Map   The Web site map allows visitors to look for specific topics or to browse content that aligns with their interests. http://www.boem.gov/Sitemap; http://www.boem.gov/Contact-Us | Email: BOEMPublicAffairs@boem.gov

For further information, contact the Office of Public Affairs, Bureau of Ocean Energy Management, Department of the Interior, 1849 C Street NW., Washington, DC 20240-0001. Phone, 202-208-6474.

Bureau of Reclamation

Department of the Interior, 1849 C Street NW., Washington, DC 20240
Phone, 202-513-0575. Internet, http://www.usbr.gov

Commissioner	ESTEVAN LÓPEZ

The Bureau of Reclamation was established pursuant to the Reclamation Act of 1902 (43 U.S.C. 371 et seq.). The Bureau is the largest wholesale water supplier and the second largest producer of hydroelectric power in the United States, with operations and facilities in the 17 Western States. Its operations and facilities also support recreation and flood control and benefit fish and wildlife. http://www.usbr.gov/main/about/mission.html

Sources of Information

Business Opportunities   The Bureau of Reclamation purchases a wide range of products and services and supports various Federal socioeconomic development programs by reaching out to and assisting businesses. The Bureau also provides financial assistance for programs related to conservation, Endangered Species Act mitigation, rural water, and water management and reclamation and reuse. http://www.usbr.gov/mso/aamd/doing-business.html

The Acquisition and Assistance Management Division is responsible for the Bureau's acquisition and financial assistance policy, acquisition and financial assistance operations, and property programs. Phone, 303-445-2431. http://www.usbr.gov/mso/aamd/org-contact.html

Career Opportunities   The Bureau relies on professionals with expertise in administration, engineering and design, environmental protection, research, wildlife management, and other disciplines to carry out its mission. Career-related information is available from the nearest regional office or the Diversity and Human Resources Office, Denver, CO. Phone, 303-445-2684. http://www.usbr.gov/hr

Environment   The Bureau maintains a list of links to online resources that provide environmental information. http://www.usbr.gov/environmental

Freedom of Information Act (FOIA)   Contact information for the Bureau's regional FOIA coordinators is available online. http://www.usbr.gov/foia/contacts.html

The Bureau maintains an electronic reading room that contains frequently requested records and documents that are currently of special interest. http://www.usbr.gov/foia/readroom.html

Glossary Definitions for terms commonly used by the Bureau are accessible in its online glossary. http://www.usbr.gov/library/glossary

The Bureau maintains a separate online glossary of recreation-related terms. http://www.usbr.gov/recreation/glossary.html

News The Bureau posts news releases and stories on its Web site, which also features congressional testimony, factsheets, photos, and speeches. http://www.usbr.gov/newsroom/newsrelease

Publications Publications for sale are available through the National Technical Information Service. Phone, 800-553-6847. http://www.ntis.gov

Reclamation Manual The Bureau's Web site has an online tool that allows users to search for keywords and terms in the "Reclamation Manual." The manual comprises a series of policy and directives and standards, which collectively assign program responsibility and establish and document agencywide methods of doing business. http://www.usbr.gov/recman

Recreation Recreation.gov provides information on all recreation facilities on Federal lands, including those owned and managed by the Bureau of Reclamation or one of its partners. Internet visitors can use Recreation.gov to make reservations at facilities that require them. http://www.recreation.gov/unifSearch.do

The Bureau's Web site features a list of publications on recreation-related topics. http://www.usbr.gov/recreation/publications.html

Regional Offices Contact information for the Washington, DC, and Denver, CO, based offices and Upper Colorado, Great Plains, Lower Colorado, Mid-Pacific, and Pacific Northwest regional offices is available on the "Addresses and Contacts" Web page. http://www.usbr.gov/main/offices.html

Water Conservation The WaterSMART program allows all Department of the Interior bureaus to work with States, tribes, local governments, and nongovernmental organizations to pursue a sustainable water supply for the Nation by establishing a framework that provides Federal leadership and assistance on the efficient use of water, that integrates water and energy policies to support the sustainable use of all natural resources, and that coordinates the water conservation activities of the various Department offices. http://www.usbr.gov/watersmart/water.html; https://www.doi.gov/watersmart; http://www.usbr.gov/main/offices.html

For further information, contact the Office of Public Affairs, Bureau of Reclamation, Department of the Interior, 1849 C Street NW., Washington, DC 20240-0001. Phone, 202-513-0575.

Bureau of Safety and Environmental Enforcement

Department of the Interior, 1849 C Street NW., Washington, DC 20240
Phone, 202-208-3985. Internet, http://www.bsee.gov

Director	Brian M. Salerno

The Bureau of Safety and Environmental Enforcement (BSEE) was created on May 19, 2010, by Secretarial Order No. 3299, as amended. https://www.bsee.gov/who-we-are/history

The BSEE promotes safety, protects the environment, and conserves resources on the Outer Continental Shelf (OCS) through regulatory oversight and enforcement. The Offshore Regulatory Program develops standards and regulations to improve operational safety and to strengthen environmental protection. The Oil Spill Preparedness Division develops standards and guidelines for offshore operators. It also collaborates with sister agencies on spill response technologies and capabilities.

Three regional offices support the Bureau. Their personnel inspect gas and oil drilling rigs and production platforms to ensure compliance with safety requirements. Inspection teams are multiperson, and the expertise of their members spans a range of disciplines. https://www.bsee.gov/what-we-do

Sources of Information

Business Opportunities Information on doing business with the BSEE is available online. http://www.bsee.gov/About-BSEE/Doing-Business-with-BSEE/index

Career Opportunities The BSEE relies on professionals with backgrounds in biology, geology, geophysics, engineering, and other fields to carry out its mission. http://www.bsee.gov/careers

Freedom of Information Act (FOIA) The FOIA gives the public the right to request Federal agency records and requires Federal agencies to make certain records available. The BSEE Web site serves as the portal to the agency's FOIA program. The FOIA is based on the principle of openness in Government: Any person has a right of access to Federal agency records, except to the extent that such records or portions of them are protected from disclosure by exemption or by special law-enforcement record exclusion. https://www.bsee.gov/newsroom/library/foia

The BSEE maintains an electronic FOIA reading room. https://www.bsee.gov/newsroom/library/FOIA-Reading-Rooom

Frequently Asked Questions (FAQs) The BSEE promotes safety, protects the environment, and conserves resources offshore through regulatory oversight and enforcement. To accomplish this mission, the Bureau relies on a wide range of world-class professionals. The Frequently Asked Questions (FAQs) Web page offers a sample of the questions that BSEE experts address and answers that they have provided. https://www.bsee.gov/newsroom/library/frequently-asked-questions | Email: webmaster@bsee.gov

Glossary This glossary contains common oil and gas exploration and leasing terms, many of which are unique to the drilling industry. https://www.bsee.gov/newsroom/library/glossary

News The BSEE newsroom contains feature stories, media advisories, news briefs, photos and videos, press releases, and posts from the Director. The briefing room contains annual reports, congressional testimony, factsheets, speeches, statements, and technical presentations. https://www.bsee.gov/newsroom

The BSEE tweets announcements and other newsworthy items on Twitter. https://twitter.com/BSEEgov

Offshore Statistics The BSEE Web sites features a section dedicated to offshore statistics and facts. https://www.bsee.gov/stats-facts

Reading Room The Bureau's Deepwater Horizon electronic reading room contains documents that deal with the BP/Deepwater Horizon explosion and ensuing oil spill and that have been cleared for public release. https://www.bsee.gov/newsroom/library/archive/deepwater-horizon-reading-room

Regional Offices Information on the BSEE's three geographic regions—Alaska OCS, Gulf of Mexico OCS, and Pacific OCS—and their respective regional offices is available on the "BSEE Regions" Web page. http://www.bsee.gov/About-BSEE/BSEE-Regions/BSEE-Regions

Site Map The Web site map allows visitors to look for specific topics or to browse content that aligns with their interests. https://www.bsee.gov/sitemap; http://www.bsee.gov/About-BSEE/Contact-Us/Contact-Us

For further information, contact the Office of Public Affairs, Bureau of Safety and Environmental Enforcement, Department of the Interior, 1849 C Street NW., Washington, DC 20240-7000. Phone, 202-208-3985.

National Park Service

Department of the Interior, 1849 C Street NW., Washington, DC 20240
Phone, 202-208-6843. Internet, http://www.nps.gov

Director   JONATHAN B. JARVIS

The National Park Service (NPS) was established in the Department of the Interior on August 25, 1916 (16 U.S.C. 1). http://www.nps.gov/aboutus/index.htm

The National Park Service protects the natural and cultural resources and values of the National Park System for the benefit of present and future generations. The National Park System comprises 401 units. These units include national parks, monuments and memorials, battlefield sites and national military parks, scenic parkways, preserves and reserves, trails and riverways, rivers and lakeshores and seashores, recreation areas, and historic sites of American or international importance. The Service also manages a variety of national and international programs to promote natural and cultural resource conservation and to expand the benefits of outdoor recreation.

The NPS develops and implements park management plans and staffs the areas under its administration. Through exhibits, films, publications talks, tours, and other interpretive media, it promotes the natural values of these areas and communicates their historical significance to the public. The NPS operates a range of visitor facilities, including campgrounds, and provides a variety of food, lodging, and transportation services.

The National Park Service also administers the State portion of the Land and Water Conservation Fund, State comprehensive outdoor recreation planning, nationwide outdoor recreation coordination and information, the National Register of Historic Places and the National Trails System, natural area programs, national historic landmarks and historic preservation, technical preservation services, the historic American engineering record and buildings survey, interagency archeological services, and planning and technical assistance for the national wild and scenic rivers system.

Sources of Information

America the Beautiful Passes   A pass may be used at more than 2,000 Federal recreation sites. A pass covers entrance fees at national parks and national wildlife refuges, as well as standard amenity fees and day use fees at national forests and grasslands and at lands managed by the Bureaus of Land Management and Reclamation and the U.S. Army Corps of Engineers. Five types of America the Beautiful passes are available: access, annual, annual fourth grade, senior, and volunteer. https://www.nps.gov/planyourvisit/passes.htm

Business Opportunities   Visit the "Doing Business With Us" Web page to find information on commercial tours, contracts and procurement, National Park concessions, and special park uses, including commercial filming. http://www.nps.gov/aboutus/doingbusinesswithus.htm

Career Opportunities   To find permanent and seasonal NPS career opportunities online, visit USAJobs, the Federal Government's official source for Federal job listings. https://my.usajobs.gov

Additional information on internships, permanent careers, seasonal opportunities, and volunteering is available on the "Work With Us" Web page. http://www.nps.gov/aboutus/workwithus.htm

Directories   An online text box allows Internet visitors to search for NPS employees by last name. https://www.nps.gov/directory

A park directory (SEP 2016) that includes park addresses, codes, phone numbers, and superintendents is available online in Portable Document Format (PDF). https://www.nps.gov/aboutus/upload/NPS-Park-Listing-09-01-16.pdf

Find a Park   Visitors to the NPS Web site may search for a park by name or by State. https://www.nps.gov/findapark/index.htm

Freedom of Information Act (FOIA)   Instructions for submitting a FOIA request to obtain NPS records are available online. https://www.nps.gov/aboutus/foia/index.htm

The NPS Web site features an electronic FOIA library. https://www.nps.gov/aboutus/foia/foia-reading-room.htm

Frequently Asked Questions (FAQs)   The NPS Web site has answers to these questions. https://www.nps.gov/aboutus/faqs.htm

Glossaries   The NPS's National Center for Preservation Technology and Training maintains an extensive glossary of building stone terms. https://ncptt.nps.gov/buildingstone/glossary

The online series "Defining the Southwest" includes a glossary of terms that are often encountered in discussions of the cultures and environments of the American Southwest. https://www.nps.gov/articles/southwest-glossary.htm

A glossary of geologic terms that the NPS and U.S. Geological Survey western Earth surface processes team compiled is available on the NPS Web site. http://www.nature.nps.gov/geology/usgsnps/misc/glossaryAtoC.html | Email: parkgeology@den.nps.gov

Grants Information is available online for grants authorized under the Land and Water Conservation Fund. Phone, 202-354-6900. http://www.nps.gov/lwcf/index.htm

Information is also available online for grants authorized under the Historic Preservation Fund. Phone, 202-354-2067. http://www.nps.gov/preservation-grants

News The NPS posts new releases online. https://www.nps.gov/aboutus/news/news-releases.htm

The NPS Web site features a multimedia section that includes audio, photographs, videos, and webcam. https://www.nps.gov/media/multimedia-search.htm

The NPS tweets announcements and other newsworthy items on Twitter. https://twitter.com/natlparkservice

The NPS maintains a Facebook page. https://www.facebook.com/nationalparkservice

Publications To explain decisions, document information, and disseminate knowledge, the NPS uses a variety of publications, many of which are accessible online. For example, "The National Parks: Index 2012–2016" can be downloaded as a PDF. The "Publications" Web page offers online access to contemporary and historic reports, periodicals, virtual stacks, and public databases. http://www.nps.gov/aboutus/publications.htm

Some publications are available for purchase in hardcopy from the U.S. Government Bookstore. Phone, 202-512-1800. Phone, 866-512-1800. https://bookstore.gpo.gov/agency/222 | Email: contactcenter@gpo.gov

Regional Offices Contact information is available online for NPS regional offices and parks and the Washington office. http://www.nps.gov/aboutus/contactinformation.htm; https://www.nps.gov/aboutus/contactus.htm

For further information, contact the Office of Communications, National Park Service, Department of the Interior, 1849 C Street NW., Washington, DC 20240. Phone, 202-208-6843.

Office of Surface Mining Reclamation and Enforcement

Department of the Interior, 1951 Constitution Avenue NW., Washington, DC 20240
Phone, 202-208-2565. TDD, 202-208-2694. Internet, http://www.osmre.gov

Director	JOSEPH PIZARCHIK

The Office of Surface Mining Reclamation and Enforcement (OSMRE) was established in the Department of the Interior by the Surface Mining Control and Reclamation Act of 1977 (30 U.S.C. 1211). http://www.osmre.gov/about.shtm

The OSMRE carries out the requirements of the Surface Mining Control and Reclamation Act in cooperation with States and tribes. The Office protects people and the environment from the adverse effects of coal mining. The OSMRE assures that land is restored to beneficial use after mining operations

cease, and it mitigates the effects of past operations by reclamation of abandoned coal mines. The Office mainly oversees State mining regulatory and abandoned-mine reclamation programs, assists States in meeting the objectives of surface mining law, and regulates mining and reclamation activities on Federal and Indian lands and in those States opting not to assume primary responsibility for regulating coal mining and reclamation activities within their borders.

The Office establishes national policy for the surface mining control and reclamation program, reviews and approves amendments to previously approved State programs, and reviews and recommends approval of new State program submissions. It also manages the collection, disbursement, and accounting of abandoned-mine land reclamation fees; administers civil penalties programs; establishes technical standards and regulatory policy for reclamation and enforcement; offers guidance for environmental considerations, research, training, and technology transfers; and monitors and evaluates State and tribal regulatory programs, cooperative agreements, and abandoned-mine land reclamation programs.

Sources of Information

Abandoned Mine Land Inventory System To provide information for implementing the Surface Mining Control and Reclamation Act of 1977, the OSMRE maintains an inventory of land and water affected by past mining. The inventory contains information on the location, type, and extent of abandoned mine land impacts, as well as information on the reclamation costs. The inventory is based on field surveys by State, tribal, and OSMRE program officials. https://amlis.osmre.gov/About.aspx

Business Opportunities Information to assist small business operators and owners is available online. For additional information, contact the Acquisition Management Branch. Phone, 202-208-2902. http://www.osmre.gov/contacts/business.shtm

Career Opportunities To find employment opportunities at the OSMRE, visit the "Jobs at OSMRE" Web page and click on the USAJobs quick link. http://www.osmre.gov/contacts/jobs.shtm

Freedom of Information Act (FOIA) A FOIA request for OSMRE records may be submitted via electronic or postal mail or by using the Department of the Interior's electronic request form and selecting "Office of Surface Mining" in the drop-down menu. http://www.osmre.gov/lrg/foia.shtm | Email: foia@osmre.gov

Frequently Asked Questions (FAQs) The OSMRE posts answers to FAQs on its Web site. http://www.osmre.gov/resources/FAQs.shtm

The OSMRE Web site also features a "How Do I?" section. http://www.osmre.gov/howdoi.shtm

Grants Information on regulatory program grants and abandoned mine land grants is available on the OSMRE Web site. http://www.osmre.gov/resources/grants.shtm

Library The general public may use the OSMRE online library catalog to locate legal and technical information. http://o10007.eos-intl.net/O10007/OPAC/Index.aspx

Mine Maps The National Mine Map Repository collects and maintains mine map information and images for the entire country. http://mmr.osmre.gov

An index that includes over 180,000 maps of closed and abandoned mines is available online. The index serves as an inventory for determining which maps are available. To obtain actual copies of maps, contact the National Mine Map Repository. Fax, 412-937-2888. http://mmr.osmre.gov/MultiPub.aspx

Most Requested Content The OSMRE Web site features a collection of links to its most frequently requested Web pages. http://www.osmre.gov/resources/mostRequested.shtm

Newsroom The newsroom features OSMRE stories and news releases. http://www.osmre.gov/resources/newsroom.shtm

The OSMRE tweets announcements and other newsworthy items on Twitter. https://twitter.com/OSMRE

The OSMRE has a Facebook page. https://www.facebook.com/Office.of.Surface.Mining.Reclamation.Enforcement

Regional Offices Appalachian Region Office. http://www.arcc.osmre.gov/contacts.shtm

Mid-Continent Region Office. http://www.mcrcc.osmre.gov/contacts.shtm

Western Region Office. http://www.wrcc.osmre.gov/contacts.shtm

Resources The OSMRE Web site features a section dedicated to electronic, informational resources. http://www.osmre.gov/resources.shtm

Site Map The Web site map allows visitors to look for specific topics or to browse content that aligns with their interests. http://www.osmre.gov/resources/sitemap.shtm

An A–Z index is also available to help visitors find the information that they seek on the OSMRE Web site. http://www.osmre. gov/resources/AtoZ.shtm

Top Priorities The OSMRE Web site features a section on the agency's top priorities. http://www.osmre.gov/ topPriorities.shtm; http://www.osmre.gov/ contacts.shtm | Email: getinfo@osmre.gov

For further information, contact the Office of Communications, Office of Surface Mining Reclamation and Enforcement, Department of the Interior, 1951 Constitution Avenue NW., Washington, DC 20240. Phone, 202-208-2565. TDD, 202-208-2694.

United States Fish and Wildlife Service

Department of the Interior, 1849 C Street NW., Washington, DC 20240
Phone, 703-358-4545. Internet, http://www.fws.gov

Director   DANIEL M. ASHE

[For the United States Fish and Wildlife Service statement of organization, see the Code of Federal Regulations, Title 50, Subchapter A, Part 2]

The U.S. Fish and Wildlife Service (USFWS) is the principal Federal agency dedicated to fish and wildlife conservation. The Service's history spans 145 years, dating from the establishment of its predecessor agency, the Bureau of Fisheries, in 1871. First created as an independent agency, the Bureau of Fisheries was later placed in the Department of Commerce. A second predecessor agency, the Bureau of Biological Survey, was established in 1885 in the Department of Agriculture. In 1939, the two Bureaus and their functions were transferred to the Department of the Interior. In 1940, they were consolidated into one agency and redesignated the Fish and Wildlife Service by Reorganization Plan No. 3 (5 U.S.C. app.). http://training.fws.gov/history/USFWS-history.html

The USFWS works with others to conserve, protect, and enhance fish, wildlife and plants and their habitats for the continuing benefit of the American people. The Service manages the 150-million-acre National Wildlife Refuge System, which comprises 563 refuges and 38 wetland management districts. It operates 72 national fish hatcheries, a historic national fish hatchery, 65 fishery resource offices, and 81 ecological service field stations. The USFWS enforces Federal wildlife laws, administers the Endangered Species Act, manages migratory bird populations, restores nationally significant fisheries, conserves and restores wildlife habitats, and assists foreign governments with conservation. It also collects excise taxes on fishing and hunting equipment and distributes the revenues to State fish and wildlife agencies.

The Service improves and maintains fish and wildlife resources by proper management of wildlife and habitat. It also helps meet public demand for wildlife dependent recreational activities by maintaining public lands and restoring native fish and wildlife populations.

Wildlife and fishery resource programs support the management of wildlife refuges on public lands. Wildlife-related activities include population control, migration and harvest surveys, and law and gaming enforcement for migratory and nonmigratory birds and mammals. Fishery-related activities include hatchery production monitoring, stocking, and fishery management. Fishery resource programs also provide technical assistance for coastal anadromous, Great Lakes, and other inland fisheries.

The USFWS identifies, protects, and restores endangered fish, wildlife, and plant species. It maintains Federal lists of endangered and threatened wildlife and plants that are published in the Code of Federal Regulations (50 CFR 17.11 et seq.), conducts status surveys, prepares recovery plans, and coordinates national and international wildlife refuge operations.

The Service protects and improves land and water environments to benefit living natural resources and to enhance the quality of human life. It administers grant programs that help imperiled species, assists private landowners restore habitat, asses environmental impact and reviews potential environmental threats, manages Coastal Barrier Resource System mapping, monitors potential wildlife contaminants, and studies fish and wildlife population trends.

Public use and information activities include preparing informational brochures and maintaining public Web sites; coordinating environmental studies on USFWS lands; operating visitor centers, self-guided nature trails, observation towers, and display ponds; and promoting birdwatching, fishing, hunting, wildlife photography, and other forms of wildlife-dependent outdoor recreation.

The Wildlife and Sport Fish Restoration Program supports the conservation and enhancement of the Nation's fish and wildlife resources. Excise taxes on sporting arms and fishing equipment fund these efforts.

Sources of Information

Blog The USFWS Web site features "Open Spaces—A Talk on the Wild Side." https://www.fws.gov/news/blog
Business Opportunities An online guide explains how to find business opportunities and to compete for them. Information is also available from regional offices and from the Division of Contracting and General Services in Falls Church, VA. Phone, 703-358-2500. http://www.fws.gov/cfm/Small%20Business/BusinessWith.html | Email: small_business_opts@fws.gov
Career Opportunities Information on careers in conservation is available on the USFWS Web site. Additional information is available from USFWS regional offices and the Human Capital Office in Falls Church, VA. Phone, 703-358-1743. https://www.fws.gov/humancapital
Climate Change The USFWS Web site provides a collection of links and informational sources for learning about climate science and conservation in a changing climate. https://www.fws.gov/home/climatechange/resources.html
Contaminants The USFWS Web site features a section dedicated to contaminants—for example, metals and pesticides—and their effects on wildlife. https://www.fws.gov/ecological-services/habitat-conservation/contaminants.html
Endangered Species The USFWS Web site features a search tool for learning about and identifying endangered species. The text boxes can search for an endangered species based on the State, U.S. Territory, or county where it lives, or according to its common or scientific name. https://www.fws.gov/endangered/?ref=topbar

An online subscription form is available to receive breaking news affecting endangered species, endangered species news stories, and the "Endangered Species Bulletin" via email. https://visitor.r20.constantcontact.com/manage/optin?v=001ip3iEJ-xkvrgM_ZzpwhxaKQXIq4Cp14J
Energy Development The USFWS Web site features a section dedicated to the development of domestic energy sources and its effect on wildlife. https://www.fws.gov/ecological-services/energy-development/energy.html
Freedom of Information Act (FOIA) The USFWS makes records available to the public to the greatest extent possible. The records that are being sought already may be posted online. If the information cannot be found online or if the location of the desired records is uncertain, consider contacting the USFWS FOIA public liaison before submitting a FOIA request. https://www.fws.gov/irm/bpim/foia.html | Email: fwhq_foia@fws.gov

The USFWS does not have a centralized records system. Most data and records are kept in field offices. Instructions on where to send a FOIA request for USFWS records are available online. https://www.fws.gov/irm/bpim/foiawhere.html
Glossaries Ecological Services maintains an online glossary of terms found in environmental legislation. https://www.fws.gov/ecological-services/about/glossary.html

The Midwest Region maintains an online glossary of terms associated with endangered species. https://www.fws.gov/midwest/endangered/glossary/index.html

The Midwest Region also maintains a glossary of terms associated with freshwater mussels of the Upper Mississippi River System. https://www.fws.gov/midwest/mussel/glossary.html

The USFWS Web site features a short glossary of National Environmental Policy Act (NEPA) terms in Portable Document Format (PDF). https://www.fws.gov/r9esnepa/Intro/Glossary.PDF

National Wildlife Refuges   For information on the National Wildlife Refuge System, including information on specific wildlife refuges and wetland management districts, visit the "National Wildlife Refuge System" Web site. Phone, 800-344-9453. http://www.fws.gov/refuges/index.html

News Media Inquiries   Journalists, reporters, and other media professionals seeking information or to arrange an interview should contact a regional public affairs officer or the Division of Public Affairs in Falls Church, VA. Phone, 703-358-2220. http://www.fws.gov/external-affairs/contacts.html

Newsroom   The USFWS posts news releases online. https://www.fws.gov/news

Permits   Visit the "Do I Need a Permit" Web page to learn the rules for importing, exporting, and reexporting protected species. Information on Convention on International Trade in Endangered Species of Wild Fauna and Flora (CITES) permits and certificates is also available from the Division of Management Authority. Phone, 800-358-2104 or 703-358-2093. http://www.fws.gov/international/permits/do-i-need-a-permit.html | Email: managementauthority@fws.gov

Publications   The USFWS national publications unit is headquartered at the National Conservation Training Center in Shepherdstown, WV. It is the primary distribution center for printed material published by the USFWS. The publications unit handles requests from Federal and State agencies, businesses, educators, and the general public. USFWS publications include booklets, brochures, posters, and reports. Phone, 800-344-9543. http://nctc.fws.gov/resources/knowledge-resources

Some publications may need to be ordered from the U.S. Government Bookstore, which the Government Publishing Office operates. Phone, 866-512-1800 (customer contact center). Phone, 202-512-0132 (store phone). https://bookstore.gpo.gov | Email: ContactCenter@gpo.gov

Regional Offices   USFWS has regional offices that represent each of its eight geographic regions: Pacific, Southwest, Midwest, Southeast, Northeast, Mountain-Prairie, Alaska, and Pacific Southwest. Contact information for each of these regional offices is available on the USFWS Web site. https://www.fws.gov/external-affairs/contacts.html

The Office of Law Enforcement, in addition to its national office in Falls Church, VA, maintains a regional office in each of the eight regions. Contact information for these offices is available on the USFWS Web site. https://www.fws.gov/le/regional-law-enforcement-offices.html

A State list of other USFWS offices and their contact information is also available online. https://www.fws.gov/offices

Report a Violation   To report a violation of wildlife laws or to learn about enforcement of them, visit the "Office of Law Enforcement" Web site, contact the nearest regional law enforcement office, or call the Office of Law Enforcement in Falls Church, VA. Phone, 703-358-1949. http://www.fws.gov/le | Email: lawenforcement@fws.gov

Social Media   The USFWS uses social media to communicate and connect with Internet users worldwide. The agency tweets from its Twitter accounts; maintains an Instagram feed and Pinterest board; posts videos on its YouTube channel and photographs on Flickr; and has Facebook, LinkedIn, and Google+ pages. http://www.fws.gov/home/socialmedia/index.html?ref=topbar

Water Resource Development   The USFWS Web site features a section dedicated to the development of water resources and its effect on wildlife. https://www.fws.gov/ecological-services/energy-development/water.html; https://www.fws.gov/external-affairs/contacts.html

For further information, contact the Division of Marketing Communications–External Affairs, U.S. Fish and Wildlife Service, Department of the Interior, 1849 C Street NW., Washington, DC 20240. Phone, 703-358-2613.

United States Geological Survey

12201 Sunrise Valley Drive, Reston, VA 20192
Phone, 703-648-4000. Internet, http://www.usgs.gov | Email: ASK@usgs.gov

Director   SUZETTE KIMBALL

The United States Geological Survey (USGS) was established by the Organic Act of March 3, 1879 (43 U.S.C. 31). Since March 3, 1879, the Survey has provided the United States with science information needed to make important land use and resource management policy decisions. http://pubs.usgs.gov/circ/c1050

The USGS serves as the Earth and natural science research bureau for the Department of the Interior. It is the only integrated natural resources research agency in the Federal Government. USGS research and data support the Department's resource and land management information needs. Other Federal, State, tribal, and local government agencies rely on USGS research and data for their biological, climate, energy, mineral resources, natural hazards, and water information needs. Emergency response organizations, natural resource managers, land use planners, and other customers use USGS research and data to protect lives and property, to address environmental health issues, and to promote the public weal. http://www.usgs.gov/about/about-us/who-we-are

The USGS conducts research, monitoring, and assessments to increase understanding of America's biological, land, and water resources. The Service informs American citizens and members of the global community by producing data, maps, and reports containing analyses and interpretations. These analyses and interpretations cover a range of topics: biological, energy, mineral, and water resources; land surfaces; marine environments; geologic structures; natural hazards; and dynamic processes of the Earth. Citizens, managers, and planners regularly use USGS data, analytical, and interpretive products to respond to and plan for changes in ecosystems and the environment.

The USGS has 135 years of experience generating science-based data. In more than 400 science centers across the United States, the Service employs 8,000 science and science-support staff, who work on locally, regionally, and nationally scaled studies, on research projects, and at sampling and monitoring sites. http://www.usgs.gov/start_with_science

Sources of Information

Business Opportunities   General information on contracting is available from the Office of Acquisition and Grants. Phone, 703-648-7376. https://www2.usgs.gov/contracts/mission.html

Email addresses and phone numbers for contacting USGS small business specialists are posted online. https://www2.usgs.gov/contracts/USGS-SmallBus.html

Career Opportunities   The USGS relies on professionals with a range of expertise and diverse skills to carry out its mission. Many of these professionals were educated and trained in the sciences: biology, chemistry, cartography, ecology, geology, geography, hydrology, and physics. https://www2.usgs.gov/humancapital/sw/careercards.html

Information on opportunities for students and recent graduates is available on the USGS Web site. https://www2.usgs.gov/humancapital/sw/studentandrecentgrads.html

Earthquakes for Kids   Earthquakes for kids provides online resources to help children and adults learn about earthquakes and earthquake science. http://earthquake.usgs.gov/learn/kids

Freedom of Information Act (FOIA)   The FOIA electronic reading room contains documents related to the Flow Rate Technical Group in response to the Deepwater Horizon oil spill. These documents have been cleared for public release, and the USGS expects to publish additional documents to this collection. Before submitting a FOIA request for agency records, an information seeker should search this reading room and other

Federal Government Deepwater Horizon electronic reading rooms for documents and information. https://www2.usgs.gov/foia

Frequently Asked Questions (FAQs)   The USGS posts answers to FAQs on its Web site. https://www2.usgs.gov/faq

Glossaries   The volcano hazards program includes an online glossary. http://volcanoes.usgs.gov/vsc/glossary

The earthquake hazards program includes an online glossary. http://earthquake.usgs.gov/learn/glossary

Grants   Information on financial assistance programs is available on the USGS Web site. https://www2.usgs.gov/contracts/faprograms.html

Landsat   The Landsat Web site features colorful images spanning the globe. https://www.usgs.gov/science/mission-areas/climate-and-land-use-change/earth-resources-observation-and-science-center?qt-programs_l2_landing_page=0#qt-programs_l2_landing_page

Libraries   Maps, publications, reports, and a variety of biological and Earth information resources and historical documents are available through the USGS library system. The USGS Web site features a tool for searching the library's catalog. http://library.usgs.gov | Email: library@usgs.gov

National Map   The National Map Web site offers Internet users a trove of topographical information. http://nationalmap.gov

Natural Hazards   Information on the programs and activities of the natural hazards mission—including information on earthquakes, volcanoes, and landslides—is available online. http://www.usgs.gov/natural_hazards

News   USGS national and State news items are posted online. https://www.usgs.gov/news/news-releases

The USGS tweets on Twitter and has a Facebook page. http://www.usgs.gov/socialmedia

Publications   The USGS publications warehouse provides access to over 130,000 publications written by USGS scientists throughout the agency's history. https://pubs.er.usgs.gov

Report a Landslide   An online form is available on the USGS Web site to report a landslide. http://landslides.usgs.gv/dysi/form.php

Science Snippets   The USGS posts fun facts and interesting snippets of science on its Web site. https://www.usgs.gov/news/science-snippets

Site Map   The Web site map allows visitors to look for specific topics or to browse content that aligns with their interests. https://www.usgs.gov/sitemap

USGS Store   Educational materials, Federal recreation passes, maps, scientific reports, and more are available from the online USGS Store. https://store.usgs.gov/b2c_usgs/b2c/start/(xcm=r3standardpitrex_prd)/.do

Volcano Notification Service   This electronic notification service keeps subscribers abreast of volcanic activity at U.S. monitored volcanoes. https://volcanoes.usgs.gov/vns2

Water Data   Reliable, impartial, and timely information on the Nation's water resources is available on the USGS Web site. Phone, 888-275-8747. http://www.usgs.gov/water

The USGS manages water information at local water resources offices located nationwide. The offices are linked through a computer network; however, each office collects data and conducts studies in a particular area. Local information is best found at a local site or at neighboring sites. http://water.usgs.gov/local_offices.html; http://www.usgs.gov/ask | Email: ASK@usgs.gov

For additional information, contact the U.S. Geological Survey, Department of the Interior, 12201 Sunrise Valley Drive, Reston, VA 20192. Phone, 703-648-4000.

DEPARTMENT OF THE TREASURY

1500 Pennsylvania Avenue NW., Washington, DC 20220
Phone, 202-622-2000. Internet, http://www.treasury.gov

Secretary of the Treasury	STEVEN T. MNUCHIN
Deputy Secretary of the Treasury	(VACANCY)
Chief of Staff	ELI H. MILLER
Chief Risk Officer	KENNETH J. PHELAN
General Counsel	BRENT J. MCINTOSH
Treasurer of the United States	JOVITA CARRANZA

Under Secretaries

Domestic Finance	(VACANCY)
International Affairs	DAVID R. MALPASS
Terrorism and Financial Intelligence	SIGAL P. MANDELKER

Assistant Secretaries

Economic Policy	(VACANCY)
Legislative Affairs	BRAD BAILEY, ACTING
Management	DAVID F. EISNER
Public Affairs	ANTHONY E. SAYEGH, JR.
Tax Policy	DAVID J. KAUTTER

Domestic Finance	
Financial Institutions Policy	KIPP KRANBUHL, ACTING
Financial Markets	(VACANCY)
Financial Stability	(VACANCY)
Fiscal Assistant Secretary	DAVID A. LEBRYK

International Affairs	
International Finance	GEOFFREY OKAMOTO, ACTING
International Markets	HEATH P. TARBERT

Terrorism / Financial Intelligence	
Intelligence / Analysis	ISABEL PATELUNAS
Terrorist Financing	MARSHALL BILLINGSLEA

https://home.treasury.gov/about/general-information/officials

Inspector General	ERIC M. THORSON

https://www.treasury.gov/about/organizational-structure/ig/Pages/Eric-M.-Thorson-Inspector-General.aspx

Treasury Inspector General, Tax Administration	J. RUSSELL GEORGE

https://www.treasury.gov/tigta/about_ig.shtml

Treasury Special Inspector General, Troubled Asset Relief Program	CHRISTY G. ROMERO

https://www.sigtarp.gov/Pages/sig.aspx

The above list of key personnel was updated 11–2018.

The Department of the Treasury enforces financial laws, manufactures coins and currency, and recommends economic, fiscal, and tax policies.

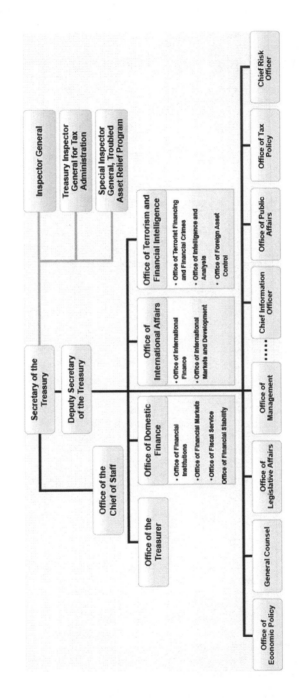

Department of the Treasury

The Treasury Department was created by act of September 2, 1789 (31 U.S.C. 301 and 301 note). Many subsequent acts have figured in the development of the Department, delegating new duties to its charge and establishing the numerous bureaus and divisions that now constitute the Treasury.

Secretary As a major policy adviser to the President, the Secretary recommends domestic and international financial, economic, and tax policy; formulates broad fiscal policies that have general significance for the economy; and manages the public debt. The Secretary oversees the activities of the Department in carrying out its major law enforcement responsibility; in serving as the financial agent for the U.S. Government; and in manufacturing coins, currency, and other products for customer agencies. The Secretary also acts as the Government's chief financial officer. https://home.treasury.gov/about/general-information/the-secretary

Activities

Domestic Finance The Office of Domestic Finance maintains confidence in the U.S. Treasury market, manages Federal fiscal operations, and strengthens financial institutions and markets; promotes access to credit; and improves financial access and education in service of America's long-term economic strength and stability. https://www.treasury.gov/about/organizational-structure/offices/Pages/Domestic-Finance.aspx

Economic Policy The Office of the Assistant Secretary for Economic Policy helps policymakers determine economic policies. The Office analyzes domestic and international economic issues and developments in the financial markets, assists in forming official economic projections, and works closely with Federal Government agencies to make economic forecasts supporting the yearly budget process. https://www.treasury.gov/about/organizational-structure/offices/Pages/Economic-Policy.aspx

Enforcement The Department's law enforcement activities are carried out by its offices and bureaus, including the Alcohol and Tobacco Tax and Trade Bureau, the Internal Revenue Service, and the Office of Terrorism and Financial Intelligence (TFI). The Office of Foreign Assets Control, which

is part of the TFI, plays an important role in controlling the assets of "blocked" countries in the United States and restricting the flow of funds and trade with these countries. https://www.ttb.gov/enforcement/index.shtml; https://www.irs.gov/compliance/criminal-investigation/criminal-enforcement; https://www.treasury.gov/about/organizational-structure/offices/Pages/Office-of-Terrorism-and-Financial-Intelligence.aspx

Financial Institutions The Office of Financial Institutions coordinates the Department's efforts regarding financial institutions legislation and regulation, legislation affecting Federal agencies that regulate or insure financial institutions, and securities markets legislation and regulation. The Office also coordinates the Department's financial education policy efforts and ensures the resiliency of the financial services sector. https://www.treasury.gov/about/organizational-structure/offices/Pages/Financial-Institutions.aspx

Financial Markets The Office of Financial Markets serves to formulate policy on Federal debt management, State and local finance (including the Federal debt), Federal Government credit policies, and lending and privatization. This Office also oversees the Federal Financing Bank, and the Assistant Secretary serves as the senior member of the Treasury Financing Group and coordinates the President's Working Group on Financial Markets. https://www.treasury.gov/about/organizational-structure/offices/Pages/Office-of-Financial-Markets.aspx

Financial Stability The Office of Financial Stability within the U.S. Treasury was created by the Emergency Economic Stabilization Act of 2008 (12 U.S.C. 5201 et seq.) to administer the Troubled Asset Relief Program (TARP). The purpose of the TARP was to help restore liquidity and stability to the U.S. financial system following the 2008 financial crisis. The Treasury's authority to make financial commitments under TARP ended on October 3, 2010. The Office continues to wind down the TARP investments in a manner that balances exit speed with maximizing taxpayer returns. It also helps homeowners prevent avoidable foreclosures. https://www.treasury.gov/initiatives/financial-stability/Pages/about-ofs.aspx

Fiscal Affairs The Office of the Fiscal Assistant Secretary provides policy oversight of the Fiscal Service bureaus and develops policy on payments, collections, debt financing operations, electronic commerce, Governmentwide accounting, Government investment fund management, and other related issues. The Office also performs two critical functions for the Department: It manages the daily cash position of the Government, and it produces the cash and debt forecasts used to determine the size and timing of the Government's financing operations. https://www.treasury.gov/about/organizational-structure/offices/Pages/Office-of-Fiscal-Service.aspx

International Finance   The Office of the Assistant Secretary for International Finance conducts macroeconomic analyses to advise the Under Secretary for International Affairs and other policymakers. The Office also helps them formulate and execute financial and economic policy affecting or involving the International Monetary Fund, the U.S.-China Strategic and Economic Dialogue, the G–20, and other major multilateral and bilateral engagements. https://www.treasury.gov/about/organizational-structure/offices/Pages/Office-Of-International-Affairs.aspx

International Markets and Development   The Office of the Assistant Secretary of International Markets and Development manages the work of the Committee on Foreign Investment in the United States and the Treasury's Office of Technical Assistance. The Office also advises the Under Secretary for International Affairs and other policymakers on financial and economic policies relevant to major bilateral and multilateral engagements, and it assists them with these engagements. The Office plays a similar role in the formulation and execution of policies affecting export finance, financial services, trade, and multilateral development, including the World Bank, the regional development banks, and emerging global issues like food security and climate finance. https://home.treasury.gov/policy-issues/international/the-committee-on-foreign-investment-in-the-united-states-cfius; https://www.treasury.gov/about/organizational-structure/offices/Pages/Technical-Assistance-.aspx

Tax Policy   The Office of the Assistant Secretary for Tax Policy advises and assists the Secretary and the Deputy Secretary in the formulation and execution of domestic and international tax policies and programs. These functions include analysis of proposed tax legislation and tax programs; projections of economic trends affecting tax bases; studies of effects of alternative tax measures; preparation of official estimates of Government receipts for the President's annual budget messages; legal advice and analysis on domestic and international tax matters; assistance in the development and review of tax legislation and domestic and international tax regulations and rulings; and participation in international tax treaty negotiations and in maintenance of relations with international organizations on tax matters. https://www.treasury.gov/about/organizational-structure/offices/Pages/Tax-Policy.aspx

Treasurer of the United States   The Office of the Treasurer of the United States was established on September 6, 1777. The Treasurer was originally charged with the receipt and custody of Government funds, but many of these functions have been assumed by different bureaus of the Department. In 1981, the Treasurer was assigned responsibility for oversight of the Bureau of Engraving and Printing and the United States Mint. The Treasurer reports to the Secretary through the Assistant Secretary for Management. https://www.treasury.gov/about/organizational-structure/offices/Pages/Office-of-the-Treasurer.aspx

Treasury Inspector General for Tax Administration   The Treasury Inspector General for Tax Administration (TIGTA), in accordance with the Internal Revenue Service Restructuring and Reform Act of 1998 (26 U.S.C. 1 note), independently oversees Internal Revenue Service programs and activities. TIGTA monitors the Nation's tax laws to ensure that the Internal Revenue Service (IRS) acts with efficiency, economy, and effectiveness; ensures compliance with applicable laws and regulations; prevents, detects, and deters fraud, waste, and abuse; investigates activities or allegations related to fraud, waste, and abuse by IRS personnel; and protects the IRS against attempts to corrupt or threaten its employees. https://www.treasury.gov/tigta

Sources of Information

Blog   Senior officials and staff post announcements, information, and news items on the blog "Treasury Notes." https://www.treasury.gov/connect/blog/Pages/default.aspx

Bureaus　The Bureaus carry out specific operations assigned to the Department of the Treasury. Bureau employees constitute 98% of its workforce. The Department's website has a "Bureaus" web page that provides easy access to the websites of each of them. https://www.treasury.gov/about/organizational-structure/bureaus/Pages/default.aspx

Business Opportunities　The Office of the Procurement Executive oversees the Department's acquisition system. It supports the use of best value, cost effective, streamlined procurement strategies and encourages achievement of socioeconomic participation goals in the Nation's business activities. For more information, contact the Office of the Procurement Executive. Phone, 202-622-1039. https://www.treasury.gov/about/organizational-structure/offices/Pages/Office-of-the-Procurement-Executive.aspx

For information on small and disadvantaged business activities, contact the Office of Small and Disadvantaged Business Utilization. Phone, 202-622-0530. https://www.treasury.gov/resource-center/sb-programs/Small Disadvantaged-Business/Pages/Small-and-Disadvantaged-Business-Utilization1.aspx

Careers Opportunities　The Department of the Treasury employs over 100,000 professionals nationwide and around the world. https://www.treasury.gov/careers/Pages/default.aspx

In 2017, the Department of the Treasury ranked number 14 among 18 large Government agencies in the Best Places To Work Agency Rankings. http://bestplacestowork.org/rankings/detail/TR00

Data / Charts　A trove of economic information—charts, data, and tables—is available online. https://www.treasury.gov/resource-center/data-chart-center/Pages/index.aspx

Educational Resources　The Department of the Treasury's website has learning resources that are suitable for children and parents, for students and teachers, as well as college students and other curious adults. https://www.treasury.gov/about/history/Pages/default.aspx

Environment　The "Office of Management and Budget Scorecard on Sustainability/ Energy" (JAN 2016) is accessible online in Portable Document Format (PDF). https://www.treasury.gov/about/budget-performance/annual-performance-plan/Documents/TREASURY%20Final%20Jan%202016%20OMB%20Scorecard.public%20version.pdf

To learn about the Department's role in supporting U.S. efforts to improve the environment and to facilitate a transition to a national and global economy powered by clean energy, see the Office of Environment and Energy's web page. https://www.treasury.gov/about/organizational-structure/offices/Pages/Environment-and-Energy.aspx

Freedom of Information Act (FOIA)　The FOIA gives a right to request access to records of the U.S. Government's executive branch to any person. The records must be disclosed unless they are shielded from request by one or more of the exempt categories of information found in the statute. https://home.treasury.gov/footer/freedom-of-information-act

The Department of the Treasury maintains an electronic reading room whose holdings are governed by the FOIA. https://www.treasury.gov/FOIA/Pages/reading_room.aspx

An electronic FOIA request form is available online. https://www.treasury.gov/foia/pages/gofoia.aspx

Frequently Asked Questions (FAQs)　The Department of the Treasury posts answers to FAQs. https://www.treasury.gov/resource-center/faqs/Pages/default.aspx

Glossary　The Department of the Treasury maintains a list of acronyms and terms that recur on its website. https://www.treasury.gov/initiatives/financial-stability/glossary/pages/default.aspx

History　A trove of historical information on the Department of the Treasury and its building is available online. https://home.treasury.gov/about/history

A visual and audio tour of the Treasury Building's points of interest is available online. The points of interest on the map are hyperlinked to brief audio descriptions. https://m.treasury.gov/about/history/m/m.html#map

Inspector General　To report the possible existence of a Treasury activity constituting mismanagement, gross waste of funds, abuse of authority, a substantial and specific danger to the public health and safety, or a violation of law, rules, or regulations—not including the Internal Revenue Service, which reports to the Treasury Inspector General for Tax Administration—contact the Treasury OIG Hotline, Office of Inspector General, 1500 Pennsylvania Avenue NW., Washington, DC 20220. Phone, 800-359-3898. http://www.treas.gov/inspector-general | Email: hotline@oig.treas.gov

Library / Reading Room   The reading room is located in the Treasury Library, Room 1428, Main Treasury Building, 1500 Pennsylvania Avenue NW., Washington, DC 20220. Phone, 202-622-0990. https://www.treasury.gov/FOIA/Pages/reading_room.aspx

Media   Members of the media may contact the Department of the Treasury by phone or email. Phone, 202-622-2960. https://home.treasury.gov/contacts-for-members-of-the-media | Email: press@treasury.gov

Organizational Chart   An organizational chart is available on the "Organizational Structure" web page. https://home.treasury.gov/about/general-information/organizational-chart

Press Releases   The Department of the Treasury posts press releases on its website. https://home.treasury.gov/news/press-releases

Site Map   The website map allows visitors to look for specific topics or to browse content that aligns with their interests. https://www.treasury.gov/Pages/site-map.aspx

Social Media   The Department of the Treasury maintains a Facebook account. https://www.facebook.com/ustreasury

The Department of the Treasury tweets announcements and other newsworthy items on Twitter. https://twitter.com/USTreasury

Tax Analysis   The staff of the Office of Tax Analysis (OTA) posts original research online in its working papers series. The OTA staff also develops datasets, methods, and models that its uses for policy analysis and estimates. The technical papers series, which is also posted online, presents documentation of these datasets, methods, and models. https://home.treasury.gov/policy-issues/tax-policy/office-of-tax-analysis

Treasury Inspector General for Tax Administration   To report fraud or waste by an Internal Revenue Service employee, as well as abuse or fraud against an Internal Revenue Service employee, contact the Treasury Inspector General for Tax Administration, P.O. Box 589, Ben Franklin Station, Washington, DC 20044-0589. Phone, 800-366-4484. https://www.treasury.gov/tigta | Email: complaints@tigta.treas.gov

The Treasury Inspector General for Tax Administration posts videos online to educate the public about fraud and impersonation scams. https://www.youtube.com/user/TIGTAVIDEOS/feed; https://www.treasury.gov/about/organizational-structure/offices/Pages/Public-Affairs.aspx

For further information, contact the Public Affairs Office, Department of the Treasury, 1500 Pennsylvania Avenue NW., Washington, DC 20220. Phone, 202-622-2960.

Alcohol and Tobacco Tax and Trade Bureau

1310 G Street NW., Box 12, Washington, DC 20005
Phone, 202-453-2000. Internet, http://www.ttb.gov

Administrator	JOHN J. MANFREDA
Deputy Administrator	MARY G. RYAN
https://www.ttb.gov/offices/executive-offices.shtml	

The above list of key personnel was updated 11–2018.

The Alcohol and Tobacco Tax and Trade Bureau (TTB) was established on January 24, 2003, by the Homeland Security Act of 2002 (6 U.S.C. 531). TTB collects Federal alcohol, tobacco, firearms, and ammunition excise taxes; regulates the production, labeling, and advertising of alcohol beverages; and investigates unfair or unlawful trade in alcohol and tobacco products. TTB regulates alcohol and tobacco producers, importers, and wholesalers. Regulation of retailers takes place on State and local levels. http://www.ttb.gov/about/index.shtml#Who

Sources of Information

Advertising, Labeling, and Formulation For information on the advertising, labeling, and formulation of alcohol beverages, contact the Advertising, Labeling and Formulation Division. Phone, 202-453-2250 or 866-927-2533. http://www.ttb.gov/advertising/alfd.shtml | Email: alfd@ttb.treas.gov

A–Z Index The website has an A–Z index to help visitors navigate its content. https://www.ttb.gov/about/a_to_z.shtml

Career Opportunities The TTB has offices nationwide, including in Puerto Rico. Many TTB employees telework full time. To carry out its mission, the Bureau relies on alcohol and tobacco tax specialists, analysts, attorneys, auditors, chemists, investigators, labeling specialists, writers, and other professionals. https://www.ttb.gov/careers/index.shtml

Among 339 agency subcomponents, the TTB placed 4th in the Partnership for Public Service's 2017 Best Places To Work rankings! https://bestplacestowork.org/rankings/detail/TR40

Consumer Complaints The TTB helps ensure that alcohol beverage products in the marketplace are safe for consumption. Complaints generally address issues of product quality: low alcohol, spoilage, unusual taste, and the presence of foreign objects. A consumer has the a right and responsibility to report a product that he or she suspects is unsafe for consumption or may have been contaminated. Phone, 202-453-2251. https://ttb.gov/consumer/filing_complaint.shtml | Email: Market.Compliance@ttb.gov

Fraud Tipline To report fraud, diversion, and illegal activity by producers, importers, or wholesalers of alcohol and tobacco, contact the Bureau's tipline. Phone, 855-882-8477. TTD, 202-882-9914. http://www.ttb.gov/tipline/index.shtml | Email: tips@ttb.gov

Freedom of Information Act (FOIA) The TTB adheres to the policy and disclosure regulations of the Department of the Treasury for implementing the Freedom of Information Act (FOIA) consistently and uniformly and for providing maximum allowable disclosure of agency records upon request. Requests are processed within the time limits defined by the FOIA. https://www.ttb.gov/foia/index.shtml

The TTB's website has an electronic reading room containing materials that the FOIA requires the Bureau to maintain. Some records are accessible, by appointment, in the public reading room located at 1310 G Street NW., Washington, DC 20005. Phone, 202-882-9904. http://www.ttb.gov/foia/err.shtml

Frequently Asked Questions (FAQs) The TTB posts answers to FAQs. http://www.ttb.gov/faqs | Email: TTBInternetQuestions@ttb.gov

Glossary The TTB maintains a glossary on its website. https://www.ttb.gov/forms_tutorials/glossary/glossary.html

National Revenue Center The National Revenue Center operates a call center that is open on weekdays, 8 a.m.–11:30 a.m. and 12:30 p.m.–5 p.m., eastern standard time. It can provide information on applications, claims, filing excise tax returns, permits, and other tax collection topics. Phone, 877-882-3277. http://www.ttb.gov/offices/nrc.shtml | Email: TTBInternetQuestions@ttb.gov

Site Map The website map allows visitors to look for specific topics or to browse content that aligns with their interests. https://www.ttb.gov/about/site_map_text.shtml; http://www.ttb.gov

For further information, contact the Administrator's Office, Alcohol and Tobacco Tax and Trade Bureau. Phone, 202-453-2000.

Bureau of Engraving and Printing

Fourteenth and C Streets SW., Washington, DC 20228
Phone, 202-874-4000. Internet, http://www.moneyfactory.com

Director   Leonard R. Olijar
Deputy Director   (vacancy)
http://www.moneyfactory.com/about/officeofthedirector.html

The above list of key personnel was updated 11–2018.

The Bureau of Engraving and Printing operates on basic authorities conferred by act of July 11, 1862 (31 U.S.C. 303), and on additional authorities contained in past appropriations made to the Bureau that are still in force. A revolving fund established in 1950, in accordance with Public Law 81–656, finances the Bureau's operations. The Secretary of the Treasury selects the Director who heads the Bureau.

The Bureau designs, prints, and finishes all of the Nation's paper currency and many other security documents, including White House invitations and military identification cards. It also is responsible for advising and assisting Federal agencies in the design and production of other Government documents that, because of their innate value or for other reasons, require security or counterfeit-deterrence characteristics.

The Bureau also operates a second currency manufacturing plant at 9000 Blue Mound Road, Fort Worth, TX. Phone, 817-231-4000. https://www.moneyfactory.gov/about.html

Sources of Information

Business Opportunities   For information on contracts and small business activities, visit the "Doing Business with the BEP" Web page or contact the Office of Acquisition. Phone, 202-874-2065. http://www.moneyfactory.com/about/dobusinesswithbep.html

Career Opportunities   The BEP relies on acquisition specialists, administrative staff, attorneys, chemists, engineers, police officers, security specialists, and other professionals to carry out its mission. http://www.moneyfactory.com/about/careers.html

Among 339 agency subcomponents, the BEP placed 94th in the Partnership for Public Service's 2017 Best Places To Work rankings. https://bestplacestowork.org/rankings/detail/TRAI

Currency Production   The production of U.S. currency involves highly trained and skilled craftspeople, specialized equipment, and a combination of traditional old world printing techniques merged with sophisticated, cutting edge technology. To learn more about the process, visit the

"How Money is Made" Web page. http://www.moneyfactory.com/uscurrency/howmoneyismade.html

Educational Resources   The U.S. currency education program offers free educational and training resources online. https://uscurrency.gov/resource-center

Freedom of Information Act (FOIA)   All Federal agencies, including the BEP, create and receive records when carrying out their missions. The FOIA gives the right to access executive branch agency records to the public. The BEP makes available, upon written request, records or extracts of records in accordance with the FOIA, the Privacy Act, and certain regulations of the Department of the Treasury. The FOIA contains, however, exemptions that shield some records from request and disclosure. Phone, 202-874-2500. Fax, 202-874-2951. http://www.moneyfactory.com/foia.html

The BEP maintains an electronic FOIA library. http://www.moneyfactory.com/bepfoialibrary.html

History   A history of the BEP and U.S. Currency is available online. http://www.moneyfactory.com/contactus.html

Mail Order Sales   Uncut sheets of currency, engraved Presidential portraits, historical engravings of national landmarks, and other souvenirs and mementos are available for purchase by phone and online. Phone, 800-456-3408. http://www.moneyfactorystore.gov

News   The BEP posts press releases online. https://www.moneyfactory.gov/presscenter/pressreleases.html

Tours   Tours of the Bureau's facilities are provided year-round according to the schedules listed below. Up-to-the-minute tour information is available online. http://moneyfactory.gov/services/takeatour.html

WASHINGTON, DC—During peak season, from March through August, 9 a.m.–10:45 a.m. and 12:30 p.m.–2 p.m., tickets are required for all tours. Tours begin every 15 minutes, with the last tour beginning at 2 p.m. The times between 11 a.m. and 12:15 p.m. are reserved for school and other groups. The ticket booth is located on Raoul Wallenberg Place (formerly Fifteenth Street) and opens at 8 a.m. Tour tickets are free. The ticket booth remains open for the morning and evening tours until all tickets have been distributed. Lines form early, and tickets go quickly, typically by 9 a.m. during peak season. Tickets are distributed on a first-come, first-served basis. Lines form on Raoul Wallenberg Place. Evening tours, running from April through August, 5 p.m.–7 p.m., are offered every 15 minutes. During nonpeak season, from September through February, 9 a.m.–2 p.m., tickets are not necessary for tours. Lines form on Fourteenth Street. No tours are given on weekends, Federal holidays, or between Christmas and New Year's Day. Phone, 202-874-2330 or 866-874-2330. http://moneyfactory.gov/washingtondctours.html

FORT WORTH, TX—During peak season, June and July, 11 a.m.–5 p.m., a new tour starts every 30 minutes. The Tour and Visitor Center opens at 10:30 a.m. and closes at 6:30 p.m. During nonpeak season, from August through May, 9 a.m.–2 p.m., the Visitor Center opens at 8:30 a.m. and closes at 3:30 p.m. No tours are given on weekends, Federal holidays, or between Christmas and New Year's Day. Phone, 817-231-4000 or 866-865-1194. http://moneyfactory.gov/fortworthtxtours.html; http://www.moneyfactory.gov/presscenter.html

For further information, contact the Office of External Relations, Bureau of Engraving and Printing, Department of the Treasury, Room 533–M, Fourteenth and C Streets SW., Washington, DC 20228. Phone, 202-874-3019. Fax, 202-874-3177.

Bureau of the Fiscal Service

401 Fourteenth Street SW., Washington, DC 20227
Phone, 202-874-6950. Internet, http://www.fiscal.treasury.gov

Commissioner	KIMBERLY A. MCCOY
Deputy Commissioners	
Accounting and Shared Services	MATTHEW J. MILLER, ACTING
Finance and Administration	STEPHEN MANNING
Financial Services and Operations	JEFFREY J. SCHRAMEK, ACTING
https://www.fiscal.treasury.gov/fsabout/fs_ourpeople.htm	

The above list of key personnel was updated 11–2018.

The Bureau of the Fiscal Service provides central payment services to Federal program agencies, operates the Federal Government's collections and deposit systems, provides Governmentwide accounting and reporting services, manages the collection of delinquent debt owed to the Federal Government, borrows the money needed to operate the Federal Government, accounts for the resulting public debt, and gives reimbursable support to Federal agencies.

Accounting The Fiscal Service gathers and publishes Governmentwide financial information that is used by the public and private sectors to monitor the Government's financial status and establish fiscal and monetary policies. These publications include the "Daily Treasury Statement," "Monthly Treasury Statement," "Treasury Bulletin," "U.S. Government Annual Report," and "Financial Report of the U.S. Government."

Collections The Fiscal Service administers the world's largest collection system, processing more than 400 million transactions through the support of six Federal Reserve Banks and a network of over 100 financial institutions. In Fiscal Year 2012, the Fiscal Service collected over $3.16 trillion in Federal revenues from individual and corporate income tax deposits, customs duties, loan repayments, fines, proceeds from leases, as well as from other revenue sources.

The Fiscal Service and Internal Revenue Service manage the Electronic Federal Tax Payment System (EFTPS), which allows individuals and businesses to pay Federal taxes online. The EFTPS website has printable acknowledgment features for documenting transactions, advance payment scheduling, and payment history access.

The Treasury Offset Program is one of the methods used to collect delinquent debt. The Fiscal Service uses the program to withhold Federal payments, such as Federal income tax refunds, Federal salary payments, and Social Security benefits, to recipients with delinquent debts, including past-due child support obligations and State and Federal income tax debt.

Debt Financing The Bureau auctions and issues Treasury bills, notes, and bonds and manages the sales and redemption of savings bonds. It provides daily and other periodic reports to account for the composition and size of the debt. In addition, the Bureau implements the regulations for the Government securities market. These regulations provide for investor protection while maintaining a fair and liquid market for Government securities.

Do Not Pay The Do Not Pay Business Center has a two-part vision for programs administered or funded by the Federal Government: to help prevent and stop improper payments from being made and to identify and mitigate fraud, waste, and abuse. The goal of the program is to integrate Do Not Pay into existing business processes by providing agencies with access to current data that are relevant for making an award or payment decision.

Electronic Commerce Through its electronic money programs, the Fiscal Service offers new payment and collection technologies to help Federal agencies modernize their cash management activities. Examples include stored-value cards used on military bases, point-of-sale check conversion, and online credit card collection programs.

Payments Each year, the Fiscal Service disburses more than one billion non-Defense payments to a wide variety of recipients, such as those individuals who receive Social Security, IRS tax refunds, and veterans' benefits. In Fiscal Year 2012, the Fiscal Service issued more than $2.4 trillion in payments, 88 percent of which were issued electronically.

Shared Services The Administrative Resource Center delivers franchise services on a reimbursable basis to more than 85 Treasury and Federal Government agencies. The Center provides services in six areas: financial management, investment accounting, human resources, information technology, procurement, and travel.

Sources of Information

A–Z Index The Fiscal Service's website has an alphabetical and comprehensive list of links to the Bureau's major programs and services. https://www.fiscal.treasury.gov/fs_a_z_index.htm

Career Opportunities The Fiscal Service relies on accountants, administrators, business and finance experts, information technology specialists, and others to carry out mission. https://www.fiscal.treasury.gov/fscareers/fs_careers.htm

Among 339 agency subcomponents, the Fiscal Service placed 118th in the Partnership for Public Service's 2017 Best Places To Work rankings. https://bestplacestowork.org/rankings/detail/TRFD

Do Not Pay The Do Not Pay Business Center supports Federal agencies in their efforts to reduce the number of improper payments. Data, information, and resources are available on its website. http://www.donotpay.treas.gov

Electronic Federal Tax Payment System (EFTPS) The EFTPS professionals post answers to frequently asked questions (FAQs) online. https://www.eftps.gov/eftps/direct/FAQGeneral.page

Freedom of Information Act (FOIA) The FOIA gives the right to request information from the Federal Government's executive branch agencies to any person. It is sometimes referred to as the law that keeps citizens in the know about their Government. The Fiscal Service posts a lot of information on its website for the public's benefit and convenience. Before submitting a FOIA request in writing, information seekers should search the website for the desired information. It may be accessible immediately and free of charge. https://www.fiscal.treasury.gov/foia/foia_home.htm

The Fiscal Service maintains an electronic reading room to support the FOIA. https://www.fiscal.treasury.gov/foia/foia_readingroom.htm

Glossaries The Fiscal Service maintains a glossary on its website. https://www.fiscal.treasury.gov/fs_glossary.htm

The EFTPS website has a glossary of terms and common acronyms. https://www.eftps.gov/eftps/direct/HelpGlossary.page

The Treasury Direct website has a glossary of terms. http://www.treasurydirect.gov/indiv/research/res_glossary/glossary.htm

Government-to-Government Shared Services The Administrative Resource Center provides Federal agencies with cost-effective, customer-focused, responsive administrative support. https://arc.publicdebt.treas.gov

History A short history of the Fiscal Service is available online. https://www.fiscal.treasury.gov/fsabout/fs_history.htm

The Treasury Direct website uses historical images to tell the story of U.S. Savings Bonds from their introduction in 1935 to the second decade of the 21st century. https://www.treasurydirect.gov/timeline.htm?src=td&med=banner&loc=consumer

News The Fiscal Service posts news items and press releases online. https://www.fiscal.treasury.gov/fsnews/fs_news.htm

Public Debt Outstanding The Treasury Direct website has an online tool that allows users to access the data on total public debt outstanding on a daily basis from January 4, 1993, onward. For example, on October 31, 2019, the total public debt outstanding was $23,008,409,564,495. http://www.treasurydirect.gov/NP/debt/current

Reports / Publications The monthly "Statement of the Public Debt of the United States" and "Treasury Statement of Receipts and Outlays of the U.S. Government," as well as the annual "Financial Report of the U.S. Government," and other publications are available on the Fiscal Service's website. https://www.fiscal.treasury.gov/fsreports/fs_reports_publications.htm

Savings Bonds Savings bonds may be purchased and held in an online account. Current rate information is available online or by calling 800-487-2663. Requests for information on all series of savings bonds, savings notes, and retirement plans or individual retirement bonds should be addressed to the Bureau of the Fiscal Service, Division of Customer Assistance, PO Box 7012, Parkersburg, WV 26106-7012. Phone, 304-480-7711. https://www.treasurydirect.gov/indiv/products/prod_eebonds_glance.htm

Treasury Securities For information on the purchase of Treasury bills, bonds, and notes, contact the Bureau of the Fiscal Service, Division of Customer Assistance, PO Box 7015, Parkersburg, WV 26106-7015. Phone, 800-722-2678. http://www.treasurydirect.gov/indiv/products/products.htm; http://www.fiscal.treasury.gov

For further information, contact the Office of Legislative and Public Affairs, Bureau of the Fiscal Service, Department of the Treasury, 401 Fourteenth Street SW., Washington, DC 20227. Phone, 202-874-6750.

Internal Revenue Service

1111 Constitution Avenue NW., Washington, DC 20224
Phone, 202 622 5000. Internet, http://www.irs.gov

Commissioner of Internal Revenue	CHARLES P. RETTIG
Chief of Staff	LIA COLBERT
https://www.irs.gov/about-irs/todays-irs-organization	
Deputy Commissioners	
Operations Support	JEFFREY TRIBIANO
Services and Enforcement	KIRSTEN WIELOBOB

The above list of key personnel was updated 11–2018.

The Office of the Commissioner of Internal Revenue was established by act of July 1, 1862 (26 U.S.C. 7802). The Internal Revenue Service (IRS) administers and enforces the internal revenue laws and related statutes, except those relating to alcohol, tobacco, firearms, and explosives. It collects the proper amount of tax revenue, at the least cost to the public, by efficiently applying the tax law with integrity and fairness. The IRS aims for the highest possible degree of voluntary compliance in accordance with the tax laws and regulations; advises the public of their rights and responsibilities; determines the extent of compliance and the causes of noncompliance; properly administers and enforces the tax laws; and continually searches for and implements new, more efficient ways of accomplishing its mission. The IRS ensures satisfactory resolution of taxpayer complaints; provides taxpayer service and education; determines, assesses, and collects internal revenue taxes; determines pension plan qualifications and exempt organization status; and prepares and issues rulings and regulations to supplement the provisions of the Internal Revenue Code.

Most of the collected revenues depend on the individual income tax and the social insurance and retirement taxes. Other major revenue sources are corporate income, excise, estate, and gift taxes. The 16th Amendment of the Constitution, ratified on February 3, 1913, gave Congress the authority to levy taxes on the income of individuals and corporations.

Sources of Information

Business Opportunities Information on and resources for doing business with the IRS are available on its "Procurement" Web page. https://www.irs.gov/uac/procurement | Email: AWSSPROCCustomerService@irs.gov

Career Opportunities To carry out its mission, the IRS relies on accountants, appeals officers, artificial intelligence analysts, attorneys, budget analysts, computer research analysts, contact representatives, data transcribers, engineers, human resources specialists, information technology specialists, internal revenue agents and officers, mathematical statisticians, operations research analysts, policy analysts, program analysts, risk analysts, special agents, tax compliance officers, tax examiners, tax law specialists, and other professionals. https://jobs.irs.gov

Among 339 agency subcomponents, the IRS placed 261st in the Partnership for Public Service's 2017 Best Places To Work rankings. https://bestplacestowork.org/rankings/detail/TR93

Charities / Nonprofits Tax information for charities and nonprofit organizations is available online. https://www.irs.gov/charities-non-profits

Forms / Publications Current forms, instructions, and publications may be downloaded from the IRS's website. https://www.irs.gov/forms-pubs

Freedom of Information Act (FOIA) In 1966, President Lyndon B. Johnson's approval of the FOIA gave the right to access documents or records belonging to the executive branch of the Federal Government to any person. The statute is based on the presumption that the Government and its information belong to the public. The IRS may withhold, however, documents or records shielded from disclosure by one of the statute's nine exemptions, and it must withhold them when disclosure is prohibited by law. https://www.irs.gov/uac/irs-freedom-of-information

The IRS maintains an electronic reading room whose contents are arranged by subject category. https://www.irs.gov/uac/electronic-reading-room

Frequently Asked Questions (FAQs) The IRS posts answers to FAQs. https://www.irs.gov/help-resources/tools-faqs/faqs-for-individuals/frequently-asked-tax-questions-answers

Identity Theft The IRS responds to tax-related identity theft with an aggressive strategy of prevention, detection, and victim assistance. The IRS continues to make progress against this crime, and it remains one of the agency's highest priorities. The IRS is committed to helping victims of identity theft resolve their cases as quickly as possible. https://www.irs.gov/individuals/identity-protection

Language Resources The IRS's home page has a drop-down menu that allows visitors to access information in Chinese, Korean, Russian, Spanish, and Vietnamese. https://www.irs.gov

News The IRS posts news items online. https://www.irs.gov/uac/latest-news

Reading Rooms Public reading rooms are located in the national office and in each territory office.

Retirement Plans The IRS website has resources for and a trove of information on retirement plans. https://www.irs.gov/retirement-plans

Tax Assistance The IRS provides taxpayers with year-round tax information and assistance, primarily through its website and toll-free telephone system. Answers to many tax-related questions can be found on the IRS's website. The toll-free telephone numbers are listed in local telephone directories and in the annual tax form packages. The telephone system can accommodate the needs of taxpayers who are deaf or hearing-impaired. Taxpayers may also visit IRS offices to find answers to their tax questions. Individual preparation is available for handicapped or other individuals unable to use the group preparation method. Tax assistance in a foreign language is also available at many locations. https://www.irs.gov/Help-&-Resources

To find the nearest taxpayer assistance center, type a ZIP Code in the text box of the online locator tool. Before going to a taxpayer assistance center for help, call and schedule an appointment. https://www.irs.gov/help-resources/contact-your-local-irs-office

Tax Statistics The IRS posts articles, data, and tables that describe and measure elements of the U.S. tax system. https://www.irs.gov/uac/tax-stats

Taxpayer Advocate Service Each district has problem resolution personnel to address taxpayer complaints that cannot be resolved through regular channels. https://www.irs.gov/advocate

Taxpayer Rights The taxpayer bill of rights is available on the IRS's website. https://www.irs.gov/taxpayer-bill-of-rights

Topics Asked About Most Information on the asked-about-most topics is available on the IRS's website. https://www.irs.gov/help-resources/telephone-assistance

Where's My Refund? Once the IRS processes a tax filer's return and approves a refund, he or she can check the refund date online. The IRS usually issues a refund in fewer than 21 days after receiving a tax filer's return. Some returns, however, require additional review and, therefore, additional time to process. https://www.irs.gov/refunds

For further information, contact the Internal Revenue Service, Department of the Treasury, 1111 Constitution Avenue NW., Washington, DC 20224. Phone, 202-622-5000.

Office of the Comptroller of the Currency

400 7th Street SW., Washington, DC 20219
Phone, 202-649-6800. Internet, http://www.occ.gov

Comptroller | JOSEPH M. OTTING
Senior Deputy Comptroller / Chief Counsel | BAO NGUYEN, ACTING
https://www.occ.gov/about/who-we-are/leadership/index-leadership.html

[For the Office of the Comptroller of the Currency statement of organization, see the Code of Federal Regulations, Title 12, Part 4]

The above list of key personnel was updated 11–2018.

The Office of the Comptroller of the Currency (OCC) was created on February 25, 1863 (12 Stat. 665), as a bureau of the Department of the Treasury. In 1929, with the issuance of the last national bank notes, the OCC essentially became an organization of national bank examiners with a singular mission: to maintain the safety and soundness of the banks under its supervision. In 2011, when the Office of Thrift Supervision integrated into the OCC, the bureau also assumed responsibility for regulating Federal savings associations, also referred to as Federal thrifts. The Comptroller of the Currency, whom the President appoints to a 5-year term with the Senate's advice and consent, administers the Federal banking system and serves as the chief officer of the OCC and as a director of the Federal Deposit Insurance Corporation.

The OCC regulates national banks and Federal thrifts by examining them; approving or denying applications for new charters, branches, capital, and other changes in corporate or banking structure; taking enforcement actions—removing officers and directors, negotiating agreements to change practices, and issuing cease and desist orders and civil monetary penalties—when national banks and Federal thrifts fail to comply with laws and regulations or when they engage in unsound practices; and issuing rules, regulations, interpretations, and corporate decisions that govern investments, lending, and other practices.

The bureau supervises nearly 1,400 national banks, Federal savings associations, and Federal branches, including their trust activities and overseas operations. A nationwide team of bank examiners works under the supervision of four district offices. National banks and Federal thrifts pay for their examinations, as well as for the processing of their corporate applications.

Assessments on national banks and Federal savings associations cover most OCC operating expenses. The OCC also benefits from some investment income, primarily from U.S. Treasury securities. https://occ.gov/about/what-we-do/mission/index-about.html

Sources of Information

Alerts The OCC posts counterfeiting, fictitious correspondence, fraudulent issuances, misrepresentation, and unauthorized banking activity alerts. https://occ.gov/news-issuances/alerts/index.html

Annual Reports The "2017 Annual Report" is available online in Portable Document Format (PDF) for downloading. Starting with the year 2003, earlier annual reports are available, too. https://www.occ.gov/annual-report/download-the-full-report/index-download-the-full-report.html

Answers / Solutions The "HelpWithMyBank" website has information and resources to help customers of national banks and Federal savings associations find answers to questions and solutions for problems. https://www.helpwithmybank.gov/index.html

Bulletins Starting with the year 1994 and continuing to the present, OCC bulletins are accessible online. Rescinded and some pre-1994 bulletins are also included in the collection. https://occ.gov/news-issuances/bulletins/index.html

Business Opportunities Procurement awards typically fall within the following service categories: computer-related services; computer facilities management services; computer systems design services; data processing, hosting, and related services; real estate agent and broker services; insurance agency and brokerage services; and administrative management and general management consulting services. https://occ.gov/about/contact-us/doing-business-with-occ/index-doing-business-with-the-occ.html | Email: OCCAcquisitionManagement@occ.treas.gov

Career Opportunities The OCC relies on accountants, attorneys, economists, financial analysts, human resources specialists, information technology specialists, project management analysts, and other professionals, particularly bank examiners, to carry out its mission. For more information, contact the Director for Human Resources Operations. Phone, 202-649-6590. Fax, 202-649-5998. http://careers.occ.gov/careers/index-careers.html

National bank examiners work to ensure the safety and soundness of America's national banking system, to provide fair access to financial services and equal treatment, and to establish and maintain a flexible regulatory framework that allows the Nation's banks to be competitive. The OCC generally hires examiners at the entry level through college recruitment. https://www.youtube.com/watch?v=RPrQmlcF0s0

In 2017, the OCC ranked 51st among 339 agency subcomponents in the Partnership for Public Service's Best Places To Work Agency Rankings. http://bestplacestowork.org/BPTW/rankings/detail/TRAJ

Consumer Protection The OCC posts information and resources on its website to protect consumers. https://occ.gov/topics/consumer-protection/index-consumer-protection.html

Customer Complaints An online form is available for submitting a complaint against a national bank or Federal savings association. https://appsec.helpwithmybank.gov/olcc_form/intro.aspx

District and Field Offices Contact information for district and field offices

is available online. https://occ.gov/about/
who-we-are/district-and-field-offices/index-
organization.html
En Español   The OCC posts information
in Spanish on its "Información para el
Consumidor" web page. https://www.
helpwithmybank.gov/espanol/index-espanol.
html
Freedom of Information Act (FOIA)   The
FOIA serves as the vehicle for obtaining
Federal agency documents and records.
The statute does contain, however,
nine exemptions and three special law
enforcement exclusions that shield some
documents and records, or parts of them,
from disclosure. https://www.occ.gov/about/
contact-us/freedom-of-information-act-
requests/index-foia.html

The electronic reading room contains
documents that attract public interest and
have been the subject of FOIA requests
in the past. https://foia-pal.occ.gov/app/
ReadingRoom.aspx
**Frequently Asked Questions
(FAQs)**   Answers to FAQs on checking
accounts, credit cards, credit reports,
mortgages, overdraft fees, and more are
posted on the "HelpWithMyBank" website.
https://www.helpwithmybank.gov/get-
answers/most-popular-faq-quesindx.html
Glossary   A dictionary of banking
terms and phrases is available on the
"HelpWithMyBank" website. https://www.
helpwithmybank.gov/dictionary/index-
dictionary.html

A list of abbreviations and acronyms is
available on the OCC's website in Portable
Document Format (PDF). https://www.occ.
gov/annual-report/download-the-full-report/
abbreviations.pdf
History   The OCC's role in the Federal
banking system started in a tumultuous year,
near the midpoint of the American Civil War.
On January 1, 1863, President Abraham
Lincoln emancipated over 3 million
men, women, and children by signing
the Emancipation Proclamation. Fifty-five
days later, he added his signature to the
National Currency Act, which established
the OCC and charged it with responsibility
for organizing and administering a system
of nationally chartered banks and a uniform
national currency. After 1913, its mission
increasingly centered on the safety and
soundness of national banks. To learn
more about the bureau's development over

the past 155 years, see the "Office of the
Comptroller: A Short History." https://www.
occ.gov/about/what-we-do/history/OCC%20
history%20final.pdf

On March 3, 1865, Congress enacted
legislation to establish the Bureau of Refugees,
Freedmen and Abandoned Lands, which came
to be known as the Freedmen's Bureau. On
that same day, it chartered the Freedman's
Savings and Trust Company, or Freedman's
Savings Bank (FSB), to meet a growing need for
financial services among African Americans.
To learn more about the intertwining histories
of the OCC and FSB, read the online article by
former OCC historian Jesse Stiller. https://www.
occ.gov/about/what-we-do/history/freedman-
savings-bank.html
News   The OCC posts news releases on
its website. https://occ.gov/news-issuances/
news-releases/index.html
Publications   An alphabetical list of OCC
publications is available online. https://occ.
gov/publications/alphabetical-listing/index-
alphabetical-listing.html
Public Information on Banks   Federal
bank regulators post public information
on individual banks. The OCC's website
provides convenient access to the websites
of these regulators. https://occ.gov/about/
contact-us/public-information/public-
information.html

The Federal Financial Institutions
Examination Council's website has a
searchable database for identifying the
Federal bank regulatory agency that oversees
a particular bank or financial institution.
https://www.ffiec.gov/consumercenter/
default.aspx
Site Map   The website map allows visitors
to look for specific topics or to browse
content that aligns with their interests.
https://occ.gov/site-map/index-site-map.html

The "HelpWithMyBank" website has its
own site map. https://www.helpwithmybank.
gov/hwmb-sitemap.html
Social Media   The OCC tweets
announcements and other newsworthy items
on Twitter. https://twitter.com/usocc

The OCC has a Facebook account. https://
www.facebook.com/US-Comptroller-of-the-
Currency-213254918823/

The OCC posts videos on its YouTube
channel. https://www.youtube.com/user/
OCCChannel#p/c/2BAA3C3A20C2630E;
https://occ.gov/about/contact-us/general-
correspondence/index-contact-us.html

For further information, contact the Communications Division, Office of the Comptroller of the Currency, 400 7th Street SW., Washington, DC 20219. Phone, 202-649-6700.

United States Mint

801 Ninth Street NW., Washington, DC 20220
Phone, 202-354-7200. Internet, http://www.usmint.gov

DIRECTOR	DAVID J. RYDER
Principal Deputy Director	(VACANCY)
https://www.usmint.gov/about/directors-office	

The above list of key personnel was updated 11–2018.

The establishment of a mint was authorized by act of April 2, 1792 (1 Stat. 246). The Bureau of the Mint was established by act of February 12, 1873 (17 Stat. 424), and recodified on September 13, 1982 (31 U.S.C. 304, 5131). The name was changed to United States Mint by Secretarial order on January 9, 1984.

The primary mission of the Mint is to produce an adequate volume of circulating coinage for the Nation to conduct its trade and commerce. The Mint also produces and sells numismatic coins, American Eagle gold and silver bullion coins, and national medals. The Fort Knox Bullion Depository is the primary storage facility for the Nation's gold bullion.

The U.S. Mint maintains sales centers at the Philadelphia and Denver Mints and at its headquarters on 9th Street in Washington, DC. Public tours are conducted, with free admission, at the Philadelphia and Denver Mints. https://www.usmint.gov/about_the_mint/index.html

Sources of Information

Artists   The artistic infusion program enriches and invigorates coin and medal designs by contracting with a pool of American artists from diverse backgrounds and having a variety of interests. These artists collaborate with the Mint's sculptor-engravers to create and submit new designs for U.S. coins and medals. https://www.usmint.gov/education/artisticInfusion/index.html

Bullion Dealers   The Mint's website has a locator tool for finding U.S. Mint bullion sellers by city and State or by ZIP Code. http://catalog.usmint.gov/bullion-dealer-locator

Business Opportunities   Contact the facility head of the appropriate field office or call the contracting and vendor department. Phone, 202-354-7820. http://catalog.usmint.gov/customer-service/contact-us.html?_ga=1.258962826.1416671245.1448488127

Career Opportunities   The Mint offers a wide range of career opportunities. An innovative, progressive bureau in the Department of the Treasury, it operates six facilities nationwide and employees professionals with backgrounds in financial management, information technology, manufacturing, protection, sales and marketing, workforce solutions, and other fields. http://www.usmint.gov/about_the_mint/careers

Among 339 agency subcomponents, the Mint placed 174th in the Partnership for Public Service's 2017 Best Places To Work rankings. https://bestplacestowork.org/rankings/detail/TRAD

Educational Resources   The Mint's website offers learning resources for children, educators, and parents. https://www.usmint.gov/education/index5105.html?action=learn

Facilities   The U.S. Mint operates four mints (CA, CO, NY, PA), one depository (KY), and maintains its headquarters in Washington, DC. http://www.usmint.gov/about_the_mint/mint_facilities

Freedom of Information Act (FOIA)   The FOIA gives the right of requesting access to documents or records maintained by the Mint to any person. Some information, however, is shielded from request and disclosure by the statute. https://www.usmint.gov/foia/index.html

The Mint's electronic reading room contains records that are commonly requested under the FOIA. https://www.usmint.gov/foia/index6dda.html?action=room

Glossary The H.I.P. Pocket Change website features a glossary. https://www.usmint.gov/Kids/campCoin/glossary.html

History The website has a section on the Mint's history and work. https://www.usmint.gov/education/historianscorner/index.html

An online timeline of the Mint that stretches from the 18th to 21st century. https://www.usmint.gov/education/historianscorner/indexf2dc.html?action=timeline

How Are Coins Made? An animated overview of the six-step coin manufacturing process—blanking, annealing, upsetting, striking, inspecting, and counting and bagging—is available online. https://www.usmint.gov/circulating_coins/indexc526.html?action=coins

Image Libraries High-resolution images of coins and medals are available on the Mint's website. For information on the use of these images, contact the Office of Licensing. Phone, 202-354-7350. Fax, 202-756-6585. https://www.usmint.gov/pressroom/indexf4a6.html?action=photo | Email: licensing@usmint.treas.gov

The high-resolution images in the historical image library represent commemorative, circulating, and bullion coins from current and previous programs. For information on the use of these images, contact the Office of Licensing. Phone, 202-354-7350. Fax, 202-756-6585. https://www.usmint.gov/about_the_mint/coinLibrary/index.html | Email: licensing@usmint.treas.gov

Medals National medals commemorate significant historical events or sites and honor individuals whose superior deeds and achievements have enriched American history or the world. Some national medals are bronze duplicates of Congressional Gold Medals that Congress authorizes under separate Public Laws, and others are produced under the Secretary of the Treasury's authority to strike them. https://www.usmint.gov/mint_programs/medals

News The Mint posts news releases online. https://www.usmint.gov/pressroom/index.html

Numismatic Services The United States Mint maintains public exhibit and sales areas at the Philadelphia and Denver Mints and at its headquarters in Washington, DC. Brochures and order forms for official coins, medals, and other numismatic items are available online. http://catalog.usmint.gov/shop/coin-programs

Production / Sales The Mint produces circulating coins for commerce, numismatic coins for collectors, and bullion coins for investors. Quantities are measured in terms of production figures when referring to circulating coins, sales figures when referring to numismatic products, and sales and mintage figures when referring to bullion. https://www.usmint.gov/about_the_mint/index83e3.html?action=coin_production

Reports Annual reports are available online in Portable Document Format (PDF). https://www.usmint.gov/about_the_mint/indexa3d5.html?action=annual_report

Special reports are available online in Portable Document Format (PDF). https://www.usmint.gov/about_the_mint/indexc390.html?action=specialreports

Seigniorage The Mint returned $550 million in seigniorage—the difference between the face value and the manufacturing cost of a circulating coin—to the Department of the Treasury's general fund in 2015. This amount was more than double the amount that it returned in 2014. The Mint publishes seigniorage information each year in its annual report.

Site Map The website map allows visitors to look for specific topics or to browse content that aligns with their interests. https://www.usmint.gov/WebsiteInfo/indexa1db.html?action=SiteMap

Sustainability The Mint has made significant progress toward achieving sustainability goals. Achievements include reducing its direct greenhouse gas emissions and water consumption and increasing its solid waste diversion rate. https://www.usmint.gov/about_the_mint/mint_facilities/indexa3d4.html?action=Sustainability; http://catalog.usmint.gov/customer-service/contact-us.html

For further information, contact the United States Mint, Department of the Treasury, 801 Ninth Street NW., Washington, DC 20220. Phone, 202-354-7200.

EXECUTIVE BRANCH: INDEPENDENT AGENCIES AND GOVERNMENT CORPORATIONS

Administrative Conference of the United States

1120 Twentieth Street NW., Suite 706 South, Washington, DC 20036
Phone, 202-480-2080. Fax, 202-386-7190. Internet, http://www.acus.gov | Email: info@acus.gov

Staff

Chairman https://www.acus.gov/staff	MATTHEW L. WIENER, ACTING
Executive Director Research Director https://www.acus.gov/contacts/matthew-l-wiener	MATTHEW L. WIENER REEVE T. BULL
Chief Financial and Operations Officer https://www.acus.gov/contacts/harry-m-seidman	HARRY M. SEIDMAN
General Counsel https://www.acus.gov/contacts/shawne-mcgibbon	SHAWNE C. McGIBBON

Council

Chair	MATTHEW L. WIENER, ACTING
Vice Chair	MATTHEW L. WIENER
Government Official	NICHOLAS T. MATICH IV
Private Citizens	RONALD A. CASS JEFFREY M. HARRIS DONALD F. McGAHN II MICHAEL H. McGINLEY THEODORE B. OLSON JANE C. SHERBURNE GEOVETTE E. WASHINGTON (VACANCY)

https://www.acus.gov/directory/council

The above list of key personnel was updated 12–2019.

The Administrative Conference of the United States develops recommendations for improving the fairness and effectiveness of procedures by which Federal agencies administer regulatory, benefit, and other Government programs.

ADMINISTRATIVE CONFERENCE OF THE UNITED STATES (ACUS)

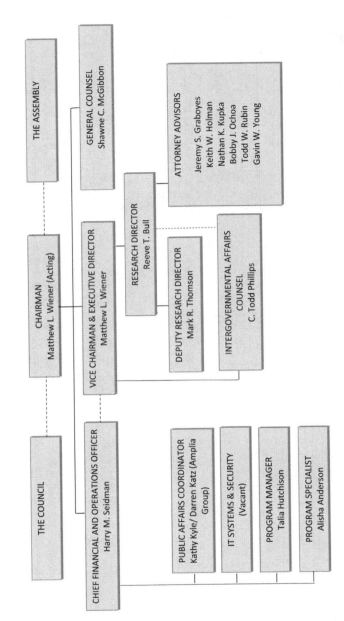

THE ASSEMBLY

GENERAL COUNSEL
Shawne C. McGibbon

ATTORNEY ADVISORS
Jeremy S. Graboyes
Keith W. Holman
Nathan K. Kupka
Bobby J. Ochoa
Todd W. Rubin
Gavin W. Young

RESEARCH DIRECTOR
Reeve T. Bull

CHAIRMAN
Matthew L. Wiener (Acting)

VICE CHAIRMAN & EXECUTIVE DIRECTOR
Matthew L. Wiener

DEPUTY RESEARCH DIRECTOR
Mark R. Thomson

INTERGOVERNMENTAL AFFAIRS
COUNSEL
C. Todd Phillips

THE COUNCIL

CHIEF FINANCIAL AND OPERATIONS OFFICER
Harry M. Seidman

PUBLIC AFFAIRS COORDINATOR
Kathy Kyle/ Darren Katz (Amplia Group)

IT SYSTEMS & SECURITY
(Vacant)

PROGRAM MANAGER
Talia Hutchison

PROGRAM SPECIALIST
Alisha Anderson

UPDATED October 2019

Establishment and Organization

The Administrative Conference of the United States (ACUS) was established as a permanent independent agency by the Administrative Conference Act (PL 88–499) enacted in 1964. The Conference is the successor to two temporary Administrative Conferences during the Eisenhower and Kennedy administrations. https://www. govinfo.gov/content/pkg/STATUTE-78/pdf/ STATUTE-78-Pg615.pdf

The Conference ceased operations on October 31, 1995, due to termination of funding by Congress. From its beginning in 1968 until its defunding in 1995, the ACUS adopted approximately 200 recommendations, based on research and the deliberations of its members in an open process that encouraged public input. The ACUS published a complete list of these recommendations in the "Federal Register" (60 FR 56312). https://www.govinfo.gov/ content/pkg/FR-1995-11-08/pdf/95-27473. pdf#page=1

Congress reauthorized the Conference in 2004 and again in 2008. The 2004 legislation expanded its responsibilities to include specific attention to achieving more effective public participation and efficiency, reducing unnecessary litigation, and improving the use of science in the rulemaking process (5 U.S.C. 591–596). Funding was approved in 2009, and the Conference was officially reestablished in March 2010. https://uscode.house.gov/view. xhtml?path=/prelim@title5/part1/chapter5/ subchapter5&edition=prelim

By statute, the Administrative Conference has no fewer than 75 and no more than 101 members, a majority of whom are Government officials. The President appoints the Chairman of the Conference with the advice and consent of the Senate for a 5-year term. The Council, which acts as an executive board, comprises the Chairman and 10 other members whom the President appoints for 3-year terms. Federal officials named to the Council may not constitute more than half of the total Council membership. The Chairman, the only full-time, compensated member of the Conference, appoints members representing the private sector with the approval of the Council for 2-year terms.

The entire membership is divided into committees. Each committee is assigned a broad area of interest such as adjudication, administration and management, judicial review, regulation, or rulemaking. The membership meeting in plenary session constitutes the Assembly of the Conference, which by statute must meet at least once, and customarily meets twice, each year. https://www.acus.gov/history

The agency's organizational chart is available in Portable Document Format (PDF) for viewing and downloading on the "Staff" web page. https://www.acus.gov/ sites/default/files/documents/ACUS%20 Organization%20Chart_Oct%202019.pdf

The Establishment and Organization paragraphs were updated 12–2019.

Activities

The Chairman develops subjects for inquiry, and the Council approves them. Government and nongovernment experts in administrative procedure often contribute to the development and approval process. The committees conduct thorough reviews of these subjects for inquiry and propose draft recommendations, which are based on supporting reports that expert consultants typically prepare for the ACUS.

Following the proposal process of the committees, the Council considers the supporting reports and the draft recommendations. The Council may then place them on the agenda for an upcoming plenary session of the Assembly. Members of the Assembly debate draft recommendations that the Council has placed on the agenda, and the Assembly's voting members then vote on their final adoption. The general public may attend deliberations of the committees and Assembly.

Recommendations adopted by the Conference may be addressed to administrative agencies, Congress, the President, or the Judicial Conference. Most recommendations call for action on the part of affected agencies or for new legislation. While a substantial number of recommendations have been implemented, implementation activities are continually ongoing.

The Chairman may make independent inquiries into procedural matters, including matters proposed by individuals inside or outside the Government. These inquiries help determine whether the problems should be made the subject of Conference study in the interest of developing fairer or more effective or efficient procedures.

Upon the request of a department or agency head, the Chairman is authorized to advise and assist on matters of administrative procedure. The Conference may collect information and statistics from departments and agencies and publish reports and sourcebooks that it considers useful for evaluating and improving administrative processes. The Conference also serves as a forum for the interchange among departments and agencies of information that may be useful for improving administrative practices and procedures.

The Activities were updated 12–2019.

Sources of Information

Archived Records   The "Guide to Federal Records in the National Archives of the United States" indicates that ACUS records have been assigned to record group 451. The Guide is accessible online, but no description is associated with this record group. https://www.archives.gov/research/guide-fed-records/groups/000.html

Assembly Membership   When the 101 statutory voting members of the ACUS meet in plenary session, they are referred to as the Assembly. The Assembly comprises three types of voting members: Council members, Government members, and public members. Nonvoting members—liaison representatives, special counsels, and senior fellows—may not make motions during plenary sessions and are not reckoned as part of the Assembly. https://www.acus.gov/members

Blog   "Administrative Fix" is the agency's official blog. https://www.acus.gov/administrative-fix-blog

Calendar   A calendar of meetings and events is available online. https://www.acus.gov/meetings-and-events/calendar

Career Opportunities   Current job openings and information on internships and the research fellow program are accessible on the "Opportunities" web page. https://www.acus.gov/opportunities

Committees   The ACUS currently has standing committees on adjudication, administration and management, judicial review, regulation, and rulemaking. https://www.acus.gov/committees

Documents   The ACUS maintains a database of electronic documents that are accessible and searchable. https://www.acus.gov/documents/advanced-search

Freedom of Information Act (FOIA)   The FOIA generally provides that any person has the right to obtain access to Federal agency records, except to the extent that those records are shielded from disclosure by the FOIA or another statute. Formal FOIA requests are unnecessary when seeking information that is publicly available. Before filing a formal FOIA request, an information seeker should search the ACUS website for relevant documents that are already accessible in the public domain and without charge. If the desired document cannot be found on the ACUS website, consider contacting the FOIA liaison. Getting assistance prior to filing a formal request may shorten the response time. Phone, 202-480-2080. https://www.acus.gov/foia

News   The ACUS posts news items on its "Latest News" web page. https://www.acus.gov/newsroom

Press Kit   The ACUS posted a press kit on its website. https://www.acus.gov/press-kit

Publications   Articles, books, papers, reports, and bibliographies are accessible online. https://www.acus.gov/publications

Recommendations   The ACUS maintains an online searchable database of recommendations. The 19 statements that the ACUS has adopted are also included in the database. A statement is adopted when the ACUS seeks to express its views on a matter without making a formal recommendation on the subject. https://www.acus.gov/recommendations

Site Map   The website map allows visitors to look for specific topics or to browse content that aligns with their interests. https://www.acus.gov/sitemap

Social Media   The ACUS maintains a Facebook account. https://www.facebook.com/ACUSgov

The ACUS tweets announcements and other newsworthy items on Twitter. https://twitter.com/ACUSgov

The Sources of Information were updated 12–2019.

Staff Directory The ACUS maintains a staff directory on its website. https://www.acus.gov/directory/staff

Central Intelligence Agency

Washington, DC 20505
Phone, 703-482-0623. Internet, http://www.cia.gov

Director	GINA C. HASPEL
Deputy Director	VAUGHN F. BISHOP
Chief Operating Officer	ANDREW MAKRIDIS
Director of Public Affairs	BRITTANY BRAMELL
General Counsel	COURTNEY SIMMONS ELWOOD
https://www.cia.gov/about-cia/leadership	

Office of Inspector General

Inspector General	CHRISTOPHER R. SHARPLEY, ACTING
https://www.cia.gov/offices-of-cia/inspector-general/index.html	

The above list of key personnel was updated 8–2019.

The Central Intelligence Agency collects, evaluates, and disseminates vital information on economic, military, political, scientific, and other developments abroad to safeguard national security.

Establishment and Organization

On July 26, 1947, President Harry S. Truman approved Public Law 80–253, which is commonly cited as the National Security Act of 1947. The Act established the Central Intelligence Agency (CIA). https://www.loc.gov/law/help/statutes-at-large/80th-congress/session-1/c80s1ch343.pdf

The President appoints the Director by the advice and with the consent of the Senate. The Director serves as the head of the CIA and reports to the Director of National Intelligence (DNI) regarding the activities of the Agency. https://www.cia.gov/about-cia/todays-cia

The National Security Act has been amended since its enactment in 1947 (50 U.S.C. 3001 et seq.). The CIA now functions under the original Act, as amended; Executive Order 12333 of December 4, 1981; the Intelligence Reform and Terrorism Prevention Act of 2004; and other laws, Executive orders, regulations, and directives. https://www.govinfo.gov/content/pkg/USCODE-2017-title50/pdf/USCODE-2017-title50-chap44.pdf

The CIA's statement of organization is found in 32 CFR 1900. https://www.govinfo.gov/content/pkg/CFR-2018-title32-vol6/pdf/CFR-2018-title32-vol6-subtitleB-chapXIX.pdf

The CIA posts its organizational graphic online in Portable Document Format (PDF). https://www.cia.gov/about-cia/todays-cia/Offices_of_CIA.pdf

Activities

The CIA uses human source collection and other means to gather intelligence; however, it neither carries out internal security functions nor exercises police, subpoena, or other law enforcement powers. The Agency correlates, evaluates, and disseminates national security intelligence. It also directs and coordinates intelligence collecting outside the United States by U.S. intelligence community elements authorized to engage in human source collection. https://www.cia.gov/about-cia

In coordination with other departments, agencies, and authorized elements of the U.S. Government, the CIA ensures that resources are used effectively and that adequate consideration is given to the risks, both to the United States and to those involved in collecting intelligence abroad. The Agency carries out other intelligence-related tasks that are necessary for safeguarding national security, as the President or the DNI may indicate. Under the direction of the DNI and consistent with section 207 of the Foreign Service Act of 1980, the CIA coordinates relationships between elements of the U.S. intelligence community and the security or intelligence services of foreign governments or international organizations in matters of national security and clandestine intelligence. https://www.cia.gov/library/publications/resources/cia-at-a-glance/what-we-do.html

Sources of Information

Agency Offices   The CIA comprises seven components: directorate of analysis, directorate of operations, directorate of science and technology, directorate of support, directorate of digital innovation, mission centers, and offices of the Director. https://www.cia.gov/offices-of-cia

At A Glance   The "CIA At-A-Glance" web page allows easy access to an overview of the Agency, a summary of its history, an introduction to working at the Agency, and explanations of what the CIA is and what it does. https://www.cia.gov/library/publications/resources/cia-at-a-glance

Bibliography of Intelligence Literature   The CIA's online bibliography contains works representing a wide spectrum of views on intelligence and the Agency. The readings cover history, opinion, technology, and some of the key figures who are associated with intelligence. https://www.cia.gov/library/intelligence-literature/index.html

Blog   The CIA maintains a blog on its website. https://www.cia.gov/news-information/blog

Career Opportunities   To carry out its mission, the CIA relies on analysts, attorneys, engineers, graphic designers, foreign language instructors, mechanics and truck drivers, physicians and psychiatrists, and other professionals. https://www.cia.gov/careers

Chiefs of State   The CIA updates its online directory of "Chiefs of State and Cabinet Members of Foreign Governments" regularly. https://www.cia.gov/library/publications/resources/world-leaders-1

Contact Information   The CIA posts contact information on its website. https://www.cia.gov/contact-cia

Foreign Languages   Abridged versions of the CIA's website content is available in several foreign languages. https://www.cia.gov/foreign-languages

Freedom of Information Act (FOIA)   The FOIA gives a right to obtain access to Federal agency records to any person, except to a fugitive from the law. Some records, or portions of them, are, however, shielded from disclosure by one or more of nine statutory exemptions or by specific harm that disclosure may cause. The CIA shields classified national security information, information relating to intelligence sources and methods, and organizational information from release under the FOIA. An information seeker may submit a FOIA request for records by sending it to the FOIA Requester Service Center, Central Intelligence Agency, Washington, DC 20505. A request also may be submitted by facsimile. Fax, 703-613-3007. https://www.cia.gov/library/readingroom/foia-annual-report

The CIA maintains an online FOIA reading room. https://www.cia.gov/library/readingroom

Frequently Asked Questions (FAQs)   The CIA posts answers to FAQs regarding employment and student programs.

History   President Harry S. Truman approved the National Security Act of 1947, creating a permanent central agency for intelligence. His approval was not the beginning of the story: 6 years prior to the formal establishment of the CIA, various renditions of an intelligence agency had occurred. To learn more of the story that underlies today's CIA, visit the "History of the CIA" web page. https://www.cia.gov/about-cia/history-of-the-cia

Kid's Zone   The "Kid's Zone" web pages contain materials that are suitable for K–5th grade, 6–12th grade, and parents and teachers. The pages also have games and related links. https://www.cia.gov/kids-page

Maps By country, maps of administration, physiography, and transportation are posted on the CIA website. https://www.cia.gov/library/publications/resources/cia-maps-publications

Museum The CIA Museum's online collection allows visitors to learn more about the Agency through an interactive timeline, historical artifacts, and stories. https://www.cia.gov/about-cia/cia-museum/experience-the-collection

Press Releases / Statements The CIA posts press releases and statements on its website. https://www.cia.gov/news-information/press-releases-statements

Site Map The website map allows visitors to look for specific topics or to browse for content that aligns with their interests. https://www.cia.gov/sitemap.html

The Sources of Information were updated 8–2019.

Social Media The CIA has a Facebook account. https://www.facebook.com/Central.Intelligence.Agency

The CIA tweets announcements and other newsworthy items on Twitter. https://twitter.com/CIA

The CIA posts videos on its YouTube channel. https://www.youtube.com/user/ciagov

World Factbook For 267 world entities, the CIA posts information on their histories, peoples and societies, governments, economies, energy sources, geographies, communications, modes of transportation, militaries, and transnational issues. https://www.cia.gov/library/publications/resources/the-world-factbook

Commodity Futures Trading Commission

1155 Twenty-first Street NW, Washington, DC 20581
Phone, 202-418-5000. 202-418-5514 (TTY). Fax, 202-418-5521. Internet, http://www.cftc.gov/index.htm

Commissioners

Chair	HEATH P. TARBERT
	ROSTIN BEHNAM
	DANIEL M. BERKOVITZ
	DAWN DEBERRY STUMP
	BRIAN D. QUINTENZ

https://www.cftc.gov/About/Commissioners/index.htm

Divisions

Directors	
Clearing and Risk	M. CLARK HUTCHISON III
Enforcement	JAMES M. MCDONALD
Market Oversight	AMIR R. ZAIDI
Swap Dealer and Intermediary Oversight	JOSHUA B. STERLING

https://www.cftc.gov/About/CFTCOrganization/index.htm

Offices

Executive Director	ANTHONY C. THOMPSON
Chief Economist	BRUCE TUCKMAN
Chief Information Officer	JOHN L. ROGERS
General Counsel	DANIEL J. DAVIS
Directors	
External Affairs	MICHAEL C. SHORT
International Affairs	MAURICIO MELARA, ACTING
Legislative and Intergovernmental Affairs	ANN WRIGHT, ACTING

Minority and Women Inclusion
https://www.cftc.gov/Contact/index.htm

Office of Inspector General

Inspector General
https://www.cftc.gov/About/OfficeoftheInspectorGeneral/
  index.htm

Sarah J. Summerville

A. Roy Lavik

The above list of key personnel was updated 8–2019.

The Commodity Futures Trading Commission avoids systemic risk; fosters open, transparent, competitive, and financially sound markets; and protects the market users and their funds, consumers, and the public from fraud, manipulation, and abusive practices related to derivatives and other products that are subject to the Commodity Exchange Act.

Establishment and Organizational
On October 23, 1974, President Gerald R. Ford approved Public Law 93–463, which is commonly cited as the Commodity Futures Trading Commission Act of 1974 (7 U.S.C. 2). The Act established the Commodity Futures Trading Commission (CFTC), which became operational in April of 1975. The U.S. Congress renewed the CFTC's authority to regulate futures trading in 1978, 1982, 1986, 1992, 1995, 2000, and 2008. https://www.govinfo.gov/content/pkg/STATUTE-88/pdf/STATUTE-88-Pg1389.pdf

In 2010, Title VII of the Dodd-Frank Wall Street Reform and Consumer Protection Act (Public Law 111–203) gave the CFTC new and expanded responsibilities and authorities for regulating the swaps marketplace. https://www.govinfo.gov/content/pkg/STATUTE-124/pdf/STATUTE-124-Pg1376.pdf

The President appoints the CFTC's five Commissioners by the advice and with the consent of the Senate. The President designates one Commissioner, also by the Senate's advice and with its consent, to serve as the Chair. The Commissioners serve staggered 5-year terms, and no more than three of them may belong to the same political party. https://www.cftc.gov/About/Commissioners/index.htm

The Commission has nine major operating components: the Divisions of Market Oversight, Clearing and Risk, Swap Dealer and Intermediary Oversight, Enforcement, and the Offices of the Executive Director, the General Counsel, the Chief Economist, International Affairs, and Data and Technology. The Office of Inspector General is an independent organizational unit at the CFTC.

The CFTC's statement of organization is found in 17 CFR 140. https://www.ecfr.gov/cgi-bin/retrieveECFR?gp=&SID=ad2cd54a43272e3456dfc1088505c4e4&mc=true&n=pt17.2.140&r=PART&ty=HTML

The CFTC posts it organizational chart online in Portable Document Format (PDF). https://www.cftc.gov/media/2261/cftcorgchart071519/download

Activities

The CFTC regulates trading on the U.S. futures and options markets that offer commodity futures and options contracts, as well as the swaps marketplace in the United States. Oversight of the derivatives marketplace is accomplished through various CFTC activities.

The CFTC oversees derivatives clearing organizations and other market participants in the clearing process, including futures commission merchants, swap dealers, major swap participants, and large traders. The CFTC oversees the registration and compliance of intermediaries and futures industry self-regulatory organizations, including U.S. derivatives exchanges and the National Futures Association. It also oversees trade execution facilities and data repositories, conducts surveillance, reviews new exchange applications, and examines existing exchanges to ensure compliance with applicable core principles. https://www.cftc.gov/About/MissionResponsibilities/index.htm

Exercising the agency's authority, its staff also investigates and prosecutes alleged violations of the Commodity Exchange Act and CFTC regulations. Potential violations include fraud, manipulation, and other abuses concerning commodity derivatives and swaps that threaten market integrity, market participants, and the general public. https://www.cftc.gov/LawRegulation/CommodityExchangeAct/index.htm

Under the Dodd-Frank Wall Street Reform and Consumer Protection Act, the CFTC develops and monitors compliance with regulations addressing registration, business conduct standards, capital adequacy, and margin requirements for swap dealers and major swap participants. https://www.cftc.gov/LawRegulation/DoddFrankAct/index.htm

Sources of Information

Business Opportunities   The Commission has recurring requirements for the following goods: furniture, office equipment and supplies, and telecommunications equipment and supplies. It also has recurring requirements for copying and printing services and minor construction. http://www.cftc.gov/About/ProcurementOpportunities/index.htm

Career Opportunities   The Commission hires professionals with strong academic records and superior analytical and problem solving skills. http://www.cftc.gov/About/Careers/Index.htm

In 2018, the CFTC ranked 23d among 29 small Government agencies in the Partnership for Public Service's Best Places To Work Agency Rankings. https://bestplacestowork.org/rankings/detail/CT00

Climate-Related Market Risk   The CFTC has established a subcommittee to prepare a report that identifies and examines climate change-related financial and market risks for the agency's Market Risk Advisory Committee. The climate-related market risk subcommittee will bring experts from academia, industry, and the public sector together to identify and examine the risks that climate change poses to the stability of the U.S. financial system. The subcommittee will propose future actions for policymakers and market participants to consider for mitigating these risks. https://www.cftc.gov/PressRoom/PressReleases/7963-19

Cotton Futures   The "Cotton On-Call Report" shows the quantity of bought or sold call cotton on which the price has not been fixed, together with the respective futures on which the purchase or sale is based. Call cotton refers to physical cotton bought or sold, or contracted for purchase or sale at a price to be fixed later based upon a specified delivery month future's price. https://www.cftc.gov/MarketReports/CottonOnCall/index.htm

Disciplinary History   Making the CFTC's disciplinary history accessible is part of the agency's ongoing effort to protect market participants and the public from fraud, manipulation, and abusive practices. https://www.cftc.gov/ConsumerProtection/DisciplinaryHistory/index.htm

Forms / Submissions   Forms and submissions information for designated contract markets, filing tips and complaints, future commissions merchants, and ownership and control reporting are available online. https://www.cftc.gov/Forms/index.htm

Freedom of Information Act (FOIA)   The FOIA gives the right to request access to Federal agency records or information to any person. All agencies of the U.S. Government must disclose records upon receiving a written request for them, except for records that the FOIA's nine exemptions and three exclusions shield from disclosure. This right of access is enforceable in court. http://www.cftc.gov/FOI/index.htm | Email: FOIAsubmissions@cftc.gov

In addition to maintaining a physical, onsite reading room in Washington, DC, the CFTC also has an electronic reading room. Information seekers should see if the records that they seek are immediately available and accessible free of charge in the electronic reading room before submitting a FOIA request. https://www.cftc.gov/FOI/foiareadingrooms.html

Frequently Asked Questions (FAQs)   The "Ask CFTC" web page provides answers to some basic questions regarding the futures markets and how they work, where to go for help, as well as answers to other FAQs. https://www.cftc.gov/ConsumerProtection/EducationCenter/index.htm

Glossary   The online glossary defines specialized words and phrases that are used in the futures industry. Standard reference works do not include some of them. http://www.cftc.gov/ConsumerProtection/EducationCenter/CFTCGlossary/index.htm

History   Futures contracts for agricultural commodities have been traded in the country for more than 150 years. The Federal Government has regulated them since the 1920s. When the CFTC was created in 1974, most futures trading took place in the agricultural sector. Over the years, the futures industry has become increasingly varied and complex. To learn more of the history of the futures trading industry and the Federal Government's role in regulating it, visit the "History of the CFTC" web page. https://www.cftc.gov/About/HistoryoftheCFTC/index.htm

LabCFTC   LabCFTC is the hub for the CFTC's engagement with financial technology innovators. https://www.cftc.gov/LabCFTC/index.htm

Learning Resources   The Office of Consumer Outreach makes information and tools available to help consumers avoid fraud. The "Learning Resources" web page has brochures, reports, videos, and a book to educate consumers on this topic. https://www.cftc.gov/ConsumerProtection/Resources/index.htm | Email: consumers@cftc.gov

The "Avoid Fraud" web page has additional resources. https://www.cftc.gov/ConsumerProtection/FraudAwarenessPrevention/index.htm

Money Laundering   A general outline of important anti-money laundering topics with links to general information and resources is available on the CFTC website. https://www.cftc.gov/IndustryOversight/AntiMoneyLaundering/index.htm

The Sources of Information were updated 8–2019.

Press Room   The press room provides convenient access to news, podcasts, press releases, remarks, statements, testimonies, webcasts, and information on public events. http://www.cftc.gov/PressRoom/index.htm

Regional Offices   The Commission maintains regional offices in Chicago, IL, and New York, NY, where many of the Nation's designated contract markets are located. Phone, 312-596-0700 (IL); Phone, 646-746-9700 (NY). A third regional office is located in Kansas City, MO. Phone, 816-960-7700.

Site Map   The Web site map allows visitors to look for specific topics or to browse content that aligns with their interests. http://www.cftc.gov/SiteMap/index.htm

Swaps Report   The "CFTC Swaps Report" is published every Wednesday at 3:30 p.m., unless otherwise noted. https://www.cftc.gov/MarketReports/SwapsReports/index.htm | Email: swapsreport@cftc.gov

Virtual Currencies   One of the most recent marketplace developments driving a lot of interest is the rise in prominence of virtual currencies, specifically bitcoin. The "Bitcoin and Other Virtual Currencies" web page has resources for market participants and customers on virtual currency and on the CFTC's role in overseeing this emerging innovation. https://www.cftc.gov/Bitcoin/index.htm

Whistleblower Program   The Commission gives monetary incentives to whistleblowers who report possible Commodity Exchange Act violations that lead to a successful enforcement action. The Commission also provides antiretaliation protections, confidentiality, and privacy. https://www.whistleblower.gov

Consumer Financial Protection Bureau

1700 G Street NW., Washington, DC 20552
Phone, 202-435-7000. Internet, http://www.consumerfinance.gov

Office of the Director

Director	KATHLEEN L. KRANINGER
Deputy Director	BRIAN JOHNSON, ACTING
Chief Communications Officer / Spokesperson	JOHN CZWARTACKI

Chief of Staff	KIRSTEN SUTTON
Principal Policy Director	BRIAN JOHNSON
Associate Director	
Equal Opportunity and Fairness	ALTHEA KIREILIS
Assistant Directors	
Civil Rights	M. STACEY BACH
Minority and Women Inclusion	(VACANCY)

https://www.consumerfinance.gov/about-us/the-bureau/about-director/

Administrative Law Judge	CHRISTINE KIRBY
Ombudsman	WENDY KAMENSHINE

Consumer Education and Engagement Division

Policy Associate Director	SHEILA GREENWOOD
Associate Director	GAIL HILLEBRAND
Assistant Directors	
Community Affairs	DANIEL DODD-RAMIREZ
Consumer Engagement	GENE KOO
Consumer Response	CHRISTOPHER JOHNSON
Financial Education	JANNEKE RATCLIFFE
Financial Education—Students and Young Consumers	(VACANCY)
Older Americans	STACY CANAN
Servicemember Affairs	PATRICK CAMPBELL, ACTING

https://www.consumerfinance.gov/about-us/the-bureau/bureau-structure/consumer-education-engagement

External Affairs Division

Policy Associate Director	ANTHONY WELCHER
Associate Director	ZIXTA MARTINEZ
Assistant Directors	
Advisory Board and Councils	DELICIA HAND
Financial Institutions and Business Liaison	DANIEL SMITH
Intergovernmental Affairs	CHERYL PARKER ROSE
Legislative Affairs	CATHERINE GALICIA
Public Engagement and Community Liaison	KEO CHEA

https://www.consumerfinance.gov/about-us/the-bureau/bureau-structure/external-affairs

Legal Division

General Counsel	MARY MCLEOD
Principal Deputy General Counsel	RICHARD LEPLEY
Deputy General Counsels	
General Law and Ethics	SONYA WHITE
Law and Policy	STEPHEN VAN METER
Litigation and Oversight	JOHN COLEMAN

https://www.consumerfinance.gov/about-us/the-bureau/bureau-structure/legal

Operations Division

Chief Operating Officer	KATE FULTON, ACTING
Chief Officers	
Administrative Officer	MARTIN MICHALOSKY

Human Capital	Jeffrey Sumberg
Information	Jerry Horton
Financial	Elizabeth Reilly
Procurement	David Gragan

https://www.consumerfinance.gov/about-us/the-bureau/bureau-structure/operations

Research, Markets, and Regulations Division

Policy Associate Director	Thomas Pahl
Associate Director	David Silberman

Assistant Directors	
Card, Payment and Deposit Markets	William Wade-Gery
Consumer Lending, Reporting and Collection Markets	John McNamara
Mortgage Markets	Mark McArdle
Small Business Lending Markets	Grady Hedgespeth
Regulations	Kelly Cochran
Research	Ron Borzekowski

https://www.consumerfinance.gov/about-us/the-bureau/bureau-structure/research-markets-regulation

Supervision, Enforcement and Fair Lending Division

Policy Associate Director	Eric Blankenstein
Associate Director	Christopher D'Angelo

Assistant Directors	
Enforcement	Kristen Donoghue
Fair Lending and Equal Opportunity	Patrice Ficklin
Supervision Examinations	Paul Sanford
Supervision Policy	Peggy Twohig

Regional Directors	
Midwest region	John Schroeder
Northeast region	Mitchell Kent
Southeast region	James L. Carley
West region	Edwin Chow

https://www.consumerfinance.gov/about-us/the-bureau/bureau-structure/supervision-enforcement-fair-lending

Office of Inspector General

Inspector General	Mark Bialek

https://oig.federalreserve.gov/the-inspector-general.htm

The above list of key personnel was updated 12–2018.

The Consumer Financial Protection Bureau (CFPB) helps consumer finance markets work by making rules more effective, by consistently and fairly enforcing those rules, and by empowering consumers to take more control over their economic lives.

The Consumer Financial Protection Bureau (CFPB) is an independent Federal agency established by title X of the Dodd-Frank Wall Street Reform and Consumer Protection Act of 2012 (12 U.S.C. 5491). The CFPB is headed by a Director whom the President appoints and the Senate confirms.

Activities

The Bureau regulates the offering and provision of consumer financial products and services under Federal consumer financial laws. It gives consumers the information they need to understand the terms of their agreements with financial companies. It also makes regulations and guidance as clear and streamlined as possible so providers of consumer financial products and services can understand and follow the rules without assistance.

The CFPB's principal activities center on writing rules, supervising companies, and enforcing Federal consumer financial protection laws; restricting unfair, deceptive, or abusive acts or practices; taking consumer complaints; promoting financial education; researching consumer behavior; monitoring financial markets for new risks to consumers; and enforcing laws that prohibit discrimination and other unfair treatment in consumer finance. http://www.consumerfinance.gov/the-bureau

Sources of Information

Blog The CFPB maintains a blog on its website. https://www.consumerfinance.gov/about-us/blog/?filter_blog_category=At+the+CFPB&filter_range_date_gte=&filter_range_date_lte=

Bureau Structure / Organizational Chart The "Bureau Structure" web page offers visitors a two-dimensional representation of the CFPB's organizational structure, which also includes the names of officials filling key leadership positions. https://www.consumerfinance.gov/about-us/the-bureau/bureau-structure

Business Opportunities Information on doing business with the CFPB is available online. http://www.consumerfinance.gov/doing-business-with-us

Career Opportunities The CFPB posts new job openings online, as well as information on the application process and opportunities for students and recent graduates. http://www.consumerfinance.gov/about-us/careers | Email: jobs@consumerfinance.gov

In 2018, the CFPB ranked 26th among 27 midsize Government agencies in the Partnership for Public Service's Best Places To Work Agency Rankings. https://bestplacestowork.org/rankings/detail/FRFT

Consumer Help The CFPB forwards financial product or service complaints to the company offering the product or service and then works to get an appropriate response. A form for filing a complaint and a searchable complaint database are accessible online. Assistance by phone is available on weekdays, excluding Federal holidays, 8 a.m.–8 p.m., eastern standard time. Phone, 855-411-2372. TTY/TDD, 855-729-2372. http://www.consumerfinance.gov/complaint

Data The CFPB publishes research and posts consumer financial marketplace information online. http://www.consumerfinance.gov/data-research

Educational Resources Resources for educators, librarians, parents, and those who manage someone else's money are available online. http://www.consumerfinance.gov/adult-financial-education

Fraud / Scams The CFPB's online resources can help consumers prevent, recognize, and report scams and fraud. https://www.consumerfinance.gov/consumer-tools/fraud

Freedom of Information Act (FOIA) A FOIA request may be submitted by email, fax, or letter. The CFPB recommends using email for making a submission. http://www.consumerfinance.gov/foia-requests/submit-request | Email: CFPB_FOIA@consumerfinance.gov

Frequently Asked Questions (FAQs) The CFPB website has clear and impartial answers to hundreds of financial questions. The topics covered include auto loans, bank accounts and services, credit cards, credit reports and scores, debt collection, families and money, money transfers, mortgages, payday loans, prepaid cards, and student loans. https://www.consumerfinance.gov/ask-cfpb | Email: info@consumerfinance.gov

Home Mortgage Disclosure Act (HMDA) The CFPB's website features a 3-minute video that explains the purpose of the HMDA. https://www.consumerfinance.gov/data-research/hmda

Invite the CFPB Send an email to invite a CFPB employee to contribute to a publication or participate in a discussion, forum, or other event. Email: invitations2cfpb@consumerfinance.gov

In Your Language In the United States, the most widely spoken foreign languages are Chinese, French, Haitian Créole, Korean, Spanish, Tagalog (Filipino), and Vietnamese. To help those who speak these languages, the CFPB provides information in them for accessing common products and making basic transactions. Assistance by phone is available in more than 180 languages. Phone, 855-411-2372. https://www.consumerfinance.gov/language

Newsroom   Blog posts, press releases, and speeches are accessible online. An online subscription form is available to receive press releases via email. http://www.consumerfinance.gov/about-us/newsroom

Open Government   The CFPB supports the Open Government initiative by promoting the principles of collaboration, participation, and transparency. http://www.consumerfinance.gov/open-government

Organizational Chart   The CFPB is currently revising its organizational chart. https://www.consumerfinance.gov/about-us/the-bureau/bureau-structure/

Plain Writing   CFPB editors and writers apply plain language principles in all of their consumer-oriented materials. They want to know if something on the CFPB website or in its printed materials is unclear. http://www.consumerfinance.gov/plain-writing | Email: CFPB_Plain_Writing_Act@consumerfinance.gov

Publications   CFPB publications, in English and Spanish, may be ordered in bulk online. http://promotions.usa.gov/cfpbpubs.html

Social Media   The CFPB maintains a Facebook account. https://www.facebook.com/CFPB

The CFPB tweets announcements and other newsworthy items on Twitter. https://twitter.com/cfpb

The CFPB posts videos on its YouTube channel. https://www.youtube.com/user/cfpbvideo

Whistleblowers   The CFPB wants to know about companies that may be breaking Federal consumer financial laws. A current or former employee of such a company, an industry insider who knows of such a company, or a competitor being unfairly undercut by such a company—people like these should report alleged violations to the CFPB. Phone, 855-695-7974. http://www.consumerfinance.gov/blog/the-cfpb-wants-you-to-blow-the-whistle-on-lawbreakers | Email: whistleblower@cfpb.gov; http://www.consumerfinance.gov/contact-us | Email: info@consumerfinance.gov

For further information, contact the Consumer Financial Protection Bureau, 1700 G Street NW., Washington, DC 20552. Phone, 202-435-7000.

Consumer Product Safety Commission

4330 East-West Highway, Bethesda, MD 20814
Phone, 301-504-7923. Internet, http://www.cpsc.gov

Commissioners

Chair https://www.cpsc.gov/About-CPSC/Chairman/Robert-Adler	ROBERT S. ADLER, ACTING
	DANA BAIOCCO ANN MARIE BUERKLE PETER A. FELDMAN ELLIOT F. KAYE
https://www.cpsc.gov/About-CPSC/Commissioners	

Independent Offices
Directors	
Communications	JOSEPH MARTYAK
Equal Employment Opportunity and Minority Enterprise	BRITTANY WOOLFOLK
Legislative Affairs	CHRISTOPHER HUDGINS
General Counsel	PATRICIA HANZ
Secretary	ALBERTA MILLS

Offices of the Executive Director
Executive Director	MARY T. BOYLE

Operations Support

Deputy Executive Director	MONICA SUMMITT
Assistant Executive Director Information and Technology Services	JAMES C. ROLFES
Chief Officers Financial Information	 JAY HOFFMAN JAMES C. ROLFES
Directors Facilities Services Financial Management, Planning, and Evaluation Human Resources Management	 MARK OEMLER JAY HOFFMAN DONNA M. SIMPSON

Safety Operations

Deputy Executive Director	DEWANE RAY
Assistant Executive Directors Compliance and Field Operations Hazard Identification and Reduction	 ROBERT KAYE DUANE BONIFACE
Directors International Programs Import Surveillance	 RICHARD O'BRIEN JAMES JOHOLSKE

Small Business Ombudsman
https://www.cpsc.gov/s3fs-public/
  cpscorgchartMM_081919_0.pdf?o.qldWd.
  ny4Xw2xhWhRJT7Ju.5KEsS_5
	SHELBY MATHIS

Inspector General https://www.cpsc.gov/About-CPSC/Inspector-General	CHRISTOPHER W. DENTEL

The above list of key personnel was updated 10–2019.

The Consumer Product Safety Commission protects the public by reducing the risk of injury and death from consumer products.

Establishment and Organization

On October 27, 1972, President Richard M. Nixon approved Public Law 92–573, which is commonly cited as the Consumer Product Safety Act (15 U.S.C. 2051 et seq.). The Act established the Consumer Product Safety Commission (CPSC) as an independent regulatory agency. The CPSC became operational on May 14, 1973. https://www.govinfo.gov/content/pkg/STATUTE-86/pdf/STATUTE-86-Pg1207.pdf

Thirty six years later, President George W. Bush approved the reauthorization and modernization of the CPSC by signing the Consumer Product Safety Improvement Act of 2008 (PL 110–314) on August 14. https://www.govinfo.gov/content/pkg/STATUTE-122/pdf/STATUTE-122-Pg3016.pdf

The Commission comprises a maximum of five commissioners. The President appoints each commissioner by the advice and with the consent of the Senate for a term of 7 years. The President also designates one commissioner to serve as Chair. No more than three of the commissioners may be affiliated with the same political party (15 USC 2053). https://uscode.house.gov/view.xhtml?path=/prelim@title15/chapter47&edition=prelim

The CPSC implements provisions of the Flammable Fabrics Act (15 U.S.C. 1191), Poison Prevention Packaging Act of 1970 (15 U.S.C. 1471), Federal Hazardous Substances Act (15 U.S.C. 1261), Children's Gasoline Burn Prevention Act (15 U.S.C. 2056 note), Virginia Graeme Baker Pool and Spa Safety Act (15 U.S.C. 8001 et seq.), and an act of 2 August 1956 (15 U.S.C. 1211) prohibiting the transportation of refrigerators without door safety devices. https://uscode. house.gov/view.xhtml?path=/prelim@ title15&edition=prelim

The CPSC's organization and functions are found in 16 CFR 1000. https://www.ecfr. gov/cgi-bin/text-idx?gp=&SID=09442eace6 033ddfb202786dac3646bf&mc=true&tpl=/ ecfrbrowse/Title16/16CIIsubchapA.tpl

The agency's organizational chart is available in Portable Document Format (PDF) for viewing and downloading on the "About CPSC" web page. https://www.cpsc. gov/About-CPSC

Activities

To protect the public from risk of injury, the CPSC requires manufacturers to report defects in products presenting substantial hazards; conducts outreach programs for consumers, industry, and local governments; collects information on consumer product-related injuries and maintains the National Injury Information Clearinghouse; conducts research on consumer product hazards; and encourages and assists in the development of voluntary standards affecting the safety of consumer products. When appropriate, the CPSC requires manufacturers to correct hazards associated with specific consumer products already in circulation, establishes mandatory consumer product standards, and bans hazardous products. http://www. cpsc.gov/en/about-cpsc/national-injury-information-clearinghouse

The Commission also has a special project to reach as many Americans as possible with lifesaving safety information. The Neighborhood Safety Network disseminates safety information to hard-to-reach populations by partnering with other organizations already active within their communities. http://www.cpsc.gov/en/safety-education/neighborhood-safety-network

Sources of Information

All-Terrain Vehicles (ATVs) ATVs are powerful, fast, and potentially dangerous. The CPSC posts ATV safety information online. http://www.cpsc.gov/en/Safety-Education/Safety-Education-Centers/ATV-Safety-Information-Center

Annual Reports The CPSC posts its annual reports online. https://www.cpsc.gov/About-CPSC/Agency-Reports/Annual-Reports

Archived Records The records of the CPSC are referenced in the "Guide to Federal Records in the National Archives of the United States." The Guide is accessible online, and CPSC records have been assigned to Record Group 424. https://www. archives.gov/research/guide-fed-records/ groups/424.html

Blog The CPSC maintains a blog on its "OnSafety" website. https://onsafety.cpsc.gov

Career Opportunities To carry out its mission, the CPSC relies on attorneys and paralegal specialists, compliance officers, economists, engineers, IT specialists, product safety investigators, program analysts, statisticians, toxicologists and pharmacologists and chemists, and other skilled professionals. http://www.cpsc.gov/ en/About-CPSC/Job

In 2018, the CPSC ranked 14th among 29 small agencies in the Partnership for Public Service's Best Places To Work Agency Rankings. http://bestplacestowork.org/BPTW/ rankings/detail/SK00

Contact Information Contact information for specific offices and other public information are available on the CPSC's website. https://www.cpsc.gov/About-CPSC/ Contact-Information/Contact-Specific-Offices-and-Public-Information

Data The CPSC makes it data, deliberations, and decisions accessible to consumers, developers, and stakeholders. https://www.cpsc.gov/Data

Fire Safety Several generations living in a home increases the need for fire safe practices. To learn more, download the multigenerational fire safety toolkit from the "Neighborhood Safety Network Toolkit" web page. https://www.cpsc.gov/safety-education/neighborhood-safety-network/ toolkits/fire-safety

Freedom of Information Act (FOIA) The Electronic Freedom of Information Act Amendments of 1996 require Federal agencies to use electronic information technology to foster access to and availability of FOIA documents. https://www. cpsc.gov/Newsroom/FOIA | Email: cpsc-foia@cpsc.gov

The CPSC informs the public by using various means: local and national media coverage, publication of booklets and product alerts, responses to FOIA requests, and the National Injury Information Clearinghouse. The agency also maintains its public information center, website, and telephone hotline for the same purpose. http://www.cpsc.gov/newsroom/foia/guide-to-public-information

Frequently Asked Questions (FAQs) The CPSC posts answers to FAQs on its website. https://www.cpsc.gov/About-CPSC/Contact-Information

Hotline The Commission operates a toll-free consumer product safety hotline in English and Spanish, on weekdays from 8 a.m. to 5:30 p.m. Phone, 800-638-2772. TTY, 301-595-7054.

Injury Statistics The CPSC posts injury statistics and technical reports by product category and by hazard category on its website. https://www.cpsc.gov/Research--Statistics

Language Assistance Read Spanish more easily than English? Visit the en Español version of the CPSC website. https://www.cpsc.gov/es/SeguridadConsumidor

Read Vietnamese more easily than English? Visit the Tiếng Việt web pages of the CPSC website. https://www.cpsc.gov/vi-VN/business-and-manufacturing-landing

Newsroom The online newsroom features CPSC data, Freedom of Information Act documents, press statements, recent news releases, videos, and a public calendar. http://www.cpsc.gov/en/Newsroom

Open Government The CPSC supports the Open Government initiative by promoting collaboration, participation, and transparency. https://www.cpsc.gov/About-CPSC/Agency-Reports/open | Email: feedback@cpsc.gov

Recalls Six Federal agencies with different jurisdictions are collaborating to make the American people more aware of defective, hazardous, and unsafe products. http://www.recalls.gov

Safety Publications Safety guides, safety alerts, and Neighborhood Safety Network posters are available online to download. https://www.cpsc.gov/Safety-Education/Safety-Guides/General-Information/Publications-Listing

Site Map The website map allows visitors to look for specific topics or to browse content that aligns with their interests. https://www.cpsc.gov/sitemap

Social Media The CPSC has a Facebook account. https://www.facebook.com/USCPSC

The CPSC tweets announcements and other newsworthy items on Twitter. https://twitter.com/USCPSC

The CPSC posts videos on its YouTube channel. https://www.youtube.com/uscpsc

Swimming Pools / Spas Pool and spas safety information is available online. http://www.poolsafely.gov

Toolkits The Neighborhood Safety Network has toolkits for all-terrain vehicle (ATV) safety, carbon monoxide (CO) awareness, child safety, multigenerational fire safety, and older adults, who are the fastest growing segment of the U.S. population. https://www.cpsc.gov/Safety-Education/Neighborhood-Safety-Network/Neighborhood-Safety-Network-Toolkits

The Sources of Information were updated 10–2019.

Corporation for National and Community Service

250 E Street NW., Washington, DC 20525
Phone, 202-606-5000. Internet, http://www.nationalservice.gov

Chair	SHAMINA SINGH
Vice Chair	DEAN A. REUTER
Member	RICHARD CHRISTMAN
Member	ROMONIA S. DIXON
Member	VICTORIA A. HUGHES
Member	ERIC P. LIU
Member	(VACANCY)

Member	(VACANCY)
Member	(VACANCY)
Member	(VACANCY)
Member	(VACANCY)
Member	(VACANCY)
Member	(VACANCY)
Member	(VACANCY)
Member	(VACANCY)
Chief Executive Officer	WENDY SPENCER
Chief Operating Officer / Chief Financial Officer	JEFFREY PAGE
Chief Human Capital Officer	SUSAN BRADBERRY
Chief Information Officer	THOMAS HANLEY
Chief of External Affairs	THEODORE S. MILLER
Chief of Program Operations	KIMBERLY MANSARAY
Chief of Staff	ASIM MISHRA
Chief Risk Officer	LORI GIBLIN
Director, AmeriCorps NCCC	GINA CROSS, ACTING
Director, AmeriCorps State and National	WILLIAM C. BASL
Director, AmeriCorps VISTA	MAX FINBERG
Director, Government Relations	KIMBERLY L. ALLMAN
Director, Office of Field Liaison	MIKEL HERRINGTON
Director, Office of Research and Evaluation	MARY HYDE
Director, Senior Corps	MIKEL HERRINGTON, ACTING
Director, Social Innovation Fund	DAMIAN THORMAN
General Counsel	JEREMY JOSEPH
Inspector General	DEBORAH J. JEFFREY

The Corporation for National and Community Service improves lives, strengthens communities, and fosters civic engagement through service and volunteering.

The Corporation for National and Community Service (CNCS) was established on October 1, 1993, by the National and Community Service Trust Act of 1993 (42 U.S.C. 12651 et seq.). The CNCS is a Federal corporation governed by a bipartisan board of directors whom the President appoints with the advice and consent of the Senate. The Board sets policies and direction for the Corporation and is responsible for all actions taken by the Chief Executive Officer with respect to standards, policies, procedures, programs, and initiatives as necessary to carry out the CNCS's mission.

As the Nation's largest grantmaker for service and volunteering, the CNCS engages millions of Americans in service through its core programs—AmeriCorps, Senior Corps, the Social Innovation Fund, and the Volunteer Generation Fund—and leads President Obama's nationwide service initiative, United We Serve. The CNCS harnesses America's most powerful resource: the energy and talents of its citizens. From grade school through retirement, the CNCS empowers Americans and fosters a lifetime of service to improve lives, strengthen communities, and foster civic engagement. http://www.nationalservice.gov/about

AmeriCorps AmeriCorps provides opportunities for more than 75,000 Americans each year to serve their communities. AmeriCorps members recruit, train, and supervise community volunteers; tutor and mentor youth; build affordable housing; teach computer skills; clean parks and streams; run afterschool programs; help nonprofit groups become self-sustaining; and assist communities responding to disasters. In exchange for a year of full-time service, AmeriCorps members earn an education award that can be used for college or graduate school tuition or for repaying qualified student loans. Since 1994 nearly 1 million Americans have served in AmeriCorps, which includes AmeriCorps State and National, AmeriCorps NCCC, and AmeriCorps VISTA.

AmeriCorps State and National supports a wide range of local service programs that engage thousands of Americans in community service each year, providing grants to a network of local and national organizations and agencies committed to using national service to address critical community needs in education, public safety, health, and the environment. Each of these organizations and agencies, in turn, uses its AmeriCorps funding to recruit, place, and supervise AmeriCorps members nationwide.

AmeriCorps State and National operates through national and local nonprofit organizations, public agencies, and faith-based and community groups. More than three-quarters of AmeriCorps grant funding goes to Governor-appointed State service commissions, which in turn award grants to nonprofit groups to respond to local needs. AmeriCorps NCCC (National Civilian Community Corps) is a team-based, residential program for men and women from age 18 to 24 that combines the best practices of civilian service, including leadership and team building. AmeriCorps VISTA (Volunteers in Service to America) members serve full-time for 1 year in nonprofit and faith-based organizations and public agencies to fight poverty, improve health services, increase housing opportunities, and bridge the digital divide. http://www.nationalservice.gov/programs/americorps

Senior Corps   Senior Corps taps the skills, talents, and experience of more than 270,000 Americans age 55 and older to meet a wide range of community challenges through three programs: Retired and Senior Volunteers Program (RSVP), Foster Grandparents, and Senior Companions. RSVP volunteers help local police departments conduct safety patrols, participate in environmental projects, provide educational services to children and adults, respond to natural disasters, and recruit other volunteers. Foster Grandparents serve as tutors and mentors to young people

with special needs. Senior Companions help homebound seniors and other adults maintain independence in their own homes. Senior Corps volunteers have served 1.5 million Americans, including 560,000 veterans and 300,000 children. http://www.nationalservice.gov/programs/senior-corps

Social Innovation Fund   The Social Innovation Fund is an approach to transforming lives and communities that allows the Federal Government to serve as a catalyst for promoting community solutions with evidence of strong results. A key White House initiative and CNCS program, the Fund identifies solutions that work and makes them work for more people. It combines public and private resources to foster innovative community-based solutions that have produced results in low-income communities in three priority areas: economic opportunity, health, and youth development. http://www.nationalservice.gov/programs/social-innovation-fund| Email: innovation@cns.gov

Other Initiatives   As the Federal agency for service and volunteerism, the CNCS carries out the Call to Service authority in multiple ways. CNCS initiatives include the Martin Luther King, Jr., National Day of Service; September 11th National Day of Service and Remembrance; President's Higher Education Community Service Honor Roll; National Mentoring Month; and United We Serve, a nationwide effort launched with the White House in 2009 to engage Americans in service to meet community needs. As a result of United We Serve, hundreds of thousands of Americans have joined with friends and neighbors to replenish food banks, provide health services, support veterans and military families, restore public lands, and more. The CNCS has also partnered with other agencies and nonprofit organizations on Let's Read! to reduce summer reading loss and Let's Move! to combat childhood obesity. Other initiatives include the Task Force on Expanding National Service, Mayors Day of Recognition, County Day of Recognition, and Joining Forces, an effort led by First Lady Michelle Obama and Dr. Jill Biden to engage Americans in supporting veterans and military families.

Sources of Information

Blog   The National Service blog features posts of interest to students, recent graduates, retirees, senior citizens, veterans, and others. The range of discussion is expansive—conservation, disaster recovery, nonprofit sector career pathways, voluntarism, and more. http://nationalservice.tumblr.com

Data   The CNCS posts datasets and other information online to support the principles of open government. http://www.nationalservice.gov/about/open-government-initiative/transparency/data-sources

Its Open Government Gallery is a demonstration of the CNCS's commitment to collaboration, participation, and transparency. http://www.nationalservice.gov/about/open-government-initiative/open-government-gallery

Employment   Most CNCS career opportunities are volunteer AmeriCorps and Senior Corps positions. The agency hires full-time employees at its Washington, DC, headquarters and at CNCS offices located across the country.

http://www.nationalservice.gov/about/careers | Email: jobs@cns.gov; https://www.usajobs.gov/JobSearch/Search/GetResults?OrganizationID=KS00

Grants   To find discretionary funding opportunities that Federal agencies have posted, visit the "Funding Opportunities" Web page. http://www.nationalservice.gov/build-your-capacity/grants/funding-opportunities

Newsroom   The newsroom features media advisories, official statements, press releases, and proclamations. http://www.nationalservice.gov/newsroom#menu-newsroom-dropdown-area

Online Courses   Self-paced instructional courses that subject matter experts created on topics aligning with CNCS strategic initiatives are available online. http://www.nationalservice.gov/resources/online-courses

Site Map   The Web site map allows visitors to look for specific topics or to browse content that aligns with their interests. https://www.nationalservice.gov/sitemap; http://www.nationalservice.gov/about/contact-us

For further information, contact the Corporation for National and Community Service, 250 E Street NW., Washington, DC 20525. Phone, 202-606-5000.

Defense Nuclear Facilities Safety Board

625 Indiana Avenue NW., Suite 700, Washington, DC 20004
Phone, 202-694-7000. Fax, 202-208-6518. Internet, http://www.dnfsb.gov

Chair	SEAN P. SULLIVAN
Vice Chair	BRUCE HAMILTON
Member	JOYCE L. CONNERY
Member	JESSIE H. ROBERSON
Member	SEAN P. SULLIVAN
General Counsel	JAMES P. BIGGINS
General Manager	GLENN SKLAR
Technical Director	STEVEN STOKES
Deputy General Counsel	(VACANCY)
Deputy General Manager	(VACANCY)
Deputy Technical Director	ADAM POLOSKI

The above list of key personnel was updated 07–2017.

The Defense Nuclear Facilities Safety Board identifies the nature and consequences of public health and safety threats at the Department of Energy's defense nuclear facilities, elevates awareness of and information on such threats to the highest levels of governmental authority, and keeps the public informed.

The Defense Nuclear Facilities Safety Board was established as an independent agency on September 29, 1988, by the Atomic Energy Act of 1954, as amended (42 U.S.C. 2286 et seq.).

The Board comprises five members whom the President appoints with the advice and consent of the Senate. Appointees to the Board must be U.S. citizens and experts in the field of nuclear safety. http://www.dnfsb.gov/about/who-we-are

Activities

The Defense Nuclear Facilities Safety Board reviews and evaluates the content and implementation of standards for the design, construction, operation, and decommissioning of the Department of Energy's defense nuclear facilities; investigates any incident or practice at these facilities that may adversely affect public health and safety; and reviews and monitors their design, construction, and operation. The Board makes recommendations to the Secretary of Energy to ensure adequate protection of public health and safety. When the Board determines that any aspect of operations, practices, or occurrences at these Department of Energy defense nuclear facilities presents an imminent or severe threat to public health and safety, the Board transmits its recommendations directly to the President. http://www.dnfsb.gov/about/what-we-do

Sources of Information

Employment Information on career opportunities is available online. http://www.dnfsb.gov/careers/opportunities |

Email: jobs@dnfsb.gov; http://www.dnfsb.gov/careers/employee-survey-results

Freedom of Information Act (FOIA) An information seeker may submit a FOIA request by email, mail, or telephone for records held or believed to be held by the Board. To make a request by mail, write to the Information / FOIA Officer, Defense Nuclear Facilities Safety Board, 625 Indiana Avenue NW., Suite 700, Washington, DC 20004. Phone, 202-694-7000. http://www.dnfsb.gov/foia-reading-room | Email: foia@dnfsb.gov

Open Government The Defense Nuclear Facilities Safety Board supports the Open Government initiative to strengthen the principles of collaboration, participation, and transparency. http://www.dnfsb.gov/open

Safety Management The Victor Stello, Jr., Award was established by the Board to recognize Department of Energy employees for exemplary leadership in promoting safety management in the Department's defense nuclear complex. http://www.dnfsb.gov/about/what-we-do/victor-stello-jr-award-safety-leadership

Site Representative Offices Site representatives produce a weekly report summarizing the pertinent activities and events that occurred during that week at their site. Five Defense Nuclear Facilities locations—Hanford, Los Alamos National Laboratory, Pantex, Savannah River Site, and Y–12 National Security Complex / Oak Ridge National Laboratory—have at least one site representative currently assigned to them. http://www.dnfsb.gov/about/where-we-work/our-site-representative-offices; http://www.dnfsb.gov/website-tools/contact

For further information, contact the Defense Nuclear Facilities Safety Board, 625 Indiana Avenue NW., Suite 700, Washington, DC 20004. Phone, 202-694-7000.

Environmental Protection Agency

1200 Pennsylvania Avenue NW., Washington, DC 20460
Phone, 202-272-0167. Internet, http://www.epa.gov

Administrator	SCOTT PRUITT
Deputy Administrator	MICHAEL FLYNN, ACTING
Assistant Administrators	
Assistant Administrator, Office of Administration and Resources Management	DONNA VIZIAN, ACTING
Assistant Administrator, Office of Air and Radiation	SARAH DUNHAM, ACTING
Assistant Administrator, Office of Chemical Safety and Pollution Prevention	WENDY CLELAND-HAMNETT, ACTING
Assistant Administrator, Office of Enforcement and Compliance Assurance	LAWRENCE STARFIELD, ACTING
Assistant Administrator, Office of International and Tribal Affairs	JANE NISHIDA, ACTING
Assistant Administrator, Office of Land and Emergency Management	BARRY BREEN, ACTING
Chief Information Officer, Office of Environmental Information	STEVEN FINE, ACTING
Chief Financial Officer, Office of the Chief Financial Officer	DAVID BLOOM, ACTING
Assistant Administrator, Office of Research and Development / Agency Science Advisor, Office of the Science Advisor	ROBERT KAVLOCK, ACTING
Assistant Administrator, Office of Water	MICHAEL SHAPIRO, ACTING
General Counsel, Office of General Counsel	AVKEVIN MINOLI, ACTING
Inspector General, Office of the Inspector General	ARTHUR A. ELKINS, JR.
Regional Administrators	
Region 1	DEBORAH SZARO, ACTING
Region 2	CATHERINE MCCABE, ACTING
Region 3	CECIL RODRIGUES, ACTING
Region 4	ANNE HEARD, ACTING
Region 5	ROBERT A. KAPLAN, ACTING
Region 6	SAMUEL COLEMAN, ACTING
Region 7	EDWARD CHU, ACTING
Region 8	DEBRA THOMAS, ACTING
Region 9	ALEXIS STRAUSS, ACTING
Region 10	MICHELLE PIRZADEH, ACTING

The Environmental Protection Agency protects human health and safeguards the environment.

The Environmental Protection Agency (EPA) was established in the executive branch as an independent agency pursuant to Reorganization Plan No. 3 of 1970 (5 U.S.C. app.), effective December 2, 1970. https://www.epa.gov/aboutepa/epa-history

The Agency facilitates coordinated and effective governmental action to protect the environment. It also serves as the public's advocate for a livable environment. https://www.epa.gov/aboutepa/our-mission-and-what-we-do

Core Functions

Air and Radiation   The Office of Air and Radiation develops air quality policies, programs, regulations, and standards, including emission standards for stationary sources, for mobile sources, and for hazardous air pollutants. It also conducts research and disseminates information on indoor air pollutants. This Office provides technical direction, support, and evaluation of regional air activities; offers training in the field of air pollution control; gives technical

ENVIRONMENTAL PROTECTION AGENCY

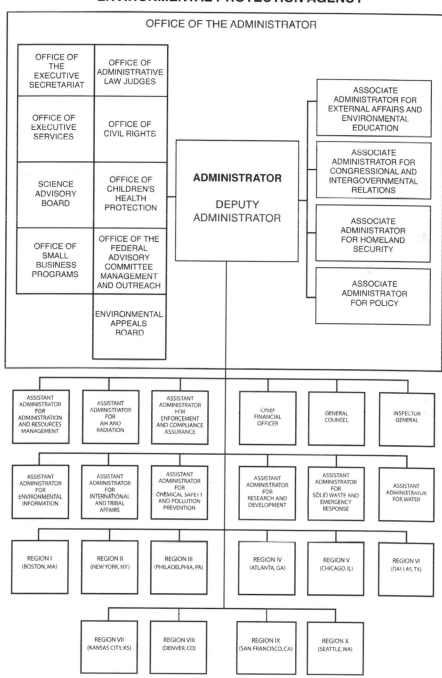

assistance to States and agencies operating radiation protection programs; and provides technical support and policy direction to international efforts to reduce global and transboundary air pollution and its effects. https://www.epa.gov/aboutepa/about-office-air-and-radiation-oar

For further information, call 202-564-7400.

Chemical Safety and Pollution Prevention   The Office of Chemical Safety and Pollution Prevention is responsible for EPA's strategies for implementation and integration of the pollution prevention, pesticides, and toxic substances programs and developing and operating Agency programs and policies for assessment and control of pesticides and toxic substances as well as recommending policies and developing operating programs for implementing the Pollution Prevention Act. The Office develops recommendations for EPA's priorities for research, monitoring regulatory and information gathering activities relating to implementation of the Pollution Prevention Act, to pesticides, and to toxic substances; and monitoring and assessing pollution prevention, pesticides and toxic substances program operations in EPA headquarters and regional offices. https://www.epa.gov/aboutepa/about-office-chemical-safety-and-pollution-prevention-ocspp

For further information, call 202-564-2902.

Enforcement and Compliance Assurance   The Office of Enforcement and Compliance Assurance serves as the primary adviser to the Administrator in matters concerning enforcement, compliance assurance, and environmental-equity efforts. It also provides the direction and review of all administrative, civil and criminal enforcement, and compliance monitoring and assurance activities. The Office manages the national criminal enforcement program as well as regulatory, site remediation, and Federal facilities enforcement and compliance assurance programs. The Office manages both administrative and judicial activities in the enforcement and compliance programs and provides case preparation and investigative expertise for enforcement activities through the National Enforcement

Investigations Center. https://www.epa.gov/aboutepa/about-office-enforcement-and-compliance-assurance-oeca

For further information, call 202-564-2440.

Land and Emergency Management   The Office of Solid Waste and Emergency Response provides agencywide policy, guidance, and direction for EPA's solid waste and emergency response programs. The Office's responsibilities include: development of guidelines and standards for the land disposal of hazardous wastes and for underground storage tanks; technical assistance in the development, management, and operation of solid waste management activities; analyses on the recovery of useful energy from solid waste; and development and implementation of a program to respond to hazardous waste sites and spills. https://www.epa.gov/aboutepa/about-office-land-and-emergency-management

For further information, call 202-566-0200.

Research and Development   The Office of Research and Development conducts leading-edge research and fosters the sound use of science and technology to fulfill EPA's mission to protect human health and safeguard the natural environment. The Office of Research and Development is responsible for the research and development needs of EPA's operating programs and the conduct of an integrated research and development program for the Agency. The Assistant Administrator serves as the Agency's principal science adviser and is responsible for the development, direction, and conduct of a national environmental research, development, and demonstration program in health risk assessment, health effects, engineering and technology, processes and effects, acid rain deposition, monitoring systems, and quality assurance. The Office participates in the development of EPA's policy, standards, and regulations; provides for dissemination of scientific and technical knowledge, including analytical methods, monitoring techniques, and modeling methodologies; and provides technical and scientific advice on agencywide technical program issues. https://www.epa.gov/aboutepa/about-office-research-and-development-ord

For further information, call 202-564-6620.

Water   The Office of Water provides agencywide policy, guidance, and direction for EPA's water quality, drinking water, groundwater, wetlands protection, marine and estuarine protection, and other related programs. The Office's responsibilities include: program policy development and evaluation; environmental and pollution source standards development; program policy guidance and overview, technical support, and evaluation of regional activities as they relate to drinking water and water programs; development and implementation of programs for education, technical assistance and technology transfer; development of selected demonstration programs; long-term strategic planning and special studies; economic and long-term environmental analysis; and development and implementation of pollution prevention strategies. https://www.epa.gov/aboutepa/about-office-water

For further information, call 202-564-5700.

Sources of Information

Blog   The EPA Web site features a blog. https://blog.epa.gov/blog

Business Opportunities   Acquisition management information, the procurement status of projects across the Agency's procurement divisions, and an acquisition forecast database of future EPA procurement opportunities are available on the EPA Web site. Contact the Office of Acquisition Management for more information. Phone, 202-564-4310. https://www.epa.gov/contracts

Education   Educators and students can access homework resources, lesson plans, and project ideas on the EPA's Web site. Environmental education incorporates a multidisciplinary approach to learning, builds critical thinking skills, and helps students make informed and responsible decisions that sustain Earth's ecosystems. https://www.epa.gov/students

EJSCREEN   The EPA Web site features an environmental justice mapping and screening tool that is based on nationally consistent data and an approach that combines environmental and demographic indicators in maps and reports. The EPA developed the tool to make the Agency a more effective protector of public health and the environment. https://www.epa.gov/ejscreen

Employment   The EPA relies on professionals from diverse backgrounds and with a wide range of skill sets to carry out its mission. The Agency posts current job openings on its Web site. For more information, contact the Office of Human Resources. Phone, 202-564-4606. http://www.epa.gov/careers | Email: recruit_inquiries@cpa.gov

Freedom of Information Act (FOIA)   The EPA is required to disclose records that the public requests, unless they are protected from disclosure by certain FOIA exemptions. https://www.epa.gov/foia/learn-about-foia | Email: hq.foia@epa.gov

The EPA participates in FOIAonline, an electronic search, submission, processing, and tracking tool. https://foiaonline.regulations.gov/foia/action/public/home

The FOIA libraries contain frequently requested information. Before making a FOIA request, search the online FOIA libraries to see if the desired information is immediately available at no cost. https://www.epa.gov/foia/foia-online-libraries

Frequently Asked Questions (FAQs)   Some EPA offices and programs have their own FAQs Web pages. The EPA maintains a list of FAQs pages that Internet users visit most often. https://www.epa.gov/home/frequent-questions-specific-epa-programstopics

Grants   Information to apply for, manage, and understand EPA grants is available online. Contact the Office of Grants and Debarment for more information. Phone, 202-564-5315. https://www.epa.gov/grants

Hotlines and Service Lines   Hotline and service line information for specific topics is available on the EPA Web site. https://www.epa.gov/home/epa-hotlines#HotlinesServiceLines4SpecificTopics

Region-specific, customer service line information is also available. https://www.epa.gov/home/epa-hotlines#RegionSpecificCustomerServiceLines

Newsroom   The EPA posts news stories on its Web site. It maintains a social media presence on Facebook and Twitter and uses RSS feeds to disseminate information. https://www.epa.gov/newsroom

The EPA produces public service announcements and materials. https://www.epa.gov/newsroom/public-service-announcements

Non-English Readers   The EPA provides information on its Web site in Chinese, Korean, Spanish, and Vietnamese. Language tags are visible at the bottom of the EPA's home page. https://www.epa.gov

Office of the Inspector General (OIG)   The OIG receives complaints of abuse, fraud, and waste in EPA programs. A complaint may be filed by email, fax, or phone. A person can expect confidentiality when filing his or her complaint by fax or phone—not by email. If the hotline is busy, leave a message and a Federal special agent will return the call. Phone, 888-546-8740. Fax, 202-566-2599. https://www.epa.gov/office-inspector-general | Email: OIG_Hotline@epa.gov

Open Government   The EPA supports the Open Government initiative by promoting the principles of collaboration, participation, and transparency. https://www.epa.gov/open

Plain Language   The EPA upholds the Plain Writing Act of 2010 by adhering to Federal plain language guidelines. EPA writers and editors want to know if a document or Web page contains content that was not written in plain language. https://www.epa.gov/home/plain-writing

Regional Offices   Ten regional offices help develop local programs for pollution abatement. https://www.epa.gov/aboutepa/visiting-regional-office

Staff Directory   The EPA maintains an online staff directory. https://cfpub.epa.gov/locator/index.cfm; https://www.epa.gov/home/forms/contact-epa

For further information, contact the Office of External Affairs and Environmental Education, Environmental Protection Agency, 1200 Pennsylvania Avenue NW., Washington, DC 20460-0001. Phone, 202-272-0167.

Equal Employment Opportunity Commission

131 M Street NE., Washington, DC 20507
Phone, 202-663-4900. TTY, 202-663-4444. Internet, http://www.eeoc.gov

Chair	Jenny R. Yang
Commissioner	Constance S. Barker
Commissioner	Charlotte A. Burrows
Commissioner	Chai R. Feldblum
Commissioner	Victoria A. Lipnic
Executive Officer	Bernadette B. Wilson, Acting
Chief Financial Officer	Germaine P. Roseboro
Chief Human Capital Officer	Lisa Williams
Chief Operating Officer	Cynthia G. Pierre
Director, Office of Communications and Legislative Affairs	Brett Brenner, Acting
Director, Office of Equal Opportunity	Erica White-Dunston
Director, Office of Federal Operations	Carlton M. Hadden
Director, Office of Field Programs	Nicholas Inzeo
Director, Office of Information Technology	(vacancy)
Director, Office of Legal Counsel	Peggy R. Mastroianni
Director, Office of Research, Information and Planning	Deidre Flippen
General Counsel	P. David Lopez
Inspector General	Milton A. Mayo, Jr.

The above list of key personnel was updated 06–2017.

The Equal Employment Opportunity Commission enforces laws prohibiting employment discrimination based on race, color, gender, religion, national origin, age, disability, or genetic information.

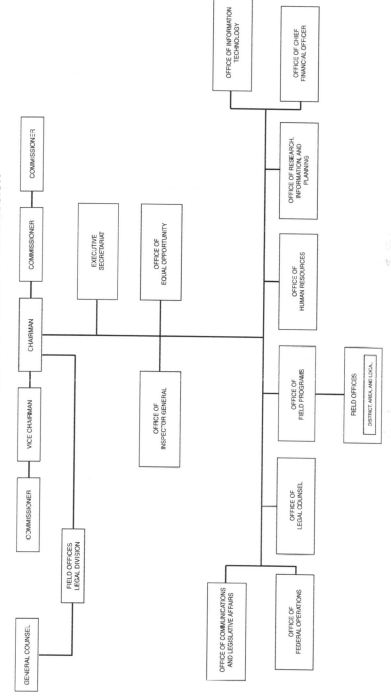

EQUAL EMPLOYMENT OPPORTUNITY COMMISSION

The Equal Employment Opportunity Commission (EEOC) was created by Title VII of the Civil Rights Act of 1964 (42 U.S.C. 2000e-4) and became operational July 2, 1965. Laws enforced by EEOC include Title VII of the Civil Rights Act of 1964 (42 U.S.C. 2000e et seq.), the Age Discrimination in Employment Act of 1967 (29 U.S.C. 621 et seq.), sections of the Rehabilitation Act of 1973 (29 U.S.C. 791 et seq.) and Civil Rights Act of 1991 (105 Stat. 1071), the Equal Pay Act of 1963 (29 U.S.C. 206), Title I of the Americans with Disabilities Act of 1990 (42 U.S.C. 12101 et seq.), and Title II of the Genetic Information Non-Discrimination Act of 2008 (42 U.S.C. 2000ff et seq.).

The EEOC is a bipartisan commission comprising five members whom the President appoints with the advice and consent of the Senate to staggered 5-year terms. The President designates a Chair and Vice Chair. In addition to the Commission members, the President appoints a General Counsel, with the advice and consent of the Senate, to support the Commission and provide direction, coordination, and supervision of the EEOC's litigation program. The General Counsel serves for a term of 4 years. http://www.eeoc.gov/eeoc/commission.cfm

Activities

Complaints Against the Federal Government   The EEOC establishes the procedures for Federal employees and job applicants to file complaints of employment discrimination or retaliation. The agency charged with discrimination is responsible for informal counseling and, if a complaint is filed and accepted, for investigating the claims raised therein. At the conclusion of the investigation, complainants may request a hearing before an EEOC administrative judge or that the agency issue a final decision on the matter. The agency's final decision or final action after a hearing may be appealed to the Commission.

In addition, the Office of Federal Operations provides oversight of and technical assistance for equal employment opportunity (EEO) complaint adjudication and Governmentwide maintenance of affirmative employment programs. Using

the guidance and principles contained in the EEOC's EEO Management Directive 715, the Commission monitors and evaluates Federal agencies' affirmative employment programs under Title VII and section 501 of the Rehabilitation Act and ensures that all Federal employees compete on a fair and level playing field. http://www.eeoc.gov/federal/fed_employees/complaint_overview.cfm

Enforcement   The EEOC enforces its statutory, regulatory, policy, and program responsibilities through its headquarters-based Office of General Counsel, Office of Field Programs, and its 53 field offices. The field offices receive charges of discrimination from the public and use a variety of resolution methods, including voluntary mediation and full-scale investigation and conciliation. The field staff is responsible for achieving a wide range of objectives that focus on the quality, timeliness, and appropriateness of individual, class, and systemic charges; for securing relief for victims of discrimination in accordance with Commission policies; for counseling individuals about their rights under the laws enforced by the EEOC; and for conducting outreach and technical assistance programs. The EEOC's Office of General Counsel litigates in U.S. District Courts and Courts of Appeal. https://www.eeoc.gov/eeoc/enforcement_litigation.cfm

Other Activities   The Commission promotes voluntary compliance with EEO statutes through a variety of educational and technical assistance activities. Its outreach and education programs provide general information on the EEOC, its mission, rights and responsibilities under the statutes enforced by the Commission, and the charge/complaint process. EEOC representatives are available, on a limited basis and at no cost, to make presentations and participate in meetings, conferences, and seminars with employee and employer groups, professional associations, students, nonprofit entities, community organizations, and other members of the general public.

The Commission offers additional training tailored to employers for a fee. The EEOC Training Institute makes this more in-depth training available to private employers and State, local, and Federal government personnel. The EEOC Training Institute helps educate managers and employees on the laws enforced by the EEOC and how to prevent and eliminate discrimination in the workplace.

The Commission publishes data on the employment status of minorities and women through six employment surveys covering private employers, apprenticeship programs, labor unions, State and local governments, elementary and secondary schools, and colleges and universities. This collection of data is shared with selected Federal agencies and is made available, in appropriate form, for public use. http://www.eeoc.gov/eeoc/index.cfm

Sources of Information

Career Opportunities The Commission hires in various job categories: attorneys, information intake representatives, investigators, mediators, office automation assistants, paralegals, program analysts, and social scientists. EEOC employment opportunities are posted on USAJobs—the Federal Government's official source for job listings and employment opportunity information. For more information, contact the Office of Human Resources. Phone, 202-663-4306. http://www.eeoc.gov/eeoc/jobs/index.cfm

District Offices The EEOC operates 15 district offices. An office list and jurisdictional map are available online. A search tool allows EEOC Web site visitors to locate field offices by using Zip Codes. http://www.eeoc.gov/field/index.cfm

Freedom of Information Act (FOIA) Contact the requester service center for FOIA-related questions. Phone, 877-869-1802. https://www.eeoc.gov/eeoc/foia/index.cfm

Internships EEOC Internships offer high school, college, and graduate and law students the opportunity to gain experience working on projects or cases involving issues of Federal antidiscrimination law. Interns work closely with experienced attorneys and specialists on assignments. Work assignments include legal research and writing, research and analysis of public policy developments, correspondence with Commission stakeholders, and assistance with charge intake and investigations. https://www.eeoc.gov/eeoc/jobs/internships.cfm

Media Inquiries Representatives of the media should contact the Office of Communications and Legislative Affairs, 131 M Street NE., Washington, DC 20507. Phone, 202-663-4191. TTY, 202-663-4494. http://www.eeoc.gov/eeoc/newsroom/index.cfm | Email: newsroom@eeoc.gov

Open Government The EEOC supports the Open Government initiative by implementing principles of collaboration, participation, and transparency. https://www.eeoc.gov/open/index.cfm

Publications The EEOC's most popular publications may be downloaded in Portable Document Format (PDF) for easy reproduction. Publications that are unavailable online may be obtained by phone or fax. Phone, 800-669-3362. TTY, 800-800-3302. Fax, 513-489-8692. http://www.eeoc.gov/eeoc/publications/index.cfm

Reading Room Contact the EEOC Library, 131 M Street NE., Washington, DC 20507. Phone, 202-663-4630.

Reports and Surveys The EEOC collects workforce data from employers with more than 100 employees. Employers who meet the reporting thresholds are required to provide the information. The data are used for enforcement, research, and self-assessment by employers. Data remain confidential; however, the public can access them in aggregate form. http://www.eeoc.gov/employers/reporting.cfm

Training Institute For information on training programs and registration, contact the EEOC Training Institute. Phone, (703) 291-0880 or (866) 446-0940. http://www.eeotraining.eeoc.gov | Email: eeoc.traininginstitute@eeoc.gov

Speakers An agency representative may be available to present an overview of the laws that the EEOC enforces and EEOC charge processing procedures—including mediation—at a conference or seminar. Contact an outreach program coordinator for more information. Phone, 800-669-4000. http://www.eeoc.gov/eeoc/outreach/nocost.cfm

Statistics The EEOC posts data, reports, and statistics online. https://www.eeoc.gov/eeoc/statistics/index.cfm; http://www.eeoc.gov/contact | Email: info@eeoc.gov

For further information, contact the Office of Communications and Legislative Affairs, Equal Employment Opportunity Commission, 131 M Street NE., Washington, DC 20507. Phone, 202-663-4191.

Export-Import Bank of the United States

811 Vermont Avenue NW., Washington, DC 20571
Phone, 202-565-3946. Fax, 800-565-3946. Internet, http://www.exim.gov

President / Chair	CHARLES J. HALL, ACTING
First Vice President / Vice Chair	SCOTT SCHLOEGEL, ACTING
Director	(VACANCY)
Director	(VACANCY)
Director	(VACANCY)
Chief Financial Officer	DAVID M. SENA
Chief Information Officer	HOWARD SPIRA
Chief Risk Officer / Executive Vice President	JEFF GOETTMAN, ACTING
Chief of Staff / Senior Vice President	JESSE LAW
Deputy Chief of Staff	RYAN CAUDELLE
General Counsel / Senior Vice President	ANGELA MARIANA FREYRE
Senior Vice President and Chief Strategy Officer	ANTHONY SCARAMUCCI
Senior Vice President, Export Finance / Chief Banking Officer	TROY FUHRIMAN
Senior Vice President, Communications	JENNIFER HAZELTON
Senior Vice President, Congressional and Intergovernmental Affairs	KEVIN WARNKE, ACTING
Senior Vice President, Credit and Risk Management	KENNETH M. TINSLEY
Senior Vice President, Policy and Planning	JAMES C. CRUSE
Senior Vice President, Resource Management	MICHAEL CUSHING
Senior Vice President, Small Business	JAMES BURROWS
Deputy Chief Banking Officer	MADOLYN PHILLIPS
Vice President, Asset Management	WALTER F. KEATING
Vice President, Business Credit	PAMELA S. BOWERS
Vice President, Business Processes, Total Enterprise Modernization	MICHELE A. KUESTER
Vice President, Communications	REBECCA ROSE
Vice President, Congressional and Intergovernmental Affairs	KEVIN WARNKE
Vice President, Controller	PATRICIA WOLF
Vice President, Country Risk and Economic Analysis / Chief Economist	WILLIAM A. MARSTELLER
Vice President, Credit Review and Compliance	WALTER HILL, JR.
Vice President, Credit Underwriting	DAVID W. CARTER
Vice President, Customer and Business Solutions	ROCHELE BARHAM
Vice President, Engineering and Environment	JAMES A. MAHONEY, JR.
Vice President, Finance / Treasurer	NATHALIE HERMAN
Vice President, International Relations	ISABEL GALDIZ
Vice President, Operations and Data Quality	NICOLE M.B. VALTOS
Vice President, Policy Analysis	HELENE WALSH
Vice President, Sales and Marketing	SEAN LUKE
Vice President, Structured Finance	HALA EL MOHANDES
Vice President, Transportation	ROBERT F.X. ROY

The Export-Import Bank helps finance the export of U.S. goods and services to international markets.

The Export-Import Bank of the United States (ExIm Bank), established in 1934, operates as an independent agency of the U.S. Government under the authority of the Export-Import Bank Act of 1945, as amended (12 U.S.C. 635 et seq.). Its Board of Directors comprises the President and Chair, the First Vice President and Vice Chair, and three directors—a total of five members. With the advice and consent of the Senate, the President appoints all of them.

The ExIm Bank helps American exporters adjust to government-supported financing competition from other countries. The assistance allows U.S. exports to compete for overseas business on the basis of price, performance, and service, which protects U.S. jobs. The Bank also fills gaps in the availability of commercial financing for creditworthy export transactions by providing a variety of financing mechanisms, including working capital guarantees, export-credit insurance, and financing for the purchase of U.S. goods and services.

The Bank is required to find a reasonable assurance of repayment for each transaction it supports. Its legislation requires it to meet the financing terms of competitor export credit agencies, but not to compete with commercial lenders. Restrictions also apply to the Bank's support for military goods and services and to its operation in some countries.

A self-sustaining agency, EXIM operates at no cost to taxpayers. Since 2009, EXIM has contributed nearly $3.8 billion to American taxpayers. http://www.exim.gov/about

Activities

The ExIm Bank is authorized to have loans, guarantees, and insurance outstanding at any one time in aggregate amount not exceeding $120 billion. A variety of Ex-Im Bank programs offered under broad export financing categories—working capital guarantees, export credit insurance, loan guarantees, and direct loans—support U.S. exporters.

The Bank's regional offices focus on small business outreach and support. Its Small Business Committee makes recommendations on and coordinates and evaluates Bank functions necessary for an effective small-business strategy. http://www.exim.gov/what-we-do#by-name

Sources of Information

Electronic Updates An online subscription form is available to sign up for email updates from the Ex-Im Bank. https://public.govdelivery.com/accounts/USEXIM/subscriber/new

Employment To carry out its mission, the Bank relies on professionals with a range of skills and expertise: attorney-advisors, business development and loan specialists, economists, engineers, and resource managers in accounting, finance, human resources, and information technology. http://www.exim.gov/about/careers

Freedom of Information Act (FOIA) A FOIA request must be made in writing. It may be submitted using the online request form or by email, fax, or postal mail. http://www.exim.gov/about/foia | Email: foia@exim.gov

News ExIm Bank posts board agendas and meeting minutes, reports, and speeches online. http://www.exim.gov/news

The Chair writes a quarterly newsletter that includes information on the Bank's performance over the previous 3 months. The newsletter also includes analysis of global economic trends, customer stories, practical export tips, upcoming Bank events, and other resources. http://www.exim.gov/learning-resources/newsletters

Office of the Inspector General (OIG) The OIG investigates complaints of abuse, fraud, and waste. Phone, 888-644-3946. http://www.exim.gov/about/oig/oig-hotline | Email: IGhotline@exim.gov

Open Government The ExIm Bank is becoming more collaborative, participatory, and transparent by making data available in an open format and by providing a mechanism for the public to submit feedback. http://www.exim.gov/open-government-directive

Project Information and Concerns The "Environmental and Social Project Information and Concerns" Web page provides an online form for expressing project-specific concerns, requesting project-specific information, or submitting information on a particular project. http://www.exim.gov/policies/ex-im-bank-and-the-environment/environmental-and-social-project-information-and-concerns

Regional Offices   The ExIm Bank operates regional export finance centers and field offices nationwide. A List of these centers, with their contact information, is available online. http://www.exim.gov/contact/regional-export-finance-centers; http://www.exim.gov/contact/headquarters

For further information, contact the Business Development Office, Export-Import Bank, 811 Vermont Avenue NW., Washington, DC 20571. Phone, 202-565-3946 or 800-565-3946.

Farm Credit Administration

1501 Farm Credit Drive, McLean, VA 22102-5090
Phone, 703-883-4000. Fax, 703-790-3260. Internet, http://www.fca.gov

Board

Chair	DALLAS P. TONSAGER
Member	JEFFERY S. HALL
Member	(VACANCY)
https://www.fca.gov/about/fca_board.html	

Officials

Chief Executive Officer	DALLAS P. TONSAGER
https://www.fca.gov/about/board/tonsager.html	
Chief Operating Officer	WILLIAM J. HOFFMAN
Designated Agency Ethics Official	PHILIP J. SHEBEST
General Counsel	CHARLES R. RAWLS
Secretary to the Board	DALE L. AULTMAN
Directors	
Office of Agency Services	A. JEROME FOWLKES
Office of Congressional and Public Affairs	MICHAEL A. STOKKE
Office of Equal Employment Opportunity and Inclusion	THAIS BURLEW
Office of Examination and Chief Examiner	S. ROBERT COLEMAN
Office of Information Technology	JERALD GOLLEY
Office of Regulatory Policy	GARY K. VAN METER
Office of Secondary Market Oversight	LAURIE A. REA
Office of the Chief Financial Officer	STEPHEN G. SMITH
https://www.fca.gov/about/offices/officials.html	
Inspector General	WENDY R. LAGUARDA
https://www.fca.gov/home/inspector.html	

[For the Farm Credit Administration statement of organization, see the Code of Federal Regulations, Title 12, Parts 600 and 611]

The above list of key personnel was updated 09–2017.

The Farm Credit Administration ensures the safe and sound operation of the banks, associations, affiliated service organizations, and other entities of the Farm Credit System, and protects the interests of the public and those who borrow from Farm Credit institutions or invest in Farm Credit securities.

The Farm Credit Administration (FCA) was established as an independent financial regulatory agency in the executive branch of the Federal Government by Executive Order 6084 on March 27, 1933. The FCA carries out its responsibilities by

conducting examinations of the various
Farm Credit lending institutions: Agricultural
Credit Associations, Farm Credit Banks,
Federal Land Credit Associations, and the
Agricultural Credit Bank.

The FCA also examines the service
organizations owned by the Farm Credit
lending institutions, as well as the National
Consumer Cooperative Bank. http://www.
fca.gov/info/organization.html#service

FCA policymaking is vested in the Farm
Credit Administration Board, whose three
full-time members the President appoints to
6-year terms with the advice and consent
of the Senate. One member of the Board is
designated by the President as Chair and serves
as the FCA's chief executive officer. The Board
approves rules and regulations, provides for the
examination and regulation of and reporting
by Farm Credit institutions, and establishes
the policies under which the Administration
operates. Board meetings are regularly held
on the second Thursday of the month and are
subject to the Government in the Sunshine Act.
Public announcements of these meetings are
published in the "Federal Register." http://www.
fca.gov/about/fca_board.html

Authority for the organization and
activities of the Farm Credit System may be
found in the Farm Credit Act of 1971, as
amended.

The lending institutions of the Farm
Credit System were established to provide
adequate and dependable credit and
closely related services to farmers, ranchers,
and producers or harvesters of aquatic
products; persons engaged in providing
on-the-farm services; rural homeowners;
and associations of farmers, ranchers, and
producers or harvesters of aquatic products,
or federations of such associations that
operate on a cooperative basis and are
engaged in marketing, processing, supply,
or business service functions for the benefit
of their members. Initially capitalized by the
U.S. Government, the Farm Credit lending
institutions are organized as cooperatives—
their borrowers completely own them. The
loan funds provided to borrowers by these
institutions are obtained primarily through
the sale of securities to investors in the
Nation's capital markets. http://www.fca.gov/
rpts/information.html

The Agricultural Credit Act of 1987, as
amended (12 U.S.C. 2279aa-1), established

the Federal Agricultural Mortgage
Corporation, commonly known as Farmer
Mac. The Corporation, designated as part
of the Farm Credit System, is a federally
chartered instrumentality of the United
States and promotes the development of a
secondary market for agricultural real estate
and rural housing loans. Farmer Mac also
provides guarantees for the timely payment
of principal and interest on securities
representing interests in or obligations
backed by pools of agricultural real estate
loans. The Administration examines and
regulates Farmer Mac to ensure the safety
and soundness of its operations. http://www.
fca.gov/info/farmer_mac.html

The FCA manages regulations under
which Farm Credit institutions operate. These
regulations implement the Farm Credit Act
of 1971, as amended (12 U.S.C. 2001), and
have the force and effect of law. Similar to
the authorities of other Federal regulators of
financial institutions, the Administration's
authorities include the power to issue
cease-and-desist orders, to levy civil
monetary penalties, to remove officers and
directors of Farm Credit institutions, and to
establish financial and operating reporting
requirements. Although it is prohibited
from participation in routine management
or operations of Farm Credit institutions,
the Administration is authorized to become
involved in these institutions' management
and operations when the Farm Credit Act
or its regulations have been violated, when
taking an action to correct an unsafe or
unsound practice, or when assuming a
formal conservatorship over an institution.

The Administration does not operate on
funds appropriated by Congress: It derives
income from assessments collected from the
institutions that it regulates and examines.
In addition to its headquarters in McLean,
VA, the Administration maintains four
field offices located in Bloomington, MN;
Greenwood Village, CO; Irving, TX; and
Sacramento, CA.

Sources of Information

A–Z Index The FCA Web site has an A–Z
index to help visitors navigate its content.
https://www.fca.gov/home/atozindex.html

Business Opportunities The Office
of Agency Services manages the FCA's

procurement opportunities. Phone, 703-883-4378. TTY, 703-883-4056. https://www.fca.gov/about/procurement.html

Career Opportunities   To carry out its mission, the FCA relies on attorneys, examiners, information technology specialists, and other professionals. Examiners play a prominent role at the FCA: They plan, organize, and conduct examinations of Farm Credit System institutions. The FCA hires examiners who hold university degrees in a variety of disciplines. The ideal candidate has a background in agriculture, business, finance, or information technology. Adaptability, teamwork, and communication skills are essential. Contact the Office of Agency Services for more information. Phone, 703-883-4135. TTY, 703-883-4056. https://www.fca.gov/browse/fca_careers.html

In 2016, the FCA ranked 10th among 29 small agencies in the Partnership for Public Service's Best Places To Work Agency Rankings. http://bestplacestowork.org/BPTW/rankings/overall/small

Cooperative Principles   Farm Credit System institutions generally adhere to three core cooperative principles: user-ownership, user-control, and user-benefits. These principles support the System's cooperative practices. To learn more about them, visit the "Cooperative Way" Web page. https://www.fca.gov/info/cooperativeway.html

Economics / Policy   FCA economists monitor conditions in the U.S. farm, national, and global economies. They write economic and policy reports that provide perspective for FCA examiners, leaders, and policy analysts. The FCA posts these reports on its Web site to make them available to a broader audience. https://www.fca.gov/rpts/economistreports.html

En Español   The FCA posts information in Spanish on its Web site. https://www.fca.gov/browse/espanol.html

Financial Indicators   The FCA posts data on selected financial performance indicators for Farm Credit System institutions. https://www.fca.gov/rpts/fcsindicators.html

Flood Disaster Protection   The FCA posts links to resources that help Farm Credit System lenders understand flood insurance rules. https://www.fca.gov/info/flooddisasterprotection.html

Freedom of Information Act (FOIA)   A written submission must clearly indicate that it is a "FOIA Request." The FCA may require payment for searching for, reviewing, and reproducing a document. A submitter must provide a detailed description—date, subject matter, title—of the record sought and indicate the maximum amount he or she is willing to pay in fees. A request may be submitted by email or fax, or by mail and addressed to the Freedom of Information Act Officer, Farm Credit Administration, 1501 Farm Credit Drive, McLean, VA 22102-5090. Phone, 703-883-4020. TTY, 703-883-4056. Fax, 703-790-0052. http://www.fca.gov/home/freedom_info.html | Email: foiaofficer@fca.gov

The FCA maintains a FOIA reading room on its Web site. Before submitting a FOIA request, search the reading room to see which documents are already accessible. https://www.fca.gov/home/FOIA_index.html

Frequently Asked Questions (FAQs)   The FCA posts answers to FAQs on its Web site. https://www.fca.gov/about/faqs.html

Glossary   The FCA maintains an online glossary. http://www.fca.gov/info/glossary.html

Handbook   The FCA Handbook database includes regulations, statutes, and FCA Board policy guidance that are applicable to the FCA, Farm Credit System, and Farm Credit System Insurance Corporation. The handbook is accessible free of charge in two formats: a searchable electronic database and files in Portable Document Format (PDF). https://www.fca.gov/exam/handbook.html

History   For centuries, North American farmers have sought reliable sources of credit to acquire land and to develop and expand farms. Their need to access long-term, fixed-rate credit has continued to the present. While 19th-century commercial banks made long-term credit available at reasonable rates to businessmen and industrial capitalists, they provided less of the same service to farmers. Presidents Theodore Roosevelt, William Howard Taft, and Woodrow Wilson saw the problem and sought solutions. To learn what they did to help 20th-century American farmers, visit the "History of FCA" Web page. https://www.fca.gov/about/history/historyFCA_FCS.html

Institution Directory and Map   The Farm Credit System institution directory contains information on each institution and its chartered territory. https://www.fca.gov/info/directory.html

Lender Locator   The Farm Credit System has 70 lending associations. To find an association, use the online locator tool by entering a street address or ZIP Code. Search results include all branch offices for a particular association. More than one lending association may serve a location. Phone, 703-883-4056. https://apps.fca.gov/Locator | Email: info-line@fca.gov

News / Events   The FCA announces events and posts news releases, rulemaking factsheets, speeches and statements, and testimonies online. http://www.fca.gov/news/index.html

Office of Inspector General (OIG)   The OIG conducts audits, evaluations, inspections, and investigations; reviews proposed legislation and regulations; informs the FCA Board and Congress of fraud or other serious problems; recommends policies to promote economy and efficiency and to prevent abuse, fraud, and waste; recommends corrective actions and reports on progress made in implementing them; and refers criminal matters to appropriate agencies for prosecution. Hotline, 800-437-7322 or 703-883-4316. Phone, 703-883-4030. https://www.fca.gov/home/inspector.html

Open Government   The FCA supports the Open Government initiative by promoting collaboration, participation, and transparency. https://www.fca.gov/home/opengovernment.html

Organizational Chart   The FCA posts its organizational chart online. https://www.fca.gov/about/offices/orgchart.html

The FCA's organizational chart is available in Portable Document Format (PDF) for viewing and downloading. https://www.fca.gov/Download/FCAorgchart.pdf

Plain Writing   Feedback on the clarity of documents and other items on the Web site helps improve the guidance that the FCA gives to institutions and the services that it offers to Americans. If a document or Web page is unclear, contact the Office of Congressional and Public Affairs. Phone, 703-883-4056. http://www.fca.gov/home/plainwriting.html

Publications   FCA documents are posted online, including publications about the Farm Credit Administration and information on the Farm Credit System. To find an older document, one that is over 5 years old, search in the archives. More information is available from the Office of Congressional and Public Affairs. Phone, 703-883-4056 (voice and TTY). Fax, 703-790-3260. http://www.fca.gov/rpts/index.html | Email: info-line@fca.gov

Site Map   The Web site map allows visitors to look for specific topics or to browse content that aligns with their interests. https://www.fca.gov/home/sitemap.html; http://www.fca.gov/home/contact.html | Email: info-line@fca.gov

For further information, contact the Office of Congressional and Public Affairs, Farm Credit Administration, 1501 Farm Credit Drive, McLean, VA 22102-5090. Phone, 703-883-4056.

Federal Communications Commission

445 Twelfth Street SW., Washington, DC 20554
Phone, 888-225-5322. TTY, 888-835-5322. Internet, http://www.fcc.gov

Commissioners

CHAIR   AJIT PAI

                                               BRENDAN CARR
                                               MICHAEL O'RIELLY
                                               JESSICA ROSENWORCEL

https://www.fcc.gov/about/leadership

Bureau Chiefs

Consumer and Governmental Affairs	PATRICK WEBRE
Enforcement	ROSEMARY HAROLD
International	THOMAS SULLIVAN
Media	MICHELLE CAREY
Public Safety and Homeland Security	LISA M. FOWLKES
Wireline Competition	KRIS MONTEITH
Wireless Telecommunications	DONALD STOCKDALE

https://www.fcc.gov/offices-bureaus#block-menu-block-4

Office Heads

General Counsel	THOMAS M. JOHNSON, JR.
Managing Director	MARK STEPHENS

Chiefs
Administrative Law Judges	RICHARD L. SIPPEL
Engineering and Technology	JULIUS KNAPP
Strategic Planning and Policy Analysis	WAYNE LEIGHTON

Directors
Communications Business Opportunities	SANFORD S. WILLIAMS
Legislative Affairs	TIMOTHY STRACHAN
Media Relations	BRIAN HART
Workplace Diversity	LARRY HUDSON

https://www.fcc.gov/about-fcc/organizational-charts-fcc

Inspector General	DAVID L. HUNT

https://www.fcc.gov/inspector-general#block-menu-block-4

[For the Federal Communications Commission statement of organization, see the Code of Federal Regulations, Title 47, Part 0]

The above list of key personnel was updated 10–2018.

The Federal Communications Commission regulates interstate and foreign communications by radio, television, wire, satellite, and cable.

The Federal Communications Commission (FCC) was established by the Communications Act of 1934 (47 U.S.C. 151 et seq.) and is charged with regulating interstate and foreign communications by wire and radio in the public interest. The scope of FCC regulation includes radio and television broadcasting; telephone and cable television operation; two-way radio and radio operators; and satellite communication.

The Commission comprises five members whom the President appoints with the advice and consent of the Senate. One of the members is designated by the President as the Chair. https://www.fcc.gov/about/overview

Activities

Consumer and Governmental Affairs Bureau   The Consumer and Governmental Affairs Bureau develops and administers the FCC's consumer and governmental affairs policies and initiatives. The Bureau facilitates public participation in the Commission's decisionmaking process; represents the Commission on consumer and Government committees, working groups, task forces, and conferences; works with public, Federal, State, local, and tribal agencies to develop and coordinate policies; oversees the Consumer Advisory Committee, the Disability Advisory Committee, and the Intergovernmental Advisory Committee;

Federal Communications Commission

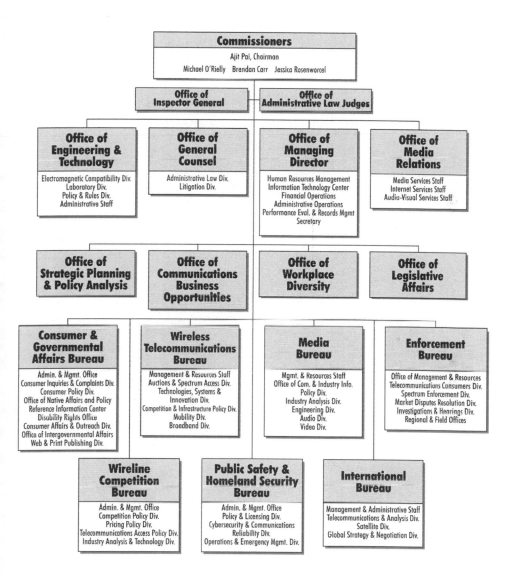

Commissioners

Ajit Pai, Chairman

Michael O'Rielly   Brendan Carr   Jessica Rosenworcel

Office of Inspector General

Office of Administrative Law Judges

Office of Engineering & Technology

Electromagnetic Compatibility Div.
Laboratory Div.
Policy & Rules Div.
Administrative Staff

Office of General Counsel

Administrative Law Div.
Litigation Div.

Office of Managing Director

Human Resources Management
Information Technology Center
Financial Operations
Administrative Operations
Performance Eval. & Records Mgmt
Secretary

Office of Media Relations

Media Services Staff
Internet Services Staff
Audio-Visual Services Staff

Office of Strategic Planning & Policy Analysis

Office of Communications Business Opportunities

Office of Workplace Diversity

Office of Legislative Affairs

Consumer & Governmental Affairs Bureau

Admin. & Mgmt. Office
Consumer Inquiries & Complaints Div.
Consumer Policy Div.
Office of Native Affairs and Policy
Reference Information Center
Disability Rights Office
Consumer Affairs & Outreach Div.
Office of Intergovernmental Affairs
Web & Print Publishing Div.

Wireless Telecommunications Bureau

Management & Resources Staff
Auctions & Spectrum Access Div.
Technologies, Systems &
Innovation Div.
Competition & Infrastructure Policy Div.
Mobility Div.
Broadband Div.

Media Bureau

Mgmt. & Resources Staff
Office of Com. & Industry Info.
Policy Div.
Industry Analysis Div.
Engineering Div.
Audio Div.
Video Div.

Enforcement Bureau

Office of Management & Resources
Telecommunications Consumers Div.
Spectrum Enforcement Div.
Market Disputes Resolution Div.
Investigations & Hearings Div.
Regional & Field Offices

Wireline Competition Bureau

Admin. & Mgmt. Office
Competition Policy Div.
Pricing Policy Div.
Telecommunications Access Policy Div.
Industry Analysis & Technology Div.

Public Safety & Homeland Security Bureau

Admin. & Mgmt. Office
Policy & Licensing Div.
Cybersecurity & Communications
Reliability Div.
Operations & Emergency Mgmt. Div.

International Bureau

Management & Administrative Staff
Telecommunications & Analysis Div.
Satellite Div.
Global Strategy & Negotiation Div.

offers expert advice on applicable disability and accessibility requirements, rules, and regulations, and assists with compliance; resolves informal complaints; and conducts consumer outreach and education programs. https://www.fcc.gov/consumer-governmental-affairs#block-menu-block-4

For further information, contact the Consumer and Governmental Affairs Bureau. Phone, 202-418-1400 or 888-225-5322.

Enforcement Bureau   The Enforcement Bureau serves as the FCC's primary agency for enforcing the Communications Act, other communications statutes, and the FCC's rules. The Bureau investigates and resolves complaints regarding common carriers (wireline, wireless, and international) and noncommon carriers subject to the Commission's jurisdiction under Title II of the Communications Act; radio frequency interference, equipment, and devices; accessibility to communications services and equipment for persons with disabilities; noncompliance with the lighting and marking of radio transmitting towers and pole attachment regulations; and unauthorized construction and operation of communication facilities and false distress signals. https://www.fcc.gov/enforcement#block-menu-block-4

For further information, contact the Enforcement Bureau. Phone, 202-418-7450 or 888-225-5322.

International Bureau   The International Bureau serves as the FCC's principal representative at international conferences and in international negotiations. The Bureau promotes procompetitive policies abroad, coordinating the FCC's global spectrum activities and advocating U.S. interests in international communications and competition. It provides advice and technical assistance to U.S. trade officials in the negotiation and implementation of telecommunications trade agreements. It also encourages the international coordination of spectrum allocation and of frequency and orbital assignments to minimize cases of international radio interference involving U.S. licenses. https://www.fcc.gov/international#block-menu-block-4

For further information, contact the International Bureau. Phone, 202-418-0437 or 888-225-5322.

Media Bureau   The Media Bureau oversees broadcast radio, television, and cable policy and licensing, as well as post-licensing matters for satellite services. The Bureau also conducts rulemaking proceedings and studies, resolves waiver petitions, and processes applications for authorization, assignment, transfer, and renewal of radio, television, and cable television relay services. https://www.fcc.gov/media#block-menu-block-4

For further information, contact the Media Bureau. Phone, 202-418-7200 or 888-225-5322.

Public Safety and Homeland Security Bureau   The Public Safety and Homeland Security Bureau develops, recommends, and administers the FCC's policies on public safety communication. This includes 911 and E911, operability and interoperability of public safety communications, communications infrastructure protection and disaster response, and network security and reliability. The Bureau also disseminates public safety communication information for emergency communication programs; alerting and warning U.S. citizens; continuity of government operations and operational planning; public safety outreach (e.g., first-responder organizations and hospitals); disaster management coordination and outreach; and studies and reports of public safety, homeland security, and disaster management issues. https://www.fcc.gov/public-safety-and-homeland-security#block-menu-block-4| Email: pshsbinfo@fcc.gov

For further information, contact the Public Safety and Homeland Security Bureau. Phone, 202-418-1300 or 888-225-5322.

Wireless Telecommunications Bureau   The Wireless Telecommunications Bureau administers all domestic commercial and private wireless communication programs and rules. It addresses present and future wireless communication and spectrum needs; promotes access, efficiency, and innovation in the allocation, licensing, and use of electromagnetic spectrum; ensures choice, opportunity, and fairness in the development of wireless communication services and markets; and encourages the development and widespread availability of wireless communication devices, facilities, and services. The Bureau also develops, recommends, administers, and coordinates policy for wireless communication services, including rulemaking, interpretations, and equipment standards; advises the public on FCC rules; serves as the FCC's principal policy and administrative resource for all spectrum auctions; and processes wireless service and facility authorization applications. https://www.fcc.gov/wireless-telecommunications#block-menu-block-4

For further information, contact the Wireless Telecommunications Bureau. Phone, 202-418-0600 or 888-225-5322.

Wireline Competition Bureau The Wireline Competition Bureau advises and makes recommendations to the FCC on policies affecting telephone landlines and fixed broadband. Its programs protect affordable communications access for health care providers, libraries, schools, and lifeline and rural consumers. The Bureau also ensures choice, opportunity, and fairness in the development of wireline communications; assesses the present and future wireline communication needs of the Nation; encourages the development and widespread availability of wireline communication services; and promotes investment in wireline communication infrastructure. https://www.fcc.gov/wireline-competition#block-menu-block-4

For further information, contact the Wireline Competition Bureau. Phone, 202-418-1500 or 888-225-5322.

Sources of Information

Blog The FCC maintains a blog. https://www.fcc.gov/news-events/blog

Business Opportunities The FCC relies on contractors for goods and services to carry out its mission. Many of these procurements are suitable for small businesses, and some offer opportunities for subcontracting. https://www.fcc.gov/about-fcc/contracting | Email: EACHelp@fcc.gov

Career Opportunities The FCC maintains a web-based recruitment system that allows employees and outside job seekers to apply for job opportunities online. https://www.fcc.gov/general/fcc jobs

In 2017, the FCC ranked 20th among 25 midsize Government agencies in

the Partnership for Public Service's Best Places To Work Agency Rankings. http://bestplacestowork.org/BPTW/rankings/detail/FC00

Consumer Assistance For general information on FCC operations, contact the FCC Consumer Center, 445 Twelfth Street SW., Washington, DC 20554. Phone, 888-225-5322. TTY, 888-835-5322. https://www.fcc.gov/consumers

Equal Employment Practices by the Communications Industry For more information, contact the FCC Consumer Center. Phone, 888-225-5322. https://www.fcc.gov/consumers

Ex-Parte Presentations For more information, contact the Commission's Office of General Counsel. Phone, 202-418-1720. https://www.fcc.gov/proceedings-actions/ex-parte

Federal Advisory Committee Management For more information, contact the Office of Managing Director. Phone, 202-418-2178. https://www.fcc.gov/about-fcc/advisory-committees-fcc

Fees Information on the FCC's fee programs is available online or from the Registration System / Fee Filer Help Desk. Phone, 877-480-3201 (option 4). https://www.fcc.gov/licensing-databases/fees | Email: ARINQUIRIES@fcc.gov

Freedom of Information Act For more information, contact the FOIA Requester Service Center. Phone, 202-418-1379. https://www.fcc.gov/general/foia | Email: foia@fcc.gov

Internal Equal Employment Practices For more information, contact the Office of Workplace Diversity. Phone, 202-418-1799. https://www.fcc.gov/workplace-diversity

Internships Information on FCC internships is available online. https://www.fcc.gov/general/internships-available-fcc

Licensing Information on the FCC's licensing systems is available online. http://www.fcc.gov/licensing

News The Office of Media Relations distributes public notices and press releases and makes them available online. https://www.fcc.gov/media-relations

Offices / Bureaus The "Offices and Bureaus" web page includes a brief description of FCC offices and bureaus, as well as links to related webpages with additional information. https://www.fcc.gov/offices-bureaus#block-menu-block-4

Organizational Chart   The FCC's organizational chart is available in Portable Document Format (PDF) for viewing and downloading. https://www.fcc.gov/sites/default/files/fccorg-06072018.pdf

The organizational charts of FCC offices and bureaus are available online in Portable Document Format (PDF) for viewing and downloading. https://www.fcc.gov/about-fcc/organizational-charts-fcc

Podcast   The official FCC podcast "More Than Seven Dirty Words" features interviews with FCC staff and others in the field of communications. https://www.fcc.gov/news-events/podcast

Public Inspection   Records that are deemed nonconfidential by law can be viewed on the FCC's Web site. Each broadcasting station maintains a current copy of its application for license, operational information, and nonconfidential FCC reports for public inspection.

Publications   The Consumer and Governmental Affairs Bureau maintains an online consumer publications library. https://www.fcc.gov/consumers

Social Media   To inform and to connect and engage with the general public, the FCC uses social media: Disqus, Facebook, Flickr, GitHub, Instagram, Scribd, Twitter, and YouTube. https://www.fcc.gov/social-media; https://www.fcc.gov/about/contact

For further information, contact the Consumer Center, Federal Communications Commission, 445 Twelfth Street SW., Washington, DC 20554. Phone, 888-225-5322. TTY, 888-835-5322.

Federal Deposit Insurance Corporation

550 Seventeenth Street NW., Washington, DC 20429
Phone, 703-562-2222. Internet, http://www.fdic.gov

Board of Directors

Chair	MARTIN J. GRUENBERG
Vice Chair	THOMAS M. HOENIG
Director (Consumer Financial Protection Bureau)	J. MICHAEL MULVANEY, ACTING
Director (Office of the Comptroller of the Currency)	JOSEPH M. OTTING
Director	(VACANCY)

https://www.fdic.gov/about/learn/board

Headquarters–Washington, DC

Chair	MARTIN J. GRUENBERG
Vice Chair	THOMAS M. HOENIG
Chief of Staff	BARBARA A. RYAN
Special Advisor for Supervisory Matters	JASON C. CAVE
Deputies	
Deputy to the Chair	KYMBERLY K. COPA
Deputy to the Chair / Chief Financial Officer	STEVEN O. APP
Deputy to the Chair / Chief Operating Officer	BARBARA A. RYAN
Deputy to the Vice Chair	MICHAEL SPENCER, ACTING
Division Heads	
Chief Information Officer / Chief Privacy Officer	HOWARD WHYTE, ACTING
Chief Information Security Officer	NOREEN PADILLA, ACTING
Director, Administration	ARLEAS UPTON KEA
Director, Corporate University / Chief Learning Officer	SUZANNAH L. SUSSER
Director, Depositor and Consumer Protection	MARK E. PEARCE
Director, Finance	CRAIG R. JARVILL
Director, Information Technology	RUSSELL G. PITTMAN

Director, Insurance and Research	Diane Ellis
Director, Resolution and Receiverships	Bret D. Edwards
Director, Risk Management Supervision	Doreen R. Eberley
General Counsel	Charles Yi

Office Heads

Chief Risk Officer	Kenyon Kilber, Acting
Deputy to the Chair for Communications	Barbara Hagenbaugh
Director, Complex Financial Institutions	Ricardo R. Delfin
Director, Legislative Affairs	M. Andy Jiminez
Director, Minority and Women Inclusion	Saul Schwartz, Acting
Ombudsman	M. Anthony Lowe

Inspector General
https://www.fdicoig.gov

Jay N. Lerner

The above list of key personnel was updated 02–2018.

The Federal Deposit Insurance Corporation preserves and promotes public confidence in U.S. financial institutions by insuring bank and thrift deposits, examining State-chartered banks, and liquidating assets of failed institutions.

The Federal Deposit Insurance Corporation (FDIC) was established under the Banking Act of 1933 after numerous banks failed during the Great Depression. The FDIC began insuring banks on January 1, 1934. The basic insurance coverage per depositor at each insured bank and savings association is $250,000. https://www.fdic.gov/about/history

The FDIC is managed by a five-member Board of Directors, all of whom the President appoints and the Senate confirms. No more than three of the Directors can be affiliated with the same political party.

The FDIC insures approximately 5,850 institutions. It receives no congressional appropriations. FDIC funding comes from insurance premiums on deposits held by insured banks and savings associations and from interest on the investment of those premiums in U.S. Government securities. FDIC has authority to borrow up to $100 billion from the Treasury for insurance purposes. https://www.fdic.gov/about/strategic/strategic/mission.html

Activities

The FDIC insures about $13 trillion of U.S. bank and thrift deposits. As required by law, the fund relies on two sources of income: premiums paid by banks and savings associations, and the interest on the investment of those premiums in U.S. Government securities. An institution's level of capitalization and potential risk to the insurance fund determines its premiums. https://www.fdic.gov/deposit

The FDIC examines about 3,600 State-chartered commercial and savings banks that are not members of the Federal Reserve System, called State nonmember banks. The FDIC also has authority to examine other types of FDIC-insured institutions for deposit insurance purposes. The two types of examinations conducted are for safety and soundness and for compliance with applicable consumer laws such as the Truth in Lending Act, the Home Mortgage Disclosure Act, the Equal Credit Opportunity Act, the Fair Housing Act, and the Community Reinvestment Act. FDIC examiners work onsite at the institution as well analyze bank data offsite. https://www.fdic.gov/regulations

A failed bank or savings association is generally closed by its chartering authority, and the FDIC is named receiver. The FDIC is required to resolve the closure in a manner that is least costly to its Deposit Insurance Fund. Ordinarily, the FDIC attempts to locate a healthy institution to acquire the failed entity. If such an entity cannot be found, the FDIC pays depositors the amount of their insured funds, usually by the next business day following the closure. Depositors with funds that exceed the insurance limit often receive an advance dividend, which is a portion of their uninsured funds that is determined by an estimate of the future proceeds from liquidating the failed institution's remaining assets. Depositors with funds in a failed institution that exceed the insurance limit receive a receivership certificate for those funds and partial payments of their uninsured funds as asset disposition permits.

As part of its insurance, supervisory, and receivership responsibilities, the FDIC approves or disapproves mergers, consolidations, and acquisitions where the resulting bank is an insured State nonmember; approves or disapproves proposals by banks to establish and operate a new branch, close an existing branch, or move its main office from one location to another; and approves or disapproves requests to engage as principal in activities and investments that are not permissible for a national bank. It also issues enforcement actions, including cease-and-desist orders, for specific violations or practices requiring corrective action and reviews changes in ownership or control of a bank.

Sources of Information

Assistance for Bank Customers   An electronic form is available for filing a complaint against a particular financial institution. The form also may be used to inquire about FDIC deposit insurance coverage or to ask a question about a particular financial institution. https://www5. fdic.gov/starsmail/index.asp

Bank Failures   The FDIC maintains a failed bank list that contains information on how accounts and loans are affected, how vendors can file claims against the receivership, and the acquiring bank—if applicable. The list covers from October 1, 2000, to the present. https://www.fdic.gov/ bank/individual/failed/banklist.html

Starting with the year 2001, the FDIC maintains a brief summary of each bank failure. For additional information on recent failures, call the customer service hotline. Phone, 888-206-4662. https://www.fdic.gov/ bank/historical/bank

A search tool is available online to help the public find the point of contact information of failed institutions. https:// www5.fdic.gov/drrip/cs/index.asp

Detailed information on bank and thrift failures since 1934 is available on the FDIC website. https://www5.fdic.gov/hsob/ SelectRpt.asp?EntryTyp=30

Bank Finder   The FDIC website has an online tool for locating insured banking institutions. https://research.fdic.gov/ bankfind

Call Center   The call center is open every day of the week: Monday–Friday, 8 a.m.–8 p.m., eastern standard time; Saturday and Sunday, 9 a.m.–5 p.m., eastern standard time. Phone, 877-275-3342. Phone, 800-925-4618 (hearing impaired).

Career Opportunities   FDIC job openings and information on career transition assistance, student employment opportunities, and submitting an application are available online. https://www.fdic.gov/ about/jobs

In 2017, the FDIC ranked 3d among 25 midsize Government agencies in the Partnership for Public Service's Best Places To Work Agency Rankings. http:// bestplacestowork.org/BPTW/rankings/detail/ FD00

Electronic Deposit Insurance Estimator (EDIE)   Consumers and bankers can use EDIE to determine, on a per-bank basis, how the insurance rules and limits apply to a depositor's specific group of deposit accounts—what is insured and what portion, if any, exceeds coverage limits. https://www. fdic.gov/edie/index.html

Enlaces en Español   Links to information and resources in Spanish are available on the FDIC website. https://www.fdic.gov/ quicklinks/spanish.html

Freedom of Information Act (FOIA)   The FDIC operates a FOIA service center that is open on weekdays, 8:30 a.m.–5:00 p.m., excluding Federal holidays. Phone, 202-898-7021. https://www.fdic.gov/about/freedom | Email: efoia@fdic.gov

The FDIC's FOIA guide offers a concise explanation of the FOIA and how it can be used to access Government records. It also explains the process for submitting a request to the FDIC. The guide also provides links to helpful reference guides and describes how additional information may be obtained from the FDIC. https://www.fdic.gov/about/freedom/guide.html

The FDIC accepts electronic FOIA requests. https://efoiarequest.fdic.gov/palMain.aspx

History "On March 3 banking operations in the United States ceased . . . the government has been compelled to step in." These words, President Franklin D. Roosevelt spoke to the U.S. Congress in 1933, 6 days after the banks had closed, when the Nation's banking system still lay dormant. The U.S. economy was in the throes of deep and widespread depression. Three months later, in response to the crisis, President Roosevelt approved the Banking Act of 1933, giving birth to the FDIC and Federal depositor protection, which the general public supported. To learn about the antecedents to Federal deposit insurance and the creation of the FDIC and its general history, see "A History of the FDIC 1933–1983." https://www.fdic.gov/bank/analytical/firstfifty

In 2008 and 2009, FDIC agents were active seizing failed banks. To learn about the process of a bank seizure and the efforts made by the FDIC to shield employees and depositors from the ill effects of a failure, watch the CBS 60 Minutes video "Your Bank Has Failed." https://www.fdic.gov/news/letters/60minutes.html

News / Events The FDIC posts conferences and events, financial institution letters, opinion editorials, press releases, speeches, and testimonies on its website. https://www.fdic.gov/news

The FDIC offers an online subscription service for email alerts. A subscriber may opt to receive various types of alerts: financial institution letters, news releases, statistical publications, and other types. https://service.govdelivery.com/accounts/USFDIC/subscriber/new

The FDIC disseminates information and news using RSS feeds. https://www.fdic.gov/rss.html

The FCC tweets news items and other information on Twitter. https://twitter.com/FDICgov

Office of Inspector General (OIG) The OIG operates a toll-free, nationwide hotline to provide a way for FDIC employees, its contractors, financial institution staff, and other members of the public to report incidents of abuse, fraud, mismanagement, and waste within FDIC programs and activities or its contractor operations. A person can file a report anonymously, confidentially, or openly by using the hotline; however, filing a report by email guarantees neither anonymity nor confidentiality. Phone, 800-964-3342. Fax, 703-562-6444. https://www.fdicig.gov | Email: ighotline@fdic.gov

Open Government The FDIC supports the Open Government initiative by promoting the principles of collaboration, participation, and transparency. https://www.fdic.gov/open | Email: opengov@fdic.gov

Plain Language The FDIC welcomes comment on it's compliance with the Plain Writing Act of 2010 and suggestions for improving communication between the agency and the public. https://www.fdic.gov/plainlanguage | Email: PlainWriting@fdic.gov

Publications The FDIC website has an online product catalog and ordering system. https://catalog.fdic.gov

Publications, press releases, congressional testimony, directives to financial institutions, and other documents are available through the Public Information Center. Phone, 877-275-3342 (press 1, then press 5). http://www.fdic.gov/news/publications/PIChardcopies.html | Email: publicinfo@fdic.gov

Site Map The website map allows visitors to look for specific topics or to browse for content that aligns with their interests. https://www.fdic.gov/sitemap

Social Media The FDIC has a Facebook account. https://www.facebook.com/FDICgov

The FDIC tweets announcements and other newsworthy items on Twitter. https://twitter.com/FDICgov

The FDIC posts videos on its YouTube channel. https://www.youtube.com/user/FDICchannel; https://www.fdic.gov/about/contact/ask | Email: communications@fdic.gov

For further information and media inquiries, contact the Office of Communications, Federal Deposit Insurance Corporation, 550 Seventeenth Street NW., Washington, DC 20429. Phone, 202-898-6993.

Federal Election Commission

999 E Street NW., Washington, DC 20463
Phone, 202-694-1100. Fax, 800-424-9530. Internet, http://www.fec.gov

Chair	Steven T. Walther
Vice Chair	Caroline C. Hunter
Commissioner	Lee E. Goodman
Commissioner	Matthew S. Petersen
Commissioner	Ellen L. Weintraub
Commissioner	Vacant
Staff Director	Alec Palmer
Chief Financial Officer	Gilbert Ford, Acting
General Counsel	Lisa J. Stevenson, Acting
Inspector General	Vacant

The Federal Election Commission provides public disclosure of campaign finance activities and ensures compliance with campaign finance laws and regulations.

The Federal Election Commission is an independent agency established by section 309 of the Federal Election Campaign Act of 1971, as amended (52 U.S.C. 30106). It comprises six Commissioners whom the President appoints with the advice and consent of the Senate. The Act also provides for three statutory officers—the staff director, the general counsel, and the inspector general—whom the Commissioners appoint. https://transition.fec.gov/about/offices/offices.shtml

Activities

The Commission administers and enforces the Federal Election Campaign Act of 1971, as amended (52 U.S.C. 30101 et seq.), and the Revenue Act, as amended (26 U.S.C. 1 et seq.). These laws provide for the public funding of Presidential elections, public disclosure of the financial activities of political committees involved in Federal elections, and limitations and prohibitions on contributions and expenditures made to influence Federal elections.

Public Funding of Presidential Elections   The Commission oversees the public financing of Presidential elections by certifying Federal payments to primary candidates and general election nominees. It also audits recipients of Federal funds and may require repayment to the U.S. Treasury if a committee has made nonqualified campaign expenditures.

Disclosure   The Commission ensures public disclosure of the campaign finance activities reported by political committees supporting Federal candidates. These committees regularly file reports disclosing the sources of campaign money and how that money is spent. The Commission places these reports on the public record within 48 hours after they are received and digitizes the data contained in them. http://www.fec.gov/ans/answers_disclosure.shtml

Sources of Information

Congressional Affairs   This Office of Congressional, Legislative, and Intergovernmental Affairs serves as the Commission's primary congressional and executive branch liaison. Phone, 202-694-1006. https://transition.fec.gov/about/offices/cong_affairs/cong_affairs.shtml | Email: congress@fec.gov

Data   Data tables summarizing campaign financial activity by filer type, election cycle, and reporting period are available online. http://www.fec.gov/press/campaign_finance_statistics.shtml

Career Opportunities   The Commission posts available positions on its Web site. Sign up online to receive email updates regarding employment opportunities. Information is also available from the Office of Human Resources. Phone, 202-694-1080. http://www.fec.gov/pages/jobs/jobs.shtml | Email: fecjobs@fec.gov

Filing Information is available online to help filers comply with the disclosure requirements of the Federal campaign finance law. http://www.fec.gov/info/filing.shtml

Freedom of Information Act (FOIA) FOIA requests may be submitted by email or fax or sent by mail to the Federal Election Commission, Attn: FOIA Requester Service Center, Room 408, 999 E Street NW., Washington, DC 20463. Fax, 202-219-1043. http://www.fec.gov/press/foia.shtml | Email: FOIA@fec.gov

General Inquiries The Information Division informs and assists Federal candidates, political committees, and the public. It answers questions on campaign finance laws, conducts workshops and seminars on these laws, and distributes publications and forms. Phone, 202-694-1100 or 800-424-9530. TDD, 202-219-3336. http://www.fec.gov/pages/contact.shtml | Email: info@fec.gov

Law Library The library contains a collection of basic legal research resources

on political campaign financing, corporate and labor political activity, and campaign finance reform. It is open to the public on weekdays, 9 a.m.–5 p.m., except on Federal holidays. Phone, 202-694-1516 or 800-424-9530. http://www.fec.gov/general/library.shtml

Media Inquiries The Press Office answers questions from media sources, issues press releases on Commission actions and statistical data, responds to requests for information, and distributes other materials. Phone, 202-694-1220. http://www.fec.gov/press/index.shtml | Email: press@fec.gov

Public Records The Public Records Branch, located at 999 E Street NW., Washington, DC, provides space for public inspection of campaign finance reports and statements after 1971. It is open to the public on weekdays, 9 a.m.–5 p.m., except on Federal holidays. Phone, 202-694-1120 or 800-424-9530. http://www.fec.gov/pubrec/publicrecordsoffice.shtml | Email: pubrec@fec.gov; http://www.fec.gov/pages/contact.shtml

For further information, contact the Information Division, Federal Election Commission, 999 E Street NW., Washington, DC 20463. Phone, 202-694-1100 or 800-424-9530 (option 6).

Federal Housing Finance Agency

400 7th Street SW., Washington, DC 20219
Phone, 202-649-3800. Internet, http://www.fhfa.gov

Director	MELVIN L. WATT
Chief Operating Officer	LAWRENCE STAUFFER, ACTING
Director, Office of Minority and Women Inclusion	SHARRON P. A. LEVINE
Deputy Director, Division of Conservatorship	BOB RYAN, ACTING
Deputy Director, Division of Federal Home Loan Bank Regulation	FRED C. GRAHAM
Deputy Director, Division of Enterprise Regulation	NINA NICHOLS
Deputy Director, Division of Housing Mission and Goals	SANDRA THOMPSON
General Counsel	ALFRED M. POLLARD
Inspector General	LAURA S. WERTHEIMER
Obmbudsman	JANELL BYRD-CHICHESTER, ACTING

The Federal Housing and Finance Agency ensures that the housing Government-Sponsored Enterprises operate safely and soundly and serve as a reliable source of liquidity and funding for housing finance and community investment.

The Federal Housing and Finance Agency (FHFA) was established by the Housing and Economic Recovery Act of 2008 (42 U.S.C. 4501 note) as an independent agency

FHFA Organizational Chart

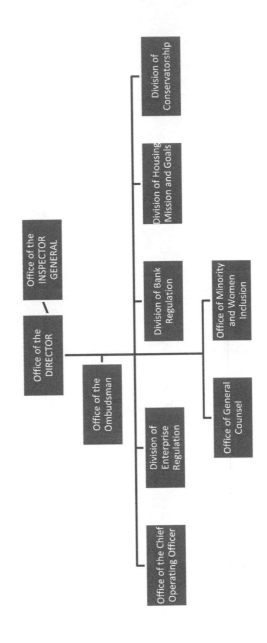

in the executive branch. The merger of the Federal Housing Finance Board and the Office of Federal Housing Enterprise Oversight, combined with the transfer of the Department of Housing and Urban Development's Government-Sponsored Enterprise mission team, formed the FHFA.

The FHFA is managed by a Director whom the President appoints and the Senate confirms. FHFA's Director also serves as the Chairman of the Federal Housing Oversight Board. The Secretary of the Treasury, the Secretary of Housing and Urban Development, and the Chairman of the Securities and Exchange Commission are also members of the Board. http://www.fhfa. gov/AboutUs

Activities

The FHFA provides research and data, supervision, and policies for strengthening and securing the U.S. secondary mortgage markets. It oversees vital components of those markets: the housing Government-Sponsored Enterprises of Fannie Mae, Freddie Mac, and the Federal Home Loan Bank System. Combined, these entities make available more than $5.6 trillion in funding for financial institutions and the U.S. mortgage markets. The FHFA also acts as the conservator of Fannie Mae and Freddie Mac. http://www.fhfa.gov/PolicyProgramsResearch

Sources of Information

Blog   Agency experts share their insights into housing finance issues on the blog "FHFA Insights." https://www.fhfa.gov/Media/Pages/Insights.aspx

Business Opportunities   FHFA contracting operations is responsible for procuring all goods and services, including information technology, that the agency requires. http://www.fhfa.gov/AboutUs/Business

Career Opportunities   The Agency's mission-critical professionals include accountants, attorneys, economists, examiners, financial analysts, and information technology specialists. The FHFA also relies on budget and procurement and human resource specialists, facilities managers, policy experts, and student interns, to fill important support roles.

The Agency advertises opportunities for employment on its "Careers" Web page. Contact the Office of Human Resources Management for additional information. Phone, 202-649-3807. http://www.fhfa.gov/AboutUs/Careers

Dodd–Frank Act Stress Tests   The FHFA requires Fannie Mae and Freddie Mac and Federal Home Loan Banks to conduct stress tests pursuant to the Dodd-Frank Wall Street Reform and Consumer Protection Act of 2010. https://www.fhfa.gov/SupervisionRegulation/DoddFrankActStressTests

The FHFA is categorized as a small agency in the Partnership for Public Service's Best Places To Work in the Federal Government rankings. In 2016, the Agency improved its index score. http://bestplacestowork.org/BPTW/rankings/detail/FY00

Freedom of Information Act (FOIA)   The FOIA established a statutory right of public access to executive branch information in the Federal Government. It gives a right to any person to obtain access to Federal agency records; however, nine exemptions and three special law enforcement exclusions shield certain records from public disclosure. https://www.fhfa.gov/AboutUs/FOIAPrivacy/Pages/FOIA.aspx | Email: foia@fhfa.gov

Frequently Asked Questions (FAQs)   The FHFA posts answers to FAQs on various topics: the Home Affordable Refinance Program (HARP), housing price index (HPI), servicing alignment initiative, as well as on conservatorship, Federal Home Loan Bank membership, principal reduction modification, and private mortgage insurer draft eligibility requirements, https://www.fhfa.gov/Media/Pages/FAQs.aspx

History   On September 6, 2008, the FHFA placed Fannie Mae and Freddie Mac into conservatorship because they could no longer carry out their mission without Government intervention. To learn more about this extraordinary action and this critical moment in the history of the Nation's mortgage market, visit the "History of Fannie Mae and Freddie Mac Conservatorships" Web page. https://www.fhfa.gov/Conservatorship/Pages/History-of-Fannie-Mae--Freddie-Conservatorships.aspx

A timeline of significant events in the history of the FHFA is available on its Web site. https://www.fhfa.gov/AboutUs/Timeline

Key Topics   These Web pages contain information on the FHFA's work on a range of national issues. They highlight relevant news releases, reports, statements, and web pages on the key topics. https://www.fhfa.gov/KeyTopics

Meet the Experts   The "Meet the Experts" page contains brief professional biographies of experienced, well-educated FHFA personnel. https://www.fhfa.gov/PolicyProgramsResearch/Pages/Meet-the-Experts.aspx

Navigate by Audience   The "Government" Web page contains consolidated resources for Federal, State, and local government personnel seeking information related to the Nation's housing finance system. https://www.fhfa.gov/Government

The "Homeowners and Homebuyers" Web page guides homeowners and buyers to resources and tools: information on avoiding foreclosure, buying a new home, refinancing an existing home, shopping for a mortgage, understanding the housing markets, and more. https://www.fhfa.gov/Homeownersbuyer

The "Industry" Web page contains consolidated resources for advocacy organizations, investors, mortgage insurers, originators, servicers, small and large companies, trade groups, vendors, and others with an interest in the Nation's housing finance system. https://www.fhfa.gov/Industry

The "Media" Web page gives members of the media and general public access to FHFA expertise on and insight into housing finance. https://www.fhfa.gov/Media | Email: MediaInquiries@fhfa.gov

News   The FHFA posts news releases on its Web site. https://www.fhfa.gov/Media/Pages/News-Releases.

aspx?k=ContentType%3APublic-Affairs%20AND%20PublicAffairsCategoryOWSCHCS%3A%22News%20Release%22%20AND%20FHFAPublishedDateOWSDATE%3D01%2F0 1%2F2017%2E%2E12%2F31%2F2017

Open Government   The FHFA supports the Open Government initiative by promoting the principles of collaboration, participation, and transparency. https://www.fhfa.gov/AboutUs/Policies/Pages/Open-Government.aspx

Plans / Reports   The FHFA posts performance and strategic plans and various types of reports on its Web site. https://www.fhfa.gov/AboutUs/reportsplans

Privacy Act of 1974   Fair information practices govern the collection, maintenance, use, and dissemination of an individual's personally identifiable information that a Federal agency maintains in a system of records—in a group of records that an agency controls and from which its staff may retrieve information by using the individual's name or an assigned identifier. https://www.fhfa.gov/AboutUs/FOIAPrivacy/Pages/Privacy.aspx | Email: Privacy@fhfa.gov

Site Map   The Web site map allows visitors to look for specific topics or to browse content that aligns with their interests. https://www.fhfa.gov/AboutUs/Sitemap

Social Media   The FHFA tweets announcements and other newsworthy items on Twitter. https://twitter.com/FHFA

The FHFA posts videos on its YouTube channel. https://www.youtube.com/channel/UCoKP7Om6nsRkEav9yInFekw

Tools   A borrower assistance map, conforming loan limits map, and housing price index (HPI) calculator and motion chart, as well as HPI maps (county, four-quarter appreciation, ZIP5) and summary tables, are available online. https://www.fhfa.gov/DataTools/Tools; https://www.fhfa.gov/AboutUs/Contact | Email: fhfainfo@fhfa.gov

For further information, contact the Office of Congressional Affairs and Communications, Federal Housing Finance Agency, 400 7th Street SW., Washington, DC 20219. Phone, 202-649-3802.

Federal Labor Relations Authority

1400 K Street NW., Washington, DC 20005
Phone, 202-218-7770. Internet, http://www.flra.gov

Chair	PATRICK PIZZELLA, ACTING
Member	ERNEST DUBESTER
Member	(VACANCY)
Executive Director	(VACANCY)
Chief Counsel to the Chairman	JAMES T. ABBOTT
Chief, Case Intake and Publication	(VACANCY)
Solicitor	FRED B. JACOB
Inspector General	DANA ROONEY
Chief Administrative Law Judge	CHARLES R. CENTER
General Counsel	PETER A. SUTTON, ACTING

Federal Service Impasses Panel

Chair	(VACANCY)
Member	(VACANCY)
Member	(VACANCY)
Member	(VACANCY)
Member	(VACANCY)
Member	(VACANCY)
Member	(VACANCY)
Executive Director	KIMBERLY D. MOSELEY

Foreign Service Labor Relations Board

Chair	PATRICK PIZZELLA, ACTING
Member	HERMAN J. COHEN
Member	STEPHEN R. LEDFORD

Foreign Service Impasse Disputes Panel

CHAIR	(VACANCY)
Member	BETTY BOLDEN
Member	WILLIAM C. HANSEN
Member	JOHN C. SULLIVAN
Member	SHAWN HOOPER

The Federal Labor Relations Authority oversees labor-management relations between the Federal Government and its employees.

The Federal Labor Relations Authority (FLRA) was created as an independent establishment by Reorganization Plan No. 2 of 1978 (5 U.S.C. app.), effective January 1, 1979, pursuant to Executive Order 12107 of December 28, 1978, to consolidate the central policymaking functions in Federal labor-management relations. Its duties and authority are specified in Title VII (Federal Service Labor-Management Relations) of the Civil Service Reform Act of 1978 (5 U.S.C. 7101-7135).

The FLRA comprises three members whom the President nominates and Senate confirms to 5-year terms. The Chair of the Authority serves as the chief executive and administrative officer. The Chair also presides over the Foreign Service Labor Relations Board. The General Counsel investigates alleged unfair labor practices, files and prosecutes unfair labor practice complaints before the Authority, and exercises other powers that the Authority may prescribe.
https://www.flra.gov/about/introduction-flra

Activities

The Authority adjudicates disputes arising under the Federal Labor-Management Relations Program, deciding cases concerning the negotiability of collective bargaining agreement proposals, appeals concerning unfair labor practices and representation petitions, and exceptions to grievance arbitration awards. It also assists Federal agencies and unions in understanding their rights and responsibilities under the program.

The Federal Service Impasses Panel, an entity within the FLRA, assists in resolving negotiation impasses between agencies and unions. The Panel can either recommend procedures to the parties for the resolution of the impasse or assist the parties in resolving the impasse through whatever methods and procedures it considers appropriate, including fact-finding and mediation-arbitration. If the parties do not arrive at a voluntary settlement after receiving Panel assistance, the Panel may take whatever action is necessary to resolve the impasse, including the imposition of contract terms.

The Foreign Service Labor Relations Board and the Foreign Service Impasse Disputes Panel administer provisions of chapter 2 of the Foreign Service Act of 1980 (22 U.S.C. 3921) concerning labor-management relations. This chapter establishes a statutory labor-management relations program for Foreign Service employees of the U.S. Government. Administrative and staff support is provided by the Federal Labor Relations Authority and the Federal Service Impasses Panel. https://www.flra.gov/about/mission

Sources of Information

Electronic Filing   To use the FLRA's electronic case filing system, register online and create a user profile. Email addresses are the case filing system's primary means of identifying electronic filers. https://flra.quickbase.com/db/bgfwmcjx4

Career Opportunities   The FLRA posts announcements for job openings on USAJobs. For more information, contact the Human Resources Division. Phone, 202-218-7979. https://www.usajobs.gov

The FLRA ranks among the best places to work in the Federal Government. http://bestplacestowork.org/BPTW/rankings/overall/small

Freedom of Information Act (FOIA)   The FLRA maintains an electronic FOIA reading room. https://www.flra.gov/elibrary

If the desired information is unavailable in the reading room or elsewhere on the FLRA's Web site, then a written FOIA request may be necessary to access the information. To learn how to submit a FOIA request, consult the "Frequently Asked Questions" section. https://www.flra.gov/foia_faq

Media   Members of the media should contact the Counsel for Regulatory and Public Affairs if they have questions or seek information. Phone, 202-218-7776. https://www.flra.gov/about/public-affairs

News   The FLRA posts press releases on its Web site. The online archives contain press releases from 2009 through 2014. https://www.flra.gov/press_releases

Open Government   The FLRA supports the Federal Government's efforts to increase collaboration, participation, and transparency. https://www.flra.gov/open-government

Plain Language   The FLRA adheres to Federal plain language guidelines. To comply with the Plain Writing Act of 2010, the agency relies on the general public. If a document or Web page is difficult to understand, alert the FLRA's writers and editors via email to the lack of clarity. https://www.flra.gov/plain_language | Email: engagetheFLRA@flra.gov; https://www.flra.gov/components-offices/offices/office-executive-director | Email: flraexecutivedirector@flra.gov

For further information, contact the Office of the Executive Director, Federal Labor Relations Authority, 1400 K Street NW., Washington, DC 20005. Phone, 202-218-7791.

Federal Mine Safety and Health Review Commission

1331 Pennsylvania Avenue NW., Suite 520N, Washington, DC 20004-1710
Phone, 202-434-9900. TTY/TDD, 202-434-4000, ext. 293. Internet, http://www.fmshrc.gov |
Email: fmshrc@fmshrc.gov

Commission

Chair	Marco M. Rajkovich, Jr.
Commissioners	William I. Althen
	Mary Lucille Jordan
	Arthur R. Traynor III
	Michael G. Young

https://www.fmshrc.gov/about/commissioners

Administration

Executive Director	Lisa M. Boyd
Chief Administrative Law Judge	(vacancy)
General Counsel	Michael A. McCord
Senior Policy Advisor	Timothy A. Greten

The above list of key personnel was updated 4–2019.

The Federal Mine Safety and Health Review Commission ensures compliance with occupational safety and health standards in the Nation's surface and underground coal, metal, and nonmetal mines.

The Federal Mine Safety and Health Act of 1977 (30 U.S.C. 801 et seq.), as amended, established the Federal Mine Safety and Health Review Commission as an independent and adjudicative agency.

The Commission comprises five members whom the President appoints and the Senate confirms. Each Commissioner serves a 6-year term, and all the terms are staggered. The President appoints one of the Commissioners to serve as the Chair. At the trial level, the FMSHRC's administrative judges decide cases. The Commissioners are responsible for appellate review of a decision made by an administrative law judge.

Activities

FMSHRC provides administrative trial and appellate review of legal disputes arising from enforcement actions taken by the Department of Labor.

The FMSHRC and its administrative law judges decide cases brought before it by the Department of Labor's Mine Safety and Health Administration, mine operators, and miners or their representatives. These cases generally involve review of the Administration's enforcement actions, including citations, mine closure orders, and proposals for civil penalties issued for violations of the act or the mandatory safety and health standards promulgated by the Secretary of Labor. The FMSHRC also has jurisdiction over discrimination complaints filed by miners or their representatives regarding their safety and health, complaints for compensation filed on behalf of miners idled as a result of mine closure orders issued by the Administration, and disputes involving mine emergency response plans.

Cases brought before the FMSHRC are assigned to a judge in the Office of Administrative Law Judges, and hearings are conducted pursuant to the requirements of the Administrative Procedure Act (5 U.S.C. 554, 556) and the FMSHRC's procedural rules (29 CFR 2700).

A judge's decision becomes a final, nonprecedential order of the FMSHRC 40 days after issuance unless it has directed the case for review in response to a petition or on its own motion. If a review is conducted, a decision of the FMSHRC becomes final 30 days after issuance unless a party adversely affected seeks review in the U.S. Court of Appeals for the District of Columbia Circuit or the circuit within which the mine subject to the litigation is located.

As far as practicable, hearings are held at locations convenient to the affected mines. In addition to its District of Columbia offices, the Office of Administrative Law Judges maintains offices in Colorado and Pennsylvania. https://www.fmshrc.gov/about

Sources of Information

Administrative Law Judges   To ask a question regarding a case before an administrative law judge, send an email to the address below or call the Office of the Administrative Law Judges. Phone, 202-434-9950. https://www.fmshrc.gov/about/aljs | Email: docket@fmshrc.gov

Contact Information   The "Contact Us" web page has contact information for the Office of the Executive Director and Office of the Administrative Law Judges. The FMSHRC maintains offices in Washington, DC; Denver, CO; and Pittsburgh, PA. Washington—phone, 202-434-9905; fax, 202-434-9906. Denver—phone, 303-844-5267; fax, 303-844-5268. Pittsburgh—phone, 412-920-7240; fax, 412-928-8689. https://www.fmshrc.gov/contact | Email: fmshrc@fmshrc.gov

Decisions   Searchable databases of FMSHRC decisions and decisions of administrative law judges are available online. http://www.fmshrc.gov/decisions

The "Cases on Review" web page includes links to cases currently on review before the FMSHRC and to decisions on appeal before the U.S. Courts of Appeals. http://www.fmshrc.gov/content/cases-review

Federal Mine Safety and Health Act   The FMSHRC has prepared a version of the Federal Mine Safety and Health Act of 1977 that reflects changes made to it by the Mine Improvement and New Emergency Response Act of 2006. This unofficial document is available in Portable Document Format (PDF) for viewing and downloading. https://

www.fmshrc.gov/content/federal-mine-safety-and-health-act-1977

Filing   Electronic filing may be done through the FMSHRC's electronic case management system (e-CMS). To use the e-CMS, a filer must register at the FMSHRC-eCMS website. The e-CMS support team is available to provide assistance. http://www.fmshrc.gov/guides/instructions-electronic-filing | Email: e-CMS.Support@fmshrc.gov

Freedom of Information Act (FOIA)   The FOIA requires Federal agencies to disclose records after receiving a properly written request. The law does include provisions that shield certain records, or parts of them, from disclosure. The FOIA Service Center assists those seeking information through the FOIA. For more information, write to the Federal Mine Safety and Health Review Commission, FOIA Service Center, 1331 Pennsylvania Avenue NW., Suite 520N, Washington, DC 20004-1710. Phone, 202-434-9935. Fax, 202-434-9944. http://www.fmshrc.gov/foia | Email: foia@fmshrc.gov

Frequently Asked Questions (FAQs)   The FMSHRC posts answers to FAQs. https://www.fmshrc.gov/guides/faq

Guidance   The "Guides" web page includes links to guidance on proceedings, case procedures, reopening a case, electronic filing, and the Freedom of Information Act. https://www.fmshrc.gov/guides

Meetings   The FMSHRC posts audio files of decisional public meetings on its website. https://www.fmshrc.gov/meetings-arguments/meetings

News   The latest FMSHRC news is available online. http://www.fmshrc.gov/about/news

Oral Arguments   The FMSHRC posts audio files of oral arguments on its website. https://www.fmshrc.gov/meetings-arguments/arguments

Organizational Chart   The FMSHRC publishes its organizational chart as part of its "Congressional Budget Justification and Annual Performance Plan." In the budget justification and performance plan for fiscal year 2020 (18 MAR 2019), the chart is on page 5. The key personnel list of commissioners and administrators, which appears at the top of this entry, relies on the organizational chart published in the budget justification and performance plan. https://www.fmshrc.gov/plans/fy2020-justification#

Procedural Rules (29 CFR 2700) The FMSHRC posts its procedural rules online in Portable Document Format (PDF) for viewing and downloading. https://www.fmshrc.gov/rules/Procedural%20Rules%20Booklet%20Jan%202014.pdf

Reports / Budget Submissions The "Reports and Budget Submissions" web page includes links to the FMSHRC's current and past strategic plans, sustainability report, reports to Congress, as well as to its budget and annual performance, buy American, and performance accountability reports. http://www.fmshrc.gov/reports-budget-submissions

The Sources of Information were updated 4–2019.

Federal Maritime Commission

800 North Capitol Street NW., Washington, DC 20573
Phone, 202-523-5707. Internet, http://www.fmc.gov

The Commission

Chair	Michael A. Khouri
Commissioners	
	Rebecca F. Dye
	Daniel B. Maffei
	Louis E. Sola
	(Vacancy)

https://www.fmc.gov/commissioners

Bureaus and Offices

Managing Director	Karen V. Gregory
Bureau Directors	
Certification and Licensing	Sandra L. Kusumoto
Enforcement	Benjamin K. Trogdon
Trade Analysis	Florence A. Carr
Office Director	
Consumer Affairs and Dispute Resolution Services	Rebecca A. Fenneman
Chief Administrative Law Judge	Erin M. Wirth
Equal Employment Opportunity Director	Ebony Jarrett
General Counsel	Tyler J. Wood
Secretary	Rachel E. Dickon

https://www.fmc.gov/about-the-fmc/bureaus-offices

Office of Inspector General

Inspector General	Jonathan Hatfield

https://www.fmc.gov/about-the-fmc/bureaus-offices/office-of-inspector-general | Email: OIG@fmc.gov

The above list of key personnel was updated 6–2019.

The Federal Maritime Commission promotes an efficient, fair, and reliable supply system of international ocean transportation; protects the public from deceptive, unfair, and unlawful practices; and contributes to the integrity and security of the Nation's supply chain and transportation system.

Establishment and Organization

The Federal Maritime Commission (FMC) was established by Reorganization Plan No. 7 of 1961 (46 U.S.C. 301–307), effective August 12, 1961. The FMC is an independent establishment, regulating shipping under the the Shipping Act of 1984, as amended (46 U.S.C. 40101–41309); Section 19 of the Merchant Marine Act, 1920 (46 U.S.C. 42101–42109); the Foreign Shipping Practices Act of 1988 (46 U.S.C. 42301–42307); and Public Law 89–777, approved on November 6, 1966 (46 U.S.C. 44101–44106). https://www.fmc.gov/about-the-fmc/fmc-regulations-statutes

The Commission is composed of five Commissioners, whom the President appoints by the advice and with the consent of the Senate. The President may not appoint more than three Commissioners who are from the same political party. The term of each Commissioner is 5 years. When his or her term ends, the Commissioner may continue to serve until a successor is appointed and qualified, but only for 1 year or less. A vacancy is filled in the same manner as the original appointment, which may be extended to include a second term. An individual appointed to fill a vacancy is appointed for the unexpired term of the person being succeeded. That individual may serve two complete terms in addition to the remainder of the term for which the predecessor of that individual was appointed. https://www.govinfo.gov/content/pkg/USCODE-2017-title46/pdf/USCODE-2017-title46-subtitleI-chap3.pdf

The FMC posts its organizational chart online. https://www.fmc.gov/about-the-fmc/organizational-chart

Activities

Adjudicatory Procedures   The FMC conducts formal investigations and hearings on its own motion and adjudicates formal complaints in accordance with the Administrative Procedure Act (5 U.S.C. note prec. 551). https://www.fmc.gov/about-the-fmc/bureaus-offices/administrative-law-judges| Email: judges@fmc.gov

Agreements   The FMC reviews agreements by and among ocean common carriers or marine terminal operators or by and among carriers and operators, which are filed under section 5 of the Shipping Act of 1984, for statutory compliance and for their likely effect on competition. It also monitors activities under all effective agreements for compliance with the provisions of law and its rules, orders, and regulations. https://www.fmc.gov/resources-services/vessel-operating-common-carriers; https://www.fmc.gov/resources-services/marine-terminal-operators

Alternative Dispute Resolution   The FMC reviews informal complaints and assists parties in resolving disputes. Mediation and other dispute resolution services are available to assist parties in achieving a more acceptable resolution to a dispute at less cost than may be possible in litigation. These services are available before and after the commencement of litigation. The Commission also provides an informal process to adjudicate certain complaints involving less than $50,000 in damages. https://www.fmc.gov/databases-services/alternative-dispute-resolution-services| Email: complaints@fmc.gov

Complaints   The FMC reviews alleged or suspected violations of the shipping statutes and rules and regulations of the Commission and may take administrative action to institute formal proceedings, to refer matters to other governmental agencies, or to bring about voluntary agreement between the parties. https://www.fmc.gov/databases-services/consumer-affairs-dispute-resolution-services| Email: complaints@fmc.gov

Economic Analyses   The FMC relies on the Office of Economics and Competition Analysis (OECA) for support in antitrust economics and competition policy. OECA staff analyzes and monitors agreements that are filed with the FMC and that are between ocean carriers or marine terminal operators or between carriers and operators. These agreements are monitored for effects that inhibit competition and for compliance with FMC regulations and U.S. shipping laws. https://www.fmc.gov/about-the-fmc/bureaus-offices/bureau-of-trade-analysis| Email: tradeanalysis@fmc.gov

Enforcement   The FMC relies on the Bureau of Enforcement (BOE) to serve as its prosecutorial component. Its attorneys participate in formal proceedings as trial counsel and, with the assistance of FMC area representatives, they investigate potential violations of the Shipping Act and FMC regulations. BOE attorneys also negotiate settlements and informal compromises of civil penalties and may participate in factfinding investigations that are initiated under the Shipping Act or the Foreign Shipping Practices Act. https://www.fmc.gov/about-the-fmc/bureaus-offices/bureau-of-enforcement| Email: boe@fmc.gov

International Affairs   The FMC conducts investigations of foreign governmental and carrier practices that adversely affect the U.S. shipping trade. In consultation with other executive agencies, the FMC takes action to effect the elimination of discriminatory practices on the part of foreign governments against shipping in the United States foreign trade and to achieve comity between the United States and its trading partners. https://www.fmc.gov/about-the-fmc/bureaus-offices/general-counsel| Email: generalcounsel@fmc.gov

Licenses   The FMC issues licenses to those persons and entities in the United States who wish to carry out the business of providing freight forwarding services and non-vessel-operating common carrier services. https://www.fmc.gov/about-the-fmc/bureaus-offices/bureau-of-certification-and-licensing| Email: bcl@fmc.gov

Non-Vessel-Operating Common Carrier Service Arrangements   The FMC receives and reviews service arrangements entered into by non-vessel-operating common carriers and their customers. Cargo moving under these service arrangements is exempt from the tariff publication and adherence requirements of the Shipping Act, on the condition that the service arrangements must be filed with the Commission. https://www.fmc.gov/resources-services/ocean-transportation-intermediaries

Passenger Indemnity   The FMC administers the passenger indemnity provisions of the act of November 6, 1966, which require shipowners and operators to obtain certificates of financial responsibility to pay judgments for personal injury or death or to refund fares in the event of nonperformance of voyages. https://www.fmc.gov/resources-services/passenger-vessel-operators| Email: pvo@fmc.gov

Rulemaking   The FMC promulgates rules and regulations to interpret, enforce, and ensure compliance with shipping and related statutes by common carriers and other persons subject to the Commission's jurisdiction. https://www.ecfr.gov/cgi-bin/text-idx?SID=77cce38e9b335eb5c0f5f515f1bbe2a2&c=ecfr&tpl=/ecfrbrowse/Title46/46cfrv9_02.tpl

Service Contracts   The FMC receives and reviews filings of confidential service contracts between shippers and ocean common carriers. It also monitors publication of certain essential terms of those service contracts. https://www.fmc.gov/about-the-fmc/bureaus-offices/bureau-of-trade-analysis

Tariffs   The FMC monitors and prescribes requirements to ensure accessibility and accuracy of electronic tariff publications of common carriers engaged in the foreign commerce of the United States. Special permission applications may be submitted for relief from statutory and/or Commission tariff requirements. https://www.fmc.gov/about-the-fmc/bureaus-offices/bureau-of-trade-analysis

Sources of Information

Career Opportunities   To carry out its mission, the FMC relies on attorneys, economists, and other professionals. https://www.fmc.gov/about-the-fmc/employment-opportunities

In 2018, the FMC ranked 9th among 29 small agencies in the Partnership for Public Service's Best Places To Work Agency Rankings. http://bestplacestowork.org/rankings/detail/MC00

Contact Information   Contact and other general information is available on the "Contact Us" web page. https://www.fmc.gov/contact | Email: Inquiries@fmc.gov

Cruise Vacations   The FMC has posted the brochure "Cruise Vacations: Know Before You Go" on its website to help potential passengers select an appropriate cruise before purchasing their tickets. https://www.fmc.gov/wp-content/uploads/2018/09/PVO2014-508.pdf

General information and additional resources to help cruise passengers are available on the FMC website. https://www.fmc.gov/resources-services/cruise-passenger-assistance

Events   The FMC posts events upcoming events on its website. https://www.fmc.gov/events

Freedom of Information Act (FOIA)   Enacted in 1966, the FOIA took effect on July 4, 1967. The law gives a right to obtain access to Federal agency records to any person, except a fugitive from the law. Some records, or portions of them, are, however, shielded from disclosure by one or more of nine statutory exemptions or by specific harm that disclosure may cause. The FMC makes a lot of information publicly available to reduce the need of filing an official FOIA request. https://www.fmc.gov/about-the-fmc/freedom-of-information-act-requests-reports | Email: FOIA@fmc.gov

The FMC maintains an electronic reading room on its website. https://www2.fmc.gov/readingroom/ProceedingSearch

Greenhouse Gas Reduction / Sustainable Development   The "Federal Maritime Commission 2017 Strategic Sustainability Performance Plan" is available online. Greenhouse gas reduction is part of the plan. https://www.fmc.gov/wp-content/upl oads/2018/10/2017SustainabilityPlan.pdf | Email: omd@fmc.gov

"The maritime industry realized years ago that sustainable development is necessary to the survival of people and businesses—whether it is related to maritime transportation, port development, or infrastructure. Any discussion in the industry now necessarily involves mention of sustainability principles. We know that a cleaner environment means economic growth, job creation, and reduced costs with greater efficiency." (excerpted from Chair Mario Cordero's statement on Earth Day 2016). https://www.fmc.gov/chairmans-statement-on-earth-day

History   In 1961, the White House and Congress made a decision that affected international liner shipping companies and the U.S. merchant marine. To learn more about that decision and the establishment of two new maritime agencies by President John F. Kennedy's Executive order, visit the "History" page on the FMC website. https://www.fmc.gov/about-the-fmc/our-history

The FMC maintains an online archive of maritime decisions that are associated with the Department of Commerce, Federal Maritime Board, U.S. Maritime Commission, U.S. Shipping Board, and itself. The archive's content begins with the year 1919. https://www.fmc.gov/fmc-reports

Library   The FMC's law and reference library contains books, directories, encyclopedias, journals, magazines, microforms, reports, and videos. It has specialized material that covers the various segments of the international shipping industry and historical and contemporary regulatory materials that cover all phases of shipping in the U.S. foreign trades. It also has material on economics, engineering, political science, and a collection of legal publications. The library's holdings comprise approximately 8,700 volumes and numerous microfiches, CD–ROMs, and online services. Members of the public may visit the library and use the collection; however, all materials must be used in the library during its hours of operation. Materials are released only through an interlibrary loan request. A librarian is available from 8 a.m. to 4:30 p.m., eastern standard time, Monday–Friday. The library is closed on weekends and Federal Holidays. Phone, 202-523-5762. https://www.fmc.gov/about-the-fmc/bureaus-offices/law-reference-library | Email: LibraryInquiries@fmc.gov

All effective vessel-operating common carrier (VOCC) and marine terminal operator (MTO) agreements on file with the FMC are accessible in its electronic agreement library. https://www2.fmc.gov/FMC.Agreements.Web/Public

Moving Overseas   The FMC posts tips for protecting property when shipping goods internationally by sea. https://www.fmc.gov/resources-services/protect-your-international-move

Before shipping a car overseas, become familiar with the laws and regulations of the United States and the destination country regarding which vehicles may be imported and the fees that must be paid. https://fmc2.fmc.gov/resources-services/shipping-your-vehicle-overseas

News   The "FMC Newsroom" posts recent headlines. https://www.fmc.gov/news-events

Notices of Agreements   Recent notices of agreements filed are posted on the "Federal Register" website. https://fmc2.fmc.gov/about-the-fmc/weekly-agreement-notices

Open Government   The FMC supports the Open Government initiative by

promoting collaboration, participation, and transparency. https://www.fmc.gov/open-government
Resources / Services The FMC has gathered its resources and services in one place, on a single web page, for its stakeholders. In the "Audiences" section, resources and services are grouped by audience: public, attorneys and litigants, ocean transportation intermediaries (OTIs),

The Sources of Information were updated 6–2019.

passenger vessel operators (PVOs), vessel-operating common carriers (VOCCs), and marine terminal operators (MTOs). https://www.fmc.gov/resources-services
Social Media The FMC tweets announcements and other newsworthy items on Twitter. https://twitter.com/FMC_gov
The FMC posts videos on its YouTube channel. https://www.youtube.com/channel/UCwKTAlGGHIA0xcN3bDt_Uqg

---

Federal Mediation and Conciliation Service

250 E Street SW., Washington, DC 20427
Phone, 202-606-8100. Internet, http://www.fmcs.gov

Office of the Director

Director	(VACANCY)
Deputy Director	RICHARD R. GIACOLONE
Assistant Director	GARY HATTAL
Attorney-Advisor	DAWN STARR
Equal Employment Opportunity Director	DENISE MCKENNEY
Senior Advisor	DAVID THALER

https://www.fmcs.gov/aboutus/agency-departments/office-of-the-director

Deputy Directors	
Field Operations	D. SCOTT BLAKE
National Representative	SCOT BECKENBAUGH
Chief Operating Officer	GREGORY GOLDSTEIN

https://www.fmcs.gov/aboutus/agency-departments

The above list of key personnel was updated 8–2019.

The Federal Mediation and Conciliation Service helps labor and management resolve disputes in industries affecting commerce, offers training in cooperative processes to promote workplace stability and economic growth, and provides alternative dispute resolution services, training, negotiated rulemaking, and public policy facilitation to government entities.

Establishment and Organization

On June 23, 1947, the "Labor Management Relations Act, 1947," became Public Law 80–101 after the Congress enacted it over a veto by President Harry S. Truman. This Act is also referred to as the Taft-Hartley Act because Senator Robert A. Taft and Representative Fred A. Hartley, Jr., sponsored the bill. The Act amended the National Labor Relations Act of 1935, commonly known as the Wagner Act, and established the The

Federal Mediation and Conciliation Service (FMCS) as an independent agency of the U. S. Government to prevent or minimize the effects of labor-management disputes on the free flow of commerce. https://catalog.archives.gov/id/299855
The FMCS "may proffer its services in any labor dispute in any industry affecting commerce, either upon its own motion or upon the request of one or more of the parties to the dispute, whenever in its judgment such dispute threatens to cause a

Federal Mediation and Conciliation Service

Denise McKenney
EEO Director

Richard Giacolone
Director Nominee, FMCS

Dawn Starr
Attorney-Advisor

David Thaler
Senior Advisor

Gregory Goldstein
Chief Operating Officer

Gary Hattal
Agency Assistant Director

Scot Beckenbaugh
*Deputy Director
(National Representative)*

D. Scott Blake
Deputy Director (Field Operations)

substantial interruption of commerce" (29 U.S.C. 173). Subsequent emendations to the original Labor Management Relations Act have expanded the scope of the agency's dispute resolution services. https://www.govinfo.gov/content/pkg/USCODE-2017-title29/pdf/USCODE-2017-title29-chap7-subchapIII-sec173.pdf

The President appoints the Director by the advice and with consent of the Senate. The Director is prohibited from engaging in any other business, employment, or vocation (29 U.S.C. 172). https://www.govinfo.gov/content/pkg/USCODE-2017-title29/pdf/USCODE-2017-title29-chap7-subchapIII-sec172.pdf

The FMCS is headquartered in Washington, DC, and it has 10 regional offices and more than 60 field and local offices. It provides mediation and conflict resolution services to industry, government agencies, and communities. https://www.fmcs.gov/aboutus

The agency's organizational chart (AUG 2019) is available in Portable Document Format (PDF) for viewing and downloading. https://www.fmcs.gov/wp-content/uploads/2019/08/FMCS-Org-Structure-August-2019.pdf

Activities

The FMCS reduces disruptions to interstate commerce and improves government efficiency by providing skilled mediators to resolve workplace disputes and conflicts arising under the statutory jurisdiction of government entities. FMCS mediators do not enforce laws: They rely on innovative mediation, communication, and relationship building techniques to help disputants achieve consensus.

The FMCS offers its labor mediation and training services in a variety of industries and sectors of the economy, including the private sector (except airlines and railroads), the Federal sector, and the public sector (in States without labor mediation agencies). The Labor-Management Cooperation Act of 1978 recognized the economic benefits of a more proactive approach to workplace stability. The FMCS awards grants to encourage the establishment of local, regional, and industrywide labor management committees to improve labor management relationships, organizational effectiveness, and economic development. The FMCS also promotes workplace innovation, productivity, and competitiveness through collaboration, good labor-management relationships, and problem solving between companies and their workers.

The Administrative Dispute Resolution and Negotiated Rulemaking Acts of 1996 recognized the broader value of FMCS conflict resolution services for government efficiency. The agency was designated as a key resource to help government entities resolve individual employment disputes, design conflict management systems, achieve stakeholder consensus on new regulations, and conduct more effective multi-stakeholder public policy dialogues. https://www.fmcs.gov/services

Mediation / Training   FMCS mediators help parties resolve workplace disputes and establish sound, stable, and enduring labor-management relations. In addition to mediating collective bargaining disputes, mediators facilitate better day-to-day workplace relations through a variety of joint training programs. FMCS mediators also assist other government entities with resolving disputes arising under their jurisdictions. https://www.fmcs.gov/services/resolving-labor-management-disputes

Arbitration   Voluntary arbitration and factfinding are widely used in labor-management relations. Upon request, the FMCS can provide panels of arbitrators who are experienced in labor relations issues. Requests can be tailored, in terms of expertise, fees, geography, and other considerations, to accommodate a variety of requirements. https://www.fmcs.gov/services/arbitration

Sources of Information

Calendar   A day-by-day listing of important FMCS events is available on online. https://www.fmcs.gov/resources/calendar

Career Opportunities   Stationed in offices nationwide, FMCS mediators are full-time excepted service employees of the Federal Government. They perform duties in five major areas: advocacy, education, and outreach; alternative dispute resolution services to government entities; collective bargaining mediation; grievance mediation; and relationship development training. The ideal applicant seeking to become an FMCS mediator has full-time experience in the collective bargaining process. U.S. citizenship is required. https://www.fmcs. gov/careers

In 2018, the FMCS ranked 1st among 29 small agencies in the Partnership for Public Service's Best Places To Work Agency Rankings! http://bestplacestowork.org/rankings/detail/FM00

Conflict Management   The FMCS Institute for Conflict Management offers practical and experience-based conflict resolution training for individuals and groups. Course descriptions and enrollment information are available online. https://www.fmcs.gov/services/education-and-outreach/fmcs-institute

Contact   To ask a question or leave a comment, use the electronic "Feedback Form." https://www.fmcs.gov/feedback

Documents / Data   Budgets and performance information, regulations and policies, speeches and presentations, publications (some in Spanish), and reports are available online. Collective bargaining notice data and work stoppage data are also posted online. https://www.fmcs.gov/resources/documents-and-data

Electronic Updates   The FMCS uses email updates to disseminate information on its dispute resolution services and to announce training opportunities. A sign-up form is available online. https://public.govdelivery.com/accounts/USFMCS/subscriber/new

Find a Mediator   An online search tool is available to find a mediator by city, State, or Zip Code, as well as by name, email, or phone number. https://www.fmcs.gov/aboutus/locations/find-a-mediator

Forms / Applications   Forms and applications needed to obtain FMCS services and funding—arbitration, Freedom of Information Act (FOIA) requests, labor-management cooperation grants, and notice of bargaining (F–7)—are available online. https://www.fmcs.gov/resources/forms-applications

Freedom of Information Act (FOIA)   The FOIA requires Federal agencies to disclose records after receiving a proper written

request for them. Certain records, however, are shielded from disclosure by provisions contained within the statute. The FMCS has an online FOIA requester center. The specific procedures for requesting its records, FOIA-related contact information, and a link to records that are already accessible online may be found on the "FOIA Requestor Center" web page. https://www.fmcs.gov/foia | Email: foia@fmcs.gov

Subsequent amendments to the FOIA of 1966 require publicly accessible, electronic reading rooms that contain FOIA response documents and other information that is routinely available to the public. Before submitting a FOIA request, see if the FMCS already has placed the desired information in its electronic reading room. https://www.fmcs.gov/resources/documents-and-data

Frequently Asked Questions (FAQs)   The FMCS posts answers to FAQs on its website. https://www.fmcs.gov/resources/faqs

History   A timeline of events in modern American labor relations is available online. The timeline starts with the first Government-mediated settlement in 1838, continues through the creation of the FMCS in 1947 and the West Coast port mediation of 2002, to end currently with President Donald J. Trump's appointment of Richard Giacolone to serve as the agency's acting Director. https://www.fmcs.gov/aboutus/our-history

News   The FMCS maintains an online news archive. https://www.fmcs.gov/news

Regional Offices   Headquartered in Washington, DC, the FMCS delivers services nationwide through its 10 regional and numerous field offices. Contact information for the FMCS national office and its regional and field offices is available online. https://www.fmcs.gov/aboutus/locations/regional-offices

Shared Neutrals   Shared Neutrals, also known as Sharing Neutrals, is an interagency mediation program in the National Capital Region, including the Washington, DC, area and Baltimore. The Shared Neutrals program assists participating Federal agencies through a pool of trained, collateral-duty Federal employees who provide mediation services to an agency, other than their own, in exchange for like services to the program from the recipient agency. https://www.fmcs.gov/sharedneutrals

Site Map The site map allows visitors to look for specific topics or to browse content that aligns with their interests. https://www.fmcs.gov/site-map

Social Media The FMCS has a Facebook account. https://www.facebook.com/fmcs.usa

The FMCS tweets announcements and other newsworthy items on Twitter. https://twitter.com/FMCS_USA

The FMCS posts videos on its YouTube channel. https://www.youtube.com/user/FMCSInfo

The Sources of Information were updated 8–2019.

Federal Reserve System

Twentieth Street and Constitution Avenue NW., Washington, DC 20551
Phone, 202-452-3000. Internet, http://www.federalreserve.gov

Board of Governors of the Federal Reserve System

Chair	JEROME H. POWELL
Vice Chair	RICHARD H. CLARIDA
Vice Chair for Supervision	RANDAL K. QUARLES
Governors	
	MICHELLE W. BOWMAN
	LAEL BRAINARD
	(VACANCY)
	(VACANCY)
Assistant to the Board and Director https://www.federalreserve.gov/aboutthefed/bios/board/default.htm	MICHELLE A. SMITH

Federal Reserve Bank Presidents

New York	JOHN C. WILLIAMS
Atlanta	RAPHAEL W. BOSTIC
Boston	ERIC S. ROSENGREN
Chicago	CHARLES L. EVANS
Cleveland	LORETTA J. MESTER
Dallas	ROBERT S. KAPLAN
Kansas City	ESTHER L. GEORGE
Minneapolis	NEEL T. KASHKARI
Philadelphia	PATRICK T. HARKER
Richmond	THOMAS I. BARKIN
San Francisco	MARY C. DALY
St. Louis	JAMES B. BULLARD
https://www.federalreserve.gov/aboutthefed/federal-reserve-system-new-york.htm	

Official Staff

Chief Operating Officer	MICHELL C. CLARK, ACTING
General Counsel	MARK E. VAN DER WEIDE
Secretary	ANN E. MISBACK
Directors Of Divisions	
Consumer and Community Affairs	ERIC S. BELSKY
Financial Management	RICARDO A. AGUILERA
Financial Stability	ANDREAS W. LEHNERT
Information Technology	SHARON L. MOWRY

International Finance
Management
Monetary Affairs
Research and Statistics
Reserve Bank Operations and Payment Systems
Supervision and Regulation
https://www.federalreserve.gov/aboutthefed/officialstaff.htm

Steven B. Kamin
Michell C. Clark
Thomas Laubach
Stacey M. Tevlin
Matthew J. Eichner
Michael S. Gibson

Inspector General
https://oig.federalreserve.gov/the-inspector-general.htm

Mark Bialek

The above list of key personnel was updated 4–2019.

The Federal Reserve System keeps the Nation's monetary and financial system flexible, safe, and stable.

Establishment and Purpose   The Federal Reserve Act (12 U.S.C. 221), approved December 23, 1913, established the Federal Reserve System (FRS).

The FRS strengthens and vitalizes the U.S. economy. By influencing the lending and investing of depository institutions and the cost and availability of money and credit, the FRS promotes the full use of human and capital resources, the growth of productivity, relatively stable prices, and equilibrium in the Nation's international balance of payments. The agency's supervisory and regulatory banking functions help maintain a commercial banking system that responds to the Nation's financial needs and objectives. https://www.federalreserve.gov/faqs/about_12594.htm

Structure   The FRS comprises the Board of Governors; the 12 Federal reserve banks and their branches and other facilities; the Federal Open Market Committee; the Federal Advisory Council; the Consumer Advisory Council; the Thrift Institutions Advisory Council; and the Nation's financial institutions, including commercial banks, savings and loan associations, mutual savings banks, and credit unions. https://www.federalreserve.gov/aboutthefed/structure-federal-reserve-system.htm

Board of Governors   The Board comprises seven members whom the President appoints by the advice and with the consent of the Senate. The President also designates a chair and two vice chairs by the advice and with the consent of the Senate. The Chair of the Board is a member of the National Advisory Council on International Monetary and Financial Policies, which is chaired by the Secretary of the Department of the Treasury. The Board determines general monetary, credit, and operating policies for the FRS as a whole and formulates the rules and regulations for carrying out the purposes of the Federal Reserve Act. The Board's principal duties consist of monitoring credit conditions; supervising the Federal reserve banks, member banks, and bank holding companies; and regulating the implementation of some consumer credit protection laws.

Within statutory limitations, the Board has the power to fix the requirements for reserves that depository institutions maintain on transaction accounts or nonpersonal time deposits (an interest-bearing bank deposit account that has a date of maturity, such as a certificate of deposit). The Board reviews and determines the discount rate charged by the Federal reserve banks. For the purpose of preventing excessive credit use for the purchase or carrying of securities, the Board regulates the amount of credit that may be initially extended and subsequently maintained on securities (with certain exceptions). http://www.federalreserve.gov/aboutthefed/bios/board/boardmembership.htm

Federal Open Market Committee (FOMC)   The Committee comprises the Board of Governors and five of the presidents of the Federal reserve banks. The Chair of the Board of Governors is traditionally the Chair of the FOMC. The president of the Federal Reserve Bank of New York serves as a permanent member. Four of the other 11 reserve bank presidents rotate annually as voting members of the FOMC.

The Federal reserve banks carry out open market operations in accordance with regulations that the FOMC adopts and pursuant to specific policy directives that it issues. Purchases and sales of securities in the open market are undertaken to supply bank reserves for supporting the credit and money needed for long-term economic growth, for offsetting cyclical economic swings, and for accommodating seasonal business and consumer demand for money and credit. These operations are carried out principally in U.S. Government obligations, but they also include purchases and sales of Federal agency obligations. The Federal Reserve Bank of New York executes transactions for the FRS open market account.

Under the FOMC's direction, the Federal Reserve Bank of New York also undertakes transactions in foreign currencies for the FRS open market account. These operations are meant to safeguard the value of the dollar in international exchange markets and facilitate growth in international liquidity in accordance with the needs of an expanding world economy. https://www.federalreserve.gov/aboutthefed/structure-federal-open-market-committee.htm

Federal Reserve Banks   The 12 reserve banks and their branches function as the operating arms of the FRS. Each reserve bank operates within its own geographic area, or district, of the United States and gathers data and other information on the businesses and the needs of local communities in that district. The FOMC and Board of Governors then factor that information into monetary policy and other decisions. https://www.federalreserve.gov/aboutthefed/structure-federal-reserve-banks.htm

Activities

In addition to implementing monetary policy, the FRS supervises and regulates banks, transfers funds, handles Government deposits and debt issues, and acts as lender of last resort. https://www.federalreserve.gov/aboutthefed/pf.htm

Conducting Monetary Policy   The FRS seeks price stability, moderate long-term interest rates, and maximum employment. Under normal economic conditions, the FOMC sets monetary policy by selecting an interest rate. To a bank, that interest rate is the cost of holding reserves. (Reserves are funds held by depository institutions as cash in their vaults or as deposits with their regional Federal reserve bank.) In recent years, the FRS has set a target, or target range, for the Federal funds rate, which is the interest rate that commercial banks charge each other for borrowing reserves for short periods. The open market desk at the Federal Reserve Bank of New York then conducts open market operations—buying or selling U.S. Treasury securities—to change the amount of reserves in the banking system to adjust the Federal funds rate. Since the Federal funds rate is the price of borrowing reserves, open market operations bring the actual Federal funds rate in line with the FOMC's target. The strategy to vary the quantity or the price of reserves in the banking system defines FRS monetary policy. https://www.federalreserve.gov/monetarypolicy.htm

Financial Supervision and Regulation   Supervision refers to the oversight and enforcement of regulations to ensure safe and sound banking behavior. The FRS's supervisory and regulatory actions help to build confidence in the banking system. Protecting the integrity of the Nation's financial institutions, fostering stability in financial markets, ensuring compliance with applicable laws and regulations, and encouraging banking institutions to meet responsibly the financial needs of their communities, promote financial stability. The FRS supervises and regulates State member banks (State chartered banks that have chosen to become members of the FRS) and bank and financial holding companies (companies that own banks). The agency also supervises overseas and international operations of regulated financial institutions. Foreign banks with U.S. branches, agencies, and nonbank operations are also subject to supervision. The FRS's banking supervision and regulation units work with other regulators and authorities to ensure that regulations are uniformly applied and consistently enforced throughout the

banking system. https://www.federalreserve.
gov/supervisionreg.htm

Payment Services   The FRS provides
payment services, including processing
checks and electronic payments, to
commercial banks and other depository
institutions. The FRS operates a nationwide
check clearing system. Traditionally,
depository institutions sent the actual paper
checks that they had received to reserve
banks, which processed and routed them
to the originating depository institution
for collection. These institutions used
their Federal reserve accounts to settle the
transactions. Since enactment of the Check
Clearing for the 21st Century Act (Check
21) in 2004, many institutions are using
electronic check clearing options. Check 21
enabled reserve banks to employ electronic
image-based solutions for the exchange of
check data between depository institutions.
Ongoing industry advances continue to
improve the process of check clearing and to
renew the FRS's role in that process.

The FRS provides two types of electronic
payment services: fund transfers (Fedwire)
and the Automated Clearinghouse (ACH).
Fedwire processes payments of all sizes
up to a maximum of just less than $10
billion. ACH is used mostly for recurring
payments, such as business payrolls,
consumer insurance payments, and the U.S.
Government's military and civilian payrolls
and Social Security benefits. https://www.
federalreserve.gov/paymentsystems.htm

Protecting and Educating Consumers   The
FRS has consumer protection
responsibilities. The agency writes consumer
protection regulations for the financial
industry and enforces consumer protection
and civil rights laws and regulations at the
banks that it supervises. Community affairs
offices across the FRS promote community
development and fair and impartial access to
credit. In each district of the FRS, economic
education offices increase the public's
understanding of the role that the FRS plays
in the economy.

**Services for the Department of the
Treasury**   As banker and fiscal agent for
the Department of the Treasury, the FRS
provides services for the Government,
primarily through depository institutions.
Federal reserve banks provide the Treasury
with a checking account. When the
Government makes a payment by check
or electronically, that payment is usually
cashed by or deposited in a commercial
bank or similar institution. The FRS
processes the payment and deducts the
amount from the Treasury's account.
Although the Treasury usually keeps the
money received from tax payments on
deposit at commercial banks, it transfers
funds to a Federal reserve bank as needed
to make payments. The Federal Government
has saved money and improved its service
to the public by using the FRS's electronic
payments network. Most regular Federal
Government payments, such as Social
Security benefits and the Government
payroll, are direct deposits made through
the FRS's automated clearinghouse service.

Acting as the U.S. fiscal agent, reserve
banks sell, transfer, and redeem Government
securities; make interest payments on these
securities; and assist the Treasury and other
Federal Government agencies with their
securities in other ways. These actions are
done electronically through a system called
"Treasury Direct." The Treasury and Federal
agencies reimburse the reserve banks for
expenses associated with these fiscal agency
functions.

Most currency enters circulation and
exits circulation through the Federal reserve
banks. As the public demands currency from
the banking system, depository institutions
draw down their accounts at the reserve
banks in exchange for additional currency.
When currency from the public flows back
into depository institutions, those institutions
deposit the surplus in their reserve banks.
The Department of the Treasury designs
and produces U.S. paper money and coin.
As the Treasury produces currency, reserve
banks put the new money into circulation
to meet public needs. The FRS also destroys
money that is no longer fit for circulation. By
crediting the Government's account, reserve
banks "buy" new paper money and coin
from the Treasury to replace the notes that
they destroy and coin that they return to the
U.S. Mint.

Sources of Information

A–Z Index   An alphabetical subject index helps visitors navigate the website's content. https://www.federalreserve.gov/azindex.htm

Beige Book   The "Summary of Commentary on Current Economic Conditions by Federal Reserve District" is published eight times per year. Each Federal reserve bank gathers anecdotal information on current economic conditions in its district through reports from bank and branch directors and interviews with key business contacts, economists, market experts, and other sources. The "Summary" or "Beige Book" summarizes this information by district and sector. The Federal Reserve Bank of Minneapolis maintains an online "Beige Book" archives whose content goes back to 1970. https://www.minneapolisfed.org/news-and-events/beige-book-archive

Business Opportunities   The FRS generally relies on competitive bidding procedures for purchasing supplies and acquiring services. The process involves issuing a solicitation. Companies respond by submitting bids. The agency awards contracts after evaluating the bidders' prices, and in some cases, their technical abilities. http://www.federalreserve.gov/aboutthefed/procurement/about.htm

Calendar   An electronic calendar of FRS events, past and future, is available online.

Career Opportunities   The FRS relies on attorneys, economists, financial analysts, research assistants, information technology experts, and other skilled professionals to carry out its mission. https://www.federalreserve.gov/careers.htm

Consumer Help   The FRS can help a consumer who is having a problem with a bank or other financial institution. Phone, 888-851-1920. TTY, 877-766-8533. Fax, 877-888-2520. https://www.federalreserveconsumerhelp.gov/

Contact Information   To speak with an FRS operator, call 202-452-3000. TDD, 202-263-4869. https://www.federalreserve.gov/aboutthefed/contact-us-topics.htm

Currency Academy   The U.S. Currency Education Program website runs the online Currency Academy, where learning about U.S. currency, or money, is fun. https://www.uscurrency.gov/educational-materials/classrooms/currency-academy

Fine Arts   Like all Federal agencies, the Board of Governors may receive gifts of artwork and funds to purchase art. In 1975, former Chairman Arthur F. Burns established the agency's fine arts program. He was responding to President Richard Nixon's urgent desire to continue the development of "the growing partnership between Government and the arts." Chairman Burns created the program to collect and care for artwork and to organize exhibitions in the historic Marriner S. Eccles building. The collection holds more than 1,000 works of art that private individuals have donated. To view a gallery of the Board's permanent collection, visit the "Fine Arts Program" page. https://www.federalreserve.gov/aboutthefed/aroundtheboard/fine-arts.htm

Freedom of Information Act (FOIA)   A request for information may be submitted online with an electronic request form; made in writing and mailed to the Information Disclosure Section, Board of Governors of the Federal Reserve System, 20th and Constitution Avenue NW., Washington, DC 20551; or sent by facsimile to the Information Disclosure Section. Fax, 202-872-7565. https://www.federalreserve.gov/foia/request.htm

The FRS has a FOIA service center to help information seekers learn about the status of a FOIA request or get answers to questions regarding the freedom of information process. The center is open from 9:00 a.m. to 5:00 p.m., Monday–Friday. Phone, 202-452-3684. https://www.federalreserve.gov/foia/servicecenter.htm

The FRS maintains electronic FOIA reading rooms. Before submitting a FOIA request, a requester should browse or search the content of the online reading rooms to ensure that the desired information is not already accessible immediately and free of charge. https://www.federalreserve.gov/foia/readingrooms.htm

Frequently Asked Questions (FAQs)   The FRS posts answers to FAQs on its website. https://www.federalreserve.gov/faqs.htm

Glossary   The Federal Reserve Bank of Richmond included a short glossary in its 16th edition (2012) of "The Federal Reserve Today." The glossary starts on page 35. https://www.richmondfed.org/-/media/

richmondfedorg/publications/education/
federal_reserve_today/frtoday.pdf

History   "Hello! This is Liberty speaking—
billions of dollars are needed and needed
NOW." That message came from Lady
Liberty, according to a World War I era
depiction of her. To learn more about the
role that the FRS played in financing World
War I, visit the "Federal Reserve History"
website. https://www.federalreservehistory.
org/essays/liberty_bonds

In 1957, shortly after the U.S. Congress
had enacted a law making "In God We
Trust" the official national motto, the first
dollar bills bearing the same four words
entered circulation. To learn more about
the history of American currency, visit the
U.S. Currency Education Program's history
section. https://www.uscurrency.gov/history

Interest Rates   As part of the "Fed
Listens" series, the Federal Reserve Bank
of Chicago hosted a conference (June
2019) on monetary policy strategy, tools,
and communication practices. Chair of
the Board of Governors Jerome H. Powell
gave the opening remarks and spoke about
the effective lower bound of interest rates
and monetary policy tools. https://www.
chicagofed.org/conference-sessions/opening-
remarks-1

Monetary Policy   The Federal Reserve
Board prepares a semiannual report that
discusses monetary policy management,
economic developments, and future
prospects. It submits this report, which is
called the "Monetary Policy Report," to the
Senate Committee on Banking, Housing,
and Urban Affairs and to the House
Committee on Financial Services. https://
www.federalreserve.gov/monetarypolicy/
mpr_default.htm

As part of the "Fed Listens" series,
Governor Lael Brainard participated in a
community listening session at the Federal
Reserve Bank of Richmond (May 2019). Her
short presentation was titled "How Does
Monetary Policy Affect Your Community?"
https://www.federalreserve.gov/newsevents/
speech/brainard20190508a.htm

News / Events   The FRS posts press releases,
speeches, and testimonies online. https://
www.federalreserve.gov/newsevents.htm

Open Government   The FRS supports
the Open Government initiative by

promoting collaboration, participation, and
transparency. https://www.federalreserve.
gov/open/open.htm

Organizational Chart   An organizational
chart is accessible in Portable Document
Format on the "Structure of the Federal
Reserve System" web page under "Board
Responsibilities." https://www.federalreserve.
gov/aboutthefed/structure-federal-reserve-
board.htm

Photo Gallery   The FRS posts
photographs on its website. High
resolution images are available on
its Flickr photostream. https://www.
federalreserve.gov/photogallery.htm

Publications   The FRS posts its publications
online. The agency's most requested
publications are its annual report, "Monetary
Policy Report," supervision manuals, and
"The Federal Reserve System Purposes and
Functions." http://www.federalreserve.gov/
publications/default.htm

Quantitative Easing   Michael T. Kiley's
working paper "Quantitative Easing and
the 'New Normal' in Monetary Policy" is
meant to stimulate discussion and critical
comment on the economic effects of
applying this monetary policy tool. https://
www.federalreserve.gov/econres/feds/
files/2018004pap.pdf

Recent Postings   The most recent postings
of the FRS are available on a single web
page. https://www.federalreserve.gov/
recentpostings.htm

Site Map   The website map allows visitors
to look for specific topics or to browse
for content that aligns with their interests.
https://www.federalreserve.gov/sitemap.htm

Social Media   The FRS maintains a
presence on Facebook, Flickr, LinkedIn,
Twitter, and YouTube. https://www.
federalreserve.gov/aboutthefed/contact-us-
topics.htm

Tariffs   "The Beige Book: Summary
of Commentary on Current Economic
Conditions by Federal Reserve District"
of May 2019 mentions tariffs 29 times.
The summary contains 29 pages of
commentary. https://www.federalreserve.gov/
monetarypolicy/files/BeigeBook_20190605.
pdf

What Is The Fed?   The Federal Reserve,
which is often referred to as "the Fed," serves
as the central bank of the United States.

The U.S. Congress created the Fed in 1913 to promote a safer and sounder monetary and financial system for the Nation. To learn more about the Fed, watch the 3-minute video. https://www.youtube.com/watch?v=wLyh5fSTLLw

The Sources of Information were updated 6–2019.

Federal Retirement Thrift Investment Board

77 K Street NE., Washington, DC 20002
Phone, 202-942-1600. Fax, 202-942-1676. Internet, http://www.frtib.gov

Board Members

Chair	MICHAEL D. KENNEDY
	DANA K. BILYEU
	WILLIAM S. JASIEN
	DAVID A. JONES
	RONALD D. MCCRAY

https://www.frtib.gov/BoardMembers/index.html

Management

Executive Director	RAVINDRA DEO
Chief Officers	
Financial	SUSAN C. CROWDER
Investment	RAVINDRA DEO, ACTING
Operating	SUZANNE TOSINI
Risk	JAY AHUJA
Technology	SUZANNE TOSINI, ACTING
Directors	
Communications and Education	JAMES COURTNEY
Enterprise Planning	RENÉE WILDER GUERIN
Enterprise Risk Management	JAY AHUJA
External Affairs	KIMBERLY A. WEAVER
Participant Operations and Policy	GUADALUPE RAMOS
Resource Management	GISILE GOETHE
General Counsel	MEGAN GRUMBINE

The above list of key personnel was updated 12–2017.

The Federal Retirement Thrift Investment Board administers the Thrift Savings Plan in the interest of its participants and beneficiaries.

The Federal Retirement Thrift Investment Board (FRTIB) was established as an independent agency by the Federal Employees' Retirement System Act of 1986 (5 U.S.C. 8351 and 8401–79). The act vests responsibility for the agency in six named fiduciaries: the Executive Director and the five members of the FRTIB.

With the advice and consent of the Senate, the President appoints two board members. The President also appoints the remaining three members and designates one of them as the Chair. Board members serve on a part-time basis, and they appoint the Executive Director, who is responsible for managing the agency and the Thrift Savings Plan (TSP).

Activities

The TSP is a tax-deferred, defined contribution plan that constitutes one of the three components of the Federal Employees' Retirement System (FERS). Employees participating in the FERS accumulate savings through the TSP and combine those savings with retirement income from the two other components: Social Security benefits and the FERS Annuity. Employees participating in the Civil Service Retirement System (CSRS) and members of the uniformed services also may take advantage of the TSP to supplement their annuities. https://www.youtube.com/watch?v=XnIQZa7g_d4

The FRTIB operates the TSP and manages the investments of the Thrift Savings Fund for the benefit of participants and their beneficiaries. These operational and management responsibilities include maintaining an account for each TSP participant, making loans, purchasing annuity contracts, and providing for the payment of benefits. https://www.tsp.gov/index.shtml

Sources of Information

Announcements / News   To keep abreast of current TSP developments, visit the "What's New" web page. https://www.tsp.gov/whatsnew/index.html

Career Opportunities   To carry out its mission, the FRTIB relies on financial experts, tax attorneys, and other professionals who possess diverse skills and expertise. https://www.frtib.gov/Careers/index.html

In 2016, the FRTIB ranked 14th among 29 small agencies in the Partnership for Public Service's Best Places To Work Agency Rankings. http://bestplacestowork.org/BPTW/rankings/overall/small

Expense Ratio   The net TSP expense ratio represents the amount that TSP administrative expenses reduce the investment returns of participants. https://www.tsp.gov/InvestmentFunds/FundsOverview/expenseRatio.html

Federal Employees' Retirement System (FERS)   The "U.S. Code" is the codification by subject matter of the general and permanent laws of the United States. Title 5, Chapter 84, of the "U.S. Code" describes the FERS. http://uscode.house.gov/view.xhtml?path=/prelim@title5/part3/subpartG/chapter84&edition=prelim

Forms   The TSP website has a collection of forms that are categorized by topic and by form number for civil service employees. Each form is available in Portable Document Format for viewing and downloading. https://www.tsp.gov/forms/civilianForms.html

The TSP website has a collection of forms that are categorized by topic and by form number for members of the uniformed services. Each form is available in Portable Document Format for viewing and downloading. https://www.tsp.gov/forms/uniformedServicesForms.html

Freedom of Information Act (FOIA)   Before making a FOIA request, consult the FRTIB's "Freedom of Information Act Guide." It is accessible online in Portable Document Format (PDF). https://www.frtib.gov/ReadingRoom/FOIA/e-read_guide.pdf | Email: foiarequest@tsp.gov

Frequently Asked Questions (FAQs)   The TSP posts answers to FAQs on its website. https://www.tsp.gov/sitehelp/content/index.html

Glossary   The TSP website has a glossary of terms. https://www.tsp.gov/sitehelp/content/glossary.html

History   In 1987, the TSP received its first participant contributions. Since that time, it has grown into the largest defined contribution retirement plan in the world. Read what former Executive Director Gregory T. Long had to say about the TSP's inception and growth during its first 30 years. https://www.tsp.gov/PDF/formspubs/high17a.pdf

The U.S. Congress established the TSP by passing the Federal Employees' Retirement System Act of 1986. The TSP offers the same types of savings and tax benefits that private corporations offer to their employees. To learn more, visit the "Purpose and History" web page. https://www.tsp.gov/PlanParticipation/AboutTheTSP/index.html

A history of TSP share prices is available online. https://www.tsp.gov/InvestmentFunds/FundPerformance/index.html

Investment Strategy   Account consolidation, compounding, and tax deferral can maximize retirement savings. Learn more about taking advantage of these benefits by visiting the "Maximize Your Retirement Savings" section of the TSP website. https://www.tsp.gov/PlanningTools/InvestmentStrategy/retirementsavings/index.html

Meeting Minutes Starting with the year 2007 and continuing to the present, minutes of the meetings of FRTIB members are available online. https://www.frtib.gov/MeetingMinutes/index.html

Newsletter Archive The TSP posts issues of its newsletter "Highlights" on its website. Beginning with the year 2009, issues are available in Portable Document Format (PDF) for viewing and downloading. https://www.tsp.gov/forms/newsletterArchive.html

Publications The TSP posts publications online in Portable Document Format (PDF) on its "All Publications" web page. https://www.tsp.gov/forms/allPublications.html

Reading Room FOIA reports, frequently requested records, press releases, regulations, reports to Congress, statements, surveys, and more are accessible in the electronic reading room. https://www.frtib.gov/ReadingRoom/index.html

Retirement Planning and Tools The TSP website has information and tools for retirement planning. https://www.tsp.gov/PlanningTools/index.html

Site Map The TSP site map allows visitors to look for specific topics or to browse content that aligns with their interests. https://www.tsp.gov/other/sitemap/siteMap.html

Social Media The TSP has a Facebook account. https://www.facebook.com/tsp4gov

The TSP tweets announcements and other newsworthy items on Twitter. https://twitter.com/tsp4gov

The TSP posts videos on its YouTube channel. https://www.youtube.com/user/tsp4gov

Website Orientation An orientation video of the TSP website is available online. https://www.tsp.gov/ParticipantSupport/Content/index.html; https://www.frtib.gov/contacts.html

For further information, contact the Office of External Affairs, Federal Retirement Thrift Investment Board, 77 K Street NE., Washington, DC 20002. Phone, 202-942-1640.

Federal Trade Commission

600 Pennsylvania Avenue NW., Washington, DC 20580
Phone, 202-326-2222. Internet, http://www.ftc.gov

Chair	MAUREEN K. OHLHAUSEN, ACTING
Commissioner	TERRELL MCSWEENY
Commissioner	(VACANCY)
Commissioner	(VACANCY)
Commissioner	(VACANCY)
Chief of Staff	SVETLANA GANS
Executive Director	DAVID B ROBBINS
Chief Administrative Law Judge	D. MICHAEL CHAPPELL
Director, Bureau of Competition	MARKUS H. MEIER, ACTING
Director, Bureau of Consumer Protection	THOMAS B. PAHL, ACTING
Director, Bureau of Economics	MICHAEL G. VITA, ACTING
Director, Office of Congressional Relations	JEANNE BUMPUS
Director, Office of Equal Employment Opportunity and Workplace Inclusion	KEVIN D. WILLIAMS
Director, Office of International Affairs	RANDOLPH W. TRITELL
Director, Office of Policy Planning	TARA ISA KOSLOV, ACTING
Director, Office of Public Affairs	PETER KAPLAN, ACTING
General Counsel	DAVID C. SHONKA, ACTING
Inspector General	ROSLYN MAZER
Secretary of the Commission	DONALD S. CLARK

[For the Federal Trade Commission statement of organization, see the Code of Federal Regulations, Title 16, Part 0]

The Federal Trade Commission protects America's consumers and enforces laws prohibiting anticompetitive, deceptive, or unfair business practices.

The Federal Trade Commission (FTC) was established in 1914 by the Federal Trade Commission Act (15 U.S.C. 41-58). The Commission comprises five members whom the President appoints with the advice and consent of the Senate for 7-year terms. No more than three of the Commissioners may be members of the same political party. The President designates one of them as Chair of the Commission to oversee its administrative management.

Activities

The FTC protects consumers and promotes competition in broad sectors of the economy. It safeguards and strengthens free and open markets and helps consumers make informed choices. The FTC carries out its mission by using a variety of tools: consumer and business education, law enforcement, research, rulemaking, and studies of marketplace trends and legal developments. The FTC envisions a vigorously competitive U.S. economy offering accessible and accurate information to consumers, an economy yielding high-quality products at competitive prices and fostering efficiency, innovation, and consumer choice. https:// www.ftc.gov/about-ftc

Competition   The FTC prevents anticompetitive mergers and works to keep the marketplace free from anticompetitive business practices. To promote competition, the FTC engages in six law enforcement-related activities: premerger notification, merger and joint venture enforcement, merger and joint venture compliance, nonmerger enforcement, nonmerger compliance, and antitrust policy. Policy initiatives, research, and business guidance and education also play a role in promoting competition. https://www.ftc.gov/about-ftc/ bureaus-offices/bureau-competition

Consumer Protection   The FTC brings a variety of consumer protection cases and works with State attorneys general and other State and local consumer protection officials. To protect consumers, it relies on five law enforcement functions: privacy and identity protection, financial practices,

marketing practices, advertising practices, and enforcement. Policy initiatives, research, and business and consumer education also enhance protection. https://www.ftc.gov/ about-ftc/bureaus-offices/bureau-consumer-protection

Enforcement   The FTC's law enforcement activities foster voluntary compliance with the law, but also include formal administrative or Federal court litigation leading to mandatory orders against offenders.

The FTC can issue an administrative complaint or authorize the filing of a Federal district court complaint charging a person, partnership, or corporation with violating one or more of the statutes that the FTC enforces. If the charges are not contested, settled by consent of the parties, or found to be true after an administrative hearing or a Federal court trial, an administrative law judge or Federal court judge will issue an order requiring discontinuance of the unlawful practices. The FTC also may request that a U.S. district court issue preliminary relief to halt allegedly unfair or deceptive practices, to prevent an anticompetitive merger or unfair methods of competition from taking place, or to prevent violations of any statute that the FTC enforces, pending the full adjudication of the matter. In Federal court, the FTC may obtain other relief, including monetary redress. An order issued after an administrative or Federal court proceeding that requires the respondent to cease and desist or take other corrective action may be appealed. https:// www.ftc.gov/enforcement

International Affairs   With other nations and international organizations, the FTC promotes sound competition and consumer protection policies and provides technical assistance to nurture competition and enable consumer protection agencies to perform their missions. https://www.ftc.gov/policy/ international

Sources of Information

Antitrust Violations   To report an antitrust violation, contact the Bureau of Competition's Office of Policy and

Coordination. Phone, 202-326-3300. https://www.ftc.gov/faq/competition/report-antitrust-violation | Email: antitrust@ftc.gov

Business Opportunities For information on contracts and procurement, contact the Assistant Chief Financial Officer for Acquisitions. Phone, 202-326-2339. Fax, 202-326-3529. https://www.ftc.gov/about-ftc/bureaus-offices/office-executive-director/financial-management-office/acquisition-branch

Career Opportunities To carry out its mission, the FTC relies on attorneys, investigators, and specialists in financial management, information technology, public affairs, public policy, and in other fields. The agency posts current job vacancies on its Web site. Information on benefits, diversity, working at the FTC, and the application process is also accessible online. For additional information, contact the Human Capital Management Office. Phone, 202-326-2021. TTY, 202-326-3422. https://www.ftc.gov/about-ftc/careers-ftc

The Partnership for Public Service categorizes the FTC as a midsize agency. In the Partnership's 2016 Best Places To Work in the Federal Government rankings, the FTC improved its index score and placed fifth in its category. http://bestplacestowork.org/BPTW/rankings/detail/FT00

Consumer Complaints The FTC relies on complaints from consumers to detect patterns of abuse and fraud. A complaint may be filed in English or Spanish and online or by phone. The FTC enters complaints into Consumer Sentinel, a secure online database that civil and criminal law enforcement agencies in the U.S. and abroad can access. Phone, 877-382-4357. https://www.ftccomplaintassistant.gov

Credit Reports The Fair Credit Reporting Act requires each of the nationwide credit reporting companies to provide a free credit report, upon request, once every 12 months. https://www.consumer.ftc.gov/articles/0155-free-credit-reports

Do Not Call Registry Register a home or mobile phone for free on the National Do Not Call Registry to eliminate most telemarketing calls. https://www.donotcall.gov

Freedom of Information Act (FOIA) Enacted in 1966, the FOIA generally provides that any Individual has the right to make a request for Federal agency records or information; all Federal Government agencies are required to disclose records upon receiving a written request for them; nine exemptions, in addition to limits to FOIA, shield certain records from disclosure. The Federal FOIA does not provide access to records that State or local government agencies hold, or that private businesses or individuals hold. https://www.ftc.gov/about-ftc/foia

History American Presidents are a part of the FTC's history. To learn which President helped pave the way toward the Commission's creation, whose signature approved the Federal Trade Commission Act, which President literally helped with the building, and which 21st-century President paid a visit to the FTC, see the "Our History" Web page. https://www.ftc.gov/about-ftc/our-history

Identity Theft Use IdentiftyTheft.gov to report identity theft and formulate a personal recovery plan. https://www.identitytheft.gov

Open Government The FTC supports the Open Government initiative by promoting the principles of collaboration, participation, and transparency. https://www.ftc.gov/site-information/open-government

Organizational Chart The FTC's organizational chart is available in Portable Document Format (PDF) for viewing and downloading. https://www.ftc.gov/system/files/attachments/about-ftc/orgchart_ftc_july_18_2017_0.pdf

Publications Blog updates, newsletters, and press releases are posted online. Free consumer and business education publications are available from the Consumer Response Center, Federal Trade Commission, Washington, DC 20580. Phone, 877-382-4357. TTY, 866-653-4261. https://www.ftc.gov/stay-connected

Regional Offices A map of the seven FTC regions—East Central, Midwest, Northeast, Northwest, Southeast, Southwest, and Western—and contact information for the regional offices representing them are available online. https://www.ftc.gov/about-ftc/bureaus-offices/regional-offices

Scam Alerts   Stay abreast of new scams with the latest information and practical tips. An online subscription form is available to receive scam alerts by email. https://www.consumer.ftc.gov/scam-alerts

Workshops   Information on conferences and workshops is available online. https://www.ftc.gov/news-events; https://www.ftc.gov/contact | Email: opa@ftc.gov

For further information, contact the Office of Public Affairs, Federal Trade Commission, 600 Pennsylvania Avenue NW., Washington, DC 20580. Phone, 202-326-2180. Fax, 202-326-3366.

General Services Administration

1800 F Street NW., Washington, DC 20405
Internet, http://www.gsa.gov

Administrator	EMILY W. MURPHY
Deputy Administrator	ALLISON F. BRIGATI, ACTING
Chief of Staff	JACK ST. JOHN
National Service Commissioners	
Federal Acquisition Service	ALAN THOMAS
Public Buildings Service	DANIEL MATHEWS
Technology Transformation Service	(VACANCY)
https://www.gsa.gov/about-us/organization/gsa-leadership-directory	

Office Heads

Associate Administrator, Civil Rights	MADELINE C. CALIENDO
Associate Administrator, Congressional and Intergovernmental Affairs	P. BRENNAN HART III
Associate Administrator, Customer Experience	ANAHITA REILLY
Associate Administrator, Government-wide Policy	GIANCARLO BRIZZI, ACTING
Associate Administrator, Mission Assurance	ROBERT J. CARTER
Associate Administrator, Small Business Utilization	CHARLES MANGER
Associate Administrator, Strategic Communication	BENJAMIN KENNEY
Chief Administrative Services Officer	CYNTHIA A. METZLER
Chief Financial Officer	GERARD BADORREK
Chief Human Capital Officer	ANTONIA T. HARRIS
Chief Information Officer	DAVID A. SHIVE
General Counsel	JACK ST. JOHN, ACTING
White House Liaison	MICHAEL R. DOWNING

Regional Service Administrators

Region 1–New England	GLENN ROTONDO, ACTING
Region 2–Northeast and Caribbean	JEFF LAU, ACTING
Region 3–Mid-Atlantic	DENA MCLAUGHLIN, ACTING
Region 4–Southeast Sunbelt	LIANA D. HENRY, ACTING
Region 5–Great Lakes	JOHN COOKE, ACTING
Region 6–Heartland	KEVIN ROTHMIER, ACTING
Region 7–Greater Southwest	GEORGE PROCHASKA, ACTING
Region 8–Rocky Mountain	PENNY GROUT, ACTING
Region 9–Pacific Rim	DAN BROWN, ACTING
Region 10–Northwest / Arctic	CHAUN BENJAMIN, ACTING

General Services Administration

Region 11–National Capital

HOUSTON TAYLOR, ACTING

Independent Office Heads

Chair, Civilian Board of Contract Appeals
http://www.cbca.gsa.gov/index.html

JERI K. SOMERS

Inspector General
https://www.gsaig.gov

CAROL F. OCHOA

[For the General Services Administration statement of organization, see the Code of Federal Regulations, Title 41, Part 105-53]

The above list of key personnel was updated 12–2017.

The General Services Administration strives to obtain the highest value in acquisition, real estate, and technology services for the Federal Government and the American people.

The General Services Administration (GSA) was established by section 101 of the Federal Property and Administrative Services Act of 1949 (40 U.S.C. 751). http://www.gsa.gov/portal/category/21354

Technology Transformation Service   The Technology Transformation Service (TTS) improves the public's experience with the Government by the application of modern methodologies and technologies. It offers services that exemplify accessibility, effectiveness, and efficiency, and it assists other Federal agencies with making their services more accessible, effective, and efficient. The TTS also builds technology applications, platforms, processes, and software solutions; it makes these products available to other agencies; and it shares technology personnel with them. The TTS comprises the Offices of Acquisitions and of Investment, the Presidential Innovation Fellowship, product and services teams, a product incubator, and the technology advisory-advocacy team. http://www.gsa.gov/portal/category/25729

USAGov helps Federal agencies develop consumer information, promote it, and disseminate it. The USAGov platform gives Americans greater ability to connect—via email, publications, social media, web sites and web chat, and phone calls to the contact center—with their Government and to access the services that it offers. USAGov makes Government information easily accessible to U.S. citizens and the public at large through a variety of resources. (See the Sources of Information below for additional USA.gov links.) https://www.usa.gov

Contract Appeals   The Civilian Board of Contract Appeals hears and decides contract disputes between Government contractors and civilian executive agencies under the provisions of the Contract Disputes Act. The Board's authority extends to all agencies of the Federal Government except the Department of Defense and its constituent agencies, National Aeronautics and Space Administration, U.S. Postal Service, Postal Regulatory Commission, and Tennessee Valley Authority. The Board promotes alternative dispute resolution as a way of resolving contract disputes efficiently, inexpensively, and promptly. When jointly

USA.Gov Web Sites	Description of Content
https://www.usa.gov	General Government information
https://kids.usa.gov	Government information for kids
http://www.publications.usa.gov	Government informational publications
http://www.digitalgov.gov	Information to help Government agencies enhance customer experience
https://www.challenge.gov/list	Government challenges that are posted for the public to help solve and win prizes
http://www.data.gov	Accessible and readable Government datasets
https://gobierno.usa.gov	General Government information in Spanish

requested by an agency and its contractor, the Board also provides alternative dispute resolution services on contract-related matters not covered by the Contract Disputes Act to executive agencies.

The Board also hears and decides other classes of cases. These other classes include cases arising under the Indian Self-Determination Act, disputes between insurance companies and the Department of Agriculture's Risk Management Agency involving actions of the Federal Crop Insurance Corporation, claims by Federal employees for reimbursement of expenses incurred while on official temporary duty travel or in connection with relocation to a new duty station, claims by carriers or freight forwarders involving actions of the GSA regarding payment for transportation services, applications by prevailing private parties for recovery of litigation and other costs under the Equal Access to Justice Act, and requests for arbitration to resolve disputes between applicants and the Federal Emergency Management Agency as to funding for public assistance applications arising from damage caused by Hurricanes Katrina and Rita. http://www.cbca.gsa.gov

For further information, contact the Civilian Board of Contract Appeals, General Services Administration, Washington, DC 20405. Phone, 202-606-8800.

Governmentwide Policy   The Office of Government-wide Policy (OGP) collaborates with the Federal community to develop policies and guidelines for the management and efficient use of Government property, technology, and administrative services. OGP policymaking authority and policy support activities cover the following areas: electronic government and information technology, acquisition, real property and the workplace, travel, transportation, personal property, aircraft, the Federal motor vehicle fleet, mail, regulatory information, energy efficiency, and the use of Federal Advisory Committees. The OGP also provides leadership to interagency groups and promotes Governmentwide management reform. Its business lines include acquisition policy; asset and transportation policy; committee and regulatory management; information,

integrity, and access; and Federal high-performance green buildings.

The Office of Acquisition Policy (OAP) leads positive change in acquisition policy through its role on the Federal Acquisition Regulation (FAR) Council as well as through GSA acquisition policy, guidance, and reporting to stakeholders. The OAP, in conjunction with the Department of Defense and NASA, writes the FAR, which serves as the rule book for all Federal agency procurements and governs the billions of dollars spent by the Federal Government every year. The OAP also hosts the Federal Acquisition Institute (FAI), which is charged with fostering and promoting the development of the Federal acquisition workforce, along with its training, certification, and warrant needs. The OAP also oversees acquisition integrity functions for the GSA. The Regulatory Secretariat Division staff prepares, compiles, and processes regulatory and general notices for publication in the "Federal Register." The OAP is headed by the Deputy Chief Acquisition Officer / Senior Procurement Executive and includes the Office of Government-wide Acquisition Policy; the Office of General Services Acquisition Policy, Integrity and Workforce; and the Federal Acquisition Institute.

The Office of Asset and Transportation Policy supports Federal agencies in the economic and efficient management of assets and specific services. It develops effective policies and guidance for travel, employee relocation allowances and entitlements, personal and real property, motor vehicles, aircraft, transportation, and mail. The Office maintains liaisons with State and local governments, industry, and professional organizations, and it participates in the work of boards, committees, and groups related to asset and transportation management. The Office also provides advice, guidance, and formal classroom training and consultation to agencies regarding establishing and managing Federal advisory committees, as mandated by the Federal Advisory Committee Act. The Office of Asset and Transportation Policy's divisions include: policy performance, aviation, transportation and mail, personal property, real property, travel and relocation, motor vehicle, and the Committee Management Secretariat.

The Office of Committee and Regulatory Management develops Governmentwide policies, guidance, performance measures, regulations, and training on the management and operation of the Federal advisory committees. It also gathers and publishes information about Federal regulations and their effect on society.

The Office of Information, Integrity, and Access develops, coordinates, and defines information technology business strategies that allow Federal agencies to improve services to American citizens. The Office also provides assistance for and develops policy in the following areas: data and acquisition management, identity credentialing and access management, information management and improvements of analysis capability and architecture development efforts on cross-agency priorities and enterprise data management strategies, Dot Gov domain registration and management, and Section 508 accessibility management.

The Office of Federal High-Performance Green Buildings helps the Federal Government operate more efficiently and effectively by minimizing the Federal footprint through efficient use of energy, water, and resources. It also helps create healthy and productive workspaces for Federal employees. Congress authorized this Office to increase Federal leadership in sustainable real property portfolio management and operations. The Office works to promote, coordinate, and stimulate environmentally friendly construction and building management practices across the entire Federal Government, which has over 400,000 owned or leased buildings containing over 3 billion square feet of space. The Office has three principal categories of activity: leading and coordinating the greening of the Federal real estate portfolio, supporting innovation and collaboration on the development of new technologies, and supplying the market with information and best practices. To accomplish its goals, the Office relies on an interdisciplinary team of energy, water, air quality, sustainable design, facilities management, budgeting, human

behavior, organizational effectiveness, and communications experts.

The Office of Executive Councils coordinates with the Office of Management and Budget and Federal management councils to identify performance improvement initiatives to pursue Governmentwide, to lead working groups to drive these initiatives, to establish performance goals, and to facilitate the adoption of new processes by Federal agencies. The Office analyzes data, diagnoses challenges, identifies best practices, and documents the benefits delivered by the initiatives. This Office also provides technical and management services to the following Federal management councils: the Chief Acquisition Officers Council, the Chief Financial Officers Council, the Chief Information Officers Council, the Performance Improvement Council, and the President's Management Council. http://www.gsa.gov/portal/content/104550

For further information, contact the Office of Government-wide Policy. Phone, 202-501-8880.

Small Business Utilization   The Office of Small Business Utilization (OSBU) promotes increased access to the GSA's nationwide procurement opportunities for small, HUBZone, and minority-, veteran-, and women-owned businesses. the OSBU engages in activities that make it possible for the small business community to meet key contracting experts and be counseled on the procurement process. The OSBU monitors and implements small business policies and manages a range of programs mandated by law. http://www.gsa.gov/portal/category/21015

For further information, contact the Office of Small Business Utilization. Phone, 202-501-1021.

Federal Acquisition

The Federal Acquisition Service (FAS) provides acquisition and procurement support services for Federal agencies to increase overall Government efficiency. FAS programs include tools and resources that aid in the acquisition of products, services, and full-service programs in information technology, telecommunications, professional services, supplies, motor vehicles, travel and transportation, charge cards, and personal property utilization and disposal.

The FAS offers customers a variety of ways to acquire the products, services, and solutions they seek. Key acquisition programs include multiple awards schedules and Governmentwide acquisition contracts that provide customers easy access to information technology, telecommunications, and professional products and services. These products, services, and tools are accessible on the GSA's Web site: GSA Advantage!; eBuy and eOffer/eMod; Schedule Sales Query; GSA eLibrary; GSA Xcess, Transportation Management Services Solutions, and other electronic tools. http://www.gsa.gov/portal/category/21305

For further information, contact the Office of the Commissioner, Federal Acquisition Service. Phone, 703-605-5400.

Public Buildings

The Public Buildings Service (PBS) is the landlord for the civilian Federal Government, providing workspace solutions to more than one million Federal employees in 2,100 communities across the Nation, stimulating local economies by designing, building, managing, and maintaining public buildings, as well as leasing from the private sector. The PBS is a leader in sustainable design, energy conservation, and green building technologies. Its portfolio consists of 378 million square feet in over 9,000 assets across all 50 States, 6 U.S. Territories, and the District of Columbia. The Service preserves and maintains 471 historic properties and commissions the country's most talented artists to produce works of art for Federal buildings, as well as preserves artwork commissioned under the Works Progress Administration. PBS collects rent from Federal tenants, which is deposited into the Federal Buildings Fund, the principal funding mechanism for the PBS. http://www.gsa.gov/portal/category/21391

For further information, contact the Office of the Commissioner, Public Buildings Service. Phone, 202-501-1100.

Sources of Information

Auctions GSA Auctions sells off Federal personal property assets—airplanes, furniture, heavy machinery, office equipment, vehicles, vessels, and other items—located nationwide to interested buyers irrespective of their location. https://gsaauctions.gov/gsaauctions/gsaauctions | Email: gsaauctionshelp@gsa.gov; GSA Auctions is accessible on Facebook. https://www.facebook.com/gsaauctions

Business Opportunities The GSA serves as the Federal Government's procurement arm. It offers facilities, products, and services that Federal agencies use to benefit the public. The GSA also gives businesses the opportunity to sell billions of dollars worth of products and services to those agencies. http://www.gsa.gov/portal/category/26754

The Office of Small Business Utilization Web pages feature information, opportunities, resources, and training for small business owners. Phone, 855-672-8472. http://www.gsa.gov/portal/category/108067

Career Opportunities The GSA relies on professionals with diverse academic backgrounds, life experiences, and skills to carry out its mission. It encourages Federal and private sector employees, Peace Corps volunteers and staff, persons with disabilities, recent retirees, students and recent graduates, and others to apply for job openings. For more information, contact the national recruitment center. Phone, 816-823-2006. http://www.gsa.gov/portal/content/105311 | Email: NRC@gsa.gov

Federal Relay (FedRelay) FedRelay provides telecommunications services to Federal agencies and tribal governments for conducting official business with people who struggle with deafness, hearing impairments, or speech disabilities. The general public—those struggling with deafness, hearing impairments, or speech disabilities—also may use FedRelay for conducting business with Federal agencies. http://www.gsa.gov/portal/content/104626

For a free copy of the Federal Government TTY Directory, write to USAGov–TTY Directory, Pueblo, CO 81009. Phone, 844-872-4681. The directory is also available online. http://www.federalrelay.us/tty

Freedom of Information Act (FOIA)   The FOIA gives the public the right to request information from Federal agencies. The GSA participates in FOIAonline, which enables users to submit a FOIA request to all participating agencies, track the status of a request, search for requests submitted by others, access previously released records, and generate agency-specific FOIA processing reports. https://foiaonline. regulations.gov/foia/action/public/home

A FOIA request also may be submitted to the GSA by fax or by sending it to the U.S. General Services Administration, FOIA Requester Service Center (H1F), 1800 F Street NW., Room 7308, Washington, DC 20405-0001. Phone, 855-675-3642. Fax, 202-501-2727. http://www.gsa.gov/portal/category/21416 | Email: gsa.foia@gsa.gov

Newsroom   The GSA Web site features an agency blog, congressional testimonies, news releases, and photo galleries. http:// www.gsa.gov/portal/category/26627 | Email: media@gsa.gov

RSS Feeds are available on the GSA Web site. http://www.gsa.gov/portal/content/102295

The GSA tweets announcements, news items, and other information on Twitter. https://twitter.com/usgsa

Office of the Inspector General (OIG)   The OIG operates a fraud hotline for reporting abuse, fraud, or waste in GSA programs and mismanagement or violations of law, regulations, or rules by GSA employees and contractors. Phone, 202-501-1780 or 800-424-5210. https://www.gsaig.gov/hotline | Email: fraudnet@gsa.gov

Open Government   The GSA supports the Open Government initiative by promoting the principles of collaboration, participation, and transparency. http://www.gsa.gov/portal/category/26751 | Email: Open. Government@gsa.gov

Per Diem Rates   The GSA sets the per diem rates for Federal travel within the continental United States. Per diem is the allowance for incidental expenses, lodging, and meals. The GSA Web site features a search tool for finding current rates in the continental United States by State or ZIP code or by clicking on a map. http://www.gsa.gov/portal/content/104877 | Email: travelpolicy@gsa.gov

The GSA offers regular travelers a mobile application that makes Federal per diem rates accessible on a smart phone. The application allows travelers to look up Federal Government per diem rates by city and State or ZIP code in locations throughout the United States and its territories. http://www.gsa.gov/portal/content/302273

Plain Language   The "Plain Writing Act of 2010" was passed by Congress and approved by the President to improve the effectiveness of Federal agencies and increase their accountability to the public "by promoting clear Government communication that the public can understand and use." The GSA is committed to writing agency documents and its Web site content in plain language. http://www.gsa.gov/portal/content/298757

Privacy Act   Privacy Act requests should be addressed to the GSA Privacy Act Officer, Office of the Chief Information Security Officer, Policy and Compliance Division, (ISP), General Services Administration, 1800 F Street, NW., Washington, DC 20405. Phone, 202-208-1317. http://www.gsa.gov/portal/content/105034 | Email: GSA.privacyact@gsa.gov

Publications   Government consumer publications on topics like avoiding scams and identity theft, managing finances and saving money, staying healthy, and understanding Government benefits are available on the USA.gov publications Web site. http://publications.usa.gov/USAPubs.php

The "Consumer Action Handbook" is a free resource guide that provides consumer rights tips and general information on shopping for goods and services. It is available in English and Spanish. A digital copy of the handbook in Portable Document Format (PDF) may be downloaded from the USA.gov Web site. A hardcopy may be ordered online; over the phone, weekdays, 8 a.m.–8 p.m., excluding Federal holidays; or by writing to USAGov–Handbook, Pueblo, CO 81009. Allow 4–6 weeks for delivery. Phone, 844-872-4681. https://www.usa.gov/handbook

The GSA maintains an electronic forms library. The library features a collection of the most frequently downloaded forms:

GSA, optional (OF), and standard (SF). http://www.gsa.gov/portal/forms/type/TOP

Real Property Disposal   Inquiries about the redistribution or competitive sale of surplus real property should be directed to the Office of Real Property Utilization and Disposal, Public Buildings Service, 1800 F Street NW., Washington, DC 20405. Phone, 202-501-0084. http://www.gsa.gov/portal/content/105035

The Office of Real Property Utilization and Disposal operates a resource center that provides information on the handling of excess real property and on properties that are being offered for sale. http://disposal.gsa.gov

Regional Offices   The GSA operates 11 regional offices. More information on these offices is available on the GSA Web site. http://www.gsa.gov/regions

Site Map   The Web site map allows visitors to look for specific topics or to browse content that aligns with their interests. http://www.gsa.gov/portal/site/map

Speakers   Requests for speakers should be directed to the nearest regional office or the Office of Communications and Marketing, General Services Administration, 1800 F Street NW., Washington, DC 20405. Phone, 202-501-1231. http://www.gsa.gov/portal/content/229943 | Email: gsaschedules@gsa.gov

Sustainable Facilities (SF) Tool   The SFTool supports the efforts of designers, facility managers, purchasing agents, tenants, and others to green buildings, operations, and purchases. https://sftool.gov | Email: sustainability@gsa.gov

USA.gov   USA.gov is an online, Governmentwide guide to information and services. https://www.usa.gov

Contact USA.gov by email, phone, or web chat for answers to Government-related questions. Web chat is available Monday–Friday, 8 a.m.–8 p.m., eastern standard time, excluding Federal Holidays. The same hours of operation apply to the USAGov contact center. Phone, 844-872-4681. https://www.usa.gov/contact USA.gov tweets on Twitter. https://twitter.com/USAgov; http://www.gsa.gov/portal/category/25728

For further information concerning the General Services Administration, contact the Office of Communications and Marketing, General Services Administration, Washington, DC 20417. Phone, 202-501-1231.

Inter-American Foundation

1331 Pennsylvania Avenue, NW., Suite 1200 North, Washington, DC 20004
Phone, 202-360-4530. Internet, http://www.iaf.gov

Chair	EDUARDO ARRIOLA
Vice Chair	JUAN CARLOS ITURREGUI
Secretary	JACK C. VAUGHN, JR.
Director	J. KELLY RYAN
Director	LUIS A. VIADA
Director	ROGER W. WALLACE
Director	(VACANCY)
Director	(VACANCY)
Director	(VACANCY)
President / Chief Executive Officer	PALOMA ADAMS-ALLEN
Chief Operating Officer	LESLEY DUNCAN
General Counsel	PAUL ZIMMERMAN
Managing Directors	
Grant-Making and Portfolio Management	MARCY KELLEY
Networks and Strategic Initiatives	STEPHEN COX
Office of External and Government Affairs	(VACANCY)

The above list of key personnel was updated 09–2017.

The Inter-American Foundation supports social and economic development in Latin America and the Caribbean.

The Inter-American Foundation (IAF) was created in 1969 (22 U.S.C. 290f) as an experimental U.S. foreign assistance program. The Foundation is governed by a nine-person Board of Directors whom the President appoints with the advice and consent of the Senate. Six members are drawn from the private sector and three from the Federal Government. The Board of Directors appoints the president of the Foundation. http://www. iaf.gov/about-the-iaf/at-a-glance-3798

In Latin America and the Caribbean, the IAF promotes equitable, participatory, and sustainable self-help development by awarding grants and giving other technical assistance directly to local organizations throughout the region. It also partners with the public and private sectors to build support and to mobilize local, national, and international resources for grassroots development. http://www.iaf.gov/about-the-iaf/more-about-the-iaf

Sources of Information

Blog   The IAF blogs in four languages: English, Kreyol, Portuguese, and Spanish. http://www.iaf.gov/resources/blog

Career Opportunities   The IAF posts employment opportunities online. http://www.iaf.gov/about-the-iaf/iaf-jobs/vacancies

The IAF posts information on student internships on its Web site. http://www.iaf.gov/about-the-iaf/iaf-jobs/internships

Corporate Partners   Contact the Office of External and Government Affairs for information on participating in the program for corporate partners. Phone, 202-688-3051. http://www.iaf.gov/partners/corporate | Email: partnerships@iaf.gov

Country Portfolios   A list of the countries where the IAF currently works is available on its Web site. Country pages include descriptions of active IAF grants. http://www.iaf.gov/our-work/where-we-work/country-portfolios

Freedom of Information Act (FOIA)   The IAF generally discloses documents or records upon receiving a properly submitted request in writing. Records, or parts of them, that one or more of the nine FOIA

exemptions shield will not be released. http://www.iaf.gov/about-the-iaf/legal-notices-and-reports/freedom-of-information-act-foia | Email: foia@iaf.gov

The IAF maintains an electronic FOIA reading room. http://www.iaf.gov/about-the-iaf/legal-notices-and-reports/freedom-of-information-act-foia/foia-e-reading-room

Frequently Asked Questions (FAQs)   The IAF posts answers to FAQs online. http://www.iaf.gov/about-the-iaf/faq

Grants   The IAF funds the self-help efforts of grassroots groups in Latin America and the Caribbean. It welcomes proposals for its grant program. http://www.iaf.gov/apply-for-grants/call-for-proposals

Multilingual Resources   Español. http://spanish.iaf.gov/home-spanish

Kreyol. http://kreyol.iaf.gov/home-kreyol

Português. http://portugues.iaf.gov/home-portuguese

News   The IAF posts news items on its Web site. http://www.iaf.gov/resources/news

The IAF posts newsletters on its Web site. http://www.iaf.gov/resources/newsletters

Open Government   The IAF's Open Government Web page has shortcuts to items of interest to the public. http://www.iaf.gov/about-the-iaf/legal-notices-and-reports/open-government-initiative | Email: inquiries@iaf.gov

Organizational Chart   The IAF includes a small organizational chart on its "Our People" Web page. http://www.iaf.gov/about-the-iaf/our-people

Project Achievements   The "From the Field" Web page presents highlights and milestones of projects that the IAF has supported. http://www.iaf.gov/our-work/results/stories-from-the-field

Publications   The IAF produces print and digital publications in English, Spanish, and Portuguese. http://www.iaf.gov/resources/publications

Site Map   The Web site map allows visitors to look for specific topics or to browse content that aligns with their interests. http://www.iaf.gov/about-the-iaf/new-advanced-components/site-map

For further information, contact the Office of the President, Inter-American Foundation, 1331 Pennsylvania Avenue, NW., Suite 1200 North, Washington, DC 20004. Phone, 202-360-4530.

Merit Systems Protection Board

1615 M Street NW., Fifth Floor, Washington, DC 20419
Phone, 202-653-7200 or 800-209-8960. Fax, 202-653-7130. Internet, http://www.mspb.gov

Chair	MARK ROBBINS, ACTING
Vice Chair	MARK ROBBINS
Member	(VACANCY)
Director, Office of Equal Employment Opportunity	JERRY BEAT
Executive Director	JAMES M. EISENMANN
Clerk of the Board	JENNIFER EVERLING, ACTING
Director, Financial and Administrative Management	KEVIN NASH
Director, Information Resources Management	WILLIAM D. SPENCER, ACTING
Director, Office of Appeals Counsel	SUSAN M. SWAFFORD
Director, Office of Policy and Evaluation	JAMES M. READ
Director, Office of Regional Operations	DEBORAH MIRON
General Counsel	BRYAN G. POLISUK
Legislative Counsel	ROSALYN L. COATES

[For the Merit Systems Protection Board statement of organization, see the Code of Federal Regulations, Title 5, Part 1200]

The Merit Systems Protection Board protects the integrity of the Federal personnel merit systems and the rights of Federal employees.

The Merit Systems Protection Board (MSPB) is a successor agency to the United States Civil Service Commission, established by act of January 16, 1883 (22 Stat. 403). Reorganization Plan No. 2 of 1978 (5 U.S.C. app.) redesignated part of the Commission as the Merit Systems Protection Board. The Board comprises three members whom the President appoints with the advice and consent of the Senate.

Activities

The Board has responsibility for hearing and adjudicating appeals by Federal employees of adverse personnel actions, such as removals, suspensions, and demotions. It also resolves cases involving reemployment rights, denial of periodic step increases in pay, actions against administrative law judges, and charges of prohibited personnel practices, including charges in connection with whistleblowing.

The Board has the authority to enforce its decisions and to order corrective and disciplinary actions. An employee or applicant for employment involved in an appealable action that also involves an allegation of discrimination may ask the Equal Employment Opportunity Commission to review a Board decision. Final decisions and orders of the Board can be appealed to the U.S. Court of Appeals for the Federal Circuit.

The Board reviews regulations issued by the Office of Personnel Management and has

MERIT SYSTEMS PROTECTION BOARD

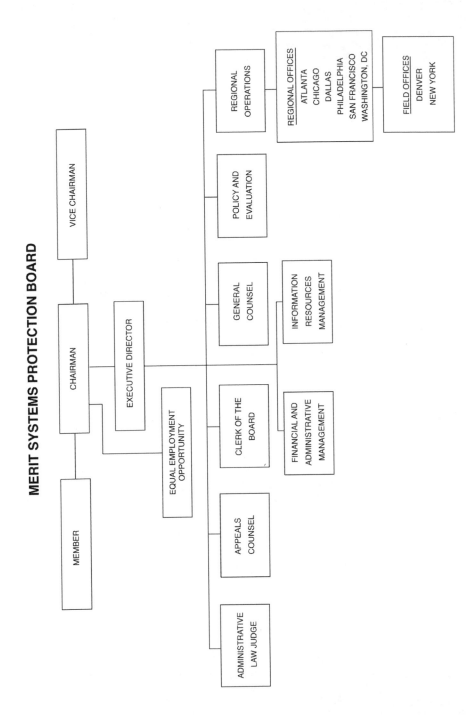

the authority to require agencies to cease compliance with any regulation that could constitute a prohibited personnel practice. It also conducts special studies of the civil service and other executive branch merit systems and reports to the President and the Congress on whether the Federal workforce is being adequately protected against political abuses and prohibited personnel practices. http://www.mspb.gov/About/about.htm

Sources of Information

Electronic Filing   An appeal may be filed online using the e-Appeal process. https://e-appeal.mspb.gov
Career Opportunities   The MSPB posts current job openings on USAJobs. http://www.mspb.gov/contact/jobs.htm
Freedom of Information Act (FOIA)   The MSPB participates in FOIAonline, which allows an information seeker to submit FOIA requests to participating agencies, track the status of requests, search for requests that others have submitted, access previously released records, and generate agency-specific FOIA processing reports. http://www.mspb.gov/foia/request.htm; https://foiaonline.regulations.gov/foia/action/public/home
Interviews   The MSPB posts external links to MSPB-related interviews on its Web site. http://www.mspb.gov/radio.htm; http://www.mspb.gov/video.htm
Public Affairs   The MSPB posts "Federal Register" notices, press releases, reports, and the results of its annual Federal Employee Viewpoint Survey online. http://www.mspb.gov/publicaffairs/publicaffairs.htm; http://www.mspb.gov/contact/contact.htm | Email: mspb@mspb.gov

For further information, contact the Merit Systems Protection Board, 1615 M Street NW., Washington, DC 20419. Phone, 202-653-7200 or 800-209-8960. TDD, 800-877-8339. Fax, 202-653-7130.

National Aeronautics and Space Administration

300 E Street SW., Washington, DC 20546
Phone, 202-358-0000. Internet, http://www.nasa.gov

Office of the Administrator

Administrator	JAMES F. BRIDENSTINE
Deputy Administrator	(VACANCY)
Associate Administrator	STEPHEN G. JURCZYK
Associate Administrator for Strategy and Plans	THOMAS E. CREMINS
Chief of Staff	THOMAS E. CREMINS, ACTING
Deputy Associate Administrator	MELANIE W. SAUNDERS, ACTING

https://www.nasa.gov/nasa-leadership

Administrator Staff Offices

Associate Administrators	
Communications	ROBERT N. JACOBS, ACTING
Diversity and Equal Opportunity	STEPHEN T. SHIH
Education	MICHAEL A. KINCAID
International and Interagency Relations	ALBERT CONDES
Legislative and Intergovernmental Affairs	REBECCA L. LEE, ACTING
Small Business Programs	GLENN A. DELGADO
Chiefs	
Engineer	RALPH R. ROE
Financial Officer	JEFFREY DEWIT
Health and Medical Officer	JAMES D. POLK
Information Officer	RENEE P. WYNN
Safety and Mission Assurance Officer	TERRENCE W. WILCUTT

Scientist	James L. Green
Technologist	Douglas A. Terrier
General Counsel	Sumara M. Thompson-King

https://www.nasa.gov/about/org_index.html

Mission Directorates

Associate Administrators	
Aeronautics Research	Jaiwon Shin
Human Exploration and Operations	William H. Gerstenmaier
Science	Thomas Zurbuchen
Space Technology	James L. Reuter, Acting

Mission Support Directorate

Associate Administrator	Daniel J. Tenney

Assistant Administrators	
Human Capital Management	Robert Gibbs
Procurement	Monica Y. Manning
Protective Services	Joseph S. Mahaley
Strategic Infrastructure	Calvin F. Williams

Executive Directors	
Headquarters Operations	Jay M. Henn
NASA Shared Services Center	Anita F. Harrell

https://www.nasa.gov/msd/msd-leadership

Centers and Facilities

Directors	
Ames Research Center	Eugene L. Tu
Armstrong Flight Center	David D. McBride
Glenn Research Center	Janet L. Kavandi
Goddard Space Flight Center	Christopher J. Scolese
Jet Propulsion Laboratory	Michael M. Watkins
Johnson Space Center	Mark S. Geyer
Kennedy Space Center	Robert D. Cabana
Langley Research Center	David E. Bowles
Marshall Space Flight Center	Joan A. Singer, Acting
Stennis Space Center	Richard J. Gilbrech

NASA Management Office	Marcus A. Watkins

https://www.nasa.gov/about/sites/index.html

Inspector General	Paul K. Martin

https://oig.nasa.gov/orgCharts/inspector_general.html

[For the National Aeronautics and Space Administration statement of organization, see the Code of Federal Regulations, Title 14, Part 1201]

The above list of key personnel was updated 9–2018.

The National Aeronautics and Space Administration advances aeronautic research, explores space, and makes scientific discoveries for the benefit of humankind.

The National Aeronautics and Space Administration (NASA) was established by the National Aeronautics and Space Act of 1958, as amended (42 U.S.C. 2451 et seq.).

Activities

Aeronautics Research Mission Directorate   The Aeronautics Research Mission Directorate conducts research, ground tests, and flight demonstrations to develop technologies and tools that reduce the adverse effects of aviation on the environment, increase efficiency while maintaining safety in skies that are becoming more crowded, and prepare the way for the emergence of new aircraft shapes and propulsion. The Directorate's four research programs partner with industry, other government agencies, and universities to develop technologies, converge breakthroughs from other fields, and ensure that the next generation workforce has the vision and skills for maintaining U.S. leadership in aviation. http://www. aeronautics.nasa.gov

For further information, call 202-358-2047.

Human Exploration and Operations Mission Directorate   The Human Exploration and Operations Mission Directorate oversees NASA space systems development and operations that support human exploration in and beyond low-Earth orbit. It also oversees low-level requirements development, policy, and programmatic oversight. The International Space Station represents the agency's exploration activities in low-Earth orbit. Beyond low-Earth orbit, exploration activities include the management of exploration systems development, human space flight capabilities, advanced exploration systems, and space life sciences research and applications. The Directorate also provides agency leadership and management of NASA space operations related to launch services and space communications and navigation in support of both human and robotic exploration programs. http://www. nasa.gov/directorates/heo/about.html

For further information, call 202-358-1562.

Science Mission Directorate   The Science Mission Directorate explores Earth and space to advance Earth science, heliophysics, planetary science, and astrophysics. Using in situ and space-based observations, the Directorate seeks a better understanding of the Sun and its influence on the solar system, climate change, the solar system's origin and evolution, whether life is limited to Earth, and the universe beyond. https:// science.nasa.gov/about-us

For further information, call 202-358-3889.

Space Technology Mission Directorate   The Space Technology Mission Directorate develops crosscutting and pioneering technologies and capabilities that the agency needs to carry out current and future missions. Through transparent, collaborative partnerships, the Directorate rapidly develops and demonstrates high-payoff technologies. It uses a merit-based competition model with a portfolio approach, spanning a range of discipline areas and technology readiness levels. http:// www.nasa.gov/directorates/spacetech/home/ index.html

For further information, call 202-358-0454.

Mission Support Directorate   The Mission Support Directorate provides overall leadership, stewardship, advocacy, integration, and optimization of Agency institutional activities. These activities include management of human capital and strategic infrastructure, procurement, protective services, headquarters operations, shared services, partnerships, external audits, and management of Agency directives. To enable successful operations, the Directorate focuses on three major goals: to provide stewardship of major institutional operations; to integrate resources, infrastructure, and processes and to advocate for institutional capabilities and needs; and to optimize mission support services through strategic analysis and business services assessments to achieve greater operational efficiency. http://msd.hq.nasa.gov

For further information, call 202-358-2789.

NASA Centers

Ames Research Center   Located in California's Silicon Valley, the Center enables exploration through selected developments, innovative technologies, and interdisciplinary scientific discovery. It provides leadership in astrobiology; small satellites; technologies for CEV, CLV, and HLV; the search for habitable planets; supercomputing; intelligent-adaptive systems; advanced thermal protection; and airborne astronomy. The Center also develops tools for a safer, more efficient national airspace, and it cultivates partnerships that benefit NASA's mission. https://www.nasa.gov/centers/ames/home/index.html

Armstrong Flight Research Center   Located at Edwards Air Force Base, CA, the Center carries out flight research and technology integration, validates space exploration concepts, conducts airborne remote sensing and science missions, enables airborne astrophysics observation missions to study the universe, and supports International Space Station operations. It also supports activities of the Agency's four Mission Directorates. https://www.nasa.gov/centers/armstrong/home/index.html

Glenn Research Center   Located on two campuses—at Lewis Field, next to Cleveland Hopkins International Airport, and at Plum Brook Station in Sandusky, OH—the Center is associated with cutting edge technologies that will enable human exploration to Mars, the design of environmentally friendlier commercial hybrid electric aircraft, and the development of more advanced high-temperature materials. Its 3,200 scientists, engineers, and other specialized employees work in partnership with U.S. companies, universities, and other Government institutions to produce and improve new technologies that are useful on and above and beyond Earth. The Center's specialized staff focuses on air-breathing and in-space propulsion, power and energy storage, aerospace communications, extreme environment materials, biomedical technologies, and high-value space experiments in the physical sciences. https://www.nasa.gov/centers/glenn/home/index.html

Goddard Space Flight Center   Located in Greenbelt, MD, the Center expands mankind's knowledge of Earth and its environment, the solar system, and the universe by observing them from space. It also conducts scientific investigations, develops and operates space systems, and advances essential technologies. https://www.nasa.gov/goddard

Johnson Space Center   Located in Houston, TX, the Center specializes in human space flight. It hosts and staffs program and project offices; selects and trains astronauts; manages and conducts projects that build, test, and integrate human-rated systems for transportation, habitation, and working in space; and plans and operates human space flight missions. This work requires a comprehensive understanding of space and planetary environments, as well as research into the effects of those environments on human physiology. It also requires development of technology to sustain and preserve life; maintenance of a supply chain to design, manufacture, and test flight products; selection, training, and provision of medical care to those who fly space missions; and ongoing administrative mission support services. The Center is currently hosting the International Space Station Program, the Multi-Purpose Crew Vehicle Program, and the Human Research Program. It plays a lead role in developing, operating, and integrating human exploration missions that include commercial, academic, international, and U.S. Government partners. https://www.nasa.gov/centers/johnson/home/index.html

Kennedy Space Center   Located on Florida's east coast, the Center is responsible for space launch operations and spaceport and range technologies. Home to the launch services program, it manages the processing and launching of astronaut crews and associated payloads. Its management activities include the International Space Station segments, research experiments and supplies, and NASA's scientific and research spacecraft. These scientific and research spacecraft range from robotic landers to Earth observation satellites and space-based telescopes on a variety of launch vehicles.

Innovative technology experts at the Center support NASA's current programs and future exploration missions by developing new products and processes that benefit the Agency and consumers. The Center remains a leader in cutting-edge research and development in the areas of physics, chemistry, technology, prototype designing, engineering, environmental conservation, and renewable energy. https://www.nasa.gov/centers/kennedy/home/index.html

Langley Research Center   Located in Hampton, VA, and established in 1917 as an aeronautics lab, the Center is renowned for its scientific and technological expertise in aerospace research, atmospheric science, systems analysis and integration, and planetary entry, descent and landing. Its researchers and engineers conduct research in structures and materials, applied sciences, space technology development, and aerosciences across the hyper, super, and subsonic flight regimes. Langley researchers and engineers have developed and validated technologies to improve the effectiveness, safety, environmental compatibility, and efficiency of the Nation's air transportation system. The Center supports space exploration and operations, and it plays a major role in expanding science-based knowledge of Earth and its environment. By determining appropriate preventative and corrective action for problems, trends, and issues across agency programs and projects, its engineering and safety personnel at the NASA Engineering Safety Center have improved mission safety and execution. https://www.nasa.gov/langley

Marshall Space Flight Center Located in Huntsville, AL, the Center oversees complex engineering, technology development, and scientific research for making human space exploration a reality. The Center is building the space launch system and developing advanced technologies that are necessary for the human journey to Mars. It also manages a number of programs and projects: the International Space Station's environmental control and life support system, its payload operations, and numerous other facilities and experiments; the Chandra X-ray Observatory; the Discovery and New Frontiers programs; space technology demonstration missions; and the Michoud Assembly Facility, where space vehicles are manufactured and assembled. https://www.nasa.gov/centers/marshall/home/index.html

Stennis Space Center Located near Bay St. Louis, MS, the Center serves as the agency's rocket propulsion testing ground. It provides test services not only for America's space program, but also for the Department of Defense and private sector. Its unique rocket propulsion test capabilities will be used for testing the engines and stages of NASA's space launch system rocket. The Advanced Technology and Technology Transfer Branch develops and licenses state-of-the-art components, processes, sensors, and software. https://www.nasa.gov/centers/stennis/home/index.html

Jet Propulsion Laboratory The Laboratory is a Federally Funded Research and Development Center (FFRDC) managed under contract by the California Institute of Technology (Caltech) in Pasadena, CA. This FFRDC is a unique nongovernment entity sponsored and funded by the Agency to meet specific long-term technical needs that cannot be met by other organizations within the Agency. As part of this special relationship, the Laboratory must operate in the public interest with objectivity and independence, avoid organizational conflicts of interest, and fully disclose its affairs to NASA. The Laboratory develops and maintains technical and managerial competencies to perform the following missions in support of the Agency's strategic goals: to explore the solar system to understand its formation and evolution; to establish a continuous and permanent robotic presence on Mars to discover its history and habitability; to make critical measurements and models to understand the global and regional integrated Earth system; to conduct observations to search for neighboring solar systems and Earth-like planets and help understand formation, evolution, and composition of the Universe; to conduct communications and navigation for deep space missions; to provide support, particularly in robotic infrastructures and precursors, that enables human exploration of the Moon, Mars, and beyond; and, under Caltech's initiative, to collaborate with other Federal and State government agencies and commercial endeavors in areas synergistic with the Laboratory's work performed for NASA. https://www.nasa.gov/centers/jpl/about/index.html

Sources of Information

A–Z Index NASA maintains an online index of all topics to help visitors browse or search for specific information. https://www.nasa.gov/topics

Business Opportunities Information on business opportunities is available on NASA's Office of Procurement website. NASA also offers small businesses opportunities to participate in prime contracts and subcontracts. Contact the Office of Small Business Programs. Phone, 202-358-2088. http://www.hq.nasa.gov/office/procurement/index.html; http://www.osbp.nasa.gov | Email: smallbusiness@nasa.gov

Career Opportunities   In addition to astronauts, the agency relies on accountants, engineers, human resources specialists, IT specialists, scientists, technicians, writers, and other skilled professionals to carry out its mission. To learn more about employment opportunities and programs, visit the NASAJobs website or contact the NASA Shared Services Center at the Stennis Space Center. Phone, 877-677-2123. http://nasajobs.nasa.gov; https://www.nssc.nasa.gov/workfornasa | Email: nssc-contactcenter@nasa.gov

In 2016 and 2017, NASA ranked number 1 among 18 large Government agencies in the Best Places To Work Agency Rankings! http://bestplacestowork.org/BPTW/rankings/detail/NN00

Freedom of Information Act (FOIA)   FOIA requests may be submitted by email or fax, delivered in person, or mailed to NASA Headquarters, 300 E Street SW., Room 5Q16, Washington, DC 20546. Phone, 202-358-2462. Fax, 202-358-4332. https://www.hq.nasa.gov/office/pao/FOIA | Email: foia@hq.nasa.gov

Glossary   The Science Mission Directorate website has a glossary. https://science.nasa.gov/glossary

History   The NASA History Office publishes a quarterly newsletter and books, hosts social media, offers fellowships, and runs the historical reference collection to assist the public with finding information on aeronautical and space history. Phone, 202-358-0384. http://www.nasa.gov/topics/history/index.html | Email: hq-histinfo@nasa.gov

The History Program Office maintains its own topical index. https://history.nasa.gov/tindex.html

Library   The NASA Headquarters Library welcomes visitors. Located in the East Lobby of NASA Headquarters in Washington, DC, the library is open Monday–Friday, 7:30 a.m.–5:00 p.m. It is closed on Federal holidays. Phone, 202-358-0168. http://www.hq.nasa.gov/office/hqlibrary | Email: library@hq.nasa.gov

Open Government   NASA supports the Open Government initiative by promoting collaboration, participation, and transparency. https://www.nasa.gov/open

Organizational Chart   NASA posts its organizational chart in Portable Document Format (PDF) for viewing and downloading. https://www.nasa.gov/sites/default/files/atoms/files/organizationchart_nov2015.pdf

Other Space Agencies   A web page of links provides convenient access to selected U.S. agencies that support aeronautics or space research and to selected international space agencies. https://www.nasa.gov/about/highlights/AN_Structure_OtherAgencies.html

Oversight   The Office of the Inspector General from NASA posts reports and data on Oversight.gov, a text-searchable repository of reports that Federal Inspectors General publish. The Council of the Inspectors General on Integrity and Efficiency operates and maintains the website to increase public access to independent and authoritative information on the Federal Government. https://oversight.gov

Picture of the Day   Discover something new about the universe each day by visiting NASA's "Astronomy Picture of the Day" web page. A professional astronomer provides a brief explanation for each daily image or photograph. A picture of the day archives is also accessible from the same page. https://apod.nasa.gov/apod/astropix.html

Plain Writing   The Plain Language Act of 2010 requires Federal agencies to communicate clearly. NASA editors and writers aim to use plain language in any document that is necessary for obtaining agency benefits or services, that provides information on agency benefits or services, or that explains how to comply with a requirement that the agency administers or enforces. https://www.nasa.gov/open/plainlanguage.html

Publications   The NASA scientific and technical information program provides access to research papers. https://www.sti.nasa.gov | Email: nasa-dl-sti-id@mail.nasa.gov

A "Find Publications" drop-down menu is available on the library web page. Additional publications are available onsite at the NASA Headquarters Library. http://www.hq.nasa.gov/office/hqlibrary

Science Missions   The mission key groups missions according to universe, solar system,

Sun, and Earth. https://science.nasa.gov/missions-page

NASA posts mission posters on its website for downloading. Posters are grouped in one of four categories: astrophysics, solar system, Sun, and Earth. https://science.nasa.gov/toolkits/nasa-science-mission-posters

Social Media NASA maintains a presence on popular social media websites. The "Social Media at NASA" page provides easy access to the agency's social media accounts. https://www.nasa.gov/socialmedia; https://www.nasa.gov/about/contact/index.html

For further information, contact the Headquarters Information Center, National Aeronautics and Space Administration, Washington, DC 20546. Phone, 202-358-0000.

National Archives and Records Administration

700 Pennsylvania Avenue NW., Washington, DC, 20408-0001
Phone, 866-272-6272. Internet, http://www.archives.gov

Archivist of The United States https://www.archives.gov/about/archivist/archivist-biography-ferriero.html	DAVID S. FERRIERO
Deputy Archivist of The United States	DEBRA STEIDEL WALL
Chief Innovation Officer	PAMELA S. WRIGHT
Chief of Staff	MARIA CAROSA STANWICH
Directors	
Congressional Affairs	JOHN O. HAMILTON
Equal Employment Opportunity Office	ERICA PEARSON, ACTING
Executive Director, National Historical Publications and Records Commission	CHRISTOPHER R. ECK
General Counsel	GARY M. STERN
Chief Operating Officer	WILLIAM J. BOSANKO
Director, Office of the Federal Register	OLIVER A. POTTS
Executives	
Agency Services	JAY A. TRAINER
Legislative Archives, Presidential Libraries, and Museum Services	SUSAN K. DONIUS, ACTING
Research Services	ANN A. CUMMINGS
Chief of Management and Administration	MICAH M. CHEATHAM
Chief Officers	
Acquisition	LA VERNE FIELDS
Financial	COLLEEN V. MURPHY
Human Capital	VALORIE FINDLATER, ACTING
Information	SWARNALI HALDAR
Executive for Business Support Services https://www.archives.gov/about/organization/senior-staff	DONNA J. FORBES
Inspector General https://www.archives.gov/oig/about	JAMES E. SPRINGS

[For the National Archives and Records Administration statement of organization, see the Federal Register of June 25, 1985, 50 FR 26270]

The above list of key personnel was updated 6–2019.

The National Archives and Records Administration safeguards and preserves the records of the U.S. Government and provides public access to them, ensuring that the American people can discover, learn from, and use their documentary heritage to support democracy.

Establishment   The National Archives and Records Administration (NARA) is the successor agency to the National Archives Establishment (NAE). On June 19, 1934, President Franklin D. Roosevelt approved Public Law 73–432, which created the Office of the Archivist of the United States and the NAE. Fifteen years later, the "Federal Property and Administrative Services Act of 1949" transferred the NAE's commitments, functions, obligations, personnel, property, and records to the General Services Administration. The new arrangement transformed the NAE into the National Archives and Records Service. More years would pass before the National Archives reemerged as an independent agency in the Federal Government's executive branch. April 1, 1985, became NARA's second birthday. On that day, the "National Archives and Records Administration Act of 1984," which President Ronald W. Reagan signed into law on October 19th, became effective. https://prologue.blogs.archives.gov/2015/04/01/happy-other-birthday-national-archives

Activities

Classified and Controlled Information Management   The Information Security Oversight Office (ISOO) oversees programs for classified national security information and controlled unclassified information in both Government and industry and reports on their status annually to the President. It receives policy and program guidance from the National Security Council and operates under the authority of Executive Orders 12829, 13549, 13587, 13526, and 13556. As a NARA component, ISOO's goals are fourfold: holding classification activities to the minimum necessary standard for protecting national security; promoting consistency and transparency in how controlled unclassified information is handled; efficiently and cost-effectively safeguarding classified national security information; and encouraging declassification of and public

access to information as soon as security considerations permit. https://www.archives.gov/isoo/about

In 2010, ISOO was named the Executive agent for administering Executive Order 13556, "Controlled Unclassified Information." The order establishes consistent information sharing and protection practices by replacing the ad hoc, agency-specific policies and procedures with an Executive branchwide program to manage unclassified information that requires safeguarding or dissemination controls pursuant to and consistent with applicable law, regulations, and Governmentwide policies. https://www.govinfo.gov/content/pkg/DCPD-201000942/pdf/DCPD-201000942.pdf; http://www.archives.gov/isoo| Email: isoo@nara.gov

For further information, contact the Information Security Oversight Office. Phone, 202-357-5250.

Declassification of Records   The National Declassification Center (NDC) was established by Executive Order 13526 and began operations in January of 2010. The Center is responsible for the timely and appropriate processing of referrals between agencies for accessioned Federal records and transferred Presidential records; general interagency declassification activities necessary to fulfill the requirements of sections 3.3 and 3.4 of the Order; the exchange among agencies of detailed declassification guidance to support equity recognition; the development of effective, transparent, and standard declassification work processes, training, and quality assurance measures; the development of solutions to declassification challenges posed by electronic records, special media, and emerging technologies; and the linkage and effective utilization of existing agency databases and the use of new technologies to support declassification activities under the purview of the Center. http://www.archives.gov/declassification| Email: ndc@nara.gov

For further information, contact the National Declassification Center. Phone, 301-837-0405.

Federal Records Storage and Retrieval NARA's Federal Records Centers Program (FRCP) stores and services active and inactive records for Federal agencies. A national network of 18 facilities, the FRCP system currently stores more than 30 million cubic feet of records. Since 1999, the FRCP system has operated as a reimbursable program that provides the Federal community with services on a fee-for-service basis. These services include storage of textual and special media records; management of classified and nonclassified records; retrieval of records needed by customers to conduct daily business or fulfill statutory requirements; expedited responses to congressional inquiries, litigation, and urgent business needs; disposition services, including the disposal of temporary records that have reached the end of their required retention period and the transfer of permanent records to the legal custody of the National Archives; and a variety of special projects based on customer needs. https://www.archives.gov/frc

The National Personnel Records Center (NPRC) in St. Louis, MO, is the largest facility in the FRCP system. This facility stores and services the civilian personnel, medical, and pay records of former U.S. Civil Service employees and the personnel, medical, and related records of discharged military personnel. The NPRC maintains research rooms where Federal employees and the general public can review official military and civilian personnel folders and other related records. It also supports Federal agencies by providing them with technical advice on and services relating to records disposition, filing and classification schemes, document conversion, and protection of civilian and military records. https://www. archives.gov/st-louis | Email: frc@nara.gov

For further information, contact the Federal Records Centers. Phone 314-801-9300.

Federal Register Publications and Services The Federal Register system is an official legal information service of the U.S. Government. The Federal Register system operates under the general authority of the Administrative Committee of the Federal Register (ACFR), as well as under statutory and regulatory authority that is specific to the Office of the Federal Register (OFR). The OFR is a component of NARA, which is obliged by statute to partner with the Government Publishing Office (GPO) to provide Federal Register publications and services to the public. The OFR's mission centers on informing citizens of their rights and obligations, documenting the actions of Federal agencies, and providing a public forum for participation in the democratic process. https://www. archives.gov/federal-register/about

The OFR makes the official text of several document types publicly accessible: administrative regulations and notices, Presidential documents, and Federal laws. In partnership with the GPO, its editors prepare and publish the "Code of Federal Regulations," "Compilation of Presidential Documents," "Federal Register," "Public Papers of the Presidents," and "United States Statutes at Large," as well as additional publications.

The OFR coordinates the functions of the Electoral College on behalf of the American people, the Archivist of the United States, the Congress, and the States. It also administers the constitutional amendment process. https://www.archives.gov/federal-register| Email: fedreg.info@nara.gov

For further information, contact Information Services and Technology, Office of the Federal Register. Phone, 202-741-6000. TTY, 202-741-6086. Fax, 202-741-6012.

Freedom of Information Act (FOIA) Compliance Established under the OPEN Government Act of 2007 (5 U.S.C. 101), the Office of Government Information Services (OGIS) works with agencies across the Executive branch to improve the Government's ability to respond to FOIA requests. OGIS serves as liaison between individuals making FOIA requests and administrative agencies, providing mediation services to resolve disputes as an alternative to litigation. It reviews policies and procedures of administrative agencies under FOIA. OGIS also reviews agency compliance with FOIA and recommends policy changes to the President and Congress. https://www.archives.gov/ogis| Email: ogis@nara.gov

For further information, contact the Office of Government Information Services. Phone, 202-741-5770.

Grant Making   The National Historical Publications and Records Commission (NHPRC) is NARA's grant-making affiliate. NHPRC supports the preservation and promotes the use of America's documentary heritage that is essential for understanding American culture, democracy, and history. NHPRC grants help State and local archives, universities, historical societies, and other nonprofit organizations preserve and manage electronic records, improve training and techniques, strengthen archival programs, preserve and process records collections, and provide access to them through the publication of finding aids and documentary editions of the papers of the Founding Era and other themes and historical figures in American history. NHPRC works in partnership with a national network of State historical records advisory boards. It also provides Federal leadership in public policy affecting the preservation of and access to America's documentary heritage. http://www.archives.gov/nhprc|
Email: nhprc@archives.gov

For further information, contact the National Historical Publications and Records Commission. Phone, 202-357-5010.

Innovation   The Office of Innovation finds innovative ways to serve its customers and to increase access to and delivery of records through all forms of media. Its mission includes demonstrating leadership in the archival and information access field. The Office coordinates NARA's efforts for Open Government and the National Digital Strategy. It comprises several divisions: digitization; digital engagement, including Internet, social media, and NARA's online catalog; business architecture, standards, and authorities; and the Innovation Hub. http://www.archives.gov/innovation-hub

National Archives Trust Fund Funding   The National Archives Trust Fund Board receives funds from the sale of historic document reproductions and publications based on historic records, as well as from gifts and bequests. The Board invests these funds and uses income to support archival functions such as the preparation of publications that make historic records information more widely available. Members of the Board are the Archivist of the United States, the Secretary of the Treasury, and the Chair of the National Endowment for the Humanities. https://www.archives.gov/files/publications/general-info-leaflets/29-trust-fund.pdf

For further information, contact the Secretary, National Archives Trust Fund Board. Phone, 301-837-3165.

Presidential Records Act Compliance   NARA operates the Libraries of Presidents Herbert Hoover through George W. Bush. While such records were once considered personal papers, all Presidential records created on or after January 20, 1981, are declared by law to be owned and controlled by the United States and are required to be transferred to NARA at the end of an administration, pursuant to the Presidential Records Act of 1978 (44 U.S.C. 2201 et seq.). The Office of Presidential Libraries within the National Archives oversees the archival, museum, and education programs of the 14 Presidential Libraries, including the fully digital Barack Obama Presidential Library. https://www.obamalibrary.gov/about-us

Through the Presidential Libraries, which are located at sites selected by the Presidents and built with private funds, NARA preserves and makes available the records, personal papers, and artifacts of a President's administration. Each Library operates a research room and offers reference services for Presidential papers and other historical materials. The Libraries display artifacts and other holdings in museum exhibits illustrating the life and times of a President. The Presidential Libraries also promote citizen engagement by providing programs for students of all ages. http://www.archives.gov/presidential-libraries

For further information, contact the Office of Presidential Libraries. Phone, 301-837-3250. Fax, 301-837-3199.

Providing Access to Archival Records   NARA maintains the U.S. Government's most historically valuable records, ranging from the Revolutionary War era to the recent past; arranges and preserves records and prepares finding aids to facilitate their use; makes records publicly accessible online and in its research rooms; answers requests for information contained in its holdings; and provides, for a fee, copies of records. NARA holdings include the records of the U.S. House of Representatives and Senate, which are preserved and administered by the Center for Legislative Archives. Many important records are available in microfilm and accessible online. Archival records are maintained in NARA facilities in the Washington, DC, area. Records of exceptional local or regional interest are maintained in NARA archives located in other parts of the country. There are also nine NARA-affiliated archives facilities that hold NARA-owned records and make them available to the public. https://www.archives.gov/research

Research Services provides world-class services to customers seeking access to NARA's accessioned Federal records. Records are available for research purposes in reading rooms at the National Archives Building (Archives I) in Washington, DC; the National Archives (Archives II) in College Park, MD; and various regional facilities throughout the Nation. https://www.archives.gov/locations#research-facilities

Records Management To ensure proper documentation of the organization, policies, and activities of the Government, NARA develops standards and guidelines for nationwide management and disposition of recorded information. It appraises Federal records and approves disposition schedules. NARA also inspects agency records and management practices, develops records management training programs, provides guidance and assistance on records management, and stores inactive records.

The Office of the Chief Records Officer assists Government agencies with their records management programs and the lifecycle management of Federal records. The Office formulates recommendations for Governmentwide policies, procedures, regulations, and guidance on the creation, management, and disposition of records in various media. It conducts inspections, evaluations, and surveys of records and records management programs in agencies; reports its findings; and recommends improvements or necessary corrective actions. The Office also provides records management services, including appraisal and scheduling, technical assistance, training, consultation, and analysis regarding policy matters, as well as identifying permanent records eligible for transfer to the National Archives. https://www.archives.gov/records-mgmt| Email: rm.communications@nara.gov

Sources of Information

A–Z Index NARA's website has an alphabetical subject index to help visitors navigate its content. https://www.archives.gov/global-pages/subject-index.html

Amending the Constitution NARA's website describes the roles played by the Archivist of the United States and the Office of the Federal Register in the ratification process of a constitutional amendment. https://www.archives.gov/federal-register/constitution

Annual Performance Plans and Reports NARA complies with the Government Performance and Results Modernization Act of 2010 by posting its annual performance plans and annual reports online. https://www.archives.gov/about/plans-reports/performance-accountability

Blogs NARA maintains multiple blogs. https://www.archives.gov/social-media/blogs

Business Opportunities Resources for doing business with NARA, as well as an inventory of service contracts awarded by the agency, are available online. http://www.archives.gov/contracts

Calendar NARA maintains a calendar of public events on its website. A recorded announcement of events in Washington, DC, and College Park, MD, also is available. Phone, 202-357-5000. TDD, 301-837-0482. http://www.archives.gov/calendar

Career Opportunities NARA has a nationwide network of facilities. The agency relies on professionals with administrative, archival, editorial, technical, and other skills to carry out its mission. For more information, visit the "Careers at NARA" web page or contact the Office of Human Capital in St. Louis, MO. Phone, 800-827-0885. https://www.archives.gov/careers

In 2018, NARA ranked 23d among 27 midsize Government agencies in the Partnership for Public Service's Best Places To Work Agency Rankings. http://bestplacestowork.org/rankings/detail/NQ00

Catalog   The National Archives catalog is accessible online. https://catalog.archives. gov

Center for Legislative Archives   The Center for Legislative Archives houses the official records of the U.S. Congress from 1789 to the present. These records are in the permanent legal custody of the Senate and House of Representatives, and their rules govern them. The Center responds to congressional committee requests for records to support congressional business needs. It is a full-service archive that assists the Senate and House archivists with managing records, that processes congressional and legislative branch records and provides public access to them, and that creates exhibits, public programs, and educational materials and workshops on the history of the Congress and representative government. Phone, 202-357-5350. Fax, 202-357-5911. http://www. archives.gov/legislative | Email: legislative. archives@nara.gov

Charters of Freedom   The Declaration of Independence, Constitution, and Bill of Rights have secured the rights of Americans for over two centuries. High resolution images of these three documents, transcriptions of their texts, and articles written on them are available online. https:// www.archives.gov/founding-docs

Congressional Affairs   The Congressional Affairs Office maintains liaison with congressional staffs and responds to their inquiries. Phone, 202-357-5100. Fax, 202-357-5959. https://www.archives.gov/ congress | Email: congress.affairs@nara.gov

Contact Information   Send postal correspondence to the National Archives and Records Administration, 8601 Adelphi Road, College Park, MD 20740-6001. Phone, 866-272-6272. https://www.archives. gov/contact | Email: inquire@nara.gov

Democracy Starts Here   The National Archives contains over 9 billion records—some frivolous, some funny, but others serious, even repellent. More than a national scrapbook, this repository of records gives Americans the opportunity to gain unfiltered, unmediated glimpses of their shared national history, to consider their Government's achievements and shortcomings, to reflect on the praiseworthy and shameful, and to engage in the civic responsibilities of renewing their Nation and fortifying and expanding its democratic institutions. In an 11-minute video, Discovery Channel captures this fundamental concept that sustains NARA's mission. https://videocast. nih.gov/sla/NARA/dsh/index.html

The National Historical Publications and Records Commission (NHPRC) awards grants for projects that publish the American story. The Commission also funds projects that preserve and make accessible the records of all types that are housed in historical repositories across the Nation. The American story is more diverse and unexpected than the Nation's Founding Fathers and 45 Presidents. It includes abolitionists, civil rights leaders, progressives, radicals, and reformers like Chief of the Cherokee Nation John Ross, Presidential candidate Eugene V. Debs of the Socialist Party of America, escaped slave and orator Frederick Douglass, freedom of speech champion and anarchist Emma Goldman, labor organizer Mary Harris "Mother" Jones, Vice President Henry A. Wallace, and Baptist minister Martin Luther King, Jr., whose collections and papers the NHPRC has made more accessible. https://www.archives.gov/publications/ prologue/2004/fall/nhprc-sidebar.html

Electoral College   The "U.S. Electoral College" web page offers a trove of information on the Electoral College, as well as external resources for learning about elections and voting in the United States. Phone, 202-741-6030. https://www.archives. gov/federal-register/electoral-college | Email: electoral.college@nara.gov

Exhibits   The National Archives in Washington, DC, and the Presidential Libraries and several regional facilities regularly host onsite exhibits. NARA also has national traveling exhibits that bring documents and records of the National Archives to communities nationwide. NARA's website features dozens of online exhibits on a range of topics: gifts that Presidents received, Government drawings, New Deal-era Federal art projects, work and the workplace in the 19th and 20th centuries, the influenza epidemic of 1918, and more. https://www.archives. gov/exhibits | Email: National_Archives_ Exhibits_Staff@nara.gov

Forms Some of the most commonly used forms for obtaining National Archives historical records—Eastern Cherokee applications, Federal census records, Federal land entry files, military pension / bounty land warrant applications, passenger arrival records, post-World War I military records, and pre-World War I military service records—are available online. https://www.archives.gov/forms

Founders Online The National Historical Publications and Records Commission and The University of Virginia Press have collaborated to create the "Founders Online" website, which gives the public free electronic access to the historical documents of the Founders of the United States. The site contains over 176,000 searchable and fully annotated documents from the Founding Fathers Papers projects. These documents include the correspondence and other writings of Benjamin Franklin, Alexander Hamilton, President John Adams and his family, and Presidents George Washington, Thomas Jefferson, and James Madison. https://founders.archives.gov/ | Email: foundersonline@nara.gov

Freedom of Information Act (FOIA) To any person, the FOIA gives a statutory right for obtaining access to Government information in the records of executive branch agencies. This right to access is limited, however, when the requested information is shielded from disclosure by any of nine exemptions contained within the statute. https://www.archives.gov/foia

Frequently Asked Questions (FAQs) NARA posts answers to FAQs on its website. https://www.archives.gov/faqs

History In the early 1930s, the Nation had a records management problem: Federal records were being housed in abandoned buildings, attics, and basements, where security and storage conditions were inadequate. In 1934, the U.S. Congress acted. To learn what it did to solve the problem, visit the "National Archives History" web page. https://www.archives.gov/about/history | Email: archives.historian@nara.gov

History Hub This crowdsourcing platform is a place for asking questions, finding people of particular experiences and interests, sharing information, and working together. The hub allows citizen archivists, American history enthusiasts, and experts from NARA and other organizations to pool their knowledge in support of historical research. https://historyhub.history.gov/docs/DOC-1012 | Email: historyhub@nara.gov

Know Your Records To assist genealogical and historical researchers with using Federal Government records held at the National Archives, NARA hosts Know Your Records events. Phone, 202-357-5260. http://www.archives.gov/calendar/know-your-records/index.html | Email: kyr@nara.gov

Museum Shops The National Archives Store sells merchandise highlighting the holdings of the National Archives. Document facsimiles, publications, and souvenirs and gifts are available for sale at each Presidential Library and at the National Archives in Washington, DC. Phone, 202-357-5271. http://www.myarchivesstore.org

News NARA posts press releases on its website. https://www.archives.gov/press

Open Government NARA supports the Open Government initiative by promoting the principles of collaboration, participation, and transparency. https://www.archives.gov/open

Organizational Chart NARA's organizational chart may be found on their website. https://www.archives.gov/about/organization

The "NARA Organization" web page allows easy access to information that complements the agency's organizational chart. https://www.archives.gov/about/organization/chart-text.html

Páginas en Español The NARA website features a collection of pages whose content is in Spanish. https://www.archives.gov/espanol

Plain Language NARA supports the Plain Writing Act of 2010 by "promoting clear Government communication that the public can understand and use." If a document or web page contains content that is unclear, please contact NARA via email and suggest a way to enhance clarity. https://www.archives.gov/open/plain-writing | Email: plainwriting@nara.gov

Publications The "Publications" web page contains a hyperlinked list of NARA's most requested publications: "Code of Federal Regulations," "Federal Register," "Guide to

Federal Records in the National Archives of the United States," "Military Service Records at the National Archives," "Prologue" magazine, and eBooks and more. https://www.archives.gov/publications

The Office of Records Services in Washington, DC, and the Office of Regional Records Services produce most of the publications on the "Publications" web page; however, other NARA offices also publish materials and a few of them do so extensively. These other offices include the Information Security Oversight Office, Office of the Federal Register, Office of Presidential Libraries, and public affairs staff. https://www.archives.gov/publications/organization.html

NARA units enter into cooperative arrangements with other organizations to produce and sell publications. To become acquainted with these partnership publications, visit the "NARA Publications" web page. https://www.archives.gov/publications/partnerships.html

"Presidential Perspectives from the National Archives" highlights modern American Presidents and the National Archives Presidential Libraries System. https://www.archives.gov/publications/presidential-materials.html

Some print versions of NARA publications are no longer in stock. To inquire about a publication, contact the National Archives Foundation. Phone, 202-357-5271. https://www.nationalarchivesstore.org/pages/contact-us

Records Management   Records management brochures and pamphlets, posters, and publications are available online. https://www.archives.gov/publications/records-mgmt.html

The national records management training program provides records management instruction to Federal employees and contractors. http://www.archives.gov/records-mgmt/training/index.html | Email: NARA.RecordsMgtTraining@nara.gov

Researcher Newsletter   "Researcher News" covers relevant and the most up-to-date information for conducting research at the National Archives. The newsletter is available online in Portable Document Format (PDF) and also disseminated via email subscription. http://www.archives.gov/research/newsletter | Email: kyr@nara.gov

Resources for Educators   NARA's website has a trove of information and resources to assist teachers. https://www.archives.gov/education

DocsTeach is an online tool that helps educators use National Archives documents for teaching their students. https://www.docsteach.org | Email: docsteach@nara.gov

Resources for Genealogists   NARA's website has a trove of information and resources to assist genealogy researchers. https://www.archives.gov/research/genealogy

Service Records   The "Veterans' Service Records" web page explains how to request service records online, to conduct research using military records, to replace lost medal and awards, and to browse World War II photographs. https://www.archives.gov/veterans

Social Media   NARA has pages on Facebook. https://www.archives.gov/social-media/facebook

NARA tweets announcements and other newsworthy items on its Twitter accounts. https://www.archives.gov/social-media/twitter

Organizations within NARA post videos on YouTube channels. https://www.archives.gov/social-media/youtube

Today's Document   Each day a different American historical document is featured on NARA's website. https://www.archives.gov/historical-docs/todays-doc

Visitors' Information   The "Visit Us" web page has a nationwide list of NARA facilities—Federal records centers, Presidential Libraries, and research facilities. The list includes directions to, hours for, and details on each facility. https://www.archives.gov/locations

The National Archives Museum is open every day of the week, 10 a.m.–5:30 p.m., except on Thanksgiving and Christmas Day, and admission is free. Directions, maps, and information on public programs and for planning a visit are available online. https://www.archives.gov/museum/visit

Volunteer Opportunities   Opportunities to volunteer are available onsite at NARA's historic building in Washington, DC, and at its modern facility in College Park, MD, as well as outside the Nation's capital at the Presidential Libraries and at NARA facilities in 11 States. Offsite opportunities are available, too. For example, volunteers can help online by editing, tagging, and transcribing. http://www.archives.gov/careers/volunteering

The Sources of Information were updated 6–2019.

National Capital Planning Commission

401 Ninth Street NW., Suite 500, Washington, DC 20004
Phone, 202-482-7200. Internet, http://www.ncpc.gov

Chair	L. Preston Bryant, Jr.
Member	Arrington Dixon
Member	Thomas Gallas
Member	Geoffery Griffis
Member	Elizabeth White
Administrator of General Services (ex officio)	Emily W. Murphy
Chair, Council of the District of Columbia (ex officio)	Philip Mendelson
Chair, House Committee on Oversight and Government Reform (ex officio)	Trey Gowdy
Chair, Senate Committee on Homeland Security and Governmental Affairs (ex officio)	Ron Johnson
Mayor of the District of Columbia (ex officio)	Muriel Bowser
Secretary of Defense (ex officio)	Jim Mattis
Secretary of the Interior (ex officio)	Ryan Zinke

Staff

Executive Director	Marcel C. Acosta
Chief Operating Officer	Barry S. Socks
Director, Office of Public Engagement / Secretary to the Commission	Julia A. Koster
Director, Physical Planning	Elizabeth Miller
Director, Policy and Research	Michael A. Sherman
Director, Urban Design and Plan Review	Diane Sullivan
Director, Office of Administration	Debra. Dickson
General Counsel	Anne R. Schuyler

[For the National Capital Planning Commission statement of organization, see the Code of Federal Regulations, Title 1, Part 456.2]

The National Capital Planning Commission conducts planning and development activities for Federal lands and facilities in the National Capital Region—the District of Columbia, the City of Alexandria, and all land areas within the boundaries of Montgomery, Prince George's, Fairfax, Loudoun, Prince William, and Arlington Counties.

The National Capital Planning Commission was established as a park planning agency by act of June 6, 1924, as amended (40 U.S.C. 8701 et seq.). Two years later, its role was expanded to include comprehensive planning. In 1952, the National Capital Planning Act designated the Commission as the central planning agency for the Federal and District of Columbia governments. https://www.ncpc.gov/ncpc/Main(T2)/About_Us(tr2)/About_Us(tr3)/History.html

In 1973, the National Capital Planning Act was amended by the District of Columbia Home Rule Act, which made

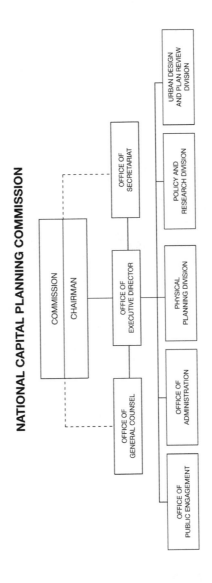

NATIONAL CAPITAL PLANNING COMMISSION

the mayor of the District of Columbia the chief planner for the District and gave the Commission specific authority for reviewing certain District decisions. The Commission continues to serve, however, as the central planning agency for the Federal Government in the National Capital Region.

The Commission comprises five appointed and seven ex officio members. Three citizen members, including the Chair, are appointed by the President. The mayor of the District of Columbia appoints the other two members. The Presidential appointees include one resident from Maryland, one resident from Virginia, and one from anywhere else in the United States. The two mayoral appointees must be District of Columbia residents. https://www.ncpc.gov/ncpc/Main(T2)/About_ Us(tr2)/AboutUs.html

Sources of Information

Business Opportunities The Commission posts contracting opportunities on its Web site. http://www.ncpc.gov/ncpc/Main(T2)/ About_Us(tr2)/About_Us(tr3)/Opportunities. html

Career Opportunities The Commission posts employment opportunities on its Web site. http://www.ncpc.gov/ncpc/Main(T2)/ About_Us(tr2)/About_Us(tr3)/Opportunities. html

Events The Commission posts upcoming events that are open to the public online. https://www.ncpc.gov/ncpc/Main(T2)/ PublicParticipation(Tr2)/Public%20 Participation(Tr3)/UpcomingEvents.html

Freedom of Information Act (FOIA) FOIA requests should be addressed to the Chief FOIA Officer, National Capital Planning Commission, 401 9th Street NW., Suite 500, Washington, DC 20004. Requests also may be submitted by fax or email. Fax, 202-482- 7272. https://www.ncpc.gov/open/home.html

Internships The Commission offers internships for students at accredited colleges and universities. Students with various educational backgrounds— architecture, communications, community planning, computer aided design, geography and geographic information systems, historic preservation, landscape architecture, law, urban design—are encouraged to apply.

http://www.ncpc.gov/ncpc/Main(T2)/About Us(tr2)/About_Us(tr3)/Opportunities.html

Memorial Map The Commission, in conjunction with the National Park Service, offers Internet users an interactive map of commemorative works in the Nation's capital. https://www.ncpc.gov/memorials

Newsletters Monthly newsletters are available online. https://www.ncpc. gov/ncpc/Main(T2)/Publications(Tr2)/ Publications(Tr3)/CompleteCatalogue. html?ccpage=1

An archive of quarterly newsletters running from 1998 to 2009 is available online. https://www.ncpc.gov/ncpc/ Main(T2)/Publications(Tr2)/Publications(Tr3)/ CompleteCatalogue.html?ccpage=3

News The Commission posts recent news releases on its Web site. Starting with the year 2001, an online archive contains releases from previous years. https://www. ncpc.gov/ncpc/Main(T2)/Media(Tr2)/ Media(Tr3)/NewsReleaseArchive.html

Open Government The Commission supports the Open Government initiative by promoting the principles of collaboration, participation, and transparency. https://www. ncpc.gov/open/home.html

Plain Language The Commission's writers and editors are committed to using plain language in new communications and revising confusing or unclear language in existing material. If a sentence or paragraph's clarity needs improvement, send them a note using the online form. https://www. ncpc.gov/open/home.html

Publications Recently released and frequently requested publications are accessible online. https://www.ncpc. gov/ncpc/Main(T2)/Publications(Tr2)/ Publications.html

Reports Starting with the year 2004, the Commission's annual reports are accessible online. https://www.ncpc.gov/ncpc/ Main(T2)/Publications(Tr2)/Publications(Tr3)/ CompleteCatalogue.html?ccpage=4

Site Map Web site visitors may use the site map to look for specific topics or to browse for content that aligns with their interests. https://www.ncpc.gov/ncpc/Main(T2)/ siteMap.html; https://www.ncpc.gov/ncpc/ Main(T2)/About_Us(tr2)/About_Us(tr3)/ Contactus.html | Email: info@ncpc.gov

For further information, contact the National Capital Planning Commission, 401 Ninth Street NW., Suite 500, Washington, DC 20004. Phone, 202-482-7200. Fax, 202-482-7272.

National Credit Union Administration

1775 Duke Street, Alexandria, VA 22314
Phone, 703-518-6300. Internet, http://www.ncua.gov

Board of Directors

Chair	J. Mark McWatters
Member	Richard T. Metsger
Member	(vacancy)

Headquarters–Washington, DC

Chair	J. Mark McWatters
Member of the Board	Richard T. Metsger
Chief of Staff	Sarah D. Vega

Office Heads	
Chief Economist	Ralph Monaco
Chief Financial Officer	Rendell L. Jones
Chief Information Officer	Edward Dorris
Director, Consumer Protection	Gail Laster
Director, Continuity and Security Management	Joy Miller
Director, Examination and Insurance	Larry Fazio
Director, Human Resources	Cheryl Eyre
Director, Minority and Women Inclusion	Monica Davy
Director, National Examinations and Supervision	Scott Hunt
Director, Public and Congressional Affairs	Alfred V. Garesché, Acting
Director, Small Credit Union Initiatives	Martha Ninichuk
Executive Director	Mark A. Treichel
General Counsel	Michael McKenna
Inspector General	James W. Hagen

https://www.ncua.gov/about/leadership/Pages/
default.aspx

[For the National Credit Union Administration statement of organization, see the Code of Federal Regulations, Title 12, Part 720]

The above list of key personnel was updated 09–2017.

The National Credit Union Administration provides a trustworthy credit union system that builds confidence in the Nation's system of cooperative credit.

The National Credit Union Administration (NCUA) was established by act of March 10, 1970 (12 U.S.C. 1752), and reorganized by act of November 10, 1978 (12 U.S.C. 226), as an independent agency in the executive branch of the Federal Government. It regulates and insures all Federal credit unions and insures State-chartered credit unions that apply and qualify for share insurance.

The Administration's Board comprises three members whom the President appoints and the Senate must confirm. Members serve staggered terms of 6 years, and no more than two of them can belong to the same political party. https://www.ncua.gov/about/leadership/Pages/default.aspx

Activities

Chartering The NCUA grants Federal credit union charters to groups sharing a common bond of occupation or association or to groups within a well-defined neighborhood, community, or rural district. Before granting a Federal charter, the NCUA conducts a preliminary investigation to determine if certain standards are met. https://www.ncua.gov/services/Pages/field-of-membership-chartering.aspx

Examinations The NCUA regularly examines Federal credit unions to assess their solvency, to ensure their compliance with laws and regulations, and to assist credit union management and improve operations.

For further information, contact the Director, Office of Examination and Insurance. Phone, 703-518-6360.

Share Insurance The act of October 19, 1970 (12 U.S.C. 1781 et seq.), provides for a program of share insurance, in which participation is mandatory for Federal credit unions. In some States, State-chartered credit unions must participate in the share insurance program. In other States, State-chartered credit unions may opt to participate in the insurance program. The National Credit Union Share Insurance Fund requires each participating credit union to place and maintain a 1-percent deposit of its insured savings with the Fund. Credit union members' accounts are insured up to $250,000. http://www.mycreditunion.gov/protect/Pages/SI.aspx

Supervision Supervisory activities are carried out through regular examiner contacts and by periodic policy and regulatory releases from the Administration. The NCUA also identifies emerging problems and monitors operations between examinations.

NCUA central offices include examination and supervision programs. Five regional offices manage the oversight of credit unions. http://www.ncua.gov/about/pages/Contact.aspx

Sources of Information

A–Z Index The NCUA Web site has an A–Z index to help visitors navigate its content. https://www.ncua.gov/Pages/SiteIndex.aspx

Business Opportunities The NCUA selects vendors who offer the best value to help the agency meet its mission. The Division of Procurement and Facilities Management is responsible for procuring goods and services. Phone, 703-518-6410. Fax, 703-518-6662. https://www.ncua.gov/About/Pages/business-opportunities.aspx | Email: ocfoprocurement@ncua.gov

Career Opportunities Career information is available from the Office of Human Resources. Phone, 703-518-6510. Fax, 703-518-6539. http://www.ncua.gov/about/Leadership/Pages/page_hr.aspx | Email: ohrmail@ncua.gov

The NCUA relies heavily on credit union examiners to carry out its mission. Watch the video "A Day in the Life of a Credit Union Examiner" to learn about the training required and the role a fully trained examiner plays in safeguarding the stability of the Nation's credit union system. https://www.youtube.com/watch?v=iP-dgprNGnw&feature=youtu.be

The NCUA ranks among the top midsize Government agencies in the Best Places To Work Agency Rankings. http://bestplacestowork.org/BPTW/rankings/overall/mid

Closed Credit Unions The Asset Management and Assistance Center conducts credit union liquidations and performs asset management and recovery. It also participates in the operational phases of a failed credit union's conservatorship and assists with record reconstruction. The Center posts up-to-date information on closed, conserved, liquidated, and merged credit unions on the NCUA Web site. https://www.ncua.gov/services/Pages/closed-credit-unions.aspx | Email: amacmail@ncua.gov

Consumer Assistance For answers to questions on credit union insurance and other consumer matters or to submit a complaint, contact the NCUA Consumer Assistance Center on weekdays, 8 a.m.–5 p.m., eastern standard time. After regular business hours, callers may leave a recorded message. Phone, 800-755-1030. http://www.mycreditunion.gov/consumer-assistance-center/Pages/default.aspx

Español Read Spanish better than English? Visit the Spanish version of the NCUA Web site. https://espanol.ncua.gov/newsroom/Pages/newsroom.aspx

Federally Insured Credit Unions A directory of federally insured credit unions that includes addresses, asset levels, and membership numbers is available online and for review at central and regional offices. Copies of the directory are available for a nominal fee: Write NCUA, Publications, 1775 Duke Street, Alexandria, VA 22314-3428. Phone, 703-518-6340. http://www.ncua.gov/Legal/GuidesEtc/Pages/CUDirectory.aspx

Financial Literacy The NCUA offers financial literacy and educational resources to help consumers increase their savings and achieve their financial goals. https://www. ncua.gov/consumers/Pages/financial-literacy- resources.aspx

Fraud Hotline   The NCUA operates a hotline for reporting illegal or suspicious activity associated with credit union employees, members, or officials in federally insured credit unions. Phone, 800-827-9650 or 703-518-6550 (Washington, DC, area). https://www.ncua.gov/services/Pages/fraud- hotline.aspx

Freedom of Information Act (FOIA)   The act allows any person to obtain records of a Federal agency. A record may be withheld only if it carries an exemption under the FOIA. The NCUA operates a FOIA requester service center to answer questions related to the FOIA process, to provide information on the status of a request, and to answer questions about documents that a requester has received from the NCUA. Phone, 703-518-6540. Fax, 703-518-6569. https:// www.ncua.gov/services/Pages/freedom-of- information-act.aspx | Email: FOIA@ncua.gov

Games / Activities   Games for testing and activities for exercising financial knowledge are available on the Web site MyCreditUnion.gov. https://www. mycreditunion.gov/tools-resources/Pages/ Games-and-Activities.aspx

Glossaries   The NCUA maintains a glossary of the common terms associated with the corporate system resolution costs. https:// www.ncua.gov/regulation-supervision/Pages/ corporate-system-resolution/glossary.aspx

The Web site MyCreditUnion.gov has a glossary of common terms associated with the share insurance coverage. http://www. mycreditunion.gov/estimator/Pages/glossary_ calculator.aspx

History   Court reporter Alphonse Desjardins knew loan sharks were charging outrageous rates of interest in Quebec. He did not like their predatory lending and responded by organizing La Caisse Populaire de Levis, the first credit union in North America, to provide affordable credit to working class families. Nearly a decade later, on April 6, 1909, with the assistance of Desjardins, the St. Mary's Cooperative Credit Association, the first credit union in the United States, opened its doors in Manchester, New Hampshire. Yet the moniker "Father of U.S. Credit Unions" would be earned by another.

To learn who this person was and what he did for credit unions, visit the NCUA "History" Web page. https://www.ncua.gov/ About/Pages/history.aspx

Learning   NCUA webinars and Learning Management Service provide free educational materials. Webinars help credit union professionals stay current on important topics affecting the credit union community. Generally 90 minutes in length, live webinars are scheduled throughout the year. Archived webinars may be viewed on demand approximately three weeks after the live event. The Learning Management Service educates people on building community partnerships, credit union operations, how credit unions are governed, how the credit union system works, and products and services. Phone, 703-518- 6610. https://www.ncua.gov/services/Pages/ small-credit-union-initiatives/learning.aspx | Email: OSCUImail@ncua.gov

Locate a Credit Union   The NCUA Web site features a credit union locator tool, which complements the research a credit union tool. The locator provides a graphical map of credit unions based on an address search. The locator also allows the user to view a credit union's contact information, the services that it offers, and directions to it. http://mapping.ncua.gov

Newsroom   The NCUA posts annual reports, events, press releases, speeches, testimonies, and its newsletter "The NCUA Report." https://www.ncua.gov/newsroom/ Pages/newsroom.aspx

Open Government   NCUA supports the Open Government initiative by promoting the principles of collaboration, participation, and transparency. The NCUA regards openness, in terms of budget, policy, and operations, as essential to fulfilling its statutory mission and maintaining public trust. https://www.ncua.gov/about/Pages/ open-government.aspx

Organizational Chart   The NCUA posts a Joint Photographic Group (JPG) file of its organizational chart online for viewing and downloading. https://www.ncua.gov/ Style%20Library/MainTheme/images/offices/ org-chart-download.jpg

Plain Language   The Plain Writing Act of 2010 promotes clear Government communication "to improve the effectiveness and accountability of Federal agencies to the public." Members of the public are welcome to comment on the NCUA's compliance with the act and to make suggestions for improving communication. Contact the NCUA via email if content in documents or on web pages is difficult to understand. https://www.ncua.gov/About/Pages/open-government/plain-writing.aspx | Email: PlainWriting@ncua.gov

Proposed Regulations The NCUA encourages the public to submit a comment on its proposed rules. Fax, 703-518-6319. https://www.ncua.gov/regulation-supervision/Pages/rules/proposed.aspx | Email: regcomments@ncua.gov

Publications To order publications, contact the Office of the Chief Financial Officer. Payment by check, credit card, or money order is acceptable and prepayment is required. Phone, 703-518-6340. https://www.ncua.gov/services/Pages/order-publications.aspx

Manuals and guides are available online to facilitate compliance with NCUA rules and regulations and with those from other agencies. The manuals and guides are not definitive and should be used in conjunction with other supervisory guidance and information provided by the NCUA and other Federal financial services regulators. https://www.ncua.gov/regulation-supervision/Pages/manuals-guides.aspx

Research a Credit Union The NCUA Web site features a credit union research tool, which complements the credit union locator. The research tool is text-based, and it can find a credit union and its profile by using a variety of search parameters. http://mapping.ncua.gov/ResearchCreditUnion.aspx

RSS Feeds / Email Subscriptions RSS services provide updates on NCUA Board actions, regulatory alerts, and supervisory guidance. Credit unions, members of the media, and general stakeholders can opt to receive notifications on Board actions, events, and general agency news. https://www.ncua.gov/Pages/rss.aspx

NCUA Express gives email users another option for receiving electronic NCUA communications. Within hours of a letter, press release, regulatory alert, or other communication being published, a message describing it and a link for downloading it are sent to a subscriber's inbox. https://www.ncua.gov/Pages/ncuaexpress.aspx

Share Insurance Estimator The Web site MyCreditUnion.gov features a share insurance estimator to help consumers, credit unions, and their members know how NCUA share insurance rules apply to member share accounts—what is insured and what portion, if any, exceeds coverage limits. http://www.mycreditunion.gov/estimator/Pages/default.aspx | Email: DCAMail@ncua.gov

Site Map The Web site map allows visitors to look for specific topics or to browse for content that aligns with their interests. https://www.ncua.gov/Pages/SiteMap.aspx

Social Media The NCUA has a Facebook account. https://www.facebook.com/NCUAgov

The NCUA tweets announcements and other newsworthy items on Twitter. https://twitter.com/TheNCUA

The NCUA posts educational videos, quarterly economic updates, and speeches on its YouTube channel. https://www.youtube.com/user/NCUAchannel

Starting a Federal Credit Union Groups interested in forming a Federal credit union may obtain free information from the appropriate regional office. Information is also available on the "How to Start a Credit Union" Web page. https://www.ncua.gov/services/Pages/field-of-membership-chartering/start-a-credit union.aspx | Email: NewFCU@ncua.gov; https://www.ncua.gov/About/Pages/contact.aspx

For further information, contact the Office of Public and Congressional Affairs, National Credit Union Administration, 1775 Duke Street, Alexandria, VA 22314-3428. Phone, 703-518-6330.

NATIONAL FOUNDATION ON THE ARTS AND THE HUMANITIES

National Endowment for the Arts

400 7th Street SW., Washington, DC 20506
Phone, 202–682–5400. TDD, 202–682–5496. Internet, http://www.arts.gov

Chair	R. Jane Chu
Senior Deputy Chairman	Mary Anne Carter
Chief Information Officer	Vacant
Chief of Staff	Mike Griffin
Deputy Chairman, Management and Budget	Vacant
Director, Accessibility	Beth Bienvenu
Director, Administrative Services	Kathy Daum
Director, Artist Communities and Presenting and Multidisciplinary Works / International Activities Coordinator	Michael Orlove
Director, Arts Education	Ayanna N. Hudson
Director, Budget	John Sotelo
Director, Civil Rights and Equal Employment Opportunity	Mike Griffin
Director, Dance	Jennifer Kareliusson, Acting
Director, Design Programs / Visual Arts Division Team Leader	Vacant
Director, Finance	Heidi Ren
Director, Folk and Traditional Arts	Clifford Murphy
Director, Grants and Contracts	Nicki Jacobs
Director, Guidelines and Panel Operations	Jillian L. Miller
Director, Human Resources	Craig M. McCord, Sr.
Director, Literature	Amy Stolls
Director, Local Arts Agencies and Challenge America	Vacant
Director, Media Arts	Jax Deluca
Director, Museums, Visual Arts, and Indemnity	Wendy Clark
Director, Music and Opera	Ann Meier Baker
Director, Public Affairs	Jessamyn Sarmiento
Director, Research and Analysis	Sunil Iyengar
Director, State and Regional Partnerships	Laura Scanlan
Director, Theater and Musical Theater	Greg Reiner
Federal Partnerships Coordinator	Tony Tighe
General Counsel	India Pinkney
Inspector General	Ronald Stith

The National Endowment for the Arts supports artistic excellence and promotes creativity and innovation to benefit individuals and communities.

Through its grants and programs, the Arts Endowment brings art to all 50 States and six U.S. jurisdictions, including rural areas, inner cities, and military bases. The Arts Endowment awards competitive matching grants to nonprofit organizations, to units of State or local government, and to federally recognized tribal communities or tribes for projects, programs, or activities in the fields of artist communities, arts education, dance, design, folk and traditional arts, literature, local arts agencies, media arts, museums, music, musical theater, opera, presenting, theater, and visual arts. It also awards competitive, nonmatching individual fellowships in literature and honorary fellowships in jazz, folk and traditional arts, and opera. Forty percent of the Arts Endowment's grant funds go to the 56 State and jurisdictional arts agencies and their regional arts organizations in support of arts projects in thousands of communities nationwide.

Sources of Information

Employment Job announcements are posted online. https://www.arts.gov/about/employment-opportunities-nea
Grants Application forms and guidelines and listings of grants recently made to

individuals and organizations are accessible online. http://www.arts.gov/grants
Podcasts Podcasts feature actors, authors, composers, musicians, playwrights, poets, and other artists and professionals who support and strengthen the arts. https://www.arts.gov/podcasts
Publications Publications, including annual reports and "NEA Arts" magazine, are available online. http://arts.gov/publications. https://www.arts.gov/about/annual-reports; https://www.arts.gov/NEARTS; https://www.arts.gov/staff

For further information, contact the Public Affairs Office, National Endowment for the Arts, 400 7th Street SW., Washington, DC 20506-0001. Phone, 202-682-5400. TDD, 202-682-5496.

National Endowment for the Humanities

400 7th Street SW., Washington, DC 20506
Phone, 202-606-8400. Fax, 800-634-1121. Internet, http://www.neh.gov | Email: info@neh.gov

Chair	Peggy Plympton, Acting
Deputy Chair	Vacant
Assistant Chair, Partnership and Strategic Initiatives	Vacant
Assistant Chair, Planning and Operations	Jeffrey Thomas
Assistant Chair, Programs	Adam Wolfson
Chief Information Officer	Brett Bobley
Chief of Staff	Vacant
General Counsel	Michael McDonald
Inspector General	Laura M.H. Davis

The National Endowment for the Humanities supports research, education, preservation, and public programs in the humanities.

According to the agency's authorizing legislation, the term "humanities" includes, but is not limited to, the study of the following: language, both modern and classical; linguistics; literature; history; jurisprudence; philosophy; archeology; comparative religion; ethics; the history, criticism, and theory of the arts; and those aspects of the social sciences that employ historical or philosophical approaches.

To increase understanding and appreciation of the humanities, the Endowment makes grants to individuals, as well as to groups and institutions: colleges, libraries, museums, nonprofit private groups, public television stations and agencies, schools, and universities. http://www.neh.gov/about

Challenge Grants The Office of Challenge Grants offers matching funds to help nonprofit institutions develop new sources of long-term support for educational, scholarly, preservation, and public programs in the humanities. http://www.neh.gov/divisions/challenge/about

For further information, call 202-606-8309.

Digital Humanities The Office of Digital Humanities supports projects that use digital technology or study how it affects education, preservation, public programming, and research in the humanities. http://www.neh.gov/divisions/odh/about | Email: odh@neh.gov

NATIONAL ENDOWMENT FOR THE HUMANITIES

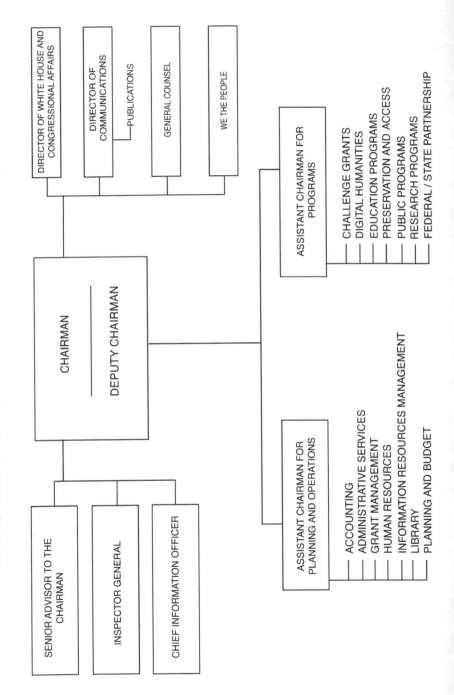

For further information, call 202-606-8401.

Education Programs   The Division of Education Programs strengthens sustained, thoughtful study of the humanities at all educational levels. It makes grants to educational institutions and gives fellowships to teachers and scholars. http://www.neh.gov/divisions/education/about

For further information, call 202-606-8500.

Federal/State Partnership   Humanities committees in each of the 50 States, the District of Columbia, Puerto Rico, the Virgin and Northern Mariana Islands, Guam, and American Samoa receive grants from the Endowment. These committees then make grants to humanities programs at the local level. http://www.neh.gov/divisions/fedstate/about

For further information, call 202-606-8254.

Preservation and Access   The Division of Preservation and Access supports creating, preserving, and increasing the availability of resources that are important for research, education, and public programming in the humanities. http://www.neh.gov/divisions/preservation/about

For further information, call 202-606-8570.

Public Programs   The Division of Public Programs supports institutions and organizations that develop and present humanities programming for general audiences. Its activities center on the Endowment's mandate "to increase public understanding of the humanities." http://www.neh.gov/divisions/public/about

For further information, call 202-606-8268.

Research Programs   The Division of Research Programs promotes original research in the humanities. It provides grants for significant research projects. http://www.neh.gov/divisions/research/about

For further information, call 202-606-8389.

Sources of Information

Employment   The National Endowment for the Humanities posts job opportunities on USAJobs, the Federal Government's official source for Federal job listings and employment opportunity information. https://www.usajobs.gov

Grants   Information on managing a grant, the application review process, and other topics is available on the "NEH Grants" Web page. http://www.neh.gov/grants

Publications   The Endowment's in-house, quarterly magazine "HUMANITIES" is available by subscription from the U.S. Government Publishing Office, P.O. Box 979050, St. Louis, MO 63197–9000. Phone, 202-512-1800. http://www.neh.gov/humanities/staff | Email: publications@neh.gov; http://www.neh.gov/about/contact | Email: info@neh.gov

For further information, contact the Office of Communications, National Endowment for the Humanities, 400 7th Street SW., Washington, DC 20506. Phone, 202-606-8400 or 800-634-1121. TDD, 202-606-8282 or 866-372-2930.

The Institute of Museum and Library Services did not meet the publication deadline for submitting updated information of its activities, functions, and sources of information as required by the automatic disclosure provisions of the Freedom of Information Act (5 U.S.C. 552(a)(1)(A)).

Institute of Museum and Library Services

955 L'Enfant Plaza North SW., Suite 4000, Washington, DC 20024-2135
Phone, 202-653-4657. Internet, http://www.imls.gov | Email: imlsinfo@imls.gov

Director	KATHRYN K. MATTHEW
Deputy Director for Library Services	MAURA MARX
Deputy Director for Museum Services	PAULA GANGOPADHYAY
Associate Deputy Director for Library Services	ROBIN DALE
Chief Financial Officer	CHRIS CATIGNANI

Chief Information Officer	STEPHANIE BURWELL
Chief Operating Officer	MICHAEL D. JERGER
Deputy Director of Digital and Information Strategy	AMMIE FARRAJ FEIJOO
Director for Grants Administration	MARY E. KENNELLY
Director of Communications and Government Affairs	JANELLE BREVARD
General Counsel	NANCY E. WEISS
Senior Museum Advisor	CHRISTOPHER J. REICH

The Institute of Museum and Library Services helps libraries and museums enhance cultural and civic engagement, embrace innovation, and further lifelong learning.

The Institute of Museum and Library Services (IMLS) was established within the National Foundation on the Arts and the Humanities by the Museum and Library Services Act of September 30, 1996 (110 Stat. 3009), which amended the Museum Services Act (20 U.S.C. 961 et seq.). The Institute combines the administration of Federal museum programs, which the Institute of Museum Services formerly managed, and Federal library programs, which the Department of Education formerly managed. The Institute's Director, whom the President appoints with the advice and consent of the Senate, is authorized to make grants to museums and libraries. The Director receives policy advice on museum and library programs from the National Museum and Library Services Board. Its 20 voting members are appointed by the President; its three nonvoting members include the Director, Deputy Director for Museum Services, and Deputy Director for Library Services.

The IMLS is the primary source of Federal support for the Nation's 35,000 museums and 123,000 libraries. Its grant making, policy development, and research help museums and libraries offer services that make people and their communities prosper. The IMLS awards grants to art, children's, general, history, natural history, science, and technology museums, as well as to aquariums, arboretums, botanical gardens, nature centers, planetariums, zoos, and historic houses. It also awards grants to academic, public, research, school, and special libraries. IMLS grants improve electronic sharing of information and expand public access to information and services. https://www.imls.gov/about-us

African American History and Culture Museum Grants   The IMLS awards these grants at two funding levels to improve

care of collections, develop professional management, and provide internship and fellowship opportunities. https://www.imls.gov/grants/available/museum-grants-african-american-history-and-culture

Laura Bush 21st Century Librarian Program   This program supports recruitment and education of library students, continuing education for those already working in the profession, and new programs and curricula. https://www.imls.gov/grants/available/laura-bush-21st-century-librarian-program

Museum Assessment Program   The IMLS supports the cost of this program through a cooperative agreement with the American Alliance of Museums. The program helps museums strengthen operations, plan for the future, and meet national standards through self-study and a site visit from a peer reviewer. https://www.imls.gov/grants/available/museum-assessment-program-map

Museums for America   The IMLS awards grants at two funding levels to help museums expand their role as lifelong learning resources, increase the vital contributions they make to livable communities, and become better stewards of the Nation's collections. https://www.imls.gov/grants/available/museums-america

National Arts and Humanities Youth Program Awards   This is a project of the President's Committee on the Arts and the Humanities in partnership with the IMLS and the National Endowments for the Arts and for the Humanities. These awards acknowledge museums and libraries for their afterschool and out-of-school arts and humanities programs for young Americans. https://www.imls.gov/grants/available/national-arts-and-humanities-youth-program-awards

National Leadership Grants for Libraries   These grants help library and archive professionals address the challenges and needs of their fields. Projects supported by these grants stimulate research, develop new tools, and produce innovative alliances, models, practices, and services that broadly affect the library and archival fields. https://www.imls.gov/grants/available/national-leadership-grants-libraries

National Leadership Grants for Museums These grants help museum professionals address the challenges and needs of their field. Projects supported by these grants promote innovation and collaboration and typically produce results that broadly affect the museum field. https://www.imls.gov/grants/available/national-leadership-grants-museums

National Medal for Museum and Library Service This award acknowledges institutions for providing exceptional and meaningful public service in their communities. https://www.imls.gov/grants/available/national-medal-museum-and-library-service

Native American and Native Hawaiian Museum Services Program These grants to federally recognized tribes and organizations that represent and serve Native Hawaiians help sustain indigenous culture, heritage, and knowledge through improved museum services. https://www.imls.gov/grants/available/native-americannative-hawaiian-museum-services-program

Native American Library Services: Basic Grants and the Education/Assessment Option These noncompetitive grants to federally recognized tribes help them purchase library materials, acquire computers and provide Internet connectivity, and fund salaries. The Education/Assessment option is supplemental to the basic grants and also noncompetitive. It funds library staff participation in continuing education courses, training workshops, and conferences. It also allows libraries to hire a consultant for an onsite professional assessment. https://www.imls.gov/grants/available/native-american-library-services-basic-grants

Native American Library Services: Enhancement Grants These grants to federally recognized tribes expand services for access to information, learning, and partnerships. https://www.imls.gov/grants/available/native-american-library-services-enhancement-grants

Native Hawaiian Library Services This program supports grants that implement new library services or enhance existing ones. https://www.imls.gov/grants/available/native-hawaiian-library-services

Sparks! Ignition Grants for Libraries These grants promote exploration and expansion of the frontiers of archival and library practices and services. https://www.imls.gov/grants/available/sparks-ignition-grants-libraries

Sparks! Ignition Grants for Museums These grants promote exploration and expansion of the frontiers of museum practices and services. https://www.imls.gov/grants/available/sparks-ignition-grants-museums

State Program Grants The Grants to States program is the largest Federal source of funding to support library services in the United States. The IMLS uses a population-based formula to distribute annual grants among the State Library Administrative Agencies—official agencies charged by law with the extension and development of library services. Each year, thousands of Grants to States projects promote the priorities and assist the purposes of the Library Services and Technology Act. https://www.imls.gov/grants/grants-states

Sources of Information

Employment The IMLS offers a unique opportunity to work with the Nation's libraries and museums at the national level and in coordination with State and local organizations. The IMLS posts employment and internship opportunities on its Web site. https://www.imls.gov/about-us/jobs-imls/employment-opportunities; https://www.imls.gov/about-us/jobs-imls/internship-opportunities

Freedom of Information Act (FOIA) An online guide answers frequently asked FOIA-related questions. https://www.imls.gov/about-us/agency-reports/freedom-information-act-foia

Grants Search tools are available online to search for available grants and awarded grants. https://www.imls.gov/grants/apply-grant/available-grants; https://www.imls.gov/grants/awarded-grants

News   The IMLS posts news releases
and project profiles online, as well as
its "UpNext" blog and "Primary Source"
monthly newsletter. https://www.imls.gov/
news-events

Open Government   The IMLS supports
the Governmentwide initiative to promote
openness in the work of Federal agencies. It
posts datasets on Data.gov and maintains a
data catalog that makes IMLS data accessible
to developers, researchers, and to the
general public. https://www.imls.gov/about-
us/open-government

Publications   Publications are accessible
in Portable Document Format (PDF) on the
"Publications List" Web page. https://www.
imls.gov/publications

ideos   A collection of IMLS videos is
available online. https://www.imls.gov/
publications/imls-videos; http://www.
imls.gov | Email: imlsinfo@imls.gov

For further information, contact the Office of Communications and Government Affairs, Institute of Museum and
Library Services, 955 L'Enfant Plaza North SW., Suite 4000, Washington, DC 20024. Phone, 202-653-4757.

National Labor Relations Board

1015 Half Street SE., Washington, DC 20570
Phone, 202-273-1000. TDD, 202-273-4300. Internet, http://www.nlrb.gov

Board

Chair	PHILIP A. MISCIMARRA
Member	MARVIN E. KAPLAN
Member	LAUREN MCFERRAN
Member	MARK G. PEARCE
Member	(VACANCY)
https://www.nlrb.gov/who-we-are/board	
General Counsel	RICHARD F. GRIFFIN, JR.
https://www.nlrb.gov/who-we-are/general-counsel/richard-f-griffin-jr	
Deputy General Counsel	JENNIFER ABRUZZO
Associate General Counsel, Division of Advice	JAYME SOPHIR
Associate General Counsel, Division of Enforcement Litigation	JOHN H. FERGUSON
Associate General Counsel, Division of Legal Counsel	BARBARA O'NEILL
Associate General Counsel, Division of Operations-Management	ANNE G. PURCELL
Chief Financial Officer	MEHUL PAREKH
Chief Information Officer	PREM ABURVASAMY
Chief Judge, Division of Judges	ROBERT A. GIANNASI
Director, Division of Administration	LASHARN HAMILTON
Director, Office of Congressional and Public Affairs	CARMEN SPELL
Director, Office of Equal Employment Opportunity	BRENDA V. HARRIS
Director, Office of Representation Appeals	(VACANCY)
Executive Secretary	GARY W. SHINNERS
Solicitor	(VACANCY)
Inspector General	DAVID P. BERRY
https://www.nlrb.gov/who-we-are/inspector-general	

[For the National Labor Relations Board statement of organization, see the Federal Register of June 14, 1979, 44 FR
34215]

*The National Labor Relations Board remedies unfair labor practices and safeguards
employees' rights to organize and to determine whether to have unions as their bargaining
representative.*

The National Labor Relations Board (NLRB) is an independent agency created by Congress to administer the National Labor Relations Act of 1935 (Wagner Act; 29 U.S.C. 167). The Board is authorized to designate appropriate units for collective bargaining and to conduct secret ballot elections to determine whether employees desire representation by a labor organization. https://www.nlrb.gov/who-we-are/our-history

Activities

In addition to preventing and remedying unfair labor practices, the NLRB conducts secret ballot elections among employees in appropriate collective-bargaining units to determine whether or not they desire to be represented by a labor organization in bargaining with employers over wages, hours, and working conditions. It also conducts secret ballot elections among employees who have been covered by a union-security agreement to determine whether or not they wish to revoke their union's authority to make such agreements. In jurisdictional disputes between two or more unions, the Board determines which competing group of workers is entitled to perform the work involved.

The regional directors and their staffs process representation, unfair labor practice, and jurisdictional dispute cases. They issue complaints in unfair labor practice cases, seek settlement of unfair labor practice charges, obtain compliance with Board orders and court judgments, and petition district courts for injunctions to prevent or remedy unfair labor practices. The regional directors conduct hearings in representation cases, hold elections pursuant to the agreement of the parties or the decisionmaking authority delegated to them by the Board or pursuant to Board directions, and issue certifications of representatives when unions win or certify the results when they lose employee elections. The regional directors process petitions for bargaining unit clarification, for amendment of certification, and for rescission of a labor organization's authority to make a union-shop agreement. They also conduct national emergency employee referendums.

Administrative law judges conduct hearings in unfair labor practice cases, make findings of fact and conclusions of law, and recommend remedies for violations found. Their decisions can be appealed to the Board for a final agency determination. The Board's decisions are subject to review in the U.S. courts of appeals. https://www.nlrb.gov/what-we-do

Sources of Information

Business Opportunities Information is available online to assist businesses that seek to sell their products and services to the NLRB. Information is also available from the agency's Acquisitions Management Branch. Phone, 202-273-4047. https://www.nlrb.gov/who-we-are/acquisitions

Electronic Filing Parties or other persons may use the e-filing program to file selected documents in unfair labor practice and representation cases with the NLRB's Office of Executive Secretary, the Division of Judges, the General Counsel's Office of Appeals, and regional, subregional, and resident offices. https://apps.nlrb.gov/eservice/efileterm.aspx

Electronic Mail Subscriptions The NLRB uses email subscriptions to disseminate various types of information: administrative law judge decisions, appellate court branch briefs and motions, board decisions, general counsel memos, news releases, operations-management memos, personnel announcements, regional election decisions, regional news, social media feeds, and a weekly summary of decisions. https://www.nlrb.gov/email-subscription-service

Employment The Board appoints administrative law judges from a register established by the Office of Personnel Management. The Agency hires attorneys for all its offices, field examiners for its field offices, and administrative personnel for its Washington and field offices. http://www.nlrb.gov/who-we-are/careers

Freedom of Information Act (FOIA) The NLRB makes available instructions online for submitting FOIA requests. Descriptions of the record types that the NLRB maintains and links to records that are accessible elsewhere on the Internet are also available on the NLRB Web site. https://www.nlrb.gov/news-outreach/foia

An e-FOIA request form is available on the NLRB Web site. https://www.nlrb.gov/news-outreach/foia/e-foia-request-form

Inspector General Hotline   Violations of laws and regulations relating to NLRB programs may be reported to the Inspector General by email or phone or by using the online form. Phone, 800-736-2983. https://www.nlrb.gov/who-we-are/inspector-general/inspector-general-hotline | Email: oighotline@nlrb.gov

Internships   At its Washington, DC, headquarters and its field offices, the NLRB offers opportunities, internships and student positions, for law and nonlegal students. https://www.nlrb.gov/who-we-are/careers/job-descriptions-and-listings/student-positions-law-non-legal

Open Government   The NLRB supports the Open Government initiative by incorporating the principles of collaboration, participation, and transparency in its plans for agency information and systems. https://www.nlrb.gov/open

Publications   Case documents and agency publications are available on the NLRB's Web site. Or, visit the NLRB's headquarters in Washington, DC, or one of its field offices to inspect case documents and read agency publications. NLRB offices offer free informational leaflets in limited quantities. http://www.nlrb.gov/cases-decisions

Regional Offices   Contact information for NLRB regional, subregional, and resident offices is available on the "Regional Offices" Web pages. http://www.nlrb.gov/who-we-are/regional-offices

Site Map   NLRB Web site visitors may use the site map to look for specific topics or to browse for content that aligns with their interests. https://www.nlrb.gov/sitemap

Speakers   To provide a better understanding of the National Labor Relations Act and NLRB policies, procedures, and services, NLRB experts are available to speak before labor and civic organizations, educational institutions, management organizations, bar associations, and other similar groups. Requests for speakers or panelists may be made online by using the online request form. http://www.nlrb.gov/news-outreach/request-speaker; https://www.nlrb.gov/who-we-are/contact-us | Email: publicinfo@nlrb.gov

For further information, contact the Office of Congressional and Public Affairs, National Labor Relations Board, 1015 Half Street SE., Washington, DC 20570. Phone, 202-273-1991.

National Mediation Board

1301 K Street NW., Suite 250 East, Washington, DC 20005
Phone, 202-692-5000. Internet, http://www.nmb.gov

Board Members	
Chair	Linda A. Puchala
Member	Harry R. Hoglander
Executive Directors	
Chief of Staff	Daniel Rainey
General Counsel, Office of Legal Affairs	Mary L. Johnson
Assistant Chief of Staff, Administration	Samantha T. Jones
Director, Arbitration Services	Roland Watkins
Deputy Chief of Staff, Mediation	Michael Kelliher

The National Mediation Board facilitates labor-management relations within the railroad and airline industries.

The National Mediation Board (NMB) is an independent agency established by the 1934 amendments to the Railway Labor Act of 1926 (45 U.S.C. 151-158, 160-162, 1181-1188). The Board comprises three members whom the President appoints and the Senate confirms. The Board designates a Chair on a yearly basis.

NMB dispute-resolution processes are designed to resolve disputes over the negotiation of new or revised collective bargaining agreements and the interpretation or application of existing agreements. The Board also effectuates employee rights of self-organization where a representation dispute exists. http://www.nmb.gov/about-nmb/nmb-overview

Activities

Mediation and Alternative Dispute Resolution   Following receipt of an application for mediation, the NMB assigns a mediator to assist the parties in reaching an agreement. The NMB is obligated to use its best efforts to bring about a peaceful resolution to the dispute. If such efforts do not settle the dispute, the NMB advises the parties and offers interest arbitration as an alternative approach to resolve the remaining issues. If either party rejects this offer, the NMB releases the parties from formal mediation. This release triggers a 30-day cooling off period. During this period, the NMB continues to work with the parties to achieve a consensual resolution. If, however, an agreement is not reached by the end of the 30-day period, the parties are free to exercise lawful self-help, such as carrier-imposed working conditions or a strike by the union or organization.

In addition to traditional mediation services, the NMB also provides voluntary Alternative Dispute Resolution (ADR) services. ADR services include facilitation, training, grievance mediation, and an online dispute resolution component, which applies technology to the dispute resolution process. The purpose of the ADR program is to assist the parties in learning and applying more effective, less confrontational methods for resolving their disputes and to help them resolve more of them without outside intervention. http://www.nmb.gov/services/mediation

Presidential Emergency Board   If the NMB determines that a dispute threatens to deprive substantially any section of the country of essential transportation service, it notifies the President. The President, at his discretion, may establish a Presidential Emergency Board (PEB) to investigate and report back within 30 days. After the PEB has been created and for 30 days after it has made its report to the President, neither party to the dispute may exercise self-help.

There are also special emergency procedures for unresolved disputes affecting publicly funded and operated commuter railroads and their employees. If the mediation procedures are exhausted, the parties to the dispute or the Governor of any State where the railroad operates may request that the President establish a PEB. The President is required to establish such a board if requested. If no settlement is reached within 60 days following the creation of the PEB, the NMB is required to conduct a public hearing on the dispute. If there is no settlement within 120 days after the creation of the PEB, either party or the Governor of any affected state may request a second, final-offer PEB. No self-help is permitted pending the exhaustion of these emergency procedures. http://www.nmb.gov/services/pebmenu

Representation   When a labor organization or individual files an application with the NMB to represent employees, the Agency assigns an investigator to conduct a representation investigation. Should the applicant meet the requirements, the NMB continues the investigation, usually with a secret telephone or Internet election. The NMB is responsible for ensuring that the requirements for a fair election process have been maintained. If the employees vote to be represented, the NMB issues a certification that commences the carrier's statutory duty to bargain with the certified representative. http://www.nmb.gov/services/representation

Arbitration   The NMB provides both grievance arbitration and interest arbitration. Grievance arbitration is a process for resolving disputes regarding the interpretation or application of an existing collective bargaining agreement. Grievances must be handled through grievance arbitration if not otherwise resolved, and they cannot be used by the parties to trigger self-help actions. The NMB has significant administrative responsibilities for grievance arbitration in the railroad industry, which includes those before the National Railroad Adjustment Board (NRAB), as well as the two types of arbitration panels established by the labor-management parties at each railroad: public law boards (PLBs) and special boards of adjustment (SBAs). Grievance arbitration in the airline industry is accomplished at the various system boards of adjustment created jointly by labor and management at the parties' expense. The NMB furnishes panels of prospective arbitrators for the parties' selection in both the airline and railroad industries. The NMB also pays the salary and travel expenses of the arbitrators for railroad arbitration proceedings. Grievance arbitration decisions are final and binding with very limited grounds for judicial review.

Interest arbitration is a process to establish the terms of a new or modified collective bargaining agreement through arbitration rather than through negotiations. Unlike grievance arbitration, its use is not statutorily required. The NMB offers the parties the opportunity to use binding interest arbitration when the agency has determined that further mediation efforts will not be successful. In addition, the parties may directly agree to resolve their collective bargaining dispute or portions of their dispute through interest arbitration. The NMB generally provides the parties with panels of potential arbitrators from which they choose an individual to resolve their dispute. In some instances, however, the parties agree to allow the NMB to appoint an arbitrator directly. Interest arbitration decisions are final and binding with very narrow grounds for judicial appeal. http://www.nmb.gov/services/arbitration

Sources of Information

Employment   Job openings are posted online. http://www.nmb.gov/about-nmb/jobs
Knowledge Store   The Knowledge Store contains over 100,000 documents—including arbitration awards, representation decisions, annual reports, PEB reports, industry contracts, and union constitutions and bylaws—in an easily searchable format. http://knowledgestore.nmb.gov/ks/build.html
Open Government   The NMB supports the Open Government initiative, which requires Federal executive departments and agencies to implement principles of collaboration, participation, and transparency. http://www.nmb.gov/resources/open
Publications   The annual reports of the National Mediation Board are available on its "NMB Documents On-Line" Web page and in the Knowledge Store. http://www.nmb.gov/resources/docs
Virtual Reading Room   Copies of collective bargaining agreements between labor and management of various rail and air carriers and NMB Determinations dating from October 1, 1998, and some even earlier, are available in the Knowledge Store. http://knowledgestore.nmb.gov/ks/build.html; http://www.nmb.gov/press-and-contacts/key-contacts

For further information, contact the Public Information Officer, National Mediation Board, Suite 250 East, 1301 K Street NW., Washington, DC 20005-7011. Phone, 202-692-5050.

National Railroad Passenger Corporation (AMTRAK)

1 Massachusetts Avenue NW., Washington, DC 20001
Phone, 202-906-3000. Internet, http://www.amtrak.com

Board of Directors

Chair	ANTHONY R. COSCIA
Vice Chair	JEFFREY R. MORELAND
Member	CHRISTOPHER R. BEALL
Member	YVONNE B. BURKE
Member	THOMAS C. CARPER
Member	ALBERT DICLEMENTE
Member	(VACANCY)
Member	(VACANCY)
Amtrak President / Amtrak Co-Chief Executive Officer (ex officio)	RICHARD H. ANDERSON
Secretary of Transportation (ex officio)	ELAINE CHAO

https://www.amtrak.com/servlet/ContentServer?c=Page&pagename=am%2FLayout&cid=1241245669142

Executive Committee

President / Co-Chief Executive Officer	RICHARD H. ANDERSON
Co-Chief Executive Officer	C. WICKCLIFFE MOORMAN IV
Executive Vice Presidents	
Administration	DONALD J. STADTLER
Chief Financial Officer	WILLIAM N. FEIDT
Chief Legal Officer / Corporate Secretary / General Counsel	ELEANOR D. ACHESON
Chief Operations Officer	SCOT NAPARSTEK
Marketing and Business Development	JASON MOLFETAS
Planning, Technology, and Public Affairs	STEPHEN J. GARDNER

https://www.amtrak.com/servlet/ContentServer?c=Page&page
   name=am%2FLayout&cid=1241245669145

Inspector General	THOMAS HOWARD

http://www.amtrakoig.gov

[For the National Railroad Passenger Corporation statement of organization, see the Code of Federal Regulations, Title 49, Part 700]

The above list of key personnel was updated 09–2017.

The National Railroad Passenger Corporation provides intercity rail passenger service in the United States.

The National Railroad Passenger Corporation (Amtrak) was created by the Rail Passenger Service Act of 1970, as amended (49 U.S.C. 241), and was incorporated under the laws of the District of Columbia. By developing, operating, and improving U.S. intercity rail passenger service, Amtrak provides a balanced nationwide transportation system.

Amtrak operates approximately 300 trains per day, serving over 500 stations in 46 States, over a system of 22,000 route miles. Of this route system, Amtrak owns about 530 route miles in the Northeast and several other small track segments elsewhere in the country.

Amtrak owns or leases its stations and owns its repair and maintenance facilities. The Corporation employs a total workforce of approximately 20,000 and provides all reservation, station, and onboard service staffs, as well as train and engine operating crews. Outside the Northeast Corridor, Amtrak has contracts with privately and publicly owned railroads to operate on their track. These railroads are responsible for the condition of the roadbed and for coordinating the flow of traffic.

In fiscal year 2016, Amtrak transported over 31 million people, 85,000 passengers traveling per day. On behalf of 21 agencies in 18 States, Amtrak is a contract operator for corridor services on 29 routes. It also runs commuter trains under contract with several commuter agencies.

Although Amtrak's basic route system was originally designated by the Secretary of Transportation in 1971, modifications have been made to the Amtrak system and to individual routes that have resulted in more efficient and cost-effective operations. Increased capital funding in recent years has allowed Amtrak to reduce its debt load and make progress in bringing its network to a state of good repair. https://www.amtrak.com/about-amtrak

Sources of Information

Business Opportunities   Amtrak provides an online procurement portal to foster business partnerships. https://procurement.amtrak.com

Career Opportunities   Amtrak employs more than 20,000 professionals in a variety of career fields. https://jobs.amtrak.com

Freedom of Information Act (FOIA)   Amtrak maintains an online FOIA library. Phone, 202-906-3741. https://www.amtrak.com/servlet/ContentServer?c=Page&pagename=am%2FLayout&cid=1241267362261

Great American Stations   The Great American Stations Project educates communities on the benefits of redeveloping train stations, offers tools to community leaders for preserving their stations, and provides the appropriate Amtrak resources. http://www.greatamericanstations.com

History   For a fast way to learn how the U.S. Congress and its passage of key legislation have affected Amtrak, how Amtrak's environmental efforts have evolved, and when Amtrak added service to a local or regional community, visit Amtrak's "Historic Timeline" web page. https://history.amtrak.com/amtraks-history/historic-timeline

Kids Depot   "The Kids Depot" website features a learning zone, park, playground, station, treehouse, workshop, and movies! https://www.amtrak.com/media/KidsDepot/KidsDepot.html

Oversight   Amtrak's Office of the Inspector General posts reports and data on Oversight.gov, a text-searchable repository of reports

that Federal Inspectors General publish. The Council of the Inspectors General on Integrity and Efficiency operates and maintains the website to increase public access to independent and authoritative information on the Federal Government. https://oversight.gov

Social Media   Amtrak has a Facebook account. http://www.facebook.com/Amtrak

Amtrak posts photos on its Instagram web page. http://www.instagram.com/amtrak

Amtrak tweets announcements and other newsworthy items on Twitter. http://twitter.com/Amtrak

Store   Official Amtrak merchandise—adult apparel, calendars, headwear, posters, and toys—may be purchased online. http://store.amtrak.com

Train Tracker   A train may be tracked online by using the train name, train number, or train station. https://www.amtrak.com/trainlocationmap; http://www.amtrak.com

For further information, contact the Government Affairs Department, Amtrak, 1 Massachusetts Avenue NW., Washington, DC 20001. Phone, 202-906-3918.

National Science Foundation

4201 Wilson Boulevard, Arlington, VA 22230
Phone, 703-292-5111. TDD, 800-281-8749. Internet, http://www.nsf.gov | Email: info@nsf.gov

National Science Board
https://www.nsf.gov/nsb/members/index.jsp

Ex officio member   France A. Córdova

Terms Expiring in 2020

                                                            John L. Anderson
                                                            Roger N. Beachy
                                                            Vicki L. Chandler
                                                            Robert M. Groves
                                                            James S. Jackson
                                                            Sethuraman Panchanathan
                                                            George P. Peterson
Chair   Diane L. Souvaine

Terms Expiring in 2022

                                                            Arthur Bienenstock
                                                            W. Kent Fuchs
                                                            W. Carl Lineberger
                                                            Victor R. McCrary
                                                            Emilio F. Moran
Vice Chair   Ellen Ochoa

JULIA M. PHILLIPS
ANNEILA I. SARGENT

Terms Expiring in 2024

MAUREEN L. CONDIC
SURESH V. GARIMELLA
STEVEN LEATH
DANIEL A. REED
GERALDINE L. RICHMOND
S. ALAN STERN
STEPHEN H. WILLARD
MARIA T. ZUBER

https://www.nsf.gov/nsb/members/terms.jsp

Executive Officer to the National Science Board   JOHN J. VEYSEY II

Inspector General   ALLISON C. LERNER
https://www.nsf.gov/staff/staff_bio.jsp?lan=alerner

National Science Foundation
https://www.nsf.gov/staff/execlist.jsp

Office of the Director (OD)

Director   FRANCE A. CÓRDOVA
Deputy Director   (VACANCY)

Chief Officers
Information   DOROTHY ARONSON
Operating   F. FLEMING CRIM

Office Heads
Diversity and Inclusion   RHONDA J. DAVIS
General Counsel   LAWRENCE RUDOLPH
Integrative Activities   SUZANNE IACONO
International Science and Engineering   REBECCA S. KEISER
Legislative and Public Affairs   AMANDA H. GREENWELL
https://www.nsf.gov/od

OAD Directorates *

Assistant Directors
Biological Sciences   JOANNE S. TORNOW
Computer and Information Science and Engineering   ERWIN GIANCHANDANI
Education and Human Resources   KAREN A. MARRONGELLE
Engineering   DAWN TILBURY
Geosciences   WILLIAM E. EASTERLING
Mathematical and Physical Sciences   ANNE KINNEY
Social, Behavioral, and Economic Sciences   ARTHUR W. LUPIA
https://www.nsf.gov/staff/orglist.jsp

OAD Offices *

Chief Officers
Financial   TERESA GRANCORVITZ
Human Capital   WONZIE L. GARDNER

Office Heads
Budget, Finance, and Award Management   TERESA GRANCORVITZ
Information and Resource Management   WONZIE L. GARDNER

---

* OAD is an abbreviation for Office of Assistant Director.

NATIONAL SCIENCE FOUNDATION

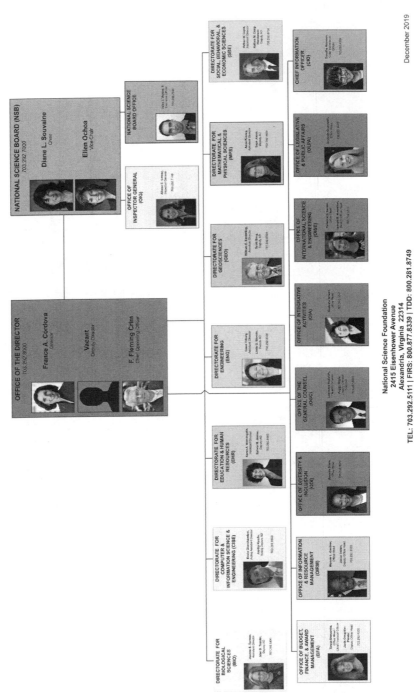

National Science Foundation
2415 Eisenhower Avenue
Alexandria, Virginia 22314
TEL: 703.292.5111 | FIRS: 800.877.8339 | TDD: 800.281.8749

December 2019

The above list of key personnel was updated 11–2019.

The National Science Foundation supports research and education to advance science and engineering.

Establishment and Organization

On May 10, 1950, President Harry S. Truman approved "an act to promote the progress of science; to advance the national health, prosperity, and welfare; to secure the national defense; and for other purposes." This statute, which is commonly cited as the National Science Foundation Act of 1950 (Public Law 81–507), established the National Science Foundation (NSF) as an independent and executive branch agency. The NSF consists of a National Science Board (NSB) and a Director. http://www.loc.gov/law/help/statutes-at-large/81st-congress/session-2/c81s2ch171.pdf

Descriptions of the NSF's establishment, composition, functions, purpose, research facilities, and other statutory information are codified in chapter 16, sections 1861–1887, of 42 U.S.C. https://uscode.house.gov/view.xhtml?path=/prelim@title42/chapter16&edition=prelim

The NSB establishes the policies of the NSF. The President appoints each of the 24 members of the Board to a term of 6 years. Appointees have earned distinguished reputations of service in the fields of agriculture, education, engineering, research management, public affairs, and the basic, medical, or social sciences. They also have an outlook that broadly represents that of national science and engineering leadership. The membership is divided into three groups of eight members; the terms of each group are staggered and expire every 2 years. Any member, other than the Director, who has served on the Board for 12 consecutive years is ineligible for reappointment during the 2-year period following the 12th year. The Board elects its Chair and vice chair every 2 years. The election takes place in an even-numbered year at the annual meeting (42 U.S.C. 1863). https://uscode.house.gov/view.xhtml?req=granuleid:USC-prelim-title42-section1863&num=0&edition=prelim

The President, by the advice and with the consent of the Senate, appoints the Director for a term of 6 years. Before making his or her selection, the President must give

the Board an opportunity to recommend candidates for consideration (42 U.S.C. 1864). As an ex officio member of the Board, the NSF Director is coordinate with the other Board members, except with respect to compensation and tenure. The Director is a voting member of the Board and is eligible to serve as its Chair or vice chair if elected (42 U.S.C. 1863). https://uscode.house.gov/view.xhtml?req=granuleid:USC-prelim-title42-section1864&num=0&edition=prelim

The NSF publishes its statements of organization in the "Federal Register" as notices:

58 FR 7587–7595 (8 FEB 1993). https://www.govinfo.gov/content/pkg/FR-1993-02-08/pdf/FR-1993-02-08.pdf#page=121

58 FR 30819 (27 MAY 1993). https://www.govinfo.gov/content/pkg/FR-1993-05-27/pdf/FR-1993-05-27.pdf#page=135

59 FR 22690 (2 MAY 1994). https://www.govinfo.gov/content/pkg/FR-1994-05-02/pdf/FR-1994-05-02.pdf#page=210

60 FR 52431 (6 OCT 1995). https://www.govinfo.gov/content/pkg/FR-1995-10-06/pdf/95-24895.pdf#page=1

The agency's organizational chart is available in Portable Document Format (PDF) for viewing and downloading on the "NSF Organization List" web page. https://www.nsf.gov/staff/organizational_chart.pdf

Activities

The NSF initiates and supports fundamental, long-term, merit-selected research in the scientific and engineering disciplines through grants, contracts, and other agreements that are awarded to universities, colleges, academic consortia, and nonprofit and small business institutions. Most of this research attempts to answer scientific and engineering questions of fundamental life processes, natural laws and phenomena, fundamental processes that influence the human environment, and the forces that affect people as members of society, as well as the behavior of society as a whole. https://www.nsf.gov/about

The NSF encourages cooperative efforts involving universities, industries, and government. It also promotes research and development for better products and services that improve the quality of life and stimulate economic growth. https://www.nsf.gov/about/what.jsp

The NSF cultivates talent by supporting undergraduate and graduate students and postdoctoral researchers. It administers special programs to identify and encourage participation of underrepresented groups in science and technology and to strengthen research capability at small institutions and businesses and at colleges and universities. https://www.nsf.gov/od/broadeningparticipation/bp.jsp

It supports major national and international science and engineering activities, including the U.S. Antarctic program, ocean drilling program, and global geoscience studies. Cooperative scientific and engineering research activities support exchange programs for American and foreign scientists and engineers, execution of jointly designed research projects, participation in international science and engineering organizational activities, and travel to international conferences. https://www.nsf.gov/dir/index.jsp?org=OISE

Contracts and cooperative agreements with national centers allow qualified scientists and engineers access to large facilities. The NSF supports national centers that are associated with astronomy and atmospheric sciences, biological and engineering research, science and technology, supercomputers, and long-term ecological research sites.

The agency's science and engineering education activities include grants for research and development of instructional materials for students and teachers and the application of advanced technologies to education. Grants also are available for teacher preparation and enhancement and informal science education activities. Funding is provided for college science instrumentation, course and curriculum improvement, faculty and student activities, and minority resource centers. The NSF also supports studies of the status of math, science, and engineering education. https://www.nsf.gov/funding/aboutfunding.jsp

The Vannevar Bush Award is given annually to an outstanding contributor to the welfare of the Nation and mankind through public service in science and technology. The Alan T. Waterman Award is given annually to a promising young scientist or engineer to support research and study. The NSF also presents its Public Service Award to one individual and to one company, corporation, or organization for increasing public understanding of science or engineering through public service in areas other than research. The NSF administratively supports the President's Committee on the National Medal of Science. https://www.nsf.gov/awards/presidential.jsp

Sources of Information

A–Z Index   An A–Z index to find funding opportunities by title is available on the NSF website. https://www.nsf.gov/funding/azindex.jsp

Archived Records   NSF records are referenced in the "Guide to Federal Records in the National Archives of the United States." The Guide is accessible online, and NSF records have been assigned to Record Group 307. https://www.archives.gov/research/guide-fed-records/groups/307.html

At a Glance   The "At a Glance" web page provides a convenient overview of NSF activities, partners, and personnel. https://www.nsf.gov/about/glance.jsp

Awards   The NSF funds science and engineering research and education through contracts, cooperative agreements, and grants. The Foundation provides approximately 20 percent of the Federal support that academic institutions receive for basic research. http://www.nsf.gov/awards/about.jsp

The abstract, institutions, names, programs, title, and other information associated with an award may be found using one search box on the NSF website. https://www.nsf.gov/awardsearch

Board and Committee Meetings   Webcasts of NSB open sessions and committee meetings that are held in Arlington, VA, remain available for at least 1 year after the event. Transcripts of closed sessions of the NSB, its committees, and other subentities are available upon request by email. http://www.nsf.gov/nsb/meetings | Email: nationalsciencebrd@nsf.gov

Business Opportunities   The NSF publicizes contracting and subcontracting opportunities in the "Commerce Business Daily" and other appropriate publications. Organizations seeking contract work should contact either the Division of Acquisition and Cooperative Support or the Division of Administrative Services, National Science Foundation, Arlington, VA 22230.

Division of Acquisition and Cooperative Support. Phone, 703-292-8240. http://www.nsf.gov/bfa/dcca/index.jsp

Division of Administrative Services. Phone, 703-292-8190. http://www.nsf.gov/oirm/das

Career Opportunities   To carry out its mission, the NSF relies on educators, engineers, mathematicians, program directors, and statisticians, as well as on professionals with administrative, business, and management backgrounds. The NSF also offers career opportunities—internship and recent graduates programs and the Presidential Management Fellows program—for students and recent graduates. http://www.nsf.gov/careers

In 2018, the NSF ranked 8th among 27 midsize Government agencies in the Best Places To Work Agency Rankings. https://bestplacestowork.org/rankings/detail/NF00

Climate Change   NSF Public Affairs publishes current research news on the effects of climate change on diverse ecosystems like coral reefs, grasslands, and the Southern Ocean of the Antarctic.

—on coral reefs. https://www.nsf.gov/discoveries/disc_summ.jsp?cntn_id=299144

—on grasslands. https://www.nsf.gov/discoveries/disc_summ.jsp?cntn_id=299102

—on the Southern Ocean. https://www.nsf.gov/discoveries/disc_summ.jsp?cntn_id=297719

Contact   The "Contact NSF" web page has email addresses and phone numbers. https://www.nsf.gov/help/contact.jsp | Email: info@nsf.gov

The NSF has a separate web page for media inquiries. Phone, 703-292-7090. https://www.nsf.gov/news/newsroom.jsp | Email: media@nsf.gov

Fellowships   Consult the online "Guide to Programs / Browse Funding Opportunities"

and appropriate announcements and brochures for postdoctoral fellowship opportunities that may be available through some NSF divisions. Beginning graduate and minority graduate students wanting to apply for fellowships should contact the Directorate for Education and Human Resources. Phone, 703-292-8600. http://www.nsf.gov/funding/browse_all_funding.jsp

Freedom of Information Act (FOIA)   A request for agency records should be submitted in accordance with the NSF's FOIA regulation (45 CFR 612). A request should be clearly labeled as "FOIA REQUEST" and be addressed to the FOIA Officer, Office of General Counsel, National Science Foundation, Room 1265, Arlington, VA 22230. Phone, 703-292-8060. Fax, 703-292-9242. http://www.nsf.gov/policies/foia.jsp | Email: foia@nsf.gov

Grants   The "Grants.gov Application Guide" helps applicants prepare NSF applications and submit them using Grant.gov. The current guide is available in Portable Document Format (PDF) for viewing and downloading. https://www.nsf.gov/publications/pub_summ.jsp?ods_key=grantsgovguide

Mobile Software Applications (Apps)   The NSF Science Zone app and Science360 Radio app are accessible through the NSF website. https://www.nsf.gov/news/special_reports/apps/index.jsp

Multimedia Gallery   The NSF maintains an online multimedia gallery. https://www.nsf.gov/news/mmg

News Search   A visitor to the NSF website may search an assortment of news types by keyword or title. https://www.nsf.gov/news/search.jsp

Office of Inspector General (OIG)   NSF employees, grantees, principal investigators, and others working on NSF programs, grants, or contracts are well-positioned to detect problems. Providing information about allegations or suspicions of abuse, fraud, mismanagement, research misconduct, unnecessary Government expenditures, and waste helps the OIG improve management and reduce fraud. https://www.nsf.gov/oig/report-fraud | Email: oig@nsf.gov

Open Government   To increase collaboration, public participation, and transparency, the NSF maintains an Open Government web page and welcomes ideas and suggestions from the public. https://www.nsf.gov/open

Proposal Status   The proposal status service of Research.gov makes a single online site available for principal investigators and sponsored projects office staff to check current status information for proposals that have been submitted to the NSF via Grants.gov or FastLane. https://www.research.gov/research-portal/appmanager/base/desktop?_nfpb=true&_pageLabel=research_node_display&_nodePath=/researchGov/Service/Desktop/grantsapplicationstatus.html

Publications   The NSF maintains an online document system to support the electronic dissemination of its documents. The online library contains thousands of documents that may be downloaded free of charge. Some NSF publications are available only in print, and others (e.g., the "Grant Proposal Guide" and "Award and Administration Guide") may be inconvenient to download. To obtain these publications in hardcopy, contact the NSF Publications Clearinghouse in Arlington, VA. Phone, 703-292-7827. http://www.nsf.gov/publications | Email: pubinfo@nsf.gov

Search or browse the online document library. http://www.nsf.gov/publications/ods

Reading Room   NSF policy documents and staff instructions, as well as current indexes, are available to the public for inspection and copying. To gain access to the collection, a visitor must schedule an appointment in advance with the library, which is open on weekdays, excluding Federal holidays, 8:00 a.m.–4 p.m. The reading room is located in the National Science Foundation Library, Room 225, Arlington, VA 22230. Phone, 703-292-7830. Email: library@nsf.gov

Small Business Support   The Office of Small Business Research and Development informs small businesses with science and technology research capabilities about NSF support that could benefit them. The Office of Small and Disadvantaged Business Utilization oversees agency compliance with the provisions of the Small Business Act and the Small Business Investment Act of 1958, as amended. Phone, 703-292-8050.

The Small Business Innovation Research and Technology Transfer program helps startups and small businesses carry out scientific research and development. http://www.nsf.gov/eng/iip/sbir/home.jsp

Social Media   The NSF uses social media sites and tools to disseminate news about research funds, funding opportunities, job openings, and more. Follow the NSF on Facebook, Instagram, LinkedIn, OpenNSF, Pinterest, Twitter, Wordpress, and YouTube. https://www.nsf.gov/social

Staff Directory   The "Staff Directory" web page has a search box that visitors can use to locate NSF employees in an electronic database. A visitor also can browse staff by NSF organization. https://www.nsf.gov/staff

The Sources of Information were updated 11–2019.

National Transportation Safety Board

490 L'Enfant Plaza SW., Washington, DC 20594
Phone, 202-314-6000. Internet, http://www.ntsb.gov

Board Members

Chair	ROBERT L. SUMWALT III
Member	T. BELLA DINH-ZARR
Member	CHRISTOPHER A. HART
Member	EARL F. WEENER

https://www.ntsb.gov/about/board/Pages/default.aspx

Office Heads Reporting to the Board

Chief Financial Officer	EDWARD BENTHALL

Directors
Office of Equal Employment Opportunity, Diversity, and Inclusion — FARA D. GUEST
Office of Safety Recommendations and Communications — SHARON BRYSON
General Counsel — KATHLEEN SILBAUGH
Managing Director — DENNIS JONES

Office Heads Reporting to the Managing Director

Chiefs
Administrative Law Judge — ALFONSO J. MONTAÑO
Information Officer — ANGEL SANTA

Directors
Office of Administration — SUSAN KANTROWITZ
Office of Aviation Safety — JOHN DELISI
Office of Highway Safety — ROBERT J. MOLLOY
Office of Marine Safety — BRIAN CURTIS
Office of Railroad, Pipeline, and Hazardous Materials Investigations — ROBERT J. HALL
Office of Research and Engineering — JAMES RITTER

https://www.ntsb.gov/about/organization/Pages/default.aspx

[For the National Transportation Safety Board statement of organization, see the Code of Federal Regulations, Title 49, Part 800]

The above list of key personnel was updated 1–2018.

The National Transportation Safety Board investigates accidents, conducts studies, and makes recommendations on safety to Government agencies, the transportation industry, and others.

The National Transportation Safety Board (NTSB) was established in 1967. On April 1, 1975, the Independent Safety Board Act of 1974 (49 U.S.C. 1111) reestablished the NTSB as an independent agency outside the Department of Transportation.

The NTSB consists of five members whom the President appoints for 5-year terms with the advice and consent of the Senate. The President designates two of these members as Chair and Vice Chair of the Board for 2-year terms. The President designates the Chair also with the advice and consent of the Senate. https://www.ntsb.gov/about/organization/Pages/default.aspx

Activities

Accident Investigation The NTSB investigates, determines probable cause, makes safety recommendations, and reports the facts and circumstances of the following types of accidents: U.S. civil aviation and certain public-use aircraft accidents; railroad accidents involving a fatality, substantial property damage, or a passenger train; pipeline accidents involving a fatality, substantial property damage, or significant harm to the environment; highway accidents (including railroad grade-crossing accidents) that the NTSB selects in cooperation with the States; major marine casualties and accidents involving a public vessel and a nonpublic vessel; certain accidents involving hazardous materials; and other transportation accidents that are catastrophic, caused by recurring problems, or otherwise should be investigated in the judgment of the Board. http://www.ntsb.gov/investigations/Pages/default.aspx

Safety Problem Identification The NTSB makes recommendations on matters of transportation safety. It reduces the severity and number of transportation accidents by conducting safety studies and special investigations; assessing accident investigation techniques and publishing recommended procedures; establishing regulatory requirements for reporting accidents; evaluating the transportation safety consciousness and efficacy of other Government agencies in

NATIONAL TRANSPORTATION SAFETY BOARD

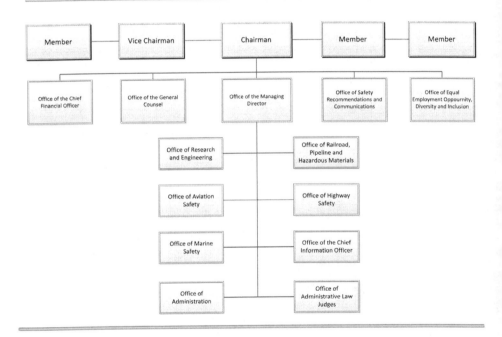

accident prevention; evaluating safeguards and procedures for the transportation of hazardous materials and the performance of other Government agencies charged with ensuring the safe transportation of such materials; and reporting annually to the Congress on its activities. http://www.ntsb.gov/safety/Pages/default.aspx

Family Assistance for Aviation Disasters The NTSB coordinates the resources of the Federal Government and other organizations to support the efforts of local and State governments and airlines to meet the needs of aviation disaster victims and their families. It assists in making Federal resources available to local authorities and airlines. http://www.ntsb.gov/tda/family/Pages/default.aspx

Certificate, Civil Penalty, and License Appeal On appeal, the NTSB reviews the suspension, amendment, modification, revocation, or denial of certain certificates, licenses, and assessments of civil penalties issued by the Secretary of Transportation. The NTSB also reviews, on appeal from the orders of any administrative law judge, decisions of the Commandant of the Coast Guard that revoke, suspend, or deny certain licenses, certificates, documents, and registers. http://www.ntsb.gov/legal/alj/Pages/default.aspx

Sources of Information

Advocacy Priorities The "Most Wanted List" raises awareness of what may be done to reduce the number of transportation accidents and the loss of life caused by them. https://www.ntsb.gov/safety/mwl/Pages/default.aspx

Career Opportunities Information on career paths at the NTSB is available on its website. For more information, contact the Human Resources Division, National Transportation Safety Board, Washington, DC 20594. Phone, 202-314-6230. http://www.ntsb.gov/about/employment/Pages/Careers.aspx

Contracts / Procurement For information on contracting and procurement opportunities, contact the Contracting Officer, National Transportation Safety Board, Washington, DC 20594. Phone, 202-314-6102. http://www.ntsb.gov

Freedom of Information Act (FOIA) Effective on July 5, 1967, the FOIA gives any person a right to obtain access to Federal agency records; however, nine exemptions and three special law enforcement record exclusions shield certain records or portions of them from public disclosure. A FOIA request may be made for any agency record. https://www.ntsb.gov/about/foia/Pages/default.aspx

History On December 17, 1903, the Wright "Flyer" became the first powered, heavier-than-air, piloted machine to achieve controlled, sustained flight. Twenty-three years later, the U.S. Congress charged the Department of Commerce with investigating the causes of aircraft accidents. Today, NTSB investigators are on call around-the-clock, every day of the year, to investigate significant aviation and surface transportation accidents wherever they may occur. To learn more of the NTSB's story, visit the "History of the National Transportation Safety Board" web page. https://www.ntsb.gov/about/history/Pages/default.aspx

Investigations The NTSB maintains a database of major aviation, highway, marine, pipeline, and railroad investigations, both ongoing and completed, on its website. https://www.ntsb.gov/investigations/Pages/All-Investigations.aspx

Open Government The NTSB supports the Open Government initiative. https://www.ntsb.gov/about/employment/Pages/open.aspx

Organizational Chart The NTSB's organizational chart is available in Portable Document Format (PDF) for viewing and downloading. https://www.ntsb.gov/about/organization/Documents/ntsb-org-chart-2016.pdf

Publications Publications are free of charge for the following categories of subscribers: Federal, State, or local transportation agencies; international transportation organizations or foreign governments; educational institutions or public libraries; nonprofit public safety organizations; and the news media. To receive copies of NTSB publications, persons in these categories should contact the Records Management Division, National Transportation Safety Board, Washington, DC 20594. Phone, 202-314-6551. All other persons may download NTSB publications from the agency's website, or purchase NTSB publications from the National Technical Information Service, 5285 Port Royal Road, Springfield, VA 22161. To place an order, call the subscription unit at 703-487-4630 or the sales desk at 703-487-4768. More information is available on the NTSB website. http://www.ntsb.gov/publications/Pages/default.aspx

Reading Room   The NTSB's public reference room is available for record inspection and photocopying. It is located on the 6th floor at the Board's Washington, DC, headquarters and is open on weekdays from 8:45 a.m. to 4:45 p.m. Requests for access to public records should be made in person at the guard desk. Phone, 202-314-6551 or 800-877-6799.

Regional Offices / Response Operations Center   Contact information for NTSB regional offices is available online. To report an accident in any transportation mode, contact the Response Operations Center. Phone, 844-373-9922. http://www.ntsb.gov/about/Pages/OfficeLocation.aspx

Site Map   The website map allows visitors to look for specific topics or to browse content that aligns with their interests. https://www.ntsb.gov/Pages/sitemap.aspx

Social Media   The NTSB has a Facebook account. https://www.facebook.com/NTSBgov

The NTSB tweets announcements and other newsworthy items on Twitter. https://twitter.com/ntsb

The NTSB posts videos on its YouTube channel. https://www.youtube.com/user/NTSBgov

Training Center   NTSB investigators and others from the transportation community improve their practice of accident investigation techniques at the training center. Its curriculum promotes independent, objective, and technically advanced accident investigations to raise levels of safety in all modes of transportation. Forums and symposia are open to the public; however, certain courses are limited to those who may be involved in an NTSB accident investigation or who are members of the emergency response community. Governmental and public organizations may reserve the training and conference center for events. Phone, 571-223-3900. https://www.ntsb.gov/Training_Center/Pages/TrainingCenter.aspx | Email: TCReservations@ntsb.gov; http://app.ntsb.gov/about/contact.html

For further information, contact the Media Relations Division, National Transportation Safety Board, 490 L'Enfant Plaza SW., Washington, DC 20594. Phone, 202-314-6100.

Nuclear Regulatory Commission

Washington, DC 20555
Phone, 301-415-7000. Internet, http://www.nrc.gov | Email: opa.resource@nrc.gov

Chair	Kristine L. Svinicki
Commissioner	Jeffrey M. Baran
Commissioner	Stephen G. Burns
Commissioner	(Vacancy)
Commissioner	(Vacancy)
Chief Administrative Judge, Atomic Safety and Licensing Board Panel	E. Roy Hawkens
Chief Financial Officer	Maureen E. Wylie
Chief Information Officer	David Nelson
Deputy Executive Director for Materials, Waste, Research, State, Tribal and Compliance Programs	Fredrick Brown
Deputy Executive Director for Reactor and Preparedness Programs	Michael R. Johnson
Director, Office of Commission Appellate Adjudication	Brooke Poole Clark

Director, Office of Congressional Affairs	EUGENE DACUS
Director, Office of International Programs	NADER L. MAMISH
Director, Office of Public Affairs	DAVID A. CASTELVETER
Executive Director, Advisory Committee on Reactor Safeguards	ANDREA VEIL
Executive Director for Operations	VICTOR M. MCCREE
General Counsel	MARGRET M. DOANE
Inspector General	HUBERT T. BELL, JR.
Secretary of the Commission	ANNETTE L. VIETTI-COOK

[For the Nuclear Regulatory Commission statement of organization, see the Code of Federal Regulations, Title 10, Part I]

The above list of key personnel was updated 06–2017.

The Nuclear Regulatory Commission licenses and regulates civilian use of nuclear energy to protect public health and safety and the environment.

The Nuclear Regulatory Commission (NRC) was established as an independent regulatory agency under the provisions of the Energy Reorganization Act of 1974 (42 U.S.C. 5801 et seq.) and Executive Order 11834 of January 15, 1975. All licensing and related regulatory functions formerly assigned to the Atomic Energy Commission were transferred to the Nuclear Regulatory Commission. http://www.nrc.gov/about-nrc/governing-laws.html

Five Commissioners whom the President appoints and Senate confirms for 5-year terms govern the NRC. The President appoints one of them to be the Commission's Chair and official spokesperson.

The NRC's major program components are the Office of Nuclear Reactor Regulation, the Office of New Reactors, the Office of Nuclear Material Safety and Safeguards, the Office of Federal and State Materials and Environmental Management Programs, and the Office of Nuclear Regulatory Research. Headquartered in Rockville, Maryland, the NRC has four regional offices.

The Commission ensures that nuclear materials and facilities for civilian use are managed in a manner consistent with public health and safety, environmental quality, national security, and antitrust laws. The NRC centers most of its efforts on regulating the use of nuclear energy to generate electric power. http://www.nrc.gov/about-nrc/organization.html

Activities

The NRC is primarily responsible for the following functions: licensing the construction, operation, and closure of nuclear reactors and other nuclear facilities, such as nuclear fuel cycle facilities, low-level radioactive waste disposal sites under NRC jurisdiction, the geologic repository for high-level radioactive waste, and nonpower test and research reactors; licensing the possession, use, processing, handling, and export of nuclear material; licensing the operators of nuclear power and nonpower test and research reactors; inspecting licensed facilities and activities; conducting the U.S. Government research program on light-water reactor safety; developing and implementing rules and regulations that govern licensed nuclear activities; investigating nuclear incidents and allegations concerning any matter regulated by the Commission; maintaining the NRC Incident Response Program; collecting, analyzing, and disseminating information on the operational safety of commercial nuclear power reactors and certain nonreactor activities; developing working relationships with the States regarding reactor operations and the regulation of nuclear material; and assuring that adequate regulatory programs are maintained by States exercising regulatory control over certain nuclear materials located within their borders. http://www.nrc.gov/about-nrc/regulatory.html

Sources of Information

Active Regulatory Guides   Regulatory guides provide guidance to licensees and applicants for implementing parts of the Commission's regulations, techniques used by NRC staff to evaluate problems or postulated accidents, and data needed by NRC staff to review applications for permits or licenses. Regulatory guides are issued in 10 broad divisions: antitrust and financial review, environmental and siting, fuels and materials facilities, materials and plant protection, occupational health, power reactors, products, research and test reactors, transportation, and general. Active regulatory guides may be downloaded from the NRC's online library. http://www.nrc.gov/reading-rm/doc-collections/reg-guides

Business Opportunities   The NRC awards contracts to commercial firms, nonprofit organizations, and universities. The agency buys products and services, including technical assistance and research in nuclear fields, information technology, facility management, and administrative support. http://www.nrc.gov/about-nrc/contracting.html

Draft Regulatory Guides   The NRC issues regulatory guides in draft form to solicit public comment and participation in developing regulatory positions. Draft regulatory guides have not received complete staff review, and, therefore, they do not represent official NRC staff positions. The public may comment on draft guides and other documents issued in draft form online. NRC staff considers all comments received during the public comment period. Draft regulatory guides may be downloaded from the NRC's online library. http://www.nrc.gov/public-involve/doc-comment.html; http://www.nrc.gov/reading-rm.html

Employment   To carry out its mission, the NRC relies heavily on engineers, scientists, and security professionals. http://www.nrc.gov/about-nrc/employment/opportunities.html; http://bestplacestowork.org/BPTW/rankings/overall/mid

Freedom of Information Act (FOIA)   To request copies of records, use the online "FOIA Request Submittal Form" or contact the FOIA / Privacy Act Officer, Mail Stop T–5 F09, Nuclear Regulatory Commission, Washington, DC 20555-0001. Phone, 301-415-7169. Fax, 301-415-5130. http://www.nrc.gov/reading-rm/foia/foia-submittal-form.html

Glossary   The NRC maintains an online glossary. http://www.nrc.gov/reading-rm/basic-ref/glossary.html

Microfiche Collections   Selected regional libraries of the U.S. Government Publishing Office Federal Depository Library Program maintain permanent microfiche collections of Nuclear Regulatory Commission documents released between January 1981 and October 1999. Contact the Public Document Room for more information. Phone, 301-415-4737 or 800-397-4209. Fax, 301-415-3548. http://www.nrc.gov/reading-rm/pdr.html | Email: pdr.resource@nrc.gov

Publications   The NRC publishes information on licensing and regulation of civilian nuclear facilities and materials, as well as annual and periodic reports. Publications and many documents are accessible on the NRC Web site. The U.S. Government Publishing Office (GPO) and the National Technical Information Service (NTIS) sell single copies of and subscriptions to NRC publications. Contact the GPO bookstore (phone, 202-512-0132) or the NTIS (phone, 888-584-8332 or 703-605-6050) for more information. http://www.nrc.gov/reading-rm.html; http://www.gpo.gov/about/bookstore.htm | Email: mainbks@gpo.gov; http://www.ntis.gov | Email: customerservice@ntis.gov

Public Documents   The Public Document Room—located on the first floor at One White Flint North, 11555 Rockville Pike, Rockville, MD—is open on weekdays, 8 a.m.–4 p.m., except on Federal holidays. The NRC maintains a large collection of documents on licensing proceedings and other significant actions. Documents issued prior to October 1999 are available in paper or microfiche. After October 1999, documents are available online from the NRC's full-text document management system. Most public documents may be reproduced on CD–ROM, microfiche, or paper for a nominal fee. Phone, 301-415-4737 or 800-397-4209. Fax, 301-415-3548. http://www.nrc.gov/reading-rm/pdr.html | Email: pdr.resource@nrc.gov; http://www.nrc.gov/reading-rm/adams.html; http://www.nrc.gov/about-nrc/contactus.html | Email: opa.resource@nrc.gov

For further information, contact the Office of Public Affairs, Nuclear Regulatory Commission, Washington, DC 20555-0001. Phone, 301-415-8200.

Occupational Safety and Health Review Commission

1120 Twentieth Street NW., Washington, DC 20036-3457
Phone, 202-606-5100. Fax, 202-418-3017. Internet, http://www.oshrc.gov

Commissioners

Chair

HEATHER L. MACDOUGALL
CYNTHIA L. ATTWOOD
JAMES J. SULLIVAN, JR.

https://www.oshrc.gov/about/Commissioners_bios.html

Administrative Staff

Executive Director

DEBRA A. HALL

Chief Administrative Law Judge
Executive Secretary
General Counsel

COVETTE ROONEY
JOHN X. CERVENY
NADINE N. MANCINI

The above list of key personnel was updated 09–2017.

The Occupational Safety and Health Review Commission ensures the timely and fair resolution of cases involving the alleged exposure of American workers to unsafe or unhealthy working conditions.

The Occupational Safety and Health Review Commission is an independent, quasi-judicial agency established by the Occupational Safety and Health Act of 1970 (29 U.S.C. 651-678).

The Commission rules on cases when disagreements arise over the results of safety and health inspections performed by the Department of Labor's Occupational Safety and Health Administration (OSHA). Employers have the right to dispute alleged job safety or health violations that OSHA inspectors find, the penalties that OSHA proposes, and the time given to correct a hazardous situation.

The Occupational Safety and Health Act covers virtually every employer in the country. Its purpose is to reduce employment-related injuries, illnesses, and deaths of working men and women in the United States. It requires employers to provide a work environment free from recognized hazards that cause or are likely to cause death or serious physical harm to their employees. It also requires employers to comply with occupational safety and health standards promulgated under the act. http://www.oshrc.gov/about/how-oshrc.html

Activities

The Commission adjudicates enforcement actions initiated under the act when they are contested by employers, employees, or representatives of employees. A case arises when a citation, issued to an employer as the result of an OSHA inspection, is contested within 15 working days of receipt of the report.

There are two levels of adjudication within the Commission. All cases are first assigned to an administrative law judge. A hearing is generally held in the community or as close as possible to where the alleged violation occurred. After the hearing, the judge issues a decision based on findings of fact and conclusions of law.

A substantial number of these decisions become final orders of the Commission. Commission members, however, will issue the final order if a party petitions the Commission members for review of the judge's decision and the petition is granted.

After a final order is issued, any party to the case may seek a review of the decision in the U.S. courts of appeals.

The Commission's principal office is in Washington, DC. Administrative law judges are also located in the Atlanta and Denver regional offices.

Sources of Information

Career Opportunities   Vacancy announcements are posted online. http://www.oshrc.gov/job_opportunities/job_opport.html

Decisions   The "Decisions" page contains two online search tools, one for the final decisions of administrative law judges and the other for the final decisions of the Commission. The administrative law judge decisions start with the year 1993, and the Commission decisions start with the year 1972. Decisions are available in the form of Hypertext Markup Language (HTML) and Portable Document Format (PDF) files. http://www.oshrc.gov/decisions/index.html

Freedom of Information Act (FOIA)   The FOIA requires Federal agencies to disclose records after receiving a proper written request for them. Certain records, however, are shielded from disclosure by provisions contained within the statute. The Commission's online FOIA information includes the specific procedures for requesting its records, FOIA-related contact information, and links to records that are already accessible online. The Commission operates a FOIA requester service center that can provide information on the status of a submitted request. Phone, 202-606-5724. Fax, 202-606-5417. http://www.oshrc.gov/foia/index.html

Frequently Asked Questions (FAQs)   The Commission posts answers to FAQs on its Web site. http://www.oshrc.gov/FAQ/index.html

News   The Commission posts press releases on its Web site. http://www.oshrc.gov/press/press.html

Open Government   The Commission supports the Open Government initiative by promoting the principles of collaboration, participation, and transparency. http://www.oshrc.gov/open.html | Email: opengov@oshrc.gov

Plain Language   The Plain Writing Act of 2010 requires all Federal agencies to write in a way that produces "clear Government communication that the public can understand and use." The Commission solicits public assistance in support of plain language: If a document or Web page is unclear, contact the Commission by email and point out the lack of clarity. The Commission seeks to ensure that any document that is necessary for obtaining services, that provides information on services, or that explains how to comply with a requirement that the Commission administers or enforces is plainly written. http://www.oshrc.gov/open/plain_writing.html | Email: plain@oshrc.gov

Publicaciónes en Español   Publications in Spanish are available online. Phone, 202-606-5400. http://www.oshrc.gov/publications/publications_spanish.html

Publications   The Commission's publications are accessible online. Copies of them and decisions are also available from the Office of the Executive Secretary. Phone, 202-606-5400. Fax, 202-606-5050. http://www.oshrc.gov/publications/index.html

Related Sites   The Commission posts helpful and informative links to State Internet and other research sites. The Commission is not affiliated with the organizations whose links are on its "Related Web Sites" page. http://www.oshrc.gov/relatedsites/relatedsites.html; http://www.oshrc.gov/about/phone-numbers.html

For further information, contact the Office of the Executive Director, Occupational Safety and Health Review Commission, 1120 Twentieth Street NW., Washington, DC 20036-3457. Phone, 202-606-5100. Fax, 202-418-3017.

Office of Government Ethics

1201 New York Avenue NW., Suite 500, Washington, DC 20005-3917
Phone, 202-482-9300. (TTY) 800-877-8339. Fax, 202-482-9237. Internet, http://www.oge.gov

Director	DAVID J. APOL, ACTING
Chief of Staff / Program Counsel	SHELLEY K. FINLAYSON

Assistant Director, Internal Operations	NELSON CABRERA, JR.
Deputy Director, Compliance	DALE A. CHRISTOPHER
General Counsel	DAVID J. APOL

[For the Office of Government Ethics statement of organization, see the Code of Federal Regulations, Title 5, Part 2600]

The above list of key personnel was updated 09–2017.

The Office of Government Ethics leads and oversees the executive branch program for preventing and resolving conflicts of interest.

The Office of Government Ethics (OGE) is an executive branch agency established under the Ethics in Government Act of 1978, as amended (5 U.S.C. app. 401).

With the advice and consent of the Senate, the President appoints the Director for a 5-year term. https://www.oge.gov/web/oge.nsf/Organization

Activities

The OGE provides overall leadership and oversight of the executive branch ethics program, which prevents and resolves conflicts of interest. To carry out its leadership and oversight responsibilities, the Office promulgates and maintains enforceable standards of ethical conduct for approximately 2.7 million employees in over 130 executive branch agencies and the White House; oversees a financial disclosure system that reaches approximately 26,000 public and 380,000 confidential financial disclosure report filers; ensures that executive branch agency ethics programs are in compliance with applicable ethics laws and regulations; provides education and training to the more than 4,500 ethics officials throughout the executive branch; conducts outreach to the general public, the private sector, and civil society; and provides technical assistance to State, local, and foreign governments and international organizations. https://www.oge.gov/web/oge.nsf/Mission+and+Responsibilities

Sources of Information

Advisories The OGE posts written guidance to executive branch ethics officials and employees online. https://www.oge.gov/web/oge.nsf/All%20Advisories

Education Educational resources for ethics officials—including Institute for Ethics in Government training videos—are available online. https://www.oge.gov/web/oge.nsf/Education%20Resources%20for%20Ethics%20Officials

Career Opportunities The OGE posts vacancy announcements on USAJobs. The Compliance Division seeks agency ethics officials to participate in rotational details for increasing financial disclosure review proficiency. A detail assignment typically lasts 4–8 weeks, and arrangements can be made to accommodate commitment and schedule. https://www.oge.gov/web/oge.nsf/Careers

Conflict of Interest The OGE Web site provides links to opinions and other guidance that interpret the conflict of interest laws. https://www.oge.gov/web/OGE.nsf/Legal%20Interpretation

Dates / Deadlines The schedule of ethics dates helps executive branch agency ethics officials identify key dates and meet important deadlines throughout the calendar year. https://www.oge.gov/web/oge.nsf/Dates%20and%20Deadlines

Executive Orders A list of Executive orders that significantly affected or continue to affect the executive branch ethics program is available on the OGE's Web site. https://www.oge.gov/web/OGE.nsf/Executive%20Orders

Financial Disclosure Appointee, nominee, Presidential, and Vice Presidential public financial disclosure reports and ethics agreements are available online. https://www.oge.gov/web/oge.nsf/Presidential%20Appointee%20&%20Nominee%20Records

Resources for public financial disclosure are available on the OGE Web site. https://www.oge.gov/web/OGE.nsf/Public%20Financial%20Disclosure/F8C35F18BF846D1C85257E96006B95B1?opendocument

Forms All forms created by the OGE and instructions for downloading them are available online. https://www.oge.gov/web/oge.nsf/OGE+Forms

Freedom of Information Act (FOIA)   Information on how to submit a FOIA request is available online. https://www.oge.gov/Web/OGE.nsf/Freedom+of+Information+Act+(FOIA)

An electronic reading room contains documents that the OGE has released after multiple FOIA requests or disclosed proactively. Before making a FOIA request, search the electronic reading room for relevant records that already may be accessible. https://www.oge.gov/web/OGE.nsf/Freedom%20of%20Information%20Act%20(FOIA)/B9B880B7B93AF8EF85257EF5006DAAB6?opendocument

Frequently Asked Questions (FAQs)   The OGE answers media FAQs on its Web site. https://www.oge.gov/web/oge.nsf/Media%20Resources/C82EAE759C7C631885257EBC0043366C?opendocument

International Support   The OGE conducts international work under the auspices of the Department of State. In addition to descriptions of its bilateral and multilateral activities and onsite briefings, the "International Activities" Web pages contain documents that international visitors most often request, international conference papers and speeches, documents prepared for anticorruption meetings, links to other information on the fight against public corruption, and a selection of documents translated into Arabic, Chinese, French, Portuguese, Russian, and Spanish. https://www.oge.gov/web/oge.nsf/International+Activities

Legislative Affairs   The OGE posts budget submissions, correspondence with Congress, information on legislation affecting the executive branch ethics program, and other legislative materials on its Web site. https://www.oge.gov/web/oge.nsf/Legislative%20Affairs%20&%20Budget

Media   The OGE posts documents and information that members of the media request often. A media liaison is available to provide additional assistance. https://www.oge.gov/web/oge.nsf/Media%20Resources | Email: ContactOGE@oge.gov

Open Government   The OGE supports the Open Government initiative by promoting the principles of collaboration, participation, and transparency. https://www.oge.gov/web/oge.nsf/OPEN+GOVERNMENT

Organizational Chart   An organizational chart is available on the "Contact Us" Web page. https://www.oge.gov/Web/OGE.nsf/Resources/Contact+Us

RSS Feeds   The dates and deadlines RSS feed streams the dates of events like training and deadlines that are relevant to the management of agency ethics programs. The latest advisories RSS feed streams new education, legal, and program management advisories. https://www.oge.gov/web/oge.nsf/Resources/RSS%20Feeds

Site Map   A site index presents document categories based on their appearance in the Web site's drop-down menus. https://www.oge.gov/web/oge.nsf/Information/Site+Index?opendocument

Social Media   The OGE tweets announcements and other newsworthy items on Twitter. https://twitter.com/OfficeGovEthics

The Institute for Ethics in Government posts videos on the OGE's YouTube channel. https://www.youtube.com/user/OGEInstitute; https://www.oge.gov/web/oge.nsf/Organization/Contact%20Us? | Email: contactoge@oge.gov

For further information, contact the Office of Government Ethics, Suite 500, 1201 New York Avenue NW., Washington, DC 20005-3917. Phone, 202-482-9300. TTY, 800-877-8339. Fax, 202-482-9237.

Office of Personnel Management

1900 E Street NW., Washington, DC 20415-0001
Phone, 202-606-1800. TTY, 202-606-2532. Internet, http://www.opm.gov

Executive Offices

Director   MARGARET WEICHERT, ACTING
Deputy Director   MICHAEL J. RIGAS

Chief of Staff — NEAL PATEL, ACTING

Chief Officers
Management — KATHLEEN M. McGETTIGAN
Privacy — KELLIE COSGROVE RILEY

Directors
Communications — ANTHONY C. MARUCCI
Congressional, Legislative, and Intergovernmental Affairs — JONATHAN BLYTHE
Executive Secretariat — JOZETTA R. ROBINSON
Strategy and Innovation — REBECCA THACKER
Chief Human Capital Officers Council
Executive Director — SARA B. RATCLIFF
General Counsel — (VACANCY)
https://www.opm.gov/about-us/our-people-organization/senior-staff-bios/#url=Directors-Office

Program Offices

Associate Directors
Employee Services — MARK D. REINHOLD
Human Resources Solutions — JOSEPH S. KENNEDY
Merit System Accountability and Compliance — MARK W. LAMBERT
Retirement Services — KENNETH J. ZAWODNY, JR.

Directors
Healthcare and Insurance — ALAN P. SPIELMAN
National Background Investigation Bureau — CHARLES S. PHALEN, JR.
Suitability Executive Agent Programs — LISA M. LOSS
https://www.opm.gov/about-us/our-people-organization/organizational-contacts/

Mission Support Services

Chief Officers
Financial — DENNIS D. COLEMAN
Information — DAVID A. GARCIA

Directors
Equal Employment Opportunity — LASHONN M. WOODLAND
Facilities, Security and Emergency Management — JAMES ONUSKO, ACTING
Human Resources / Chief Human Capital Officer — ANDREA J. BRIGHT
Small and Disadvantaged Business Utilization — DESMOND BROWN

Senior Procurement Executive — JUAN I. ARRATIA
https://www.opm.gov/about-us/our-people-organization/senior-staff-bios/#url=Support-Function-Leaders/

Office of the Inspector General

Inspector General — NORBERT E. VINT, ACTING
https://www.opm.gov/our-inspector-general/staff-biographies/

Federal Prevailing Rate Advisory Committee

Chair — JILL L. NELSON
https://www.opm.gov/about-us/our-people-organization/organizational-contacts/federal-prevailing-rate-advisory-committee/

[For the Office of Personnel Management statement of organization, see the Federal Register of Jan. 5, 1979, 44 FR 1501]

The above list of key personnel was updated 10–2018.

The Office of Personnel Management administers a merit system to ensure compliance with personnel laws and regulations and assists agencies with recruiting, examining, and promoting on the basis of skills and knowledge irrespective of race, religion, sex, political influence, or other factors not based on merit.

The Office of Personnel Management (OPM) was created as an independent establishment by Reorganization Plan No. 2 of 1978 (5 U.S.C. app.), pursuant to Executive Order 12107 of December 28, 1978. Many of the functions of the former United States Civil Service Commission were transferred to OPM. https://www.opm.gov/about-us/our-people-organization/

Activities

Employee Benefits   OPM manages numerous activities that directly affect the well-being of the Federal employee and indirectly enhance employee effectiveness. These include health benefits, life insurance, and retirement benefits. https://www.opm.gov/healthcare-insurance

Examining / Staffing   The OPM provides departments and agencies with technical assistance and guidance in examining competitive positions in the Federal civil service for General Schedule grades 1 through 15 and Federal Wage system positions. In addition, OPM is responsible for the following duties: providing testing and examination services, at the request of an agency, on a reimbursable basis; establishing basic qualification standards for all occupations; certifying agency delegated examining units to conduct examining; providing employment information for competitive service positions; and providing policy direction and guidance on promotions, reassignments, appointments in the excepted and competitive services, reinstatements, temporary and term employment, veterans preference, workforce planning and reshaping, organizational design, career transition, and other staffing provisions. https://www.opm.gov/services-for-agencies/recruiting-staffing-solutions/

Executive Resources   OPM leads in the selection, management, and development of Federal executives. OPM provides policy guidance, consulting services, and technical support on Senior Executive Service (SES) recruitment, selection, succession planning, mobility performance, awards, and removals. It reviews agency nominations for SES career appointments and administers the Qualifications Review Boards that certify candidates' executive qualifications. It manages SES, senior-level, and scientific and professional space allocations to agencies, administers the Presidential Rank Awards program, and conducts orientation sessions for newly appointed executives. In addition, OPM manages three interagency residential development and training centers for executives and managers. https://www.opm.gov/policy-data-oversight/senior-executive-service

Investigations   The Office of the Inspector General conducts comprehensive and independent audits, investigations, and evaluations relating to OPM programs and operations. It is responsible for administrative actions against health care providers who commit sanctionable offenses with respect to the Federal Employees' Health Benefits Program or other Federal programs. https://www.opm.gov/our-inspector-general/

For further information, contact the Office of the Inspector General. Phone, 202-606-1200.

Oversight   OPM assesses human capital management Governmentwide and within agencies to gather information for policy development and program refinement, ensure compliance with law and regulation, and enhance agency capability for human resources management accountability. Agency accountability systems help ensure that human capital decisions are consistent with merit principles and that human capital strategies are aligned with mission accomplishment. OPM also works with agencies to find better and more strategic ways to manage Federal human capital. https://www.opm.gov/policy-data-oversight/oversight-activities

Personnel Systems   OPM provides leadership and guidance to agencies on systems to support the manager's personnel management responsibilities. These include the following: white- and blue-collar pay systems, including SES and special occupational pay systems; geographical adjustments and locality payments; special rates to address recruitment and retention problems; allowances and differentials, including recruitment and relocation bonuses, retention allowances, and hazardous duty/environmental pay; and premium pay; annual and sick leave, court leave, military leave, leave transfer and leave bank programs, family and medical leave, excused absence, holidays, and scheduling of work, including flexible and compressed work schedules; performance management, covering appraisal systems, performance pay and awards, and incentive awards for suggestions, inventions, and special acts; classification policy and standards for agencies to determine the series and grades for Federal jobs; labor-management relations, including collective bargaining, negotiability, unfair labor practices, labor-management cooperation, and consulting with unions on Governmentwide issues; systems and techniques for resolving disputes with employees; quality of work-life initiatives, such as employee health and fitness, work and family, AIDS in the workplace, and employee assistance programs; human resources development, including leadership and administration of the Human Resources Development Council and the Government Performance and Results Act interest group; the Training and Management Assistance program, to help agencies develop training and human resources management solutions, including workforce planning and succession management strategies, e-learning applications, traditional classroom training materials, compensation and performance management systems, and other customized products; information systems to support and improve Federal personnel management decisionmaking; and Governmentwide instructions for personnel processing and recordkeeping and for release of personnel data under the Freedom of Information Act and the Privacy Act.

OPM also provides administrative support to special advisory bodies, including the Federal Prevailing Rate Advisory Committee, the Federal Salary Council, and the Presidential Advisory Committee on Expanding Training Opportunities.

Workforce Diversity   OPM provides leadership, direction, and policy for Governmentwide affirmative recruiting programs for women, minorities, individuals with disabilities, and veterans. It also provides leadership, guidance, and technical assistance to promote merit and equality in systemic workforce recruitment, employment, training, and retention. In addition, OPM gathers, analyzes, and maintains statistical data on the diversity of the Federal workforce and prepares evaluation reports for Congress and others on individual agency and Governmentwide progress toward full workforce representation for all Americans in the Federal sector. https://www.opm.gov/policy-data-oversight/diversity-and-inclusion/

Other Programs

OPM coordinates the temporary assignment of employees between Federal agencies and State, local, and Indian tribal governments, institutions of higher education, and other eligible nonprofit organizations for up to 2 years, for work of mutual benefit to the participating organizations. It administers the Presidential Management Intern Program, which provides 2-year, excepted appointments with Federal agencies to recipients of graduate degrees in appropriate disciplines. In addition, the Office of Personnel Management administers the Federal Merit System Standards, which apply to certain grant-aided State and local programs.

Federal Executive Boards   Federal Executive Boards (FEBs) were established by Presidential memorandum on November 10, 1961, to improve internal Federal management practices and to provide a central focus for Federal participation in civic affairs in major metropolitan centers of Federal activity. They carry out their functions under OPM supervision and control.

FEBs serve as a means for disseminating information within the Federal Government and for promoting discussion of Federal policies and activities of importance to all Federal executives in the field. Each Board is composed of heads of Federal field offices in the metropolitan area. A chairman is elected annually from among the membership to provide overall leadership to the Board's operations. Committees and task forces carry out interagency projects consistent with the Board's mission.

Located in places where Federal activity is concentrated, FEBS can be found in 28 metropolitan areas. Federal executive associations or councils, which are locally organized, can be found in approximately 65 other metropolitan areas. They perform functions similar to the FEBs, but on a lesser scale of organization and activity. https://www.feb.gov/board-locations/

For further information, contact the Director for Federal Executive Board Operations. Phone, 202-606-1000.

Sources of Information

A–Z Index   The OPM's website has an alphabetical subject index to help visitors navigate its content. https://www.opm.gov/a-z-index/

Blog   The OPM has a blog on its website. https://www.opm.gov/blogs/Director/

Business Opportunities   The "Doing Business with OPM" web pages provide information on finding contracting opportunities, registering to do business with the OPM, and connecting with the OPM's small business program. https://www.opm.gov/about-us/doing-business-with-opm

Staff contact information is available online. https://www.opm.gov/about-us/doing-business-with-opm/contact-us/

Career Opportunities   To help fulfill its mission, the OPM relies on a professional workforce with energy, expertise, personality, and skill. https://www.opm.gov/about-us/careers-at-opm/

In 2017, the OPM ranked 17th among 25 midsize Government agencies in the Partnership for Public Service's Best Places To Work Agency Rankings. http://bestplacestowork.org/BPTW/rankings/overall/mid

Electronic Questionnaires for Investigations Processing (e-QIP)   The National Background Investigations Bureau manages e-QIP—a web-based, automated system—to facilitate the processing of standard investigative forms that are used when conducting background investigations for Federal security, suitability, fitness, and credentialing purposes. The system allows the user to enter, update, and transmit his or her personal investigative data over a secure internet connection to a requesting agency. https://nbib.opm.gov/e-qip-background-investigations/

Federal Holidays   Federal law (5 U.S.C. 6103) establishes the public holidays for Federal employees. Most Federal employees work on weekdays. For these employees, when a holiday falls on a nonworkday— Saturday or Sunday—the Federal holiday usually is observed on Friday or Monday. https://www.opm.gov/policy-data-oversight/snow-dismissal-procedures/federal-holidays/#url=Overview

Forms   The "Forms" web page serves as the single source of information for forms belonging to and used by the OPM. Links are also available to browse forms used by other Federal agencies. https://www.opm.gov/forms | Email: formsmanager@opm.gov

Freedom of Information Act (FOIA)   A FOIA request must be made in writing and clearly labeled "Freedom of Information Act Request." Instructions for making a request are available online. https://www.opm.gov/information-management/freedom-of-information-act

Frequently Asked Questions (FAQs)   The OPM posts answers to FAQs on its website. https://www.opm.gov/FAQs/

Glossaries   A glossary is available on the "Healthcare—Reference Materials" web page. https://www.opm.gov/healthcare-insurance/healthcare/reference-materials/reference/glossary/

A glossary is available on the "Benefits Officers Center—Reference Materials" web page. https://www.opm.gov/retirement-services/benefits-officers-center/reference-materials/#url=Glossary

An insurance glossary of terms that are used on the "Federal Benefits Programs" website is available online. If a term is absent from the glossary, please email a request for its inclusion. https://www.opm.gov/healthcare-insurance/insurance-glossary | Email: fehb@opm.gov

History   On October 27, 1992, the agency's Washington headquarters was dedicated to a former Civil Service Commissioner, who later became the 26th President of the United States. To find out more about this dedicated civil servant, visit the "Theodore Roosevelt" web page. https://www.opm.gov/about-us/our-mission-role-history/theodore-roosevelt/

Insurance Information on the Federal health benefits open season; flexible spending accounts; and dental and vision, health, life, and long-term care insurance programs, is available online. https://www.opm.gov/healthcare-insurance

Integrity / Efficinecy The Office of the Inspector General from the OPM posts reports and data on Oversight.gov, a text-searchable repository of reports that Federal Inspectors General publish. The Council of the Inspectors General on Integrity and Efficiency operates and maintains the website to increase public access to independent and authoritative information on the Federal Government. https://www.oversight.gov/about

News The OPM posts news items on its website. https://www.opm.gov/news/latest-news/

Open Government The OPM supports the Open Government initiative by promoting the principles of collaboration, participation, and transparency. The agency is committed to increasing accountability, effectiveness, efficiency, and innovation; building trust with American citizens; empowering the public; fostering a culture in which everyone's contribution is valued; making better decisions; and tracking how agency money is used. https://www.opm.gov/about-us/open-government

Operating Status—Washington, DC, Area The OPM sponsors the Operating Status listserv. Subscribers receive an email when the operating status of the Federal Government within the Capital Region changes. https://apps.opm.gov/listserv_apps/list-sub.cfm?targetlist=operatingstatus

Organizational Chart The OPM included an organizational chart on page 13 of its Annual Performance Report—Fiscal Year 2017, which was published in February of 2018. Please note: The Office of Planning and Policy Analysis no longer exists; its functions were transferred to the Office of Strategy and Innovation. https://www.opm.gov/about-us/budget-performance/

performance/2017-annual-performance-report.pdf

Publications An electronic database allows users to search for operating manuals, periodicals, and other OPM publications. For more information on Federal personnel management publications, contact OPM Publications Management. Phone, 202-606-1822. http://www.opm.gov/news/reports-publications/publications-database

Reading Room The electronic reading room contains documents that the FOIA identifies for inclusion. This electronic collection also contains records that FOIA users have requested multiple times. https://www.opm.gov/information-management/freedom-of-information-act#url=Electronic-Reading-Room

Retirement Information Center The Retirement Information Center provides information on retirement benefits for current, new, and prospective Federal employees, as well as for Federal retirees, their survivors, and benefits officers. The information includes recent changes, events, and other issues affecting Federal retirement benefits. https://www.opm.gov/Blogs/Retire/

Salaries / Wages General schedule locality pay tables are posted online. https://www.opm.gov/policy-data-oversight/pay-leave/salaries-wages/2018/general-schedule/

Social Media The OPM maintains a Facebook account. https://www.facebook.com/USOPM/

The OPM tweets announcements and other newsworthy items on its Twitter account. https://twitter.com/usopm

Telework The OPM maintains the Federal Government's official telework program website. https://www.telework.gov/about/ | Email: teleworkpolicy@opm.gov

Unlocking Federal Talent In partnership with other Federal agencies, the OPM developed the website UnlockTalent.gov to tap current talent in the Federal workforce and to shape the workforce that the future requires. The website serves as an interactive tool that enables agency leaders and practitioners to make decisions based on data and to design initiatives for creating a work culture of engagement and excellence. https://www.unlocktalent.gov/about; https://www.opm.gov/about-us/contact-us

For further information, contact the Office of Communications, Office of Personnel Management, 1900 E Street NW., Washington, DC 20415-0001. Phone, 202-606-2402. TTY, 202-606-2532.

Office of the Director of National Intelligence

Washington, DC 20511
Phone, 703-733-8600. Internet, http://www.dni.gov

Director	DAN COATS
Principal Deputy Director	SUE GORDON
Deputy Director, Intelligence Integration	MICHAEL DEMPSEY
Assistant Deputy Director, Intelligence Integration	EDWARD GISTARO
Assistant Director, Acquisition, Technology and Facilities	KEVIN MEINERS
Assistant Director, Partner Engagement	LT. GEN. THEODORE C. NICHOLAS
Assistant Director, Policy and Strategy	DAWN EILENBERGER
Assistant Director, Systems and Resource Analyses	TROY MEINK
Chief Financial Officer	TREY TREADWELL
Chief Human Capital Officer	DEBORAH KIRCHER
Chief Information Officer	JOHN SHERMAN
Civil Liberties Protection Officer	ALEXANDER W. JOEL
Director, Cyber Threat Intelligence Integration Center	TONYA UGORETZ
Director, Equal Employment Opportunity and Diversity	RITA SAMPSON
Director, National Counterintelligence Security Center	RUSSELL TRAVERS, ACTING
Director, National Counterproliferation Center	ANNETTE TOTTEN
Director, National Counterterrorism Center	NICHOLAS RASMUSSEN
Director, Public Affairs	BRIAN HALE
General Counsel	JASON KLITENIC
Inspector General	MICHAEL ATKINSON
Principal Deputy General Counsel	SUSAN GIBSON
Program Manager, Information Sharing Environment	KSHEMENDRA PAUL

The Office of the Director of National Intelligence oversees and coordinates the foreign and domestic activities of the Intelligence Community across the Federal Government.

The Office of the Director of National Intelligence (ODNI) was established by the Intelligence Reform and Terrorism Prevention Act of 2004 (50 U.S.C. 403). It began operation on April 21, 2005.

The Office is headed by the Director of National Intelligence whom the President appoints with the advice and consent of the Senate. The Director reports directly to the President and is the principal intelligence adviser.

The ODNI ensures that the President, the heads of departments and agencies of the executive branch, the Chairman of the Joint Chiefs of Staff and senior military commanders, and the Congress receive timely and objective national intelligence. It also establishes goals and priorities for collection, analysis, production, and dissemination of national intelligence; ensures the availability of and access to intelligence information within the Intelligence Community; develops the annual budget for the National Intelligence Program; oversees coordination of relationships with the intelligence or security services of foreign governments and international organizations; ensures that accurate analysis of intelligence information is derived from all sources to support national security needs; develops personnel policies and programs to enhance the capacity for joint operations and to facilitate staffing of community management functions; and jointly oversees the development and implementation of an acquisition program management plan with the Secretary of Defense.

Sources of Information

Career Opportunities The ODNI hires acquisitions and financial managers, engineers, foreign language experts,

OFFICE OF THE DIRECTOR OF NATIONAL INTELLIGENCE

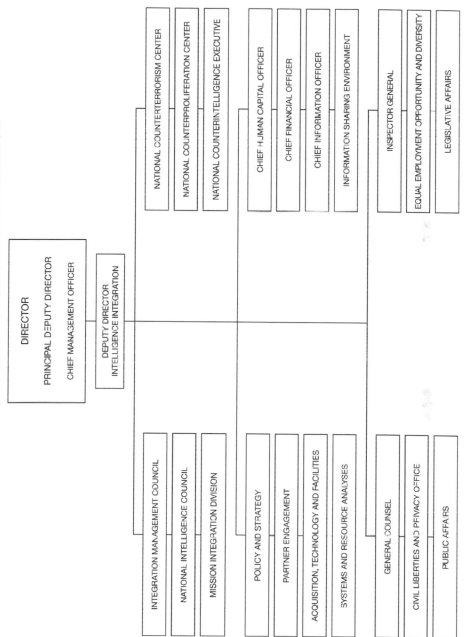

scientists, security experts, software and hardware developers, technology specialists, and other career professionals. http://www.dni.gov/index.php/careers/careers-in-the-ic

Publications   Reports and other publications are available online. http://www.dni.gov/index.php/newsroom/reports-and-publications; http://www.dni.gov/index.php/contact-us

For further information, contact the Office of the Director of National Intelligence, Washington, DC 20511. Phone, 703-733-8600.

Overseas Private Investment Corporation

1100 New York Avenue NW., Washington, DC 20527
Phone, 202-336-8400. Fax, 202-336-7949. Internet, http://www.opic.gov

President / Chief Executive Officer	DEV J. JAGADESAN, ACTING
Executive Vice President	(VACANCY)
Chief Information Officer	ROBERT DELUCA
Chief of Staff	CAMERON ALFORD, ACTING
Director, Office of Accountability	WILLIAM KENNEDY
Vice President, Department of Legal Affairs / General Counsel	CINDY SHEPARD, ACTING
Vice President, Department of Management and Administration	MICHELE PEREZ
Vice President, Financial and Portfolio Management	MILDRED CALLEAR
Vice President, Human Resources	MICHELE PEREZ, ACTING
Vice President, Investment Funds	LYNN NGUYEN, ACTING
Vice President, Office of External Affairs	EDWARD BURRIER
Vice President, Office of Investment Policy	MERRYL BURPOE, ACTING
Vice President, Small and Medium Enterprise Finance	JAMES C. POLAN
Vice President, Structured Finance and Insurance	TRACEY WEBB

[For the Overseas Private Investment Corporation statement of organization, see the Code of Federal Regulations, Title 22, Chapter VII]

The above list of key personnel was updated 07–2017.

The Overseas Private Investment Corporation promotes economic growth and job opportunities both at home and abroad by encouraging U.S. private investment in developing countries and emerging markets.

The Overseas Private Investment Corporation (OPIC) was established in 1971 as an independent agency by the Foreign Affairs Reform and Restructuring Act (112 Stat. 2681-790). The Corporation helps U.S. businesses invest overseas, fosters economic development in new and emerging markets, complements the private sector in managing risks associated with foreign direct investment, and supports U.S. foreign policy. It charges market-based fees for its products and operates on a self-sustaining basis at no net cost to American taxpayers. https://www.opic.gov/who-we-are/overview

Activities

The agency serves as the U.S. Government's development finance institution. It mobilizes private capital to help solve critical development challenges. This mobilization of capital advances U.S. foreign policy and national security objectives. Working with the U.S. private sector, the agency helps U.S. businesses gain footholds in emerging markets thereby catalyzing revenues, jobs, and growth opportunities both at home and abroad. Consistent with its mission, the Corporation provides financing guarantees, insures against political risk, and supports private equity investment funds to stimulate investment. https://www.opic.gov/what-we-offer/overview

OPIC projects adhere to high environmental and social standards and uphold human rights. By its adherence to high standards, the agency tries to raise the industry and regional standards of the countries where it operates. OPIC services are available for new and expanding business enterprises in more than 160 countries. https://www.opic.gov/opic-action/overview

Sources of Information

Eligibility   To determine whether a business owner or company is eligible for OPIC insurance or finance products, visit the online applicant screener. Some eligibility requirements are the same across all OPIC products; however, some vary by product. https://www.opic.gov/doing-business-us/applicant-screener

Employment   Most OPIC career opportunities fall within the following professional categories: attorney-advisors, business development specialists, economists, finance specialists, and managers. New hires must be U.S. citizens. https://www.opic.gov/who-we-are/careers

In 2015 and 2016, the OPIC was ranked number two among small Government agencies in the Best Places To Work Agency Rankings. http://bestplacestowork.org/BPTW/rankings/overall/small

Media   Annual reports, newsletters, and public notices, as well as the OPIC blog and media library are available online. https://www.opic.gov/media-events/media-library

Workshops   Participants learn how American small businesses use OPIC finance and insurance products to gain access to emerging markets overseas, as well as how they can take advantage of OPIC products to expand their businesses abroad and support growth at home. https://www.opic.gov/outreach-events/upcoming-workshops; https://www.opic.gov/doing-business-us/contact-us | Email: info@opic.gov

For further information, contact the Overseas Private Investment Corporation, 1100 New York Avenue NW., Washington, DC 20527. Phone, 202-336-8400. Fax, 202-336-7949.

Peace Corps

1111 Twentieth Street NW., Washington, DC 20526
Phone, 855-855-1961; 202-692-2000. Fax, 202-692-2231. Internet, http://www.peacecorps.gov

Director	JOSEPHINE K. OLSEN
Deputy Director	(VACANCY)
Chief of Staff	MICHELLE K. BROOKS
https://files.peacecorps.gov/documents/jody-olsen-bio.pdf	
Chief Officers	
Financial	RICHARD SWARTTZ
Information	SCOTT KNELL
Director	
Civil Rights and Diversity	JOHN W. BURDEN
Victim Advocacy	DA SHAWNA TOWNSEND
General Counsel	ROBERT SHANKS
White House Liaison	MATTHEW MCKINNEY
Associate Directors	
Global Operations	PATRICK YOUNG
Health Services	KAREN BECKER
Safety and Security	SHAWN BARDWELL

Volunteer Recruitment and Selection	DAVID WALKER
Directors	
Global Health and HIV	MARIE MCLEOD
Overseas Programming and Training Support	STEPHANIE RUST
Peace Corps Response	KWEKU BOAFO
Strategic Information, Research, and Planning	JEFFREY KWIECINSKI, ACTING
Regional Directors	
Africa	JOHNATHAN MILLER
Europe, Mediterranean and Asia	JEANNETTE WINDON
Inter-America and the Pacific	GREGORY HUGER
Associate Directors	
External Affairs	RACHEL KAHLER
Management	JEFFREY HARRINGTON
Chief Compliance Officer	ANNE HUGHES
Directors	
Communications	MATTHEW SHEEHEY
Congressional Relations	NANCY HERBOLSHEIMER
Grants and Gifts Management	KAREN ROBERTS
Strategic Partnerships and Intergovernmental Affairs	SHANNON KENDRICK
Third Goal and Returned Volunteer Services	KEITH HONDA
Executive Secretary	SYLVIE MORTIMER, ACTING
https://www.peacecorps.gov/about/leadership	
Inspector General	KATHY A. BULLER
https://www.peacecorps.gov/about/inspector-general	

The above list of key personnel was updated 8–2019.

The Peace Corps gives the peoples of host countries increased access to volunteers who are qualified, skilled, and trained, and it strengthens mutual understanding between Americans and the peoples of the countries served.

Establishment and Organization

President John F. Kennedy approved the Peace Corps Act on September 22, 1961. This Public Law became effective on that same day. Its declaration of purpose states: "It is the policy of the United States and the purpose of this Act to promote world peace and friendship through a Peace Corps, which shall make available to interested countries and areas men and women of the United States qualified for service abroad and willing to serve, under conditions of hardship if necessary, to help the peoples of such countries and areas in meeting their needs for trained manpower, and to help promote a better understanding of the American people on the part of the peoples served and a better understanding of other peoples on the part of the American people." https://www.govinfo.gov/content/pkg/STATUTE-75/pdf/STATUTE-75-Pg612.pdf

The Peace Corps Act has been amended since its enactment (22 U.S.C. 2501). Title VI of the International Security and Development Cooperation Act of 1981 (22 U.S.C. 2501–1) made the Peace Corps an independent agency. https://www.govinfo.gov/content/pkg/USCODE-2017-title22/pdf/USCODE-2017-title22-chap34.pdf

The President appoints the Director and Deputy Director of the agency by the advice and with the consent of the Senate.

Activities

The Peace Corps consists of a Washington, DC, headquarters, six regional offices, and overseas operations in 62 countries, relying on more than 7,350 volunteers and trainees.

To fulfill the Peace Corps mandate, men and women are trained for a 9- to 14-week period in the appropriate local language, the technical skills necessary for their particular jobs, and the cross-cultural skills needed to adjust to a society with traditions and attitudes different from their own. Volunteers serve for a period of 2 years, living among the people with whom they work. Volunteers are expected to become a part of the community through their service.

Thousands of volunteers serve worldwide and work in six program areas: agriculture, business development, education, environment, health and HIV/AIDS, and youth development. Community-level projects are designed to match the skills of volunteers with the resources of host-country agencies and other international assistance organizations to solve specific development problems, often in conjunction with private volunteer organizations.

In the United States, the Peace Corps is working to promote an understanding of people in other countries. Through its World Wise Schools program, volunteers partner with elementary and junior high school students in the United States to encourage an exchange of letters, pictures, music, and artifacts. Participating students increase their knowledge of geography, languages, and different cultures, while gaining an appreciation for voluntarism.

The Peace Corps offers other domestic programs that rely on former volunteers. Working together with universities, local public school systems, and private businesses and foundations, these former volunteers help solve some of our Nation's most pressing domestic problems. http://www.peacecorps.gov/about

Sources of Information

Age Limit   The Peace Corps does not have an upper age limit, and spouses and partners can serve together. To learn more, visit the "Volunteering at 50–Plus" web page. https://www.peacecorps.gov/volunteer/is-peace-corps-right-for-me/50plus

Becoming a Volunteer   The volunteer program has an online application portal. http://www.peacecorps.gov/apply

Career Opportunities   Peace Corps vacancy announcements are posted online. Additional information is available from the Office of Human Resource Management. Phone, 202-692-1200. http://www.peacecorps.gov/about/jobs

The Peace Corps consistently ranks high among midsize agencies in the Partnership for Public Service's Best Places To Work Agency Rankings. In 2018, it ranked 6th among 27 midsize agencies. http://bestplacestowork.org/rankings/detail/PU00

Climate Change / Sustainability   The 2016 Strategic Sustainability Performance Plan identifies greenhouse gas reduction as one of its principal goals and includes an appendix on climate change resilience. https://files.peacecorps.gov/documents/open-government/2016_Strategic_Sustainability_Performance_Plan.pdf

Contact Information   The "Contact Us" web page has key phone numbers and email addresses for contacting the Peace Corps. https://www.peacecorps.gov/contact/#email_form | Email: dcinfo@peacecorps.gov

Countries   Peace Corps volunteers serve in more than 60 countries. https://www.peacecorps.gov/countries

Donate   The "Donate" web page lists and describes projects that donors can support. https://www.peacecorps.gov/donate

Educator Resources   The Paul D. Coverdell World Wise Schools program provides online educational resources based on the Peace Corps experience. https://www.peacecorps.gov/educators/resources/?search_text=climate&list=educators-resources

Events   The "Events" web page has a search tool for locating a nearby event by ZIP Code. https://www.peacecorps.gov/events

Facts   Curious to know how many Americans have been in the Peace Corps? On which continent most volunteers serve? To learn the answers to these questions and others, visit the "Fast Facts" web page. https://www.peacecorps.gov/news/fast-facts

Freedom of Information Act (FOIA)   The FOIA (5 USC 552) gives the public right to request records from a Federal agency. An agency must disclose the requested record as long as one of the law's nine exemptions does not shield the information from public disclosure. https://www.govinfo.gov/content/pkg/USCODE-2017-title5/pdf/USCODE-2017-title5-partI-chap5-subchapII.pdf

The Peace Corps posts certain types of records that it creates on its website. A formal FOIA request is not necessary to access them. The Peace Corps also maintains a FOIA requester service center that can provide information on the status of a person's FOIA request. https://www.peacecorps.gov/about/open-government/foia

Frequently Asked Questions (FAQs)   The Peace Corps posts answers to FAQs on its website. https://www.peacecorps.gov/faqs/all

Global Initiatives   These programs promote AIDS relief, work to eliminate malaria, help local people assure their own food security, economically empower women, and support development projects in local communities. https://www.peacecorps.gov/about/global-initiatives

History   At 2 a.m., before a crowd of 10,000 students, then Senator and Presidential candidate John F. Kennedy launched a new experiment in public service from the steps of the Michigan Union at the University of Michigan in Ann Arbor. To learn more about what happened early that morning of October 14, 1960, visit "The Founding Moment" web page. https://www.peacecorps.gov/about/history/founding-moment

News   The Office of Press Relations posts news—agency statements, media advisories, and press releases—on the Peace Corps website. https://www.peacecorps.gov/news | Email: pressoffice@peacecorps.gov

The Sources of Information were updated 8–2019.

Open Government   The Peace Corps supports the Open Government initiative by promoting the principles of collaboration, participation, and transparency. https://www.peacecorps.gov/about/open-government

Oversight   The Office of the Inspector General from the Peace Corps posts reports and data on Oversight.gov, a text-searchable repository of reports that Federal Inspectors General publish. The Council of the Inspectors General on Integrity and Efficiency operates and maintains the website to increase public access to independent and authoritative information on the Federal Government. https://oversight.gov/reports

Recruitment Offices   Contact information for Peace Corps recruitment offices is available online. http://www.peacecorps.gov/recruiters/offices

Social Media   The Peace Corps tweets announcements and other newsworthy items on Twitter. https://twitter.com/peacecorps

The Peace Corps has a Facebook account. https://www.facebook.com/peacecorps

The Peace Corps posts videos on its YouTube channel. https://www.youtube.com/peacecorps

Stories   Peace Corps volunteers have stories to tell. Read and listen to them on the Peace Corps' website. https://www.peacecorps.gov/stories

---

Pension Benefit Guaranty Corporation

1200 K Street NW., Washington, DC 20005
Phone, 202-326-4000. Fax, 800-400-7242. Internet, http://www.pbgc.gov

Board of Directors

CHAIR (Secretary of Labor)	ALEXANDER ACOSTA
Member (Secretary of the Treasury)	STEVEN MNUCHIN
Member (Secretary of Commerce)	WILBER ROSS

Officials

Director	THOMAS REEDER
Chief, Benefits Administration	DAVID FOLEY
Chief Counsel	ISRAEL GOLDOWITZ
Chief Financial Officer	PATRICIA KELLY
Chief Information Officer	ROBERT SCHERER

PENSION BENEFIT GUARANTY CORPORATION

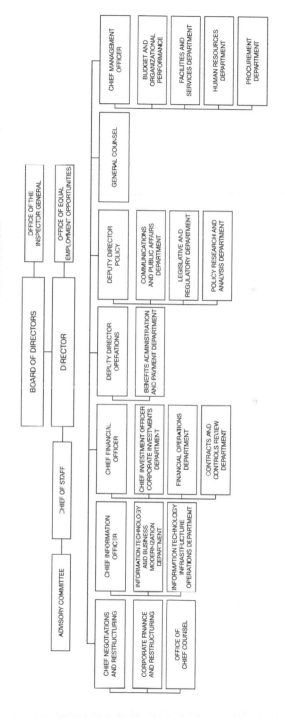

Chief Investment Officer	JOHN GREENBERG
Chief Management Officer	ALICE MARONI
Chief, Negotiations and Restructuring	KAREN MORRIS
Chief of Staff	ANN ORR
Chief Policy Officer	(VACANCY)
Deputy Chief, Benefits Administration	(VACANCY)
Deputy Chief, Negotiations and Restructuring	(VACANCY)
Deputy Chief Policy Officer	MICHAEL RAE
Deputy General Counsel	PHILIP HERTZ
Director, Department of Budget	EDGAR BENNETT
Director, Department of Communications Outreach and Legislative Affairs	MARTHA THREATT, ACTING
Director, Department of Corporate Controls and Reviews	MARTIN BOEHM
Director, Department of Corporate Finance and Restructuring	ADI BERGER, ACTING
Director, Department of Financial Operations	THEODORE WINTER
Director, Department of Human Resources	ARRIE ETHERIDGE
Director, Department of Information Technology and Business Modernization	VIDHYA SHYAMSUNDER
Director, Department of Information Technology Infrastructure Operations	JOSHUA KOSSOY
Director, Department of Policy Research and Analysis	CHRISTOPHER BONE
Director, Department of Procurement	STEVE BLOCK
Director, Department of Quality Management	DIANE BRAUNSTEIN
Director, Department of Workplace Solutions	ALISA COTTONE
General Counsel	JUDITH STARR
Inspector General	ROBERT A. WESTBROOKS

The Pension Benefit Guaranty Corporation protects the retirement incomes of American workers in private-sector defined benefit pension plans.

The Pension Benefit Guaranty Corporation (PBGC) is a self-financing, wholly owned Government corporation subject to the Government Corporation Control Act (31 U.S.C. 9101–9109). The Corporation, established by title IV of the Employee Retirement Income Security Act of 1974 (29 U.S.C. 1301–1461), operates in accordance with policies established by its Board of Directors.

The Board comprises the Secretaries of Labor, Commerce, and the Treasury. The Secretary of Labor serves as Chair of the Board. A seven-member advisory committee, comprising two labor, two employer, and three general public representatives whom the President appoints, advises the PBGC on investment issues. The President also appoints the PBGC's Director, whom the Senate then confirms. http://www.pbgc.gov/about/who-we-are.html

Activities

Coverage The Corporation insures most private sector defined-benefit pension plans that provide a pension benefit based on factors such as age, years of service, and salary.

It administers two insurance programs, separately covering single-employer and multiemployer plans. More than 40 million workers and retirees participate in nearly 24,000 covered plans.

Single-Employer Insurance Under the single-employer program, the Corporation guarantees payment of basic pension benefits if an insured plan terminates without sufficient assets to pay those benefits. The law limits, however, the total monthly benefit that the PBGC may guarantee for one individual to $5,011.36 per month for a 65-year-old individual in a pension plan that terminates in 2015. The law also sets other restrictions on PBGC's guarantee, including limits on the insured amount of recent benefit increases. In certain cases, the Corporation may pay some benefits above the guaranteed amount depending on the funding level of the plan and amounts recovered from employers.

A plan sponsor may terminate a single-employer plan in a standard termination if the plan has sufficient assets to purchase private annuities to cover all benefit liabilities. If a plan does not have sufficient assets, the sponsor may seek to transfer the pension liabilities to the PBGC by demonstrating that it meets the legal criteria for a distress termination. In either termination, the plan administrator must inform participants in writing at least 60 days prior to the date the administrator proposes to terminate the plan. Only a plan that has sufficient assets to pay all benefit liabilities may terminate in a standard termination. The Corporation also may institute termination of underfunded plans in certain specified circumstances. http://www.pbgc.gov/wr/benefits/guaranteed-benefits.html

Multiemployer Insurance Under title IV, as revised in 1980 by the Multiemployer Pension Plan Amendments Act (29 U.S.C. 1001 note), which changed the insurable event from plan termination to plan insolvency, the Corporation provides financial assistance to multiemployer plans that are unable to pay nonforfeitable benefits. The plans are obligated to repay such assistance. The act also made employers withdrawing from a plan liable to the plan for a portion of its unfunded vested benefits. http://www.pbgc.gov/prac/multiemployer.html

Premium Collections All defined-benefit pension plans insured by the PBGC are required to pay premiums to the Corporation according to rates set by Congress. The per-participant flat-rate premium for plans starting in 2015 is $57.00 for single-employer plans and $26.00 for multiemployer plans. Underfunded single-employer plans must also pay an additional premium equal to $24 per $1,000 of unfunded vested benefits. A termination premium of $1,250 per participant per year applies to certain distress and involuntary plan terminations, payable for 3 years after

the termination. http://www.pbgc.gov/prac/prem/premium-rates.html

Sources of Information

Blog The PBGC Web site features the "Retirement Matters" blog. http://www.pbgc.gov/about/who-we-are/retirement-matters

Business Opportunities The PBGC tries to give a fair share of its procurement awards and subcontracting opportunities to small businesses. The PBGC regularly procures accounting, actuarial, auditing, benefits administration, legal, and information technology services.

The agency utilizes various types of contract vehicles that are outlined in the "Federal Acquisition Regulation". These types of contract vehicles include agreements, commercial contracts, major contracts, orders against other Government contracts, and purchase orders. http://www.pbgc.gov/about/procurement.html

Career Opportunities The PBGC relies on accountants, actuaries, administrative personnel, analysts, attorneys, auditors, employee benefits law specialists, information technology experts, public affairs specialists, and other professionals to carry out its mission. http://www.pbgc.gov/about/jobs.html

Fraud Alerts The PBGC, with support from its Office of the Inspector General, posts fraud alerts to spread awareness of scams. http://www.pbgc.gov/wr/other/pg/fraud-alerts.html

Freedom of Information Act (FOIA) The PBGC participates in FOIAonline, which allows information seekers to submit electronic FOIA requests, to track the status of requests, to search for requests submitted by others, to access released records, and to generate agency-specific processing reports. https://foiaonline.regulations.gov/foia/action/public/home

FOIA requests must be in writing and may be submitted also by email, fax, or by regular mail to the Disclosure Officer, Pension Benefit Guaranty Corporation, 1200 K Street NW., Suite 11101, Washington, DC 20005. Fax, 202-326-4042. http://www.pbgc.gov/about/pg/footer/foia.html | Email: disclosure@pbgc.gov

Glossary The PBGC maintains a glossary of terms with simplified definitions. Some terms and their definitions are PBGC-specific in usage. http://www.pbgc.gov/about/pg/header/glossary.html

Insured Pension Plans   A list of pension plans that recently paid premiums to the PBGC is available online. http://www.pbgc.gov/wr/find-an-insured-pension-plan/pbgc-protects-pensions.html

Open Government   The PBGC posts datasets that are useful for increasing agency accountability, public knowledge of the agency and its operations, and economic opportunity. http://www.pbgc.gov/open/index.html | Email: opengov@pbgc.gov

Plain Language   PBGC writers and editors are committed to using plain language in new communications and revising confusing or unclear language in existing material.

Send them a note via email if a sentence or paragraph's clarity could be improved. http://www.pbgc.gov/about/pbgc-in-plain-english.html | Email: webmaster@pbgc.gov

Press Room   The PBGC posts press releases on its Web site. http://www.pbgc.gov/news/press.html

An online subscription form is available to sign up for the latest news, delivered via email, from the PBGC. http://www.pbgc.gov/about/stay-informed.html

Site Map   PBGC Web site visitors may use the site map to look for specific topics or to browse for content that aligns with their interests. http://www.pbgc.gov/pbgc-sitemap.html; http://www.pbgc.gov/about/pg/contact/contact.html

For further information, contact the Pension Benefit Guaranty Corporation, 1200 K Street NW., Washington, DC 20005-4026. Phone, 202-326-4000 or 800-400-7242.

Postal Regulatory Commission

901 New York Avenue NW., Suite 200, Washington, DC 20268-0001
Phone, 202-789-6800. Fax, 202-789-6861. Internet, http://www.prc.gov

Chair	Robert G. Taub
Vice Chair	Mark Acton
Commissioner	Nanci E. Langley
Commissioner	Tony Hammond
Commissioner	(vacancy)
Director, Office of Accountability and Compliance	Margaret Cigno
Director, Office of Public Affairs and Government Relations	Ann Fisher
Director, Office of Secretary and Administration	Stacy L. Ruble
General Counsel	David A. Trissell
Inspector General	John F. Callender

[For the Postal Regulatory Commission statement of organization, see the Code of Federal Regulations, Title 39, Part 3002]

The above list of key personnel was updated 06–2017.

The Postal Regulatory Commission develops and implements a modern system of postal rate regulation.

The Postal Regulatory Commission is the successor agency to the Postal Rate Commission, which was created by the Postal Reorganization Act, as amended (39 U.S.C. 101 et seq.). The Commission was established as an independent agency in the executive branch of Government by the

Postal Accountability and Enhancement Act (39 U.S.C. 501). It comprises five Commissioners, appointed by the President with the advice and consent of the Senate, one of whom is designated as Chair.

The Commission promulgates rules and regulations, establishes procedures, and takes other actions necessary to carry out its obligations. It considers complaints received from interested persons relating to United States Postal Service rates, regulations, and services. The Commission also has certain reporting obligations, including a report on universal postal service and the postal monopoly. http://www.prc.gov/about

Sources of Information

Case Information   Active cases and daily listings are accessible online. A docket search tool is also available. http://www.prc.gov/dockets/active; http://www.prc.gov/dockets/daily; http://www.prc.gov/dockets/search | Email: prc-dockets@prc.gov

Employment   The Commission relies on the professional services of accountants, attorneys, economists, industrial engineers, marketing specialists, statisticians, and administrative and clerical personnel to fulfill its mission. http://www.prc.gov/employment-opportunities

Freedom of Information Act (FOIA)   A FOIA request form is available online. http://www.prc.gov/foia/onlinerequest

Newsroom   The Commission posts congressional submissions, papers, press releases, speeches, and upcoming events online. http://www.prc.gov/press-releases

Reading Room   Facilities for inspection and copying of records, viewing automated daily lists of docketed materials, and accessing the Commission's Web site are located at 901 New York Avenue NW., Suite 200, Washington, DC. The room is open on weekdays, excluding legal holidays, 8 a.m.–4:30 p.m.

Practice / Procedure   Practice and procedure rules governing the conduct of proceedings before the Commission may be found in parts 3001, 3010, 3015, 3020, 3025, 3030, 3031, 3050, and 3060 of title 39 of the "Code of Federal Regulations." http://www.ecfr.gov/cgi-bin/text-idx?SID=a34266c229a4a7b3c470845f8da08605&node=39:1.0.2.15.2&rgn=div5; http://www.prc.gov/offices/osa

For further information, contact the Secretary, Postal Regulatory Commission, 901 New York Avenue NW., Suite 200, Washington, DC 20268-0001. Phone, 202-789-6840.

Railroad Retirement Board

844 North Rush Street, Chicago, IL 60611-1275
Phone, 312-751-4777. Fax, 312-751-7154. Internet, http://www.rrb.gov | Email: opa@rrb.gov

Chair	VACANT
Labor Member	WALTER A. BARROWS
Management Member	STEVEN J. ANTHONY
Inspector General	MARTIN J. DICKMAN
Director, Administration	KEITH B. EARLEY
Director, Equal Opportunity	LYNN E. COUSINS
Director, Human Resources	MARGUERITE V. DANIELS
Director, Public Affairs	MICHAEL P. FREEMAN
Chief, Acquisition Management	PAUL T. AHERN
Facility Manager	SCOTT L. RUSH
General Counsel	ANA M. KOCUR
Director, Legislative Affairs / Legislative Counsel	BEVERLY BRITTON FRASER
Director, Hearings and Appeals	RACHEL L. SIMMONS
Secretary to the Board	MARTHA P. RICO
Chief Actuary	FRANK J. BUZZI
Chief Information Officer	RAM MURTHY
Chief Financial Officer	VACANT
Director of Field Service and Senior Executive Officer	DANIEL J. FADDEN
Director, Programs	MICHAEL A. TYLLAS

Director, Policy and Systems	KIMBERLY PRICE-BUTLER
Director, Program Evaluation and Management Services	JANET M. HALLMAN
Director, Retirement and Survivor Benefits	VALERIE F. ALLEN
Director, Disability Benefits	SHERITA P. BOOTS
Director, Unemployment and Programs Support	MICHEAL T. PAWLAK

[For the Railroad Retirement Board statement of organization, see the Code of Federal Regulations, Title 20, Part 200]

The Railroad Retirement Board administers comprehensive retirement-survivor and unemployment-sickness benefit programs for the Nation's railroad workers and their families.

The Railroad Retirement Board (RRB) was originally established by the Railroad Retirement Act of 1934, as amended (45 U.S.C. 201-228z-1).

The RRB derives statutory authority from the Railroad Retirement Act of 1974 (45 U.S.C. 231-231u) and the Railroad Unemployment Insurance Act (45 U.S.C. 351-369). It administers these acts and participates in the administration of the Social Security Act and the Health Insurance for the Aged Act insofar as they affect railroad retirement beneficiaries.

The RRB comprises three members whom the President appoints with the advice and consent of the Senate: one upon the recommendations of representatives of railroad employees; one upon the recommendations of railroad employers; and one, the Chair, as a public member.

Activities

The Railroad Retirement Act provides for the payment of annuities to individuals who have completed at least 10 years of creditable railroad service, or 5 years if performed after 1995, and have ceased compensated service upon their attainment of specified ages or at any age if permanently disabled for all employment. In some circumstances occupational disability annuities or supplemental annuities are provided for career employees.

A spouse's annuity is provided, under certain conditions, for the wife or husband of an employee annuitant. Divorced spouses may also qualify.

Survivor annuities are awarded to the qualified spouses, children, and parents of deceased career employees, and various lump-sum benefits are also available under certain conditions.

Benefits based upon qualifying railroad earnings in a preceding 1-year period are provided under the Railroad Unemployment Insurance Act to individuals who are unemployed in a benefit year, but who are ready and willing to work, and to individuals who are unable to work because of sickness or injury.

The RRB maintains, through its field offices, a placement service for unemployed railroad personnel.

Sources of Information

Benefit Inquiries   The RRB provides personal assistance to railroad employees and railroad retirement beneficiaries through its field offices. Staff can explain benefit rights and responsibilities on an individual basis, assist employees in applying for benefits, and answer questions about benefit programs. (Railroad labor groups and employers also help railroad personnel stay informed about benefit programs.) Most field offices are open to the public during the week, 9 a.m.–3:30 p.m. They close at noon on Wednesdays, however, and do not open on Federal holidays. To locate an office, see "Field Offices" below and use the online Zip Code locator or call the automated phone system. Phone, 877-772-5772. http://www.rrb.gov/mep/ben_info.asp

Congressional Inquiries   Members of Congress or their staff may inquire about constituents, benefit claims, and filed applications by contacting the Congressional Inquiry section of the Office of Administration. Phone, 312-751-4970. Fax, 312-751-7154. https://www.rrb.gov/opa/rrbcongress_contacts.asp | Email: opa@rrb.gov

Data   The RRB posts actuarial, financial, and statistical data on its Web site. It also publishes datasets on the Web site Data. gov. https://www.rrb.gov/act/historical.asp; https://www.rrb.gov/data

Employment Contact the RRB's Bureau of Human Resources. Phone, 312-751-4580. Email: recruit@rrb.gov

The RRB posts online railroad job vacancies that have been reported to its field offices. https://www.rrb.gov/PandS/Jobs/rrjobs.asp

Field Offices Field offices are located throughout the country. Staff members answer questions about Medicare and Social Security benefits for railroad workers and their families, retirement benefits, sickness and unemployment benefits, survivor benefits, and tax withholding and statements. A Zip Code locator is available online for finding the nearest field office. https://www.rrb.gov/field/field.asp

Freedom of Information Act (FOIA) A FOIA request may be made by fax, letter, or online request form. A record description must contain sufficient detail—author, date, subject matter, type of record—to allow RRB staff to locate the record with reasonable effort. https://www.rrb.gov/blaw/foia/foia_guide.asp; https://secure.rrb.gov/efoia

Glossary A glossary of RRB terms is available online. https://www.rrb.gov/general/glossary.asp

Hotline To report the illegal receiving of RRB benefits or to file a complaint about misconduct relating to the RRB, its programs or employees, contact the Office of Inspector General. Phone, 800-772-4258. Fax, 312-751-4342. https://www.rrb.gov/OIG/hotline.asp | Email: hotline@oig.rrb.gov

Legislative Affairs For information on legislative matters, contact the Office of Legislative Affairs. Phone, 202-272-7742. Fax, 202-272-7728. The office is open Tuesday–Thursday, 9 a.m.–3:30 p.m., eastern standard time, except on Federal holidays. http://www.rrb.gov/org/ogc/ola.asp | Email: ola@rrb.gov

Publications Booklets, pamphlets (English and Spanish), and forms of interest to beneficiaries and railroad workers are available online. Pamphlets also are available from the RRB's field offices and Chicago headquarters. https://www.rrb.gov/mep/ben_forms.asp | Email: opa@rrb.gov

Telecommunications Devices for the Deaf (TDD) The RRB provides TDD services: beneficiary inquiries (Phone, 312-751-4701); equal opportunity inquiries (Phone, 312-751-4334). https://www.rrb.gov/general/contact_us.asp | Email: opa@rrb.gov

For further information, contact Public Affairs, Railroad Retirement Board, 844 North Rush Street, Chicago, IL 60611-1275. Phone, 312-751-4777. Fax, 312-751-7154.

Securities and Exchange Commission

100 F Street NE., Washington, DC 20549
Phone, 202-551-7500. Internet, http://www.sec.gov

Chair	W. Jay Clayton
Commissioner	Michael S. Piwowar
Commissioner	Kara M. Stein
Commissioner	(VACANCY)
Commissioner	(VACANCY)
Division Heads	
Codirector, Enforcement	Stephanie Avakian
Codirector, Enforcement	Steven Peikin
Director, Corporation Finance	William Hinman
Director, Economic and Risk Analysis / Chief Economist	Jeffrey Harris
Director, Investment Management	Dalia Blass
Director, Trading and Markets	Heather Siedel, Acting

Office Heads

Associate Executive Director, Human Resources	LACEY DINGMAN
Chief Accountant	WESLEY BRICKER
Chief Administrative Law Judge	BRENDA P. MURRAY
Chief Financial Officer	CARYN KAUFFMAN, ACTING
Chief FOIA Officer	BARRY D. WALTERS
Chief Operating Officer	KENNETH JOHNSON, ACTING
Chief Technology Officer	PAMELA DYSON
Director, Acquisitions	VANCE CATHELL
Director, Compliance Inspections and Examinations	PETER DRISCOLL, ACTING
Director, Credit Ratings	THOMAS BUTLER
Director, Equal Employment Opportunity	PETER HENRY, ACTING
Director, International Affairs	PAUL LEDER
Director, Investor Education and Advocacy	LORI J. SCHOCK
Director, Legislative and Intergovernmental Affairs	KEITH CASSIDY
Director, Minority and Women Inclusion	PAMELA GIBBS
Director, Municipal Securities	JESSICA KANE
Director, Public Affairs	JOHN NESTER
Director, Strategic Initiatives	MARK AMBROSE
Director, Support Operations	BARRY D. WALTERS
Ethics Counsel	SHIRA P. MINTON
General Counsel	ROBERT STEBBINS
Inspector General	CARL W. HOECKER
Investor Advocate	RICK A. FLEMING
Secretary	BRENT J. FIELDS

[For the Securities and Exchange Commission statement of organization, see the Code of Federal Regulations, Title 17, Part 200]

The above list of key personnel was updated 09–2017.

The Securities and Exchange Commission protects investors, facilitates capital formation, and maintains efficient, fair, and orderly markets.

The Securities and Exchange Commission (SEC) was created under authority of the Securities Exchange Act of 1934 (15 U.S.C. 78a–78jj) and was organized on July 2, 1934. The Commission serves as adviser to United States district courts in reorganization proceedings for debtor corporations in which a substantial public interest is involved. The Commission also has certain responsibilities under section 15 of the Bretton Woods Agreements Act of 1945 (22 U.S.C. 286k-1) and section 851(e) of the Internal Revenue Code of 1954 (26 U.S.C. 851(e)). https://www.sec.gov/about/laws.shtml

The Commission is vested with quasi-judicial functions. Persons aggrieved by its decisions in the exercise of those functions have a right of review by the United States courts of appeals. https://www.sec.gov/about/whatwedo.shtml

Activities

Full and Fair Disclosure   The Securities Act of 1933 (15 U.S.C. 77a) requires issuers of securities and their controlling persons making public offerings of securities in interstate commerce or via mail to file registration statements containing financial and other pertinent data about the issuer and the securities being offered with the SEC. There are limited exemptions, such as government securities, nonpublic offerings, and intrastate offerings, as well as certain offerings not exceeding $1.5 million. The effectiveness of a registration statement may be refused or suspended after a public hearing if the statement contains material misstatements or omissions, thus barring sale of the securities until it is appropriately amended.

Regulation of Investment Advisers   Persons who, for compensation, engage in the business of advising others with respect to securities must register with the Commission. The Commission is authorized to define what practices are considered fraudulent or deceptive and to prescribe means to prevent those practices.

Regulation of Mutual Funds and Other Investment Companies The Commission registers investment companies and regulates their activities to protect investors. The regulation covers sales load, management contracts, composition of boards of directors, and capital structure. The Commission must also determine the fairness of various transactions of investment companies before they actually occur.

The Commission may institute court action to enjoin the consummation of mergers and other plans of reorganization of investment companies if such plans are unfair to securities holders. It may impose sanctions by administrative proceedings against investment company management for violations of the act and other Federal securities laws. It also may file court actions to enjoin acts and practices of management officials involving breaches of fiduciary duty and personal misconduct and to disqualify such officials from office.

Regulation of Securities Markets The Securities Exchange Act of 1934 assigns to the Commission broad regulatory responsibilities over the securities markets, the self-regulatory organizations within the securities industry, and persons conducting a business in securities. Persons who execute transactions in securities generally are required to register with the Commission as broker-dealers. Securities exchanges and certain clearing agencies are required to register with the Commission, and associations of brokers or dealers are permitted to register with the Commission. The act also provides for the establishment of the Municipal Securities Rulemaking Board to formulate rules for the municipal securities industry.

The Commission oversees the self-regulatory activities of the national securities exchanges and associations, registered clearing agencies, and the Municipal Securities Rulemaking Board. In addition, the Commission regulates industry professionals, such as securities brokers and dealers, certain municipal securities professionals, Government securities brokers and dealers, and transfer agents.

Rehabilitation of Failing Corporations In cases of corporate reorganization proceedings administered in Federal courts, the Commission may participate as a statutory party. The principal functions of the Commission are to protect the interests of public investors involved in such cases through efforts to ensure their adequate representation and to participate in legal and policy issues that are of concern to public investors generally.

Representation of Debt Securities Holders The Commission safeguards the interests of purchasers of publicly offered debt securities issued pursuant to trust indentures.

Enforcement Activities The Commission's enforcement activities are designed to secure compliance with the Federal securities laws administered by the Commission and the rules and regulations adopted thereunder. These activities include measures to do the following: compel compliance with the disclosure requirements of the registration and other provisions of the relevant acts; prevent fraud and deception in the purchase and sale of securities; obtain court orders enjoining acts and practices that operate as a fraud upon investors or otherwise violate the laws; suspend or revoke the registrations of brokers, dealers, investment companies, and investment advisers who willfully engage in such acts and practices; suspend or bar from association persons associated with brokers, dealers, investment companies, and investment advisers who have violated any provision of the Federal securities laws; and prosecute persons who have engaged in fraudulent activities or other willful violations of those laws.

In addition, attorneys, accountants, and other professionals who violate the securities laws face possible loss of their privilege to practice before the Commission.

To this end, private investigations are conducted into complaints or other indications of securities violations. Established evidence of law violations is used in appropriate administrative proceedings to revoke registration or in actions instituted in Federal courts to restrain or enjoin such activities. Where the evidence tends to establish criminal fraud or other willful violation of the securities laws, the facts are referred to the Attorney General for criminal prosecution of the offenders. The Commission may assist in such prosecutions. https://www.sec.gov/litigation.shtml

Sources of Information

Business Opportunities   The Office of Acquisitions' web page features links to help those who seek business opportunities with the SEC. Phone, 202-551-7300. https://www.sec.gov/oacq

Career Opportunities   The SEC relies on accountants, attorneys, economists, examiners, industry specialists, information technology specialists, and other professionals to carry out its mission. Applicants must apply for a specific vacancy and complete a process of competitive selection. This process does not apply, however, to attorney vacancies. The Commission runs a college and law school recruitment program that relies on campus visits and student interviews. http://www.sec.gov/careers

For more information, contact the Office of Human Resources. Phone, 202-551-7500. Fax, 202-777-1028. https://www.sec.gov/ohr

Electronic Data Gathering, Analysis, and Retrieval (EDGAR)   The EDGAR database provides free public access to corporate information such as prospectuses, registration statements, and quarterly and annual reports. https://www.sec.gov/edgar.shtml

Events   A schedule of upcoming SEC meetings, public appearances by SEC officials, and public hearings is available online. http://www.sec.gov/about/upcoming-events.htm

Fast Answers   The SEC maintains a list of the terms for which SEC website visitors search most frequently. https://www.sec.gov/fast-answers

Freedom of Information Act (FOIA)   The Office of Freedom of Information Act Services makes SEC records available to the public to the greatest extent possible under the FOIA. The Office receives nearly 17,000 requests per year for Commission documents and records. For more information, contact the FOIA public service center. Phone, 202-551-7900. Fax, 202-772-9337. https://www.sec.gov/page/foia

Many records—no-action and interpretive letters, public comments on proposed rules, registration statements and reports filed by regulated companies and individuals, SEC decisions and releases, and staff manuals—can be read and printed for free by using the SEC online search feature. An electronic request form is available for obtaining nonpublic records: consumer complaints, records compiled in investigations, and staff comment letters. The SEC will release nonpublic records, except when they are protected by a FOIA exemption. The electronic request form may be used also for obtaining older records that the SEC has not posted on its website—records usually dated before 1996. https://tts.sec.gov/cgi-bin/request_public_docs

Glossary   The Office of Investor Education and Advocacy maintains an online glossary. https://investor.gov/glossary

Investment Adviser Public Disclosure   The SEC provides an online tool to search for an investment adviser firm and to view the registration or reporting form (Form ADV) that the adviser filed. The tool also allows an investor to search for an individual investment adviser representative and to view his or her professional background and conduct. http://www.adviserinfo.sec.gov/IAPD/default.aspx#

Investor Education   The Office of Investor Education and Advocacy offers services to and provides tools for investors. The Office cannot tell an investor how or where to invest money, but it can help him or her invest knowledgeably and avoid fraud. Phone, 800-732-0330. Fax, 202-772-9295. https://www.investor.gov | Email: help@sec.gov

The Office of Investor Education and Advocacy tweets on Twitter. https://twitter.com/SEC_Investor_Ed

The SEC maintains a list of external educational websites. https://www.sec.gov/investor/links.shtml

The SEC maintains a list of investor calculators and tools that are available on external websites. https://www.sec.gov/investor/tools.shtml

Links   The SEC web page "Other Links" contains links to other websites—government and nongovernment—that may be of interest to Internet visitors. https://www.sec.gov/links

Newsroom   The SEC posts press releases, public statements, speeches, testimonies, and webcasts on its website. A subscription form is available online to receive news alerts via email. https://www.sec.gov/news | Email: news@sec.gov

Open Government   The SEC supports the Open Government initiative by promoting the principles of collaboration, participation, and transparency. https://www.sec.gov/open | Email: opengov@sec.gov

Organizational Chart   The SEC's organizational chart is available in Portable Document Format (PDF) for viewing and downloading. https://www.sec.gov/images/secorg.pdf

A text version of the SEC's organizational chart also is available. https://www.sec.gov/about/orgtext.htm

Plain Language   Like other Federal agencies, the SEC must compose documents in plain writing. According to the Plain Writing Act of 2010, writing should be "clear, concise, well-organized" and follow "other best practices appropriate to the subject or field or audience." SEC writers and editors want to know if agency documents and web pages are difficult to understand. Contact them by email to leave a comment or make a suggestion. https://www.sec.gov/plainwriting.shtml | Email: PlainWriting@sec.gov

Publications   SEC publications are available in Chinese, English, and Spanish in Portable Document Format (PDF). https://www.investor.gov/publications-research-studies/publications

Regional Offices   Regional offices can provide investors with information and assist them with complaints. Contact information for the SEC's 11 regional offices is available online. https://www.sec.gov/page/sec-regional-offices

RSS Feeds   RSS feeds are an online resource for keeping abreast of the most recent materials posted to the SEC website. https://www.sec.gov/about/secrss.shtml

Site Map   The website map allows visitors to look for specific topics or to browse content that aligns with their interests. https://www.sec.gov/sitemap.shtml

Small Business Activities   Information for small businesses—information on legal obligations when they sell securities and on financial and other reporting obligations when their securities are traded publicly—is available online. Contact the Office of Small Business Policy for more information. Phone, 202-551-3460. http://www.sec.gov/info/smallbus.shtml

Social Media   The SEC maintains a presence on Flickr, LinkedIn, Pinterest, Twitter, and YouTube. https://www.sec.gov/opa/social_media.html

Tips / Complaints   Members of the public can inform the SEC of possible violations of U.S. securities laws by completing the online questionnaire. https://www.sec.gov/complaint.shtml

Votes   The final votes of SEC Commissioners on decisions, orders, rules and similar actions are posted online. https://www.sec.gov/about/commission-votes.shtml; https://www.sec.gov/contact.shtml

For further information, contact the Office of Public Affairs, Securities and Exchange Commission, 100 F Street NE., Washington, DC 20549. Phone, 202-551-4120. Fax, 202-777-1026.

Selective Service System

National Headquarters, Arlington, VA 22209-2425
Phone, 703-605-4100. Internet, http://www.sss.gov

National Headquarters—Arlington, VA

Director	DONALD M. BENTON
Deputy Director	JOHN P. PRIGMORE
Chief Officers	
Financial	RODERICK R. HUBBARD
Information Security	ANTHONY CLARK
Chief of Staff	WADI A. YAKHOUR

General Counsel	RUDY G. SANCHEZ, JR.
https://www.sss.gov/About/Directors-Biography	
Associate Directors	
Information Technology	ANTHONY CLARK
Operations	CRAIG T. BROWN
Public and Intergovernmental Affairs	MATTHEW H. TITTMANN
Support Services	RODERICK R. HUBBARD
Data Management Center—Palatine, IL	
Manager	NICOLE F. HARRIS
Regional Headquarters	
Directors	
Region I—North Chicago, IL	THOMAS J. KENNEY
Region II—Marietta, GA	CARLOS M. PEREZ
Region III—Denver, CO	JOHN J. WILBER
https://www.sss.gov/About	

The above list of key personnel was updated 7–2019.

The Selective Service System supplies the Armed Forces with manpower in an emergency and operates an Alternative Service Program for men classified as conscientious objectors.

Establishment and Organization

On June 24, President Harry Truman approved the Selective Service Act of 1948, which established the Selective Service System. https://www.loc.gov/rr/frd/Military_Law/Morgan-Papers/Vol-I_PL-759.pdf

The SSS is an independent agency within the executive branch. The President appoints the Director, who is directly responsible to the President. The agency is not part of the Department of Defense. The agency's statement of organization is found in the Code of Federal Regulations (32 CFR 1605). https://www.govinfo.gov/content/pkg/CFR-2018-title32-vol6/pdf/CFR-2018-title32-vol6-part1605.pdf

By the enactment of a later amendment, the original Act became known as the Military Selective Service Act (50 U.S.C. 3801 et seq.). It requires the registration of male U.S. citizens and other male persons who are in the United States. The Act exempts members of the active Armed Forces and nonimmigrant aliens. https://www.sss.gov/About/Agency-Mission/Military-Selective-Service-Act

From 1948 until 1973, men were drafted to fill Armed Forces vacancies that could not be filled through voluntary means. When the authority of induction expired in 1973, the SSS continued and maintained readiness to support the all-volunteer force in case an emergency should require Congress to authorize a resumption of inductions. Registration was suspended early in 1975, and the SSS assumed a standby posture. Beginning in late 1979, efforts were made to upgrade the System's capability for rapid mobilization in an emergency. In the summer of 1980, the registration requirement was reinstated. https://www.sss.gov/About/History-And-Records/Background-Of-Selective-Service

Proclamation 4771 of July 20, 1980 (45 FR 45247), requires, unless exempted by the Military Selective Service Act, male citizens and other males residing in the country born on or after January 1, 1960, and who have attained age 18, but have not attained age 26, to register. A young man may register at a post office within the United States and at a U.S. Embassy or consulate outside the United States. Today, registering online at the SSS's website is also possible. https://www.govinfo.gov/content/pkg/FR-1980-07-03/pdf/FR-1980-07-03.pdf#page=1

Activities

The Selective Service System (SSS) is a proven way to expand the U.S. Armed Forces in a national emergency. The SSS operates at low cost; it ensures that a future draft will be fair and equitable; and it can respond to the Nation's needs for manpower in a timely manner. Registration is the only mission component that is publicly visible during peacetime; however, readiness to respond is crucial. It fosters timeliness, fairness, and the equity that is expected of the agency if it is directed to reestablish conscription.

The Military Selective Service Act imposes liability for training and service in the Armed Forces upon registrants who are ages 18–26, except those who are exempt or deferred. Persons who have been deferred remain liable for training and service until age 35. Aliens are not liable for training and service until they have remained in the United States for more than 1 year. Conscientious objectors who are opposed to all service in the Armed Forces are required to perform civilian work in lieu of induction into the Armed Forces. https://www.sss.gov/About

Readiness The SSS maintains readiness to manage a conscription program for the U.S. Armed Forces if authorized by Congress and directed by the President. The agency must be ready to execute a national draft lottery, to issue induction orders to those registrants who are selected through the lottery, and to arrange transportation to relocate them to a military entrance processing station for testing and evaluation before induction into military service. The agency also must maintain the ability to operate an alternative service program for the men who request and are granted conscientious objector status.

Three regional headquarters keep the agency connected with its hundreds of part-time employees and thousands of volunteers throughout the country and U.S. Territories. The regional headquarters maintain the SSS's readiness at the grassroots level. They manage the activities of the agency's 56 State directors; conduct training for them, regional field offices, and civilian board members; and ensure that the local and district appeals boards have sufficient numbers of people serving on them. They also directly support the agency's goal of increasing registration compliance through local registration awareness programs.

The board member program relies on uncompensated civilian volunteers who serve as local, district, and national appeals board members. The SSS trains board members to prepare them for adjudicating claims filed by registrants seeking postponements, exemptions, and deferments in accordance with the Military Selective Service Act, the Code of Federal Regulations, and other policies and procedures. Readiness training, operational planning, and policies for the agency are continually updated to reflect changes that may be occurring in real-time.

Registration Registration is a critical component of readiness. The agency is responsible for providing trained and untrained manpower to the Department of Defense in the event of a national emergency. If conscription becomes necessary, the maximum number of eligible men must be registered to assure the public of a fair and equitable lottery and induction process. By registering, male citizens comply with Federal law and remain eligible for student financial aid, job training, and Government employment opportunities. Immigrant men protect their eligibility for U.S. citizenship by being registered.

Data Management Center employees process registrations and operate the agency's database system. If directed by Congress and the President, the SSS's registration database would be used to facilitate the induction of men into the U.S. Armed Forces. The agency's database is constantly maintained to ensure accuracy, accessibility, and network security.

Sources of Information

Alternative Service The "Alternative Service Program" brochure is available online. https://www.sss.gov/Portals/0/PDFs/ASP%20Brochure%20-%20Web.pdf

Annual Reports The SSS posts it annual reports to the U.S. Congress online. https://www.sss.gov/Reports/Annual-Report-to-Congress

Career Opportunities The Selective Service System offers competitive wages, the Thrift Savings Plan with matching funds, health care benefits, paid vacation time, and work-life benefit options that include telework, as well as alternate and flexible work schedules for most positions. https://www.sss.gov/Careers

In 2018, the SSS ranked 26th among 29 small agencies in the Partnership for Public Service's Best Places To Work Agency Rankings. http://bestplacestowork.org/rankings/detail/SS00

Contact Information   The SSS posts helpful email addresses and phone numbers for contacting the agency. https://www.sss.gov/About/ContactInformation | Email: information@sss.gov

Facts / Figures   Quick facts and figures are available online. https://www.sss.gov/About/Quick-Facts-and-Figures

Forms   Frequently requested forms are available online. https://www.sss.gov/Forms

Freedom of Information Act (FOIA)   Enacted in 1966, the FOIA took effect on July 4, 1967. The law gives a right to obtain access to Federal agency records to any person, except a fugitive from the law. Some records, or portions of them, are, however, shielded from disclosure by one or more of nine statutory exemptions or by specific harm that disclosure may cause. https://www.sss.gov/Reports/FOIA

The electronic reading room contains documents that the SSS has posted proactively. Before making a FOIA request, search the electronic reading room for relevant records that may be accessible without a formal FOIA request. https://www.sss.gov/Reports/FOIA/FOIA-Electronic-Reading-Room

Frequently Asked Questions (FAQs)   The SSS posts answers to FAQs. https://www.sss.gov/QA

Newsletter   The SSS posts its quarterly newsletter "The Register" online. https://www.sss.gov/Public-Affairs/The-Register-Newsletter

Noncitizens / Dual Nationals   U.S. noncitizens and dual nationals are required by law to register with the SSS. More information is available on the "Non-Citizens and Dual Nationals" web page.

https://www.sss.gov/About/History-And-Records/Non-Citizens-and-Dual-Nationals

Performance / Accountability   The agency's performance and accountability reports are available online. https://www.sss.gov/Reports/Financial-Reports/Performance-Accountability-Report

Plain Language   The Selective Service System adheres to Federal plain language guidelines. If a document or web page contains poorly written prose or is difficult to understand, contact the agency by email. https://www.sss.gov/Reports-and-Notices/Plain-Language | Email: Information@sss.gov

Registration   Men, age 18–25, with a valid social security number, may register online using an electronic form. A fillable registration form that can be returned by mail is also available for immigrant males (documented or undocumented), for men who cannot use the online registration form because of a faulty social security number, and for men without a social security number. https://www.sss.gov/Home/Registration

Registration resources that have been adapted for various audiences and made suitable for blogs, websites, and electronic and print newsletters, are available on the agency's website. https://www.sss.gov/Resources/Resources

Return to the Draft   Learn how the SSS would conduct a return to the draft. https://www.sss.gov/About/Events-after-Draft

Social Media   The SSS has a Facebook account. https://www.facebook.com/SSSregistration?ref=ts&fref=ts

The SSS tweets announcements and other newsworthy items on Twitter. https://twitter.com/SSS_gov

The SSS posts videos on its YouTube channel. https://www.youtube.com/user/SelectiveServ?feature=watch

Women   Women are not required to register with the SSS. To learn the reasons for their exemption, visit the "Women and the Draft" web page. https://www.sss.gov/Registration/Women-And-Draft

The Sources of Information were updated 7–2019.

Small Business Administration

409 Third Street SW., Washington, DC 20416
Phone, 202-205-6600. Fax, 202-205-7064. Internet, http://www.sba.gov

SBA Headquarters

Administrator	CHRISTOPHER M. PILKERTON, ACTING
Deputy Administrator	(VACANCY)
Chief Counsel	MAJOR CLARK, ACTING
Senior Advisor	PATRICIA GIBSON
https://www.sba.gov/person/chris-pilkerton	

Associate Administrators	
Capital Access	WILLIAM MANGER
Communications and Public Liaison	JIMMY F. BILLIMORIA
Congressional and Legislative Affairs	MICHAEL HERSHEY
Disaster Assistance	JAMES RIVERA
Entrepreneurial Development	ALLEN GUTIERREZ
Field Operations	MICHAEL VALLANTE, ACTING
Government Contracting and Business Development	ROBB WONG
International Trade	DAVID M. GLACCUM
Investment and Innovation	JOSEPH SHEPARD
Small Business Development Centers	GEORGE KOKLANARIS
Veterans Business Development	LARRY STUBBLEFIELD

Assistant Administrator	
Hearings and Appeals	DELORICE PRICE FORD

Chief Officers	
Financial	DORRICE ROTH
Information	MARIA A. ROAT
Operating	(VACANCY)
General Counsel	CHRISTOPHER M. PILKERTON
National Ombudsman	STEFANIE WEHAGEN
https://www.sba.gov/about-sba/organization/sba-leadership	

Regional Administrators

Regions	
I	WENDELL G. DAVIS
II	STEVE BULGER
III	MICHELLE CHRISTIAN
IV	ASHLEY DANIEL BELL
V	ROBERT SCOTT
VI	JUSTIN CROSSIE
VII	THOMAS SALISBURY
VIII	DANIEL NORDBERG
IX	MICHAEL VALLANTE
X	JEREMY FIELD

https://www.sba.gov/local-assistance/find/?type=SBA%20
    Regional%20Office&pageNumber=1

Office of Inspector General

Inspector General	H. MIKE WARE
https://www.sba.gov/content/hannibal-mike-ware	

The above list of key personnel was updated 6–2019.

The Small Business Administration aids, assists, and counsels entrepreneurs and protects their business interests; preserves free and competitive enterprise; and maintains and strengthens the overall economy.

Establishment and Organization

On July 30, 1953, President Dwight D. Eisenhower approved Public Law 83–163, which is also cited as the "Small Business Act of 1953." This Act created the Small Business Administration (SBA), whose present existence and authority are derived from the Small Business Act (15 U.S.C. 631 et seq.) and the Small Business Investment Act of 1958 (15 U.S.C. 661). https://www.govinfo.gov/content/pkg/STATUTE-67/pdf/STATUTE-67-Pg230.pdf

For the SBA statement of organization, see the Code of Federal Regulations, Title 13, Part 101. https://www.ecfr.gov/cgi-bin/text-idx?SID=d38ae405ec8120025c2a65388e249f57&mc=true&node=pt13.1.101&rgn=div5

The SBA included an organizational chart in its "Agency Financial Report—Fiscal Year 2018" on page 12. https://www.sba.gov/sites/default/files/2018-11/SBA%20FY%202018%20AFR.pdf

Activities

Advocacy   The Office of Advocacy (OA) promotes the views and elevates the concerns of small business before Congress, White House officials, representatives of Federal agencies, Federal court judges, and policymakers on the State level. Within the Federal government, the OA speaks independently on behalf of small business and is the source of small business statistics. The OA also has watchdog responsibilities, ensuring that small business receives the support and consideration that the "Regulatory Flexibility Act of 1980" (Public Law 96–354), as amended, provides. https://advocacy.sba.gov | Email: advocacy@sba.gov

For further information, contact the Office of Advocacy. Phone, 202-205-6533.

Bonding for Contractors   The Surety Bond Guarantee program helps small and emerging contractors obtain the bonding necessary for bidding on and receiving non-Federal contracts up to $6.5 million and Federal contracts up to $10 million. The SBA guarantees bonds that participating surety companies issue and reimburses between 70–90 percent of losses and expenses incurred should a business default on the contract. Construction, service, and supply contractors are eligible for the program if they meet certain standards. https://www.sba.gov/funding-programs/surety-bonds

For further information, contact the Office of Surety Guarantees. Phone, 202-205-6540.

Business Development   The Office of Business Development (OBD) oversees the 8(a) Business Development program. The Office assists with contracts and loans, counsels, expands access to capital and credit, gives technical guidance, and offers training workshops. Eligible 8(a) program participants may receive Federal surplus property on a priority basis. One of the OBD's principal development tools is the Mentor-Protégé program, which allows participants to benefit from business development assistance provided by successful companies. https://www.sba.gov/offices/headquarters/obd/resources

For further information, contact the Office of Business Development. Phone, 202-205-5852.

Capital Access   The Office of the Associate Administrator for Capital Access increases the availability of capital through banks and other lending partners. It oversees SBA programs that help small businesses gain access to capital. These programs include the 7(a) general business guarantee, 504 Certified Development Company, SBA surety bond guarantee, and microlending. https://www.sba.gov/offices/headquarters/oca

For further information, contact the Office of Capital Access. Phone, 202-205-6657.

Disaster Assistance   The SBA serves as the Federal disaster bank for nonfarm, private sector losses. It lends money to disaster survivors for repairing or replacing their most damaged property. The agency makes direct loans with subsidized interest rates to individuals, homeowners, businesses of all sizes, and nonprofit organizations. https://www.sba.gov/content/disaster-assistance | Email: disastercustomerservice@sba.gov

For further information, contact the Office of Disaster Assistance. Phone, 202-205-6734.

Field Operations The Office of Field Operations is responsible for the provision of SBA services and availability of its products: It serves as the critical link between SBA policymakers and businessmen and women who operate small businesses. The Office provides policy guidance and oversight to regional administrators and district directors for achieving agency goals and objectives and for solving problems in specific operational areas. It plays a liaison role and expedites issues for the regional and district offices when dealing with the central office, coordinating the presentation of views from the field. It also establishes and monitors district performance goals and organizes reviews of the field offices. https://www.sba.gov/about-sba/sba-locations

For further information, contact the Office of Field Operations. Phone, 202-205-6808.

Financial Assistance The SBA does not lend money directly to owners of small businesses, but it supports lenders in their efforts to make loans to them. The SBA sets guidelines for loans made by lending partners, community development organizations, and micro-lending institutions. The SBA reduces the risk of lending and makes it easier for lenders to access capital, which allows owners and operators of small business to receive loans more easily. The SBA gives its guarantee to lending institutions and certified development companies that make loans to small businesses. Small businesses use the borrowed money for working capital and financing the acquisition of land and buildings, for constructing new and improving existing facilities, and for purchasing equipment and machinery. https://www.sba.gov/funding-programs/loans

For further information, contact the nearest Small Business Administration district office.

Government Contracting Through various programs and services, the SBA assists small businesses—including HUBZone certified firms and disadvantaged, women-owned, and service-disabled veteran owned small businesses—with receiving Government procurement. The contracting liaison helps small-scale entrepreneurs secure an equitable share of the natural resources that the Federal Government sells. The Administration also works with the Office of Management and Budget and other Federal agencies to establish policy and regulations affecting small business access to Government contracts. https://www.sba.gov/category/navigation-structure/contracting

For further information, contact the nearest Office of Government Contracting. Phone, 202-205-6460.

Historically Underutilized Business Zone Development The Historically Underutilized Business Zone (HUBZone) program was part of the Small Business Reauthorization Act of 1997. The program fosters economic development and employment in HUBZones, which include Indian reservations, through the establishment of preferences. The program provides greater access to Federal contracting opportunities for qualified businesses. The SBA regulates and implements the program, determining which businesses are eligible to receive contracts, maintaining a list of qualified businesses that Federal agencies may use for locating vendors, adjudicating protests of eligibility, and reporting to the Congress on the program's effect on employment and investment. https://www.sba.gov/content/understanding-hubzone-program | Email: HUBZone@sba.gov

For further information, contact the HUBZone Help Desk. Phone, 202-205-8885.

International Trade The Office of International Trade (OIT) makes American small businesses more competitive worldwide by developing international trade opportunities for them. It collaborates with other Federal agencies and with public and private sector groups to promote the exports of small businesses and to help entrepreneurs who seek export opportunities. Through 21 U.S. Export Assistance Centers, SBA district offices, and service-provider partners, the OIT coordinates and directs the Administration's export initiatives. https://www.sba.gov/offices/headquarters/oit

For further information, contact the Office of
International Trade. Phone, 202-205-6720.

Local Assistance   The SBA supports
business centers for women (WBCs),
business outreach centers for veterans
(VBOCs), small-business development
centers (SBDCs), and the Service Corps of
Retired Executives (SCORE). These programs
and others help the SBA further its reach
beyond the regional, to the local level.
https://www.sba.gov/local-assistance

For further information, contact the Small Business
Administration. Phone, 202-205-6600.

Native American Affairs   The Office
of Native American Affairs assists and
encourages the creation, development, and
expansion of small businesses that Native
Americans own. It develops and implements
initiatives designed to address specific
business challenges encountered by Native
American entrepreneurs. https://www.sba.
gov/offices/headquarters/naa

For further information, contact the Office of Native
American Affairs. Phone, 202-205-7364.

Regulatory Fairness   Congress established
the National Ombudsman and 10 Regulatory
Fairness (RegFair) Boards in 1996 as part of
the Small Business Regulatory Enforcement
Fairness Act. The National Ombudsman
assists owners of small businesses when
they experience excessive or unfair Federal
regulatory enforcement action. The National
Ombudsman receives comments from small
businesses and acts as a liaison between
them and Federal agencies. These comments
are forwarded to the appropriate Federal
agencies for review and consideration of
the fairness of the enforcement actions. The
National Ombudsman sends a copy of an
agency's response to the business owner. In
some cases, fines are reduced or eliminated
and decisions changed in favor of the owner.
   Each of the RegFair Boards comprises
five volunteer members who are owners,
operators, or officers of small enterprises.
The SBA Administrator appoints board
members for 3-year terms. Each RegFair
Board meets at least annually with the
Ombudsman, reports to the Ombudsman on
substantiated instances of excessive or unfair
enforcement, and comments on the annual
report to Congress prior to its publication.

https://www.sba.gov/ombudsman |
Email: ombudsman@sba.gov

For further information, contact the Office of the
National Ombudsman. Phone, 888-734-3247.

**Research Investment / Technology
Transfer**   The Office of Investment and
Innovation manages the Small Business
Investment Research (SBIR) and Small
Business Technology Transfer (STTR)
programs. Together, they provide billions
of dollars each year for small enterprises
to participate in federally funded research
and development and to cooperate with
Government agencies and research
institutions and universities. The SBIR and
STTR programs stimulate the creation of
intellectual property with potential for
commercialization and with applications
in a broad range of sectors in the Nation's
economy. https://www.sba.gov/offices/
headquarters/ooi/about-us

For further information, contact the Office of
Investment and Innovation. Phone, 202-205-6510.

Small Business Development   The
Office of Small Business Development
Centers funds, oversees, and supports the
nationwide Small Business Development
Center (SBDC) network. The SBDC program
provides one-stop management assistance
to current and prospective owners of small
businesses in central and easily accessible
branch locations. The program relies on
the cooperation of the private sector, the
educational community, and Federal, State,
and local governments.
   The SBDC program delivers up-to-date
counseling, technical help, and training in
all aspects of managing a small business. Its
services include assistance with feasibility
studies and with engineering, financial,
marketing, organization, production, and
technical challenges. SBDC activities
include international trade assistance,
procurement assistance, rural development,
venture capital information, and technical
assistance. https://www.sba.gov/offices/
headquarters/osbdc

For further information, contact the Office of Small
Business Development Centers. Phone, 202-205-6766.

Venture Capital   The Small Business
Investment Company (SBIC) program was
created in 1958 to connect venture capital

with the needs of startups and expanding small businesses. SBICs are privately owned and managed venture capital funds, which the SBA licenses and regulates. They use their own capital, combined with SBA guaranteed funds, to make equity and debt investments in qualifying small businesses. Fund managers may invest up to 75 percent of total capital in small businesses that have no more than 49 percent of their employees oversees, a tangible net worth of between $6 and $19.5 million, and an aftertax income averaged over the previous 2 years of between $2 and $6.5 million. At least 25 percent of the fund's total capital must be invested in smaller U.S. enterprises that have no more than 49 percent of their employees oversees, a tangible net worth of less than $6 million, and an aftertax income averaged over the previous 2 years of less than $2 million. https://www.sba.gov/partners/sbics/apply-be-sbic#section-header-6 | Email: askSBIC@sba.gov

For further information, contact the Investment Division. Phone, 202-205-6510.

Veterans Business Development The Office of Veterans Business Development (OVBD) formulates, executes, and advances policies and programs that provide assistance to small businesses that veterans own and control. Exclusively promoting veteran entrepreneurship, the OVBD helps veterans, service-disabled veterans, reservists, active-duty servicemembers, transitioning servicemembers, and their dependents or survivors, to avail themselves of all SBA programs and their benefits. The OVBD is involved in each SBA program, ensuring that veterans receive special consideration in each program's operation. The Veterans Business Outreach Program is an OVBD initiative that oversees Veterans Business Outreach Centers nationwide. https://www.sba.gov/content/veteran-service-disabled-veteran-owned

For further information, contact the Office of Veterans Business Development. Phone, 202-205-6773.

Women's Business Empowerment The Office of Women's Business Ownership (OWBO) enables and empowers female entrepreneurs through advocacy, education, outreach, and support. OWBO programs provide business training and counseling,

access to credit and capital, and marketing opportunities, including Federal contracts. The Women's Business Center (WBC) program offers SBA services in almost every State. A WBC tailors its services according to the needs of its individual community. Each WBC provides training in finance, management, marketing, and the Internet, as well as offering access to all financial and procurement assistance programs of the SBA. https://www.sba.gov/offices/headquarters/wbo | Email: owbo@sba.gov

For further information, contact the Women's Business Ownership representative in your SBA district office. Phone, 202-205-6673.

Sources of Information

Blog The SBA blog offers information, news, and perspectives that deal with doing business on a small scale. https://www.sba.gov/blogs
Business Opportunities Information on selling to the Government and qualifying for Government contracts is available online. The SBA also provides online resources for small businesses and posts information on Government contracting programs on its Web site. https://www.sba.gov/contracting
Career Opportunities To carry out its mission, the SBA relies on professionals who are culturally astute, have strong communication and presentation skills, can write effectively, and posses technological proficiency. https://www.sba.gov/about-sba/sba-team/jobs-sba

In 2018, the SBA ranked 20th among 27 midsize agencies in the Partnership for Public Service's Best Places To Work Agency Rankings. http://bestplacestowork.org/BPTW/rankings/detail/SB00
Climate / Sustainability The SBA's Strategic Sustainability Performance Plan (effective, 30 June 2017) presents a blueprint and a framework for the agency to carry out its mission in a way that helps the biosphere and demonstrates a commitment to the creation of a clean energy economy The plan addresses reducing greenhouse gases, pollution, waste, and water use. It also discusses strategies, targets, and metrics for climate change adaptation and resilience planning. https://www.sba.gov/document/support--strategic-sustainability-performance-plan

Contact Information Email addresses and phone numbers are available on the "Contact the SBA" web page (and on the "SBA Locations" web page). https://www.sba.gov/about-sba/organization/contact-sba?interiorpage2015

The SBA public affairs team responds to questions from the media and general public, arranges interviews with appropriate program staff, and provides referrals and other information. To find an SBA local or regional spokesperson, visit the "Regional and Local Media" web page. https://www.sba.gov/about-sba/sba-newsroom/regional-local-media

The Press Office team's contact information is available on the "Press Office Contacts" web page. That team includes staff from the Office of Communications and Public Liaison, Office of Advocacy, Office of Inspector General, and the Freedom of Information Act Office. https://www.sba.gov/about-sba/sba-newsroom/press-office-contacts

Events The "Find Events" page lists upcoming SBA events nationwide. https://www.sba.gov/events/find/?dateRange=all&distance=200&pageNumber=1

Glossary The SBA maintains an online glossary. https://www.sba.gov/offices/headquarters/obd/resources/13240

Freedom of Information Act (FOIA) Enacted in 1966, the FOIA took effect on July 4, 1967. The statute makes all existing Federal Government records available to the public; however, a record may be shielded from disclosure by one or more of nine exemptions or by specific harm that its disclosure may cause. Any person, except a fugitive from the law, has a right to request access to Federal agency records. https://www.sba.gov/about-sba/sba-performance/open-government/foia | Email: FOIA@sba.gov

Introduction to the SBA A short video explaining the SBA's principal services is available online. https://www.sba.gov/videos/introduction-sba?interiorpage2015

Learning Center The SBA offers online courses to help entrepreneurs start and run businesses. https://www.sba.gov/learning-center

Locations The "SBA Locations" page helps visitors find contact and other information for disaster offices, district offices, headquarters offices, regional offices, and loan and guaranty centers. https://www.sba.gov/about-sba/sba-locations

Newsroom The SBA newsroom features congressional testimonies, disaster press releases, media advisories and other press releases, speeches, and weekly lending reports. https://www.sba.gov/about-sba/sba-newsroom

Open Data The SBA makes data resources and application programming interfaces (APIs) available to the public. The "Open Data Sources" web page lists all the SBA datasets that the general public can access. https://www.sba.gov/about-sba/sba-performance/open-government/digital-sba/open-data/open-data-sources

Open Government The SBA supports the Open Government initiative by promoting the principles of collaboration, participation, and transparency. https://www.sba.gov/about-sba/sba-performance/open-government

Plain Language SBA writers and editors are committed to communicating in plain language. If a document or web pages lacks clarity or is difficult to understand, contact the SBA by email. https://www.sba.gov/about-sba/sba-performance/open-government/other-plans-reports/plain-language-page | Email: plain.language@sba.gov

Resource Guide The Winter 2019 edition of the "Small Business Resource Guide" is available online in Portable Document Format (PDF). https://www.sba.gov/about-sba/what-we-do/resource-guides

Site Map The Web site map allows visitors to look for specific topics or to browse content that aligns with their interests. https://www.sba.gov/sitemap

Social Media The SBA maintains social media accounts on Facebook, Instagram, LinkedIn, Twitter, and YouTube. https://www.sba.gov/about-sba/open-government/about-sbagov-website/social-media

Videos The SBA has a collection of online videos. The collection includes a 2-minute video series and other videos that are grouped by topic: financing, Government contracting, managing a business, marketing, and starting a business. https://www.sba.gov/videos

The Sources of Information were updated 6–2019.

Social Security Administration

6401 Security Boulevard, Baltimore, MD 21235
Phone, 410-965-1234 / 800-772-1213. 800-325-0778 (TTY). Internet, http://www.socialsecurity.gov

Commissioner	NANCY A. BERRYHILL, ACTING
Deputy Commissioner	(VACANCY)
Chief of Staff	BEATRICE M. DISMAN, ACTING
Counselor to the Commissioner	(VACANCY)
Director, Equal Employment Opportunity	CLAUDIA J. POSTELL, ACTING
Executive Secretary	DARLYNDA K. BOGLE
https://www.ssa.gov/org/coss.htm	

Offices

Chief Actuary	STEPHEN C. GOSS
General Counsel	ASHEESH AGARWAL
Deputy Commissioners	
Analytics, Review, and Oversight	PATRICIA A. JONAS
Budget, Finance, Quality, and Management	MICHELLE A. KING
Communications	JAMES C. BORLAND, ACTING
Hearings Operations	THERESA L. GRUBER
Human Resources	MARIANNA LACANFORA
Legislation and Congressional Affairs	ROYCE B. MIN, ACTING
Operations	MARY L. HORNE, ACTING
Retirement and Disability Policy	MARK J. WARSHAWSKY
Systems / Chief Information Officer	RAJIVE K. MATHUR
https://www.ssa.gov/org/ssachart_access.pdf	
Inspector General	GALE S. STONE, ACTING
http://oig.ssa.gov	

[For the Social Security Administration statement of organization, see the Code of Federal Regulations, Title 20, Part 422]

The above list of key personnel was updated 02–2018.

The Social Security Administration manages the retirement, survivors, and disability insurance programs that are known as Social Security; it administers the Supplemental Security Income program for the aged, blind, and disabled; and it assigns Social Security numbers to U.S. citizens and maintains earnings records based on those numbers.

The Social Security Administration (SSA) was established by Reorganization Plan No. 2 of 1946 (5 U.S.C. app.), effective July 16, 1946. It became an independent agency in the executive branch by the Social Security Independence and Program Improvements Act of 1994 (42 U.S.C. 901), effective March 31, 1995. https://www.ssa.gov/history

The SSA is headed by a Commissioner whom the President appoints with the advice and consent of the Senate.

The Deputy Commissioner assists in administering the programs necessary to accomplish the Administration's mission. The Deputy Commissioner performs duties that the Commissioner, Chief Financial Officer, Chief Information Officer, General Counsel, Chief Actuary, and Inspector General assign or delegate to him or her. https://www.ssa. gov/OP_Home/ssact/title07/0702.htm

The Administration's operations are decentralized to provide local services. Each of the 10 SSA regions has a network of field offices and call centers. These offices and centers provide liaison between the SSA and public. The Administration operates 10

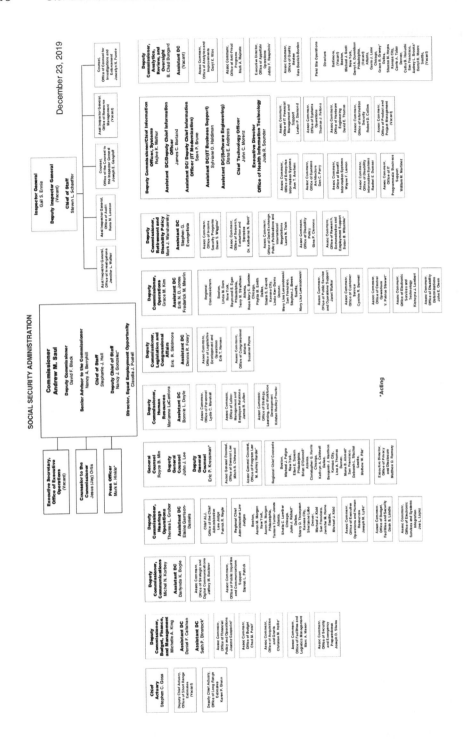

SOCIAL SECURITY ADMINISTRATION

December 23, 2019

regional offices, approximately 1,230 field offices, 33 teleservice centers, 15 Social Security card centers, 6 processing centers, and 2 additional processing centers in its central office. https://www.ssa.gov/org/index.htm

Activities

Black Lung By agreement with the Department of Labor, the SSA assists in the administration of the black lung benefits provisions of the Federal Coal Mine Health and Safety Act of 1969, as amended (30 U.S.C. 901). https://www.ssa.gov/OP_Home/rulings/di/09/SSR73-24-di-09.html

Hearings and Appeals The SSA administers a nationwide hearings and appeals program that offers a way for those who are dissatisfied with determinations affecting their rights to and amounts of benefits or their participation in programs to seek remedy through the Social Security Act. The act allows for administrative appeals of these determinations in accordance with the requirements of the Administrative Procedure and Social Security Acts. The SSA operates approximately 166 hearing offices, including 2 satellite offices; 5 national hearing centers; and 4 national case assistance centers within in its 10 administrative regions. http://www.ssa.gov/appeals/about_odar.html

Medicare While the administration of Medicare is the responsibility of the Centers for Medicare and Medicaid Services, the SSA provides Medicare assistance to the public through SSA field offices and call centers. It adjudicates requests for hearings and appeals of Medicare claims. http://www.ssa.gov/medicare

Old-Age, Survivors, and Disability Insurance The SSA administers social insurance programs that provide monthly benefits to retired and disabled workers, to their spouses and children, and to survivors of insured workers. Financing is under a system of contributory social insurance, whereby employees, employers, and the self-employed pay contributions that are pooled in special trust funds. When earnings stop or decrease because the worker retires, dies, or becomes disabled, monthly cash benefits are paid to supplement the family's reduced

income. https://faq.ssa.gov/ics/support/splash.asp

Supplemental Security Income The SSA administers this needs-based program for the aged, blind, and disabled. A basic Federal monthly payment is financed by general revenue, rather than from a special trust fund. Some States, choosing to provide payments to supplement the benefits, have agreements with the Administration under which it administers the supplemental payments for those States. http://www.ssa.gov/disability/ssi/ssi.html

Sources of Information

Business Opportunities The Office of Acquisition and Grants serves as the SSA's principal procurement office. http://www.ssa.gov/oag

Career Opportunities The SSA offers opportunities for various career paths: acquisitions, contracts, and grants; administrative support; facilities and physical security; finance and accounting; human resources; information technology; law enforcement; legal; and public contact. http://www.ssa.gov/careers

In 2017, the SSA ranked 12th among 18 large agencies in the Partnership for Public Service's Best Places To Work Agency Rankings. http://bestplacestowork.org/BPTW/rankings/detail/SZ00

Fraud Hotline The Office of the Inspector General (OIG) operates a toll-free hotline, 10 a.m.–4 p.m., eastern standard time, for reporting allegations of abuse, fraud, and waste affecting SSA programs and operations. Phone, 800-269-0271. TTY, 866-501-2101. Fax, 410-597-0118. https://oig.ssa.gov/report-fraud-waste-or-abuse

An online form also is available to file a report. https://www.ssa.gov/fraudreport/oig/public_fraud_reporting/form.htm

Freedom of Information Act (FOIA) An online guide discusses important FOIA-related topics: how to request information and records, information that the SSA cannot disclose, and the fees associated with making a request. https://www.ssa.gov/foia

Frequently Asked Questions (FAQs) The SSA posts answers to FAQs and offers information on popular help-topics. https://faq.ssa.gov/ics/support/default.

asp?deptID=34019&_referrer=https://www.ssa.gov/ask

Glossary   A glossary of Social Security terms is available online. https://www.ssa.gov/agency/glossary

History   In 1795, the unflagging colonial and revolutionary pamphleteer Thomas Paine wrote about Americans entering adulthood and their welfare in retirement. To the new Republic, he issued a challenge: Establish a public system of economic security that would give a one-time stipend to each citizen upon attaining age 21, as well as annual benefits starting at age 50. To learn more about this patriot's bold proposal, see the "Historical Background and Development of Social Security" web page. https://www.ssa.gov/history/briefhistory3.html

Multilanguage Gateway   The SSA tries to eliminate or reduce, as much as possible, barriers of language that impede the delivery of its services. Social Security information is available on the SSA website in the following languages: American Sign Language, Arabic, Armenian, Chinese, Farsi, French, Greek, Haitian Creole, Hmong, Italian, Korean, Polish, Portuguese, Russian, Somali, Spanish, Tagalog, and Vietnamese. The SSA provides free interpreter services for conducting Social Security-related business. https://www.ssa.gov/multilanguage

News   The SSA posts press releases online. https://www.ssa.gov/news/press/releases

An online newsletter also is available. https://www.ssa.gov/news/newsletter

Online Services   The SSA offers a growing number of services electronically through its website. https://www.ssa.gov/onlineservices

Open Government   The SSA supports the Open Government initiative to create a more open and transparent Government by promoting the principles of collaboration, participation, and transparency. https://www.ssa.gov/open | Email: open.government@ssa.gov

Organizational Chart   The SSA's organizational chart is available in Portable Document Format (PDF) for viewing and downloading. https://www.ssa.gov/org/ssachart.pdf

Plain Language   The Plain Writing Act of 2010 requires Federal agencies to communicate in a manner that the public can understand and use. SSA writers and editors welcome suggestions for improving agency forms, notices, pamphlets, or pages from its website. https://www.ssa.gov/agency/plain-language | Email: PlainWriting@ssa.gov

Publications   Many SSA publications in English, Spanish, and other languages are accessible online. http://www.socialsecurity.gov/pubs

Site Map   The website map allows visitors to look for specific topics or to browse content that aligns with their interests. https://www.ssa.gov/sitemap.htm

Speakers   Under certain circumstances, the SSA can provide a speaker free of charge, generally available during business hours, to explain benefits, programs, and services. An online form is available to initiate a request. http://www.ssa.gov/agency/ask-for-a-speaker.html https://www.ssa.gov/agency/contact | Email: OPI.Policy.Coordination@ssa.gov

For further information, contact the Office of Public Inquiries, Social Security Administration, 6401 Security Boulevard, 1106 West High Rise Building, Baltimore, MD 21235. Phone, 410-965-0709. Fax, 410-965-0695.

Surface Transportation Board

395 E Street SW., Washington, DC 20423
Phone, 202-245-0245. Internet, http://www.stb.gov/stb/index.html

Board

Chair	Ann D. Begeman, Acting
Vice Chair	Debra L. Miller
Member	(Vacancy)
Member	(Vacancy)

Member	(VACANCY)
https://www.stb.gov/stb/about/board.html	

Directors

Office of Economics	WILLIAM J. BRENNAN
Office of Environmental Analysis	VICTORIA J. RUTSON
Office of Proceedings	SCOTT ZIMMERMAN, ACTING
Office of Public Assistance, Governmental Affairs, and Compliance	LUCILLE L. MARVIN
Office of the General Counsel	CRAIG KEATS
Office of the Managing Director	RACHEL D. CAMPBELL, ACTING

The above list of key personnel was updated 2–2018.

The Surface Transportation Board adjudicates and resolves railroad rate and service disputes and reviews proposals for railroad mergers.

The Surface Transportation Board (STB) is the successor agency to the Interstate Commerce Commission (ICC), which was created in 1887. The ICC Termination Act of 1995 established the STB as an independent adjudicatory body within the Department of Transportation. It remained administratively aligned with the Department for nearly two decades. On December 18, 2015, the Surface Transportation Board Reauthorization Act of 2015 established the STB as a wholly independent Federal agency (49 USC 1301 et seq.). https://www.stb.gov/stb/about/overview.html

The STB comprises five members whom the President appoints and the Senate confirms for 5-year terms. The President also designates one of the members to serve as the Board's chair. https://www.stb.gov/stb/about/board.html

Activities

The STB adjudicates disputes and regulates interstate surface transportation through various laws governing the different modes of surface transportation. Its general responsibilities include the oversight of firms engaged in interstate and foreign commercial transportation—to the extent that it takes place within the United States, or between or among points in the contiguous United States and points in Alaska, Hawaii, or U.S. Territories or possessions. The STB's jurisdiction generally extends over railroad rate and service issues, rail restructuring transactions, including mergers and line abandonments, construction, and sales, and labor matters related thereto; some moving van, trucking, and noncontiguous ocean shipping company rate matters; some intercity passenger bus company financial, operational, and structural matters; and pipeline matters that the Federal Energy Regulatory Commission does not regulate.

The STB promotes substantive and procedural regulatory reform, provides a forum for the resolution of disputes, and facilitates appropriate market-based business transactions. Through rulemakings and case disposition, it develops improved and efficient ways of analyzing problems, reducing costs associated with regulatory oversight, and encouraging private sector negotiations and resolutions.

Sources of Information

Annual Reports The STB posts activity reports that it prepares for Congress every few years and annual reports on its website. https://www.stb.gov/stb/about/annual.html

Career Opportunities Current job openings are posted online. https://www.stb.gov/stb/about/jobs.html

In 2017, the STB ranked 18th among 28 small Government agencies in the Partnership for Public Service's Best Places To Work Agency Rankings. http://bestplacestowork.org/BPTW/rankings/detail/TX00

Electronic Filing   As an alternative to submitting paper filings, consider filing electronically. E-filing may not be used for initial filings in a proceeding, filings requiring a fee (with the exception of recordations), and large evidentiary filings. https://www.stb.gov/stb/efilings.nsf

Environment   The Office of Environmental Analysis's web page features links to cases, correspondence, rules, and other resources related to environmental matters. https://www.stb.gov/stb/environment/sea.html

Freedom of Information Act (FOIA)   The STB website features an online form for submitting FOIA requests. Phone, 202-245-0271. Fax, 202-245-0464. https://www.stb.gov/stb/efilings.nsf/FOIARequest?OpenForm | Email: FOIA.privacy@stb.gov

Frequently Asked Questions (FAQs)   The STB posts answers to FAQs on its website. https://www.stb.gov/stb/faqs.html

Glossary   The STB website has a glossary of terms associated with environmental issues. https://www.stb.gov/glossary.nsf/emletterweb?OpenView&RestrictToCategory=a

Historic Preservation   The National Environmental Policy and National Historic Preservation Acts and other Federal environmental laws require the STB to consider the impact of its licensing decisions on historic properties. The Office of Environmental Analysis develops guidance that clarifies the STB's historic preservation review requirements and posts it on the STB's website. https://www.stb.gov/stb/environment/preservation.html

Industry Data   The STB posts financial and statistical reports containing economic data on its website. https://www.stb.gov/stb/industry/econ_reports.html

Rail carriers must file a summary of each contract entered into for the transportation of agricultural products. Beginning with the first quarter of 2008, filed contract summaries are available on the STB's website in Portable Document Format (PDF) and grouped by railroad. https://www.stb.gov/econdata.nsf/8B5F6EFB897D7C2185257434003D44A2 | Email: rcpa@stb.gov

Library   The library is open to the public on weekdays, excluding Federal Holidays, 10 a.m.–3 p.m. Phone, 202-245-0406. http://www.stb.dot.gov/stb/public/inquiries_library.html | Email: rcpa@stb.gov

The STB's website has an electronic library whose resources can be accessed by opening the "E–Library" drop-down menu on the home page. https://www.stb.gov/stb/index.html

Maps   The Railroad Map Depot features links to railroad maps. The railroad map information is based on publicly available maps and data that government agencies, railroads, and other stakeholders produce. https://stb.maps.arcgis.com/home/index.html

News   The STB posts announcements and other noteworthy items on its "What's New" web page. https://www.stb.gov/stb/news/whatsnew.html

Organizational Chart   An organizational chart is available in the "About STB" section of its website. https://www.stb.gov/stb/about/orgchart.html#

Publications   Consumer pamphlets are available in Portable Document Format (PDF) from the electronic library. http://www.stb.dot.gov/stb/elibrary/epubs.html

Railroad Rates   Experts in the Office of Economics monitor patterns of average rail rates that the Nation's railroads charge. Multiyear studies address the key factors behind rate increases and decreases and assess the effects on consumers, shippers, and the Nation as a whole. A small collection of rail rate studies in Portable Document Format (PDF) is available on the STB website. https://www.stb.gov/stb/industry/econ_rateindex.html

Testimony / Speeches   The Office of Public Assistance, Governmental Affairs, and Compliance posts the testimony and speeches of STB officials online. https://www.stb.gov/stb/news/speeches_testimony.html; https://www.stb.gov/stb/contact.html | Email: rcpa@stb.gov

For further information, contact the Surface Transportation Board, Office of Public Assistance, Governmental Affairs, and Compliance, 395 E Street SW., Washington, DC, 20423. Phone, 202-245-0238.

Tennessee Valley Authority

400 West Summit Hill Drive, Knoxville, TN 37902
Phone, 865-632-2101. Internet, http://www.tva.com

Board of Directors

Chair	JAMES R. THOMPSON III
Directors	
	KENNETH E. ALLEN
	A.D. FRAZIER, JR.
	RICHARD C. HOWORTH
	VIRGINIA T. LODGE
	JOHN L. RYDER
	JEFFREY W. SMITH
	RONALD A. WALTER
	(VACANCY)

https://www.tva.com/About-TVA/Our-Leadership/Board-of-Directors

Executive Leadership

President / Chief Executive Officer	JEFFREY J. LYASH
Chief Operating Officer	MICHAEL D. SKAGGS
Executive Vice Presidents	
Chief Financial Officer	JOHN M. THOMAS III
External Relations	VAN M. WARDLAW
General Counsel	SHERRY A. QUIRK
Senior Vice Presidents	
Chief Communications and Marketing Officer	JANET J. BREWER
Chief Human Resources Officer	SUSAN E. COLLINS
Resources and Operations Support	JOSEPH STOWE

https://www.tva.com/About-TVA/Our-Leadership/Executives

Inspector General	RICHARD W. MOORE

http://oig.tva.gov/igmoore.html

The above list of key personnel was updated 5–2019.

The Tennessee Valley Authority conducts a unified program of resource development to advance economic growth in the Tennessee Valley region.

Establishment and Members of the Board

The Tennessee Valley Authority Act of 1933 created the Tennessee Valley Authority (TVA). This act of May 18, 1933 (16 U.S.C. 831-831dd), established the TVA as a wholly owned Government corporation. https://www.tva.com/file_source/TVA/Site%20Content/About%20TVA/TVA_Act.pdf

All functions of this public corporation are vested in its nine-member Board of Directors, whose members the President appoints by the advice and with the consent of the Senate. At least seven of the nine members must be legal residents of the TVA's service area. The Board designates one of its members to serve as the Chair. https://www.tva.com/About-TVA/Our-History

Activities

TVA activities range from economic development and environmental stewardship to electric power production and transmission; to flood control, navigation, and recreation improvement; and to water supply and water quality management.

The TVA's electric power program is financially self-supporting and operates as part of an independent system with the Authority's system of dams on the Tennessee River and its larger tributaries. These dams provide flood regulation on the Tennessee River and contribute to regulation of the lower Ohio and Mississippi Rivers. The system maintains a continuous 9-foot-draft navigation channel for the length of the 650-mile Tennessee River main stream, from Paducah, KY, to Knoxville, TN. The dams harness the power of the rivers to produce electricity. They also provide other benefits, notably outdoor recreation and water supply.

The Authority operates the river management system and provides assistance to State and local governments in reducing local flood problems. It also works with other agencies to encourage full and effective use of the navigable waterway by industry and commerce.

The TVA is the wholesale power supplier for 154 local municipal and cooperative electric systems serving customers in parts of 7 States. It supplies power to 60 industries and Federal installations whose power requirements are large or unusual. Power to meet these demands is supplied from dams, coal-fired powerplants, nuclear powerplants, natural gas combined-cycle powerplants, combustion turbine and diesel installations, solar energy sites, wind turbines, a methane gas facility, and a pumped-storage hydroelectric plant; U.S. Corps of Engineers dams in the Cumberland Valley; and Brookfield Renewable Energy Partners dams, whose operations are coordinated with the TVA's system.

Economic development is at the heart of the TVA's mission of making the Tennessee Valley a better place to live. A healthy economy means quality jobs, more investment in the region, sustainable growth, and opportunities for residents in the southeastern region to build more prosperous lives. TVA economic development takes a regional approach to economic growth by partnering with power distributors and both public and private organizations to attract new investments and quality jobs, supporting retention and growth of existing businesses and industries, preparing communities for leadership and economic growth, and providing financial and technical services. https://www.tva.com/About-TVA

Sources of Information

Birdwatching   With birds living in and migrating through the area year-round, TVA lands offer plenty of opportunities for birdwatchers. https://www.tva.com/Environment/Recreation/Bird-Watcher%27s-Paradise | Email: plic@tva.gov

Business Opportunities   The TVA partners with power distributors, suppliers, and other individuals and organizations. It seeks business relationships with firms offering reliable products and services at competitive prices. The TVA encourages businessmen and women of diverse backgrounds—minorities, service-disabled-veterans, veterans, as well as small business owners and entrepreneurs in historically underutilized business zones—to learn about available opportunities. For more information, contact Supply Chain, BR 4A–C, 1101 Market Street, Chattanooga, TN 37402. Phone,   423-751-7903. https://www.tva.com/Information/Doing-Business-with-TVA

Career Opportunities   The TVA is a service-oriented agency whose mission covers 86,000 square miles and depends on professionals with expertise in diverse fields. Some of those fields include archaeology, aviation, economics, engineering, environmental law, hydrology, law enforcement, library science, marketing, program management, water quality, and zoology. https://www.tva.com/Careers | Email: careers@tva.gov

In 2018, the Office of Inspector General ranked first among 415 agency subcomponents in the Partnership for Public Service's Best Places To Work Agency Rankings! http://bestplacestowork.org/BPTW/rankings/detail/TV01

Climate Change   Carbon performance is a matter of growing concern for companies. Consumers and investors alike are paying more attention to the amount of carbon dioxide that commercial activities release into the atmosphere. To increase the competitiveness of Tennessee Valley companies, the agency helps them more accurately account for the carbon released into the atmosphere from the generation of TVA electricity that they purchase. https://www.tva.com/Newsroom/News-Features/Carbon-Competitiveness

Contact Information The TVA benefits from engaged citizens. It encourages comments, feedback, and input. Contact TVA Communications, 400 W. Summit Hill Drive, Knoxville, TN 37902-1499. Phone, 865-632-2101. https://www.tva.gov/About-TVA/Contact-Us | Email: tvainfo@tva.gov

Economic Development TVA Economic Development serves the seven States of the TVA service area—AL, GA, KY, MS, NC, TN, and VA. Through partnerships with other economic development organizations, the TVA fosters capital investment and job growth in its service area. Information is available online, or contact TVA Economic Development, 26 Century Boulevard, Suite 100, Nashville, TN 37214. Phone, 615-232-6051. https://www.tva.com/Economic-Development

Environmental Reviews The TVA conducts environmental reviews to consider the effects of its proposed projects on the human and natural environment before making final decisions. The TVA's environmental projects are open for public review. https://www.tva.com/Environment/Environmental-Stewardship/Environmental-Reviews

Fishing Tips The TVA helps ambitious fishermen and women meet their numbers. The "Where the Sport Fish Are" page lists the largest populations of Tennessee Valley sport fish and the reservoirs that they inhabit. https://www.tva.com/Environment/Recreation/Where-the-Sport-Fish-Are | Email: plic@tva.gov

Anglers developed the "Angler's Aquatic Plant ID" as a guide for anglers. The online guide contains seasonal tips for fishing near aquatic plants, starting with American Lotus and ending with Southern Naiad. https://www.tva.com/Environment/Environmental-Stewardship/Anglers-Aquatic-Plant-ID

Freedom of Information Act (FOIA) Like all Federal agencies, the TVA is required to disclose records that any person requests in writing. The statute contains, however, nine exemptions and three exclusions that may shield some records or parts of them from disclosure. The TVA operates a FOIA requester service center. Phone, 865-632-6945. https://www.tva.com/Information/Freedom-of-Information | Email: foia@tva.gov

Green Power The Green Power Providers program offers Tennessee Valley homeowners and businessmen and women an opportunity to help the TVA generate clean, renewable energy. Participants in the program agree to install a small-scale renewable energy system on their property, and the TVA pays them for every kilowatt hour generated by that system. https://www.tva.com/Energy/Valley-Renewable-Energy/Green-Power-Providers

Historic Photographs From the earliest days of the TVA, photographers captured images of the agency's work and the cultural changes that followed. The TVA collection contains over 20,000 black-and-white negatives and over 5,000 original file prints. Its images span half a century, from 1933 to 1983. https://www.tva.com/Environment/Environmental-Stewardship/Land-Management/Cultural-%2B-Historic-Preservation/TVA-Historic-Photograph-Collection

Lake Levels Current information on ecological health ratings, fish population surveys, planned generation releases at the dams, recreation facilities, reservoir operations, today's levels, and predicted elevations for each TVA reservoir is available online. https://www.tva.com/Environment/Lake-Levels

Library Services Visitors may use the TVA Research Library by appointment. Contact the TVA Research Library, 400 W. Summit Hill Drive, Knoxville, TN 37902-1499. Phone, 865-632-3464. https://tva.com/Our-TVA-Story/Nancy-Proctor | Email: corplibknox@tva.gov

Native American Tribes Native Americans have a cultural and historical interest in the Tennessee Valley. The TVA consults with 18 federally recognized tribes when it undertakes projects that could affect their cultural sites. https://www.tva.com/Environment/Environmental-Stewardship/Land-Management/Cultural-%2B-Historic-Preservation/Native-Americans

Newsroom The TVA posts news stories and press releases online. https://www.tva.com/Newsroom

Oversight   The Office of the Inspector General from the TVA posts reports and data on Oversight.gov, a text-searchable repository of reports that Federal Inspectors General publish. The Council of the Inspectors General on Integrity and Efficiency operates and maintains the website to increase public access to independent and authoritative information on the Federal Government. https://oversight.gov

Public Relations   The TVA Public Relations team is available to help representatives of the media. https://www.tva.com/Newsroom/Media-Contacts

Site Map   The website map allows visitors to look for specific topics or to browse content that aligns with their interests. https://www.tva.com/Index

Social Media   The TVA has a Facebook account. https://www.facebook.com/TVA

The TVA posts photos and short videos on Instagram. https://www.instagram.com/TVA/

The TVA publishes business-oriented information on LinkedIn. https://www.linkedin.com/company/tva

The TVA tweets announcements and other newsworthy items on Twitter. https://twitter.com/tvanews

The TVA posts videos on its YouTube channel. https://www.youtube.com/user/TVANewsVideo

TVA Kids   The TVA maintains the website tvakids.com, which is a colorful online resource for students and teachers. The site covers topics like green power, making electricity, and saving energy. It also has a section of "Cool Stuff" that includes games, videos, and warnings about energy vampires. https://www.tvakids.com

The Sources of Information were updated 5–2019.

Trade and Development Agency

1000 Wilson Boulevard, Suite 1600, Arlington, VA 22209-3901
Phone, 703-875-4357. Fax, 703-875-4009. Internet, http://www.ustda.gov

Director	Enoh T. Ebong, Acting
Deputy Director	Enoh T. Ebong
Administrative Officer	Carolyn Hum
Chief of Staff	Vacant
Chief, Office of Acquisition Management	Garth Hibbert
Director, Congressional Affairs and Public Relations	Thomas R. Hardy
Director, Finance	Kathleen Neumann
General Counsel	Kendra Link, Acting
Chief Information Officer	Benjamin Bergersen
Special Advisor to the Director	Clark Jennings

Regional Directors

East Asia	Carl B. Kress
Latin America and Caribbean	Nathan Younge
Middle East, North Africa, Europe and Eurasia	Carl B. Kress
South and Southeast Asia	Henry D. Steingass
Sub-Saharan Africa	Lida Fitts
Director, Global Programs	Andrea Lupo
Director, Office of Program Monitoring and Evaluation	Diana Harbison

---

The Trade and Development Agency advances economic development and U.S. commercial interest in developing and middle-income countries.

TRADE AND DEVELOPMENT AGENCY

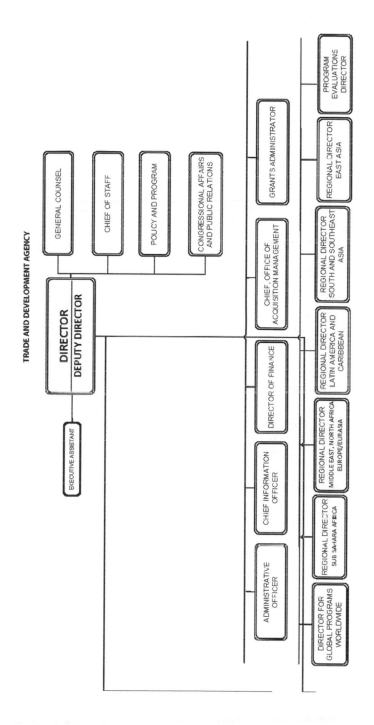

The Trade and Development Program was established on July 1, 1980, as a component organization of the International Development Cooperation Agency. Section 2204 of the Omnibus Trade and Competitiveness Act of 1988 (22 U.S.C. 2421) made it a separate component agency. The organization was renamed the Trade and Development Agency (USTDA) and made an independent agency within the executive branch of the Federal Government on October 28, 1992, by the Jobs Through Exports Act of 1992 (22 U.S.C. 2421).

The USTDA is a foreign assistance agency that delivers its program commitments through overseas grants and contracts with U.S. firms. The Agency helps companies create U.S. jobs through the export of U.S. goods and services for priority development projects in emerging economies. The Agency links U.S. businesses to export opportunities by funding project planning activities, pilot projects, and reverse trade missions while creating sustainable infrastructure and economic growth in partner countries.

The USTDA provides grant funding to overseas project sponsors for the planning of projects that support the development of modern infrastructure and an open trading system. The hallmark of USTDA development assistance is building partnerships between U.S. companies and overseas project sponsors. These partnerships facilitate the application of proven private sector solutions to developmental challenges.

The Agency works with other U.S. Government agencies to bring their particular expertise and resources to a development objective. These agencies include the Departments of Commerce, Energy, State, Transportation, and the Treasury; Office of the U.S. Trade Representative; Export-Import Bank of the United States; and Overseas Private Investment Corporation. https://www.ustda. gov/about/mission

Activities

The USTDA funds various forms of technical assistance, training, early investment analysis, reverse trade missions, and business workshops that support the development of a modern infrastructure and a fair and open trading environment. The Agency works closely with foreign project sponsors and makes its funds available to them for contracting with U.S. businesses. This arrangement gives American firms market entry, exposure, and access to information. It helps them establish positions in markets that are otherwise difficult to penetrate. The USTDA is involved in many sectors, including energy, transportation, and information and communications technologies.

USTDA-funded studies evaluate the technical, economic, and financial aspects of a development project. They provide the host nation with information on the availability of U.S. goods and services. Financial institutions also use these studies for assessing the creditworthiness of an undertaking. Grants are based on an official request for assistance: Either the sponsoring government or a private sector organization in a developing or middle-income nation can make the request. https://www.ustda. gov/program

Sources of Information

Business Opportunities   Overseas project sponsors can select U.S. firms to carry out USTDA-funded work through a competitive proposal process that relies on the Federal Business Opportunities Web site (FedBizOpps.gov) or through "sole-source" grants, which allow an overseas project sponsor to identify a U.S. firm as a partner or preferred supplier. More information is available on the "Project Proposals" Web page. https://www.ustda.gov/program/project-proposals

Employment   Job openings and information on internships are posted online. https://www.ustda.gov/about/career-opportunities https://www.ustda.gov/about/career-opportunities/internships

Freedom of Information Act (FOIA)   A FOIA request must be submitted in writing by email, fax, or mail, and clearly identified as a "FOIA REQUEST." Staff is available to answer questions and help formulate a request over the phone; however, the USTDA does not accept phone requests. Mail a request to the FOIA Requester

Service Center, U.S. Trade and Development Agency, 1000 Wilson Boulevard, Suite 1600, Arlington, VA 22209-3901. Phone, 703-875-4357. Fax, 703-875-4009. https://www.ustda.gov/about/resources/foia | Email: foia@ustda.gov

Library The USTDA maintains a collection of reports on infrastructure development projects from emerging economies worldwide. Contact the library by email to obtain a report: Most reports can be sent electronically. These reports are accessible also online. Phone, 703-875-4357. https://www.ustda.gov/ustda-library | Email: library@ustda.gov

Newsletter To provide timely information on Agency supported activities, the USTDA distributes an electronic newsletter containing business opportunities, events, and updates. A subscription form is available online. https://www.ustda.gov/connect/subscribe-ustda-news-and-alerts

Regional Programs The USTDA is organized into five international regions. Information on each region is available on the Agency's Web site. Questions should be addressed to the appropriate regional director or country manager. Phone, 703-875-4357. http://www.ustda.gov/program/regions/index.asp; https://www.ustda.gov/about/contact | Email: info@ustda.gov

For further information, contact the U.S. Trade and Development Agency, 1000 Wilson Boulevard, Suite 1600, Arlington, VA 22209-3901. Phone, 703-875-4357. Fax, 703-875-4009.

United States Agency for Global Media

330 Independence Avenue SW., Washington, DC 20237
Phone, 202-203-4545. Internet, http://www.usagm.gov

Broadcasting Board of Governors

Chair	KENNETH WEINSTEIN
Members	
	LEON ARON
	RYAN C. CROCKER
	MICHAEL W. KEMPNER
	KAREN KORNBLUH
	JEFFREY S. SHELL
	(VACANCY)
	(VACANCY)
Ex officio	SECRETARY OF STATE MICHAEL R. POMPEO
https://www.usagm.gov/who-we-are/board	

Management

Chief Executive Officer / Director	JOHN F. LANSING
Deputy Director for Operations	MATTHEW WALSH
https://www.usagm.gov/who-we-are/the-ceo	
Chief Strategy Officer	SHAWN POWERS, ACTING
Managing Director	OANH TRAN
Chief Officers	
Financial	GRANT TURNER
Information	P. TERRY BALAZS
Directors	
Congressional Affairs	ELLONA FRITSCHIE
Global Communications and Public Affairs	NASSERIE CAREW
Internet Freedom	CHAD HURLEY
Management Services	MARIE LENNON

Policy and Research	(VACANCY)
Technology, Services, and Innovation	P. TERRY BALAZS
General Counsel	DAVID KLIGERMAN
https://www.usagm.gov/who-we-are/management-team	

Networks

Presidents of Grantee Networks	
Middle East Broadcasting Networks	ALBERTO M. FERNANDEZ
Radio Free Asia	LIBBY LIU
Radio Free Europe / Radio Liberty	DAISY SINDELAR, ACTING
Directors of Federal Networks	
Office of Cuba Broadcasting	TOMÁS P. REGALADO
Voice of America	AMANDA BENNETT
https://www.usagm.gov/networks	

Office of Inspector General

Inspector General for the U.S. Department of State	STEVE A. LINICK
https://www.stateoig.gov/about/IG	

The above list of key personnel was updated 7–2019.

The U.S. Agency for Global Media informs, engages, and connects people around the world in support of freedom and democracy.

Establishment and Organization

The first Broadcasting Board of Governors (BBG) was sworn in on August 11, 1995. Four years later, on October 1, 1999, the BBG became an independent and autonomous entity as a result of the Foreign Affairs Reform and Restructuring Act of 1998 (22 U.S.C. 6501 note). On August 22, 2018, as part of a modernization effort, the agency changed its name from the BBG to the United States Agency for Global Media (USAGM). The USAGM still uses the name BBG to refer to its nine-member board. https://www.usagm.gov/who-we-are/history

The BBG comprises nine members who are experts in the field of broadcast media, international affairs, or mass communications. The President appoints eight of the members, and the Senate must confirm them. The ninth member, who is the Secretary of State, serves on the board in an ex officio capacity. https://www.usagm.gov/who-we-are/board

The USAGM posts an organizational chart on its website. https://www.usagm.gov/who-we-are/organizational-chart

All USAGM broadcast services adhere to the broadcasting standards and principles of the International Broadcasting Act of 1994. These principles and standards support reliable, accurate, and comprehensive news; balanced and comprehensive presentations of U.S. thought, institutions, and policies, as well as discussions on those policies; information on developments throughout the world; and a variety of opinions from nations around the world. https://www.usagm.gov/who-we-are/oversight/legislation/international-broadcasting-act

Activities

Middle East Broadcasting Networks   The Middle East Broadcasting Networks, Inc. (MBN) is a nonprofit news organization that operates Alhurra and Alhurra-Iraq Television, Radio Sawa, and MBN Digital under a grant from the USAGM. Alhurra Television, Radio Sawa, and MBN Digital offer an open line of communication between the people of the Middle East and the United States. These networks deliver accurate information on the United States, its policies, and its people, from a range of perspectives and with an exchange of ideas on relevant issues. They reach an audience of nearly 25 million Arabic-speakers in 22 countries across the

Middle East and North Africa. https://www.usagm.gov/networks/mbn; Alhurra TV; http://www.alhurra.com; Radio Sawa; https://www.radiosawa.com

Office of Cuba Broadcasting The Office of Cuba Broadcasting operates the Martís from its headquarters in Miami, FL. The Martís are a multimedia hub of news, information, and analysis that provides the people of Cuba with interactive programs each day of the week. To broadcast their message, the Martís rely on a combination of high- and low-tech approaches: DVDs, emails, flash drives, Internet, satellite television, shortwave and AM radio, and SMS text. Combined with martinoticias.com, they constitute a unique service that brings accurate information to the Cuban people. https://www.usagm.gov/networks/ocb; Martinoticias http://www.martinoticias.com

Radio Free Asia Radio Free Asia (RFA) is a private nonprofit news organization that operates under a grant from the USAGM. Broadcasting daily in nine languages to Asian audiences whose governments restrict media, RFA delivers award-winning, reliable news and information. It also allows a range of voices and opinions from within Asia to be heard as a demonstration of freedom of expression over the airwaves, on television, and online. Through shortwave, medium wave, satellite and transmission television, social media, and the Internet, RFA broadcasts in Cantonese, Khmer, Korean, Lao, Mandarin, Myanmar, Uyghur, Vietnamese, and in three Tibetan dialects. Headquartered in Washington, DC, it has eight overseas bureaus and a network of correspondents around the world. https://www.usagm.gov/networks/rfa; Radio Free Asia—English. https://www.rfa.org/english

Radio Free Europe / Radio Liberty Radio Free Europe/Radio Liberty (RFE/RL) is a private nonprofit multimedia broadcasting corporation whose funding comes from a USAGM grant. It reaches nearly 34 million people in 23 countries—including Afghanistan, Iran, Pakistan, Russia, and Ukraine—in 26 languages. Its journalists provide what many people cannot get locally: uncensored news, responsible discussion, and open debate. RFE/RL uses digital technologies—the Internet, SMS text messaging, online video, satellite radio, and popular social media networks—and conventional broadcast radio to reach people in some of the most closed societies on Earth. With nearly 70 years of surrogate broadcasting experience, it continues to bring diverse, immediate, and interactive content to audiences. https://www.usagm.gov/networks/rferl; Radio Free Europe / Radio Liberty—English; https://www.rferl.org

Voice of America The Voice of America (VOA) is a multimedia international broadcasting service funded by the U.S. Government through the USAGM. It began broadcasting in 1942 and now reaches more than 275 million people worldwide. The VOA provides accurate, comprehensive, and trustworthy news and information, as well as informed discussion on the United States and the world. It engages audiences in regions deemed critical to the United States through whatever medium—radio, television, Internet, or digital media—the people of those regions prefer. It broadcasts approximately 1,800 hours of news, information, educational, and cultural programming every week to a global audience. Programs are produced in 46 languages. https://www.usagm.gov/networks/voa; Voice of America—English; https://www.voanews.com

Sources of Information

At a Glance The "Who We Are" web page features a 60-second video that captures the essence of USAGM core activities: informing people, engaging them in support of democracy, and connecting with them on a global scale. https://www.usagm.gov/who-we-are

Awards The USAGM has won awards for its productions in a variety of categories: documentary, education, investigative journalism, promotional programming, special reporting, video, and more. https://www.usagm.gov/awards

Business Opportunities Information on contract opportunities and instructions on how to do business with the USAGM are available online. https://www.usagm.gov/who-we-are/partnerwithus/contract-opportunities

Career Opportunities The USAGM work environment is diverse, multicultural, and professional. In addition to American citizens, the agency also hires non-U.S. citizens for positions that require foreign language skills. Internships are available in the fields of engineering, public affairs, public diplomacy, and research. https://www.usagm.gov/work-with-us

The USAGM provides training opportunities for reporters and students of media on five continents. https://www.usagm.gov/our-work/media-development

In 2018, the USAGM ranked 25th among 27 midsize agencies in the Partnership for Public Service's Best Places To Work Agency Rankings. http://bestplacestowork.org/rankings/detail/IB00

Climate Change   The USAGM is committed to developing a better understanding of the effects of climate change and to addressing climate change adaptation. https://www.usagm.gov/our-work/strategy-and-results/strategic-priorities/research-reports/strategic-sustainability-performance-plan

The USAGM has provided media training aimed at equipping journalists in the Latin America and the Caribbean region with skills and practices needed to report accurately and effectively on changes in the climate. https://www.usagm.gov/2016/09/29/covering-climate-change

Freedom of Information Act (FOIA)   The FOIA provides a statutory basis for public access to official agency information previously restricted from public view. Through the FOIA, Congress affirmed that citizens have the right to know what their Government does. Under the act, official information is available to "any person" without regard to need for or interest in the material. The USAGM and its FOIA staff are committed to ensuring the fullest possible disclosure that is consistent with the letter and spirit of the law. https://www.usagm.gov/foia | Email: foia@usagm.gov

The FOIA requires agencies to disclose, proactively and electronically, certain categories of records to the public. Records that the USAGM has previously released to the public under the FOIA and that are the subject of subsequent requests or likely to be the subject of subsequent requests are proactively disclosed in the USAGM's electronic reading room for public access.

Records that the USAGM determines are of sufficient public interest to warrant automatic disclosure are also proactively disclosed in the electronic reading room. https://www.usagm.gov/foia/electronic-reading-room

History   "The news may be good for us. The news may be bad. But we shall tell you the truth." These words, American journalist and writer William Harlan Hale spoke during the Voice of America's first radio show. For 75 years, U.S. international media have been broadcasting to audiences abroad. Visit the "History" web page to learn more about a story that continues to be heard around the world today. https://www.usagm.gov/who-we-are/history

Learn English   The Voice of America's website features resources for learning American English. https://learningenglish.voanews.com

Legislation / Congressional Committees   The USAGM receives its mandate to supervise all broadcasting activities and to provide strategic management for the agency from various public laws. The U.S. Congress oversees the USAGM, which is an independent executive branch agency, by monitoring, reviewing, and supervising its activities, programs, and policy implementation. https://www.usagm.gov/who-we-are/oversight

Networks   The USAGM's website provides convenient access to the home pages of all of its networks. https://www.usagm.gov/networks

News   USAGM-related news and information are available online. https://www.usagm.gov/news-and-information

Open Government   The USAGM supports the Open Government initiative by promoting collaboration, participation, and transparency. https://www.usagm.gov/our-work/strategy-and-results/strategic-priorities/research-reports/open-government | Email: opengov@bbg.gov

Press Releases   The latest press releases from the USAGM and its networks are available online. https://www.usagm.gov/news-and-information/press-releases

Site Map   The website map allows visitors to look for specific topics or to browse content that aligns with their interests. https://www.usagm.gov/sitemap

Social Media   The USAGM has a Facebook account. https://www.facebook.com/USAGMgov

The USAGM tweets announcements and other newsworthy items on Twitter. https://twitter.com/USAGMgov

The USAGM posts videos on its YouTube channel. https://www.youtube.com/channel/UCvYge67D7cpRJ6aYn2E9pPw

Students and Youth Worldwide   Voice of America's "Student Union" section offers students and youth international news that relates to them. https://www.voanews.com/student-union

Technology and Services To Evade Censorship   The Office of Internet Freedom provides anticensorship technology and services to journalists and citizens around the world. The technology and services enhance people's ability to access and share digital news and information without fear of repercussions or surveillance. https://www.usagm.gov/worldwide-operations/office-internet-freedom

The Sources of Information were updated 7–2019.

United States African Development Foundation

1400 I Street NW., Suite 1000, Washington, DC 20005
Phone, 202-233-8800. Fax, 202-673-3810. Internet, http://www.usadf.gov

Board of Directors

Chair	JOHN W. LESLIE, JR.
Vice Chair	JOHN O. AGWUNOBI
Board Member	WARD BREHM
Board Member	MORGAN M. DAVIS
Board Member	IQBAL PAROO
Board Member	(VACANCY)
Board Member	(VACANCY)

http://www.usadf.gov/board-of-directors

Staff

President / Chief Executive Officer	C.D. GLIN
General Counsel	JUNE B. BROWN
Managing Director, Finance and Administration	MATHIEU ZAHUI, ACTING

http://www.usadf.gov/leadership

[For the United States African Development Foundation statement of organization, see the Code of Federal Regulations, Title 22, Part 1501]

The above list of key personnel was updated 09–2017.

The United States African Development Foundation promotes development in Africa to empower marginalized and underserved communities.

The United States African Development Foundation was established by the African Development Foundation Act (22 U.S.C. 290h) as a Government corporation to support African-led development. The Foundation is led by the Board of Directors, which comprises the Chair, the Vice Chair, and five Board Members whom the President nominates with the advice and consent of the Senate. http://www.usadf.gov/adfact

The Foundation invests in private and nongovernmental organizations in Africa to promote and support innovative enterprise development, generate jobs, and increase incomes of the poor. It seeks to expand local institutional and financial capacities to foster entrepreneurship, ownership, and community-based economic development among marginalized and underserved populations in sub-Saharan Africa.

Sources of Information

Blog The United States African Development Foundation has a blog. http://www.usadf.gov/blog

Career Opportunities Vacancy announcements are posted online. http://www.usadf.gov/open-positions

Country Portfolios The Foundation has 20 country programs and special initiatives that extend its reach to a total of 30 African countries. http://www.usadf.gov/wherewework

Events Information on Foundation-related events is available online. http://www.usadf.gov/events

Frequently Asked Questions (FAQs) Answers to FAQs are posted on the Foundation's Web site. http://www.usadf.gov/faq

Grants Information on grants is available online. An applicant may download an application in English or French. Once completed, the application may be submitted by email or postal mail. http://www.usadf.gov/apply

News Press releases are available online. http://www.usadf.gov/pressreleases

Resources / Results Information on the Foundation's effectiveness, efficiency, investment return, and successful enterprises is included in its 2016 impact sheet. http://www.usadf.gov/results

Sectors The Foundation supports African-led agricultural development that benefits community enterprises. http://www.usadf.gov/agriculture

The Foundation supports the development of affordable and renewable energy to benefit rural African communities. http://www.usadf.gov/off-grid

The Foundation invests in the next generation of youth-led African enterprises. http://www.usadf.gov/youth

Social Media The United States African Development Foundation has a Facebook account. https://www.facebook.com/USADF

The Foundation tweets announcements and other newsworthy items on Twitter. https://twitter.com/USADF

The Foundation posts videos on its YouTube channel. https://www.youtube.com/channel/UCvhwYYAN6WGK4rlmiWAfEAA http://www.usadf.gov/contact-us | Email: info@usadf.gov

For further information, contact the Office of the President, U.S. African Development Foundation, 1400 I Street NW., Suite 1000, Washington, DC 20005-2248. Phone, 202-673-3916. Fax, 202-673-3810.

United States Agency for International Development

1300 Pennsylvania Avenue NW., Washington, DC 20523
Phone, 202-712-0000. Internet, http://www.usaid.gov

Administrator	MARK GREEN
Deputy Administrator	BONNIE GLICK
Chief of Staff	WILLIAM R. STEIGER
Chiefs	
Financial Officer	REGINALD W. MITCHELL
Information Officer	JAY MAHANAND
Directors	
Acquisition and Assistance	MARK A. WALTHER, ACTING
Executive Secretary / Senior National Security Advisor	ADRIEL HARVEY
General Counsel	DAVID H. MOORE
https://www.usaid.gov/who-we-are/organization/leadership-listing	

Central Bureaus

Assistant Administrators
Foreign Assistance (VACANCY)
Legislative and Public Affairs EDDY ACEVEDO, ACTING
Management ANGELIQUE M. CRUMBLY, ACTING

Assistant to the Administrator
Policy, Planning and Learning JAMES RICHARDSON

Executive Director
U.S. Global Development Lab HARRY BADER, ACTING

Functional Bureaus

Assistant Administrator
Democracy, Conflict and Humanitarian Assistance TIMOTHY ZIEMER, ACTING

Assistant to the Administrator
Food Security / Deputy Coordinator for Development, Feed BETH DUNFORD
the Future

Senior Deputy Assistant Administrators
Economic Growth, Education and Environment MICHELLE BEKKERING
Global Health ALMA CRUMM GOLDEN

Geographic Bureaus

Assistant Administrators
Europe and Eurasia BROCK BIERMAN
Latin America and the Caribbean STEVE OLIVE, ACTING
Middle East MICHAEL T. HARVEY

Assistant to The Administrator *
Afghanistan and Pakistan Affairs KAREN L. FREEMAN

Senior Deputy Assistant Administrators
Africa RAMSEY DAY
Asia GLORIA STEELE
https://www.usaid.gov/who-we-are/organization/bureaus

Independent Offices

Directors
Budget and Resource Management PETER WIEBLER, ACTING
Civil Rights and Diversity KIMBERLY A. LEWIS
Security JOHN VOORHEES
Small and Disadvantaged Business Utilization MAURICIO P. VERA

Chief
Human Capital Officer ROBERT LEAVITT
https://www.usaid.gov/who-we-are/organization/independent-
offices

Office of Inspector General

Inspector General ANN CALVARESI BARR
https://oig.usaid.gov/leadership

[For the Agency for International Development statement of organization, see the Federal Register of Aug. 26, 1987, 52 FR 32174]

---

* an independent office that functions like a geographic bureau

The above list of key personnel was updated 4–2019.

The United States Agency for International Development seeks to eradicate extreme global poverty and enables resilient and democratic societies to realize their potential.

The United States Agency for International Development (USAID) is an independent Federal agency established by 22 U.S.C. 6563. Its principal statutory authority is the Foreign Assistance Act of 1961, as amended (22 U.S.C. 2151 et seq.). The Agency serves as the focal point within the Government for economic matters affecting U.S. relations with developing countries. It administers international economic and humanitarian assistance programs. The Administrator is under the direct authority and foreign policy guidance of the Secretary of State. https://www.usaid.gov/who-we-are/mission-vision-values

Programs

The Agency works in over 100 countries to promote broadly shared economic prosperity, strengthen democracy and good governance, protect human rights, improve global health, advance food security and agriculture, increase environmental sustainability, further education, help societies prevent and recover from conflicts, and provide humanitarian assistance in the wake of natural and manmade disasters. https://www.usaid.gov/what-we-do

Democracy   The Agency promotes the transition to and consolidation of democratic regimes throughout the world. Programs focus on such problems as human rights abuses; misperceptions of democracy and free-market capitalism; lack of experience with democratic institutions; the absence or weakness of intermediary organizations; nonexistent, ineffectual, or undemocratic political parties; disenfranchisement of women, indigenous peoples, and minorities; failure to implement national charter documents; powerless or poorly defined democratic institutions; tainted elections; and inability to resolve conflicts peacefully. https://www.usaid.gov/democracy

Economic Growth   The Agency promotes broad-based economic growth by addressing factors that enhance the capacity for growth and by working to remove obstacles that obstruct individual opportunity. Programs concentrate on strengthening market economies, expanding economic opportunities for the disadvantaged in developing countries, and building human skills and capacities to facilitate broad participation. http://www.usaid.gov/what-we-do/economic-growth-and-trade

Environment   Environmental programs support two strategic goals: 1) reducing long-term threats to the biosphere, particularly loss of biodiversity and change in climate; 2) promoting sustainable economic growth locally, nationally, and regionally by addressing shortsighted economic, environmental, and developmental practices. Globally, USAID programs focus on reducing sources of greenhouse gas emissions and enhancing greenhouse gas sinks and on promoting innovative approaches to the conservation and sustainable use of Earth's biological diversity. The approach adopted to address national environmental problems differs from county to country, depending on its environmental priorities. Strategies may include improving agricultural, industrial, and natural resource management practices; strengthening public policies and institutions; being in dialogue with governments and international agencies; and environmental research and education. http://www.usaid.gov/what-we-do/environment-and-global-climate-change

Global Health and Population   The Agency improves access and quality of services for maternal and child health, nutrition, voluntary family planning, and reproductive health. It prevents and treats HIV/AIDS, malaria, and tuberculosis. It assists countries in the design and implementation of state-of-the-art public health approaches to end preventable child-maternal deaths and achieve an AIDS-free generation. The Agency takes advantage of economies of scale in procurement, technical services, and commodities. To promote sustainability, the Agency helps expand health systems and the health workforce by adopting and scaling-up proven health interventions across programs and countries. It also contributes to a cooperative global effort to stabilize world population growth and support women's reproductive rights. The types of population and health programs supported vary with the particular needs of individual countries and the kinds of approaches that local communities initiate and support. http://www.usaid.gov/what-we-do/global-health

Humanitarian Assistance / Post-Crisis Transitions   The Agency gives humanitarian assistance to save lives, reduce suffering, help victims return to self-sufficiency, and reinforce democracy. Programs focus on disaster prevention, preparedness, and mitigation; timely delivery of disaster relief and short-term rehabilitation supplies and services; preservation of basic institutions of civil governance during a disaster crisis; support for democratic institutions during periods of national transition; and building and reinforcement of local capacity to anticipate disasters and better cope with their aftermath. http://www.usaid.gov/what-we-do/working-crises-and-conflict

Overseas Organizations   USAID country organizations are located in countries where a bilateral program is being implemented. The in-country organizations are subject to the direction and guidance of the chief U.S. diplomatic representative in the country, usually the Ambassador. The organizations report to the appropriate assistant administrators according to geographic bureaus: Africa, Asia and the Near East, Europe and Eurasia, and Latin America and the Caribbean.

Overseas program activities that involve more than one country are administered by regional offices. These offices may also have country organizational responsibilities for assigned countries. Generally, the offices are headed by a regional development officer.

Coordination and representative offices for development assistance provide liaison with various international organizations and represent U.S. interests in development assistance matters. These offices may be only partially staffed by USAID personnel and may be headed by employees of other U.S. Government agencies. http://www.usaid.gov/where-we-work

Sources of Information

Blog   "Impact" is the name of the official USAID blog. https://blog.usaid.gov/

Bureaus   Geographic bureaus are responsible for the overall activities in countries; functional bureaus conduct Agency programs that are worldwide in nature or that cross geographic boundaries. https://www.usaid.gov/who-we-are/organization/bureaus

Business Opportunities   Through worldwide partnerships, USAID seeks to find innovative and cost-effective ways of addressing global challenges. The Agency partners with educational institutions, faith-based and community organizations, nongovernmental organizations, and individuals and organizations in the private sector. https://www.usaid.gov/work-usaid/how-to-work-with-usaid

Career Opportunities   USAID employs professionals with a variety of managerial, operational, and technical skills to achieve its international development goals. Its workforce includes direct-hire and contract employees based in the United States and at field missions worldwide. http://www.usaid.gov/careers

The Partnership for Public Service ranked USAID 13th among 27 midsize agencies in its Best Places To Work in the Federal Government 2018 rankings. https://bestplacestowork.org/rankings/detail/AM00

Climate Change   Deforestation and reliance on fossil fuels accelerate climate disruption. As the climate changes, it undermines the efforts of poor communities to be self-supporting. USAID shares data, knowledge, and tools with developing countries to help people predict, prepare for, and adapt to more frequent and more destructive weather-related events. The Agency also helps countries grow in sustainable ways by promoting clean and reliable energy and healthy landscapes. Watch the 3-minute video to learn more about USAID global climate action. https://www.usaid.gov/climate/usaid-global-climate-action

Comments   Comments, complaints, feedback, ideas, questions, and recommendations may be submitted by using an online form. https://www.usaid.gov/contact-us | Email: open@usaid.gov

Foreign Aid Explorer   The Foreign Aid Explorer website offers a multidimensional picture of U.S. foreign assistance to help users find and retrieve the data that they seek. Interactive maps and graphics displaying the historical details of U.S. foreign assistance allow users to explore foreign aid data across countries, sectors, and over time. Advanced users can quickly download data by using data query tools or by selecting a prepared file. https://explorer.usaid.gov/aid-dashboard.html

Forms   An electronic forms page features a selection of up-to-date USAID forms that are arranged according to form number. https://www.usaid.gov/forms

Freedom of Information Act (FOIA)   FOIA requests must be submitted in writing: email, fax, mail, or via the Public Access Link web portal. The Agency does not accept verbal FOIA requests. USAID Government information specialists are available to answer questions. Phone, 202-712-0960. Fax, 202-216-3070. https://www.usaid.gov/foia-requests | Email: foia@usaid.gov

USAID adds records that information seekers request repeatedly to its electronic FOIA library. If the desired record or document is not part of the FOIA library, consider submitting a written FOIA request to obtain the desired information. Please search the electronic reading room before submitting an official request for information. https://foiarequest.usaid.gov/app/ReadingRoom.aspx

History   President John F. Kennedy approved the Foreign Assistance Act of 1961 and created USAID by Executive order. Two years later, in a commencement address, he proclaimed: "Our problems are man-made; therefore, they can be solved by man. For in the final analysis, our most basic common link is that we all inhabit this small planet; we all breathe the same air; we all cherish our children's futures—and we are all mortal." President Kennedy's actions and words helped characterize the years of his administration and the one that followed, years that became known as the "decade of development." To learn more about the role that USAID played in expanding international development assistance opportunities, visit the "USAID History" web page. https://www.usaid.gov/who-we-are/usaid-history

Mission Directory   The online mission directory allows users to filter their searches by region: Afghanistan and Pakistan, Africa, Asia, Europe and Eurasia, Latin America and the Caribbean, and the Middle East. https://www.usaid.gov/mission-directory

News   USAID posts news and information: congressional testimonies, events, factsheets, photographs and videos, podcasts, press releases, speeches, and success stories, as well as its "Frontlines" magazine, "Impact" newsletter, and "Impact" blog. https://www.usaid.gov/news-information

Offices   USAID has several independent offices that carry out discrete functions. https://www.usaid.gov/who-we-are/organization/independent-offices

Open Government   USAID supports the Open Government initiative by posting data, records, and reports online. https://www.usaid.gov/open

Organizational Chart   USAID posts its organizational chart online. The chart includes independent offices and central, functional, and geographic bureaus. https://www.usaid.gov/who-we-are/organization

Plain Language   USAID adheres to the principles of transparency and openness that the Plain Writing Act of 2010 promotes. Plain writing plays a key role in achieving Open Government initiative goals and in improving collaboration, public participation, and transparency. https://www.usaid.gov/plain-writing

SERVIR Global   A joint initiative of USAID and the National Aeronautics and Space Administration, SERVIR partners with leading regional organizations worldwide to help developing countries use information from Earth observing satellites and geospatial technologies for managing climate risks and land use. SERVIR products, services, and tools empower decisionmakers to act locally on agriculture, ecosystems, land use, natural disasters, water, and other climate-sensitive issues. https://servirglobal.net/

Social Media   USAID maintains a YouTube channel and has a presence on Facebook, Twitter, and other social media. https://www.usaid.gov/stayconnected

Staff Directory   USAID maintains an electronic staff directory that allows users to search for personnel contact information by entering a first name, last name, or both. https://www.usaid.gov/staff-directory

Water / Sanitation Nearly 2.1 billion people cannot access safe drinking water in their homes, and about 4.4 billion people live exposed to sewage, trash, or both. Inadequate water and sanitation and poor hygiene combine to spread disease and elevate death rates worldwide. https://www.usaid.gov/what-we-do/water-and-sanitation

"Global Waters" magazine is accessible online. https://www.usaid.gov/global-waters https://www.usaid.gov/work-usaid/take-action

For further information, contact the U.S. Agency for International Development, 1300 Pennsylvania Avenue NW., Washington, DC 20523-0001. Phone, 202-712-0000.

United States Commission on Civil Rights

1331 Pennsylvania Avenue NW., Suite 1150, Washington, DC 20425
Phone, 202-376-8128. Fax 800-977-8339 (FedRelay). Internet, http://www.usccr.gov

Chair	CATHERINE E. LHAMON
Vice Chair	PATRICIA TIMMONS-GOODSON
Commissioner	DEBO P. ADEGBILE
Commissioner	GAIL HERIOT
Commissioner	PETER N. KIRSANOW
Commissioner	DAVID KLADNEY
Commissioner	KAREN K. NARASAKI
Commissioner	MICHAEL YAKI
Staff Director	MAURO A. MORALES

[For the Commission on Civil Rights statement of organization, see the Code of Federal Regulations, Title 45, Part 701]

The Commission on Civil Rights informs the development of national civil rights policy and enhances enforcement of Federal civil rights laws.

The Commission on Civil Rights was first created by the Civil Rights Act of 1957, as amended, and reestablished by the United States Commission on Civil Rights Act of 1994, as amended (42 U.S.C. 1975). http://www.usccr.gov/about/index.php

Activities

The Commission conducts hearings on important civil rights issues, including issuing subpoenas for the production of documents and the attendance of witnesses; publishes studies and reports on a wide range of civil rights issues to inform and advise policymakers; holds public briefings, issues press releases, makes information publicly available online, and provides a complaint referral service to promote greater public awareness of civil rights issues, protections, and enforcement; and sustains advisory committee involvement in the national program planning to strengthen factfinding. http://www.usccr.gov/about/powers.php

Regional Programs The Commission maintains 51 State Advisory Committees (SACs), one for each State and the District of Columbia. Each SAC is composed of citizen volunteers who are familiar with local and State civil rights issues. SAC members assist the Commission with factfinding, investigating, and disseminating information. The Commission ensures that advisory committees are diverse and represent a variety of backgrounds, skills, experiences, and perspectives. This diversity promotes debate and broadens exploration of the issues. All appointments are made in a nondiscriminatory manner. http://www.usccr.gov/about/sac.php

Sources of Information

Complaints The complaint referral service helps place individuals in contact with the appropriate office for obtaining information on the complaint process. Phone, 202-376-8513 or 800-552-6843. http://www.usccr.gov/filing/complaint.php | Email: referrals@usccr.gov

Employment   Career opportunities—vacancy announcements and available internships—are posted online. Contact the Human Resources Division for more information. Phone, 202-376-8364. http://www.usccr.gov/about/careers.php | Email: careers@usccr.gov

Freedom of Information Act (FOIA)   Information on how to file a FOIA request is available online. A request may be sent by email or fax, or by mail to the FOIA Officer, U.S. Commission on Civil Rights, 1331 Pennsylvania Avenue NW., Suite 1150, Washington, DC 20425. Phone, 202-376-8351. Fax, 202-376-1163. http://www.usccr.gov/foia/index.php | Email: foia@usccr.gov

Library   The Robert S. Rankin Memorial Library welcomes visitors. It is open on weekdays, 10 a.m.–4 p.m. (except on Federal holidays). For more information,

contact the Robert S. Rankin Memorial Library, 1331 Pennsylvania Avenue NW., Washington, DC 20425. Phone, 202-376-8110. Fax, 202-376-7597. http://www.usccr.gov/about/library.php | Email: publications@usccr.gov

Publications   For a complete list of Commission publications, consult the online catalog. It includes briefings; clearinghouse publications; hearings, consultations, and conferences; periodicals; publications in Spanish; staff reports; State advisory committee reports; and statutory and interim reports. To order a publication, contact the U.S. Commission on Civil Rights, 1331 Pennsylvania Avenue, NW., Suite 1150, Washington, DC 20425. Phone: 202-376-8128. http://www.usccr.gov/pubs/index.php | Email: publications@usccr.gov

Regional Offices   A list of the six regional offices—including addresses, telephone numbers, and areas served—is available online. http://www.usccr.gov/contact/regional.php; http://www.usccr.gov/contact/index.php

For further information, contact the Office of the Staff Director, U.S. Commission on Civil Rights, 1331 Pennsylvania Avenue NW., Suite 1150, Washington, DC 20425. Phone, 202-376-7700. Phone, 800-977-8339 (FedRelay).

United States International Trade Commission

500 E Street SW., Washington, DC 20436
Phone, 202-205-2000. Internet, http://www.usitc.gov

Commissioners

Chair	DAVID S. JOHANSON
Vice Chair	(VACANCY)
	MEREDITH M. BROADBENT
	JASON E. KEARNS
	RHONDA K. SCHMIDTLEIN
	IRVING A. WILLIAMSON
https://www.usitc.gov/press_room/bios.htm	
Chief Administrative Law Judge	CHARLES E. BULLOCK
Chief Information Officer	KEITH B. VAUGHN
General Counsel	DOMINIC L. BIANCHI

Administrative Services Offices

Chief Administrative Officer	STEPHEN MCLAUGHLIN
Directors	
Human Resources	ERIC MOZIE
Security and Support Services	ROBERT N. RIESS

Secretary to the Commission	LISA R. BARTON

Financial Offices

Chief Financial Officer	JOHN M. ASCIENZO
Directors	
Budget	CHRIS SWETZ
Finance	DEREK HENDERSON
Procurement	DEBRA BRIDGE

Independent Offices

Directors	
Equal Employment Opportunity	ALTIVIA R. JACKSON
External Relations	JENNIFER ANDBERG

Operating Offices

Director of Operations	CATHERINE B. DEFILIPPO
Chief Data Officer	JEREMY WISE
Directors	
Analysis and Research Services	JEREMY WISE
Economics	WILLIAM M. POWERS
Industries	JONATHAN R. COLEMAN
Investigations	NANNETTE M. CHRIST
Tariff Affairs and Trade Agreements	JAMES R. HOLBEIN
Unfair Import Investigations	MARGARET D. MACDONALD

Office of Inspector General

Inspector General	PHILIP M. HENEGHAN
https://www.usitc.gov/oig.htm	

The above list of key personnel was updated 7–2019.

The United States International Trade Commission provides the President, the U.S. Trade Representative, and the Congress with independent analysis of and information on tariffs, international trade, and the Nation's competitiveness; makes determinations in proceedings involving imports that may harm a domestic industry or violate U.S. intellectual property rights; and maintains the Harmonized Tariff Schedule of the United States.

Establishment and Organization

The United States International Trade Commission (USITC) is an independent agency created by the Revenue Act (39 Stat. 795) and originally named the United States Tariff Commission. The name was changed to the United States International Trade Commission by section 171 of the Trade Act of 1974 (19 U.S.C. 2231). https://www.govinfo.gov/content/pkg/USCODE-2017-title19/pdf/USCODE-2017-title19-chap12.pdf

With the advice and consent of the Senate, the President appoints six commissioners for 9-year terms, unless the appointment is made to fill an unexpired term. The Chair and Vice Chair are designated by the President for 2-year terms, and succeeding Chairs may not be of the same political party. The Chair generally is responsible for the administration of the Commission. Not more than three Commissioners may be members of the same political party (19 U.S.C. 1330). https://www.govinfo.gov/content/pkg/USCODE-2017-title19/pdf/USCODE-2017-title19-chap4-subtitleII.pdf

The USITC posts its organizational chart (2017) online. https://www.usitc.gov/documents/usitc_org_2017_revised.pdf

Activities

The USITC engages in various activities pursuant to the previously mentioned statutes. Under the Tariff Act of 1930, it has broad powers of investigation to scrutinize the following competitive factors: U.S. customs laws and those of foreign countries; the proportional relationship between the volume of imported articles and domestic production and domestic consumption; the conditions, causes, and effects of foreign industries competing with U.S. industries; and any other factor affecting competition between imported articles and U.S. articles. Upon request, the USITC is required to convey its available information to the President, the House Committee on Ways and Means, and the Senate Committee on Finance. The President, the Congress, or the two committees mentioned can direct the USITC to undertake investigations and studies. To carry out its research and conduct its specialized studies, the USITC maintains expertise in all matters relating to the commercial and international trade policies of the United States. https://www.usitc.gov/press_room/about_usitc.htm

Foreign Subsidization / Selling at Less Than Fair Value   The USITC conducts preliminary-phase investigations to determine whether imports of foreign merchandise that are alleged to be subsidized or sold at less than fair value injure or threaten to injure an industry in the United States. If its determination is affirmative and the Secretary of Commerce concludes that unfair practices are occurring or suspects that they may be occurring, then the USITC conducts final-phase investigations to determine the injury or threat of injury to an industry. https://www.usitc.gov/press_room/usad.htm

Under the Uruguay Round Agreements Act, the USITC also conducts sunset reviews. In these reviews, the it evaluates whether material injury to a U.S. industry would continue or recur if the antidumping duty or countervailing duty order under review were revoked. Injury reviews must be conducted on all antidumping duty and countervailing duty orders every 5 years for as long as the orders remain in effect. https://www.usitc.gov/press_room/us_sunset.htm

Generalized System of Preferences   With respect to articles that may be considered for preferential removal of the duty on imports from designated developing countries, the USITC advises the President of the economic consequences that removal may have on the domestic industry and on consumers. https://www.usitc.gov/glossary/term/generalized-system-preferences-gsp

Harmonized Tariff Schedule   The U.S. Congress enacted the "Harmonized Tariff Schedule of the United States" (HTS). The HTS became effective on January 1, 1989, replacing the Nation's former tariff schedules. The USITC publishes the HTS, which contains the U.S. tariff schedules and related matters. The agency also considers questions affecting the arrangement of tariff schedules and the classification of articles. https://www.usitc.gov/tariff_affairs/about_hts.htm

Import Relief for Domestic Industries   The USITC conducts global safeguard investigations upon petition, on behalf of an industry, a firm, a group of workers, or other entity representative of an industry, to determine whether an article is being imported in increased quantities that injure, or threaten to injure, the domestic industry producing a similar article or an article that competes with the imported one. If its determination is affirmative, the USITC recommends to the President action that would address the threat and be most effective in facilitating positive adjustment by the industry to import competition. The President determines if import relief is an appropriate response. The USITC also reports on developments within an industry that has been granted import relief. It advises the President of the probable economic effect of reducing or eliminating the tariff increase that was previously granted. The President may continue, modify, or terminate the import relief. https://www.usitc.gov/press_room/us_safeguard.htm

Imports From NAFTA Countries   Pursuant to section 302 of the NAFTA Implementation Act, the USITC conducts bilateral safeguard investigations. https://www.govinfo.gov/content/pkg/BILLS-103hr3450enr/pdf/BILLS-103hr3450enr.pdf

These investigations seek to determine whether, as a result of the reduction or elimination of a duty that the North American Free Trade Agreement (NAFTA) facilitates, a Canadian or Mexican export to the United States in increased quantities and under certain conditions may damage, or threaten to damage, a U.S. industry that produces a similar article competing with the Canadian or Mexican export. If the USITC makes an affirmative determination, it advises the President on the relief needed to prevent or to remedy serious harm. USITC investigations of this kind resemble procedurally investigations that are conducted under the global safeguard-action provisions of the Trade Act of 1974. https://www.usitc.gov/press_room/us_safeguard.htm

Interference With Agricultural Programs   The USITC conducts investigations, at the direction of the President, to determine whether products are being imported into the United States under conditions and in quantities that render, or tend to render, ineffective or that materially interfere with a Department of Agriculture program. The USITC communicates its findings to the President and makes recommendations. The President then may impose a fee or quota on the imports in question; however, no fee or quota may be imposed on any article that a member of the World Trade Organization produces. https://www.usitc.gov/press_room/statutory_resp.htm

Market Disruption From Communist Countries   The USITC conducts investigations to determine whether increased imports of an article produced in a Communist country are causing market disruption in the United States. If the USITC'S determination is in the affirmative, the President may take the same action as in the case of serious injury to an industry, except that the action would apply only to imports of the article from the Communist country. Commission investigations conducted under this provision are similar procedurally to those conducted under the global safeguard action provisions. https://www.usitc.gov/press_room/statutory_resp.htm

Trade Negotiations   When duties and other trade barriers are being considered for modification as part of a proposed trade agreement with a foreign county, the USITC advises the President of the potential economic consequences on U.S. industries and on consumers. https://www.usitc.gov/press_room/statutory_resp.htm

Unfair Import Trade Practices   The USITC applies U.S. statutory and common law of unfair competition to the importation of products into the United States and their sale. If it determines that there is a violation of law, it will direct that the articles involved be excluded from entry into the United States, or it may issue cease-and-desist orders directing the person engaged in such violation to stop. https://www.usitc.gov/intellectual_property/about_section_337.htm

Uniform Statistical Data   The USITC cooperates with the Secretary of the Treasury and the Secretary of Commerce to establish an enumeration of articles imported into and exported from the United States for statistical purposes. It also seeks to establish comparability of these statistics with statistical programs for domestic production. https://www.usitc.gov/press_room/statutory_resp.htm

Sources of Information

Business Opportunities   Most USITC contract opportunities are reserved for small businesses. They are typically for experienced contractors in the areas of administrative services, facilities management, information technology, and management consulting. The Office of Procurement oversees all procurements. Phone, 202-205-2252. https://usitc.gov/procurement/doing_business_with_usitc.htm

Career Opportunities   The USITC relies on accountants, analysts and specialists, attorneys, economists, and other professionals to carry out its mission. For more information, contact the Director, Office of Human Resources. Phone, 202-205-2651. https://www.usitc.gov/employment/positions.htm | Email: hr@usitc.gov

The USITC ranked 2d among 29 small agencies in the Partnership for Public Service's 2018 Best Places To Work Agency Rankings. http://bestplacestowork.org/rankings/detail/TC00

Contact Information   The USITC website has an electronic form for submitting a comment or question. https://www.usitc.gov/contact_us.htm

External Links The "Related External Links" web page has a collection of external links to make locating additional information more convenient. https://www.usitc.gov/related_sites.htm

Freedom of Information Act (FOIA) Enacted in 1966, the FOIA took effect on July 4, 1967. The statute makes all existing Federal Government records available to the public; however, a record may be shielded from disclosure by one or more of nine exemptions or by specific harm that its disclosure may cause. Any person, except a fugitive from the law, has a right to request access to Federal agency records. The FOIA strengthens democratic governance by giving access to Government records to anyone who submits a proper FOIA request. https://www.usitc.gov/secretary/foia/index.htm

The USITC posts answers to frequently asked FOIA-related questions. https://www.usitc.gov/secretary/foia/foia_faq.htm

Glossary The USITC maintains an online glossary. https://usitc.gov/glossary.htm

The "USITC Acronyms" web page enables the nonspecialist to navigate in an acronym-rich environment. https://www.usitc.gov/acronyms.htm

Harmonized Tariff Schedule The "Harmonized Tariff Schedule of the United States," which includes general notes and rules of interpretation, is available online in Portable Document Format (PDF). The HTS is used to classify imported merchandise for rate of duty and statistical purposes. https://hts.usitc.gov/current

History The USITC has developed a timeline of U.S. tariffs and trade and posted it online. https://www.usitc.gov/flash/dynamic_timeline.htm

The USITC celebrated its 100th birthday in September of 2016. To mark that milestone, it published a 453-page history of the agency called "A Centennial History of the United States International Trade Commission" (2017). The entire history is available online in Portable Document Format (PDF). https://www.usitc.gov/documents/final_centennial_history_508_compliant_v2.pdf

How To Find It Try the "How Do I Find" web page, which has a collection of links to help online visitors use the USITC website. https://www.usitc.gov/press_room/how_to_find.htm

Investigations A list of active antidumping and countervailing duty investigations is available online. https://www.usitc.gov/trade_remedy/731_ad_701_cvd/investigations.htm

337Info is an information retrieval system containing data on USITC Section 337 investigations. https://pubapps2.usitc.gov/337external | Email: 337InfoHelp@usitc.gov

The Electronic Document Information System (EDIS) contains all documents that have been filed in relation to USITC investigations. EDIS provides the capabilities to file documents for an investigation and to search for documents that have been submitted to the USITC. https://edis.usitc.gov | Email: EDIS3Help@usitc.gov

Low-Carbon Energy / Sustainable Products European Union climate regulations, which treat wood pellets as a low-carbon energy source, play a principal role in supporting the wood pellet industry's growth. To learn more, see Robert Ireland's 2018 executive briefing, in which he expresses his views on international trade in this energy source. https://www.usitc.gov/publications/332/executive_briefings/wood_pellets_ebot_final.pdf

In their 2018 working paper "Exporting Ecolabels: Is Demand for Certified Sustainable Products Affecting International Trade?" coauthors Renee Berry and Marin Weaver explore the influence of sustainability certifications on trade patterns in food and agricultural products. USITC working papers express the views of their authors and may not represent the views of the U.S. International Trade Commission or its individual Commissioners. https://www.usitc.gov/publications/332/working_papers/exporting_ecolabels_final_with_cover_mjs_071718.pdf

News The USITC posts news releases on its website. https://www.usitc.gov/press_room/news_release/news_release_index.htm

Open Data The USITC helps increase the Federal Government's efficiency and transparency by making its operational information more accessible and useful. https://www.usitc.gov/data/index.htm

Reading Rooms Reading rooms are open to the public in the Office of the Secretary and the USITC Main Library. The USITC Law Library is publicly accessible by prior arrangement. Call 202-205-3287 to schedule a visit.

Popular Topics The "Popular Topics" web page has links to frequently visited USITC pages. Popular topics include calendar events, commissioner biographies, "Federal Register" notices, hearing protocols, jobs, and news releases. https://usitc.gov/popular_topics.htm

Publications The Commission publishes results of investigations on various commodities and subjects. Other publications include an annual report

to the Congress on the operation of the trade agreements program and an annual review of Commission activities. Specific information on these publications may be obtained from the Office of the Secretary. https://usitc.gov/research_and_analysis/commission_publications.htm

Site Map The USITC site map allows visitors to look for specific topics or to browse content that aligns with their interests. https://www.usitc.gov/sitemap

Trade Seminars The research division of the Office of Economics posts the International Trade Seminar Series on the USITC website. https://www.usitc.gov/research_and_analysis/seminars_economics.htm

The Sources of Information were updated 7–2019.

United States Office of Special Counsel

1730 M Street NW., Suite 218, Washington, DC 20036-4505
Phone, 202-804-7000, 800-872-9855, 202-653-5151. Internet, http://www.osc.gov

Leadership Tables

Special Counsel	HENRY J. KERNER
Principal Deputy Special Counsel	ELLEN C. EPSTEIN
Deputy Special Counsels	
Legal Affairs	PATRICK HARTOBEY
Public Policy	TRAVIS MILLSAPS
General Counsel	SUSAN K. ULLMAN

https://osc.gov/Pages/Leadership.aspx

Administrative Services Division

Chief Operating Officer	BRUCE GIPE
Chief Officers	
Administrative Services	DERRICK MCDUFFIE
Data	SMITA PATEL
Financial	KARL P. KAMMANN
Human Capital	KATHY MCDUFFIE
Information	SMITA PATEL
Clerk	MAHALA DAR

General Law Division

Associate Special Counsel	ANNE WAGNER
Unit Chiefs	
Alternative Dispute Resolution	JANE JULIANO
Complaints Examining	BARBARA J. WHEELER
Disclosure	CATHERINE A. MCMULLEN
Diversity, Outreach, and Training	SHIRINE MOAZED

Investigation and Prosecution Division—Field

Associate Special Counsel	Bruce D. Fong
Field Office Chiefs	
Dallas	Anne Gullick
Detroit	Christopher T. Tall
San Francisco Bay Area	Joseph Siegelman

Investigation and Prosecution Division—Headquarters

Associate Special Counsel	Louis Lopez
Division Chiefs	Kimberley Baxter
	Emilee Collier
	Darshan Sheth
	Rachel Venier
Unit Chiefs	
Hatch Act	Ana Galindo-Marrone
Retaliation and Disclosure	Elizabeth McMurray
Uniformed Services Employment and Reemployment Rights Act	Patrick H. Boulay

The above list of key personnel was updated 11–2019.

The United States Office of Special Counsel investigates allegations of certain activities prohibited by civil service laws, rules, or regulations and litigates before the Merit Systems Protection Board.

Establishment and Organization

The U.S. Office of Special Counsel (OSC) was established on January 1, 1979, by Reorganization Plan No. 2 of 1978 (5 U.S.C. app.). https://uscode.house.gov/view.xhtml?req=granuleid:USC-prelim-title5a-node84-leaf186&num=0&edition=prelim

Public Law 95–454, which is also cited as the Civil Service Reform Act of 1978, was approved on October 13, 1978, and became effective on January 11, 1979. This statute enlarged the agency's functions and powers (92 Stat. 1112). https://www.govinfo.gov/content/pkg/STATUTE-92/pdf/STATUTE-92-Pg1111.pdf

Pursuant to provisions of Public Law 101–12, which is also cited as the Whistleblower Protection Act of 1989, the OSC functions as an independent investigative and prosecutorial executive branch agency that litigates before the Merit Systems Protection Board (103 Stat. 16). https://www.govinfo.gov/content/pkg/STATUTE-103/pdf/STATUTE-103-Pg16.pdf

Statutory material associated with the OSC is codified in sections 1211—1219 of 5 U.S.C. https://uscode.house.gov/view.xhtml?path=/prelim@title5/part2/chapter12/subchapter2&edition=prelim

Additional statutory material that affects the OSC and that derives from the Civil Service Reform Act of 1978 is codified in section 1101, note, of 5 U.S.C. https://uscode.house.gov/view.xhtml?path=/prelim@title5/part2/chapter11&edition=prelim

The OSC included an organizational chart in its "Performance and Accountability Report for Fiscal Year 2018" on page 107. https://osc.gov/Documents/Resources/Statutory%20Reports%20and%20Notices/Performance%20and%20Accountability%20Reports%20(PAR)/Performance%20Reports/FY%202018%20Performance%20and%20Accountability%20Report.pdf

Activities

The OSC safeguards the merit system in Federal employment by protecting employees and applicants from prohibited personnel practices, especially from reprisal for whistleblowing. The Office operates a secure channel for Federal whistleblower disclosures of gross waste of funds or mismanagement, substantial and specific danger to public health and safety, and violations of laws, regulations, or rules. The OSC also issues advice on the Hatch Act and enforces its restrictions on political activity by Government employees. It protects the civilian employment and reemployment rights of military servicemembers under the Uniformed Services Employment and Reemployment Act. The OSC enhances Government accountability and performance by the realization of a diverse, inclusive Federal workplace where employees embrace excellence in service, uphold merit system principles, are encouraged to disclose wrongdoing, and are protected against reprisals and other unlawful employment practices. https://osc.gov/Services

Sources of Information

Archived Records   The "Guide to Federal Records in the National Archives of the United States" indicates that OSC records have been assigned to record group 481. The Guide is accessible online, but no description is associated with this record group. https://www.archives.gov/research/guide-fed-records/groups/000.html

Business Opportunities   The OSC relies on the Department of Interior for performing assisted procurements. The OSC posts contract opportunities online by using Government acquisition vehicles like GSA Ebuy. It posts open market opportunities on the Federal Business Opportunities Web site. https://osc.gov/Careers

Career Opportunities   The agency employs approximately 110 employees who work in Washington, DC, or in the Dallas, Detroit, and Oakland field offices. To carry out its mission, the OSC relies heavily on attorneys, investigators, and personnel management specialists.

The OSC seeks law students year-round for internships in Dallas, TX; Detroit, MI; Oakland, CA; and Washington, DC. https://osc.gov/Careers

In 2018, the OSC ranked 14th among 29 small agencies in the Partnership for Public Service's Best Places To Work Agency Rankings. http://bestplacestowork.org/BPTW/rankings/detail/FW00

Contact Information   The "Contact OSC" web page has postal and email addresses and phone numbers. https://osc.gov/Pages/contact.aspx | Email: info@osc.gov

Electronic Filing   The E–Filing System makes filing a complaint with the OSC easier and faster. https://osc.gov/pages/file-complaint.aspx

En Español   The OSC posts information in Spanish on its "Para Información En Español" web page. https://osc.gov/Espanol

Freedom of Information Act (FOIA)   FOIA requests must be submitted in writing by email, fax, or U.S. postal mail or other delivery service. The OSC provides a Public Access Link portal that allows information seekers to submit a request online and to receive confirmation of and updates on a pending request. https://osc.gov/Pages/FOIA-Resources.aspx

Frequently Asked Questions (FAQs)   The OSC posts answers to FAQs on its website. https://osc.gov/FAQ

Hatch Act Advisory Opinions   Advice that the OSC has given to individuals on the Hatch Act is publicly accessible online. https://osc.gov/Services/Pages/HatchAct-AdvisoryOpinion.aspx

News   The OSC posts press releases online. https://osc.gov/PressReleases

Open Government   The OSC supports the Open Government initiative by promoting the principles of collaboration, participation, and transparency. https://osc.gov/OpenGov

Prohibited Personnel Practices   The OSC provides information on personnel practices that are prohibited within the Federal workplace. https://osc.gov/Services/Pages/PPP.aspx

Reports   The OSC posts reports on its website. https://osc.gov/Reports

Site Map   The website map allows visitors to look for specific topics or to browse content that aligns with their interests. https://osc.gov/Pages/SiteMap.aspx

Social Media   The OSC tweets announcements and other newsworthy items on Twitter. https://twitter.com/US_OSC

Speakers   To request a speaker, contact the OSC by phone or fax. Phone, 202-804-7000. Fax, 202-254-3711.

Whistleblower Files   The OSC posts documents from closed investigations on its website. These documents are based on whistleblower disclosures. https://osc.gov/PublicFiles

2302(c) Program Certification   The White House has required all Federal agencies to certify that they are educating their employees about the rights of whistleblowers. Phone, 703-466-0259. https://osc.gov/Services/Pages/Outreach-2302Cert.aspx | Email: 2302c@osc.gov

The Sources of Information were updated 11–2019.

United States Postal Service

475 L'Enfant Plaza SW., Washington, DC 20260
Phone, 202-268-2000. Internet, http://www.usps.gov

Board of Governors

Chair	(VACANCY)
Vice Chair	(VACANCY)
Governor	(VACANCY)
Governor	(VACANCY)
Governor	(VACANCY)
Governor	(VACANCY)
Governor	(VACANCY)
Governor	(VACANCY)
Governor	(VACANCY)
Postmaster General / Chief Executive Officer	MEGAN J. BRENNAN
Deputy Postmaster General / Chief Government Relations Officer	RONALD A. STROMAN
Secretary	JULIE S. MOORE

http://about.usps.com/who-we-are/leadership/board-governors.htm

Officers

Postmaster General / Chief Executive Officer	MEGAN J. BRENNAN
Deputy Postmaster General / Chief Government Relations Officer	RONALD A. STROMAN
Executive Vice Presidents	
Chief Customer and Marketing Officer	JACQUELINE KRAGE STRAKO, ACTING
Chief Financial Officer	JOSEPH CORBETT
Chief Human Resources Officer	JEFFREY C. WILLIAMSON
Chief Information Officer	KRISTIN SEAVER
Chief Operating Officer	DAVID E. WILLIAMS
General Counsel	THOMAS J. MARSHALL

http://about.usps.com/who-we-are/leadership/pmg-exec-comm.htm#p=1

Chief Postal Inspector	GUY COTTRELL

https://postalinspectors.uspis.gov/aboutus/Chief.aspx

Judicial Officer	GARY E. SHAPIRO

http://about.usps.com/who-we-are/judicial/welcome.htm

Vice Presidents

Chief Information Security Officer	GREGORY S. CRABB
Controller	MAURA A. McNERNEY
Corporate Communications	JANICE D. WALKER
Delivery Operations	KEVIN L. McADAMS
Employee Resource Management	SIMON STOREY
Engineering Systems	MICHAEL J. AMATO
Enterprise Analytics	ISAAC S. CRONKHITE
Facilities	THOMAS SAMRA
Finance and Planning	LUKE GROSSMANN
Information Technology	JEFFREY C. JOHNSON
Labor Relations	DOUGLAS TULINO
Mail Entry and Payment Technology	PRITHA MEHRA
Marketing	STEVEN W. MONTEITH
Network Operations	ROBERT CINTRON
Pricing and Costing	SHARON OWENS
Product Innovation	GARY C. REBLIN
Retail and Customer Service Operations	KELLY M. SIGMON
Sales and Customer Relations	CLIFF RUCKER
Supply Management	SUSAN M. BROWNELL

Vice Presidents—Area Operations	
Capital Metro Area	LINDA M. MALONE
Eastern Area	JOSHUA D. COLIN
Great Lakes Area	ERICA BRIX, ACTING
Northeast Area	EDWARD PHELAN, JR.
Pacific Area	LARRY MUÑOZ
Southern Area	SHAUN E. MOSSMAN
Western Area	GREGORY GRAVES

http://about.usps.com/who-we-are/leadership/officers.htm

Inspector General	TAMMY L.,WHITCOMB, ACTING

https://www.uspsoig.gov

[For the United States Postal Service statement of organization, see the Code of Federal Regulations, Title 39, Part 221]

The above list of key personnel was updated 02–2018.

The United States Postal Service provides the American public with affordable, reliable, and universal mail service.

The Postal Service was created as an independent establishment of the executive branch by the Postal Reorganization Act (39 U.S.C. 101 et seq.), approved August 12, 1970. The present United States Postal Service commenced operations on July 1, 1971.

In Fiscal Year 2016, the Postal Service had approximately 508,908 career employees and handled over 153 billion pieces of mail. The chief executive officer of the Postal Service, the Postmaster General, is appointed by the nine Governors of the Postal Service. The President appoints the nine Governors with the advice and consent of the Senate. The Governors and the Postmaster General appoint the Deputy Postmaster General, and these 11 appointees constitute the Board of Governors.

In addition to the national headquarters, area and district offices oversee more than 35,000 post offices, branches, stations, contract postal units, village post offices, and community post offices throughout the United States. http://about.usps.com/welcome.htm

Activities

To expand and improve service to the public, the Postal Service engages in customer cooperation activities, including the development of programs for both the general public and major customers. The consumer advocate, a postal ombudsman, represents the interests of the individual mail customer in matters involving the Postal Service. The advocate brings complaints and suggestions to the attention of top postal management and solves the problems of individual customers. To provide services responsive to public needs, the Postal Service operates its own planning, research, engineering, real estate, and procurement programs, and it maintains close ties with international postal organizations.

The Postal Service is the only Federal agency whose employment policies are governed by a process of collective bargaining under the National Labor Relations Act. Its Office of Human Resources, including the Labor Relations Division, administers labor contract negotiations that affect bargaining unit personnel, as well as personnel matters involving employees not covered by collective bargaining agreements.

The U.S. Postal Inspection Service, a Federal law enforcement agency, has jurisdiction in criminal matters affecting the integrity and security of the mail. Postal inspectors protect all postal employees and enforce more than 200 Federal statutes involving mail fraud, mail bombs, child pornography, illegal drugs, mail theft, and other postal crimes. http://about.usps.com/what-we-are-doing/welcome.htm

Sources of Information

Business Opportunities   Suppliers can learn about doing business with the Postal Service online. Information on rights and permissions (the use of trademarked material) and licensing products is also available online. http://about.usps.com/doing-business/welcome.htm

Career Opportunities   Information on careers—including information for veterans and reservists, for students and recent graduates—is available on the Postal Service's Web site or at the nearest post office. http://about.usps.com/careers/welcome.htm

The U.S. Postal Inspection Service posts career opportunities on its Web site. https://postalinspectors.uspis.gov/employment/positions.aspx

Consumer Information   For general information, call the "ASK USPS" line. Phone, 800-275-8777. To buy stamps, calculate postage prices, change addresses, find answers to frequently asked questions, locate ZIP Codes, print postage, shop at the Postal Store, and track packages, visit the Postal Service's Web site. http://about.usps.com/news/welcome.htm

Fraud / Theft   Postal inspectors can be located by Zip Code on the U.S. Postal Inspection Service's locator Web page. http://locator.uspis.gov/locator

Complaint forms to report identity and mail theft, mail fraud, and unsolicited sexually oriented advertising are accessible online. Phone, 800-275-8777. https://postalinspectors.uspis.gov/contactUs/filecomplaint.aspx

Freedom of Information Act (FOIA)   Information and guidance on the Freedom of Information and the Privacy Acts and on Postal Service records management, as well as access to an electronic FOIA reading room are available online. http://about.usps.com/who-we-are/foia/welcome.htm

The Postal Service maintains an online FOIA reading room. Before submitting a FOIA request to access records, check the electronic reading room to see if the desired information is immediately available. https://about.usps.com/who-we-are/foia/readroom/welcome.htm

History   Benjamin Franklin and the Postal Service, what was the nature of their association? Visit the "Postal History" Web page to learn just how close it was. http://about.usps.com/who-we-are/postal-history/welcome.htm

The National Postal Museum houses one of the largest and most significant philatelic and postal history collections in the world and one of the most comprehensive library resources on philately and postal history. The museum's exhibition galleries present America's postal history from Colonial times to the present. Its collections contain prestigious international and U.S. postal issues and specialized collections, archival postal documents, and three-dimensional objects. https://postalmuseum.si.edu

Inspector General   The Office of Inspector General has a toll-free hotline and online complaint form for reporting fraud, mismanagement, and waste. Phone, 888-877-7644 or 866-644-8398 (hearing impaired). Complaints also may be sent to the U.S. Postal Service, Office of Inspector General Hotline, 10th Floor, 1735 N. Lynn Street, Arlington, VA 22209-2020. https://www.uspsoig.gov/hotline | Email: hotline@uspsoig.gov

Newsroom   The Postal Service maintains an online newsroom that features broadcast and audio downloads, leadership biographies, national and local news, service alerts, testimonies and speeches, and a photo gallery. http://about.usps.com/news/welcome.htm

Organizational Chart   The "Postal Leadership" page has links leading to two Portable Document Format (PDF) files containing organizational charts, one with leadership photographs and the other without them. http://about.usps.com/who-we-are/leadership/officers.htm

Passports   Thousands of post offices accept passport applications on behalf of the Department of State. These post offices offer the products and services needed to acquire a first-time passport or renewal. At some locations, a passport photograph can be taken for an additional fee. https://www.usps.com/international/passports.htm

Philatelic Sales   For information on available stamps, philatelic items, and collectibles, visit the "Stamps" Web page. https://www.usps.com/stamps

Publications   Information on mailability, on postage rates and fees, and on other topics is available at the nearest post office. Most postal regulations affecting domestic and international mail, employee and labor relations, and purchasing can be found in Postal Service manuals and in the "Code of Federal Regulations." A wide range of publications—including annual reports to Congress, handbooks, manuals, notices, periodicals, and posters—is available online. http://about.usps.com/periodicals-publications/welcome.htm

Reading Areas   Reading areas are maintained in the library at USPS Headquarters on the 11th Floor. The library's holdings include historic, legal, regulatory, and other documents. Visitors must schedule an appointment—weekdays, 9 a.m.–4 p.m. (except Federal holidays)—before accessing the library. Phone, 202-268-2906.

Site Map   The Web site map allows visitors to look for specific topics or to browse content that aligns with their interests. http://about.usps.com/sitemap.htm

Social Media   The Postal Service has a Facebook account. https://www.facebook.com/USPS

The Postal Service tweets announcements and other newsworthy items on Twitter. https://twitter.com/usps

The Postal Service posts videos on its YouTube channel. https://www.youtube.com/user/uspstv/custom; https://www.usps.com/help/contact-us.htm

For further information, contact the U.S. Postal Service, 475 L'Enfant Plaza SW., Washington, DC 20260. Phone, 202-268-2000.

QUASI-OFFICIAL AGENCIES

Legal Services Corporation

3333 K Street NW., Washington, DC 20007
Phone, 202-295-1500. Fax, 202-337-6797. Internet, http://www.lsc.gov

Board of Directors

Chair	JOHN G. LEVI
Vice-Chair	FR. PIUS PIETRZYK, O.P.
	ROBERT J. GREY, JR.
	MATTHEW KEENAN
	ABIGAIL LAWLIS KUZMA
	VICTOR B. MADDOX
	JOHN G. MALCOLM
	LAURIE MIKVA
	FRANK X. NEUNER, JR.
	JULIE A. REISKIN
	GLORIA VALENCIA-WEBER

https://www.lsc.gov/about-lsc/board-members

Leadership

President	JAMES J. SANDMAN
Chief of Staff	REBECCA FERTIG COHEN
Vice Presidents	
Government Relations and Public Affairs	CAROL A. BERGMAN
Grants Management	LYNN A. JENNINGS
Legal Affairs	RONALD S. FLAGG
Corporate Secretary	RONALD S. FLAGG
General Counsel	RONALD S. FLAGG
Treasurer	DEBORAH MOORE

Chief Officers

Data	CARLOS MANJARREZ
Financial	DEBORAH MOORE
Information	JADA BREEGLE

Office Directors

Compliance and Enforcement	LORA RATH
Data Governance and Analysis	CARLOS MANJARREZ
Human Resources	TRACI HIGGINS
Institutional Advancement	NADIA ELGUINDY
Program Performance	JOYCE MCGEE

https://www.lsc.gov/about-lsc/lsc-leadership

Inspector General   JEFFREY E. SCHANZ
https://www.oig.lsc.gov/about-oig/meet-the-ig

The above list of key personnel was updated 10–2019.

The Legal Services Corporation promotes equal access to justice and provides civil legal assistance to low-income persons.

Establishment and Organization

On July 25, 1974, President Richard M. Nixon approved Public Law 93–355 "to amend the Economic Opportunity Act of 1964 to provide for the transfer of the legal services program from the Office of Economic Opportunity to a Legal Services Corporation." The Legal Services Corporation Act of 1974, as amended (42 U.S.C. 2996 et seq.), established a private, nonprofit corporation to promote equal access to justice under the law for all Americans. https://www.govinfo.gov/content/pkg/ STATUTE-88/pdf/STATUTE-88-Pg378.pdf

The President appoints, by the advice and with the consent of the Senate, the 11 members who constitute the Board of Directors, which heads the LSC. By law, it is bipartisan and no more than six members may be of the same political party. A member is appointed to a term of 3 years. A majority of the Board members must be members of the bar of the highest court of any State. The Board meets four or more times per year. https://www.govinfo.gov/ content/pkg/USCODE-2017-title42/pdf/ USCODE-2017-title42-chap34.pdf

An organizational chart is available on the "LSC Leadership" web page. https://www. lsc.gov/about-lsc/lsc-leadership

Activities

Congressional appropriations fund the LSC to provide legal services through grants to independent, local legal services provider programs. These programs are selected through a system of competition. In 2017, the LSC funded 133 programs. Together, they serve every county and congressional district in the Nation, as well as the U.S. Territories. Some of these programs address the particular needs of Native Americans and migrant farmworkers. http://www.lsc. gov/what-legal-aid/how-we-work

The legal services delivery system is based on several principles: local priorities, national accountability, competition for grants, and a strong public-private partnership. Local programs are governed by their own boards of directors, which set priorities and determine the types of cases that will be handled subject to restrictions set by Congress. A majority of each local board is appointed by local bar associations, and one-third of each local board is composed of client representatives appointed by client groups. Each board hires its own executive director. Programs may supplement their LSC grants with additional funds from State and local governments and other sources. They further leverage Federal funds by involving private attorneys in the delivery of legal services for the poor, mostly through volunteer pro bono work.

LSC-funded programs neither handle criminal cases nor accept fee-generating cases that private attorneys are willing to accept on a contingency basis. In addition, in 1996, a series of new limitations were placed upon activities in which LSC-funded programs may engage on behalf of their clients, even with non-LSC funds. All programs must comply with laws enacted by Congress and the implementing regulations promulgated by the LSC. http://www.lsc.gov/ about-lsc/what-we-do

Sources of Information

Blog   The LSC maintains a blog. http:// www.lsc.gov/media-center/blog

Board Meetings   Board meeting documents and information are available online. http://www.lsc.gov/about-lsc/board/board-meetings

Business Opportunities   The LSC regularly seeks the assistance of vendors to purchase products and contractors to carry out special projects. The LSC is eligible for General Services Administration schedule pricing and posts requests for proposals on eBuy and FedBizOpps.gov. http://www.lsc.gov/about-lsc/doing-business-lsc-rfps

Career Opportunities The LSC is an organization of socially aware professionals who serve the unrepresented and promote equal justice. Information on career opportunities and working at the LSC is available online. http://www.lsc.gov/about-lsc/careers

Civil Legal Outcomes The LSC developed its civil legal outcomes toolkit to help legal aid programs with defining, collecting, and reporting on metrics that describe their effectiveness. The toolkit includes detailed instructions, electronic learning modules, examples, and additional resources for implementing an outcomes management system. https://www.lsc.gov/grants-grantee-resources/civil-legal-outcomes

Client Success Stories An interactive map allows website visitors to browse client success stories by State. http://www.lsc.gov/what-legal-aid/client-success-stories

Contact Us To make a media inquiry, submit a Freedom of Information Act request, ask a grant submission question, or need to contact the LSC for another reason, use the electronic form on the "Contact Us" web page. https://www.lsc.gov/about-lsc/contact-us

Data Detailed national and local level information on client characteristics, expenditures, funding, private attorney involvement, service area demographics, services provided, staffing, and the use of technology is available on the "Grantee Data" web pages. http://www.lsc.gov/grants-grantee-resources/grantee-data

Donations Tax-deductible donations to the LSC support the use of technology innovations in legal services, provide law fellows for civil legal aid programs in need, raise public awareness of the legal aid system crisis, and support research into the effectiveness and need of civil legal aid. http://www.lsc.gov/support-lsc/donate-now

Events A list of upcoming events is available online. http://www.lsc.gov/meetings-and-events/calendar

Facts What percentage of the population is eligible for LSC-funded assistance? What is the average annual salary of LSC grantee staff attorneys? To learn the answers to these questions and others, visit the "Quick Facts" web page. http://www.lsc.gov/quick-facts

Find Legal Aid An online search tool is available to find the nearest LSC-funded legal aid organization by address, city, or ZIP Code. http://www.lsc.gov/what-legal-aid/find-legal-aid

Freedom of Information Act (FOIA) The FOIA grants any person the right to request access to Federal agency records or information. U.S. Government agencies are required to disclose records after they receive a written request for them; however, the statute shields certain records from disclosure. The LSC complies with the FOIA and releases records to information seekers, as long as the desired records are not shielded. A FOIA request must be made in writing and may be submitted by electronic submission form, email, fax, or postal service. The request should be clearly marked: "Freedom of Information Act Request." Fax, 202-337-6519. http://www.lsc.gov/about-lsc/foia | Email: FOIA@lsc.gov

The LSC maintains a FOIA reading room online. Before submitting a FOIA request, information seekers should search the reading room for records that are immediately accessible. http://www.lsc.gov/about-lsc/foia/foia-electronic-public-reading-room

Grant Programs Descriptions of the LSC's seven grant programs basic field, disaster relief emergency, technology initiative, and veterans appeals pro bono grants; leadership development and loan repayment assistance programs; and pro bono innovation fund—are available online. http://www.lsc.gov/grants-grantee-resources/our-grant-programs

Justice Gap The justice gap represents the difference between the level of civil legal assistance that is available and the level that is necessary to meet the legal needs of low-income individuals and families. To learn more about the justice gap, visit the "The Unmet Need for Legal Aid" web page. http://www.lsc.gov/what-legal-aid/unmet-need-legal-aid

Maps The LSC posts maps that provide a visual representation of nationwide statistics on poverty, disaster risks, flood zones, social vulnerability, and on other topics. https://www.lsc.gov/what-legal-aid/maps

News   The LSC posts press releases on its website. http://www.lsc.gov/media-center/press-releases

Oversight   The Office of the Inspector General from the LSC posts reports and data on Oversight.gov, a text-searchable repository of reports that Federal Inspectors General publish. The Council of the Inspectors General on Integrity and Efficiency operates and maintains the website to increase public access to independent and authoritative information on the Federal Government. https://oversight.gov

Publications   Annual reports, budget requests, factbooks, and reports are accessible online. http://www.lsc.gov/media-center/publications

Public Commentary   The LSC seeks public comments on a variety of proposals affecting grants and operations. https://www.lsc.gov/about-lsc/matters-comment

Sharing Best Practices   The "Best Practices Corner" web page has a collection of resources: ideas, innovations, projects, and best practices. The legal aid community has contributed these resources as examples, models, or guidance in the quest to provide the highest quality and most effective legal services to low-income communities. https://www.lsc.gov/grants-grantee-resources/best-practices-corner

Social Media   The LSC has a Facebook account. https://www.facebook.com/LegalServicesCorporation

The LSC tweets announcements and other newsworthy items on Twitter. https://twitter.com/lsctweets

The Sources of Information were updated 10–2019.

Smithsonian Institution

1000 Jefferson Drive SW., Washington, DC 20560
Phone, 202-633-1000. Internet, http://www.si.edu

Board of Regents
Citizen Regents

Chair	DAVID M. RUBENSTEIN
Vice Chair	STEVE M. CASE
	BARBARA M. BARRETT
	JOHN FAHEY
	ROGER W. FERGUSON
	MICHAEL GOVAN
	RISA J. LAVIZZO-MOUREY
	MICHAEL M. LYNTON
	JOHN W. MCCARTER, JR.

Congressional Regents

Representatives	THOMAS J. COLE
	SAMUEL JOHNSON
	DORIS MATSUI
Senators	JOHN BOOZMAN
	PATRICK J. LEAHY
	DAVID PERDUE

Ex Officio Regents

Chief Justice of the United States	JOHN G. ROBERTS, JR.
Vice President of the United States	MICHAEL R. PENCE
Chief of Staff to the Regents	PORTER WILKINSON
https://www.si.edu/regents/members	

Senior Executives

Secretary https://www.si.edu/about/secretary-david-skorton	DAVID J. SKORTON
Chief Financial Officer	ALBERT G. HORVATH
Provost	JOHN H. DAVIS, ACTING

Assistant Secretary, Advancement	ZULLY DORR, ACTING
Assistant Secretary, Communications and External Affairs	CAROLYN MARTIN, ACTING
Assistant Secretary, Education and Access	PATTY BARTLETT, ACTING
Director, Equal Employment and Minority Affairs	ERA L. MARSHALL
General Counsel	JUDITH E. LEONARD

Administration / Program Directors

Under Secretary for Finance and Administration	ALBERT G. HORVATH

Chief Information Officer	DERON BURBA
Chief Investment Officer	AMY CHEN
Director, Contracting and Personal Property Management	THOMAS DEMPSEY
Director, Finance and Accounting	JEAN GARVIN
Director, Human Resources	WALTRUNETTE GARDNER, ACTING
Director, Planning, Management and Budget	DAVID VOYLES
Director, Policy and Analysis	H. WHITNEY WATRISS, ACTING
Director, Smithsonian Exhibits	SUSAN ADES
Director, Smithsonian Facilities	NANCY BECHTOL
Director, Sponsored Projects	TRACEY FRASER
President, Smithsonian Enterprises	CHRIS LIEDEL

Museums / Research Centers

Under Secretary for Museums and Research	JOHN H. DAVIS, ACTING

Directors

Anacostia Community Museum	LORI D. YARRISH, ACTING
Archives of American Art	KATE HAW
Center for Astrophysics	CHARLES R. ALCOCK
Center for Folklife and Cultural Heritage	MICHAEL A. MASON
Cooper Hewitt, Smithsonian Design Museum	CAROLINE BAUMANN
Freer Gallery of Art and Arthur M. Sackler Gallery	JULIAN RABY
Hirshhorn Museum and Sculpture Garden	MELISSA CHIU
National Air and Space Museum	JOHN R. DAILEY
National Museum of African American History and Culture	LONNIE G. BUNCH III
National Museum of African Art	CHRISTINE KREAMER, ACTING
National Museum of American History	JOHN GRAY
National Museum of Natural History	KIRK JOHNSON
National Museum of the American Indian	KEVIN GOVER
National Portrait Gallery	KIM SAJET
National Postal Museum	ELLIOT GRUBER
National Zoological Park	DENNIS KELLY
Smithsonian American Art Museum and Renwick Gallery	STEPHANIE STEBICH
Smithsonian Asian Pacific American Center	LISA SASAKI
Smithsonian Environmental Research Center	ANSON H. HINES
Smithsonian Institution Archives	ANNE VAN CAMP
Smithsonian Institution Traveling Exhibition Service	MYRIAM SPRINGUEL
Smithsonian Latino Center	EDUARDO DÍAZ
Smithsonian Libraries	NANCY E. GWINN
Smithsonian Marine Station	VALERIE J. PAUL

Smithsonian Museum Conservation Institute Smithsonian Tropical Research Institute https://www.si.edu/about/people	ROBERT J. KOESTLER MATTHEW LARSEN
Inspector General https://www.si.edu/oig	CATHY L. HELM

The above list of key personnel was updated 09–2017.

The Smithsonian Institution increases the fund of human knowledge and diffuses that knowledge among people.

The Smithsonian Institution was created by an act of Congress on August 10, 1846 (20 U.S.C. 41 et seq.), to carry out the terms of the will of British scientist James Smithson (1765–1829), who in 1826 had bequeathed his entire estate to the United States "to found at Washington, under the name of the Smithsonian Institution, an establishment for the increase and diffusion of knowledge among men." On July 1, 1836, Congress accepted the legacy and pledged the faith of the United States to the charitable trust.

In September 1838, Smithson's legacy, which amounted to more than 100,000 gold sovereigns, was delivered to the mint at Philadelphia. Congress vested responsibility for administering the trust in the Secretary of the Smithsonian and the Smithsonian Board of Regents, composed of the Chief Justice, the Vice President, three Members of the Senate, three Members of the House of Representatives, and nine citizen members appointed by joint resolution of Congress. To carry out Smithson's mandate, the Institution executes the following functions: conducts scientific and scholarly research; publishes the results of studies, explorations, and investigations; preserves for study and reference more than 137 million artifacts, works of art, and scientific specimens; organizes exhibits representative of the arts, the sciences, American history, and world culture; shares Smithsonian resources and collections with communities throughout the Nation; and engages in educational programming and national and international cooperative research.

The Smithsonian Institution is an independent trust instrumentality of the United States that comprises the world's largest museum and research complex. It includes 19 museums and galleries, the National Zoo, and nine research facilities in several States and the Republic of Panama. The Institution is dedicated to public education, national service, and scholarship in the arts, sciences, history, and culture. Smithsonian activities are supported by its trust endowments and revenues; gifts, grants, and contracts; and funds appropriated to it by Congress. Admission to the museums in Washington, DC, is free. http://www.si.edu/About/History

Activities

Anacostia Community Museum   The Museum, located in the historic Fort Stanton neighborhood of Southeast Washington, serves as a national resource for exhibitions, historical documentation, and interpretive and educational programs relating to the impact of history and contemporary social issues on urban communities. http://anacostia.si.edu; | Email: ACMinfo@si.edu

For further information, contact the Anacostia Community Museum, 1901 Fort Place SE., Washington, DC 20020. Phone, 202-633-4820.

Archives of American Art   The Archives contains the Nation's largest collection of documentary materials reflecting the history of visual arts in the United States. On the subject of art in America, it is the largest archives in the world, holding more than 16 million documents. The Archives gathers, preserves, and microfilms the papers of artists, craftsmen, collectors, dealers, critics, and art societies. These papers include manuscripts, letters, diaries, notebooks, sketchbooks, business records, clippings, exhibition catalogs, transcripts of tape-recorded interviews, and photographs of artists and their work. http://www.aaa.si.edu

For further information, contact the Archives of American Art, Suite 2200, 750 Ninth Street NW., Washington, DC 20001. Phone, 202-633-7940.

Arthur M. Sackler Gallery   This Asian art museum opened in 1987 on the National Mall. Changing exhibitions drawn from major collections in the United States and abroad, as well as from the permanent holdings of the Sackler Gallery, are displayed in the distinctive below-ground museum. The Gallery's growing permanent collection is founded on a group of art objects from China, South and Southeast Asia, and the ancient Near East that were given to the Smithsonian by Arthur M. Sackler (1913–1987). The Museum's current collection features Persian manuscripts; Japanese paintings; ceramics, prints, and textiles; sculptures from India; and paintings and metalware from China, Korea, Japan, and Southeast Asia. The Sackler Gallery is connected by an underground exhibition space to the neighboring Freer Gallery. http://www.asia.si.edu; | Email: publicaffairsAsia@si.edu

For further information, contact the Arthur M. Sackler Gallery, 1050 Independence Avenue SW., Washington, DC 20560. Phone, 202-633-4880.

Center for Astrophysics   The Smithsonian Astrophysical Observatory and the Harvard College Observatory have coordinated research activities under a single director in a cooperative venture, Harvard-Smithsonian Center for Astrophysics. The Center's research activities are organized in the following areas of study: atomic and molecular physics, radio and geoastronomy, high-energy astrophysics, optical and infrared astronomy, planetary sciences, solar and stellar physics, and theoretical astrophysics. Research results are published in the Center Preprint Series and other technical and nontechnical bulletins and distributed to scientific and educational institutions around the world. http://www.cfa.harvard.edu/sao

For more information, contact the Smithsonian Astrophysical Observatory, 60 Garden Street, Cambridge, MA 02138. Phone, 617-495-7463.

Center for Folklife and Cultural Heritage   The Center is responsible for research, documentation, and presentation of grassroots cultural traditions. It maintains a documentary collection and produces Smithsonian Folkways Recordings, educational materials, documentary films, publications, and traveling exhibits, as well as the annual Smithsonian Folklife Festival on the National Mall. Recent Folklife festivals have featured a range of American music styles, a number of State tributes, and performers from around the world. Admission to the festival is free. The 2-week program includes Fourth of July activities on the National Mall. http://www.folklife.si.edu

For further information, contact the Center for Folklife and Cultural Heritage, Capital Gallery, Suite 2001, 600 Maryland Avenue SW., Washington, DC 20024. Phone, 202-633-1000.

Cooper Hewitt, Smithsonian Design Museum   The Museum is the only museum in the country devoted exclusively to historical and contemporary design. Collections include objects in such areas as applied arts and industrial design, drawings and prints, glass, metalwork, wallcoverings, and textiles. Changing exhibits and public programs seek to educate by exploring the role of design in daily life. http://cooperhewitt.org

For further information, contact the Cooper Hewitt, Smithsonian Design Museum, 2 East Ninety-First Street, New York, NY 10128. Phone, 212-849-8400.

Freer Gallery of Art   The building, the original collection, and an endowment were the gift of Charles Lang Freer (1854–1919). The Gallery houses one of the world's most renowned collections of Asian art, an important group of ancient Egyptian glass, early Christian manuscripts, and works by 19th- and early 20th-century American artists. The objects in the Asian collection represent the arts of East Asia, the Near East, and South and Southeast Asia, including paintings, manuscripts, scrolls, screens, ceramics, metalwork, glass, jade, lacquer, and sculpture. Members of the staff conduct research on objects in the collection and publish results in scholarly journals and books for general and scholarly audiences. http://www.asia.si.edu | Email: publicaffairsAsia@si.edu

For further information, contact the Freer Gallery of Art, Jefferson Drive at Twelfth Street SW., Washington, DC 20560. Phone, 202-633-4880.

Hirshhorn Museum and Sculpture Garden   From cubism to minimalism, the Museum houses major collections of modern and contemporary art. The nucleus of the collection is the gift and bequest of Joseph H. Hirshhorn (1899–1981). Supplementing the permanent collection are loan exhibitions. The Museum houses a collection research facility, a specialized art library, and a photographic archive, available for consultation by prior appointment. The outdoor sculpture garden is located nearby on the National Mall. There is an active program of public service and education, including docent tours, lectures on contemporary art and artists, and films of historic and artistic interest. http://www.hirshhorn.si.edu | Email: hmsginquiries@si.edu

For further information, contact the Hirshhorn Museum and Sculpture Garden, Seventh Street and Independence Avenue SW., Washington, DC 20560. Phone, 202-633-4674.

Museum Conservation Institute   The Institute researches preservation, conservation, and technical study and analysis of collection materials. Its researchers investigate the chemical and physical processes that are involved in the care of art, artifacts, and specimens and attempt to formulate conditions and procedures for storage, exhibit, and stabilization that optimize the preservation of these objects. In interdisciplinary collaborations with archeologists, anthropologists, and art historians, natural and physical scientists study and analyze objects from the collections and related materials to expand knowledge and understanding of their historical and scientific context. http://www.si.edu/mci

For further information, contact the Museum Conservation Institute, Museum Support Center, Suitland, MD 20746. Phone, 301-238-1240.

National Air and Space Museum   Created to memorialize the development and achievements of aviation and spaceflight, the Museum collects, displays, and preserves aeronautical and space flight artifacts of historical significance, as well as documentary and artistic materials related to air and space. Among its artifacts are full-size planes, models, and instruments.

Highlights of the collection include the Wright brothers' "Flyer," Charles Lindbergh's "Spirit of St. Louis," a Moon rock, and Apollo spacecraft. The exhibitions and study collections record the human leap into the air, the sky, and space beyond. They offer a concentrated presentation of flight craft of all types, spaceflight vehicles, and propulsion systems. The Museum's IMAX Theater and domed Einstein Planetarium are popular attractions. The Museum's Steven F. Udvar-Hazy Center, at Washington Dulles International Airport, features artifacts that include a space shuttle and the "Enola Gay" World War II bomber. http://airandspace.si.edu | Email: NASMVisitorServices@si.edu

For further information, contact the National Air and Space Museum, Sixth Street and Independence Avenue SW., Washington, DC 20560. Phone, 202-633-2214.

National Museum of African American History and Culture   Established in 2003, the Museum is the first national museum that documents exclusively African American art, culture, history, and life. http://www.nmaahc.si.edu | Email: NMAAHCinfo@si.edu

For further information, contact the National Museum of African American History and Culture, Capital Gallery, Suite 7001, 600 Maryland Avenue SW., Washington, DC 20024. Phone, 202-633-1000.

National Museum of African Art   This is the only art museum in the United States that portrays exclusively Africa's creative, visual traditions. Its research components, collection, exhibitions, and public programs make the Museum a primary source for the examination and discovery of African arts and culture. The collection includes works in wood, metal, fired clay, ivory, and fiber. The Eliot Elisofon Photographic Archives includes slides, photos, and film segments on Africa. There is also a specialized library. http://africa.si.edu

For further information, contact the National Museum of African Art, 950 Independence Avenue SW., Washington, DC 20560. Phone, 202-633-4600.

National Museum of American History   In pursuit of its fundamental mission to inspire a broader understanding of the United States and its people, the Museum provides learning opportunities, stimulates the imagination of visitors, and presents challenging ideas about the Nation's past. The Museum's exhibits provide a unique view of the American experience. Emphasis is placed upon innovative individuals representing a wide range of cultures, who have shaped our heritage, and upon science and the remaking of our world through technology. Exhibits draw upon strong collections in the sciences and engineering, agriculture, manufacturing, transportation, political memorabilia, costumes, musical instruments, coins, Armed Forces history, photography, computers, ceramics, and glass. Classic cars, icons of the American Presidency, First Ladies' gowns, the Star-Spangled Banner flag, Whitney's cotton gin, Morse's telegraph, the John Bull locomotive, Dorothy's ruby slippers from "The Wizard of Oz," and other American icons are highlights of the collection. http://www.americanhistory.si.edu | Email: info@si.edu

For further information, contact the National Museum of American History, Fourteenth Street and Constitution Avenue NW., Washington, DC 20560. Phone, 202-633-1000.

National Museum of Natural History
Dedicated to understanding the natural world and the place of humans in it, the Museum's permanent exhibitions focus on human cultures, Earth sciences, biology, and anthropology, with the most popular displays featuring gem stones such as the Hope Diamond, dinosaurs, insects, marine ecosystems, birds, and mammals. In 2010, the Museum celebrated its 100th anniversary with the opening of a new permanent exhibition, the David H. Koch Hall of Human Origins. An IMAX theater offers large-format films. The Museum's encyclopedic collections comprise more than 126 million specimens, making the Museum one of the world's foremost facilities for natural history research. The Museum's seven departments are anthropology, botany, entomology, invertebrate zoology, mineral sciences, paleobiology, and vertebrate zoology. Doctorate-level staff researchers ensure the continued growth and value of the collection by conducting studies in the field and laboratory. http://www.mnh.si.edu | Email: naturalexperience@si.edu

For further information, contact the National Museum of Natural History, Tenth Street and Constitution Avenue NW., Washington, DC 20560. Phone, 202-633-1000.

National Museum of the American Indian
The Museum was established in 1989, and the building on the National Mall opened September 2004. Much of the collection of the Museum is comprised of the collection of the former Heye Foundation in New York City. It is an institution of living cultures dedicated to the collection, preservation, study, and exhibition of the life, languages, literature, history, and arts of the Native peoples of the Americas. Highlights include Northwest Coast carvings; dance masks; pottery and weaving from the Southwest; painted hides and garments from the North American Plains; goldwork of the Aztecs, Incas, and Maya; and Amazonian featherwork. The National Museum of the American Indian also operates the George Gustav Heye Center at the Alexander Hamilton U.S. Custom House in New York City. http://americanindian.si.edu | Email: NMAI-info@si.edu

For further information, contact the National Museum of the American Indian, Fourth Street and Independence Avenue SW., Washington, DC 20560. Phone, 202-633-1000.

National Portrait Gallery
The Gallery was established in 1962 for the exhibition and study of portraiture depicting men and women who have made significant contributions to the history, development, and culture of the United States. The Gallery contains more than 19,000 works, including photographs and glass negatives. The first floor of the Gallery is devoted to changing exhibitions from the Gallery's collection of paintings, sculpture, prints, photographs, and drawings as well as to special portrait collections. Featured on the second floor are the permanent collection of portraits of eminent Americans and the Hall of Presidents, including the famous Gilbert Stuart portrait-from-life of George Washington. The two-story American Victorian Renaissance Great Hall on the third floor of the Gallery houses an exhibit of 20th-century Americans and is used for special events and public programs.

The Gallery shares a large library with the Smithsonian American Art Museum and the Archives of American Art. The education department offers public programs; outreach programs for adult groups; and walk-in and group tours. http://www.npg.si.edu | Email: npgnews@si.edu

For further information, contact the National Portrait Gallery, Eighth and F Streets NW., Washington, DC 20001. Phone, 202-633-8300.

National Postal Museum   The Museum houses the Nation's postal history and philatelic collection, the largest of its kind in the world, with more than 13 million objects. The Museum is devoted to the history of America's mail service, and major galleries include exhibits on mail service in colonial times and during the Civil War, the Pony Express, modern mail service, automation, mail transportation, and the art of letters, as well as displays of the Museum's priceless stamp collection. Highlights include three mail planes, a replica of a railway mail car, displays of historic letters, handcrafted mail boxes, and rare U.S. and foreign-issue stamps and covers. http://postalmuseum.si.edu

For further information, contact the National Postal Museum, 2 Massachusetts Avenue NE., Washington, DC 20001. Phone, 202-633-1000.

National Zoological Park   The National Zoo is an international leader in wildlife conservation, education, and research. Home to more than 2,000 animals, the Zoo encompasses 163 acres along Rock Creek Park in Northwest Washington. Exhibits include the David M. Rubenstein Family Giant Panda Habitat, where the giant pandas Mei Xiang and Tian Tian reside with their cub Bao Bao. Built to mimic the animals' natural habitat in China, it is part of the Zoo's Asia Trail, which also takes visitors through the habitats of red pandas, Asian small-clawed otters, fishing cats, sloth bears, and clouded leopards. Other highlights include the Elephant Trails, home to the Asian elephant Kandula, who was born at the Zoo in 2001; Amazonia, a 15,000-square-foot rain forest habitat; the Reptile Discovery Center, featuring African pancake tortoises and the world's largest lizards, Komodo dragons; and the Great Ape

House, home to gorillas, orangutans, and other primates. http://nationalzoo.si.edu

For further information, contact the National Zoo, 3001 Connecticut Avenue NW., Washington, DC 20008. Phone, 202- 633-4888.

Renwick Gallery   The Gallery, a branch of the Smithsonian American Art Museum, is dedicated to exhibiting crafts of all periods and to collecting 20th-century American crafts. It offers changing exhibitions of American crafts and decorative arts, both historical and contemporary, and a rotating selection from its permanent collection. The Gallery's grand salon is elegantly furnished in the Victorian style of the 1860s and 1870s. http://www.americanart.si.edu/renwick | Email: AmericanArtRenwick@si.edu

For further information, contact the Renwick Gallery, Seventeenth Street and Pennsylvania Avenue NW., Washington, DC 20006. Phone, 202-633-7970.

Smithsonian American Art Museum   The Museum's art collection spans centuries of American painting, sculpture, folk art, photography, and graphic art. A major center for research in American art, the Museum has contributed to such resources as the Inventory of American Paintings Executed Before 1914, the Smithsonian Art Index, and the Inventory of American Sculpture. The library, shared with the National Portrait Gallery, contains volumes on art, history, and biography, with special emphasis on the United States. The Donald W. Reynolds Center for American Art and Portraiture is home to the Smithsonian American Art Museum, the National Portrait Gallery, and the Archives of American Art. Hundreds of images from the collection and extensive information on its collections, publications, and activities are available on the Museum's Web site. http://www.americanart.si.edu | Email: AmericanArtInfo@si.edu

For further information, contact the Smithsonian American Art Museum, Eighth and F Streets NW., Washington, DC 20006. Phone, 202-633-7970.

Smithsonian Asian Pacific American Center   The Center seeks to enrich the appreciation of America's Asian Pacific heritage and empower Asian Pacific American communities in their sense of

inclusion within the national culture. http://
smithsonianapa.org | Email: apac@si.edu

For further information, contact the Asian Pacific
American Center's administrative office, Capital Gallery,
Suite 7065, MRC 516, P.O. Box 37012, Washington, DC
20013-7012. Phone, 202-633-2691.

Smithsonian Environmental Research
Center (SERC)
The Center is the leading
national research center for understanding
environmental issues in the coastal zone.
SERC is dedicated to increasing knowledge
of the biological and physical processes
that sustain life on Earth. The Center,
located near the Chesapeake Bay, trains
future generations of scientists to address
ecological questions of the Nation and the
globe. http://www.serc.si.edu

For further information, contact the Smithsonian
Environmental Research Center, 647 Contees Wharf
Road, Edgewater, MD 21037. Phone, 443-482-2200.

Smithsonian Institution Archives
The
Smithsonian Institution Archives acquires,
preserves, and makes available for research
the official records of the Smithsonian
Institution and the papers of individuals and
organizations associated with the Institution
or with its work. These holdings document
the growth of the Smithsonian and the
development of American science, history,
and art. http://siarchives.si.edu

For further information, contact the Smithsonian
Institution Archives, Capital Gallery, Suite 3000, 600
Maryland Avenue SW., Washington, DC 20024. Phone,
202-633-5870.

Smithsonian Institution Traveling Exhibition
Service (SITES)
Since 1952, SITES has
been committed to making Smithsonian
exhibitions available to millions of people
who cannot view them firsthand at the
Smithsonian museums. Exhibitions on art,
history, and science travel to more than 250
locations each year. http://www.sites.si.edu

For further information, contact the Smithsonian
Institution Traveling Exhibition Service, Suite 7103, 470
L'Enfant Plaza SW., Washington, DC 20024. Phone,
202-633-3120.

Smithsonian Latino Center
The Center
promotes Latino presence within the
Smithsonian Institution. It is not represented
in one physical location; rather, it works
collaboratively with the Institution's
museums and research centers to ensure that
the contributions of the Latino community

in the arts, history, national culture, and
scientific achievement are celebrated,
explored, presented, and preserved. The
Center supports collections and archives,
exhibitions, public and educational
programs, research, and Web-based content
and virtual platforms. It also manages
leadership and professional development
programs for emerging scholars, museum
professionals, and Latino youth. http://latino.
si.edu/Home

For further information, contact the Smithsonian Latino
Center at Capital Gallery, 600 Maryland Avenue SW.,
MRC 512, Washington, DC 20013-7012. Phone, 202-
633-1240.

Smithsonian Libraries
The Smithsonian
Institution Libraries include more than 1
million volumes (among them, 40,000 rare
books) with strengths in natural history, art,
science, humanities, and museology. Many
volumes are available through interlibrary
loan. http://library.si.edu

For further information, contact the Smithsonian
Institution Libraries, Tenth Street and Constitution
Avenue NW., Washington, DC 20560. Phone, 202-633-
2240.

Smithsonian Marine Station at Fort
Pierce
The research institute features a
state-of-the-art laboratory where Station
scientists catalog species and study marine
plants and animals. Among the most
important projects being pursued at the site
is the search for possible causes of fishkills,
including Pfiesteria and other organisms.
http://www.sms.si.edu

For further information, contact the Smithsonian Marine
Station–Fort Pierce, 701 Seaway Drive, Fort Pierce, FL
34949. Phone, 772-462-6220.

Smithsonian Tropical Research Institute
(STRI)
The Institute is a research
organization for advanced studies of tropical
ecosystems. Headquartered in the Republic
of Panama, STRI maintains extensive
facilities in the Western Hemisphere
tropics. It is the base of a corps of tropical
researchers who study the evolution,
behavior, ecology, and history of tropical
species of systems ranging from coral reefs
to rain forests. http://www.stri.org

For further information, contact the Smithsonian
Tropical Research Institute, 1100 Jefferson Drive SW.,
Suite 3123, Washington, DC 20560. Phone, 202-633-
4700. Phone, 011-507-212-8000 (Panama).

Sources of Information

Business Opportunities   Information on procurement of supplies, property management and utilization services for Smithsonian Institution organizations, and construction contracts may be obtained from the Director, Office of Contracting, Smithsonian Institution, 2011 Crystal Drive, Suite 350, Arlington, VA 22202. Phone, 202-633-7290. http://www.si.edu/se/seproductsubmissions.aspx

Career Opportunities   Employment information is available from the Office of Human Resources, Smithsonian Institution, Capital Gallery, Suite 5060, 600 Maryland Avenue SW., Washington, DC 20560. Phone, 202-633-6370. http://www.sihr.si.edu

In 2016, the Smithsonian Institution ranked 7th among 27 midsize Government agencies in the Best Places To Work Agency Rankings. http://bestplacestowork.org/BPTW/rankings/detail/SM00

Education / Research   Write to the Directors of the following offices at the Smithsonian Institution, Washington, DC 20560: Office of Fellowships and Internships, Smithsonian Center for Folklife and Cultural Heritage, Smithsonian Science Education Center, and Smithsonian Center for Learning and Digital Access. http://www.smithsonianofi.com; http://www.folklife.si.edu; https://ssec.si.edu; http://smithsonianeducation.org

Frequently Asked Questions (FAQs)   The Smithsonian Institution posts answers to FAQs on its website. https://www.si.edu/faqs

Media Affairs   Members of the press may contact the Smithsonian Office of Public Affairs, 1000 Jefferson Drive SW., Washington, DC 20560. Phone, 202-633-2400. http://newsdesk.si.edu/contacts

Memberships   For information on the Friends of the Smithsonian, write to PO Box 37012, MRC 712 Washington, DC 20013-7012. Phone, 202-633-6300. http://smithsonianmembership.com | Email: membership@si.edu

For information on the Resident Associate Program, write to Smithsonian Associates, PO Box 23293, Washington, DC 20026-3293. Phone, 202-633-3030. http://residentassociates.org

For information on the Smithsonian National Associate Program, call 800-766-2149. http://www.si.edu/Membership

For information on the National Air and Space Society, call 202-633-2603. http://www.nasm.si.edu/getinvolved/membership | Email: MembershipNASM@si.edu

For information on the Friends of the National Zoo, call 202-633-3038. http://nationalzoo.si.edu/Audiences/Members

For information on National Museum of the American Indian membership, call 800-242-6624. http://americanindian.si.edu | Email: NMAImember@si.edu

Organizational Chart   The Smithsonian Institution's organizational chart is accessible online in Portable Document Format (PDF) for viewing and downloading. https://www.si.edu/Content/Pdf/About/Smithsonian-organizational-chart.pdf

Photographs   Photographs and slides from the Smithsonian photographic archives are available to researchers, publishers, Government agencies, and the general public. A searchable database of images is available online. Purchase or use of images may require permission from the Smithsonian curatorial unit that holds copyright. For assistance, contact Smithsonian Photographic Services. Phone, 202-633-1933. http://www.si.edu/Collections | Email: photos@si.edu

Publications   The Smithsonian Institution's annual reports, starting with the year 2004, are available online as Portable Document Format (PDF) files. For information on acquiring hardcopies of reports, call 202-633-1000. http://www.si.edu/About/Annual-Report | Email: info@si.edu

Smithsonian Books, in collaboration with the Smithsonian Institution, publishes narrative nonfiction books on culture, history, science and technology, and the arts, as well as signature illustrated books based on Smithsonian museums and their collections. Random House Publisher Services distribute these titles. http://www.smithsonianbooks.com

Smithsonian Institution Scholarly Press, in conjunction with Rowman and Littlefield Publishing Group, Inc., publishes the research and other scholarly contributions of Smithsonian authors. http://www.scholarlypress.si.edu

Subscribe to the "Smithsonian Magazine" online. Phone, 800-766-2149. http://www.smithsonianmag.com | Email: smithsonian@customersvc.com

Subscribe to "Air and Space Magazine" online. Phone, 800-513-3081. http://www.airspacemag.com/?no-ist | Email: airandspace@customersvc.com

Social Media The Smithsonian Institution has a Facebook account. https://www.facebook.com/Smithsonian

The Smithsonian Institution tweets announcements and other newsworthy items on Twitter. https://twitter.com/smithsonian

The Smithsonian Institution posts videos on its YouTube channel. https://www.youtube.com/user/SmithsonianVideos

Tours For information on museum and gallery tours, contact the Smithsonian Information Center, 1000 Jefferson Drive SW., Washington, DC 20560. Phone, 202-633-1000. School groups are welcome. The benefits of various memberships and their levels include special guided tours. http://www.si.edu/Visit/GroupTours

Visitor Information The Smithsonian Information Center, located in the original Smithsonian building, commonly known as The Castle, provides general orientation through films, computer interactive programs, and visitor information specialists to help members and the public learn about the national collections, museum events, exhibitions, and special programs. Write to the Smithsonian Information Center, 1000 Jefferson Drive SW., Washington, DC 20560. Phone, 202-633-1000. http://www.si.edu/Visit/Hours

An accessibility map of Smithsonian museums on and near the National Mall is available online. https://www.si.edu/content/ovs/accessmapsindd.pdf

Volunteer Opportunities The Smithsonian Institution welcomes volunteers and offers a variety of service opportunities. For information, write to the Office of Visitor Services, 1000 Jefferson Drive SW., Washington, DC 20560. Phone, 202-633-1000. http://www.si.edu/Volunteer; http://www.nga.gov/content/ngaweb/contact-us/department-list

For further information, contact the Smithsonian Information Center, 1000 Jefferson Drive SW., Washington, DC 20560. Phone, 202-633-1000. TDD, 202-357-1729.

John F. Kennedy Center for the Performing Arts

John F. Kennedy Center for the Performing Arts, Washington, DC 20566
Phone, 202-467-4600. Internet, http://www.kennedy-center.org

Chair	DAVID M. RUBENSTEIN
President	DEBORAH F. RUTTER
http://www.kennedy-center.org/pages/about/ourpeople	

National Symphony Orchestra

Music Director	GIANANDREA NOSEDA
http://www.kennedy-center.org/artist/A58901	

The Suzanne Farrell Ballet

Artistic Director	SUZANNE FARRELL
http://www.kennedy-center.org/sfb/biography	

Washington National Opera

Artistic Director	FRANCESCA ZAMBELLO
http://www.kennedy-center.org/wno/MTO/ArtDir	

The above list of key personnel was updated 09–2017.

The Kennedy Center is the only official memorial to President John F. Kennedy in Washington, DC. The Center presents a year-round program of dance, drama, music, and opera from the United States and abroad.

Sources of Information

Business Opportunities   Opportunities are posted on the Federal Business Opportunities Web site. For more information, contact The John F. Kennedy Center for the Performing Arts, Washington, DC 20566. https://www.fbo.gov

Career Opportunities   Job descriptions of open positions are available online. http://www.kennedy-center.org/jobs

The John F. Kennedy Center for the Performing Arts offers internships for undergraduate and graduate students and for recent college graduates. http://education.kennedy-center.org/education/internships/overview.html

In partnership with American University, the Center offers a merit-based, 9-month fellowship in art management. http://education.kennedy-center.org/education/internships/fellowships.html

Education / Research   For information on education programs, contact The John F. Kennedy Center for the Performing Arts, Washington, DC 20566. Phone, 202-416-8000. http://www.kennedy-center.org/education

Free Performances   Free performances are given every day at 6 p.m. on the Millennium Stage in the Grand Foyer. https://www.kennedy-center.org/video/upcoming

History   In January of 1964, not long after the death of President John F. Kennedy, Congress designated the National Cultural Center as a "living memorial" to the slain President and authorized 23 million dollars to help build what is known today as the John F. Kennedy Center for the Performing Arts. Before the end of that year, enough artwork, building materials, and additional funds had been donated to start construction. With a gold-plated spade that had been used to break ground at both the Lincoln and Jefferson Memorials, President Lyndon B. Johnson symbolically removed the first soil from the new site. The Center opened to the public in 1971, more than a decade after President Dwight D. Eisenhower and legislators, from both parties, had taken initial steps toward realizing this vision. To learn more about the people who imagined a cultural center for the Nation, those who supported its realization, and the emergence of the John F. Kennedy Center for the Performing Arts as an iconic institution of the arts, visit the "History" Web page. http://www.kennedy-center.org/pages/about/history

Live Streaming   The Center live streams artists while they perform. http://www.kennedy-center.org/video/live

Memberships   For information on national and local activities, including the bimonthly "Kennedy Center News" for members, visit an information desk inside The John F. Kennedy Center for the Performing Arts. Or, contact Member Services, The John F. Kennedy Center for the Performing Arts, Washington, DC 20566. Phone, 202-416-8310. http://www.kennedy-center.org/membership | Email: membership@kennedy-center.org

Social Media   John F. Kennedy Center for the Performing Arts has a Facebook account. https://www.facebook.com/KennedyCenter

The Center tweets announcements and other newsworthy items on Twitter. https://twitter.com/KenCen

The Center posts videos on its YouTube channel. https://www.youtube.com/user/TheKennedyCenter

Special Functions   For information on using the facilities for special functions, contact the Office of Special Events, The John F. Kennedy Center for the Performing Arts, Washington, DC 20566. Phone, 202-416-8000. https://www.kennedy-center.org/rental

Theater Operations   For information on using the theaters, contact the booking manager at The John F. Kennedy Center for the Performing Arts, Washington, DC 20566. Phone, 202-416-8032. http://www.kennedy-center.org/pages/theaterrental

Tickets   Tickets for admission to performances may be purchased at the box office, by mail, by phone using instant-charge, or online. Phone, 202-467-4600. TTY, 202-416-8524. https://www.kennedy-center.org/tickets

The Center posts answers to frequently asked ticket-related questions. http://www.kennedy-center.org/contact/topic/1

Tours   The Friends of the Kennedy Center volunteers provide visitor services. Tours are available free of charge on weekdays, 10 a.m.–5 p.m., and on weekends, 10 a.m.–1 p.m.

https://www.kennedy-center.org/pages/visitor/tours

Videos   The Center regularly posts short videos of artists performing. Its Web site has an expanding collection of over 2,000 selections. http://www.kennedy-center.org/Video/recentVideos

Volunteer Opportunities   For information on volunteer opportunities, contact Friends of the Kennedy Center, 2700 F Street NW, Washington, DC 20566. Phone, 202-416-8000. http://www.kennedy-center.org/support/volunteers; http://www.kennedy-center.org/contact

For further information, contact The John F. Kennedy Center for the Performing Arts. Phone, 202-467-4600.

National Gallery of Art

4th and Constitution Avenue NW., Washington, DC 20565
Phone, 202-737-4215. Internet, http://www.nga.gov

President	FREDERICK W. BEINECKE
Director	EARL A. POWELL III

Activities

The National Gallery of Art administers a world-class collection of painting, sculpture, and the graphic arts. The West Building includes European (13th–early 20th century) and American (18th–early 20th century) works. An extensive survey of Italian painting and sculpture, including the only painting by Leonardo da Vinci in the Americas, is on display in the Gallery. Rich in Dutch masters and French impressionists, the collection offers superb surveys of American, British, Flemish, Spanish, and 15th- and 16th-century German art, as well as Renaissance medals and bronzes, Chinese porcelains, and about 117,000 works of graphic art from the 12th century to the present day. The East Building collections and Sculpture Garden contain important works by major 20th-century artists. The Gallery relies on public and private resources. Federal appropriations support its operations and maintenance. Private donations and funds allow it to acquire artwork, as well as to offer a variety of special programs. For example, a fellowship program promotes graduate and postgraduate research, an extension service provides free education resources to millions of people each year, and other programs educate schoolchildren and the public.

Sources of Information

Business Opportunities   For more information, contact the National Gallery of Art, Office of Procurement and Contracts, 2000B South Club Drive, Landover, MD 20785. Phone, 202-842-6745. Fax, 202-312-2792. https://www.fbo.gov/index?s=main&mode=list&tab=list

Calendar   The full calendar of events is available online. To subscribe to the quarterly brochure of seasonal exhibition and programming highlights, visit the Gallery's Web site or call 202-842-6662. http://www.nga.gov/content/ngaweb/calendar.html | Email: calendar@nga.gov

Career Opportunities   The National Gallery of Art relies on approximately 1,000 employees to carry out its mission. Some positions require a background in art history or design; however, other positions—like salesperson, security guard, and visitor services aide—support the museum's daily operations and are less specialized. The National Gallery of Art also employs accountants, administrators, facilities managers, fundraisers, information systems specialists, librarians, and other professionals with technical expertise. Phone, 202-842-6282. http://www.nga.gov/content/ngaweb/opportunities/employment-opportunities.html | Email: staffing@nga.gov

The National Gallery of Art offers internships and opportunities for fellows. Conservation and curatorial fellowships are available, as well as Center for Advanced Study in the Visual Arts (CASVA) fellowships. http://www.nga.gov/content/ngaweb/opportunities/interns-and-fellows.html

The National Gallery of Art offers a range of volunteer opportunities. Volunteers serve as docents, manage the information desks at the entrances to the East and West Buildings, work in the library, and help in the horticulture division. Local high school students can participate in the teen volunteer program. http://www.nga.gov/content/ngaweb/opportunities/volunteer-opportunities.html

Center for Advanced Study in the Visual Arts (CASVA)   The CASVA is a research institute that supports study of the production, use, and cultural meaning of architecture, art, artifacts, film, photography, and urbanism. It offers fellowships, organizes scholarly meetings, produces publications, and supports research. These activities are privately funded through endowments and grants to the National Gallery of Art. Phone, 202-842-6480. http://www.nga.gov/content/ngaweb/research/casva.html | Email: casva@nga.gov

Concerts   Concerts by accomplished musicians are open to the public without charge. Seating starts 30 minutes before the performance on a first-come, first-seated basis. Phone, 202-842-6941. http://www.nga.gov/content/ngaweb/calendar/concerts.html

Educational Resources   The Gallery's free loan program allows community groups, educational institutions, individuals, and nonprofit television stations nationwide to borrow teaching packets and DVDs. Dozens of lessons and activities are also accessible on the Gallery's Web site. For more information, including the free catalog of education resources, contact the Department of Education Resources, National Gallery of Art, 2000B South Club Drive, Landover, MD 20785. Phone, 202-842-6273. http://www.nga.gov/content/ngaweb/education/learningresources.html | Email: edresources@nga.gov

Family Programs   The Gallery offers free family programs—children's films, music

performances, storytelling, and workshops— that are suitable for children ages 4 and up. Phone, 202-789-3030. http://www.nga.gov/content/ngaweb/education/families.html | Email: family@nga.gov

Films   An ongoing program of classic cinema, documentary, avant-garde, and area premieres takes place each weekend. Seating is on a first-come, first-seated basis, and admission is free. Doors open approximately 30 minutes before each show. Visiting filmmakers and scholars discuss films with the audiences following some screenings. Phone, 202-842-6799. http://www.nga.gov/content/ngaweb/calendar/film-programs.html | Email: film-department@nga.gov

Frequently Asked Questions (FAQs)   The National Gallery of Art posts answers to FAQs on its Web site. http://www.nga.gov/content/ngaweb/contact-us.html

Ice-Skating Rink   Each winter, the National Gallery of Art opens its ice rink in the Sculpture Garden. The seasonal skating schedule is posted online in November. http://www.nga.gov/content/ngaweb/visit/ice-rink.html

Image Collections   The Department of Image Collections serves as the National Gallery of Art's research center for images of Western art and architecture. The collections now contain over 14 million digital images, microforms, negatives, photographs, and slides, making this resource one of the largest of its kind. Gallery staff, Center for Advanced Study in the Visual Arts (CASVA) members, visiting scholars, and serious adult researchers regularly use the collections. The library is accessible by appointment every Monday, noon–4:30 p.m., and Tuesday– Friday, 10 a.m.–4:30 p.m., except on Federal holidays. Phone, 202-842-6026. http://www.nga.gov/content/ngaweb/research/library/imagecollections.html

Lectures   Lecture events are open to the public, and admission is free. Seating is available on a first-come, first-seated basis. http://www.nga.gov/content/ngaweb/calendar/lectures.html

Library   The National Gallery of Art Library maintains a collection of more than 400,000 books and periodicals on the history, theory, and criticism of art and architecture. The collection's holdings emphasize Western art from the Middle Ages to the present and American art from the colonial era to the present. The library is accessible by appointment every Monday, noon–4:30 p.m., and Tuesday–Friday, 10 a.m.–4:30 p.m., except on Federal holidays. Phone, 202-842-6511. http://www.nga.gov/content/ngaweb/research/library/About.html

Memberships The Gallery offers three membership levels of annual giving: The Circle, The Tower Project, and The Exhibition Circle. Circle members contribute to conservation programs, special exhibitions, and research. Tower Project members promote contemporary artists by supporting modern and contemporary exhibitions in the Tower Gallery of the East Building. Exhibition Circle members provide funding for exhibitions. For more information on membership levels and their benefits, contact The Circle, National Gallery of Art, 2000B South Club Drive, Landover, MD 20785. Phone, 202-842-6450. Fax, 202 789-4577. http://www.nga.gov/content/ngaweb/support/membership.html | Email: circle@nga.gov

News The National Gallery of Art posts recent news releases on its Web site. http://www.nga.gov/content/ngaweb/press.html | Email: pressinfo@nga.gov

An online subscription form is available to sign up for announcements, newsletters, notifications, and updates on acquisitions and exhibitions; activities, projects, and programs; and other topics. http://subscribe.nga.gov/subscription_form_ngart.cfm

NGAkids NGAkids offers interactive activities and adventures with artwork from the Gallery's collection and an animated tale set in the Gallery's Sculpture Garden. http://www.nga.gov/content/ngaweb/education/kids.html

Photographs Photographs that are not on display may be viewed by appointment. Phone, 202-842-6144. Email: photographs@nga.gov

Publications The Gallery Shops sell publications on the Gallery's collections and quality reproductions of artwork. Purchases may be made online or by calling 800-697-9350. https://shop.nga.gov

Public Wi-Fi Wireless internet service is available throughout the Gallery to visitors who are 18 years old and older or at least 13 years old with permission from a parent or guardian. The network name is "NGA_Public_WiFi," and a password is not needed. A user must, however, supply his or her own Internet device and agree to the "Terms and Conditions of Use." http://www.nga.gov/content/ngaweb/visit/public-wifi.html

Tours The education division offers daily guided talks and tours in the galleries. Phone, 202-842-6247. http://www.nga.gov/content/ngaweb/visit/tours-and-guides.html

Visitor Services The Visitor Services Office assists those with special needs, responds to written and telephone requests, and helps visitors plan their stay in the Washington, DC, area. For more information, contact the National Gallery of Art, Office of Visitor Services, 2000B South Club Drive, Landover, MD 20785. Phone, 202-842-6691. http://www.nga.gov/content/ngaweb/visit.html

Works on Paper Works of art on paper that are not on display may be viewed by appointment. Phone, 202-842-6380 (European works). Phone, 202-842-6605 (American works). http://www.nga.gov/content/ngaweb/research/make-an-appointment.html | Email: printstudyrooms@nga.gov; http://www.nga.gov/content/ngaweb/contact-us.html

For further information, contact the National Gallery of Art. Phone, 202-737-4215.

Woodrow Wilson International Center for Scholars

Scholar Administration Office, Woodrow Wilson Center, One Woodrow Wilson Plaza, 1300 Pennsylvania Avenue NW., Washington, DC 20004-3027
Phone, 202-691-4000. Fax, 202-691-4001. Internet, http://www.wilsoncenter.org

Director / President / Chief Executive Officer   JANE L. HARMAN
https://www.wilsoncenter.org/person/jane-harman

The above list of key personnel was updated 10–2017.

Activities

Created by an Act of Congress in 1968, the Woodrow Wilson International Center for Scholars is a national, living memorial honoring the legacy of President Woodrow Wilson. The Wilson Center, headquartered in Washington, DC, and supported by both public and private funds, provides a strictly nonpartisan space for scholars and policymakers to interact. By conducting relevant, timely research and promoting dialogue from diverse perspectives, the Center works to address critical current and emerging challenges confronting the United States and the world. https://www.wilsoncenter.org/about-the-wilson-center

Sources of Information

Career Opportunities   Career opportunities at the Center are posted online. For more information, contact the Office of Human Resources, One Woodrow Wilson Plaza, 1300 Pennsylvania Avenue NW., 3d Floor, Washington, DC 20004-3027. http://www.wilsoncenter.org/opportunities/Job | Email: jobs@wilsoncenter.org

Donations   An online form is available for making tax-deductible contributions to support dialogue and scholarship in public policy. Gifts may be directed to a specific program by using the "Designation" drop-down menu. "Unrestricted" gifts allow the Center to build its overall capacity and meet areas of greatest need. Phone, 202-691-4171. https://support.wilsoncenter.org/donation_form | Email: development@wilsoncenter.org

Fellowships   The Center offers residential fellowships that allow academics, public officials, journalists, business professionals, and others to pursue their research and writing at the Center while interacting with policymakers in Washington. The Center also invites public policy scholars and senior scholars from a variety of disciplines to conduct research for varying lengths of time in residence. Phone, 202-691-4000. http://www.wilsoncenter.org/fellowships-grants

Internships   The Center has a year-round need for interns to assist the program and projects staff and to act as research assistants for scholars and fellows. Phone, 202-691-4053. http://www.wilsoncenter.org/opportunities/Internship

Media Affairs   Members of the press may contact the Center at 202-691-4217. http://www.wilsoncenter.org/media-access-to-the-wilson-center

Multimedia   Wide ranging in scope, "Wilson Center On Demand" serves as a hub for insightful analysis of and commentary on ideas and issues. https://www.wilsoncenter.org/wilson-center-demand

Presidential Memorial Exhibit   The Center houses the Woodrow Wilson Presidential Memorial Exhibit, which features memorabilia, historical information, photographs, several short films, and a memorial hall with quotations. The exhibit is open weekdays, 8:30 a.m.–5 p.m. Admission is free. Phone, 202-691-4000. http://www.wilsoncenter.org/woodrow-wilson-presidential-memorial-exhibit-and-learning-center | Email: wwics@wilsoncenter.org

Publications   The Center publishes policy briefs and research reports, as well as books written by staff and visiting scholars and fellows, through the Wilson Center Press. Phone, 202-691-4000. http://www.wilsoncenter.org/publications

Every 3 months, "The Wilson Quarterly" magazine releases a cluster of content exploring a single topic from diverse perspectives. This free, online magazine examines culture, current events, ideas, and the people affected by them. http://wilsonquarterly.com/quarterly | Email: wq@wilsoncenter.org

Research   The Center's "Research" Web page allows visitors to explore the pressing global challenges confronting the U.S. policy community and general public today. https://www.wilsoncenter.org/research
Social Media   The Center maintains an account on Facebook. https://www.facebook.com/woodrowwilsoncenter

The Center posts openings for jobs and internships on its LinkedIn page. https://www.linkedin.com/company/woodrow-wilson-international-center-for-scholars

The Center tweets announcements, news, and other noteworthy items on Twitter. https://twitter.com/thewilsoncenter

The Center posts videos on its YouTube channel. https://www.youtube.com/user/woodrowwilsoncenter
Visitor Services   Events, unless otherwise noted, are free and open to the public. Photo identification is required for entry. A listing of events at the Center is available online. http://www.wilsoncenter.org/events; http://www.wilsoncenter.org

For further information, contact the Woodrow Wilson International Center for Scholars, One Woodrow Wilson Plaza, 1300 Pennsylvania Avenue NW., Washington, DC 20004-3027. Phone, 202-691-4000. Fax, 202-691-4001.

State Justice Institute

11951 Freedom Drive, Suite 1020, Reston, VA 20190
Phone, 571-313-8843. Internet, http://www.sji.gov | Email: contact@sji.gov

Board of Directors
Judges

Treasurer	DAVID V. BREWER
	JONATHAN LIPPMAN
	WILFREDO MARTINEZ
Chair	JOHN D. MINTON, JR.
Secretary	GAYLE A. NACHTIGAL
	CHASE T. ROGERS
Public Sector Members	
	ISABEL FRAMER
	MARSHA J. RABITEAU
	HERNÁN D. VERA
	(VACANCY)
State Court Administrator	
Vice Chair	DANIEL J. BECKER
http://www.sji.gov/about-sji/board-of-directors	
Executive Director	JONATHAN D. MATTIELLO
http://www.sji.gov/about-sji/executivedirector	

The above list of key personnel was updated 10–2019.

The State Justice Institute supports the Nation's judicial system and the public that it serves.

Establishment and Organization

On November 8, 1984, President Ronald W. Reagan approved Public Law 98–620. Title II of that statute, which is commonly cited as the State Justice Institute Act of 1984, established the State Justice Institute as a private nonprofit corporation whose purpose is "to further the development and adoption of improved judicial administration in State courts in the United States" (98 Stat. 3336). http://www.sji.gov/wp/wp-content/uploads/SJI_Authorization.pdf

Statutory descriptions of the SJI's duties, Board of Directors, officers and employees, grants and contracts, activities, administrative provisions, Presidential coordination, records and reports, and audits, are codified in chapter 113, sections 10701–10713, of 42 U.S.C. https://uscode. house.gov/view.xhtml?path=/prelim@title42/ chapter113&edition=prelim

A Board of Directors that comprises 11 members—six judges, a State court administrator, and four members from the public sector— supervises the SJI. The President appoints the members, by the advice and with the consent of the Senate, to 3-year terms. A member cannot be reappointed to more than two consecutive terms immediately following his or her initial term. The Chair of the Board is selected from among the members, by the members. No more than two of the public sector members can affiliate with the same political party. https://uscode.house.gov/ view.xhtml?req=granuleid:USC-prelim-title42-section10703&num=0&edition=pr elim

The SJI does not post an organizational chart on its website.

Activities

The SJI develops solutions to common issues faced by State courts; provides practical products to judges and court staff; ensures that effective approaches in one State are quickly and economically shared with other courts nationwide; and supports national, regional, and instate educational programs to accelerate the transfer of solutions. To accomplish these broad objectives, the SJI is authorized to provide funds through grants, cooperative agreements, and contracts to the State courts and to organizations that support them. http://www.sji.gov/about-sji

The Sources of Information were updated 10–2019.

Sources of Information

Archived Records   "Records of the State Justice Institute, 1990 - 2013" have been accessioned by the National Archives and Records Administration. The collection identifier is SJI. https://catalog.archives.gov/ id/7459146

Budget Request   The SJI posted its "Fiscal Year 2019 Budget Request" to Congress in Portable Document Format (PDF) on its website. http://www.sji.gov/wp/wp-content/ uploads/FY-2019-SJI-Budget-Request.pdf

Forms   Documents to view and print are posted online in Portable Document Format (PDF). These documents include a number of forms: assurances, consultant rate, disclosure of lobbying activities, grant application, project budget, reimbursement request, and State approval certificate. http://www.sji.gov/forms

Grants   Information on various award and grant types—curriculum adaptation and training grants, the education support program, project grants, and technical assistance grants—is available online. http:// www.sji.gov/grants

History   In 2014, the SJI published its 30th Anniversary Report, which offers a retrospective overview of achievements over the past three decades. http://www. sji.gov/wp/wp-content/uploads/SJI-30th-Anniversary-Report.pdf

Investment   The SJI has posted its priority investment areas for fiscal year 2020. http:// www.sji.gov/priority-investment-areas

News   The SJI posts news items on its website. http://www.sji.gov/news

Newsletter   Readers may subscribe to the monthly "SJI Newsletter" online. http://www. sji.gov/newsletter-archives

Social Media   The SJI has a Facebook account. https://www.facebook.com/SJI.gov

The SJI tweets announcements and other newsworthy items on Twitter. https://twitter. com/statejustice

---

United States Holocaust Memorial Museum

100 Raoul Wallenberg Place, SW., Washington, DC 20024-2126
Phone, 202-488-0400. TTY, 202-488-0406. Internet, http://www.ushmm.org

U.S. Holocaust Memorial Council

Arizona

Andrew M. Cohn
Susan G. Levine

California

Laurence M. Baer
Susan E. Lowenberg
Deborah A. Oppenheimer
Eric P. Ortner
Elliot J. Schrage
Clemantine Wamariya
Jeremy M. Weinstein
Daniel G. Weiss

District of Columbia

Vice Chair Allan M. Holt

Joshua B. Bolten
Norman L. Eisen
Raffi Freedman-Gurspan
David M. Marchick
Benjamin J. Rhodes

Florida

Walter R. Allen, Jr.
Jeffrey P. Feingold
Murray J. Laulicht
Andrew J. Weinstein

Illinois

Jordan T. Goodman
Samuel N. Gordon
Priscilla Levine Kersten
Tamar Newberger
Michael P. Polsky
Richard S. Price
Maureen Schulman

Indiana

Lee A. Feinstein
Cindy Simon Skjodt

New Jersey

Ethel C. Brooks
Betty Pantirer Schwartz

New York

Chair Howard M. Lorber

Tom A. Bernstein
Michael S. Bosworth
Jonathan W. Burkan
Sara Darehshori
Helene Feldman
David M. Flaum

Michael H. Posner
Daniel J. Rosen
Menachem Z. Rosensaft
Howard D. Unger

Maryland

Edward P. Lazarus
Bradley D. Wine

Other States

Massachusetts
Missouri
New Hampshire
Ohio
Texas
Virginia
Washington
West Virginia

Jonathan S. Lavine
Sam M. Devinki
Daniel Benjamin
Ronald Ratner
Fred S. Zeidman
Melissa Rogers
Eric A. LeVine
Irvin N. Shapell

England

Stuart A. Levey

https://www.ushmm.org/information/about-the-museum/council

Congressional Members

Florida
Georgia
Illinois
New York
Tennessee

Rep. Theodore E. Deutch
Rep. John R. Lewis
Rep. Bradley S. Schneider
Rep. Lee M. Zeldin
Rep. David F. Kustoff

Florida
Maryland
South Carolina
Vermont

Sen. Marco A. Rubio
Sen. Benjamin L. Cardin
Timothy E. Scott
Sen. Bernard Sanders
(vacancy)

Ex Officio Members—Nonvoting

Executive Branch Departments
Education
Interior
State

Philip H. Rosenfelt
(vacancy)
Thomas K. Yazdgerdi

General Counsel to the Council

Gerard Leval

Council Staff

Museum Director
Internal Auditor
https://www.ushmm.org/information/about-the-museum/
    executive-biographies/bloomfield

Sara J. Bloomfield
Mel Schwartz

Museum Administration

Museum Director
Deputy Museum Director

Sara J. Bloomfield
Sarah Ogilvie

General Counsel
Senior Advisors

Ronald F. Cuffe

Marketing

Michelle Stein

Strategy	CAMERON HUDSON
Chief Officers	
Development	JORDAN TANNENBAUM
Financial Officer	POLLY POVEJSIL HEATH
Information	JOSEPH KRAUS
Museum Operations	TANELL COLEMAN
Program Officer	SARAH OGILVIE
Directors	
Constituency Engagement	DIANE SALTZMAN
International Affairs	PAUL SHAPIRO
Levine Institute for Holocaust Education	YARIV LAPID
Mandel Center for Advanced Holocaust Studies	WENDY LOWER, ACTING
National Institute for Holocaust Documentation	MICHAEL GRUNBERGER
Planning	DARA GOLDBERG
Simon-Skjodt Center for the Prevention of Genocide	JILL SAVITT, ACTING

The above list of key personnel was updated 7–2019.

The United States Holocaust Memorial Museum promotes documentation, study, and interpretation of the Holocaust and maintains a permanent living memorial to its victims.

Establishment and Organization

On October 7, 1980, President James E. Carter approved Public Law 96–388, which established the U.S. Holocaust Memorial Council. This Act made the Council responsible for planning, constructing, and overseeing "the operation of, a permanent living memorial museum to the victims of the holocaust." It established the United States Holocaust Memorial Museum (USHMM) (36 U.S.C. 1401-1408). https://www.govinfo.gov/content/pkg/STATUTE-94/pdf/STATUTE-94-Pg1547.pdf

The United States Holocaust Memorial Council, which serves as a board of trustees, governs the USHMM. The Council's 55 members are appointed by the President to staggered 5-year terms. Additionally, five members are appointed from each Chamber of the Congress. There are also three nonvoting ex-officio members from the Departments of Education, State, and the Interior.

On October 12, 2000, President William J. Clinton approved Public Law 106–292 "to authorize appropriations" for the USHMM and "for other purposes." The Act gave the Museum permanent authorization as an independent establishment (36 U.S.C. 2301 et seq.). https://www.govinfo.gov/content/pkg/STATUTE-114/pdf/STATUTE-114-Pg1030.pdf

The USHMM operates as a public-private partnership. Its activities and programs are supported by planned giving, endowments, and revenues; gifts, grants, and contracts; and Federal funding. https://www.ushmm.org/information/about-the-museum

The Museum's organizational chart is available in its "Performance and Accountability Report—FY 2018" on page 35. https://www.ushmm.org/m/pdfs/20181116-ushmm-par-fy18.pdf

Activities

Advanced Holocaust Studies   The Jack, Joseph and Morton Mandel Center for Advanced Holocaust Studies works with the United States Holocaust Memorial Council's Academic Committee to support research projects and publications on the Holocaust, provide access to Holocaust-related archival materials for study and new research, sponsor fellowship opportunities for pre- and postdoctoral researchers, and offer seminars, summer research workshops, conferences, lectures, and symposia. https://www.ushmm.org/research/about-the-mandel-center

For further information, contact the Jack, Joseph, and Morton Mandel Center for Advanced Holocaust Studies. Phone, 202-488-0400. TTY, 202-488-0406.

Holocaust Education   The William Levine Family National Institute for Holocaust Education promotes a variety of resources and programs to help educators, professionals, and students increase their knowledge of Holocaust history and understand its relevance today. Educational outreach programs provide teachers with classroom strategies and resources for teaching students about the Holocaust. http://www.ushmm.org/educators/teaching-about-the-holocaust

For further information, contact the National Institute for Holocaust Education.

Prevention of Genocide   The Simon-Skjodt Center for the Prevention of Genocide raises awareness of genocide, influences policymaking on genocide prevention, and stimulates worldwide action to prevent genocide and related mass atrocities. It seeks to make genocide prevention a national and international priority by increasing public awareness and mobilizing worldwide support to avert these crimes against humanity. http://www.ushmm.org/confront-genocide/about | Email: genocideprevention@ushmm.org

For further information, contact the Simon-Skjodt Center for the Prevention of Genocide. Phone, 202-488-0400. TTY, 202-488-0406.

Programs

Civic and Defense Initiatives   This program explores the ways in which the military can work to prevent genocide today. http://www.ushmm.org/professionals-and-student-leaders/military-professionals

Ethics, Religion, and the Holocaust   These programs focus on the response of churches to the Holocaust and the ways in which religious institutions, leaders, and theologians have addressed this history and its legacy. https://www.ushmm.org/research/about-the-mandel-center/initiatives/ethics-religion-holocaust

For further information, contact the Programs on Ethics, Religion, and the Holocaust.

Law Enforcement and Society: Lessons of the Holocaust   This program examines the role that law enforcement professionals played in the Holocaust. It also challenges them to reflect on their professional and personal responsibilities in a democracy today. http://www.ushmm.org/professionals-and-student-leaders/law-enforcement

For further information, contact the Lessons of the Holocaust Program.

Law, Justice, and the Holocaust   This program examines the decisions German jurists made and the pressures they faced under the Nazi regime. This is a one-day program for judges, prosecutors, and court administrators. http://www.ushmm.org/professionals-and-student-leaders/judiciary

For further information, contact the Law, Justice, and the Holocaust Program.

Youth and Community Initiatives   This program introduces students to Holocaust history and helps them develop leadership skills for confronting hatred and promoting human dignity. http://www.ushmm.org/professionals-and-student-leaders/student-leaders

For further information, contact the Student Leaders Program.

Sources of Information

Café   The Museum Café is open daily, 8:30 a.m.–4:30 p.m., except on Yom Kippur and Christmas Day. Visitors may not bring food into it or the Museum. The café serves breakfast, salads, sandwiches, and soups, including vegetarian and kosher options. Kosher food is prepared and sealed offsite under rabbinical supervision. https://www.ushmm.org/information/visit-the-museum/museum-cafe

Calendar of Events   For information on upcoming events, see the Museum's online calendar. http://www.ushmm.org/online/calendar

Career Opportunities   The museum employs people with diverse professional experience: collections, education, exhibits, fundraising, marketing, programming, and other areas. A list of current job openings is available on the "Careers" web page. https://www.ushmm.org/information/career-volunteer-opportunities/careers

Paid and unpaid internship opportunities are available. https://www.ushmm.org/information/career-volunteer-opportunities/internships

Collections / Exhibitions The Museum's holdings include art, books, pamphlets, advertisements, maps, film and video historical footage, audio and video oral testimonies, music and sound recordings, furnishings, architectural fragments, models, machinery, tools, microfilm and microfiche of government documents and other official records, personal effects, personal papers, photographs, photo albums, and textiles. The self-guided permanent exhibition spans three floors and presents a narrative history of the Holocaust with historical artifacts, photographs, and film footage. Special exhibitions include Remember the Children: Daniel's Story (for children 8 and up) and Some Were Neighbors: Collaboration and Complicity in the Holocaust. The Museum's traveling exhibitions have gone to numerous cities, States, and countries. These exhibitions extend the history of the Holocaust beyond the Museum's walls. More information on the Museum's collections and exhibitions is available on its website. http://www.ushmm.org/information/exhibitions

Contact Information The "Press Room" web page has phone numbers and email addresses for contacting the Museum's communications staff. https://www.ushmm.org/information/press

Encyclopedia An encyclopedia of the Holocaust is available on the Museum's website. https://www.ushmm.org/learn/holocaust-encyclopedia

Frequently Asked Questions (FAQs) The Museum posts answers to FAQs on its website. https://www.ushmm.org/research/ask-a-research-question/frequently-asked-questions

Multilingual Resources At the top of the Museum's home page is a "Language" drop-down menu that allows non-English readers to access resources in a number of languages: Arabic, Bahasa, Chinese, French, Greek, Hungarian, Italian, Japanese, Korean, Portuguese, Russian, Spanish, and Turkish. https://www.ushmm.org

News The Museum posts press releases on its website. https://www.ushmm.org/information/press/press-releases

To receive electronic Museum news, invitations to special programs and exhibitions, and updates on genocide prevention and other initiatives, subscribe using the online form. https://engage.ushmm.org/subscribe.html

Plan a Visit The Museum is open every day, except on Yom Kippur and Christmas. Admission is free; however, timed passes are required to enter the permanent exhibition from March through August. No passes are required for other Museum exhibitions. The "Plan Your Visit" web pages contain a trove of useful information on accessibility, admission and tickets, group reservations, hours, location, transportation, and more. https://www.ushmm.org/information/visit-the-museum/plan-your-visit

Reports Strategic plans and annual, budget, and FAIR Act reports are available on the "Reports" web page. https://www.ushmm.org/copyright-and-legal-information/annual-reports

Starting with the year 2004, performance and accountability reports are available online. https://www.ushmm.org/copyright-and-legal-information/performance-and-accountability

Social Media The Museum relies on social media to share information on its programs and resources; to memorialize the victims of Nazism; to launch discussion on the Holocaust and its relevance today; and to raise awareness that antisemitism, genocide, and hatred are persistent threats and that everybody has a role in combating them. https://www.ushmm.org/information/connect-with-the-museum#guidelines

Support the Mission Annual membership gifts help the Museum confront antisemitism and answer Holocaust denial, expand educational outreach, and preserve historical artifacts. https://www.ushmm.org/support

The Museum uses its resources to confront hatred and genocide, to educate students and provide classroom resources for teachers, and to rescue Holocaust evidence and make additional historic documents available in digital format. An online contribution, one-time or monthly, supports these activities immediately and directly. https://engage.ushmm.org/support.html

Volunteer Opportunities   The Museum welcomes volunteers and offers a variety of service opportunities. http://www.ushmm.org/information/career-volunteer-opportunities/volunteering

The Sources of Information were updated 7–2019.

United States Institute of Peace

2301 Constitution Avenue NW., Washington, DC 20037
Phone, 202-457-1700. Fax, 202-429-6063. Internet, http://www.usip.org

Board of Directors

Chair	STEPHEN J. HADLEY
Vice Chair	GEORGE E. MOOSE
Member	JUDY ANSLEY
Member	ERIC S. EDELMAN
Member	JOSEPH ELDRIDGE
Member	KERRY KENNEDY
Member	IKRAM U. KHAN
Member	STEPHEN D. KRASNER
Member	JOHN A. LANCASTER
Member	JEREMY A. RABKIN
Member	J. ROBINSON WEST
Member	NANCY ZIRKIN
Secretary of State (ex officio)	REX W. TILLERSON
Secretary of Defense (ex officio)	GEN. JAMES MATTIS, USMC
President, National Defense University (ex officio)	MAJ. GEN. FREDERICK M. PADILLA, USMC
President, U.S. Institute of Peace (ex officio)	NANCY LINDBORG

Officials

President	NANCY LINDBORG
Executive Vice President	WILLIAM B. TAYLOR
Director, Congressional Relations	ANNE HINGELEY, ACTING
Director, Public Affairs and Communications	LIZ CALLIHANACTING
Vice President, External Relations	DIANE ZELENY

The United States Institute of Peace prevents, mitigates, and resolves violent conflicts around the world.

The United States Institute of Peace (USIP) is an independent nonprofit corporation established by Congress pursuant to title XVII of the Defense Authorization Act of 1985, as amended (22 U.S.C. 4601-4611), to develop, apply, and foster cost-effective strategies and tools to prevent, mitigate, and resolve violent international conflicts, particularly those that threaten or harm America's strategic and security interests.

The United States Institute of Peace Act defines the organization's mission: "to serve the people and the government through the widest possible range of education and training, basic and applied research opportunities, and peace information services on the means to promote international peace and the resolution of conflicts among nations and peoples of the world without recourse to violence."

http://www.usip.org/vision-mission-core-principles

With the confirmation of the Senate, the President appoints the Institute's bipartisan Board of Directors. It comprises 12 members from outside the Federal service—plus four ex officio members, three from the State Department, Department of Defense, and National Defense University, and the fourth is the President of the Institute. The Board governs the Institute and appoints its President. No more than eight voting members may be from the same political party. http://www.usip.org/aboutus/board.html

Activities

The Institute supports U.S. national security and foreign affairs through conflict management and peacebuilding operations, training in conflict management and peacebuilding tradecraft and best practices, and conflict research and analysis. The USIP operates on the ground in conflict zones. It facilitates dialogue among parties in conflict, builds conflict management skills and capacity, identifies and disseminates best practices in conflict management, promotes the rule of law, reforms and strengthens education systems, strengthens civil society, and educates the public through media and other outreach activities. The USIP works in partnership with the State and Defense Departments, the U.S. Agency for International Development, nongovernmental organizations, higher and secondary educational institutions, foreign governments, and international organizations to promote collaborative problemsolving through conflict management operations, training and analysis, facilitated dialogue, Track 1.5 diplomacy, and special events. The Institute conducts practitioner training in conflict management, including mediation and negotiating skills for government and military personnel, civil society leaders, and staff of nongovernmental and international organizations. The Institute extends its reach through grants, fellowships, and scholarships to nonprofit organizations in the United States and overseas. http://www.usip.org/issue-areas

Sources of Information

Employment   The USIP relies on knowledgeable, talented professionals to carry out its mission. A recent graduate typically starts as a program assistant. The ideal candidate is a high academic achiever; has a background in international relations or a related field; and possesses administrative, computer, research, and writing skills. Regional specialization and language skills may be required for some positions. http://www.usip.org/jobs

Grants / Fellowships   Information on USIP grants and fellowship programs is available online. http://www.usip.org/grants-fellowships

Publications   USIP articles, publications, and tools are accessible online. http://www.usip.org/publications; http://www.usip.org/newsroom

For further information, contact the U.S. Institute of Peace, Office of Public Affairs and Communications, 2301 Constitution Avenue NW., Washington, DC 20037. Phone, 202-457-1700.

INTERNATIONAL ORGANIZATIONS

African Development Bank

Avenue Jean-Paul II, 01 BP 1387, Abidjan 01, Côte d'Ivoire
Phone, +225 20 26 10 20. Internet, http://www.afdb.org | Email: afdb@afdb.org

President   AKINWUMI ADESINA
https://www.afdb.org/en/about-us/organisational-structure/the-president

The above list of key personnel was updated 09–2017.

The African Development Bank stimulates sustainable economic development and social progress in regional member countries to mitigate poverty and its effects.

The African Development Bank (AFDB) was established in 1964. By charter amendment, the AFDB expanded its membership to include nonregional countries in 1982. The admission of nonregional countries boosted AFDB capital resources by more than twofold.

The Bank's mandate centers on the economic development and social progress of its regional members. AFDB membership totals 80 countries: 54 African and 26 nonregional countries.

The African Development Fund, established in 1972 and operational in 1974, complements AFDB operations by providing concessional financing for high-priority development projects. Contributing countries provide the Fund with resources to improve economic and social conditions in beneficiary countries. These beneficiaries include countries that are increasing in economic capacity and en route to becoming the new emerging markets or that are regarded as fragile states and require special assistance for basics levels of service delivery. http://www.afdb.org/en/about-us/mission-strategy

Sources of Information

Career Opportunities   Grade and salary data and information on current job vacancies are available online. http://www.afdb.org/en/about-us/careers

Documents   The AFDB posts documents on its website. http://www.afdb.org/en/documents

Environmental and Social Assessments   The AFDB website features relevant documents in a database that may be filtered and sorted by country, topic and sector, or both. https://www.afdb.org/en/documents/environmental-social-assessments/cop

Field Offices   Contact information for AFDB field offices is available online. http://www.afdb.org/en/about-us/organisational-structure/complexes/country-regional-programs-policy/field-offices/field-office-contacts

Français   The AFDB website offers information and resources for visitors who read French. https://www.afdb.org/fr

Frequently Asked Questions (FAQs)   The AFDB posts answers to FAQs on its website. http://www.afdb.org/en/about-us/frequently-asked-questions

Glossary   The AFDB website features a glossary of acronyms. http://www.afdb.org/en/glossary

News / Events   The AFDB website features events, interviews, loan and grant announcements, multimedia, news, press releases, project stories, and speeches. http://www.afdb.org/en/news-and-events

Organizational Chart   The AFDB's organizational chart is available in Portable Document Format (PDF) for viewing and downloading. https://www.afdb.org/fileadmin/uploads/afdb/Documents/Generic-Documents/AFDB_ORGANIZATION_CHART_2_MAY_2017.pdf

Site Map   The website map allows visitors to look for specific topics or to browse content that aligns with their interests. http://www.afdb.org/en/sitemap

Social Media   The AFDB has a Facebook account. https://www.facebook.com/AfDBGroup/?ref=ts

The AFDB tweets announcements and newsworthy items in English and French on Twitter. https://twitter.com/AfDB_Group

Statistics   Defining achievable goals and setting realistic targets, as well as evaluating the effects of projects, depend heavily on reliable data. The AFDB promotes improvement in the quality and quantity of statistical data on all aspects of development. https://www.afdb.org/en/knowledge/statistics

Web TV   The AFDB's Web TV features programs in English and French. http://www.afdb.tv

Where the AFDB Works   The AFDB's website features a list of African countries where the Bank is active. http://www.afdb.org/en/countries

---

Asian Development Bank

Headquarters: 6 ADB Avenue, Mandaluyong City, 1550 Metro Manila, Philippines
Phone, +632 632-4444. Fax, +632 636-2444. Internet, http://www.adb.org | Email: information@adb.org

ADB North American Representative Office: 900 17th Street NW., Suite 900, Washington DC 20006
Phone, 202-728-1500. Fax, 202 728 1505

President   Takehiko Nakao
https://www.adb.org/about/management/takehiko-nakao

The above list of key personnel was updated 09–2017.

The Asian Development Bank stimulates sustainable economic development and social progress in member countries to mitigate poverty and its effects.

The Asian Development Bank (ADB) commenced operations on December 19, 1966. It comprises 67 members: 48 regional and 19 nonregional countries.

The ADB works to eradicate poverty in Asia and the Pacific. As a multilateral development finance institution, it provides grants, loans, and technical assistance. The Bank serves its member countries, which are also its shareholders. Through equity investments and loans, the ADB also provides direct assistance to private enterprises of developing member countries.

To maximize the effects of its assistance on development, the ADB facilitates policy dialogues, offers advisory services, and mobilizes financial resources through cofinancing operations involving official,

commercial, and export sources of credit. ABD operations promote three complementary agendas: environmentally sustainable growth, inclusive economic growth, and regional integration. The Bank's core areas of development activity are education, environment, finance, infrastructure, and regional cooperation and integration. http://www.adb.org/print/node/179940

Sources of Information

Business Opportunities   ADB projects rely on the goods and services of consultants, contractors, manufacturers, and suppliers. http://www.adb.org/site/business-opportunities/main

Career Opportunities   The "Careers" Web page features access to the ABD career and employment system, information on its young professional program and internships, descriptions of current job vacancies, and a summary of what the ADB looks for in a potential employee. http://www.adb.org/site/careers/main

Chinese   The ADB website offers information and resources for visitors who read Chinese. https://www.adb.org/zh

Climate Change   Production and use of energy from nonrenewable sources and the unsustainable development and consumption of other natural resources destabilize the climate and undermine long-term prosperity in Asia and the Pacific. Devastating storms, droughts, floods, and rising sea levels disproportionately affect poor communities. While climatologists forecast that extreme climate events will become more frequent and intense, the ADB continues its support of sustainable growth in the region through financing and innovative technologies. https://www.adb.org/themes/climate-change-disaster-risk-management/main

History   Conceived in the early 1960s as a financial institution that would be Asian in character and foster economic growth and cooperation in one of the poorest regions in the world, the ADB opened in the Philippine capital of Manila in 1966. To learn about the Bank's initial achievements and those of more recent decades, visit the "ADB History" web page. https://www.adb.org/about/history

Members   The ADB posts a list of its regional and nonregional members and descriptions of them on its website. https://www.adb.org/about/members

Organizational Chart   The ADB's organizational chart is available in Portable Document Format (PDF) for viewing and downloading. https://www.adb.org/sites/default/files/page/203876/adb-org-chart-20170720.pdf

Publications   The ADB website offers information on books, brochures and flyers, conference proceedings, guides, papers and briefs, policies and plans, reports, and statutory reports and official records. http://www.adb.org/publications

Social Media   The ADB has a Facebook account. https://www.facebook.com/AsianDevBank

The ADB tweets announcements and other newsworthy items on Twitter. https://twitter.com/ADB_HQ

The ADB posts videos on its YouTube channel. https://www.youtube.com/user/AsianDevelopmentBank

Statistical Database System   The ADB maintains a central statistical database to store macroeconomic and social data of its developing member countries. https://sdbs.adb.org/sdbs | Email: sdbs@adb.org

European Bank for Reconstruction and Development

One Exchange Square, London EC2A 2JN, United Kingdom
Phone, +44 20 7338 6000. Internet, http://www.ebrd.com

President	SIR SUMA CHAKRABARTI
http://www.ebrd.com/who-we-are/ebrd-president-sir-suma-chakrabarti.html	

The above list of key personnel was updated 09–2017.

The European Bank for Reconstruction and Development develops open and sustainable market economies in democratic countries.

The European Bank for Reconstruction and Development (EBRD) is a multilateral development bank that supports projects in over 30 countries, from central Europe to central Asia and to the southern and eastern Mediterranean. Investing primarily in private sector clients whose needs cannot be met fully by commercial credit and equity markets, the EBRD promotes entrepreneurship and fosters transition toward open and sustainable market economies.

The London-based EBRD has a political mandate: It assists countries that are committed to and apply the principles of multiparty democracy and pluralism. The Bank also conducts its affairs with a commitment to environmental protection and sustainable energy development. In addition to benefiting the countries that receive its investments, the Bank also serves its shareholders' interests: 66 countries from five continents, the European Union, and the European Investment Bank. http://www.ebrd.com/who-we-are/history-of-the-ebrd.html

Sources of Information

Business Opportunities   Information on opportunities for consultants, contractors, and suppliers is available on the EBRD website. http://www.ebrd.com/work-with-us/procurement.html

Career Opportunities   Information on job locations and types, benefits and rewards, and internships is available on the EBRD website. http://www.ebrd.com/careers-at-the-ebrd.html

Contact Information   Department and country contacts are listed on the "EBRD Contacts" Web page. http://www.ebrd.com/contacts.html

Economic Data   Economic teams publish macroeconomic and structural data series, and they survey data affecting the Bank's countries of operation. http://www.ebrd.com/what-we-do/economic-research-and-data/data.html

Environmental and Social Sustainability   EBRD financing supports sustainable development projects that are designed and operated in compliance with good international practices. To help clients meet sustainability goals, the EBRD posts downloads and resources on its website. http://www.ebrd.com/key-sustainability-downloads.html

Green Economy Transition (GET)   By 2020, the GET approach seeks to increase the volume of green financing to 40 per cent of EBRD annual business investment. Safeguarding the environment and strengthening ecosystems help market economies function better and, therefore, are central to the transition process that the EBRD has promoted since its inception. http://www.ebrd.com/what-we-do/get.html

History   In October of 1989, a month before German citizens dismantled parts of the Berlin Wall, President François Mitterrand of France proposed the establishment of a European bank to meet the challenges of emergent economic and political realities. In less than 2 years, the EBRD opened for business with its headquarters in London. To learn more about the role played by the EBRD in the transition from the end of the Cold War to a new European era, visit the "History of the EBRD" web page. http://www.ebrd.com/who-we-are/history-of-the-ebrd.html

Organizational Chart   The EBRD's organizational chart is available on the "Structure and Management" web page in Portable Document Format (PDF) for viewing and downloading. http://www.ebrd.com/who-we-are/our-structure.html

Products / Services   Information on the EBRD's advisory services, policy reform dialogue services, and financial products is available online. http://www.ebrd.com/what-we-do/products-and-services.html

Reports   The EBRD posts annual, donor, financial, sustainability, and transition reports on its website. http://www.ebrd.com/news/publications.html

Sectors / Topics   The EBRD website features a section that brings together the topics that most concern the Bank and the sectors in which it is most active. http://www.ebrd.com/what-we-do/sectors-and-topics.html

Social Media   The EBRD tweets announcements and other newsworthy items on Twitter. https://twitter.com/ebrd

The EBRD maintains a Facebook account. https://www.facebook.com/ebrdhq

Where EBRD Works   The EBRD website features the list of countries where the Bank is active. http://www.ebrd.com/where-we-are.html

Inter-American Defense Board

2600 Sixteenth Street NW., Washington, DC 20441
Phone, 202-939-6041. Fax, 202-319-2791. Internet, http://iadb.jid.org | Email: protocol@jid.org

Chair	VICE ADM. GONZALO NICOLÁS RÍOS POLASTRI

The Inter-American Defense Board is the oldest permanently constituted, international military organization in the world. It was founded by Resolution XXXIX of the Meeting of Foreign Ministers at Rio de Janeiro in January 1942. The Board is governed according to Statutes that the General Assembly of the Organization of American States approved in March 2006. Senior armed forces officers from the member nations staff the various agencies of the Board. Its three major components are the Council of Delegates, the Secretariat, and the Inter-American Defense College. http://iadb.jid.org/quienes-somos/resena-historica-de-la-sede-de-la-jid

The Board studies and recommends to member governments measures it deems necessary for the safety and security of the hemisphere. It also acts as a technical military adviser for the Organization of American States and is involved in projects such as disaster preparedness and humanitarian demining programs in Central and South America.

Established in 1962, the Inter-American Defense College is located on Fort Lesley J. McNair, whose buildings and furnishings the United States Government donated. The United States hosts the College, which prepares senior military officers and civilian functionaries for positions in their respective governments. The College offers an 11-month, professionally-oriented, and fully accredited Masters of Science degree. Multidisciplinary in content, the curriculum centers on the Western Hemisphere's most pressing defense and security issues. http://www.colegio-id.org/index.php

Sources of Information

Documents Documents are posted online to increase the transparency of Inter-American Defense Board activities. http://iadb.jid.org/documents-and-publications
Events Symposia and seminars are posted on the Board's Web site. A calendar of meetings also is available on the Web site's home page. https://sites.google.com/a/jid.org/iadb/eventos/simposios-y-seminarios
News News items are available on the home page of the Board's Web site. http://iadb.jid.org
Regional Organizations Links to regional organizations are accessible on the "Strategic Links" Web page. http://iadb.jid.org/strategic-links; http://iadb.jid.org/quienes-somos/contactos | Email: jid@jid.org

For further information, contact the Inter-American Defense Board, 2600 Sixteenth Street NW., Washington, DC 20441. Phone, 202-939-6041. Fax, 202-319-2791.

Inter-American Development Bank

Headquarters: 1300 New York Avenue NW., Washington, DC 20577
Phone, 202-623-1000. Fax, 202-623-3096. Internet, http://www.iadb.org

President	LUIS A. MORENO
http://www.iadb.org/en/about-us/office-of-the-president,19639.html	

The above list of key personnel was updated 09–2017.

The Inter-American Development Bank (IDB) was established in 1959 to help accelerate economic and social development in Latin America and the Caribbean.

The Bank has 48 member countries, 26 of which are borrowing members in Latin America and the Caribbean. http://

www.iadb.org/en/about-us/about-the-inter-american-development-bank,5995.html

Sources of Information

Business Opportunities   IDB projects in Latin America and the Caribbean create contract opportunities for businesses and consultants. http://www.iadb.org/en/projects/project-procurement,8148.html

Career Opportunities   The IDB relies on professionals with expertise in economics, education, energy, environmental sustainability, financial markets, institutional capacity, investment funds, rural development and disaster risk, science and technology, social protection and health, transport, water and sanitation, and other fields to carry out its mission. http://www.iadb.org/en/careers/careers-at-the-idb,1165.html

Data   The IDB posts datasets on its Web site. https://data.iadb.org

Glossary   The IDB maintains a glossary on its Web site. http://www.iadb.org/en/projects/glossary,18952.html

Key Facts   To learn at glance who leads the IDB, how many people it employs, how many countries are members, who are its clients, and recent annual levels of its approved lending, visit the "Key Facts" section. http://www.iadb.org/en/about-us/key-facts,18246.html

Learning Resources   Online courses are accessible on the IDB Web site. http://www.iadb.org/en/courses/home,20468.html

Looking for Something?   Try finding it by using the "What Are You Looking For" Web page. http://www.iadb.org/en/projects/what-are-you-looking-for,18944.html?

Publications   A variety of publications—annual reports, books, catalogs and brochures, databases and datasets, discussion and working papers, journals, magazines, monographs, newsletters—is available online. https://publications.iadb.org/facet-view?field=type_view

Social Media   The IDB tweets announcements and other newsworthy items on Twitter. https://twitter.com/the_IDB

The IDB has a Facebook account. https://www.facebook.com/IADB.org

---

Inter-American Investment Corporation

Headquarters: 1350 New York Avenue NW., Washington, DC 20577
Phone, 202-623-3901. Internet, http://www.iic.org/en

Chair, Board of Executive Directors   Luis A. Moreno
Chief Executive Officer   James P. Scriven
http://www.iic.org/en/who-we-are/structure-and-management#.
WYiXZOauhs0

The above list of key personnel was updated 09–2017.

The Inter-American Development Bank promotes development in Latin America and the Caribbean through the private sector.

The Inter-American Investment Corporation (IIC), an affiliate of the Inter-American Development Bank based in Washington, DC, was established in 1985 to promote the economic development of its Latin American and Caribbean members by financing small- and medium-size private enterprises. The IIC provides project financing in the form of direct loans and equity investments, lines of credit to local financial intermediaries, and investments in local and regional investment funds. http://www.iic.org/en/who-we-are/about-us#.WGLh5H0rLIU

The IIC has 45 member countries, of which 28 are in the Western Hemisphere, including Canada and the United States, and 17 are outside the region. http://www.iic.org/en/what-we-offer#.VumT0H0rLIU

Sources of Information

Career Opportunities The ICC relies on talent and experience to carry out its mission. It recruits, hires, and maintains a staff of diverse, motivated, and qualified professionals with expertise, leadership potential, and strong interpersonal and teamwork skills. Current job opportunities are posted online. http://www.iic.org/en/about-us/careers

History A three-part history, from 1985 to 1999, from 2000 to 2012, and from 2013 to the present, is available on the IIC's Web site. http://www.iic.org/en/who-we-are/our-history-timeline#.WD9-D30rLIV

Key Initiatives The IIC's Web site features a section on its most important initiatives. http://www.iic.org/en/initiatives

Library The IIC's Web site features a photo library. http://www.iic.org/en/media/photo-library#.WD94730rLIU

Member Countries The IIC Web site features two lists of member countries: regional members and other members. An interactive map complements the two lists. http://www.iic.org/en/countries

News The IIC posts news items on its Web site.

Projects IIC projects may be searched by country or year. http://www.iic.org/en/projects

Publications Brochures, factsheets, and reports—some in English and Spanish, some also in French and Portuguese—are available online. http://www.iic.org/en/media/publications#.VumPI30rLIU

Transaction Cycle A description of the five stages of a successful IIC transaction—business origination, eligibility review, due diligence and approval, closing and disbursement, and supervision and evaluation—is available online. http://www.iic.org/en/what-we-offer/transaction-cycle#.WD9_p30rLIU

Social Media The IIC tweets announcements and other newsworthy items in Spanish on Twitter. https://twitter.com/GrupoBID_CII

The IIC has a Facebook account. https://www.facebook.com/CIIGrupoBID

International Monetary Fund

700 Nineteenth Street NW., Washington, DC 20431
Phone, 202-623-7000. Fax, 202-623-4661. Internet, http://www.imf.org

Managing Director / Chair of the Executive Board https://www.imf.org/external/np/omd/bios/cl.htm	DAVID LIPTON, ACTING
First Deputy Managing Director https://www.imf.org/external/np/omd/bios/dl.htm	DAVID LIPTON
Chief Administrative Officer	CARLA GRASSO
Deputy Managing Directors	
	MITSUHIRO FURUSAWA
	CARLA GRASSO
	TAO ZHANG
https://www.imf.org/external/np/sec/memdir/officers.htm	

The above list of key personnel was updated 7–2019.

The International Monetary Fund fosters global monetary cooperation, secures financial stability, facilitates international trade, promotes employment and sustainable economic growth, and reduces poverty worldwide.

Establishment and Organization

The Final Act of the United Nations Monetary and Financial Conference, signed at Bretton Woods, NH, on July 22, 1944, set forth the original Articles of Agreement of the International Monetary Fund (IMF). The Agreement became effective on December

27, 1945, when the President, authorized by the Bretton Woods Agreements Act (22 U.S.C. 286), accepted membership for the United States in the IMF. The inaugural meeting of the Board of Governors was held in March 1946, and the first meeting of the Executive Directors was held May 6, 1946. https://www.govinfo.gov/content/pkg/USCODE-2017-title22/html/USCODE-2017-title22-chap7-subchapXV-sec286.htm

On May 31, 1968, the Board of Governors approved an amendment to the Articles of Agreement for the establishment of a facility based on Special Drawing Rights (SDR) and for modification of certain rules and practices. The amendment became effective on July 28, 1969, and the Special Drawing Account opened on August 6, 1969. The Special Drawing Rights Act (22 U.S.C. 286 et seq.) authorized the United States to accept the amendment and participate in the Special Drawing Account. https://www.imf.org/en/About/Factsheets/Sheets/2016/08/01/14/51/Special-Drawing-Right-SDR

On April 30, 1976, the Board of Governors approved a second amendment to the Articles of Agreement, which became effective on April 1, 1978. This amendment gave members the right to adopt exchange arrangements of their choice while placing certain obligations on them regarding their exchange rate policies, which the IMF was to monitor closely. The official price of gold was abolished, and the Special Drawing Account was promoted as the principal reserve asset of the international monetary system. The Bretton Woods Agreements Act Amendments (22 U.S.C. 286e-5) authorized the United States to accept this amendment. https://www.govinfo.gov/content/pkg/USCODE-2017-title22/pdf/USCODE-2017-title22-chap7-subchapXV-sec286e-5.pdf

On June 28, 1990, the Board of Governors approved a third amendment to the Articles of Agreement, which became effective on November 11, 1992. Under this amendment, a member's voting rights and certain related rights may be suspended by a 70-percent majority of the executive board if the member country has been declared ineligible to use the Fund's general resources and persists in its failure to fulfill any of its obligations under the Articles.

The IMF posts its organizational chart online. https://www.imf.org/external/np/obp/orgcht.htm

Activities

The IMF has 189 member countries. It promotes international monetary cooperation through a permanent forum for consultation and collaboration on international monetary problems; facilitates the expansion and balanced growth of international trade; promotes exchange rate stability; assists in the establishment of an open multilateral system of payments for current transactions among members; and gives confidence to members by making IMF resources temporarily available to them under adequate safeguards.

The IMF helps member countries correct imbalances in their international balances of payments. It periodically examines the economic developments and policies of its members, offers policy advice, and at a member's request and upon executive board approval, provides financial assistance through a variety of financial facilities designed to address specific problems. These financing mechanisms provide access to the Fund's general resources and offer short-term assistance during crises of market confidence, compensatory financing to countries suffering declines in export earnings, emergency assistance for countries recovering from natural disasters or armed conflict, and low-interest rate resources to support structural adjustment and promote growth in the poorest countries. The IMF also provides technical assistance and training to member countries. https://www.imf.org/en/About

Sources of Information

A–Z Index   The IMF's website has an alphabetical index to help visitors search for specific topics or browse content that aligns with their interests. https://www.imf.org/external/siteindex.htm

Archives   A catalog of the IMF's archives is available online. https://archivescatalog.imf.org/search/simple

At a Glance   Fast facts and an overview of the IMF's founding and mission, governance and organization, and core activities are available on "The IMF at a Glance" web page. https://www.imf.org/en/About/Factsheets/IMF-at-a-Glance

Blog   The IMF's blog offers insightful and analytical posts on economics and finance. https://blogs.imf.org

Career Opportunities   In addition to economists and research assistants, the IMF relies on professionals with skills and expertise in a range of other fields: communications, facilities management, finance and accounting, human resources, information technology, language services, law, library science and archives, office assistance, procurement, security, and transportation and hospitality. Information on careers, current job vacancies, and recruitment programs is available online. http://www.imf.org/external/np/adm/rec/recruit.htm

Climate Change   The IMF counts "Climate Change" as one of its six key issues. https://www.imf.org/external/np/fad/environ/index.htm

Commodity Prices   The "IMF Primary Commodity Prices" web page offers easy access to data on primary commodity prices, the interactive commodity data portal, and the commodity terms of trade database. https://www.imf.org/en/Research/commodity-prices

Contact Information   Contact information for general, media, and other types of inquiries is available online. https://www.imf.org/external/np/exr/contacts/contacts.aspx | Email: publicaffairs@imf.org

Country Information   The IMF is an organization comprising 189 countries that, together, work to promote monetary cooperation, financial stability, international trade, employment and sustainable economic growth, and to reduce poverty. An alphabetical index of the participating countries and information on those countries are available on the IMF's website. https://www.imf.org/en/Countries

Data   The IMF publishes data on IMF lending, exchange rates, and other economic and financial indicators. https://www.imf.org/en/Data

Gender   The IMF counts the division along gender lines in labor markets worldwide as one of its six key issues. https://www.imf.org/external/themes/gender/

Glossary   The IMF maintains an online glossary of financial terms and acronyms. http://www.imf.org/external/np/exr/glossary/index.asp

History   James M. Boughton's "Silent Revolution: The International Monetary Fund 1979–1989" is accessible online. https://www.imf.org/external/pubs/ft/history/2001/index.htm

A chronological history of the IMF is available online. https://www.imf.org/external/np/exr/chron/chron.asp

Language Resources   The IMF provides information on its website in Arabic, Chinese, French, Japanese, Russian, and Spanish. Language tags are visible at the top and bottom of the IMF's home page. https://www.imf.org

Negative Interest Rate Policy   IMF Working Papers describe research in progress and are published to elicit comments and encourage debate. The views expressed in working papers belong to the authors and do not necessarily represent the views of the IMF, its executive board, or IMF management. In their recent working paper "Enabling Deep Negative Rates to Fight Recessions: A Guide" (April 2019), Ruchir Agarwal and Miles S. Kimball wrote that "the option to enable deep negative rates will be critical for central banks to maintain effectiveness of monetary policy in the future and will help mitigate the hardships associated with prolonged recessions" (page 84). https://www.imf.org/en/Publications/WP/Issues/2019/04/29/Enabling-Deep-Negative-Rates-A-Guide-46598

News   The IMF posts podcasts, newsworthy items about various countries, and the latest news on its website. https://www.imf.org/en/news

The "What's New Archive" allows easy access to recently posted items of interest. https://www.imf.org/external/what/whatsnewenglish/what.aspx

Publications   The IMF's "Finance and Development" magazine and "Fiscal Monitor" biannual report are available online in Portable Document Format (PDF). Its "New and Noteworthy" newsletter and other publications are also accessible online. https://www.imf.org/en/publications

Site Map   The IMF site map allows visitors to look for specific topics or to browse

for content that aligns with their interests. https://www.imf.org/external/sitemap.htm
Social Media   The "IMF Social Hub" allows easy access to the IMF's Facebook page, Instagram photos and videos, LinkedIn account, Tweets and replies, and YouTube channel. https://www.imf.org/external/social.htm
Special Drawing Rights (SDRs)   A 5-minute video explaining the SDR, the international reserve asset that the IMF created to supplement the official reserves of its member countries, is available online. https://www.imf.org/external/mmedia/view.aspx?vid=5027851809001
U.S. Economy   On June 24, 2019, the IMF published its "United States: 2019 Article IV Consultation." The staff report for the consultation noted that the U.S. economy is undergoing the longest expansion in

recorded history, unemployment is low, real wages are rising, and inflationary pressures remain subdued. It also notes that "the benefits from this decade-long expansion have not been shared as widely as they could. . . . Average life expectancy is falling, income and wealth polarization have increased, poverty has fallen but remains higher than in other advanced economies, social mobility has steadily eroded, and education and health outcomes are discouraging." https://www.imf.org/en/Publications/CR/Issues/2019/06/24/United-States-2019-Article-IV-Consultation-Press-Release-Staff-Report-and-Statement-by-the-47019
Videos   The IMF posts videos in Arabic, Chinese, English, French, Russian, and Spanish on its website. http://www.imf.org/external/mmedia/index.aspx

The Sources of Information were updated 7–2019.

International Organization for Migration

Headquarters: 17 Route des Morillons, C.P. 17, CH–1211 Geneva 19, Switzerland. Mailing address, P.O. Box 71, CH–1211, Geneva 19, Switzerland
Phone, 011–41–22–717–9111. Internet, http://www.iom.int | Email: hq@iom.int

Washington Office: Suite 700, 1752 N Street NW., Washington, DC 20036
Phone, 202-862-1826. Email: IOMWashington@iom.int

New York Office: 122 E. 42d Street, 48th Floor, New York, NY 10168
Phone, 212-681-7000. Email: newyork@iom.int

Director General	WILLIAM LACY SWING
Deputy Director General	LAURA THOMPSON
Chief of Mission–Washington, DC	LUCA DALL'OGLIO
Director, IOM Office to the United Nations	ASHRAF EL NOUR

The above list of key personnel was updated 09–2017.

The International Organization for Migration addresses the underlying issues of migration, answers the operational challenges of migration management, promotes economic and social development through migration, champions the dignity and well-being of migrants, and challenges the xenophobic narrative directed at them.

Established in 1951, the International Organization for Migration (IOM) is the leading intergovernmental organization in the field of migration. With 166 member states, an additional 8 states holding observer status, and offices in over 100 countries, the IOM promotes humane and orderly migration for the benefit of all. It does so by providing services and advice to

migrants and governments, while working in close cooperation with governmental, intergovernmental, and nongovernmental partners. The IOM has observer status to the United Nations.

The Organization works with its partners in the following areas: meeting the operational challenges of migration management, increasing understanding of

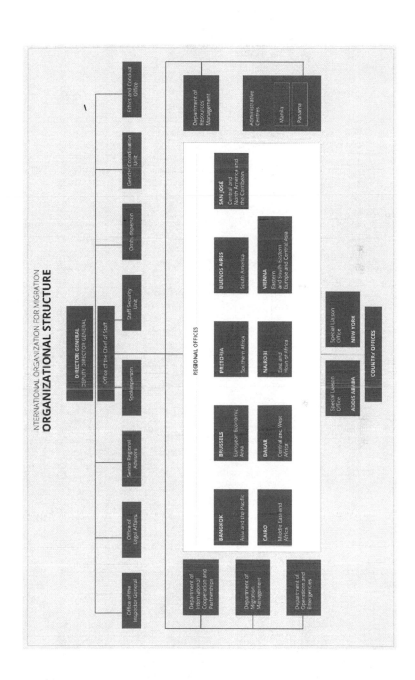

INTERNATIONAL ORGANIZATION FOR MIGRATION
ORGANIZATIONAL STRUCTURE

migration issues, encouraging social and economic development through migration, and upholding the human dignity and well-being of migrants.

The Organization has been at the forefront of emergency response to ensure assistance and protection to stranded migrants and displaced persons. It has a lead role under the UN Cluster Approach in camp coordination and management in natural disasters and is a key partner in emergency shelter, logistics, health, protection, and early recovery.

IOM expertise and services support the following activities: secure, reliable, and cost-effective assistance for migrating persons; humane and orderly management of migration and the effective respect for migrants' human rights; technical cooperation and operational assistance for building national capacities and facilitating cooperation on issues relevant to migration; helping states to integrate migrants into their new environment and to engage diasporas as development partners; advising states in the development and delivery of programs and technical expertise to combat migrant smuggling and human trafficking; working with national health systems to reduce mortality, morbidity, and disabilities and to enhance access to rights-based health and well-being services throughout the migration cycle; and partnering with states to address labor migration. http://www.iom.int/about-iom

Sources of Information

Blog   The IOM maintains a blog on its Web site. http://weblog.iom.int
Business Opportunities   Information on procurement opportunities is available online. https://www.iom.int/procurement-opportunities
Career Opportunities   Current job vacancies in various countries are posted online. https://recruit.iom.int/sap/bc/webdynpro/sap/hrrcf_a_unreg_job_search?sap-client=100&sap-language=EN&sap-wd-configid=ZHRRCF_A_UNREG_JOB_SEARCH#
Countries   IOM maintains more than 480 country offices and sub-offices worldwide. http://www.iom.int/countries

Español / Français   Spanish and French versions of the Web site can be accessed by using language links at the top of the home page. http://www.iom.int
Glossary   A list of key migration terms that is based on the IOM's "Glossary on Migration" is available online. http://www.iom.int/key-migration-terms
History   Originally known as the Provisional Intergovernmental Committee for the Movement of Migrants from Europe, the IOM got its start amidst the chaos and displacement caused by WWII. Today, the IOM is the leading international agency working to advance the understanding of migration issues, encourage social and economic development through migration, and uphold the human dignity and well-being of migrants. To learn more of the IOM story, which began in 1951, visit the "IOM History" page. http://www.iom.int/iom-history
Organizational Chart   The IOM's organizational chart is available in Portable Document Format (PDF) for viewing and downloading. http://www.iom.int/sites/default/files/Organigram.pdf
Press Room   The IOM posts featured stories, news, radio and television interviews, and more on its Web site. http://www.iom.int/press-room
Publications   Visit the online bookstore to see IOM publications in English, French, and Spanish. http://publications.iom.int
Regional Geographic Coverage   A map of IOM regional geographic coverage is available online. http://www.iom.int/sites/default/files/about-iom/IOM_Regional_Geographical_Coverage.jpg

A list of IOM regional geographic coverage also is available online. http://www.iom.int/sites/default/files/about-iom/Coverage-of-ROs-Feb2016.pdf
Regional Offices   Regional office staff reviews and endorses projects and provides technical support to Country Offices. Descriptions of and contact information for the IOM's nine regional offices are available online. http://www.iom.int/regional-offices
Social Media   The IOM has a Facebook account. https://www.facebook.com/IOM

The IOM tweets announcements and other newsworthy items on Twitter. https://twitter.com/UNmigration

The IOM posts videos on its YouTube channel. https://www.youtube.com/user/IOMMigration

United Nations Information on the IOM's Office to the United Nations is available online. http://unofficeny.iom.int | Email: unofficeny@iom.int; http://www.iom.int/contact-us | Email: hq@iom.int

For further information, contact the International Organization for Migration–Headquarters, P.O. Box 71, CH–1211, Geneva 19, Switzerland.

Organization of American States

Seventeenth Street and Constitution Avenue NW., Washington, DC 20006
Phone, 202-370-5000. Fax, 202-458-3967. Internet, http://www.oas.org/en

Secretary General http://www.oas.org/en/about/secretary_general.asp	LUIS ALMAGRO LEMES
Assistant Secretary General http://www.oas.org/en/about/assistant_secretary_ general.asp	NESTOR MENDEZ

The above list of key personnel was updated 9–2018.

The Organization of American States seeks an order of peace and justice among its member states, promotes their solidarity and strengthens their collaboration, and defends their sovereignty, territorial integrity, and independence.

The Organization of American States (OAS) brings together the countries of the Western Hemisphere to strengthen cooperation and advance common interests. At the core of the OAS mission is a commitment to democracy. Building on this foundation, OAS works to promote good governance, strengthen human rights, foster peace and security, expand trade, and address the complex problems caused by poverty, drugs, and corruption. Through decisions made by its political bodies and programs carried out by its General Secretariat, OAS promotes greater inter-American cooperation and understanding.

OAS member states have intensified their cooperation since the end of the cold war, taking on new and important challenges. In 1994, the region's 34 democratically elected presidents and prime ministers met in Miami for the First Summit of the Americas, where they established broad political, economic, and social development goals. They have continued to meet periodically since then to examine common interests and priorities. Through the ongoing Summits of the Americas process, the region's leaders have entrusted the OAS with a growing number of responsibilities to help advance the countries' shared vision.

With four official languages—English, Spanish, Portuguese, and French—the OAS reflects the rich diversity of peoples and cultures across the Americas. The OAS has 35 member states: the independent nations of North, Central, and South America, and of the Caribbean. Since 1962, Cuba has been barred from participation by resolution of the Eighth Meeting of Consultation of Ministers of Foreign Affairs. Countries from all around the world are permanent observers, closely following the issues that are critical to the Americas and often providing key financial support for OAS programs.

Member states set major policies and goals through the General Assembly, which gathers the hemisphere's foreign ministers once a year in regular session. The Permanent Council, made up of ambassadors appointed by member states, meets regularly at OAS headquarters in Washington, DC, to guide ongoing policies and actions. The chairmanship of the Permanent Council rotates every 3 months, in alphabetical order of countries. Each member state has an equal voice, and most decisions are made through consensus.

Also under the OAS umbrella are several specialized agencies that have considerable autonomy: the Pan American Health Organization in Washington, DC; the Inter-American Children's Institute in Montevideo, Uruguay; the Inter-American Institute for Cooperation on Agriculture in San Jose, Costa Rica; and the Pan American Institute of Geography and History and the Inter-American Indian Institute, both in Mexico City.

In 1948, at the Ninth International Conference of American States, 21 nations of the hemisphere signed the OAS Charter: Argentina, Bolivia, Brazil, Chile, Colombia, Costa Rica, Cuba (barred from participation), Dominican Republic, Ecuador, El Salvador, Guatemala, Haiti, Honduras, Mexico, Nicaragua, Panama, Paraguay, Peru, United States of America, Uruguay, and Venezuela.

Subsequently, 14 other countries joined the OAS by signing and ratifying the Charter. They were Barbados, Trinidad and Tobago, Jamaica, Grenada, Suriname, Dominica, Saint Lucia, Antigua and Barbuda, Saint Vincent and the Grenadines, the Bahamas, Saint Kitts and Nevis, Canada, Belize, and Guyana. This brings the number of member states to 35. http://www.oas.org/en/about/who_we_are.asp

Sources of Information

A–Z Index   The "Topics" web page presents a collection of popular topics in alphabetical order. http://www.oas.org/en/topics/default.asp

Career Opportunities   Information on employment, consultancies, and internships is available online. http://www.oas.org/dhrs/dhr/employment_opportunities.asp

Conferences   A calendar of conferences is available online. http://www.apps.oas.org/oasmeetings/default.aspx?Lang=EN

Documents   The most important OAS documents, including its founding Charter and the Inter-American Democratic Charter, are available on its website. Along with these essential documents, links to other key reference material—such as annual reports of the Secretary General, OAS resolutions, agreements, and treaties—are also available. http://www.oas.org/en/information_center/default.asp

History   A short history of the OAS is available. http://www.oas.org/en/about/our_history.asp

Language Assistance   The OAS maintains English and Spanish versions of its website. Some web pages are also available in French and Portuguese. Language tags appear above the search box in the top right corner of most of the site's pages. http://www.oas.org/en

Media Center   Newsletters, press releases, and speeches by OAS leaders are posted in the media center. http://www.oas.org/en/media_center/press_releases.asp

Members States   Information on the 35 independent states of the Americas—all of which have ratified the OAS Charter and are member states—is available on the OAS website. http://www.oas.org/en/member_states/default.asp

Organizational Chart   The OAS posts its organizational chart in Portable Document Format (PDF) online. http://www.oas.org/legal/english/organigramaOEAeng.pdf

Organizational List   The "Organizational List" web page brings informational resources on the OAS's component parts together in one place. http://www.oas.org/en/about/organizational_list.asp

Permanent Representatives   A list of permanent representatives to the OAS is available on its website. http://www.oas.org/en/about/authorities.asp

Publications   OAS publications in English and Spanish are available online. http://www.oas.org/en/information_center/publications.asp

Scholarships   Information on OAS scholarships is available online. http://www.oas.org/en/scholarships

Social Media   The OAS tweets announcements, news, and other noteworthy items on Twitter. https://twitter.com/oas_official

The OAS has a Facebook account. https://www.facebook.com/OASofficial

The OAS posts video news on its Vimeo channel. https://vimeo.com/channels/oasvideonews

Staff Directory   The OAS maintains an online staff directory. To see the complete directory, leave all fields blank and click on the search button. http://www.oas.org/teldir; http://www.oas.org/en/contactus.asp

For further information, contact the Organization of American States, Seventeenth Street and Constitution Avenue NW., Washington, DC 20006. Phone, 202-370-5000. Fax, 202-458-3967.

United Nations

United Nations, New York, NY 10017
Phone, 212-963-1234. Internet, http://www.un.org

United Nations Office at Geneva: Palais des Nations, 1211 Geneva 10, Switzerland

United Nations Office at Vienna: Vienna International Centre, P.O. Box 500, A-1400, Vienna, Austria

Washington, DC: United Nations Information Centre, Suite 500, 1775 K Street NW., Washington, DC 20006
Phone, 202-331-8670. Fax, 202-331-9191. Internet, http://www.unicwash.org | Email: unicdc@unic.org

Secretary–General https://www.un.org/sg/en/content/sg/biography	ANTÓNIO GUTERRES
Deputy Secretary-General https://www.un.org/sg/en/dsg/index.shtml	AMINA J. MOHAMMED
Director-General, United Nations Office at Geneva	TATIANA VALOVAYA
Director-General, United Nations Office at Vienna https://www.un.org/sg/en/content/senior-management-group	YURY FEDOTOV
Director, Washington DC Information Centre http://www.unicwash.org/staff	MARY KIRTLEY WATERS

The above list of key personnel was updated 12–2019.

The United Nations supports tolerance and peaceful coexistence among the nations; seeks to maintain peace and security among them; opposes the use of armed force, except in the common interest; and promotes the economic and social advancement of all peoples.

The United Nations is an international organization that was set up in accordance with the Charter drafted by governments represented at the Conference on International Organization meeting at San Francisco. The Charter was signed on June 26, 1945, and came into force on October 24, 1945, when the required number of ratifications and accessions had been made by the signatories. Amendments increasing membership of the Security Council and the Economic and Social Council came into effect on August 31, 1965.

The United Nations now consists of 193 member states, of which 51 are founding members.

The purposes of the United Nations set out in the Charter are to maintain international peace and security; to develop friendly relations among nations; to achieve international cooperation in solving international problems of an economic, social, cultural, or humanitarian character and in promoting respect for human rights; and to be a center for harmonizing the actions of nations in the attainment of these common ends.

The principal organs of the United Nations are the Economic and Social Council, General Assembly, International Court of Justice, Secretariat, Security Council, and Trusteeship Council. http://www.un.org/en/sections/about-un/overview/index.html

Economic and Social Council   This organ is responsible, under the authority of the General Assembly, for the economic and social programs of the United Nations. Its functions include making or initiating studies, reports, and recommendations on international economic, social, cultural, educational, health, and related matters; promoting respect for and observance of human rights and fundamental freedoms for all; calling international conferences and preparing draft conventions for submission to the General Assembly on matters within its competence; negotiating agreements with the specialized agencies and defining their relationship with the United Nations; coordinating the activities of the specialized agencies; and consulting with nongovernmental organizations concerned with matters within its competence. The Council consists of 54 members of the United Nations elected by the General Assembly for 3-year terms; 18 are elected each year.

The Council usually holds two regular sessions a year. It has also held a number of special sessions. https://www.un.org/ecosoc/en

General Assembly   All states that are members of the United Nations are members of the General Assembly. Its functions are to consider and discuss any matter within the scope of the Charter of the United Nations and to make recommendations to the members of the United Nations and other organs. It approves the budget of the organization, the expenses of which are borne by the members as apportioned by the General Assembly.

The General Assembly may call the attention of the Security Council to situations likely to endanger international peace and security, may initiate studies, and may receive and consider reports from other organs of the United Nations. Under the "Uniting for Peace" resolution adopted by the General Assembly in November 1950, if the Security Council fails to act on an apparent threat to or breach of the peace or act of aggression because of lack of unanimity of its five permanent members, the Assembly itself may take up the matter within 24 hours—in emergency special session—and recommend collective measures, including, in case of a breach of the peace or act of aggression, use of armed force when necessary to maintain or restore international peace and security.

The General Assembly normally meets in regular annual session from September through December. It also has met in special sessions and emergency special sessions. http://www.un.org/en/ga

International Court of Justice   The International Court of Justice is the principal judicial organ of the United Nations. It has its seat at The Hague, the Netherlands. All members of the United Nations are ipso facto parties to the Statute of the Court. Nonmembers of the United Nations may become parties to the Statute of the Court on conditions prescribed by the General Assembly on the recommendation of the Security Council.

The jurisdiction of the Court comprises all cases that the parties refer to it and all matters specially provided for in the Charter of the United Nations or in treaties and conventions in force.

The Court consists of 15 judges known as members of the Court. They are elected for 9-year terms by the General Assembly and the Security Council, voting independently, and may be reelected. http://www.icj-cij.org/homepage/index.php?lang=en

Secretariat   The Secretariat consists of a Secretary-General and "such staff as the Organization may require." The Secretary-General, who is appointed by the General Assembly on the recommendation of the Security Council, is the chief administrative officer of the United Nations. He acts in that capacity for the General Assembly, the Security Council, the Economic and Social Council, and the Trusteeship Council. Under the Charter, the Secretary-General "may bring to the attention of the Security Council any matter that in his opinion may threaten the maintenance of international peace and security." http://www.un.org/en/sections/about-un/secretariat/index.html

Security Council   The Security Council consists of 15 members, of which 5—the People's Republic of China, France, Russia, the United Kingdom, and the United States of America—are permanent members. The 10 nonpermanent members are elected for 2-year terms by the General Assembly. The primary responsibility of the Security Council is to act on behalf of the members of the United Nations in maintenance of international peace and security. Measures that may be employed by the Security Council are outlined in the Charter.

The Security Council, together with the General Assembly, also elects the judges of the International Court of Justice and makes a recommendation to the General Assembly on the appointment of the Secretary-General of the organization.

The Security Council first met in London on January 17, 1946, and is so organized as to be able to function continuously. http://www.un.org/en/sc

Trusteeship Council   The Trusteeship Council was initially established to consist of any member states that administered trust territories, permanent members of the Security Council that did not administer trust territories, and enough other nonadministering countries elected by the General Assembly for 3-year terms to ensure that membership would be equally divided between administering and nonadministering members. Under authority of the General Assembly, the Council considered reports from members administering trust territories, examined petitions from trust territory inhabitants, and provided for periodic inspection visits to trust territories.

With the independence of Palau, the last remaining United Nations trust territory, the Trusteeship Council formally suspended operations after nearly half a century. The Council will henceforth meet only on an extraordinary basis, as the need may arise. http://www.un.org/en/decolonization/trusteeship.shtml

Sources of Information

A–Z Index An alphabetical index is available on the United Nations' website to help visitors search for specific topics or browse content that aligns with their interests. http://www.un.org/en/sections/about-website/site-index/index.html

Career Opportunities United Nations staff members coordinate relief in humanitarian crises, disarm child soldiers, monitor elections, provide administrative and logistical support for carrying out complex mandates, and carry out a host of other functions around the world. https://careers.un.org/lbw/Home.aspx

Children in Detention Many children are held in inhuman conditions and in adult facilities—in violation of their human rights—where they are at high risk of violence, rape, and sexual assault, including acts of torture and cruel, inhuman, or degrading treatment or punishment. The Office of the High Commissioner for Human Rights recently released the "Global Study on Children Deprived of Liberty" (OCT 2019). https://www.ohchr.org/EN/HRBodies/CRC/StudyChildrenDeprivedLiberty/Pages/Index.aspx

Climate Change While speaking at the United Nations, Secretary-General António Guterres addressed the crisis of climate change, the demands of science to mitigate its effects, and the urgent need for leaders to act with greater ambition. https://www.youtube.com/watch?feature=youtu.be&v=VNe-jBVij-g&app=desktop

Contact the Public Inquiries Team The public inquiries team answers general questions about the UN and its website. Questions are submitted by using the electronic form on the "Contact Us" web page. Quick links to the "United Nations Careers" and "Dag Hammarskjöld Library" websites are also available on the web page. https://www.un.org/en/contact-us/index.html

Documents Launched in 1993 and updated in 2016, the Official Document System (ODS) is an online database of United Nations documents that has full-text, born-digital documents published from 1993 onward. The ODS also includes scanned documents that were published between 1946 and 1993. Documents are available in the official languages of the United Nations. Some documents are also available in German. https://documents.un.org/prod/ods.nsf/home.xsp

Free Trade The secretariat of the United Nations Conference on Trade and Development (UNCTAD) has released its "Trade and Development Report—2018." In the report's foreword, Secretary-General of UNCTAD Mukhisa Kituyi wrote: "The growing mountain of debt . . . is symbolic of [the failure to address the inequities and imbalances of a hyperglobalized world since 2008]. While the public sector in advanced economies has been obliged to borrow more since the crisis, it is the rapid growth of private indebtedness, particularly in the corporate sector, which needs to be monitored closely; this has, in the past, been a harbinger of crisis." https://unctad.org/en/PublicationsLibrary/tdr2018_en.pdf

Frequently Asked Questions (FAQs) The United Nations posts answers to FAQs on its website. http://www.un.org/en/sections/about-un/frequently-asked-questions/index.html

Global Issues The "Global Issues Overview" web page offers convenient access to a trove of information on aging, atomic energy, children, climate change, decolonization, democracy, food, population, refugees, water, women, and more. http://www.un.org/en/sections/issues-depth/global-issues-overview/index.html

Human Rights   The Universal Declaration of Human Rights and a short history of this document are posted on the United Nation's website. http://www.un.org/en/universal-declaration-human-rights

High Commissioner for Human Rights Michelle Bachelet Jeria presented the United Nations Human Rights Report—2018. As part of that presentation, she explained: "At a time when humanity faced many serious challenges [including climate change, technological developments, civilian suffering in armed conflicts, displacement, youth unemployment, structural economic injustices, xenophobia and hate speech, and gross inequalities] . . . inequalities in income, wealth, access to resources, and access to justice constituted fundamental challenges to the principles of equality, dignity and human rights for every human being. . . . Even in prosperous States, people felt excluded from the benefits of development and deprived of economic and social rights, leading to alienation, unrest and sometimes violence." https://www.ohchr.org/EN/HRBodies/HRC/Pages/NewsDetail.aspx?NewsID=24269&LangID=E

Library   The Dag Hammarskjöld Library is accessible online. https://library.un.org

Mine Awareness   The United Nations Mine Action Service observes International Mine Awareness Day each year on April 4th. To hear the United Nation's global advocate's 2019 message, watch the 3-minute video. https://www.youtube.com/watch?v=LcWiyvxpkwE

Multimedia   United Nations Radio is accessible online. In addition to English, listeners may opt to hear programs in Arabic, Chinese, French, Russian, Spanish, and other languages. http://www.unmultimedia.org/radio/english

United Nations Video is accessible online and features documentaries, as well as coverage of events, news developments, and issues at the United Nations. http://www.un.org/en/sections/news-and-media/un-video/index.html

News   The News Centre provides breaking news coverage of developments around the United Nations system, offering quick access to news-related products and resources. http://www.un.org/News

Non-English Readers   The United Nations provides versions of its website in Arabic, Chinese, French, Russian, and Spanish. Language options are available on the site's welcome page. http://www.un.org

Organizational Chart   A chart of the United Nations System's principal organs is available online. https://www.un.org/en/pdfs/18-00159e_un_system_chart_17x11_4c_en_web.pdf

Publications   Books, reports, and data are available from the online bookshop. https://shop.un.org

Resources by Audience   The United Nations groups information and resources on its website according to categories of people who may be interested in them. Audiences include academics, businessmen and women, delegates, job seekers, journalists, representatives of civil society, students, and visitors. http://www.un.org/en/sections/resources-different-audiences/index.html

Social Media   Official United Nations social media include Facebook, Flickr, Tumblr, Twitter, YouTube, and other accounts. http://www.un.org/en/sections/about-website/un-social-media/index.html

Sustainable Development   The United Nations promotes 17 sustainable development goals to end poverty, to ensure prosperity for all people, and to protect Earth's biosphere as part of a development agenda. http://www.un.org/sustainabledevelopment/sustainable-development-goals

System Organizations Directory   The Charter of the United Nations established the organizations that constitute the United Nations system. The directory presents these organizations in categories with links to their web pages. Viewing these organizations in alphabetical order is also an option. https://www.unsceb.org/directory

Where We Work   The United Nations is a global organization that affects billions of people. It and the components comprising the United Nations system have a worldwide presence to ensure that timely assistance can reach people who most need it. The activities of the United Nations are divided into five geographical regions: Africa, Americas, Asia and the Pacific, Europe and Central Asia, and the Middle East. An overview of each area and links to relevant offices, agencies, and programs are available on the "Where We Work" web page. http://www.un.org/en/sections/where-we-work/index.html

The Sources of Information were updated 12–2019.

World Bank Group

Headquarters: 1818 H Street NW., Washington, DC 20433
Phone, 202-473-1000. Fax, 202-477-6391. Internet, http://www.worldbank.org

President	JIM YONG KIM
http://www.worldbank.org/en/about/leadership/managers	

The World Bank Group's personnel tables were updated 07–2018.

The World Bank Group promotes shared global prosperity and seeks to end extreme poverty.

The World Bank Group (WBG) comprises five institutions: the International Bank for Reconstruction and Development (IBRD), the International Development Association (IDA), the International Finance Corporation (IFC), the Multilateral Investment Guarantee Agency (MIGA), and the International Centre for the Settlement of Investment Disputes (ICSID). These WBG institutions work together to help developing countries find answers to tough global and local development challenges that range from climate change adaptation to food security, to fighting corruption and more. http://www.worldbank.org/en/about/what-we-do

The IBRD and the IDA serve as the WBG's primary economic and social development institutions. Together, these two development banks constitute the World Bank. Donor countries and countries with borrowing rights, a total of 189 countries, support and benefit from the World Bank. The activities of the IFC, MIGA, and ICSID complement those of the IBRD and IDA. http://www.worldbank.org/en/about/leadership

Sources of Information

A–Z Topics An alphabetical list of topics helps visitors learn about the WBG's many and diverse activities. http://www.worldbank.org/en/topic

Access to Information In 2010, the World Bank adopted its landmark disclosure policy: The World Bank Policy on Access to Information. It also has undertaken numerous initiatives to inform and educate the public. These open access initiatives include Open Data, Open Finances, and Open Knowledge Repository. http://www.worldbank.org/en/access to information

Blog The World Bank posts items by featured bloggers on its website. http://blogs.worldbank.org

Career Opportunities The WBG typically hires people with strong academic backgrounds, a broad understanding of development issues, and international work experience. In more than 170 countries, it employees professionals who specialize in economics, education, engineering, finance, public health, and many other fields. About 40 percent of World Bank staff members work in more than 110 developing countries. http://www.worldbank.org/en/about/careers

Climate Investment Funds Since the inception of this climate finance mechanism, donor countries have contributed over 8 billion dollars in support of scaling up mitigation and adaptation action in developing and middle-income countries. The World Bank holds these public resources in trust and disburses them as grants, concessional loans, and risk mitigation instruments to recipient countries through multilateral development banks. https://www.climateinvestmentfunds.org/

Climate Migration The World Bank report "Groundswell: Preparing for Internal Climate Migration" (2018) found that by midcentury the adverse effects of climate change in three densely populated regions of the world could force more than 140 million people to relocate within their respective countries. Concerted action, including global reductions in greenhouse gas emissions and development planning, could reduce internal migration by as much as 80 percent. http://www.worldbank.org/en/news/feature/2018/03/19/meet-the-human-faces-of-climate-migration

Contact Information General information for contacting the World Bank is available on its website. http://www.worldbank.org/en/about/contacts

Countries / Regions The "Where We Work" web page allows visitors to browse WGB locations by region or country group. http://www.worldbank.org/en/country

Data The World Bank's website allows free and open access to global development data. http://data.worldbank.org

The microdata library facilitates access to data collected through sample surveys of households, business establishments, and other facilities. These sets of microdata may also be derived from agricultural, housing, or population censuses or through an administrative data collection processes. The Library also contains supporting documentation from censuses and surveys that the World Bank and other international organizations, statistical agencies, and other agencies in low and middle-income countries conducted or supported. http://microdata.worldbank.org/index.php/home

History Founded in 1944, and not long thereafter referred to as the World Bank, the International Bank for Reconstruction and Development (IBRD) expanded to become a group of five development institutions. In the aftermath of World War II, IBRD loans helped countries overcome the devastation and rebuild. Over time, the Bank's focus shifted from reconstruction to development, particularly to development of infrastructure: dams, electrical grids, irrigation systems, and roads. To learn more about the inception and growth of the World Bank, visit the "History" web page. http://www.worldbank.org/en/about/history

The "World Bank Group Archives" website supports the institutional memory of the World Bank Group and provides access to records of the International Bank for Reconstruction and Development and the International Development Association. The website also features online historical resources and information products: exhibits on the Archives' collection and World Bank history, General International Standard Archival Description (ISAD(G)) finding aids, and transcripts of oral history interviews. http://www.worldbank.org/en/about/archives

Indicators The WBG's Global Indicators Group produces indicators and datasets. http://www.doingbusiness.org/about-us/global-indicators

Libraries The WBG and International Monetary Fund libraries collaborate to provide information services and make available resources to World Bank Group and International Monetary Fund staff. These libraries provide limited services to external researchers and visitors. http://jolis.worldbankimflib.org/external.htm

News The World Bank posts press releases and other newsworthy items on its website. http://www.worldbank.org/en/news

Open Learning Campus The Open Learning Campus offers educational opportunities that allow diverse audiences to learn at their own pace. It helps prepare people seeking to address the tough development challenges of the 21st century. https://olc.worldbank.org

Organizational Chart The World Bank posts its organizational chart in Portable Document Format (PDF) for viewing and downloading. http://pubdocs.worldbank.org/en/404071412346998230/wbg-org-chart.pdf

Partnerships The World Bank participates in global partnerships. Visit the "Partners" web page to learn about some of them. http://www.worldbank.org/en/about/partners

Podcasts The World Bank's "All Multimedia" web page allows visitors to access a trove of podcasts on diverse topics: climate change, energy development, food, indigenous communities, immigration

Organizational Chart
Effective November 4, 2019

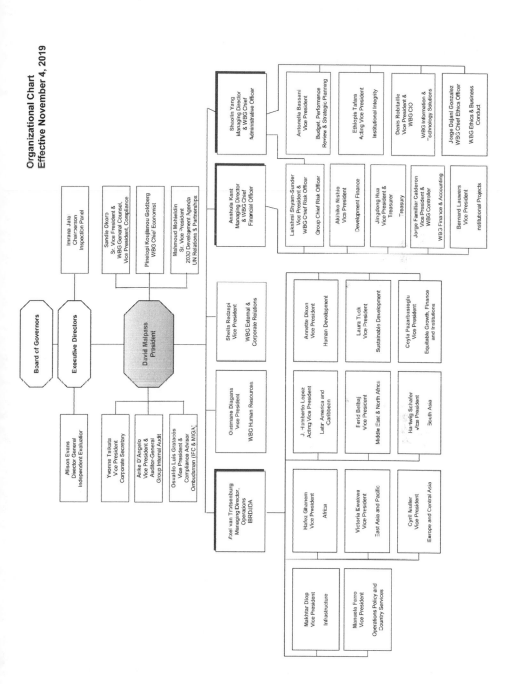

and forced displacement, pollution, sanitation, sustainability, tourism and more. http://www.worldbank.org/en/news/multimedia?multimedia_class_exact=Audio&qterm=&lang_exact=English

Poverty and Equity The "Poverty and Equity Data Portal" web page allows visitors to access the World Bank Group's most recent data on inequality, poverty, and shared prosperity. http://povertydata.worldbank.org/poverty/home/

Projects The "Projects and Operations" web page allows visitors to browse or search for projects by country or area, sector, or theme. http://projects.worldbank.org

Publications / Research The "Open Knowledge Repository" allows users to browse and search for thousands of publications. http://www.worldbank.org/en/publication/reference

Social Media The World Bank tweets announcements and other newsworthy items on Twitter. https://twitter.com/worldbank

The World Bank has a Facebook account. https://www.facebook.com/worldbank

The World Bank posts videos on its YouTube channel. https://www.youtube.com/WorldBank

Speaker's Bureau The Speaker's Bureau serves as the official liaison between the World Bank Group and its visitors, who include business leaders, governmental representatives, students and teachers, youth organizations, and other professionals. http://www.worldbank.org/en/about/speakers-bureau | Email: speakersbureau@worldbank.org

International Bank for Reconstruction and Development

The International Bank for Reconstruction and Development (IBRD) officially came into existence in 1944. It promotes economic, social, and environmental progress in developing nations by reducing poverty.

The Bank lends funds at market-determined interest rates, provides advice, and serves as a catalyst to stimulate outside investments. Its resources come primarily from funds raised in the world capital markets, its retained earnings, and repayments on its loans. http://www.worldbank.org/en/about/what-we-do/brief/ibrd

Sources of Information

Activities and Achievements The IBRD helps countries craft policies and shape investments, manage crises and prevent them, and create markets and access additional resources. To learn about the results of these IBRD activities, visit the "Results" web page. http://www.worldbank.org/en/who-we-are/news/campaigns/2018/ibrd-results-page

Countries The Governments of the 189 member countries own the IBRD. http://www.worldbank.org/en/about/leadership/members

Organizational Chart The IBRD and International Development Association are represented on the World Bank's organizational chart, which is available in Portable Document Format (PDF) for viewing and downloading. http://pubdocs.worldbank.org/en/404071412346998230/wbg-org-chart.pdf

International Centre for Settlement of Investment Disputes

Headquarters: 1818 H Street NW., MSN J2-200, Washington, DC 20433
Phone, 202-458-1534. Fax, 202-522-2615. Internet, http://icsid.worldbank.org/en |
Email: ICSIDsecretariat@worldbank.org

President   JIM YONG KIM
Secretary-General   MEGAN KINNEAR
https://icsid.worldbank.org/en/Pages/about/Secretariat.aspx

The International Centre for Settlement of Investment Disputes (ICSID) is an autonomous international institution and a World Bank Group affiliate that provides an independent forum for conciliation and arbitration of international investment disputes. By providing an impartial system for dispute settlement, it facilitates foreign investment. The Convention on the Settlement of Investment Disputes Between States and Nationals of Other States established the ICSID, setting forth its mandate, organization, and core functions. The executive directors of the International Bank for Reconstruction and Development formulated this multilateral treaty, which entered into force in 1966, to further the World Bank's goal of promoting international investment.

The ICSID has a composite structure comprising an administrative council and secretariat. Each member state holds one seat on the Administrative Council, whose mandate is to address organizational matters related to ICSID's institutional framework. The Secretariat consists of about 70 professionals who administer arbitration and conciliation cases and support other ICSID activities. https://icsid.worldbank.org/en/Pages/about/default.aspx

Sources of Information

Archives The ICSID archives contain annual reports, events, featured videos, model clauses, and news and announcements. https://icsid.worldbank.org/en/Pages/resources/Archives.aspx

Contact Information General information for contacting ICSID is available online. https://icsid.worldbank.org/en/Pages/about/Contact-us.aspx

Convention The ICSID Convention is available in 20 languages; however, its official version is available in 3 languages: English, French, and Spanish. https://icsid.worldbank.org/en/Pages/resources/ICSID-Convention-in-other-Languages.aspx

Member States A database of ICSID member states is available online. https://icsid.worldbank.org/en/Pages/about/Database-of-Member-States.aspx

Publications The ICSID publishes specialized texts on international investment law and investment dispute resolution procedures. https://icsid.worldbank.org/en/Pages/resources/ICSID-Publications.aspx

Related Websites A list of links to public and commercial websites that may be useful for research in the field of international investment law and practice is available on the ICSID website. https://icsid.worldbank.org/en/Pages/resources/Other-Related-Websites.aspx

Resources Overview The ICSID Secretariat promotes greater awareness of the ICSID dispute settlement process and the development of international law on foreign investment by posting information resources on its website. https://icsid.worldbank.org/en/Pages/Resources/default.aspx

Social Media The ICSID tweets announcements and other newsworthy items on Twitter. https://twitter.com/icsid

Structure This separation of functions within the ICSID enhances impartiality and independence in the resolution of disputes. https://icsid.worldbank.org/en/Pages/about/Structure.aspx

International Development Association

Established in 1960, the International Development Association (IDA) reduces poverty by providing loans, or "credits," and grants for programs that boost economic growth, improve living conditions, and reduce inequalities. The IDA complements the International Bank for Reconstruction and Development (IBRD), which is the original lending arm of the World Bank.

The IDA and IBRD share the same staff and headquarters and evaluate projects using the same standards.

The IDA lends money on concessional terms, which means that IDA loans, or credits, have a zero or very low interest charge and repayments extend from 25 to 38 years. The IDA also provides grants to countries at risk of debt distress. In addition to loans and grants, the IDA provides significant levels of debt relief. http://ida.worldbank.org/about/who-we-are

Sources of Information

Articles of Agreement   The IDA's Articles of Agreement became effective in 1960. They are available online in Portable Document Format. http://ida.worldbank.org/sites/default/files/IDA-articles-of-agreement.pdf

Climate   Climate change threatens poorer people globally, with the potential to force more than 100 million people back into poverty by 2030. The IDA is making plans to help manage this threat of enormous scope and scale. http://ida.worldbank.org/theme/climate

Countries   Seventy-five countries are eligible to receive IDA resources. http://ida.worldbank.org/about/borrowing-countries

A list of the approximately 50 contributor countries is available on the IDA's website. http://ida.worldbank.org/about/contributor-countries

Crisis Financing   The IDA has a history of involvement in various aspects of crisis response, including providing financial support. http://ida.worldbank.org/financing/crisis-financing

History   Australia, Canada, China, Germany, India, Italy, Malaysia, Norway, Pakistan, Sudan, Sweden, Thailand, United Kingdom, United States, and Vietnam launched the IDA on September 24, 1960, with an initial funding of 912.7 million dollars. http://ida.worldbank.org/about/history

News / Publications   The IDA posts press releases and other newsworthy items online. http://ida.worldbank.org/news

Organizational Chart   The IDA and International Bank for Reconstruction and Development are included on the World Bank's organizational chart, which is available in Portable Document Format (PDF) for viewing and downloading. http://pubdocs.worldbank.org/en/404071412346998230/wbg-org-chart.pdf

Resources / Policy   Every 3 years, donors meet to replenish IDA resources and review its policy framework. The replenishment process typically consists of four formal meetings over the course of 1 year. Four IDA18 replenishment meetings were held in 2016. http://ida.worldbank.org/financing/replenishments/ida18-overview

Results   The IDA's website features an overview of the results of the IDA's efforts in the world's poorest countries by country, theme, and topic. http://ida.worldbank.org/results

Social Media   The IDA has a Facebook account. https://www.facebook.com/IDA.WBG/?ref=nf

The IDA posts videos on its YouTube channel. https://www.youtube.com/playlist?list=PL6A79B12D02618711&feature=plcp

---

International Finance Corporation

Headquarters: 2121 Pennsylvania Avenue NW., Washington, DC 20433
Phone, 202-473-7711. Fax, 202-974-4384. Internet, http://www.ifc.org

President	JIM YONG KIM
Executive Vice President / Chief Executive Officer	PHILIPPE LE HOUÉROU
http://www.ifc.org/wps/wcm/connect/CORP_EXT_Content/IFC_External_Corporate_Site/About+IFC_New/Leadership	

The International Finance Corporation (IFC), a World Bank Group institution, was established in 1956 to promote productive private enterprise in developing member countries.

The Corporation pursues its objective principally through direct debt and equity investments in projects that establish new businesses or expand, modify, or diversify existing businesses. It also encourages cofinancing by other investors and lenders.

Additionally, to developing member countries, the IFC provides advisory services and technical assistance in capital market development, corporate restructuring, foreign investment, and privatization. https://www.ifc.org/wps/wcm/connect/corp_ext_content/ifc_external_corporate_site/about+ifc_new

Sources of Information

Articles of Agreement The official version of the IFC Articles of Agreement is the English version that each member country signs. Translations of the official version are available in Arabic, Chinese, French, Japanese, Portuguese, Russian, and Spanish. https://www.ifc.org/wps/wcm/connect/CORP_EXT_Content/IFC_External_Corporate_Site/About+IFC_New/IFC+Governance/Articles/

Bonds In 2013, the IFC helped transform the green bond market by issuing a 1 billion dollar global benchmark green bond. The IFC is currently investing in the Green Cornerstone Bond Fund, which buys green bonds issued by banks in Africa, Asia, Central Asia, Eastern Europe, Latin America, and the Middle East. The Green Cornerstone Bond Fund is a partnership involving the IFC and the European asset manager Amundi. http://www.worldbank.org/en/results/2017/12/01/green-bonds

Career Opportunities The IFC posts career opportunities. http://www.ifc.org/wps/wcm/connect/Careers_Ext_Content/IFC_External_Corporate_Site/IFC+Careers

Climate The IFC is increasing its climate-related investments to address climate change—a fundamental threat to development, with the potential to impact millions, threatening agricultural livelihoods, increasing the incidence of natural disasters and affecting water, energy, and food supplies. http://www.ifc.org/wps/wcm/connect/Topics_Ext_Content/IFC_External_Corporate_Site/Climate+Business

Contact Information General information is available on the IFC's website. http://www.ifc.org/wps/wcm/connect/corp_ext_content/ifc_external_corporate_site/about+ifc_new/contacts

Countries The IFC operates in more than 100 countries. http://www.ifc.org/wps/wcm/connect/corp_ext_content/ifc_external_corporate_site/about+ifc_new/Where+We+Work

Expertise The IFC's areas of expertise include agribusiness and forestry; financial institutions; funds; health and education; infrastructure; manufacturing; oil, gas, and mining; public-private partnerships; telecoms, media, and technology; and tourism, retail, and property. https://www.ifc.org/wps/wcm/connect/CORP_EXT_Content/IFC_External_Corporate_Site/solutions/expertise

Frequently Asked Questions (FAQs) The IFC posts answers to FAQs online. https://www.ifc.org/wps/wcm/connect/corp_ext_content/ifc_external_corporate_site/about+ifc_new/faqs

Funding The IFC raises funds for lending activities by issuing debt obligations in international capital markets. IFC borrowings are diversified by country, currency, source, and maturity to enhance flexibility and cost effectiveness. https://www.ifc.org/wps/wcm/connect/CORP_EXT_Content/IFC_External_Corporate_Site/About+IFC_New/IFC+Governance/Funding/

History Opened in 1956 with $100 million in capital, the IFC has been creating jobs and raising living standards for six decades. https://www.ifc.org/wps/wcm/connect/CORP_EXT_Content/IFC_External_Corporate_Site/About+IFC_New/IFC+History/

Media The "Communications Contacts" page contains communications and public affairs contact information, as well as contact information associated with IFC accountability and the various spheres of IFC expertise and regional activity. https://www.ifc.org/wps/wcm/connect/NEWS_EXT_CONTENT/IFC_External_Corporate_Site/News+and+Events/Media+Contacts/

Organizational Chart The IFC posts its organizational chart in Portable Document Format (PDF) for viewing and downloading. https://www.ifc.org/wps/wcm/connect/7973ac004a4483708622bf10cc70d6a1/IFC+organization+chart.pdf?MOD=AJPERES

Press Releases The IFC posts press releases in Arabic, Bahasa Indonesia, Chinese, English, French, German, Japanese,

Montenegrin, Portuguese, Russian, Spanish, Tajik, Turkish, and Ukranian. https://ifcextapps.ifc.org/ifcext/pressroom/ ifcpressroom.nsf/MorePressReleases/?OpenV iew&Start=1&Count=25

Publications   A search tool allows visitors to search IFC publications by language, region, and topic. The advanced option allows users to refine their search by IFC department, industry, and publication type. https://www.ifc.org/wps/wcm/connect/ publications_ext_content/ifc_external_ publication_site/publications

Social Media   The IFC has a Facebook account. https://www.facebook.com/IFCwbg

The IFC tweets announcements and other newsworthy items on Twitter. https://twitter. com/IFC_org

The IFC posts videos on its YouTube channel. https://www.youtube.com/user/ IFCvideocasts

Stories   The IFC posts stories highlighting the achievements of its clients who affect people's lives in a favorable and notable way. https://www.ifc.org/wps/wcm/connect/ NEWS_EXT_CONTENT/IFC_External_ Corporate_Site/News+and+Events/News/ Impact-Stories

Sustainability   The IFC partners with industry and other stakeholders to find ways that open opportunities for economically, socially, and environmentally sustainable private investment. https://www.ifc.org/ wps/wcm/connect/Topics_Ext_Content/IFC_ External_Corporate_Site/Sustainability-At-IFC

Multilateral Investment Guarantee Agency

Headquarters: 1818 H Street NW., Washington, DC 20433
Phone, 202-458-2538. Fax, 202-522-0316. Internet, http://www.miga.org

President	JIM YONG KIM
Executive Vice President / Chief Executive Officer	KEIKO HONDA
https://www.miga.org/who-we-are/senior-management	

The Multilateral Investment Guarantee Agency (MIGA), a World Bank Group institution, was formally constituted in 1988.

Working with public and private insurers, MIGA promotes foreign direct investment in developing countries to support economic growth, reduce poverty, and improve the quality of people's lives. Due to its status as a World Bank Group institution, MIGA's guarantees protect investments against noncommercial risks and help investors gain access to funding sources with improved financial terms and conditions. https://www. miga.org/who-we-are

Sources of Information

Access to Information   MIGA's policy on accessing information defines its obligations to disclose information on itself and its activities. https://www.miga.org/projects/ access-to-information/

Career Opportunities   The MIGA advertises available positions on the World Bank's job

vacancies page. https://www.miga.org/who-we-are/careers

Contact Information   General information is available on the MIGA's website. https:// www.miga.org/contact

Convention   The "Convention Establishing the Multilateral Investment Guarantee Agency" went into effect on April 12, 1988. The Council of Governors amended it in 2010. The Convention is available online in Portable Document Format (PDF). https:// www.miga.org/who-we-are/miga-convention

Frequently Asked Questions (FAQs)   The MIGA posts answers to FAQs on its website. https://www.miga.org/who-we-are/ frequently-asked-questions

History   A timeline and short history of the MIGA are available on its website. https:// www.miga.org/who-we-are/history

Member Countries   The names of the 181 member countries—156 developing, 25 industrialized—are available on the MIGA's website. https://www.miga.org/who-we-are/ member-countries

Organizational Chart
Effective December 16, 2019

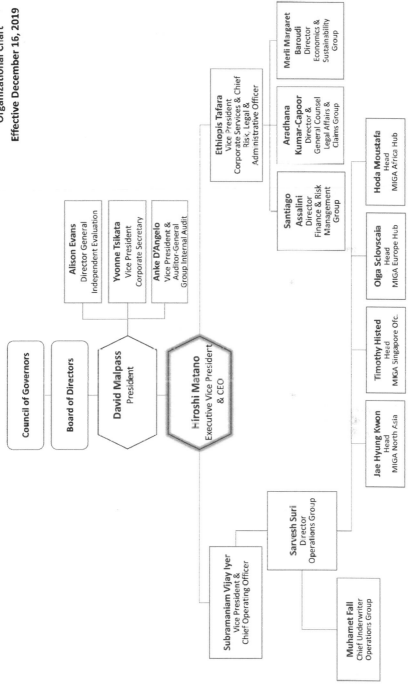

Council of Governors

Board of Directors

David Malpass
President

Hiroshi Matano
Executive Vice President
& CEO

Alison Evans
Director General
Independent Evaluation

Yvonne Tsikata
Vice President
Corporate Secretary

Anke D'Angelo
Vice President &
Auditor-General
Group Internal Audit

Ethiopis Tafara
Vice President
Corporate Services & Chief
Risk, Legal &
Administrative Officer

Merli Margaret
Baroudi
Director
Economics &
Sustainability
Group

Aradhana
Kumar-Capoor
Director &
General Counsel
Legal Affairs &
Claims Group

Santiago
Assalini
Director
Finance & Risk
Management
Group

Hoda Moustafa
Head
MIGA Africa Hub

Olga Sclovscaia
Head
MIGA Europe Hub

Timothy Histed
Head
MIGA Singapore Ofc.

Jae Hyung Kwon
Head
MIGA North Asia

Subramaniam Vijay Iyer
Vice President &
Chief Operating Officer

Sarvesh Suri
Director
Operations Group

Muhamet Fall
Chief Underwriter
Operations Group

News   The MIGA posts press releases on its website. https://www.miga.org/news/press-releases

Organizational Chart   The MIGA posts its organizational chart in Portable Document Format (PDF) for viewing and downloading. http://pubdocs.worldbank.org/en/268791412196376513/miga.pdf

Projects   The MIGA provides investment insurance, or guarantees, for projects in a variety of sectors, covering all regions of the world. https://www.miga.org/projects

Reports   The MIGA posts its annual reports online. https://www.miga.org/Pages/Resources/Reports/AnnualReports.aspx

Small Investment   The small investment program facilitates investment in small and medium-size enterprises that are active in the agribusiness, finance, manufacturing, and services sectors. This MIGA program has a streamlined approval process, which allows investors to acquire MIGA coverage quickly. https://www.miga.org/investment-guarantees/small-investment-program/

The application for the small investment program is available online. https://www.miga.org/Documents/SIP_Application.pdf#search=SIP%20Application

Social Media   The MIGA tweets announcements and other newsworthy items on Twitter. https://twitter.com/miga

The MIGA posts videos on its YouTube channel. https://www.youtube.com/migaworldbank